Gun Digest

38th Anniversary

1984 Deluxe Edition

EDITED BY KEN WARNER

D1470469

DBI BOOKS, INC., NORTHFIELD, ILL.

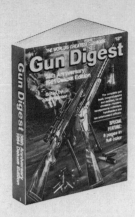

OUR COVER GUNS

For the American hunting public, as well as the international hunting community, the name Weatherby has come to symbolize the epitome of power, style and custom quality. The editors and staff are indeed pleased to have Weatherby products on the covers of this, the 38th Edition of GUN DIGEST.

On the front, you'll see Weatherby's all-time great Mark V Magnum big game rifle, in 300 Weatherby Magnum, together with the all-new Weatherby Athena over-under 12-gauge shotgun, a strong boxlock design complete with decorative sideplates. On the back cover is the new Fibermark Mark V Magnum rifle—24 ounces lighter than the standard with its fiberglass stock—and the Weatherby Model Eighty-Two auto-loading shotgun, available with Weatherby's Multi-Choke tube system.
Photos by John Hanusin

K.W.

GUN DIGEST STAFF

EDITOR-IN-CHIEF
Ken Warner
ASSISTANT TO THE EDITOR
Lilo Anderson
SENIOR STAFF EDITOR
Harold A. Murtz
ASSOCIATE EDITOR
Robert S. L. Anderson
PRODUCTION MANAGER
Pamela J. Johnson
CONTRIBUTING EDITORS
Bob Bell
Dean A. Grennell
Rick Hacker
Edward A. Matunas
Layne Simpson
Larry S. Sterett
Hal Swiggett
Ralph T. Walker
D. A. Warner
J.B. Wood
EUROPEAN CORRESPONDENT
Raymond Caranta
EDITOR EMERITUS
John T. Amber
GRAPHIC DESIGNS
Mary MacDonald
PUBLISHER
Sheldon L. Factor

DBI BOOKS INC.

PRESIDENT
Charles T. Hartigan
VICE PRESIDENT & PUBLISHER
Sheldon L. Factor
VICE PRESIDENT — SALES
John G. Strauss
TREASURER
Frank R. Serpone

ISBN 0-910676-57-7   Library of Congress Catalog #44-3588

NRA Settled For Now

After months of politicking, charging, and counter charging, the members of NRA settled their executive brouhaha in just a few hours with a two-thirds vote at the 1983 Members Meeting. The bid of the Federation for NRA to change the by-laws to limit terms of office and further open up election procedures was thumped hard. So were the hopes of Neal Knox, who was elected, nonetheless, to the Board of Directors. The tenure of Harlon Carter was assured; the vote is also seen as a vote of confidence in Carter personally.

Revolvers Only, Please

Omark Industries has discovered that 357 Blazer ammunition which works well and safely in modern revolvers may not be compatible with all rifles and has put out a WARNING NOTICE, and will affix warnings to all Blazer 357 Magnum packages. Blazer 357 conforms to the industry's SAAMI specs, but some rear-locking lever-action rifles and some oversize chambers apparently permit the aluminum cases to stretch beyond the yield point.

NMLRA Is Over 50

There are not many independent organizations that last 50 years, but the folks from Friendship have done it and are on their way to the other half-century.

There were 30 or so names on the first sheet of paper; now there are 25,000 members, 200 shooting matches a year, and a monthly magazine. That's good going.

ARMY JOINS FLAYDERMAN

Sharing Savage Profits

New (1981) Savage owners Lt. Gen. Robert J. Friedman (Ret.) and F. J. Renkowicz have moved toward digging in, in Westfield, Mass. The firm has signed a profit-sharing contract with its union. Workers get a 20 percent share of pre-tax profits. Both sides were happy with the new deal.

More and More SHOT Show

Having to avoid San Francisco and go to Dallas didn't hurt this 1983 behemoth of ballyhoo. The fifth annual event was again the biggest ever (three times the size of the first one). There were 740 exhibitors and 160,000 sq. ft. of displays—you get the idea. It was so good they're going back to Dallas for 1984.

Second SCI Rifle: $43,500

Safari Club International's "Big Five" series looks like going strong. The second gun, a 375 H&H labelled "Rhino," was built by Champlin Firearms and stocked by Maurice Ottmar, with engraving by Dan Goodwin. At auction, it brought $43,500.

New Owl Heads

Iver Johnson is now a new company with a history that goes back to 1871. A new group of investors acquired the firm. Walter Gleason, former manager of the Colt Custom Shop heads a team which includes Lewis Sharp, Frank Foley and Les Kimmel. One of the first major moves is to a manufacturing facility in Arkansas.

L. R. Wallack, Jr.
1919-1983

Bob Wallack died following heart surgery in the early spring. He was a square-shouldered vital kind of fellow and we hoped he would make it to some more years with the help of a bypass, but it didn't happen.

He had been a gunsmith, shooter, advertising man, writer, husband, father and a good friend to many in the business and the hobby of firearms. He will be missed on many levels in many places.

Here he'll be missed because in a world and at a level where most answers are routine, one was not always quite sure what Bob might say. Or have found out, but not told you yet. There are not so many interesting people in the world we can afford to lose the ones that write about guns, even if they have left their marks, as Bob Wallack did.

Shelley Braverman

Famed firearms consultant Shelley Braverman died at age 72, July 1, 1982, after a long illness. A member of 10 or more collector associations, he was active until well along in years, but eventually passed his business along to Robert S. Krauss. He died at home.

The Eleventh Man

J. D. Jones, well-known shooter of hot handloads, was chosen the 11th Outstanding American Handgunner in Phoenix, AZ, during the NRA meetings.

It took five generals to invest Norm Flayderman with his new distinction: He is a Civilian Aide to the Secretary of the Army, and is in basic civilian blue here.

CONTENTS

DEPARTMENTS

RATING HANDGUN POWER

This Power puts, finally, cartridges proper **Index Rating all handgun in their places.**

by **EDWARD A. MATUNAS**

For A LONG TIME the best possible way to estimate the potential effectiveness of handgun ammunition has been to compare the kinetic energy developed by a given round of ammunition with the kinetic energy of other rounds. As you may know, kinetic energy figures are expressed in *foot pounds*. This method is a reasonable approach to the problem as it is very objective and it is supported by the laws of physics. It is, however, not without its shortcomings.

For example, the kinetic energy system shows us that a 38 Special using a 158-grain round nose bullet, travelling at 755 ft/s, has 200 foot pounds of energy. It also tells us that a 158-grain semi-wadcutter's bullet travelling at the same speed has the same energy. And while it is true that both bullets possess the identical energy, the semi-wadcutter is a superior performer. This performance superiority can be proven by shooting into gelatin blocks or by examining rec-

ords based on actual shootings involving police officers.

The vagaries of the kinetic energy system for rating handgun ammunition are numerous. No knowledgeable shooter would expect a full metal jacket 9mm bullet to perform as well as an expanding bullet of the same caliber and weight traveling at the same velocity. The expanding bullet is vastly superior. And despite the similarities in energy, a factory 9mm Luger with a 124-grain full-metal case bullet at 339 foot pounds of energy will not perform as well as a factory 45 Auto with a 230-grain full metal case bullet at 335 pounds of energy.

A number of systems have been devised over the years to express a handgun bullet's ability to get the job done. One of the most publicized expressed the bullet's performance by listing its momentum. The various methods tried have failed because they have ignored or played down the bullet's kinetic energy.

In some circles, extensive testing has been conducted in various media to get the bullet to perform as it would in tissue. These tests, usually conducted by or for a well financed police department, have resulted in some very elaborate charts which graphically depict bullet performance. These charts have been a giant step forward as they indeed show the superiority of expanding bullets over otherwise identical non-expanding bullets, but the drawbacks are very real. First, they are not readily available to most shooters; Second, they are useless when a new round is being considered; Third, they are subject to errors created when test performance is nontypical, caused by a lot of ammunition with velocity above or below nominal velocity or by a firearm that produced nontypical results.

The shooter therefore has been left to choose ammunition using the objective value of the kinetic energy of the round combined with his intuitive and subjective reckoning on the per-

Here are a Speer 158-gr. round nose 38 Special bullet, unfired, and a 158-gr. Speer semi-wadcutter, fired and unfired. The PIR System clearly shows the superiority of the semi-wadcutter over the round nose. Both are non-expanding, carry different energy transfer values.

These are 158-gr. lead hollow point bullets. They were fired from a 2-inch revolver. These were loaded by Winchester as +P ammunition, and expansion was obviously perfect. Such bullet performance gains high ratings in the PIR System.

Classic expansion was obtained in a 3-inch 38 Special with these Sierra 125-gr. hollow points. These newest Sierra bullets feature jacket cuts at the nose. It is these cuts which allow such perfect expansion.

These are Speer 110-gr. 38-caliber hollow points fired from a 2-inch 38 Special revolver. While the nose lead smeared to some extent these bullets do not qualify as expanding bullets when fired from this length barrel at the tested velocity.

Shown are Winchester 85-gr. Silvertips fired from a 380 Auto. The bullets on either side were fired into thoroughly soaked phone book pages. The bullet in the middle was fired into identical material which had not yet become completely soaked. The importance of using 100% saturated phone books is clear.

Even the 140-gr. Sierra hollow points expanded when fired from a 2-inch S&W Chiefs Special. While expansion of this heavy bullet is not tremendous in such a short barrel, it is sufficient to give the bullet a maximum energy transfer value in the PIR System.

This is the Sierra 125-gr. jacketed hollow point unfired. There are notches or cuts in the jacket at the nose end, and it is these notches that make these new Sierra bullets predictably good expanders.

This shows an unfired 125-gr. Sierra soft point 38/357 bullet alongside of a fired bullet of the same make and style. No expansion took place when this bullet was fired in a 4-inch revolver, which is why each style and type of bullet needs to be tested for expansion.

formance of a particular bullet style. As often as not, this has led to a great many misconceptions. For instance, most handgunners feel the 45 Auto will outperform any 38 Special round. This simply is not so. A number of 38 Special high speed rounds which use expanding bullets are far superior to the standard 230-grain full-metal case 45 Auto bullets.

Of course, a shooter can resort to testing each and every interesting round in gelatin blocks. Or if he has great influence he could perhaps examine 5-6,000 case histories from a major police department's records of shootings. Neither approach is very practical.

I have devised a method that fully takes into account the bullet's kinetic energy, its shape, its ability to expand and its basic diameter. I have been working with the basic idea for almost 20 years and I have reworked the idea many more times than I care to admit. Each time I discovered a discrepancy it was back to the drawing board. The system now, in my opinion, is what it was intended to be—a reliable indicator of handgun bullet performance, regardless of the bullet style, caliber, velocity or weight being considered. I call this new system *Power Index Rating* or PIR. *(Note: I call it the Matunas Number. Editor.)*

Any system which purports to express the ability to reflect an accurate representation of a bullet's capability to get the job done must somehow incorporate the bullet's kinetic energy. The formula for kinetic energy is, as you may know:

$$K.E. = \frac{V^2 Bg}{450240}$$

In this formula: V = the velocity in feet per second; and Bg = the weight of the bullet in grains.

A 9-inch pile of soaked phone books stops all expanding bullets up to 115-gr. 9mm Luger rounds. For heavier calibers substantially greater thickness is required to stop the bullet in the books.

Bullet performance can, of course, be tested in clay blocks. However, such testing is very time-consuming and very costly. The author feels wet phone books are quicker, cheaper, and just as reliable.

By measurement, the weight of the bullet and its actual velocity can be determined. It is then a very simple matter to square the velocity, multiply the resulting figure by the bullet weight and divide all this by the constant 450240. The basis of the above formula has been verified and explained in a great number of places including my book, *American Ammunition and Ballistics*. Kinetic energy remains an important part of the PIR formula.

Any system to rate bullet performance must also address itself to the bullet's ability to expand because, as stated, an expanding bullet is far more effective than an identical non-expanding bullet at an identical velocity. And flat nosed, non-expanding

bullets are better performers than other shapes of non-expanding bullets.

Since expansion is a vital part of bullet performance, I have tested a great number of bullets. As you may have expected, a number of bullets purported to be expanding turned out to be non-expanding. As an example, note the accompanying photo of three factory bullets fired from a 380 Auto PPK/S Walther. One is a Remington 88-grain Hollow Point, one is a Federal 90-grain Hollow Point, and one is a Winchester 85-grain Silvertip Hollow Point. Neither the Remington nor the Federal bullet expanded, while the Winchester bullet expanded in a classic style. Obviously in this case, with

three almost identical bullets at nearly identical velocities, the expanding bullet is a far superior performer. All of my bullet tests were 15-round tests, at minimum.

You can easily duplicate my expansion tests. It is not necessary to prepare elaborate blocks of ordnance gelatin. All you need is a good supply of thoroughly soaked telephone books. It will speed up the soaking process if you remove the covers and backing which hold the books together. Before testing flip through the pages to make certain all the pages are completely wet.

WARNING: Bullets will penetrate through a much greater thickness of dry pages than through wet pages.

Left to right: Remington 88-gr. hollow point, Federal 90-gr. hollow point, Winchester 85-gr. Silvertip, and Speer 100-gr. hollow point (a reload). Only the Silvertip proved to be a reliable expanding bullet from a PPK/S pistol. The PIR System rates the Winchester load considerably higher than any of the other loads.

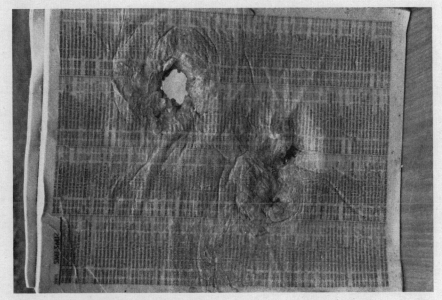

Holes in these pages were made with a 380 Auto. The large hole was made by an 85-gr. Winchester Silvertip which expanded perfectly. The others were made by Federal 90-gr. hollow point and a Remington 88-gr. hollow point. The channel created by the expanding bullet is much larger than its expanded diameter. The PIR System will accurately reflect such differences in bullet performance.

And bullet expansion in dry pages will be extremely poor. Be certain that the book pages are completely soaked.

A 9 to 10-inch stack of wet phone books will stop expanding bullets up to and including the 9mm Luger. For heavier calibers or for non-expanding bullets you will have to increase this thickness notably. Be certain your bullets stop inside the wet paper. Bullets which completely penetrate can be severely expanded against your backstop.

For my testing I dug a hole in the ground about 24 inches deep. I poured a concrete floor some 5 inches thick in the bottom of the hole. The concrete aided in holding water and insured that the book pages would lie flat. At the beginning of my tests I failed to use enough paper and two different bullets hit the concrete and flattened out to about the thickness of a quarter. Expansion looked tremendous. Both bullets however, completely failed to expand when they hit an adequate thickness of wet pages. A bullet in tissue will perform very differently than a bullet hitting a very hard object.

The wet phone books produce a very visual impression of a bullet's performance. The hole from a high velocity expanding bullet will be considerably larger than the bullet's actual expanded diameter. The holes left by non-expanding bullets will be quite small. Good expanding bullets will actually cause an eruption of tiny wet particles out of the bullet hole. The width and depth of the bullet hole will be a good indicator of bullet performance. However, for our purposes you simply need to determine if a bullet will reliably expand shot after shot. Therefore I suggest that you test no less than 5 and preferably as many as 15 bullets.

Establishing expansion is essential, as my formula for determining the bullet's Power Index Rating applies a factor for expanding bullets and a different factor for non-expanding, flat nosed bullets and still a different factor for non-expanding, non-flat nosed bullets. My formula also allows for the increased performance of larger diameter bullets. Be certain that you test for expansion at the range (velocity level) for which you wish to determine performance. Some bullets expand well at 7 yards or from a given barrel length, but fail to expand at longer ranges or from shorter barrels.

The formula for the Power Index Rating of handgun ammunition started out as:

$$PIR = \frac{V^2 ETvBg}{(450240 \times 269)} \times Dv$$

In this formula: V = Velocity in feet per second; ETv = an Energy Transfer value; Bg = the Weight of the Bullet in Grains; Dv = A Bullet Diameter value.

The PIR formula retains all the factors involved in obtaining kinetic energy figures $\left(\frac{V^2 Bg}{450240}\right)$, plus it allows for bullet shape and expansion or lack thereof (ETv) and also for basic caliber size (Dv). Additionally, it allows a factor (269) that will bring a specific level of cartridge performance to a value of 100. Most handgun ammunition performance is geared to defensive use, so I have used a constant that will result in a value of 100 for any cartridge/bullet combination that would prove to be highly effective as a man-stopper at short ranges and neither lighter nor heavier than needed.

This value was assessed equal to a 38-caliber bullet of 158 grains, capable of expansion at a muzzle velocity of 875 feet per second. This level of performance is generally accepted by a large number of progressives who have adopted the 38 Special +P 158-grain lead hollow-point load. It is important to realize that if you disagree with this performance level the formula still remains completely accurate. You can simply select a value higher than 100 to represent your minimum acceptable level of cartridge performance.

In the interest of making the formula easier to use, the original values for ETv (Energy Transfer Value) were modified simply by moving the decimal position. This allowed for the constant factor of (450240 × 269) to be reduced to 12111, thus giving a more manageable formula of:

$$PIR = \frac{V^2 ETvBg}{12111} \times Dv$$

As in the earlier formula: V = Velocity in feet per second; ETv = Energy Transfer Value; Bg = Bullet Weight in Grains; Dv = Bullet Diameter Value.

The ETv values were arrived at only after years of research and trial and error applications. These values now used have been proven correct in every conceivable application. They are as follows:

Bullet Type	ETv Value
Bullets that actually expand	.0100
Non-expanding flat-nose bullets	.0085
Other non-expanding bullets	.0075

A bullet qualifies as a non-expanding flat-nosed bullet only if it has a total flat area equal to 60% or more of its diameter. All wadcutter and semi-wadcutter bullets that I have examined qualify for the flat nosed ETv. Almost all other non-expanding bullets have an ETv of .0075. To any "expanding" bullet that does not actually expand should be applied one of the non-expanding ETv's. For instance, the 88-grain Remington Hollow Point 380 Auto bullet that failed to expand in our tests received an ETv of .0075. The Federal 90-grain bullet for the 380 Auto also failed to expand. But it had a relatively flat profile and therefore received an ETv of .0085.

It is vital to the application of the formula that you determine whether or not a bullet expands in your use. You can do so from the included data chart or by actual firing into wet phone books. If the barrel length of your gun is shorter than our test firearm then, due to reduced velocity, a bullet that expanded in our test gun may fail to expand in your shorter barrel. *You must apply the correct ETv value if the formula is to express the real potential of any particular gun/cartridge combination.* For a shorter or longer barrel, an appropriate velocity correction must be made. For my tests and charts I used four-inch barrels for most of the data collection. In some calibers, I have included data for other lengths.

The Dv values for bullet diameters have been proven to be correct in application as follows:

Actual Bullet Diameter	DV Value
.200" to .249"	0.80
.250" to .299"	0.85
.300" to .349"	0.90
.350" to .399"	1.00
.400" to .449"	1.10
.450" to .499"	1.15

Obviously some very fine lines were drawn when establishing the Dv values. However, the values used have been carefully checked against actual performance records. I am unaware of any case where a Power Index Rating derived from the formula did not accurately reflect the performance of a bullet in actual usage.

As an example of the formula's application, let's run through a simple exercise.

Question: How does the 38 Special 95-grain SJHP Remington Factory +P load compare to the 38 Special 158-grain LHP Winchester factory +P load in a three-inch barrel? By measurement, the 95-grain Remington bullet delivers a velocity of 1100 ft/s and the Winchester 158-grain bullet delivers a velocity of 875 ft/s.

To determine our answer we have the following:

$$PIR = \frac{V^2 ETvBg}{12111} \times Dv$$

Remington Bullet

(As specified in a 3" barrel)

$$PIR = \frac{1100^2 \times .0100 \times 95}{12111} \times 1.0$$

$$PIR = \frac{1149500}{12111} \times 1.0$$

Here are a fired and an unfired Speer 100-gr. 9mm bullet, and Winchester 115-gr. Silvertip 9mm's also unfired and fired. Most 9mm Luger expanding bullets perform very well but these two types afford classic expansion every time at all practical ranges.

At extreme ranges, even the superb Winchester 9mm Silvertip hollow point will fail to expand. Here are a 158-gr. 38 Special semi-wadcutter and two 115-gr. 9mm Silvertips. These bullets were loaded to 125-yard velocity; the results illustrate that when velocity gets low enough even the best of expanding bullets fail to work.

PIR = 94.913715 × 1.0
(Round to nearest whole number)

Power Index Rating = 95

Winchester Bullet

(As specified in a 3″ barrel)

$$PIR = \frac{875^2 \times .0100 \times 158}{12111} \times 1.0$$

$$PIR = \frac{1209687.5}{12111} \times 1.0$$

PIR = 99.88337 × 1.0
(Round to nearest whole number.)

Power Index Rating = 100

Therefore, the Winchester load in question will perform at a somewhat (5.3%) higher level than the Remington load. Obviously, in a shorter barrel the results would be somewhat different. In a two-inch barrel, the results would be as follows, given a velocity of 990 ft/s for the Remington bullet, which will still expand, and a velocity of 790 ft/s for the Winchester bullet which also still expands:

Remington Bullet

(As specified in a 2″ barrel)

$$PIR = \frac{990^2 \times .0100 \times 95}{12111} \times 1.0$$

$$PIR = \frac{931095}{12111} \times 1.0$$

PIR = 76.880109 × 1.0

PIR = 76.880109
(Rounded to nearest whole number.)

Power Index Rating = 77

Winchester Bullet

(As specified in a 2″ barrel)

$$PIR = \frac{790^2 \times .0100 \times 158}{12111} \times 1.0$$

$$PIR = \frac{968078}{12111} \times 1.0$$

PIR = 81.42003 × 1.0

PIR = 81.42003
(Rounded to nearest whole number.)

Power Index Rating = 81

Thus a two-inch barrel, in this caliber and with the ammunition being considered, is some 23% less effective than a three-inch barrel.

It can be seen from the above that our formula fully allows for velocity changes, kinetic energy changes, expansion (or lack of expansion) and basic bullet diameters. The formula shows that the heavy lead bullet load was superior to the other in both barrels.

Earlier we stated that the 124-grain FMC 9mm Luger factory load (velocity of 1110 ft/s) possessed almost identical kinetic energy (339 foot pounds) to a 45 Auto 230-grain FMC factory load (velocity of 810 ft/s) with 335 foot pounds. We said that in actual usage the 45 Auto round would outperform the Luger round. Let's apply the PIR formula to both of these loads to see if it reflects the superiority of the 45 load.

$$PIR = \frac{V^2ETvBg}{12111} \times Dv$$

9mm Luger Bullet

(As specified)

$$PIR = \frac{1110^2 \times .0075 \times 124}{12111} \times 1.0$$

$$PIR = \frac{1145853}{12111} \times 1.0$$

PIR = 94.612584 × 1.0

PIR = 94.612584
(Round to nearest whole number)

Power Index Rating = 95

PIR

Formula and Values for Power Index Rating of Handgun Ammunition

$$\text{Power Index Rating: } PIR = \frac{V^2ETvBg}{12111} \times Dv$$

In which:
V = Velocity in feet per second
ETv = Energy Transfer Value
Bg = Bullet Weight in Grains
Dv = Diameter Value of Bullet

ETv Values:

For all bullets that actually expand[1]	= .0100
For non-expanding bullets with a flat nose equal to 60% of diameter	= .0085
For all other non-expanding bullets	= .0075

[1]Determined by actual test at range and velocity for which Power Index Rating is desired.

Dv Values

Actual Bullet Diameter	Value
.200″ to .249″	0.80
.250″ to .299″	0.85
.300″ to .349″	0.90
.350″ to .399″	1.00
.400″ to .449″	1.10
.450″ to .499″	1.15

These three fired Speer 100-gr. 9mm Luger hollow points were recovered from wet phone books at 7 yards. They perform as well or better than most of the bullets the author has tested and so are favorites for hunting varmints with a handgun. They would, of course, attain very high ratings in the PIR System.

45 Auto Bullet

(As specified)

$$PIR = \frac{810^2 \times .0075 \times 230}{12111} \times 1.15$$

$$PIR = \frac{1131772.5}{12111} \times 1.15$$

$$PIR = 93.449963 \times 1.15$$

$$PIR = 107.46746$$
(Round to nearest whole number.)

Power Index Rating = 107

The clear advantage of the 45 Auto in actual usage is indicated by the formula showing it 12.6% more efficient. To further prove our point let's consider a 9mm Luger round loaded with a 115-grain Silvertip Hollow Point to a velocity of 1255 ft/s (a Winchester factory load). This bullet does expand remarkably well.

$$PIR = \frac{V^2ETvBg}{12111} \times Dv$$

$$PIR = \frac{1255^2 \times .0100 \times 115}{12111} \times 1.0$$

$$PIR = \frac{1811278.7}{12111} \times 1.0$$

$$PIR = 149.5564 \times 1.0$$

$$PIR = 149.5564$$
(Round to nearest whole number.)

Power Index Rating = 150

The difference in barrel length with regard to bullet expansion is clearly shown by these photos. The bullets above were fired from a 4-inch revolver and those below from a 3-inch revolver. The loads are identical. The velocity gain in the longer barrel produced classic expansion while the shorter barrel results were almost marginal for expansion, as evidenced by the third bullet.

PIR GUIDELINES

Level	PIR Values	Application
1	24 or less	Loads within this value range should never be used for personal protection. They are suitable only for target shooting and plinking.
2	25 to 54	Loads in this value grouping would require very exact bullet placement if used for personal defense. If a killing shot was not made, your antagonist might only be further enraged. Loads in this group could prove satisfactory for small game but must be considered less than satisfactory for personal defense.
3	55 to 94	Loads within this PIR grouping are somewhat popular as personal defense weapons. However, the experience of many people shows these cartridges to be marginal even when good hits are made. Many police departments are armed with cartridges in this group. However, more than one police officer has lost his life when he was unable to stop an assailant with a load from this group. Loads in this category must be considered at best marginal.
4	95 to 150	Loads fitting in this category will meet the requirements of most military applications. They will also prove adequate for police departments that wish to arm personnel with weapons that are likely to prove effective under almost any situation. These are ideal loads for personal protection. Many police departments are now equipping their men with loads from this grouping.
5	151 to 200	Loads in this range will usually take the fight out of any opponent with only fairly placed hits. However, loads of this power level are difficult to control and most shooters have trouble scoring hits due to the recoil and noise levels. With extensive practice they can be mastered and prove useful to a highly skilled shooter.
6	201 or more	Loads in this category are best described as overkill in self-defense. They are hunting loads best used for protection from bears gone crazy rather than against human opponents. Few shooters can develop the necessary skills to handle the very heavy recoil and noise levels of cartridges with PIR values in the 200 plus range.
PLEASE NOTE:		It is impossible to suggest specific values for any specific application unless all the criteria are known. The above table is offered as a general guideline.

POWER INDEX RATING CHART

CALIBER	BULLET Wgt./Grs.	Brand	Style	POWDER Type	Wgt./Grs.	Barrel Length (Inches)	Velocity in ft/s	Bullet Expansion	Kinetic Energy in Foot Pounds	Power Index Rating
22 Short SV	29	all	LRN	Factory Load		6	865	No	48	11
22 Short HV	29	all	LRN	Factory Load		6	1010	No	66	15
22 Long HV	29	all	LRN	Factory Load		6	1095	No	77	17
22 Long Rifle SV	40	all	LRN	Factory Load		6	950	No	80	18
22 Long Rifle HV	40	all	LRN	Factory Load		6	1060	No	100	22
22 Long Rifle HV	37	CCI	LHP	Factory Load		6	1080	Yes	96	29
22 MRF	40	all	JHP	Factory Load		6½	1480	Yes	195	58
22 Jet	40	Rem.	JSP	Factory Load		8⅜	2100	Yes	392	117
25 Auto	45	Win.	EP	Factory Load		2	835	Yes	70	22
25 Auto	50	Rem.	FMC	Factory Load		2	810	No	73	17
30 Luger	93	all	FMC	Factory Load		4½	1220	No	307	77
32 Short Colt	80	all	LRN	Factory Load		4	745	No	99	25
32 Auto	71	Win.	FMC	Factory Load		4	905	No	129	32
32 Auto	60	Win.	STHP	Factory Load		4	970	Yes	125	42
32-20 WCF	100	Win.	LFN	Factory Load		6	1030	No	237	67
9mm Luger	95	Win.	JSP	Factory Load		4	1355	Yes	387	144
9mm Luger	115	Win.	FMC	Factory Load		4	1155	No	341	95
9mm Luger	115	Win.	STHP	Factory Load		4	1255	Yes	402	150
9mm Luger	115	Fed.	JHP	Factory Load		4	1165	Yes	347	129
9mm Luger	124	Rem.	FMC	Factory Load		4	1110	No	339	95
9mm Luger	100	Speer	JHP	231	5.8	4	1300	Yes	375	140
9mm Luger	125	Speer	JSP	231	5.6	4	1150	Yes	367	136
38 Special + P	95	Rem.	JHP	Factory Load		2	990	Yes	207	77
38 Special + P	95	Rem.	JHP	Factory Load		3	1100	Yes	255	95
38 Special + P	95	Rem.	JHP	Factory Load		4	1175	Yes	291	108
38 Special + P	95	Win.	STHP	Factory Load		2	945	Yes	188	70
38 Special + P	95	Win.	STHP	Factory Load		3	1050	Yes	233	86
38 Special + P	95	Win.	STHP	Factory Load		4	1100	Yes	255	95
38 Special + P	110	all	JHP	Factory Load		2	880	Yes	189	70
38 Special + P	110	all	JHP	Factory Load		3	975	Yes	232	86
38 Special + P	110	all	JHP	Factory Load		4	1020	Yes	254	94
38 Special + P	110	Sierra/Speer	JHP	231	5.9	6	1090	Yes	290	108
38 Special + P	110	Sierra/Speer	JHP	Bullseye	5.4	6	1090	Yes	290	108
38 Special	110	Sierra	JHP	800-X	7.2	3	950	Yes	220	82
38 Special + P	125	all	JHP	Factory Load		4	945	Yes	248	92
38 Special + P	125	Sierra/Speer	JHP	231	5.6	6	990	Yes	272	101
38 Special	125	Sierra	JHP	800-X	6.9	3	875	Yes	213	79
38 Special + P	140	Sierra/Speer	JHP	231	5.5	6	935	Yes	272	101
38 Special + P	158	Win.	LHP	Factory Load		2	790	Yes	219	81
38 Special + P	158	Win.	LHP	Factory Load		3	875	Yes	269	100
38 Special + P	158	all	LHP	Factory Load		4	915	Yes	294	109
38 Special	148	all	LWC	Factory Load		2	525	No	91	29
38 Special	148	all	LWC	Factory Load		3	575	No	109	34
38 Special	148	all	LWC	Factory Load		4	710	No	166	52
38 Special	148	all	LWC	231	3.0	2	550	No	99	31
38 Special	148	all	LWC	231	3.0	3	600	No	118	37
38 Special	148	all	LWC	231	3.0	6	750	No	185	58
38 Special	158	all	LRN	Factory Load		2	630	No	139	39
38 Special	158	all	LRN	Factory Load		3	700	No	172	48
38 Special	158	all	LRN	Factory Load		4	755	No	200	56
38 Special	158	all	LSWC	Factory Load		2	630	No	139	44
38 Special	158	all	LSWC	Factory Load		3	700	No	172	54
38 Special	158	all	LSWC	Factory Load		4	755	No	200	63
38 Special	158	Speer	LSWC	231	4.3	2	655	No	151	48
38 Special	158	Speer	LSWC	231	4.3	3	725	No	184	58
38 Special	158	Speer	LSWC	231	4.3	6	850	No	254	80
38 Special	158	Rem.	LSWC	800-X	5.9	6	880	No	272	86
38 Special	200	all	LRN	Factory Load		2	545	No	132	37
38 Special	200	all	LRN	Factory Load		3	600	No	160	45
38 Special	200	all	LRN	Factory Load		4	630	No	176	49
38 Special	200	Rem.	LRN	800-X	4.6	6	725	No	233	65
38 S & W	145	all	LRN	Factory Load		4	685	No	151	42
357 Magnum	110	all	JHP	Factory Load		4	1295	Yes	410	152
357 Magnum	110	Speer	JHP	231	8.8	6	1370	Yes	459	170
357 Magnum	125	all	JHP	Factory Load		4	1450	Yes	584	217
357 Magnum	125	Speer	JHP	231	8.6	6	1310	Yes	476	177
357 Magnum	140	Speer	JHP	231	8.0	6	1200	Yes	448	166
357 Magnum	158	all	JHP	Factory Load		4	1235	Yes	535	199
357 Magnum	158	Speer	JHP	Unique	8.2	6	1200	Yes	505	188
38 Super + P	130	all	FMC	Factory Load		5	1245	No	448	125
38 Super + P	125	Win.	JHP	Factory Load		5	1280	Yes	455	169
380 Auto	85	Win.	STHP	Factory Load		3	1000	Yes	189	70
380 Auto	88	Rem.	JHP	Factory Load		3	990	No	192	53
380 Auto	90	Fed.	JHP	Factory Load		3	1000	No	200	63
380 Auto	95	all	FMC	Factory Load		3	955	No	192	54
41 Magnum	210	all	JSP	Factory Load		4	1300	Yes	778	322
41 Magnum	210	all	LSWC	Factory Load		4	965	No	434	151
44 Special	246	all	LRN	Factory Load		4	755	No	311	96
44 Magnum	240	all	JHP	Factory Load		4	1180	Yes	742	304
44 Magnum	240	all	LSWC	Factory Load		4	1350	Yes	971	397
44 Magnum	200	Speer	JHP	2400	23.0	7½	1475	Yes	966	395
45 Auto	185	Win.	STHP	Factory Load		5	1000	Yes	411	176
45 Auto	230	all	FMC	Factory Load		5	810	No	335	107
45 Auto	185	all	JWC	Factory Load		5	770	No	244	89
45 Auto	200	Speer	JHP	231	6.3	5	950	Yes	401	171
45 Colt	225	Win.	STHP	Factory Load		5½	920	Yes	423	181
45 Colt	225	Fed.	LHP	Factory Load		5½	900	Yes	405	173
45 Colt	255	all	LRN	Factory Load		5½	860	No	419	134

Abbreviations used for bullet style: **LRN** = Lead Round Nose; **LHP** = Lead Hollow Point; **JSP** = Jacketed Soft Point; **FMC** = Full Metal Case, Round Nose; **STHP** = Silvertip Hollow Point; **LFN** = Lead Flat Nose; **JHP** = Jacketed Hollow Point; **LWC** = Lead Wadcutter; **LSWC** = Lead Semi-Wadcutter; **JWC** = Jacketed Wadcutter; **EP** = Expanding Point.

In this example we find the expanding 115-grain bullet load in the 9mm Luger vastly superior to the 124-grain non-expanding bullet load in the same caliber and also greatly superior to the 45 Auto 230-grain non-expanding bullet. And this is a very real reflection of the various loads' effectiveness in actual usage.

Because the PIR formula takes every possible aspect into account, the use of a wrong value or a wrong velocity can cause serious errors. For this reason, if you wish to compare the Power Index Rating of any given load at 25 or 50 yards (or any other range) you must first determine if your chosen load will offer bullet expansion at the range in question and then apply the correct ETv value. You will also need to know the exact velocity of your load at the range in question. Velocities may be obtained by actual measurement with a chronograph or from various data sources. After you have used it, the Power Index Rating system will prove itself to you as an unfaltering, easy-to-use system that will reflect a bullet's actual performance. *(Please keep in mind that everything connected with the PIR system is copyrighted. Any one is free to use the system; however no commercial application of the PIR may be made without the written consent of the author.)*

The Power Index Rating system has been applied to rifle cartridges wherein a value of 1000 equals an adequate amount of power to kill game of 300 pounds. However, almost all rifle bullets are of the expanding type, so the current kinetic energy levels continue to be fairly accurate appraisals of a load's worth.

I cannot over-stress establishing the actual velocity obtained with your handgun. This is particularly true in guns with three-inch or shorter barrels. In such guns, actual firearm dimensions can cause significant changes in velocities from one handgun to another, even the same brand, model and barrel length.

In testing two two-inch 38 Special revolvers, I found one would give consistent expansion with a 110-grain hollow point load while the other revolver wouldn't expand that or any other tested load. Results in four-inch or longer barrels are far more consistent and one can usually count on similar results from one gun to the next. Velocity averages should be taken from 15-shot strings, at least; 5-shot strings do not reveal average velocities sufficiently.

Bullet expansion does not always occur when one might expect. For example, the new Sierra 125-grain Hollow Point bullets will reliably expand in my three-inch S & W Chief's Special when pushed by 6.9 grains of Du-Pont 800-X. The Sierra 125-grain Soft Point bullet will not show the slightest trace of expansion with the same powder charge. In fact, there is no load that will cause expansion of the Soft Point bullet in that gun. The new Sierra 38/357 Hollow Point bullets with notches cut into the jacket nose have proven to be the very best expanding handgun bullets normally available to reloaders.

In two-inch 38 Specials one must stay with 95 to 110-grain bullets if positive expansion is desired. Very few will offer any expansion with heavier bullets and none of those I

have tested would offer expansion with bullets over 125 grains unless +P loads are used. In three-inch 38 Specials bullets up to 125 grains can usually be made to expand reliably *if* you select the proper bullet and powder charge. +P loads will offer expansion regardless of bullet weight. And in four-inch 38 Specials, bullets up to 140 or 158 grains will often expand if good bullets are used with appropriate powder charges.

Other calibers are equally affected by changes in barrel length.

Please keep in mind +P loads must be avoided in any aluminum frame revolver. Many shooters have found the Speer 110-grain Hollow Point 38 Special ammunition loaded to standard pressures, will offer expansion in three-inch or longer 38 Specials when no other standard pressure ammunition will. This load is worth investigating when you want maximum performance from an alloy frame revolver.

There are a number of good bullets which offer good expansion in handguns of various calibers, properly used. The accompanying chart lists many popular loads for you. If you want to select maximum performance ammunition for your handgun it is up to you to assure, by testing, that the bullet you use will expand. The Power Index Rating system clearly shows only expanding bullets get the maximum potential from a handgun. If a load that interests you is not in the table, apply the PIR formula after determining if the bullet will expand in your gun. ●

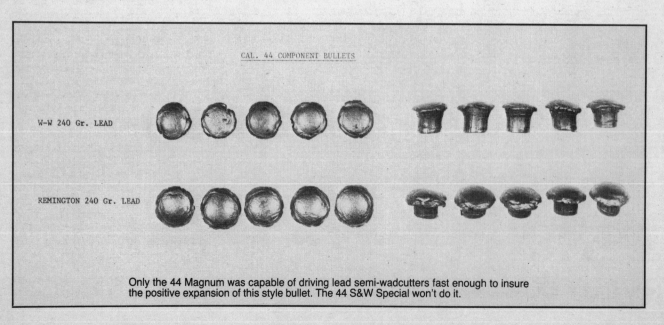

CAL. 44 COMPONENT BULLETS

W-W 240 Gr. LEAD

REMINGTON 240 Gr. LEAD

Only the 44 Magnum was capable of driving lead semi-wadcutters fast enough to insure the positive expansion of this style bullet. The 44 S&W Special won't do it.

AFTER WE WON THE WAR

The next 30 years were a lot easier.

by ROY DUNLAP

AFTER WE saved the world for the democrats the second time, calling it World War Two—the last one we won—99 percent of the two million in uniform wanted out now, and most did not want to go back to the old pre-war jobs, which screwed up things a bit. The incredible total-war organization stopped; the old workers, men and women, wanted out; reconversion to peace-time production meant changing equipment and training workers to replace the ex-soldiers who wanted different occupations now. Everything was in short supply up into 1948—if you wanted a new car, a stove, a Winchester Model 70, forget it for now, get on the list, find a friend in the business. Stores were empty.

I wrote a book for Tom Samworth (Small Arms Publishing Co.) called *Ordnance Up Front.* I think it was his title, not mine. I wrote it while waiting for my new car that my service-manager buddy in Chicago was getting me. Sam proudly showed the manuscript to an army general friend, who confiscated it and held for over a year as having too much information for the public. When it was published, it became a text in all the assorted military survival schools.

Finally, I got the car, accumulated tools, rented a garage in Chicago to work in, made a couple rifles for army friends, and then took off west looking for a climate like that in Egypt. Like, for example, southern Arizona. I took a store gunsmith job in Tucson, rented a room next door to Jack O'Connor's home, traded him out of a 22-250 with one of Keith Stegall's first stocks, and took up varmint hunting, meaning I learned to shoot running jackrabbits at 200 yards and further. It's not as hard as it sounds. I got so I hit one out of three first shot, which broke Jack of his habit of sitting down to shoot. By the time he was planted, I had fired three shots and anything I got three shots at was hit.

The factories were slow getting back into sporting arms and ammunition production, having few experienced workmen. I must have made a few thousand 8x57mm cartridges from 30-06 cases and Vernon Speer's first bullets for the Mausers brought back by the soldiers. Lots of actions used for sporters, of course. Parker Ackley was making barrels in 1947 and had a batch of GI trainee gunsmith students. Some of whom were good stock men, including John Hearn who was very good. He was a young veteran with some war disabilities and quit stock work for health reasons after a few years. I remember shortening a Springfield action to 250-3000 length so he could make himself a small-scale deer rifle in the early 1950s.

The BRNO (Czech) sporters were first imports, I believe—available in 1947. They were very good rifles, first to have integral dovetails on receivers for scope mounting. Lots of ex-servicemen were interested in gunsmithing, so Ackley, Pfeifer, a few others started GI Bill training deals. I think P.O. started the first college program at

$15 to $25, retail. Handguns were $14 to $40, all sorts, from Colt revolvers to Broomhandle Mausers. Lots of custom rifles were made, many not too great in style or finish. And lots of barrel makers started up, learning on the job.

From a weak start in 1948, International shooting slowly grew. I looked at it, and—after realizing that I was probably the best-known gunsmith in the U.S. at the moment and was averaging about $65 a week—said goodbye to the metal work and the

Matches became very popular, and the service rifle, then the M1 Garand, was lacking somewhat in accuracy. So everybody—the Army, the Marines and me—began working on it. I picked the brains of all the experimenting armorers, put those things together, and started from there. I worked out a good system with glass bedding, tight handguards, waterproofed stocks, clearance on metal parts, and so on. I could make the M1's shoot nearly as good as bolt actions.

Ft. Benning sent their shop chief, WO/Glenn Baker, to me for three weeks; the Air Force decided to get into shooting, found a sergeant in Japan who was a good amateur gunsmith on his own time, and sent him in to me. Leon Johnson was head of the Lackland shop until he retired from service and went promptly to Remington's custom shop to make beautiful stocks on the special-order arms. The Marines had their own shop training.

We all swapped information, tools, and parts. My principal point was knowing the shrinkage of the fiberglass resins and milling wood surfaces away to uniform depths so there would be full support when the bedding shrank a little. You couldn't allow high and low spots.

At one and the same time, I was accurizing M1s for service units, base teams, and civilians; I was making free rifles, match rifles and accessories; I was importing from Europe, everything from Finnish leather coats to Russian rapid-fire pistols.

Colt made match auto pistols in 38

I rented a room next to Jack O'Connor's house, traded him out of a 22-250 . . .

Trinidad State Junior College in Colorado, which is still one of the very best gunsmithing schools.

Samworth wanted me to update Baker's *Modern Gunsmithing*, which was the only usable gunsmithing text; Howe's fine two-volume job was nice to look at, but nearly worthless to the average shop or to the amateur. Only, from experience, I knew Baker's book was not so good. Formula might say '30 minutes' when correct time was about 45 seconds. Clyde Baker was never a professional. He was a good amateur, greatly interested, and an advertising writer by trade. I refused to compound the errors, and spent several months writing my own book *Gunsmithing* which pretty well covered the subject. It must be OK as it's now in about the 12th printing. I wish I had royalties on it, but I sold it outright to Samworth for $5,000 in advance, good money in 1948. I was just married and broke.

After 1950, we were in pretty good shape. Fabrique Nationale, Husqvarna, other European makers were sending in good rifles; Beretta was furnishing pistols; U.S. makers were back in production. Remington brought out the 721 and 722 rifles, their first self-designed bolt actions. The 722 was instantly popular, being the first medium-length since the Savage 1920, long gone. Both lengths sold well having good triggers, not too heavy, and the price was right. I found I could remodel the hinged forged trigger guards from Japanese 6.5mm Arisaka rifles to fit the 722 and made a few presentable custom rifles from them.

Foreign surplus came in an ever-increasing flood. Rifles, actions, were

sporters and went into target equipment. I went to the world matches in Venezuela in 1954, wrote them up for *The American Rifleman* (February, 1955). However, the *Rifleman* did not print the second half of my writeup, which proved a mistake. In it, I foresaw the building boom around cities and recommended that all shooters—handgun, rifle, shotgun—form associations, financed to buy large tracts of land so that all types of safe ranges could be built with recreational facilities for family participation.

The Great Western firm in California put out a copy of the Colt Single Action Army revolver, a very good copy of very good steel, which I believe eventually prompted Colt to get back into production on the model.

Foreign surplus came in an ever-increasing flood. Rifles, actions, were $15 to $25 . . .

Ruger was making his 22 auto and 22 single action, getting set to become one of the great arms makers. High Standard was flourishing, showing new models yearly. Smith & Wesson began their good revolvers again, and target shooting boomed. I was a Referee on pistol, smallbore, and high power except when I was shooting myself. I was mainly in high power, fighting with top experts twenty years younger than I, with better eyes to begin with. I set a few national records, but on the whole, I was the country's top second-rater for twenty years.

In the middle 1950s, the National

Special and 38 AMU as well as 45 caliber that would really shoot. The revolvers faded from the firing lines. Smith & Wesson came out with a 22 match pistol that was good; High Standard had several models, too; and the Colt 22s could not compete. Today a Match Woodsman is just a plinking pistol or an item for a Colt collector.

Winchester began to go downhill in the '60s. Sales people evidently dominated the engineers. There were a lot of new and not-so-good 22s. In 1964, the Model 70 was discontinued, but the model number kept for a cheaper replacement type. They weren't selling as many rifles as was Remington, and it did not occur to the idiots to keep the old 70, double the price, make it a premium rifle, like the deluxe FN's, and such.

Cheaper materials were experimented with and there are people now wondering why their 94 won't take a reblue job, or why the carbine they bought at the discount house has some stamped parts inside while the ones from the gun store have forged ones. Today, under new management, it appears that the good features of the original M70 rifle are slowly returning. The feeble extractor on the Winchester post-64 70—and Remington 700, for that matter—have finally surfaced through the advertising to reach public awareness. The old M70 Winchester rifle was not perfect, but it was the highest development of the Mauser system, with locking, extractor and trigger system superior to any other manually-operated rifle.

The companies have a spotty track record for service as well as products. Around 1949 or 1950 they decided that reloading was cutting into their profits too much, so Winchester, Remington, Western all quit selling primers and other components. Dick Speer immediately announced he was preparing to make cases and primers. And did. The company is now CCI. Federal started selling primers, too.

The late 1960s saw the 1968 restrictive gun law come into effect, the start of inflation in Europe and the beginning of steady raises in gun and ammunition prices. The Viet Nam war went on for a decade, influenced the military small-arms thinking of the

Metallic Silhouette rifle match in Tucson. Today the sport has more competitors than all other rifle and pistol shooting sports combined. Now rifles, handguns and scopes are made especially for it.

Except for the high cost of everything, resulting from the worldwide inflation, I think the shooter of the 1980s pretty well off. He has by far the greatest variety of arms of all types available since modern shooting began. Even loading equipment gives so many choices everyone can be confused. Superb optical equipment like the positive-adjusting Weaver T system, imported scopes like the matchless Kahles and Zeiss models, and the vast choice of U.S.-made scopes make catalog-browsing a pleasure. On mounts, we ain't so well off. Nothing as good as the Tilden of 25 years ago is being made. We have a half-dozen or more skilled barrelmakers, plus even more specializing in muzzleloader barrels.

In gunsmithing, I think we have a bad gap. We have many, many more top-grade custom men, such as Fred Wells, who can actually make actions and complete rifles of superb quality, custom makers of all sorts of modern arms, and in the muzzle-loading field, men such as Bivens, Mandarino,

Consider that a union carpenter makes over $16 per hour, that a custom stock can take 100 hours of highly-skilled labor. And an engraver's pay-per-hour isn't going to figure out a hell of a lot more than a tool and die man, or even a master machinist.

I mentioned a gap: We have a great shortage of good everyday gunshop repair gunsmiths, men who can put a broken gun back into using condition, fix trigger pulls on all types of arms, make repeaters repeat. I was both, and I think it takes longer to learn general gunsmithing than custom work. You work on old, often unfamiliar rifles, pistols, shotguns. And make parts that cannot be bought. You make flat springs.

The gunsmithing schools turn out capable smiths, but we have a new semi-pro would-be gunsmith type that often doesn't even buy gunsmithing books. They don't even know how to take an unfamiliar arm apart, or where to find obsolete parts or make them. Or even where to get gunsmithing tools and supplies. They scar up a lot of good guns: The post-WW II gunsmith population of 1950-60-70 working years, like me, just died off or retired.

Shooting for fun—plinking, groups from bench, etc., is a big thing now. Formal target shooting has become a very expensive game—match 22 cartridges can cost you fourteen cents each, for example. Hunting is not too great in most areas of the country, as of course it is seasonal, and the number of hunters increases yearly, making good hunting grounds pretty crowded. The metallic silhouette game, (high-power rifle, 22 rifle and handgun of many types) seems a great outlet, and does not have to cost as much as many of its participants believe—custom equipment is not really needed.

One thing the handgun silhouette program has done is to produce some hitherto unheard-of power. Rifle calibers, no limit, come in bolt action and single-shot type arms; now there are super-magnum revolver and auto cartridges. I'm not sure if they are really worthwhile, but they sure can be fun to try! It all was before.

... it did not occur to the idiots to keep the old 70, double the price ...

Personally, I don't think survival necessarily means guerilla warfare.

world, and made a generation of young men believe in paramilitary weapons and firepower. Witness the vast number of semi-auto military type "rifles" such as the AR-15, Mini-14, the countless foreign-made ones, even the AK-47, available. And all these arms sell—we got a lot of weekend commandoes and survival types buying them. Personally, I don't think survival necessarily means guerilla warfare.

Scope sights became universal on everything, even handguns for hunting, and metallic silhouette shooting. In April, 1968, I ran a Mexican-type

Alexander and a half-dozen others are artists equal if not superior to Manton, Nock and Egg, the original English masters, and far better than the American colonial gunsmiths who, after all, weren't trying to be artists, just gunmakers. There are a hundred men in the country who can make top-quality "using" replica antiques. We got better tools and better barrels than the old-timers had.

We have so many super-good custom stockmakers and gun engravers I wouldn't try to mention even one. Prices on both engraving and stock work are high, but not out of reason.

●

NEW SHARPS RIFLE INFORMATION INSIDE!

J THOMPSON

From the beginning, Swanson evoked the
Sharps heritage. This picture is the cover
of the first brochure.

the Colt

SHARPS Story

The old name had a chance once again, but it didn't go.

by LES BOWMAN

On SEPTEMBER 12, 1848, a patent was granted to Christian Sharps for a single shot breech-loading rifle, the forerunner of the Sharps rifle later so important in the West. Nearly 100 years later, the West saw the Sharps reborn.

As a young boy in Eastern Kansas, Arthur L. Swanson's interest in hunting and shooting started with ownership of some 22 rifles and in single-barrel shotguns. An uncle who lived near Bly, Oregon where Swanson spent his summers and other visiting periods encouraged him. The uncle, a collector of all makes and types of guns, never failed to answer the endless stream of questions about firearms. By the age of six, Swanson could quote ballistics though he could not read, and had been well instructed in gun safety, handling, and use. And in 1968, after working at it for 15 years, he incorporated the new Sharps Arms Co.

Swanson's compelling reason for pursuing this dream was to see one of the most famous names in firearms history, a company instrumental in the development of the cartridge rifle as we know it today, return to production. Sharps rifles had been involved with nearly every event in the settlement of the West from the California Gold Rush to the passing of the Indian, the buffalo, and the open range. Sharps was also a winner at International matches and had continued to win at Creedmoor long after the first company was out of existence. It was a very worthwhile rifle, Swanson believed.

Swanson had studied engineering and drafting in college. He worked in civilian life in unrelated fields for the most part, except when he ran a sporting goods store. He read and studied firearms design and ballistics and was an active hunter, shooter and handloader.

In 1966, while working on the Pacific Coast as a marketing and sales consultant, Swanson met some people connected with a national sales organization based in Salt Lake City. The company was called EMDEKO, and the president was interested in adding a line of firearms and related equipment. With the legal aspects cleared in 1967, the new Sharps Arms Co. was incorporated with the financial backing of Emdeko Corporation and with the agreement that Emdeko Corp. would finance the Sharps project. Swanson was in Salt Lake City in early 1968 to work out plans for setting up the new company, and met P. O. Ackley, one of America's best-known, most knowledgeable gun men. Swanson asked Ackley if he knew of any local engineering firms that might make up prototypes based on his drawings and plans.

A firm was suggested, a meeting with heads of the organization arranged, and a decision to proceed with the prototype work was made. The company tried, to the extent of their knowledge, to fulfill the contract and did produce five working actions, but they just did not have the expertise for the job. Two of the actions shot acceptably well, the other three only fairly well.

After this setback, Ackley and Swanson made a fast trip to the eastern United States. This time, the shop which agreed to accept the work was one of the best in the country—Bellmore-Johnson. With a modern new shop and equipment, excellent engineers and a world of past experience they were given the top priority job of design: the interior of the action. Special emphasis was placed on the extractor and ejection system.

The late Carl Coliander and Bob Hillberg, both engineers, were responsible for the rolling cam mechanism, turning in needle bearings, and for the extractor and lever cam arrangement. The work would leave space for the trigger Matt Canjar designed. Swanson had done the specifications for all the other action work. And the stock work and design, originally attempted by a midwest stocker, finally was done by Wysowski Bros. of Connecticut.

The plan was to introduce the new Sharps at the National Sporting Goods Association show in January, 1969, in Houston, a very short period of time for such a project. From May, 1968, with the formation of the corporation, to the 1969 Houston show, all of the work and assembly was accomplished. This included organizing a staff, setting up manufacturing facilities and a proposed sales organization, assembling all advertising and promotion—even travelling to show prototypes—for the initial showing as well as future use. Plans were also in the making for the development of a line of Sharps cartridges, handloading components and other spin-off products. Swanson was almost solely responsible for all these operations

Bowman, making field tests, shot rock chucks in Wyoming with a production model Sharps 78 rifle assembled in Salt Lake City plant.

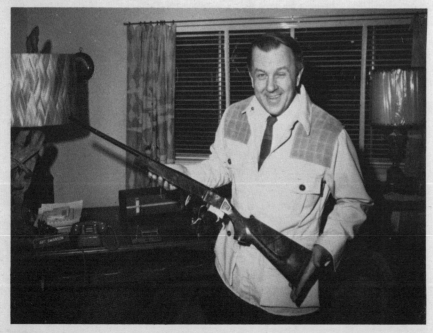

Happy Art Swanson, the man responsible for the Sharps resurrection, holds a presentation rifle from Colt.

and was the one who put together the advertising brochures and advance information.

Six prototypes had been planned for the Houston show. They were numbered from 001 to 006, and were to be 30-40 Krag, 220 Swift, 45-75 Sharps, 30-06 Gov't, 375 H&H, 9.3x74R. All except the 30-40 Krag had 30-inch barrels; it was 26 inches. As it turned out, #006 in 9.3x74R was the only gun for which all parts were available in the allotted time. The advertising photos and the Houston showing featured this #006 rifle.

The forend supports were changed after the first group of six rifles to get a better looking fit. The second group of six prototype rifles numbered from 2001 to 2006, and were respectively: 17 Sharps Magnum, 26-inch barrel; 22-250, 26-inch barrel; 220 Swift, 30-inch barrel; 25-06 Remington, 30-inch barrel; 50-70 Sharps, 30-inch barrel; 30-06, 36-inch barrel. The last rifle, #2006, was originally planned as a 300 H&H, but was changed to 30-06 Gov't when a chamber reamer in 300 H&H proved defective.

The barrel contours were Swanson's design, as he states, "For better or for worse." All rifles made at the Emdeko plant in Salt Lake City had Ackley barrels. These twelve were the last guns put together in Salt Lake City. Except for the barrel work, all the manufacturing of the guns was done in Connecticut.

When Swanson joined forces with Emdeko to build the Sharps rifles he had anticipated the company being able to supply sufficient finances to equip a small factory. Plans were to have most parts made in the East by specialty shops, and to put machines, workers and expertise to do all the barrel work and assembly in Salt Lake City. P. O. Ackley owned his relatively small shop for barrel making and general gunsmithing. It was located on his personal property in the Dalt Lake area. It was, however, not large enough to handle the necessary barrel making, assembly work, and such which would be required if the new Sharps rifle became as popular as expected.

Emdeko made P. O. Ackley a proposition to buy the P. O. Ackley Company, including the name, which was well known throughout North America. They would hire Ackley to run the factory end. This deal was consummated and the industrial machine tools which P. O. had were moved to a large section of the Emdeko Company's warehouse. A large section of offices were set aside there for the use of Sharps personnel. New barrel making machines were procured to make barrels by the button rifling process for the Sharps rifles in all calibers planned to be produced. Also, barrel making for the gun trade was anticipated.

Swanson wanted to make the new Sharps rifles, particularly the ones chambered for modern cartridges, very accurate. He had drawn up accuracy specifications covering most of the modern calibers and they were very close to what the best top factories or custom gunmakers would offer on custom made and finished rifles, not production guns.

Swanson had been collecting single-shot rifles and had nearly a hundred of them. A primary reason was that he wanted to make comparative tests to determine what could be expected from a single shot in the areas of accuracy and maximum load performance. Included in this collection were four highwall actions, two Remington Hepburn actions, a Stevens 44½, all in excellent condition; and he had two dozen Model 1902 Remington Rolling Block actions in "like new" condition.

These were part of the basis for test work over a twelve-year period. Tests, using the long-barreled rifles, were made with Dupont and Hercules cannister powders and with early Hodgdon powders, including 4831. Swanson was convinced that using the longest barrel possible while keeping over-all length at usable proportions was highly desirable.

His tests showed there is a general increase or decrease of velocity in all cartridges in barrel lengths from 18 inches on the short side to 26 inches on the long end of the scale. Such velocities would vary from as little as 6 to 10 feet per inch of increased barrel length to as much as 70 feet per inch. In barrel lengths over 26 inches, particularly from 28 to 32 inches, with certain high intensity cartridges and slow burning powder, velocities could be increased as much as 100 feet per added inch of barrel length. All these tests were not concerned with accuracy, but with velocity.

Swanson was also encouraged by similar barrel length tests which P. O. Ackley had made and included in his published handbooks. Most of these high velocity gains were made with barrel lengths of from 28 to 31 inches. The author has also personally made many such velocity tests using barrels of 31 and occasionally 32 inches. My long-barrel late model Colt-Sharps rifle in 270 caliber will deliver

The Bellmore-Johnson Tool Company plant at Hamden, Connecticut. Their engineers were responsible for the high quality action of the Sharps rifle.

The author did some bench time on the project. Here he is assembling a rifle in Salt Lake City.

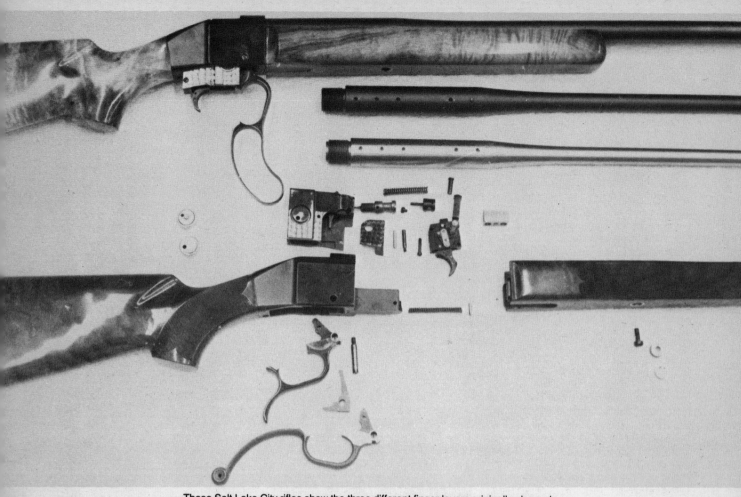

These Salt Lake City rifles show the three different finger levers originally planned.

3,500 fps with a 130-grain bullet and no apparent excessive pressure.

By using the shortest possible action, it was determined the Sharps Model 78 could achieve an advantage over standard length bolt actions of between 5½-inch to six inches. The Sharps with a 30-inch barrel, has the same approximate length over-all as the standard Winchester Model 70 or a Remington Model 700 with 24-inch barrel.

With the original few new Sharps rifles it was apparent that barrel quality was going to be a problem. It was thought, however, that all this could be taken care of in due time.

Unfortunately, it soon became apparent the Emdeko financing would be far short of what was really necessary for the production of this rifle, or any of the ammunition and components as planned. The money situation became acute and friction developed among management.

Fortunately, a prospective buyer for the company had materialized. Shortly after the first 12 rifles were completed, Colt's Firearms Division of Colt Industries had become inter-

ested. Swanson had his first meeting with Colt people in May, 1969. Colt Firearms Division sent management personnel to Salt Lake City to look the company over and report. Gordon Walker, then President of Colt's Firearms Division, made a special trip to Salt Lake City to talk with Emdeko Company's management and make a final on-the-spot evaluation.

The result was the purchase of the Sharps Rifle Company; all development so far accomplished, most of the prototype rifles, and especially the Sharps name and all patents which had been developed by the engineers of Bellmore-Johnson and assigned to the Sharps Company and owners.

They did not buy the barrels or other parts made for the Sharps in Salt Lake City by the P. O. Ackley Company. And they did not buy any machine tools or equipment. All the equipment in the Salt Lake plant was the property of Emdeko and their P. O. Ackley Company.

Only two employees of the Emdeko Company were hired by Colt's Firearms Division as consultants for the newly formed Sharps Rifle Company

Division of Colt's Firearms. One was Art Swanson and the other was Les Bowman.

The modern Sharps rifle as assembled and sold by Colt's Firearms Division was definitely not a revamped Borchardt. The only real similarity was the pure falling block action. The action externally followed the line of the Borchardt. Internally, it was and still is the most modern single-shot rifle in the United States. Expensive needle bearings at the most crucial point in the new action prevent friction; it is the slickest and easiest to operate of any ever made: and it was made from the finest 4140 steel, beefed up in the walls. It was amply strong enough to take any cartridge made in the United States up to and including the 458 Winchester.

The rush to get the rifle in production had frozen the design; the possible upgrading of the extractor and one or more other improvements were planned for later development.

Any rifle made for modern United States ammunition must really have as near perfect as possible material, design, and workmanship in the bar-

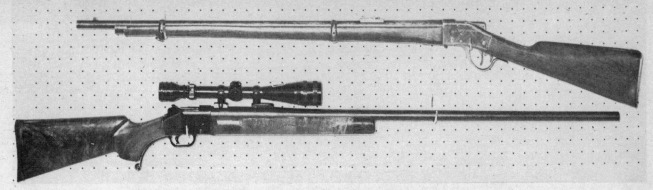

The first Emdeko Sharps (bottom) produced for the 1969 Houston Show is shown with an old Sharps Borchardt. The family resemblance was intentional.

A Colt Sharps with the forend off and the lever down. Bowman was never happy with the forend hanger you see here.

rel. Swanson had visualized using premium quality barrels made by Ed Shilen or made and used by Remington Arms Company on their custom rifles.

One of the first things Colt's did was send men to one or more barrel makers to secure prices on barrels for the various planned Sharps calibers, in fair quantities. Although very strict on external specifications and measurement, Colt's purchasing department admitted, later, that no internal specifications for barrels were stressed, other than caliber and chambering. Price was of primary importance, with no quality requirements. Internal specifications were not included in any orders given to the barrel makers nor did they suggest any.

Gordon Walker and Paul Benke, top Colt officials, were both excellent shooters. They were very interested in the new Sharps and shared Swanson's desire that the new rifle should be one of the most accurate in the field. Barrel quality would be the main factor to achieve this goal.

In the meantime, barrel shipments from one company were received and readied for use. Parts from Bellmore-Johnson were in stock in quantities sufficient to start assembling rifles in different calibers as soon as they were polished and blued. To test the assembled rifles, it was necessary to drive to a range. Subsequently, a one-bench 100-yard shooting tube was made available at West Hartford. It proved invaluable in finding out exactly what the accuracy limits of the newly assembled rifles were because shooting conditions through the tube were always perfect.

Some of the barrels in shipments from one of the companies were rejected after inspection at the Colt's factory by experts using the best of checking equipment. Barrels from another barrel maker were checked, in several different calibers, and proved excellent.

On assembly, the rifles with action parts from Bellmore-Johnson which were exactly the dimensions and tolerances asked for on the Colt drawings for these parts proved them to be entirely too loose. It was found Colt factory men had polished those parts down considerably before blueing. The people in charge of that department were over-zealous in trying to get a quality finish on all parts. This severe polishing was particularly noticeable on the critical action parts, such as the falling block.

The plan had been to send demonstration rifles to all the principal firearms editors and writers for their tests and evaluations. Complimentary write-ups in gun and outdoor magazines were anticipated, and the guns had been sent. Shortly, letters began to come back about the critical action parts and it was too late to do anything. Assemblers did pick and choose parts from the supply which would minimize the error. The drawings given to Bellmore-Johnson should have carried a notation that certain surfaces must accommodate the polishing procedure.

When the project was first started at Emdeko, a questionnaire survey of the firearms writers/editors group had been made, asking them for their criticism, their preferences, and such.

The survey produced the following answers and suggestions:

Les Bowman, P. O. Ackley, firearms and ballistics expert, and the late Warren Page, shooting editor for *Field & Stream* (left to right) are here inspecting several modern Sharps rifles at the Chicago NSGA Show in the first year.

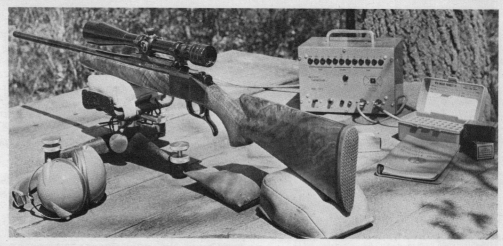

This set-up was for John Amber's Creedmoor Farm test of the Colt Sharps rifles in the 1972 GUN DIGEST. Three rifles looked good, but Amber's test crew did not shoot up to the Sharps' guarantee.

In May of 1969, Art Swanson (left) on his rounds called on John Amber's Chicago office to show the Sharps 78 samples.

- Most of the group felt single-shot rifles could be used on game as well as for varmints and targets.
- Most of them also felt a top rated single-shot could be used for all classes of game, except for dangerous game.
- Many felt a single stage quality trigger, fully adjustable, was necessary for either varmints or game.
- Most answers signified a very accurate nine-pound rifle was not too heavy.
- Almost all wanted varmint calibers to shoot well under one minute of angle. From 25-06 on up, most wanted minute of angle performance. The consensus was a desire for accuracy regardless of price.
- None of the group wanted an automatic safety.
- And none wanted barrels on such a gun any shorter than 26 inches.

This indicated accuracy had to be considerably better than for production bolt action rifles, therefore it was necessary to plan on quality barrels. Run of the mill production barrels would not do. After a thorough study, it was agreed that varmint calibers should shoot in the minute of angle class. Hunting rifles, from 25-06 to 30-06 calibers, should hold groups to an average of 1¼-inch, none wider than 1½-inch. These specifications were to be met with properly assembled handloads using the best grade and make bullets, as the Remington Custom Shop did.

Because of an unexpected problem during inspection of incoming barrels, a rush order to the tooling department was made by the inspectors and engineering officers for a special rifling twist gauge which would inspect the consistency and twist of rifling all the way through the length of a barrel. Such a tool was made up at considerable expense. With this tool it was discovered that some barrels showed a gain or loss, and in a few cases both, within the length of a barrel. This caused considerable furor and a cancellation of the entire order. The manufacturer flew into Hartford, and his first statement to management and engineers was to the effect that no such design as the Sharps could ever be made to produce accuracy as indicated by the writers/editors group.

When the barrel problem was found, some of the Sharps staff had asked another barrel maker to visit the factory and give his opinions and advise. This man was Ed Shilen, of Shilen Rifles, Inc., who is considered a very knowledgeable accuracy authority. After considerable discussion and conversation, Ed Shilen stated he would withhold his opinion until he could make his own tests. He arranged to take several actions and stocks home with him. There he would install his own barrels to do the testing.

He stated at the time that he was doubtful any run-of-the-mill barrels, directly from the machines, would "cut the mustard." He also indicated he was uncertain how much additional handwork (lapping) would be necessary or what the cost would be to obtain the required results.

At his shop he made several barrels in different calibers, and had one of his employees, experienced in hand-lapping, smooth them out. This took an average of 45 minutes handwork per barrel. These were installed on the actions he had brought from the factory and then tested on the bench.

One of the actions was setup in 222 Remington caliber, with a barrel which received the same short handlap treatment as the other barrels. Ed Shilen took it to a benchrest meet at Dallas, Texas and personally shot the rifle. He made five groups of .511—.497—.395—.432—.273 at 100 yards, for an average of .471-inch.

Off-the-machine barrels, given an average of 45 minutes of hand work, could definitely be counted upon to produce the fine quality, consistent accuracy which was desired for the new Sharps rifles. And at an advance in barrel cost of less than ten dollars.

The late Warren Page had been asked to write a critique on the first three Sharps rifles sent to him for evaluation. Page was an experienced and winning National benchrest shooter. His report stated he believed Sharps barrels should come from companies like Hart or Shilen.

The foregoing is not a first person account. My participation in all this started in 1969, when a representative for Swanson and the Emdeko Company brought two prototype modern Sharps rifles to Cody, Wyoming, where my wife and I were living. From this point on, though, I will be writing about my personal participation and observations relative to the new Sharps rifle project.

To pick up on the barrel problems and situation: I knew Remington Arms Co. could make very acceptable barrels which would meet Sharps' most stringent specifications. However, they had never taken outside jobs of this nature for anyone. I went to Ilion, New York, to spend the night and talk with Mike Walker, a top engineer for Remington, in whose province this was.

We discussed the problem. There were only two barrel makers, we agreed, likely to fill such specifications consistently. Then Walker completely surprised me by stating that if I would submit specifications, interior and exterior, he would see that a quotation was made to Sharps for such barrels.

I reported to Gordon Walker, of Colt-Sharps, about my talk with Mike and he was very pleased. When he presented the idea to the Colt engineers, however, they promptly vetoed it, I was told. They felt if the word got out in the industry that Remington barrels were used, this would work against Colt's prestige. They flatly refused the offer.

I felt certain Gordon Walker was as disappointed as I was. Remington, at the time, were making some of the finest barrels in the country for their own rifles, both production and custom guns as well as recognized excellent competition 40-X rifles. Remington's prices would no doubt have been equal to or above Shilen's charge for his work. It may have been well worth the price, but we'll never know.

The Colt-Sharps rifle was and is a more expensive rifle to build than any other single-shot so far produced. The needle bearings and other costly parts in the action and the fine custom trigger by Matt Canjar assured a quality product. These would have been out of place on an ordinary production rifle with run-of-the-mill accuracy and mediocre stock wood.

To bolster my contentions, I called the late Lenard M. Brownell. He had operated his gun business near Sheridan, Wyoming, when Martie and I had our Cody ranch, and Len had worked for me a number of times as a big game guide. He was then a gunstock maker by trade and one of the very best. His custom gun metal work was also top rank.

Lenard had met Bill Ruger, of Sturm, Ruger & Co., when Bill came to our ranch for a pack-in big game hunting trip. Some years later, Ruger hired Brownell to move east and take over Ruger stock work and stock design for all Ruger rifles. Lenard was living in the east during our phone visit.

I told Lenard I was having trouble getting barrels. When I asked him what size groups run-of-the-mill barrels on the Ruger Number One would produce, he said, "Darn it, Les, from one half inch to four inches."

And then he explained:

The most accurate twist gauge Bowman ever saw, designed by Colt and built by their tool men. It could read gain or loss (or both) of twist the length of the barrel.

Bob Hillberg (left), engineer and Howard Johnson, co-owner of Bellmore Johnson, inspecting a Colt Sharps rifle and action.

The dealer price list really rang the Western chimes, showing a happy Sharps-toting Indian watching a new Sharps being unpacked.

Bowman with his 270 Sharps Presentation rifle, given to him by Gordon Walker of Colt.

"For instance," he said, "the first gun sent to Warren Page for his own use shot well under one inch, consistently."

Lenard had to test more than a dozen to get that one. In answer to my question of what happened to the other barrels, he told me they went on production guns. Such a procedure was necessary in order to produce a low-cost rifle.

Clyde Hart was making his famous benchrest barrels, all in stainless steel, and all fully hand lapped to bench rest quality. He had a small shop and his barrel prices nearly doubled that which Sharps could reasonably afford to put on their proposed single-shot. So our search for a barrel maker of quality work left Ed Shilen as the only real source of affordable supply. Sharps was getting the run-of-the-mill barrel from the one company they were dealing with at about half the price Shilen would have to charge for a barrel with interior specifications which would meet all of Sharps requirements.

In getting together a considerable supply of different caliber Sharps rifles for the editor/writer group, I personally shot over 100 rifles. I was able to pick out about 35 to 40 which would qualify. Using the best bullets available in handloads, I was able to stay well under one-inch groups for the varmint calibers and under 1¼-inch for the hunting calibers. Some of these guns shot in the half-inch to ¾-inch category consistently. In the year and some months I was in Hartford with Colt, I put a total of 35,000 rounds through Sharps rifles in one year of testing.

Swanson and I both knew that ultimately a new or double extractor would be a great improvement. It would undoubtedly require a large and costly change in the basic action. It could come later. Also, an entirely different forend hanger was desirable. Ed Shilen and I discovered that eliminating the then-current two-piece hanger and using two screws through escutcheons, directly into the barrel, worked much better. Indeed, early Salt Lake Sharps were put together that way.

Friction between Colt management and personnel in engineering and related departments had been growing. Long entrenched engineers did not want any "come latelies" interfering. No one in these departments was what could be called a shooter and top-flight rifle accuracy was practically unknown to any of them. The old crowd appeared to resent the Presi-

dent, Gordon Walker, for buying the Sharps program. Swanson was getting the cold shoulder, and had little or no help to further his various proposed projects such as the ammunition program for the old Sharps calibers.

I had personally gone East for an expected three or four months as a consultant. Martie was at our home in Utah. The commuting was tiresome and time-consuming. I was happy to finish my work and return to the West.

Bellmore-Johnson had made up enough parts for approximately 450 rifles. When I left, the company planned to assemble these rifles and then survey the program before going further. Colt's engineers were interested in a new German-made bolt action by Sauer, to be manufactured entirely in Germany. They were putting a lot of emphasis on this project.

Prices of everything had started rising and a single-shot which was originally planned to sell for $200.00 to $300.00 was now probably going to have a price tag of $750.00 to $800.00, maintaining the quality as projected for the modern Sharps. Interest in a single-shot rifle was strong, although it had not caught the public fancy as it has now in the 1980's.

Apparently no one knows if Colt will ever re-establish the Sharps program. My last contact with the company revealed they had no idea what they would do with the project, but that it was not for sale at that time. Top management has changed several times since the Sharps was in the making.

Most owners are probably holding those 450 rifles as investments. The last I have heard, the going price was upward from $2,500.00. In any caliber, the Sharps is a top using rifle and will no doubt appreciate in value from now on, wither as an excellent hunting rifle or a valuable collectible.

One of the last projects before I completed my work was to build 12 presentation rifles. These were assembled from carefully picked action parts which did, by careful work, polish out for bluing without developing any noticeable looseness when assembled. They had benchrest quality barrels by Shilen, of standard steel, not stainless. The stocks were of carefully selected California Claro or California Walnut woods in excellent pattern.

The twelve rifles were in different standard calibers from 17 up to and including 458. They had some engraving on the actions and the trap door

butt plates. With 28-inch barrels these rifles all shot excellent groups.

Knowing that I was a strong fan of the 270 Winchester, Gordon Walker presented me with the only 270 in the bunch. It has been a consistent minute of angle rifle during the 12 years I have owned and used it.

The only changes I made to it was to free the rear of the forend from the action and to add escutcheons and screws, spaced three inches apart to hold the forend on. As it was originally, the rifle threw occasional flyers. It no longer does that. In fact, I have taken this rifle on trips to Northern British Columbia for sheep and goat and it has yet to be shot twice at any one animal.

One more fine point for the gun and barrel: I have always used 130-grain bullets in 270s. The velocity as shown by either of my reliable Oehler chronographs, using factory 130-grain Winchester Silvertip loads, is right at 3,275 fps. Careful handloads register an even 3,500 fps.

For the record, this fine Colt-Sharps rifle is not for sale, not in my lifetime. It is one of my two or three all-time favorites. ●

Editor's Note

In the summer of 1969, the staff of *Gunfacts Magazine* entertained Art Swanson and three Sharps 78 rifles at Fairfax Rod and Gun Club in Virginia. It was a nice party, duly reported in the magazine.

The guns were out of that first Salt Lake six—a 30-06, a 220 Swift and a 9.3x74mm. The 30-06 shot remarkably well. One staffer—this writer—shot a 5-shot ¾-inch group with it. Everybody went under an inch; indeed, down to ⁹⁄₁₆-inch.

And we took them apart and the late Fred Davis and Chuck Lanham and I were most impressed all around. The plans Swanson had would have been simply marvelous, but it didn't work out.

It *was* possible to say, back then in '69, of the hoped-for Sharpses to come: "If those rifles measure up to the standards of these sample rifles, we will have a worthy successor to the original Sharps-Borchardt in the technical sense, and a rifle worth calling a Sharps from any point of view one cares to take."

And so it might have been, but wasn't.   *Ken Warner*

The engraved silver buttplate
of the story.

There is a 101st Gentleman!

"C'est moi, c'est moi, it is I," as Lancelot
so modestly proclaimed as he entered
stage right in "CAMELOT."

by ROGER BARLOW

This depiction of Hornsey Wood Shooting Ground in the late 1850s shows a competitor with a
flintlock, to judge from the flash at the breech area. It is unlikely many shooters used such guns,
fast flying birds being far too difficult to hit with such a slow-to-ignite gun. The breech-loading pinfire gun was just coming into use but was thought to be less "hard shooting" than the solid-breech
muzzleloader.

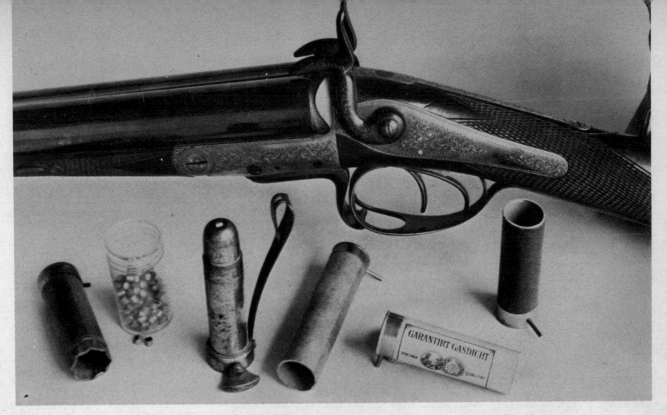

The Purdey pinfire is in remarkably good condition after well over a century. At a time when virtually every American shotgunner was still using a percussion muzzleloader, Europeans were shooting with breech-loading pinfires. The invention was largely the creation of Lefaucheux, a Paris gunmaker. In the 1840s another Frenchman, Houllier, invented the base wad to render this type of cartridge case more gas-tight, and it has been doing this for every shotshell since then up to the advent of the plastic hull of today. Pinfire cases are still available in many parts of Europe and reloads, and the author reloads his fired cases with a modern crimp closure. The tool (third item from left) is a device for repriming fired cases with the little percussion caps. (Black powder only for this gun.)

I CLAIM, quite reasonably, to be the 101st gentleman because I own a very special 120-year-old pinfire Purdey double that was presented in 1863 to Mr. Frank Heathcote by a group of English shooting men who called themselves "The 100 Gentlemen," and also admitted to being "The Crack Shots of England." Some of this information is engraved upon the silver buttplate of the gun I have; more is to be found in English shooting literature of the last century.

Those 100 gentlemen, some I suspect of even more dubious character than myself but all undoubtedly impressive performers with a shotgun, were participants in mid-19th century live pigeon shoots in the London area. Live bird shooting, frowned upon in this humanitarian nuclear age, had its origins as a moving-target sport in ancient times. Homer, the "Iliad," says doves were the marks. The birds were allowed a limited range of movement by being secured to a pole by a cord. Obviously, the arm of the day would have been a bow or possibly a sling.

In the 1700s, in England, the Toxo-philite Society held frequent meetings for popinjay shooting. The "popinjay" usually was a stuffed bird, but sometimes was a tethered live sparrow. This was an archery contest. And, no doubt, other popinjays were falling to missiles fired from flintlock guns.

During the early 1800s, the shooting of released live birds (now mainly pigeons) was enthusiastically practiced by the frequenters of what were known as "low public houses" in many of the larger English towns. It was all very informal with few if any rules and guns and loads were those a shooter felt he could do best with.

Then, about 1850, Lord Huntingfield, the Earl of Stamford, and other noblemen took up the sport, quickly rendering it more respectable and even more popular. The first of the new and more fashionable pigeon shooting establishments near London was the "Old Hats," a public house on the Uxbridge Road. It came by its name because the birds used were released from holes in the ground covered by old top hats.

The "Red House," at Battersea, was the next great metropolitan resort for this sport, which by then had formed the basis for much heavy betting by both shooters and spectators. Hundreds of pounds changing hands on a single match. It wasn't only the wagers that were heavy—the guns were 10, 8 and even 6 gauge! However, the preponderance of such large bore guns and heavy loads resulted in a reduced interest on the part of many shooters and so, with the eventual destruction of the "Red House" to make way for a new bridge, the sport fell into something of a decline for a few years.

It revived with the advent of the first true club for pigeon shooters, set up at Hornsey Wood with a restricted membership. New and extensive formal rules were adopted governing all aspects of the sport, including weight of gun as well as shot and powder charges. The maximum load was fixed at 1¼ ounces or 5, 6, 7 or 8 shot with no more than 4 drams of powder (black, of course). Gun weight could not exceed eight pounds, with no bore larger than 11 gauge.

Soon Mr. Frank Heathcote argued

"Old Hemlock Parker," this dignified English setter, has a pedigree that clearly establishes *his* antecedents, but the writer's best claim to gentility rests with the unique pinfire he holds.

This Purdey of 1862 is a true snap-action gun. The convenient thumb-operated underlever retracted a bolting plate similar to that made more famous when actuated by a top lever. Note that the hammers must be drawn to half cock before the breech end of the barrels can be raised.

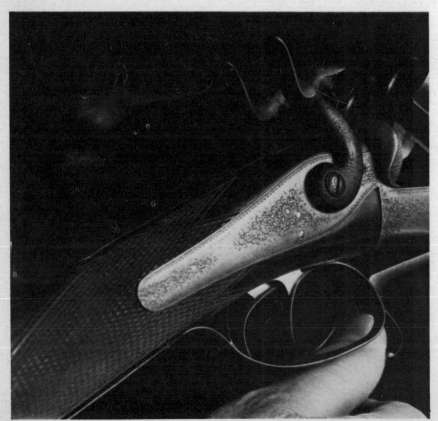

for even lighter loads, instigating special matches having 1⅛ oz. as the basic shot charge. Anyone wishing to use heavier loads could do so by moving back a yard for each additional ⅛th ounce of shot. Shooters were now also handicapped for many matches on the basis of their past performances and firing from a greater or lesser distance to make for more entertaining competition. Interest, prize money and betting continued to grow.

In 1863, with the loss of the Hornsey Wood Grounds, the very posh and exclusive Hurlingham Club came into existence with even more comprehensive shooting regulations which specified a maximum gun weight of 7½ pounds. This was also the final home of that informal club-within-a-club, The 100 Gentlemen, who were by then already making annual awards to outstanding members. The pinfire breechloader, that long suspect and much reviled *French* invention so despised by the famous Col. Hawker, was, as made by Purdey, Lang, Holland & Holland, Greener, et al, very near to displacing that *British* invention, the percussion muzzleloader, except in the affections of the most diehard of the old-timers. Indeed, the centerfire cartridge that would soon replace the once-revolutionary pinfire was already on the scene.

In commenting upon well-known shooters of the day, Lord William Lennox had this to say in print about some of those "100 Gentlemen" whose names appear on the buttplate of my Purdey: "A. Walsh, steady; Stirling Crawford, shoots beautiful; the Hon. A. Fraser, quiet; Lord Bective, good; Col. Carlton, steady, cool and good; the Hon. H. Wyndom, shoots steady and well; the Hon. H. Annesley, will become Number 1, Letter A; F. Heathcote, than whom a more honorable gentleman and excellent sportsman does not exist." Obviously the 100 Gentlemen, besides being the crack shots of England, were also the Salt of the Earth!

This latter-day, possible 101st gentleman can make no claim to being a "Number 1, Letter A" pigeon shooter, but with this historical presentation Purdey, here in Virginia, 3000 miles and 120 years removed from Hornsey Wood, I have shot many quail and ruffed grouse, using it with respect, admiration and affection. Often, I am quite certain, I have been in the company of the amiable spirit of its original owner. Certainly, I have raised a glass in friendly salute across the years. I hope it's accepted in the spirit it is offered. ●

THE ASSAULT RIFLE SYNDROME

Editor tries out fearsome Franchi SPAS-12.

The hue and cry is up over military style rifles and shotguns and pistols—and a lot of associated gear as well. This stuff annoys people, particularly gun industry people who view it all as an image problem.

Certainly all of us involved with firearms have an image problem in certain circles. We have had that problem since the 1920s; it is a manufactured image, and the worst thing is it was and is manufactured by anti-gun people. We will have the problem so long as we accept the image. And it has little to do with the presence of what are called assault rifles.

They're here. There is no blinking it—the semi-military, semi-police guns are around in such profusion as to confuse everyone but the true believers.

The true believers, however, know them all. They know them as boys used to know batting averages and teens used to know cars. They know them as your 8th grader knows Pac-Man. And they like them.

There are several generations of shooters now shooting who don't like assault rifles, but these new people don't care. They have the money and this is the United States and please step out of the way, sir, so I can decide whether or not I really want an AUG or will I settle for another Mini-14?

Remember—they say please, most of them. They were baptized in different places, maybe, but they are all your sons and daughters and nephews and cousins and maybe even uncles.

Somehow, somewhere, a whole batch of American shooters got the idea that large capacity, military-rugged centerfire rifles are sound merchandise. They find such guns shoot well—and make no mistake about it, they do shoot well; the guns, that is—and build confidence. So they buy them, blissfully unaware of any public-relations problem, or cantankerously intent on suiting themselves regardless.

Whatever you do, don't view this with alarm. These are the heirs of those fellows who soaked up about a million M1 Carbines 20 years ago. You know, those old carbines have not held up many liquor stores. They have just been there for two decades, just in case.

Following are two views of the matter, presented at length.

Ken Warner

Who Needs an Assault Rifle?

Not this writer, who plans a different kind of scenario.

THERE IS A growing and rather large market in this country for the quasi-military assault type rifles, often semiautomatic versions of automatic arms in use by the military in one or more countries. Such rifles, as a whole, are well-made, positive functioning, heavy, and very expensive, though there are individual exceptions to these four criteria. The Ruger Mini 14, for example, is relatively lightweight and inexpensive. It is not uncommon to see figures in excess of $1000 on other assault rifle price tags. Moreover, a host of aftermarket accessories which include such items as folding stocks, extra large capacity magazines, bayonets, bipods, flash hiders, and a multitude of similar items, can up the basic price.

by **EDWARD A. MATUNAS**

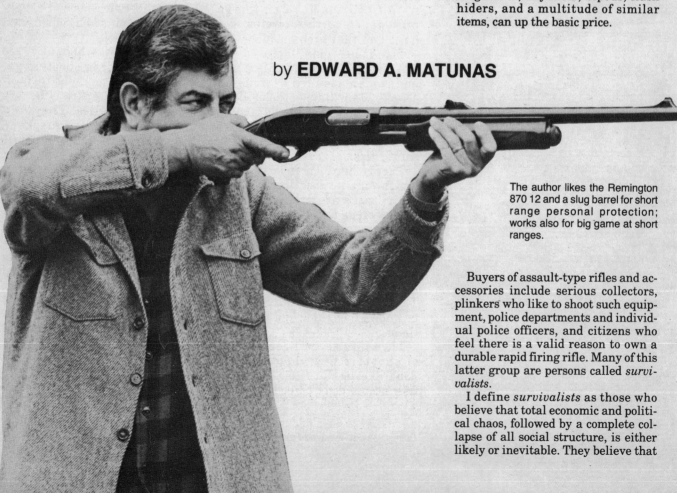

The author likes the Remington 870 12 and a slug barrel for short range personal protection; works also for big game at short ranges.

Buyers of assault-type rifles and accessories include serious collectors, plinkers who like to shoot such equipment, police departments and individual police officers, and citizens who feel there is a valid reason to own a durable rapid firing rifle. Many of this latter group are persons called *survivalists.*

I define *survivalists* as those who believe that total economic and political chaos, followed by a complete collapse of all social structure, is either likely or inevitable. They believe that

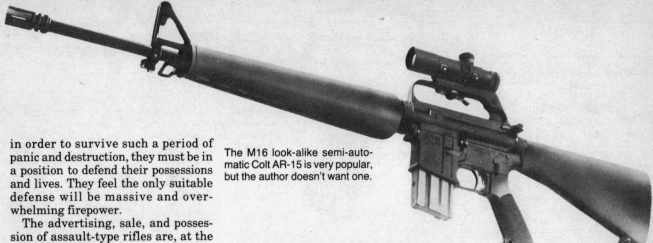

The M16 look-alike semi-automatic Colt AR-15 is very popular, but the author doesn't want one.

in order to survive such a period of panic and destruction, they must be in a position to defend their possessions and lives. They feel the only suitable defense will be massive and over-whelming firepower.

The advertising, sale, and possession of assault-type rifles are, at the same time, of deep concern to a great many people, among them both anti-gun and pro-gun people. Most all of the pro-gun faction who object to the assault-type rifles believe the assault rifle's image doesn't support the rec-reational and sporting image of fire-arms. They believe no useful sporting purpose is served by such firearms. Others claim legitimate applications for the rifles. They believe no rifle should be legislated against or out-lawed because it *looks* military. Maybe so!

Perhaps it should be mentioned at this point that there are a great number of M1 carbines in the hands of ci-vilians, a very great number indeed. However, such guns, in my opinion, are not assault-type rifles. These lit-tle carbines were designed to replace handguns and as such make fair per-sonal defense firearms. They are small, light and rugged. With the most common magazine (15 rounds) they make excellent personal home defense arms. Recoil is light and accu-racy is acceptable for short ranges.

Besides those who bought them for home defense, a great many ex-GI's keep carbines because they used them in the service. Relatively inexpensive, M1 carbines proved quite popular with those wishing a memento of their military years. And at one time surplus ammunition for the carbine was available at very inexpensive prices.

Certainly, collectors and students of military weapons have legitimate reasons for owning para-military ri-fles, as do serious collectors of semi-automatic firearms and police depart-ments or individual peace officers. How strong is the argument, howev-er, for ownership of assault rifles by the non-collector or non-peace officer? Are they even practical or useful?

The plinker claims an afternoon on the range with such a rifle is enjoy-

ment, but no serious shooter I know enjoys a rifle that is less than accu-rate. And most assault rifles are best described as highly inaccurate when compared to many sporting rifles, es-pecially modern bolt action sporting rifles. There are some very accurate semiautomatic military target rifles, but such rifles do not fit into the as-sault category.

Anyone who claims he likes to shoot a lot and thus likes assault rifles has simply got to be kidding himself or putting the rest of us on. The only way to shoot a *lot* of centerfire ammunition is to be able to afford to do so. This means you are a millionaire, you re-load your own ammunition, or you simply don't care how you blow your money. The 30 rounds of 308 ammo required to fill a magazine could, at retail prices, cost a staggering $22.50. A similar quantity of 223 ammo could cost $16.50. Reloading seems the only sensible way to go, but reloading for the assault-type semi-automatic is at best extremely challenging.

Most of these rifles throw the fired case out so violently it is a monumen-tal task to retrieve any usable cases. Some are thrown as far as 20 yards. One particular assault rifle I shot put most of the empty cases 10 yards in front, 20 yards to the right and literal-ly in the woods. I could recover no more than 20 percent. Besides, as-sault rifles eject with such violent force they bounce cases vigorously off surrounding pieces of landscape and range. As a result most show serious deterioration in the form of nicks, gouges and dents. These casualties of the firing process are not what most reloaders would consider prime candi-dates for new primers, powder, and bullets.

No, for an afternoon's shooting at the range, there are more accurate, less expensive to own and feed, and more satisfying tools to punch holes in

paper targets or tin cans. The only thing assault rifles can do better at the range than conventional rifles is to make a great deal more noise. This doesn't include the noise created when an ejected case ricochets off the bench of the next shooter and slaps him smartly on the forehead.

The survivalist has his own argu-ments. He may well have not only an assault rifle but also hundreds of rounds of ammunition. This ammuni-tion is often carefully loaded in large capacity magazines to guarantee rap-id reloads during life and death strug-gles.

Practice sessions with the chosen assault rifle I have seen take on al-most a religious tone. After all, the survivalist must be the match for any soldier or group of crazed civilians who may wish to separate him from his food, clothing, fuel, or even his shelter. That such groups may num-ber from a half-dozen to possibly two dozen or more is not a concern since he has at least a half-dozen large ca-pacity magazines, fully loaded.

Personally, I think anyone who thinks a semiautomatic assault rifle and a stack of loaded magazines will enable him to get the best of any mili-tary squad or armed group of civilian crazies is not using his grey matter. No one civilian survivalist or small group of survivalists will ever be the match of even a fair squad of military personnel. When a military squad un-leashes its full automatic fire power, it will, in most circumstances, make short work of the situation. Even if the survivalist won a given encoun-ter, his next group of opponents would simply release a barrage of heavier weapons. The single survivalist or even a large group cannot expect to cope. There may be something said for

The collapsible stock AR-15 is popular with police officers who want a small, compact, lightweight semi-auto, but the author can't imagine needing one.

not giving up without a fight, but certain death is not a viable option, not for a *survivalist*.

OK. Let's skip the civilian/military engagement. Let's say a mob of hostile civilians want food, guns, ammo, shelter, wife, or you name it. Under such assault, a heavily armed civilian may put a semiautomatic assault rifle to deadly, practical and efficient use, for a while at least. Sooner or later, though, a stray round, a ricochet or a well-directed projectile will find its mark.

It just isn't college-level-thinking to assume any individual or group can best a similar or larger number of persons better trained, armed and equipped, as would be any military group. Nor is it smart to think that one could hold off large numbers for more than a brief period. It may be heroic, but imprudent (read *stupid*).

In history, it has been obvious that freedom fighters fail, despite being on the side of right, whenever they are outgunned, outmanned, or outmaneuvered. To survive such troubles, I think one must remain mobile and able to hide. A real survivor is going to be a fast-moving pro who is not where everyone is looking for him, a master at hiding. All the while he must be able to feed and shelter himself and perhaps others. Backed into a corner, he will be able to shoot his way out, but simply to escape and hide again.

One of the ways to manage this will be to keep his opponents far enough away. A highly accurate long-range rifle can hit long before opponents get to assault rifle range. We are thus talking about a 350- to 500-yard rifle.

The only type of rifle that will deliver hits at such long ranges is a good scope-equipped, well-tuned bolt action. It had best be a lightweight, if one has to carry it on long and arduous treks.

A smart survivalist knows his entire kit had best fit into the family transportation, but he should also know that at some point his vehicle will run out of fuel or be stopped at a road block. True survival will then depend on how fast he and his can get into the woods and put a hill or two between them and his antagonists. A loaded assault rifle at 10 or more pounds, and a half-dozen or so loaded magazines to boot, are simply more than he can handle. A light bolt action with 20 to 40 cartridges will be about the maximum, especially if he attempts to take a sleeping bag, a bit of food and some medical supplies, let alone some spare clothing. A few semiautomatic assault models are light enough, but won't provide the long range hits required. And none are chambered for a cartridge large enough to anchor big animals when only a single shot should be expended.

Who then needs an assault rifle? Certainly not you or I. Something like a Model 70 Featherweight in 270 Winchester, 308 Winchester or 30-06 Springfield would make far more sense. Equipped with a good, rugged, all-purpose scope in sturdy mounts with a sling and a full magazine of cartridges, it will weigh no more than about 7¾ pounds. That's light enough to be carried all day, day after day, even without the breakfast of champions.

The author's selection for a "survival" rifle would be a lightweight sporter with scope, chambered for a long range cartridge such as this Model 70 Featherweight in 270 with its 1.5-5x Leupold scope.

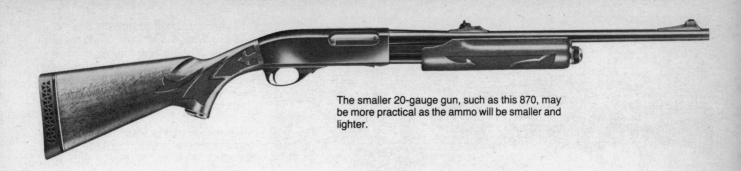

The smaller 20-gauge gun, such as this 870, may be more practical as the ammo will be smaller and lighter.

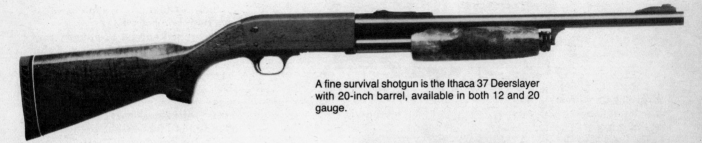

A fine survival shotgun is the Ithaca 37 Deerslayer with 20-inch barrel, available in both 12 and 20 gauge.

This close-up shows some of the body dents caused during violent ejection of these 308 cases from a semi-automatic assault rifle.

The author favors a hunting-class rifle for emergencies because he uses one well.

A short, lightweight rifle is best for anyone who needs to go over the hills and far away.

The survival shotgun should be stored with 10 rounds of buckshot, 10 rifled slugs, and 25 rounds of bird shot.

A good choice for a second gun is a compact, lightweight belt gun with a large magazine capability such as this S&W Model 59. This pistol has a capacity of 15 9mm Luger rounds.

Cartridges such as the 38 Special and the 9mm Luger are about ideal with the 357 Magnum being the upper limit. Accuracy will always remain paramount. I would choose the 9mm cartridge as it is smaller and lighter than most cartridges in its class.

I would probably load 40 or 50 cartridges into clips for my Model 59 Smith & Wesson. With one in the chamber, it holds 15 rounds. Two extra loaded magazines provide 43 rounds at the ready. I would carry it in a flap style holster.

Everyone knows a 12-gauge pump gun would also prove mighty useful especially if equipped with a short barrel and rifle-type sights. With such a gun you could either hunt big game (with slugs) or small game and birds (with shot loads). And a magazine full of 00 buckshot would make you a top contender in any alley-cleaning situation. No better short range defensive weapon could be found. I would select either an Ithaca Model 37 or Remington 870 because both are extremely reliable. The 870 is a bit easier to load and hence may be somewhat preferable in a stress situation.

From this point of view, assault rifles only make sense for collectors, police, and military personnel. I think the shooter who just enjoys banging away on the range will be better off with almost any other rifle. And the fellow or couple who really wants to survive will have a long range rifle and either a handgun with a large capacity magazine or a pump shotgun. Such equipment would allow anyone to survive wherever possible, and a semiauto assault rifle would, in all probability, prove to be a liability in most situations. I consider them too cumbersome, heavy and inaccurate, not to mention those that are insufficiently powerful or don't work with soft point ammunition.

I won't be setting aside a semiautomatic assault rifle and hundreds of rounds if I ever decide there may be a problem. Instead, it will be a lightweight 270 with two boxes of carefully loaded ammunition and a good 15-shot 9mm auto with two spare magazines and a box of ammo. If someone goes over the hill with me, I'll hope he's brought along a 12-gauge pump shotgun with a magazine full of 00 buckshot, 25 rounds of birdshot and maybe a handful of slugs. If his belt gun is the same as mine, I'll figure we really are increasing our chances of survival. ●

I would choose the 270, but if you prefer the 30-06 I would not even start to try and change your mind. The 308 also will get the job done, even though its trajectory is somewhat more curved. My Winchester Model 70 Featherweights, when any of the three suggested cartridges are properly handloaded, will group between an inch and one and a half inches at 100 yards, or three to six times better than most assault rifles.

A good belt pistol is a definite plus. The belt gun is important because it is *always* there. It is never set aside even for "just a moment," nor is it inside when you are outside or vice versa.

YOU DON'T NEED A BASS BOAT EITHER

by KEN WARNER

This surrealistic bazaar shows 13 goodies from the assault rifle shelves: two in 308, four in 223, five 12-gauges, a 45 ACP, and a 20-bore.

Big boats or pricey guns— if you got it, flaunt it.

THERE'S a fellow you have read about who has a lot of African experience. When he went out to Kenya in the '50s and stayed for years, he carried along two Model 70s and a Model 69, all stocked alike. With 375 H&H and 30-06 and 22 rimfire, he did it all. His battery was classic; indeed, the stocks were by Keith Stegall, I believe.

He yearns to go back. He tells me when and if he does, he's going to carry a military-style 308 rifle as his only arm. If it's really to do, he figures that is the way to go. And he plans to do nine whole yards of elephant if he can get at them.

There are many thousands of shooters without his experience who share his views. And they spend real money to back their opinions.

It is not cheap, this assault rifle battery. The whole survival thing seems to call for a considerable capital investment, in fact.

It's not the gun that costs, necessarily, although I was looking at a little $2500 number from Finland in 308 the other day. It's all the rest of it— spare magazines at $20 to $40 apiece, web gear to hold them, bipods, extra stocks, carrying cases in SWAT-black Cordura, cleaning and maintenance kits—there's no end. I saw a rather special European scope at the SHOT Show at $3200, shuddered and passed on to neater and more accessible items.

I am here to attest there is real

Some assault rifles, like this H-K93, are entirely suitable for scoped sniping.

The bull-pup Valmet, on the other hand, is more in the fire-and-movement class.

The short shotgun, this one a Kimel KPR-20, provides uncomplicated firepower, even in 20-gauge.

And especially in 20-gauge, guns like the KPR-20 provide easy-toting and easy handling.

money on the board here. To get pictures, experience, and such, I check guns out from the importers. It was illuminating to review my indebtedness to three gun company computers—about six guns ran right around $7000 on the printouts, but, of course, several were relatively cheap models.

You will notice I have not mentioned ammunition. Most guys who spend an afternoon at the range with their assault rifle do that instead of taking a plane to Vegas or bus to Atlantic City to drop a few bucks at blackjack. The scale of expense is similar, and the shooting range is not so far from home and mother.

Or so it seems to this older fellow who paid $200 for a box of 1000 308 cartridges a couple years ago. I guess it works out at maybe $20 an afternoon for plinking, or less than it takes to fill up the Chevvie anymore. That's five 20-round magazines for one person. If you take a kid or your wife, well, the price of fun goes up. It is not out of the question as entertainment. It's not like plinking with a 22 used to be, but neither is plinking with a 22 like it used to be.

There is no denying the entertainment quotient of the assault rifle, but that is not what they are about, those cammie-clad hordes of upright (and maybe even uptight) citizens. They want good guns for time-honored and legitimate reasons and regard military-level designs as arms of choice.

In fact, there is widespread belief that such firearms as you see here are state-of-the-art designs, guns better than any ever built. They are believed more reliable, more accurate in the field, more rugged, and better suited to a wide range of firearms needs than, for instance, bolt-action sporting rifles. That's speaking of the assault rifles in 308 Winchester, for the most part. The Heckler & Koch HK91, the Belgian FAL, the Finnish light machine gun (LMG) on the Kalashnikov action modified into an infantry rifle in 308, the M1A—a U.S.-made civilian M14—the various Swiss, Spanish, Italian renditions in semi-auto mode of what every foot soldier needs.

The equivalent 223s have a slightly different audience, and a couple of far more accessible guns—the Colt AR-15, which is the civilian version of our military's M16, and the Ruger Mini-14, which is Ruger's version of Everyman's U.S. military rifle—at far more affordable prices. And you can have Israeli and Egyptian and Austrian models as well.

The rest of it—the pseudo-submachine guns, the much-doctored combat shotguns, the jazzy combat pistols in your choice of magazine capacity and calibers—sort of falls in place around assault rifles. Those lesser guns are there for shooters who don't want to take an assault rifle to raise, but want to go with the flow.

Certainly, none of us are going to object to proficiency at arms in our fellow citizens, are we? The time is gone when a 50-shot prone series at 50 yards with a 10-pound 22 through a 20x scope passed for para-military training. In a world which includes El Salvador, Lebanon, Afghanistan and, I am told, 40 other places at war, who is to say a U.S. citizen ought not know how with current technology? Not this writer, for one.

And with these guns one can be proficient. The good ones shoot where they look. They are lots different to manage; they are not, in 308, lightweights; they do not offer a lot of optional chamberings; they are not guns for experimental handloaders, or one shot at a time varminters—that's all true. Just never ever make the mistake of thinking they don't shoot well. They almost all do.

Personally, the assault rifle is not my choice; indeed, I don't much like large-capacity 9mm pistols or submachine guns. I do have a vast respect for short shotguns for many purposes. So I would not be your average good witness for the assault rifles, right?

Wrong!

I know of one such semi-auto in 30-06 I fired three times, bagging one fox and one deer, neither at close range. I know another I shot on varmints three times—three hits on three critters. I know another I was able to hit four out of five 200-meter steel chickens with, shooting offhand. Since my only claim to fame as a shot is that it generally doesn't make much difference what I'm shooting, it appears to me those guns shoot very well. Bench and match and training results agree with me.

If you can afford them and like them, you may not be the country club type, but you are likely a good shooter and citizen. In a world which fondly regards $100 sneakers and $12,000 bass boats and $200 tennis rackets and $2000 home entertainment computers and video arcades that eat 20 quarters per hour per kid, how wrong can you be with your $800 rifle and $1000 ammo cache and $2000 kit? I'd prefer you to skip the cammies when you come for cocktails, but that's just because of the neighbors. Your guns are OK. ●

Most recognized profile of the bunch is the Tommy gun, here in the 1927 Carbine semi-auto version, which has all the charm it ever had.

WARNING
TRESPASSERS
WILL BE SHOT
SURVIVORS
WILL BE SHOT AGAIN

NEVER MIND THE DOG. BEWARE OF OWNER!

The sardonic humor in signs like these finds a ready market today among people who are maybe a little serious about the sentiment. From Delta Ltd.

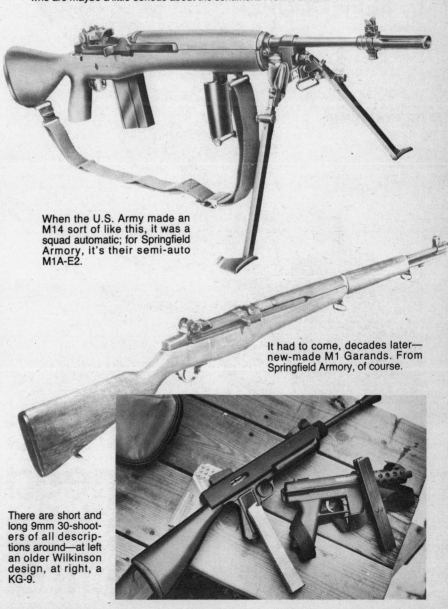

When the U.S. Army made an M14 sort of like this, it was a squad automatic; for Springfield Armory, it's their semi-auto M1A-E2.

It had to come, decades later—new-made M1 Garands. From Springfield Armory, of course.

There are short and long 9mm 30-shooters of all descriptions around—at left an older Wilkinson design, at right, a KG-9.

THE SCOUT RIFLE IDEA

by **JEFF COOPER**

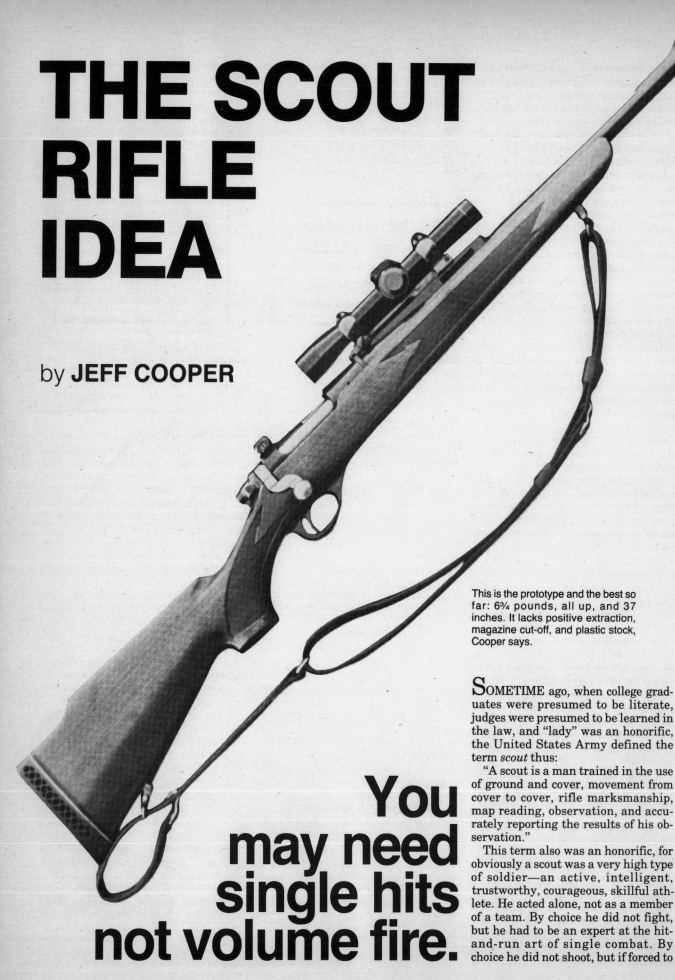

This is the prototype and the best so far: 6¾ pounds, all up, and 37 inches. It lacks positive extraction, magazine cut-off, and plastic stock, Cooper says.

You may need single hits not volume fire.

SOMETIME ago, when college graduates were presumed to be literate, judges were presumed to be learned in the law, and "lady" was an honorific, the United States Army defined the term *scout* thus:

"A scout is a man trained in the use of ground and cover, movement from cover to cover, rifle marksmanship, map reading, observation, and accurately reporting the results of his observation."

This term also was an honorific, for obviously a scout was a very high type of soldier—an active, intelligent, trustworthy, courageous, skillful athlete. He acted alone, not as a member of a team. By choice he did not fight, but he had to be an expert at the hit-and-run art of single combat. By choice he did not shoot, but if forced to shoot he shot quickly, carefully, and as little as possible. "One round, one hit—and then vanish!"—that was his motto. He did not need an assault rifle. He needed a *scout rifle*.

Times have changed, and the true scout is no longer found (Or, at any rate, *cataloged:* Editor) in today's armies. The enemy is located from the air, pinned by artillery, and then smashed by mechanized infantry and tanks. The scout's rifle has been replaced by the *Sturmgewehr,* and the character and qualities of the rifle for use by a lone rifleman have been all but forgotten. The hunter-rifleman still exists (in diminishing number), but since he does not hunt to save his life, even he loses sight of certain essentials which a true scout rifle should embody.

We have been fortunate at Gunsite Ranch, in Arizona, in that we teach practical riflery to clients who are not likely ever to use their rifles as fire-team members, and who consequently seek their highest level of *individual* competence, with the instrument best suited to the task.

But what *is* the task of a rifle? In an age of specialization it is easy to say, "Just tell me what you want it for and I'll tell you what sort of rifle you should have."

That is too easy. What do you say when the response is, "I don't know what I may want to do with it. I want a *general purpose* rifle?"

That is a much more interesting question.

One of the Eternal Truths is this: *The purpose of shooting is hitting.* By extension we may say that the purpose of the rifle is to enable the rifleman to strike a decisive blow to the limit of his vision. Let us call a "decisive blow" one which can be relied on instantly to incapacitate any unarmored animal of 500 pounds or less, with one solid hit in the vital zone. Such a blow will provide good probability to twice that weight, or more with careful placement. Let us further say that the "limit of vision" is the greatest distance at which 20-20 eyes, unaided, can clearly discern the vital zone of the animal engaged.

These parameters suffice well for both human adversaries and medium big game, and there are all sorts of rifles which will suit them. That, however, is not the whole story. There is the quality of handiness. We work so much at the target range (to which we drive in motor vehicles) that we tend to forget that the natural habitat of the general-purpose rifle is the field, the forest, the desert and the moun-

tain—not the shooting shed with its bench rest. To be really useful a rifle must be as short, light and quick to use as is technically compatible with adequate power and useful accuracy. Adequate power may be had with any of the 20-caliber family of military cartridges, the best of which was probably the 30-06, now largely pre-empted by its compacted offspring the 308. Useful accuracy is that which the shooter can put to use.

We properly use the bench to test the intrinsic accuracy of barrel, action, bedding, cartridge, and sighting system. And we often forget that what matters is not what the equipment can do, but rather what it will do in the hands of its operator under field, rather than laboratory, conditions. One enlightening test is a series of five two-shot pairs, standing-to-sitting, 100 yards, Option target, 10 seconds per pair. Any combination of man and rifle which can keep all ten shots in five inches in this exercise demonstrates excellent *practical* accuracy. Whether the equipment is bench-capable of a one-inch group or a 1½-inch group or a two-inch group at that range is irrelevant.

If we consider that the "range probable error" of a rifle—the distance of the best 50% of hits from the mathematical point of aim—is one-fourth group diameter, it is clear that the advantage of a one-minute rifle over a two-minute rifle is a matter of one-half inch at 200 yards. Under field conditions this is insignificant. Thus the general-purpose rifle should be good for two minutes, and 2½ will do very well.

At this point a certain kind of purist will snort that we are talking about a "scatter gun." Not so. We are talking about accuracy we can use, for that which we cannot use is only theoretically interesting.

Let us proceed on the assumption that we need a two-inch-shooting 308 as a base. There are plenty of those. The next goal is compactness, and for that we think at once of a short barrel. A short barrel reduces velocity somewhat, and it increases blast. The shortest popular barrel measures 18½-inches. In such a barrel a charge of 43 grains of IMR3031 will start a 150-gr. bullet at right about 2700 fps. Those were the ballistics of the old original 30-06 in a 24-inch barrel, and they sufficed very well for Theodore Roosevelt and Stewart Edward White in Africa. A 30-caliber, 150-grain spitzer at 2700 fps may not be a "magnum," but it has been logging one-shot kills all over the world for so long

that one may well ask why anything more is necessary, unless one's target weighs over 1000 pounds.

It is true that the blast of an 18-inch 308 is impressive, especially on a dark day, but a lone rifleman need not worry much about tell-tale flash. If he shoots carefully—once—and moves, it doesn't matter.

Along with a short barrel we should have a short action, both as to cartridge length and also over-all. The most compact actions that come to mind are the new Remington Model Seven and the Remington 600, now out of production, and the curious Mauser also called 600. By compressing the action, an extra inch or more of over-all length can be deleted.

The scout rifle now evolving will be a bolt gun, as the semi-autos are overly long, heavy, and bulky, and the volume of fire they afford is of little consequence to a true scout. One might construct a quite good scout rifle with a Savage 99, but it would still be a couple of inches longer than a comparable bolt gun.

Modern bolt actions all fall somewhat short of ideal, the best features of some being offset by corresponding drawbacks. Completely shrouded case heads, for instance, all seem to come with weak extraction systems. Reduced bolt rotation makes for stiff bolt work, especially with a fired case in the chamber. Bolt handles which are tacked on rather than forged integrally with the bolt will sometimes detach themselves under hard use. This may produce an elegant dueling scar on the right cheek, but it definitely sidelines the rifle for the duration of the game. Actions which are enclosed against foreign matter are difficult to load from the top, eyes off, in a hurry; whereas those that facilitate single loading do not feature a magazine cutoff to take full advantage thereof.

Detachable box magazines are, except for the Mannlicher, of reduced capacity, and experimental modifications taking the 20-round M-14 magazine are awfully clumsy with the big box in place. At this time nobody except Mannlicher offers point protection for reserve rounds in the magazine. Nearly all modern bolt guns come with a roughened bolt knob, when what is needed for proper bolt work is a smooth and round ball bearing.

On the good side, most of the new bolt actions come with very nice triggers. Though many are set on the heavy side for reasons of product-liability intimidation, they normally can be reduced down to a marksman-

Scouts move and a scout rifle needs to be easy in the grasp for tough-country hurrying.

The forward scope permits eyes-off loading and manipulation, and alternate iron sights as well.

like three pounds. The consensus of the masters is that a fine trigger is the single most important *desideratum* in any rifle.

A short bolt action, in combination with a short barrel, can bring over-all length down to about 37 inches without serious loss in performance. For optimum handiness and portability we should now seek a weight ceiling of seven pounds, all up. The scout rifle should weigh less than seven pounds, with scope and sling in place, but unloaded. The best way to meet this limit is by means of a plastic stock. There are all sorts of plastics, but the best sort can produce a stock that is both lighter and stronger than wood. Fine wood is prohibitive in price and common wood is no prettier than plastic, so plastic would seem to be the wave of the future. Stamped checkering is rather like instant wine (better than nothing, but not much), so perhaps some sort of blast-roughening is the answer.

In styling the stock should be plain and straight, a "classic" without bumps, flanges, notches, or cheekpieces, since the gun must be comfortably operable from either shoulder. It should be high enough at comb to support a low scope line. No butt cushion is necessary, but the heel should be rounded to encourage quick mounting for a snap shot. A thin rubber skidplate should finish the butt.

The short, light barrel of the scout rifle heats up quickly. This is no problem in the field but has been known to blister hands during practice. It can be partially shrouded by a full-length stock of the pattern popularly termed "Mannlicher"—which need not, incidentally, have any adverse affect

upon accuracy, contrary to rumor. (I have a Model L that shoots like a match rifle.)

The sling fittings should be of the Pachmayr flush design, metal reinforced, and the sling itself must provide loop support. Bipods are certainly helpful under certain conditions but they constitute a dangerous crutch if a shooter comes to depend on them. On the range they work fine, but in rough and broken terrain they are almost useless, and those presently available are ugly. The loop sling remains more generally useful than the bipod, and no bipod design should interfere with proper sling mounting.

To this point the scout rifle is fairly easy to assemble. Sights, however, are another matter. A scout rifle should be equipped with both iron and optical sights, but neither is easily available at this time in a configuration which suits it for the scout rifle concept.

The iron sights for a scout should consist of a square front post, possibly red filled, and a large-aperture, small-rim rear sight mounted on the receiver bridge—popularly referred to as a "ghost ring." Most over-the-counter rifles come with a front bead and a rear notch, since it is assumed that they will be quickly fitted with a telescope and therefore nothing very good in the way of iron sights is necessary or desirable. It is no great problem to knock out the gold bead and install a proper front post. The square post gives all the speed afforded by a bead, plus a distinctly better index of elevation in precise shooting.

On the other hand, rear aperture sights are rarely fitted to rifles at the factory, and those available as acces-

sories are often both bulky and unsightly. Possibly the best option was the integral and retractable rear aperture that came as standard equipment on the ZKK 600 Series actions from Brno in Czechoslovakia. The aperture in this sight was too small, but it could be easily drilled out, and the neatness and compactness of the entire assembly are not duplicable with currently available accessory equipment.

Those who do not understand the ghost ring or its usages should try it sometime, on both paper targets and thrown clay birds. Locations where one can shoot trap with the rifle with safety are scarce, but the skeptic is well advised to try this, even at considerable difficulty, in order to learn how the rifle is properly used in a hurry.

The vast majority of currently available telescope sights are too big and have too little eye relief for proper use as we are learning to use a scout rifle. And most mounting systems place the sight axis too high above the bore. The best combination so far was available only for a short time during which Leupold produced a 2x compact glass of ten-inch eye relief, and Buehler produced a mount which would fit this glass very low over the bore of the Remington 600 series and mounted so as to place the ocular lens directly flush with the front end of the magazine well. This combination, sight and mount, is the fastest ever to appear at Gunsite, and it loses nothing in precision when used for careful shots at long range. We have even heard it dubbed "unfair," and no higher compliment can ever be paid to any piece of equipment than that.

The virtues of this sight system are three:

First, it obscures very little of the shooter's vision as the piece is cheeked. This enables him to keep both eyes open while mounting the rifle, with a full view of his entire target area, and to place the cross wires instantly with his shooting eye while keeping track of the target with his non-shooting eye. The closer the glass is to the eye, the more of the shooter's field of view is obscured.

Second, the forward-mounted scope allows instantaneous eyes-off loading from the top, without obstruction by the scope tube.

Third, the forward-mounted glass allows the rifle to be grasped at the balance during running, jumping and violent exercise much more conveniently than any weapon with the glass mounted rearward.

There are several extended-eye-relief telescopes available, but they are primarily designed for pistols and come with an eye relief of about 14 inches, making it necessary to place them so far forward on the piece that no secure portion of the action is available for a base. The classic quarter-rib sometimes found on venerable bolt action rifles forms an excellent base for a forward-mounted telescope, but only if the glass may be mounted far enough to the rear to take advantage of it. Of course, until there is perfection, a good low conventional scope will serve.

The notion that a rifle must be long and heavy in order to suit it for any sort of serious work at distance is a myth which has been with us for a long time. The most frequent comment heard about the prototype scout rifles is that they are all very well as brush guns, but are not suited for general use. This charge is best met by taking the rifles to a field trial exercise and examining the results. It is clearly true that smaller groups may be fired at 500 meters with a properly designed bull gun than with a scout rifle. But the difference is less than one might think, and certainly too little to matter when the goal is achieving hits in the vital zones of big game animals, or in human adversaries.

Long testing has led to the conclusion that the ability to achieve a first-shot hit, on a 10-inch disc at ranges varying from 50 to 550 yards, is far more a matter of the skill of the shooter than of the size or weight of his rifle. The scouts hold their own with the big guns on any practical field test we have been able to devise, and they are so much easier to pack around and to use quickly, that our more traditional rifles are spending more and more time on the rack.

Consider this observation from H. W. McBride, quoted from his classic, *A Rifleman Went to War:*

"The neatest and handiest military rifle I have ever seen was one I took from one of these German *Jägers,* and when I held it up beside my Ross for comparison, the cocky little rascal actually laughed in my face, and he had a bullet through his arm at that. It did look ridiculous, I admit—that is, the Ross did; a great big long heavy club beside the trim little sporter which he had been using. His rifle had been made for something other than a handle for a bayonet."

At this time it would seem that the best cartridges for the scout rifle are three, with possibly one more if extra power is important. We have already discussed the virtues of the 308, and nearly all of our experimental and

Conventional scope placement obscures a lot of country and covers the best place to grab the piece.

Steyr's quick-switch potential means a lot in the scout concept, but the forward scope can't be had easily.

pioneer models are made for this cartridge. For those who are recoil shy, or lightly built, the 243 is an acceptable option, although since the 243 is a "velocity cartridge" its barrel should not probably be cut much under 22-inches in order to retain the virtues of the round. The 7mm-08 may be of no particular interest to the American shooting public, but it has much to recommend it in those jurisdictions where the 308 cartridge is forbidden as a "military caliber." There are more places like this than you might suspect. All three—the 308, the 7mm-08, and the 243—are of the same length on the same basic case.

The additional cartridge in the scout family, which makes up into what may be called a "super scout," is the 350 Remington Magnum. This is one of the very few *short* magnum cartridges, and is certainly useful in places where its 250-grain bullet may be desirable for extra knockdown effect on large animals. I have taken my own to many strange and far-away places, and always my host wanted to buy it from me. The super scout, incidentally, runs to 7½ pounds, and 39 inches.

The scouts, as now built in prototype form, do have certain drawbacks. They heat up quickly, they are noisy, and they kick somewhat more than conventional rifles of similar type. Also, finding sights for them is a frustrating enterprise. Their virtues, however, outnumber their vices, or so it seems to me.

In C. S. Forester's heroic tale, *Brown on Resolution,* one Able Seaman Brown, on the beach with a Mauser rifle in a battle port, is able to forestall the repairs necessary on a German cruiser for long enough for the British fleet to arrive, thus winning the battle:

"But Brown was only powerful in consequence of his rifle; the handiest, neatest, most efficient piece of machinery ever devised by man."

That was in 1915, and, though fictional, realistically drawn from life. Now we have a handier, neater, and more efficient piece of machinery than that. Actually, of course, we don't quite have it, but there are designs, prototypes and ideas. When we are satisfied with our concept, we may prevail upon some established maker to produce it.

Perhaps some year soon, you will be able to walk into a store and buy a scout rifle over the counter. As Max Beerbohm says, "It is a contingency furiously to be hoped." ●

THE ASSAULT RIFLE AND SURVIVAL SHOPPER

Data from Larry S. Sterett

Really a light machine-gun design, the Valmet 78 is a Finnish Kalashnikov enlarged to 7.62 NATO. From Odin Intl.

Dressed up as a sniper, the M78/83S has a real Star Wars profile. It's only $1595 as you see it in 308.

Egypt's AKM is a Kalashnikov in 7.62x39mm. It's made semi-auto and imported here by Steyr and is really real and rugged.

The Galil is a jazzy Israeli Kalashnikov in 223, highly thought of in the extra-rugged category.

People are even finding and shooting the AR-10, a 308 predecessor of the AR-15.

An old favorite is the Beretta BM-59, shown here in the Alpine version. Gun is essentially an updated Garand.

Experimental Valmet 223 in bullpup design, thought about ready, is not to be marketed for a while.

The Austrian AUG-SA has settled in at Interarms. A technically advanced arm in 223, it sells for $1195, is an all-out bullpup.

Shotgunning can be very simple with the effective Stevens 311-R 12-gauge guard gun.

(Right) Mossberg aims to please in this market and here are six versions of their 500 pump gun, with the pistol-gripped Cruiser not shown.

If you are perhaps diffident about the all-out assault rifle, then either the 223 H-K SL-6 (left) or the scoped Ruger Ranch Rifle (below), also in 223, will suit.

THE RIGHT STUFF

Here's the real thing—an all-out CETME belt-fed MG in 223. It's a state-of-the-art automatic and it will all fit in a 3-inch attache case with 100 rounds belted in a box. From Odin Intl.

ACCESSORIES, OF COURSE:

Federal Ordnance offers this flash hider for Mini-14s.

If you want all your ammo in one satchel, this Fed. Ord. web rig will haul a 45 drum and four rifle magazines.

Drum magazine for 30 rounds of 45? Certainly. This one's from Taylor, distributed by Bingham.

This is not a picture of a scoped H&K rifle, but of a snap-on Cherokee Cheekpiece to make scope work easier.

The Ruger 10/22 is a favorite for spiffing up with extra-capacity magazines. The Condor (above) holds over 25; the Mitchell's unusual configuration gives it a 50-round charge.

Choice of camo or black is usually afforded in protective web gear like this shotgunner pouch from Assault Systems.

S&K will scope most anything and this is how their Insta-Mount looks on the AKM.

Understandably, there is a certain vogue for brass catchers. This one works on a variety of arms. From Auto Strip Pak.

THE CULTURAL HERITAGE OF HUNTING

by STUART M. WILLIAMS

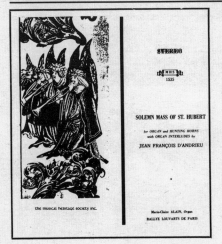
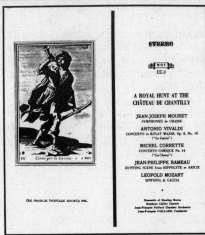

Record jackets are not trophies, but they can hold symbols of the heritage of hunting, nonetheless.

TWO THINGS our forefathers came here to escape were the abuses of feudalism, and royal and aristocratic privilege. In the case of hunting, kings and nobility had virtually exclusive access to game—at least, all big game—and poaching was punishable by death or long imprisonment. In fact, poachers were generally shot on sight.

Eliminating the evils of a system that allocated hunting rights strictly to title and the possession of land in favor of a democratic system, however, eliminated much of the cultural heritage of hunting. This heritage is rich, and remains largely intact in Europe, but few American hunters are aware of its existence. It is high time we turned back.

The essence of the problem is that in our democratic society there are too many hunters. As such, the average level of hunting skill, love of and knowledge of the game, and felt responsibility toward game and landowner, is low. The only people who love hunters in large numbers are the manufacturers of arms, ammunition, and hunting accessories. As they say back in West Virginia, hunters have become as common as pig tracks.

How different from our much less numerous counterparts in Scandinavia, Belgium, Germany, Switzerland, or Austria. Whether titled noblemen or commoners, hunters there still are in that same hunting culture which has been their heritage for centuries. Essentially, they believe hunting is a unique and exquisite privilege which involves as many responsibilities as it offers pleasures.

The visible heart of this heritage of hunting is the cult of St. Hubert, the patron saint of hunters. St. Hubert was converted to Christianity in the Ninth Century when he saw a magnificent stag bearing a radiant crucifix between its antlers while he was hunting in the Ardennes forest in Belgium. St. Hubert is feted annually on November 3 by Catholic and Protestant hunters alike throughout Europe with large trophy displays, exhibitions of hunting art and fine firearms, and by concerts of hunting music.

The piéce de résistance of St. Hubert's Day is the competition of the hunting horn groups. These groups flourish in France, Belgium, Germany, Austria, and Switzerland. The occasions attract thousands of people and are excellent public relations for

hunting. They are certainly not intended for that purpose, however, because they are not necessary for that purpose. Hunters in most Central European countries are highly respected members of the community.

How has this hunting culture been perpetuated down the generations? By law, by folklore and tradition, and by the arts, principally literature, painting, and music. It is these last that I am concerned with, since they are readily accessible to us all.

Of the three, literature is the least rich in works motivated primarily by the hunt. (Here I am concerned only with imaginative literature, and not with memoirs or technical literature on hunting or philosophy such as Gaston Phebus' *The Master of Game* or Ortega y Gasset's *Meditations on Hunting.)*

The earliest of such works is *Sir Gawain and the Green Knight,* which is one of the treasures of Middle English literature. There is perhaps no better picture of how hunting was conducted in the Middle Ages than the hunting scenes from *Sir Gawain.* In a modernized version, it still affords great entertainment and profit.

Much the same can be said of the boar-hunting scenes from Shakespeare's *Venus and Adonis*. Legend has it that Shakespeare had to flee from Stratford-on-Avon because he had been poaching deer. There are allusions to hunting scattered throughout his work.

In Book II of his *Travels* Marco Polo describes the Cecil B. DeMille-scale hunting expeditions mounted by Kubla Khan. He also describes some of the earliest conservation measures on record.

In the Epilogue to *The Hunting Sketches* Turgenev has provided a very lyrical description of the joys of hunting, and Leo Tolstoy, in *Anna Karenina,* has given us a partridge-hunting scene that is no less lyrical.

For sheer excitement of the chase, the stag-hunting scene that opens Sir Walter Scott's *Lady of the Lake* is without peer:

Waken, lords and ladies gay!
On the mountain dawns the day;
All the jolly chase is here
With hawk and horse and hunting-
    spear;
Hounds are in their couples yelling,
Hawks are whistling, horns are
    knelling,
Merrily merrily mingle they,
'Waken, lords and ladies gay!' . . . .

In his extraordinary *Alexandria Quartet* Lawrence Durrell has given us a duck-shooting scene that is worth any dozen such scenes from the popular sporting press: "Their wings purr, as they feather the sky, their necks reach. Higher again in mid-heaven, there travel the clear formations of mallard, grouped like aircraft against the light, plowing a soft, slow flight. The guns squash the air and harry them as they pass, moving with a slow curling bias towards the open sea . . ."

e. e. cummings has recreated a medieval hunting scene in a most striking modern manner. It is, I think, the most outstanding poem ever written on the subject of hunting:

all in green went my love riding
on a great horse of gold
into the silver dawn.

Four lean hounds crouched low and
    smiling
the merry deer ran before.

fleeter be they than dappled dreams
the swift sweet deer
the red rare deer.

four red roebuck at a white water
the cruel bugle sang before.

horn at hip went my love riding
riding the echo down
into the silver dawn.

softer be they than slippered sleep
the lean lithe deer
the fleet flown deer.

four fleet does at a gold valley
the famished arrow sang before . . . .

We can't mention all the works motivated to a greater or lesser extent by hunting. Homer and Vergil, Plato and Xenophon, Cicero, Chaucer, Shakespeare, Milton, Cervantes, Fielding, de Maupassant, Kipling, Lawrence Durrell, and John Masters all contain extensive hunting scenes or significant references to hunting.

All these men hunted or admired hunting. They all recognized hunting as an indispensable ingredient of a free and noble lifestyle. And they recognized wild creatures—in the strictest Old Testament sense—as God's gift to man, for nourishment and for delight in the chase: "Thou madest him (man) to have dominion over the works of thy hands; thou hast put all things under his feet: all sheep and oxen, yea, and the beasts of the field; the fowl of the air, and the fish of the sea . . . " (Psalms 8:6-8)

These are names to conjure with. Yet to most American hunters, they are about as familiar as the far side of Betelgeuse. *(Neither are they all that familiar to current college graduates of any persuasion, nor to many Americans considered cultured. K.W.)* Certainly a familiarity with the great cultural heritage of hunting would make us all better hunters—more sensitive to our great heritage, more conscientious, more responsible, and worthier of respect from the anti-hunters who despise us so thoroughly.

As far as hunting literature is concerned, the palm has passed in the twentieth century from the Old World to the New. The works of men like Van Campen Heilner, Havilah Babcock, Corey Ford, and Nash Buckingham have become minor classics. Ernest Hemingway's *Short Happy Life of Francis Macomber* is an absolutely flawless gem of a short story and his *Green Hills of Africa,* although not among his more successful works, is still the best account we have of an African safari.

It is, however, William Faulkner's *The Bear* that stands supreme among all the works of imaginative literature about hunting produced by American authors. In it Faulkner describes hunting as "the best game of all, the best of all breathing and forever the best of all listening."

The visual arts are even more richly endowed than literature for transmitting the hunting heritage. Hunting art began as far back as ancient Egypt: there is a monumental relief of Pharaoh Rameses II hunting ducks with a boomerang. There are also well-preserved reliefs of the Assyrian king Assurbanipal hunting lions in his

chariot, while richly conceived scenes of the hunt dominate much of Persian miniature painting. However, the most—and the best—hunting art is concentrated in 17th-century France —thanks to the patronage of Louis XIV and XV—and in Flanders, which corresponds approximately to present-day Belgium.

The Nonesuch recording of the Bach hunting cantata shows his patron riding to the hunt.

One man—the great diplomat and cosmopolite Peter Paul Rubens—bestrode Flemish painting like a colossus. Although justly more famous for his voluptuous nudes, Rubens has left us some half-dozen hunting canvases. I admire especially his *Boar Hunt,* his *Lion Hunt,* and his *Wolf Hunt.* In each there is a tremendous vortex of energy centered on the hunters, their spears, and their dogs, and converging upon the prey. All of this is set amid apocalyptic landscapes.

Rubens refutes like no other the charge that hunting art is irrelevant today because the circumstances of hunting have changed. The fierce, primitive energy of these scenes and the tremendous will-to-survive of the animal at bay, make it very clear that although circumstances have changed, the spirit remains the same. Prints of these paintings may be bought or ordered from any better art museum, art supply store, or book store.

At Antwerp, Rubens had a school of painting at which it is believed he had up to 400 pupils. Accordingly, many later Flemish paintings and foreign painters came under his influence there.

Among the most accomplished of them, for our purposes, was Paul de

Vos. De Vos specialized in paintings of wild animals and of hunting scenes. He carefully eliminated the hunters from his works, concentrating strictly on the dogs baying their quarry. The radial lines of force in the paintings flow up through the dogs and on into the beast at bay near the center. The overall impression is one of tremendous energy held under control. The rendering of the shapes of the animals' bodies, their hair, and their texture, is meticulous. Perhaps his two finest paintings are *The Deer Hunt* and *The Stag Pursued by Hounds* (originals in the Prado, Madrid).

Under the patronage of King Philip IV and his brother Fernando, the Cardinal-Infante, both zealous hunters, paintings of hunting scenes became extremely fashionable in the Flanders of the first half of the 17th century. Frans Snyders, Jan Wildens, Jan Siberechts, and Roeland Saevery turned out many delightful canvases devoted to the subject. Regrettably, few of their works have been printed.

In neighboring Holland, pictures dealing with hunting motifs took on a very different form, namely the still life. This 17th-century Dutch painting was dominated by themes of bourgeois domesticity, and instead of scenes of the chase, there are beautiful still-lifes of dead game in the kitchen or in the larder. Roedeer, hares, pheasants, ducks, woodcock, and even swans are hung alongside domestic fowl, fruits, and vegetables in cornucopious profusion. With the great masters—Rembrandt, Jan Weenix, Jan Fyt, Adriaen van Utrecht, and Willem van Aelst—the compositions are harmoniously arranged in a kind of calculated chaos. Among the lesser painters they are carelessly arranged.

The striking thing about all these painters is that they took dead game —that sad cliché of most hunting photography—and transformed it into something rich and strange, making it more beautiful dead than alive. Plainly these men had great respect and love for the animals and birds they portrayed.

The greatest collections of hunting art are found at Drottningholm, Sweden; Kranichstein Castle, Darmstadt, Germany; the Hunting Museum in Munich; and the Musée de la Chasse et de la Nature, Hotel Guenégaud, 60 Rue des Archives, Paris. I would suggest that anyone seriously interested in the subject consult the November and December, 1977, issues of *The Connoisseur,* of London, which are devoted in their entirety to the theme: "The Chase in Art."

Music is the most accessible of the arts which bring down to us the glories of European hunting traditions. For much of the greatest hunting music we must look again to the Bourbon dynasty of 16th and 17th century France, namely Louis XIII, Louis XIV, and Louis XV, but most especially to *le Roi Soleil,* the Sun King, Louis XIV.

Absolute monarch of France for 72 years, one of the most indefatigable and certainly the most eminent huntsman of all time, he was among the *grands seigneurs* of all history. Louis XIV wore his music as he wore his magnificently royal robes, throughout the day and on into the night through the endless succession of stylized ceremonies occasioned by every move he made. He had three different orchestras, of which the *Grande Ecurie* (the Great Stable) was designated to play the music that accompanied his daily departure for the hunt, at precisely 2:30 p.m.

It was under the patronage of Louis XIV that such great composers of hunting music as Jean-Baptiste Lully, Andre Danican-Philidor, and Jean-Baptise Morin flourished. Perhaps greatest of them all, Marc-Antoine, Marquis de Dampierre, was Commandant of Louis XV's hunt. Jean-Joseph Mouret, who wrote the rondeau that is now the theme music for Masterpiece Theater, also composed under the patronage of Louis XV. Collectively, these men wrote hundreds of marches, fanfares, and symphonies to accompany various stages of the hunt. Though many of them have been lost, many still survive in all their glory. It is largely due to the efforts of the Musical Heritage Society, 14 Park Road, Tinton Falls, N.J. 07724 that we can relive the splendor of those glorious hunts. I especially recommend MHS records #1080, #1137, and #CC-3, also Deutsche Grammophon #13931, Nonesuch #71009, and EMI CO6128815. These records contain some of the peaks of Western musical achievement. For example, the hunting scene from Jean-Phillipe Rameau's *Hippolyte et Aricie* ranks right up with Mozart's *Don Giovanni* or Bach's Brandenburg Concertos.

Louis XIV established a lifestyle of such grandeur that he was the envy of kings and noblemen all over Europe, emulated by many but equalled by none. Among those noblemen of the baroque era who emulated *le Roi Soleil* was Duke Christian of Sachsen-Weissenfels, Germany. The celebration of his birthday extended over several weeks, and usually included a series of hunts. In 1713 he

called upon the solid paternal, God-intoxicated Johann Sebastian Bach to provide music appropriate to these hunts. Bach responded to the call with the earliest of the very few secular cantatas that he wrote, *Was mir behagt is nur die muntere Jagd* (My one delight is a lively hunt), BWV 208. Bach was only 28 at the time, and the work shows a youthful freshness and vigor that is very appropriate to the subject. It is available in excellent recordings on several labels, among them Nonesuch #H71147.

As in the case of literature, many of the greatest composers turned their hand to music with a hunting motif. Most notable among them are Franz Joseph Haydn (Symphonies #31 "Hornsignal" and #73 "La Chasse"); Antonio Vivaldi (Violin Concerto op. 8 #10, "La Caccia," and the third concerto, "Autumn," from *The Four Seasons;* Mozart (The Hunting Quartet, K. 458); his father Leopold, (Sinfonia di Caccia); and Georg-Phillip Telemann (Suite in F). MHS #CC-3 and 759M contain several of these selections.

Hunting music had its second great efflorescence during the romantic period. There are hunting motifs in several of Richard Wagner's operas *(Siegfried* and *Tannhäuser);* in Albert Lortzing's *Der Wildschütz;* and in Carl Maria von Weber's *Der Freischütz* and *Euryanthe.* (Some of these are available on MHS #1224.) Rossini wrote an original composition for Parforce-Horns entitled "Le Rendez-Vous de Chasse;" Schumann wrote Five Hunting Songs (opus 137), and Schubert wrote several others. Finally, Mendelssohn has given us a lovely "Hunter's Farewell." Originating in the same period were a large group of German folksongs and artsongs done in the folk manner (Lieder), many of them hunting songs. If anything, they are even more exhilirating than the more formal compositions with hunting motifs from the same period. The one indispensable collection of these songs is sung by the great black bass of the Hamburg Opera, Gottlob Frick, on Angel #S-36610.

This article could only give a cursory glance to a subject that is worthy of a book. I hope I have, nevertheless, demonstrated that we hunters have a heritage to be proud of, a heritage of great but neglected riches. I would urge you to explore those "realms of gold." I cannot help but think that a familiarity with them will make us better exemplars of our kind—more aware, more responsible, to the sport, and better able to defend it. ●

To protect politicians the French came to prefer revolvers and, inevitably, built their own.

THE FRENCH MR-73

The standard MR 73—this one a 9mm—has service sights, heavy three-inch barrel, short oversize grips.

by **RAYMOND CARANTA**

Ten YEARS ago in 1973, the huge French Manurhin concern, located in Mulhouse near the German border, disclosed a compact double-action revolver chambered in 357 Magnum, the MR 73 "Police et Défense," intended for police use. That gun, proudly considered by its Alsatian designers and some French police officials as the "best in the world," displayed, in fact, an *internal* workmanship well above the average, a three-inch ribbed barrel (then a rarity) and several original features such as the yoke and the leaf spring-and-roller rebound slide and trigger return.

The MR 73 was tested at length by many government agencies, issued at first in limited quantities to some Police departments, anti-gang brigades and *Gendarmerie nationale* units, exported to various countries of the Middle East and Africa and, since then, several variations have been marketed and widely distributed.

It's a situation of rare standardization. Up to World War II, most French police departments were communal and therefore their equipment was bought by the municipalities to which they were bound. At the turn of the century, there was a hodge-podge of miscellaneous local armaments ranging from the Gras rifle sword-bayonet to the large obsolete 45 service revolver, Model 1873.

The *Gendarmerie nationale,* as a military organization, was already perfectly standardized. Its sidearm was the newly issued swing-out revolver Model 1892, chambered in 8mm and firing a long and heavy flat-nose jacketed bullet. Then, during the first ten years of the century, a new revolver, also chambered in 8mm Model 1892, but more compact and less expensive than the Army service model, and made in Saint-Etienne, was quite successful among police forces. Called the "Municipal," it looked like a British constabulary revolver and was available with rod or with simultaneous ejection.

In 1911, when the *"Bande à Bonnot"*, infamous *"bandits à l'automobile,"* ransacked the country in their stolen cars, armed with Browning 32 ACP pistols, many police departments shifted to automatic pistols of that caliber. After World War I *(la Grande guerre),* the move was complete and revolvers fell into oblivion for quite 50 years, except for target shooting.

Further to the creation of the *Police nationale,* a new force for France, dur-

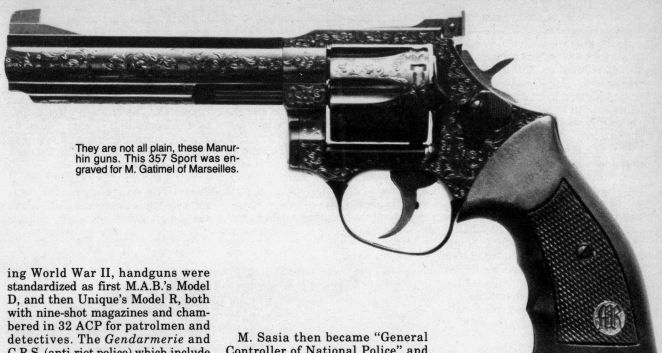

They are not all plain, these Manurhin guns. This 357 Sport was engraved for M. Gatimel of Marseilles.

ing World War II, handguns were standardized as first M.A.B.'s Model D, and then Unique's Model R, both with nine-shot magazines and chambered in 32 ACP for patrolmen and detectives. The *Gendarmerie* and C.R.S. (anti-riot police) which include the highway brigades, were equipped with the 9mm Luger service pistol Model 1950.

Such was the situation in 1960, when the Algerian war was nearly finished: little guns for street cops and heavier artillery for police shock troops.

When General de Gaulle, President of France, started to negotiate with the Algerian rebels, the O.A.S. *(organisation de l'Armée Secrète)* clandestine organization made several attempts on his life. The Government sent a specialist in close-range protection, Raymond Sasia, to the F.B.I. Academy in Virginia, USA, in May, 1962.

M. Sasia then became "General Controller of National Police" and created a National Training Center in Paris where many French, European and African police officers have learned the art of practical shooting. But—this is more important for our story—he also came back from the United States as a true wheelman. He had the Presidential guards equipped with Smith & Wesson revolvers, and started a crusade to convince the Police ordnance people that revolvers were the best for their purpose.

It took quite ten years to succeed. Meanwhile, several prototypes were bought from Smith & Wesson, and Ruger quoted and was favored by many due to its field-stripping capability and economical construction.

Indeed, a fixed-sight round-butt version of the Smith & Wesson Model 19, chambered in 357 Magnum, with a ribbed three-inch barrel, was under consideration when Manurhin proposed to design a French revolver "as good as it can be," tailor-made to the Police nationale requirements.

This led to the MR 73.

The French police shooting champions and instructors who advised the Manurhin engineering staff wanted a sturdy, compact, well-balanced, accurate and comfortable-to-shoot revolv-

MR 73 SPECIFICATION

Model	Police & Defense	Sport	Match (Special grip)	MR 9″ Long Range MR 10¾″ Silhouette
Caliber	38 Special 357 Magnum 9mm Luger	38 Special 357 Magnum 9mm Luger	32 SW Long 38 Special	357 Magnum
Number of shots	6	6	6	6
Barrel length	2½″ - 3″ - 4″	4″ - 5¼″ - 6″ 8″-	6″	9″ -10¾″
Length over-all	8.07″ (3″)	10.82″ (5¼″)	11.73″	14.2″ - 16.7″
Height	4.9″	5.12″	5.7″	5.3″
Thickness	1.5″	1.5″	1.89″	1.5″
Empty weight	32 oz. (3″)	36.42 oz. (5¼″)	40 oz. (.32)	46.42 oz. (9″ plain)
Sight radius	4.4″ (3″)	6.9″ (5¼″)	8.2″	11.53″ (9″)
Normal S.A. pull	5 lbs.	3 lbs.	3 lbs.	3 lbs. (standard)
Normal D.A. pull	85. lbs.	8.5 lbs.	Nil	8.5 lbs. (optional)
Sights	Fixed	Click adjustable	Click adjustable	Click adjustable

er. All worked together to meet these drastic requirements.

As the gun was to be sturdy, a solid frame with a swing-out cylinder along the S&W Military & Police system was selected. The steels were the best available and critical surfaces were to be as smooth as possible. Manurhin are mostly machine-tool manufacturers, so this was an easy task for them.

For the compactness, a medium round-butt frame was drawn and the barrel length of the French police model was set to 74mm (2.91 inches) with a resulting length of 8.07 inches. The cylinder diameter is similar to that of the Smith & Wesson Model 19, i.e. 1.5-inch against 1.45-inch. An excellent balance was obtained with a ribbed barrel fitted with an ejector rod housing, a cross between those of the Colt Python and S&W Magnums.

Accuracy is very good. Manurhin has a long experience in the making of barrels for automatic cannons, military rifles and Walther pistols. For the MR 73 barrel, the Manurhin staff selected a tight boring, similar to that of some Colt revolvers, in view of producing later a 9mm Luger variation with interchangeable cylinders. This is generally good for accuracy, but sometimes increases leading with handloads or even some commercial ammunition.

With excellent workmanship and close tolerances, the cylinder alignment and gap are as perfect as possible. An original yoke was designed for the cylinder, with a view to reducing both play resulting from possible abuses and the entrance of sand or other foreign materials.

The sights are conventional—⅛-inch wide, square ramp style for the front and a square notch for the rear sight. Under poor light conditions, they are just as bad as their American counterparts. The barrel rib is sandblasted.

The French police advisers were critical about the double-action pull, and Manurhin engineers tried to improve over Smith & Wesson, not an easy bet as everybody will agree. In that time, when the only double action revolvers featuring coil-type mainsprings were Colt's Trooper and Lawman, the small frame Smith & Wessons, the first generation Rugers and the German Arminius, leaf springs were generally thought better for providing smooth double-action pulls. This was later demonstrated as an error by the Spanish Astra 357 Magnum revolver, among others.

All that was not known yet and Manurhin took another path. Their approach mounted the rebound slide on rollers to avoid jolts during the trigger return stroke, and set-up an adjustable small leaf, also acting on rollers, for the same return function. The result is extremely positive and double-action pulls are usually about 14 oz. lighter than those of similar S&W revolvers for the same hammer strike. Manurhin MR 73's are now famous for this smoothness, combined with crisp single action pulls. Just as for revolvers of other makes, however, misfires occur when trigger pull weights are too low.

To improve shooting comfort, special care was devoted to the grip. However, in my opinion, too much consideration was given to instinctive shooting with low-power ammunition as the backstrap is too canted, without anything to prevent the gun from slipping in the hand in rapid fire with hot loads, a defect shared with modern Colt revolvers. (Again, my opinion.) Using wadcutters at the shooting range, this grip is very pleasant for those who have small hands and it is also quite short for better concealment and affords good support to the second finger.

The empty weight is just two pounds, which is good for the average shooter and the sights are relatively low over the hand, also an excellent feature. Among the minor weak points of the gun are the small square spur of the hammer and the poorly shaped thumbpiece of the cylinder latch.

When the gun entered in service, small bugs developed, but were soon corrected. The M 73 "Police & Défence" is now highly appreciated by French police officers. And it is also commercially available with 2½-inch or 4-inch barrels.

Before the MR 73 was issued, when everything was ready for the final competition between the MR 73 and the foreign models, somebody had the

Manurhin largely followed the Smith & Wesson path, but some engineer balked at the crane and so this massive arrangement was born.

bright idea to require that the new French Police and *Gendarmerie nationale* revolver be capable of shooting the 9mm Luger cartridge. This would unify the supply of handgun and submachine gun ammunition and to exhaust the existing stocks available in this caliber, they said.

There and then started a long race between Manurhin, Smith & Wesson and Ruger.

Manurhin engineers eventually invented and patented a clever extractor for rimless cartridges and the 9mm Luger was introduced at the beginning of 1977, both as a caliber option and as a spare cylinder for converting existing revolvers. This writer shot it in October, 1976, and

The standard Sport MR 73 offers micrometer sights, 5¼-inch barrel, full-length under-rib, and a bigger butt profile than the standard.

was favorably impressed. The factory had done a tremendous work from the reliability and interchangeability standpoints. A Manurhin tester, M. Pflieger, shot offhand, in front of me, a 1.53 x 2-in. single-action group and a 1.77 x 2.16-in. double-action group, five rounds each, at 25 meters.

However, once the 9mm was in service, several quite insuperable problems were met, brought on by the diversity of the ammunition available. Beside the steel-case military ammu-

nition, primers were not intended for revolvers, cases were not really adapted to revolver use, cannelures were very different, brand to brand, and there are two significantly different case lengths, those made in the United States being longer than most European production.

After five years of playing and testing, the French ordnance seems to have definitely abandoned this nice dream, and only the 357 Magnum remains in government service.

When the MR 73 was ready for the commercial market, a target version was immediately introduced in 38 Special, 357 Magnum and, since 1977, 9mm Luger. While 4, 6, and 8-inch barrels were available, the basic Sport model had a 5.12 inch heavy

This is the 32 Match MR 73. The barrel weight slides; the sight and hammer spur are oversize; the grips may be individually fitted.

barrel especially designed so as to give the same balance as a 6-inch barrel, but with a shorter sight radius. An adjustable backlash stop was added behind the trigger and the gun was fitted with target sights.

The .13-inch square front sight is undercut and mounted on a knurled ramp. The rib is identical to that of the service model. The micrometer rear sight is outstanding and original with its very large undercut dull blade (.94-inch wide; .39-inch high). The square notch is .12-inch wide and sight radius is 6.9-inch long with the 5.12-inch basic barrel. In the same configuration, the empty weight is 36.42 ounces. The gun is slightly more muzzle-heavy than a conventional 6-inch K38 Masterpiece, balanced .39-inch in front of the trigger. The top of the rear sight is .12-inch higher over the hand than that of the K38.

As a target revolver, the grip is a little short for big hands and the hammer spur is small and too square for the swinging silhouette of I.S.U. competition.

The MR 73 "Sport" is well thought of among French big bore target shooters. It was only the dream of many while the dollar rate oscillated between four and five French francs; good American guns were cheaper. At seven francs for a dollar, it became cheap for the workmanship provided

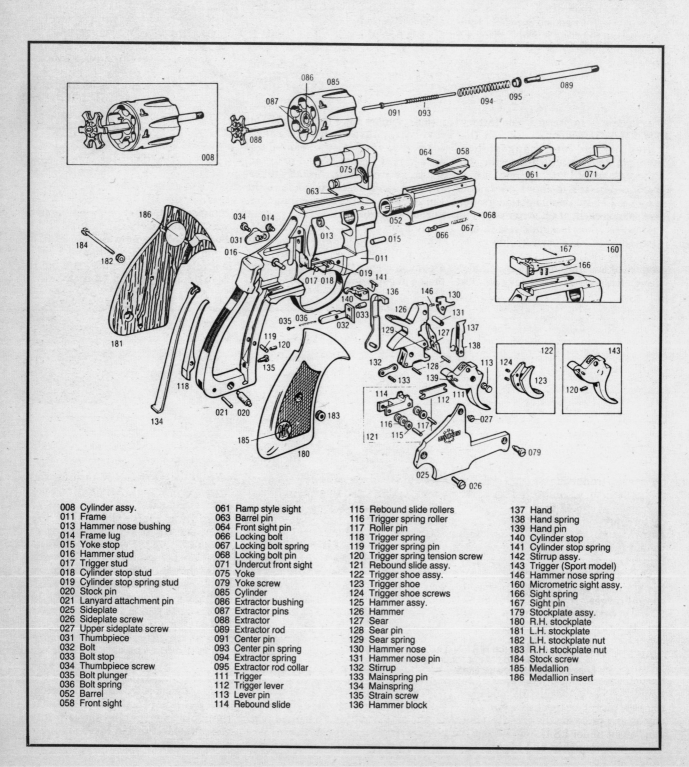

008 Cylinder assy.	061 Ramp style sight	115 Rebound slide rollers	137 Hand
011 Frame	063 Barrel pin	116 Trigger spring roller	138 Hand spring
013 Hammer nose bushing	064 Front sight pin	117 Roller pin	139 Hand pin
014 Frame lug	066 Locking bolt	118 Trigger spring	140 Cylinder stop
015 Yoke stop	067 Locking bolt spring	119 Trigger spring pin	141 Cylinder stop spring
016 Hammer stud	068 Locking bolt pin	120 Trigger spring tension screw	142 Stirrup assy.
017 Trigger stud	071 Undercut front sight	121 Rebound slide assy.	143 Trigger (Sport model)
018 Cylinder stop stud	075 Yoke	122 Trigger shoe assy.	146 Hammer nose assy.
019 Cylinder stop spring stud	079 Yoke screw	123 Trigger shoe	160 Micrometric sight assy.
020 Stock pin	085 Cylinder	124 Trigger shoe screws	166 Sight spring
021 Lanyard attachment pin	086 Extractor bushing	125 Hammer assy.	167 Sight pin
025 Sideplate	087 Extractor pins	126 Hammer	179 Stockplate assy.
026 Sideplate screw	088 Extractor	127 Sear	180 R.H. stockplate
027 Upper sideplate screw	089 Extractor rod	128 Sear pin	181 L.H. stockplate
031 Thumbpiece	091 Center pin	129 Sear spring	182 L.H. stockplate nut
032 Bolt	093 Center pin spring	130 Hammer nose	183 R.H. stockplate nut
033 Bolt stop	094 Extractor spring	131 Hammer nose pin	184 Stock screw
034 Thumbpiece screw	095 Extractor rod collar	132 Stirrup	185 Medallion
035 Bolt plunger	111 Trigger	133 Mainspring pin	186 Medallion insert
036 Bolt spring	112 Trigger lever	134 Mainspring	
052 Barrel	113 Lever pin	135 Strain screw	
058 Front sight	114 Rebound slide	136 Hammer block	

and domestic sales boomed.

During 1979, the Manurhin management decided to design, upon the suggestion of French Army and *Fédération Francaise de Tir* officials, two improved target versions of the Sport model intended for sporting handgun shooting under ISU regulations. One gun was chambered in 38 Special and the other one in 32 SW Long.

They were introduced in 1980 and the 32 Match took the National title the same year. The Match models differ from the Sport as follows: • Single action only with wide serrated trigger. • Longer sight radius (8.18-inch instead of 6.9-inch). • Lower rear sight. • Interchangeable sights. •

beautiful, even when compared to yesteryear standards. The very large interchangeable blades of the rear sight are without peer on a modern revolver; trigger pull is extremely clean with convenient backlash adjustment; and the sliding balance weight is a marked improvement over all competitive models. Finally, when custom fitted to the shooter's hand, the optional walnut target grip significantly reduces both fatigue and jerks, particularly at the turning I.S.U. "silhouette."

The latest Manurhin achievement in the MR 73 line was released in January, 1981. It is the MR 9-inch Long Range, designed in accordance with the regulations of both the Inter-

easy field stripping. Accordingly, Manurhin contracted with the Southport manufacturer for the supply of frame castings and fitted them with French 3 and 4-inch barrels, 357 Magnum cylinders and walnut stockplates similar to those of the fine MR 73 *Police & Defense*.

The new revolver, called "Special Police," was introduced as a substitute police model featuring a better workmanship and a smoother action than direct imports. Three grip sizes were scheduled in walnut: Sport for big hands; Police for average; and *Tir rapide* or small, for fast shooting. There were special rubber stockplates.

The empty weight was 33.6 oz. and

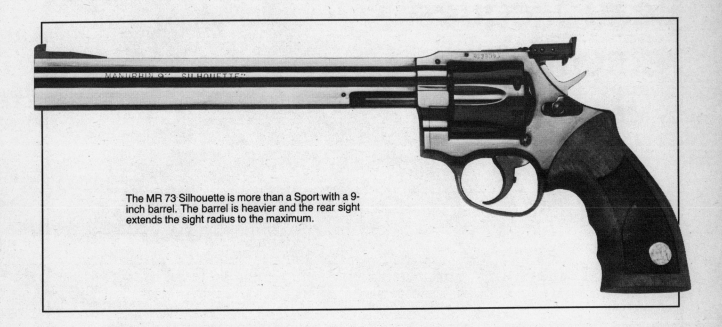

The MR 73 Silhouette is more than a Sport with a 9-inch barrel. The barrel is heavier and the rear sight extends the sight radius to the maximum.

Shorter cylinder matching the cartridge length. • Longer barrel (5.9-inch instead of 5.12-inch). • New barrel forcing cone, improving the bullet entrance. • Sliding 3.57-oz. balance weight (four positions). • Grooved enlarged trigger.

The guns are available with either the standard sport stockplates or a special target grip. Empty weight is 38.6-oz. with the Sport stockplates and 40-oz. with the special target grip.

An MR 38 Match under test in our facilities appealed to all the seasoned French shooters who had the chance to use it. They consider this model as the best target *revolver* available today at any price for the "Sport handgun" event under I.S.U. regulations.

The workmanship and bluing are

national Handgun Silhouette Association (IHMSA) and the International Handgun Long Range Association (IHLRA).

This special version of the 357 Magnum MR 73 Sport is fitted with either a 9 or a 10¾-inch (called the Silhouette Model) heavy barrel, rifled at a 18¾-inch R.H. pitch for long range shooting with 160 to 220-grain full jacketed bullets. A 2.85-oz. lead balance weight is available as an option. With the basic 9-inch barrel, the plain revolver weighs 46-oz. and is 14.2-inch long. Otherwise, it is strictly similar to the Sport model.

Meanwhile, the Ruger service revolver, recently improved as far as the double action pull is concerned, was also scoring high. Police circles like its low cost production potential and

over-all length was 8.15-inch for the three-inch barrel. All "Police Specials" are blued.

Unfortunately, the cost of the American components increased so sharply during the year 1982 that the whole project was cancelled. Now, the rare "Special Police" revolvers are highly desirable collector's pieces.

That's quite a lot of activity for 10 years. While the MR 73 is controversial as a service revolver, where its nice workmanship and smooth double action result in quite a high price tag and internal sophistication, as a sporting handgun, it becomes a superb specimen of modern engineering. In the recent Match and Silhouette configurations, I believe it certainly one of the best target revolvers in its class. ●

Gun Collecting's
HEYDAY

This is Beau Jacques, and Beau Jacques remembers . . .

by **R. C. HOUSE**

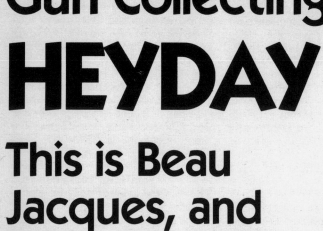

In the mid-50s, nobody went shooting in buckskins and fur hats unless he was looking for wisecracks or guys in white coats.

THE YEAR is 1948.

The man looking over the fullstock Kentucky rifle he has come across resting in a corner of an antique shop has no notion that he—or anyone ever again—might fire it. He considers himself only a collector. In these times, he knows of very few people interested in shooting the old guns.

Thus, instead of bringing it to his shoulder and looking down the sights, he carefully turns it over and over, studying its lines, its graceful primitive sculpture, the wedding of metal to wood still crisp after 100 years. He marvels at the tiger-stripe grain of the wood which, like a fine polished gem, shows new rippling facets each time the light catches them at a slightly different angle.

He can scarcely afford the $15 price tag, but he knows he has to have it to add to his collection.

World War II seems to have been the catalyst that brought gun collecting to its finest hour. There had, it seemed, always been gun collectors, but they were something of a quiet minority. There had also been state gun collecting associations and a Na-

tional Muzzle Loading Rifle Association for some years, but it still was a hobby and a sport shared by a relative few.

Those of us who rode the crest of the postwar boom in black powder guns still don't know exactly why or how it happened. It is difficult to put your finger on what caused it, or what the motivations were that brought us into this flood of interest and to go with that tide of growing sport and hobby for 30-plus years now.

Somehow the fates decreed that I should be in it, this postwar black powder boom. Gun shows began simply as get-togethers of people, mostly men, with similar interests. At the start, they were not sales events, though some selling and trading went on. Mostly, the great guns were hauled off the walls and carried to some central meeting place, tables were set up and people wandered around and looked at one another's collections. And the hot air flowed.

Even as I entered the hobby as a quite young man, I sensed the winds of change. I remember particularly— and this was probably in the early

'50s—listening to Virginia Kindig speak of what she considered sadly significant trends in gun collecting. She was the wife of Wes Kindig, founder of the Log Cabin Sport Shop, now a nationally known shop owned and operated by the sons of Wes and Virginia.

Hers was a kind of wistful sadness at the changing aspects of collecting. The big eastern dealers were making pilgrimages to the Ohio shows, and probably to others I was not aware of. All day Saturday and on Sunday morning, they roamed up and down the aisles of the shows as collections were uncovered, almost stalking the bargain gun buy. They had seemingly endless supplies of ready cash. In retrospect after more than 30 years, it is easy to see they were shrewdly investing in gun collecting "futures."

They saw the big boom coming and were already preparing for it. All day long the stacks of newly bought Kentuckies, rare muskets and other long guns and handguns piled up behind their display tables. They, too, had brought along things to sell. Along about Sunday noon, however, their blankets and padded wrappers came out and the mass of guns was carefully wrapped and tied for the long trip home.

Virginia observed this and decried the change. For a long time, she told me, the Ohio guns had stayed in Ohio. Sure, they were traded, and a gun from a Cincinnati collection might wind up on a wall in Cleveland, but Cleveland guns were also showing up in Cincinnati. Now, those same guns were leaving the state, and others from other regions were coming into Ohio. Virginia probably failed to see that gun collecting was growing out of a state and regional adolescence, and maturing into a national hobby.

Those of us who were on the scene wish now with hindsight that we had had some of the foresight of those eastern dealers—men like Bob Abels, Tony Fidd, Herb Glass, Norm Flayderman and others. Anyone who has an old Abels or Flayderman catalog from the 50s becomes quickly aware of that. Through their shrewd buying and business savvy, their catalogs grew fatter by the year.

Those same guns are now in collections across the country; they are the ones that today show up on gun show tables with $700 and $800 price tags. They served as the prototypes for the beautiful proliferation of fine replicas on the market today.

But in those days, there were only originals. I ran with a pack of collec-

tors who had, in my estimation, the true collector spirit. Our collections grew and diversified, but nobody I spent much time with ever had many more than five or ten guns at any time. Most of us had to sell something from our collection before we could invest in others. We often parted with precious possessions with great anguish.

We quickly adopted the philosophy that we didn't "own" these guns. Sure, our money gave us temporary stewardship, but these were the things of history and of the future—larger than ourselves. Lofty and egotistical as it may sound, we considered ourselves merely "curators." It was our duty to restore and preserve these symbols of early American craft and art in as near their venerable condition as possible, at the same time respecting their antiquity.

Thus we cringed, rebelled and sometimes got downright nasty when someone "refinished" an old gun stock to a high-gloss varnish. We despised the mindless grinding away of fine age-brown patina on the flats of a barrel, followed by cold blueing. Senseless as it sounds, it happened; so help me, it happened!

In the long history of these guns that carved a nation out of an inhospitable and sinister backwoods frontier, we, the sensitive ones, were the restorers and the preservers. It behooved us to treat these ancients with dignity; we had an obligation to the long-gone original owners to restore them to something of their original glory. We also owed it to future generations.

The motivation of the "true" collectors and restorers of those days was not money, though the improvement of the product surely heightened its market value. But that, to most of us, was a secondary benefit. In a much larger sense, there was a personal connection we had with a glorious past as we held in our hands these wood and metal objects of our heritage. In finding original beauty under the neglect and abuse of years, we were truly reaching back to meet and greet those bygone giants. In handling and restoring their guns, our lives truly intersected theirs as surely as though we had breathed the same woodland air and drank from the same mountain streams.

Call it fantasy, call it day-dreaming, there was much, much more to it than that. In our embrace of the solid substance of America, we operated from a totally realistic point of view.

But where does it all begin? What

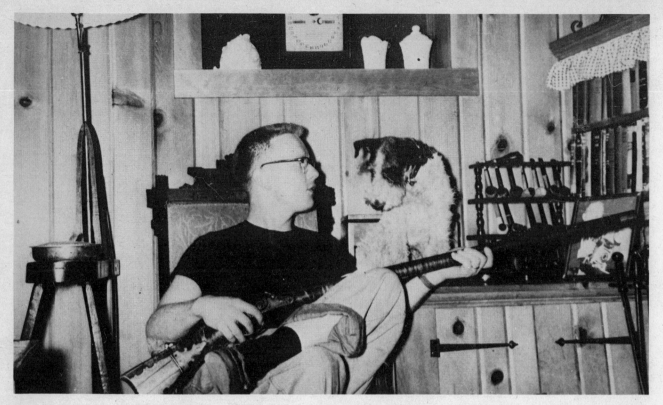

In the early '50s, the author's collection was highlighted by this original 32 fullstock by S. Stout, Lancaster; he had more pipes and books than guns.

makes a muzzleloader man? Is it possible to put your finger on the surges of mystic force within an individual that makes this one a sports fan, that one a classic violinist, this one a stamp collector, that one a gun nut?

Out of any given number of babies born, a certain percentage, I am sure, are bound to be gun collectors. I've talked with a lot of people down through the years about it, and the consensus is pretty strong. Early on in their lives, they become aware of a growing need, a consciousness of beautiful old shooting pieces, and their compulsion to have some on their walls begins to grow.

Once this realization dawns, the twig becomes bent, the tree is inclined, and a lifetime is shaped around his mania. No escaping it; it's there. Once caught, like the gambling or the alcohol sickness, it seldom goes away; it only becomes stronger. It lurks there in the blood, always demanding the nourishment of another gun to own, another shop or show to go to, another rendezvous, another sunny afternoon of burning powder.

My own early influences are easy to trace. A Cleveland, Ohio, newspaper had a Sunday rotogravure section—a magazine supplement. It was mostly photographs and in those days, in the early '30's, was on slick paper in brown ink, called sepia-tone.

One picture when I couldn't have been a day over six or seven, was of an early American fireplace with logs blazing on the hearth, and tall candlesticks and three-legged kettles and all sorts of old-timey things around it. What hurled a spear of delight into my heart was a fullstock Kentucky rifle resting on pegs above the mantle, with a horn and pouch dangling beneath—the symbol of early American readiness and rugged independence.

I recall cutting out the picture in my childish way and pasting it in a scrapbook with Lepage's wheat paste—the kind of gunk that dried thoroughly after three days and the pictures fell out. I remember hours of staring at that picture, a compulsion growing within my chubby little baby fat that some day I would own a rifle just like that one, and maybe even a cabin with a hearth like that to hang my longrifle over.

Seeing he had a gun nut for a kid, my old man finally gave up his cherished dream of having a big-league ballplayer in the family and began preparing me for ownership of my first real gun—his little Stevens 22 Crackshot. He would not allow me the intermediate step of a BB gun. With him you went from boy to man in one quick jump. He complained that a lot of fathers allowed their boys to have BB guns like pacifiers. They weren't play guns or real guns, but the father could consider them a toy and turn the kid loose without much training. My dad was right; a few eyes were lost in our town from improper training with a BB gun.

With him, by gum, when you were man enough to have a gun, you got it, but you sure as hell had also done your homework. He brought home a thick oak plank and set it against the basement wall and on cold winter nights we poured 22 Shorts at targets from across the room. If I missed hitting the board—I don't remember missing—or violated some elementary safety rule, I'd get a smart cuff up 'side the head. When he thought I was ready, I got permission to haul the Crackshot on my regular forays into the woods and along the creek banks. If I got paid for chores, or had an allowance, the money for cartridges had to come from that; 22 Longs in those days were 35 cents a box.

The Christmas I was 10, there was a long, flat box under the tree. After I pulled off the colorful wrapping, the Winchester logo appeared on the box and inside it was a Model 61 pump 22 with an octagon barrel, a comparative rarity, I've been told.

I still have it and after 40 and more

years, and tens of thousands of rounds through it, most of its blue is intact, the stock still gleams, and it still shoots true as a maiden's vow.

I hunted squirrel with it, while the old man lugged along his old Stevens 12-gauge double with outside hammers. One day when we were out among the shocked corn and the oaks and hickories, he had me heft his gun and take aim at a pile of dead leaves. The recoil sent my red corduroy cap dangling on my cowlick. The kick was like that of a mule, but I remember the feeling as being as sweet as a caress. When he got a new shotgun, I got the old Stevens to hang on my wall with the Winchester and the Crackshot. In the days ahead they would be joined by many frontstuffers.

One day the old man got the commander of his Legion post to take me in and show me their gun locker. Somehow, instead of 03's, they had come into possession of enough brand new, unfired, 1873 Springfield trapdoor rifles to equip the entire post for drilling and salute squads. I don't remember the Legion using them, but I do remember that guncase door whining open and seeing that regiment of rifles standing at attention all beautiful blue metal barrels and case-hardened breeches, and brown wood marked only by clear oval inspector's marks.

I became aware of an ache to own one of them. Not merely to own it, but to heft and feel and fondle it, keep it cleaned and oiled, to study on it and dream and learn of the history and the events and the drama it had seen. My consolation came a few months later when a pal and I, on a long bike trip, stopped at a country repair garage run by a man who loved guns and took them in on trade sometimes for his work on Model As and Plymouths and such. He had a couple Civil War guns for sale cheap and we rushed home to get our dads' permission and loan of a few bucks to get them, promising to work like hell in the yard to pay for them.

His dad was more easily swayed and went right out. For five bucks, my buddy got an original Zouave musket, as best I can remember its lines. When my old man and I went out, he shelled out two bucks for a contract Civil War musket by Jas. D. Mowry. The rear sight was gone and a nub of copper wire served for a front sight. The stock was docked half its length, and only one band remained. Someone had also tried to checker the wrist and fore-end.

No matter. I had my first antique.

C. H. Spriggle, the Ohio country gunsmith who got the author started in black powder, posed in 1951 with just a small sample of his enormous collection in which Kentuckies were predominant.

By 1952, the author's collection amounted to this sorry-looking hodgepodge. It was a start.

Even the worst basket case plays a true collector like a harp, invoking his sympathies, spurring him to work some kind of restoration, regardless how futile. The pal and I sent off to Bannerman's in New York for original Civil War forage caps at 50 cents each, and a tin of original top-hat musket caps, and went out in the woods and played Civil War.

One day he tore a shotgun shell apart (I wasn't around or might have cautioned better judgment), poured it in the muzzle, and followed it with a marble. I don't have to tell you the rest. When the smoke cleared, the beautiful Zouave was in two pieces with the breech area totally gone, and my friend almost minus his arm.

Our barber, an inveterate coon-hunter and shooter, penned a poem to my pal in the hospital, and somehow I never forgot the rhyme:

"I was never any sicker, than when I heard you'd pulled the trigger, on your old muzzle loader of yore; When the doc removes the bandage, I hope that you will manage, to never pull that trigger anymore!"

World War II came and toward the end of it, I got in, qualifying with my issue M1, as well as with the pistol, the water-cooled machine gun, and that big stovepipe three-man 81mm mortar. I never had to use the M1 for blood, but the shooting germ got into mine forever.

I am sure the fates were at work with evil design when in one of my first college classes, I worked at a geology lab table with a guy who had spent a lifetime collecting 18th and 19th century martial pistols. We became pals and on numerous weekends, we drove to his folks' home to sit by the hour in his gunroom and talk guns and hold guns and look them over, his cabinets and walls loaded with prime examples.

He had the wherewithal to buy collections just to get a particular piece to round out his collection. Once he took me into his basement to show me his "trade goods" — Kentuckies and other rifles, pistols and revolvers, sabers, a significant mess of all kinds of goodies. He offered me the lot for $1,000 to get me started in collecting and dealing. I had $800 in the bank and three years of college facing me—with a little help from Uncle Sam. I was tempted, but helpless.

He introduced me to my first gun show—this one at the grand Neil House in Columbus, Ohio, in the spring of 1948. The night before we left, we went out and got swakked on 3.2 beer in one of the local college-boy

hangouts. Outside in the cold early spring night with the grey slush turning crunchy again with chill, he lifted the car trunk lid to show me the guns he planned to take to the show. From the bunch I bought a North flintlock pistol for $13. When I sold it two years later for $18, I felt I had made the deal of a lifetime!

That show was a fabulous eye-opener. My pal Bob knew nearly everyone in the Ohio Gun Collectors Association. We hobnobbed with Bob Abels and Tony Fidd—big-time dealers out of New York. I met a rather eccentric character named Miller Bedford whose claim to fame was a home-

On July 4, 1961, Detroit's Loomis Battery—the author a member—filled the air with smoke and roar at the Centennial Re-Enactment of the Battle of the First Bull Run.

made lubricant and preservative called "Gunjuice." We talked with Bill Large and Wes Kindig, names to become nationally famous, and the proprietor of the Military Inn in Dearborn, Michigan, Andy Palmer. Andy's establishment boasted one of the largest gun collections in the world. He also put out a newspaper called "Great Guns."

Andy also alleged to be the owner of "The Gun That Killed Long-Nose Kate," and I heard the story that weekend. It took Andy the better part of an hour to tell it. Some years later, when I was living in Dearborn, I often saw the gun when I went to Military Inn for dinner. It was a rusted little derringer-style revolver, the original "Saturday Night Special." Andy's purported research tended to indicate that Long-Nose Kate was leaning

way over the Tombstone, Arizona, bar for a glass of water when a gun went off in an argument at a poker table. She fell dead. According to Andy, it was Doc Holliday, who, finding no wounds in the comely prostitute's body, determined that the bullet, at that angle, had entered a prefabricated orifice!

The facts proved Andy a 14-karat liar, but it made a hell of a yarn!

Out of college, I took a reporter-photographer job on a small-town, Ohio, paper. In the course of things, I ferreted out an oldtime country gunsmith for a feature story. He built and repaired all manner of rifles, but his

greatest love was Kentuckies. I'll bet he had several hundred.

His workshop was in a 9x12 shed behind the house, and it was hard to move around in there for the guns stacked everywhere, with dusty old powderhorns and hunting bags and sabers and Bowie knives encrusting the walls and stacked around in the floor space. His house was equally packed with gun cabinets, cases and racks, mostly Kentuckies. I bought a fine old Lancaster style rifle by S. Stout from him for $49—about the equivalent of a week's pay for me, before taxes! He painstakingly took the time to teach me all he knew about the care and feeding of muzzleloaders. I was hooked.

For the essentials, the old gunsmith steered me to a man who was just getting started in a business of supplying to the muzzleloader trade. He lived nearby in Lodi, Ohio. I went over to see him to get my first supply of caps and balls and other fixings for my fullstock. He was Wes Kindig whom I had met a few years earlier in Columbus, and who founded the now well-known Log Cabin Sport Shop. After Wes' death, the shop was taken over by his sons, Dan and Rick, who really converted it to national prominence. Then they were just little fellows hanging around behind the counter and learning the ropes.

For things Wes couldn't supply, he referred me to another man who had a pretty good business starting up down in Union City, Tennessee. It had to be in the early '50s that I sent my first

actions, and ornate silver crescent buttplates.

The name H.M. POPE stamped on top of the barrels meant absolutely nothing. A dozen or so of the moulds and tong tools in the drawers also bore Pope's name. I heard of a grocer in nearby Akron who bought guns. Figuring I could pick up a few bucks against my bill to the antique dealer, I paid him a visit with the Pope-marked hardware and guns in the car.

He took great pains to explain how the bores were worn, the finish gone and the stocks in such disrepair, and he didn't have any idea how he'd move those tong tools and moulds. He grudgingly gave me $40 for the lot.

And the very next issue of "The

grin much later. That copy should have been in a museum.

Despite my bungling, gun shows were great. True wheeling and dealing went on. Original Kentuckies, fullstocks at that, seemed to be the most prized, sought-after pieces. It was common to go to a show and see dozens of them lining the tables, and damned few with price tags over $100.

Hindsight is a distressing thing. Anyone who has been collecting more than 20 years kicks himself over the prices that Civil War muskets and 45-70s were going for, usually no more than $25 for a musket and $10 to 15 for the trapdoors; rifles, that is. Carbines were a bit higher. '03 Springfields were worse. My brother-in-law got one unfired, mint, for five bucks.

But how we wheeled and dealed. A table rented for about two bucks at the Swiss Club in Canton or at the Fairgrounds in Ashland, or the hall the OGCA used in Chagrin Falls, Ohio. One weekend at the Swiss Club, I dealt so high and mighty that I came away after much buying and swapping and selling and taking boot with a fullstock Kentucky I had wanted, and a near-mint 1873 Winchester. I managed my hotel room, eats and beers, and my buddy and I had taken in dinner and a show on Saturday night, and I brought home extra cash besides.

I had the rare Midas touch that weekend. It went away after that and never came back.

Years passed, more and more collectors were joining the circuit, driving the prices up. What had started as a laid-back, carefree hobby began to take on overtones of viciousness in making bucks rather than enjoying to the fullest the guns themselves, and the fun of driving a bargain. Even rusty Belgian frontstuffer shotguns were starting to command a price over $10. Once somebody outright gave me one—with the left-hand lock missing—and I hauled it along to a show to see what I could get for it, and I don't mean the missing lock!

A buddy from work drove down for his first show. I was short of funds and figured to hit him up for a fiver to have a few beers at the show and buy lunch. By the time we got there, his car was about out of gas and he asked to borrow five for gas and beer and lunch.

Oops! We were both broke, the tank was nearly empty. All that stood between us and disaster was that Belgian shotgun.

I threw it into the pot, telling him to play dumb and try to find a buyer for

The Loomis Battery—with one green recruit named House hopelessly out of uniform—parades in Battle Creek, Michigan. Aside from the jackets and trousers, everything was original issue.

mail order to Turner Kirkland of Dixie Gun Works.

Soon my fullstock had a companion. I picked up a nice little small caliber halfstock in an antique shop for $18. I was on my way. Word of my eccentric hobby got around. An antique dealer whose story I had written up for the paper called one night. He had just taken in trade five old guns, a big oak gun cabinet with a row of small drawers down the side—all of them loaded with moulds and tong tools and such.

I looked the stuff over and agreed to $200 for the lot, without any idea where the money was coming from. The guns included a halfstock Kentucky, a 45-70 1873 Springfield rifle, a Russian bolt-action military rifle, and a couple of things I learned from reading were Schuetzen rifles. They had fish-belly stocks and drop-block

American Rifleman" carried a full-page obituary on Harry M. Pope, the greatest barrel-maker and gunsmith of them all. The story said as much as that any gun or piece of equipment with Pope's name on it was worth about twice its weight in gold. I bowed my head and offered a prayer to deliver me from such stupidity on my part.

I should have learned a lesson, but didn't. Also in the mess was a book, "The Bullet's Flight" by Franklin P. Mann. It was obviously even earlier than a first edition because little slips of paper were glued right into the binding pointing out errors in the text that were to be corrected before final publication. At a gun show soon after, I persuaded a man to part with two bucks for the book—one of the earliest and most prized treatises on ballistics, a fact I was to learn to my chait. My face was known, so it would be impossible for me to pull off the scam. He was a personable, persuasive guy and I figured with the right line, he might be able to peddle it. I told him to walk up and down the aisles and talk with anyone who showed interest. He was to tell them it had been in the family for years, he didn't know what it was worth, but that he needed money to mend some fences or get a new tractor tire—anything. After his first pass, he caught up with me with a grin on his face like he'd been set up. He still had the shotgun.

"You S.O.B.," he said, "this gun's not worth a dime!"

"I know," I said, "but we gotta sell the damned thing today, or we don't get home tonight."

He saw my line of reasoning. It took us most of the day, but we finally

At Ford's Greenfield Village Muzzle Loader Festival, the Loomis Battery team competes at far left, the author third from left, digging into his pouch.

found a buyer with $15. In the twilight, we headed happily for home with a full tank of gas, bellies full of beer. We stopped off at a roadhouse for chicken-fried steak and home fries and felt on top of the world!

A Belgian shotgun was responsible for another hilarious episode. I was visiting another buddy when his phone rang. Knowing he was up on his guns values, a local antique dealer wanted to bring by a gun she had bought at an auction for his "appraisal." He hemmed and hawed, reluctant to get involved, but finally gave in. In about ten minutes, the doorbell rang and in popped this woman with her Belgian shotgun. If I'm not mistaken, the left-hand lock was missing. (Why always the left-hand lock?)

She was a typical antique dealer who should have stayed with her

Windsor chairs, depression glass, crystal decanters and tiny lavalieres. She wore mannish shoes, a tweed skirt, and a knobby sweater over a plain blouse. Her greying hair was wadded up in a bun on top of her head—a great place to hide pencils—and her glasses dangled from a brass chain around her neck.

More hemming and hawing.

My buddy looked her shotgun over and over, trying to find some way to ease the pain; she had bought something that with a little fixing up could sell for junk. After many long pauses and false starts, he said, "Well, gee, I suppose . . . well, you might be able to get 30 dollars for it."

"Thirty dollars" she screamed. "Thirty dollars?! I paid $50!"

A lot of collectors today probably aren't aware that the first replica antique guns were fakes. A lot of collectors got stung with these.

By the early '60s, though, I became aware of the first acknowledged replicas coming on the market. A tall, rawboned Lincolnesque man named Cap Cole from Pittsburgh began showing up at the Ohio shows with replica Kentuckies.

I was touring the show with another buddy, and we stopped by and I wanted to compliment Cole on the quality of his work.

"What I like," I said, "is that you don't stick in a brass inlay every time the knife slips."

Cole really didn't take a good look at us. He wore a broad-brimmed hat with a beaded band and was looking down at something he was working on. "Naw," he drawled, "some of them inlays are about as out of place as a

wart right on the end of your nose."

My companion, a good-natured guy with a rapier wit, did indeed have a prominent beak with, coincidentally, a dark brown mole slightly off center of the very tip.

"Sir," he said, sounding haughty as hell, "I'll remind you not to joke about warts on other people's noses."

Cole's eyes came up and fixed on the blob on the pal's nose. His look said he wished for a larger than normal crack in the floor in which to hide.

"Well," he said, by way of apology and appraisal, "ah, gee, yours ain't so big, y'know."

I also had handgun fever. Three of us were heading for a gun show early one Saturday morning. The guy riding in front said he was taking along a little percussion revolver to sell; he handed it back to me. What I hefted was an original Colt New Belt Model in top shape. Most of the blue was gone leaving the mellow grey-silver on frame, barrel and cylinder. There was still a little plating on the brass trigger guard and backstrap.

You know the style—a virtual honey in 36 caliber, short barrel, fluted cylinder. Colt recently has gone back into production of them because of the big hue and cry for them among collectors and shooters.

Get this conversation, and it is almost word for word:

"How much you going to ask for it?"

"Oh, I'll probably ask fifty, but I'd take twenty-five."

"Would you take twenty-five now?"

"Well . . . O.K."

Along about then, six-shooters got to be the craze, probably a lot of it stemming from the writings of Elmer Keith. Everybody thought at least once that he'd like to have a Buntline Special. The fast-draw fad also hit about then, and everybody got a single-action along with a buscadero cartridge belt and holster.

There were simply not enough Colt SAA's around to fill the need. An outfit calling itself Great Western began making them; also a guy named Hy Hunter. The Ruger outfit also got on the bandwagon.

Colt got wind of this and soon the announcements were out that they were going to tool up for the Single-Action Army—the Peacemaker, Old Equalizer, hogleg, plowhandle, six-shooter, sixgun, etc. In continuous production after the patent of the model in 1873, Colt discontinued the SAA in 1943 because of war production. Now the Colt was back and was coming on the market in a variety of calibers and barrel lengths at $125.

This, to my mind, was the start of the replica movement. Colt's almost overnight success with the new line of SAAs prompted others to realize there was, indeed, a massive market out there waiting to be tapped.

I fired off my pre-production order for a 6½-inch barrel in a 38 Special, and began pinching pennies. Soon I had it—serial number 2695SA, the SA denoting the new production run and to avoid confusion with the hundreds of thousands of original models. About a year later, I had persuaded my brother-in-law to get one. Coincidentally, his number was 12695SA, identical to my number but 10,000 higher—in just a year's time.

I was fortunate in those days, on a photography assignment, to meet the popular crooner, Mel Torme, a well-known collector of SAAs, who was appearing at a local auto show.

When I got close to the Velvet Fog for one of my pictures, I mentioned my interest in guns; we quickly found our way to a quiet corner of the bar for a couple drinks and some palaver. Among other things, he told me that he had managed to acquire a Colt SAA in the new series numbered 1873SA—a fitting number not that many ahead of mine.

As the years began pushing toward the Civil War Centennial, I got that bug, accumulating several nice muskets and at various times, I believe I owned quite good examples of most of the Civil War breechloading experimental carbines.

I also wanted a heavy-duty handgun of that period for a shooter. One Monday morning a pal strolled into the office asking if I'd seen the old Colt advertised in the Sunday paper. Fortunately he had the paper and I made a quick call and told the guy I'd be out to see it at noon.

When a shooting buddy and I arrived at his place, he took us into his basement and hauled out—not a Colt—but a battered 1858 Remington Army from a musty-dusty tool box. My heart skipped a beat. My mind had been on toggling up a big 44 for a shooter, but thought I might find a battered frame and cannibalize a gun from parts from dealers here and there, and maybe carve out a set of grips.

This find was too good to be true. Some frame bolts were missing and the timing was shot—and thus playful kids had snapped the hammer down between the nipples. Otherwise it was OK.

He wanted $30. Deciding to haggle for the fun of it, I offered $25.

"Nothing doing," he said. "A guy called after you did and said he'd take it sight unseen, but first money talks."

I made a dive for my roll.

I knew I'd have to skip lunch in the plant cafeteria for a while, but I had my Remington Army—a style I had long admired. As my pal and I strolled down the man's driveway as he stood at his front door counting his money, my pal whispered out the side of his mouth, "And they called Jesse James a thief! You stole that SOB."

"I know," I said. "Ain't it great?"

Soon after, Ford transferred me from the Cleveland plant to Central Staff in Dearborn, near Detroit, and somehow that change marked the end of the wheeling-dealing days for me, and I guess, for the hobby. It was 1960. Prices really started sky-highing. In Michigan I joined a uniformed Civil War unit, and fired two years in the Greenfield Village Muzzle Loader Festivals. With my gang of uniformed buffs, I went down and played soldier at the July 4, 1961, re-enactment of the First Bull Run—or First Manassas, depending on your persuasion.

In those days, I was buying excellent grade muskets and carbines and seldom paid more than $50—usual going price was $35 or $40. But I was becoming disillusioned with the East. It seemed to me it was progressively harder and harder to find a place to shoot. Every place I went, it seemed, the land was posted—and I had grown up in country where you could hike around and hunt and shoot on any man's land as long as you conducted yourself with some degree of consideration.

The West, they kept telling me, was still the country of wide, open spaces, breathtaking ranges, and a man could still find miles and miles of land with no fences and damned little of it posted. I took a bit of a dive, professionally and pay-wise, winding up in Arizona, and I got out in the desert to shoot black powder. Other than that, the trends in black powder collecting were passing me by. In that time, and my jump a year later to the West Coast, things were changing dramatically. Prices are going clear out of reason and with this, the need for replicas was making itself known.

I saw some of those early mass-produced replicas and was disillusioned. I largely went underground with my gun interests, stayed away from shows and clubs. I couldn't afford originals any more, and I wouldn't have the replicas, what few I had seen.

I did now and then try L.A. area gun shows, but came away thinking gun shows had changed for the worst. They were held in giant convention halls and there were seemingly hundreds of exhibitors and thousands of spectators. What interesting antiques I saw had price tags that would have jarred even King Farouk.

I had always been critical of people who looked at an old gun and saw only dollar signs. In my early days when I was having guys stop by to see my stuff, I quickly lost interest in a bozo who could only ask "How much is it worth?" I wanted him to see the fine inlay work on a patchbox, the magnificent patina I had tried so hard to preserve, the soul-satisfying twists in a fine piece of old tiger-stripe. I know that sometimes I paid less than a piece was worth, but more often than not, I paid more. There were some things I knew I could afford, and some things I couldn't, and only hoped I had the good sense to know the difference. Actual dollars were inconsequential.

By the early 70s, when I had conversations with people about old guns, the words "buckskinner" and "Hawken" began cropping up. I learned that a small bunch of men across the country were trying to develop quality replicas of the old Hawken style, and turning with viciousness on importers of shoddily built shooting merchandise from overseas. Since coming West, the mountainman period had gained great appeal to me; I admired the lifestyle and the guns they carried and had read a great deal about the fur-trade period. It sounded like it was right down my alley, so I made some inquiries. Before long I was a columnist for a magazine calling itself "The Buckskin Report," and I continued at it on a monthly basis for five or six years.

So there you have it, the making of a muzzle-loader man—one of the good *old* boys now, but one fortunate enough to have been around during the true glory days of antique gun collecting.

Those were the days, as Archie Bunker warbles. Days when for 25 dollars you could make somebody happy who found they had an old flintlock frontstuffer tucked away up under the rafters, or one that was gathering dust in the corner of an antique shop. Through it, we strived to preserve the dignity of those tangible objects of a grand heritage—and to do it with respect and sensitivity.

T'was so good to be young then . . . ●

HANDLING

by **DAVE REYNOLDS**

MINI-REVOLVERS

Arms tightly against body help hold gun on point while thumbing hammer for rapid fire. This shooter is left-handed.

I DON'T KNOW how big the first gun in the world was, but I'll bet that the second one was smaller. Much of our technology is devoted to getting more performance from smaller units, and the basic idea of the gun is a lot of power in a little package.

However, as packages get smaller, control gets more difficult and requires specialized knowledge and skill. That's certainly the case with currently available mini-revolvers. Tiny external controls and internal parts place a special burden on the user to become attuned to the gun's needs. Failure to do so will result in less than satisfactory performance.

If you do it right, though, your mini might give you two-inch five-shot groups at 50 feet. See the picture here.

If you buy a mini to carry, your first decision is to determine (for you) the best carry condition. Since the guns are all conventional style single actions, you have three options: 1) All chambers loaded, hammer in safety notch; 2) All chambers loaded, hammer down, with firing pin resting between two rounds; 3) Hammer down on an empty chamber. Each condition has merit, but each also has disadvantages.

The safest carry condition is with hammer down on an empty chamber, just like they did in the old West. Since the minis hold only five rounds—four for the Freedom Arms Magnum—cartridge capacity becomes four or three repectively. If you feel that you must trade some safety for another round, let the hammer rest on firing pin so it protrudes between case heads. If you choose this mode, be certain that when you thumb the hammer back the cylinder will rotate. I have seen several guns that were not 100% reliable at this.

The internal parts are so tiny that if cylinder isn't close to its proper position, the hand may not pick up the ratchet. When this happens, the cylinder won't rotate and the gun is tied up. The situation can be corrected by rotating the cylinder into place manually, but this may take a few precious seconds that you can't spare. It may occur when the gun is empty, and not when it's loaded. The cartridge heads may help to guide the hand into the ratchet. Use fired cases to check this function, and do it thoroughly. It doesn't happen on many guns.

Your last option is to carry the gun with hammer in the safety or loading notch. Because of the very light weight of the mini-revolvers, the loading notch is relatively much stronger than the same feature on full size guns. The possibility of an accidental discharge from a blow on the hammer still exists, so be warned.

Ways to transport the mini-revolver range from dropping it in a pocket to wearing it on a belt buckle. In between there are stainless steel neck chains, ankle holsters, boot holsters, and many others. All do not offer equal security. Your method of carry should influence carry condition as outlined above, and let your circumstances be your guide.

Shooting a mini for the first time will surprise you. Recoil is sharp. With not much to hold, you have to hang on tight. A conventional one-hand hold leaves much to be desired—you discover that right away. Your hand tends to obliterate the sights and you can't get a secure grip. Consequently, the minis have an undeserved reputation for poor accuracy.

For accurate shooting, the mini-revolvers require a two-hand hold. Maybe you think it's strange that a gun which is too small to hold in one hand can be handled well with two, but it's a fact. You hold the gun with one hand and operate the hammer and trigger with the other. It's that simple.

Newest versions of guns made by Freedom Arms come with oversize

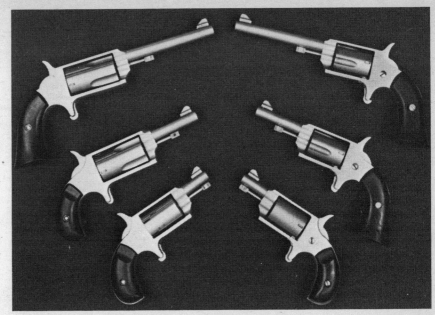

At top are Freedom Arms Boot Guns—4-shot 22WMR at left; below them are 1¾-inch models; at bottom, the 1-inch gun at left is a 22 percussion; that on the right, a 22LR.

Author shoots mini-revolvers at 50 feet and not just for the exercise—see the groups.

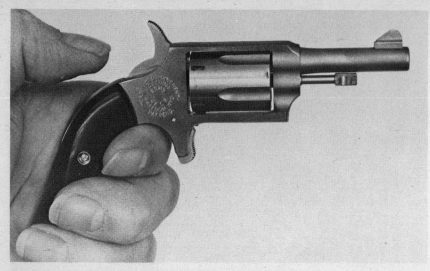

Good shooting starts with tucking the gun tightly into the pointing hand. (Posing here is a southpaw; switch hands if you are right-handed, of course.)

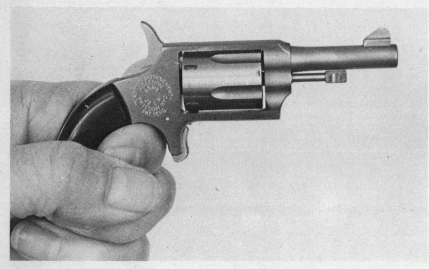

A tight wrap-up with the thumb is essential, particularly with 22WMR guns.

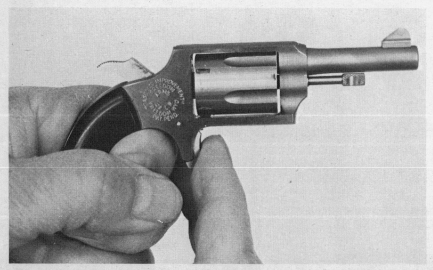

The other hand then functions the trigger; also handles the hammer.

stocks, which are also available separately. With these on the gun, one hand operation is easier, but two hands still produce better results.

My two-hand hold begins by wrapping index finger of holding hand around butt *behind* trigger spur. With the oversize stock, you'll probably be able to use two fingers. Squeeze butt tightly into palm and press thumb solidly against fingers. This firm hold will minimize bounce from recoil. The other (shooting) hand operates hammer and trigger.

This method of holding places the sights high enough above your hand that you can see them. On earlier guns, the rear sight notch was covered by the solid firing pin that protruded from hammer face, but the latest Freedom Arms guns have floating pins and flat-faced hammers. On these, sighting is more precise, because the rear notch is clearly visible above the cocked hammer.

Few minis shoot to point of aim. As with all fixed sight guns, some correction can be made by filing the sights, but you may have to hone up on Kentucky windage techniques too. How you hold the gun also affects point of impact.

Rapid-fire work offers another surprise. Using the two-hand technique, but point shooting, with arms tight against sides for support, 5 shots can be fired in about 2 seconds. With a little practice, you can dump five into a basket ball at 10 feet at that speed. Just point at the target, hold the trigger down with index finger of shooting hand, and thumb the hammer. Shades of the Single Action Colt! I've thought about removing the trigger, or tying it back, but I'll probably never do so. Loading would be hazardous without a trigger to hold the hammer in loading position.

The presently available assortment of mini-revolvers began with the Rocky Mountain Arms 5-shot 22 Short model. When it arrived on the scene several years ago, it was considered by most to have no practical value. At least one person—a James Bond type—thought otherwise. He safety-pinned a 22-caliber cleaning brush under the lapel of his coat, then pushed the brush into the gun's muzzle. The gun dangled there until he needed it. His report stated, " . . .I screwed the barrel into his ear and pulled the hammer back . . ."

Most people still consider the minis to be virtual contact weapons. I did, too, until a couple of years ago when I needed to chronograph the then new 1¾-inch barrel Freedom 22 Magnum.

Not wanting to blow away the screens of my Oehler Chronotach, I began experimenting with holding and sighting techniques, which resulted in the methods described above. The test report, which appeared in January, 1982, *Guns Magazine*, prompted the Freedom Arms folks to develop the 3-inch barrel Boot Guns and the oversize stocks. They hadn't previously explored the gun's accuracy potential.

Experiments in speed shooting began after Freedom sent me a pair of Boot Guns—22LR and 22 Magnum—for testing. The larger grip gives the stability of hold needed for rapid hammer manipulation. The Freedom folks hadn't tried this, either, until I told them about it.

Properly handled, the mini-revolvers turn in a very respectable performance. If I had to grab one gun and head for the hills, it probably wouldn't be a mini, but if I could take two, one might be. •

Minis have good accuracy potential. This 2-inch group was fired at 50 feet with 22LR Boot Gun and the technique described here.

Minis do not always shoot to point of aim. This 5-shot group by percussion gun printed at bottom of paper at 15-foot distance.

Freedom Arms Mini at top is not alone. The North American models offer bigger basic handle, five-shot 22 Magnums, and respond to same shooting technique.

If you shoot them enough, handling gets much easier, according to author Reynolds, but they stay very small regardless.

SCOPES AND MOUNTS

The compacts are coming

by BOB BELL

Bob Bell with first chuck shot with first click-adjusted 6.5-20x Leupold out of the plant. 55-gr. Sierra went in one ear orifice, out the other, at 225 long steps. M700 Remington 22-250.

Bell believes the trend is toward smaller simpler scopes. Here are Leupold's 3-9x variable (front) and 6x Compacts.

Small Scope Scoop

Burris	Actual X	Field	Eye Relief	Length	Weight
Mini 4	3.6	24	3.75	8.25	7.8
Mini 6	5.5	17	3.75	9.0	7.8
Mini 2-7	2.5-6.9	32-14	3.75	9.4	10.5
Mini 3-9	3.6-8.8	25-11	3.75	9.8	11.5
Leupold					
Compact 2.5	2.3	42	4.3	8.5	7.4
Compact 4	3.6	26.5	4.1	10.3	8.5
Compact 6	5.7	16	3.9	10.7	8.5
Compact 3-9	3.2-8.5	34.5-13.5	3.8-3.1	11	9.5

I'M NOT CERTAIN about the last head of big game I shot with iron sights. I think it was an elk in Idaho in 1947. Since then, it's been scopes all the way on my big game guns, and even more emphatically on varmint rifles. As many have, I've run the gamut from the low power ¾-inch hunting Weavers of the '30s to the 3-9x, 4-12x hunting jobs and even bigger varmint and target models of today. Ignoring the latter fields, which require king-size optics for the most part, it seems time to give some consideration to the hunting scope situation. Maybe it's time to reverse our steps. In a sentence, I feel that most of today's big game scopes are too big, too heavy, too bulky, too complicated.

I'm not advocating a return to the simple designs of the '30s. There have been enormous advances in scope optics and durability in the last 50 years, and it would be stupid to give them all up. I could do without some of the frills, the needless extras that run up size and weight and ultimately result in a tail-wagging-the-dog look as the scope overpowers the gun on which it's riding. It was inevitable that we would reach this point, of course. The if-it's-bigger-it's-better syndrome is genetic with Americans, so it naturally follows that if a little

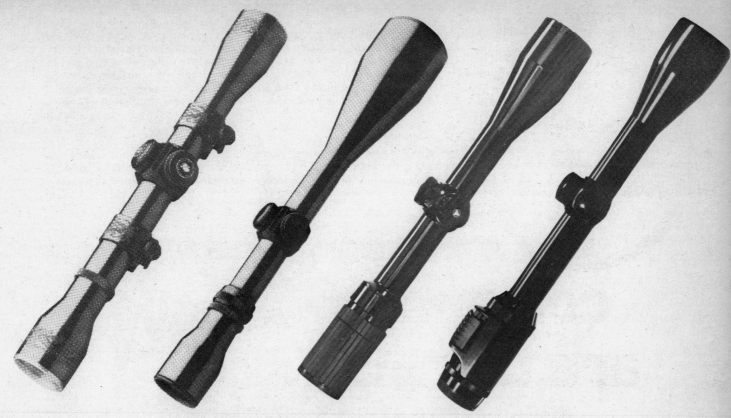

From the left—Weaver's celebrating K4-50, their V856; Bausch & Lomb's new 3-9x with 40mm objective; Bushnell's 3-9x-40 Lite-Site scope.

2½x scope is a big aid to shooting, a 6-18x variable must be a tremendous aid, the improvement increasing at least as the square of the magnification.

The scopemakers responded to our demands and gave us what we wanted. They probably scratch their heads in amazement when their sales records indicate that the 3-9x variable is the top choice of buyers the country over, as they're sure most of them are going onto rifles to pop whitetails at 40 yards in the choppings or elk in the black timber at 50. Yet, if that's what we want, that's what we'll get. The makers' goal is to sell scopes, not argue with customers. There are few firearms stranger looking than a 742 Remington carbine, say, with a king-size variable weighing a pound or more perched atop it, and few things more likely to spoil the easy-handling qualities of this and similar brush guns.

In recent years, there has been a slight reversal. Or, more accurately, an option in the other direction. Perhaps this is a result of all niches in the big scope lineup being filled. Or perhaps, after almost a half-century of steady growth, some makers have come to realize that enough is enough, and that a growing number of hunters have gone the route and are ready to

back off a little and look at things sensibly for a change.

Whatever the reason, a few years back two of our leading scopemakers introduced several smaller than what had come to be normal models. Burris, the Colorado company which had offered its first scopes only four years earlier, in 1979 hit the market with three new small ones called Mini models, in 4x, 6x, and 8x. The same year, up in the Pacific Northwest, Leupold marketed a pair of compact scopes called, strangely enough, the Compacts. Shooters had a choice of 2½x or 4x from Leupold.

I don't know what either company's sales figures were on these small models, but they must have been reasonable for all except the 8x Burris are still with us, this power being dropped in 1982. (That I don't find surprising, as an 8x is probably the least chosen magnification nowadays. It's more than is needed for big game use, and not enough for most varmint shooting.) Before the 8x vanished, though, a Mini 3-9x variable came on the market in 1980, and it was followed two years later by a 2-7x.

Leupold, too, has continued to market the 2½x and 4x, and this year offers a pair of new Compacts, a straight 6x and a 3-9x, the variable being available in either conventional

black or a new silver finish, probably intended to complement stainless steel guns.

This means eight high quality small scopes, five straight powers and three variables, are available right now for those of us who want good optics but prefer to keep the rifle/scope relationship in perspective. To make it easier to visualize these, their specs are charted here.

It is possible to save both inches and ounces with one of the small models. Such savings don't come free. Nothing does, in optics. The most noticeable loss is in field of view. So anyone considering a small scope should try to visualize how they'll fit into his usual hunting situations. If the somewhat reduced field in the 4x and 6x is no problem, a lot of arguments can be made for these small models. All are built on one-inch tubes, and all have long eye relief that will permit use with magnum loads without getting smacked on the eyebrow, when properly mounted.

All else aside, these Minis and Compacts look great on sporter-size hunting rifles; they look as if they belong, a sensible and integral part of a well-planned outfit. Don't think that isn't important, either. All of us spend an awful lot more time looking at our rifles than we do shooting them. Maybe we'd prefer it otherwise, but that's the way it actually is.

My personal feeling, in regard to the big game use we started talking about in the beginning of this, is to skip the variables here and go with the lightest weight and biggest field available. Most of the critters I've killed for quite a few years have fallen to a variable set at 1½x, so I feel 2½x is enough for almost all my big game shooting. Thus, the little 2.5x Compact would be my first choice, every-

give a field suitable for fast moving game in thick cover, high enough to quarter a sheep's ribcage at 400 yards. It should be built on a straight ⅞-inch tube, big enough to give an unobstructed objective lens of 18 millimeters, and an exit pupil of 6mm, which in turn is big enough to supply all the light the eye can use and big enough for fast aim if the rifle fits at all well. Eyepiece should be large enough to get a field of close to 40 feet, and eye relief should be at least 3½

can choose among hundreds of glass types which didn't exist back then. Computers design lens surfaces far quicker and more accurately, reducing aberrations of all types. Today, all air-glass surfaces of scopes from the better makers are magnesium fluoride coated. A few of them—and this is what we'd like on this hunting scope we're talking about—have multiple-layer coating with five, six, even seven layers. Each coat contributes in its own way to that perfect optical im-

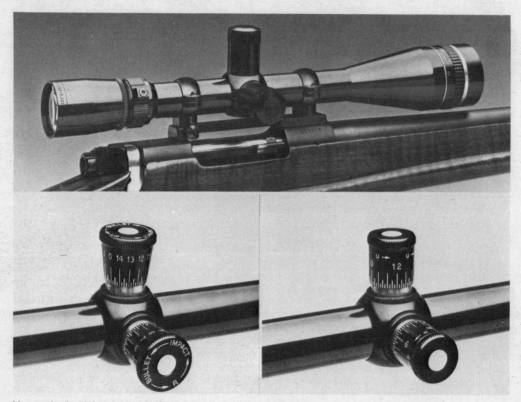

You get it all with Leupold's Vari-X III 6.5x20 scope—it comes with both sets of knobs pictured.

thing considered, with its adequate power and 42-foot field. The 4x Mini would get the nod if I lived in plains country.

I could settle for either of these, but since I've gone this far with my opinions I might as well go a step further and describe what I'd like to have:

I don't think the scope I want exists now, but there's no reason it couldn't, and I've got a hunch a lot of guys my age, who have eased through the black timber and climbed the granite hills for decades, would welcome it with quiet smiles and say, "Well, they've finally made a scope for a hunter."

In this scope that I'd like to have, the power should be 3x, low enough to

inches and noncritical. Adjustments must be internal, but they don't have to be the click variety. Hunting rifles don't get adjusted more than once or twice a year, and friction types are easier to build, less complicated and thus less likely to get out of whack.

I was chewing this idea around with Bob Wise, enumerating the points just listed, and he said, "Sounds great. All of a sudden it's 1940 again and we've got the Lyman Alaskan."

Well, not really. The Alaskan was a great scope in its time, but this one would be better, as Bob agreed after he gave me time to list some more requirements.

Today's lenses are better than those of pre-WW II days. Optical designers

age we're trying to get.

The reticle will be the type popularized by Leupold as the Duplex. Everything considered, the Duplex has more advantages and fewer disadvantages than any other type in a big game scope. Its dimensions should be such that the "open space" in the center, the crosshair part between opposing posts, should subtend 12 minutes of angle. That means there would be 6 minutes between the CH intersection and any post, and that's a convenient measurement for use as a rangefinder and for two-range zeroing (CH intersection and top of 6-o'clock post) with many of today's high velocity loads. Zeroed conventionally with the crosshair, the post zero will come somewhere around 400 or 500 yards, the precise distance depending upon the individual shooting at game.

This ideal hunting scope will not have any trick range-estimating reticle, nor any illumination so we can aim in the dark. Nor will it have a built-in windage gauge. And its eyepiece will be round, and no larger than necessary to get a reasonable field. I just can't get used to a TV-shaped eyepiece, I don't see any need for one, and they're harder to seal

Now, for what's been happening in the real world, I'm told:

Weaver Scope Co. is celebrating its 50th anniversay this year. It's the American hunter who should be celebrating, for it's doubtful any other person did as much to benefit hunting riflemen as the late Bill Weaver. A Kentucky-born engineer with a passion for hunting and shooting, a sharp inquisitive mind and a gift for getting things done, he started designing scopes and building them in his spare

to be pondered, but at least it was possible if a hunter's heart was set on a glass sight, and enough of them liked that "needle-sharp picture" that Weaver, it is said, now makes half the scopes in the world, out there in that big El Paso plant.

The 3-30 evolved into the famed 330, relied on by everyone from back-of-the-barn hunters like you and me to true experts such as Elmer Keith. There were other models back then, numerous designs intended mostly for

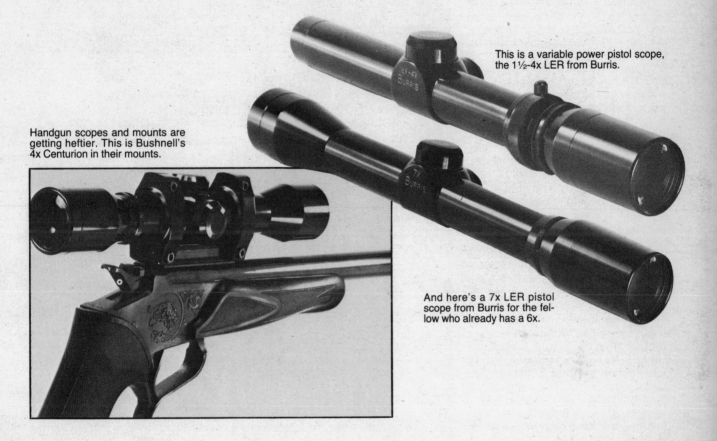

This is a variable power pistol scope, the 1½-4x LER from Burris.

Handgun scopes and mounts are getting heftier. This is Bushnell's 4x Centurion in their mounts.

And here's a 7x LER pistol scope from Burris for the fellow who already has a 6x.

against moisture and to keep lenses solidly in than round ones.

To wrap this up, it should have an aluminum alloy tube. Not because it's prettier than steel, for it should be dull-matte finished, nor because it's stronger, for it isn't, but it's strong enough and the alloy will save a few ounces. And that means we can wind up with a rough-country, durable, practical big game rig that weighs six ounces or less, sits right down on the gun in simple ring/block mounts that add maybe 2 ounces more, and will do the job on anything we point it at.

Anyone who thinks that isn't an improvement over a pound and a quarter of 3-9x variable just ain't climbed enough mountains.

time. He might have been influenced by a near-vacuum in the marketplace. In the early 1930s, you could buy a good American bolt action rifle for 40 or 50 bucks but an imported Zeiss or Hensoldt scope cost several times that. So he tinkered together a small, light, efficient hunting scope and a mount to go with it, and ran his first ad ever. That was in the September 1933 *American Rifleman,* and it said: "The sighting post held on target, squirrel, woodchuck or deer forms a gratifying needle-sharp picture." The scope was the Weaver 3-30 and the price, including "grasshopper" mount, was $19.

That was the beginning. During the Depression, even $19 was an amount

rimfires, the little 29S (my first scope ever), and the 330's slightly longer brother, the 440, a 4x which Jack O'Connor liked for varmints.

Then came WW II, and the 330 was rebaptized the M73B1 and bedded in the Redfield Jr. mount atop the '03-A4 Springfield for sniping duty. Old competitive riflemen who had cut their teeth on National Match '03s became apoplectic at sight of the "battle baby" A4, and the few who had gazed into heaven through Zielviers whined that a little Weaver didn't have enough magnification or light transmission for sniping. But young cold-eyed GIs who didn't know any better went on aiming and squeezing, aiming and squeezing—up through Italy, across Northern Europe, at places like Guadalcanal and Okinawa. We didn't really have many snipers, but the ones we had proved their worth, as did that little GI 330. Truth is, I expect a few of them are still giving service on these same old A4's in the forgotten corners of the world, as cold-eyed teenagers go on aiming and squeezing.

World War II was scarcely over before Weaver was offering the new brilliant K2.5 and the model which has become one of the true legends in the field, the best selling big game scope ever, the K4. There have been a lot of models since—the current line includes more than three dozen—but we don't have space to go into them here. Chances are, we've done that in past editions. But I did want to take a few paragraphs for this quick review. Fifty years of American-made scopes deserves something.

The K4 has been chosen to commemorate their 50 years in business. A limited edition, the K4·50, is being produced this year. The adjustment caps carry the anniversary dates and Bill Weaver's silhouette, and the enlarged tube ends have some restrained engraving.

There are two other additions. The recently introduced K856 (8x, with 56mm objective), is now made in variable power form. Called the V856, its power range is 3-8x, with a field of 35-13 feet. Eye relief is about 4 inches, so it can be used on anything you want to shoot from the shoulder. I haven't used this new scope yet, but did carry a K856 for a few days last December, on an old favorite long-range rig, a 7x61 Sharpe & Hart Magnum. As it turned out, except for a couple of zeroing groups at 200x yards—just shading 2 inches with 154-gr. Hornadys at better than 3000 fs—I got no shooting those days. But I did get a chance to put the Dual X reticle on a number of does at maybe 400 yards, resting over a windfall pine, and this big scope provided all the aiming ability necessary, even in dim, late afternoon light. That, of course, is what it's designed to do.

For handgunners there's a new Weaver 4x stainless steel model, the PS4. That's its actual magnification, not a simplified monicker, and it has eye relief of 12 to 18 inches, a field of 6½ feet. Dual X is the only reticle choice; adjustments are Micro-Trac; it's on a one-inch tube with enlarged objective; it weighs 12½ oz. and is a scant 10 inches long.

Leupold has two new scopes this

(Continued on page 74)

Shepherd's Scope: A Real Switch

The basic 3-9x Shepherd scope (above) shows extra hardware, but nothing really unusual. Inside, however, it offers the unusual reticle at right, plus really easy zeros, as below: With two reticles aligned, you fire a shot, hold one reticle on the point of aim and shift the other to the bullet hole, then shift the second into alignment—that's it.

Hi-power reticles have 18" stadia circles up to 1000 yards for deer - antelope - sheep - black bear, etc.

Adjust secondary reticle toward impact point of first round.

Adjust secondary to realign with primary

Shepherd Scope Ltd. is the newest company on the rifle scope field, and they're off to an impressive start, with an entry that will grab the attention of anyone concerned about making hits over long unknown ranges. Out of the blue of a town called Waterloo, Nebraska, has come a design which a number of other scopemakers said couldn't be made on a production basis. I first heard about the new Shepherd several years ago, but got no response to queries until the day before this was written—in mid-February 1983—when there was a knock on the door and Shepherd reps Terry Clark and Rene Anderson stood there, clutching assorted Remington rifles, each mounted with the new Shepherd 3-9x scope.

Obviously, another 3-9x is no great news, but what we have here is a Dual Reticle System that permits a long range rifleman to hold dead on at any range up to 1000 yards. With any of the conventional high velocity loads, he can expect to hit within 1 MOA of his aiming point, so far as elevation is concerned. (And if his rifle will do it.)

Shooters have been using multiple Lee Dots, as an example, for decades, but with a dot system, you must determine the range separately. The Shepherd has that built-in.

In any scope there are two image planes, the first at the focal length of the objective lens system (at the front end of scope), the second at the focal length of the erector system (the lenses which get the image right side up and focus it on a vertical plane ahead of the ocular lens). These image planes are the only places within a scope where anything is visible from the user's end. Therefore, the reticle has to be installed in one or the other. There are advantages and disadvantages to both. Normally, there is only one reticle; the Shepherd has two.

The one Shepherd calls the Primary Reticle is a crosswire and it is installed in the focal plane of the erectors, as are most reticles in variable power scopes nowadays. It gets smaller as the scope's power is increased, as American shooters prefer, and it's constantly centered. The Shepherd is screw-adjusted, but can be seen moving against reference marks on a lens surface, so it's easy to get the desired correction.

The other Shepherd reticle, called the Secondary Reticle, is installed in the focal plane of the objective lens, thus there can be no impact shift when scope power is varied. It is an independently adjustable, range-finding, bullet drop compensating

unit. It consists of a vertical line with a tiny circle near the top and a series of larger circles, all photo-etched on a glass surface, one below the other. Each circle is of a size that will enclose an 18-inch target at consecutive 100-yard units from 300 to 1000 yards.

To use the system, you zero in at 100 yards with the Primary CH reticle. You can do this with one shot, providing it's somewhere on the target and you know your first shot is normally in the group. Assume the bullet hole is out at 5 o'clock. Holding the CH on the original aiming point, you move the tiny top circle of the Secondary Reticle to enclose the bullet hole. Now holding the Secondary unit on the hole, you move the CH reticle to the same point. The gun is now zeroed at 100 yards.

To use over long unknown ranges, you find the circle which will enclose an 18-inch measurement of the target—long assumed to be the body depth of a big whitetail or average mule deer—and the center of that circle is your aiming point.

How does it accommodate for bullets having different drops? Well, when you examine the paths of bullets of different ballistic coefficents and muzzle velocities, you find that most of them fall into two or three groups. Therefore, if you have aiming points appropriate to these several groups, you can handle them all. So, instead of having only one Secondary Reticle, this Shepherd scope has three with different vertical spacings. You just dial one to match your ballistics. Here's how they came up with the multiple unit:

The Secondary Reticle is photo etched on one surface of a cube measuring .5000 on a side and made of the highest quality optical glass. Two more Secondary Reticles are etched on two of the remaining three vertical faces of the cube, and these can be rotated into view as desired via a knob atop the turret housing. Incoming light passes through the cube as if it were a plane lens, but since an image forms only at a precise distance from the objective lens, you see only the reticle on the surface that lies in the focal plane; the reticle on the far side of the cube simply doesn't exist, so far as the viewer is concerned.

Development work showed that in order to get both the Primary Reticle and Secondary Reticle in exact focus simultaneously, the fore-and-aft position of the latter had to be accurate within .002-inch. Ultimately, it was found necessary to hold the cube di-

mensions to a "zero" tolerance, at least by normal measuring procedures. Cube dimensions are closer than can be measured with a mechanical micrometer.

Currently, two SR's are calibrated for high velocity centerfire loads. The third is for 22 Long Rifle, using range-finding circles of 9-inch diameter at 100, 150, 200 and 250 yards.

The fourth surface of the cube is blank. It is the one turned into position when the hunter is using his scope at 3x for woods use so only the Primary CH Reticle is visible. If there were an SR on the fourth surface also, it would be faintly visible against the bottom half of the vertical Primary wire, and this might be annoying to some users. Personal observation indicates it could be faintly seen against snow-covered ground on a bright day; I don't think it would be visible in the woods on a dark day at 3x. If this is found to be no problem, the fourth cube can be used for another Secondary Reticle. Actually, there is little need for this, as Rene Anderson has worked out the impacts of many loads to 1000 yards and the two current centerfire SR's handle most.

Use of the Dual Reticle System also eliminates parallax. If the eye doesn't always align precisely the same for each shot, an angle is introduced and the CH intersection of the Primary Reticle doesn't snug inside the tiny top circle of the Secondary. The shooter then actually sees that an eye adjustment is necessary and makes it.

Terry Clark recommends that this Shepherd scope be used in mounts having windage adjustments, such as the Redfield, to make gross corrections. Internal adjustments total 40 minutes in each plane—20 left, right, up and down from center. Scopes are made in Japan by Hako Shoji to Shepherd specifications. Tubes are of one-piece aircraft aluminum, one-inch diameter between the enlarged ends, with a blocky looking turret to house all the machinery. Both glossy and matte finishes will be available, with a neoprene-armored version to come.

The first 1000 scopes, scheduled for delivery here in April, 1983, will have objectives adjustable from 15 feet to infinity, according to Anderson. The scope has an 11-lens system, counting the cube as one lens, and all air/glass surfaces are to be multi-coated. Length 13 inches, weight 13½ oz., clear objective 40mm, eyepiece 34mm, field approximately 40 - 13 feet, eye relief 3.3 inches. Projected retail price at this writing is something like $600.

The guy who came up with the idea—Dan Shepherd—is a carpenter out in Nebraska. Went to Redfield, Weaver, Burris, Leupold, they say, and maybe others and got laughed at. Shepherd says he had a *dream* with lines of light lining up when he looked through his deer scope; and got the idea for the revolving cube when a hunk of board he was drilling got away from him and went round and round on the drill.

Clark and Anderson arrived at my home shortly after our biggest snowfall in years—over 24 inches in the front yard—so it was impossible to get to the range to actually shoot this scope. All I can say is that this looks like a most interesting approach to the problem of long range hits. Everything about the several scopes I examined indicated high quality as well as original thinking in the Secondary Reticle area. That part is all to the good. Having a series of circles subtending that traditional 18-inch measurement at various ranges eliminates the need of a third hand for bracketing a critter with stadia wires, as many other rangefinder reticles require. And I have to admit that the SR reticle, which is not very wide or heavy, doesn't clutter up the field any more than other RF designs; it has a transparent look to it which doesn't bother me as much as some I've used.

However, it has to be pointed out that this Dual Reticle System has the same weakness as all so-called rangefinder reticles—which are actually range-estimating units. They all assume that 18-inch measurement is valid, and much—actually most—of the time it isn't. I've never measured a deer that came out exactly at 18 inches. One Idaho mulie I killed measured 22 inches, lying on its side—call it 21 inches live measurement. That's 17 percent greater than the popular assumption.

That's one problem. Another is that simply having a rangefinder reticle tempts countless hunters to try shots they should pass up. Even if we get the range and the bullet drop perfect, how do we deal with wind? Suppose you hold for a 10 mph wind and it's actually 20 mph? Drift is maybe 30 inches at 500 yards, and instead of a lung-shot elk you've got a gutshot one, or a miss off the front end. And if you get a chest hit, will the bullet expand enough to make it quickly fatal?

We ought not borrow trouble, I suppose. The Shepherd seems a fair try at solving one real problem. If it brings other problems, there are probably solutions for those. *Bob Bell*

Golden oldies like the Krag need love and affection and scope mounts, too, and can get the latter as shown from S&K Mfg.

(Continued from page 72)

year—the 6x and 3-9x Compacts mentioned earlier. And another improvement: You might remember that last year, when discussing the then-new 6.5-20x as a varmint scope, we said it would be much more effective with target-type internal adjustments, rather than the friction design. These would permit in-the-field changes for range, so the shooter could take full advantage of the top end of this scope's power settings. This year, quarter-minute clicks are available and they work fine. Fact is, they sent the first such scope out of the plant and I put it on a HB700 22-250 and went for chucks. My first opportunity wasn't at ultra-long range—maybe 225—but the 55-gr. Sierra went in one ear orifice and out the other, which was an auspicious beginning as that was my aiming point. For typical chuck and crow shooting, this 6.5-20x is awfully hard to beat.

A new scope concept, borrowed from the camera world, is the idea of closing down the aperture (objective lens) to sharpen the image. To effect this, Leupold is now offering three screw-on discs with successively smaller diameter openings. Though this reduces light, it increases depth of field, and there are times when this is desirable.

For those hunters wanting non-glare scopes, the Leupold 4x, Vari-X II 3-9x and Vari-X III 2.5-8x are now made with a flat-black matte finish as well as the regular high-gloss look. And a two-piece version of the Leupold STD mount is also new. It can be used on long or short actions, either right- or left-handed versions, without any fuss. Currently available for M700 Remington, M70 Winchester and Mauser-type actions. Reversible front and/or rear bases are also being made; these accommodate different action lengths and different length scopes.

Burris has added two handgun scopes to what has become a rather extensive line. New are a 1½-4x LER (Long Eye Relief) variable and a 7x IER (Intermediate Eye Relief). Both are built on one-inch tubes with a choice of Plex or Dot reticles. The 7x weighs 10 oz., the variable an ounce more, due to its internal machinery. The 7x, which has an enlarged objective, was developed for long range use with two-handed hold or for rest shooting, as few one-hand handgunners have the ability to utilize this much magnification. Its eye relief is 10 inches minimum, 16 max. Because these scopes are on the heavy side for their type, Burris recommends their mounts be used.

B-Square has so many mounts it's had to keep up with them. New this year is a design to attach an Aimpoint sight to assorted military rifles, shotguns and handguns, including but not limited to the UZI, M-1A, AR 15/16, AK47, Remington 870/1100, Python, Redhawk, Contender and X-Caliber. Most versions have elevation adjustments; none require drilling, tapping or sight removal.

The shotgun mount has both w. and e. adjustments. It's installed by removing the trigger plate pins and replacing them with B-Square socket head screws to hold a mounting plate. A large knurled clamp knob makes this a QD unit.

S&K Mfg. Co. has added an Insta Mount for the Russian AK-47 (AKM) and is now in production with one for the 98 Krag which was in preparation when last year's GD went to press. These two employ S&K rings only (some Insta Mount bases accept Weaver rings).

The Krag mount installs without drilling or tapping; it offsets the scope to the left to clear ejected cases. The AK-47 mount requires removal of one rivet, which is replaced by a special bolt. This one permits use of iron sights. Insta Mounts are no longer made for the 94 and 64 Winchester, and the Mini 14 Shell Ketcher has been discontinued.

Bausch & Lomb is back in the scope business again with two brand new models, a 4x and a 3-9x. When talking to one of the engineers a year or so ago, he casually said they would be the best hunting scopes in the world, which takes in quite a bit of territory. I don't know if that's so or not, but it suggests the way B&L is

Zeiss, in Germany.

These scopes are on the heavy side, 14½ and 17 oz., 12.7 and 13 inches in length, with eye relief of 3.2 inches. Fields are 28 feet for the 4x, 36 - 12 for the variable. Adjustments are said to be extremely accurate, with no loss of zero when switching power. $219.95 for the 4x, $339.95 for the 3-9x.

Kahles scopes, imported from Austria by Del-Sports, have long been admired for their fine optics, but many American shooters objected to the way their reticles moved off-center if

instructions, the shooter turns the magnification ring until the conventional 18-inch target equals the thickness of one of the reticle post ends. The scope is then in zero at the range in question. The scope has distinctive military look, utilitarian rather than slick, but it works.

Redfield has an extensive line of scopes—several lines, actually,—primarily hunting models but also including fine choices for benchrest, MS, and varmints. They make so many that they didn't have an open slot to insert any new ones this year. That gives me a bit of space to mention that last fall I installed a little 1½-5x Redfield on a whittled-down 788 Remington 7mm/08 and took it deer hunting in a couple of states. Almost at dark, down in South Carolina's Santee-Cooper country, a 7-point appeared against the treeline maybe 135 yards across a field. I had the power set at 3x and figured I might as well boost it, as he was standing motionless. But I twisted it the wrong way, so ended up with the 1½x setting. No matter. The 140-gr. Hornady smashed the spine at shoulder top for an instant kill. My Pennsylvania whitetail was dead just as quickly with another spine shot—also at dark—also at 1½x. I snuck within 40 yards of that one, so the low power was plenty. But then, isn't it usually?

Interesting Stith-style straddle mount from Orchard Park Enterprises is called saddle-proof.

aiming.

These are decidedly different looking than any previous B&L's I recall, particularly at the aft end where the eyepiece is a fairly long cylindrical unit that drops abruptly to the one-inch tube. Both have 40mm objectives, which gives a 10mm exit pupil with the 4x (unusually large for a B&L design), 4.4 - 13.3mm for the variable. These result in a new spec called Relative Light Efficiency, with ratings of 150 for the 4x, 267 - 30 for the 3-9x. The traditional relative brightness figure, obtained by squaring the diameter of the exit pupil, obviously does not account for such ratings, so I asked how they were derived. The response was that these two new scopes have multi-coated lenses, rather than the old single magnesium fluoride coating. This improves light transmission, resulting in more light through a given size exit pupil. To make people aware of this, some calculating was done and the new RLE specification resulted: a figure which is 1½ times the conventional RB rating. Few American scopes have multi-coated lenses; only Burris comes to mind. The leader has been

a large correction had to be made. (Might say I have an older 1½-4½x on a rough-country 338, and this has been no problem at all at bottom power, where I usually carry it, but is noticeable at top power when the field decreases.) Regardless, the problem is now eradicated because the new Kahles scopes have the centered reticles. Americanized, I guess.

Del-Sports is also importing an extensive line of EAW Pivot Mounts (so-called because the rear mount ring can be adjusted horizontally, pivoting around a "foot" in the front mount. There is also some vertical adjustment in the front mount, but this is used primarily to relieve tension on the scope which might acrue from accumulated manufacturing tolerances in the rifle action/mount/scope.

Leatherwood Enterprises is involved primarily with manufacturing sniping scopes for the military, but they do supply one or two models for hunters. The ART (Auto-Ranging Telescope) II is a 3-9x which compensates for bullet drop via a cam of varying thickness which is rotated around the rear of the tube to tilt the scope up or down. Once zeroed according to

Beeman Precision Scopes is offering a pair of short, military-looking models, the look possibly deliberate as they are readily installed on such quick-shooters as the Mini-14, HK91/93, AR15/16, UZI and similar outfits. The SS-1 is a 2.5x16, with 22mm tube (rubber armored), 29-foot field, and 3-inch eye relief. It is only 5.5 inches long and 6.9 oz. The SS-2 is a 3x21mm with 35mm tube, black matte finish, 30-foot field, 3.5-inch eye relief. The objective can be instantly dialed for range, to eliminate parallax. Length, 6.7 inches, weight 13.5 oz. The maker says it will withstand even machinegun recoil, but I have no way of testing that. SS-1, $119.95; SS-2, $189.95.

Wasp Shooting Systems is a relatively new mount manufacturer. They currently have models for the Mini-14, H&K 91/93, UZI, and S&W K-22 revolver. All mounts are machined from steel, and all are designed to allow the use of iron sights as a backup. The Mini-14 mount has a backup aperture built into it to get the scope as low as possible. The K-22 mount employs no base, locking directly to the barrel rib to save weight. ●

The Mobile

A sling can be an indispensable accessory when covering rugged terrain.

SINCE THE FIRST ramrod pushed a lead ball down a barrel on this continent, muzzle-loading riflemen have had an ongoing evolutionary problem in how to transport shooting gear safely, conveniently, and efficiently. Much paraphernalia has evolved in this quest: powder horns and shooting bags are just two obvious items needed by the mobile muzzleloader.

The stationary target shooter has no real need for such. He can easily pack his black powder belongings in an apple crate and then spread everything out on his shooting bench at the range. The black powder sportsman faces, however, the same challenges his pathfinding forefathers dealt with: he must carry enough powder, lead, reloading equipment and emergency items to assure his effectiveness, yet these items must not hinder his stride or weigh him down.

Fortunately, there are as many "solutions" for the muzzle-loading hunter afield as there are schools of thought. The most popular of these is that all black powder progress stopped in the 19th century. That is, whatever they were wearing and doing in 1840 is the *only* way to wear and do it in 1983.

If that were true, then Kit Carson would have never given up Colt Patersons for the harder-hitting Dragoons and Jim Bridger would not have retired his graceful Kentucky for a stouter, bigger-bored plains rifle. In their day, it was survival. In most cases today, we simply blend convenience with tradition, a combination that, ironically enough, goes well with muzzleloading.

The buckskin possibles bag, for example, is just as viable today as it was for the hunter 150 years ago. Well-made, compartmentalized bags put out by such firms as Dixie, Uncle Mike's and October Country are convenient packages for caps or flint, short-starter, patches, balls, and nipple wrench or vent pick all in one place, plus the convenience of being able to take off all these accoutrements *en masse* and hange them up on a tent peg when the hunt is over.

However, there are alternatives to the handcut, handsewn, and costly leather shooting bag. The first alter-

Muzzle Loader

by RICK HACKER

Even personal items can be carried conveniently and still be "traditional." Tedd Cash capbox is ideal for pills or vitamins, while soft leather pouch holds an extra pair of glasses.

Two excellent means of carrying premeasured charges that keep your powder dry and speed up reloading time are made by J&S Sales (top) and Butler Creek (bottom).

Leather "cow's knee" lock cover helps keep your powder dry in rain or snow, a time-proven method that has been used for hundreds of years.

Shooting and maintaining your flintlock can be made easier with (L. to R.) stainless steel short-starter from Uncle Mike's, a leather flint-and-pick pouch from Dixie, and an authentically-styled shooting bag.

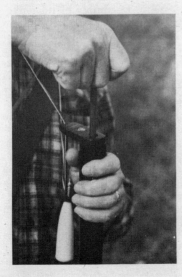

(Left) For the patched ball, this home-made 2-shot loading block is ideal. Worn around the neck, it is both fast and convenient.

For flintlocks in the field, the pan charger is an extra item to carry, but provides a convenient way to get FFFFg.

The English-style leather shot pouch is a handy but heavy way to transport a day's worth of shot in the field. Spout is adjustable from 1 oz. to 1½ oz.

Traditional-garbed hunters are most often encountered at rendezvous and in primitive hunting areas. More conventional clothing is the norm for regular big game seasons.

native came about as soon as the Army began issuing cloth haversacks to its foot soldiers. These over-the-shoulder pouches were lighter than leather, did not crack when they were dried in the sun after a thorough soaking, and were less costly to make. The same holds true today and authentic white canvas 1841 Mexican War and 1861 Civil War haversacks are available from Winchester Sutler for less than $15 each. Most leather bags of equal quality start at close to $30 apiece. In addition to being inexpensive, these haversacks also make ideal small game and bird bags.

Carrying one shooting bag alternative still farther and into the 20th century, I have found that an extremely practical method for transporting a muzzle-loading hunter's supportive shooting gear is the bush jacket—or for that matter, any jacket that has at least four roomy, easy-to-reach pockets. In those pockets, the hunter's valuables are kept and he becomes a walking possibles bag himself. It is virtually impossible to separate a hunter wearing a bush jacket from his shooting necessities.

An even more modern substitute for the shooting bag is the belt pouch or fanny pack, as sold to backpackers by firms such as Eddie Bauer and L. L. Bean. These handy water-proofed mini-packs are usually worn on the belt, snugged up against the small of your back, where they are out of the

This West Texas flintlock hunter transports his complete shooting gear over his shoulder and around his neck, via a 19th Century possibles bag and leather-thonged pan charger.

Blending the old with the new, author wears traditional coonskin cap for warmth, while opting for the multi-pocketed modern bush coat for mobility.

way and can actually help maintain your balance while walking. The only two criticisms I have of this alternative is that the zippers on the packs I have tested are rather noisy in a wilderness environment, and the fact that the pack is, after all, *behind* you. Still, they do let your arms swing naturally at your side and they keep your possibles out of the way of your canteen, belt knife and rifle butt.

Because of the nature of our muzzle-loading guns, transporting powder and lead deserves serious contemplation. Without them, the black powder outdoorsman becomes just an observer of nature, not a participant in the sport of hunting. Many traditionalists opt for the powderhorn; I have never found this to be a satisfactory or safe method while in the field. Originally, powderhorns were the most readily obtainable material that could hold up to a month's worth of powder for a cautious hunter. Nowadays, most muzzle-loading hunters do not stay out in the field for more than two weeks, with three days being the norm for most deer hunts.

No matter what the length of the hunt with modern bag limits, chances are one or two shots will be all that are fired in any given hunt. Besides, for me, there is something unnerving about having a half-pound of powder banging around at my side or hanging near the redhot embers of a campfire. Lewis and Clark must have had the

same concern, for on their famous 1804-06 trek, they had their men divide their ration of precious black powder into individual pre-measured charges. Troops in the Revolutionary War also used pre-measured charges as a timesaving reloading measure during the pressure of battle.

Anticipating the pressures of a hunt, where a fast follow-up shot may be needed, I find it practical to divide my powder supply up into carefully pre-measured charges. I rarely carry more than six hunting charges with me at one time, which cuts down considerably on weight and bulk; I have never fired more than three times during any single hunt. Thus, the rest of my powder is stored safe and dry. As a safeguard, I will leave five to six additional pre-measured charges back in camp, in case my field charges become lost.

Because of the methods I use in storing pre-measured charges, I have never had them become wet. Basically the only surefire (*good* choice of words!) way to carry your charges in the field is in airtight, waterproof containers. Today, instead of using paper or wax-coated leather and wood as our forefathers did, we have a variety of tight-fitting plastic or brass containers to do the job. I have personally had excellent results with pre-measured black powder containers manufactured by Butler Creek, Blue & Gray Products, Winchester Sutler and

J&M Sales. All these containers are waterproof and can hold over 140 grains of black powder or Pyrodex. Flintlock shooters will also need a separate pan charger, such as those put out by Dixie and Uncle Mike's.

When hunting with a percussion rifle, I always wear my capper around my neck, attached by a leather thong and tucked into my shirt. For me, this has proven to be the fastest way of getting a new cap on the nipple.

Black powder shotgunners have a slightly more complex problem than muzzle-loading riflemen, for their scatterguns require more components per shot. In addition to powder and caps (no one makes a commercially available flintlock shotgun so problems of extra flint and leather are not encountered), thick over-powder wads and thin over-shot wads are required, along with enough 1- to 1½-oz. loadings of lead shot to make the trip pay off. This translates into more bulk and weight than the rifleman normally carries. Whether using bush coat or shooting bag, I keep a handful of thin cardboard over-powder wads, and the thick cork over-powder wads (pregreased with Crisco or a commercial patch lube to make them easier to start down the bore) in separate plastic bags, which are carried in my shooting bag, or more often in a separate pocket of my bush coat. Pre-measured loadings of shot can be conveniently transported to the field in one

Hunters planning extended stays in the wilderness can transport literally everything they will need in one of two containers: the large MTM storage box (L.) or a standard fishing tackle box. Dixie's 3-compartment pistol flask contains powder, balls, and caps all in one leather-and-brass container.

Mowrey, among others, has recognized the muzzle-loading hunter's need for compactness and lightness in a rifle with a shortened version of their standard Plains Rifle.

Author likes the strength and utility of belt knives: (L. to R.) small Sheffield Bowie from Navy Arms in a custom, beaded Plains Indian sheath, Randall knife with whetstone in sheath, El Paso Saddlery's Green River knife and Buffalo Hunter sheath, CVA's new Arkansas toothpick.

Muzzleloaders need extra care in transport. For around-the-camp protection, the cloth case by CVA is economical. Rare guns go in the lockable aluminum case made by Alco. My beaded deerskin cover is used on horseback, and Uncle Mike's stalking case comes along in the woods.

of the compartments of the Butler Creek, J&M or Winchester Sutler speed-loaders, a technique that works extremely well. Of course, a more traditional way to carry shot is via the hard leather English and Irish-style shot pouches, which come complete with adjustable 1- to 1½-oz. measuring cut-offs, and are available from Dixie Gun Works and Navy Arms.

Weather plays an important part in every hunter's life and I can recall more than one hunt when I started out during the birth of a warm sunny day and a few hours later watched black and ominous storm clouds roll in and obscure every patch of blue above me. I've had it rain and sleet and snow on me and my rifle, all within 30 minutes. Thus, when I venture more than 100 feet from car or cabin, I always tie a lightweight poncho to my belt or fit it in with the shooting equipment. A wet hunter is not a happy hunter and the poncho will keep those silvery tricklets of water from leaking into your firing mechanism, thereby rendering your smokepole useless.

Unlike modern guns, all the igniting action of a muzzleloader takes place on the outside. Therefore, it is imperative that you take extra care to protect the hammer/nipple area of the caplock and the hammer/pan/frizzen area of the flintlock. Through my "practical experience" (i.e., getting my gun thoroughly rainsoaked) I helped Butler Creek devise a replaceable nipple cover that helps keep your percussion's powder dry.

One of the newest and most unique wet-weather aids for flintlock shooters out in the elements is a substance called Raincoat, put out by Mountain State Muzzleloading Supplies. By coating your priming powder with this stuff, it will actually repel moisture and remain dry! I've tried it and it works, although you will still have to keep water off of your frizzen pan and breech area. Dixie sells a ready-made leather lock cover for both flinters and percussions that adequately keeps rain and snow out.

I have also successfully used plastic kitchen-wrap around the lock portion of my guns, although this self-adhesive material is darn hard to tear off when you are in a hurry and I once fired my caplock with the stuff still clinging to the gun. The 54 Hawken fired okay, but afterwards it had a strange plastic odor to it that got me some strange glances when I got back into camp.

To be sure, muzzleloaders are more vulnerable to the elements and hazards of travel than today's self-contained guns. Our longer barrels are more likely to get knocked into trees, ramrods are prone to break, the Kentucky's slender stock is subject to crack at the wrist area, and dovetailed sights can be accidentally driven or dinged out of alignment. But by realizing this, we can take precautions to safeguard our valuable hunting rifle, especially while traveling to and from the hunting site. By far the best overall protective device for a rifle in transit is a high-quality aluminum case, such as that made by firms such as Alco. Next comes the reinforced fiberglass, padded cases, such as those put out by Doskocil. Although these two firms guarantee their cases for airline travel, I like the added protection even for automobile use. It should be mentioned that although most muzzle-loading rifles will fit into standard full length hunting cases, Alco is the only firm of which I am aware that makes an aluminum case long enough to hold a 40"-barreled Kentucky.

Both Connecticut Valley Arms and Uncle Mike's make soft leather cases that will keep dust and scratches from marring your rifle. For in-the-field use, Uncle Mike's makes a superb

Belt holsters are traditional, but these long-barreled guns ride better higher on the body. El Paso Saddlery produces this historically correct shoulder holster.

Choice of pistol can save weight. The short Euroarms 1860 44 at top is one way—grip is chopped, too. The 1861 Navy 36 from CVA is less bulky. The standard 1860 is at bottom.

In the rain, a standard Army-type poncho can be dropped over the entire gun to keep lock and muzzle moisture-free, which you can't do with a coat.

fires). For game I've hunted before or may hunt again, such as deer or bear, I will usually take one rifle in flintlock and the other in caplock, but both in the same caliber. I get the luxury of being able to choose my style of ignition, depending on the weather and my frame of mind. A less expensive but equally practical protection consists of having an extra lock and, for caplocks, an extra nipple, or in the case of flintlocks, extra flints and leather.

I also never go afield, even for a few hours, without taking a pocket-sized emergency rifle repair kit with me. This home-assembled package consists of a small screwdriver, a paper clip or small piece of wire to use as a touch hole/nipple vent pick, a worm for pulling hung-up patches or balls, extra flints and leather or spare caps and nipple, and extra pre-cut patches, usually of the Ox-Yoke prelubed variety for convenience sake. These items easily fit in your pocket or possibles bag. I like a small pouch, but they will also fit into an empty band-aid can, which rattles. Some rifles sport a patchbox big enough to hold your emergency kit, but wrap it to prevent game-spooking sounds.

As long as you are assembling an emergency kit for your rifle, why not assemble one for yourself? The whims of fate and nature are far too unpredictable to take any chances. Into your personal emergency kit should go a few band-aids of various sizes, water purification tablets, a small container of waterproofed wooden matches, a small vial of iodine, insect repellent in warm weather, tweezers and some string. All this takes up less space than a Tedd Cash Tinder Box and in fact will fit into one.

No hunter should be without a knife. Although well-made pocket-knives with 3- to 4-inch blades are preferred by many, I tend to lean more towards the more traditional sheath knives. Their blades are stronger and, for me, at least, they have proven to be more versatile as camp, cooking and skinning tools.

Whether mounted on horseback or on foot, concealed behind a log or cautiously moving through the woods, there are certain items that every black powder hunter must take along, and by planning ahead and examining each of these basics described in this article, he will find that his effectiveness as an outdoorsman will be greatly enhanced. A truly mobile muzzleloader keeps alive a tradition started in this country over 200 years ago.

Stalking Case for muzzleloaders, a ¾-length leather cover that protects your rifle's barrel and action from the elements, but leaves the wrist and butt stock exposed so you can quickly slide the gun out for instant use. I have treated mine with a water repellent spray and it has served a variety of rifles well over the past few years.

Everything the black powder hunter carries centers around the muzzleloading gun itself. Because of the key importance it plays on a hunt, I normally make it a point to transport *two* rifles to the base camp, just in case

one of my guns malfunctions. This simple insurance has given me great peace of mind over the years and on more than one occasion has enabled me to continue hunting, rather than spend valuable time in camp trying to repair a temporarily inoperable front-stuffer.

The type of rifle I select for a backup will vary. On a once-in-a-lifetime big game hunt in a faraway, distant place, I will opt for two rifles of the same caliber (usually 54 for big game and almost always a percussion, which affords the least chance for mis-

AMERICAN AIR POWER TODAY

by **J. I. GALAN**

One favorite CO₂ rifle by Sheridan gives superb workmanship and performance for under $100.

As AMERICA moves deeper into the decade of the 1980s, we find that many of the old problems that plagued us way back in the sixties are still around. In addition to familiar nasties such as inflation, high crime, the threat of gun control, vanishing wilderness, urban destabilization, et cetera, we are now faced with some new situations which, interestingly enough, should cause a rebirth of good ol' Yankee inventiveness and productivity.

The field of adult airguns, for instance, has been dominated by foreign manufacturers for more than two decades. West German companies, in particular, have been at the forefront of the airgun invasion that began in the early 60s. In recent years, there have been added large numbers of British and Spanish models. Japan's small airgun industry is looking to the U.S.A. with increasing interest. A smattering of miscellaneous airguns get here from a variety of countries such as Italy and Red China. Our homegrown airgun industry, in short, is under severe pressure to rise up to the challenge of the adult airgun from overseas.

A parallel of sorts could be drawn between the American automotive industry and the American airgun industry, as far as each group's initial attitude and response toward the influx of competitive foreign products. For years, Detroit chose to ignore foreign cars, until eventually a few token changes were effected in American cars. The disastrous results are well-known to all; too little almost too late.

In domestic airguns the situation is not quite that bad. The American airgun industry was never particularly preoccupied with the adult market. If adults wanted to purchase American airguns, so much the better, but by and large the entire domestic industry was geared toward the youth market. This had been the case since around 1886, when the Markham BB gun first appeared, heralding a new and uniquely American era in the saga of the airgun. As the variety of BB guns increased—eventually led by the company which for decades has been synonymous with *BB gun*, Daisy—all the attention was focused on the tremendous potential of the kid BB gun market.

Thus, the spring-piston airgun advances incorporated into 19th century adult gallery guns and later improved upon by Henry Quackenbush took two very different roads. One went to

Europe, where the spring-piston gun eventually blossomed into the superb precision products we see today. The second road led straight through several generations of American youngsters raised believing that since BB guns are airguns, and since BB guns are toys, to be eventually discarded in favor of firearms, all airguns are, therefore, toys.

The American airgun industry, of course, was itself largely responsible for the propagation of this concept. Why, everybody knew that most BB guns did not possess any great accuracy and lacked enough power to kill anything bigger than a sparrow. BB guns were only the first phase of a boy's association with guns, an initial and short-lived step before going on to bigger and better *real* guns. The prevailing attitude on the part of the American airgun industry until fairly recently, it seems, was to remain in the background of the firearms industry.

All that is changing fast, though the American adult airgun industry still has a long road to travel before it catches the Europeans. There are tangible examples already of that time when match shooters may be able to use American-made Olympic-grade air rifles or air pistols instead of foreign models.

The Daisy Model 777 air pistol two years ago signified America's first effort. Based largely on the popular Daisy Model 717 air pistol, the Model 777 is a full-fledged match air pistol in the strictest sense of the term. Its single-stroke pneumatic powerplant is not really a new concept. Walther and two Italian companies use the same powerplant. The Model 777 sells for less than half the price of most of its European contenders, but its fine performance and reliability make it a wise choice indeed.

The next logical step down the road to bigger and better things should be, of course, an American-made match air rifle. If rumors are to be believed—and I found out long ago that in the airgun industry rumors usually *follow* after the fact—a homegrown match air rifle is just around the corner. The target date was supposed to be early to mid-1983 in order for the thing to be totally debugged and ready for the 1984 Olympics. The recession, or anything from a business slowdown to technical difficulties with the project, apparently has put the brakes on the project and we are going to have to wait a bit longer for this hot new gun. At any rate, when it gets here it will enhance the status of

the American airgun industry in the eyes of our foreign competitors as well as those of American shooters themselves.

Coming back into the present, however, let's take a look at those serviceable American airgun models that are currently available and suitable for

adult use. The list, as might be anticipated, is not too long. Only four companies produce adult airguns in the U.S. at this time; in alphabetical order: Benjamin, Crosman, Daisy, and Sheridan.

The Benjamin Air Rifle Company was the first American company to

The Spartan Benjamin 3100-3120 magazine rifles still offer American walnut.

Crosman's Model 1 pneumatic rifle offers excellent performance, good looks, moderate price.

The Daisy single-stroke pneumatic Model 851 sports a decent, full-sized hardwood stock.

The Crosman 2100 Classic has a MV of approximately 790 fps with 177-caliber pellets and 10 pumps.

Crosman's new Model 66 pneumatic has a big-game rifle style for an economy-priced plinking airgun.

The Daisy 977 pneumatic rifle is one of the most accurate of all American air rifles, despite its multi-pump action.

Crosman 38T and 38C CO₂ revolvers are currently in training use with some law enforcement agencies.

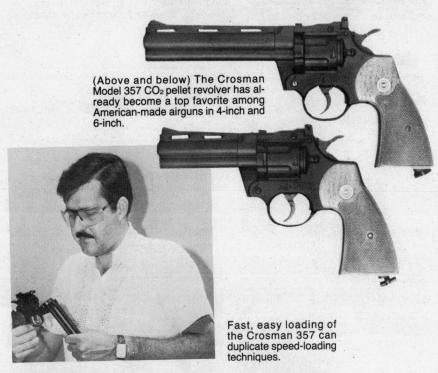

(Above and below) The Crosman Model 357 CO₂ pellet revolver has already become a top favorite among American-made airguns in 4-inch and 6-inch.

Fast, easy loading of the Crosman 357 can duplicate speed-loading techniques.

Daisy has introduced handy belt packs for pellets.

calibers, respectively. I have tested and used several Benjamin air rifles over the years and can attest to their ruggedness and accuracy. The second basic Benjamin rifle model is a repeater, also available in two versions, the No. 3100 smoothbore for BBs and the No. 3120 with rifled bore for 22-cal. lead balls. Both have piggy-back gravity feed magazines that can take up to 100 BBs in the No. 3100 and 85 balls in the No. 3120.

While the BB gun is not terribly accurate due to the absence of rifling and the light weight of BBs, the 22 is capable of fine field accuracy at up to 25 yards or so. It also packs quite a punch and there is no need to fumble in a pocket for a pellet after each shot. Simply tilt the muzzle up after pumping and open the bolt to cock the action. This automatically will feed a ball from the tube magazine down into the breech. All current Benjamin air rifle models come with American walnut stocks.

The lone Benjamin air pistol also comes in three different versions: the No. 130 smoothbore for BBs and the rifled No. 132 in 22 and No. 137 in 177. The basic profile of this pistol has changed little during the past 50 years, which says a lot about both its sound design as well as the ultra-conservative outlook in management of the company that produces it.

Crosman Air Guns has been around since the mid-1920s. At that time the Crosman Model 100 pneumatic rifle became the first in a line of models that would challenge Benjamin in the field of adult airguns.

The present Crosman lineup includes eight long guns and nine handguns. Five of the rifles, including a spring-piston model imported from Germany, are accurate and powerful enough to be considered adult guns. The handguns, by their very nature, I would definitely consider "light fun" adult air pistols, as opposed to formal target or match air pistols. The last couple of years alone have seen the introduction of two new Crosman CO² pellet revolvers and three pneumatic rifles, as well as a full-range of no-nonsense airgun accessories. These include metallic silhouette targets scaled down for airgun distances, a pistol shoulder stock, pellet trap, tele-sights, etc. The introduction of the Crosman Model 1 pneumatic rifle in early 1981 signaled a genuine effort to push a basically good, serviceable pellet rifle (the Model 2200 Magnum), into a higher sphere where it could compete with the Benjamin and Sheridan models on a more or less

produce and market a pneumatic (pump up) gun, back in 1882. Today's Benjamins are made in almost the same traditional style that made them popular almost since the company's beginnings. In recent years, however, the number of different Benjamin airgun models has been drasti- cally reduced, and now there are only two basic pneumatic rifles and one pneumatic air pistol.

Of the two rifles, the single-shot model seems to be the most popular. It comes in three versions: the smooth- bore No. 340 for BB's and the finely ri- fled Nos. 347 and 342, in 177 and 22

equal footing. There is no doubt that the Model 1 has met with success in this regard. The wooden stock and Williams open rear sight, coupled with creditable accuracy and a superb feel definitely make the Model 1 an adult air rifle.

Early in 1983, Crosman brought out the Model 2100 Classic and the Model 66 Powermaster. The former replaces the older Model 766, while the latter is a cross between the aforementioned Model 766 and the highly popular Model 760. After that mouthful of digits, the facts are as follows. The 2100 Classic is Crosman's highest m.v. rifle, reaching up to 790 fps with a 177-caliber pellet in front of ten pumps. The Model 66 Powermaster is more sedate, but it still manages to push a 177-cal. pellet at 675 fps. Both models also have BB magazines and plastic stocks, a concession to the younger set. As a result, it could be said that both of these models are not true adult air rifles. Not so at all. If you erase from your mind anything to do with BBs, both models will handle and perform in a very grownup manner.

In the handgun department, Crosman's most recent addition (fall of 1982) was the Model 357 revolver. This CO_2-powered 177-caliber copy of the Colt Python comes in 6-inch or 4-inch. There may be a healthy number of Crosman 357s in the hands of young shooters, but I suspect the majority are bought by adults who simply want an economical look-alike home-practice substitute for the real 357 Magnum cannon. Law enforcement agencies are looking with great interest at this model, so the Crosman 357 is an adult pellet gun.

Daisy, the BB-gun giant, has not really had the same activity in new guns as Crosman. With the major exception of the aforementioned Daisy

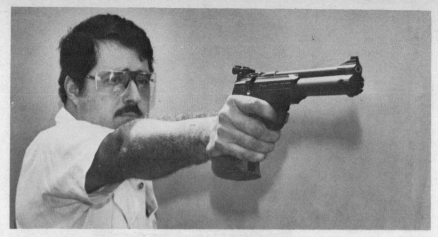
Author putting the Daisy 777 Match pistol through its paces.

Bright Daisy 41 Magnum CO_2 pistol was originally introduced by S&W.

The Daisy 777 air pistol is America's first serious attempt to grab a piece of the world-class air pistol action.

Currently available from Sheridan is the Model E CO_2 pistol; it's compact, yet powerful.

777 match air pistol, the gang from Rogers, Arkansas, has kept relatively quiet (or so they would have us believe) during the past couple of years. The Powerline 790—brought in from the cold after Smith & Wesson decided to chuck airguns back in 1980—is definitely an adult sized CO_2 pistol capable of excellent performance for its price. A fairly recent variant of this model is the Model 41 Magnum pistol, which is nothing but a 790 with a nickel-plated finish and black grips. Performance specs are the same for the 790 and the 41 Magnum models.

The Daisy 851 is a wood-stocked version of the 850, a single-stroke pneumatic rifle that was introduced a couple of years ago. While the 850/851

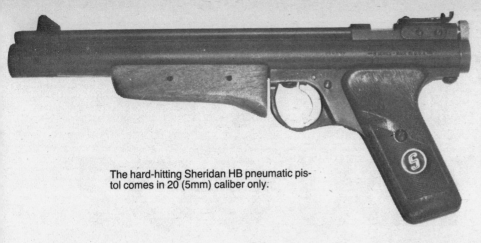

The hard-hitting Sheridan HB pneumatic pistol comes in 20 (5mm) caliber only.

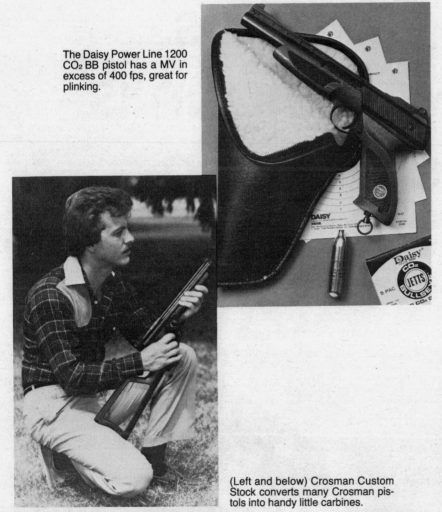

The Daisy Power Line 1200 CO_2 BB pistol has a MV in excess of 400 fps, great for plinking.

(Left and below) Crosman Custom Stock converts many Crosman pistols into handy little carbines.

is not exactly a powerhouse (480 fps of m.v. with 177-cal. pellets), it does offer entirely acceptable over-all quality and enough precision for plinking and informal target shooting.

The fourth firm is Sheridan Products. This company, long considered the Rolls Royce of American airgun producers, was purchased by Benjamin a few years ago. Sheridan pneumatic rifles, which first appeared back in 1946 with the now much-sought-after Model A, have earned a well-deserved reputation for hard-hitting accuracy with Sheridan's own bullet-shaped Bantam 20-cal. pellets. The Sheridan CO_2 rifle, introduced in 1976, is another excellent model that's still doing very well. Since then, Sheridan has also added a CO_2 pistol and the Model HB pneumatic pistol. Both handguns fall squarely within the field of adult air pistols, right along the Sheridan rifles.

There are thoroughly valid reasons for hoping that the American airgun industry will continue to improve. First, interest in airguns is increasing at a very rapid pace. This interest encompasses everything from expensive imported match models to cheap airguns used for plinking. Keep in mind, however, that the most expensive of all the American-made air rifles, the Sheridan Pneumatic models, currently retail for a little over $100. Compared to many of the hot spring-piston rifles from Europe, that's still cheap. Granted, there's all that pumping to be done, but you really don't have to pump those guns up more than 3 times for most plinking or target shooting.

A second reason as to why the future looks bright for American airguns is the fact that there is a lot of money to be made in a market that is still largely untapped, despite its growth during the past decade. Like Detroit automakers, our airgun producers realize only too well that if they are going to keep and expand a large share of their domestic market, their products must reflect the quality and sophistication that the American consumer demands and expects.

America has the technical know-how to become a leader in the production of adult airguns just as good as those made in Europe. Until now, we have concentrated mainly upon the pneumatic and CO_2 powerplants. To be honest, we have not done too badly at all; but, who knows? In time we may even beat the Europeans at their own game in the adult spring-piston airgun field as well. ●

HOW HIGH CAN YOU GO?

Getting 2000 fps from a wheelgun is possible and fun.

by **CLAUD S. HAMILTON**

Author sets Model 29 S&W in adapter of his Ransom Rest. C-clamps were really unnecessary since light bullets generate little recoil.

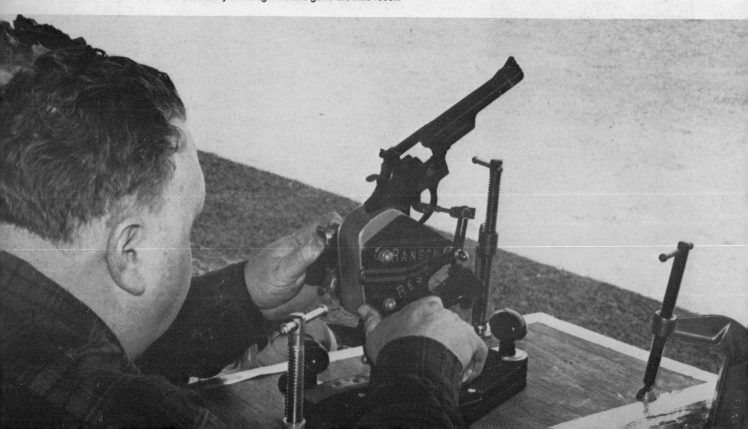

HAVE YOU ever wondered just how much velocity you can wring out of a conventional handgun? I have, and I enjoy taking an occasional excursion "into the unknown" just to see what's out there. So, during 1982, I set out in a very slow and easy fashion to see just what I might discover.

The only ways I know to get more velocity out of a handgun are: 1) use heavier charges of powder; or 2) use lighter bullets; or 3) a combination of both. In practice the problem is a lot simpler. Factory ammunition and the loads prescribed in the loading manuals are already pretty close to the maximum pressures allowable for the combination of bullet and charge, so there is not much point in adding more powder. Lighter bullets will, in fact, give faster velocity, but only up to a point. Sooner or later, you run out of the energy content of the charge and gain nothing more. The only workable approach lies in the combination of light bullets and increased powder charges.

Making light bullets for testing requires a little imagination. I have access to a Corbin Mity Mite bullet swaging press. It is a great help in such matters, and I used it to make all of the special bullets used in this shooting.

I began with the 41 Magnum. Later, as things developed, I changed to the 44 Magnum and finally the 45 Colt due in part to technical problems with the particular dies I have for the press, and other minor problems. I could make lighter and better bullets in the largest caliber than I could in any of the others.

The beginning test bullets for the 41 were all of conventional jacketed hollow point type. Weight reduction was achieved simply by making smaller and smaller lead cores. I had jackets in but one size, and was not equipped to modify them. Later, as I went up in caliber, my solutions for cores grew more "exotic."

The roughest problem I encountered was computation of safe starting charges for light bullets. Study of the loading manuals, and plain dumb logic, told me that as bullet weight got lighter, heavier powder charges could be accommodated, *but how much heavier?* First, I charted the loading manuals, plotting varying weights and powder charges shown for and extending these down to the weights I was working with. Next, I tried comparing sectional densities of known bullets and my super light weights, and working up inverse ratios so that as weight went down, charges would increase. None of these approaches gave very satisfactory results—the frightening thing for me was that well before reaching my selected very light bullet weights the plotted charges were often larger than the capacity of the cartridge case.

Finally, I went back to the time-honored approach: "start with the known and proceed toward the unknown . . ." In this way, with the 41, I began with charges that were surely safe for the lightest bullet shown in Speer's Manual No. 10 and then added to the charge 1/10th grain at a time, until I reached a point past which I did not wish to venture. After a year of shooting, I know of no other approach to take.

I am not well versed in handgun powders, and so am sure that my choices were not the best. I began with an old personal favorite, Blue Dot, but soon found it not well suited to such light bullets. I progressed through AL-7, 2400, the new Hi-Skor 800X, and Unique. As I worked my way down to the lighter and lighter bullets in each caliber, usually a point would come where I'd get a blinding flash coupled with sudden, erratic variations in velocities over the chronograph. I felt I was burning about 80% of the charge out there in the air about a foot in front of the muzzle, but not always.

AL-7 did not give great flash or erratic velocity variations. It simply reached a velocity level with the lightest bullet past which it could not go. I added 2.5 grains more powder and gained not one foot per second.

Here are the steps I went through in more or less chronological order, and by caliber. My three 41-caliber bullets were conventional lead core jacketed hollow points, and for lack of better data I began with a charge of 14.2 grains of Blue Dot for the heaviest bullet of the three, based upon Speer's entry for the 200-grain JHP in Manual No. 10. I was quite cautious; here is what I got:

The Mity Mite bullet swage with long and short jackets in 45 caliber together with cores ready for seating.

Bullet (grs.)	Powder (grs.)	Velocity (fps)
170	Blue Dot/16.7	1560
140	Blue Dot/20.2	1740
120	Blue Dot/23.6	1880

At this point I discovered that I could not make uniform lead cores any lighter for the 41. Also I was running short of 41 jackets, which are a very rare commodity these days. A move up to the 44 seemed wise.

With the 44 Magnum I began to use some imagination with respect to bullet cores. I built three different bullets once again, this time using No. 4 shot, oil-based modelers' clay, and balsa wood for the cores.

I began with AL-7. Here is what I got:

Bullet (grs.)	Powder (grs.)	Velocity (fps)
95; shot core	AL-7/19.7	1790
65; clay core	AL-7/20.2	2005
46; balsa core	AL-7/21.5	1942

The 46-grain bullet illustrates what I have said earlier about AL-7. It "topped out" at 19 grains of powder and 2.5 grains more made no velocity difference whatsoever.

All shooting was done off the Ransom Rest over a Speed Meter chronograph. One thing that surprised me was the accuracy I got with the clay and balsa cored bullets; they grouped quite well on the paper at 25 yards. The shot core bullets were a joke. There was no way to spin balance them, and so they refused to group at all, as I should have expected. Worse yet, one of them managed to free a single No. 4 shot upon encountering the rifling, and that shot holed both my sky screens. Fortunately, it passed through just above the "works" and the chronograph continued to function.

The third and final phase of my shoot was done with the 45 Colt. I increased the number of bullets to five this time, and changed to 800X powder to start. I didn't really have much of a feel for this new powder and it seemed like a good chance to see what it could do.

The first 45 bullet was a 162-gr. conventional JHP; next came a 142-gr. bullet having both lead and balsa as a core; then there was the 108-gr. conventional JHP made using a special shorty jacket. Finally, I made up 66-gr. and 60-gr. bullets using clay and balsa cores, respectively.

Here's what I got:

A complete set-up on a roofed handgun range, with the S&W Model 25-5 in 45 Colt ready to be test-fired.

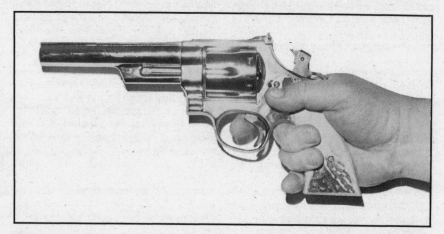

The author began his search for super velocities in handguns with this S&W Model 57 41 Magnum revolver.

Spent cases for the 44 loads were carefully placed so each might be examined for signs of excess pressure, but none were seen.

Bullet (grs)	Powder (grs.)	Velocity (fps)
162	800X/19.0	1598
142/lead-balsa	800X/20.5	1691

At this point I could tell that 800X was not going to be the powder to do the job, so I added Unique for the remaining bullets:

Bullet/grs.	Powder/grs.	Vel./fps
108; short jacket	800X20.5	1841
	Unique/19.0	1918
66; clay core	800X/22.0	1691
	Unique/20.0	1961
60; balsa core	Unique/21.0	2249

All along I had had 2000 fps as my secret goal, and it was fun to have made it. There was, however, a problem. The 66- and 60-gr. bullets with their clay and balsa cores simply vanished out there somewhere beyond the forward sky screen. They gave fine velocity readings, but they never reached the 25-yard target.

This caused me a good deal of thought. The clue was provided by what had happened with the shot core bullets. When a bullet passes through a revolver chamber throat it jumps the barrel gap and encounters the rifling. This causes a considerable deceleration and my light cores were simply disintegrating and exiting the hollow noses of the bullets. The result was that jackets alone were being shot out and they are like practice golf balls—they go nowhere.

My final move was to go to hardwood dowel as a core to replace the balsa. In such small sizes there really is little difference in weight. My final light bullet weighed in at 66 grains and gave me 2275 fps ahead of 21.5 grains of Unique. *And* this bullet holds together and groups. Oh, it's nothing to write home about, but at least it behaves like a bullet.

I tested these loads in heavy oil-based modelers' clay to see what their effect might be on a target and found that they tend to explode within about the first inch of penetration. They leave a ball shaped cavity of 2 to 3 inches maximum diameter in the clay, and do not penetrate further.

So, I made my goal of 2000 fps out of conventional handguns. I am proud to be able to say that I did it without once encountering signs of excessive pressure, hard extraction, flattened primers, *et al.* If you decide to do a little experimenting in this direction, remember that your gun and mine are not the same. Work up from well below the charges I have chosen and watch carefully for pressure signs. ●

Martha Penso shows where a single No. 4 birdshot got loose from its bullet jacket and holed the sky screen neatly.

In search of the lightest possible bullets, the author settled upon these three. From left—46-grain balsa wood core, 65-grain clay core, and 95-grain shot core. All are for 44 Magnum.

The light wood and clay core bullets produce ball-shaped "explosive" cavities in modelers' clay. Penetration was slight and only bits of jacket metal were found.

RIFLE REVIEW

by **LAYNE SIMPSON**

Shorter and lighter is better for today's market.

HAVE YOU noticed how many short-barreled bolt action rifles are available nowadays? We had quite a selection last year, some of domestic manufacture, others from vendors abroad; and in half-stocks, full-stocks, you name it. Now, in 1983, Remington and Ruger are offering us two more choices with the Model Seven and Model 77 Ultra Light.

What's spooking such designs out of the bushes? One thing, I think, is the steady, albeit almost noiseless invasion of bolt action rifles onto sacred grounds, heretofore dominated by rifles of lever action, pump and autoloading persuasion. I'm speaking, of course, about woods hunting.

Another factor of great influence is the advanced sophistication of today's hunter, as compared to yesteryear. No longer will he tolerate light-caliber rifles weighing an arch-busting ten pounds or better, when outfitted with scope, sling and a magazine full of cartridges. The best way to lighten up a rifle is by removing metal. We are thus going to thinner and shorter barrels; as seen in the Models Seven and Ultra Light, or to the lesser extreme of merely reducing outside dimensions of a barrel, as Smith & Wesson has done with their new Classic Hunter.

A less conventional method of reducing a rifle's heft is to substitute a synthetic material for wood in rifle stocks—fiberglass, for example. Chet Brown and Lee Six are credited with perfecting such an application for benchrest rifles quite some time back and they, as well as several other small gun shops, have offered same for

The Model 600 fan club will quickly recognize a "cover piece" extending over the forward part of the Model Seven bolt.

Here's the Model 94 with a Monte Carlo buttstock; it Angle-Ejects for over-the-bore scope mounting. Cartridges like 307 and 356 Winchester are even newer ideas.

hunting rifles during these past years. But, until Roy Weatherby unveiled his Mark V Fibermark in 1983, our larger rifle producers had steered clear of this type of stock. We'll never come up with a synthetic to match the warmth and beauty of a piece of walnut but in this case, we're talking about working rifles and not looking rifles.

Until the late 1940s, most bolt action rifles, both commercial and custom, were commonly fitted with stocks of what is now known as classic configuration, a style which more or less originated in Europe about the turn of this century. During the 1950s and 1960s, so-called California style stocks, with their exaggerated dimen-

Editor's Note: Layne Simpson did last year's Long Gun Report. That and Sporting Arms of the World have been discontinued in favor of reports more simply titled Rifles for one and Shotguns for the other. Simpson is now the rifle writer and will tell us of virtually everything with a rifled bore, even in this banner year for rifles, as reading this and the Testfires will quickly show. K.W.

Remington's 6½-pound Model Seven, in 222, 243, 6mm, 7mm-08 and 308, has 18½-inch barrel and hinged steel floorplate nestled in a classic-style stock.

After six years of development, Homer Koon's six-pound, medium action, Alpha I rifle is flowing steadily out to woods hunters; and mountain hunters; and plains hunters.

The Ruger M77RL Ultra Light will offer a 20-inch barrel in all calibers. The long action will be chambered for 257, 270, and 30-06; the short for 22-250, 243, 250/3000, 7mm-08 and 308. Price is $455.

New Ruger 22 rimfire will look like big game rifle, has double lugs, three-position safety, good looks. New gun uses 10/22 magazine, Ruger mounts, is promised in 22 LR for 1984. 22 WMR version is to come.

At 6½ pounds, S&W's lightweight Classic Hunter will appeal to those who like a trim stock, schnabel forend and detachable magazine. It's chambered in 243, 270 or 30-06.

Thompson/Center's remarkable Model 83 single shot, featuring optional, interchangeable barrels in 223, 22-250, 243, 30-06 and 7mm Remington Magnum, is built for scope-mounting.

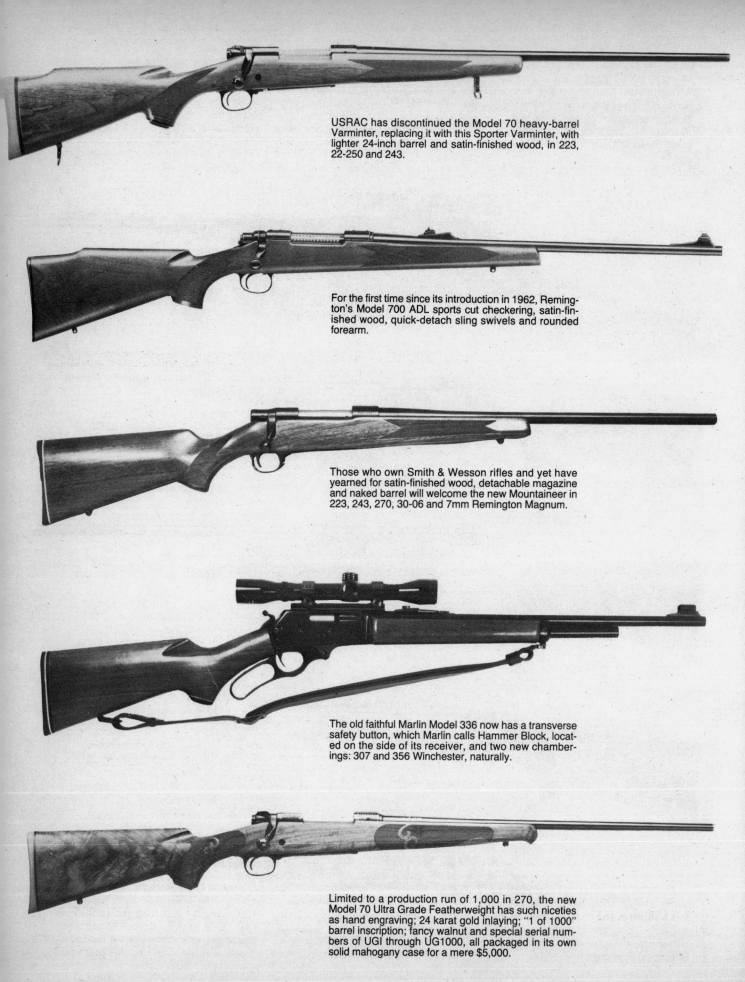

USRAC has discontinued the Model 70 heavy-barrel Varminter, replacing it with this Sporter Varminter, with lighter 24-inch barrel and satin-finished wood, in 223, 22-250 and 243.

For the first time since its introduction in 1962, Remington's Model 700 ADL sports cut checkering, satin-finished wood, quick-detach sling swivels and rounded forearm.

Those who own Smith & Wesson rifles and yet have yearned for satin-finished wood, detachable magazine and naked barrel will welcome the new Mountaineer in 223, 243, 270, 30-06 and 7mm Remington Magnum.

The old faithful Marlin Model 336 now has a transverse safety button, which Marlin calls Hammer Block, located on the side of its receiver, and two new chamberings: 307 and 356 Winchester, naturally.

Limited to a production run of 1,000 in 270, the new Model 70 Ultra Grade Featherweight has such niceties as hand engraving; 24 karat gold inlaying; "1 of 1000" barrel inscription; fancy walnut and special serial numbers of UGI through UG1000, all packaged in its own solid mahogany case for a mere $5,000.

sions, appeared and the race was on to see who could produce a rifle stock with the most game-spooking shine to its finish. The classic style was all but dead, commercially, and now it's not. Most of our manufacturers have at least three of their wheels out of this rut.

Companies like Ruger (who led the

Impressed checkering, a Remington development, lasted for twenty years, but it's gone now, missed by no one and replaced by cut checkering, compliments of computer technology. Even Remington's working rifle, the Model 700 ADL, sports cut checkering in 1983.

Two other changes taking place

afield grows tougher with each new season, prompting deer hunters to seek cartridges which drop deer a bit quicker. And, even though most whitetails are killed inside a hundred paces, occasional long shots across clearings call for a flatter trajectory than can be found with the 30-30 class of cartridges.

With its 19¾-inch barrel, the Anschutz Model 1433D in 22 Hornet and 222 Remington, with full stock and bufflo-horn tip, will be pounced on by turkey hunters and varmint shooters alike. It's also available in 22 LR and 22 WMR.

(Above and below) Marlin's neat little lever-action Model 1894M, which has been available in 357 and 44 Magnum, is now offered in 22 WMR, as is their Model 25M bolt action. All new Marlin centerfire rifles, and the Model 1894M as well, will have a transverse-type safety button on the receiver, which Marlin calls Hammer Block.

Stoeger reintroduces the Sako Model 78 in 1983 and chambers this little varmint-small game-turkey rifle in 22 LR, with standard or heavy barrel, as well as 22 Hornet.

pack), USRAC, Remington, Smith & Wesson, Harrington & Richardson and Browning, are pointing much of their efforts toward classic styling, while glossy finishes on wood are all but a thing of the past, as they should be. However, with the exception of Anschutz, this message seems to be falling on deaf ears in Europe.

since the 1950's are a tremendous increase in the use of rifle scopes and woods hunters turning toward rifles of more power and inherent accuracy. Whether they always need scopes or not is beside the point; today's hunting majority will have nothing to do with iron sights.

Competition from other hunters

Finally, more people are realizing what some of us have known for a long time; attempting to drive a bullet through thick brush is somewhat risky business, as compared to threading it twixt twig and limb. This calls for a greater degree of accuracy than was once considered quite acceptable in woods rifles. All these fac-

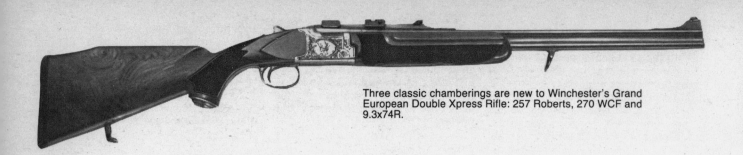

Three classic chamberings are new to Winchester's Grand European Double Xpress Rifle: 257 Roberts, 270 WCF and 9.3x74R.

tors have caused many woods hunters to turn toward bolt actions, pumps and autoloaders, as well as lever actions such as the 99 Savage, while leaving the old 94 Winchester back home hanging on the wall.

In 1983, USRAC beckons them back with the Model 94 Angle Eject and its greater power, better accuracy and scope mounts that hug glass sights low and centrally over the bore.

I see some things happening with 22-caliber centerfires too, with varmint shooters headed back toward full circle with the 22 Hornet and gunmakers responding to the demand. We now have available to us more rifles in this chambering than during any period since its introduction almost 53 years ago. Anschutz, for example, now offers three Hornets with a Mannlicher-style carbine added in 1983, and Sako is reintroducing their little Model 78, not to mention the Kimber Model 82 Hornet, available in three grades.

No, the 22 Hornet will never replace the 22-250 for serious work afield, but for every bullet sent toward a varmint, literally thousands punch holes in nothing but paper. The Hornet punches a 22-size hole in targets. Jacketed bullets for the Hornet are the cheapest we can buy and a pound of powder is good for about 600 shots.

For another example of what I'm talking about, we can look at the number of rifles chambered in 223 Remington and in 1983, we have yet another choice, the Remington Model 700 BDL. Based on reloading die sales, RCBS lists the 223 as our most popular 22 centerfire, even ahead of the 22-250 and 220 Swift.

Though our present economic situation is playing havoc with some things within our industry (which tends to add risk to new ventures), it will serve to swiftly boot a brand-new rifle to immediate stardom, mainly due to a rather unique concept in high intensity rifles. Being able to buy two rifles for the price of 1.33 rifles will cause train loads of Thompson/Center's new TCR 83 to be added to gun cabinets all across our country.

On the darker side, we have among us those who will try, by most any means, to get something for nothing and for this reason, our rifle manufacturers are spending more and more in effort to idiot-proof their wares. Good examples are warnings stamped on barrels by Ruger, and now Remington, as well as a two-finger safety on the TCR 83. And, of course, Marlin has their Hammer Block.

Here, in neat little nutshells, is what else we'll see in 1983:

Alpha Arms

According to Homer Koon, his little lightweight Alpha I rifles are flowing out to distributors as fast as he can make them. During 1982, rifles in 243 were produced, to be followed by 308 and 7mm-08 in 1983. Actions and barreled actions are also available for those who prefer to stock their own. The Alpha I action, by the way, is medium in length and works with longer cartridges such as the 257 Roberts and 7x57mm Mauser.

Anschutz

Thanks, in good part, to the accuracy of Anschutz rifles, Conrad Bernhardt of Olympia, Washington won the 1982 National Small Bore championships. Anschutz rifles were also used by the first, second and third place overall winners at the Camp Perry smallbore matches. New for 1983 is the Model 2000, described as a match rifle for intermediate competition and the Model 520, an autoloading takedown 22 rifle, with ten-shot clip.

Bighorn Rifle Co.

A new company with a relatively old idea has introduced the Bighorn, a Mauser action sporter with interchangeable barrels in most standard and magnum calibers, as well as several wildcats. For a base price of $1995.00 you get: classic-style custom stock; two Douglas premium barrels, with wrench and headspace gauge; targets with test groups and load data, along with several other choice goodies. For more money, you have a choice of 16 options, which include: extra-fancy wood and checkering; engraving; matte-finished metal; trapdoor buttplate; Mannlicher-type or fiberglass stock; etc., etc.

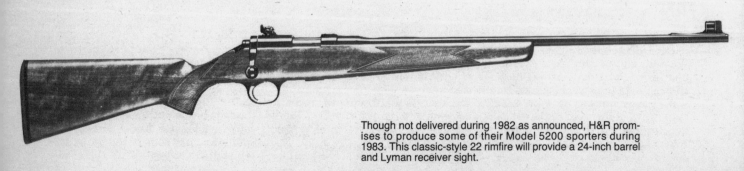

Though not delivered during 1982 as announced, H&R promises to produce some of their Model 5200 sporters during 1983. This classic-style 22 rimfire will provide a 24-inch barrel and Lyman receiver sight.

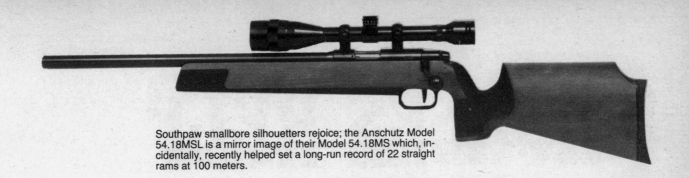

Southpaw smallbore silhouetters rejoice; the Anschutz Model 54.18MSL is a mirror image of their Model 54.18MS which, incidentally, recently helped set a long-run record of 22 straight rams at 100 meters.

Browning

The BLR is, to my knowledge, the first lever action repeater to be chambered in 257 Roberts and the second in 7mm-08 Remington, while a new caliber in the BBR is the 338 Winchester Magnum. A new short action BBR is available in 22-250, 243, 7mm-08 and 308, with 22-inch standard weight or 24-inch heavy barrels or in 257 Roberts in standard only. Obviously, Monte Carlo humps have bit the dust in Morgan, Utah, because these new rifles show not the slightest trace of either.

Chipmunk

Now there's a Chipmunk in 22 WMR which adds a bit more bite to this diminutive little rifle. Tiny little scope bases are also available, as is a tiny little gun case. No, the Chipmunk isn't made on an island called Lilliput; it's made by relatively normal-size people in a tiny little factory in a tiny little Oregon town called Medford.

Harrington & Richardson

Due to H&R's contract with Uncle Sam to manufacture military versions of their Model 5200 target rifle, as well as replacement parts for the old Winchester Model 52, only a few commercial versions managed to trickle into the hands of civilian shooters during 1982. This situation is supposed to improve in 1983. I have also been told to look for ISU and metallic silhouette rifles in the near future, but I surely won't hold my breath—this time.

Interarms

The Mark X (Ten) Whitworth rifle is now available in eleven chamberings, from 222 Remington to 458 Winchester Magnum. Rossi's 5¾ pound Model 92 SRC lever action holds ten 44 Magnums or 44-40s, both of which are introduced in 1983. Also new from Rossi are a 22 WMR chambering and octagon barrel in their pump action gallery rifle.

Kimber

Kimber has announced a new Model 82 Super America grade, replete with select walnut, quarter rib and Brownell-designed side lever scope rings, to which they now own manufacturing rights. Design changes to be incorporated in all Model 82 rifles are a Brownell-designed bolt handle and a new bolt release, located on the left side of the receiver. Next, for late 1983, is a heavy-barrel Model 83 in 22 Hornet. My flash-in-the pan award goes to Kimber for announcing and showing their Silhouette rifle in 1982 but discontinuing it before it got beyond the prototype stage.

Remington

Continuing their limited runs of classic cartridges in the Model 700 Classic, Remington has chosen the venerable old 300 H&H for 1983, which is good because the Classic has been available on special order in 375 H&H since mid-1982. The 7mm Express which, for a very short time, was called 7mm-06, is now called 280 Remington, just as it was when first introduced in 1957, and now it has disappeared from the Model 700 and is only available in pump and autoloading persuasion. The 223 Remington is now available in the Model 700 BDL and in case you haven't noticed, the two-position safety on all Remington bolt action centerfires no longer locks the bolt.

Ruger

In a 1982 Ruger brochure, received in January, 1983, I see caliber revisions in three rifles which, to my knowledge, were not announced, so I don't know exactly which took place when; Model 77, 358 dropped, 257 Roberts and 7mm-08 added; Number One, 223, 257 and 280 added; Number 3, 22 Hornet and 375 Winchester dropped, 44 Magnum added. At the NRA meetings in May, Ruger announced their new 22 sporter, pictured here and added a No. 1 in International styling. That's quite a rifle year for Ruger.

U.S.R.A.C

Latest in a seemingly endless stream of Winchester Commemorative Rifles are the Model 9422 Annie Oakley in 22 WMR and the Model 94 Chief Crazy Horse, in 38-55 caliber. The 32 Winchester Special is back, in the handy little Model 94 Trapper, except it's called Wrangler because of its roll-engraved receiver and oversized finger loop. ●

Precision Sports has unveiled the latest in their line of BSA rifles, the CFT target, in 7.62mm NATO caliber. Designed to meet ISU specifications, there is a solid-bottom receiver, full-length dovetail for scope mounting, and an accessory rail in the forearm.

HORSES HELP the MOUNTAIN RIFLE-MAN

by MELVIN P. ESPY

A CENTURY AND A HALF ago, a unique breed of rifleman had begun to spread across the vast high plains and nearly limitless mountains of the American West. Their daring and highly venturous travels and explorations have rightly become a part of the American legend and particularly the legends of the West. Names like the following come to mind: John Colter, William Ashley, Tom Fitzpatrick, Jim Beckworth, Milton Sublette, Zenas Leonard, Jim Bridger. Furs, principally beaver, were their main objective.

The rifles they carried were of a general type, gradually evolving to meet their special need; muzzleloading, heavier calibers than their forebears (the Pennsylvania or Kentucky rifles), relatively shorter, quite sturdy and dependable, flintlock during the early years and principally percussion lock later. Best known among their makers were men or firms like H. E. Dimick, Reno Beauvais, J. Henry, Henry Leman, and the well renowned J. & S. Hawken brothers. As most every rifleman knows, modern but more or less authentic versions of these rifles, their accessories and their use have been receiving enthusiastic and rapidly growing attention over the last few years by numerous groups and individuals.

It is obvious that horses and expert use of those horses were a vital part of the travel and very existence of the early mountain men, but the horse part of the early mountain man's activities has received very little attention. However the early writer Washington Irving said of the Mountain Man: "With his horse and his rifle, he is independent of the world, and spurns all its restraints."

Great skills with horses they must have had for they survived (at least the good ones did, for some years) among thousands of potential bitter enemies, in a really hostile environment over very great distances in which they were either completely alone or in small parties of two or three or a half dozen, very limited usable water over great areas, often very little sheltering cover, extremes of weather from heat and dry to vicious blizzards. Dependable mobility they had to have for without it they would have been finished. Expert use of horses was therefore mandatory if they were to stay alive.

The Mountain Men were largely illiterate and only a small portion of their activities was ever chronicled.

The portion regarding horses, being strictly an everyday thing to them from childhood on, particularly received little attention in their writings. However, today, at least one of the "buckskin" clubs incorporates horse activities along with the black powder enthusiasm. Coming from the "Cowboy" State, they may later contribute specialties in early horse techniques. I refer to the Yellowstone Mountain Men of Cody, Wyoming.

The horse activities described here are not researched into Mountain Man methods as they took place in the years just preceding the current rising interest. They did however involve traveling, hunting and for rather long periods, living in large part out of contact with other humans. More or less present day equipment of simple types was used, adapted, developed and added-to by the writer to permit camping and hunting and at times just waiting out bad weather, but with a surprising degree of comfort to both myself and horses in tough country. Often, that weather was indeed severe.

In addition to adapted equipment and good horses, it took a lot of knowhow, some of it worked out as I went along. It is obvious to me that the mountain men must have used similar techniques and no doubt had indeed numerous "wrinkles" of their own.

Some readers will already know that, over and above the obvious utility, a smart saddle horse can be an excellent companion if the two of you are alone way back in the rugged canyons and hidden high-up timbered valleys. Knowledgeable use of horses can greatly extend the rifleman's ability to get into country where he can really use high-performance rifles, their accessories, and his skill with them. And the horse can extend the years when the man can do this by ten or more, at a time past middle life where his enjoyment can be most keen and deeply appreciated. Horse travel readily permits the rifleman to use the heavier armament that will perform best when he really needs top performance at long range under tough circumstances.

Back about 1962 and 1963, I used to backpack into some beautiful hunting country on the east slope of Washington's Cascades for deer but principally elk. I was fifty then and didn't really mind lugging a fifty-pound backpack, ten and a half pound 30-06 (modified U.S. Model 1917, Bishop stock, Weaver K2.5) with gilt edge accuracy and 24-oz. 8x40 binoculars. My favorite trek involved five miles upstream to nicely isolated mountain meadows.

The effect of years was beginning then to make itself felt, but giving up my treasured lone-wolf hunting "way back in" was something I couldn't take. I switched to horses, my own horses, and in the twelve or thirteen years following, I ranged deeper and farther into even more remote and challenging country.

Horses weren't new to me as I worked with horses all the years I was growing up on my Dad's farm in the Pennsylvania mountains. Also I was by then raising and training sassy quarter horses and Appaloosa's on my small ranch in the stock country of the northern Olympic Peninsula. However I've worked out a practical and useful method or routine of teamwork between my shooting equipment, horses and horse gear and myself which have added very greatly to my use and enjoyment of that equipment in remote and highly attractive country.

Most hunters and riflemen have heard of Elmer Keith who did a lot of hunting in the northern Rockies, principally Idaho, and has written countless articles and a number of books on hunting and shooting. He has been a great advocate of heavy calibers, and weapons heavy enough to perform really well and to help the hunter shoot better by "steadying him down."

Back when his articles were so popular, a lot of serious hunters accepted his thesis of heavy weapons, but I notice in recent years a continuingly greater use and acceptance of the lightweight rifle even though the calibers and cartridges may be decidedly potent. I don't ever recall his explaining how he managed to get his heavy armament around the mountains. But knowing what I know now I expect his horse or horses did 95 percent of the carrying.

Most of you have read of hunters in remote western and northwestern mountains using spotting scopes in serious trophy hunting. Again, I think horses did most of the lugging of those relatively bulky and heavy scopes and stands.

I spoke earlier of teamwork between the rifleman, his gear and the horse. It's obvious there is a wide range or degree of experience that big game hunters will have had with horses— many near zero, then on up. There is also a very great range of horse characteristics that will be encountered. There also are a number of ways by which the hunter might obtain his horses. Generally, the information given here fits best the hunter who owns at least one of his horses, therefore likely is well acquainted with one or all of them.

Since this article will cover details of the horse angle per se only superficially, readers with less than expert knowledge are referred to *Horses, Hitches and Rocky Trails,* by Joe Back, Swallow Press, Chicago. Even the top experts can pick up a kink or two in this interesting little book. However, while it covers packing and horses rather well, it discusses very little of the actual riding or hunting.

Another very excellent text, dealing in detail with riding and handling horses, is *Breaking and Training the Stock Horse,* published by the Caxton Printers Ltd., Caldwell, Idaho. It was written by the highly respected Charles O. Williamson, DVM, of Hamilton, Montana, former Wyoming and Montana cowboy, registered guide and packer, expert trainer and exhibitor of saddle horses.

In general, the hunter with very little horse experience will tie up his horse sooner, while hunting, and walk longer. The experienced horse hunter, however, is apt to walk only the last ten to fifty feet, or after he's cut fresh sign and close foot stalking is in order.

In addition to packing the hunter and his heavy rifle, binoculars, cameras, filled canteen, lunch and emergency gear right up to where the game is, the horse serves several other useful purposes. Many people know or have heard that elk and particularly deer can be approached much more closely by a horse and rider. It is very true. Over several years I saw numerous elk while mounted and never spooked one. On one occasion, about 10 A.M. in a very isolated snow covered basin, fairly well timbered, I rode slowly through a herd of some forty feeding elk looking for a legal bull. The bulls were shy and kept behind the timber, but the horse and I were within 30 feet of a number of unconcerned cows and calves. The horse kept signaling to me position of elk hidden from my view.

Another time, a couple miles away, as I angled toward a wide open strip, an avalanche blowdown, I spotted through a thin evergreen screen a big bull facing me possibly 200 yards away. I stepped down off the mare, tied her, took my rifle from the scabbard, moved quietly to my right possibly a hundred feet past a strip of swamp to where I could look out over the blowdown and discovered the bull was only fifty yards away, walking from my left toward my

right. I eased quietly to one knee, placed a single 165-gr. Sierra B.T. open point, ahead of 61 grains of 4831, at the base of the neck. I had lugged that 10½ lb. 30-06 only 100 feet.

A smart horse can be trained rather easily to help a hunter find game. The type that will do it best is somewhat shy, lively and alert. The shy type is always looking for something far or near to be a bit afraid of. Accordingly his sharp eyes, ears and sensitive nose will locate anything unusual that's moving or whose scent is blowing his way. His manner will tell the rider, and if the rider knows him well, can tell where and possibly what. He can be trained to take a dozen slow steps, stop and check, take a dozen slow steps, stop and check, and continue that for a time. A horse that whinnies to locate other horses can be taught not to do so by jiggling the bit somewhat sharply each time and teaching the command "quiet."

A quarter horse gelding that fit this description once signaled to me that there were elk on the opposite slope of a small wooded valley. As we moved along slowly I kept watching and he kept signaling. We moved over slowly and it then turned out from signs in the snow that a half dozen elk had passed that way, migrating down the mountain valley not more than a half hour earlier. The horse had

scented their trail from over a hundred feet away.

Another time, coming out of thick timber this same horse signaled elk up on a semi-open hillside. Sure enough, there were a dozen there, preparing to move off slowly, apparently all cows. So, now dismounted with rifle in hand, I led the horse slowly into the open, then discovered a bull among them. I started to drop to the snow for a more certain shot at over 300 yards, but the bull moved into the timber and the entire herd then moved off. To a meat hunter this would have been a disappointment but to a long-time varmint hunter, habitually used to identifying the target carefully and placing the bullet precisely, it became simply a most interesting incident.

Under most circumstances a horse can be a great help in getting back to camp. In my favorite hunting area there was a promising elk crossing some 2½ miles below camp, down along a very steep sided mountain valley, that I liked to work late in the afternoon. Since the horse would be tied a little way from the stand, incidentally somewhat masking my personal scent, it was easy to have all the desirable gear close at hand. At those times I used a capable and dependable mare which permitted me to stay on the stand until the last possible minute. In the rapidly gathering dusk

Old-time closeness is still possible with 20th century horses, Espy claims, and adds tremendously to hunter skills and thrills.

I then loaded gear onto the horse, stepped aboard, and she then threaded her way up over the steep trailless, partly-timbered, gullied and ridged slope for a mile or so until she reached the narrow trail. By then it would be absolute black dark, with little if any snow to help locate the twisting treacherous trail which wound along the very steep valley-side. However the mare could easily negotiate the 1½ miles of trail with no help from me. On the very few occasions when we encountered someone else along the trail, I'd switch my flashlight on briefly, pointing it backward while switching on, to avoid startling her, then using it very sparingly to avoid dulling her night vision. Very obviously, this arrangement gave me at least an added hour, the most likely productive hour, at the stand, and with all the desirable gear. Also, I arrived at camp relatively fresh instead of dead beat.

Had I killed an elk at the stand at dusk the added capability of having the horse and equipment right at hand would have been very welcome indeed. This is particularly true since the only sensible routine is to build a fire and stay overnight while at least partially butchering the elk.

The emergency gear which the horse was carrying would be useful indeed, for instance: Rope and cord, dry blanket or light tarp, slicker or poncho, mountaineers' light axe, thin plastic tarp and, very comforting indeed, several spare sandwiches, chocolate bars and filled canteen with metal cup.

There have also been times when, uncertain as to my most direct way back out of a basin or to the trail and with no snow on the ground, the horse sniffed out the back trail in fairly short order. Also I've seen smart horses dead reckon their way back to camp or trails over rough terrain they'd never covered before. Considering the work that would have entailed on foot, with heavy rifle, binoculars and rucksack, the advantages of using the horse and its sharp senses were great indeed.

Still another advantage to doing it all by horse is that it provides a great deal of flexibility in making hunting trips. You don't have to arrive at an agreement with the horse or horses as to where or when the two or three of you (yourself and horse or horses) hunt. You go where you want, whenever you can personally arrange it. Now, mind you, I'm not recommending this as the safest possible arrangement, since two men together, equally equipped, is a better deal. But there's another side of the coin. Five or ten miles back in, with only two good horses for companions, in 2 feet of snow, provided the horseman is really experienced and woods-experienced, is no problem. But three backpackers in the same situation could be in real trouble.

Three horsemen I knew in Washington packed into the Okanogan country for deer each year. Each would drive his own pick-up with double horse trailer, two horses, equipment, necessary feed, etc. They packed in and camped together. I had the impression this worked very well.

Incidentally, all the hunting I've described was done in primitive areas where motorized vehicles were prohibited. This has really been the way to go. I should mention too that the horseman back in alone except for his horses has no need to feel alone. Horses and man quickly develop a camaraderie and self-sufficiency.

Here are a few cautions to keep in mind while hunting by horse. If you don't already know, check your horse beforehand for sensitivity to nearby gunfire. Start with a .22 pistol forty feet away, then work closer and up to bigger calibers as the horse's actions indicate.

While afield use a stout lead and tie rope, like a good ½-inch hemp, attached at the horse's head and eighteen to twenty feet long, that can be unstowed quickly. With a bowline knot, fashion a loop in the free end, into which you can slip an arm when you step down to shoot or to use binoculars: A loose horse that refuses to be caught is no fun whatever. Reason for the extra long rope is to permit you to shoot while standing some ten feet or more from the horse. Also if he gets to pulling at any time you can "play" him a great deal better on a long rope.

There are extremely few cases where a hunter is justified in shooting while mounted and even then should be attempted only by an expert. Under no circumstances should a shot be fired out over the horse's head since the concussion will be, at the very least, painful to his eardrums and will likely cause some real excitement.

It must be kept in mind some number of horses will get to bucking if greatly excited or startled in strange places. So the real trick is to know what to do so they won't start bucking. First let me reassure the reader by explaining that none of my horses with a bucking potential ever tried to do so when loaded down with gear and rider while hunting. This applies to the gelding I mentioned earlier who bucked like a fiend on a couple other occasions, to the mare who had bucked some as a youngster and still had plenty of spirit, and also to a big,

You don't have to fear a horse coming unglued if you follow Espy's rules, pay attention to the horse's needs, and stay alert.

strong black gelding used all one winter who showed he could cut some real high jinks when summer came.

For precautions, first of all don't be afraid to step down quickly and calm the horse before he gets too upset, but hang onto the reins for dear life. I nearly lost a beautiful Appaloosa stallion down a 1000-foot long, steep slide bank a couple years ago and would have but for hanging onto the reins. Most horses will automatically stay quiet where the trail-side is precipitous, but not all.

If you're on ground anywhere near level, mounted, and you sense the horse is getting too excited, spin him quickly around with the reins two or three complete turns to either left or right, but keep his head up without pulling back too far on the reins. If he starts to rear somewhat, quickly get one hand down on top of his neck some twelve inches ahead of the saddle. Bat down on his neck a couple times quickly with that hand, to get his attention, then keep the hand there, reassuring him. This will keep him from coming up, also help calm him down. I notice that the Montana cowboys, instead of spinning a horse round and round will spin him a half turn one direction, then a half turn the other, which seems to work.

If a horse has any degree of bucking mystique, he's likely to use it just at starting out, particularly if you do it too quickly. After saddling but before loading expensive gear, lead him around for a minute or two, then step up in the saddle and walk him around for a couple minutes. Then move slowly while loading your gear, particularly if you have to lift your rifle high to get it in a somewhat vertical scabbard secured at his shoulders. Then when you leave camp, mounted, don't let him break from a walk to a trot for the first couple hundred yards. In hunting you'll practically never have occasion to go faster than a trot.

Earlier I mentioned holding on to the reins "for dear life." However getting into a tug of war isn't the best way to do it, since the harder you pull, the harder the horse will pull back, usually. Instead, as he backs away, step with him leaving the reins fairly slack. After several backward steps he'll usually stop and can then be easily kept under control. This is an important point that I learned the hard way.

You'll find it quite helpful if you can mount and dismount from the right side in addition to the usual left. In fact, on a narrow trail along a steep hillside, with the uphill at your right

shoulder, the right side is often the only choice for mounting or dismounting. It's a good idea to check your horse out on this point very early in the hunt. Even if a horse is sensitive about this right side mount or dismount, you can gradually train him to it by stepping off quickly but smoothly on the right on a high bank or rock. Do this several times before mounting on the right side in the same smooth way. If he has only a second or two to think about it, he's not likely to react.

An earlier writer has cautioned to remove the rifle from the scabbard promptly upon stopping to avoid horses rolling on and ruining the former. Saddle bags, if adequate in size will normally contain cameras, canteens, possibly binoculars and should

Carrying a hard scabbard for a varmint rifle: 1—Top, barrel end; 2—straps to pommel, horn; 3—back surface curves to clear scope, mounts; 4—secured to breast strap, front and rear, and pad inside of breast strap; 5—pad here under scabbard may be needed; 6—lower end rides out, away from horse's foreleg. (Author's sketch)

be rigged for easy removal and installation. They will readily permit similar removal upon stopping.

If any of this sounds dangerous, remember you were taking chances equally great or much more so while driving to the trail head, particularly if roads were slippery. It's just that with cars and trucks, you're used to taking the chances most every day. One advantage attached to horse excitement is that you can talk about it for years. Chances are he only meant to do some mild crow hopping anyway, but don't tell your listeners that.

My favorite place for securing the rifle scabbard is at the horse's right shoulder with the end of the barrel below my right heel, rifle butt up and forward and telescope forward. This puts the bolt away from the horse. In removing the rifle it's most easily done from the ground while standing on the opposite or left side of the horse, taking it over the horse's shoulders or neck, swinging the bottom end of scabbard away from the horse for a favorable assisting angle. I could also remove it from the horses's right side, but it requires a somewhat higher vertical lift, also some horses are nervous about a person standing on their right.

A scabbard and rifle secured similarly but on the horses's left side will be

in the way of your hands and reins while mounting and dismounting, will also pre-empt the spot for stowing your lead rope, which you need to be able to undo quick as a flash.

You'll need unobtrusive scope lens covers front and rear. The most practical I've found for use in even a roomy leather scabbard is a quickly contrived homemade rig. Its a ten to fifteen inch long leather thong secured at its midpoint midway of the scope barrel, with a rubber band secured by an overhand knot at each end. Each lens cover proper is simply a 4- or 6-inch square of

1- or 1½-mil clear flexible plastic secured over that end of the scope by the rubber band. Carry a couple square feet of spare plastic in your pocket for ready replacement of a lost square. Sandwich bag plastic is pretty good material for this.

To keep snow or rain out of the scabbard, use a spare cloth tucked into the open spaces at the top. Also, a large canvas boot can be sewn, to slip down over rifle butt and openings.

A word or two is in order regarding footwear while hunting by horse. In cowboy country you can buy pointy toed five-buckle galoshes to go over western boots. Feet can be surprisingly warm if leather boots are large enough to accept fairly heavy woolen socks and if the galoshes (they're nearly all fleece lined) are big enough to accept a full half inch thickness of dense felt insoles. The pointy toes are very functional in letting the toes come clear of the stirrups quickly if needed. If you wear any of the usual types of bulky hunting boots, and particularly if they have the lug soles, be very careful to put only the first several inches of toe in the stirrups. It's pretty important for the feet to come clear instantly when needed.

Let's take a look now at a new and choice type of varmint hunting rapidly opening up all over the northern Rockies. Since use of the poison 1080 for coyote control was outlawed five or more years ago, the coyote population has been going up very rapidly. The greatly increased predation has caused very great difficulties for sheep ranchers all over the West, driving many out of business. Coyotes are now putting pressure on the cattle industry by having learned to attack cattle and calves at special times when they are vulnerable. The general reduction of populations of deer, antelope and smaller game may also be attributable to the large number of coyotes.

Result of this is that the responsible coyote hunter, with proper equipment, can now obtain permission to hunt coyotes on many of the large ranches in the northern Rockies that were previously entirely closed to hunting by outsiders. I've only done a small amount of this particular type of hunting but can readily envisage methods and equipment. Much of this can employ really long-range varmint shooting equipment that will put the impact points into a seven-inch circle at 500 to 600 yards under rather poor weather conditions. The poor weather conditions come from the most desirable seasons, November into April, resulting from the value of the pelts ranging

up to $40 to $60 or more when prime.

I'll not get into calibers, bullets and loads here. However, having posed the requirements, the reader can start calculating and experimenting as to how best to fill those requirements. Spelling out the requirements rather than giving the solutions may seem unusual, but, among other things, that's what a broad-based system engineer does. To start passing out answers I must put on my other hat which is labeled development engineer: The "broad base" mentioned has nothing to do with seating capacity.

How does all this tie in to using a horse for coyote hunting? First of all the horse-mounted hunter can get permission to hunt on a larger number of ranches. Also, mounted, he'll likely get some number of shooting opportunities at 400 to 600 yards while riding along. Obviously he's going to shoot from prone after extracting his long-range rifle and slipping one arm into his horse's tie rope loop.

Unless the hunter has exceptional skill with the mouth-blown varmint call, he'll find that the best method of calling will use one of the recordings with speaker equipment. I'm sure that a couple of the various types of these will lend themselves to being carried on horseback by a modest sized saddle-bag type deal. In any event, using good calling equipment and techniques, a reasonable amount of shooting at ranges like 200 to 400 yards should be afforded. The hunter will need to tie or hobble his horse out of sight when he wants to start calling.

Coyotes will be out and most easily found without calling at dawn and, particularly, dusk. They'll also respond best to calling at these times although, with a good call, in a lightly hunted area, they'll also respond during the day. They can also be found abroad without calling during the day but the likelihood is smaller. Again, the horse is very handy in getting hunter and equipment out several miles to likely areas before dawn or back after dusk. It is granted, however, that it takes pretty enthusiastic early risers to feed, saddle and ride horses in time to get out to a likely area by dawn.

Note that the hunter's camp, with pick up(s) and horse trailer(s), would likely be near water on ranch grounds and he would be essentially self-sufficient.

For coyote hunting as described, it is granted that the hunter could employ a varmint rifle with large internal adjusted scope, like a 3x-9x variable,

in a conventional scabbard, carrying it on the horse on the right front as previously described. However, to maintain the gilt edge shooting capability necessary for coyotes at 600 yards, particularly if the scope has the desirably large forward optics, it may be advisable to use a more protective type scabbard.

This is by no means all that might be written about teamwork between the hunter, his horse, rifle and various supporting gear. At the very least it points out one way for the dedicated rifleman to obtain more and better opportunities to test his skills and under a greatly widened range of circumstances.

If one will stop to think a bit, it's obvious that personal enjoyment is the main motivation for hunting for most persons. Enjoyment can take many forms and, particularly as one grows older, the ability to get into and thoroughly enjoy a lot of beautiful, unspoiled mountain hunting country, to get easily into the remote, game-likely higher country, can be a major reward. Possibly many, like myself, would prefer to traverse many, many miles of such near-primeval country alone except for an alert mount, the mount close-tuned to the wild and, by nature, but little removed from there.

Let me mention a few points of pure enjoyment that I recall particularly: Late one afternoon on a remote, deserted winter-wonderland valley trail, my favorite saddle horse traveling for miles at a delightful slow jog trot, bridle hardware and saddle leather sounding faintly, putting in mind holiday tunes soon to come. Another time: I and heavy gear snugged down well on a young mare at her unbelievably smooth long trot, on the trail to a miles-away special hunting spot. Or, mounted, leading a pack horse carrying a huge elk head and a couple of man-tied quarters downtrail through wild and splendid mountain country, horses at the single-foot, leather and pack saddle squeaking out a faint, rhythmic, primal mountain "tune." Still another time: With the stout young mare, an enthusiastic mountain climber, topping out on our own personal faint-blazed trail up a steep butte-side, into a snowy, primeval jumble of rocks, cliff-tops and stunted firs, untouched elk country with a view of wintry peaks and ridges stretching a hundred miles to the north and far to the east to lower rounded sagebrushed ridges, but in that vast alpine expanse, not the faintest sign of man or his works. •

MURATA TYPE 22:

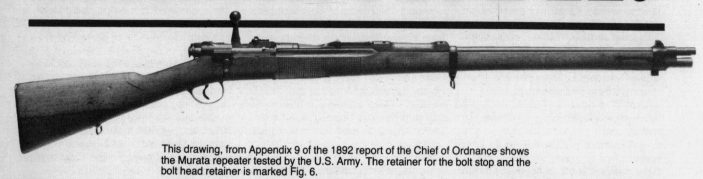

This drawing, from Appendix 9 of the 1892 report of the Chief of Ordnance shows the Murata repeater tested by the U.S. Army. The retainer for the bolt stop and the bolt head retainer is marked Fig. 6.

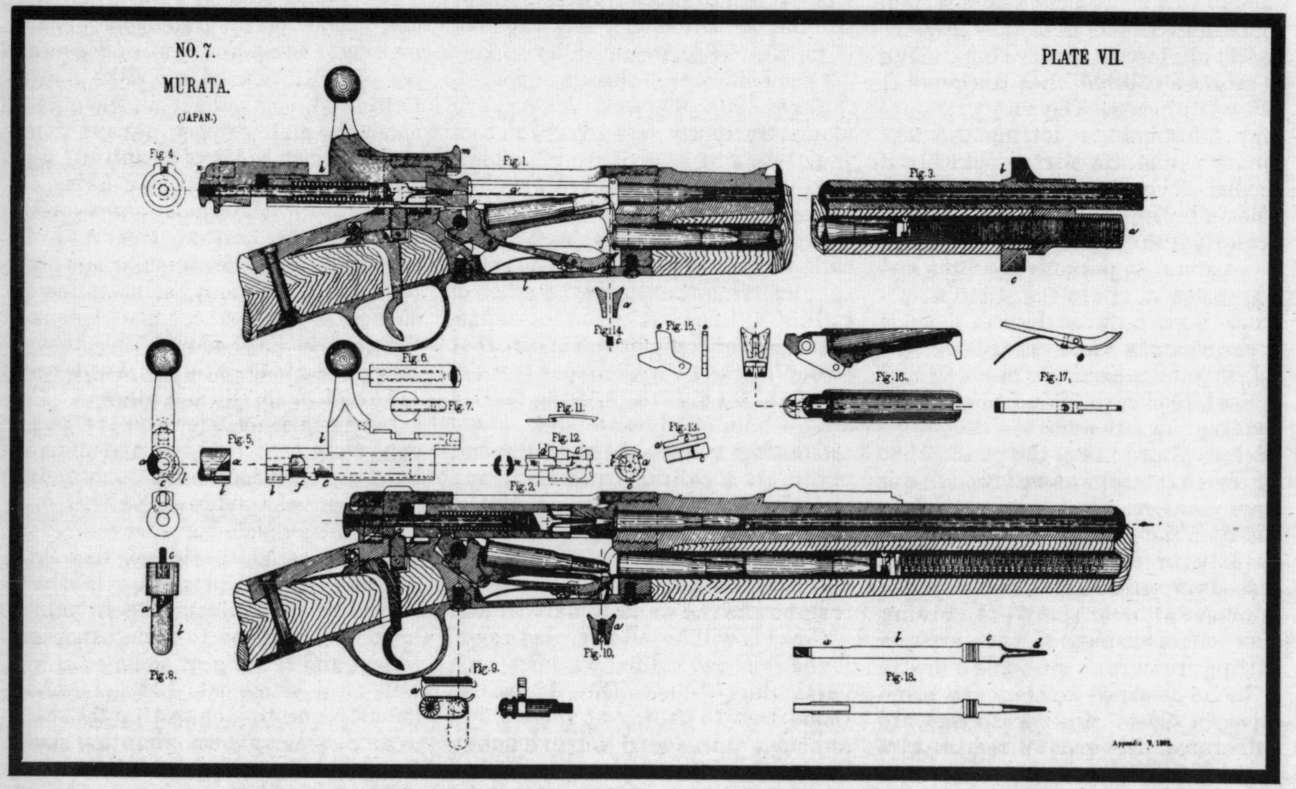

NO. 7.
MURATA.
(JAPAN.)

PLATE VII

Fig. 4.

Fig. 1.

Fig. 3.

Fig. 6.

Fig. 14.

Fig. 15.

Fig. 16.

Fig. 17.

Fig. 7.

Fig. 5.

Fig. 11.

Fig. 12.

Fig. 13.

Fig. 2.

Fig. 8.

Fig. 10.

Fig. 9.

Fig. 18.

Appendix 9, 1892.

This 1889 repeater offered small-bore advantages, but tubular magazine liabilities.

by CHARLES S. SMALL

JAPAN COMMENCED its entry into the modern world when Emperor Meiji ascended the throne in 1867. The newly formed Imperial Japanese Army inherited from the preceding regime a motley collection of surplus European firearms. This collection included the 1853 Enfield, the Snider conversion of the old Enfield, the French Miné muzzle loader, the Tabatiere conversion of the Miné rifle, the Chassepot needle gun, the Braedlin-Albini trap-door from Holland, the Peabody, the Martini, and others.

Getting out of this mess and developing shoulder arms made at home was the life work of Tsuneyoshi Murata, who by the time of his retirement in 1890, had risen to the rank of General. Three of his designs were produced at the Tokyo Arsenal. The first two were single shot bolt action arms, 11mm caliber, designs approved in 1880 and 1885. The third was an 8mm repeater adopted in 1889. All three have his name on their receivers.

The first two contained no startling design innovations but were a combination of ideas gained from the European rifles of the 1870s. Technically they were behind the best European design concepts and about equal to the average. This article is about his last design.

The 1889 Murata combines their own turnbolt action with the Kropatschek repeater mechanism with its associated tubular magazine under the barrel. Kropatschek was an Austrian ordnance officer who himself ended his career as a General.

The Kropatschek repeating mechanism was first used in 1878 for a French Navy rifle which was manufactured at Steyr in Austria. The French then built two more versions in their own arsenals. The final French Kropatschek was the Lebel of 1886.

Also in 1886, a Kropatschek 8mm repeater was made at Steyr for the Portugese. The only really significant difference between the Steyr-manufactured repeating mechanism and the Japanese version is the omission in the latter of the ejector stud on the cartridge lifter. The ejector stud had to be omitted to make room for the single locking lug on the bolt body.

The Murata bolt is conventional having three pieces with a non-rotating bolt head. Because the ejector was omitted from the cartridge lifter, an ejector was provided in the bolt head. It slides in a groove, half of which is cut into the left receiver wall with the other half being in the bolt head. Its basic design is similar to the ejector of the 71/84 Mauser.

The only unusual feature of the Murata design was the combination of the bolt stop and the bolt head retainer. The circular bolt stop, when the bolt is pulled all the way back, contacts a circular cut on the top of the rear receiver walls. This design came from the 71 Mauser. The forward part has a hook which, projecting downward, retains the bolt head. This stop/retainer has its own retainer. It is dovetailed to the top of the stop/retainer piece and has a cylindrical projection at the back which fits into a hole at the root of the bolt handle. This was the original design and very few of the existing rifles retain this peculiar arrangement.

The one real invention was the manufacture of the stock using a separate piece of wood for the bottom of the butt. This was an economy measure for it enabled more stocks to be made from a given quantity of beech wood. This system endured right through the last of the Arisaka designs.

In 1890 the U.S. Army finally decided that the time had come for the replacement of Allin's ancient trapdoor design. Accordingly, a board was convened in that year to test potential replacements. A total of fifty-one repeaters were entered. Two Springfield trap-doors were converted to a 30 caliber against which the others were to be measured. The Murata was number 7 on the list of entries. The testing was done on Governors Island in New York harbor during 1891. The Chief of Ordnance reported on the tests in his 1892 report. This is a very thick volume and makes interesting reading for those interested in old repeaters.

The U.S. Army had a poor opinion of the Murata. During the 500-shot endurance test, there were failures to eject and load in the repeater mode. If the bolt was pulled back gently, the spent cartridge case would fail to eject and when the bolt was recycled there would be a loading jam. If, on the other hand, the bolt was brought back with considerable force the cartridge lifter would be snapped up with such energy that it flipped the loaded cartridge out of the rifle. If the cartridge was not flipped out it would be displaced sufficiently that it would not enter the chamber when the bolt was returned to the firing position. Neither of these problems exist with the Steyr-manufactured Kropatschek.

With my own rifle I find that the ejector jams in its slot. If the jam occurs in the ejection position, that is, with the ejector protruding from the bolt head, then the next round will not chamber because the bolt can not close. If the ejector jams in the retracted position then the spent round will not eject. Once the bolt head is removed from the rifle there is nothing to hold the ejector in place and it can easily drop out and become lost. None of these problems exist with Mauser's design for the 71/84 rifle.

If a jam occurs in the under-the-barrel magazine tube, you have to take the rifle apart to free it. On both the Steyr and Mauser tubular repeaters there is a removable cap at the end of the tube at the muzzle. This feature was omitted in the Murata design.

The Steyr-designed Portugese rifle's magazine cut-off lever can easily be removed by turning it to the forty-five degree position and then pulling it out. This frees the cartridge lifter and its operating cam for cleaning. To get these parts out of the Murata you need a punch and a hammer. This is another of the negative improvements.

The original Murata repeater bolt had a very cumbersome device for retaining the bolt stop/bolt head retainer. It faced forward with a dovetail on the bottom and a pin which fitted into a hole on the bolt handle.

Facing forward it would loosen under recoil. If this piece were lost the bolt stop/bolt head retainer would fall out and the rifle could not be fired. Further, it left little room for the soldier's fingers on the front grasping surface of the bolt handle.

At some time either during manufacturing or later the design was changed. A deep U-shaped cut was made in front of the bolt handle and the bolt stop/bolt head retainer was fastened to the body of the bolt with a screw.

There are not enough Murata repeaters in existence to determine when the change was made nor whether the original bolts were reworked, replacements made, or the rifles were originally made with the second design bolt. About 125,000 repeaters were manufactured and examples with serial numbers from the 30,000 to 122,000 have been examined. There are a few with the bolt head serial matching the rifle's serial and one of these has no number on the bolt. There are others—the author's rifle is in this category—with mismatched bolt heads and *katakana* plus unrelated digits stamped on the bolt body. One rifle in the 122,000 serial range has a second-type bolt marked in the 35,000 range with a bolt head in

A close-up of the right side of the receiver. The inscription, read vertically from the muzzle end down, translated is "Meiji 22 Year Authorized." This picture clearly shows the second bolt form with the bolt head retainer fastened by a screw. It also shows the serial number, not matching, on the bolt head.

the 45,000 range. About all that can be concluded is that the original design was defective.

The Murata barrel has the deep .0075-inch grooves which are characteristic of the rifles made at Steyr right up to and including the 1895 Austrian Army model. It is difficult to understand why this manufacturer continued to use deep grooves and undersized jacketed bullets for so long. The deep grooves fill up with fouling which is very difficult to remove with ordinary field cleaning. American rifles of this period managed very nicely with grooves of half of this depth. The deep grooves were one of the Steyr design features that Murata should not have copied.

Had Murata simply bought the complete Steyr design he would have had a better rifle, but then national honor would not have been served. This is also true of Mauser's 1884 rework of the 1871 single shot. The Mauser design is more complex and more expensive to manufacture, but

again national honor would not have been served.

When I acquired my Murata 8mm repeater it had a replacement bolt with the bolt stop/bolt head retainer missing. It also appeared to have no firing pin. Upon disassembly I found that the firing pin end of the striker had been broken off, probably by someone's attempt to disassemble the bolt. A replacement stop unit was easy to make. A new tip was welded on to the end of the striker and its length adjusted to today's primers. These two repairs put the rifle back into a fully operable condition.

To disassemble the bolt you need a piece of ½-inch steel rod with a ¼-inch hole drilled in the center. Take the bolt assembly out of the gun by removing the bolt stop/bolt head retainer. Rotate the cocking piece clockwise to the fired position to reduce the tension on the striker spring. Place the flat guide rib of the striker against the rim of the ½-inch rod and push the bolt and the cocking piece down until the notch of

the striker nut is clear of the hook shaped lug at the rear of the cocking piece. The nut can then be unscrewed. This method protects the firing pin end of the striker for it is down in the ¼-inch hole.

When the first Murata 11mm single shot rifle was designed the choice of a cartridge case was not very difficult. The current European 11mm military rifles used cartridges whose dimensions were about the same and all were loaded with between 75 and 78 grains of black powder.

The French military influence was strong in Japan during the 1870s and there was a resident French military training mission. Murata had toured Europe for most of 1875 with one of the French Mission officers. A large number of Chassepot paper cartridge needle guns had been purchased. Concurrently with the manufacture of the Murata 1880 rifle, these Chassepots were converted to fire metallic cartridges. It is not surprising, therefore, that the 11mm Murata cartridge re-

A close-up of the left side of the receiver. This inscription, also read vertically from the muzzle end down, translated is "Imperial Japan Murata Repeater Toyko Arsenal Small Arms Factory."

sembles the French Gras cartridge.

By 1888, when the 8mm repeater was being designed, the guidelines were not so clear. The 8mm cartridges in existence varied in length from 50 to 60mm and their base diameters from 12 to 14mm.

The standard American reference books are confusing as to the components of the Murata 8x52.5 (or 52.7) ammunition. One says it was a smokeless load from the beginning. Another says that the first ammunition was loaded with black powder and used a lead bullet. One gives the black powder load as 39 grains which is the figure usually quoted for the smokeless powder charge.

The chances that the Japanese had developed a satisfactory smokeless powder by 1888, when the prototype was being tested, are very small. Almost everyone knew that by nitrating an organic compound, such as cotton or wood, you could produce an explosive. The problems were to control the rate of combustion which, in turn,

would control the temperature and pressure and to be able to make successive batches with the same characteristics.

Both the 1886 Portugese Kropatschek and the 1888 Austrian Mannlicher cartridges were loaded with black powder. The probabilities are very compelling that the Murata 8mm case was originally loaded with from 62 to 63 grains of black powder. This powder charge with a 230 grain bullet would have produced a velocity of not more than 1700 fps.

Of the three 8mm cartridges of the 1886-1888 period, the Kropatschek, Lebel, and Mannlicher, the Murata case is closest to the Mannlicher. This 8x50R round was not loaded with true smokeless powder until 1895.

One Japanese source indicates that the first attempt to make smokeless powder was in 1889 at the Tokyo Arsenal. This source also says that the manufacture of smokeless powder commenced in 1894. When the Murata was tested by the U.S. Army during

1891, the cases were loaded with Wetteren smokeless powder manufactured by Coöpale in Belgium and imported into the United States by DuPont.

If you have a Murata 8mm and wish to fire it, making cases is quite simple. The starting point is the 7.62 Russian case made by Norma. Assuming that the cases are new it is prudent to anneal the neck and shoulder area. No dies are necessary. Just prime the cases, load with 10 grains of Bullseye, a tissue paper wad, Cream of Wheat as a filler, and a closing tissue paper wad.

When the fireformed case is extracted you will find that the neck has been blown out to .365″ outside diameter. This is too large to hold the original diameter bullet which was .3295″ in diameter. The use of a bullet equal to the groove diameter is quite surprising. Europeans during this period were using undersized bullets with the expectation that they would be upset during firing to fit the bore.

Proper .330″ bullets are difficult to

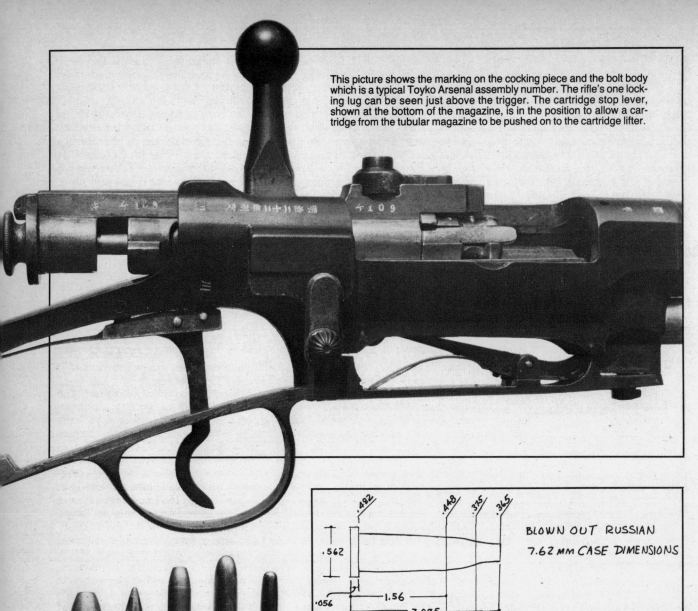

This picture shows the marking on the cocking piece and the bolt body which is a typical Toyko Arsenal assembly number. The rifle's one locking lug can be seen just above the trigger. The cartridge stop lever, shown at the bottom of the magazine, is in the position to allow a cartridge from the tubular magazine to be pushed on to the cartridge lifter.

norma **NO. 27634**
(INDEX NO. 819)

7.62 RUSSIAN UNPRIMED CASES

Contemporary cartridges. Left to right—45-70 USG, French 8mm Lebel, the author's reformed 7.62 Russian case for the Murata, Portuguese 8mm Kropatschek, 6mm USN Winchester-Lee.

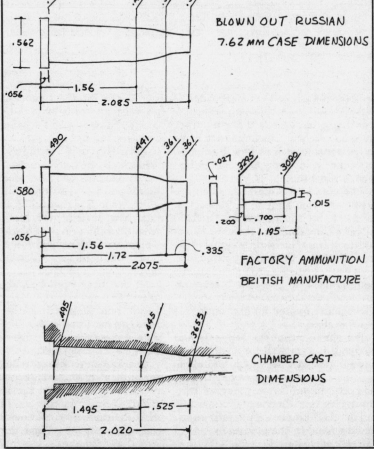

BLOWN OUT RUSSIAN
7.62 MM CASE DIMENSIONS

FACTORY AMMUNITION
BRITISH MANUFACTURE

CHAMBER CAST
DIMENSIONS

obtain. When faced with the .330″ bullet problem during my experiments with the Portuguese Kropatschek, I obtained a custom mould from Richard Hoch of the Gun Shop at Montrose, Colorado. The bullet from this mould, cast in linotype metal, weighs 255 grains and is 1.25 inches long. Accuracy was excellent, backed by 12 grains of Unique, using the bullet as cast. Although it is 20 grains heavier than the Murata bullet, it is close enough to approximate the original lead bullet performance. Neck sizing, expanding and bullet seating were done with a set of RCBS Kropatschek dies.

I have an undated drawing which originated at RSAF at Enfield Lock which gives the following Murata 8mm ammunition dimensions:

Rim diameter	.561″
Head diameter	.490″
Shoulder diameter	.441″
Neck diameter-outside	.361″
Rim thickness	.056″
Length to shoulder	1.56″
Length to neck	1.72″
Length of neck	.335″
Over-all length	2.075″

The drawing shows a bullet, material not specified, with a .3295″ base, .200″ long. It then tapers to .309″ at a distance of .900″ from the base. Then there is a very short nose. The over-all length is 1.195″. Under the bullet there is a .027″ thick cardboard wad. The primer was protected by a copper disc. Although they went to all of this trouble the bullet nose, .15 inches in diameter, was smaller than the disc.

The drawing represents the Murata ammunition made in England. One can only imagine that this ammunition was used by whomever bought the rifles as surplus from the Japanese.

A chamber cast revealed a long smooth curve starting at the shoulder and extending into the beginning of the rifling. At the point where the rifling begins the bore diameter is .330″ and the groove diameter about .340″. This long throated area must have been provided to keep the pressures down with smokeless powder.

The exterior of my Murata 8mm repeater is close to being perfect. There are no deep gouges on the stock, no exterior pitting, and the original blueing is intact. A rifle which had seen wartime service would not be in such good condition. The only part of the gun in poor condition is the interior of the barrel. There are deep scratches on the lands and in the grooves.

Based on my experience with the Kropatschek, the initial load was 11.5 grains of Unique covered with a .5 grain synthetic fiber wad and the 255-grain .331″ linotype bullet. The muzzle velocity measured with an Oehler chronograph averaged 1220 feet per second. Using the rifle's iron sights, at 100 yards, the groups ran around six inches with the shots nicely scattered. The recoil with this load was negligible.

At the end of each five-shot group a patch was run through the barrel and it came out covered with extremely thin flakes of bullet metal. There was no leading of the bore in the conventional sense.

In an attempt to overcome the problem of the rough bore a test was made with the linotype bullets dipped in undiluted Bullet Master lube. At the same time the powder charge was increased to 12½ grains of Unique. The increased powder charge resulted in an average velocity of 1453 fps. There was a marked reduction in the lead shaving due to the rough bore. The group size was reduced to the four-inch level. Recoil was still mild and there were no excess pressure signs.

The documentation of the Murata 8mm repeater available in the United States is confusing. Smith and Smith in their 1948 book which is now called *The Book Of Rifles* lists a Murata Type 20 (1887) as an 8mm repeater. Such a rifle would be marked on the right rear of the receiver with = + which is the Japanese symbol for twenty. I have been unable to locate such a rifle in the United States or in the excellent military collections maintained by the government small arms factories in Europe. Every Murata repeater which I have examined is marked = + = which is the rendition of twenty two. Most subsequent authors seem to have accepted Smith and Smith as gospel, but there is no Type 20 rifle or carbine.

The error comes from the only Japanese source which has been translated into English and which is widely available at libraries. The book is called *The Military Industries Of Japan*. It was published in 1922 by the American Branch of the Oxford University Press.

This book was edited by Baron Sakatani, written by Norimoto Masuda, and has a foreword by Ushisaburo Kobayashi. It is not a technical book on firearms but rather covers the full range of Japanese war industries through the period of the 1905/6 war with Russia. It is full of all sorts of interesting information. For example, the Army had their own corned beef operation commencing with a slaughter house and finishing with putting the finished product in the cans which they had made. The Army also made all of their own uniforms in a large clothing factory.

There is not too much information on rifles. The book lists the Murata Meiji 13 (1880) 11mm single shot. It states that in 1883 the Tokyo Arsenal converted 8000 Chassepot and manufactured 7000 Muratas.

On page 44 of this book it states that the Murata repeater was adopted in Meiji 22 (1887). The 1887 is a typographical error. To convert from the Japanese calendar of the Meiji regime you add 1867. Evidently most authors subtracted the 1867 from 1887 and arrived at 20.

All of the American authors state that the Murata 8mm repeater was used in the 1894/1895 war with China. On the basis of its adoption in 1889 this was a good guess except that it seems not to be true.

This war was hardly a contest. The decaying Manchu dynasty had little effective control. The various warlords who actually controlled the armies were too busy fighting each other to bother with the upstart Japanese.

I have read General Murata's biography which was published serially in Japan during 1897 and 1898. It is in the Japanese Diet Library at Tokyo. His biographer who states in the introduction that he talked to General Murata (Murata lived until 1921), states categorically that the 8mm repeater was not used in the war with China. Its first use was during the 1900 Boxer rebellion. It was also used by rear echelon troops during the 1905 war with Russia.

This definite statement raises the question of why it was it not used? At this late date the question will never be answered. One can speculate indefinitely and I could think of at least six reasons but the fact remains that neither I nor anyone else really knows.

The Murata Meiji 22 8mm repeater was the last of the military under-the-barrel tubular repeaters to be designed and the first of this breed to be taken out of service.

When Murata was retired in 1890 he was heaped with honors by the Emperor. Although he was an indifferent small arms designer, Murata was instrumental in starting the small arms development of the growing Japanese war machine. Interestingly, the honors were not for his three rifle designs but for his services during the suppression of the civil war which was started when Emperor Meiji ascended the throne in 1867. ●

Jim O'Meara shot a 54-caliber percussion CVA rifle over chronograph screens and proved it got the same velocity with single patch, with double patch and naked ball.

SECRETS OF BLACK POWDER PATCHES

by **SAM FADALA**

Shooting through a chronograph screen sheds new light.

A BARE BALL, bereft of any cloth patch as a newborn babe, can obtain the same muzzle velocity as a patched round ball, provided the naked projectile is not terribly undersize for the bore. While that information may not be exciting enough to make the headlines, it does have important implications for the black powder shooter.

First, there's general curiosity. We would imagine an unpatched lead ball going poosh! from the barrel and dropping 30 feet in front of the shooter, which is hardly the case. We'd also think of the undressed ball going random, unable to hit even a large target. That isn't entirely true, either.

Second, the flight of the unpatched ball has historical significance. Documentation shows that in the heat of battle, when a hostile was trying to make decoration of a frontiersman's hair, the old-timer simply poured a dose of powder downbore, flopped a round ball in after it, leveled the rifle and fired. We assumed the ball flew wherever fate took it, and at a greatly reduced velocity. The chronograph says that isn't so. The ball, instead, took off at a reasonable rate of speed, and in a somewhat straight line.

Third, the patch is supposed to serve as a gasket, sealing the hot expanding gases of the burning powder behind the missile. Does it? If so,

rounds each. Maybe this phenomenon has nothing to do with patching; however, there is a theory which suggests the possibility of early bore destruction when streams of jetting hot gas flames escape past the projectile, causing extensive metal erosion.

Perhaps, just perhaps, if indeed gasses that go in front of the ball do cause a lot of wash, then a properly arranged patching setup that kept at least a large portion of these gasses behind the ball might increase barrel life. We should add that in the three test barrels, though best accuracy was gone after about 1,000 shots with safe, moderate loads, some of the lost accuracy was regained by going up in ball size. All barrels were 50's. All were tested with .490″ balls. After accuracy fell off, .495″ balls were used and finally .498″ balls until, at about 2,000 shots, even the larger balls were inaccurate.

Finally, when we found a bare ball getting standard velocity with standard loads, that led to an experiment with double patching, in an attempt to better seal the bore and perhaps up the velocity of the ball over either single patching or, of course, no patching. By double-patching, we mean seating an over-powder patch before seating a patched ball. One can use a regular patch, or something special—

has been proved to my satisfaction that despite some tests showing otherwise a separated ball/charge can mean trouble, with a possibility of a "rung" bore (a bulge in the barrel) or even a fracture of a barrel. The no-patch trials were run to learn something. All round balls should be patched in the bore to stay put until firing.

The tests coming up showed that the value of the patch lay in: 1. some extent of bore sealing, especially with proper patch selection and use; 2. the patch does take up the windage in the bore and makes for optimum accuracy; 3. leading can be prevented by the use of a patch; and, 4., of course, the safety factor already mentioned.

The highest velocities, as will be seen in the data, were achieved when the patch was kept intact. Double patching paid off when there was patch burnout—in other words, when the hot gasses ate holes in a single patch, which is not uncommon with hunting loads. Ten rifles were tested with hunting loads. These were safe maximum charges suggested by the manufacturer, and in all cases slightly *under* the top recommended loads. Of the ten rifles, nine gave top velocity with double patching. One did not, but fired single patches from that rifle probably gave the answer; the patches were intact. Therefore, adding an-

This pillow ticking patch does not clearly show abuse until it is held to the light. Then, light seems to come through at many places where holes have burned or worn through the material during firing.

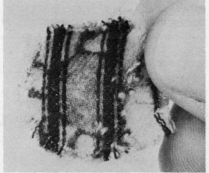

This patch appears to have held up quite adequately, but it does have some burned out areas. When a patch looks marginal, as this one does, the best bet is to chronograph with one and with two patches.

This pillow ticking patch was down on top of the powder charge, backing up an Irish linen patch surrounding the ball. The ball patch was totally intact; however, the powder patch in this case was not intact.

when does the patch serve as a gasket and when does it fail? How is a truly decent gasket made from cloth patching?

Fourth, black powder rifles, in spite of relatively low velocity and pure lead projectiles, have a rather short-lived barrel life in terms of top grade accuracy. In my own tests on bore longevity with round patched ball, three high quality rifle barrels faded in gilt-edged accuracy after about 1,000

we have found hornet nests really superior—and can seat it all the way as a separate operation or can stuff it in the muzzle and seat it with the patched ball.

Warning—the shooting of unpatched balls was for experimentation only. Great care was taken to ram the ball on the powder charge and never have it depart from the charge before firing. While some may not agree, it

other patch on top of the powder charge did nothing.

The reasons for that patch not burning, when others did burn, are not entirely clear. Maybe the bore was smoother, with lands that were rounded instead of sharp. Recovered patches did have tiny holes burned through them, but in spite of this, one single patch still gave optimum velocity in this particular 54-caliber firearm. A full 120-grain volume charge

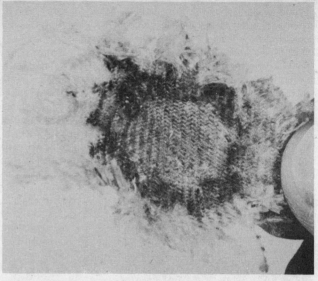

Here, some pure Irish linen has been dyed to get a close-up photograph. The photo shows the close weave of this cloth, and that the edges tend to fray. It is a good idea to make the Irish linen patch just a little bit oversize.

This Irish linen patch shows tremendous fraying at the edges. It is not necessarily burning out, but may well be failing to protect the lead ball in the bore. The way to check for this condition is to shoot single and double patch loads against each other.

of FFg GOI brand black powder did not eat into the patch. There was nothing unique about the lube or the patch material, either.

Most interesting of all were the data collected from firing the ten rifles. While there is hardly room here to duplicate it all, a sampling is possible. In all cases, RIG was used as a lube, since a grease tends to promote optimum velocity. RIG also served as an anti-flame agent, retarding the effect of the hot gases on the patch.

RIFLE: Navy Arms Ithaca Hawken, 50-caliber, firing Speer .490″ swaged round ball over 100-grain volume, FFg, GOI.

Patching Arrangement	Velocity
One .015″ Irish linen	1,897 fps
NO PATCH	1,741 fps
Two patches	1,898 fps

The figures are taken from five-shot tests, averaged, and the figures were very close together. There were no readings which were not in the group.

It might appear from this data that the theory of the bare ball and optimum velocity is a flop. However, two factors were at play. First, the 100 volume charge (about 95 grains weight) of FFg was not destroying the single patch. Second, the .490″ ball fairly rattled down the bore without a patch. With the .015″ patch of Irish linen, the .490″ worked well in general shooting and is to be recommended, but see what happened when a .495″ ball was used with 110 volume FFg, GOI brand black powder, same rifle:

Patching Arrangement	Velocity (MV)
One Irish linen .015″	1,902 fps
NO PATCH	1,963 fps
Two Patches*	2,002 fps

*One undersize pillow ticking patch on the powder charge, Irish linen .015″ on the ball, both lubed with RIG.

It would appear that the single thickness patch might be succumbing to the powder charge at the 110 volume level, that is, the Uncle Mike's powder measure set for 110 grains by volume. So what would happen if we changed from the Irish linen to a commercial type patch, trying different thicknesses of this patching with a .535″ ball in a 54-caliber rifle?

Patching Arrangement	Velocity (MV)
.005″ patch, commercial	1,223 fps
.010″, same material	1,628 fps
.015″, same material	1,600 fps
NO PATCH	1,647 fps
Double patching*	1,790 fps

*Same as double patching above

The recovered commercial single patches were quite destroyed after shooting, and this last test, while interesting, could be discounted because of this factor. It is interesting that after going to the double patch, and getting away from the more perishable cloth, velocity went up 143 fps average. Speculation is always dangerous, but it would seem that the .005″ patch was in effect an anti-gasket. The bare ball did better. Velocity

with the .005″ patch was consistently terrible. Perhaps it thwarted proper ball obturation, allowing gases to escape around the ball, and the bare ball obturated better. Perhaps a single patch that burns out is, in fact, an anti-gasket.

The .010″ patch ups the velocity considerably. It would appear that this patch does a much better job of sealing than the .005″ patch; however, it does no better than no patch at all. The .015″ patch functioned in the same general domain as the .010″ patch, with an inconsequential difference of 28 fps average. The bare ball obturates well enough in the bore of this rifle, thereby gaining slightly on the patched balls so far, though not significantly so. The double-patched load, with the pillow ticking patch on the powder and the Irish linen patch on the ball, both lubed with RIG churned up better velocity than any other arrangement in this run.

I had mentioned a rifle which did not respond to double patching, and its data might be interesting:

RIFLE: CVA 54-caliber drum/nipple percussion rifle, 32-inch barrel, 1-72 twist, 120 volume FFg, GOI.

Patching Arrangement	Velocity (MV)
white sail cloth .015″	1,812 fps
	1,858*
	1,866
	1,856
	1,868
NO PATCH	1,854
Double patching	1,842

*Changed chargers after first shot, got slightly heavier charge at same setting.

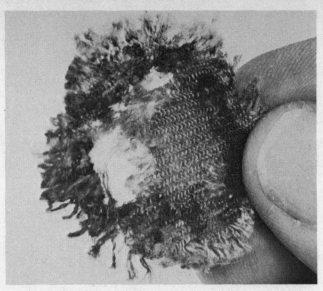 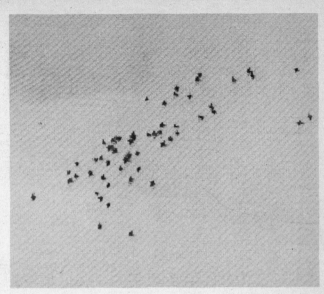

This Irish linen patch shows definite abuse with clear, large holes. The gasket sealing ability has been destroyed. This condition calls for a trial run of double patching.

Buying the best patching is not the only problem; storing it is another. This Irish linen was left out to be damaged. Patching should be washed, rinsed, dried in a home drier and put away.

In going to a .535" ball with the same CVA rifle and the same charge of FFg, GOI black powder, the 120-grain load with a single patch gave 1,896, while the same charge with double patching gave a muzzle velocity of 1,892. No patch at all with the .535" ball earned a MV of 1,874, or about the same as either single or double patching, for all practical purposes. Just for fun, we tried a light tanned leather patch soaked with Bullet Lube No. 103 (well saturated) and the velocity was 1,895.

Again, drawing conclusions becomes guesswork. However, in another 54, going to double patching and switching from a watery lube to a grease lube, raised the muzzle velocity about 150 fps, and in a 36-caliber Mowrey Squirrel Rifle, 30 grains volume of FFFg, GOI earned an average velocity of 1,604 fps at the muzzle, while the same charge double patched bumped velocity to an average of 1,722 fps. Using 40 grains volume of the same powder in the same rifle, the single patch got 1,730 fps at the muzzle, while the double patch read out at 1,865 average.

As for accuracy, it was best with a patch, and the differences between double and single patching were slight, with any favor going to double patching. With no patch at all, we got accuracy suitable for hitting large targets. At 50, 100 and 150 yards, a man-sized figure would have been struck with decent aim and a no-patch load, so the old mountain man was not totally helpless in the accuracy de-

partment when he was forced to load without benefit of a patch.

Our tests seem to indicate that when a patch is burning out to any large degree, accuracy must suffer, and velocity goes down as well. We can also state the converse—if a single patch is not burning out, adding another patch to the load will probably have little value. It's a matter of trial and error, of course, to find out whether or not to use a double patch or not. Much is to be learned from picking up fired patches. However, it seems that slight holes are a rule, even with good patches. So, the shooter should not panic when he holds his expired patch up to the light and spreads the fibers to find that there are burned out places, tiny holes.

It would seem that a tough, close weave material, such as the sailcloth or fine Irish linen makes for better patching material than flimsy fabrics. A good lube should be used, too. Saliva seems to work fine in preventing burnout. However, left loaded for a time, the saliva could dry out and leave the patch virtually unlubed. If the charge is for hunting, then a grease lube could be better than saliva for that purpose, helping to prevent burnout.

It's worth repeating that with the popular round ball, the patch should always be used, for the reasons already stated. Although it may be an imperfect gasket, it does seem to have some sealing ability when used properly, and, of course, it takes up the windage in the bore for accuracy and

it does not prevent proper obturation of the ball, which is essential to accuracy. The patch can be square or round. Either works, although a square which is oversize can tend to get hung up on the ramrod at times.

Patching is nothing new, and it is certainly not an invention of the 19th century. In an interesting book, *Espingarda Perfeyta,* written in the Portuguese language and printed in 1718, the authors explained one way to patch the ball, when they said: "Others made barrels with rifling inside, some with more, and others with less rifling, all of them deep and twisted in the form of a spiral. These were loaded by putting the bullet in a little piece of leather of a thin glove, folded only once, dipped in oil, and thus it was pushed down to the bottom in such a manner that the bullet may not lose its roundness."

Although black powder is indeed an agent of antiquity, it is again with us to stay, it's sure, for a long, long while. Dormant before the Age of Science, many of the precepts about shooting were derived from guesswork and even superstition. Now, we are looking at black powder in the light of modern times, testing anew and retesting the old, and, in many instances, arriving at some pretty interesting findings. These findings can hardly be called "fact" yet, but we have to start somewhere. So, we'll keep on shooting the charcoal burners, trying to move toward friendship instead of acquaintance with the old style guns. ●

A GOOD

For a handy fellow, can be a

by RAY ORDORICA

MOST OF US HAVE felt pangs when a good gun comes back from a hunting trip with new scratches. Some, who spend only a small amount of time in the outdoors, can put up with a few nicks in a fancy gun to enjoy its company. Those who spend a lot of time outdoors with a rifle may often be better served with a rather plain companion.

The 1893 Mauser, also called the Spanish Mauser, is one of many that offer advantages to those in need of a good down-and-dirty working rifle, not the least of which is a usually modest price. They cock on closing, which is not really a problem; they are usually chambered for the 7x57 round, an effective all-round cartridge. It is factory loaded to moderate pressure levels and adequate ballis-

tics. The rifle has one of the best forms of extractor, and with luck or a little tuning, the two-stage military trigger can be very good. You *can* fit custom triggers and sights and safeties, but for the best bargain, use what's on it. All the standard issue equipment has been proven in war, the hardest test of a rifle.

The little rifle pictured here is an example of a good working tool that fills a need and didn't cost much in either time or money. Other than the checkering and time for the finish to dry, it took less than two hours to complete, starting from a military configuration. It cost me less than $50 and I even got some ammo with it.

Years ago, back in Michigan, a friend gave me the idea of having an alternate rifle for use in the really bad

weather that so often accompanies hunting season in Michigan. He uses some pretty fancy rifles, but always keeps a rough weather rifle handy. It is usually some form of Mauser, with most of the military trim left on: a good weapon underneath some protective wood and unfancy iron that, if dinged up or banged around, will not be any major cause for alarm.

In succeeding years I spent a lot of time hunting in Michigan, Colorado, and Montana, and put my share of nicks in various rifles, and even broke the stock of one when it (and I) went over a cliff, but I never got around to a rough-use rifle. Looking back, I admit I could have used guns lots less fancy and I would have done just as well in my hunting efforts.

We are often, for example, obsessed

Rough work, if it's solid, is OK on a rifle expected to take a beating. Writer did not waste time on this ramp.

Getting it in the middle, and getting a good sight picture was more important than a fine finish.

ROUGH RIFLE

nearly any military rifle sound trail companion.

with a desire for accuracy in a rifle that will never be needed. I am as guilty as anyone of the unreasonable desire for less-than-MOA rifles, but I have now come to admit that a whole lot less accuracy than that will do just fine for most of my shooting needs.

When I came to Alaska to live I brought nice rifles along. Shortly after I got settled, I started living the outdoor life with a vengeance. I was spending most of my time outdoors in the company of one or more firearms, and I discovered that none of my rifles was at all suited to the rough use of such a life. I cared too much for them. They were all too nice to endure the vicissitudes of a long Alaskan winter riding a thousand miles or more on a snowmobile under my foot.

We use snowmobiles some seven months out of the year as our main form of transportation in the Alaskan bush. I wanted a rifle along at all times for use against fur critters, and in case I came upon a grizzly or black bear while exploring some new country, so I started looking for a rifle to use for this rough work.

One day, a friend hauled this Mauser up from the floor of his pickup truck and handed it over to me to examine. He had no more use for it, and thought I might like to buy it. The rifle looked like it had spent its entire life in places a lot worse than the floor of my friend's pickup, especially the bore. I said so, but was told in good faith that the rifle shot very well indeed. I took that with a grain of salt, but its origin—Deutsche Waffen und Munitionsfabriken, or DWM—and a

*Editor's Note: Writer Odorica has been living in the Alaskan bush where one learns to weld and use a chainsaw and make a snowmobile go, or one moves to town. Readers with less training or aptitude for metalwork who want a rifle like this should see they hire a gunsmith for the following chores: Cut and crown barrel; install ramp front sight; drill and tap for receiver sight; bend bolt handle. With no polish or finish needed, these shouldn't be expensive. **K.W.***

good trigger pull decided the matter. I gave him $40 and got the rifle with most of a box of ammo.

It was in pretty much original military trim with 29-inch barrel and a bolt handle that stuck out at a right angle to the stock, pointing east if you

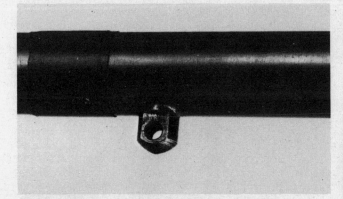

The front sling lug, silver-soldered in place, was made from a standard one, cutting off the screw and shaping the base with a file. That's muzzle tape behind it.

This old Lyman aperture sight is the kind of thing gun people keep just in case, and before your very eyes is a case.

Checkering was a mid-winter chore; the shape was rasped into the stock. Note the cut-down area at the ejector port.

Rear view shows the tight bolt bend, which makes a slim rifle. Military safety is retained: there's a good-sized aperture in the sight.

faced north. It had the original military tangent rear sight and barley-corn front. With hacksaw, files, and an oxy-acetylene torch, a piece of scrap steel for a front sight ramp, and a few odd parts that I had scrounged over the years I made what you see.

I cut nine inches off the barrel, bent the bolt down, fitted aperture rear and sourdough front sights, and trimmed the military stock to a handy size. Metal parts were touched up with cold blue. I didn't spend a lot of time making the bolt bend to the "per-fect" angle. I didn't file the front sight ramp to match any "perfect" custom ramp. And I didn't spend hour after hour sanding and whiskering and finishing a fancy stock or polishing metal. I knew that this rifle would get rusty, scuffed, and scratched and did only enough busywork to make the rifle a little handier, so it would therefore tend to always be there.

I got lucky with the rear sight, in that I already had a unit that was custom made for slipping over Mauser bolt releases with very little fitting required. I picked it up years ago at a gun show, figuring it might come in handy someday. It is a Lyman unit, patented in 1905. Iron sights are far less likely to break than even the most durable scopes, and never fog up. I gave the stock a quicky oil finish using Lin-Speed. Then, after the rifle had seen a little use and I knew it was worth the effort, I did a simple job of checkering it during some long Alaskan winter nights.

None of this "custom" work was at all difficult to one accustomed to working with hand tools. There are certainly plenty of suitable old rifles around. In fact, many of these would be used more with this treatment in place of costly rebarreling and restocking. There are many barrels prematurely consigned to the scrap heap that could provide years of acceptable service. As long as the basic unit is sound and the barrel at all usable, why not have at it? A few inquiries at used gun parlors, gun shows, or pawn shops should give you the makings in short order. The military stocks are excellent walnut and fine practice pieces for the beginning checkerer.

If in doubt as to the suitability of a rifle, take it to a qualified gunsmith for a careful appraisal. He can tell you if the gun in question will be suitable for modification into a knock-around hunting rig, and may be able to suggest some short cuts to getting the job done. One caution is in order: Many old military or other rifles are now valued collector items, and either your gunsmith or perhaps a collector friend can tell you if you plan to cut up a museum piece. Make haste slowly.

Fears concerning my rifle barrel's rough condition were groundless, and the little rifle shoots fully as well as I can hold. This is my second custom rifle based on this action. The first was a 257 Roberts I traded off, but I think this new one will be with me for a long time.

Testing it at a remote Alaskan lake with a good hill to back up stray bullets, I picked out a rock some 300 yards away just above the shoreline. The rock sat in an area where I could spot hits against a dirt bank. Now 300 yards was stretching both this rifle's sights and my eyes to the limit. However, I was able to keep all my shots within an area that would approximate the vitals of a deer or caribou at that range.

Continuing my testing at targets of opportunity at closer range, I rediscovered the great speed possible when using a large rear aperture combined with a good visible post front sight. Picking out a tomato can or a clump of dirt at 25 yards, I'd throw the rifle to my shoulder, put the post on the target, and cut loose, trying for a good combination of speed and accuracy. The little M93 was fully up to it, and when the front sight was on target as the shot broke, the target broke. I saw no bear, but it took my share of ptarmigan and rabbit, all I asked of it.

It is always there at the side of my snowmobile in its scabbard with a piece of tape over the muzzle to keep out water, and a bread wrapper loose around the action to keep it from freezing shut. I don't worry about rust, stock damage, or a fogging scope. While it is no Rigby Mauser, this working tool does have a certain amount of elegance in its simplicity of form and function. It does a job I'd never ask of any fine and valuable custom rifle—day in and day out service under very harsh conditions.

You don't have to run an Alaskan trapline to have a need for such a handy little rifle. You can do a lot of hunting, fun shooting, practicing, and even instructing with a good solid and plain Mauser. Part of the money you save over a more costly rifle can be used for loading dies, powder, and bullets and you can therefore get in lots of shooting with the rifle. A bit of regular practice will go a long way toward overcoming any accuracy deficiency the rifle may have. Military Mausers deserve a lot of consideration if you are in the market for a good rough rifle. ●

This clip-loading hump was filed down to clear the unique old Lyman sight. The lever unlocks it.

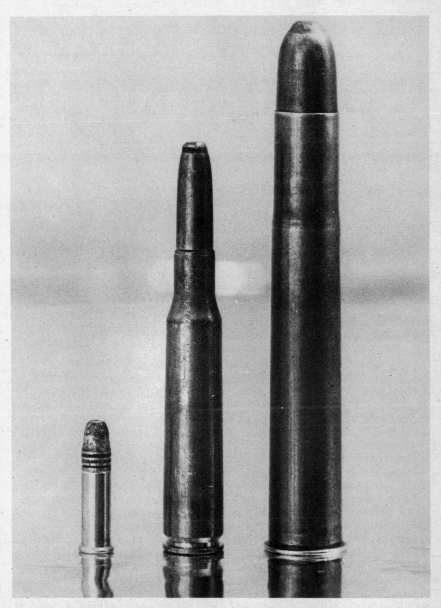

The 7x57mm at center overshadows both the 22 Long Rifle and the 470 Nitro when it comes to versatility. It's enough gun for Alaska's bush.

IT WAS MOSTLY my mother's fault, but James Oliver Curwood had a hand in it. She gave a young and impressionable boy a set of books of adventure in the Far North. Mr. Curwood was the author, I was the boy, and his writing hooked me on books and a life of vicarious adventure. At a very tender age, a book collector was born.

People collect books for many reasons—investment, information, pleasure and profit. I do it for pleasure. Books opened the door to a whole new world of adventure.

who specialized in out-of-print and rare sporting books.

Those catalogs were a revelation to me, showing almost every book ever printed on outdoor subjects. The only drawback was the price level.

Limited finances and a desire for the rarer and finer books led me to a self-inflicted financial crisis. The law of supply and demand applies to books, and the fact that a book is harder to find after it goes out of print usually means that it's more expensive. I found that I could not afford the books I wanted without major sacri-

was always looking for books for his stock and for his customers, and he was willing to work out trades with me.

From then on, I used his catalog as a shopping guide and began to pick up books from every inexpensive source I could find, and traded them to the dealer for books I wanted. He would give me from thirty to sixty percent of his selling price as trade credit.

With judicious shopping and a lot of footwork, I was able to build up an excellent library for a cash outlay of only a few cents on the dollar of its ac-

How to Collect SPORTING BOOKS

There's a way to realize the many pleasures of fine books without going broke.

For a few years, a voracious appetite for the printed word was satisfied by local libraries and indulgent neighbors and relatives. I read everything I could find about guns and hunting and outdoor adventure until I exhausted the nearby supply.

Eventually, I joined a book club that specialized in the kind of books I loved, and other authors and titles joined Curwood on my bookshelves. The club offered a good selection of the sporting books in print at reasonable prices, and I took full advantage of their offerings.

My acquisitive urges were growing, though, and the discovery that many of the most desirable books were no longer in print resulted in a flurry of outbound letters and a mailbox stuffed with catalogs from the dealers

by JAMES HANDCOCK

fices. I had to find a more lucrative grindstone for my nose or do without books I badly wanted.

The solution I worked out over a period of time has proven both effective and enjoyable. I learned specialty book dealers usually charge more for a given book than any other source does, so I began to haunt rummage sales and second-hand stores. On rare occasions, I found books I wanted, but I passed up many I already had. Then I visited a local gun show and met a dealer who specialized in outdoor books and I realized that passing up some of these books was a mistake. He

tual value. I also learned some very valuable lessons about the art of dealing with used books.

The most important of these was the effect of condition on the value and collectibility of the books I found. Condition is the main criterion for determining the desirability of a given book, but it is often overlooked.

Most book dealers use the standards that the *AB Bookman's Weekly*, a trade publication for antiquarian book dealers, recommends. Grades run from "as new" to "poor" somewhat like the used gun standards established by the N.R.A.

A book described as being "as new" or "mint" is as perfect as the day it left the publisher. It has absolutely no flaws. Books in this condition are sought after by people who collect for investment value or are trying to upgrade the condition of their collections.

The next step down in value and condition is "fine." Such a book is close to new, but has been read. It still has no defects, but is not as crisp or shiny as a new book.

"Very good" refers to a copy that shows small signs of wear on the jacket, binding or paper, but has no tears or other defects.

"Good" is the conditon of the average used and worn book that still has all of its pages intact and present.

books at such unlikely places as rummage sales, thrift shops, Salvation Army stores, second-hand stores, department store sale tables, junk dealers, consignment houses, antique stores, sporting goods stores, gun shows and flea markets. Making the rounds of these places was time-consuming, but very worthwhile. I even found general used book stores to be worth shopping. They often had excellent books in my field at prices a lot lower than the specialty dealers.

Most general book stores have the stock divided into categories, and the

source for information about scarcity, collectibility and value of sporting books. The best I could get was the assortment of dealer's catalogs I had already accumulated.

Most books found in my scouting had been listed at one time in one of the catalogs. By taking into account the edition, condition, and the age of the listing, I was usually able to get a close estimate of the retail value of the book. From this, I could make an accurate estimate of what I could get for it in trade and what I should spend on it. When several dealers had listed

The author with his own books, hundreds of them.

"Good" and "very good" books are the ones usually sought out and purchased by the average collector who is as much interested in the contents of the book as he is in the book for its own sake.

A "fair" book is one that still has all of the pages of text intact. End-papers, half-title pages, etc., may be missing. Its value is minimal.

A "poor" book is often referred to as a reading copy. The text is complete and readable, but can be smudged, torn and tattered. Its only value is in its contents—you may want to read it, but you won't want to display it on your shelves.

Another lesson I learned was that hard work could pay dividends in book scouting. I found an amazing number of inexpensive but desirable

first and most obvious place to look is the section titled "Guns & Hunting" or "Outdoor Sports." I found that it pays to check other sections, too! Many larger stores have sections on Africa, Asia, India, Alaska, and the like, and they often file hunting books there; Travel, Geography and Natural History often contain good outdoor titles, as well; Technical sections may contain books on firearms and reloading; Biography often has works by or about hunters and explorers; even Fiction can be lucrative since works by Jack O'Connor, Robert Ruark, Nash Buckingham and Stewart Edward White are frequently found there.

I learned that a good reference library was one of the most important things I needed. There is no single

a given book at differing prices, I either used the catalog of the dealer I traded with or took the average of the prices as a true value.

One good reference I found and used was Ray Riling's excellent work, *Guns And Shooting—A Bibliography.* This originally came out in a limited edition of 1500 copies and is the standard work on the subject of sporting books. First published in 1951 and long out of print, it has been recently republished and is available from Ray Riling Arms Books.

Guns And Shooting is not a price guide. It is a very definitive bibliography of virtually every sporting book published in a major European language between 1521 and 1950. Book listings are given by year of publication and by author: pertinent data on

A complete set of GUN DIGEST isn't easy to get, but it's valuable year-to-year post-World War II history.

You can pick a technical subject like handloading and realize a wide range of books on it.

You can pick a man and places far away, Selous and Africa, for instance, on which to focus.

size, publisher, contents and related facts are given. For the serious collector, it is an invaluable reference:

Another lesson I learned was the advantage of doing a majority of my business with one dealer. I found that there were many benefits in working with one dealer instead of several. Doing so allows you and the dealer to get to know each other and build up a relationship of mutual trust, and trust is a key factor in any business.

Mutual trust means a dealer can ship a book out to you without worrying about bouncing checks or other maneuvers on your part that can leave him with no book and no money. Mutual trust also means that you can ship off a box of books to him in trade and be confident that you will get a fair deal.

No dealer will buy from or trade with anyone for books sight unseen unless they know them well. Too often have they heard a book described as "real nice!" or "really fine!" and then found it to be a very mediocre copy.

Every dealer has his own idiosyncrasies, especially in the area of judging the condition of books. This is a subjective art to a large extent, and what one man honestly calls "very good," another dealer with equal hon-

A man and familiar places—like Elmer Keith and our own West—can add up to a collection all to themselves.

esty may call "fine" and a third dealer may call "good." When you and a dealer do enough business together, you learn to speak the same language and to see things the same way. This makes for a much smoother relationship.

Another area of potential friction between you and a dealer that mutual trust can eliminate is search requests. Most dealers offer a search service for a title you want. A search costs the dealer time and money, and he will hesitate to invest them if he thinks you are not serious or you have made the same request to another dealer. The majority of search services go through the same channels, and one man asking several dealers to find a certain book results in competition between searchers that drives up the price of the book and costs everyone involved more than it should, which is why mimeographed "want" lists sel-

dom get results. Dealers assume several other dealers got the lists, so it would be a waste of time to search actively for the books.

Establishing a good relationship with a dealer has other advantages. If he knows that you are a serious collector or that you are especially interested in a certain category or subject, he will probably be willing to notify you if he gets a book that you might be interested in. He might even send a book to you for you to examine and decide if you want to buy it or not.

A friendly dealer can also give you good advice if you are interested in buying books as an investment. Like artwork and other collectibles, rare books are going up in value much faster than the inflation rate. Wise buying can be a good hedge against inflation, and your dealer's help and advice are invaluable. He is in a position to know the best books for you to buy.

Whether you collect for pleasure or profit or a combination of the two, having a good relationship with a dealer can make your quest much easier and cannot fail to benefit you.

Most of all, I learned that book collecting can be an insidious malady. It is no respecter of persons or of ages. It

Antlers can take you into books that will take you to more and better antlers.

Sometimes you can make money. This book by Mellon has appreciated greatly.

Above all there is the pleasure of reading what thoughtful men have said about things to know.

Books can span centuries. They have been writing of Africa in English for almost two.

can start easily like a fire and be harder to quench than any conflagration Smoky warns us against.

I have found it rewarding: educational, pleasant, and fun. A good library can be built up without great expense, and scavenging and trading and working to get the books I want gives me both thrill and sport.

My mother's gift started me on a long and enjoyable road: I have never regretted traveling it. ●

Mail Order Sporting Book Dealers

Angler's Shooter's Bookshelf, Goshen, CT 06576
Berkshire Collection, P.O. Box 891, Pittsfield, MA 01202
Blacktail Mountain Books, 42 1st. Avenue West, Kalispell, MT 59901
Cabinet of Books, P.O. Box 195, Watertown, CT 06795
Chestnut Ridge Books, P.O. Box 353, Rutherford, NJ 07070
Charles Daly Collection, 66 Chilton St., Cambridge, MA 02138
Gary L. Estabrook, P.O. Box 61543, Vancouver, WA 98666
Gallery of the Old West, P.O. Box 556, Bigfork, MT 59911
Gunnerman Books, P.O. Box 4292, Auburn Heights, MI 48057
Melvin Marcher, 6204 N. Vermont, Oklahoma City, OK 73112
Gerald Pettinger, Rte. 2, Russell, IA 50238
Pisces & Capricorn, 302 S. Berrien St., Albion, MI 49424
Ray Riling Arms Books, P.O. Box 18925, Philadelphia, PA 19119
Rutgers Book Center, 127 Raritan Ave., Highland Park, NJ 08904
James Tillinghast, Box 405, Hancock, NH 03449
Trophy Room Books, 4858 Dempsey Ave., Encino, CA 91436
Ken Trotman, 2-6 Hampstead High Street, London NW3 1QQ England

Most of these issue catalogs are free, but it is courteous to enclose one or two dollars to cover the dealer's expense when you request a catalog.

References

Margaret Haller, 1976: *Book Collector's Fact Book,* Arco Publishing, N.Y.
Joe Riling: "The Arms Library" annually in GUN DIGEST.
Ray Riling, 1951: *Guns And Shooting - A Bibliography,* Greenberg, N.Y.
Jean Peters, Ed. 1977: *Book Collecting - A Modern Guide,* Bowker, N.Y. & London
Jack Tannen, 1976: *How To Identify And Collect American First Editions,* Arco, N.Y.
Bookman's Yearbook — The 1966 AB - Old and New

Useful Terminology

Book sizes
Folio—over 13″ high
Quarto (4to)—about 12 ″ high
Octavo (8vo)—about 9″
Duodecimo (12mo)—7″-8″ high
Sextodecimo (16mo)—6″-7″ high
Vigesimoquarto (24mo)—5″-6″ high
Trigesimosecundo (32mo)—4″-5″ high

Book defects, features, etc.
Chipped—very small pieces torn or gouged out.
Derrydale Press—the Ne Plus Ultra of collecting. Derrydale operated during the Depression, producing limited editions of sporting books in deluxe bindings. They generally demand top prices from collectors.
Ex-Lib—formerly a library book. Generally in good condition, but not very desirable to serious collectors.
Faded—usually a cloth binding that has been exposed to the sun until the original color is bleached out.
Foxing—light brown spots caused by the aging of paper. Common in older books.
Hinge cracked—the paper which acts as the hinge for the cover has begun to crack, but still functions.
Hinge separated—the hinge has completely torn and the cover—front or rear, depending on which hinge—is loose. If both hinges are separated, then the cover is completely detached.
Shaken—hinges have loosened to the point where the cover is not tightly attached to the book. This is a common condition in older, heavier books. Generally any book with faulty hinges is only "good" in condition.

BENELLI'S B76:

by DONALD M. SIMMONS

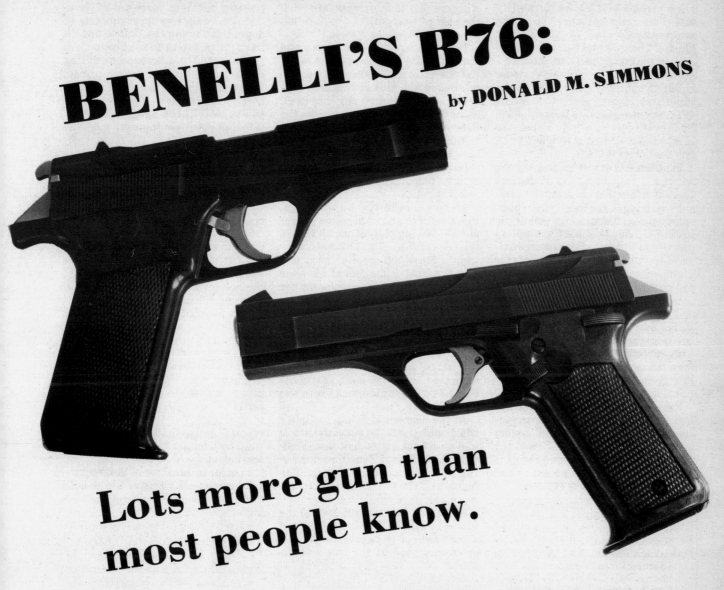

Lots more gun than most people know.

THE AUTOMATIC pistol world has for the past couple of decades turned to making copies. In high-power recoil-operated autos, we have generally seen copycats of the Walther or Browning systems. In many cases, the two systems have been intermarried, giving us Walther-like pistols with double-action hammers and hammer-drop safeties with Browning's locking system. An example would be the line of Smith & Wesson automatics which are now offered with two magazine capacities and three different frame materials — aluminum, steel and stainless steel.

One obvious reason for this lack of originality was the U.S. Army's recent interest in replacing the perennial Colt 45 with a 9mm handgun.

Their specifications just about spelled out a Walther-like recoil-operated automatic pistol.

Regardless of all this, a small Italian manufacturer has come up with an entirely unique system of locking. Senor Giovanni Benelli of Urbino is the inventor and applied for an Italian patent granted in February of 1972, ten years ago. The U.S. patent was applied for in 1973 and was granted on July 8, 1975, U.S. patent number 3,893,369.

In 1976, Sile, Inc., 7 Centre Market Place, New York, New York became the exclusive U.S. distributor for Benelli's automatic pistols, and the first Benellis imported by Sile were not 9mm. They were blowback 32 ACPs. In addition to the 9mm and that handful of early 32 ACPs, Benelli has been

offered in 30 Luger, 9mm Ultra and, in prototype form, in 38 Super and 9mm Largo. There is a target B-76T with adjustable sights. The regular B-76 sold in 1983 for $349.95 which will only buy you half a Walther P-38.

The B-76 has an eight-round magazine with an exposed double action hammer. The firing pin is a Browning inertia-operated type. The extractor doubles as a loaded chamber indicator. The hammer has three positions — down, full cock and half cock; in any of these positions the safety will lock the hammer. It will lock the slide in open or closed position. The sights are non-adjustable and have a very low profile. The front sight has a broad white stripe on it and the rear sight has two thinner outline marks making sighting much easier in bad light. The slide and frame are blued over a sandblasted finish and the working internal parts are given a hard chrome plating for durability and corrosion resistance. The grips are checkered wood, or ribbed black plastic. The fore and back straps are scored longitudinally to provide a good handgrip. The magazine release is thumb operated and located in the same area as that of the Colt Model 1911, but operated by a forward push. Its over-all length is $8\frac{1}{16}$ inches; the height is $5\frac{3}{8}$ inches; it weighs 34 ozs. and the barrel is $4\frac{1}{2}$ inches long.

In automatic or self-loading pistols, we find — in general — two distinct types of action. Pistols using low pressure cartridges are mostly blowback operated, i.e., the cartridge case at the instant of firing becomes a gas sealing piston and is driven by pressure rearward from a fixed barrel. Pistols for high pressure cartridges employ recoil operation. In this case, the barrel is locked to the breech at a discharge and the two move rearward together. If this rearward locked movement is less than the cartridge length, we call it short recoil; if it is as long or longer than the cartridge, we call it long recoil. These then represent the conventional systems.

Examples of blowback pistols are legion, and the Walther PP is an outstanding one. The short recoil system is found in the Walther P-38 and the Colt Model 1911. The long recoil is rather rare and can be seen in the Frommer Stop pistols of Hungary.

Over the years there have been other systems tried: the Savage automatic pistol with a turning barrel, the Remington 51 and 53 with a blowback-recoil system, and the ill-fated

Kimble Arms floating barrel blowback system. These hybrid systems approached straight blowback to such a degree that to all intents, except to the engineering purists, they are felt to be of the blowback system.

Into this background comes one Benelli Model B-76 claiming to be recoil operated, but having a fixed barrel. Before any all knowing soul says it is impossible, let me say that in all of the tests that I could improvise, the indication is that it may not be recoil in the purest sense but it sure isn't blowback either!

Here is how the B-76 works — from both its patent information and from test firing it:

The slide is in two basic pieces. Piece number one is the slide proper and its locking closure which blocks the rear of the slide. This assembly weighs about $8\frac{1}{4}$ ozs. Enclosed in a square tunnel at the rear of the slide is the bolt assembly, piece number two. The bolt assembly consists of the bolt, the extractor, the guide stud, the firing pin and the link (toggle). The bolt assembly weighs $2\frac{3}{4}$ ozs. The rest of the pistol is the frame into which the barrel and subframe unit are mounted rigidly. The lower rear of the bolt has a lug which locks into the subframe.

At the moment of firing, the gases which push the bullet out of the barrel also push back on the bolt face. Visualize the slide on a Benelli as unmoving at the moment of firing. The frame and the barrel and subframe move rearward, while the slide is in effect forced forward, relative to the frame, by inertia. This causes the link at an angle of 45 degrees to exert a downward push on the bolt and mo-

mentarily locks the bolt to the subframe. As the forward inertia of the heavy slide is overcome and residual pressure begins its rearward acceleration, the link pivots approximately 15 degrees allowing the bolt to unlock from its groove in the subframe. All this happens in microseconds during the critical high pressure phase. There is still blowback action from this point on, as is often found in short-recoil-locked systems, and residual pressure continues to push the bolt and, through it, the slide, rearward.

The detail action around the bolt is interesting. At the moment of firing, the link at 45 degrees exerts a downward push — from the forward inertia of the slide — keeping the bolt locked to the subframe. As the pressure drops to a safe level the bolt cams itself out of the subframe as the slide starts to move backwards. The front of the link pivots, leaving the link at 30 degrees. This means that the bolt moves forward $\frac{3}{64}$-inch in the slide while both are also moving rearward. The guide on the top of the bolt engages in an undercut keeping the bolt in a high position within the slide.

The unusual thing about Benelli's design is that the more powerful the cartridge, the better the lock up of the several parts, due to the increased inertial impulse forcing the slide forward for a longer dwell time. That's it and it does work!

In order to test some of the theories, I did some field firing of the Benelli and these are the results of my testing:

First, if a pistol is operating like a Pedersen-designed Remington 51 blowback recoil action, you can re-

Remington Model 51, 380 ACP having a separate bolt and slide like the Benelli.

Post-war Berlin Police Walther P-38, a gun with short recoil lock.

move the extractor and the shell case will not be ejected. This is because with Pedersen's action the bolt, also independent of the slide, moves rearward a small distance at the moment of firing. Then it locks to the frame and the slide proper continues rearward under the momentum acquired from the movement of the bolt. When the slide has thus moved a small distance, it unlocks the bolt and they travel together to full recoil position. The delays built into Pedersen's system are such that the pressure in the barrel is almost over by the time the bolt unlocks and therefore the shell casing without the help of the extractor is left protruding from the chamber of the barrel.

Is this the case with an extractorless B-76?

NO! When the extractor is removed from a Benelli, it acts more like a blowback design. The shell casing is driven to the rear by the residual chamber pressure, strikes the ejector, and is in most cases thrown from the gun.

To test the validity of this, a blowback Astra 600 9mm Luger was used without an extractor and consistently also ejected and operated as though it had an extractor. Truly, in a pure blowback pistol, there is no need for an extractor during firing. It only serves to remove a live cartridge from the chamber if the shooter wishes to stop firing and clear the arm.

As a further check, a recoil-operated Walther P-38 with a recoiling barrel and a fully locked system was fired without its extractor. Here, as we might predict, the shell casing after each firing was left partially pushed out of the chamber. Because of the

small amount of pressure left after unlocking, the Walther's action requires an extractor.

In the Benelli then, we have a fully locked breech for micro-seconds, but there is still blowback action from this point on as residual pressure pushes the bolt and through the link pushes the slide rearward. The fact that the extractor can be removed and the action is not changed proves the point that there is pressure exerted on the shell casing pushing the recoiling parts of the pistol to the rear.

There is nothing wrong in the design of the Benelli — what was desired was a locked delay while the chamber pressure was at its peak and that is just what was accomplished. I think it is interesting to note that the United States patent office, during the examination of Benelli's claim, cited the Pedersen Patent 1,391,496. It had to do with a Remington Model 51 which had a toggle-like link but still had the Model 51's "blowback-recoil" action. The two actions while appearing similar are anything but the same, as shown above. If a quick term were to be applied to the action of the Benelli B-76, it might be "recoil-blowback" or "inertia-locked blowback" which of course could be applied to many other so-called recoil operated pistols.

(Another set of tests involve fixing the frame in a vise. If you then push forward lightly on the slide while trying to push the bolt back with a rod down the bore, you will find the breech locked. When you lift the pressure from the slide, the rod down the bore will open the breech easily. The first test shows you the inertial locking; the sec-

ond test demonstrates response to residual blowback. Editor)

Someone might ask: If the B-76 depends on its link for locking action, what would happen if the link was removed? Well, I am here to tell you that is just what I wanted to know so I removed the link and fired the Benelli from a rest. There is no doubt in my mind now that the toggle serves a purpose; in fact a very important purpose. When I fired without the toggle, the bolt was blown rearward, shearing the bolt guide stud's upper surface and also shearing the nose of the extractor from its body. The shell case showed slight signs of swelling but no rupturing was evident. The important point is that no one would have been hurt by this abuse of a well-designed system. By the way, the link can't be removed, even when disassembling the pistol, without turning the firing pin about 180 degrees and withdrawing the firing pin from the rear.

What is new about the concept of the Benelli system? Several patents exhibit the same idea but they were applied to shoulder arms where Benelli's was applied to a handgun. John L. Lochhead patented a shotgun with the same type of recoil system except for the fact that he added weight to his inertia block to further slow down the action of the shotgun. He also had a separate spring to drive the inertia block rearward after the chamber pressure had fallen to a safe figure. Lochhead's U.S. patent number 2,466,902 also shows a positively locked bolt which has to wait until the inertia block has been driven rearward by its spring for it to unlock from the receiver (frame).

Colt Combat Commander in 45 ACP, the familiar Browning short recoil lock.

Astra 600, circa 1945, used by Germans, a straight blowback 9mm.

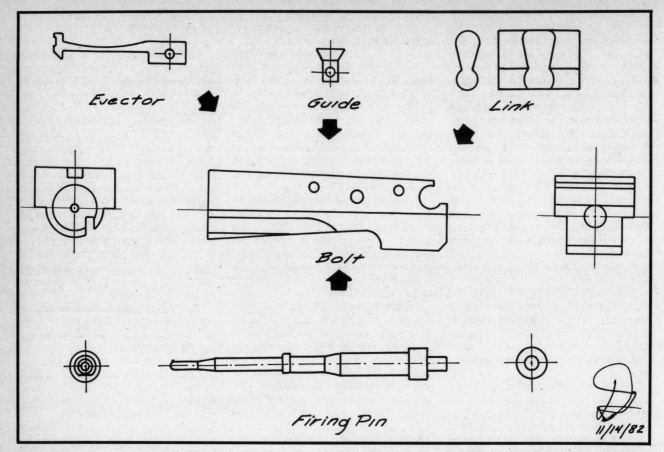

Benelli bolt showing all the component parts.

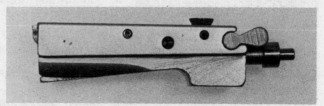

Benelli B76 bolt assembly in assembled position.

The frame of the B-76 Benelli is made up of two clam shells of .080-inch alloy sheet steel welded together. This construction is reminiscent of the Ruger 22 automatic pistol and, before that, the obscure German Jaeger 32 automatic pistol. After welding, the bead is carefully ground off leaving, to all intents and purposes, a forged-machined frame. The only external point at which the sheet metal construction can be noticed, is the inside of the trigger guard. Where strength was needed, a reinforcing slug of steel was welded into the frame assembly. Where the four grip screws thread into the frame, heavy extrusions are formed to give the screws adequate threads. In back of the trigger, a small Allen screw is threaded to act as an adjustable trigger stop (the Allen Wrench for this screw is shipped with each pistol). The grip of the Benelli is set at a Luger-like 65 degrees to the frame and

makes the pistol much more self-pointing than some of its more square contemporaries.

The barrel and subframe are made from bar stock and are then completely machined. After machining, the parts are hard chrome-plated including the bore. During my testing, I used some of the most corrosive ammunition I could find. I had World War II Italian Beretta submachine gun ammo, German World War II steel case tungsten core ammo, and some very tough-primered Yugoslavian ammo which was also corrosive. After firing, without any attempt at cleaning, the Benelli was put away for a month in a very humid area for at least two of those weeks and in Arizona dryness for two more weeks. The bore, on final examination, showed absolutely no evidence of this abuse, which is quite a testimonial to hard-chroming the bore of a barrel.

One unusual thing about the Ben-

elli is the chamber. The forward part of the chamber has a series of grooves running with the axis of the barrel. These grooves, during firing, allow a small amount of gas to slip by the throat of the case of the cartridge. The pressure inside and outside of the case mouth equalized and this tends to float the cartridge, allowing easy extraction of a wide variety of ammunition. The fired case does not show any grooves because they are so small. This system helps prevent any welding of the case to the chamber wall during firing which can lead to case rupture and other ills.

The barrel is threaded into the subframe and the subframe is attached to the frame by four roll pins. I know, I know — why four roll pins? The average shooter is as allergic to roll pins as he is to poison ivy, but is this prejudice right? No! I don't think so — a roll pin because of its springiness will hold better than a solid pin. These roll

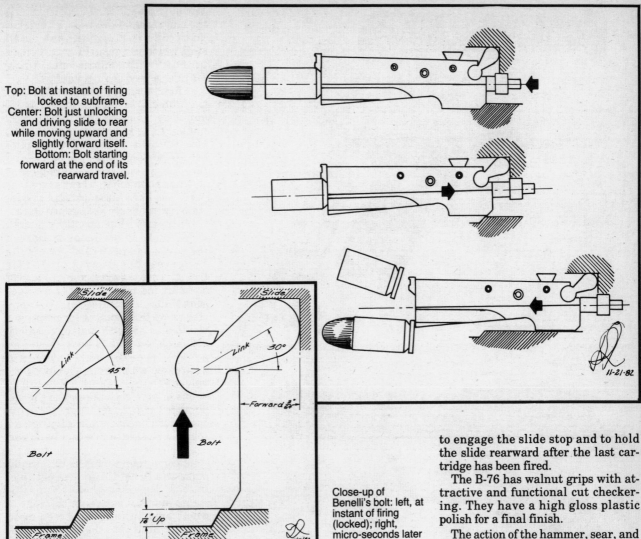

Top: Bolt at instant of firing locked to subframe.
Center: Bolt just unlocking and driving slide to rear while moving upward and slightly forward itself.
Bottom: Bolt starting forward at the end of its rearward travel.

Close-up of Benelli's bolt: left, at instant of firing (locked); right, micro-seconds later (unlocked).

pins in the Benelli are all hidden from view so no one is the wiser.

When the subframe has been removed from the frame, the tension on the hammer spring can be adjusted. Sile pointed out that the pistols as sold are set up for NATO-specified 9mm Luger ammo. U.S. commercial primers require a much less vigorous hit and the entire action — single and double — of the hammer can be improved by reducing its spring tension.

It is thought erroneously by many that a heavy recoil spring will materially help in keeping the breech closed in a blowback automatic pistol. Even the Benelli patent says that "strong recoil springs" are needed to lock the breech in a blowback pistol. This is not true. There are only two functions of a recoil spring in any automatic pistol. The primary function is to store energy during the recoil of the slide in order that the slide can return to battery using this energy. The second

function is that in the final movement, it will soak up any excessive recoil velocity and avoid pounding other parts. The recoil spring on the Benelli serves both functions admirably. The recoil spring collapses into a steel cylinder during recoil. A guide which slides on the main assembly pin limits the height of this spring and prevents over stressing. The buffer function of the assembly is accomplished by six sets of Belleville washers which take up the final movement of the recoil of the slide. This entire assembly is held together by a snap ring.

The magazine has a continuous slot on both sides — this allows finger holding sections of the plastic follower to be grasped from the outside. The body of the magazine is made of .032-inch through-hardened steel with a reinforcing rib at the rear wall. The floorplate is secured in the conventional manner by a second dimpled plate. The plastic follower has a notch

to engage the slide stop and to hold the slide rearward after the last cartridge has been fired.

The B-76 has walnut grips with attractive and functional cut checkering. They have a high gloss plastic polish for a final finish.

The action of the hammer, sear, and trigger is interesting. The three parts are all mounted in the subframe. The hammer and the sear are controlled by the trigger through a spring-loaded trigger bar which also acts as a disconnector à la Walther. But here the similarity ends since the trigger bar in the Benelli pushes either the hammer as in double action or the sear as in single action. In double action, the trigger bar's nose engages a stud mounted on the hammer; the hammer is forced back until the stud slides under the trigger bar and this allows the hammer to fly forward. In single action, a leg of the trigger bar engages the lower surface of the sear and pivots it about its mounting pin, allowing the hammer to fall.

Other than the parts already mentioned, the hammer, sear, trigger, link, manual safety, slide stop, and magazine catch all appear to be investment castings of, we're told, chrome-moly alloy. With the exception of the combination spring which tensions the sear and manual safety, all springs are of the durable coil type.

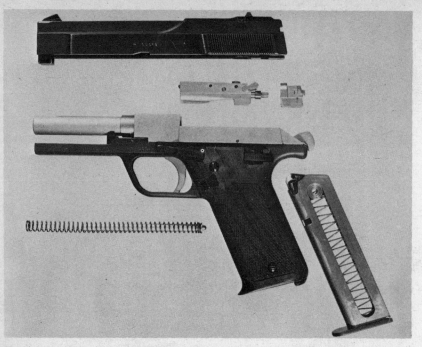

Early—pre-production—prototype B76 stripped. Note very plain recoil spring and heavy slide.

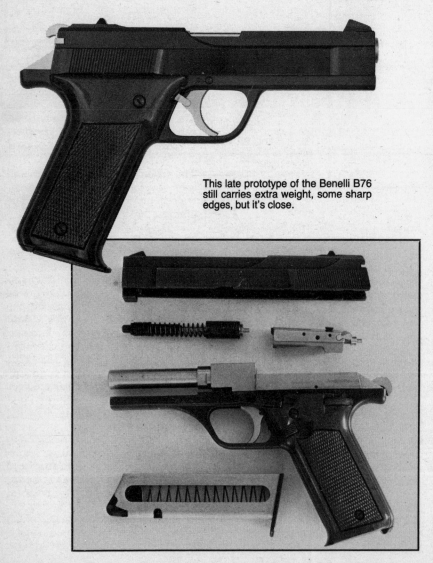

This late prototype of the Benelli B76 still carries extra weight, some sharp edges, but it's close.

Current Benelli B76 showing the slide over the recoil spring assembly left and the bolt assembly over the frame and barrel assembly.

The only plastic in the entire gun is the magazine follower. Benelli makes much of the fact that their pistol is all steel which is unusual today. Benelli uses a 17-4PH stainless steel firing pin, also a good selling point.

In most modern pistols, we find only the frame is serial numbered as required by U.S. laws. The Benelli B-76 not only has the frame serialed but also marked with the full serial number are the subframe, the barrel and the slide. Strangely, the all-important bolt has no number. These same four parts also have the smokeless powder Italian proof house acceptance marks.

What don't I like about the Benelli B-76? Well, in all honesty there is very little that I don't like. One of the things that has always griped me is trying to use the extractor as a loaded chamber indicator. The idea is to get something for nothing but what one ends up with is nothing for nothing. I would also prefer a magazine safety although few pistols have them any more. This device makes the pistol unfireable when the magazine is removed. To me, this valuable safety seems to have gone the way of the un-lamented grip safety. A great deal is heard today about the manual safety that can be used with either hand and can drop the hammer without firing a chambered round. This feature would make the Benelli more competitive. In today's market where 13 and 15-round magazines are all the rage, I would have liked to have seen more capacity built into the Benelli B-76. The slide stop is hard to release with the shooting hand's thumb. Lastly, why does the Benelli have a complicated "recoil-blowback" system when the successful Astra 600 whose recoiling parts weigh a scant couple of ounces more is straight blowback?

What is good about the Benelli? Well, almost everything. It has a very attractive appearance — square and robust. It points well and there is a non-glare rib between the two sights. Its magazine can be released with one hand and will be ejected from the pistol. The trigger stop is adjustable. It can fire all kinds of old corrosive ammo with no ill effects.

The bottom line is that the Benelli is sold for a reasonable amount of money. A lot of planning and knowledge went into the Benelli and it pays off for you, its owner. Would I buy a Benelli B-76 again? You bet I would. ●

An aggressive manufacturer/importer, F.I.E. has recently added some unique products to its well known line of sporting firearms. The centerpiece of this page is F.I.E.'s special purpose, combination pump/auto 12-gauge shotgun called the SPAS 12. It features a folding stock and selective (pump or semiauto) fire. To the right is F.I.E.'s KG-99 semiauto, 9mm handgun, complete with large capacity 36-round magazine. On the bottom is the new TZ-75, a double action, 9mm, semiauto pistol.

Crosman continues to offer new and better products for the fast-growing airgun market. Featured here, from top to bottom, are three top flight Crosman airguns—the 66 Powermaster .177-caliber pellet gun and BB repeater, the 2100 Classic .177 pellet/BB rifle and the Crosman 357, .177-caliber pellet revolver. Also shown are Crosman Copperhead® CO₂ Powerlets™, pellets and BBs.

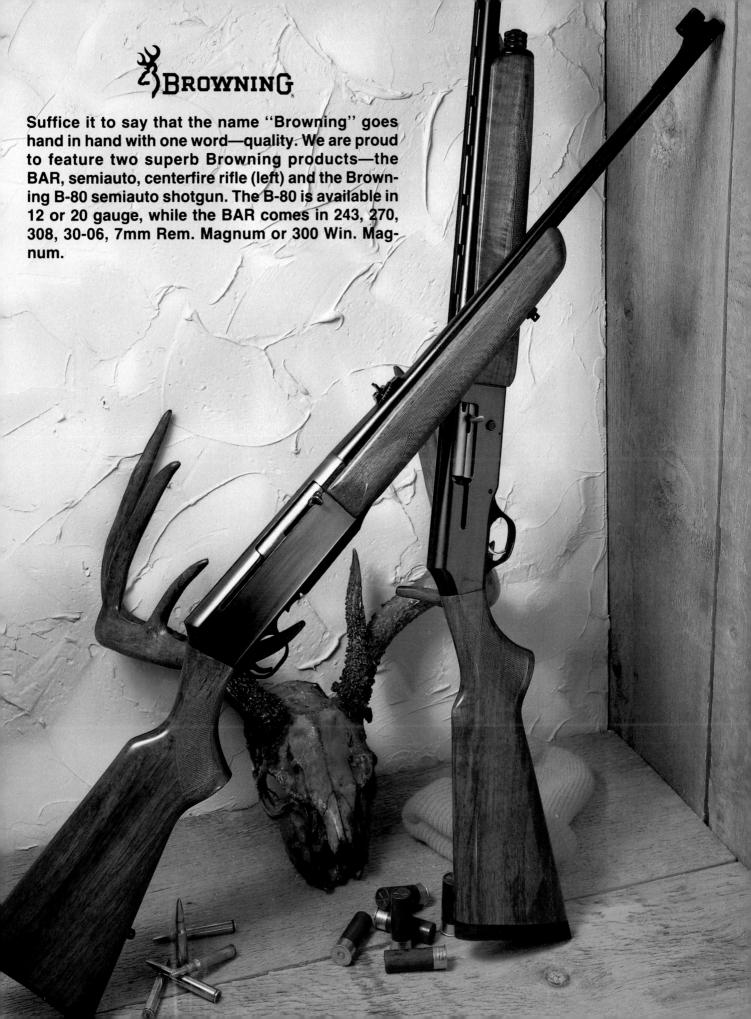

BROWNING

Suffice it to say that the name "Browning" goes hand in hand with one word—quality. We are proud to feature two superb Browning products—the BAR, semiauto, centerfire rifle (left) and the Browning B-80 semiauto shotgun. The B-80 is available in 12 or 20 gauge, while the BAR comes in 243, 270, 308, 30-06, 7mm Rem. Magnum or 300 Win. Magnum.

CCI / SPEER / RCBS / OUTERS
OMARK INDUSTRIES

The good news about the Good Old Boys is that their product line just gets bigger and better. In the center of this photo is the new RCBS Reloader Special 2 surrounded by CCI primers, Speer bullets, an RCBS primer tray and an RCBS powder funnel. In the background is a new offering from Outers. It's their Field Target Holder, a fully portable yet compact target frame.

Remington DUPONT

While Remington is America's oldest firearms manufacturer, their products always represent the latest in style and engineering. The guns shown here represent Remington's newest offerings. On the left is the new lightweight 1100 Special Field semiauto shotgun complete with 21-inch barrel, straight grip buttstock and cut checkering. It's available in 12 or 20 gauge. To the right is the new Model 7, lightweight bolt action centerfire. Weighing in at 6¼ pounds, the Model 7 is chambered for 222 Rem., 243, 6mm Rem., 7mm '08 Rem. and 308.

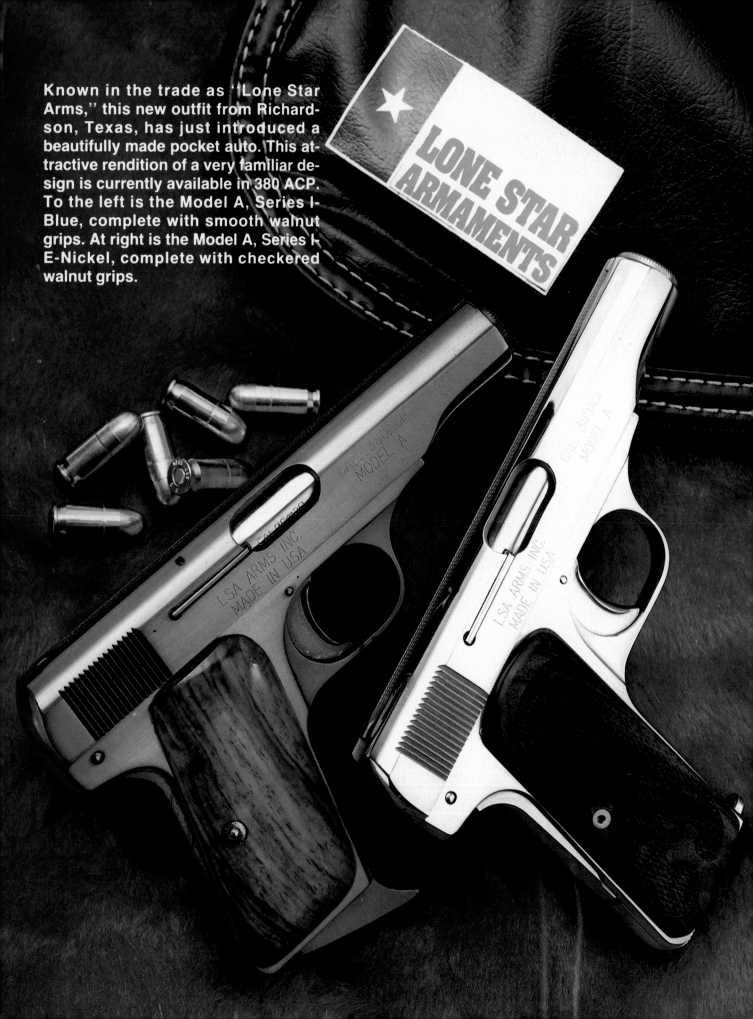

Known in the trade as "Lone Star Arms," this new outfit from Richardson, Texas, has just introduced a beautifully made pocket auto. This attractive rendition of a very familiar design is currently available in 380 ACP. To the left is the Model A, Series I-Blue, complete with smooth walnut grips. At right is the Model A, Series I-E-Nickel, complete with checkered walnut grips.

LONE STAR ARMAMENTS

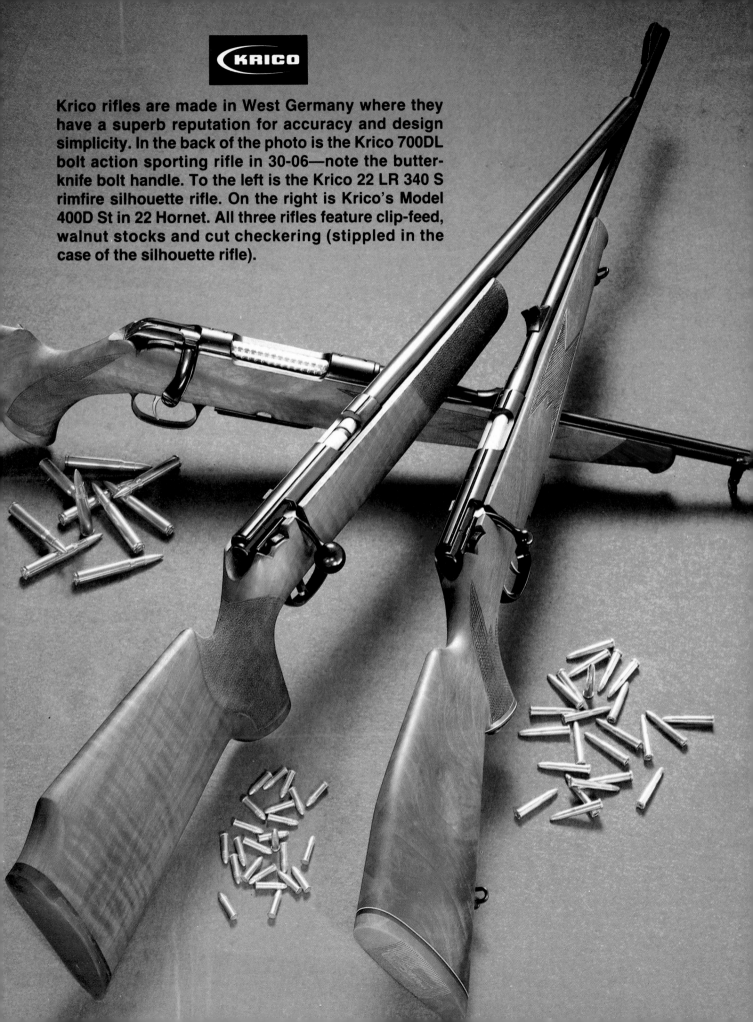

Krico rifles are made in West Germany where they have a superb reputation for accuracy and design simplicity. In the back of the photo is the Krico 700DL bolt action sporting rifle in 30-06—note the butter-knife bolt handle. To the left is the Krico 22 LR 340 S rimfire silhouette rifle. On the right is Krico's Model 400D St in 22 Hornet. All three rifles feature clip-feed, walnut stocks and cut checkering (stippled in the case of the silhouette rifle).

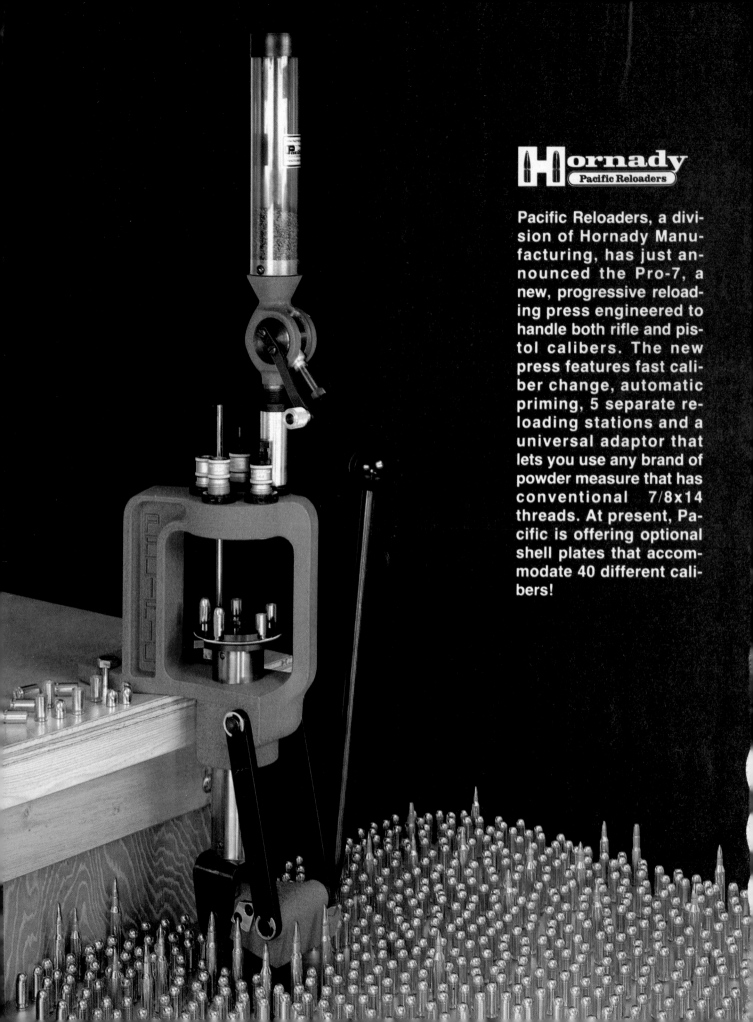

Hornady
Pacific Reloaders

Pacific Reloaders, a division of Hornady Manufacturing, has just announced the Pro-7, a new, progressive reloading press engineered to handle both rifle and pistol calibers. The new press features fast caliber change, automatic priming, 5 separate reloading stations and a universal adaptor that lets you use any brand of powder measure that has conventional 7/8x14 threads. At present, Pacific is offering optional shell plates that accommodate 40 different calibers!

PRE-WINCHESTERS:

by JAMES E. SERVEN

The guns that brought the greats together

F EW MODERN arms can trace their origins to men born in 1796, yet if we are to credit the idea that led to Winchester repeating cartridge rifles, we must look back to Walter Hunt, an ingenious fellow who lived near Martinsburg, New York. Hunt's "rocket-ball" patent relating to firearms came to notice in August of 1848 when he patented this strange self-contained ammunition.

The rocket-ball appealed to mechanic Lewis Jennings, who then designed a gun to use it. He called it a "Volition Repeater." Jennings worked for George A. Arrowsmith of New York City, from whom Hunt had sought financial assistance. Thus, by 1850 there was developed a combined effort which produced a Hunt-Jennings firearm. This promised prospects for developing a lever-worked repeating rifle employing self-contained cartridges. Meanwhile Arrowsmith had interested a well-to-do hardware merchant named Courtland C. Palmer.

Palmer, having secured a major interest in producing the Hunt-Jennings designed gun, was instrumental in engaging the well-regarded Robbins & Lawrence gunmaking firm of Windsor, Vermont, to produce the rifles collectors generally have come to refer to today as the Jennings rifles. We note that a talented young man named B. Tyler Henry was then a foreman at the Robbins & Lawrence plant.

C. P. Dixon of New York City was engaged as sales agent, and the Windsor-made rifles will often be found marked "Patented 1849. C. P. Dixon, Agent, New York."

It soon became apparent to the owners that the gun, even with a 54-caliber bore, had too little power and was mechanically much too complicated. Sales were so slow that manufacture was discontinued in 1852. Even the addition of Horace Smith's patent, obtained in 1851, had failed to win popular acceptance for the rifles.

The total made at Windsor was relatively small. Strangely enough, the price of those guns today, when one can be found, has risen to several thousand dollars.

Horace Smith's belated interest in the Jennings rifles, while not in time to stem the poor sale the gun had attracted, was nevertheless an important step in the arm's progression. Smith was convinced that the system had good chances of success. He interested a friend, Daniel B. Wesson, and the two went to work to see how it could be improved. Wesson was seventeen years younger than Smith, but both had considerable gunmaker's experience. In 1854 they formed a partnership and produced a plan to manufacture (at Norwich, Conn.) and sell two models of rocket-ball repeating pistols.

Although he had suffered financially from the demise of the Jennings rifles, Courtland Palmer still had faith in the system and entered into an agreement with Smith and Wesson to form a company.

The products turned out at Norwich were a No. 1—pocket size—31-caliber

repeating pistol with 4-inch barrel and a No. 2—Navy size—pistol with 6-inch or 8-inch barrels about 41-caliber. They were made with lightly engraved, flat-sided iron frames. The barrels were part round and octagon. No. 1 barrel pistols had a rounded bag-type grip with rosewood stocks and the No. 2 pistols had a larger grip, flat at the butt.

It is not clear why Smith, Wesson and Palmer decided to reorganize after only about a year at Norwich. Their pistols were well made, but we can speculate that even for pistols the rocket-ball was too weak. Whatever the reasons, a new company was formed in June of 1855 with 6000 shares at $25 each. There were 27 subscribers, among them men from widely diversified fields of endeavor, including a shirt manufacturer of New Haven named Oliver F. Winchester.

The new company was named THE VOLCANIC REPEATING ARMS CO., the first time the word *Volcanic* had been employed. Probably of greater importance was the fact that Oliver F. Winchester had become an active investor in the new firm. At this juncture Courtland Palmer withdrew from the company. Horace Smith and Daniel Wesson also prepared to withdraw for they had great plans to develop new repeating pistols which used self-contained metallic 22-caliber ammunition.

Some have said that they made a mistake in giving up those vital lever-action patents which helped to gain such great success for Winchester, but the development of the Smith & Wesson Company was also a great suc-

(Above) Volcanic pistols with shoulder stock are scarce. A few had barrels as long as 16 inches.

WALTER HUNT
AMERICAN INVENTOR

In Walter Hunt's patent application he claimed: "The construction of a ball for firearms, with a cavity to contain the charge of powder for propelling said ball, in which cavity the powder is secured by means of a cap enclosing the back end."

W. HUNT.
Cartridge.

Patented Aug. 10 1848

Horace Smith, 1808-1893, partner in the Smith & Wesson production of lever-action repeating pistols.

Daniel B. Wesson, 1825-1906, member of a gunmaking family, became a partner with Horace Smith.

Oliver F. Winchester, 1810-1880, whose talents and great faith in the lever action Volcanic mechanism produced a great success story.

cess. And this change of direction by the Smith & Wesson principals made it possible for Oliver Winchester to start his great climb to success with the acquisition of their Volcanic patents.

New directors of the Volcanic company decided that New Haven would be a better manufacturing location, and in 1856 operations were started there with great hopes and expectations. They enlarged their offerings to include a repeating rifle with 24-inch barrel and carbines with 16-inch and 20-inch barrels.

One major change was to use brass for the frame. It was easier to work and free of rust. No. 1 pistols now offered octagon barrels at either four or six inches. The No. 2 pistols conformed with 6-inch and 8-inch octagon barrels. All had flat butts.

Their price list later included these listings:

Pocket Pistol (31-cal.)	4"—	6 shots	$12.00
Target Pistol (31-cal.)	6"—	10 shots	13.50
Navy Pistol (41-cal.)	6'—	8 shots	18.00
Navy Pistol (41-cal.)	8"—	10 shots	18.00
Carbine (41-cal.)	16"—	20 shots	30.00
Carbine (41-cal.)	20"—	25 shots	35.00
Rifle (41-cal.)	24"—	30 shots	40.00

Additional charges of $1.50 for 31-caliber pistols, $2.00 for Navy pistols, or $3.00 for carbines were made if the arms were to be plated or engraved. The No. 1 cartridges sold for $10.00 per M and were 130 to the pound. No. 2 cartridges were priced at $12.00 per M and ran 64 to the pound. Special order guns might be had as No. 2 pistols with shoulder stocks; the barrel length on these rare pistols sometimes was 16 inches.

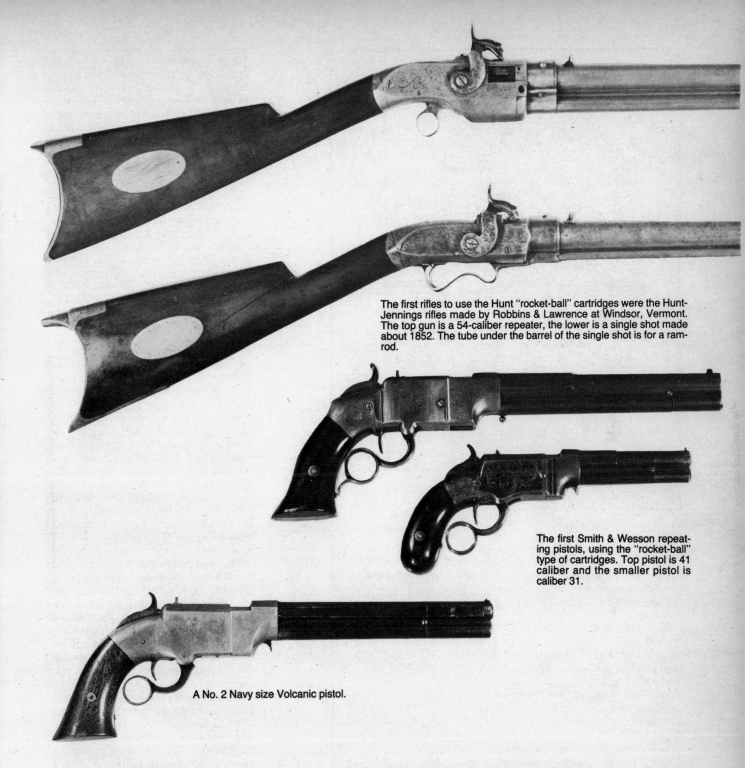

The first rifles to use the Hunt "rocket-ball" cartridges were the Hunt-Jennings rifles made by Robbins & Lawrence at Windsor, Vermont. The top gun is a 54-caliber repeater, the lower is a single shot made about 1852. The tube under the barrel of the single shot is for a ramrod.

The first Smith & Wesson repeating pistols, using the "rocket-ball" type of cartridges. Top pistol is 41 caliber and the smaller pistol is caliber 31.

A No. 2 Navy size Volcanic pistol.

It is strange that collectors had ignored the rarity of these arms for a long time. Almost a century later, in 1950, an arms dealer offered a lot of *seven* lever-action Smith & Wesson and Volcanic pistols, all different and in very good condition, for only $195.00!

Sales at the New Haven plant struggled valiantly along after 1856. Nelson B. Gaston died in December, and Oliver Winchester was elected president to succeed him, having become the most important stockholder.

The company was skating on thin ice, and in 1857 was forced into court and declared insolvent. Oliver Winchester was the largest creditor and in due time the court awarded him the major assets of the company.

It should be said that Oliver Winchester was not a man to give up easily, once he was convinced he had a promising product. He was determined that they would find proper, self-contained ammunition which would make their product a winner.

As a gesture of civic pride Winches-

ter reorganized the company under the name NEW HAVEN ARMS CO. Firmly in control, he made careful plans. A major step forward was to engage B. Tyler Henry, an experienced and imaginative machinist, whom we have mentioned before in his former employment with Robbins & Lawrence. Henry was instructed to develop a suitable metallic cartridge for the lever-action repeating arms, no small task.

At some cost and with great tenacity Winchester held on for those try-

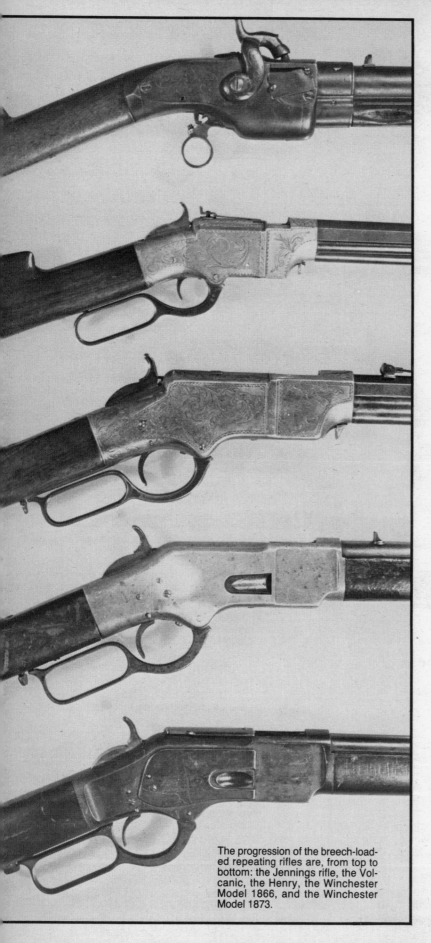

The progression of the breech-loaded repeating rifles are, from top to bottom: the Jennings rifle, the Volcanic, the Henry, the Winchester Model 1866, and the Winchester Model 1873.

ing few years until 1860 when B. Tyler Henry finally succeeded in developing the 44 Henry rimfire metallic cartridge and a heavier Volcanic-type repeating action to accommodate it. It was the occasion of a great breakthrough in Winchester arms manufacture. They proceeded to give it wide publicity and no time was lost in tooling up.

The introduction of a new repeating rifle, with a self-contained 44-caliber cartridge to use with it, was not something the public accepted blindly. Careful advertisements had to be placed, demonstrations made, and the many advantages claimed for the rifle demonstrated.

It was 1862 before the NEW HAVEN ARMS CO. was ready to put the rifles on the market. Their advertisements read: "The most effective weapon in the world . . . Sixty shots per minute . . . can be discharged 16 times without loading or taking down from the shoulder, or even losing aim . . . For a house or sporting arm, it has no equal . . . A resolute man, armed with one of these rifles, particularly if on horseback, cannot be captured."

Some of the advertisements claimed that the new 44 rimfire ammunition, fired from the 24-inch Henry rifle barrel, had sufficient force to kill at 1000 yards! It is now enough to say that the Henry's patent rifle employed ammunition far superior to the rocket-ball.

The war between the Union and Confederacy made an opportunity for Winchester. He succeeded on May 16-17, 1862, in arranging a test at the Washington Navy Yard. The "so-so" report of Lieut. W. Mitchell, U.S.N., did not discourage him, nor did Brig. Gen. Ripley's prejudice against the use of repeating rifles dampen his enthusiasm.

Despite General Ripley's objections, in fact, the government purchased 1731 Henry patent rifles during the war, and the government was not the only buyer. The company manufactured 10,000 Henry rifles during the war. Many were purchased by state regiments, volunteers, and others who had realized the great advantages of this repeating rifle. The four-story building at 9 Artizan Street in New Haven was kept humming.

In the summer of 1865, as the war neared its end, Oliver Winchester and his Board of Directors gave serious thought to a change in the Henry rifle's design, and to a change in the company's corporate name.

The rifle's 15-shot magazine offered a number of weak places:

Packed in a tin box with Oliver Winchester's design were the 41-caliber Volcanic cartridges known as the No. 2 size.

There were several names along the road to the Winchester label, including both New Haven Arms Co. and a brief stint as Henry Repeating Arms Co.

VOLCANIC
REPEATING FIRE ARMS,
MANUFACTURED BY THE
NEW HAVEN ARMS COMPANY,
NEW HAVEN, CONN.
(PATENTED, 1854.)

The above named Company having purchased all the Patent rights on this Arm and its ammunition, (some eight or ten in number,) the inventions of as many of the most ingenious mechanics of the country, who have spent years in bringing this wonderful triumph of genius to perfection, are now prepared to manufacture them in a perfect manner, and offer them for sale as the most powerful and effective weapon of defense ever invented. They are made of all sizes, from a four inch Pocket Pistol, carrying six balls, to a twenty-four inch Rifle, carrying thirty balls.

The rapidity of execution of this Arm places it beyond all competition. The thirty shooter can be loaded and fired in less than one minute—a quickness and force of execution which is as much superior to the best revolvers, as they are to the old muzzle loading single shooters.

The Ammunition is water-proof, hence it can be used in any weather, or loaded and hung up for months, or laid under water, and then fired with certainty.

Its safety from accidental discharge is a great consideration in its favor; for while the magazine (a tube running the whole length of the barrel) may be filled with balls, and thus the gun, in fact, be loaded from breech to muzzle, it is yet impossible, from any carelessness in handling, to discharge it. *Its construction* is simple and its workmanship most perfect, hence it is not easily got out of repair.

Its proportions are light, elegant and compact, and the barrels are all rifled with great exactness. It requires no cap nor priming, no bullet mould nor powder flask. The powder and cap is contained in a loaded "minnie" ball of the best form and proportions, and is as sure as the best percussion caps.

It shoots *with accuracy and greater force* than any other Arm can with double the powder used in this. Directions for use accompany each Arm. Balls are packed in tin cases, 200 each.

LIST OF MANUFACTURERS' PRICES.

No. 1.	4 inch Pocket Pistol,	$12.00, Plated and Engraved, $13.50, Carrying	6 Balls.
" 1.	6 " for Target Practice,	13.50, " 15.00, "	10 "
" 2.	6 " Navy Pistol,	18.00, " 20.00, "	8 "
" 2.	8 " "	18.00, " 20.00, "	10 "
" 2, 16	" Carbine,	30.00, " 33.00, "	20 "
" 2, 20	"	35.00, " 38.00, "	25 "
" 2, 24	"	40.00, " 43.00, "	30 "

Plating and Engraving, from $2.50 to $5.00 extra, per Arm.

AMMUNITION.

No. 1 Balls, 130 to the Pound, $10 per M. No. 2 Balls, 66 to the Pound, $12 per M. (No. 1 Arms, require No. 1 Balls. No. 2 Arms, require No. 2 Balls.)

The numbers 1 and 2 designate the size of the bore, and the Balls are numbered to correspond.

A liberal discount to the trade.

We select the following from numerous testimonials, as the service to which the Arms were subjected was most severe, from the rapid action of salt water upon all metals.

New York, March 10th, 1855.

GENT.—I consider the Volcanic Repeating Pistol the *ne plus ultra* of Repeating or Revolving Arms, and far superior in many respects to Colt's much extolled Revolver. I have fired, myself, over 200 shots from it without even wiping the barrel—this is an advantage which no other Arm I know of possesses. I have had the Pistol with me at sea for more than eighteen months, on a voyage around the world, and find that, with the most common care, it will keep free from rust, far more so than Colt's. I find the Balls as good now as when I left New York. I have shown the Pistol to my friends in San Francisco, Hong Kong, Manilla, Canton and Shanghae, and they were much pleased with it.

C. F. W. BEHM, Late of Clipper Ship Stag Hound.

New York, 23d November, 1856.

GENT.—I have used a Volcanic Repeating Pistol for some months, on my last voyage to San Francisco, and in all that constitutes a good Pistol or Fire Arm, it has no equal, and excels all others I have over seen in rapidity, efficiency and certainty of execution. Its peculiar merit for sea service is in the nature of the Ball, which containing the Ammunition, is water-proof, and cannot be damaged by any change of climate, but is sure fire even after having been loaded for months.

Signed, FRED'K A. STALL, Commander Ship Star of the Union.

All orders may be addressed to

NEW HAVEN ARMS COMPANY,
New Haven, Conn.

October, 1859.

This 1859 broadside lists the Volcanic arms and their ammunition. Courtesy the Winchester Company files.

SIXTY SHOTS PER MINUTE
HENRY'S PATENT
REPEATING
RIFLE
The Most Effective Weapon in the World.

This Rifle can be discharged 16 times without loading or taking down from the shoulder, or even loosing aim. It is also slung in such a manner, that either on horse or on foot, it can be **Instantly Used**, without taking the strap from the shoulder.

For a House or Sporting Arm, it has no Equal;
IT IS ALWAYS LOADED AND ALWAYS READY.

The size now made is 44-100 inch bore, 24 inch barrel, and carries a conical ball 32 to the pound. The penetration at 100 yards is 8 inches; at 400 yards 5 inches; and it carries with force sufficient to kill at 1,000 yards.

A resolute man, armed with one of these Rifles, particularly if on horseback, **CANNOT BE CAPTURED.**

"We particularly commend it for ARMY USES, as the most effective arm for picket and vidette duty, and to all our citizens in secluded places, as a protection against guerilla attacks and robberies. A man armed with one of these Rifles, can load and discharge one shot every second, so that he is equal to a company every minute, a regiment every ten minutes, a brigade every half hour, and a division every hour."—*Louisville Journal.*

Address   JNO. W. BROWN,
Gen'l Ag't., Columbus, Ohio,
At Rail Road Building, near the Depot.

By 1862, the Henry rifle was ready to begin its remarkable career on behalf of resolute men who did not want to be captured.

The barrel had to be reduced in thickness to accommodate the movable collar which controlled loading in the throat of the tubular magazine. This was said to have an undesirable effect on the rifle's accuracy.

A long spiral spring inside the tubular magazine pushed the cartridges toward the breech. In order to load the gun, the spring had to be compressed to five inches. To accomplish this, the thumbpiece of a metal plunger traveled in an open slot. And this open slot not only weakened the tube, making it more liable to denting, but admitted dirt or other foreign matter.

Rusting, dirt or an accidental heavy blow could clog the tube and render the gun inoperative. Cartridges could not be effectively fed into the barrel in any other way. In an effort to make the action of the spring pass the cartridges smoothly down the tube to the receiver, most Henry cartridges were

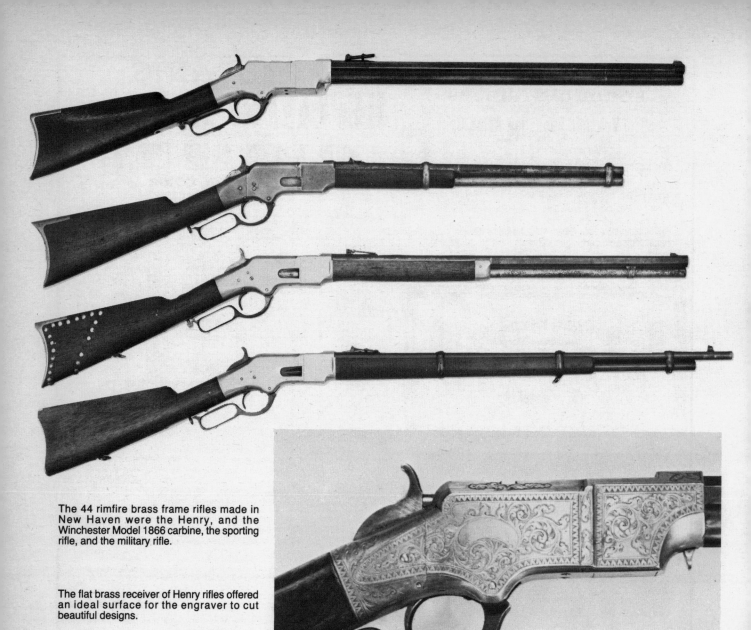

The 44 rimfire brass frame rifles made in New Haven were the Henry, and the Winchester Model 1866 carbine, the sporting rifle, and the military rifle.

The flat brass receiver of Henry rifles offered an ideal surface for the engraver to cut beautiful designs.

made with a flattened nose and were referred to as the *44 Henry Flat*.

The Henry rifle, however, measured up well against its major competition—the Spencer repeating rifle. The Spencer was produced in several models and different calibers. While the Henry was quite streamlined, the Spencer was bulky. The Spencer magazine, inserted through the buttstock, held about half as many cartridges as the Henry. For rapid firing the Henry was cocked automatically when the lever was worked; the Spencer must be cocked by a separate hand operation. From a manufacturing standpoint, the Henry had the advantage of one model, one barrel length, one caliber.

Because of these and other evident facts, the Henry became very popular, especially in the West. Its self-contained 15 cartridges gave it a great advantage over muzzleloaders in a region where fast, repeated shots could mean a difference between life and death. The later barrels were usually marked HENRY'S PATENT OCT. 16, 1869 *over* MANUFACTURED BY THE NEW HAVEN ARMS CO. NEW HAVEN, CT.

Nelson King succeeded B. Tyler Henry as shop superintendent, and it was he who superintended the Winchester progression from the Henry rifle to the Winchester Model of 1866. Other changes were taking place. On July 7, 1865, the company name had

been changed briefly to HENRY REPEATING ARMS CO., but in less than two years the company was given its more familiar name WINCHESTER REPEATING ARMS COMPANY. For an interval of four years, the company moved its operation to Bridgeport, occupying a portion of the Wheeler & Wilson sewing machine plant.

The Winchester Model of 1866 had been developed by Nelson King. It changed the basic Henry from a frontloader to a sideloader. It was loaded through a spring-controlled port in the right side of the brass receiver. This eliminated some of the complaints about the Henry magazine, which was now partly protected from

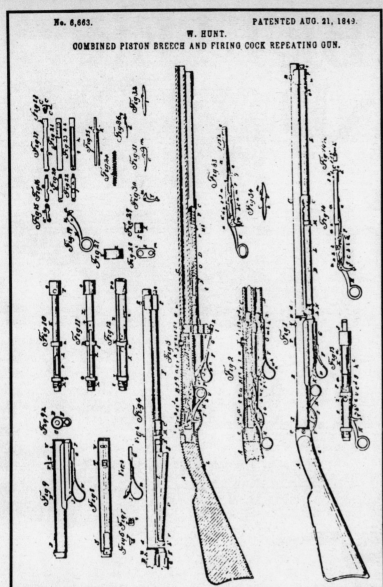

No. 6,663.   PATENTED AUG. 21, 1849.

W. HUNT.

COMBINED PISTON BREECH AND FIRING COCK REPEATING GUN.

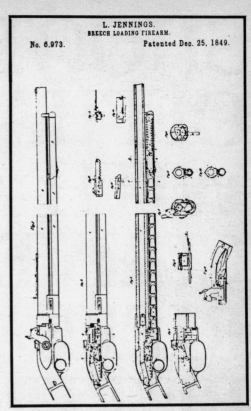

L. JENNINGS.
BREECH LOADING FIREARM.

No. 6,973.   Patented Dec. 25, 1849.

An improvment of the Hunt patent was issued to Lewis Jennings only four months later in 1849. The rifles were made by Robbins & Lawrence at Windsor, Vermont.

Walter Hunt's August, 1849, patent led to Lewis Jennings improved patent in December of 1849.

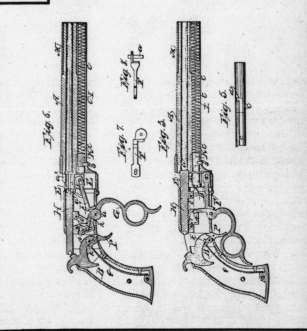

H. SMITH & D. B. WESSON   2 Sheets—Sheet 2.

MAGAZINE FIREARM.

10,535.   Patented Feb. 14, 1854.

damage by a wooden forestock and was freed from dirt.

The Model 1866, the first Winchester, was the last of the brass-framed rifles. With the preceding Henry rifle, it offered a great surface for the engraving artist, and many fine scenes are to be found on the deluxe specimens. It was also the last of the rimfire models, a 44 rimfire. Soon would come the Model 1873 with centerfire cartridges. Soon would come a succession of excellent Winchester rifles to elevate the company. What Oliver Winchester liked to call his "machine to throw balls" succeeded greatly over the years, but we don't always remember that those years stretch all the way back to 1848.   ●

Employing the Hunt "rocket-ball" cartridges, Horace Smith and Daniel Wesson invented a lever-action repeating pistol in 1854.

SHOOT BETTER OFFHAND WITH A CURVED RIFLE BUTTPLATE

Brass muzzle-loading rifle buttplate rough-fitted to a Winchester.

by FRANCIS E. SELL

It may be heresy, but it works for the writer in the woods of the Northwest.

A RIFLE buttplate isn't for every rifle, but at woods ranges, where the time for a shot is seconds and fractions of a second, it can certainly improve the chances of scoring. Before examining this modern application of a rifle buttplate in heavy cover, there's a bit of early woods history to mention.

When those early day riflemen had only one shot, it seems obvious to me they wouldn't handicap themselves with equipment that didn't make a direct contribution. Early day Indian fighters didn't go in for rifle fads beyond a bit of decoration. Those rifles had rifle buttplates and long barrels

nection between these two on flint-lock rifles.

Just about any schoolboy familiar with early American history knows that both Indians and Indian fighters of Kentucky, Ohio, and Virginia "treed" at the first sign of hostility. Either took his shot, if target were presented, standing straight behind his tree. Maybe the long barrel and rifle buttplate made a contribution. First, the smoke haze of his firing was well away from his tree. Second, the inertia of the long barrel compensated for the slow ignition. The rifle buttplate enabled him to keep on target during the time the primer powder sparked

snapshooting deer in heavy cover. It is closely associated with the early Marlin, Winchester, and Savage lever actions, the most popular hunting rifle types ever made.

Once, I had the very pleasant job of keeping a large backwoods ranch in venison from late summer to early winter. I was 14 years old at the time and each hunter was allowed five deer. The ranch hands turned over their tags to me, and I did all the hunting. I used a 25-35 Winchester Model 94, 26-inch barrel. The rifle carried the standard crescent-shaped buttplate. Shooting, for the most part, was offhand in the oak groves,

Author's Marlin Model 336-A, adapted to a 257 wildcat. Buttplate was made from a steel shotgun-type. The stock, by the author, is built for offhand snapshooting in heavy cover.

as a matter of course.

Once, here at my wilderness hideout, several hunters were examining an old flintlock muzzleloader for which I had traded a hunting knife. This rifle had a 50-inch barrel, a rifle buttplate and a stock with plenty of drop. As the discussion became more involved, with several of those learned riflemen pointing out the handicaps of the long barrel, crooked stock and rifle buttplate, I suggested we take the evaluation of the rifle out to the woods.

We found a grove of trees in my reforesting about the size of those trees in the early day wilderness where the old flintlock was originally used. Maybe we could find some of the reasons for the rifle buttplate and long barrel. I always felt there was a con-

in the pan until the rifle fired, an interval more like a hangfire.

That crooked stock, with its great drop, enabled this early day rifleman to take his shot with a minimum exposure. It also kept his face well back from the exploding powder in the flash pan. The extremely long barrel put the task of reloading at eye level, without exposure—powder pouring, patching and ramming home the round lead ball.

Later, when the lever action breech-loaders came in, barrels became shorter. The rifles, however, were mostly used in the offhand position, so the rifle buttplate was retained. It was used on all the early day pump actions and autoloaders, as well as the lever actions. It is still a good choice if these rifles are to be used offhand,

where the deer fattened on acorns.

That crescent-shaped rifle buttplate made a direct contribution to the shooting. The rifle always came to shoulder at exactly the same point, not governed by comb height, but by the exact buttplate positioning. I recall that if I killed less than 18 deer with the 20-round box of ammo the ranch furnished, the boss threatened to put me to repairing fence until I learned how to shoot.

The very popular 20-inch barrel, Winchester and Marlin, pushed the longer barrels out of the picture. These early carbines had a rifle buttplate, more or less.

Col. Townsend, who had a mission in life—to make the country again a nation of riflemen, bolt action riflemen—condemned anything in the way of stocking that didn't have the so-called shotgun buttplate. Obviously, a crescent rifle butt was out of place on a bolt action rifle for two reasons. First, many of the big game bolt actions had heavy recoil, very noticeable in the prone, sitting and kneeling positions. Second was a matter of working the bolt.

I can still remember my gravel voiced U.S. Marine rifle instructor saying, "This here Springfield is a straightpull bolt action, and by the Holy Old Khaki, that is the way you'll use it."

What he was putting across to us skinheads was the fact that you didn't turn up the bolt with the right hand to open the action. You canted the Springfield to the right to clear your aiming eye, brought the bolt straight back, then straight forward with the right hand. The left hand canted the rifle to the left closing and bringing it into eye alignment. No matter how you cut it, you had to take the aiming eye away from the sights. Obviously, it was no place for a crescent-shaped rifle buttplate, even though the first post-World War I Remington sporter bolt action, the Model 30, had one.

Col. Whelen, in one of his books, *The Modern Rifle*, has this to say about the rifle buttplate, an indirect endorsement: "There is only one place where the rifle buttplate is efficient. That is in the offhand position, the target on a level with the rifleman."

Nice going! For this is the usual position of rifleman and target in the brush.

Even if the snapshooting rifleman is shooting uphill or downhill a bit, the good Col. Whelen's proposition still holds. How about rifles of heavy recoil, with the crescent butt? Whelen is silent on this phase of the question. But it must be pointed out that recoil is much less felt in the offhand position than it is shooting in the other positions. Any shotgunner can testify to this.

Several years ago, Savage Arms offered a fairly heavy-barreled lever action, the Model 99A. It had a 24-inch barrel, crescent rifle butt and weight around 7¼ lbs. Today, among wilderness riflemen, most of whom haven't seen a benchrest, this model Savage commands a premium price—not as a collector's item, but as a good efficient offhand snapshooting deer rifle.

Here, where ranges are always short, and where 98% of all deer are taken, the shooting is always offhand, with the opportunity measured in seconds and fractions of seconds. If the first shot is a miss, or a wounding hit, there is usually a chance for a second shot provided the butt hasn't slipped during the reloading.

With all this in mind, I recently custom-stocked a rifle for offhand snapshooting in heavy cover, deer the quarry. It's a 257-caliber wildcat made up on the Marlin 336 lever action.

First thing I learned the hard way is that you cannot put a rifle buttplate on a factory stock. The stock would be shortened about ⅝-inch. So it was a matter of custom work.

There are few rifle buttplates available, and mostly for muzzleloaders, so I bypassed them and adapted the Brownell steel plate to my requirements. This Brownell plate measures 5⅛-in. long, 1⁹⁄₁₆-in. wide. It is shaped like a shotgun buttplate, but is well checkered and blued.

It is mild steel, so I found no problem in cold shaping it to the dimensions of a rifle buttplate by careful bending. The concavity is ⅝-in., measured from a straight edge heel to toe. In bending the Brownell plate to fit, I shortened the distance from heel to toe by ⅜-inch. This gave me a very trim stock, and a beautifully handling rifle.

How well did it work out? I have had no big game seasons, but I have made several dry runs on deer about my cabin. Snapping the rifle to my shoulder, the sights come up ready aligned. These sights, incidentally, are a Marble tang sight made for the Model 336 that a friend picked up at a gun show, complemented by a ³⁄₁₆-inch white bead front sight. On target, I would work the empty gun as if chambering a second round, and always I could continue to look through those sights, the white bead on target.

My only chance to use this wildcat

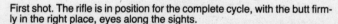

First shot. The rifle is in position for the complete cycle, with the butt firmly in the right place, eyes along the sights.

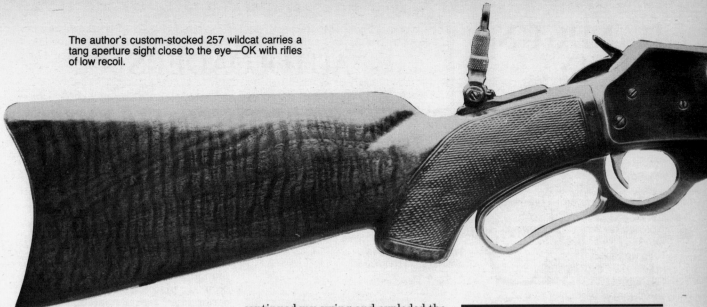

The author's custom-stocked 257 wildcat carries a tang aperture sight close to the eye—OK with rifles of low recoil.

much as it will be used on deer was a good test of the rifle buttplate:

I flushed two ravens out of my garden and caught them at about 45 yards, flying between the garden and my reforesting. The reforesting gave me a safe background for aerial shooting.

I caught the rearmost raven with my first shot, exploding him with a 117-grain round nose Hornady bullet, and, without my eyes being distracted by any rifle shifting when I snapped the lever down and back to reload, I continued my swing and exploded the second raven. No pain, no strain. Later, in my garden I shot the head off a running cottontail at about 30 yards. These three shots confirmed my dry runs on deer.

Using this Marlin Model 336 lever action wildcat seemed like going home to the early days with the 25-35 Winchester and shooting venison for that backwoods ranch. This is much more dynamic, however, and that will count unconditionally when I am cat-footing along a deer trail, a trophy buck in mind.

Seems to me those so-called shotgun buttplates have a place on some

SELL'S STOCK DIMENSIONS
Length to center of stock from trigger .... 12⅞"
Length to heel of stock from trigger ...... 13¾"
Length to toe of stock from trigger......... 14"
Drop at comb .... 1⅝"
Drop at heel........................ 2⅝"
Cast off at butt of stock................ ¼"
Rifle: Wildcat 257-cal. on Marlin 336

modern rifles, but not on the hind end of a rifle to be used for offhand snap-shooting in heavy cover. Here, there is a definite payoff in going back to the rifle buttplate, such as Dan Boone and Louis Wetzel used when so much depended on an accurate shot. ●

Chambering a second shot, eyes are still on sights and target; fast enough to hit big birds flying slow up close.

HANDGUNS TODAY:

AUTOLOADERS

by J. B. WOOD

The MAB Model P-15 pistol in 9mm chambering.

Charter Arms Model 79K double action 380 stainless steel pistol. Length 6.5-inch; magazine capacity 7 rounds; weight 24½ oz.

The new Detonics 9mm pocket pistol.

THIS YEAR brought no startling new mechanisms among the automatic pistols, but there were still a few surprises. A revolver maker announced its first true self-loading pistol, and an auto pistol maker is going to produce a revolver. Otherwise, several manufacturers improved their existing models by making small but significant changes in the designs. One major manufacturer produced a drastic re-design that made one of their pistols a match for the size-reduction jobs done by the custom pistolsmiths. With no further preamble, and in no particular order, let's look at what's new:

Benelli

One of my favorite pistols. The Benelli B-76 has had some subtle alterations. The slide sculpturing was changed slightly, and the trigger guard now has a graceful sweep at the front. Internally, there is an entirely new recoil spring unit. This is a real re-design, as the new system will not work in the early guns. An adjustable rear sight, previously available only on the full target model, is now an option on the standard model. In either configuration, the Benelli is an eerily accurate pistol, and its quality and performance are outstanding.

Charter

Known primarily for revolvers, Charter already had an autoloader in its Explorer II pistol, a reduced version of their AR-7 carbine. Now, Charter has moved into the real auto pistol field with three new designs. The Model 40 is a small 22 double action in blue finish, and the Model 79K is a similar centerfire pistol, a 380, in stainless steel. There will also be a new 22 target pistol, the Model 42TGT, in blue finish. On all three, grips are of checkered walnut. Mechanically, these pistols use design elements by Erma of Germany.

Detonics

Going the other way, the Detonics company has a new revolver design, a top-break with a Webley-style latch. Since this interesting piece is not really in my department, I'll leave a more complete description to my esteemed colleague Hal Swiggett. Three other new guns from Detonics, though, are definitely in my category. The one that will be seen first on the market is a very small 9mm Parabellum double action auto in stainless steel. The prototype I've seen has an external ring-type hammer and an ambidextrous slide-mounted safety that blocks the firing pin. Another new pistol is their "Scoremaster", a full-sized stainless target/competition gun in 45 Auto or 451 Detonics Magnum. This gun is a basic 1911-pattern pistol, with adjustable sight, ambidextrous safety, and other custom features. Also in the works for later this year is a full-sized double action in stainless steel, in the same two chamberings. Detonics, it appears, will soon be known for a lot more than their fine little 45 single action pistol.

H & K

The word from Heckler & Koch is that there are no immediate plans to produce the large-capacity version of the P7 pistol, the P13A1, that was made in prototype for the U.S. military test program. There is, however, some substance added to the rumor of a possible P7 in 45 Auto chambering. This version is "under consideration" at the present time. If it's done, I believe it will be a real winner.

Bren Ten

After their initial offering of the Bren Ten as a Jeff Cooper Special Edition, Dornaus & Dixon have begun regular production of the Standard Model. This is good news for shooters who may have found the price of the commemorative version a bit much. For those who came in late, the Bren Ten combines the best features of the CZ75, the SIG P-210, and the Browning HP, with chambering for a new 10mm cartridge. The cartridge, by the way, will be made by Super Vel. In addition to the Standard Model, the Bren Ten will also be offered in a Military/Police Model (all matte black finish), and in a reduced-size Pocket Model.

F.I.E.

Speaking of the CZ75, the Italian-made version of this fine Czech pistol is now in production. Called the TZ-75, it's produced by Tanfoglio Giuseppe, and imported by F.I.E. Availability is projected for mid-1983. Also from F.I.E. is the re-designed version of the Interdynamic KG-9 "Assault Pistol." Now named the KG-99, the new gun fires from a closed bolt, and has several other improvements. I've fired this one extensively, and it's a fine and reliable piece. A vertical front grip that was originally supplied with the gun apparently made it look too "machine-gunnish," and by government order it is no longer sold with the pistol.

Arminex

Jim Mongello of Arminex, Ltd. is an absolute perfectionist, and would not allow production of his Trifire pistol until everything was exactly right. In the spring of 1983, the Arminex factory officially went into operation, and the new pistol will be available soon. Those who missed last year's announcement will be interested to know that the Trifire has an external appearance similar to the Government Model pistol, and has an innovative recoil spring unit and a slide-

mounted firing pin block safety. It is also easily convertible from 45 Auto to 38 Super and 9mm Parabellum. With the Trifire in production, Arminex is now developing a small 45 pistol, probably with a double action trigger system. The prototype I've examined is beautifully made, and has a superb grip shape. Since it's still in the R&D stage, I'll save a precise description until next year.

The Egyptian Helwan pistol (below) is an exact copy of the Beretta Model 1951 right.

The TZ-75, a copy of the Czech 75 by Tanfoglio Giuseppe, imported by F.I.E.

357 Magnums

The two pistols that were announced last year in 357 Magnum chambering are both in production now, and are just a few months away from general availability. The Eagle, designed by Magnum Research and made by IMI in Israel, is gas-operated, with a rotating-bolt locking system. The other 357 auto, by Coonan

A 15-yard one-hand firing of the ODI Viking Combat pistol delivered this commendable group.

The ODI Viking Combat pistol.

Arms, has a Browning-type falling-barrel system. These are interesting pistols, and both have solved the mechanical problems of a rimmed revolver cartridge in an automatic. In the process of doing this, Coonan Arms also developed a unique magazine loading system.

Helwan/Steyr

Some shooters who do not insist on double action have long admired the elegant lines and fine balance of the now-discontinued Beretta Model 1951, once sold in America as the Brigadier. It is the standard military pistol of Italy, Israel, and Egypt. In Egypt, it was made under license from Beretta by the Maadi company, and last year the pistol was offered on the commercial market as the Helwan. It is imported into the U.S. by Steyr, and in recent months I've fired a Helwan pistol frequently. While its external finish is not quite as beautiful as an original Beretta, it is otherwise identical, and this includes accuracy and reliability.

The other big news from Steyr is the on-market availability of their gas-locked Model GB pistol. A version of this 18-shot 9mm was attempted a few years ago by a U.S. manufacturer, and it didn't turn out well. The Model GB, though, is the genuine article, made with the precision you expect from Steyr. I haven't fired this one yet, but I'm confident that it will work perfectly.

Lone Star Arms

One of the few real surprises for me, at the 1983 SHOT Show, was seeing what appeared to be, at first glance, a classic Browning Model 1910 pistol. Unavailable for many years, this sleek little true hammerless gun has always been well-liked as a personal defense piece. Now, thanks to a new Texas company called Lone Star Arms, the little Browning has been beautifully re-created as the "Lone Star .380, Series A." It is available in blue or electroless nickel, and the prototypes I examined showed very precise engineering. According to Don Maloney of Lone Star, the company also has other guns in the works.

Grizzly 45 Magnum

Introduced last year under another name, the "Grizzly" by L.A.R. Manufacturing Company is a large pistol of basic Government Model pattern, chambered for the 45 Winchester Magnum cartridge. Other chamberings, including the 9mm Winchester Magnum, are to be added later, and the same pistol will easily be convertible to the different rounds. The gun has a heavy, sculptured slide with a fully-adjustable rear sight, a tangent-type that resembles the one used on early Browning HP pistols. The frame-mounted safety is ambidextrous. In addition to the two chamberings mentioned, conversion units are planned for 45 Auto, 38 Super, 357 Magnum, and others to be announced later.

MAB/Howco

Several years ago, a Chicago firm briefly imported the fine MAB Model PA-15 from France. In the years between, there has been no U.S. agent for MAB, and I've lamented the unavailability of this great 9mm pistol with the unique turn-barrel locking system. In the past year, the Howco company of Maryland has become the U.S. importer for MAB, and I'm pleased to note that the gun is back. It's now called the P-15, and there's more good news: It's also available in 45 Auto chambering. This is a single action pistol in what seems to be an age of double actions, but serious handgunners should check out its fantastic accuracy. Another advantage is that its turn-barrel locking system allows the use of a wide range of load levels, without any adjustments.

Viking/ODI

Over the past few months, I have really wrung out a Viking Combat pistol by O.D.I. (Omega Defensive Industries), and I can't find anything to criticize. It has functioned flawlessly with several loads, and its out-of-the-box accuracy is outstanding. For those who haven't heard of it, it's a Commander-sized 45 of traditional 1911-pattern, in stainless steel, with the well-known Seecamp double action trigger system. A full-sized version is planned soon, and a little later, a much smaller version in 9mm Parabellum will be made.

Seecamp/Sile

Speaking of Larry Seecamp, his neat little DA-only stainless steel 25, initially being marketed by Sile, Incorporated, had a few improvements between the prototypes and the regular production model. Among these, the most notable is a small scooped-out area on top, at the edge of the breech face on the slide. The rim of a

A re-creation of the Browning 1910 pistol by Lone Star Arms of Texas.

The stainless Model 659 S&W.

The Smith & Wesson Model 469 pistol.

The Star Model 28 pistol, right side.

The Star Model 28 pistol, left side.

chambered cartridge is visible there, a quick non-mechanical means of showing that the chamber is loaded. The takedown system was also simplified, and the trigger pivot was changed to a fixed post. It's a fine little pistol, and one that I carry with some frequency.

Baby Brownings

While we're in the small pistol category, there are some odd developments concerning the stainless steel version of the Browning "Baby" 25 Auto, until recently made only by Bauer, Now, there are identical pistols by Fraser Firearms Corporation (RB Industries, Ltd.), a firm formerly connected in some way with Bauer. I have examined and fired the Fraser pistol, and it's essentially the same little gun, the only apparent difference being a blued-steel magazine. Meanwhile, in California, the transplanted Michigan Armament Company has announce production of *their* version of the same small pistol, Three models are planned: A two-tone Custom, a Nightshade model in all black, and a satin stainless. Another Michigan Armament endeavor, the resurrection of the former Indian Arms 380 stainless steel double action pistol, will also be offered in these three finish patterns. The 380 pistol is called the Guardian, while the 25 is named the Protector.

Jennings/Johnson

Other small pistol news includes the offering of the Jennings J-22 in matte black, a test-run to see if buyers of this popular 22 will want the dark

Charter Arms Model 42, 22 LR competition double action target pistol. Length 10.4-inch; magazine capacity 10 rounds; weight 38½ oz.

The Beretta Model 20 pistol.

The Iver Johnson TP-22 pistol.

The Fraser 25 Auto.

finish. I believe that a large number will. Iver Johnson is now well along in production of their Erma-designed TP-22, a 22 LR version of their earlier small 25 DA pistol. Both guns now have a patented automatic firing pin block safety, cleared only when the trigger is fully to the rear. A steel stop-pin has also been added beside the manual safety lever on the slide, to prevent any peening at that point. I've tested the Iver Johnson in both calibers, and it's a *very* well-engineered little pistol.

Beretta U.S.A.

The most recent news from Beretta includes pistols in both the small-frame and medium-frame categories. The Model 20 in 25 caliber is essentially a double action version of the Model 950-series guns, with an altered grip shape that is a perfect complement to the new trigger system. The Model 20 has been available in Europe for several years, but because

of its size we had to wait for it to be made at Beretta's U.S. facility in Maryland. It's a little jewel. The medium-frame gun is the 380 Model 85, a flatter version of the popular Model 84, with a single-line 8-round magazine.

Interarms

Interarms continues to offer its always impressive panorama of Walther, SIG/Sauer, Astra, Bernardelli, and Star. The last named has special significance for me, as I've lately been trying out the new 9mm Star double action Model 28. Those who know some of the more esoteric pistols might imagine a combination of the experimental SIG SP-44/16 and the CZ75, with several added innovations. The Star Model 28 has an ambidextrous firing pin lock safety, an adjustable rear sight, and a modular firing system that is easily removable from the frame for cleaning. The double action trigger system is unbelievably smooth. Of all the new 9mm pis-

tols I've tested this year, this one has impressed me the most.

S&W

Now that Smith & Wesson has their 9mm automatics in alloy frame, steel, and stainless steel, they've turned their attention to developing a "reduced" version of the Model 459, a gun with size and features previously available only from the custom pistolsmiths. It has an alloy frame with a combat-styled guard, and a 12-round magazine. The front sight is a serrated yellow ramp, and the rear sight is a simple dovetail-mounted square notch. The finish is matte blue, and the grips have a pebble-grain surface. The magazine floorplate has a finger extension, and the hammer spur is bobbed. Its designation is Model 469, and a factory spokesman says it should be available by late 1983.

Randall Firearms

Among the 45 pistols of Government Model type, there's a new all-

J. B. Wood with the KG-99 pistol. The front handgrip shown is no longer supplied with the gun.

Charter Arms Model 40 22 LR double action pistol. Length 6.3"; magazine capacity 8 rounds; weight 21½ oz.

The stainless steel Randall 45 Auto.

stainless gun of impressive quality, and it also has several special features. Among these are a ten-groove barrel and black combat-style sights, a custom safety and wide-spur hammer, and a choice of long or short triggers. The grips are of checkered walnut, and 38 Super and 9mm Parabellum chamberings will be available. It's made by Randall Firearms of Sun Valley, California. I haven't tried it yet, but the samples I examined were *very* nicely made.

Bernardelli

While Interarms imports the Bernardelli 22 and 380 pistols, this Italian firm has opened an American agency for the marketing of their new double action 9mm pistol. This is a stagger-magazine type that has an external resemblance to the SIG/Sauer pattern, but it has several unique Bernardelli design touches. By the time we get together here next year I will have fired one, and can tell you more. ●

The large-frame double action auto from Detonics, to be made in 45 and 451 Detonics Magnum.

HANDGUNS TODAY:

SIXGUNS AND OTHERS

by HAL SWIGGETT

Roy Jinks of S&W goes over finer points of the new Model 29 Silhouette 10⅝-inch barrel 44 Magnum with Hal Swiggett (left).

A single grain of Bullseye produces this much smoke and even a little recoil in Freedom Arms' 22 muzzle-loader.

Freedom Arms percussion mini 5-shot revolver.

World's most powerful handgun—the 454 Casull—will weigh 50 ounces, require handloading.

MORE THAN 3,000 years ago David, the little fellow, and Goliath, the giant, were in opposing armies and the little fellow slew the giant. The David and Goliath of today's revolvers are in the same camp. Freedom Arms builds the tiniest new revolver, a percussion mini-22 shooting a 29-grain bullet over two grains of FFFFH black powder (or one grain of Bullseye), and the largest, the 454 Casull which spews forth a 200-grain bullet at 2,100 feet per second (fps).

The mini is cute. What other word could describe a watch fob-sized revolver, particularly one that is fed black powder and set off with #11 percussion caps? The one I shot has 1¾ inches of barrel, a 5-shot cylinder, and weighs 5 ounces. Being an old black powder shooter, this correspondent opted for the smokeless option. Instructions with the little revolver said black powder, 2 grains; or Pyrodex, 1.6 grains; or Bullseye, 1 grain. All, it said, could be dipped with the same measure provided. Bullseye wouldn't need the cleaning and anyway it was an entirely new medium for percussion shooting.

Jim Riggs and I dipped and shot until we ran out of bullets. It doesn't reload very fast, but then neither do any other percussion revolvers: Remove the cylinder; pour powder in each chamber; seat a bullet over that powder (I do one chamber at a time); put a percussion cap on each of the five nipples; place the cylinder back in the revolver; and do it all over again.

It's a fun gun and I think that's all it's supposed to be.

Goliath now, the 454 Casull, that's another matter. Not yet in production but positively to be out by the time you read this the 454 by Dick Casull has been kicking around for a long time. All stainless steel, barrel lengths of 7½, 10, and 12 inches, 5-round capacity, brushed stainless finish, hardwood grips, and 50 ounces of weight. The flaw, if there is one, is sighting. Here is a modern revolver chambered for a hot modern load and blessed with 100-plus-year-old sights—a blade front and notched rear.

The 454 Casull with 41 grains of Winchester 296 will kick a 200-grain jacketed bullet out at 2100 fps. That same powder, 25.5 grains, will do likewise to a 350-grain bullet for 1390 fps. Either way, it's going to smart when it hits.

The "R's" of Connecticut, Remington and Ruger, put their heads together and the 357 Remington Maximum is the result. Remington designed the cartridge but had data on hand supplied years ago by Elgin Gates. Elgin heads up the International Handgun Metallic Silhouette Association. He determined, at the first match in 1975, the regulation 357 Magnum wasn't enough gun for silhouette shooting and went to work lengthening cases by welding parts of two 357 Magnum cases together. The outcome is this new .315 inches longer 357 Remington Maximum cartridge.

Ruger—after all there had to be something to shoot it in—went to work on their Blackhawk. No current production revolver was long enough of cylinder to house the 1.605-inch case length of this new 357 Remington Maximum.

The Blackhawk frame was extended to take the necessary cylinder length. In addition, the new revolver has the long Super Blackhawk type square-back Dragoon style grip frame and the wide hammer spur and serrated trigger of the Super BH.

There are two models—7½-inch standard has a ramp style front sight; 10½-inch bull barrel an undercut target front sight. Both are provided with Ruger's adjustable for windage and elevation rear sight.

Remington's 357 Maximum is loaded with their 158-grain SJHP bullet to 1825 fps from a 10½-inch vented test barrel. This provides muzzle energy of 1168 ft. lbs. At 100 yards the velocity is 1381 fps with 669 ft. lbs. of energy. It was here, with this bullet, that Remington fumbled. Federal picked up the ball and headed for the end zone. Their 357 Remington Maximum has a new 180-grain jacketed hollow point bullet starting at 1550 fps from a Ruger 10½-inch Blackhawk. This churns up 960 ft. lbs of energy at the muzzle, 515 at 100 meters and 365 at 200 where those iron rams stand.

Federal ballistics figures are more in keeping with the intent—that of duplicating, as near as possible, the effectiveness of the 44 Magnum with 357 Magnum recoil.

Whichever route taken, Remington's light bullet velocity or Federal's hunting weight the Ruger 357 Maxi-

Elgin Gates, president, International Handgun Metallic Silhouette Association, checking 357 Maximum case length.

Ruger New Model Blackhawk 357 Maximum revolver. This is the 10½-inch bull barrel model.

Remington 357 Maximum 158-grain SJHP beside their 357 Magnum 125-grain SJHP.

The new 180-grain hollow point 357 Maximum from Federal keeps energy way out there.

Jim Riggs said the Ruger 357 Blackhawk Maximum didn't kick, but this photo—and his expression—tell a little different story.

Close-up of the four-position Silhouette front sight.

Smith & Wesson Model 29 44 Magnum Silhouette gun has 10⅝-inch barrel and four-position front sight.

Ruger Redhawk double action 44 Magnum with integral scope mounting system.

Colt Python stainless steel 357 Magnum revolver; its new guarantee doesn't show, but it's there.

Hal Swiggett likes the heavy Dan Wesson stainless steel 44 Magnum (above) and so does Basil Bradbury (below) who slew this javelina with one.

mum Blackhawk will find quick use. Long range varmint hunters are going to love it.

Handloaders can have their cake and eat it too. I'm already using Pacific's carbide dies, loading 110-to 180-grain bullets, and having a ball.

Popular demand forced Ruger to add a Redhawk with integral scope mounting bases and stainless steel rings. The Redhawk is their double action behemoth weighing 3¼ pounds. Six shot and 44 Magnum this

Charter Arms stainless Police Bulldog 38 Special—a six-shot snub with pocket hammer.

(Left) Smith & Wesson 22 Magnum Kit Guns—Model 650 is considerably heavier than the Model 651.

Smith & Wesson 22 Magnum Kit Guns: The Model 651 (top) has adjustable sights; the 650 has fixed sights.

Colt Agent in 38 Special is a lightweight version of the Detective Special.

Davis Industries D-22 and D-25 (here) derringers are made in California.

big DA revolver has been a hit with both hunters and silhouette shooters. It is only in 7½-inch barrel and stainless steel throughout.

Smith & Wesson

Smith & Wesson offers four new revolvers:

The Model 29 Silhouette wears 10⅝-inches of barrel, weighs 58 ounces, has all the standard Model 29 goodies plus a great new four-position adjustable front sight. Designed specifically for the silhouette shooter, one can set the #1 position on 50 meters, the #2 at 100, #3 for 150 and #4 at 200 meters. All this without touching the rear sight once it is set for that first distance. All of the elevation is out front.

Hunters are also going to like S&W's four-position sight. My test M29 has been set at 75 yards, 150 yards, and 300 yards. I'm using only three of the positions. Others will prefer varied settings. It is a viable solu-

tion to "Kentucky windage"—one of those "Why didn't I think of that" things.

Billed as "an old favorite returns," the Model 24 in 44 Special is again in S&W's catalog. Popular demand with Skeeter Skelton as possibly the inspiration caused pause for thought and the result is a schedule for limited production. There will be 7,500 guns made. Both 4-inch and 6½-inch barrels are available; it's blue only.

The Model 24 has all the S&W N-frame features. There are those shooters preferring 44 Special and 45 Colt in a 43-ounce gun over the far more boisterous 44 Magnum. True, the lighter cartridge could be shot in 44 Magnum guns, but the weight of the big gun is unnecessary. The Model 25-5 was given back to 45 Colt fans a few years ago. Now 44 Special Model 24 is the icing on that cake.

The S&W Models 651 and 650 Kit Guns are chambered for 22 Magnum. The 651 is an adjustable-sight 4-inch; the 650 a fixed sight 3-incher. Both are stainless steel. The magnum Kit Gun is a reintroduction as it was in the line from 1960 to 1974.

The Model 651 has a red ramp front sight; weighs 24½ ounces; has a checkered walnut square butt. The Model 650 with its 3-inch heavy barrel weighs 23½ ounces; its handle is checkered walnut in round butt form. A 22 Long Rifle cylinder is available on special order as a component part of a new revolver or purchased through the service department.

Dan Wesson

Dan Wesson stainless steel 22, 357, 41 and 44 double action revolvers are making big waves wherever they show up. Fast becoming a favorite of silhouette shooters, DW 357s and 44s regularly appear in the winners circle. My stainless 44 has seen a good deal of use. It was instrumental in bagging another handgun hunting supporter. Basil Bradbury, editor of Petersen's Hunting Magazine and hunter of note (Weatherby Award winner), saw mine, asked to borrow it while on a South Texas deer hunt, made a great 60-yard shot on a javelina and now he's one of us.

There is a new Dan Wesson. The big 44 has been modified, lightened a bit, and turned into a 357 Maximum. But then we knew it would happen—didn't we?

Detonics

Detonics isn't setting a production date, but will one day have an interchangeable barrel/cylinder top-break

Detonics top-break Modular 7-shot revolver will have interchangeable barrel/cylinder units, even single shot barrels.

Jim Riggs shot the prototype M.O.A. "Maximum" falling block pistol with a Bushnell 2.5 scope.

"Maximum" by M.O.A. is a falling block single shot with interchangeable barrels. This one is 223.

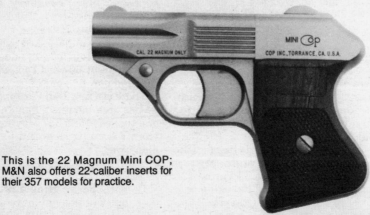

This is the 22 Magnum Mini COP; M&N also offers 22-caliber inserts for their 357 models for practice.

double action revolver in all stainless steel. The Modular 7-shot I saw had a 5-inch barrel, was 10 inches in length and weighed 53 ounces. It will be made in 357, 41 and 44 Magnum and 45 Colt. There is also a single shot barrel for calibers up to 45. Sights are on each barrel/cylinder unit. Single shot barrels are tapped for scope mounting.

This Modular 7-shot from Detonics is the first really new double action in a long time, entirely its own design.

M.O.A Corporation

Another new design to watch and again not scheduled for production with a specific date, the Maximum is being shot by two or three of us, checking for bugs obviously and offering suggestions before final production design is set. The gun could easily be mistaken for a single action from the trigger guard back, but it's a single-shot falling block.

My test pistol, one of only two out, is in 223 Remington. With 10½-inch barrel and Bushnell 2.5 scope mounted, its weight is 66 ounces. Accuracy with Federal ammunition, the only brand tried so far, is good. The other copy, manufactured by the M.O.A. is a 308 Winchester.

Available calibers will be most anything between these two test guns. Barrels are interchangeable but have to be factory fitted. Once that is done, a spanner wrench is shipped with the barrel for quick changing as the shooter desires.

United Sporting Arms

They're in full production in Arizona, turning out Seville single actions, both stainless steel and blued. There are models from 10½-inch Silhouette down to 3½-inch Sheriff. Calibers include all the usual plus 357 Maximum, 45 ACP, 45 Winchester Magnum, and 454 Casull.

USA's "Quick Kit Conversion System" features all usual calibers with a barrel and cylinder for each interchangeable on the same frame. Barrel lengths are 4⅝ to 7½ inches. Available in brushed satin stainless or high lustre blue.

Butler

Butler has a new Quad-4. The 4-barreled derringer, with 2.6-inch barrels, is 4.6 inches in length. Both 22 Magnum and 22 Long Rifle versions can be had in either stainless or blue. There is a police model with an open trigger guard. Grips are a choice of hard rubber, plain or checkered walnut.

HJS Industries

The Frontier "FOUR" 4-barreled derringer from HJS is 22 Long Rifle and stainless steel. It weighs 5½ ounces, has a positive rotating firing pin and can fire only in battery position. The firing pin position is readily visible to indicate the next barrel to be fired.

A stablemate, the Lone Star 38 S&W single-shot derringer is stainless steel and weighs 6 ounces. It features a beryllium copper firing pin and a unique "hammer-down" carry position.

Colt

An economically priced 2-inch Agent is back with us. This 6-shot 38 Special, quoting Colt's release, is "for those more concerned with dependability and reliability than with a highly finished revolver." The Agent is a derivative from the well-known Detective Special. It differs only in the external finish, a non-glare combat finish, which eliminates much of the polishing normally associated with Colt firearms.

More news from Colt comes in the form of a stainless steel Python. Not much can be said about the famous "Snake" as all who know or have even heard of revolvers know about the Python. All this writer can say is—a fine revolver made finer.

There is more, however: Beginning January 1, 1983, all newly-purchased Python revolvers carry 10 years of free service. This is for Python only and excludes accidents, misuse, damage by overpressure ammunition and Python revolvers which have been worked on outside of the Colt factory or one of their authorized gunsmiths.

Also noted is the absence of the Trooper MK III from this year's catalog along with a notation, "Colt MK V Trooper now sells for under $300.00. Colt, realizing the impact of the current recession on the firearms industry and the consumer, has reduced the price of the MK V revolvers and will hold this price through 1983.

Charter

Charter Arms is deeply into stainless this year, almost across the board. There are several Police Bulldog models with various grips and ground-off hammer spurs. This columnist is a long-time fan of the Pathfinder 22. The personal involvement goes so far back mine is a Pocket Target, the name it started with, so the new stainless steel 3-inch 22 LR Pathfinder means they still have the outdoorsman in mind, not just police and

Seville 357 Super Mag 357 Maximum by United Sporting Arms was fast off and running.

Seville also has a conversion system. Your choice of calibers can be shot with the same frame by changing the cylinder and barrel.

Frontier FOUR derringer in 22 Long Rifle from HJS Industries weighs 5½ ounces.

Swiggett's office fun gun—the Crosman 357 CO_2 pellet revolver, even shoots like a Python. That is an 18-foot 6-shot group.

personal protection. The Charter Pathfinder in 22 Magnum is again in the catalog.

Interarms

Interarms catalogs a new Rossi Model 88 stainless steel 38 Special. My first impression, on opening the box, that I had a S&W Kit Gun with bigger holes in the cylinder and barrel—the same size and shape frame and trigger guard. GD's test Model 88 has a 3-inch barrel and weighs 22 ounces. The side plate fits so perfectly only a hair line shows and the cylin-

Rossi Model 88 stainless 38 Special from Interarms has familiar Kit Gun lines, but bigger holes.

New Weaver 4x handgun scope in SSK mounts on SSK custom 300 Savage barrel. Note the Mag-na-port slots.

der cannot be moved with the fingers, no matter how hard you try, with the trigger back. It locks up right. The trigger pull is a mite heavy at five pounds, but breaks crisp. Double action pull is a smooth 11½ pounds.

Thompson/Center

There's nothing new for the great Contender, but we have to expect 357 Maximum barrels, both bull and Super 14. Continuous updating on the assembly line means you might never be able to get two identical T/C's but all parts are interchangeable without a hitch and no fuss made about upgrading. It is all a credit to Warren Center, a master in his field.

M&N

COP, the 4-barreled double action derringer, was available in two 22-caliber versions last year: an all-stainless steel 22 Magnum that weighs 16 ounces, and an aluminum frame 22 Long Rifle in royal blue at the same weight. The all-stainless 38/357 COP weighs 28 ounces.

There is something new now for that 38/357: M&N has adapters in sets of four, making it possible to shoot 25 ACP or 22 LR in the 38/357, though not in the same adapter set, of course. There is also an adapter set for Long Rifle ammo in the Magnum 22 version.

Davis Industries

Here is a little O-U derringer in 25 ACP or 22 Long Rifle. Barrel length is 2.4 inches and weighs in at 9.5 ounces. Grips are simulated ivory and the finish a choice of nickel or chrome. Jim Davis finishes off his description with, "Made entirely in California."

Miscellaneous

Earle Harrington, Harrington & Richardson executive, said, "Nothing new from us—we're just trying to catch up on orders." And American

Derringer's Robert Saunders bore similar tidings—no new guns, no new calibers, just trying to keep up with orders. At North American Arms, manufacturers of mini revolvers, there is a new gun on their agenda, but they're not ready to talk about it yet.

Sterling Arms recent X-Caliber is doing well. Nothing's new except maybe a caliber or two added. And Mossberg's U.S. Arms Abilene is still cataloged in 357 and 44 Magnum and 45 Colt.

Trapper Gun Inc. lists spring kits for most handguns and rifles. It's the least expensive way I know to get a trigger job. I've tried them in several guns. In every instance—Ruger single action, Ruger Redhawk, T/C, Dan Wesson—they have made a better trigger.

Weaver has a new stainless 4x handgun scope. Dan Flaherty asked me to try and destroy it. At the same time my SSK 300 Savage barrel for the T/C contender showed up. They were teamed together. They are still together.

It's been six weeks. Five boxes of Federal 150-grain and five of their 180-grain plus an even hundred handloads featuring Hornady's 165-grain spire point. You're right, that is only 300 rounds but it is 300 rounds of a fair-to-middlin' rifle caliber through a handgun and all is still well. I'm trying, Dan. I'm still trying.

Crosman

I have a new "fun gun." At least once a day, a fresh business card is taped to an old telephone directory leaning against a closet door 18 feet from my desk chair. The cylinder (pellet clip) of my Crosman 357 Six is loaded with six 177 Crosman Super Pells and business ceases for a while. Using Crosman Copperhead CO_2 Powerlets each corner of the card gets a clip full of pellets. Twenty four shots and it's back to work.

Don't know what it is doing for my handgun shooting but it sure helps keep my morale up.

The Six stands for barrel length and there is also a 357 Four. It looks like a Colt Python. It even feels like a Colt Python. So far, and this has been going on for months, there has been no indication of any leaking of the Powerlets.

Some days the six pellets would easily hide under a nickel. Other days a silver dollar wouldn't cover them which says it shoots about as good as I do. ●

Shotgun Review

by RALPH T. WALKER

The year of the multi-choke . . .

First in repeaters, then in over-unders, now Winchester puts choke tubes in the Model 23 side-by-side double.

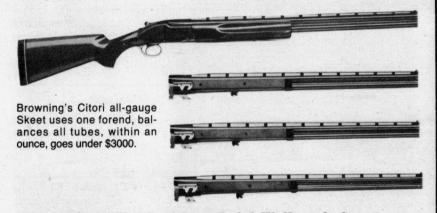

Browning's Citori all-gauge Skeet uses one forend, balances all tubes, within an ounce, goes under $3000.

Editor's Note: This introduces Ralph Walker who knows something of shotguns and here keeps track of what's happening for you in that field. It is not quite correct to say he's a man of few words, since DBI Books has just published his Gun Digest Book of Shotgun Gunsmithing, but he kept this year's report short and sweet. K.W.

Beretta

Beretta, like many other manufacturers, has expanded the versatility of their line to incorporate everything from slug guns to skeet and trap versions and, naturally, the high-priced engraved versions as well. The firm has held to the quality of manufacture which is synonymous with their name. It's too bad they dropped the lightweight field action of their over-under that made them famous in the

U.S. They have switched all models to the much heavier competition action.

Breda

This well-known Italian shotgun manufacturer has been around for quite a few years, but owners and customers have lately had trouble locating the importer. The correct name and address is Diana Import Co., 842 Vallejo St., San Francisco, CA 94133 which imports the Breda semi-autos

and their over-under shotguns. Diana also imports and distributes the Andromeda side-by-side, the Aquila nickel plated shot used for competition in Italy, a well-rounded line of Italian shotgun shooting accessories, game bags, shell bags and belts.

Browning

First among Browning's new stuff is a special screw-in choke tube system of their own design. While not interchangeable with the well known Winchoke style tube, it is nevertheless first class in appearance and performance. It will be available on three guns: The Citori, the BPS, and the BT99. The system offers choke constriction ranging from cylinder to full throughout a six-tube selection. This will allow the Browning shooter to have virtually an unlimited choice of choke to meet changing game and range requirements.

The Browning B-80 gas semi-auto was chosen by Ducks Unlimited as the shotgun of the year and 3,000 copies will be made for distribution throughout D.U.'s chapters for fund raising. Browning will also produce 500 special American Pintail Commemoratives in their Superposed 12 gauge.

For those who lean toward the side-by-side gun in the classic tradition with a straight grip stock, slim forend and two triggers, I would suggest a close inspection of the new Browning 12 gauge which incorporates a feature close to classic shotgunners hearts—real functioning sidelocks. This is not a boxlock with fake side locks to provide engraving space, but a beautiful shotgun in true English tradition. With 2¾-inch chambers the 26-inch barrel length is available in improved cylinder and modified choke, or modified and full. The 28-inch barrel choice offers only modified and full choke. The stated retail price is $1,500.00.

Gastinne Renette

This company, dating back to 1812 in France, recently opened shop in the U.S. In essence, the Renette shotguns are of the British best gun class but with a few unique French innovations. They build only four basic models, but all with various extras.

The Model 105 with a basic price tag of $1,800.00 is a boxlock side-by-

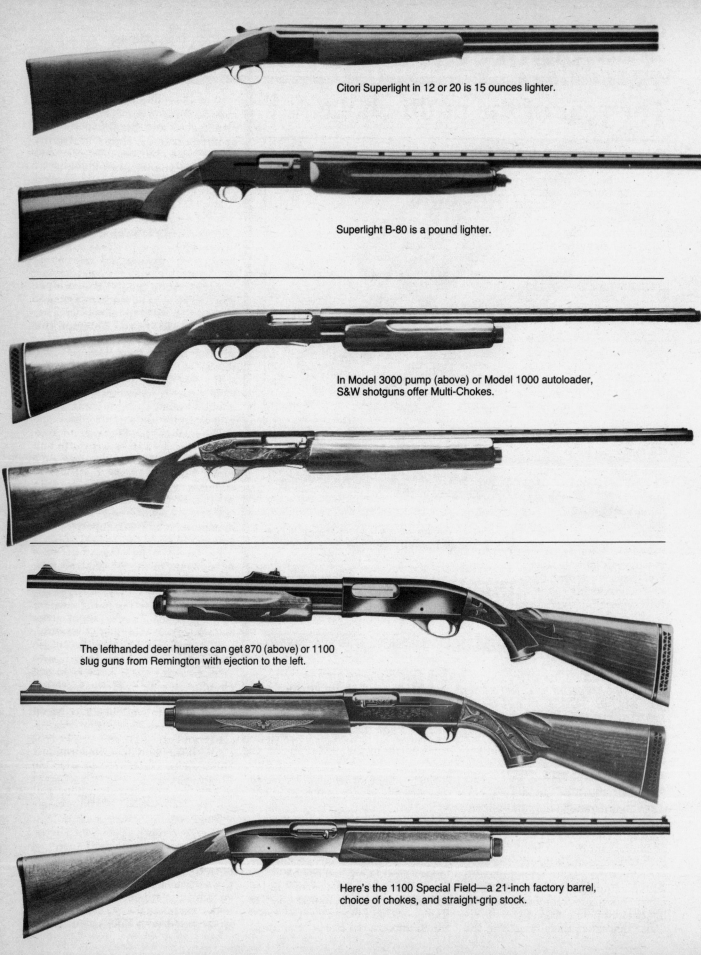

Citori Superlight in 12 or 20 is 15 ounces lighter.

Superlight B-80 is a pound lighter.

In Model 3000 pump (above) or Model 1000 autoloader, S&W shotguns offer Multi-Chokes.

The lefthanded deer hunters can get 870 (above) or 1100 slug guns from Remington with ejection to the left.

Here's the 1100 Special Field—a 21-inch factory barrel, choice of chokes, and straight-grip stock.

side with auto ejectors, etc., but dual triggers, in 12 or 20 gauge with 2¾-inch chambers. It goes 6 pounds 8 ounces in weight for the 12 gauge. Next up the line is the Model 98 with a $2,500.00 price tag. Then the Model 202 is a sideplate gun built on a Purdey-type action at $3,325.00. Top of the line is the Model 353 true sidelock with hand-detachable locks at $8,900.00 for the basic gun.

I once had the pleasure of owning and shooting a Renette and can best sum it up in one word—CLASS.

The firm also markets a very interesting line of shotgun accessories with French accents. Such items as shell belt, shell bags, game bags, leather trunk cases and such are of first class materials and workmanship.

Harrington & Richardson

One would have thought that there was no caliber or gauge or option left for H&R to manufacture utilizing their time-proven single shot action for they carry in their line about everything but a sling shot on this action. Somehow this year they succeeded in adding two more that should have wide appeal. The first is their basic single shot shotgun with a 3-inch chamber in 12, 20 and 410 and the 16 with the 2¾-inch chamber with standard barrel lengths. The difference is that the new version, designated the Model 099 Deluxe, has every metal part—which includes the barrel—finished in the well-received matte electroless nickel finish. The metal is thus virtually rust free and will take abundant abuse and is rightfully termed the "work horse."

Their second new offering, also with the same nickel finish throughout, is the Model 258 Handy Gun II and should have good reception with the boat, RV and survival people. It comes with a 20 or 22-inch 20-gauge 3-inch chambered modified barrel to which is added a choice of 22 Hornet, 30-30, 357 Mag (or 38 Spl.) or 44 Magnum rifled barrels. The rifle barrels are predrilled for scope mounts. The receiver and two barrels are packed in a factory furnished heavy duck takedown carrying case.

Benelli/Heckler & Koch

The Benelli, a recoil operated semi-auto, is gaining on the U.S. market primarily due to wise marketing by Heckler & Koch within the market where they have the most influence and strength. That is the police, para-military and survival-oriented group. The newest versions of the Benelli are

models and variations that appeal to these customers.

Ithaca

The big news from Ithaca last year was the 4¾-pound 20-gauge and 5¼-pound 12-gauge straight-gripped Model 37 pump termed the English UltraLite. The latest version is the same gun, but equipped with the more American buttstock with a pistol grip. This adds ¼-pound to each gauge but still allows Ithaca to claim title to "The world's lightest pump shotgun." Also added is a youth or ladies' model with pistol grip, but with 12½-inch pull instead of the standard 14 inches.

Taking a page from their past, Ithaca now offers "Customizing Unlimited" on any model for those who want something a wee bit different than the next guy. The sort of direction this might take was seen in a splendid cased set of 20-gauge stakeout shotguns shown at this year's SHOT Show and elsewhere.

Lanber

Lanber, new in the USA, showed a full line of over-under shotguns last year ranging from a two-trigger extractor version to a single selective trigger, ejector and screw-in choke equipped model. Theirs is a rugged well-built gun at an affordable price. This year's news is that they have listened to field reports and made slight modifications that "Americanize" their guns.

La Paloma

This marketing firm made news a couple of years ago with the introduction on the U.S. market of the K.F.C. semi-auto with a unique gas system that drastically reduces recoil. Latest poop is that LaPaloma will offer a "modified in America" version that meets the one-gun concept head on. The barrel incorporates a ten choke tube selection ranging from Cylinder to Maximum Full and with a new multi-use vent rib. The buttstock is unique in that it is adjustable for comb height by the shooter and so is a new recoil absorbing pad. Two barrel lengths come with the unit, a 26 and a 30-inch, and all are in a fitted trunk case.

LaPaloma has added the Ameria shotgun line made in Spain, formerly imported by Leland Firearms, consisting of a made-to-order side-by-side in the various gauges, chokes and barrel lengths. Another addition is the prestigious W & C Scott shotgun line, absent from the U.S. market for several years.

Marlin

One of the success stories of current shotguns is the Model 120 pump in 12 gauge. This all-steel pump with modern design sells about as fast as Marlin can turn them out. Welcome news is the plain jane version sporting the Glenfield name, a walnut-stained birch stock sans checkering and an aluminum trigger guard that allows a retail price under the $100.00 level. The Glenfield Model 778 and a choice between 8 barrel configurations should earn Marlin even more of the pump shotgun market.

Mossberg

Few companies have developed more variations of one pump shotgun as Mossberg has with their 500. They offer 16 choices in 12 gauge, which may be why the average shooter has boosted sales so high. They have left no stone unturned in variations to suit the police, para-military and survival market, including adding two more this year.

Big news is their brand-spanking-new gas operated semi-auto, the Model 5500 which will be available initially in 12 gauge only, but with instant shooter choice of either the 2¾-inch or 3-inch length barrel with no changes necessary for feeding. The gas system differs considerably as the energy derived from the gas ports are directed to an inertia weight which in turn functions the action instead of the more common gas cylinder with piston attached to the mechanism. An extra plus is the placement of the safety directly on top of the receiver as with the 500 pumps. "Right under the thumb" says Mossberg literature.

The 5500ADV comes with vent rib barrel and with three Accu-Choke screw-in chokes in full, modified and improved cylinder. There are standard barrels with or without vent rib. And the 5500AS sports a slug barrel with rifle sights and sling swivels.

We can look forward to the new 5500 being produced in just about any configuration for which a market potential exists. Mossberg's general price structure places their guns well within the so-called "workingman's pay bracket."

Perazzi

Competition shotguns by Perazzi are well known for quality of product. Perazzi is now offering a line of field or hunting versions, with the over-under versions, the SC series, based on the well-known MX8 action. There is a line of top-drawer side-by-side field guns, as well, termed the DHO series. Both offer a seemingly unlimited choice of engraving and other foibles. If you have the bucks on hand, you should consider the new Perazzi hunting shotguns.

AYA/Precision Sports

The Aquirre y Aranzabal (AYA) line of shotguns Precision imports naturally includes the Matador side-by-side in the 10-gauge 3½-inch magnum. This has been a big hit with the turkey hunting crowd and also with deer hunters where buckshot is a must, since the 10 gauge delivers more pellets than any other. The Mat-

Remington

A couple of years ago Remington ran a few 26-inch barrels with full choke and the end result was this length barrel in full, modified and improved cylinder chokes for the M-1100. The news is they have gone one step further due to public demand and offer this choke selection in a 21-inch barrel. The new version of the M-1100 mated to these barrels is the "special field model." It has a straight grip stock and matching slimmed forend and it's chambered for the 2¾-inch 12-gauge shell. The same gun will be manufactured in a 20-gauge version, same chamber length, same

with some short variations of the Savage over-under combination gun.

Smith and Wesson

While S&W built its reputation with their handguns, they are boosting their image with the Model 1000 gas operated semi-auto and the model 3000 pump shotguns. This year they have added the 1000 in 20 gauge equipped with their screw-in Multi-Choke system. The new choice comes with three tubes, full, modified and improved cylinder. An interesting little goodie that comes with all Multi-Choke guns is a neat two-tube pouch. If you prefer a 20-gauge pump over a semi-auto, not to worry: the same 20-

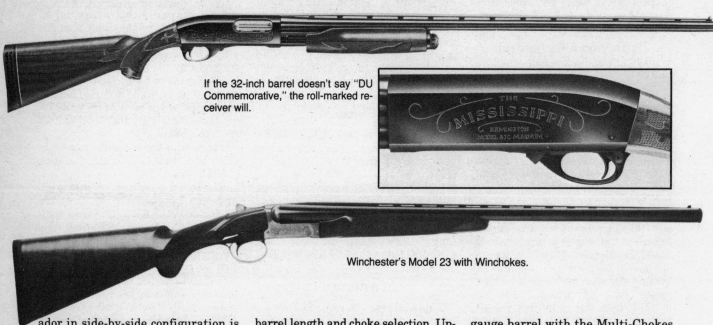

If the 32-inch barrel doesn't say "DU Commemorative," the roll-marked receiver will.

Winchester's Model 23 with Winchokes.

ador in side-by-side configuration is one of the better choices as it is specifically built to absorb the heavy recoil, both to gun and shooter. In recent years, it has simply not been available and should receive a good revival with bigbore sportsmen. The other AYA models are made in just about any style or gauge and choke selection, of course.

L. Joseph Rahn, Inc.

This small import company has an interesting line of shotguns. Among them is the Astra, in field, skeet and trap styles and a price range from about $500 to $850 with a lot of desirable features. They also have the top-grade Garbi line in which you can order just about anything your wallet will stand, from $350 to $3,800, and fulfill your classic shotgun dreams. There is the Secolo which is a trap-style gun only, and the Falco over-under shotgun in 410 gauge with all components scaled down.

barrel length and choke selection. Upland game hunters should find this new version of the proven M-1100 just the ticket.

For the lefthanded shooter, Remington offers both the M1100 and M870 pump with port side ejection. This year the same lefthand ejection is made available in the deer gun models, or one can buy the barrels as separate items.

Savage

For the past few years this firm has been undergoing some internal changes with the new management stressing quality of manufactured products. They have not, however, been asleep as evident by this year's introduction of a screw-in choke tube system on their Model 67 pump shotgun, and several models for the police military crowd. For one, the 311R, which is a short double-12 used by detectives on several police forces, is now in the standard catalog, along

gauge barrel with the Multi-Chokes is also available this year with the Model 3000.

Smith and Wesson is also making a serious run at the competition shotgun market. This year they have added the 20-gauge Model 1000 with the superskeet barrel that has proven popular in 12 gauge. This is the so called "Tula Choke" system which is a recessed form of choke allowing the shot load to expand internally and deliver a more widely dispersed shot pattern for skeet purposes.

Stoeger

A shotgun line at an affordable price consists of two basic models:

The side by side, in 12, 20 and 28 gauge with 2¾-inch chambers and the 410 with three inch chambers provides choke selection of full and full in the 410 and modified and full or improved cylinder and modified in the other three. Barrel length is 28-inch and 26-inch in the 12 and 20, 26-inch in the others plus a 20-inch barrel version in 12 and 20 termed the "Coach" for upland game shooting.

The over-under, also available in the four gauges, is made in two styles. The lower-priced version has an extractor and two triggers, while the other has a non-selective single trigger. Barrel length and choke selection is the same as the side-by-side except for the 20-inch barrel.

Called the IGA, both guns are manufactured in Brazil under contract.

U.S. Repeating Arms

Last year, USRAC tried their Ranger series of shotguns with birch stocks and lower prices. It worked and

Don Allen, with the deluxe version being returned to Europe for sale. That speaks well for American craftsmen.

Weatherby

Like many other manufacturers bowing to public demand, Weatherby last year began marketing their semi-auto shotgun with a screw-in choke. Their tubes are fully interchangeable with all those based upon the field-proven Winchoke dimensions. This is in the best interest of the American sportsman who will undoubtedly accumulate various constrictions and desire to use them in more than one shotgun.

velvet lined trunk type case complete with lock.

Advanced Stocking Systems

Every shotgunner who knows and loves walnut, but has wanted a more scratch-resistant and virtually indestructible handle can get one here. Advance produces a synthetic material stock so tough that part of their advertisement has a photo of a stock being used to drive a large nail.

Nothing is required in the way of finishing and the stocks and forends bolt right on to factory guns. Three color choices are available—black, brown and green. The hollow-core model duplicates the factory stock in

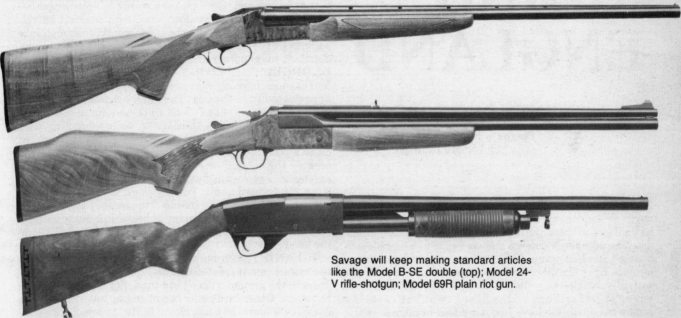

Savage will keep making standard articles like the Model B-SE double (top); Model 24-V rifle-shotgun; Model 69R plain riot gun.

USRAC now offers virtually the whole shotgun line under this name with corresponding price reductions. There is the semi-auto in both 12 and 20 gauge, with Winchoke and ventilated barrel, plain barrel and Winchoke, or plain barrel with built-in choke. The same system in their pump shotguns includes a package deal of a deer barrel and a Winchoke-vent rib barrel in 12 gauge.

Another introduction is the Winchester pump 12 in a Defender version with 8-shell capacity. And there is a marine model with open sights, 7-shot capacity, and a triple chrome finish on all metal parts. The Police model is about the same, sans the sights.

Valmet

Following the shooting system theme, Valmet this year introduced an engraved version with a deluxe stock. An interesting side note is that the receivers are engraved by Ken Hurst and the deluxe stock made by

Winchester

The whole concept of the screw-in choke tube originated with Winchester in their Model 59 semi-auto shotgun in 1959 and the WinLite tubes. Later, using gained experience, they originated the Winchoke upon which most screw-in tubes are patterned. This system was installed in both the 1400 and 1200 shotguns now manufactured by U.S. Repeating Arms. The next step was to lead the pack with the introduction of the screw-in choke tubes in their Model 101 over-under.

This year they scored another first by offering the time-proven Win-Choke system in the well-accepted Model 23 side-by-side shotgun. It's the only side-by-side production shotgun with such a wide choice of chokes. There will be six of the tubes with the 12 gauge and four with the 20 gauge. Included with the suggested retail price of $1,300.00 is a cloth covered,

weight, while the solid-core model is 40% heavier and stout enough for door-busting. Currently it is available for 12 different semi-auto and pump shotguns.

Pennsylvania Arms Company

This company displayed at the 1982 SHOT Show a rather unique conversion of the AR10 into a clip-fed shotgun with a rifled barrel. In the following year, they found little acceptance of the conversion but a strong interest in their rifled shotgun barrel. Consequently, they now offer a new rifled barrel for virtually any shotgun with a detachable barrel system. This is not a standard shotgun barrel with rifling cut into it but a completely new barrel. Accuracy with slugs is way above the normal accuracy when they are fired in the regular smooth standard barrel. This should be of interest to sportsmen in states that allow only slugs for large game, and permit them in a rifled bore. ●

HUNTING IN GEORGIA AND ENGLAND

by SIDNEY DU BROFF

Photos by Sidney Du Broff
and Nedra Du Broff

ENGLAND: It's Bedfordshire, England, about 60 miles north of London, on a Saturday in November. The cars, half a dozen of them, pull off the road, onto the grass shoulder. The occupants emerge and we begin to assemble our double-barrel shotguns. The dogs, two springers—one belongs to Eric, the other to Doc—greet each other enthusiastically, while the yellow Lab owned by Ian acknowledges the existence of the other two, but remains somewhat aloof. We have had our ritual breakfast at the hotel in town, where we meet every two weeks prior to the shoot.

GEORGIA: In the USA, we are at Pinewood, a 1350-acre plantation not far from Albany, owned by Harold Weatherbee, who drives the jeep over the rough road. We are seated on the dog box built into the back of the jeep, and holding tight. It's the middle of January, but down here in south Georgia it's pleasant and mild. I'm a Northerner; it's my first Southern hunt; and I can feel the excitement growing. My companions, besides Harold, are Sonny and Lamar, both from Albany. The dogs—there are two teams of them—are all English pointers.

ENGLAND: It's a familiar field; we know the procedure without Doc, who is the shoot captain, having to go into too much detail. Three of the other guns and myself take positions along our boundary, behind which is a wood. The remaining guns, in addition to the two beaters, start across the field from the opposite side, along with the dogs, and move slowly in our direction. A cock pheasant gets up in the distance, well ahead of the advancing guns, struggles to gain height and flies forward towards us, somewhere between Ron and Geoffrey. Ron fires, with the first barrel, then with the second, but the bird is unscathed and only seconds from the safety of the woods. Geoffrey throws his double to his shoulder and fires.

GEORGIA: Harold brings the jeep to a stop. The dogs, four of them, barking, whimpering, eager to be in the field, are released from the box. They make a dash for the field and range widely. Sonny and I are moving in behind. It doesn't take long before the dogs are on to something. One of them freezes to a point. The other three back him up, go on to a point, too, even though they have not necessarily scented the birds themselves, or are even aware of their existence. I move in; I'm nervous. It's been a long time since I've hunted quail. There's going to be an explosion. It's going to happen any second. This second? The next? In two seconds? It's now. A covey of bobwhites burst out and spread in every direction, including two that fly back over my head.

ENGLAND: The bird is hit hard, probably stone dead, but the momentum it created carries it into the wood, where it drops to the ground with a hard thud. For the moment it is left there. Other birds may be getting up any second. One does. It's a hen this time, closer to the approaching guns. Doc swings on her and brings her down with the first barrel. His springer rushes forward. The advancing line stops.

GEORGIA: Hunting partner, Ginger Taylor, from Americus, GA, downs one at Calloway Gardens.

ENGLAND: Our beaters at work, scuffling over every square foot.

ENGLAND: Having worked one field, we proceed to another, guns open for reassurance.

GEORGIA: Moving into the field by jeep at Pinewood, where we shot coveys, not singles.

In triumph, the springer returns with the hen pheasant in his mouth. "Drop," Doc says firmly. Still the dog clings to it. "Drop!" he says again, and this time the dog complies.

GEORGIA: Which one do I shoot at first? Pick one out! I do. I swing the double and fire, but the bird keeps going. I pick out another and miss it, too. There's a shot off to my right and a bobwhite drops in the tall grass. Sonny has downed the first bird. He wants the dogs to find it and bring it to him. They'd just as soon go on and look for another covey, and let Sonny find his own bird. "Dead!" he commands. "Dead!" The dogs scramble around and eventually find the bird, which Sonny puts in his game pocket. We don't go after the singles here. There are enough coveys about not to have to bother.

ENGLAND: Doc picks up the bird, and hands it to one of the beaters, who puts it in his game bag. The line resumes its forward trek, but no more birds get up. The drive is over. We all break open our doubles. The dogs are directed into the woods to pick up the dead pheasant. It's been a dis-

appointing drive. On previous shoots we put up as many as 20 birds in this field; admittedly some of them must have originated from the adjacent shoot. The birds they stock, driven over the standing guns, take refuge on our land. But the full-time gamekeeper employed there induces his birds to return by feeding them regularly, which also encourages ours to go over and stay. We have the right to retrieve the dead bird from the wood, though it is not our land, but no one can enter carrying a gun. Hen pheasants are also fair game, though toward the end of the season some shoots may terminate, or severely restrict, the killing of hens.

GEORGIA: It isn't long before we're onto another covey. They get up. I hear a shot go off. It's from my gun and a bird drops. That comes as something of a surprise, so much so that I forget to shoot again. But two shots from Lamar's autoloader account for two birds. We take turns with the coveys, providing alternate opportunities to move in on the birds. The jeep goes where it can, following the dogs

ENGLAND: Firing at pheasant, flushed by the beaters or the walking guns.

GEORGIA: Du Broff takes a shot over German shorthair pointer at Calloway Gardens.

ENGLAND: Later in the season we're bound to get some snow, but one tries, you know.

GEORGIA: Sonny, Harold and Du Broff holding quail at Pinewood on a sunny January day.

when possible. Some of the terrain is pretty rough. Well, the quail like it. By lunchtime we've put up seven or eight coveys, and the bag is pretty fair. I'm eager to get back, but things don't get rushed down here. The birds will still be there. And they are. By the end of the day we've put up 12 or 13 coveys. That's a lot of birds.

ENGLAND: Now we cross the road into another field, a much smaller one. We move forward together, closer to each other than I like, a characteristic of an English rough shoot, where the fields are often small, and fragmented. We have leased the shooting rights here, and no one else, including the farmer who owns the land, may go shooting on it. The farms are small—300 acres is a large one—and the land we use belongs to several farmers. We have almost a thousand acres, half of it here, the rest ten miles away, which we will shoot in the afternoon.

GEORGIA: I'm at Calloway Gardens, Pine Mountain, Georgia, 80 miles south of Atlanta, and still after bobwhites. Here they put 'em down, and you try to put 'em up.

You pick out a team of dogs, and with the handler, and another hunter, go out into the field. A couple of German shorthairs for me, please. They've got 1100 acres set aside for hunting. Here, too, you take turns walking in on them—they're singles, rather than coveys, though several times there were doubles, and once a triple.

ENGLAND: Pheasants are by far the most important game bird in England, initially imported, as they were in the United States. In most of the country there is little by way of natural breeding, so stocking must take place to insure that there is game in the field at which to shoot. The season begins on October 1st and runs to February 1st, with no bag limit, since each shoot is a separate entity and responsible only to itself. If, toward the end of the season, the birds are scarce, the last one or two shoots may be cancelled.

On our shoot the game is divided each day, hopefully two birds for each gun, which may become one later in the season. On the driven shoots, they may kill a hundred, 200, or

ENGLAND: It's lunchtime on our shoot. Weather permitting, we eat in the field, all of us.

ENGLAND: Some of our guns moving through the field. There's generally a brisk walk or two.

GEORGIA: Dogs on point at Pinewood. One may be on quail, the other two backing.

GEORGIA: Dog handler John Salle at Calloway Gardens takes a bird from a German shorthair pointer.

even more birds in the course of a day. The guns are presented with two pheasants each; the rest are sent to market. With game being sold legally, at six or seven dollars for a pheasant—depending upon market fluctuations—there invariably results the problem of poaching and illegal sales. For us, a day in the field works out to something like $60.00 per man. The cost of raising a pheasant is figured at about $16.00.

GEORGIA: The quail at Pine Wood are all native and none are put down. Conditions have been created in which they can thrive. Never more than half the birds are taken from a covey during a shoot. They soon regroup and once again become a covey that will sit tight before a team of dogs. The birds hold up through the whole of the season, though they are fairly heavily hunted. Statewide, quail opens on the 20th of November and runs through the 28th of February, with a daily bag limit of 12 and 36 in possession.

Pine Wood is private, and one hunts there by invitation, though there is plenty of place in Georgia for the hunter on his own. At Calloway Gardens, you put down your money and you can take up to ten birds, which works out to about $7.50 a bird. If you're really keen, you can put down some more of your money and shoot another ten. The birds belong to you. Accommodations are also available, with help-yourself Southern food. If you want to get in practice before the hunt, there is Skeet and trap shooting. This quail hunting does not conform to the state season, but begins October 1st and continues until the 31st of March.

SUMMING UP: For me the Southern experience was a satisfying one, and the hospitality remarkable. Our American way of hunting is essentially more satisfying than what I have come to know in England; the whole country would fit into the state of Georgia, with plenty of room to spare. England, with about 50 million people trying to live in it, is acutely short of space, and the hunting that exists must reflect that unalterable condition. ●

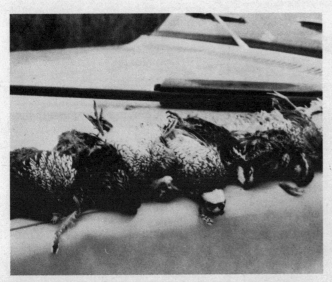

GEORGIA: Part of the bag at Calloway Gardens, slightly larger than strictly wild birds.

ENGLAND: Tallying up the game after the shoot reveals this was not a better day.

BLACK POWDER REVIEW

by RICK HACKER

Lee Allen (left) gives Rick Hacker firsthand look at the new Allen Fire Arms Henry replica in 44-40.

The Allen Fire Arms Henry is a near-perfect replica of the original, but is offered in sensible 44-40.

The Allen Fire Arms black powder SAA, showing screw-type lock for cylinder pin and rounded bull's-eye ejector rod head.

IT IS NO GREAT secret that 1983 was economically hard for the country. The black powder industry, with the rest of the "modern" world, felt the financial squeeze. Companies such as Sile opted to downplay their muzzle-loading imports, and Browning decided this was the year to discontinue their extremely well-made but underrated Mountain Rifle.

However, for every player that left the stage, a new one entered, with firms such as Traditions, Inc. and Gibson Products emerging upon the black powder shooting and collecting scene for the first time this year. Of course, the industry's leaders—Dixie Gun Works, Navy Arms and CVA—offer the sort of new items that keep the muzzle-loading sport interesting and very much alive. Judging from the amount of new plunder and my own observations, it looks like another booming year for the muzzle-loading fraternity, hunters, match shooters, collectors and all.

Allen Arms

Allen (formerly Western) Fire Arms cap and ball revolvers are among the finest of reproductions in terms of fit, finish and historical accuracy, and will continue to be despite the death of the founder Leonard Allen. Leonard's son Lee has taken over the reins, of his father's firm, and is both maintaining the old line and introducing some rather exciting new shootables.

High on this list is the Allen reproduction of the Henry rifle. Only 13,500 original Henrys were made between 1860 and 1865 and they are highly sought-after collectibles today. Allen is chambering them for the shootable 44-40, and duplicating the original, right down to its sling swivels and unique loading system.

Another resurrection of note from Allen Arms is their copy of the black-powder frame Colt Single Action Army. Fully proofed to accept modern 45 and 44-40 factory loads, it has the bullseye ejector rod and cylinder base pin screw. Allen has also introduced a complete line of stainless steel replicas of the Colt 1851 Navy, 1860 Army, 1862 Police and 1862 Pocket.

Dixie's Magnum 12 and 10-gauge shotguns (10-ga. shown here) have more steel and wood in their design and can handle beefier loads.

Dixie Gun Works is offering their versatile 74-caliber smoothbore British Trade Gun, which can handle shot or round ball.

The Frontier Scout is an economically priced half-stocked, scaled down boy's hunting rifle in 45 or 50 caliber from Traditions, Inc.

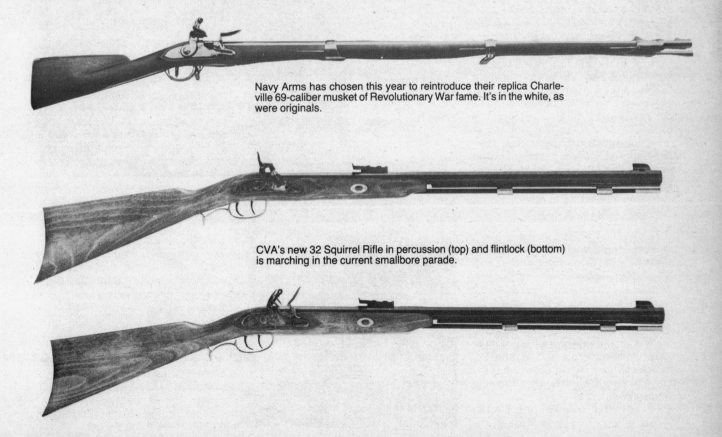

Navy Arms has chosen this year to reintroduce their replica Charleville 69-caliber musket of Revolutionary War fame. It's in the white, as were originals.

CVA's new 32 Squirrel Rifle in percussion (top) and flintlock (bottom) is marching in the current smallbore parade.

The Gibson Products Oklahoma Diamond Jubilee commemorative is a replica 1866 with fancy wood, decorated sideplates and a diamond.

Dixie Gun Works

Dixie has chosen this year to introduce guns for any buckskinner's rack. First is their 10-gauge—they call it "magnum"—shotgun, a double with super thick 30-inch barrels. There's also a "magnum" version of their 12 gauge, with heavier steel tubes than the standard 12. Both are cylinder bored and have a sturdy, hefty feel in the hand. With the 12 gauge I dropped four pheasants last fall (that's good shotgunning for *me*!) and I find the 10 gauge patterns even better than the 12.

Another form of scattergunning is possible with Dixie's Flint Trade Gun, actually a cut-down Brown Bess with a 30-inch barrel. This 74-caliber smoothbore comes with chocolate browning, 1762 pattern lockplate and polished brass furniture. It is close to the classic English pattern trade gun of the early 1800s, and with a few brass tacks in its walnut stock, would look good in the hands of any voyager. And their version of the Model 1806 Harper's Ferry pistol is a formidable flinter in 58 caliber.

Shooters wanting handgunning accuracy, however, might well check out Dixie's Tornado muzzle-loading target pistol, a 45-caliber single shot percussion pistol reminiscent of the old Tingle and B.W. Southgate pistols of the '50s and '60s. The gun comes with adjustable rear sights and trigger pull and oversized walnut target grips that can be custom-fitted to the shooter's hand. This one is built strictly to win matches.

Navy Arms

Navy is now producing many black powder arms completely in the U.S., reversing the former policy that had all of their replicas made in Europe. New in the Navy Arms line this year is a limited edition of 2,500 specially marked 58-caliber Harper's Ferry flintlock pistols, Model of 1806, made for the U.S. Military Police Commission. Also new is a U.S.-made 12-gauge shotgun barrel designed to fit the Thompson/Center Hawken and Renegade rifles.

Of particular interest to me is the return of the Charleville Musket, the

Detail of Oklahoma Commemorative frame with 5-point Diamond. Gun is engraved both sides.

Tornado Target Pistol from Dixie Gun Works features oversized free-pistol grip which may be carved to fit shooter's hand.

Safe-N-Dry Kap Kover is a novel waterproofing device in which a brass cap makes a snug fit over an O-ringed Hot Shot nipple.

Buckskinners looking for personalized scrimshawed powder horns can get them from D. J. Whitehead, sold through Tennessee Valley Manufacturing of Corinth, Mississippi.

69-caliber French flintlock of the American Revolution. Navy first brought this brightly-polished musket to shooters during the Bicentennial celebration back in '76 and demand has been strong enough to warrant its return. Navy is also getting heavily involved with the commemorative line and is creating a special shotgun for the Wild Turkey Federation and a Ned Kelly Commemorative for the Australian market.

Gibson Products

Yes, this does seem like the Year of the Commemoratives and one of the nicest I have seen (and most realistically priced) is the Oklahoma Diamond Jubilee Rifle, a deeply etched replica of the brass-framed Model 66 lever action. This new replica, assembled in the U.S., is chambered for 44-40. Limited to a run of only 1,000 guns, each rifle has a diamond embedded in the left side of its frame, and features deluxe hard-rubbed walnut stock and forearm. Produced by Bill McDuff of Gibson Products in Chickasha, Oklahoma, each of the 1,000 rifles may be purchased with walnut case or gun rack and matching serial-numbered belt buckle, and with a small Bowie-style knife, diamond-inlaid, by Mike England.

Hawken Armory

Ted Jennings did not go out of business, but he did get flooded out in one of those Arkansas squalls Crockett used to tell about. Jennings lost everything—wood, barrels, locks and orders—but now has re-established his gunmaking firm and is back in production with his famed Hawken, Jennings, Dimmick and Cattaraugus County rifles. His frontloaders are strictly for hunting and represent an extremely good value for the money.

He is also one of those gunmakers willing to offer personalized service, such as lengthening or shortening barrel lengths to meet a customer's preference.

Hatfield

Ted Hatfield, whose extremely well-made, attractive and straight-shooting squirrel rifles grace many a small-game hunter's camp is now offering 32, 36, 45 and 50-caliber rifles in percussion as well as flintlock. Like his flinters, the new caplocks are all finely tuned and have fast actions. Half-stock variations of his collector's quality squirrel rifles are also available, as is a new custom service: Ted's shop will build a rifle for you according to blueprints, which you may inspect and augment before the first chisel hits wood. His metal engraving, patchbox work and inlays, all skillfully executed by Dennie Pitts, are among the best for shooters desiring to create an extra fancy personalized muzzle-loading collectible for field or wall.

Traditions Inc.

This new company has a complete line of muzzle-loading rifles and single shot pistols economically priced. Most notable are their Frontier Scout and Kentucky Scout—shortened "Boy's Rifle" versions of full-sized mountain rifles and Kentucky longrifles. Seem to be just the things to get your youngster started in muzzleloading.

Michigan Arms, Euroarms, CVA

Something for non-traditionalists is found in the Wolverine, a unique new muzzleloader produced by Michigan Arms Corporation. For ignition, this bolt-action-looking in-line rifle fires a shotgun primer instead of a percus-

sion cap. A target version with adjustable sights is also available. Euroarms has added a brass-framed 1860 Army to their already extensive line. CVA has an economically priced 32-caliber squirrel rifle in either flint or percussion and a 12-gauge double-barreled percussion shotgun, somewhat British in appearance as it has no buttplate.

Accessories

Trail Guns Armory has seen a need and filled it by creating replacement parts kits for the '51 Navy, '60 Army, the Walker, all models of the Dragoon, the '61 Navy and the 1858 Remington. These kits each contain extra set of nipples, mainspring, trigger, bolt, hand—in short, most of the internal parts that eventually wear out or break at the most inopportune times. Blue and Gray Products have come out with a waterproof plastic form-fitting breech and lock covering called Weatherguard, designed to help keep your powder dry. Also new from B&G are their regular and magnum Speed Shell loaders for shotguns, giving muzzle-loading scattergunners the same quick-reloading convenience that riflemen have enjoyed for decades. K&M Industries has a rather well-thought-out waterproofing device for caplock shooters called Safe-N-Dry Kap Kover (their spelling, not mine), consisting of a brass cover that tightly fits over an Uncle Mike's Hot Shot nipple with a friction-tight "O"-ring in it and very effective. Uncle Mike's #9 Sidekick holster will fit most medium frame cap and ball revolvers with 7½-inch barrels and comes in both black and camouflage for you turkey hunters. Mountain State Muzzleloading now supplies their unbreakable Super-Rod for practically every muzzle-loading longrifle on today's market. ●

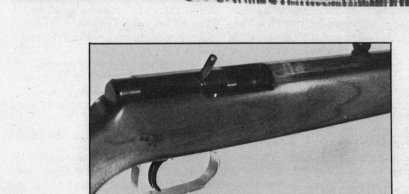

A modern muzzleloader in 45, 50 or 54 caliber is available from Michigan Arms Corp. This is the peep-sighted Friendship Match Special Wolverine. At left is the in-line breech action.

the peep sight

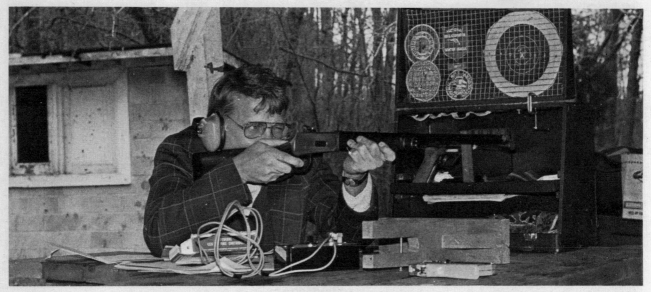

Running accuracy and velocity tests on a Winchester Model 94 that isn't quite like the other 5,000,000 model 94s.

For very little weight, you get a lot more sighting capacity.

by **MARSHALL R. WILLIAMS**

NOT LONG AGO I loaded up some 30-30's with a new load I wanted to try out. I don't have a 30-30 now, but I called my brother and asked to borrow the 30-30 I gave him. When he pulled it out of his car, the receiver sight was missing. He said his son had taken it off because neither of them liked "peep" sights and they didn't understand why I ever put it on the gun. I decided I ought to tell him.

I bought this Model 94 Winchester 30-30 in good used condition some years ago. As 30-30's go it is a pretty good little gun. Its attributes are light weight, adequate power for the deer it is intended to shoot, and very tolerable accuracy. It came with an open U-notch rear sight which had a little step elevator for rather coarse elevation adjustment and the typical bead front sight with cover. Windage adjustment could be made only by hammering one of the sights to the side in its little dovetail.

I got satisfactory accuracy with the gun and with 170-grain bullets it shot more or less to point of aim at 100 yards. With other bullets and loads it shot to different points of aim and there was no satisfactory method for quickly adjusting the sights. I wanted to use the gun for other types of hunting than deer hunting. This included small game with reduced loads and lead bullets and varmints with a fairly fast lightweight bullet. These latter loads didn't shoot near the sight setting of each other or the 170-grain deer load.

The problem had been easily and neatly solved on my other guns by installing a good little low or medium power scope. Unfortunately, the Model 94 ejects its empties out the top of the receiver right where a scope ought to be mounted. There were two possibilities for scope mounting. One involved a scope mount offset about an inch to the left. Such a mount was rig-

id and could use an ordinary scope. However something would have to be done to offset my head so my eye would line up with the scope when the gun was shouldered. Normally this is done by padding the cheekpiece of the stock. I didn't like this arrangement much. It wasn't pretty for one thing. For another you couldn't shoot left-handed and I find it convenient to be able to shoot left-handed occasionally. The other possiblity was to mount a long eye relief scope ahead of the receiver. This would work with the stock as it was and could be used left-handed. On the negative side the field of view of these scopes is limited. Either arrangement would add nearly a pound to the weight of the gun and tend, by that amount, to negate the advantage of light weight.

The obvious solution was a receiver sight. This would give me the ready adjustability I wanted and would improve accuracy somewhat, although not to the degree a scope would. It would add only an ounce or two to the weight of the gun.

At that time a large selection of receiver sights was available from a number of manufacturers. I chose a Lyman Model 66 for its ready availability as much as for any other reason. It is a very good sight but others are probably just as good. Today you can get, in addition to the Lyman 66, a similar sight called the Model 57. Williams makes their excellent "Foolproof" in both a sporting and a target mode along with a bargain called the "5D Economy." It isn't click adjustable but it is a good sight.

The Model 94 receiver comes from the factory already drilled and tapped for this sight so installation took all of about three minutes with a small screwdriver. After installing the receiver sight I adjusted it so it lined up with the U-notch and front sight. I then removed the U-notch part of the rear sight. This would save time and ammunition when I sighted in the gun later.

When I ordered this sight, probably in 1968, it was available with a choice of knurled adjusting knobs you could turn with your fingers or coin-slotted smooth knobs you couldn't. I chose the former on the theory I might not always have a coin. This worked out in practice as I have been penniless much of my adult life. I have never had one of these knobs get accidentally turned so the convenience hasn't cost me any missed shots either.

These knobs have audible clicks for adjusting the sight aperture for both windage and elevation. Elevation and windage adjustments are clearly marked. The current Lyman catalog no longer lists these adjustable knobs so I assume they have been discontinued. The coin adjustable knobs were designed to prevent accidental changing of your sight settings by curious children at home or other shooters at the range.

Each click of adjustment is supposed to be ¼ minute or approximately ¼-inch at 100 yards. These click adjustments make sighting in the gun a fairly simple affair. I usually take my first shots at 25 yards to see if the gun is shooting in the right general direction. At this distance the clicks of adjustment will only have one-fourth of their 100 yard value. Therefore you will need 16 clicks to move your bullet's impact one inch. Once the gun is sighted in at 25 yards I move the targets out to 100 yards for my final sighting. Here you need four clicks for each inch you want your group to move. If you find your 100-yard group centered two inches low and one inch to the right, you raise your rear sight eight clicks and move it four clicks to the left.

These adjustments are fairly consistent and repeatable. Therefore if you wish to shoot two different loads in the gun which don't group to the same point of aim, you may sight it in for one load, and then sight it in for the other load, keeping track of the

adjustments. Then, if you can remember which load the gun is sighted in for, and which load you are using, you can easily make any necessary corrections. If you are like me, however, I recommend you write down the information and tape it to the stock. That way you can look it up when you need it.

What all those clicks are moving around is the sight disc. This has a small hole or aperture drilled in its center and is what you look through. When I bought the Lyman sight, Lyman offered a choice of sight discs ranging in diameter from 5/16-inch up to one inch with a choice of apertures from .040-inch up to .093-inch as standard and for thirty cents extra you could get apertures in any standard drill size from .040-inch to .140-inch. Generally, the small discs and large apertures are for hunting rifles and the large discs and small apertures are for target shooting. As the discs were interchangeable you could get one for hunting and another for target shooting.

I got a ⅜-inch disc with .062-inch aperture as a sort of compromise. It seemed to work fine. If I want a larger aperture I remove the disc altogether and use the socket it screws into. This hole must be about 5/32-inch in diameter and it really adds to the speed with which your sight picture can be picked up.

There probably is some slight loss in precision accuracy with an aperture this large but it is a lot less than

Assuming we wanted to shoot a hog, these illustrations show about what we would see of the pig using a peep sight vs. an open U-notch. In actual use, you would not see the ring of the aperture except as a blur.

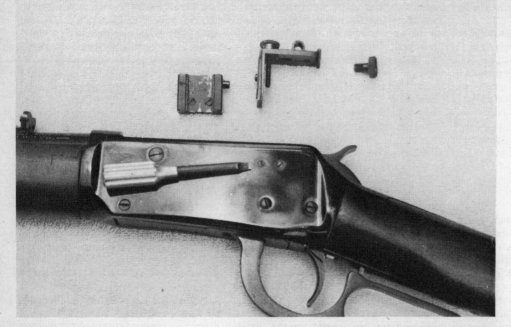

It doesn't take much to install an aperture sight like Lyman's 66—just a screwdriver. And you can use the same front sight.

Author likes the target version, never had click trouble. And he can keep adequate track of several different zeros on the Lyman's slide.

It takes several different zeroes to accommodate a good range of 30-30 loads—the 100-gr. varmint pill at left, the cast load that anchors squirrels, the 170-gr. jacketed game bullet are all useful.

you might expect. On the Model 94 I expected groups on the order of 2½ to 3 inches at 100 yards with the small aperture. With no disc and the large hole I probably got 3 to 3½-inch groups. In contrast, my groups with the open U-notch which came on the gun ran 4 to 6 inches.

I do not know what the accuracy potential of receiver sights is but it is high. I once owned an Anschutz Model 54 match rifle with the Anschutz receiver sight and target front sight. The front sight insert was shaped like a Life Saver lollipop—a post with a circle on top. There was also a lens in the front sight. I was bench-resting some scoped rifles and decided to try the Anschutz. I fired five shots at 100 yards using Federal Champion standard velocity ammunition. Through the spotting scope, I couldn't see but two holes so I walked down for a closer look. To my surprise the two holes were a double and triple and formed a ⅝-inch group. This rifle had a three ounce trigger which didn't hurt my shooting any. That is one of the best 100-yard groups I ever shot with any rifle.

Aperture type sights over the years have come in a variety of styles. The old Lyman No. 1 and Marble's sights were tang sights rather than receiver sights. They mounted on the top tang of older rifles like the Remington and Winchester single shots and the lever-action Winchester. The top tangs of some of these old rifles provide screw holes for mounting the tang sights. Such sights were closer to the shooter's eye than the receiver sights and gave a slightly longer sight radius. I have never used one but many older shooters regarded them highly. These sights normally only adjusted for elevation and it was necessary to make windage adjustments with the front sight. They folded down on the stock when not in use, but I think they were relatively fragile. I have seen a number of rifles with the base for these sights broken off at the joint where the sight folded down.

A very old variation of this is the aperture sight which mounted on the heel of the buttstock of long-range target rifles such as were used by the American and Irish teams at Creedmoor. The shooters used a number of supine positions which allowed the head to be behind the buttstock. This gave the longest possible sight radius and some truly remarkable shooting was done using these. These sights were for very specialized uses and certainly wouldn't be practical for modern shooting.

Another variation was the tang type, only mounted on the cocking piece of bolt action rifles like the Mauser, Mannlicher, and Springfield. This put the sight very close to the eye and no less an authority than Jack O'Connor said it was the fastest sight he had ever used. I have never used one, but I would think it was a little less accurate because it is mounted on the cocking piece which jumps when the firing pin falls and is not rigid in relation to the front sight.

Another variation, one I have used, is on a muzzleloader I made. It is simply a flat piece of spring steel with one end turned up and a hole drilled in it. It screws to the top of the barrel and can be adjusted for elevation. While it isn't much to look at, I can get 3 to 4-inch groups at 100 yards when this gun is properly loaded.

Aperture sights are used a little differently than open sights. With the aperture all you do is look through and place the front sight on your target. There is no need to line up anything as you must with open sights. Instead, when you look through the aperture your eye has a natural tendency to look through the center, where the light is best. It assures that your eye is at the same level no matter where your cheek may be resting on the comb of the stock.

Among the advantages of aperture sights is the speed with which you can aim. I didn't believe the aperture sight was faster until I used one trying for speed of aimed shots but it's true, especially so with a large aperture. With open sights I have to line up the front sight deliberately with the rear sight and then aim this sight picture at the target. With the aperture, you just put the front sight on the target. It's very much like pointing a shotgun. In fact, I believe a large aperture sight on a shotgun would be a good idea. It should cure the problem of moving your head off the stock, a major cause of misses.

Another advantage is that there is no exposed surface on the rear sight to pick up reflections of sunlight and blur one side of your notch. Our local shooting range happens to face southwest and on sunny afternoons it is very difficult to get a clear open sight picture because the sun glares on the left side of your rear sight notch. If I'm going to shoot open sights there I generally make a cardboard sunscreen, but you can't always do this when you are hunting. And you don't have to, with a "peep."

The aperture sights are supposed to be an advantage for older eyes which are losing the ability to focus rapidly. With the aperture one doesn't have to focus on a sight picture made up of a rear sight sitting 18 inches or so behind a front sight and then get them both on a distant target. Instead you simply look through the hole and put the front sight on the target.

Another problem prevented by the aperture is high shooting in poor light. This is a phenomenon mentioned in practically all books on deer hunting. The hunter gets into a brushy area on the shady side of a hill on an overcast day and shoots over top of his quarry. The problem seems to be caused by trying to see the front sight in poor light. Since the sights are harder to see, the shooter raises his head slightly in order to see the front sight clearly. The result is a high shot with a sight picture that looks right. Obviously with the aperture you can't see the front sight or anything else if your head is too high.

Finally, the aperture lets you see more of your target. All types of open rear sights obscure everything below the line of sight. Some, like the full buckhorn design, blot out a good bit on the sides as well. With the aperture you can see everything not covered by the front sight and barrel.

To summarize, a good receiver sight is readily adjustable for both windage and elevation; it is easily installed on most rifles because the required holes are usually drilled and tapped at the factory; you can get different apertures to fit all your shooting needs; it improves accuracy over open sights; it speeds up sight alignment; it eliminates sun glare and low shooting in poor light; it works better for older eyes; and it lets you see more of your target. While it won't do these things quite as well as a scope, it does it with a lot less weight.

All of that, of course, is theory. In practice, I used that old Model 94 with the Lyman peep sight to kill groundhogs at a more or less honest 200 yards, using a 100 grain half-jacket bullet at about 2700 feet per second; I filled a stewpot or two with squirrels using a cast bullet at about 1200 feet per second; and while I never did kill a deer with it, I stoned a couple of coyotes and a javelina; and, finally, I loaned the gun to a friend who promptly went out and won an informal bullseye shoot with it.

So, now, older brother and nephew, you know why I put the receiver sight on the gun. And if it ain't back on the gun the next time I want to borrow it, I ain't gonna borrow it no more.

You hear me, boy? ●

A ten-pound rifle that swats hard saves steps, author contends.

The 45-70 In The Brush . . .

. . . cuts down the trailing for the old feller on the stump.

by FRANK MARSHALL, JR.

This is the gun—it takes scopes two ways and the irons are always there.

THANKS TO THE four-wheel-drive miracle, many of us over-the-hill gang still hang in there. Hunters like us still make it up on the mountain come the magic dawn of new opening day.

Most still go with light-totin', snapshot, so-called deer rifles, our carry-over from the days of the long trekking, usually up hill or hollow all the way, and then the stalk, or stand, or drive in turn. We went light. We had to, but, however attractive the easy carrying misnamed deer rifle, it was never adequate. And it can no longer be justified under today's mobile methods of hunting and especially not in the hands of the stump-standing old codger. Those experienced legs and tickers may not bear up under the rough rundown of the buck not well shot.

After the anxiety of one of those acts, I got real religious suddenly about deer rifles and loads. I needed a no-compromise outfit to minimize or eliminate that chase 'em down bit.

I am assigned, usually, to the so-called flatwoods stand about halfway between up and down. To see the game is a chore, much less shoot it, but the flatwoods stand is typical of most eastern slopes deer coverts.

One way of helping any bullet to the big stag under such a revolting but normal situation is to use the scope to place the shot to avoid the visible obstacle course. That works if the quarry cooperates to any degree, usually unlikely.

Another method uses the heavy, large caliber, smashing brushcutter concept of rifle and cartridge with some disregard allowed for the light twigs and bush intervening, although the target may appear clearly enough at the moment of truth. The latter obviously requires a margin of overkill, for the often less-than-10-ring-area perfect hit, or what is referred to as the "knock 'em anyhow" factor and not to be found in the foot pounds figures of merit. Those fail to consider favorable diameter effect.

In-depth appraisal of pros and cons solely relevant to conditions most applicable to my thick rolling flatwoods

stand indicated a combination of both scope sight and most accurate heavy-for-steady large-caliber rifle for a big can-do cartridge. Not ordained to safari class affluence, nor at my best under the recoil of their Big Bertha rifles and cartridges, which do qualify as candidates for my needs, I went from scratch with economy and fulfillment of the objective given equal priority. Accuracy required a bolt rifle along with the fact that after 50 years on range and afield with a bolt action my natural reaction under duress for a repeat shot would be best served. Further, due to my choice of the old but new solid head 45-70 cartridge and the reload area of whump I expected to work with, the bolt lock was a must.

Coincident to my musings, the Siamese Mauser barreled action came on the scene and in 45-70 caliber. Anxious investigation revealed also a utility grade sporter stock for same, soon available from Fajen and forthwith I had these main ingredients in hands of friendly gunnery smiths. Involved was bolt alteration for scope, express sights and a configuration copied somewhat from British big bore magazine Mausers.

I like to lounge on my old log first class as I leisurely contemplate the wonder of it all. Wood fit and glass work by McNutt and iron work by Lanham resulted in a product over-all equal functionally to any and at cost commensurate to one with twice as much time and half as much money, not to mention the ravages of infla-

tion. From those in the retired ranks, thanks again, guys.

Reloading, both from the economic and requirement aspects, was mandatory since factory loads just wouldn't cut it on the flatwoods stand, and the price of factory was out of my reach. Testing loads, sighting in and the considerable familiarization courses of fire I like to shoot uses up a lot of cartridges.

Jacketed 405-grain bullets were in for a few sessions because I had some from an old trade deal and I had moulds of several weights and forms from round balls to 500-gr. Cached also was a keg and a half of lead secured solely by scrounging the backstops.

Cases, powder and primers were all I'd need. Time and tools I had to suffice.

With the reincarnation of the 45-70 recently, so it showed up at Sighting-In days at the club range, I even managed to boil down my needs to only powder and caps. That is, I scrounged the cases, too.

The powder best by test for both accuracy and ornery with 405-grain jacketed bullets was IMR 3031, allowing over 1800 fps and 3000-plus ft. lbs. of wallop at the muzzle. Through judicious experiment I managed to get the cast gas-check #457483 economy load to match that. This cast slug seated to touch lands, is long-loaded, but still functions through this particular Siamese Mauser magazine. Its accuracy will shade the jacketed loads if I use match load reload procedures.

Pressure signs as loaded and in this rifle are moderate at any time of the year. The barrel is 24″ long .458″ groove, .45″ bore with a close concentric chamber. I size this cast bullet to .459″ in the Lyman #450, Alox lubed.

This outfit, I found, is not hard to handle at 10 pounds. Accuracy with either load is above average, even for rifles considered as top choice sporters.

I conducted brush and branches tests in the thick flatwoods parallel to my private test range on the lower slopes of the Blue Ridge. A running deer target pasted to a piece of plywood was shot at through brush, branches, bushes and twigs, since my flatwoods stand offers the same obstacles.

The scope sight under such conditions reveals many small branches and twigs that would go unnoticed with open sights. Shooting with loads duplicating the factory 405-grain jacketed at 1300 fps quickly revealed why this ancient and honorable load

You can expect to get kidded about your thumb-sized cartridges until one of those 400-gr. bullets hits a deer.

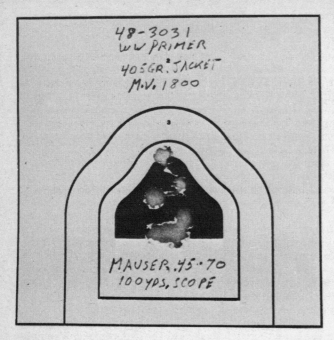

48-3031
WW PRIMER
405GR. JACKET
M.V. 1800

MAUSER .45-70
100 YDS, SCOPE

Steadied down, Marshall can deliver the 100-yard goods when his 45-70 is scoped.

And, when his scope is in his other suit, Marshall can manage with iron sights.

has survived all comers over a century of brush and woods work. Tests of the revived 300-grain factory fast loads were notable unless the shot had to get through more than 50 yards of light twigs. The slower 405-grain load punched on through some pretty heavy stuff for 75-yard hits.

It is most significant that very little is required to deflect any bullet from a deer-size target even at close range. The 405-grain jacketed or cast at 1800 fps proved best both for brush work and my ability to shoot it well which is equally necessary.

This is not for shooting through nine Christmas trees in a line, but for normal woods and brushy deer cover common to little 'ol Virginia white-tails, the most hunted big game species on this continent. Knowing the shots fired under what conditions, with what calibers and rifles, would be very revealing from the gunnery viewpoint. As of now, only data on bagged game is given.

If a buck comes to the checking point, brought to bag with a 30-06, then it was adequate, right? Wrong as hell most of the time, pardner. We get no count on wounded, missed and/or brush-deflected shots. Shooter error is one thing; inadequate armament is the other and most easily corrected.

When you can't chase 'em down no more, and you face up to the facts, you get nitty gritty as to how it is and what it takes. Unless you do, you got no business on that flatwoods stump

at opening dawn unless you go for fresh air and prayer.

A couple of old grizzled gunny-writers have been voices in the wilderness dispensing down to earth advice, but alas, the flat-out flamethrower 1000-yard match-type cartridges have held the limelight too long.

When I first tracked my new rifle into camp, I got the usual comments like "Where's the wheels?" Or, "How much yuh pay gun bearers these days, Duke?" Or "Ol' Duke just shoots for kicks anyhow, with firewood cuttin's thrown in, no charge."

Of course, I loved it all.

The one I liked best was, "Duke decks 'em, guts 'em, cuts a trail to 'em and has plenty of firewood to fricassee the pieces, if any."

I did not get into this 45-70 Express special project wet behind the ears, having witnessed the merits of this great one over a half a hundred years. Even at lower level for trapdoor rifles, no so-called modern deer rifle can match that old 500 grain standard looping along through at 1150 fps or so.

In fact, I would have gone gladly with the heavier, longer 500-grain cast bullet but I could not get the steam up for my velocity ideas in this 45-70 case, and I had the quantity of factory jacketed bullets which I wanted to mate up to a 400-grain cast load as to approximate impact and power. Those two bullets seem suited to this twist rate at 1800 fps. The 500-grain

would need a couple hundred more fps, not very plausible in a 45-70 case.

Factory loads of 300 grains at 1800 fps and 405 grains at 1300 fps are available with the 1800 fps loads probably suited only to certain reproduction rifles along with the Ruger, Marlin and Navy Arms Mauser. Smokeless jacketed loads of any type should simply not be fired in the old original black powder rifles, well distributed in this country. With the variety of 45-70 rifles around today as new offerings, why strain the old and priceless family heirloom?

All in all, the rifle and load concept jelled perfectly. However, I am getting that urge again, with ideas forming around a down-loaded 458 Winchester with cast loads. Could I go 1800 with 500 grains for openers and work up?

Mine hospitable hosts down in the deer woods didn't get to own two mountains with an airstrip between them by being dummies. They notice a good proposition right now.

My meat on the table 80-yard (paced) shot under previously considered "not possible even with luck conditions" won me the gunnery wizardry award my first outing with 45-70 chain saw. It also, the very next season, put a few more 45-70s on the camp rack and more venison on the poles with less huffin' puffin', and moanin' and groanin'. In the doin', it's fun again. ●

Rimfires and hickory trees go together in squirrel season.

REMINGTON 513-S:

A man-sized rimfire sporter from a while ago worth searching for today.

by KENNETH BOLIN

I BECAME interested in guns and hunting back in the 1950s as a teenager. At that time, I overlooked bolt-action rimfires because one could buy a good slide-action or autoloader like Winchester's 61 or 63 for comparable sums of money. And I thought in terms of firepower. Experience taught me that stalking ability and shot placement is what gets the squirrels and rabbits.

After I owned several fine bolt-action centerfire rifles, my attention turned to better grade bolt-action rimfires. When I saw an illustration of the Remington 513-S in the reprinted edition of the 1951 GUN DIGEST, I knew it was the one I wanted. An extensive search of old stores, pawn shops, garage sales, and gun shows finally produced one.

Fancy bolt-action 22s were never very common nor big sellers. They have only in the last few years gained the attention from shooters they deserve. The Remington 513-S was manufactured from 1941 to 1956 but was little advertised; at least, it was not advertised as much as its direct counterpart, the 513-TR. The 513-TR was reasonably popular, being used during World War II as a training arm, and later by rifle clubs for the less serious junior shooters.

The 513-S looks like a genuine big-

game gun. It hefts a good seven pounds without scope or sling. It is decidedly muzzle heavy, and that extra weight aids steady holding for those demanding long-range shots. The muzzle heavy balance stems from the 27-inch barrel, .700-inch in diameter at the counterbored muzzle. The barrel, labeled "Matchmaster," is the same length as that on the 513-T target rifle and is no doubt from the same stock, only slimmed down a bit. The potential for accuracy is there in that barrel, and I'll discuss it later.

The stock of the 513-S is, to me, the most attractive feature of the rifle. It is truly classic in every way. Arms companies are just discovering that many American gun lovers adore the classic look. The stock comb is high enough for scope mounting, although few scopes were used on sporter 22s when it was built. I imagine the design was intended for use with higher iron target sights.

Incidentally, the 513-S barrel originally came with a raised ramp front sight and a Marble No. 63 step-adjustable rear sight. The receiver was tapped for the Redfield 75 receiver peep and a slot was provided under the ramp for use of a globe target sight. One version was offered with Remington's own economical receiver sight and designated the 513-SP.

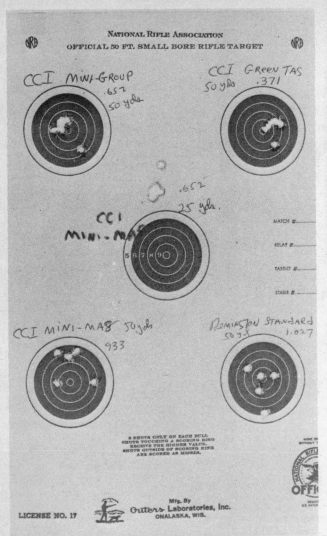

Very few brands are very bad in Bolin's 513-S, but some are, as usual, better than others.

For the fellow who sits it out to make one shot count, the 513-S is ideal, author feels.

The mechanical underpinnings of the 513-S are plenty stout, provide no problems over long use.

It's the game rifle heft of this model that gives it its glamour for the writer.

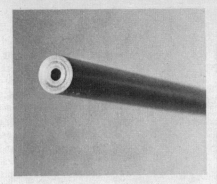

Very special crowning on Matchmaster class barrel is one of extra 513-S touches.

The big-gun metal buttplate provides a look you can't get another way.

When deer—or bigger game—seasons come, a good bolt-action rifle is no stranger to the 513-S owner.

The steel buttplate shows the look of quality. The grip and fore-end are generously hand-checkered. This adds both beauty and utility. The contour of the forearm is nicely slimmed with very little wood from stock edge to barrel. Though I have not seen enough samples to say for sure, I can verify that the wood in my rifle's stock is superb for a production made 22 and is better than that on many 52 Winchester sporters and other famous makes.

The detachable sling swivel studs must have almost been a first to come on a 22. I was unsure they were original until I checked it out in a 1941 Remington brochure and parts price list. The trigger guard, magazine plate, and magazine are metal. Thank goodness, the rifle has no plastic about it anywhere. The six-shot magazine fits nearly flush with the stock, providing a clean profile.

Though not as heavy as the receiver of a Winchester 52, the action of the 513-S is a good one and plenty strong for a 22 rimfire. The bolt has twin extractors and the firing pin is painted red on the end making it easy to tell when it's cocked. The side safety is rocker type. The beehive-shaped bolt handle is amply large and easily grasped. Bolt handles on most 22s are too small.

Triggers are one of the most important features of a rifle. The 513-S has the same adjustable trigger as the 513-T. It's a simple design that moves pressure on and off the sear, and it works very well. The trigger of my rifle, with all pressure removed is about 2-2½ pounds without creep or backlash.

Creditable performance is mandatory for a rifle that will be used rather than merely admired in the gun rack. The heavy target-type barrel of the 513-S will deliver that commendable accuracy. Like any 22 rifle, different brands of ammo must be tested to find which vibrates the best in a particular barrel. I found high-velocity ammo delivered acceptable though not outstanding accuracy. Five-shot groups with this ammo generally averaged a little over an inch at 50 yards. Standard velocity brands such as Federal Champion, Remington standard, and CCI Mini-group did much better, with groups averaging ¾-inch. As might be expected, match-grade ammo performed best. CCI Green Tag averaged about ½-inch consistently. One grade of famous brand match ammo, which I will not name, performed horribly to the tune of 2-inch groups. That incident graphically illustrates how critical certain barrels react to certain ammunition.

It takes a good scope to wring the ultimate accuracy from the 513-S. The receiver must be drilled and tapped to accommodate top mounts for a good full-sized scope. I chose Weaver top mounts for my rifle. The receiver can be drilled forward and rear, or the barrel can be drilled for the front mount. Weaver specifications call for a barrel-mounted front base and provide the No. 44 forward and No. 43 rear.

I personally prefer to use two No. 43 bases, both on the receiver. I have had scopes with front mounts on barrel and rear mount on receiver that would not group well. One would think a 22 rimfire would not heat up nor vibrate enough to make a difference, but I believe they can. With minor exceptions, the receiver-mounted one-inch scope will have plenty of latitude for proper eye-relief positioning.

Remington 513-S models are hard to find. The shooter and hunter wanting a fancy "big-caliber looking" bolt action 22 today may have to be satisfied with a substitute. The new Kimber 82 or Savage-Anschutz 54 come to mind as such. If, however, you should stumble into a 513-S in a shop, attic, or gun show, you'll know from reading this what one 22 afficionado thinks you should do—buy it! ●

One Good Gun

Good balance, combined with fast repeat shots make the Model 63 a natural for hunting big, Idaho jackrabbits in sagebrush flats.

THEY CAME OUT of the brush just after midnight for the third time that night. In the light from the full moon their dark bodies made shadows against the whiteness of the snow; their padded feet thudded on the icy crust. Pushing off the safety, I quickly picked up a big one in the rifle scope running straight at me; the tapered post recticle black against his chest. At the shot he tumbled. Quickly, I fired the remaining nine cartridges in the magazine, dropping one with each round. But, I was all alone, and they were at battalion strength. Before I could reload, they reached my position and started eating the hay.

It was January 8, 1982, near Mud Lake, Idaho during one of the worst jackrabbit epidemics in history; so bad that it gained national attention both in the press and on TV news. Concentrations of jackrabbits during the wintertime are a common problem throughout much of the sagebrush West, but nothing like this! This one began in August, after a severe, summer drought forced the rabbits to migrate out of the sagebrush uplands of the Snake River Plains down to the irrigated farms along the Snake River.

Like a swarm of locusts, they chewed down the alfalfa and ripening wheat, and every ten rabbits ate as much as a big steer. By Christmas, 1981, deep snows covered the raped cropland and only the haystacks were left. And I was up on a haystack trying to keep them off it with my old Winchester Model 63.

This was old hat to me and my 63

WINCHESTER 63
The real classics never get old

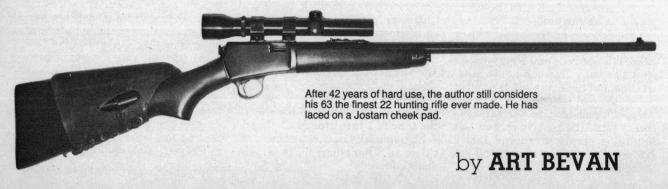

After 42 years of hard use, the author still considers his 63 the finest 22 hunting rifle ever made. He has laced on a Jostam cheek pad.

by ART BEVAN

model. Since 1940, the two of us have spent time every winter shooting rabbits off farmlands. After firing thousands of rounds at rabbits, often in bitter cold weather, without a single breakdown, I'm convinced that the Winchester Model 63 is the finest 22 semi-auto rifle ever produced by anyone, and I'm here to talk about it:

Back in 1904, Winchester introduced their first semi-auto, the Model 1903, chambered for a brand-new rimfire cartridge, the 22 Winchester Automatic Smokeless, firing a 45-grain bullet at 1055 feet per second. This new rifle was designed by Thomas Crossley Johnson, a design genius with Winchester, who created many famous guns, including such greats as the Model 12 pump shotgun, the Model 52 target rifle, and the Model 54, forerunner of the famous Model 70. So, designed by a genius, the new Model 1903 had a lot going for it right from the start. Then, in 1933, after thirty years and a production run of 126,000 rifles, Winchester redesigned the old Model 1903 to handle the more popular, efficient, and cheaper high velocity, 22 Long Rifle cartridge. They called this revamped rifle the Model 63.

In their 1933 catalog, Winchester described the Model 63 action as having *A Balanced Breech Bolt Recoil Operated Mechanism,* but most folks know it simply as *a blow-back action.* The Model 63's breech bolt's weight is carefully proportioned to the weight and velocity of the bullet, so that the recoil movement activates the action just as the bullet is leaving the barrel. Blow-back actions don't use part of the gas pressure to activate the ac-

tion, so you get a simple design without loss of velocity or energy. But the blow-back action only works well with one specific cartridge, and so the Model 63 cannot be used with shorts and longs. On balance as I see it, the Model 63 has the simplest, and most efficient type action for 22 rimfire, semi-auto rifles.

The second outstanding design feature of the Model 63 has to be the cartridge feeding system, with the tubular magazine located inside the buttstock. Indeed, after considering all the advantages of this design, one wonders why tubular magazines were ever stuck under the forearm.

First, consider reliability of feeding, which is surely the most important consideration of any semi-auto's loading system; the Model 63 seems to be as reliable and smooth-working as a much-used Colt Match Target, or High Standard Supermatic target pistol, and that's just about 100%. The forward end of the Model 63's magazine is formed into a massive loading ramp extending right up to the chamber entrance. The breech bolt slides each cartridge out of the magazine, up the loading ramp, and straight into the chamber. It's a very short, straight-line, solid feeding path, from the big loading port in the buttstock to the chamber.

In sharp contrast, consider all the under-barrel tubular magazines, where the cartridges enter the receiver butt-end first; then each cartridge has to be lifted up to the correct loading elevation by mechanical fingers before the breech bolt can strip them off the fingers, and then push them into the chamber. This is a much long-

er and more complicated loading path. The Model 63 just slides them straight in and that's why it hardly ever misses.

Other advantages of the tubular magazine in the butt are that it is better protected from the weather, and from accidental damage. Loading the Model 63 is safer, too, because the end of the barrel is tipped down. You just turn it on its side, point the barrel towards the ground, and then pour the cartridges into the big porthole in the buttstock. It's much faster than fingering individual cartridges into a tiny loading slot out under the barrel.

The Model 63 seems to shoot a little better than other 22 rifles with two-piece stocks. Certainly, the tubular magazine in the butt stiffens the joint where the buttstock joins the receiver. Naturally, a manufacturer always does its best work on the more expensive rifles in its line, and the Model 63 was always an expensive rifle. Even forty years ago, my rifle cost more than a brand-new Model 94 30-30. Replacement barrels for the Model 63 once cost more than any other Winchester 22, except for the Model 52 target rifle. Whatever the reason, after tens of thousands of rounds, my old 63 still groups into less than 1½-inches at 50 yards.

The Model 63's breech bolt is manually activated by a push-rod extending out 1¼-inches from the steel forearm tip. By pushing this rod all the way in, and then turning it slightly clockwise, the action is locked open. This push-rod is much neater than the common, awkward, unsightly knob projecting out from the breech bolt that catches on brush, scabbards, etc.

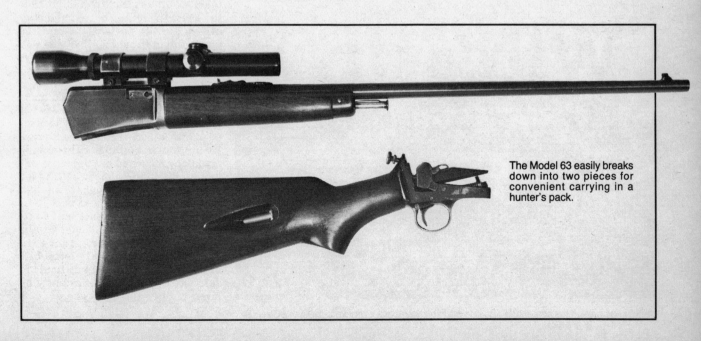

The Model 63 easily breaks down into two pieces for convenient carrying in a hunter's pack.

The safety on the Model 63 is a small, neat, push-button located in the rear of the trigger guard. It is very positive in action, and almost impossible to brush off accidently. Also, the trigger finger can't push on the safety and pull on the trigger at the same time.

The Model 63 ejects its hot empties out to the side, rather than down into the crook of your elbow, as is the case with some other 22 semi-autos. This side ejection, combined with its flat, rather massive receiver, makes the Model 63 well adapted to scope use. Thirty years ago, I had my rifle's receiver milled-out to accept a dovetail scope mount. I then mounted a Weaver K 2.5 scope very low; almost down on top of the receiver. Next, I laced-on a Jostam Number 2 leather cheek pad to raise the stock comb up to scope height. This combination has worked out perfectly for me, as I can cheek the stock comb very hard which helps me greatly on offhand running shots.

The Model 63 is conveniently taken-down by means of the slotted-screw located at the rear of the receiver, and the cartridges feed right straight up that big spout.

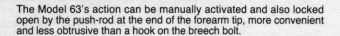

The Model 63's action can be manually activated and also locked open by the push-rod at the end of the forearm tip, more convenient and less obtrusive than a hook on the breech bolt.

Like all truly classic rifles, the Model 63 is constructed entirely of steel and walnut; there isn't a piece of plastic or aluminum on it anywhere! Even the buttplate is made of checkered steel! Although the action can be taken-down by means of a large, slotted screw located at the rear of the receiver, the two parts of the receiver are so finely fitted together that one can barely discern the joint. Truly, this is old-time factory workmanship at its finest!

In 1958, Winchester stopped making the Model 63 because the cost of production became too great to compete with other, cheaper semi-autos. Even though 174,692 of them were made, the Model 63 has become a collectors item today, often selling for well over $300.00. Perhaps it was just good luck, or perhaps it was T. C. Johnson's design genius, but whatever the reasons, the Model 63 has that certain something, that rare combination of materials, form, balance, and workmanship difficult to describe, but recognized instantly by lovers of fine rifles everywhere. ●

Author has proven his contention with hundreds of jackrabbits every year for over 40 years.

This is the very Bearcat of which the cowboy speaks.

RUGER'S LITTLE BEAUTY...

... caught this cowboy early.

by ROBERT K. SHERWOOD

SOMETIMES the young are dazzled by looks alone. I was young in 1958, and easily dazzled. I leaned on the display case in Bill Ives's sporting goods store in St. Anthony, Idaho, and leered in dumbstruck wonder at a precise and petite beauty down there on the green felt. It was a very youthful Ruger Bearcat 22 revolver, and it had me for good and all. I couldn't see another firearm in the store. I pulled out my checkbook, hoped my expense check would beat Bill's deposit, and surrendered myself to $49.95 worth of sheer folly—I thought.

After I finished showing off the lovely little gun, I took several boxes of 22 Long Rifles and one of 22 shorts and went out to see what the little handgun might do. It took a while to determine this; the 17-ounce weight and the small grip made for difficult holding in the beginning. It was tricky, but one can forgive the right gun a lot of eccentricities. I did ease up the pull a little with a point file across the dog. When I adjusted to the size, shape and weight I found the little gun to be as accurate as any production 22 short iron built for service and sport.

The short sight radius limited effective range at first—another whim to adjust to—but 150 rounds saw a lot of improvement, and it was never the complication that the two-inch barrel of a snubbie was. I could keep them all on the shiny end of a beer can at 15 yards, and I asked no more than that from a 22 sidearm. I couldn't shoot any better than that anyway.

So for years thereafter, I wandered around with the unobstrusive Bearcat in my belt or boot. Once in a while I'd take it out just to look at it, always to be impressed by the neat and graceful lines. Perhaps because of its attractiveness and certainly because of its convenience, I found myself carrying the Bearcat more waking hours than not.

I had a field job with the Idaho Fish & Game Department, which meant I had constant opportunity to shoot

It doesn't take much leather or room, so it has gone along with Sherwood for 25 years.

The point is that a working fellow wants to carry not even a little bit more than he absolutely has to.

varmints on the job, and small game for meat in season. In those days a Department officer rarely carried a big sidearm on duty; it was a kindlier time when the most lawless of violators were little inclined to make a $25.00 misdemeanor into a full-fledged felony, and there was always room on my belt for a rabbit gun.

Rabbits it got. For several years following my purchase of the Bearcat, Idaho was inundated by certain millions of black-tailed jackrabbits and any time one cleared the city limits he was in sight of potential targets. They were shot on sight and slaughtered in drives by nearly everyone, which made them a bit spooky. However, I'd often jump one out of thick greasewood or a pile of tumbleweed and get a close range shot at him. I learned to point the Bearcat and took a surprising number of bouncing bunnies without bothering with the sights.

In the fall, cottontails were legal game and the Idaho fluffbutts kept me from starving the first year I worked that hardluck job. The Bearcat was always on my belt, on the job and off, whenever I was in the field. It was certain insurance that I wouldn't pass

Small as it is, the Bearcat gives a full four-inch barrel's worth of 22 ballistics, which is a long way beyond being unarmed.

up any cottontails over the price of shotshells when bird hunting and it was the prime grouse and snowshoe hare collector for big game camp skillets.

It eventually turned out that a lot of deer, elk, bears, antelope, and mountain goats got their final mercy bullet in the ear from the Bearcat. A 22 bullet ruins nothing in the way of cape or meat when applied to ear orifice or to the back of the skull between the antler pedicels. I guided for a number of seasons in Montana and here the handy gun really proved its worth, both as a camp meat collector and as a finisher for big critters. There isn't much need for a guide to carry any sidearm other than a 22; bigger ones are surplus on power for blue grouse and finalizing shots, and their ammunition presents a bulk problem. The Bearcat was all the 22 handgun I needed in that time.

Now, many will say, and they are right or nearly so, that any reliable 22 revolver would have served me well through the years, and that a lot of autoloaders in that caliber would have, too. I don't suppose I could have done anything with the little Ruger that I couldn't duplicate with a heftier Ruger 22, or with a Colt or S&W. It's been a somewhat harried 26 years, though, and the dainty Bearcat was made to order for man leading a more-than-active outdoor life. Most handguns of that weight and size are much less efficient. Larger ones offer problems that offset their value to me. Generally, they require extra leather; the Bearcat is no problem hung on a pants belt. You hardly know it's there. My duty tours involved falls, plenty of them, and the cylinders of the larger revolvers are sometimes bone bruisers. On long back-pack trips, one counts ounces; the Bearcat was the least weight I could carry and still say I was armed.

A hunter, or anyone else out in the timber just for fun, can carry any arm or arms he wants to without too much undue inconvenience. He really doesn't have anything to do but carry guns and shoot them. A working guide and packer needs a sidearm quite as much as does his recreational cronie, perhaps more so, but he must have a convenient and compact one. He can afford neither weight nor bulk; he has many functions other than being an arms rack and firing device; and he can't afford much firearm consideration until he needs one. The Bearcat was what I needed.

The alloy frame and low price might indicate a gun with short effective life. It didn't. My neat companion held up through a lot of rough and tumble, and certainly it fired something over 20,000 rounds during all that time and travail, and it shoots very well today. In all the miles and rounds I had but one malfunction. The little Allen screw that secures the plunger bearing on the cylinder hand backed out and fell somewhere in the soft duff of the Madison River drainage, and I finished the season out turning the cylinder with my front foot for next shots. It was inconvenient, but not a catastrophe. I suggest that Bearcat owners Loc-tite this particular screw.

The Bearcat and I continue; I carry it now, more days than not. It still has the same uses and convenience, and I'll wear out before it does. Now and then I draw it and look at it to be sure it looks as good as it did in '58. It does, every time. ●

Given the inclination and enough opportunities like this, Sherwood says, and even a running jack isn't safe.

Dinner can be, for any passerby with a 22 revolver, almost any cottontail that will sit tight at ten yards.

SEEING THE array of short-barreled sporting and military rifles being made today, a shooter is forced to wonder if long barrels are obsolete. The trend in modern rifles seems to be to shorter and ever shorter barrels. In some ways this seems strange, as long-barreled rifles were an American tradition for some time.

The earliest uniquely American rifle was the Kentucky or Pennsylvania rifle. It was characterized by a long barrel, generally 40 to 44 inches in length. The long barrel made the rifle muzzle heavy, giving greater steadiness for the offhand shots usually taken. The balance point was well forward of the lock mechanism for easy carrying while traveling through the woods on foot.

As America moved westward, horseback travel increased, and the long slender Kentucky was awkward on a horse. Barrels shortened to about 32 to 36 inches, still long by modern standards.

The first U.S. military rifle was the Model 1803 Harpers Ferry. The rifle was adopted just in time to be used on the Lewis and Clark expedition of 1804. Barrel length was approximately 32 inches. This was later felt to be too short, and was increased to 36 inches in 1814.

By the time of the Civil War, the standard military arm was the rifle-musket, with a 40-inch barrel. A group of infantry armed with such rifles had little to fear from a cavalry unit armed only with the traditional sabers and pistols. Perhaps this situation led to extensive arming of cavalry with carbines. Carbines were short, allowing them to be hung from a saddle or slung on the rider's side from a shoulder strap. Yet they were adequately powerful to give the cavalry firepower approaching that of the infantry. Thus, about the time of the Civil War, the short-barreled carbine came into extensive use in America for the first time.

The concept of long rifles and short carbines carried on for some time. Trapdoor Springfields were made in several barrel lengths—the standard was 32 inches for rifles and 22 inches for carbines. The adoption of the Krag in 1892 saw a 30-inch rifle and a 22-inch carbine. The contemporary military rifles of other countries were long-barreled, and only to cavalry were short carbines issued.

Sporting rifles followed suit and were offered in rifle and carbine lengths. By the 1890s certain lengths had become more or less standard—rifles had 26-inch barrels and carbines had 20-inch barrels.

During the development of the 1903 Springfield, early experimental versions had 30-inch barrels. It was decided that, rather than develop two different lengths for cavalry and infantry uses, one length could suffice for both.

In 1902 a special lot of 100 Krag rifles had been made with 26-inch barrels, "splitting the difference" between the 30-inch rifle and the 22-inch carbine. This length was acceptable to infantry units, but was felt to be still too long for mounted use. The final Springfield barrel of 24 inches was a compromise between the 22-inch carbine and the 26-inch experimental Krag barrels.

The Germans apparently were impressed with the performance of the then-short Springfield in World War I.

An Italian Carcano rifle (30.7-inch barrel) is 36 percent longer than a Carcano carbine, with muzzle blast 54 percent farther from the shooter's face. The long one is much more comfortable to shoot.

Everywhere you turn, barrels are getting shorter...

Are Long Barrels Obsolete?

by JOHN MALLOY

The short gun, here a Carcano carbine, does have transportation and storage and weight advantages, but offers few shooting benefits.

After the war, the barrel length of their 1898 Mauser rifle was shortened from 29 inches to 23.5 inches.

Within a few years after the First World War, mounted troops were no longer important, but the United States never went back to long barrels. When we entered World War II, the M1 Garand rifles carried by our troops had 24-inch barrels. The M1 was superceded by the M14, with a 22-inch tube. It in turn was superceded by the M16, with a 20-inch barrel as standard.

Sporting rifles shrank along with the military rifles. Standard barrel lengths for rifles went from 26 to 24 to 22 inches. Carbines remained stable at 20 inches, but a trend to 18½ inches has become apparent in the last few years.

Early in 1980, Remington announced 18½ inches as the standard length for all its Model 788 rifles in big game calibers. About the same time, Winchester re-introduced an even-shorter 16-inch barrel version of its Model 94 Carbine as a trapper carbine. The trend to ever shorter barrels is clear, and only a few reversals can be seen.

Some years ago, Winchester revived 24- and 26-inch versions of its Model 94, but they were soon discontinued. Marlin offered the 336A, a 24-inch version of its Model 336 recently, but has withdrawn it.

A few bolt-action target rifles still have long barrels. Strangely enough, 22 target rifles are offered with barrels up to 28 inches, whereas the longest barrel available on a high-power target rifle is 26 inches. For sporting rifles, several makers list 24-inch barrels. The Weatherby Mark V is available in 26 inches for all calibers, as are some custom and import rifles.

Modern single-shot rifles by Browning and Ruger have 26-inch versions,

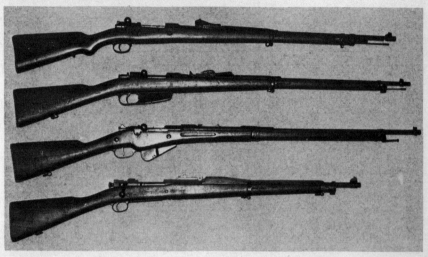

The 1903 Springfield (bottom) was the shortest standard rifle used in the First World War. It set a pattern of short-barrel rifles for the years to come. The others are, from the top: German 1898 Mauser, 29-inch barrel; Italian 1891 Carcano, 30.7-inch barrel; French 1916 Berthier, 31.4-inch barrel.

and Harrington & Richardson produced its 45-70 Shikari as a 28-incher.

But these few exceptions constitute only a tiny fraction of the rifles produced today. Clearly, the trend is to short barrels.

Consider this: Almost all modern rifles would have been classed as carbines at the turn of the century. Even as we experience this trend, we should ask ourselves whether short barrels really are superior. Are long-barrel rifles obsolete?

At one time, long barrels were thought to be more accurate. This is not really true; there is no difference in inherent accuracy between long and short barrels. However, there may be a difference in practical accuracy for iron-sighted rifles because a longer barrel allows a longer sight radius, with greater sighting precision possible.

A long barrel gives some appreciable gain in velocity and a corresponding gain in energy. Many sources indi-

cate a velocity increase of about 25 to 30 feet per second per additional inch of barrel length, or an equivalent loss for shorter barrels. This rule of thumb generally considers a 24-inch, 30-06-class rifle as a standard, however scarce such a rifle may be. The exact figure depends on caliber of the rifle used, powder type and charge, and of course varies with individual rifles. Caliber for caliber, though, a long barrel on a rifle gives a finite increase in velocity.

In practical terms this velocity increase means it is possible to get the power of a large cartridge by using a smaller cartridge in a longer barrel. With equivalent bullets, a 26-inch 270 would come very close to the power of a 22-inch 264 Winchester Magnum or 7mm Remington Magnum. Of these three, the long-barrel 270 would have the least recoil, blast and noise.

To carry this line of thinking further, consider the old 30-40 Krag with its 30-inch barrel. Such a rifle can ap-

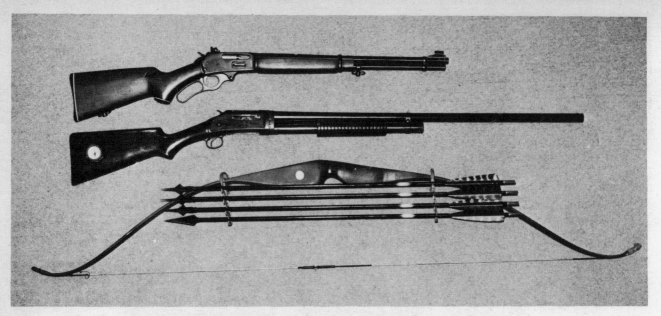

All these were used by the author on Louisiana and Texas deer hunts. The 12-inch difference in barrel length is of little significance compared with the size of the bow. Only the bow was difficult to maneuver in heavy brush.

proximate the power of a 308 with a 20-inch barrel or a 30-06 with an 18-inch shorty. Imagine how pleasant to shoot a long 30-40 would be compared to the punishment of firing the stubby carbines with the bigger cartridges.

Still, tortured logic can argue that with modern powders, short rifles can duplicate velocities of early powders in longer barrels, so performance is not really less than before, though less than it could be. Even if we accept this, short barrels can deliver standard performance only at the expense of increased noise and muzzle blast.

This increased noise and blast is perhaps the greatest disadvantage of short-barrel rifles. If no ear protection is worn during extensive shooting with a modern high-power rifle with a short barrel, hearing damage is almost sure to occur. For sensitive ears, even ear plugs and muffs may not be able to attenuate all the harmful effects of this noise and blast. Any great amount of shooting with short-barrel rifles and big cartridges produces discomfort to the shooter and may cause some permanent hearing loss. A long barrel allows more powder burning time inside the bore, and less beyond the muzzle. This not only subdues noise and blast, but gets the harmful effects farther from the shooter's ears and face.

So there are some benefits to long barrels! It seems evident that, caliber for caliber, a long-barrel rifle will be somewhat more powerful than a

short-barrel rifle. Also, while shooting enough to really be proficient, one is subjected to less discomfort and stands less chance of suffering hearing loss with a long barrel.

With such obvious advantages of long barrels, why are barrels getting shorter and shorter?

Well, a short rifle is required for hunting in the brush, isn't it? There is no denying that short rifles are fast handling in or out of the woods, but they are not appreciably better than longer firearms. I realized this on Louisiana deer hunts, where brush was heavy and firearms used fell into two general categories—30-30 carbines with 20-inch barrels and 12-gauge shotguns with 28 and 30-inch barrels. Both short rifles and long shotguns seemed to perform in the brush adequately, and deer were killed with both types.

It doesn't take much thinking to explain this situation. Hunting from a stand or a fixed position, a hunter will choose a spot that affords clear zones of fire, and barrel length is of little importance.

Still hunting or stalking is a slow process, with the hunter moving slowly, picking his position with each step. A careful hunter will avoid getting tangled in briars or thick brush, and will allow room to maneuver his gun as well as himself.

There are places where short-barrel rifles are truly better than their long-barrel counterparts. One instance is

in the hunting of dangerous game at close range, particularly wounded dangerous game. From what I've read, tracking a wounded bear in the Alaskan alders or stalking a lion or buffalo in the dense African bush would make me yearn for the fastest-handling, most powerful rifle I could carry. In these cases, muzzle blast would be the least of the hunter's worries.

Short rifles also come into their own in the realm of transport. A short carbine will ride in a saddle scabbard or nestle into a gun rack in a pickup window as no long-barreled rifle ever can.

Still, if the average shooter is honest with himself, he will probably admit that very little of his hunting is done in places where a longer barrel would be a handicap. The instances in which a short barrel is needed are far fewer than the number of short barrels in use.

When all the facts are in, long barrels have definite advantages: They offer a real increase in velocity and energy. Comfort and hearing protection are greatly improved. With metallic sights, practical accuracy may be better.

Rather than following the trend to short barrels, consider whether a longer barrel on your next rifle might not serve your needs better. You may find you have a more effective rifle that you enjoy shooting more, because in terms of practical advantages, long-barreled rifles are definitely not obsolete.

THE BOLT ACTION STOPPER STOCK

by **JACK LOTT**

Author's stock for big-bore Mauser: Less wood behind recoil lug; but plenty in the web behind the magazine. He uses original triggers.

FEW AMERICAN hunters now indulge in African safaris, but the popularity of production and custom big-bore bolt action and double rifles continues well in excess of any hunting requirements. North America is the home of some large and dangerous game such as the great bears of Alaska and Canada, all as dangerous potentially as lions or tigers, and heavier. Their thick coats, especially when wet, combined with heavy muscle and bone make them more resistant to expanding bullets than their African and Asian feline rivals. Bison, elk and moose, though less often dangerous,

Late Holland & Holland Modele de Luxe in 375 H&H Magnum on pre-war flat-top commercial Mauser action showing good lines for recoil and fast-handling.

Gil Van Horn's and the late Walter Abe's stock design for hard-kickers, including straight combs, laid-back pistol grips, short forearms and steel recoil bolts.

Winchester Model 70 375 H&H Magnum showing twin recoil bolts and Keith-type Monte Carlo comb—a workable recoil solution.

Three-slot 458 Mauser by author, with straight comb, long pistol grip, internal recoil bolts and sight base with integral recoil lug.

Author with post-68 Winchester Model 70 458 African in full recoil. Sling stud can't strike forefinger, and there's still clearance between the trigger guard and second finger.

are also tough and large. Thus based on size and/or danger, there is no logical reason to use lighter-powered rifles on these species than on lion, tiger or even Cape buffalo.

Many medium to heavy bolt action express rifles are owned by shooter-collectors who enjoy handloading cast or jacketed bullets to full or near-full power for rock and bullseye punching. I know several such shooters who will never see Africa. They have funds, but they are happiest when busting wild—never pet—rocks. These heroes of the petrified shoulder blast away with 375 Magnums, 458s, 460s and 505s at targets, rocks, and even ground squirrels or jackrabbits, brushing aside any suggestion their ordnance might be inadequate. Others are excellent hunters of my acquaintance who use 375 Magnums with full-power loads for mule deer or elk. One friend and excellent hunter uses large-bore double rifles on elk each year, with almost 100% success, claiming minimal meat damage and two holes for easy blood-spooring if needed, which it seldom is.

The better contemporary gunsmiths have, on the whole, done well at crafting handsome and outstandingly functional rifles up to about 338 Winchester Magnum. I have never seen previously such a profusion of beautifully finished rifles, both in wood and metal work. In some instances, though, the most exquisite and lavish craftsmanship is reduced to mere junk, or at best a repaired vestige of original appearance, because its maker constructed an "elephant" rifle as a scaled-up 270 deer rifle.

When we go up from the powerful 375 H&H Magnum through the 458 Winchester Magnum and into the 460 Weatherby or 500 belted wildcats we are a quantum jump above the 270 in recoil. This pertains as much to the strength of the stock to withstand this recoil force as it does for shooters to control it and be as comfortable with it as possible. Stock self-destruction isn't always a matter of life and death. Usually, it is simply the needless destruction of a costly and lovely creation; sometimes it includes the loss of a fine trophy.

My views in the matter are based on extensive experience here, in Africa and Southeast Asia with a variety of heavy express Mausers, Model 70s and modified Enfields. Here are a few personal experiences and my proven methods of preventing the recoil-induced stock split as well as repairing it when the damage hasn't gone too far. You can make serviceable field repairs in Africa or elsewhere, far away from gunsmiths, if you carry along some epoxy stock bedding compound and some reinforcing machine screws with a few chisels to clear slots for them. However, as with all problems, prevention is both cheaper and better than cure. Unfortunately, prevention is in short supply when the cookie crumbles.

When I first hunted Africa in 1959, I carried an early Winchester 458 and a pre-war Holland 375 Magnum Mauser, both with open sights only. Before departing for Mozambique, I tested them both and installed a quarter rib and "V" express sight on the 458 with a platinum line inlaid in its face. I filed this sight until the rifle placed its shots under the bead at 50 yards.

Both the 458 and the 375 had single steel recoil bolts through the stock, bearing against the integral receiver recoil lug. A couple of weeks before departure, the 458 split the web behind the recoil lug, the split then jumping the magazine mortise to split the small web between magazine and trigger as well. Those early Winchester 458 Africans lacked the sweat-on extra recoil lug attached to the forearm area of barrel, as well as the second steel recoil bolt through the stock between magazine and trigger.

Winchester offered to replace the stock, but it was a beautiful fiddleback specimen with fine color and contrasting dark stripes so I refused the offer and set about to repair the splits, which fortunately had not reached the grip. I also determined to preclude any repetition and cleared out enough wood behind the recoil lug to surround the recoil bolt with epoxy. Through the web between magazine and trigger I installed a chrome-moly Allen bolt in ¼-20 size with the head turned to a flat, slotted form and made a special nut for the opposite side. I surrounded it with epoxy, dressing it off after it hardened. I test-fired the rifle over 100 times with full factory-equivalent handloads before departing and I satisfied myself that no trace of further splitting had occurred.

The Mauser '98's receiver recoil lug, even that of its variants like the original Mauser Magnum action, is shallow and barely adequate to contain the recoil thrust of 30-06s even when closely bearing. Mauser intended this recoil lug to bear against a heavy square recoil bolt extending through the stock. Many sporters, including those by Mauser, however, omitted these recoil bolts as on my original Mauser Type A 404 (10.75x73). This caused many otherwise good stocks to split. Even their square recoil bolt is no panacea for the recoil of truly powerful rifles such as the 375 Magnum and on up, since it must have some clearance around it for installation, and wood fiber is only wood fiber. With continued heavy hammering, many such recoil bolts in these calibers can be pounded back until they compress the wood, create excessive clearance and split the wood behind the recoil lug.

Through the experience of the English gunmakers over decades of producing Mauser-actioned heavy expresses for African and Indian dangerous game, it was finally seen that the Mauser steel recoil bolt alone would not stand, so the extra recoil lug forward on the barrel was born, though by no means universally applied. When custom makers here began producing 458-caliber wildcats based on the full-length 375 H&H

Magnum case, in the '40s and '50s, some of the more astute installed these secondary lugs plus two bolts through the stock, one behind the recoil lug of the receiver, and the second between the trigger and magazine. If done with precise inletting of dense wood and a .020-inch clearance behind the receiver tang, such an arrangement would stand continued hammering of full loads without splitting, providing you kept the guard screws tight.

I owned such a rifle on a Remington-Enfield 1917 action with barrel by Atkinson & Marquart, featuring an integrally-turned barrel recoil lug, the over-all job completed by Paul Jaeger of Jenkintown, Pa. I used that 458 during 1962 and 1963 in Rhodesia and Nyasaland (Malawi) with nary a stock-splitting problem and it is still going strong. It was for all practical purposes a solid unit of steel and French walnut.

I also recall a custom Enfield in 458 Watts which had been on safari, and had recoiled itself into splinters due to porous wood, sloppy inletting and inadequate reinforcement. A common complaint is the upper tang area grip split caused by a receiver tang wedging inexorably rearwards, unstopped at the recoil lug. Accordingly, I invariably surround all steel recoil bolts in epoxy bedding compound, and create an unyielding shoulder of ample thickness of bedding compound between the receiver lug and the recoil bolt behind it.

My friend, gunsmith-photographer-hunter Gil Van Horn, an expert in making stocks for his African express rifles, has devised his own system: He fits a sturdy steel yoke around the lug to increase the bearing surface, and extends it along the forearm in epoxy bedding.

A seldom-recognized problem with original Mauser Magnum actions is that their guard screw spacing is identical with that of the standard '98. Since the Magnum action's magazine is longer, and the receiver recoil lug on both is identically placed, there is less wood behind the Magnum action's lug. In view of the heavier recoil of cartridges used in the Magnum action, the reinforcement for recoil must be greater.

The design of the secondary or barrel-mounted recoil lug presents opportunities for originality, including the integral lug turned on the barrel from an extra-large diameter blank, dovetailing, milling a flat on the underside of barrel and silver soldering a lug on, or combining the lug and express

This Original Mauser Type "A" 9.3x62mm with British express sights and ribbed half-octagonal barrel was stocked by author; note unaltered bolt for iron sight use and stronger stock. Stock is now ready for checkering.

F.N.-actioned 450 Lott belted magnum has five-shot magazine, Browning trigger and side safety, but British express sights and Hensoldt scope for versatility. Wood is California English.

A six-shot Mauser Magnum 375 H&H, formerly a 350 Rigby Magnum, follows author's prescription in California English walnut. It still needs rebluing and checkering. Again, bolt has been left unaltered.

sight base with a barrel band. Of all these systems, I have rejected all but the combined barrel band sight base and lug. This form is strongest, since once sweated on, there is no chance of recoil loosening it if the fit is right and the joint is fully bonded. Since I find the open "V" express sight essential on such a rifle, the integral base coincides with a suitable recoil lug position on the barrel, to be epoxy bedded into a cavity inletted in the forearm. I always file a slight draft angle of about one degree on the sides of the lug and slightly radius the corners for easy disassembly of barreled action from stock.

Integrally-turned recoil lugs on the barrel are obviously permanent, but for them to be deep enough, the barrel blank must be outsize, and most late examples I've seen tend to be very shallow since few barrel makers want to turn down all that extra stock or carry a stock of extra-large blanks. The milled flat system requires cutting into the barrel, which on principal is undesirable, and it is less permanent than the band lug in theory since it has no mechanical retention. I have seen a factory 458 of popular make with such a lug attached to a flat which blew out, almost destroying the shooter's left hand. Some machine operator had milled the flat too deep. Doubtless the operator dialed one turn beyond the zero setting of his milling machine's finish depth, a not

uncommon error when the operator is distracted. Such a thing is, however, rare, and this is the only such case I know of.

Less rare, however, is shearing off a badly bonded sweat-on recoil lug such as occurred to professional hunter Norman Sparrow's post-64 Model 70 458. He had killed close to 200 elephants with it on culling operations in Rhodesia's Wankie National Park, when one day during a difficult hunt, the stock exploded in a shower of splinters along the right side of receiver—where the stock is weakened by the bolt slot—the entire tang area and part of the forearm. I removed the stock and both Norman and I were surprised to find the cause to be separation of the sweat-on barrel lug and not gaps behind the recoil lugs. When the lug gave away, the recoil bolts and the main lug were unable to contain the thrust. Close inspection revealed the cause. The silver solder was $1/32$-inch thick and had contacted the barrel flat only in four small round pad-like spots. The workman who had done the job must obviously not have clamped the lug on before soldering.

The best way to do such a job is to cut a silver solder shim and apply flux on both sides of the shim and then clamp and apply heat. Such a job will last for centuries. I cleaned the surfaces and re-soldered with hard solder, then reconstructed the missing parts of the stock with Micro-Bedding

until a replacement stock could be obtained. Though rare, such a case shows how such seemingly small details can at worst place us in danger during a hunt for dangerous game, and at best ruin a fine stock or cause a lost trophy.

Many stockmakers refuse to use epoxy bedding on the recoil lug areas, even on heavy-recoil rifles—regarding such use as a reflection on their ability. I can understand and sympathize with such pride, but such pride goeth before a fall. When repeated hammering of wood fibers compresses and shifts the line of an originally precise inletting it becomes clear that wood is only wood, even the densest walnut. It is, however, hard to compress at the end grain. To remove my doubts, I insist all recoil thrust surfaces in my heavy rifles be bedded with suitable epoxy bedding compound. There are more important things than stock splits on my mind when hunting Cape buffalo in thick bush.

There is porous and dense walnut in all varieties, but American black and California Claro are not often dense enough for such stocks. The better California English, French, New Zealand, Yugoslavian, Turkish, Pakistani and Indian walnuts are the premium walnuts. The California Claro/English hybrid Bastogne is an ultra-dense wood which is uniquely suited to hard-recoiling rifles. Other tough woods, such as screw bean mesquite, have been successfully used for such rifles, but none so outstandingly as the better Old World walnuts. Such woods combine strength with moderate weight, clean, across-the-grain inletting, and the ultimate in color and figure, when of premium quality.

The fancy grain structures so favored for fine custom stocks, though enhancing the stock's beauty, are not always the best for the heavy express. I recommend wood that is as nearly straight-grained as possible in dense heart wood. Try for grain esthetics from contrasting lengthwise striping or fiddleback and rich color, rather than natural artistic twistings and turnings.

One vital admonition in epoxy bedding your stock is in order: Micro-Bed is one of my favorite compounds, but no release agent is furnished, so you must provide. The one sure release agent is a couple coats of superior paste wax, such as Johnson's floor wax. Don't forget to coat the guard

screws and their female threads. This part of the release agent application is vital to success unless you enjoy permanently assembled rifles. Use cotton swabs or similar applicators to coat these internal threads. Always apply the release agent wax over a much wider area than you expect to bed. It is amazing how epoxy can spread under the pressure of assembly. If the receiver area of the stock, especially the bottom, is true to the receiver itself, you may only want to apply the compound around the recoil lug or lugs.

In the halcyon pre-war days, all heavy tropical express rifles were custom-made, invariably on Mauser actions and stocked of the best European walnut, usually with recoil bolts. Invariably the triggers were original Mauser military-type triggers modified to a single-stage pull. Such triggers required minimal wood removal and left a rather massive web of walnut between the magazine and the trigger. Beginning with the 1937 debut of Winchester's great Model

70, a new factory trigger concept appeared—the override trigger with its adjustable pull. Never topped by subsequent override trigger designs, especially for ruggedness, the Model 70 trigger required more wood removal than the converted military type. This leaves the web between trigger and magazine somewhat reduced in size under that of a hand-inletted Mauser or Springfield with original military-type trigger, converted or not. This did not create a problem with very light calibers, but from 30-06 on up to 375 Magnum, factory stocks would often develop splits through this web. Naturally a hand-inletted Model 70 stock would retain more of the original wood at this point, but the remedy for many owners of Model 70s was to install steel recoil bolts behind the recoil lug and between trigger and magazine, using epoxy bedding behind the recoil lug. Thusly reinforced, the factory stocks usually remained serviceable.

After World War II, with the flood

Author filing-in express sights of 458 on original Mauser action. Note the lack of slot for unaltered bolt to increase strength, and note the height of comb which almost touches bolt's cocking piece. Rear sight base incorporates an integral forearm-mounted recoil lug.

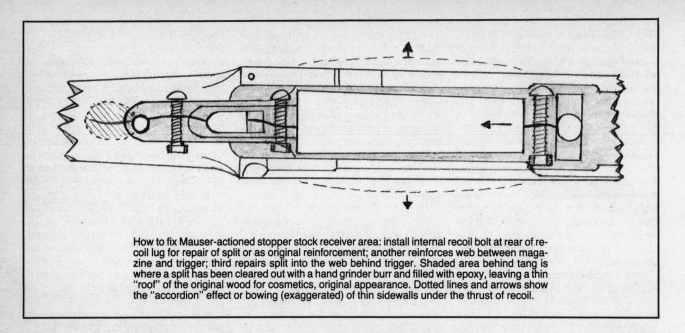

How to fix Mauser-actioned stopper stock receiver area: install internal recoil bolt at rear of recoil lug for repair of split or as original reinforcement; another reinforces web between magazine and trigger; third repairs split into the web behind trigger. Shaded area behind tang is where a split has been cleared out with a hand grinder burr and filled with epoxy, leaving a thin "roof" of the original wood for cosmetics, original appearance. Dotted lines and arrows show the "accordion" effect or bowing (exaggerated) of thin sidewalls under the thrust of recoil.

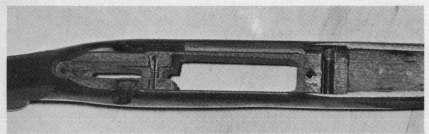

Model 70 stock shows reinforcing bolts before epoxy is placed.

Center—the traditional Mauser recoil bolt. At either side are bolts used by author.

of sporters on Mauser and other military actions came a flood of ready-to-install accessories, including adjustable override triggers of relatively massive proportions. Installing these is easier by far than grinding off the two-stage fulcrum of the issue trigger, then grinding away the excess sear engagement and stoning sear, cocking piece and all rubbing surfaces to a clean, crisp pull. Not all such trick triggers were or are Spartan in ruggedness compared to the few parts of the forged issue trigger, nor can they be with so many springs, compound leverage and a series of screws and nuts attached to stamped sideplates.

The most negative result of such triggers on heavy-recoiling rifles is a tiny, useless web between trigger and magazine. When stock rigidity goes at this point, the inevitable next stage is splitting through the grip. It must be understood how the receiver area of the stock reacts under recoil. The magazine takes out a lot of wood, leaving but two thin sidewalls, the weakest and most flexible area of the Mauser-type stock. When the rifle is shouldered and fired, the force of re-coil drives the stock against the shoulder. It is the receiver recoil lug that does the driving. The shooter's shoulder almost stops the rear movement of the buttstock, but the thin sidewalls don't move straight back without bending or bowing. They simply lack the rigidity to retain their shape and the thin walls of the magazine box do not add reinforcement. The sidewalls bow outwards, shortening the inletted receiver portion of stock, but the receiver doesn't bow or shorten with recoil, so unless the inletting at the upper tang is cleared behind the metal by from .020- to .030-inch, the tang will often wedge into the grip area, causing a split.

Before this grip split occurs, the bowing or accordion effect will always split the web between trigger and magazine. This is why steel bolts are essential through this web. The recoil begins behind the receiver recoil lug, it must present a totally solid and unyielding stop, created by epoxy-bedding a steel recoil bolt of ample dimensions at that point.

When Browning Safari Grade F.N. Mausers appeared in the '60s in 375 and 458, they had enormous clearances machined from their stocks for the excellent Browning modification of the Winchester Model 70 override trigger. This trigger is bulkier than the Model 70 trigger, largely because it incorporates a side safety. Browning wisely installed steel recoil bolts through the thin web between trigger and magazine and behind the receiver lug as well as employing a second recoil lug attached to the barrel on their heaviest recoiling calibers such as the 458. I have heard of little trouble with these Brownings splitting, despite so much wood removal by machining and for the somewhat bulky trigger. This is to the credit of both Browning engineers and Fabrique Nationale.

One day a prominent gunsmith asked me to sight-in and testfire a fancy 458 custom Mauser. I asked him if the barrel contained a second recoil lug and if so, was it and the receiver lug epoxy-bedded. He declared that such a setup was unnecessary "if the stockmaker did his job." I demurred and said that I was reluctant to preside over the suicide of his rifle's fancy stock, but he was unworried.

Five shots of factory soft-nosed 510-grain loads and the stock split from the wood behind the receiver lug, through the web between magazine and trigger and well into the upper grip. I felt lucky that it had not been worse and driven splinters into my right hand, but I also felt badly that a beautiful stock, the result of weeks of fine handwork, had been wiped out needlessly. Its owner took the result lightly, saying it was the only way the stockmaker would learn. I knew this wasn't so because if he had listened to me and installed a second lug on the barrel and epoxy bedded both recoil lugs, the splitting would not have occurred. To be done right, of course, there should also have been two steel recoil bolts installed.

A Sako Safari Model 375 H&H Magnum on the long action with quarter rib, express sight and French walnut classic stock was testfired and a box of factory ammo run through it. I disassembled the rifle, after noting a small crack behind the tang, finding the stock had split through the wood behind the recoil lug, the miniscule web between trigger and magazine and then into the upper grip. The recoil lug only contacted the recoil bolt at the lug's bottom edge and this recoil bolt face was round. The guard screws weren't tight and the round face of the bolt and the tangential contact with the recoil lug's tip, allowed the lug to cam upwards and back, thereby driving the tang into the upper grip.

A steel recoil bolt through the web after epoxying the split at upper grip cured that problem, for the time being, at least. I removed the recoil bolt, filed it square and reinstalled surrounded by epoxy bedding. Due to the excessive wood removed for the receiver, there was no real bedding, so I "glass"-bedded the receiver and the first inch of barrel shank. Previously, the rifle would group with scope at 100 yards within 3½ inches. After

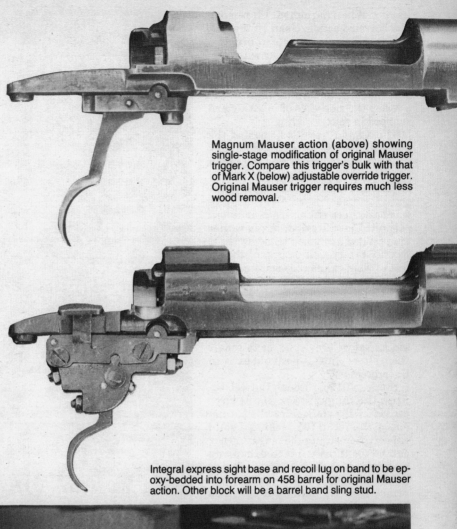

Magnum Mauser action (above) showing single-stage modification of original Mauser trigger. Compare this trigger's bulk with that of Mark X (below) adjustable override trigger. Original Mauser trigger requires much less wood removal.

Integral express sight base and recoil lug on band to be epoxy-bedded into forearm on 458 barrel for original Mauser action. Other block will be a barrel band sling stud.

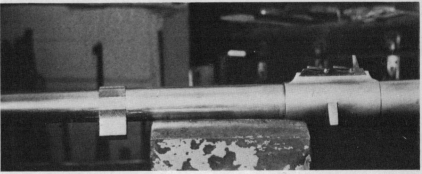

this treatment it made three, three-shot groups under an inch at 100 yards. Such extreme wood removal at receiver should never have been done. for strength and for accuracy's sake.

I recently bought an English-made Whitworth Mark-X Mauser sporter in 7mm Remington Magnum, with an excellently shaped stock of French walnut. It is, of course, a copy of the F.N. Supreme action and has a side safety and an adjustable override trigger assembly. I was, however, surprised to see that excessive wood removal to accommodate the trigger

had all but eliminated the web which was merely a sliver of walnut some ⅛-inch thick and obviously too thin for installing an anti-split bolt at that point. The rifle came with a steel recoil bolt behind the recoil lug, but the amount of wood removed for it and the receiver left no real bedding. Before I shoot this rifle, I will reinforce the trigger mortise by covering the trigger with modeling clay corresponding to the amount of clearance I estimate it requires. Then I will fill that excessive mortise with epoxy bedding to reinforce and to reduce the size of the cavity. When hardened, I'll remove the barreled action, clean off the clay and test for adequate clearance. If it lacks clearance I will clear with chisels and files. I may also install a cadmium-plated #10 machine screw and nut—the latter locked in place—to overlap the sidewalls of inletting and trapped in epoxy bedding.

The original recoil bolt behind the lug will also be trapped with epoxy since it fits too loose and too much wood has been machined out around the lug and receiver. Such gross disregard for essential receiver bedding and basic stock strength has no cost or technical justification, but is rather the result of a common tendency these days to pretty well disregard the effect of what cannot be seen when the rifle is merely handled. Fortunately, the availability of excellent bedding compounds and ordinary hardware items such as machine screws and nuts, enables us to reinforce such stocks before they split, or to repair them after splitting, if caught early in the process.

Stock splitting through the web behind the magazine is not always caused by the stock sidewalls bowing out or the recoil lug lacking a solid support. Sometimes the magazine box can be too tightly inletted, causing wedging which can be as damaging as in the aforementioned instances. I prefer that my Mauser magazines bear solidly, but not under tension, against the wood behind the recoil lug to its front, but the rear corners of the box ought not bind. Too loose a magazine can also create problems as when a clearance exists in front of the forward wall of the box and this gets dented by recoiling into steel-jacketed solids. To cure this problem, especially with magazines on 375 Magnums on up, which are merely thin sheet metal liners, I silver-solder a reinforcing piece of tool steel on the outside front face and "glass" in place.

The traditional Mauser stock recoil bolt has been successfully used for over 80 years, but I do not prefer them because they rust and because I prefer the uninterrupted grain of fine walnut to the bolts visible on either side of an otherwise unbroken vista of Nature's handiwork. Mind you, I have several fine rifles with such bolts, and I will doubtless acquire others which I shall cherish, but I no longer install them as they are unnecessary.

I put a heat-treated chrome-moly ¼-20 Allen screw with its head turned flat and a nut squeezed on tight in a vise or riveted in place at the end opposite the head behind the

Looking down at inletting of Whitworth stock in 7mm Remington Magnum rifle, showing plenty of machining clearance for the receiver. The web between the magazine and trigger is but ⅛-inch thick.

Bottom view shows—at the white paint—a very thin web remaining.

lug with essentially the same system I use in repairing split stocks. The threads and head and nut are trapped in bedding compound, in a permanent relationship with the wood with no clearance around it. This is easier and does not show from outside. I have never had a stock with such a recoil bolt and another through the web behind the magazine split, even on the heaviest-recoiling of rifles. Of course, I always put a second recoil lug sleeved on the barrel for calibers over 375 Magnum. Under these, the two recoil bolts and .020-.030-inch clearance behind the tang will make the stock quite indestructible to recoil.

When a stock splits through both webs and has visibly begun its path of destruction into the upper grip, there is also a repair available which usual-

A split through the web of a 350 Rigby stock runs almost invisibly into the upper grip area. Also there's a split running from the bolt stop-release position forward. The author repaired this stock with epoxy-trapped bolts.

ly will cure the problem. After installing the epoxy-trapped recoil bolts in the webs, undercut the wood around the split with a rotary file burr on a hand grinder, leaving a thin shell at top for cosmetics. Clear out a sizeable cavity which appears to go beyond the split. This can be then filled with epoxy bedding, or it can also be filled after installing a #10 machine screw and affixed nut, positioned to straddle the former split line.

I did this to a 350 Rigby Mauser, also adding hidden recoil bolts behind the recoil lug and between trigger and magazine. Nothing is visible from the outside, only the trace of that hairline crack behind the tang, which will now never spread. The rifle has been fired with many full loads since then.

That about covers the reinforcement and repair of the heavy bolt action express stock, but there remain some peculiarities of design to be discussed. One of these is the positioning of the forward sling stud, which can badly "bite" the forefinger on the forearm. Such a position is OK on a deer or antelope rifle, but on the heavy express, it had better be on the barrel in a band. Combined with a short English forend, this also allows the rifle's muzzle to drop below the head when the rifle is carried shoulder-slung through thick bush. Winchester wisely adopted this placement for their 458 African Model, preferring to oven-braze a wide base, rather than a band, to the underside of barrel.

The Browning, on the other hand, has its forward sling stud mounted on the forearm where it can and does sometimes catch the left forefinger. The remedy is to remove and replace with a Pachmayr sling swivel or to plug, and shorten the forend, then to install a barrel band sling stud.

Winchester set the trend for factory stocks for heavy rifles with the African Model 458 stock, an excellent design for recoil in its final form with barrel recoil lug and two recoil bolts. The conservative Monte Carlo of this stock, the ample but not cramped pistol grip, and the slightly pear-shaped forearm section with barrel-mounted sling stud is a practical approach to the large-bore stock. An even more gradual curve to the pistol grip which lays the hand well back from the rear of trigger guard will reduce the tendency of the hand to slam into the guard during recoil.

An abrupt pistol grip which permits a firm grip on a 270 or similar powered rifle, can cause painful injury to the second finger as it is slammed against the trigger guard in rifles of from 375 Magnum caliber on up. I prefer the traditional, long English semi-pistol grip as found on 416 Rigby Mausers, but coupled with a straight comb just barely clearing the bolt. This combined with a deep and wide butt pad works best for me to keep recoil in a reasonably straight line and to cushion it by spreading it over as wide a shoulder area as possible. I find that this lack of drop and a wide and deep pad is more effective in reducing the feel of "kick" than increasing weight. Many shooters are amazed at the mild apparent recoil of heavy rifles thusly stocked, even eight-pound 458s.

The Keith Monte Carlo comb is also favored by many, and is a moderate Monte Carlo which slopes away from the cheek and cheekbone, losing contact with the face during recoil. Whereas this is liked by many experienced men, I prefer for the face to retain contact and control during recoil. The three point-contact of face forearm and grip is essential to my control of rifle upchuck. The straight comb doesn't wedge against the cheek during recoil, but it does maintain contact.

The practice of welding or forging bolts to clear scopes is one I avoid for the heavy express to be used solely with open sights. This eliminates the deep, weakening slot on the right side of receiver which almost cuts the stock in half. By leaving the bolt simply bent down at a suitable angle, with no deep slot for its clearance, the heavy express stock gets a big measure of strength, at lower cost of time, effort and money. If, at some future date you decide to mount a low-powered scope, the bolt can then be lowered, but meanwhile the unaltered bolt works in your favor.

In the case of the non-scoped heavy rifle we naturally don't want the comb to be scope height, but it can still be kept straight, or nearly so, if a bit lower for rapid alignment of the open or peep sights. A forearm section which is slightly pear-shaped and of moderate width, makes for firm control. One which is too narrow or of outsize "beavertail" form reduces the grip needed for good control. Length of pull should be based on what comes up best with light clothing, if the rifle is to be used mainly in the tropics. If for Alaska or Canada, allow for heavy garments. Neck length, as well as arm length, musculature and other bulk affect correct length of pull, and a shorter pull aids rapid working of the bolt. Too short a pull can drive the thumb into the nose. For the heavy bolt rifle I prefer a stock slightly longer than that of the light rifle, by about ½-inch.

These factors can make or break your stock for the "heavy." What I have attempted to do is to show that such ultra-powerful rifles demand special dimensional and structural considerations, compared to light rifles. Heavy recoil goes with your "heavy's" power. You won't even notice it during that exciting hunt, and you don't have to flinch because its kick disturbs you, if you begin with a correctly dimensioned stock with a deep and wide one-inch recoil pad such as made by Pachmayr. Your rifle cannot take recoil when the barreled action recoils *faster* than the stock. You now know how to keep that from happening. ●

The Sporting Martini

Early Swiss Martini in 11mm caliber marked "F. von Martini & Co. Frauenfeld."

Rimfire, centerfire, shotguns—this rugged single-shot action did it all and still does.

by JOHN MC CADDEN

FREDERICH von Martini's action design of 1868 was an immense improvement on the complex falling blocks of its day. It stood out from them all in simplicity, strength and dependability. For these qualities, it became Britain's Service rifle after thorough and punishing tests. Wedded to the Henry rifled barrel in 450, this was the rifle of the Sudan and the Victorian brush wars.

It's a strong design. The solid rear bulkhead and stout block with gas escape vents in the base is eminently safe. This was illustrated to perfection in early trials when very poor Swiss ammunition repeatedly ruptured, enveloping the firer in clouds of black powder smoke, but leaving him unharmed. The gases were vented downward away from his face, showing the strength and safety of the breech, which impressed the British military.

This is an accurate rugged breech, ideal for modern sporting calibers. It has chambered many of these, among them the 22/303, 25/300, 25 Roberts, 25 Winchester, 30-06, in addition to the African 45's of the old black powder and cordite era. The light Cadet action suits the 22 Hornet, 218 Bee, 25/35 Improved, 222 Remington and 357 Magnum. For the 458 Winchester, Greener's massive forged steel G P shotgun breech is the obvious choice.

The early English sporters simply chambered a commercial version of the military cartridge. This was a .577 brass case, necked to .450 with a 480-grain bullet and 85 grains of RFG black powder at 1,350 fps. This was considered a small bore in its day. In the 1870's this and the straight cased 3¾-inch Henry Boxer cartridge, using the same bullet and charge were very popular and reliable in British rifles for big game. The second military/sport chambering was for the Mk. II .303 of 1893 with a 215-grain flat-nosed jacketed bullet at 1,970 fps.

With the military pattern cartridges alone, all kind of softskinned game from Eland and Leopard to Red Deer has been taken with the Martini. Even now, there are more than a few of these rifles behind the doors of South African and English farms. Up to World War II and even after, the half-stocked Martini in .303 British and .30-06 was a good stalker over the barren Scottish moors, dropping many a Red Deer. It balances well between the hands and the extra weight helps accurate shooting. A single shot, yes, but an accurate second shot and even third, are quick and easy with a little practice using the old trick of a couple of cartridges held between the fingers of the left hand. The author's partner shot his first elephant years ago as a laddie using this technique with a .45 Martini sporter and the 480-grain lead bullet.

At 300 yards such rifles are entirely accurate with .303 British, .30-06 and .22/303 grouping within five inches. They are fine with reloads and both thirties are best with the heavy Lyman 210-grain cast bullet No. 311299.

The British Army's adoption of the Martini assured its success in Europe and it was very popular in Germany and Switzerland in set trigger rifles and in carbines, mostly in 10.5 mm both rim and center fire. English makers turned out many sport/target and hunting rifles on the military pattern, distinguishable by quality chequering and flat, or sometimes recessed muzzles, such as by Webley and the Field's Rifle Co.

Many English makers also made Martinis for Express cartridges of the African and Indian safari days. Some of the names on these guns are Rigby, Westley-Richards, Fields Rifle Co., Blanch and Sons, Silver and Co., Webley & Sons, Cogswell & Harrison, Hollis & Sons, Gibbs, London Small Arms Co., and from Scotland D.J. Frazer and Alex. Henry both of Edinburgh, and Martin of Glasgow. These and many others also made little gems of Rook rifles on the Martini action. The quick detachable trigger mechanism of the Westley-Richards model made it very popular, and it still is.

Plenty of Martinis survive with the original Henry barrels. This is Alexander Henry of Edinburgh, Scotland. His barrel has deep square cut rifling, one turn in 22 inches; right hand twist, with seven grooves, .009 inches deep at the breech and .007 inches deep at the muzzle. Width of the lands is .003 inches. Rifling is progressive for the

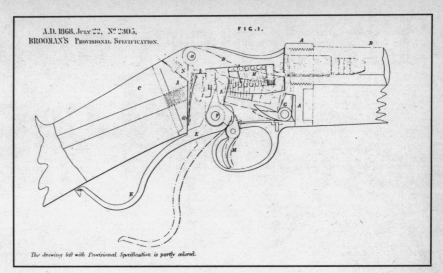

The drawing left with Provisional Specification is partly colored.

(Right and below) The original 1868 patent captured all the essentials, though there were many, many modifications to come.

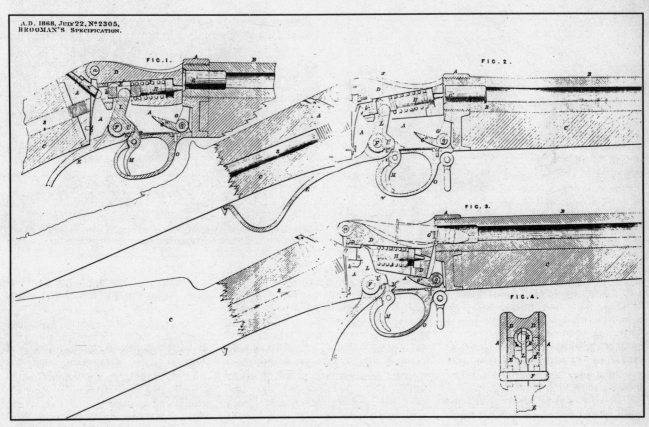

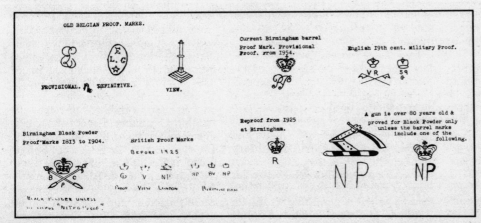

Proofmarks are essential to understanding any individual Martini. Here are some key marks.

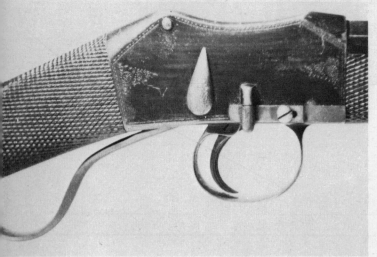

Breech of a lightweight octagonal-barreled rook rifle in 360 (No. 5) by the Braendelin Co. of Belgium. It shows the original 1869 safety.

Mk.II Martini-Henry rifle converted to 22 rimfire for clubs—very large. for the cartridge but accurate in use.

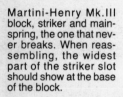

Martini-Henry Mk.III block, striker and mainspring, the one that never breaks. When reassembling, the widest part of the striker slot should show at the base of the block.

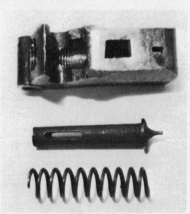

Martini Metford Artillery Mark III originally in 303, much later converted to 22 rimfire for the National Rifle Association (of Britian). (Courtesy F. Evans)

first eleven inches. This rifling is on the polygonal system. A section shows a seven sided polygon. Down each angle formed by the intersection of planes runs a raised rib. Consequently barrel and bullet have fourteen bearing points. This barrel effectively minimized black powder fouling and remained accurate despite any buildup of residue which in any event would be slight with most sporting use. An uncommon but by no means rare Martini barrel is Lancaster's smooth oval bore, no rifling at all, favored for a time by long range target shots and another answer to the fouling problem.

In the 1870's the most popular British game cartridge for the bigger stuff was the bottlenecked .577/.450. Its 480-grain bullet was one part tin to 12 parts lead, 1.27 inches long, .439-inch at the shoulder and .450 at the slightly hollow base with 2 cannelures, one for crimping. Two turns of fine white parchment paper around the bullet from right to left untwisted in the bore preventing leading. A thick wad of beeswax was behind the bullet.

Literally thousands of obsolete military Martinis were converted to .22 rimfire, mostly by Bonehill; with others by Greener and B.S.A. for civilian rifle clubs about 1900. These actions show the inspection marks and crossed pennants of the original government manufacture and military proof. The .22 barrels have either the London or, usually, Birmingham View and Proof marks required by law for all arms sold within the realm. Plenty more ex-military Martinis were converted to half stocked short rifles that still see use today.

Ex-military models usually bear the following marks on the breech body and block: Opposed Broad Arrows indicating ex-government property; backed capital R's mean unsafe barrels; D P denotes a Drill Purpose only arm usually made up of odd components and not for shooting. The British military proof mark was a simplified crown over crossed pennants. Black Powder Express rifle proof was first for Black Powder, then a definitive Proof for Cordite to give a pressure between 30%

and 45% over the standard working load. These Black Powder/Cordite barrels show the Crowned Proof marks and in figures and words the cartridge for which proved, the maximum weight of powder and bullet in grains, and if these are the maximum to be used, the word MAXIMUM. A crowned Capital R means that a barrel has been reproved which can be a good sign in conjunction with corresponding proof marks.

It is often said that the original .22 Black Powder barrels are bound by now to be eroded and inaccurate from having had a few hundred modern nitro loaded cartridges through them. This is not borne out from personal experience. The author's gun by Greener in .22 Long Rifle has been a work horse for the past 50 years with nitro cartridges. In the thirties you could shoot the family dinner for less than a dime, many a time. From a rest, this rifle gives a dime-sized group at 50 yards with a 'scope.

Many such rifles do have poor barrels for a host of reasons. Most were never cared for after a time, so what can be expected of them. But a lot perform

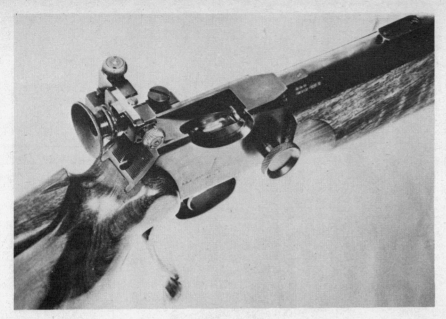

The flats under the barrels of a typical English double rifle show the sort of proofmark jungle one must penetrate. (Courtesy of the Historical Firearms Society of South Africa.)

(Left) The B.S.A. Martini International with Parker Hale Micro rear sight. Every part is machined from solid metal. (Courtesy: BSA Guns Ltd.)

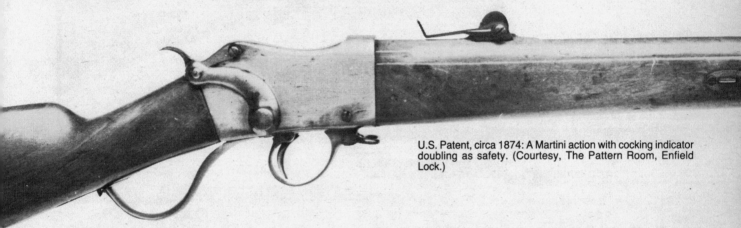

U.S. Patent, circa 1874: A Martini action with cocking indicator doubling as safety. (Courtesy, The Pattern Room, Enfield Lock.)

well, all shots touching or at least sociable at 50 yards even offhand. The conversions are all overstrong Victorian stalwarts. With a .22 pistol cartridge they are virtually noiseless in the field and do not alert squirrel, rabbit or fox.

In the Martini, the coil mainspring does all the work. Since 1870 none have been known to snap. Some very early ones did so but this was not apparent and the actions continued working normally. Only when stripped was it realized that the springs had snapped. They were too brittle which was easily remedied. This coil spring was unique at a time when vee springs were *de rigeur* for the best rifles. The coil was easier to mass produce.

Through the middle of the block is a massive striker with the coilspring around it. The underside of the block is slotted for the tumbler to engage the striker. The block is operated by an underlever. Correct operation is a sharp jerk down on the lever. Forked arms on the end of the lever fit into slots at the sides of the block. As the lever moves

down, the arms cam the block down cocking back the striker. As the block drops, it hits the L-shaped arm of the extractor which is shaped to give primary extraction, then ejects the case smartly over the right shoulder. The original safety was in front of the trigger inside the guard and omitted from many later models.

There is no friction between the breechblock and the rear of the barrel. The face of the block is parallel to the base of the chambered cartridge. The two faces are each tangential to one curve struck out from the block hinge. On opening, the block immediately drops down away from the rear of the barrel. The socket for the block axis pin is made slightly larger than the pin so that recoil is taken by the shoulders of the breech body and not by the pin. Pins made of lead have been substituted in the cocking lever and block hinges and after loading and firing these pins were not deformed or marked, showing that they take no stress.

The early cocking indicator on the

right of the action body was on a squared internal axis which moved with the tumbler. Later models had a round axis and no indicator. Many sporters have Francotte's indicator working in a slot in top right of the block. The very early Frauenfeld action had a pin protruding vertically at the rear of the breech where it could be felt by the thumb.

The G P shotgun, Greener's single barrel general purpose gun has for a long time been renowned for rugged dependability and hard hitting in the wilder and remote parts of the world and has been a regular standby and meatgetter of great versatility on safaris, on expeditions and in overseas postings. This gun has withstood hard service, rough use, even positive neglect. It is probably the simplest and most foolproof shotgun action ever designed. It balances very well. The safety catch operates automatically when the underlever is dropped to load. A great advantage of this gun is the quickly removable barrel.

In competition, the Greener Trap

Martini cartridges, old and new: 45-70 rimfire, 222 Remington soft point, 22 Long Rifle, 36-caliber Bulleted Cap, 410 revolver, 303 British with cast 150-gr. bullet, 410 shotgun, 12 gauge, 2½ inch.

The massive forging of the GP action by Greener, which will hold the largest of rifle cartridges safely.

The Greener, fitted with multichoke or not, served in rough duty for British overseas for generations.

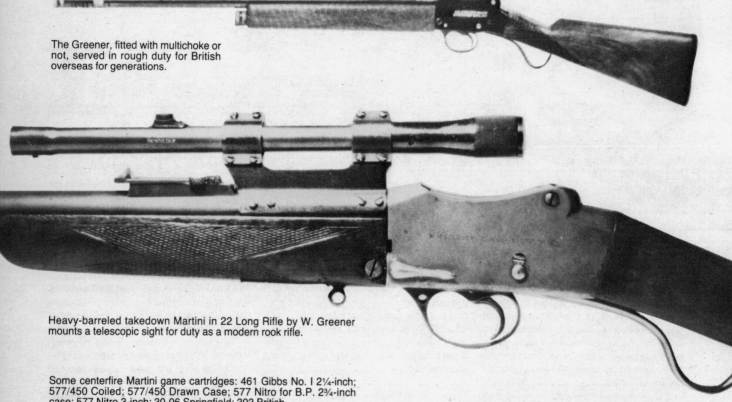

Heavy-barreled takedown Martini in 22 Long Rifle by W. Greener mounts a telescopic sight for duty as a modern rook rifle.

Some centerfire Martini game cartridges: 461 Gibbs No. I 2¼-inch; 577/450 Coiled; 577/450 Drawn Case; 577 Nitro for B.P. 2¾-inch case; 577 Nitro 3-inch; 30-06 Springfield; 303 British.

The Greener Multichokes were approximately halfway in size and function and between the contemporary Cutts Compensator and Poly-Choke. (Courtesy Webley & Scott Ltd.)

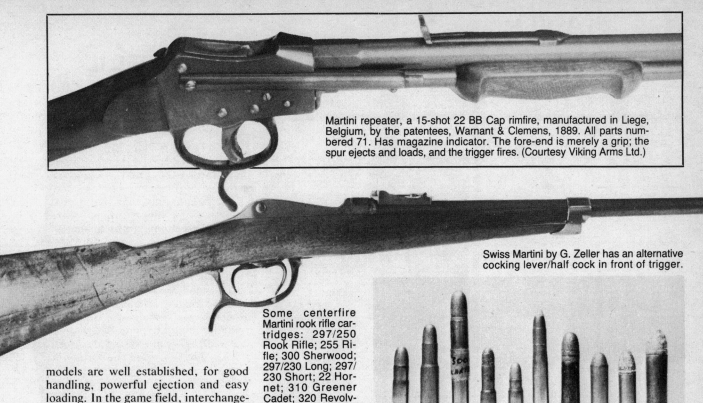

Martini repeater, a 15-shot 22 BB Cap rimfire, manufactured in Liege, Belgium, by the patentees, Warnant & Clemens, 1889. All parts numbered 71. Has magazine indicator. The fore-end is merely a grip; the spur ejects and loads, and the trigger fires. (Courtesy Viking Arms Ltd.)

Swiss Martini by G. Zeller has an alternative cocking lever/half cock in front of trigger.

Some centerfire Martini rook rifle cartridges: 297/250 Rook Rifle; 255 Rifle; 300 Sherwood; 297/230 Long; 297/230 Short; 22 Hornet; 310 Greener Cadet; 320 Revolver; 320 Long; 380 Long.

models are well established, for good handling, powerful ejection and easy loading. In the game field, interchangeable multichoke tubes give wide versatility and the convenience of four spare barrels carried in one pocket.

The G P action is also eminently suitable for the bigger African cartridges. Based on the 1886 Martini, this is a very massive breech. The excellent safety is easily operated by the knuckle without moving the trigger finger, and lifts the sear clear of the trigger which is far superior to simply relying on blocking the trigger.

Martini and Peabody, two patentees, suddenly stopped feuding back then. Avarice won and they amalgamated. These guns were made at Providence, Rhode Island, the Peabody stable. After 1874, it was the 1869 Martini action that was manufactured and sold in the U.S. by and under the established Peabody name. All had a safety in front of the trigger and cocking indicator at right of the action identical with the British Army trials model of 1869.

The original Peabody proper was neither the first falling block nor the best. It was more complex and weaker than the Martini, needing a combination of six different springs, rollers and screws to keep the breech closed. The Martini is not, therefore, a plagiarism of the Peabody action. It is so improved a falling block it is virtually a new action. In fact, the two function quite differently. The Martini is far simpler. There is a U.S. patent of 1862, but the relevant patent is 1092 of 1865 taken out in England for von Martini by G. Bousefield, a patent agent.

The amalgamated Peabody and Martini guns appeared after the sidehammer rimfire Army model. There was a long line of target guns, many of which were also suitable for sporting or were converted. Many of the original safeties on these guns have been removed.

The sporting models were the 1875 No. 1 Midrange Target Model, first of the henceforth hammerless models. Body marked: Peabody & Martini Patents. Some of these must have been immediately and nicely sporterised. The 1881 was reputedly the most accurate gun for the government .45/70 cartridge. Weight: 10 pounds with a half-octagonal barrel, 32 inches long. Some of these, too, have been professionally made into handy sporters.

The Creedmoor model of about 1880 was a very successful long range target gun in England. The cartridge was .44-100-550 2¼ inches long. The gun came in various grades and in types and lengths of barrel. Some of these and the pistol-gripped 1887 model were much more popular for sporting use in England, Germany and Switzerland than in the U.S. The exception was the "Kill Deer" model in .45/70 with half stocked round barrel and elevating leaf rearsight over the chamber.

In Belgium and Britain, many quality rifles were turned out for the now obsolete, shortrange, heavy bulleted rook rifle calibers in such black powder loadings as the .380 Long with 125-grain bullet and 10 grains of FFFg; the .360 No. 5 with 145-grain bullet and about 12 grains of black powder; the .44 Webley with 200-grain bullet and 15 grains of black, and various other .32's and 38's. Little beauts these rifles are, nicely balanced, crisply chequered. A shame to convert them to modern calibers, I think.

U.S. teams once took the Martini rifle to at least two Olympics and many international competitions, and still use it in handguns. It is still produced after well over 100 years.

The B.S.A. Company's Mk. V target rifle is a highly refined Martini. The very successful and sophisticated Greener Trap gun harks back to the improved Martini of 1886. The most well known pistol version is the Hammerli Free Pistol.

This wide range of Martinis, by many makers in many countries, in a variety of breech weights and sizes from the old military to the sport/target models produced since 1900 to the present day, is suitable for any sporting caliber from varmint/wildcatters to big game. We have the modern 12 Gauge 3-inch Magnum, and the contrasting dainty light .360 black powder "rook" rifle by the Braendlin Co., of Belgium. Over 110 years of continuing production and use is adequate testimonial to the astounding, long lived Martini. ●

HAND-LOADING UPDATE

by DEAN A. GRENNELL

Happy Steve Hornady hawks the Pro-7 at the SHOT Show.

DETAILS ON reloading components—bullets, powder, primers, wads, shot, hulls, cases and the like—are discussed in the ammunition section. That leaves us the basic operational hardware and supporting software and there are numerous such items on which to report.

LOADING PRESSES

RCBS has two new presses for metallic cartridges since last year's discussion here. There is the Big Max, weighing in at a brawny 27½ pounds and wearing—you guessed it—green trunks. There is also the Reloader Special 2, at a mere 8¾ pounds taking the place of the larger and considerably heavier original Reloader Special that, in turn, was introduced as a contemporary of the Rockchucker.

The Big Max was briefly termed the A-4 but they seem to have dropped that designation. Like the old A-2, it has a hollow ram so the expelled primers drop down through it instead of onto the floor. A small plastic cup snaps onto the lower end of the ram to catch them. The chassis is a monolithic O-frame, flat-on to the operator. It is possible to get at the shell holder with either hand. There is a universal shell holder or, if you prefer, a turn-on head to accept conventional shell holders. The handle is a lengthy affair with spade grip.

Both the Big Max and RS-2 do away with the pivoting primer arm—a gadget I've loathed all my reloading career—and substitute priming punches that go in the end of the ram and an adapter for universal shell holders that is installed in place of the die. It is similar to a setup that Fred Huntington offered out of RCBS in the latter Sixties. Properly adjusted, it's faster than the swinging arms and gives an excellent feel for the seating operation.

Discussed here last year, the RCBS Green Machine can now be had for 9mm Luger, 44 Special/Magnum or 45 ACP in addition to the original offering for 38 Special/357 Magnum.

Hornady/Pacific now has a progressive loader for metallics in the form of the Hornady Pro-7. It has a five-station turret to hold a powder

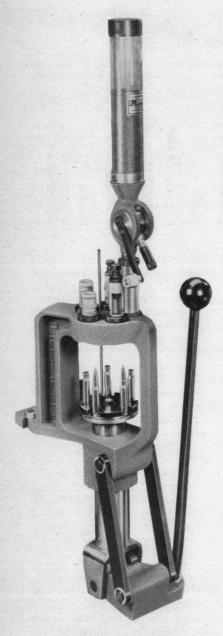

The Hornady Pro-7 progressive press for metallic cartridges.

RCBS Big Max weighs over 27 pounds, dressed in green.

measure and four dies, permitting the use of a roll or taper crimping die after the bullet seater. It uses reloading dies of conventional design with the ⅞-14 thread but requires a shell plate—retailing at $25—instead of the usual shell holders. Most of the shell plates will handle a number of different cartridges having identical head dimensions and the cost of the shell plate isn't much if any worse than having to buy four more conventional shell holders.

The shell plate advances automatically as the handle is worked and priming is performed automatically. Manual operations performed for each cycle include putting an empty case in the plate, working the handle, operating the powder measure and inserting the bullet. Naturally, it employs the compound leverage system that Hornady terms Power-Pac, to ease the effort for performing all those operations simultaneously. Suggested retail price with one shell plate of your choice, but without dies, is $425.

Dillon has a new four-station press, the Model RL 450, with three dies and the powder measure installed in fixed holes at the top. The case carrier head is advanced manually, the primer is fed manually by a push rod and the powder measure is operated in a like manner. Complete with primer feed and powder measure in the caliber of your choice, less dies, it's $365, $310 without the measure, and extra shell plates with locator buttons are $35.50 each. Dillon also has an electric case trimmer for use on their presses, available only in 223 Remington or 308 Winchester at $225 for the standard sizing die or $425 with tungsten carbide die. As I understand, they recommend lubricating the case for use with the carbide die, also.

Lyman has their Orange Crusher press with compound-toggle leverage system and the option of switching the handle from right to left and their T-Mag press with a six-station turret and a conventional leverage system that is entirely adequate for just about any reloading operation that comes to mind. Both come with priming arm and a plastic hopper designed to snare the spent primers. Price of the press with arm and catcher is $109.95 for the Orange Crusher, $139.95 for the T-Mag. Add another $25 and they come complete with a set of dies in the caliber of your choice. If your choice is 9mm Luger, 38/357, 41 Magnum, 44 Special/Magnum, 45 ACP or 45 Colt, the dies are supplied with a tungsten carbide resizing die at no extra cost.

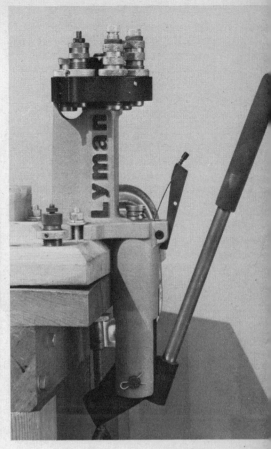
Lyman's T-Mag, in orange, has a six-station turret.

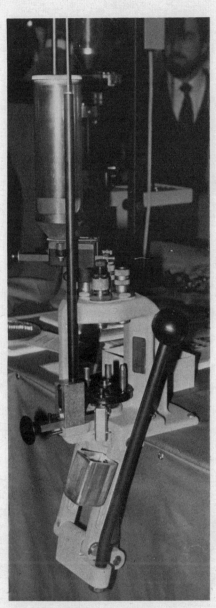
The Dillion 450 four-station press offers fast manual operation.

Huntington's version of the old Decker is better.

C-H Tool & Die Corporation came up with what they call their 105-Z die set in 38 and 44 sizes for swaging bullets with a zinc washer base locked in place by extruded bullet metal. They can also supply the zinc washers in small sacks holding one thousand. The system can be used quite nicely in any reasonably sturdy and competent reloading press such as the C-H Heavyweight CHamp. It offers a simple and economical alternative to casting or swaging with gilding metal bullet jackets since the zinc-based bullets are ready to load and shoot as they come from the basic production, without need for further sizing or lubrication. C-H also has added a taper-crimp die in 223 Remington that goes far to improve the feeding reliability of that cartridge in various autoloading rifles of that caliber.

Do you happen to recall the little Decker loading press? Well, it's back in a new and improved version and **Huntington Die Specialties** is producing it for about $50. That's Fred Huntington, of course, of RCBS fame and legend. He's added a priming punch so you can seat primers on the same rig—a feature notably lacking on the first version—and he cranked in another welcome feature for good measure.

Have you ever seen a picture of the Hindu goddess they call Siva, the one with eight arms or so? She is perhaps

Lee's Auto Disk Powder Measure, here on his Turret, measures uniform charges.

the only entity capable of seating bullets easily with the original Decker press, but Fred has added a small steel plate to the base of the press, permitting it to be secured to any solid surface with a C-clamp to free both your hands for bullet seating and such. I fastened mine to a small piece of hardwood so it can rest on one thigh while seated and find it remarkably convenient to use as modified to the

current pattern. Although small enough to pack in your pocket—without the mounting board, that is—the basic W-frame design of the Decker/HDS press gives it a surprising amount of leverage and the ability to reload large rifle cartridges without undue strain and fuss. This makes a highly satisfactory rig to take along to the shooting site for assembling ammo as you go.

Lee Precision has further aces and rabbits up their corporate sleeve to embellish their turret press discussed in last year's edition. Quite possibly available shortly is an Auto Index accessory probably—but not yet positively—available as a retrofit item for presses now in the field. This will index the turret that carries the dies, with the shell holder remaining stationary.

Then there's the new Lee Precision unit they call the Auto Disk Powder Measure which, at this stage in its development, is geared to the case neck expander. A letter from Dick Lee says, "Whenever a case is pushed against the expander, the charge bar is moved to the dump position. Powder will not dump if no case is pushing on the expander. Keeps things nice and neat. [. . .] We call it that because the charge bar is a disk with six holes for metering powder. Each hole is 7.5% larger than the last. To change holes or disks, just push the disk completely through the measure

NEW ROUNDS FOR THE 1911 PISTOL

41 Avenger

J. D. Jones, head of SSK Industries, worked up this 41-caliber wildcat round as an alternative load for the M1911A1 auto, cannily arranging things so as to give it a fairly broad spectrum of performance in terms of velocity and energy. Having butted my head to the bone and beyond in various grapplings with the 38-45 round for the old auto, I found the 41 Avenger a real piece of cake—angel food, to be specific—in comparison.

Forming the brass is simple and easy. A set of three Pacific reloading dies is supplied with the kit. Merely lube a 45 ACP case, run it up into the resizing die, then into the decap/mouth-expand die, reprime it, drop the powder charge, seat the bullet and away you go. Wipe off the case lube, of course, and, if you wish to turn in the slight flare at the case neck, just back out the resizing die and give the loaded round a chug up into that after it's adjusted properly.

That gives a cartridge subject to the pressure limits of the 45 ACP parent case, as discussed earlier. In dimensioning the chamber, Jones allowed sufficient room to perform the same operations on a longer case, such as the 451 Detonics Magnum and, when using that stronger-headed brass, you can turn up the wick a bit and shove the .410-inch diameter bullets forth at pretty brisk paces. As with

and reinstall through the side pushed against. No tools needed. The measure comes with four disks and 24 metering holes. I can honestly say that it dispenses the most uniform charges I have ever seen. This is due to the uniform actuation of the charge bar by the stroke of the press during the time of greatest mechanical advantage. Using the Auto Index in combination with the Auto Disk makes loading pistol and rifle cartridges 223 size and shorter surprisingly fast. Just keep adding a case, primer, bullet and three pumps of the handle."

Lee notes they hope to have these in production by the summer of 1983 and will also have a comparable and similar measure available for use as a separate accessory off a mounting stand. Lee supplied photos of the prototypes with the note that they may vary somewhat from final production in appearance.

For the roving reloader or those with space at a premium, the Reload-a-stand is a compact, lightweight, sturdy three-piece mounting base that works gratifyingly well at a trifle over $50; the pieces are storable in nooks and crannies. It's from **Accessory Specialty Company**

BULLETMAKING EQUIPMENT

Recall the French Arcane ammo discussed in the firearms press a year or so ago? **Hensley & Gibbs** now has their No. 938 mould for turning out 45 bullets that fairly well duplicate the shape and size of the 45 ACP Arcane in the casting alloy of your choice. It has a conical nose with included angle of 70 degrees and weighs about 174 grains when cast in an alloy of 80 percent linotype metal and 20 percent

Lee also will offer an Auto Index unit for the Turret to speed loading.

lead. It has a single, fairly broad grease groove and, when seated with the bullet shoulder even with the 45 ACP case mouth, feeds with notable reliability through every autoloader of that caliber in which I've tried it to date and it does equally well in revolvers or the Thompson/Center Contender if you've a barrel for that in the discontinued 45 ACP chambering.

Being lighter than most bullets for the 45 ACP, the recoil is correspondingly milder, although it can be driven to respectable velocities. As but one example, it would be a good performer for bowling pin competition, given anything better than a glancing hit.

Corbin Manufacturing & Supply now can furnish a flux that enables the home swager of jacketed bullets to solder the core securely to the jacket in somewhat the manner of the Speer *Hot-Cor* bullets. They have a dip lube that can be used in lieu of other lubricants in driving bullets to about 1100 fps without fouling the bore and a production canneluring tool of high capacity.

The Corbin Bullet Press, formerly called the Mity-Mite, soon will be available with a frame of a specialized bronze alloy that looks like gold and is more resistant to stress than cast iron. Also under development, and perhaps in production by the time you read this, are several other items of

Stiff clay test medium reacts like this to mild 44 Avenger load with Sierra 170-gr. hollow point.

The 41 Avenger feeds well, delivers the goods. Bullet is 170-gr. Sierra HP.

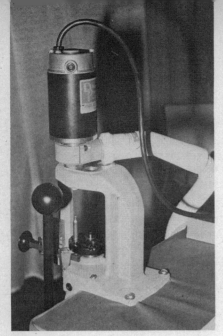

This Dillion electric case trimmer is $225 with standard sizing.

Grennel uses the Rust Guardit on stored moulds; uses RIG 3 to remove it before using them.

Rust Free and Q-tips are the Grennell prescription for cleaning mould cavities.

bulletmaking equipment including equipment for casting your own cores or extruding lead wire in any desired diameter.

For those with a need for tough-jacketed, large-bore bullets, Corbin can furnish dies to make bullets with jackets made from copper pipe or, at the other extreme, they can set you up to produce jacketed bullets that use spent 22 rimfire cases as the jacket

material. Most of these items can be furnished, Corbin says, as automated systems, ready to plug in and put into production.

A few quick tips for fellow casting enthusiasts: Rust on the working surfaces of moulds can be removed quite easily by means of Rust Free applied with a cotton swab or Q-Tip. Once cleaned up and ready for storage, Rust-Gardit provides the best protec-

tion against corrosion of any material I've encountered to date. To get the preservative off and the mould ready for further use, RIG 3 degreaser is wondrously effective and, to make the casting alloy flow almost as readily as hot skim milk, try stirring a small amount of Marvelux casting flux into the hot mixture. Marvelux is available from Brownell's, and a little goes a long but useful way.

the D-Mag, you can work up some cases out of the 308 Winchester brass as yet another alternative and Jones can supply the needed reamer and so on.

My favorite load for the 41 Avenger—working with the same old Remington-Rand used with the D-Mag—is 10.6 grains of Blue Dot behind the 170-grain Sierra JHC bullet, made up with 45 ACP brass. In point of fact, I find it a splendid way to make good use of all the thin-necked cases with the R-P headstamp that are inclined to hold .452-inch bullets a bit casually. When necked down, the neck thickens and they work just fine. I use the CCI-300 standard large pistol primer and the quoted load averages 1120 fps/474 fpe from the five-inch barrel. Hits stay in a patch the size of a playing card at 25 yards and the recoil is delightfully mild.

Fired into a block of the stiff, oil-base clay that I use as a ballistic test medium, that particular load makes an entrance opening nearly four inches across, coning on down to near bullet diameter about five inches deeper. It feeds as an undernourished piranha might; that is, voraciously and with great reliability. The fired primers look healthy and untroubled.

SSK Industries can provide bullet moulds, custom-built for them by NEI Industries, to turn out flat-point or round-nose bullets at around 180-185 grains, depending upon the alloy. I tried the flat-point, at 181 grains, with progressive charges of Hercules Herco powder from 5.6 to 8.0 grains. Velocity/energy figures spanned from 910/333 to 1160/541

Here's how SSK marks the 41 Avenger units. Seems quite clear—not much room for error.

The Saeco #351 at 200 grains is designed for the 357 Maximum cartridge.

These are the new RCBS designs for cast bullets for the silhouette games.

Hensley & Gibbs #938 mimics the French Arcane pistol bullet. Shown also in 45 ACP round.

RCBS has added moulds for four new cast bullets specifically designed for metallic silhouette competition. The 7mm 145-grain and 308 165-grain bullets have long, bore-riding forward shanks and the rear shank is short enough to be seated entirely in the case neck so the bullet heel and gas check do not protrude into the powder space in small-volume cases such as the 7mm T/CU or 30 Herrett.

Also with gas checks are a 180-grain 357 and 240-grain 44 bullet, both with the same anti-skid nose designs used on the 7mm and 308 designs. All are available in double-cavity moulds at a list price of $35 each.

Saeco has been busily on the go with a host of new products and improvements on the older ones. They've moved to Torrance, California and the firm was bought out by John Adams,

a dedicated combat competitor and silhouette shooter of many years experience. I look for a lot of good things out of this firm in coming years and some are here already. For example, Catalog No. 30004 is a modification kit for the Saeco lubri-sizer, available only as a factory direct item, enabling you to use top punches from Lyman, RCBS or Star. They have a truncated-point mould design in 44 available in

and the latter should be regarded as maximum, to be approached with caution, if at all. That was still with the R-P 45 ACP brass and CCI-300 primers.

The mentioned load with 5.6 grains of Herco is purely a purring pussycat to fire. The spent cases slide out lazily and usually remain on the shooting bench, saving wear and tear on the back in recovery. The recoil is ridiculously diffident and the groups are gratifying. Boost the charge to 6.2 grains of Herco and switch back to the 170-grain Sierra JHC and you have much the same state of affairs. It turns the old thumb-buster into a real fun-gun, the likes of which you find hard to believe.

You can shift over to using D-Mag brass, or cobble it from 308 stock, or trim it down from 45 Winchester Magnum if you wish, and pack in more propellant within the limits of the data sheet that Jones supplies. In so doing, the 41 Avenger becomes considerably more vengeful but still hardly worse than a bad cold.

In discussing all this, I feel I've yet to more than scratch the surface of this cartridge's promising potential. I've the capability for making .410-inch jacketed bullets of reassuring appearance clear on down to around 136 grains and I've yet to try promising powders such as DuPont's new 800-X in it although that has turned in ballistics I can hardly believe when applied to the 41 Magnum out of the ten-inch Contender barrel. In my book, the 41 Avenger still has a lot of untapped promise to explore, but the early results are warmly encouraging.

451 Detonics Magnum

For its whole seventy-odd-year career, the 45 ACP gun and cartridge have been throttled in performance by the fact that a crescent-shaped portion of the chambered case head hangs unsupported over the lower part of the feed ramp. There is nothing between the burning powder and the magazine well but a layer of brass, and the thickness of the brass dictated the maximum pressures not exceed 19,900 copper units of pressure.

The debut of the 45 Winchester Magnum cartridge of a few seasons back featured a thicker, considerably stronger case head design that proved capable of coping with remarkable pressures and of delivering impressive performance in guns such as the T/C Contender. The design staff at Detonics took a thoughtful look at the new case with its external dimensions the same as the 45 ACP, except for case length. Obviously, it could give the M1911-pattern pistol a badly needed boost, but there was the usual problem—what if such a hot load were to get into some gun of marginal strength, into a Model 1917 revolver, for example?

So Detronics trimmed the 45 Winchester Magnum case from its original 1.198 inches back to about .941-.943-inch (as checked on a pair of virgin factory cases), thereby creating the 451 Detonics Magnum case. Nominal case length for the 45 ACP is .898-inch, although few measure quite that long. Routine production of the D-Mag case is from scratch, headstamped 451 DET / MAGNUM, rather than

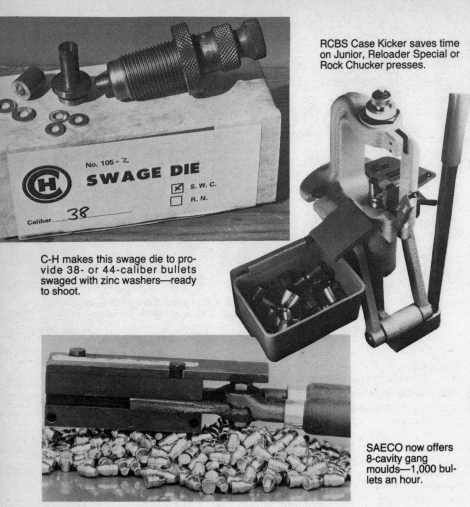

RCBS Case Kicker saves time on Junior, Reloader Special or Rock Chucker presses.

C-H makes this swage die to provide 38- or 44-caliber bullets swaged with zinc washers—ready to shoot.

SAECO now offers 8-cavity gang moulds—1,000 bullets an hour.

plain base at 195 grains (No. 448) or 240 grains with gas check (449) that work great in the 44 Special or Magnum. In addition to the two-cavity and four-cavity moulds traditional to the line, Adams has added eight-cavity gang moulds that roll forth the bullets at somewhere around one hundred every six minutes. These are available in any design Saeco offers and the delivery time is suprisingly prompt. Several new designs have been added in recent times and most if not all are illustrated in the brochure that's free on request.

The jargon of computers seems to be leaking into the language, as you may have just noticed. Software, in this instance, refers to the *Lyman Reloading Handbook,* 46th Edition and now available at $16.95 the copy at the better emporia of reloading wares. As the previous edition appeared in late 1970 and the new one has 164 additional pages, all of them larger, it seems a suitable topic.

There are 79 headings for rifle cartridges and 41 for handgun rounds, and 16 of the latter give specific performance in the Thompson/ Center Contender pistol. Discussion is included on muzzleloading, but they've dropped coverage of reloading shotshells.

Another useful data source, of special interest to those who reload for

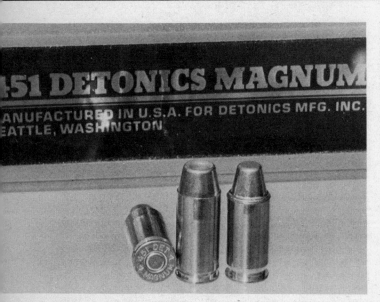

Just a little more room makes a lot more poop in the 451 Detonics Magnum cartridge.

by trimming Winchester cases, of course, but the cross-sections at the head are closely comparable. As a result, there is no way the D-Mag case or load can be chambered in a gun intended for sole use of the 45 ACP round. That whole problem is thereby side-stepped in much the manner of the 357 Magnum vs. 38 Special. Suffice to say, the 451 D-Mag case can cope with peak pressures considerably higher than the 45 ACP's limit of 19,900 CUP and, as you crack on the steam, some interesting ballistics begin to appear.

I did my D-Mag testing by means of a conversion kit installed in a Model 1911A1 made by Remington-Rand in 1945. The kit is supplied with a good set of instructions and I encountered no noteworthy problems. The sheet stresses that installation should be on modern guns in good condition. The complete kit consists of a barrel with recoil link and pin; a barrel bushing; a recoil spring assembly including recoil plug; an extractor; a firing pin spring; and a small reamer from Forster Brothers with which cases can be produced from 308 Winchester brass.

Since the 451 D-Mag is not as yet in production as a loaded factory round, the kit also included a reloading manual listing loads for the 185-grain Sierra JHC and 200-grain Speer JHP bullets. Respective maximum listed velocities are 1353 fps for the 185-grain bullet and 1281 fps for the 200-grain; respective energies are 752 and 729 fpe.

Curiously enough, conventional 45 ACP ammo can be fired with the conversion kit installed and it seems to work

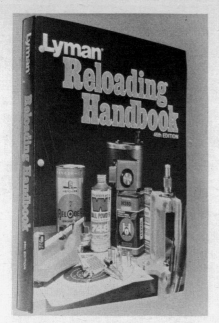

This edition is 164 pages bigger, gets into everything but shotshells.

Priming system of new RCBS RS 2 press is favored by Grennell.

Reload-a-stand offers three-piece rigidity and storage benefits—from Accessory Specialty Co.

handgun metallic silhouette competition, has been published by the International Handgun Metallic Silhouette Association (IHMSA) and it's available from IHMSA headquarters at $9.95 a copy. The title is *Reloading Guide for Handgun Accuracy* and it's a gold mine of useful lore for the bang-clang aficionado.

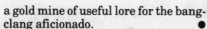

From left: The 41 Avenger, standard model; the 41 Avenger in 451 Detonics Magnum brass; the 451 Detonics Magnum.

through the action quite nicely, with decent accuracy, although it should be fed up through the magazine rather than singly hand-chambered. The recoil spring assembly supplied with the kit is quite powerful, to the point that even the hotter D-Mag loads rarely if ever lock the slide open on firing the last shot.

I did most of my firing with Hercules Blue Dot powder and did not work up to the maximum loads listed in the reloading booklet. With 14.1 grains of Blue Dot behind the 200-grain Speer JHP, the five-shot average was 1216 fps/657 fpe and the center spread for the five-shot group at 25 yards was barely as much as two inches. Other loads grouped even closer than that and all groups compared quite favorably with accuracy out of the same gun set up to fire 45 ACP exclusively. Accuracy was viewed as no problem. The plain truth is that when you start unleashing that many foot-pounds out of the M1911A1 recoil gets fairly fierce, prompting me to terminate the tests before getting to the top of the listed loads in the Detonics booklet.

The compact Detonics pistol can be had in the 451 D-Mag chambering and, like the converted M1911A1, it will handle standard 45 ACP loads out of the magazine. All in all, now that the scabs have healed from the first session, I want to get a grip safety with a broad tang installed and try it again. It is an interesting concept, giving the venerable auto a punch roughly equal to that of the 357 Magnum out of fairly long revolver barrels, with a capacity of seven or eight shots instead of six.

At his first stop on a long night's ride, Queen's Prize-winner G. R. Graham arrives at the English VIII Club, whose members provide the Elcho team.

After two seasons of bottomless ignominy, the 1978 Oxford University Rifle Team pulled it together for a four-trophy grand slam.

In England shooting is the . . .
INVISIBLE

The traditional British target pistol lives on, if precariously. This elegant single shot is by Jurek of Birmingham.

THERE IS NONE like the Intelligence Service for inflicting old school loyalty. If ever you were good enough, so legend and fiction has it, they will contrive a way to maneuvre you back in. The scenario of the reluctant spy's being dragged back into the cold is recurrent in espionage fiction and appeared most recently, perhaps, in Ted Allbeury's *A Choice of Enemies,* where the "Service" manages to blackmail public relations executive Ted Bailey back into the fold for a one-off job. His retraining, after a thirty-year layoff, began immediately:

"The next day I spent down in the basement of St. Alphage House on the firing range of the Marylebone Pistol Club where a guy from the Special Branch worked on me for hours on the 25-meter range with an automatic .22. By mid-afternoon the clusters of fifteen were getting closer and closer together and he was satisfied. They had chosen a Browning 9 mm for me, and we practised loading and unloading and then we stripped it down. The next day I had a felt holster that fitted neatly under my left armpit and we both knew that provided the other guy wasn't too good and missed with his first two shots, I'd survive."

St. Alphage House is an office block in Fore Street near Moorgate, next to the Barbican. Curiosity took us there and a discreet sign reading MRPC + SERC directed us to the sub-basement and a door festooned with heavy locks. Behind the door, the chatter of gunfire reverberated down a corridor from the left which, to the right, opened into a well-appointed club room with a bar and restaurant service. MRPC stands for the Marylebone Rifle and Pistol Club, where we were greeted courteously and ushered into the Committee Room. A few moments later, a uniformed police sergeant appeared from Wood Street station, examined our press credentials and conducted a low-key interrogation. Sergeant Hunter, we later learned, is one of Britain's finest Rapid Fire Pistol shots, and represented Scotland at the recent Commonwealth Games.

"You'll have to pardon the big security act," said Jan Stevenson, a Marylebone member and former top pistol shot for Oxford University. "We tend to be a bit froggy these days."

Once past the gauntlet, we found Marylebone congenial and impressive. The bar offers all the potables, plus Swiss cuisine at lunch and dinner. A firearms library occupies one corner while lighted cabinets display a small fortune in silver trophies currently held by Marylebone teams. The club often represents Britain abroad, *de facto* if not *de jure,* and recent excursions have included matches in the Netherlands, Germany, Switzerland, Rumania and the Bahamas. These were all pistol competitions. The club occasionally shoots fullbore rifle, but never smallbore, and discourages applications from rifle shooters. There would appear to be no shortage of handgunners. Membership is limited to 550 and there is always a waiting list of fifteen or so despite the £20 subscription.

SPORT
by EDWARD BAXTER

The mighty Elcho Shield, of sculpted steel with gold and silver embellishment, stands five feet and was donated by Lord Elcho in 1862. It is fired for at 1,000, 1,100, and 1,200 yards and goes to the winning team of eight from England, Scotland or Ireland. The Welsh, for some remote historical reason, are not invited, but may shoot for hundreds of pounds of other silver as individuals.

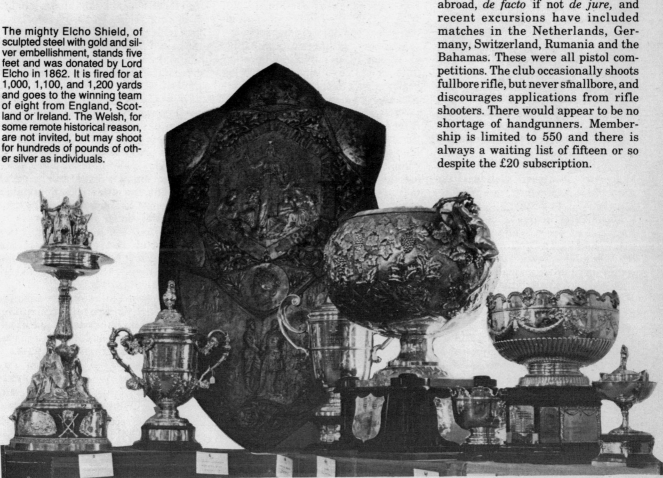

Victoria de Korda, firearms curator at the Imperial War Museum, arriving at Marylebone Club—MRPC, for short.

The Marylebone bar. Pistol-shooter Julia Goulding, at center left, is a London lawyer. Facing the camera in coat and tie is a National Centerfire Pistol Champion, Phillip Klein.

Committee member Alan Warner showed us around. An electrician by profession, he made one of the trophies in the cabinet and is perpetually attired in jeans and a tee shirt.

"What sort of people belong to Marylebone?" we asked.

"All sorts. We have members from every trade and profession. You can't read a class slant into pistol shooting, or any of the shooting sports."

This could be recent egalitarianism. The club was founded at the turn of the century by Sir Samuel Scott, Bart., M.P., a decade after the National Rifle Association had moved from Wimbledon Common to Bisley.

Major Peter Pearson, the NRA (of England) archivist, told us: "Competitive shooting in Britain grew out of the Volunteer movement of the 1860s, which was quite fashionable for a long time. Queen Victoria fired the opening shot at our first prize meeting, as did Princess Alexandra at the 1890 meeting which was our first at Bisley. The Prince of Wales, later King Edward VII, was very much a Bisley man and I have found a number of his scores in our records. Back then a member of the NRA Council would rarely be less than a Marquess and Earls were three the ha'penny. The occasional Esquire was conspicuous. Today it is the other way round."

The peerage on the NRA's Council today is in fact represented only by a brace of barons, Lord Swansea and Lord Cottesloe, and Sir Ronald Melville, K.C.B., the Chairman, does not likely feel apologetic of his station.

A century ago, there was probably a clear social distinction between fullbore and smallbore rifle shooting. Fullbore was the sport of Volunteers, who enjoyed a measure of money and leisure, while the National Smallbore Rifle Association, founded in 1901, was the successor to the Society of Working Men's Rifle Clubs. Today things have changed. Lord Swansea manages to assemble eleven peers for the annual match against the Commons, but aside that, Lords are thin on the line. Many regret their absence, for the aristocracy, if nothing else, has traditionally nurtured entertaining eccentricity. One peer is fondly remembered for having his manservant standing by on sunny days with a wet cabbage leaf on a silver salver, which his Lordship would periodically place on his head as a palliative for the heat.

Back to Marylebone:

Jan Stevenson said, "Of the members I know, there are two architects, several cops, three museum curators, a garagist, a guy who services housing estates, a forensic ballistician, a 'London best' gunmaker, a banker, a literary agent, a fashion model, a construction worker, a Sunday newspaper editor, a school teacher, a chemist and a heating contractor—sort of middle class on the whole, but then I'm sort of middle class and I don't make a habit of asking people what they do for a living. If you go by accent and demeanor, I imagine a class breakdown would show us to be as accurate a microcosm of British society as you'll likely find. The extremes of rich and poor would be absent and we would seem paragons of punctillious law observance, but aside that, dead average. Being City, we find farmers under-represented. And there is a bit of an Oxbridge scent to the place, since both universities have strong pistol traditions and when a team member comes down to London, he or she usually slides down the grapevine to Marylebone rather than joining another club. But in a membership of 550 they don't bulk large."

"What about spies?" we asked, recalling Allbeury's book.

"None that I know of. One assumes they have their own training facilities. And although our range is one of the most sophisticated in Britain and easily adaptable to any small arms use, a fledgling spook with a funny gun would have us all crowded round to watch. This is a club after all, and people get to know each other. A new face arouses curiosity, as you discovered. If spooks need firearms training, I'm sure they have their own range. Everyone else has, why not they?"

"Who else?"

Silver by the ton, a legacy of Empire, circulates among British shooters each year, especially in the classic shoots.

The Marylebone range has six points at 25 meters, with automatic target controls. The backstop will handle anything short of anti-tank weapons.

"Well, there is a range at the Bank of England and another at the British Museum. The House of Lords has one that is used three nights a week, mostly by Palace of Westminster staff. There is a primitive one at the Treasury and a pukkah one at the Department of the Environment and an unused one at the Tower of London, occupied by ghosts, no doubt. London Transport has one at Baker Street tube station. There must be at least a hundred firing ranges in London. There is a fair chance to find one underneath any large building, St. Alphage House for one, the Shell building for another.

"Shooting is very much a subterranean affair in London, both in the sense that underground is a good place for an indoor range and in the sense that shooting is an invisible sport. The legitimate side of firearms use is ignored by the general press and the media with the result that most people have no concept of the extent and complexity of it, of the diversity of disciplines and the numbers who compete. The impression given is that firearms equals violence equals crime, which is a grotesque distortion. One could as well associate Grand Prix racing with driving getaway cars for a bank raid. The difference is that most people have a personal acquaintance with automobiles and can keep things in perspective. People fear and misunderstand the unknown, and most people today have no personal familiarity with firearms. The sum of their knowledge consists of a jumble of bizarre impressions from American television programs. Some source!"

We found ourselves repeatedly compelled in the course of our research to jettison large chunks of shooting sports information to keep the subject to manageable dimensions. The Services understandably promote sport shooting and each service has a rifle association and a busy competitive program. Most TA units, OTC's and CCF's (training establishments) have their own ranges and clubs. Shooting is a fast-growing sport in the police and the Police Athletic Association has separate sections devoted to shotgunning on the one hand and rifle and pistol on the other. Last year's annual PAA rifle and pistol meeting at Bisley attracted some six hundred competitors and police teams often compete against civilian clubs. Shotgunning and airgun shooting are tremendously popular. There are over 800,000 shotgun owners in Britain, and the National Air Rifle and Pistol Association claims a quarter million members for its affiliated clubs.

There are seven shooting events at the Olympic Games and in terms of total individual membership of the affiliated national federations, shooting is the foremost Olympic sport. In Britain, shooting ranks second as a club sport, a fly cast behind fishing and a long drive ahead of golf. Leaving shotgunning and airgun shooting aside, there are some 3,500-4,000 rifle and pistol clubs in Britain. The NRA has about 3,000 individual members, while the NSRA numbers over 43,000. There are some 220,000 holders of rifle and pistol certificates in Britain, virtually all of whom are members of one club or another, and many club members do not hold certificates.

One can understand when shooters complain that their sport suffers from a *de facto* press blackout. By contrast, 80 reporters from the leading daily and provincial newspapers and London agencies covered the NRA's 1905 meeting, and the Bisley telegraph office transmitted over a million words of news text. Today, only two of the dailies cover competitive shooting and with an almost tabular laconism, often unintelligible to all but shooters themselves. And they scarcely need to turn to the *Times* or the *Telegraph* for the results, for they have a well-developed press of their own.

There are five newsstand firearms magazines published in Britain. *Shooting Times and Country,* which covers shotguns, stalking and field sports, circulates a phenomenal 58,000 copies a week. The remaining four are monthlies and circulate from 20,000 to 40,000 copies. Two are de-

Thin on the line: Lord Swansea, far right, finishing the 600-yard stage of the Vizianagaram on Century Range. Standing, in tweed, among the House of Commons is Sir Ronald Melville, KCB, Chairman of the NRA.

A member of the Athelings, in distinctive hat and blazer, keeps score during the Vizianagaram. Lord Brocket is leading, but Lord Swansea finished first overall, as usual.

British Sporting Rifle Club and the Muzzle Loaders' Association of Great Britain, which circulate at several hundred copies.

When looked at closely, British shooting fragments into a mosaic of specialized interests, each administered by an independent association or "subcontracted" by a parent association to a national club. There are some twenty or thirty such groups, including a half-dozen or so coordinating committees or councils which endeavor to foster some sort of coherence. The cries for amalgamation of all shooting interests into a central association are constant, but not unanimous. The editor of the U.K. Practical Shooting Association *Newsletter* recently wrote, "I am not much sold for the moment on the desirability of all shooters' amalgamating into a single, unified, lethargic, incompetent, gutless association."

Jan Stevenson explained, "We are in the midst of a massive crisis of confidence. Shooters, almost to a man, regard the leadership of the national associations as incompetent and out of touch with political reality. We are being done in by the Chief Constables and the Home Office bureaucracy and the associations are still preaching compromise. When you are sentenced to hang by the neck until dead, you don't gain a hell of a lot by negotiating a compromise for a short rope. Shooters are fast figuring this out; the leadership has not got the word. The problem with the amalgamation movement is that there is no trusted figure to build it around. It will be a close race as to whether the associations will clean up their act and swing round to fight for the survival of the sport before the Home Office succeeds in killing it."

Meantime, the associations regard their purpose as promoting competitions and coping with the incredible administrative detail that goes into an annual competitive program culminating in a national championship for each discipline.

Competitive rifle shooting is broadly divided into smallbore (.22 caliber rimfire) administered by the National Smallbore Rifle Association in Southwark and fullbore (.30 caliber centerfire) administered by the National Rifle Association at Bisley Camp, Surrey.

Smallbore rifle on the grand championship level is fired outdoors

Smallbore rifle on the grand championship level is fired outdoors at 50 yards, 50 meters and 100 yards, but it lends itself ideally to indoor ranges

voted to shotguns, one to airguns and the fourth, *Guns Review*, is a general firearms journal. *(Note: There is now also a bimonthly for handgunners. KW)*

Then there are about a dozen publications produced by and distributed to the members of the shooting associations, national clubs and collector's societies. These range from *WAGBI*, the Wildfowlers' Association journal, a slick, professional magazine distributed to a membership of 40,000, to the newsletters of the U.K. Practical Shooting Association, the Long Range Pistol Shooters' Association, the

where it is fired throughout the year at 25 yards. There is an international competition called the English Match in honor of the British rifleman's renowned disinclination to fight gravity—it is fired entirely from prone position. Generally though, smallbore rifle is a 3-position exercise: prone, which is soporific; kneeling, which is painful; and standing, which is demoralizing. It is a tremendously exacting sport, for the 10-ring is a pinprick dot which must be obliterated by the bullet. The International Running Boar event is fired standing from 50 meters on a porcine silhouette which hurtles from side to side at varied speeds. The shooter fires one shot per pass.

Fullbore rifle on the Continent is a 3-position exercise fired exclusively at 300 meters. The British have never been keen on this, for fullbore rifle here is a richer tapestry. The Queen Mary's, for example, is fired with the self-loading rifle on snapshooting silhouettes on exposure during a 500-yard to 100-yard run-forward. It is a spectacular event, and fun, but a bit outside the mainstream.

When we speak of British fullbore rifle shooting, we generally mean shooting from prone or supine position with great deliberation at ranges from 300 to 1,200 yards. The Continentals never do this; the Americans, except for the Wimbledon Cup and the Palma Match against Britain, rarely venture beyond 600 yards, and the Commonwealth usually pack it in at 900. Twelve hundred is the limit in Britain only because Bisley's Stickledown Range stops there. For given his inclination, the Englishman will shoot from as far away as he can get. Sometimes he will go to Scotland to do it, for rifle shooting British style reached its apogee in the late 1950s at Barry, Angus, where a series of competitions were conducted at 2,100 yards—almost a mile and a quarter.

Each shooter went to the line armed with a battery of graphs and calculations to assist him in getting a bullet to the almost-invisible 4½-foot bullseyes on the horizon. Admiral Fitzroy Hutton, one of the most famous of Bisley riflemen and an organizer of the Barry shoots, determined that the bullets were taking four seconds in flight, that their trajectory carried them to a height of 130 feet above the ground, and that they entered the targets at a 7° downward angle. A 25 mile per hour cross-wind—not unusual—would drift the bullets 54 minutes of angle, or 100 feet at the targets. Since this far exceeded the windage adjustments on

Stickeldown's terraced 1,000-yard firing line attracts a throng of spectators for the Queen's final. The giant scoreboard is kept current shot-by-shot. (Photo: Robin Peters)

No apologies—G. R. Graham of Australia leaves Stickledown in 1978, a Digger who has done it all. (Photo: Robin Peters)

the backsight, the targets were placed a careful 30 feet center to center. Wind was read by an anemometer on a 40-foot tower at 1,200 yards and the readings relayed electrically to the firing line. The shooter would aim one or two targets up the line from his own, and take the incremental adjustment on his sights. In these circumstances, with winds varying to 18 miles an hour, Major Crawford managed a string of five straight bulls, but was tied at the end of two days by Wing Commander Whitelock for first place.

Need it be said that the Barry range stopped at 2,100 yards only because the terrain permitted no more?

The British rifleman's year consists of a series of club, county and regional competitions culminating in the Queen's Prize match during the NRA's Annual Meeting at Bisley the middle fortnight of July, which is still known, albeit informally now, as the Imperial Meeting. The Queen's is a three-stage match, and the first stage, fired at 300, 500 and 600 yards on Century range, is restricted to 1,200 shooters. The top-scoring 300 are passed to fire the second stage, again at 300, 500 and 600 yards on Century. The top 100 are then passed to fire the third stage on Stickledown at 900 and 1,000 yards, itself a signal honor for which many riflemen spend a lifetime striving.

Stickledown is a difficult range. The terrain undulates back from the targets and at about 800 yards tilts downward so abruptly that the 900-yard shooting takes place from a sort of dike at the downhill side of the line, which terminates in a wood. The wind sweeps in, bounces off the trees, hooks through the hollow and corkscrews down the range. Either that or it sweeps downslope, bounces off the face of the wood and does a backflip on everybody. Or it comes in over the trees, leaves the hollow becalmed and ricochets off the up-slope firing points. Ninety percent of long range shooting is wind doping. Americans hate Stickledown; the Colonials merely look dazed and practice a Pommy upper lip. They have all come up judging the wind from downrange mirage, and there is rarely enough heat at Bisley to generate any. The wind has to be read from the flags, which likely as not point different ways at different distances and bearing in mind that the trajectory of the bullet carries it well above the midrange flags into an invisible wind pattern. One has but to watch the Queen's third stage to sense the fascination of the sport.

The match is decided at 1,000 yards. In case of a tie, the shooting continues until it is broken. The winner is declared on the spot, climbs into the traditional chair with his rifle, and is carried in triumph from Stickledown to the NRA headquarters to the acclamation of a thousand spectators and behind a military band playing "See the Conquering Hero Comes." It is a tremendously moving event.

"I'm not a rifleman," said Alan Keller, "but I have been watching the third stage of the Queen's for four years now. It is fantastic. The blokes who win all look as if they had been

Oxford's pistoleers, above, fared up and down, but had more fun most years.

NRA headquarters, (opposite page top) built in 1902, reflect a tweedy, squirearchical outlook shooters begin to find galling.

(Opposite page middle) Flanked by chariots, is the ornate and fiendishly heavy National Trophy. The Vizianagaram pilgrim jugs and the Grand Aggregate Shield, presented by Canada in 1877 and second only to the Queen's Prize in prestige, may also be seen.

Expatriate Jan Stevenson (opposite page bottom) of Marylebone and Roanoke, Alabama, with—on the horizon at 1,100 yards—the Stickledown target line where the wind deceives.

Jim Cairns' (below) concentration had just slipped. Commiserating is former British women's champion Trudy Henry. (Photo: Col. T. W. Whitaker)

dragged by the foot behind the machine of time, like Hector after the horses got tired. Charles Trotter, who won in 1975, is a grey, grizzled, bearded Gurnseyite who walks with two canes as a result of a motor accident. Seeing him in the chair with the two canes across one knee and his rifle across the other, looking out over the band and the crowd, knowing he was the best in the Empire was splendid.

"Walter Magnay, who won in 1976, looks like a cross between Charles Laughton and Charles Bronson who just walked out of the Sahara and hit a string of pubs on the way, though I understand his personal drinking habits are moderate. David Friend, who won in '77 looks as if he spent his life behind a rifle in bad weather. G.R. Graham, who won this year, is a grey-haired, sun-baked Digger. The Australian national council overruled his state association, who had not selected him to come to Bisley. He rode down from Stickledown knowing he had no apologies to make back home. All the guys who win the Queen's have spent decades stockpiling the expertise and the luck it takes. They are hard, leathery old dudes who earned their victory. Seeing them in the chair getting the recognition they deserve is glorious. Think what it must be like for them. What a way to cap a life!"

The ride in the chair is a longer one than most realize. There are some two dozen clubs resident at Bisley. After the awards ceremony in late afternoon, the Queen's prize winner begins a tour of the clubs which ordinarily terminates about midnight, depending on stamina. Relays of chair bearers wilt by the wayside and at the end of the ride the winner himself is often in rare condition. More than one, we suspect, has seen the sun rise from the randomly parked chair. He is carried to the steps of each club and is followed in by the bearers, where he is greeted with applause by the committee and assembled membership and shown to the bar for a drink and some ritual shooting of the breeze. The drink downed and the stories recounted, he climbs back in the chair to a round of cheers for the voyage to the next club.

Shooting is a traditional sport and Bisley is a skein of custom.

"I once paid the ten bob fee to lodge a protest with the Bisley Committee," Jan Stevenson recalled. "I'd have reconsidered if I had realized that the signal for the Committee to meet was raising a black flag above NRA headquarters and hoisting a black drum to the top of the Clock Tower on Stickledown."

The most popular pistol event—with as many as 700 entries—in Britain is the Advancing Men, a simulated bayonet charge in which the shooter places two hits on each of three silhouettes. Here Richard Munday of Oxford fires it in Fairbairn Cup competition against Cambridge.

Not selected for the National Squad one year, Vic Kelston rubbed it in by winning the British Centerfire Championship Cup, the Granet Cup (duelling), and the ISU Aggregate Cup. He nearly grand-slammed the year.

Traditions come in hierarchies and none stands in the way of the winner's boozy, chairborne, nighttime promenade. In 1930 the King's prize, as it was then, was won by the elegant Marjorie Foster. That night, she became the first woman ever to enter the bar of the North London Rifle Club. The President of the North London, traumatized by the prospect, declined to greet her and locked himself in his office with a stiff drink. But it never occurred to him that *anything* could qualify the prize winner's right of access to the bar. Nothing could.

Two years ago petite Libby Felton, the Australian national champion, almost became the second woman to win the Queen's. She won the second stage on a shoot-off, and when the smoke cleared at 1,000 yards she was in a three-way tie for the prize, but this time lost the shoot-off. This year she did not qualify for the second stage. "I went back to 600 yards having dropped only two points," she said, "but it all came apart at 600." Six hundred yards left prestigious litter this year. Besides Libby Felton, Lord Swansea, one of Britain's finest and most experienced riflemen, was left there.

Bisley is a shooting man's Mecca. The camp boasts perhaps the richest profusion of Victorian ersatz-colonial architecture extant. Several of the buildings were dismantled in 1890 and moved from Wimbledon. The trophies, on view during the Imperial Fortnight, constitute one of the world's most magnificent collections of silver—tons of it. The National Trophy takes six men to carry and some of the cups are large enough for a woman to bathe in. The China Vase, made in Hong Kong in 1864 by a silversmith named Lee Ching, stands four feet high and a yard across and every square centimeter of surface is engraved. It was said at the time that if Ching were to die, the vase could not be finished. The House of Commons and the House of Lords compete each year for an exquisite pair of silver pilgrim jugs presented by the Maharaja of Vizianagaram, whose invitation to become a vice-president of the NRA arrived posthumously, to the embarrassment of everyone save the late Maharaja himself.

In response to our question, Mr. P.E. Bowerbank of the NRA said, "I would be pleased to tell you the insurance value of the trophies, but it would bear no relation to the value of the collection, for the policy was negotiated on the understanding that the trophies come together only once a year, and throughout this period they are under constant armed military guard."

In fact, the value of the collection is incalculable.

Shooters meet and marry at Bisley. They spend their honeymoons and their annual holidays there. Rendered redundant, (that is, laid off a job) they retreat to Bisley and shoot until a job application proves successful. They die there and, if riflemen, have their ashes spread across Stickledown. Pistol shooters have theirs spread on Cheylesmore.

"I get embarrassed to go down and change targets," said Jed Frobisher. My upbringing must have been strong on cemetery etiquette, and I have friends underfoot here."

Bisley is devoted to the rifle. The Imperial Fortnight is a celebration of riflery and the silver in its vast majority goes to riflemen. Behind the scenes, pistol shooters fight their contests almost unnoticed. When one delves into it though, one discovers a sub-sport of kaleidoscopic diversity, Byzantine complexity and extreme fascination.

"I actually prefer pistol," said a former Cambridge University rifleman, "but the consequences of going out of training are so painfully conspicuous. With the rifle, your group may open by 50%. With the pistol it is more like 300%."

There are approximately ten pistol disciplines practiced in Great Britain, each administered by an association or national club. Together they comprise some thirty different events, most of which require a different, specialized weapon. These range from bog standard battle pistols to late 18th century flintlocks to late 19th century revolvers to the International Free Pistol, an ornate single shot that fits onto the hand like a glove, with a hair trigger that adjusts so finely that a change of temperature can set it off. Distances vary from the occasional absolute pointblank shot in Practical Pistol to 300 yards with big revolvers in Long Range. Pocket pistols, in these competitions, are shot at 100 yards and service pistols at 100 and 200.

The "International" events are shot at 25 meters, except for Free Pistol, which is sixty excruciating rounds in 2½ hours against a target at 50 meters with a 2-inch 10-ring. Police Pistol is fired at ranges varying from 7 yards to 50 yards from standing, kneeling, prone and barricade positions. Service pistol is fired from 25 yards down to 10 yards on a ferocious target with scoring zones so small that the 25-yard stage is the equivalent of firing from 125 yards on a Practical Pistol silhouette. This calls for extremely fine shooting from standing position with an unmodified service pistol.

If fullbore rifle is largely a question of wind judgment, pistol is a game of nerves and concentration. The pistol shooter is embarked on a lifelong struggle for an extra increment of self-control.

"We used to worry," said Jeff Cooper, an American authority, "about the technique of the pistol falling into the wrong hands. But we have found that the criminal almost by definition lacks the self-control required for mastery of the handgun and will with rare exception be a mediocre shot no matter what."

Dr. David Bartram of the Department of Psychology of the University of Hull, said, "To me, as a psychologist, the interesting question is: How do people develop the remarkably high degree of control which is necessary for accurate shooting?"

He has devoted a considerable amount of study to determining the minimum group it is theoretically possible to fire with a handheld weapon, taking physiological and neurological factors into account. Such a group would not win a match.

"Somehow," Dr. Bartram continues, "the expert marksman manages to overcome this and shoot, it seems, beyond his physical capabilities."

What kind of people then win at pistol?

"You get the occasional child prodigy who illuminates the sky like Haley's Comet, and on about the same frequency," said Frobisher, "the occasional *Wunderkind* who barnstorms his way from one horizon to the other, but usually on the lower tier. When the dust settles, everyone is still grubbing away. The guy with conspicuous talent is a bit of a freak. Mastery of the pistol usually comes from decades of hard work."

The question is clouded by the fact that there are about two dozen national pistol champions at any one time. Some cut a wider swath or cast a longer shadow than others, but the effect is usually cumulative. There is no Queen's prize in pistol which can catapult an unknown visitor onto a popular pedestal.

"If any single event commands universal respect at the moment," said Alan Keller, "it is probably the National Centrefire Championship, which is fired at the Imperial as a two-stage event, 30 shots precision at 25 meters and 30 shots duelling, repeated for a total of 120 rounds. The match was won last year by John Gough, a retired paratroop major who is generally classed alongside Olympian John Cooke as one of the two finest all-around classical pistol shots in Britain. Classical means they stick to the old-line events.

"This year's match was won by a crusty old Polak named Victor S. Krzyszkowski-Kelston, who came to Britain during the war. He did the Battle of Poland in 1939 in a volunteer infantry unit and later, after a working over by the Gestapo, escaped, walked to Palestine and joined the Carpathian Brigade. Eventually he made it to Britain via South Africa and spent the war in the R.A.F. as a gunner and co-pilot. Afterwards he moved to the Northcountry and settled down as a chiropodist.

"Vic has always been a fine shot, but has had a pernicious habit of placing several slots down the scoresheet and claims a run of second places worthy of *Guiness*. He has been grinding away at pistol marksmanship for more than a quarter century and meantime became taken for granted as part of the scenery. This year he was not selected for the National Squad and has been exacting vengeance ever since."

At the Imperial, the Centrefire Championship settled into a duel between the old Pole and Jim Cairns, the British Army's top pistol shot, whose concentration is legendary.

"I once saw Jim picking cartridges up from the table and loading his pistol," said Captain Dave Thomas of the Army team, "and said to him, 'Why are you picking those cartridges up? With your concentration you should be able to think them off the table and into the gun.' I really believe that within a few years Cairns will literally be able to levitate objects by force of concentration."

The Championship balanced on a razor's edge until the 118th shot. Cairns threw it to the 6-ring.

"It was the third from the last shot on the final set of duelling," he said, "My concentration faltered."

Kelston's didn't.

"Damned shame we don't chair the pistol champion," said Keller. "Vic Kelston would have looked great up there. He's a shooting champion from the rough old mold most of them are." ●

(NOTE: This entertaining report only touches the tip of the classic iceberg. UK shooting is as varietal as their terriers, of which there are several dozen breeds. *KW*)

TESTFIRE

M6 22/410 Survival Gun

You can shoot the M6 wearing mittens.

The M6 buttstock holds 19 rounds under the comb.

The M6 by Springfield Armory is a short range survival gun, intended mainly for small game, such as rabbits. Thus, the rifle barrel was checked out for accuracy and point-of-impact at 25 yards, using CCI, Federal, Remington, and Winchester Long Rifle ammunition. From a standing position, with rest, 3-shot groups were fired. High speed cartridges tended to open the groups over 3 inches at 25 yards. Best groups were obtained using the Federal Power-Flite, Winchester T22, and Remington Hi-Speed Golden cartridges. The smallest group—1 3/32 inches—was obtained with the Federal load, although the other two brands produced groups as small as 1 9/16 inches.

With the new Federal 410 Super Slug load, the M6 produced 3-shot groups at 25 yards measuring as small as 3½ inches, hardly useful for taking any game which the 22 couldn't handle better, but with other useful potential. The 410 barrel was patterned at 25 yards using 3-inch Remington Express shells with ¾-ounce of No. 7½ shot, and at 20 yards using the Winchester AA Skeet load containing ½-ounce of No. 9 shot. The

Remington load produced a 5-shot pattern average of 51.3 percent, with 31.1 percent of this total inside the 15-inch diameter center circle. The AA load produced a 5-shot average of 80.2 percent at 20 yards, with 36.6 percent of this total inside the 15-inch diameter center circle.

Over-all length of the M6 test gun was 32 inches, with a length of pull of 10 9/16 inches, measured from the center of the grooved firing lever. Four versions are available—the 22/410 which was tested, plus a 22 WRM/410, a 22 Hornet/410, and the 22 LR/45 Colt.

Basically the M6 consists of a 22-caliber rifle barrel over a 410-bore smoothbore barrel, both sleeved into a forged monobloc, hinged at the bottom to a buttstock/receiver assembly and locked by a top latch. All metal parts have a gray Parkerized finish, including the optional quick-detachable swivels and studs. The outside hammer is a rebounding design; in its face is a movable push/pull block which serves as a barrel selector.

The stamped steel buttstock assembly has the breech block, hammer spring retainer, etc., riveted in place

while the rebounding firing pins are retained by screws. One excellent feature of the M6 is the method of ammo storage in the buttstock. The neoprene-covered comb of the stock is hinged at the heel, with a push-button latch on the left side near the nose. Raising the comb reveals recesses in the plastic insert for 15 rimfire cartridges and four 3-inch 410-bore cartridges. On the test gun these recesses were a very snug fit with some brands of 410 shells: it would pay to check this feature and use only those shell brands which are easily removed.

The 22 and 410 barrels on the test gun shot to different points. The rifle barrel shot 5½ to 6½ inches below the aiming point; the 410 barrel shot from 6½ to 10½ inches low, and from 5 to 7 inches to the right as well. Anyone planning on using the M6 for survival better do a lot of shooting with it first.

The M6 has definitely been field tested, by the U.S. Air Force no less in the original design. The latest version is just as rugged. It is doubtful a more rugged survival gun can be obtained for the same price, which is less than $150, as this is written.

Larry S. Sterett

Benelli B76: The Thinking Man's 9mm?

Several years ago, when first the Benelli pistol was marketed, I borrowed one and shot it some and then sent it on to J. B. Wood. And I wrote something but never published it. Here's what I wrote:

"I suppose we fired a couple of hundred rounds through the Benelli, between myself and some other fellows. It was a very nicely behaved gun,

The Benelli fits in standard holsters; rides well on the hip.

brand-new and possibly even from a pre-production run, but you had the feeling that you could certainly solve the accuracy problem with it. That is, if you had an accuracy problem. It just feels right, all the way around.

In all the normal handling procedures, it handled normally. It fits the hand and is particularly adapted to the two-hand hold we all use these days.

I guess it just isn't possible to write what I am trying to say and I hope you get it from the pictures. The Benelli 9mm is a very gunny gun. Its manufacturers have created a set of machining lines and general configuration that make great visual sense."

Now, much later, Donald Simmons' article in this issue piqued my interest and I got another one. And it's more appealing now than it was then, even though I have met a number of good pistols since.

Talking to other shooters, I find their responses are quick—they like it or they don't. I'm convinced this opinion is based on the Benelli's looks; there's something about its squared-up front end some don't like. Personally, I like it.

There can be little exception to the

rest of the Benelli's looks. It reminds me, overall, of the SIG-210, though it has a slicker grip angle and somewhat easier controls—except that bolt release—and good trigger feel, either double-action or single.

There are two things I really like about the Benelli and these are enough to tilt me toward it:

First, the grip suits me in terms of bulk and cross-section, and most of all in terms of grip angle. The gun points well and quickly and comfortably and that is a hard to buy feature in any class of gun.

Second, it shoots quick. It shoots the first one quick because of the grip angle and decent trigger. It shoots the next couple quick because it doesn't bounce as much as a lot of service autoloaders do.

You see, I have little need for a service-class autoloader in 9mm or 45 or 10mm or whatever. When I do need one though, it has to be one that helps me put the rounds where I want them fast; until then, it should not get in the way.

I find the Benelli 76 is a very friendly pistol that does just that, so I'm going to keep this one.

Ken Warner

That grip angle is wonderful, even if it forces geometry that insists on full-length cartridges.

The gun simply behaves well

It takes a lot of stuff to test a T/C 83.

Thompson/Centers' New Single Act

Mention single shot, centerfire rifles in about any crowd and, most likely, the name Thompson/Center won't enter the conversation. However, that will change because they've introduced another winner, the TCR 83. For now, it's available in 223, 22-250, 243, 30-06 and 7mm Remington Magnum.

The barrel pivots down, exposing its breech for loading a cartridge into the chamber, or removing a fired case. Thus, in both form and function, the TCR closely resembles the common single-barrel shotgun.

The breech end of the barrel is a 2⅞-inch long monobloc, replete with a husky bolting lug in its bottom to engage a locking bolt protruding through the standing breech face. Swinging the top lever *either* left or right cocks the striker and retracts the locking bolt, allowing the barrel to pivot down on its hinge pin. As the barrel swings down, an "L" shaped dog, standing in the receiver floor,

cams rearward a case extractor, located in a raceway in the monobloc.

As a rimless cartridge is pushed into the chamber, the spring-loaded extractor snaps into the extractor groove and, as the breech is closed, the extractor is cammed forward, along with the cartridge, by the standing breech face. When the rifle is closed, the bottom of the monobloc trips a latch, allowing the locking bolt to move forward into engagement with the bolting lug. One gets a solid feel when closing the TCR.

Forward in the trigger bow are two buttons; one locks the sear and another locks the button which locks the sear. Thus it takes both the thumb and index finger to coax the safety over to its "fire" position. It only takes one to do the rest, however, either by first pulling the rear trigger to set the front trigger, or by pulling the front trigger alone.

Taking down the TCR is simple enough. The forearm is removed by

swinging its latch down, allowing the barrel to pivot off its hinge pin. What we end up with is a suitcase-size package measuring 23 inches, the barrel length. Fresh from its box, the test rifle in 243 weighed 7 lbs., 4 oz.

Atop the monobloc are four holes for scope mounting, filled with slave screws which can be utilized for filling four holes out on the barrel if one chooses to remove the iron sights. The stock and forearm are walnut, both adorned with cut checkering of a modest but adequate pattern. The rubber padded buttstock has a small European-type cheekpiece and is attached to the receiver by means of a through-bolt. Surprisingly, the TCR does not have sling swivels.

During my accuracy tests, B-Square mounts held a Weaver KT-10 atop the 243 and after a couple hundred rounds I expressed my disappointment with its accuracy to Bob Gustafson of T/C. Since the test rifle was a pilot model, he was kind enough to replace its barrel with another from standard production. I'm glad he did because the replacement 243 shoots like a house afire. Federal's 100-grain Premium ammunition absolutely refuses to place three of its bullets farther apart than 1¼-inch, while Winchester's 80-grain loads hover at minute of angle. Thus far, the best performance with handloads has come from 100-grain spitzers from Sierra, Speer and Nosler, all pushed by either IMR-4831 or WW-760. The most accurate varmint loads are the 85 Sierra and 75 Nosler, combined with IMR-4064.

I foresee a very bright future for the TCR 83, mainly because of its interchangeable barrels. Thanks to the folks at T/C, a fellow can buy a 223 or 22-250 in the spring and later in the year take $140 to his local gun shop and easily transform his varmint rifle into a big game rifle. Also, I like the idea of flying off on a hunting trip with a TCR in my suitcase or duffle bag, which does not advertise its presence to thieves, as does a gun case.

And, of course, we must not overlook the possibility of taking a second barrel, replete with scope, as back-up on an extended hunt. A trip to Africa with a bolt action heavy for the nasty stuff and a TCR with barrels in 243, 30-06 and 20 gauge sounds good but we'll have to wait awhile on the smoothbore, or so Warren Center says.

I like the new TCR 83, for both its concept and its performance. I also like its lifetime guarantee.

Layne Simpson

Simpson shoots and tells all.

Model 94 Angle-Eject for Scopes

Of course, it's long been possible to mount glass sights on Winchester's Model 94, if you don't mind side mounts, with the scope sitting over toward Aunt Hattie's hen house, but now things have changed, and here's why: The bolt face of this newest 94 has an extractor positioned at eleven o'clock and an ejector at five o'clock.

Rather than flipping a fired case skyward, as with the standard Model 94, the Model 94 Angle Eject propels it right and slightly rearward through an ejection slot milled from the top of the right receiver wall. What we have here is a Model 94 which allows a scope to be mounted low and centrally over the bore. Neat idea. It works without a hitch too.

Scope mounts come with the 94AE, the rear base straddling the bolt and attached with two screws into the top of the receiver walls. The front base is also attached with two screws at the receiver ring.

There is more good news: In addition to the fine 375 Winchester, the 94AE is available in two new cartridges called 307 and 356 Winchester. They are made up by leaving 30-30 size rims on what look like 308 and 358 Winchester cases and despite their names, the new rounds hold .308 and .358-inch bullets. The names have been changed in effort to avoid confusing the semirimless with the rimless. Four new flat-nose Power Point bullets were also introduced with these cartridges—150- and 180-grain in the 307, while the 356 has 200- and 250-grain loads.

With the 180-grain factory loads, my 307 test rifle, with Redfield 1-4x scope attached, shot like Model 94s are not supposed to shoot: 0.92 to 2.00 inches for three-shot groups at 100 yards. On the other hand, at 1.66 to 3.36 inches, the 150-grain load made the Angle Eject act like any other Model 94. However, other rifles may like this load better. Despite its dislike for the lighter factory load, a few handloads with Sierra's 180-grain round nose say that this Angle Eject is the most accurate 94 I've ever worked with. It likes to stay around an inch and a half and when I do my part it will, on occasion, break the one-inch barrier. Such accuracy will allow one to thread a bullet between twig and limb, which is a nice thing to have in a woods rifle.

Yes, you can believe your eyes; the Angle Eject has a Monte Carlo type buttstock. Once past the initial shock, you'll probably learn to like it, especially at the bench. It does add some weight, though, as does the relatively heavy barrel. Fresh from its box, the test rifle weighed seven pounds, three ounces. That's 13 ounces more than my Big Bore, which, by the way, has been discontinued. I find felt recoil with the 307 to be no greater than the lighter Model 94 in 30-30.

From a 24-inch pressure barrel, Winchester rates their new cartridges about 100 feet per second shy of the 308 and 358 Winchester with all bullet weights—a result of boosting chamber pressures to over 50,000 CUP. Realistically speaking, if we deduct about 100 fps to allow for a pressure barrel's minimum chamber and bore dimensions, and maybe another 100 fps for the 4-inch shorter barrel, we're talking close to 300 Savage velocities with the 307 and somewhere this side of the 358 Winchester with the 356.

I don't think the 94AE is a long range rifle, because its tubular magazine requires blunt-nose bullets, which shed velocity awfully fast. It

Alpha I Is Fun

Homer Koon's Alpha I rifle has taken awhile in coming, with its initial development starting around 1976. Several years later, a few prototypes in various calibers were made up for field testing; Hal Swiggett put a 284 Winchester through its paces on Texas whitetails while Larry Sterrett wrote about his 243 in GUN DIGEST 35.

Though the reputation was before them, Alpha rifles and I didn't actually meet, face to face, until January 1982 at the Atlanta SHOT Show. I liked what I saw a lot, as I mentioned in GUN DIGEST 37. Within eight months after that, an Alpha and I began a long relationship.

Plain means sleek if you're talking Alpha.

My Alpha's statistics read: walnut stock; 13½″ pull; solid rubber pad; adjustable trigger; recessed bolt face; three-lug locking system; sixty degree bolt lift; matte finish on a medium-length action and 20-inch barrel, all neatly done up in a ready-to-go, seven pound, four ounce, package. That includes a Leupold 2½x Compact scope in Conetrol mounts; Uncle Mike's nylon sling and four 243 cartridges. A 7mm-08 or 308 will probably go a few ounces less.

Obviously, a great deal of thought was put into handling pressures in this action. In the event of a blown primer, or ruptured case, gas is exhausted out through four ports, one on either side of the receiver ring and two more in the right side of the bolt body. Any gas making its way rearward should be deflected away from the eye by a massive bolt shroud

surely does increase the 94's killing power at woods ranges beyond that of the 30-30 class of cartridges and adds about another half hour per day of hunting by making the 94 suitable for scope mounting. *Layne Simpson*

which actually caps off the end of the bolt.

The two-position safety does not lock the bolt, which is the way to have it if your design does not include a three-position safety. The safety lever, when pulled to the rear, actually lifts the sear off the trigger, a la 700 Remington. A red dot tells us when the safety is off and a red tail, riding on the cocking piece, indicates whether or not the firing pin is cocked.

Unique in a sporter, to my knowledge, is Koon's bedding system. The round bottom of the receiver rests in two aluminum "U" blocks, inletted into the receiver channel. Two screws, fore and aft of the nonhinged floorplate, hold barreled action and stock together. With this bedding system, a tang screw is unnecessary.

The barrel doesn't thread directly into the receiver. Alpha's receiver ring holds a separate barrel extension, replete with integral locking lug abutments. The barrel shank is screwed into this barrel extension or, as Homer prefers to call it, receiver insert. Homer does this to assure that those critical abutments are heat-treated to his satisfaction, or so he tells me.

The staggered-cartridge magazine box is a bit unconventional too. Cartridge travel is controlled by lips formed in its top side, instead of utilizing the receiver rails for this purpose. It might best be described as a nondetachable clip. Mine hasn't bobbled yet and Homer says it won't—ever. That is, of course, an awfully long time.

Alpha's stock is well done with proper grain flow and inletting less than perfect, but a notch or two above what is usually seen on mass-produced rifles. I would like to feel some checkering but then, if Alpha rifles had such we might not like the price.

After spending a little over three months with this Alpha, four days of which were in the woods, here's what I've logged: for best accuracy, both guard screws must be kept extremely tight; fired 60 three-shot groups with handloads—smallest group, 0.551 MOA; largest group, 2.175 MOA; loves Federal Premium 100-grain loads (1.231 average); tolerates Remington and Winchester and hates Frontier; Teflon coating on trigger guard/floorplate is easily nicked and scratched; hunted one day in rain; grain in wood should be more thoroughly raised and dewhiskered before finish is applied; Alpha's a joy to carry; Alpha's an honest rifle; Alpha's cute; Alpha killed a whitetail.

Layne Simpson

MODEL SEVEN: A Really New Look

There is nothing wrong with rifles or ladies that are lady-like.

(EDITOR'S NOTE: Believe it or not, testing rifles is not always exciting. Thus, Contributing Editor Simpson was not able to resist concocting this conversation between two Remington employees. KW)

"Let's build a new bolt action rifle."

"You got to be kidding; we already offer more options than a dog does fleas."

"No; I mean something so new and exciting that it'll have all the mountain stumblers, saddle bums, woods rats and even ladies and kids slavering at our doorstep."

"But we already have the Model 788 carbine and it puts most of its bullets in one ragged hole at a hundred paces."

"No argument there, but let's build a pretty one. In fact, let's sort of resurrect the old Model 600."

"Now I know you're playing with less than a full deck—they almost burned us at the stake for its ventilated rib alone."

"Forget the past and think about this; what would we get if we took the old Model 600; removed its squarish stock; threw away its Delrin trigger guard; turned out its ribbed barrel; discarded its fire-control system and knocked off its dog-leg bolt handle?"

"We'd have a Model 600 receiver and bolt body."

"Right; and we'd also have the foundation for building a rifle which would do everything the Model 600 did and more; and it could be prettier to boot. Here's how we'll do it:

"We'll keep the front section of the Model 600's receiver wall extended out over the bolt, and we'll redesign for smoother bolt operation by keeping the follower from contacting the bolt body.

"Let's see now, the Model 600's tang is not so shapely so let's flatten it down a bit. Next, we eliminate that dumb bolt release, and we'll can the safety thumb-piece which is a bit larger than it has to be."

"How do we do all of that without busting the design budget?"

"It's easy; we just fit a Model 700 fire-control system which has a bolt release just forward of its trigger piece, as well as a much neater safety lever. And, we'll fix the safety so it doesn't lock the bolt so the fellows can unload with the safety on."

"Now what do we do with the bolt?"

"That's easy too; we merely use one from a Model 700 except we leave the checkering off its knob. Looks kinda nice, doesn't it? Just for good measure, the bolt body might as well be engine turned, and we'll make it a real lightweight by chopping the barrel at 18½ inches and tapering it to a .550-inch muzzle. We can top it off with adjustable rear and ramped front sights.

"Now, what about the trigger guard/floorplate assembly, will it be blind or hinged, or aluminum or, heavens forbid, steel?"

"Blind magazines are not quite so popular as hinged floorplates while steel is awfully expensive and besides, only a few old die-hards complain about "pot metal" in rifles anymore, sooo; wait a minute, what if we stamped the unit of steel and yet did such a neat job, it would not be recognized as such from over two feet away? Hey, looks even better than we thought it would. Pretty isn't it?"

"Sure beats the heck out of aluminum."

"Now let's really get fancy and conceal the front guard screw by shifting the floorplate hinge forward. Nice, huh? Wonder what the boys over in Southport will think about that?"

"Oops, you forgot about the floorplate latch."

"Time's awasting, let's just stand on our heads and throw something together. Besides, everything else will be so pretty, who would notice such a minor detail? See, you just push right here with the end of your fingernail and — — well I'll be darned, it worked a minute ago."

"Heck, if we make it perfect, gun writers won't be able to sound objective in their reviews."

"Let's go pure classic with the wood and put a little less drop in its buttstock. We won't even think about such things as Monte Carlo humps and cheek rests. We'll really bug their eyeballs with a cute schnabel forend. How about those smoothly flowing lines? We'll leave off the shine and cut checkering at 18 lines per inch is plenty.

"Holy Ilion, what a beauty we've built, and it weighs less than six and a half pounds too. It handles like greasy lightning. We'll sell zillions of them. What will we chamber it for?"

"222, 243, 6mm, 7mm-08 and 308 Winchester."

"What's the 222 for?"

"Haven't you ever heard of a walking varmint rifle? Let's get tough and strap a 16x Model-T on the 7-08 and see how she does on paper."

"Hey, not bad at all. What should we say when they ask how well it shoots?"

"Oh, I think maybe two minutes of angle with factory loads and one to one and a half with handloads."

"But what about those that measure well under an inch?"

"We'll keep those under our hats because they wouldn't believe us anyhow. Let them find out for themselves."

"What's left to do?"

"We've got to name her. Got any ideas?"

"I don't know; it's the seventh bolt action carbine we've built and all our centerfire models start with Seven——"
Layne Simpson

As Un-single or as Combo, the 72 AAT breaks birds.

Rottweil's 72 AAT With Adjustable Rib

Manufactured in Italy for distribution in the U.S. by Dynamit Nobel of America, the 72 AAT was introduced in January, 1979. It is based on the Rottweil 72 action, which has been available for a decade. The receiver is machined from a solid steel forging for maximum durability.

The Rottweil 72 design features a receiver having a lower tang milled to house interchangeable trigger assemblies. A selective single pull trigger is standard, although other assemblies are available.

Weight of the test gun, which was the 72 AAT Single 34, was 7 pounds, 15 ounces. The barrel measured $33^{13}/_{16}$ inches in length, giving the AAT an over-all length of $51^{11}/_{16}$ inches with the ventilated rib adjustment collar in the center position.

The barrel on the AAT is fitted into a steel monobloc as an under barrel; the shoulders on the monobloc wedge tightly against the shoulder portion of the receiver walls. The upper portion of the monobloc, into which the over barrel would normally be fitted on an over-under shotgun, is fitted with a solid aluminum false barrel section measuring $13^{1}/_{16}$ inches long.

Extending forward and above from the false barrel section is the adjustable-impact ventilated rib. Milled from a solid piece of aluminum stock, anodized glossy black, the rib has a top, middle, and bottom section. Between these sections, oval-shaped ventilating areas—each measured 1.525 inches long—have been milled.

The forearm and Monte Carlo buttstock on the 72 AAT are of French walnut, with an oil finish. On the test gun the length of pull measured $14^{1}/_{2}$ inches, with drops at the comb, heel of the Monte Carlo, and heel of the stock of $1^{11}/_{32}$, $1^{11}/_{32}$, and $1^{27}/_{32}$ inches, respectively. The comb was rounded on the nose, wide, and deeply fluted on each side. The pistol grip has a slight flare at the bottom, but there is no pistol grip cap or palm swell; circum- ference of the grip at its smallest measured an even five inches.

Following the examination, the 72 AAT was taken to the patterning range to check it out at 40 yards, using Winchester-Western's AA Plus light ($2^{3}/_{4}$, $1^{1}/_{8}$, 8) trap load. The five-shot pattern average was 79.6 percent, with the patterns centered just over nine inches high, and slightly more than four inches to the left of the point-of-aim. (The ventilated rib was set in the standard or center position.) The ventilated rib was then raised by sliding the ventilated barrel collar to the rearmost position, and the 72 AAT patterned again with the same load. This time the patterns were centered four inches below the point-of-aim, but less than an inch to the left.

Maximum adjustment of the impact-point for the test gun was nearly two feet, using the AA Plus load. Other loads, or different shot sizes, might shoot to different impact points, but regardless, the 72 AAT adjustments will be adequate for most shooters.

Several hundred rounds of assorted handloads and factory loads were put through the 72 AAT test gun. No problems were encountered, with the handloads or the factory loads, and all fired shells were ejected with authority. The 72 AAT has an automatic selector ejector, located on the upper right side of the barrel, and it takes a good 0.625-inch bite on the shell rim. Unfired shells are lifted approximately $^{7}/_{16}$-inch for removal with the fingers, and fired shells are ejected three to four paces to the rear.

The Rottweil Adjustable American Trap is a first class singles gun. It handled well on the range—the center of gravity for the test gun with the 34-inch barrel was $1^{5}/_{8}$ inches forward of the center of the trunnions—produced some excellent targets, and broke the clay targets with authority.
Larry S. Sterett

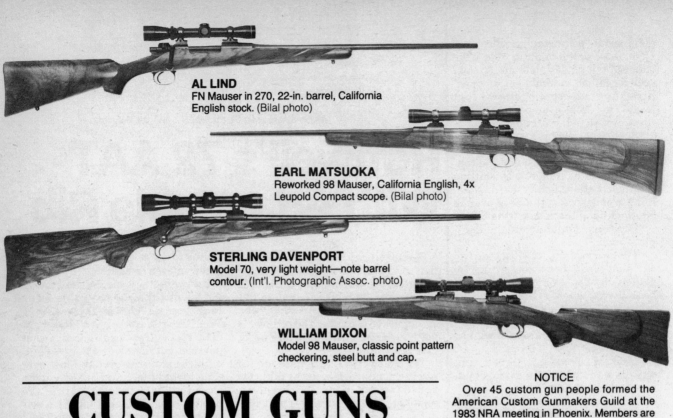

AL LIND
FN Mauser in 270, 22-in. barrel, California English stock. (Bilal photo)

EARL MATSUOKA
Reworked 98 Mauser, California English, 4x Leupold Compact scope. (Bilal photo)

STERLING DAVENPORT
Model 70, very light weight—note barrel contour. (Int'l. Photographic Assoc. photo)

WILLIAM DIXON
Model 98 Mauser, classic point pattern checkering, steel butt and cap.

CUSTOM GUNS

NOTICE
Over 45 custom gun people formed the American Custom Gunmakers Guild at the 1983 NRA meeting in Phoenix. Members are approved by other members as in the old, old days. Details: Write group's president, Don Allen, at Rt. 4, Northfield, MN 55057.

PHILIP D. LETIECO
Classic 1909 Mauser lightweight special quarter-rib, ebony tip.
(C. Hadley Smith photo)

S. L. BILLEB
Mauser 98 with very special wood, fleur-de-lis pattern.

STANLEY KENVIN
Clean big bore with side mount, express sights, dense wood.

MAURICE OTTMAR
Model 70 with almost everything—octagonal barrel, shotgun trigger guard and all. (Bilal photo)

JERE D. EGGLESTON
Light barrel and graceful schnabel and much refinement in this sporter.

PAUL JAEGER INC.
Texas Magnum lefthand action developed into a 270 sporter.

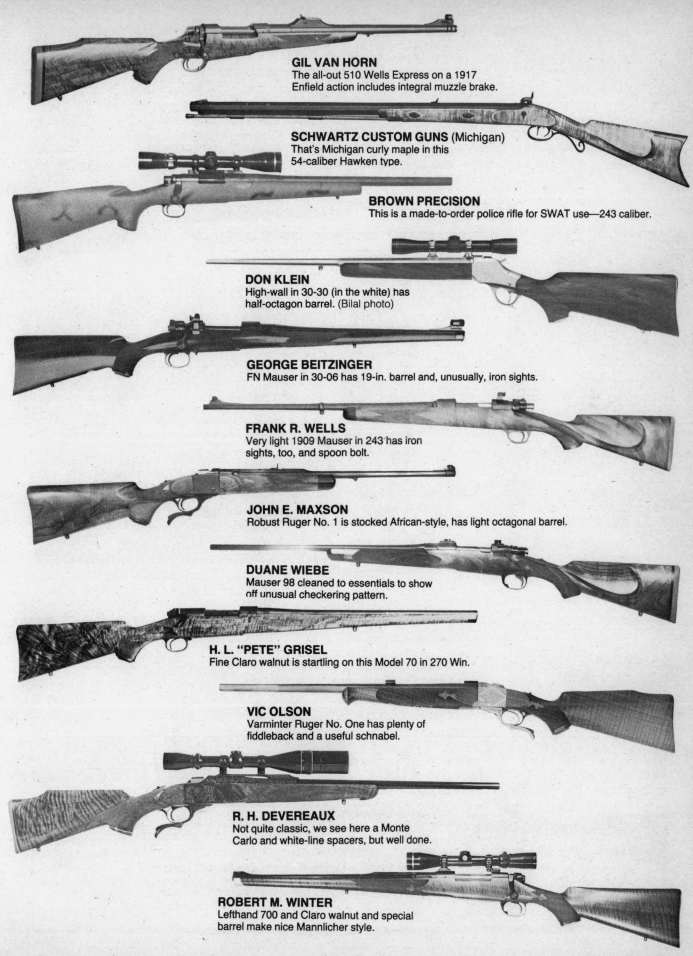

GIL VAN HORN
The all-out 510 Wells Express on a 1917
Enfield action includes integral muzzle brake.

SCHWARTZ CUSTOM GUNS (Michigan)
That's Michigan curly maple in this
54-caliber Hawken type.

BROWN PRECISION
This is a made-to-order police rifle for SWAT use—243 caliber.

DON KLEIN
High-wall in 30-30 (in the white) has
half-octagon barrel. (Bilal photo)

GEORGE BEITZINGER
FN Mauser in 30-06 has 19-in. barrel and, unusually, iron sights.

FRANK R. WELLS
Very light 1909 Mauser in 243 has iron
sights, too, and spoon bolt.

JOHN E. MAXSON
Robust Ruger No. 1 is stocked African-style, has light octagonal barrel.

DUANE WIEBE
Mauser 98 cleaned to essentials to show
off unusual checkering pattern.

H. L. "PETE" GRISEL
Fine Claro walnut is startling on this Model 70 in 270 Win.

VIC OLSON
Varminter Ruger No. One has plenty of
fiddleback and a useful schnabel.

R. H. DEVEREAUX
Not quite classic, we see here a Monte
Carlo and white-line spacers, but well done.

ROBERT M. WINTER
Lefthand 700 and Claro walnut and special
barrel make nice Mannlicher style.

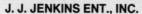

J. J. JENKINS ENT., INC.
Angelo Bee "upgraded" this Parker, and J. P. Mazur stocked it.

MIKE YEE
Trap guns can be graceful. Note elaborate checkering. (Bilal photo)

SHANE CAYWOOD
Winchester 21 has 10 inlays, French walnut, extra barrels.

DON WILLS
Two buttstock treatments worth looking at.

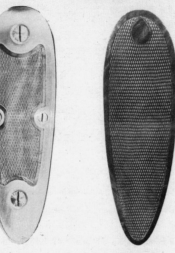

SHANE CAYWOOD
The teardrop is a small skid plate.

FRED WELLS
Perfectly ordinary Model 98 double square bridge made lefthanded and 100% titanium.

J. KORZINEK
A Ruger No. One can be a 22 rimfire and can convert back to centerfire.

WAYNE SCHWARTZ CUSTOM GUNS
Falling Block Works action is the center of this 32-40 Schuetzen rifle.

DO THEY HUNT WITH THEM?

Yes. Southpaw Curt Crum here took this splendid David Miller rifle out for elk for 10 days in Colorado. He works with Miller, true, but that's a mighty expensive hunting rifle.

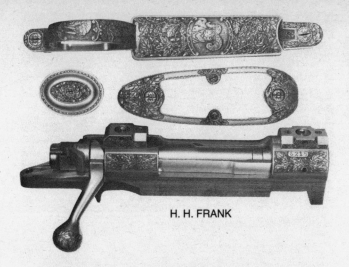

H. H. FRANK

HEIDEMARIE
HIPTMAYER

HENRY "HANK"
BONHAM

GEORGE SHERWOOD

The Art of The Engraver

NOTICE
The Firearms Engravers Guild of America, from first beginnings in June, 1980, at the Sahara Gun Show, now numbers over 200 engravers and patrons. Details: Robert Evans, Sec., 332 Vine St., Oregon City, OR 97045.

MARTIN RABENO

RICHARD D. ROY

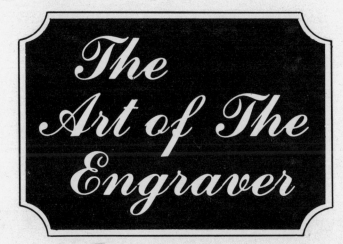

WAYNE RENO

F. R. GURNEY

E. C. PRUDHOMME

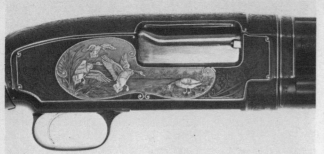

CECIL J. MILLS

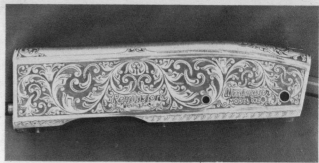

HARVEY MCBURNETTE

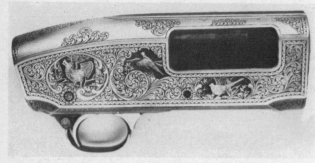

H. V. GRANT

GEORGE SHERWOOD

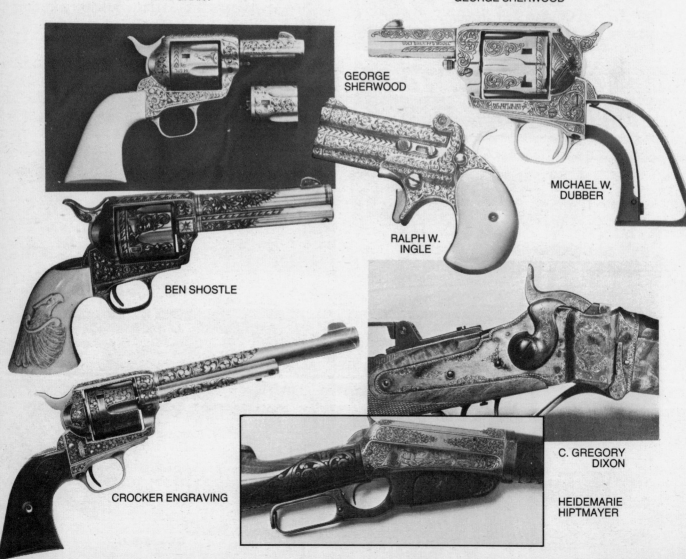

GEORGE
SHERWOOD

MICHAEL W.
DUBBER

RALPH W.
INGLE

BEN SHOSTLE

CROCKER ENGRAVING

C. GREGORY
DIXON

HEIDEMARIE
HIPTMAYER

ED PRANGER

NEIL HERMSEN

HANS OBILTSCHNIG

WILLIAM H. MAINS

ANGELO BEE

STEVE
LINDSAY

H. V. GRANT

LEONARD
FRANCOLINI

MEL WOOD

CARL BLEILE

SHOOTER'S SHOWCASE

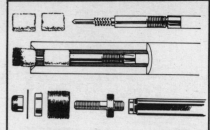

Blackpowder Bullpup

Yep—that's a muzzleloader called the Predator. It has a 30-in. barrel, 33-in. over-all length, enclosed primer system, easy takedown, just two moving parts. In calibers 45, 50 or 54 from Provider Arms Inc.

Goodie from Goodwin

Young old-timer John Goodwin is doing it again. His Pecos Valley Armory is to produce a U.S.-made (breeched in Carlsbad, NM) half-stock muzzleloader, a dull-browned lightweight. Goodwin helped produce Ithacagun's handsome plains rifle back a ways.

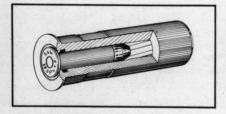

38 Special/12-Gauge Fun

This well-made Cherry Converter makes it easy to shoot a 38 Special with some accuracy—say, bunnies at 20 yards—from your 12-gauge shotgun. It's pretty quiet, pretty simple—you push out the empty with a stick. From Amimex, Inc.

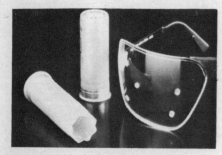

The Eyes Can Have It

These Gargoyle shooting glasses are tough enough to bounce 7½ shot from a 12-bore at 15 yards so it's no surprise they resist scratching. From Pro-tec, Inc.

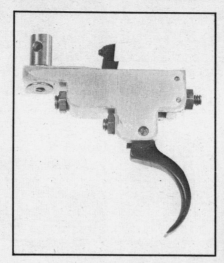

Adjust your Ruger 77

This NOC Industries trigger for the Ruger bolt-action uses the factory safety and sear, adjusts for pull weight, engagement, overtravel.

Before You Shoot a 22

This gauge—you drop a loaded round in and slide the bar 'til it stops—sorts rimfire ammunition by rim thickness. And that, when you shoot the batches separately, improves grouping a good deal. From Neil A. Jones.

Kimber/Brownell Mounts

Lenard Brownell's double-lever scope mounts are now to be made and sold by Kimber of Oregon, Inc. Still for most fine rifles, of course.

Make It Beeman-Clean

Shotgun and rifle cleaning systems from Beeman work better, Beeman says, because they get most of the dirt out with the first pass. The rifle system uses felt cylinders; the shotgun system adds a hard paper disk.

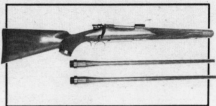

Two-Barreled Rifle

Bighorn Rifle Co. doesn't make double-barreled rifles, but every rifle it makes has two barrels—different calibers. As shown, about $2,000.

The 9x35 Returns

Canny Leupold picked 7x30 and 9x35 for their Porro-shaped hunter binoculars. Shades of pre-War Bausch & Lomb!

Right From The Can

This Phyl-Mac brass charger fits one-pound DuPont or Goex cans, throws accurate charges. About $20.

Both Sides Match

That's the least of it, Russwood says—grips are hand made to work all the way around. Exotic woods are normal; so is fitting to the individual hand.

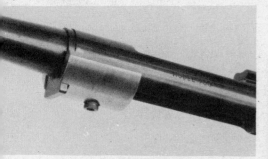

Locate Your Lug

K. W. Kleinendorst makes this tool for people who replace Remington 700 barrels. It's $19.95.

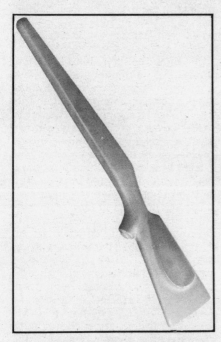

Drop-In Glass Stock

Accuracy Products makes fiberglass stocks that need no fitting on factory rifles. That's why they call them "drop-ins."

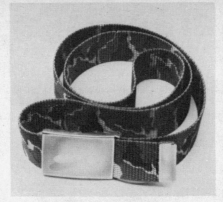

Camo Web Belt

If you must coordinate everything, here's the last link—your camouflaged trousers belt from Michaels of Oregon.

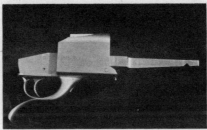

The Hauck Also Rises

Matteson Firearms is making the highly regarded Hauck patent action the old way—machined from chromemoly. About $265 buys an action as shown.

Pump a Pachmayr

The well-dressed police shotgun can sport a Pachmayr pistol grip and matching pump handle in the black rubber we have all learned to love. Call it Vindicator.

W & C Scott Research

Somebody will tell you what you don't know about your W&C Scott British gun if you tell them what you do know about it. Contact Information Service, P.O. Box 1924, Corvallis, OR 97339.

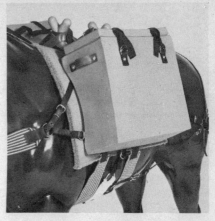

Make Happy Horses

Here's a whole trail-ready packing system that eliminates ropes, diamond hitches and tarps. They say it makes a wrangler out of a dude. From Ralide-West (Box 998, W. Yellowstone, MT 59758).

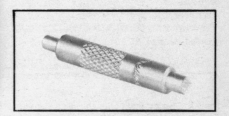

Bites At Both Ends

That's why they call this J. Dewey primer pocket cleaner for both large and small pockets the "Baby Crocogator." It's hardened steel and under $5.

Tough Is First

Kalispell cases are made tough first, their makers say, because all other features don't count if your stuff doesn't get there. They make 13 sizes in aluminum.

1983:
IWA, Hunfishow

The Safariland booth at IWA 83; thanks to their plastic-faced holsters, the California firm is now a supplier to the Munich Police Department.

Mauser 66 with ramped rear sight for quick shooting (above) and a more classic sporter on the Mauser 98 action were both shown at IWA.

New Zeiss compact 10x40B binoculars with rubber coating caught the eye at IWA 83.

WiTH 480 exhibitors IWA 83 unquestionably dominated European gun shows in 1983. There were so many items it was practically impossible to review all in the four days of the show.

The small Italian Air Match company revealed an impressive free pistol, extremely light (just above 29 ozs., including the balance weight) but amazingly well balanced, as their Model 500. Anschütz had a nice moving target version of their Model 380 air rifle and Armerie Italiane Fratelli Gamba, showed a most attractive side-by-side shotgun featuring a patented removable lock. The Argentine Bersa and Mahely Companies introduced the Europeans to their 22 rimfire guns; while the Brazilian Taurus company had also a big success. And new *lighter* 177 pellets for match air pistols at RWS reduce the bullet time in the barrel.

If the Czech pistol CZ 83 highly impressed Hunfishow visitors, the Hungarian booth had a similar effect at IWA 83 when the FEG concern from Budapest, in turn, displayed three new pistols: firstly, the FP9 is a direct copy of the Browning High Power, also in 9mm Luger with a 13-shot magazine; then, a brand new P9R (steel receiver) or P9RA (light alloy receiver) *selective double action* model looking also like the Browning High Power, *but much more sophisticated* and featuring a drop hammer safety; and the third new Hungarian pistol is called "Self-Defense"—it is *very small and flat,* a double-action automatic.

The Finns, on their side, revealed a particularly compact and efficient 9mm Luger submachine gun which is claimed to have no climb. Called the Jati-Matic, this gun is particularly attractive for detectives and security staff. And a revolutionary rimfire caseless ammunition patented by Mr. Fiocchi himself is available in 9mm only, intended for use in a special Benelli submachine gun.

The Italian firm of Davide Pedersoli is now making a complete line of Remington Rolling Block replicas chambered in 357 Magnum and 45-70 Government. Mauser had a 300-meter free rifle and several short sporting bolt action carbines. Remington raised much interest with Models Seven and 700 bolt action rifles. In an entirely different style, the Israelis showed an Uzi semi-automatic pistol looking like a mini-submachine gun and their Eagle gas-operated pistol in 357 Magnum or 44 Magnum for silhouette shooting. Perazzi had perhaps the most expensive over-under of the show with their "DHO Extra" costing exactly $56,700.

THE eleventh Hunfishow was in Paris and will be held there, where it is supported by the leading French gun manufacturers, henceforth. There were about 100 exhibits, quite twice that of the previous show in Monte Carlo. This year, no gold medal was awarded by the Press Jury as a new regulation is in preparation.

The Czech Merkuria Company selected Paris for introducing perhaps the best gun in its class—the CZ 83 15-shot double-action automatic pistol chambered in 32 ACP; versions in 9mm Makarov and 30 Luger are also planned. This all-steel pistol looks quite like a scaled down CZ 75, but the inside is different.

The thumb safety and magazine stop can be readily operated with both hands and a slide stop for southpaws will be available. The square sights feature a vertical white strip between two white dots for quick alignment under poor light conditions. The gun size and weight are similar to those of the Walther PP.

An Austrian maker of fine quality replicas, Mr. F. Hebsacker, displayed his Siber percussion pistol (1200 have been made to date), an impressive matchlock and a brace of Manton flintlock pistols made in a very limited quantity in view of the Muzzle-Loaders World Championship which will be held in Bordeaux next September. The Spanish maker Azhur had an original removable lock fitted on his new line of shotguns. And a new French Company located in St.-Etienne, Bouchet, has resumed the manufacture of the once famous Darne shotguns.

Lanber from Eibar had a new Spanish automatic shotgun called the Victoria. To this editor's knowledge, it is the first Spanish automatic made during the recent years. Manurhin now makes the SIG gas-operated military rifle in a semi-automatic version chambered in 222 Remington and 243 Winchester for the civilian market. They had also a new MR 73 Sport revolver called the "Gendarmerie model" fitted with a compact micrometric rear sight and sold to the Services.

Ruger, Safariland, Remington and Winchester France had impressive stands attracting many visitors. New French body armor and a clever night sight were displayed by SEMA, a Nanterre Company, while S.F.M., the former Gevelot, enjoyed a big success with their new Alia high performance handgun ammunition. ●

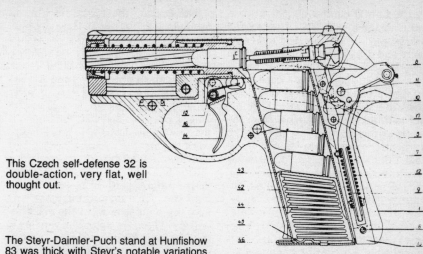

This Czech self-defense 32 is double-action, very flat, well thought out.

The Steyr-Daimler-Puch stand at Hunfishow 83 was thick with Steyr's notable variations on the hunting rifle theme.

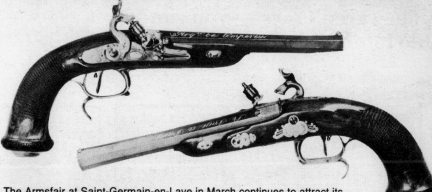

The Armsfair at Saint-Germain-en-Laye in March continues to attract its thousands of French men and guns.

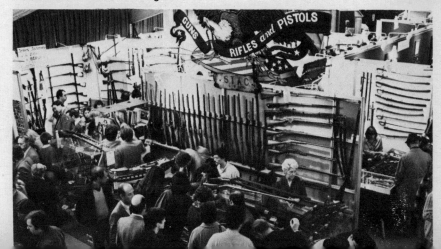

THE EMCO Unimat 3—the universal machine tool for metal, wood and plastic work—is being used to handle more and more gunsmithing work as a first lathe for the hobbyist or beginning gunsmith and as a second lathe for the professional. At first glance, the Unimat 3 may appear to be a toy, but nothing could be further from the truth. Although small in size, it's an authentic, scaled-down version of the real thing—a universal machine for longitudinal turning, taper turning, thread cutting, drilling, milling, dividing, grinding, cutting, polishing, sawing, woodturning, planing and routing. In fact, it can do all the things in skilled hands *in miniature* that would require an entire machine shop to handle in larger numbers and sizes.

The cost of the basic machine is around $400, but by the time you purchase the extra accessories necessary for gun repair work you'll be shelling out around $1000. No wonder I was hesitant about purchasing one of these machines when I needed a small lathe some months ago, but it didn't take long. I have decided that for the hobbyist or professional who has enough work to keep the machine busy, it's a worthwhile investment.

The following illustrated how-to-do-it details of performing some of the most common gunsmithing tasks will give you an idea of what the machine will do. Then, by applying your own imagination and knowledge, you're certain to come up with a host of other gunsmithing applications.

TURNING FIRING PINS

Recently, a customer brought in a Raven .25 auto pistol for repair. It had a broken firing pin and, since there was no time to order a new one, I decided to turn one on the Unimat 3. A small piece of round stock was found in my junk pile, and after measuring and marking the centers of each end, the piece was chucked into a 3-jaw chuck and turned at a speed of 1500 rpm. A combination center drill and countersink was used for drilling the center holes.

The existing, broken firing pin was used as a guide; that is, measurements were taken to apply to the new work. The pin point was, of course, broken and exact dimensions of the point were unknown. However, this could be es-

by JOHN E. TRAISTER

MINI-LATHE GUNSMITHING

They aren't toys — you can do lots of things to guns with them.

Unimat set up for milling operation. The work is clamped with T-nut screws and flat clamps on the milling table.

Modified base tried on the gun for fit prior to drilling and tapping holes in the action.

timated and fitted perfectly later on by trial and error. The dimensions and rough shape of the firing pin were marked on the work piece with an outside thread cutting tool, and then turned to approximate dimensions with a roughing tool.

At a point in the work where the firing pin began to take shape, a round nosed tool was used to smooth the surface and bring the work to final shape. Then, a parting off tool was used to cut one end of the firing pin away from the shaft. Since the work was now getting to the point of having only very thin metal to support the piece, one slight mistake could ruin the entire project. Therefore, the remaining work was held only by the 3-jaw chuck around a part of the pin that had sufficient metal to support it.

Once the pin was shaped, except for rounding the nose, the pin was tried in the gun to insure a perfect fit. Then the only remaining work was to shape the firing pin nose and heat treat the part by heating it to cherry red, then dipping and cooling in conventional motor oil.

DOVETAILING BARRELS FOR SIGHT BASES

Dovetailing a rifle barrel for a front sight is just pushing the little tool to its limits, but if you're willing to be patient, it can be done—regardless of the barrel length.

You'll need the vertical drill and milling attachment that sells for about $275 extra and also a milling and fixture table. Mount these attachments on the Unimat and then remove the tailstock. The muzzle of the barrel is then mounted directly under the milling chuck and clamped securely to the milling and fixture table, so that the barrel is parallel to the lathe bed. You'll have lots of barrel hanging beyond the lathe bed, and although the Unimat will hold it securely, it is recommended that some means of support be provided on the bench adjacent to the machine.

An end mill cutter is then chucked into the drill chuck to remove all the metal possible before making a pass with the sight base (dovetail) cutter. This will be the toughest operation and you are going to have to take it slow, very slow! The cross-feed is then used to move the muzzle across the lathe bed so the end mill cutter will cut a smooth notch (of the proper depth) in the barrel. I've found that by cutting not more than $1/16''$ at a pass and by feeding not faster than about .002'' per second, binding problems will not be experienced. Any faster, watch out!

Once the notch is cut with the end mill cutter, a standard sight base cutter with 60° shoulder by .359'' base is used to cut the dovetail. The drill chuck will not take the shanks of these cutters, so the 3-jaw chuck will have to be used to hold the dovetail cutter. Two cutting passes with this, and the job is done.

OTHER ACCESSORIES

A threading attachment is also available for this mini-lathe, but I've found little use for it in gun repair work to date. I did try threading a junk handgun barrel just to see what it would do, but after 30 minutes and about 1000 passes, the threads were still not deep enough, so I gave up on this project.

One attachment that I do recommend is the collet attachment for holding drills, milling cutters and round workpieces when the highest accuracy and concentric running are demanded. This attachment is fitted onto the spindle nose by means of a specially machined flange to obtain the highest concentricity. Ten collets for gripping diameters of $1/32''$ to $5/16''$ are available.

There are many other attachments, but I'd recommend that you write directly to the manufacturer and request their catalog for a complete listing.

SUMMARY

So just what will the little Unimat 3 do? It will turn firing pins, drift pins and similar items all day with the accuracy of a $3000 machine. If you know how to take extremely accurate measurements, you can make all the headspace gauges you need from scrap brass stock. Milling an occasional handgun trigger guard or hammer is within the reach of this machine, but be prepared to spend a couple of hours on each. Fitting scope mounts to an unusual rifle is a whiz for the Unimat as well as fitting replacement bolts for 22-caliber single-shot rifles. The 3.6'' swing over the bed will allow most .22 bolts to be centered between the head and tailstock with enough room for the bolt to turn without hitting the bed. A bolt facing lathe bit may then be used to open up the bolt face.

By now you have probably thought of several other applications where the Unimat can be used. Just remember to take it slow, and you'll be surprised at what this little machine can do. ●

Finished job. Note that the scope ring knobs are positioned to the left of the action rather than conventionally on the right. This is to prevent ejection problems.

Dovetailing a rifle barrel for front sight—a precision cut is made on the second pass with the ⅜'' sight base cutter.

Ammunition, Ballistics and Components

by EDWARD A. MATUNAS

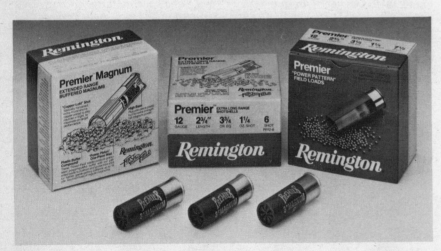

Remington's new Premier line of magnum, high velocity, and field loads features copper plated, extra hard shot.

A NUMBER OF this year's products are direct descendants of consumer wishes. An example is the improved 257 Roberts ammunition being offered by one of the industry biggies. Handloaders have been matching the *new and improved* velocities for years, so it's about time a major ammunition manufacturer saw the light. Keep asking the manufacturer for what you want. It may just come to pass.

Remington

Remington has made important additions to its ammunition line. The most noteworthy, this writer feels, is the new line of shotshells called *Premier*. These are the highest grade shotshells offered by Remington, assembled with premium grade copper-plated shot. Copper plating greatly reduces shot's tendency to deform during its passage through the bore. It was first offered by Winchester years ago. Remington uses granulated plastic shot buffering in Premier magnums for long range performance. Premier shells are also offered in high velocity and standard velocity loadings.

Also new from Remington is the

greatly enlarged Nitro Magnum line of shotshells. This line becomes Remington's popular priced offering for high velocity magnum shells. Extra hard shot and granulated poly shot-buffering material are used in all the Nitro Magnum loads. These new shells will effectively add a number of yards to the practical range of previous magnum shells. Remington claims an 80% pellet count in a 30-inch circle at 40 yards from a full choke shotgun.

With but two exceptions, all non-buffered magnum loads have been discontinued. The exceptions are the 10-gauge 3½" and the 16-gauge 2¾" Express Magnum loads. One could speculate that either sales volumes are low in these loadings or that they will be incorporated into the Nitro Magnum line sometime in the future.

Remington has also introduced a 12-gauge target load under the Peters label. Called simply the *Peters Target* load it replaces the Peters Blue Magic load. It is available in both 2¾ and 3 dram (light and heavy) powder equivalents with 1⅛ ounces of shot. Shot sizes include 7½, 8 and 9. This load has seen extensive field testing by some very qualified target shooters.

One of the changes in this new target load is the primer which incorporates a covered flash hole and a hotter mix. Remington suggests that the new primer results in superior ignition and more uniform ballistics. Extra hard shot and Power Piston wads are retained.

Of importance to the reloader is the change in the hull construction of the new Peters Target load. Hull strength and hence its reloading life have been notably increased. The color remains blue.

Also available in Peters Target is a 1-ounce shot load offering the shooter reduced recoil and, equally important, reduced cost. This load uses an entirely new Power Piston wad designed specifically for the new Target case. Muzzle velocity is 1145 ft/s, the same as the 2¾ dram equivalent 1⅛ ounces loads, and therefore the lightest recoiling one ounce factory 12-gauge target load now available to the shooter. Shot size is No. 8, suitable for Skeet, trap and small upland birds.

Few changes have been made in Remington's metallic cartridge line of ammunition. One item has been discontinued—the 300 Savage 180-grain pointed soft point load. The 180-grain round nose and 150-grain pointed soft point bullets continue to be available in this caliber.

Announced is a new 125-grain load-

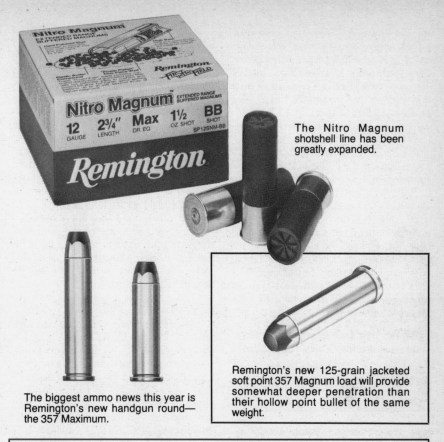

The Nitro Magnum shotshell line has been greatly expanded.

The biggest ammo news this year is Remington's new handgun round—the 357 Maximum.

Remington's new 125-grain jacketed soft point 357 Magnum load will provide somewhat deeper penetration than their hollow point bullet of the same weight.

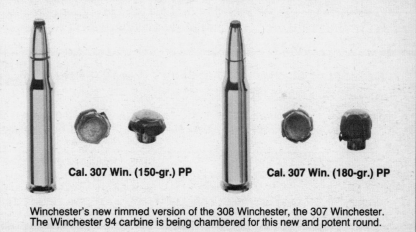

Cal. 307 Win. (150-gr.) PP

Cal. 307 Win. (180-gr.) PP

Winchester's new rimmed version of the 308 Winchester, the 307 Winchester. The Winchester 94 carbine is being chambered for this new and potent round.

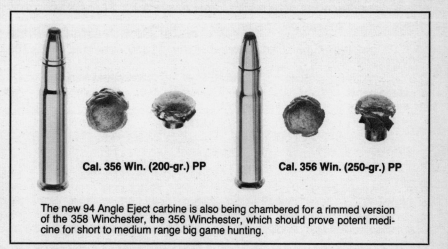

Cal. 356 Win. (200-gr.) PP

Cal. 356 Win. (250-gr.) PP

The new 94 Angle Eject carbine is also being chambered for a rimmed version of the 358 Winchester, the 356 Winchester, which should prove potent medicine for short to medium range big game hunting.

ing for the 357 Magnum. This new bullet uses a short jacket soft point, offering somewhat deeper penetration than Remington's hollow point load of the same weight. The consumer now has a choice of two different bullet styles in the popular 125-grain weight. Ballistics are identical in either load.

A notable addition in Remington's metallic cartridge line is the new 357 Remington Maximum. This handgun cartridge is similar to the 357 Magnum except its case is a third of an inch longer. This lengthening (and strengthening) of the 357 Magnum case has allowed for a substantial increase in ballistic performance. It will be offered only in one bullet weight at this time, a 158-grain short jacket hollow point. Ballistics for this new load are as follows:

357 Remington Maximum Ballistics
obtained in a 10½″ barrel, 158-gr. bullet

	Velocity (fps)	
Muzzle	50 yds.	100 yds.
1825	1588	1381

	Energy (ft. lbs.)	
Muzzle	50 yds.	100 yds.
1168	885	669

Energy levels are in the 44 Magnum range but perceived recoil is lower. This new cartridge is mated with a Ruger single action revolver especially designed for it.

The 7mm Remington Express name is gone. First came the 280 Remington; then the 280 was renamed the 7mm Remington Express; now the surviving name is the 280 Remington! Current loads for the 280 include a 150-grain bullet at 2970 ft/s and a 165-grain bullet at 2820 ft/s. Thus the early 280 165-grain load and the 7mm Express 150-grain load have been incorporated under one name. Remington no longer chambers bolt action rifles in either name. Only pumps and autoloaders are now chambered for the 280 Remington.

Winchester

Two new Winchester rifle calibers will be used in USRAC's redesigned Winchester 94, the Angle Eject. These new cartridges have the same over-all length as the 375 Winchester and are designated the 307 Winchester and the 356 Winchester. Basically, they are rimmed versions of the 308 Winchester and the 358 Winchester.

The 307 Winchester is loaded with 150-grain and 180-grain Power Point bullets. The 180-grain is the more efficient loading. The 150-grain load has sufficient energy to take deer to about 250 yards while the 180-grain load has ample energy to 300 yards. The 356 Winchester is offered in 200- and 250-grain bullet weights. These Power Point bullets will easily best the ballistics of the 35 Remington, the 30-30 Winchester and the 375 Winchester.

Accuracy and trajectory will be the limiting factors with both loads. Bullet expansion has been tested to ranges of 250 yards and appears to be excellent with all four bullets.

A table comparing the ballistics of both new cartridges with other lever action cartridges is shown nearby.

Also new from the ammo folks at East Alton are two slightly beefed-up 257 Roberts loads. The 100-grain Silvertip has had 100 ft/s added to its muzzle velocity bringing it to 3000 ft/s. The 117-grain Power Point has been pumped to 2780 ft/s, a 130 ft/s increase. While these loads will certain-

Ballistics of Winchester 257 Roberts + P and 257 Roberts
Shot in 24-inch barrel

Bullet		Velocity in ft/s						Energy in Foot-Pounds					
Wt. Grs.	Type	Muzzle	100	200	300	400	500	Muzzle	100	200	300	400	500
					Yards						Yards		
100+P	ST	3000	2633	2295	1982	1697	1447	1998	1539	1169	872	639	465
100	ST	2900	2541	2210	1904	1627	1387	1867	1433	1084	805	588	427
117+P	PP(SP)	2780	2411	2071	1761	1488	1263	2009	1511	1115	806	576	415
117	PP(SP)	2650	2291	1961	1663	1404	1199	1824	1363	999	718	512	373

Winchester Silvertip 200-gr. Hollow Point 44 S&W Special

Velocity,
Muzzle:	900
50 Yards:	860
100 Yards:	822

Energy, Foot-Pounds,
Muzzle:	360
50 Yards:	328
100 Yards:	300

MRT, Inches,
50 Yards:	1.4
100 Yards:	5.9

Barrel Length: 6½ inches

Winchester Comparative Ballistics
307 Winchester, 30-30 Winchester, 356 Winchester, 35 Remington, and 375 Winchester

Cartridge	Bullet Wt. Grs.	Type	Barrel Length Inches	Velocity in ft/sec Muzzle	100	200	300	400	500	Energy in foot-pounds Muzzle	100	200	300	400	500
						Yards						Yards			
1) 307 Winchester	150	PP	24	2764	2325	1928	1578	1291	1093	2545	1801	1238	830	555	398
2) 30-30 Win.	150	PP(SP)	24	2390	2018	1684	1398	1177	1036	1902	1356	944	651	461	357
3) 307 Winchester	180	PP	24	2506	2175	1870	1596	1360	1175	2511	1891	1398	1018	739	552
4) 30-30 Win.	170	PP(SP)	24	2200	1895	1619	1381	1191	1061	1827	1355	989	720	535	425
5) 356 Winchester	200	PP	24	2455	2109	1793	1513	1281	1111	2677	1976	1428	1017	729	548
6) 35 Remington	200	PP(SP)	24	2020	1646	1335	1114	985	901	1812	1203	791	551	431	360
7) 375 Winchester	200	PP(SP)	24	2200	1841	1526	1268	1089	980	2150	1506	1034	714	527	427
8) 356 Winchester	250	PP	24	2162	1914	1684	1478	1300	1160	2595	2034	1575	1213	938	747
9) 375 Winchester	250	PP(SP)	24	1900	1647	1424	1239	1103	1011	2005	1506	1126	852	676	568

ly improve the performance of factory loaded 257 Roberts cartridges, they are, unto themselves, no startling news. Reloaders have been pushing 100-grain bullets from the 257 Roberts at 3000+ ft/s for a long, long time. Also, reloaders have and will continue to best the new 117-grain load. At 2780 ft/s it comes not too close to the 2900 ft/s that the Roberts will deliver at pressures of 46,000 to 47,000 CUP's with this weight bullet.

These new 257 loads are being called 257 Roberts +P. The name suggest more results than the actual performance. But any increase is welcome. The same bullets are used for the new loadings as were used in the earlier rounds, therefore bullet expansion will continue to be superb. The new loads will prove useful to about 250 yards on deer, antelope and similar game. It is a shame that the heavier weight bullet isn't available in a Spitzer style.

Now, if Winchester will reintroduce a varmint load in the 257 Roberts, using either a 75- or 87-grain bullet, this cartridge would be a nice choice for many a hunter. It's no problem to push the 75-grain bullet at velocities of 3200 to 3300 ft/s at modest pressure levels. Such a load would make a flat shooting load and such a total offering could best the 6mm's.

Once again Winchester has expanded its line of Silvertip handgun loads. The aluminum jacketed Silvertip hollow point handgun rounds offer the very best expansion obtainable in pistols or revolvers. Accuracy is usually not quite as good as traditional loads but the positive expansion of this type of bullet makes a good trade-off.

This year, the 44 Special has been added to the list of Silvertip handgun ammunition. This load incorporates a 200-grain Silvertip bullet at 900 ft/s for a muzzle energy of 360 foot pounds. Even when fired from a 3″ barrel it offers splendid expansion.

When it comes to expansion in handgun cartridges, the Winchester Silvertip, in my opinion, has no competitors. I have experienced a few core jacket separations with these loads, but I far prefer this to the zero expansion I have gotten from some other handgun loads.

Following Federal and Remington, Winchester is adding a hollow point to their shotgun slugs—no change in ballistics, just a large dimple in the front end of the slug. I have always found that soft lead slugs expand as well as could be expected. I can't see that the hollow points being offered will add a great deal to the slug's al-

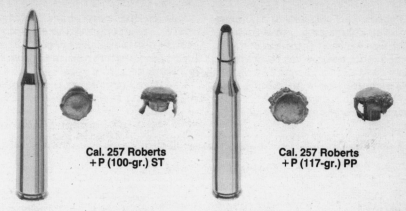

Cal. 257 Roberts +P (100-gr.) ST   **Cal. 257 Roberts +P (117-gr.) PP**

Winchester has upgraded the ballistics on the 257 Roberts and now calls it the 257 Roberts +P.

Cal. 44 S&W Special (200-gr.) STHP

A welcome addition to the Silvertip line of handgun ammo is Winchester's new 200-grain STHP 44 Special round.

Winchester has followed their competitors and added a hollow point to their shotgun slugs.

20-ga. Rifled Slug   **12-ga. Rifled Slug**

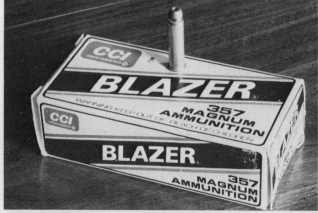

CCI's line of aluminum-cased Blazer ammunition is selling very well and has been broadened to include the 357 Magnum, 25 Auto and 9mm Luger.

ready fine performance. My samples of the new slugs gave a good showing of themselves, grouping 2½ to 3 inches at 50 yards from two slug barrels.

Winchester has announced a new 22 Long Rifle cartridge with a heavy weight bullet designed for higher re-tained energies down range. Reportedly, this new round will be advantageous for silhouette shooting. The cartridge is not yet in its finalized form and therefore nothing further can be stated except that it will probably deliver a 45-grain bullet at 1100 to 1200 ft/s.

Federal 32 S&W Long

Bullet Wt. & Style	Velocity in ft/s		Energy in Foot-Pounds		Mid-Range Trajectory
	Muzzle	50 yds.	Muzzle	50 yds.	50 yds.
98-gr. wadcutter	780	630	130	85	2.2"
98-gr. round nose	705	670	115	98	2.3"

Federal 223 Remington
Hollow Point Boattail

Range (yards)	Velocity (ft/s)	Energy (ft/lbs)	Drop Inches	Drift 10 mph Crosswinds (in.)	Inches Above Line of Sight if Sighted In at 200 yards
0	3240	1280	—0—	—0—	
100	2880	1010	1.8	1.0	+ 1.7
200	2550	790	7.8	4.2	—0—
300	2240	610	19.2	10.0	− 7.0
400	1950	460	37.6	19.1	−21.1

Federal 22 LR Spitfire

Range yards	Velocity (ft/s)	Energy (ft/lbs)	Mid-Range Trajectory Inches	Drop Inches	Drift 10 mph Wind
0	1500	165	—0—	—0—	—0—
50	1240	110	.6	2.2	1.9
100	1080	85	2.8	10.0	7.3
150	980	70	7.2	24.7	15.5
200	900	60	14.4	47.5	26.0

Federal 338 Winchester Magnum
210-gr. Nosler Partition

Range (yards)	Velocity (ft/s)	Energy (ft/lbs)	Drop Inches	Drift in 10 mph Wind (inches)
0	2830	3735	—0—	—0—
100	2590	3130	2.3	.8
200	2370	2610	9.8	3.5
300	2150	2155	23.5	8.3
400	1940	1760	44.8	15.4
500	1750	1435	75.3	25.4

Sierra Bullets

A number of new bullets have been announced by Sierra. Some were available early in the year and some are yet to come. Several serve definite needs, while others are simply responses to competition.

To meet demands from 25 Auto, 32 Auto, 30 Luger and 30 Mauser users, Sierra is now making full metal case bullets for them. They have also announced a 95-grain .355 inch diameter bullet for 9mm fans. Other new full metal jacket bullets are for the 38 Super, the 6mm rifle, and a .311 inch diameter bullet for the SKS and AK-47.

It will probably take a full year to test all of these new Sierra bullets. I am already convinced of the superiority of the new Sierra handgun bullets which feature the two-year-old *Power Jacket* design. I can see little reason for the 140-grain bullet in 270 diameter, but some shooters who are torn between 130- or 150-grain bullets are finding this weight to their liking. The number of new items announced by Sierra for this year is quite impressive.

Omark (CCI and Speer)

Omark has broadened its Blazer ammunition to include, among others, a 125-grain and a 158-grain loading in the 357 Magnum. You may remember that we reported on the then new Blazer ammunition in these pages last year. The Blazer ammunition incorporates a non-reloadable, Berdan primed, aluminum cartridge case. The appeal of this ammo is that it sells for 35% less (at suggested retail pricing) than conventional ammunition using brass cases. If you don't reload it doesn't make sense to pay for expensive brass cases, which are simply thrown away, when Speer's lower cost aluminum cased Blazer ammo will perform equally well.

Also introduced into the Blazer line is a 50-grain FMJ 25 ACP round, a 115-grain FMJ 9mm Luger round, a 150-grain FMJ 38 Special +P round, a 158-grain lead semi-wadcutter hollow point 38 Special round, and finally a 158-grain JHP 38 Special +P round. If non-reloading shooters continue to agree that saving money with Blazer ammo makes sense, I would expect this line to be further broadened next year.

During the past months I have had the opportunity to range test Speer's three new boattail rifle bullets. These included a 100-grain 6mm, a 100-grain 25 caliber, a 130-grain 7mm caliber. All three shot with a fine level of accuracy. Those who want extra flatness in trajectory will appreciate these three new bullets.

Also new from Speer are two very interesting full metal cased bullets designed especially for handgun silhouette shooting. Unlike most full metal jacket bullets which expose the lead core at the base, their cores are completely encased by the gilding metal jacket. I tried both the 180-grain 38/357 caliber and the 240-grain 44 caliber bullets. Accuracy was exceptional. These bullets are bound to become popular with the handgun crowd that enjoys toppling steel animals.

Also new to the Speer handgun bullet line are a 115-grain 9mm FMJ bullet, a 150-grain FMJ 38/357 bullet and, happily, a lead 158-grain semi-wadcutter hollow point bullet. This last style should prove extremely popular, as it is, in my opinion, the most practical style lead bullet made for the 38 Special or the 357 Magnum.

Speer has also added a number of match grade bullets to be companions to their 168-grain HPBT 30-caliber bullet which we reported on last year. These will include a 7mm 145-grain HPBT and a 30-caliber 190-grain HPBT.

Nosler

I have shot a lot of Nosler bullets during the past year. The Nosler Partition bullets, which enjoy an enviable reputation as premium big game bullets, shoot very well indeed. The accuracy of the solid base bullets tested was excellent, making them ideal candidates for consideration when selecting popularly priced bullets.

The new items from Nosler include the following:

Caliber	Weight (Grs.)/Type
25	120/spitzer Partition
8mm	200/spitzer Partition
22	45/Hornet solid base
22	50/Expanded solid base
22	52/spitzer solid base

The 25-caliber 120-grain spitzer Partition bullet replaces the 115 and 117-grain bullets of the same caliber. This new bullet provides a high level of accuracy in my 257 Winchester Model 70 Featherweight. Expansion is positive and because of the dual core construction, core/jacket separations are impossible. Even if the entire front half of the bullet was completely expended, the rear core would remain intact, thus ensuring ade-

Federal 180-Grain JHP 357 Magnum

From 10-inch standard barrel:

Range Yards	Velocity Ft/s	Energy Ft./lbs.	Momentum lb/s	Mid-Range Traj. (in.)
0	1450	840	1.15	—0—
50	1220	595	.97	.6
100	1070	460	.85	2.9
150	990	390	.79	7.3
200	910	330	.72	14.5

From 18-inch standard barrel:

Range Yards	Velocity Ft/s	Energy Ft./lbs.	Momentum lb/s	Mid-Range Traj. (in.)
0	1550	960	—0—	—0—
50	1330	700	.5	2.0
100*	1160	535	2.5	8.9
150	1050	445	6.3	22.0
200	980	385	12.5	42.2
250	920	295	21.5	70.5

Speer's new boat-tail bullets (100-grain 6mm, 100-grain 257 and 130-grain 7mm) shot very well. The new 180-grain FMJ 38/357 bullet will prove ideal for silhouette shooting.

Nosler's new 120-grain Partition .257″ diameter bullet is the only 25-caliber bullet the author recommends for big game hunting.

Speer's new 180-grain 38/357 FMJ bullet is unique in that the core is completely enclosed by the jacket.

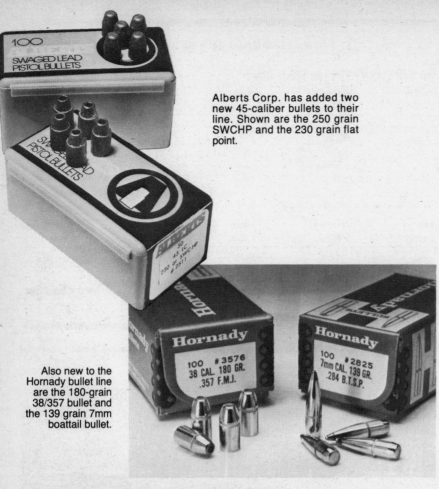

Alberts Corp. has added two new 45-caliber bullets to their line. Shown are the 250 grain SWCHP and the 230 grain flat point.

Also new to the Hornady bullet line are the 180-grain 38/357 bullet and the 139 grain 7mm boattail bullet.

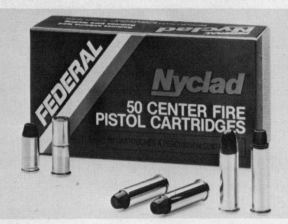

Federal's new Nyclad ammunition takes away the smoke and soot of indoor shooting and is very accurate.

Hornady's new 140-grain 38/357 bullet expands well at high velocities.

quate penetration. For big game hunting with the small calibers (6mm, 25 caliber and 6.5mm) Nosler Partition bullets are the only bullets I can recommend without reservation.

I fired more than a few of the 8mm Partition bullets through a Remington Model 700 8mm Magnum. The results were quite gratifying. Additionally, I fired several hundred of each of the three new 22-caliber solid base bullets in a Remington Model Seven 222 and a Kimber Model 82 22 Hornet. Accuracy was outstanding and all of the bullets that I fired at varmints expanded perfectly.

Alberts Corp.

Alberts has added a new 45 Colt 250-grain semi-wadcutter bullet to their line of swaged lead bullets. This bullet incorporates a good sized hollow point. If velocities are kept to a moderate level, this bullet will not lead the bore. Alberts bullets lack a crimping groove but reloaders simply crimp into the smooth side of the bullet or where possible on the leading edge of the nose profile. Also new to the Alberts bullet line is a 230-grain flat nosed bullet for the 45 ACP.

Hornady Manufacturing Co.

The 140-grain 357 diameter bullet has proven quite popular. During the past year, Hornady added such a bullet to their product line. The 140-grain weight will usually afford improved expansion over the 158-grain bullets in the 357 Magnum without running into the limited penetration problems of the 125-grain bullets. This bullet should prove a good choice in both rifles and handguns.

Hornady has also introduced a full metal case 180-grain 38/357 bullet for use on steel silhouettes. And they have added a boattail version of the popular 139-grain 7mm spire point. This bullet should prove useful in a number of applications including silhouette shooting, especially in the 7mm-08 Remington cartridge.

Federal Cartridge

The new Federal Cartridge item that most catches my interest is Nyclad handgun ammunition. Nyclad ammo was originally offered by Smith & Wesson. However, when S & W closed down its ammunition efforts, they sold the Nyclad line to Federal.

In brief, Nyclad ammunition offers nylon coated lead bullets. Providing all the velocity and accuracy of conventional lead bullets, Nyclad eliminates, or nearly so, gun fouling, bore leading and lubricant smoke. Most important is the drastic reduction of airborne contaminant lead particles. For indoor ranges, Nyclad ammunition should, in my opinion, be mandatory. The very high level of lead in the air on even the best ventilated of indoor ranges is a potential health hazard. Nyclad ammunition can greatly reduce the risk of harmful effects from airborne lead. This new ammunition will be offered in the following loads during 1983:

Caliber	Weight & Type
38 Special	148 gr. WC
38 Special	158 gr. RN
38 Special	158 gr. SWC HP
38 Special	125 gr. SWC HP

The 125-grain semi-wadcutter hollow point load is called the "Chief's Special." The big appeal for this round is that it will provide positive bullet expansion when fired from a 2 inch barrel but is not a +P load.

The developing interest of very serious target shooters in the 32 S & W Long cartridge has not, until now, gotten much of a reaction from the ammunition manufacturers. Federal has, however, decided to try it. The folks at Federal have added two loads in this caliber to their line. The first is a conventional 98-grain lead round nose bullet which, in most aspects, duplicates the loadings offered by the other ammunition biggies. However, they have also introduced a 98-grain lead hollow base wadcutter loading. This load leaves the muzzle some 75 ft/s faster than the round nose bullet and arrives at the 50-yard mark going a mere 40 ft/s slower. In international competition, because of its light recoil, the 32 caliber has almost completely replaced the 38 Special as the preferred target caliber. Federal's new load should, therefore, generate worldwide interest.

Federal has introduced a 180-grain jacketed hollow point 357 Magnum load. Suited to the short barreled rifles being chambered for this cartridge, this round may prove of interest to those who wish to hunt deer with these somewhat low power rifles. The new load will also undoubtedly be tried by handgunners for hunting and also on silhouette.

A 55-grain boattail hollow point bullet loading in 223 Remington has been added to Federal's centerfire ammo offerings. This load is said to duplicate the ballistics of the military M193 ball round. It should prove a popular varmint loading. Another new item in Federal's centerfire car-

Federal Nyclad Ballistics

38 Special 148-grain wadcutter

muzzle velocity	710 ft/s
muzzle energy	166 foot-pounds

38 Special 158-grain round nose

muzzle velocity	755 ft/s
muzzle energy	200 foot-pounds

38 Special 158-grain SWCHP +P

muzzle velocity	915 ft/s
muzzle energy	294 foot-pounds

***38 Special 125-grain SWCHP non +P**

muzzle velocity	825 ft/s
muzzle energy	190 foot-pounds

*All the above are based on a 4-inch vented test barrel, except the Chief's Special is derived in a 2-inch revolver.

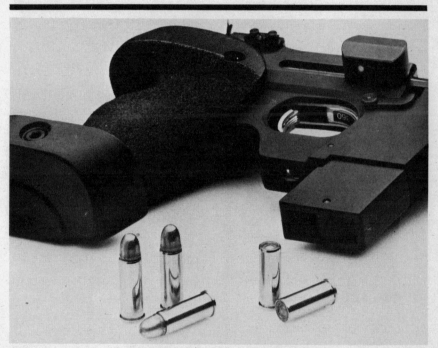
Two new 32 S&W Long rounds have been added to the Federal line.

Federal's new 180-grain 357 Magnum round is an addition to their handgun ammunition line.

A 55-grain hollow point bullet with a boat-tail has been added to Federal's C.F. rifle rounds.

Federal has also added a new monster masher—a 210-grain Nosler Partition bullet loaded in the 338 Winchester caliber.

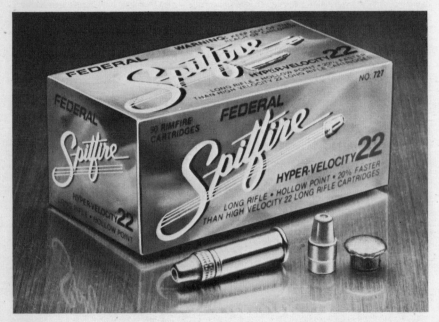

Federal's answer to Remington's Yellow Jacket is the 22 Long Rifle Spitfire which delivers a sizzling 1500 ft/s muzzle velocity.

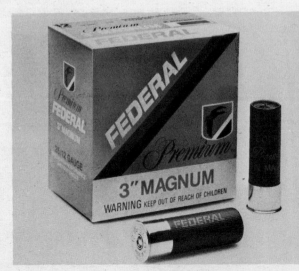

Federal's new Premium 12 gauge magnum load may prove useful for turkey hunting.

tridge line is their Premium load of a 210-grain Nosler Partition bullet in the 338 Winchester Magnum caliber.

To duplicate Remington's Yellow Jacket 22 rimfire load, Federal has introduced the 22 Long Rifle "Spitfire." This load uses a 33-grain hollow point truncated cone bullet. Leaving the muzzle at a blistering 1500 ft/s, it however slows to 1080 ft/s at 100 yards. Thus, its real advantage, as with all such loads, is at ranges less than 50 yards.

Federal now loads a shotshell line, Premium 3-inch 12 gauge 1⅛ ounce shell in No. 6 size shot. It incorporates extra hard plated shot and a buffering material. There is one addition to Federal's component line—a new 1 ounce 12-gauge wad, item #12SO. This wad will enable the reloader to assemble cost-efficient 1 ounce target loads in Federal cases.

Hercules Powder Co.

Hercules has upgraded their Handloaders Guide, adding a notable amount of new data. However, the rumored impending announcement of new products has not yet been made. Those interested in new propellants are, however, waiting for what many feel to be inevitable—an expanded line of Hercules rifle powders.

PMC

Patton and Morgan Corp. has announced the broadening of its ammunition line. Newcomers for this year include: a 55-grain 222 Remington load in FMC and PSP configurations; two loads for the 243 Winchester, an 80-grain PSP and a 100-grain PSP—plus two loads for the 270 Winchester—130 and 150-grain PSP's. Also new are the 140 and 160-grain PSP loads for the 7mm Remington Magnum and the 150 and 170-grain flat nose soft points for the 30-30 Winchester.

New handgun cartridges include the 25 ACP (a 50-grain FMC), the 380 Auto (90-grain FMC and JHP) and the 44 Remington Magnum (180-grain JHP and 240-grain semi-wad-cutter). Ballistics for all these new loads are shown in the following charts. All PMC ammo is loaded with Ball Powder manufactured in Korea under license from OLIN. All PMC ammo is priced substantially below domestic counterparts.

Estate Cartridge Inc.

Estate Cartridge Inc. is a new shotshell ammunition producer located in Conroe, Texas and headed up by Paul Butaud. Estate is scheduled, by the time you read this, to be producing a full line of 12 and 20-gauge shot-shells. Everything from buckshot to target loads, several unique offerings, and private label loadings are all in Estate's plans.

This new loader is not manufacturing his own cases; rather he is importing cases from Italy. Both standard shot and extra hard shot are loaded by Estate. For private label business, corporate logos or other brand information can be printed on the shell case at the customer's option.

Estate is using an Oehler Model 82 system to check ballistics. This system not only measures velocity but also records pressure via a transducer method. I examined the printout results of a test on a pilot lot of ammunition and they were very uniform. On an average pressure of 8,500 PSI an extreme spread of 790 PSI was obtained with a standard deviation of only 250 PSI. The same run of ammo produced an average velocity of 1136 ft/s (vs. nominal velocity of 1145 ft/s) with an extreme spread of only 12 ft/s and a standard deviation of 4.2 ft/s. If this kind of uniformity can be maintained on production runs the resulting ammunition will be delivering some of the most uniform velocities and pressures ever to come from a mass producer.

Norma

The Norma line as offered in the U.S. is not as broad as the total offerings available in Europe. Fred Lawson of Outdoor Sports Headquarters, Inc., Dayton, OH advised me that a strong representative line of Norma rifle and pistol ammunition is currently available. Unprimed cases and Norma powders are also available from Outdoor Sports, who are the exclusive agents for Norma in the U.S. O.S.H. is a distributor and sells through a wide distribution of retailers throughout the U.S. The Norma line apparently is stabilizing in this country through the efforts of O.S.H. Your dealer can obtain all available Norma products by contacting this outfit whose home office address is P.O. Box 1327, Dayton, OH 45401. ●

Sierra's New Bullets

Caliber	Weight & Style	Comments
25	50 gr. FMJ	For 25 ACP
32	71 gr. FMJ	For 32 ACP
30	93 gr. FMJ	For 30 Luger & 30 Mauser
9mm	95 gr. FMJ	For 380 Auto & 9mm Luger
38	130 gr. FMJ	For 38 ACP & 38 Super
38	125 gr. JWC	A jacketed hollow base wadcutter
6mm	90 gr. FMJ/BT	Good for fur bearers
270	140 gr. HP/BT	
303	125 gr. FMJ	For SKS and AK-47 (.311″ diameter)
38	158 gr. JHP	Replaces similar 150 gr. bullet
38	110 gr. JHP	Blitz design
9mm	90 gr. JHP (Power Jacket)	Excellent expander
9mm	115 gr. JHP (Power Jacket)	Excellent expander
45	185 gr. JHP (Power Jacket)	Excellent Expander

New PMC Handgun Cartridge Ballistics

Caliber	Bullet Wgt. and Style	Velocity (ft/s) at:		Energy (ft/lbs) at:	
		Muzzle	50 yds.	Muzzle	50 yds.
25 ACP	50-gr. FMC	810	775	73	63
380 ACP	115-gr. FMC	1155	1047	341	280
380 ACP	115-gr. JHP	1160	1060	345	285
44 Rem. Mag.	180-gr. JHP	1610	1365	1036	745
44 Rem. Mag.	240-gr. SWC	1350	1186	971	749

FMC—full metal case; **JHP**—jacketed hollow point; **SWC**—semi-wadcutter

PMC Rifle Cartridge Ballistics

Caliber	Bullet Wgt. and Style	Muzzle	Velocity in ft/s at:			Muzzle	Energy in foot-pounds at:		
			100 yds.	200 yds.	300 yds.		100 yds.	200 yds.	300 yds.
222 Rem.	55 gr. FMC or PSP	3000	2544	2130	1759	1099	790	554	378
243 Win.	80 gr. PSP	3350	2955	2593	2259	1993	1551	1194	906
243 Win.	100 gr. PSP	2960	2697	2449	2215	1945	1615	1332	1089
270 Win.	130 gr. PSP	3110	2823	2554	2300	2791	2300	1883	1527
270 Win.	150 gr. PSP	2900	2550	2225	1926	2801	2165	1649	1235
7mm Rem. Mag.	140 gr. PSP	3200	2997	2803	2605	3183	2791	2442	2109
7mm Rem. Mag.	160 gr. PSP	3000	2830	2657	2487	3197	2844	2507	2197
30-30 Win.	150 gr. FSP	2390	1973	1605	1303	1902	1296	858	565
30-30 Win.	170 gr. FSP	2200	1895	1619	1381	1827	1355	989	720

FMC—full metal case; **PSP**—pointed soft point; **FSP**—flat nose soft point

CENTERFIRE RIFLE CARTRIDGES—BALLISTICS AND PRICES

(R) = REMINGTON; (W) = WINCHESTER-WESTERN); (F) = FEDERAL; (H) = HORNADY-FRONTIER; (PMC) = Patton & Morgan Corp.

Cartridge	BULLET Wt. Grs.	BULLET Type	Bbl. (in.)	VELOCITY (fps) Muzzle	VELOCITY 100 yds.	VELOCITY 200 yds.	VELOCITY 300 yds.	ENERGY (ft. lbs.) Muzzle	ENERGY 100 yds.	ENERGY 200 yds.	ENERGY 300 yds.	BULLET PATH† 100 yds.	BULLET PATH† 200 yds.	BULLET PATH† 300 yds.	Price Per Box
17 Remington (R)	25	HPPL	24	4040	3284	2644	2086	906	599	388	242	+0.5	– 1.5	– 8.5	$12.65
22 Hornet (R) (W)	45	PSP	24	2690	2042	1502	1128	723	417	225	127	0.0	– 7.7	– 31.3	*23.35
22 Hornet (R)	45	HP	24	2690	2042	1502	1128	723	417	225	127	0.0	– 7.7	– 31.3	*23.35
22 Hornet (W)	46	OPE	24	2690	2042	1502	1128	739	426	230	130	0.0	– 7.7	– 31.3	*23.80
218 Bee (W)	46	OPE	24	2760	2102	1550	1155	778	451	245	136	0.0	– 7.2	– 29.4	*35.20
222 Remington (R) (W) (F) (H)	50	PSP, SX	24	3140	2602	2123	1700	1094	752	500	321	+2.2	0.0	– 10.0	9.95
222 Remington (R)	50	HPPL	24	3140	2635	2182	1777	1094	771	529	351	+2.1	0.0	– 9.5	10.90
222 Remington (R) (PMC)	55	MC	24	3000	2544	2130	1759	1099	790	554	378	+2.3	0.0	– 10.0	9.95
222 Remington (W)	55	FMC	24	3020	2675	2355	2057	1114	874	677	517	+2.0	0.0	– 8.3	9.95
222 Remington (F)	55	MC BT	24	3020	2740	2480	2230	1115	915	750	610	+1.9	0.0	– 7.7	10.20
222 Remington Magnum (R)	55	PSP	24	3240	2748	2305	1906	1282	922	649	444	+1.9	0.0	– 8.5	11.35
222 Remington Magnum (R)	55	HPPL	24	3240	2773	2352	1969	1282	939	675	473	+1.8	0.0	– 8.5	12.10
223 Remington (R) (W) (F) (H)	55	PSP	24	3240	2747	2304	1905	1282	921	648	443	+1.9	0.0	– 8.5	10.90
223 Remington (R) (PMC)	55	HPPL	24	3240	2773	2352	1969	1282	939	675	473	+1.8	0.0	– 8.2	11.75
223 Remington (R) (H)	55	MC	24	3240	2759	2326	1933	1282	929	660	456	+1.9	0.0	– 8.4	10.90
223 Remington (W) (F) (PMC)	55	FMC, MC BT	24	3240	2877	2543	2232	1282	1011	790	608	+1.7	0.0	– 7.1	10.90
225 Winchester (W)	55	PSP	24	3570	3066	2616	2208	1556	1148	836	595	+1.2	0.0	– 6.2	12.10
22-250 Remington (R) (W) (F) (H) (PMC)	55	PSP	24	3730	3180	2695	2257	1699	1235	887	622	+1.0	0.0	– 5.7	10.90
22-250 Remington (R)	55	HPCL	24	3730	3253	2826	2436	1699	1292	975	725	+0.9	0.0	– 5.2	11.75
22-250 Remington (F) — Premium	55	BTHP	24	3730	3330	2960	2630	1700	1350	1070	840	+0.8	0.0	– 4.8	11.80
220 Swift (H)	55	SP	24	3630	3176	2755	2370	1609	1229	927	686	+1.0	0.0	– 5.6	14.70
220 Swift (H)	60	HP	24	3530	3134	2763	2420	1657	1305	1016	780	+1.1	0.0	– 5.7	14.70
243 (W) (R) (F) (H) (PMC)	80	PSP, HPPL, FMJ	24	3350	2955	2593	2259	1993	1551	1194	906	+1.6	0.0	– 7.0	13.60
243 Winchester (F) — Premium	85	BTHP	24	3320	3070	2830	2600	2080	1770	1510	1280	+1.5	0.0	– 6.8	14.55
243 Winchester (W) (R) (F) (H) (PMC)	100	PPSP, PSPCL, SP	24	2960	2697	2449	2215	1945	1615	1332	1089	+1.9	0.0	– 7.8	13.60
243 Winchester (F) — Premium	100	BTSP	24	2960	2760	2570	2380	1950	1690	1460	1260	+1.4	0.0	– 5.8	14.55
6mm Remington (R) (W) (Also, 244 Rem.)	80	PSP, HPPL	24	3470	3064	2694	2352	2139	1667	1289	982	+1.2	0.0	– 6.0	13.60
6mm Remington (R) (W) (F)	100	PSPCL, PPSP	24	3130	2857	2600	2357	2175	1812	1501	1233	+1.7	0.0	– 6.8	13.60
25-20 Winchester (W) (R)	86	SP	24	1460	1194	1030	931	407	272	203	165	0.0	–23.5	– 79.6	*22.10
256 Winchester (W)	60	OPE	24	2760	2097	1542	1149	1015	586	317	176	0.0	– 7.3	– 29.6	*28.45
25-35 Winchester (W)	117	SP	24	2230	1866	1545	1282	1292	904	620	427	0.0	– 9.2	– 33.1	15.45
250 Savage (W)	87	PSP	24	3030	2673	2342	2036	1773	1380	1059	801	+2.0	0.0	– 8.4	14.10
250 Savage (W)	100	ST	24	2820	2467	2140	1839	1765	1351	1017	751	+2.4	0.0	– 10.1	14.10
250 Savage (R)	100	PSP	24	2820	2504	2210	1936	1765	1392	1084	832	+2.3	0.0	– 9.5	13.80
257 Roberts (W)	100	ST	24	2900	2541	2210	1904	1867	1433	1084	805	+2.3	0.0	– 9.4	15.25
257 Roberts (W) (R)	117	PPSP, SPCL	24	2650	2291	1961	1663	1824	1363	999	718	+2.9	0.0	– 12.0	15.55
25-06 Remington (R)	87	HPPL	24	3440	2995	2591	2222	2286	1733	1297	954	+1.2	0.0	– 6.3	14.80
25-06 Remington (W) (F)	90	PEP, HP	24	3440	3043	2680	2344	2364	1850	1435	1098	+1.2	0.0	– 6.1	14.80
25-06 Remington (R)	100	PSPCL	24	3230	2893	2580	2287	2316	1858	1478	1161	+1.6	0.0	– 6.9	14.80
25-06 Remington (F)	117	SP	24	3060	2790	2530	2280	2430	2020	1660	1360	+1.8	0.0	– 7.3	14.80
25-06 Remington (R) (W)	120	PSPCL, PEP	24	3010	2749	2502	2269	2414	2013	1668	1372	+1.9	0.0	– 7.4	14.80
6.5mm Remington Magnum (R)	120	PSPCL	24	3210	2905	2621	2353	2745	2248	1830	1475	+1.3	0.0	– 6.6	23.00
264 Winchester Magnum (W) (R)	100	PSP, PSPCL	24	3320	2926	2565	2231	2447	1901	1461	1105	+1.3	0.0	– 6.7	19.10
264 Winchester Magnum (W) (R)	140	PPSP, PSPCL	24	3030	2782	2548	2326	2854	2406	2018	1682	+1.8	0.0	– 7.2	19.10
270 Winchester (W) (R)	100	PSP	24	3480	3067	2690	2343	2689	2088	1606	1219	+1.2	0.0	– 6.2	14.80
270 Winchester (W) (R) (F)	130	PPSP, BP, SP	24	3110	2849	2604	2371	2791	2343	1957	1622	+1.7	0.0	– 6.8	14.80
270 Winchester (W) (R) (H) (PMC)	130	ST, PSPCL	24	3110	2823	2554	2300	2791	2300	1883	1527	+1.7	0.0	– 7.1	14.80
270 Winchester (F) — Premium	130	BTSP	24	3110	2880	2670	2460	2790	2400	2050	1740	+1.6	0.0	– 6.5	15.80
270 Winchester (W) (H)	150	PPSP	24	2900	2632	2380	2142	2801	2307	1886	1528	+2.1	0.0	– 8.2	14.80
270 Winchester (F) — Premium	150	BTSP	24	2900	2710	2520	2350	2800	2440	2120	1830	+1.6	0.0	– 7.0	15.80
270 Winchester (R) (F)	150	SPCL, SP	24	2900	2550	2225	1926	2801	2165	1649	1235	+2.2	0.0	– 9.3	14.80
270 Winchester (F) — Premium	150	NP	24	2900	2630	2380	2140	2800	2310	1890	1530	+2.1	0.0	– 8.2	19.40
7mm Mauser (R) (W)	175	SP	24	2440	2137	1857	1603	2313	1774	1340	998	0.0	– 6.8	– 23.7	15.35
7mm Mauser (F)	175	SP	24	2470	2170	1880	1630	2370	1820	1380	1030	0.0	– 6.6	– 23.0	15.05
7mm-08 Remington (R)	140	PSPCL	24	2860	2625	2402	2189	2542	2142	1793	1490	+2.1	0.0	– 8.1	14.80
7mm Express Remington (R)	150	SPCL	24	2970	2699	2444	2203	2937	2426	1989	1616	+1.9	0.0	– 7.8	14.80
280 Remington (R)	165	SPCL	24	2820	2510	2220	1950	2913	2308	1805	1393	+2.3	0.0	– 9.4	14.80
284 Winchester (W)	150	PPSP	24	2860	2595	2344	2108	2724	2243	1830	1480	+2.1	0.0	– 8.5	17.45
7mm Remington Magnum (W)	125	PPSP	24	3310	2976	2666	2376	3040	2458	1972	1567	+1.2	0.0	– 6.5	18.30
7mm Remington Magnum (R) (W) (F)	150	PSPCL, PPSP, SP	24	3110	2830	2568	2320	3221	2667	2196	1792	+1.7	0.0	– 7.0	18.30
7mm Remington Magnum (F)	150	BTSP-Prem.	24	3110	2920	2750	2580	3220	2850	2510	2210	+1.6	0.0	– 6.2	19.40
7mm Remington Magnum (F)	165	BTSP-Prem.	24	2860	2710	2560	2420	3000	2690	2410	2150	+1.6	0.0	– 6.9	19.40
7mm Remington Magnum (R) (W) (F) (H)	175	PSPCL, PPSP	24	2860	2645	2440	2244	3178	2718	2313	1956	+2.0	0.0	– 7.9	18.30
7mm Remington Magnum (F)	160	NP	24	2950	2730	2520	2320	3090	2650	2250	1910	+1.8	0.0	– 7.7	22.80
30 Carbine (R) (W) (F) (H)	110	SP, HSP, SP, RN	20	1990	1567	1236	1035	967	600	373	262	0.0	–13.5	– 49.9	*23.75
30 Carbine (W) (F) (H) (PMC)	110	FMC, MC, FMJ, FMC	20	1990	1596	1278	1070	967	622	399	280	0.0	–13.0	– 47.4	*23.75
30 Remington (R) (W)	170	SPCL, ST	24	2120	1822	1555	1328	1696	1253	913	666	0.0	– 9.7	– 33.8	15.55
30-30 Accelerator (R)	55	SP	24	3400	2693	2085	1570	1412	886	521	301	+2.0	0.0	– 10.2	12.90
30-30 Winchester (F)	125	HP	24	2570	2090	1660	1320	1830	1210	770	480	0.0	– 7.3	– 28.1	11.60
30-30 Winchester (W) (F) (PMC)	150	OPE, PPSP, ST, SP	24	2390	2018	1684	1398	1902	1356	944	651	0.0	– 7.7	– 27.9	11.60
30-30 Winchester (R) (H)	150	SPCL	24	2390	1973	1605	1303	1902	1296	858	565	0.0	– 8.2	– 30.0	11.60
30-30 Winchester (W) (R) (F) (PMC)	170	PPSP, ST, SPCL, SP, HPCL	24	2200	1895	1619	1381	1827	1355	989	720	0.0	– 8.9	– 31.1	11.60
300 Savage (R)	150	SPCL	24	2630	2247	1897	1585	2303	1681	1198	837	0.0	– 6.1	– 21.9	14.95
300 Savage (W)	150	PPSP	24	2630	2311	2015	1743	2303	1779	1352	1012	+2.8	0.0	– 11.5	15.25
300 Savage (W) (F) (R)	150	ST, SP, PSPCL	24	2630	2354	2095	1853	2303	1845	1462	1143	+2.7	0.0	– 10.7	14.95
300 Savage (R) (W)	180	SPCL, PPSP	24	2350	2025	1728	1467	2207	1639	1193	860	0.0	– 7.7	– 27.1	14.95
300 Savage (R) (W)	180	PSPCL, ST	24	2350	2137	1935	1745	2207	1825	1496	1217	0.0	– 6.7	– 22.8	14.95
30-40 Krag (R) (W)	180	SPCL, PPSP	24	2430	2098	1795	1525	2360	1761	1288	929	0.0	– 7.1	– 25.0	15.60
30-40 Krag (R) (W)	180	PSPCL, ST	24	2430	2213	2007	1813	2360	1957	1610	1314	0.0	– 6.2	– 21.1	15.60
303 Savage (W)	190	ST	24	1940	1657	1410	1211	1588	1158	839	619	0.0	–11.9	– 41.4	15.25
308 Accelerator (R)	55	PSP	24	3770	3215	2726	2286	1735	1262	907	638	+1.0	0.0	– 5.6	16.40
308 Winchester (W)	110	PSP	24	3180	2666	2206	1795	2470	1736	1188	787	+2.0	0.0	– 9.3	15.10
308 Winchester (W)	125	PSP	24	3050	2697	2370	2067	2582	2019	1559	1186	+2.0	0.0	– 8.2	14.80
308 Winchester (W)	150	PPSP	24	2820	2488	2179	1893	2648	2061	1581	1193	+2.4	0.0	– 9.8	14.80
308 Winchester (W) (R) (F) (H) (PMC)	150	ST, PSPCL, SP	24	2820	2533	2263	2009	2648	2137	1705	1344	+2.3	0.0	– 9.1	14.80
308 Winchester (PMC)	147	FMC-BT	24	2750	2473	2257	2052	2428	2037	1697	1403	+2.3	0.0	– 9.1	9.34
308 Winchester (F) (H)	165	BTSP, SPBT	24	2700	2520	2330	2160	2670	2310	1990	1700	+2.0	0.0	– 8.4	14.80
308 Winchester (W) (R)	180	PPSP, SPCL	24	2620	2274	1955	1666	2743	2086	1527	1109	+2.9	0.0	– 12.1	14.80
308 Winchester (W) (R) (F) (PMC)	180	ST, PSPCL, SP	24	2620	2393	2178	1974	2743	2288	1896	1557	+2.6	0.0	– 9.9	14.80
308 Winchester (W)	200	ST	24	2450	2208	1980	1767	2665	2165	1741	1386	0.0	– 6.3	– 21.4	14.80
30-06 Springfield (W)	110	PSP	24	3380	2843	2365	1936	2790	1974	1366	915	+1.7	0.0	– 8.0	14.80
30-06 Springfield (W) (R) (F)	125	PSP, PSP, SP	24	3140	2780	2447	2138	2736	2145	1662	1269	+1.8	0.0	– 7.7	14.80
30-06 Springfield (W)	150	PPSP	24	2920	2580	2265	1972	2839	2217	1708	1295	+2.2	0.0	– 9.0	14.80
30-06 Springfield (W) (R) (F) (H) (PMC)	150	ST, PSPCL, SP, SP	24	2910	2617	2342	2083	2820	2281	1827	1445	+2.1	0.0	– 8.5	14.80
30-06 Springfield (R)	150	BP	24	2910	2656	2416	2189	2820	2349	1944	1596	+2.0	0.0	– 8.0	15.75
30-06 Springfield (PMC)	150	FMC (M-2)	24	2810	2555	2310	2080	2630	2170	1780	1440	+2.2	0.0	– 8.8	9.34
30-06 Accelerator	55	PSP	24	4080	3485	2965	2502	2033	1483	1074	764	+1.0	0.0	– 5.0	16.40
30-06 Springfield (R)	165	PSPCL	24	2800	2534	2283	2047	2872	2352	1909	1534	+2.3	0.0	– 9.0	14.80
30-06 Springfield (F) (H)	165	BTSP	24	2800	2610	2420	2240	2870	2490	2150	1840	+2.1	0.0	– 8.0	15.80
30-06 Springfield (R) (W) (PMC)	180	SPCL, PPSP	24	2700	2348	2023	1727	2913	2203	1635	1192	+2.7	0.0	– 11.3	14.80
30-06 Springfield (R) (W) (F) (H) (PMC)	180	PSPCL, ST, NOSLER	24	2700	2469	2250	2042	2913	2436	2023	1666	+2.4	0.0	– 9.3	14.80
30-06 Springfield (R)	180	BP	24	2700	2485	2280	2084	2913	2468	2077	1736	+2.4	0.0	– 9.1	15.75

CAUTION: PRICES CHANGE. CHECK AT GUNSHOP.

Cartridge	Wt. Grs.	Bullet Type	Bbl. (in.)	Velocity Muzzle	100 yds.	200 yds.	300 yds.	Energy Muzzle	100 yds.	200 yds.	300 yds.	Bullet Path 100 yds.	200 yds.	300 yds.	Price Per Box
30-06 Springfield (F)	200	BTSP	24	2550	2400	2260	2120	2890	2560	2270	2000	+2.3	0.0	− 9.0	14.80
30-06 Springfield (W) (R)	220	PPSP, SPCL	24	2410	2130	1870	1632	2837	2216	1708	1301	0.0	− 6.8	− 23.6	14.80
30-06 Springfield (W)	220	ST	24	2410	2192	1985	1791	2837	2347	1924	1567	0.0	− 6.4	− 21.6	14.80
300 H & H Magnum (W)	150	ST	24	3130	2822	2534	2264	3262	2652	2138	1707	+1.7	0.0	− 7.2	18.85
300 H & H Magnum (W) (R)	180	ST, PSPCL	24	2880	2640	2412	2196	3315	2785	2325	1927	+2.1	0.0	− 8.0	18.85
300 H & H Magnum (W)	220	ST	24	2580	2341	2114	1901	3251	2677	2183	1765	+2.7	0.0	− 10.5	18.85
300 Winchester Magnum (W) (R)	150	PPSP, PSPCL	24	3290	2951	2636	2342	3605	2900	2314	1827	+1.3	0.0	− 6.6	19.35
300 Winchester Magnum (W) (R) (F) (H)	180	PPSP, PSPCL, SP	24	2960	2745	2540	2344	3501	3011	2578	2196	+1.9	0.0	− 7.3	19.35
300 Winchester Magnum (F) Premium	200	BTSP	24	2830	2680	2530	2380	3560	3180	2830	2520	+1.7	0.0	− 7.1	20.40
303 British (R)	180	SPCL	24	2460	2124	1817	1542	2418	1803	1319	950	0.0	− 6.9	− 24.4	15.20
303 British (W)	180	PPSP	24	2460	2233	2018	1816	2418	1993	1627	1318	0.0	− 6.1	− 20.8	15.20
32-20 Winchester (W) (R)	100	SP	24	1210	1021	913	834	325	231	185	154	0.0	−32.3	−106.3	*22.30
32-20 Winchester (W) (R)	100	L	24	1210	1021	913	834	325	231	185	154	0.0	−32.3	−106.3	*18.00
32 Winchester Special (F) (R)	170	SP	24	2250	1920	1630	1370	1911	1390	1000	710	0.0	− 8.6	− 30.5	12.40
8mm Mauser (R) (W)	170	SPCL, PPSP	24	2360	1969	1622	1333	2102	1463	993	671	0.0	− 8.2	− 29.8	15.25
8mm Mauser (F)	170	SP	24	2510	2110	1740	1430	2380	1677	1140	770	0.0	− 7.0	− 25.7	15.25
8mm Remington Magnum (R)	185	PSPCL	24	3080	2761	2464	2186	3896	3131	2494	1963	+1.8	0.0	− 7.6	22.90
8mm Remington Magnum (R)	220	PSPCL	24	2830	2581	2346	2123	3912	3254	2688	2201	+2.2	0.0	− 8.5	22.90
338 Winchester Magnum (W)	200	PPSP	24	2960	2658	2375	2110	3890	3137	2505	1977	+2.0	0.0	− 8.2	23.65
338 Winchester Magnum (W)	250	ST	24	2660	2395	2145	1910	3927	3184	2554	2025	+2.6	0.0	− 10.2	23.65
348 Winchester (W)	200	ST	24	2520	2215	1931	1672	2820	2178	1656	1241	0.0	− 6.2	− 21.9	27.20
351 Winchester S.L. (W)	180	SP	20	1850	1556	1310	1128	1368	968	686	508	0.0	−13.6	− 47.5	38.60
35 Remington (W)	150	PSPCL	24	2300	1874	1506	1218	1762	1169	755	494	0.0	− 9.2	− 33.0	13.65
35 Remington (R) (F)	200	SPCL, SP	24	2080	1698	1376	1140	1921	1280	841	577	0.0	−11.3	− 41.2	13.65
35 Remington (W)	200	PPSP, ST	24	2020	1646	1335	1114	1812	1203	791	551	0.0	−12.1	− 43.9	13.65
358 Winchester (W)	200	ST	24	2490	2171	1876	1610	2753	2093	1563	1151	0.0	− 6.5	− 23.0	20.90
350 Remington Magnum (R)	200	PSPCL	20	2710	2410	2130	1870	3261	2579	2014	1553	+2.6	0.0	− 10.3	22.15
375 Winchester (W)	200	PPSP	24	2200	1841	1526	1268	2150	1506	1034	714	0.0	− 9.5	− 33.8	18.00
375 Winchester (W)	250	PPSP	24	1900	1647	1424	1239	2005	1506	1126	852	0.0	−12.0	− 40.9	18.00
38-55 Winchester (W)	255	SP	24	1320	1190	1091	1018	987	802	674	587	0.0	−23.4	− 75.2	16.75
375 H & H Magnum (R) (W)	270	SP, PPSP	24	2690	2420	2166	1928	4337	3510	2812	2228	+2.5	0.0	− 10.0	22.95
375 H & H Magnum (W)	300	ST	24	2530	2268	2022	1793	4263	3426	2723	2141	+2.9	0.0	− 11.5	22.95
375 H & H Magnum (R) (W)	300	FMC, MC	24	2530	2171	1843	1551	4263	3139	2262	1602	0.0	− 6.5	− 23.4	22.95
38-40 Winchester (W)	180	SP	24	1160	999	901	827	538	399	324	273	0.0	−33.9	−110.6	28.80
44-40 Winchester (W) (R)	200	SP, SP	24	1190	1006	900	822	629	449	360	300	0.0	−33.3	−109.5	29.80
44 Remington Magnum (R)	240	SP, SJHP	20	1760	1380	1114	970	1650	1015	661	501	0.0	−17.6	− 63.1	11.35
44 Remington Magnum (F) (W)	240	HSP	20	1760	1380	1090	950	1650	1015	640	485	0.0	−18.1	− 65.1	11.35
444 Marlin (R)	240	SP	24	2350	1815	1377	1087	2942	1755	1010	630	0.0	− 9.9	− 38.5	16.45
444 Marlin (R)	265	SP	24	2120	1733	1405	1160	2644	1768	1162	791	0.0	−10.8	− 39.5	16.65
45-70 Government (F)	300	HSP	24	1810	1410	1120	970	2180	1320	840	630	0.0	−17.0	− 61.4	16.80
45-70 Government (W)	300	JHP	24	1880	1559	1294	1105	2355	1619	1116	814	0.0	−13.5	− 47.1	17.15
45-70 Government (R)	405	SP	24	1330	1168	1055	977	1590	1227	1001	858	0.0	−24.6	− 80.3	16.80
458 Winchester Magnum (W) (R)	500	FMC, MC	24	2040	1823	1623	1442	4620	3689	2924	2308	0.0	− 9.6	− 32.5	47.00
458 Winchester Magnum (W) (R)	510	SP, SP	24	2040	1770	1527	1319	4712	3547	2640	1970	0.0	−10.3	− 35.6	31.00

*Price for 50. †Bullet Path based on line-of-sight 0.9″ above center of bore. Bullet type abbreviations: BP—Bronze Point; BT—Boat Tail; CL—Core Lokt; FN—Flat Nose; FMC—Full Metal Case; FMJ—Full Metal Jacket; HP—Hollow Point; HSP—Hollow Soft Point; JHP—Jacketed Hollow Point; L—Lead; Lu—Lubaloy; MAT—Match; MC—Metal Case; NP—Nosler Partition; OPE—Open Point Expanding; PCL—Pointed Core Lokt; PEP—Pointed Expanding Point; PL—Power-Lokt; PP—Power Point; Prem.—Premium; PSP—Pointed Soft Point; SJHP—Semi-Jacketed Hollow Point; SJMP—Semi-Jacketed Metal Point; SP—Soft Point; ST—Silvertip; SX—Super Explosive. PMC prices slightly less.

WEATHERBY MAGNUM CARTRIDGES—BALLISTICS AND PRICES

Cartridge	Wt. Grs.	Bullet Type	Bbl. (in.)	Velocity Muzzle	100 Yds.	200 Yds.	300 Yds.	Energy Muzzle	100 Yds.	200 Yds.	300 Yds.	Bullet Path 100 Yds.	200 Yds.	300 Yds.	Price Per Box
224 Weatherby Magnum	55	PE	26	3650	3214	2808	2433	1627	1262	963	723	+2.8	+3.6	0.0	22.95
240 Weatherby Magnum	70	PE	26	3850	3424	3025	2654	2305	1823	1423	1095	+2.2	+3.0	0.0	22.95
240 Weatherby Magnum	87	PE	26	3500	3165	2848	2550	2367	1935	1567	1256	+2.8	+3.6	0.0	22.95
240 Weatherby Magnum	100	PE	26	3395	3115	2848	2594	2560	2155	1802	1495	+2.8	+3.5	0.0	22.95
240 Weatherby Magnum	100	NP	26	3395	3068	2758	2468	2560	2090	1690	1353	+1.1	0.0	− 5.7	30.95
257 Weatherby Magnum	87	PE	26	3825	3470	3135	2818	2827	2327	1900	1535	+2.1	+2.9	0.0	23.95
257 Weatherby Magnum	100	PE	26	3555	3256	2971	2700	2807	2355	1960	1619	+2.5	+3.2	0.0	23.95
257 Weatherby Magnum	100	NP	26	3555	3242	2945	2663	2807	2335	1926	1575	+0.9	0.0	− 4.7	32.95
257 Weatherby Magnum	117	SPE	26	3300	2853	2443	2074	2830	2115	1551	1118	+3.8	+4.9	0.0	23.95
257 Weatherby Magnum	117	NP	26	3300	3027	2767	2520	2830	2381	1990	1650	+1.2	0.0	− 5.9	32.95
270 Weatherby Magnum	100	PE	26	3760	3341	2949	2585	3140	2479	1932	1484	+2.4	+3.2	0.0	23.95
270 Weatherby Magnum	130	PE	26	3375	3110	2856	2615	3289	2793	2355	1974	+2.8	+3.5	0.0	23.95
270 Weatherby Magnum	130	NP	26	3375	3113	2862	2624	3289	2798	2365	1988	+1.0	0.0	− 5.2	32.95
270 Weatherby Magnum	150	PE	26	3245	3012	2789	2575	3508	3022	2592	2209	+3.1	+3.8	0.0	23.95
270 Weatherby Magnum	150	NP	26	3245	3022	2809	2604	3508	3043	2629	2259	+1.2	0.0	− 5.4	32.95
7mm Weatherby Magnum	139	PE	26	3300	3037	2786	2546	3362	2848	2396	2001	+3.0	+3.7	0.0	23.95
7mm Weatherby Magnum	140	NP	26	3300	3047	2806	2575	3386	2887	2448	2062	+1.1	0.0	− 5.4	32.95
7mm Weatherby Magnum	154	PE	26	3160	2928	2706	2494	3415	2932	2504	2127	+3.3	+4.1	0.0	23.95
7mm Weatherby Magnum	160	NP	26	3150	2935	2727	2528	3526	3061	2643	2271	+1.3	0.0	− 5.8	32.95
7mm Weatherby Magnum	175	RN	26	3070	2714	2383	2082	3663	2863	2207	1685	+1.6	0.0	− 7.5	23.95
300 Weatherby Magnum	110	PE	26	3900	3465	3057	2677	3716	2933	2283	1750	+2.2	+3.0	0.0	23.95
300 Weatherby Magnum	150	PE	26	3545	3248	2965	2696	4187	3515	2929	2422	+2.5	+3.2	0.0	23.95
300 Weatherby Magnum	150	NP	26	3545	3191	2857	2544	4187	3392	2719	2156	+1.0	0.0	− 5.3	33.95
300 Weatherby Magnum	180	PE	26	3245	3010	2785	2569	4210	3622	3100	2639	+3.1	+3.8	0.0	23.95
300 Weatherby Magnum	180	NP	26	3245	2964	2696	2444	4210	3512	2906	2388	+1.3	0.0	− 6.0	33.95
300 Weatherby Magnum	220	SPE	26	2905	2578	2276	2000	4123	3248	2531	1955	+1.9	0.0	− 8.6	23.95
340 Weatherby Magnum	200	PE	26	3210	2947	2696	2458	4577	3857	3228	2683	+3.2	+4.0	0.0	25.95
340 Weatherby Magnum	210	NP	26	3180	2927	2686	2457	4717	3996	3365	2816	+1.3	0.0	− 6.2	40.65
340 Weatherby Magnum	250	SPE	26	2850	2516	2209	1929	4510	3515	2710	2066	+2.0	0.0	− 9.2	25.95
340 Weatherby Magnum	250	NP	26	2850	2563	2296	2049	4510	3648	2927	2331	+1.8	0.0	− 8.2	40.65
378 Weatherby Magnum	270	SPE	26	3180	2796	2440	2117	6064	4688	3570	2688	+1.5	0.0	− 7.3	40.95
378 Weatherby Magnum	300	SPE	26	2925	2564	2234	1935	5700	4380	3325	2495	+1.9	0.0	− 9.0	40.95
378 Weatherby Magnum	300	FMJ	26	2925	2620	2340	2080	5700	4574	3649	2883	+4.9	+6.0	0.0	46.95
460 Weatherby Magnum	500	RN	26	2700	2395	2115	1858	8095	6370	4968	3834	+2.3	0.0	− 10.3	44.95
460 Weatherby Magnum	500	FMJ	26	2700	2416	2154	1912	8095	6482	5153	4060	+2.2	0.0	− 9.8	51.95

†Bullet Path based on line of sight 1.5″ above center of bore. Bullet type abbreviations: FMJ—Full Metal Jacket; NP—Nosler Partition; PE—Pointed Expanding; RN—Round Nose; SPE—Semi-Pointed Expanding.

CAUTION: PRICES CHANGE. CHECK AT GUNSHOP.

NORMA C.F. RIFLE CARTRIDGES—BALLISTICS AND PRICES

Cartridge	Wt. Grs.	Bullet Type	Bbl. (in.)	Velocity (fps) Muzzle	100 Yds.	200 Yds.	300 Yds.	Energy(ft. lbs.) Muzzle	100 Yds.	200 Yds.	300 Yds.	Bullet Path† 100 Yds.	200 Yds.	300 Yds.	Price Per Box
222 Remington	50	SP	24	3200	2650	2170	1750	1137	780	520	340	+1.6	0.0	− 8.2	$10.95
222 Remington	50	FJ	24	3200	2610	2080	1630	1137	756	480	295	+1.9	0.0	−10.1	10.95
222 Remington	53	SpPSP	24	3117	2670	2267	1901	1142	838	604	425	+1.7	0.0	− 8.7	10.95
22-250 Remington	53	SpPSP	24	3707	3192	2741	2332	1616	1198	883	639	+1.0	0.0	− 5.7	11.80
220 Swift	50	SP	24	4110	3611	3133	2681	1877	1448	1090	799	+0.6	0.0	− 4.1	15.85
22 Savage Hi-Power (5.6 x 52R)	71	SP	24	2790	2296	1886	1558	1226	831	561	383	+2.4	0.0	−11.4	21.00
22 Savage Hi-Power (5.6 x 52R)	71	FJ	24	2790	2296	1886	1558	1226	831	561	383	+2.4	0.0	−11.4	21.00
243 Winchester	100	SP, FJ	24	3070	2790	2540	2320	2090	1730	1430	1190	+1.4	0.0	− 6.3	14.55
6.5mm Carcano	139	PPDC	24	2576	2379	2192	2012	2046	1745	1481	1249	+2.3	0.0	− 9.6	21.95
6.5mm Carcano	156	SP	24	2430	2208	2000	1800	2046	1689	1386	1123	+2.9	0.0	−11.7	21.00
6.5mm JAP	139	SPBT	24	2430	2280	2130	1990	1820	1605	1401	1223	+2.7	0.0	−10.8	21.00
6.5mm JAP	156	SP	24	2065	1871	1692	1529	1481	1213	992	810	+4.3	0.0	−16.4	21.00
6.5mm Norma (6.5 x 55)	77	SP	29	2725	2362	2030	1811	1271	956	706	562	+2.4	0.0	−10.9	21.00
6.5mm Norma (6.5 x 55)	139	PPDC	29	2790	2630	2470	2320	2402	2136	1883	1662	+1.8	0.0	− 7.8	21.95
6.5mm Norma (6.5 x 55)	156	SP	29	2495	2271	2062	1867	2153	1787	1473	1208	+2.6	0.0	−10.9	21.00
270 Winchester	130	SPBT	24	3140	2884	2639	2404	2847	2401	2011	1669	+1.4	0.0	− 6.6	15.80
270 Winchester	150	SPBT	24	2800	2616	2436	2262	2616	2280	1977	1705	+1.8	0.0	− 7.7	15.80
7mm Mauser (7 x 57)	150	SPBT	24	2755	2539	2331	2133	2530	2148	1810	1516	+2.0	0.0	− 8.4	16.55
7 x 57 R	150	SPBT, FJ BT	24	2690	2476	2270	2077	2411	2042	1717	1437	+2.1	0.0	− 8.9	—
7 x 64	150	SPBT	24	2890	2598	2329	2113	2779	2249	1807	1487	+1.7	0.0	− 7.5	18.95
7mm Rem. Express (280 Rem.)	150	SPBT	24	2900	2683	2475	2277	2802	2398	2041	1727	+1.7	0.0	− 7.4	—
7mm Remington Magnum	150	SPBT	26	3250	2960	2638	2440	3519	2919	2318	1983	+1.2	0.0	− 5.8	19.40
30 Carbine U.S.	110	SP	18	1970	1595	1300	1090	948	622	413	290	0.0	−12.4	−45.7	10.45
30-30 Winchester	150	SPFN	20	2410	2075	1790	1550	1934	1433	1066	799	0.0	− 7.0	−26.1	12.75
30-30 Winchester	170	SPFN	20	2220	1890	1630	1410	1860	1350	1000	750	0.0	− 8.1	−29.2	12.75
7.5 x 55 Swiss	180	SPBT	24	2650	2441	2248	2056	2792	2380	2020	1690	+2.1	0.0	− 8.9	22.00
7.62 x 39 Short Russian	125	SP		2385				1580							18.95
7.62 Russian	180	SPBT	24	2625	2415	2222	2030	2749	2326	1970	1644	+2.2	0.0	− 9.1	22.35
308 Winchester	130	SPBT	24	2900	2590	2300	2030	2428	1937	1527	1190	+1.9	0.0	− 8.6	15.80
308 Winchester	150	SPBT	24	2860	2570	2300	2050	2725	2200	1760	1400	+1.9	0.0	− 8.5	15.80
308 Winchester	180	PPDC	24	2610	2400	2210	2020	2725	2303	1952	1631	+2.3	0.0	− 9.4	15.80
30-06	130	SPBT	24	3205	2876	2561	2263	2966	2388	1894	1479	+1.4	0.0	− 6.7	15.80
30-06	150	SPBT	24	2970	2680	2402	2141	2943	2393	1922	1527	+1.7	0.0	− 7.8	15.80
30-06	180	SP	24	2700	2477	2261	2070	2914	2430	2025	1713	+2.1	0.0	− 8.7	15.80
30-06	180	PPDC	24	2700	2494	2296	2109	2914	2487	2107	1778	+2.0	0.0	− 8.6	15.80
303 British	150	SP	24	2720	2440	2170	1930	2465	1983	1569	1241	+2.2	0.0	− 9.7	16.75
303 British	180	SPBT	24	2540	2340	2147	1965	2579	2189	1843	1544	+2.4	0.0	−10.0	16.75
308 Norma Magnum	180	PPDC	26	3020	2798	2585	2382	3646	3130	2671	2268	+1.3	0.0	− 6.1	27.90
7.65mm Argentine	150	SP	24	2920	2630	2355	2105	2841	2304	1848	1476	+1.7	0.0	− 7.8	21.95
7.7mm JAP	130	SP	24	2950	2635	2340	2065	2513	2004	1581	1231	+1.8	0.0	− 8.2	22.50
7.7mm JAP	180	SPBT	24	2495	2292	2101	1922	2484	2100	1765	1477	+2.6	0.0	−10.4	22.50
8 x 57J (.318)	196	SP	24	2525	2195	1894	1627	2778	2097	1562	1152	+2.9	0.0	−12.7	—
8mm Mauser (8 x 57JS)	196	SP	24	2525	2195	1894	1627	2778	2097	1562	1152	+2.9	0.0	−12.7	19.65
9.3 x 57mm	286	PPDC	24	2065	1818	1595	1404	2714	2099	1616	1252	0.0	− 9.1	−32.0	—
9.3 x 62mm	286	PPDC	24	2360	2088	1815	1592	3544	2769	2092	1700	+3.3	0.0	−13.7	—

†Bullet Path based on line of sight 1.5″ above center of bore. Bullet type abbreviations: BT—Boat Tail; DC—Dual Core; FJ—Full Jacket; FJBT—Full Jacket Boat Tail; FP—Flat Point; HP—Hollow Point; MC—Metal Case; P—Pointed; PP—Plastic Point; RN—Round Nose; SP—Soft Point; SPFN—Soft Point Flat Nose; SPSBT—Soft Point Semi-Pointed Boat Tail; SPSP—Soft Point Semi-Point; SpPSP—Spire point Soft Point.

RIMFIRE CARTRIDGES—BALLISTICS AND PRICES

Cartridge Type	Wt. Grs.	Bullet Type	Velocity (fps) 18½″ Barrel Muzzle	50 Yds.	100 Yds.	Energy (ft. lbs.) Muzzle	50 Yds.	100 Yds.	Velocity (fps) 6″ Barrel Muzzle	50 Yds.	Energy (ft. lbs.) Muzzle	50 Yds.	Price Per Box 50 Rds.	100 Rds.
22 CB Short (CCI & Win. only)	29	Solid	727	667	610	34	29	24	706	—	32	—	$N.A.	$4.25
22 CB Long (CCI only)	29	Solid	727	667	610	34	29	24	706	—	32	—	N.A.	4.25
22 Short Standard Velocity	29	Solid	1045	—	810	70	—	42	865	—	48	—	2.17	N.A.
22 Short High Velocity (Fed., Rem., Win.)	29	Solid	1095	—	903	77	—	53	—	—	—	—	2.17	N.A.
22 Short High Velocity (CCI only)	29	Solid	1132	1004	920	83	65	55	1065	—	73	—	N.A.	4.20
22 Short High Velocity HP (Fed., Rem., Win.)	27	Hollow Point	1120	—	904	75	—	49	—	—	—	—	2.30	N.A.
22 Short High Vel. HP (CCI only)	27	Hollow Point	1164	1013	920	81	62	51	1077	—	69	—	N.A.	4.47
22 Long Standard Vel. (CCI only)	29	Solid	1180	1038	946	90	69	58	1031	—	68	—	N.A.	4.47
22 Long High Velocity (Fed., Rem., Win.)	29	Solid	1240	—	962	99	—	60	—	—	—	—	2.30	N.A.
22 Long Rifle Stand. Velocity (CCI only)	40	Solid	1138	1046	975	115	97	84	1027	925	93	76	N.A.	4.77
22 Long Rifle Stand. Velocity (Fed., Rem., Win.)	40	Solid	1150	—	976	117	—	85	—	—	—	—	2.46	4.91
22 Long Rifle High Vel. (CCI only)	40	Solid	1341	1150	1045	160	117	97	1150	1010	117	90	N.A.	4.77
22 Long Rifle High Velocity (Fed., Rem., Win.)	40	Solid	1255	—	1017	140	—	92	—	—	—	—	2.46	4.91
22 Long Rifle High Velocity HP (CCI only)	37	Hollow Point	1370	1165	1040	154	111	89	1190	1040	116	88	N.A.	5.27
22 Long Rifle High Velocity HP (Fed., Rem., Win.)	36-38	Hollow Point	1280	—	1010	131	—	82	—	—	—	—	2.74	5.45
22 Long Rifle Yellow Jacket (Rem. only)	33	Hollow Point	1500	1240	1075	165	110	85	—	—	—	—	3.08	N.A.
22 Long Rifle Spitfire (Fed. only)	33	Hollow Point	1500	1240	1075	165	110	85	—	—	—	—	2.70	N.A.
22 Long Rifle Viper (Rem. only)	36	Solid	1410	1187	1056	159	113	89	—	—	—	—	2.67	N.A.
22 Stinger (CCI only)	32	Hollow Point	1687	1300	1158	202	120	95	1430	1100	145	86	3.18	N.A.
22 Winchester Magnum Rimfire (Win. only)	40	FMC or HP	1910	—	1326	324	—	156	—	—	—	—	6.81	N.A.
22 Winchester Magnum Rimfire (CCI only)	40	FMC or HP	2025	1688	1407	364	253	176	1339	1110	159	109	6.43	N.A.
22 Long Rifle Pistol Match (Win., Fed.)	40	Solid	—	—	—	—	—	—	1060	950	100	80	5.38	10.75
22 Long Rifle Match (Rifle) (CCI, Fed.)	40	Solid	1138	1047	975	116	97	84	1027	925	93	76	N.A.	7.53
22 Long Rifle Shot (CCI, Fed., Win.)	—	#11 or #12 shot	1047	—	—	—	—	—	950	—	—	—	5.00	N.A.
22 Winchester Magnum Rimfire Shot (CCI only)	—	#11 shot	1126	—	—	—	—	—	1000	—	—	—	3.95(1)	N.A.
22 Short Match (CCI only)	29	Solid	830	752	695	44	36	31	786	—	39	—	N.A.	4.55

Please note that the actual ballistics obtained in your gun can vary considerably from the advertised ballistics. Also, ballistics can vary from lot to lot even within the same brand. All prices were correct at the time this table was prepared. All prices are subject to change without notice.
(1) 20 to a box

CAUTION: PRICES CHANGE. CHECK AT GUNSHOP.

CENTERFIRE HANDGUN CARTRIDGES—BALLISTICS AND PRICES
Win.-Western, Rem.-Peters, Norma, PMC, and Federal

Most loads are available from W-W and R-P. All available Norma loads are listed. Federal cartridges are marked with an asterisk. Other loads supplied by only one source are indicated by a letter, thus: Norma (a); R-P (b); W-W (c); PMC (d); CCI (e). Prices are approximate.

Cartridge	Gr.	Bullet Style	Muzzle Velocity	Muzzle Energy	Barrel Inches	Price Per Box
22 Jet (b)	40	SP	2100	390	8⅜	$27.05
221 Fireball (b)	50	SP	2650	780	10½	11.50
25 (6.35mm) Auto*	50	MC	810	73	2	14.40
25 ACP (c)	45	Exp. Pt.	835	70	2	15.45
256 Winchester Magnum (c)	60	HP	2350	735	8½	28.45
30 (7.65mm) Luger Auto	93	MC	1220	307	4½	23.65
32 S&W Blank (b, c)	No bullet	—	—	—		13.75
32 S&W Blank, BP (c)	No bullet	—	—	—		13.75
32 Short Colt	80	Lead	745	100	4	13.85
32 Long Colt IL (c)	82	Lub.	755	104	4	14.40
32 Auto (c)	60	STHP	970	125	4	18.20
32 (7.65mm) Auto*	71	MC	905	129	4	16.55
32 (7.65mm) Auto Pistol (a)	77	MC	900	162	4	—
32 S&W	88	Lead	680	90	3	13.90
32 S&W Long	98	Lead	705	115	4	14.40
32-20 Winchester	100	Lead	1030	271	6	18.35
32-20 Winchester	100	SP	1030	271	6	22.75
357 Magnum	110	JHP	1295	410	4	21.70
357 Magnum	110	SJHP	1295	410	4	21.70
357 Magnum	125	JHP	1450	583	4	21.70
357 Magnum (d)	125	JHC	1450	583	4	21.70
357 Magnum (e)	125	JSP	1900	1001	—	21.70
357 Magnum (e)	140	JHP	1775	979	—	21.70
357 Magnum (e)	150	FMJ	1600	852	—	21.70
357 Magnum*	158	SWC	1235	535	4	18.35
357 Magnum (b) (e)	158	JSP	1550	845	8⅜	21.70
357 Magnum	158	MP	1410	695	8⅜	21.35
357 Magnum	158	Lead	1410	696	8⅜	18.35
357 Magnum	158	JHP	1450	735	8⅜	21.70
9mm Luger (c)	95	JSP	1355	387	4	20.90
9mm Luger (c)	115	FMC	1155	341	4	20.50
9mm Luger (c)	115	STHP	1255	383	4	21.95
9mm Luger*	115	JHP	1165	349	4	20.50
9mm Luger*	125	MC	1120	345	4	20.50
9mm Luger (e)	125	JSP	1100	335	—	20.50
38 S&W Blank	No bullet	—	—	—		16.65
38 Smith & Wesson	145	Lead	685	150	4	15.50
38 S&W	146	Lead	730	172	4	15.50
38 Special Blank	No bullet	—	—	—		16.75
38 Special (e)	110	JHP	1200	351	—	19.80
38 Special IL +P (c)	150	Lub.	1060	375	6	17.65
38 Special IL +P (c)	150	MP	1060	375	6	19.80
38 Special	158	Lead	855	256	6	15.60
38 Special	200	Lead	730	236	6	16.65
38 Special	158	MP	855	256	6	19.80
38 Special (b)	125	SJHP	Not available			19.80
38 Special WC (b)	148	Lead	770	195	6	16.25
38 Special Match, IL	148	Lead	770	195	6	16.25
38 Special Match, IL (b)	158	Lead	855	256	6	16.25
38 Special*	158	LRN	755	200	4	15.60
38 Special	158	RN	900	320	6	15.60
38 Special	158	SWC	755	200	4	16.75
38 Special Match*	148	WC	710	166	4	16.25
38 Special +P (c)	95	STHP	1100	255	4	21.20
38 Special +P (b)	110	SJHP	1020	254	4	19.80
38 Special +P	125	JSP	945	248	4	19.80
38 Special +P	158	LRN	915	294	4	15.60
38 Special +P	158	LHP	915	294	4	17.30
38 Special +P*	158	SWC	915	294	4	17.30
38 Special +P*	158	SWCHP	915	294	4	17.30
38 Special +P*	158	LSWC	915	294	4	17.30
38 Special +P (e)	140	JHP	1275	504	—	16.95
38 Special +P (e)	150	FMJ	1175	461	—	—
38 Special +P*	110	JHP	1020	254	4	19.80
38 Special +P*	125	JHP	945	248	4	19.80
38 Special Norma +P (a)	110	JHP	1542	580	6	21.75
38 Short Colt	125	Lead	730	150	6	15.20
38 Short Colt, Greased	130	Lub.	730	155	6	15.20
38 Long Colt	150	Lead	730	175	6	23.35
38 Super Auto +P (b)	130	MC	1280	475	5	17.85
38 Super Auto +P (b)	115	JHP	1300	431	5	20.80
38 Auto	130	MC	1040	312	4½	18.40
38 Auto +P	130	FMC	1280	475	5	17.85
380 Auto (c)	85	STHP	1000	189	3¾	18.00
380 Auto*	95	MC	955	190	3¾	16.90
380 Auto	88	JHP	990	191	4	16.90
380 Auto*	90	JHP	1000	200	3¾	16.90
38-40 Winchester	180	SP	975	380	5	28.80
41 Remington Magnum	210	Lead	1050	515	8¾	24.30
41 Remington Magnum	210	SP	1500	1050	8¾	28.50
44 S&W Spec.*	200	LSW	960	410	7½	21.80
44 S&W Special	246	Lead	755	311	6½	21.80
44 Remington Magnum*	180	JHP	1610	1045	4	25.80
44 Remington Magnum (e)	200	JHP	1650	1208	—	—
44 Remington Magnum (e)	240	JSP	1625	1406	—	11.35
44 Remington Magnum (b)	240	SP	1470	1150	6½	11.35
44 Remington Magnum	240	Lead	1470	1150	6½	27.70
44 Remington Magnum	240	SJHP	1180	741	4	11.35
44 Remington Magnum (a)	240	JPC	1533	1253	8½	25.80
44 Auto Mag (a)	240	JPC	1350	976	6½	—
44-40 Winchester	200	SP	975	420	7½	30.40
45 Colt*	225	SWCHP	900	405	5½	20.85
45 Colt	250	Lead	860	410	5½	22.15
45 Colt, IL (c)	255	Lub., L	860	410	5½	22.15
45 Auto (c)	185	STHP	1000	411	5	9.70
45 Auto (e)	200	JHP	1025	466	—	23.70
45 Auto	230	MC	850	369	5	22.60
45 ACP	230	JHP	850	370	5	23.70
45 Auto WC*	185	MC	775	245	5	23.70
45 Auto*	185	JHP	950	370	5	23.70
45 Auto MC	230	MC	850	369	5	22.60
45 Auto Match (c)	185		775	247	5	23.70
45 Winchester Magnum (c)	230	FMC	1400	1001	5	24.65
45 Auto Rim (b)	230	Lead	810	335	5½	24.00

IL—Inside Lub.; JSP—Jacketed Soft Point; WC—Wad Cutter; RN—Round Nose; HP—Hollow Point; Lub—Lubricated; MC—Metal Case; SP—Soft Point; MP—Metal Point; LGC—Lead, Gas Check; JHP—Jacketed Hollow Point; SWC—Semi Wad Cutter; SJHP—Semi Jacketed Hollow Point; PC—Power Cavity

SHOTSHELL LOADS AND PRICES
Winchester-Western, Remington-Peters, Federal

In certain loadings one manufacturer may offer fewer or more shot sizes than another, but in general all makers offer equivalent loadings. Sources are indicated by letters, thus: W-W (a); R-P (b); Fed. (c). *Prices are approximate, list is a random sampling of offerings.*

GAUGE	Length Shell Ins.	Powder Equiv. Drams	Shot Ozs.	Shot Size	PRICE PER BOX
MAGNUM LOADS					
10 (a)	3½	4½	2¼	BB, 2, 4	$25.50
10 (a¹, b)	3½	Max	2	BB, 2, 4	17.70
12 (a, b, c)	3	Max	1⅞	BB, 2, 4	16.35
12 (a¹, b)	3	4	1⅝	2, 4, 6	14.80
12 (a¹, b)	2¾	Max	1½	2, 4, 5, 6	14.05
16 (a, b, c)	2¾	Max	1¼	2, 4, 6	13.70
20 (a, b, c)	3	Max	1¼	2, 4, 6, 7½	12.95
20 (a¹, b, c)	2¾	2¾	1⅛	4, 6, 7½	12.15
LONG RANGE LOADS					
10 (a)	2⅞	4¾	1⅝	4	16.35
12 (a¹, b, c)	2¾	3¾	1¼	BB, 2, 4, 5, 6, 7½, 8, 9	11.40
16 (a, b, c)	2¾	3¼	1⅛	4, 5, 6, 7½, 9	10.90
20 (a¹, b, c)	2¾	2¾	1	4, 5, 6, 7½, 8, 9	10.05
28 (a, b)	2¾	2¼	¾	6, 7½, 8	10.10
410 (b)	2½	Max	½	6, 7½	7.95
410 (b)	3	Max	11/16	4, 5, 6, 7½, 8	9.40
FIELD LOADS					
12 (a, b, c)	2¾	3¼	1¼	7½, 8, 9	10.70
12 (a, b, c)	2¾	3¼	1⅛	4, 5, 6, 7½, 8, 9	9.80
16 (a, b, c)	2¾	2¾	1⅛	4, 5, 6, 7½, 8	9.70
20 (a, b, c)	2¾	2½	1	4, 5, 6, 7½, 8, 9	8.85
SKEET & TRAP					
12 (a, b, c)	2¾	3	1⅛	7½, 8	7.85
12 (a, b, c)	2¾	2¾	1⅛	7½, 8, 9	7.85
20 (a, b, c)	2¾	2½	⅞	9	7.35
28 (a)	2¾	2	¾	9	8.65
410 (a)	2½	Max	½	9	7.15
BUCKSHOT					
10 (c)	3½	Sup. Mag.	—	4 Buck—54 pellets	5.10
12 (a, b, c)	3 Mag.	4½	—	00 Buck—15 pellets	4.10
12 (a, b, c)	3 Mag.	4½	—	4 Buck—41 pellets	4.10
12 (b)	2¾ Mag.	4	—	1 Buck—20 pellets	3.55
12 (a, b, c)	2¾ Mag.	4	—	00 Buck—12 pellets	3.55
12 (a, b, c)	2¾	Max	—	00 Buck— 9 pellets	3.20
12 (a, b, c)	2¾	3¾	—	0 Buck—12 pellets	3.20
12 (a, b, c)	2¾	Max	—	1 Buck—16 pellets	3.20
12 (a, b, c)	2¾	Max	—	4 Buck—27 pellets	3.20
12 (a)	2¾ Mag.	—	—	000 Buck— 8 pellets	3.20
12 (a)	3 Mag.	—	—	000 Buck—10 pellets	4.10
16 (a, b, c)	2¾	3	—	1 Buck—12 pellets	3.20
20 (a, b, c)	2¾	Max	—	3 Buck—20 pellets	3.20
RIFLED SLUGS					
10	3½"	Mag.	1¾	Slug 5-pack	6.45
12 (c)	2¾	Max	1¼	Slug 5-pack	4.60
12 (a, b, c)	2¾	Max	1	Slug 5-pack	3.70
16 (a, b, c)	2¾	Max	⅘	Slug	3.70
20 (b)	2¾	Max	⅝	Slug	3.40
20 (a, b)	2¾	Max	¾	Slug	3.40
410 (a, b)	2½	Max	⅕	Slug	3.20
STEEL SHOT LOADS					
10 (c)	3½	Max	1⅝	BB, 2	23.95
12 (c)	2¾	3¾	1⅛	1, 2, 4	15.60
12 (a, c)	2¾	Max	1¼	BB, 1, 2, 4	17.15
12 (b)	3	Max	1¼	1, 2, 4	18.85
12 (b)	2¾	Max	1⅛	1, 2, 4	14.25
20 (c)	3	3¼	1	4	13.65

CAUTION: PRICES CHANGE. CHECK AT GUNSHOP.

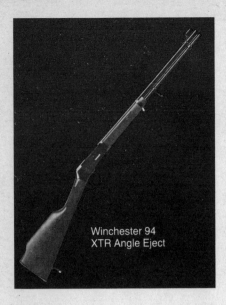

Winchester 94
XTR Angle Eject

Ruger No. 1 International

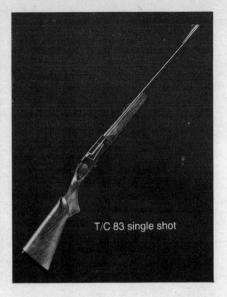

T/C 83 single shot

THE COMPLETE COMPACT

It's not a trick phrase, you know. This really is a complete catalog of legal firearms available through trade channels in the U.S. It shows them all in just 155 pages, which is certainly compact.

So you definitely are looking at a complete compact catalog. And this year it's different from last year's in some significant ways:

For one thing, there's quite a bit more of it, even if it is compact.

For another, its "look" is changed. It's packed a little tighter, and there are some better headlines to help guide you to the material you want to find.

And there's the GUNDEX® — eight pages of a really new service.

There's more catalog because there are more and more models of guns out there, particularly rifles. It seems a factory just can't make too many different models.

A catalog like this one, even a 38-year-old catalog, is not an automatic perennial. It does not just happen each year; it's made to happen.

We start with last year's catalog and we send tear-sheets to all the gun sources listed. We ask for new model notes, for new photos, for the manufacturer to tell us what he's discontinued. As soon as we hear of a new gun, its maker goes on this list.

Some years we get as high as 85% return on this mailing. We then chase the rest of them on the phone. With the data in our offices, the work starts— it all has to get into its proper place. That's called, in publishing, "production work." However, in this case, it can't be turned over to what, in publishing, are called "production people." To get such a gun catalog straight takes what we all call "gun people."

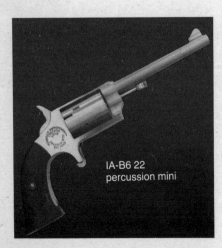

IA-B6 22
percussion mini

I.M.I. 357 Magnum
Eagle pistol

Coonan Arms
357 pistol

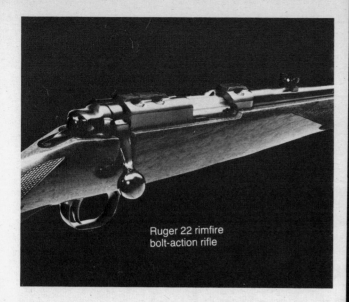

Ruger 22 rimfire
bolt-action rifle

CATALOG

We have them and they do it.

You get to be gun people by shooting, by owning guns, by talking to the industry, by reading a lot. You have to go to the big trade shows and the little gun shows. You have to be interested. We are.

That many—there are 150 or so here—pages of dense-pack information has to be organized properly or it's useless. And what worked fine in 1974 when there were 118 pages does not serve in 1984. We make new categories; we combine old ones; we change the order of things—the change is constant.

Last year was a big year for that—we put military-style rifles in their own classification, and police shotguns, too, and we grouped competition guns differently. This year we didn't do much of that, but we did a big job of changing how it all looks.

We want you to depend on it and use it—like always—and enjoy it—like always. *The Editors*

Ruger 357-cal. Maximum

GUNDEX®

This new feature of our catalog may very well speed up the chore of finding the basic facts on a given firearm for the experienced. And it may make the contents of the catalog far more available to the inexperienced.

That is our intention.

To use it, you need the manufacturer's name and model designation. That designation might be a number, as in Winchester Model 94, or it might be a name, as in Colt Python. And you need to know the alphabet.

The manufacturers are listed alphabetically and the entry under each manufacturer is arranged in the quickest way—numbers are in numerical order, names are alphabetical.

It's all very straightforward. It is all pretty voluminous, as well. There are nearly 1500 entries. At 255 lines per page, what with headings and all, the GUNDEX® is eight pages long.

We have tried to make it easy to find, too—just look for the black GUNDEX® label along the edge of the page, flip to there, and get your page number in short order.

GUNDEX®

A listing of all the guns in the catalog, by name and model, alphabetically and numerically.

Beeman/FAS 602

BEEMAN/FAS 602 MATCH PISTOL
Caliber: 22 LR, 5-shot.
Barrel: 5.5″.
Weight: 41 oz. **Length:** 11.02″ over-all.
Stocks: Full target stocks; adjustable, one-piece. Left hand style avail.
Sights: Match. Blade front, open notch rear fully adj. for w. and e. Sight radius is 8.66″.
Features: Line of sight is only $1\frac{1}{32}$″ above centerline of bore; magazine is inserted from top; adjustable and removable trigger mechanism; single lever takedown. Full 5 year warranty. Imported from Italy by Beeman Inc.
Price: **$1,295.00**

Beeman/FAS 601 Match Pistol
Similar to SP 602 except has different match stocks with adj. palm, shelf, 22 Short only, weighs 40 oz., 5.6″ bbl., has gas ports through top of barrel and slide to reduce recoil, slightly different trigger and sear mechanisms.
Price: **$1,295.00**

Bernardelli Model 100

BERNARDELLI MODEL 100 PISTOL
Caliber: 22 LR only, 10-shot magazine.
Barrel: 5.9″.
Weight: 37¾ oz. **Length:** 9″ over-all.
Stocks: Checkered walnut with thumbrest.
Sights: Fixed front, rear adj. for w. and e.
Features: Target barrel weight included. Heavy sighting rib with interchangeable front sight. Accessories include cleaning equipment and assembly tools, case. Imported from Italy by Interarms.
Price: With case... **$425.00**

BERETTA MODEL 76 PISTOL
Caliber: 22 LR, 10-shot magazine.
Barrel: 6″.
Weight: 33 ozs. (empty). **Length:** 8.8″ over-all.
Stocks: Checkered plastic.
Sights: Interchangeable blade front (3 widths), rear is fully adj. for w. and e.
Features: Built-in, fixed counterweight, raised, matted slide rib, factory adjusted trigger pull from 3 lbs. 5 ozs. to 3 lbs. 12 ozs. Thumb safety. Blue-black finish. Wood grips available at extra cost. Introduced 1977. Imported from Italy by Beretta Arms Co.
Price: With plastic grips **$370.00**
Price: With wood grips **$415.00**

Beretta Model 76

> Consult our Directory pages for the location of firms mentioned.

BRITARMS 2000 MK.2 TARGET PISTOL
Caliber: 22 LR, 5-shot magazine.
Barrel: 5⅞″.
Weight: 48 oz. **Length:** 11″ over-all.
Stocks: Stippled walnut, anatomically designed wrap-around type with adjustable palm shelf.
Sights: Target front and rear. Interchangeable front blades of 3.2mm, 3.6mm or 4.0mm; fully adjustable rear.
Features: Offset anatomical and adjustable trigger, top loading magazine. Satin blue-black finish, satin hard chrome frame and trigger. Introduced 1982. Imported from England by Action Arms Ltd.
Price: **$1,200.00**

Britarms 2000 MK.2

CAUTION: PRICES CHANGE. CHECK AT GUNSHOP.

COLT GOLD CUP NAT'L MATCH MK IV Series 70
Caliber: 45 ACP, 7-shot magazine.
Barrel: 5″, with new design bushing.
Weight: 38½ oz. **Length:** 8⅜″
Stocks: Checkered walnut, gold plated medallion.
Sights: Ramp-style front, Colt-Elliason rear adj. for w. and e., sight radius 6¾″.
Features: Arched or flat housing; wide, grooved trigger with adj. stop; ribbed-top slide, hand fitted, with improved ejection port.
Price: Colt Royal Blue **$560.95**

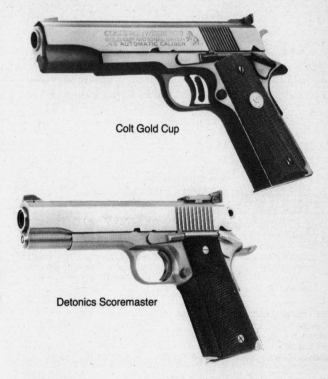

Colt Gold Cup

DETONICS SCOREMASTER TARGET PISTOL
Caliber: 45 ACP, 451 Detonics Magnum, 7-shot clip.
Barrel: 5″ heavy match barrel with recessed muzzle; 6″ optional.
Weight: 41 oz. **Length:** 8¾″ over-all.
Stocks: Pachmayr checkered with matching mainspring housing.
Sights: Blade front, Low-Base Bomar rear.
Features: Stainless steel; self-centering barrel system; patented Detonics recoil system; combat tuned, ambidextrous safety; extended grip safety; National Match tolerances; extended magazine release. Introduced 1983. From Detonics.
Price: Either caliber **$995.00**

Detonics Scoremaster

Hammerli Model 150 Free Pistol

HAMMERLI MODEL 230 RAPID FIRE PISTOL
Caliber: 22 Short.
Barrel: 6.3″, 6-groove.
Weight: 43.8 oz. **Length:** 11.6″.
Stocks: Walnut.
Sights: Match type sights. Sight radius 9.9″. Micro rear, click adj. Interchangeable front sight blade.
Features: Semi-automatic. Recoil-operated, 6-shot clip. Gas escape in front of chamber to eliminate muzzle jump. Fully adj. trigger from 5¼ oz. to 10½ oz. with three different lengths available. Designed for International 25 meter Silhouette Program. Imported from Switzerland by Mandall Shooting Supplies.
Price: Model 230-1 . . . . **$1,295.00**
Price: Model 232 . . . . **$1,395.00**

Hammerli Model 230 Rapid Fire Pistol

HAMMERLI STANDARD, MODELS 208 & 211
Caliber: 22 LR.
Barrel: 5.9″, 6-groove.
Weight: 37.6 oz. (45 oz. with extra heavy barrel weight). **Length:** 10″.
Stocks: Walnut. Adj. palm rest (208), 211 has thumbrest grip.
Sights: Match sights, fully adj. for w. and e. (click adj.). Interchangeable front and rear blades.
Features: Semi-automatic, recoil operated. 8-shot clip. Slide stop. Fully adj. trigger (2¼ lbs. and 3 lbs.). Extra barrel weight available. Imported from Switzerland by Mandall Shooting Supplies.
Price: Model 208, approx. **$1,295.00**
Price: Model 211, approx. **$1,195.00**
Price: Model 215, approx. **$1,195.00**

HAMMERLI MODEL 120-1 FREE PISTOL
Caliber: 22 LR.
Barrel: 9.9″.
Weight: 44 oz. **Length:** 14¾″ over-all.
Stocks: Contoured right-hand (only) thumbrest.
Sights: Fully adjustable rear, blade front. Choice of 14.56″ or 9.84″ sight radius.
Features: Trigger adjustable for single- or two-stage pull from 1.8 to 12 oz. Adjustable for length of pull. Guaranteed accuracy of .98″, 10 shots at 50 meters. Imported from Switzerland by Mandall Shooting Supplies.
Price: Model 120-1 . . . . **$995.00**
Price: Model 120-2 (same as above except has walnut target grips with adjustable palm-rest RH or LH) **$1,195.00**

HAMMERLI MODEL 150 FREE PISTOL
Caliber: 22 LR. Single shot.
Barrel: 11.3″
Weight: 43 ozs. **Length:** 15.35″ over-all.
Stocks: Walnut with adjustable palm shelf.
Sights: Sight radius of 14.6″. Micro rear adj. for w. and e.
Features: Single shot Martini action. Cocking lever on left side of action with vertical operation. Set trigger adjustable for length and angle. Trigger pull weight adjustable between 5 and 100 grams. Guaranteed accuracy of .78″, 10 shots from machine rest. Imported from Switzerland by Mandall Shooting Supplies.
Price: About **$1,500.00**
Price: With electric trigger (Model 152), about **$1,650.00**

HECKLER & KOCH P9S COMPETITION PISTOL
Caliber: 9mm Para.
Barrel: 5.5".
Weight: 32 oz. **Length:** 9.1" over-all.
Stocks: Stippled walnut, target-type.
Sights: Blade front, fully adjustable rear.
Features: Comes with extra standard 4" barrel, slide and grips, as well as the target gun parts and tools and is fully convertible. Imported from West Germany by Heckler & Koch.
Price: **$990.00**

H&K P9S Competition

HIGH STANDARD X SERIES CUSTOM 10-X
Caliber: 22 LR, 10-shot magazine.
Barrel: 5½" bull.
Weight: 44½ oz. **Length:** 9¾" over-all.
Stocks: Checkered walnut.
Sights: Undercut ramp front; frame mounted fully adj. rear.
Features: Completely custom made and fitted for best performance. Fully adjustable target trigger, stippled front- and backstraps, slide lock, non-reflective blue finish. Comes with two extra magazines. Unique service policy. Each gun signed by maker.
Price: **$714.00**

High Standard X Series Custom 10-X

HIGH STANDARD SUPERMATIC CITATION MILITARY
Caliber: 22 LR, 10-shot magazine.
Barrel: 5½" bull, 7¼" fluted.
Weight: 46 oz. **Length:** 9¾" (5½" bbl.)
Stocks: Checkered walnut with thumbrest.
Sights: Undercut ramp front; frame mounted rear, click adj.
Features: Adjustable trigger pull; over-travel trigger adjustment; double acting safety; rebounding firing pin; military style grip; stippled front- and backstraps; positive magazine latch.
Price: 5½" barrel **$341.00**
Price: 7¼" barrel **$362.50**

HIGH STANDARD VICTOR
Caliber: 22 LR, 10-shot magazine.
Barrel: 5½".
Weight: 47 oz. **Length:** 9⅝" over-all.
Stocks: Checkered walnut with thumb rest.
Sights: Undercut ramp front, rib mounted click adj. rear.
Features: Vent. rib, interchangeable barrel, 2 - 2¼ lb. trigger pull, blue finish, back and front straps stippled.
Price: **$415.00**

HIGH STANDARD SUPERMATIC TROPHY MILITARY
Caliber: 22 LR, 10-shot magazine.
Barrel: 5½" bull, 7¼" fluted.
Weight: 44½ oz. **Length:** 9¾" (5½" bbl.)
Stocks: Checkered walnut with thumbrest.
Sights: Undercut ramp front; frame mounted rear, click adj.
Features: Grip duplicates feel of military 45; positive action mag. latch; front- and backstraps stippled. Trigger adj. for pull, over-travel
Price: 5½" barrel **$362.50**
Price: 7¼" barrel **$385.00**

High Standard Supermatic Citation Military

M-S Safari Arms Matchmaster Pistol

M-S SAFARI ARMS MATCHMASTER PISTOL
Caliber: 45 ACP, 7-shot magazine.
Barrel: 5".
Weight: 45 oz. **Length:** 8.7" overall.
Stocks: Combat rubber or checkered walnut.
Sights: Combat adjustable.
Features: Beavertail grip safety, ambidextrous extended safety, extended slide release, combat hammer, threaded barrel bushing; throated, ported, tuned. Finishes: blue, Armaloy, Parkerize, electroless nickel. Also available in a lightweight version (30 oz.) and stainless steel. Made by M-S Safari Arms.
Price: **$631.80**

M-S Safari Arms Model 81 Pistol

M-S Safari Arms Model 81NM Pistol

Similar to the Matchmaster except weighs 28 oz., is 8.2″ over-all, has Ron Power match sights. Meets all requirements for National Match Service Pistols. Throated, ported, tuned and has threaded barrel bushing. Available in blue, Armaloy, Parkerize, stainless steel and electroless nickel. From M-S Safari Arms.

Price: **$818.00**

M-S Safari Arms Model 81 Pistol

Similar to Matchmaster except chambered for 45 or 38 Spec. mid-range wadcutter; available with fixed or adjustable walnut target match grips; Aristocrat rib with extended front sight is optional. Other features are the same. From M-S Safari Arms.

Price: **$818.00**
Price: Model 81L long slide **$945.00**

M-S Safari Arms Model 81BP

Similar to the Matchmaster except designed for shooting the bowling pin matches. Extended slide gives 6″ sight radius but also fast slide cycle time. Combat adjustable sights, magazine chute, plus same features as Matchmaster.

Price: **$906.00**
Price: BP Super model has the heavier slide extension with a shorter, lighter slide **$995.00**

M-S Safari Arms Enforcer

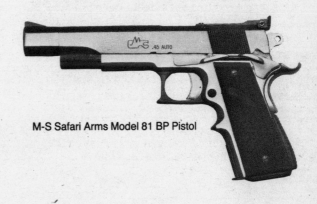

M-S Safari Arms Model 81 BP Pistol

M-S Safari Arms Enforcer Pistol

Shortened version of the Matchmaster. Has 3.8″ barrel, over-all length of 7.7″, and weighs 40 oz. (standard weight), 27 oz. in lightweight version. Other features are the same. From M-S Safari Arms.

Price: **$631.80**

M-S Safari Unlimited Silhouette

M-S SAFARI ARMS UNLIMITED SILHOUETTE PISTOL

Caliber: Any caliber with 308 head size or smaller.
Barrel: 14¹⁵⁄₁₆″ tapered
Weight: 72 oz. **Length:** 21½″ over-all.
Stocks: Fiberglass, custom painted to customer specs.
Sights: Open iron.
Features: Electronic trigger, bolt action single shot. Made by M-S Safari Arms.
Price: **$895.00**
Price: Ultimate model, heavy fluted barrel, shorter action **$895.00**

Navy Grand Prix Silhouette

NAVY GRAND PRIX SILHOUETTE PISTOL

Caliber: 44 Mag., 30-30, 7mm Spacial, 45-70; single shot.
Barrel: 13¾″.
Weight: 4 lbs.
Stocks: Walnut fore-end and thumb-rest grip.
Sights: Adjustable target-type.
Features: Uses rolling block action. Has adjustable aluminum barrel rib; matte blue finish. Made in U.S. by Navy Arms.
Price: **$375.00**

Remington XP-100 Silhouette

RUGER MARK II TARGET MODEL AUTO PISTOL
Caliber: 22 LR only, 10-shot magazine.
Barrel: 6⅞" or 5½" bull barrel (6-groove, 14" twist).
Weight: 42 oz. with 6⅞" bbl. **Length:** 10⅞" (6⅞" bbl.)
Stocks: Checkered hard rubber.
Sights: ⅛" blade front, micro click rear, adjustable for w. and e. Sight radius 9⅜" (with 6⅞" bbl.). Introduced 1982.
Price: Blued, either barrel length................................ **$196.00**

REMINGTON XP-100 SILHOUETTE PISTOL
Caliber: 7mm BR Remington, single-shot.
Barrel: 14¾".
Weight: 4⅛ lbs. **Length:** 21¼" over-all.
Stocks: Brown nylon, one piece, checkered grip.
Sights: None furnished. Drilled and tapped for scope mounts.
Features: Universal grip fits right or left hand; match-type grooved trigger, two-position thumb safety.
Price: **$381.95**

Ruger Mark II Target Model

SIG/Hammerli P-240

SIG/HAMMERLI P-240 TARGET PISTOL
Caliber: 32 S&W Long wadcutter.
Barrel: 6".
Weight: 34¼ oz. **Length:** 10" over-all.
Stocks: Walnut, target style, unfinished.
Sights: Match sights; ⅛" undercut front, ⅛" notch micro rear click adj. for w. and e.
Features: Semi-automatic, recoil operated; meets I.S.U. and N.R.A. specs for Center Fire Pistol competition; double pull trigger adj. from 2 lbs., 15 ozs. to 3 lbs., 9 ozs.; trigger stop. Comes with extra magazine, special screwdriver, carrying case. Imported from Switzerland by Mandall Shooting Supplies and Waidmanns Guns International.
Price: About.. **$1,500.00**
Price: 22 cal. conversion unit................................... **$750.00**

SEVILLE "SILHOUETTE" SINGLE ACTION
Caliber: 357, 41, 44, 45 Win. Mag.
Barrel: 10½".
Weight: About 55 oz.
Stocks: Smooth walnut thumbrest, or Pachmayr.
Sights: Undercut Patridge-style front, adjustable rear.
Features: Available in stainless steel or blue. Six-shot cylinder. From United Sporting Arms of Arizona, Inc.
Price: Stainless **$400.00**
Price: Blue.. **$325.00**

SMITH & WESSON 1955 Model 25, 45 TARGET
Caliber: 45 ACP and 45 AR, 6 shot.
Barrel: 6" (heavy target type).
Weight: 45 oz. **Length:** 11⅞".
Stocks: Checkered walnut target.
Sights: ⅛" Patridge front, micro click rear, adjustable for w. and e.
Features: Tangs and trigger grooved; target trigger and hammer standard, checkered target hammer. Swing-out cylinder revolver. Available with or without presentation case.
Price: Blue only.. **$437.00**
Price: Without presentation case **$391.00**

Smith & Wesson K-38 S.A. M-14

SMITH & WESSON 22 MATCH HEAVY BARREL M-41
Caliber: 22 LR, 10-shot clip.
Barrel: 5½" heavy. Sight radius, 8".
Weight: 44½ oz. **Length:** 9".
Stocks: Checkered walnut with modified thumbrest, usable with either hand.
Sights: ⅛" Patridge on ramp base. S&W micro click rear, adj. for w. and e.
Features: ⅜" wide, grooved trigger; adj. trigger stop.
Price: S&W Bright Blue, satin matted top area **$390.00**

SMITH & WESSON K-38 S.A. M-14
Caliber: 38 Spec., 6-shot.
Barrel: 6".
Weight: 38½ oz. **Length:** 11⅛" over-all.
Stocks: Checkered walnut, service type.
Sights: ⅛" Patridge front, micro click rear adj. for w. and e.
Features: Same as Model 14 except single action only, target hammer and trigger.
Price: 6" bbl..................................... **Special Order only**

SMITH & WESSON MODEL 29 SILHOUETTE
Caliber: 44 Magnum, 6-shot.
Barrel: 10⅝".
Weight: 58 oz. **Length:** 16⅛" over-all.
Stocks: Over-size target-type, checkered Goncalo Alves.
Sights: Four-position front to match the four distances of silhouette targets; micro-click rear adjustable for windage and elevation.
Features: Designed specifically for silhouette shooting. Front sight has click stops for the four pre-set ranges. Introduced 1983.
Price: Without presentation case **$423.50**
Price: With presentation case **$469.50**

Smith & Wesson 29 Silhouette

> Consult our Directory pages for
> the location of firms mentioned.

SMITH & WESSON 22 AUTO PISTOL Model 41
Caliber: 22 LR, 10-shot clip.
Barrel: 7⅜", sight radius 9⁵⁄₁₆".
Weight: 43½ oz. **Length:** 12" over-all.
Stocks: Checkered walnut with thumbrest, usable with either hand.
Sights: Front, ⅛" Patridge undercut; micro click rear adj. for w. and e.
Features: ⅜" wide, grooved trigger with adj. stop; wgts. available to make pistol up to 59 oz.
Price: S&W Bright Blue, satin matted bbl. **$390.00**

Smith & Wesson Model 41

SMITH & WESSON 38 MASTER Model 52 AUTO
Caliber: 38 Special (for Mid-range W.C. with flush-seated bullet only). 5-shot magazine.
Barrel: 5".
Weight: 41 oz. with empty magazine. **Length:** 8⅝"
Stocks: Checkered walnut.
Sights: ⅛" Patridge front, S&W micro click rear adj. for w. and e.
Features: Top sighting surfaces matte finished. Locked breech, moving barrel system; checked for 10-ring groups at 50 yards. Coin-adj. sight screws. Dry firing permissible if manual safety on.
Price: S&W Bright Blue. **$573.50**

Smith & Wesson Model 52

TAURUS MODEL 86 MASTER REVOLVER
Caliber: 38 Spec., 6-shot.
Barrel: 6" only.
Weight: 34 oz. **Length:** 11¼" over-all.
Stocks: Over size target-type, checkered Brazilian walnut.
Sights: Patridge front, micro. click rear adj. for w. and e.
Features: Blue finish with non-reflective finish on barrel. Imported from Brazil by International Distributors.
Price: About. **$187.00**
Price: Model 96 Scout Master, same except in 22 cal., about. **$187.00**

Taurus Model 86 Master

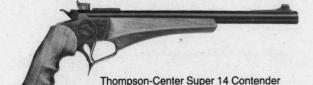

Thompson-Center Super 14 Contender

THOMPSON-CENTER SUPER 14 CONTENDER
Caliber: 22 LR, 222 Rem., 223 Rem., 6.5 TCU, 7mm TCU, 30 Herrett, 357 Herrett, 30-30 Win., 35 Rem., 41 and 44 Mag., 45 Win. Mag. Single shot.
Barrel: 14".
Weight: 45 oz. **Length:** 17¼" over-all.
Stocks: Select walnut grip and fore-end.
Sights: Fully adjustable target-type.
Features: Break-open action with auto safety. Interchangeable barrels for both rimfire and centerfire calibers. Introduced 1978.
Price: **$285.00**
Price: Extra barrels **$125.00**

CAUTION: PRICES CHANGE. CHECK AT GUNSHOP.

Unique D.E.S. 69

UNIQUE D.E.S. 69 TARGET PISTOL
Caliber: 22 LR.
Barrel: 5.91".
Weight: Approx. 35 oz. **Length:** 10.63" over-all.
Stocks: French walnut target style with thumbrest and adjustable shelf; hand checkered panels.
Sights: Ramp front, micro. adj. rear mounted on frame; 8.66" sight radius.
Features: Meets U.I.T. standards. Comes in a fitted hard case with spare magazine, barrel weight, cleaning rod, tools, proof certificate, test target and two year guarantee. Fully adjustable trigger; dry firing safety device. Imported from France by Solersport.
Price: Right-hand..$675.00
Price: Left-hand..$705.00

Unique D.E.S. VO 79

UNIQUE D.E.S. VO 79 TARGET PISTOL
Caliber: 22 Short.
Barrel: 5.85", Four gas escape ports, one threaded with plug.
Weight: 44 oz.
Stocks: French walnut, target style with thumbrest and adj. palm shelf. Hand stippled.
Sights: Low, .12" front, fully adj. rear.
Features: Meets all UIT standards; virtually recoil free. Four-way adj. trigger, dry-firing device, all aluminum frame. Cleaning rod, tools, extra magazine, proof certificate and fitted case. Imported from France by Solersport.
Price: Right hand..$675.00
Price: Left hand..$705.00

VIRGINIAN DRAGOON STAINLESS SILHOUETTE
Caliber: 357 Mag., 41 Mag., 44 Mag.
Barrel: 7½", 8⅜", 10½", heavy.
Weight: 51 oz. (7½" bbl.) **Length:** 11½" over-all (7½" bbl.).
Stocks: Smooth walnut; also comes with Pachmayr rubber grips.
Sights: Undercut blade front, special fully adjustable square notch rear.
Features: Designed to comply with IHMSA rules. Made of stainless steel; comes with two sets of stocks. Introduced 1982. Made in the U.S. by Interarms.
Price: Either barrel, caliber....................................$425.00

WALTHER FREE PISTOL
Caliber: 22 LR, single shot.
Barrel: 11.7".
Weight: 48 ozs. **Length:** 17.2" over-all.
Stocks: Walnut, special hand-fitting design.
Sights: Fully adjustable match sights.
Features: Special electronic trigger. Matte finish blue. Introduced 1980. Imported from Germany by Interarms.
Price: $1,375.00

WALTHER GSP MATCH PISTOL
Caliber: 22 LR, 32 S&W wadcutter (GSP-C), 5-shot.
Barrel: 5¾".
Weight: 44.8 oz. (22 LR), 49.4 oz. (32). **Length:** 11.8" over-all.
Stocks: Walnut, special hand-fitting design.
Sights: Fixed front, rear adj. for w. & e.
Features: Available with either 2.2 lb. (1000 gm) or 3 lb. (1360 gm) trigger. Spare mag., bbl. weight, tools supplied in Match Pistol Kit. Imported from Germany by Interarms.
Price: GSP...$950.00
Price: GSP-C...$1,075.00
Price: 22 LR conversion unit for GSP-C.........................$645.00
Price: 22 Short conversion unit for GSP-C......................$695.00

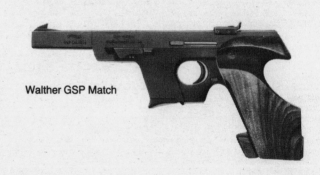

Walther GSP Match

Walther OSP Rapid-Fire Pistol
Similar to Model GSP except 22 Short only, stock has adj. free-style hand rest.
Price: $950.00

WICHITA MK-40 SILHOUETTE PISTOL
Caliber: 7mm IHMSA, 308 Win. F.L. Other calibers available on special order. Single shot.
Barrel: 13", non-glare blue; .700" dia. muzzle.
Weight: 4½ lbs. **Length:** 19⅜" over-all.
Stocks: Metallic gray fiberthane glass.
Sights: Wichita Multi-Range sighting system.
Features: Aluminum receiver with steel insert locking lugs, measures 1.360" O.D.; 3 locking lug bolts, 3 gas ports; flat bolt handle; completely adjustable Wichita trigger. Introduced 1981. From Wichita Arms.
Price: $640.00

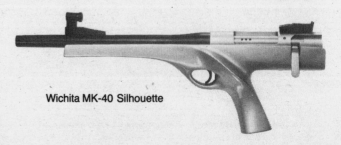

Wichita MK-40 Silhouette

COMPETITION HANDGUNS

WICHITA SILHOUETTE PISTOL
Caliber: 7mm IHMSA, 308, 7mm x 308. Other calibers available on special order. Single shot.
Barrel: 14¹⁵⁄₁₆″ or 10¾″.
Weight: 4½ lbs. **Length:** 21⅜″ over-all.
Stocks: American walnut with oil finish, or fiberglass (yellow or black). Glass bedded.
Sights: Wichita Multi-Range sight system.
Features: Comes with either right- or left-hand action with right-hand grip. Fluted bolt, flat bolt handle. Action drilled and tapped for Burris scope mounts. Non-glare satin blue finish. Wichita adjustable trigger. Introduced 1979. From Wichita Arms.
Price: Center grip stock **$750.00**
Price: As above except with Rear Position Stock and target-type Lightpull trigger. (Not illus.) **$780.00**

Wichita Silhouette Pistol

WICHITA CLASSIC PISTOL
Caliber: Any, up to and including 308 Win.
Barrel: 11¼″, octagon.
Weight: About 5 lbs.
Stock: Exhibition grade American black walnut. Checkered 20 lpi. Other woods available on special order.
Sights: Micro open sights standard. Receiver drilled and tapped for scope mount.
Features: Receiver and barrel octagonally shaped, finished in non-glare blue. Bolt has three locking lugs and three gas escape ports. Completely adjustable Wichita trigger. Introduced 1980. From Wichita Arms.
Price: **$1,615.00**
Price: Engraved, in walnut presentation case **$3,500.00**

Wichita Classic Pistol

HANDGUNS—AUTOLOADERS, SERVICE & SPORT

American Arms TP-70

AMT 45 ACP HARDBALLER LONG SLIDE
Caliber: 45 ACP.
Barrel: 7″.
Length: 10½″ over-all.
Stocks: Checkered walnut.
Sights: Fully adjustable Micro rear sight.
Features: Slide and barrel are 2″ longer than the standard 45, giving less recoil, added velocity, longer sight radius. Has extended combat safety, serrated matte rib, loaded chamber indicator, wide adjustable trigger, custom fitted barrel bushing. From AMT.
Price: **$625.00**

Consult our Directory pages for
the location of firms mentioned.

AMERICAN ARMS TP-70
Caliber: 22 LR, 25 ACP
Barrel: 2.6″
Weight: 12.6 oz. **Length:** 4.72″ over-all.
Stocks: Checkered, composition.
Sights: Open, fixed
Features: Double action, stainless steel. Exposed hammer. Manual and magazine safeties. From M & N Distributors.
Price: About **$199.95**

AMT "BACKUP" AUTO PISTOL
Caliber: 22 LR, 8-shot magazine; 380 ACP, 5-shot magazine
Barrel: 2½″
Weight: 17 oz. **Length:** 5″ over-all.
Stocks: Smooth wood.
Sights: Fixed, open, recessed.
Features: Concealed hammer, blowback operation; manual and grip safeties. All stainless steel construction. Smallest domestically-produced pistol in 380. From AMT.
Price: 22 LR or 380 ACP **$250.00**

AMT 45 ACP HARDBALLER
Caliber: 45 ACP.
Barrel: 5″
Weight: 39 oz. **Length:** 8½″ over-all.
Stocks: Checkered walnut.
Sights: Adjustable combat-type.
Features: Extended combat safety, serrated matte slide rib, loaded chamber indicator, long grip safety, beveled magazine well, grooved front and back straps, adjustable target trigger, custom-fitted barrel bushing. All stainless steel. From AMT.
Price: **$450.00**

American Derringer 25 Auto

AMERICAN DERRINGER 25 AUTO

Caliber: 25 ACP or 250 Magnum; 7-shot magazine.
Barrel: 2.1".
Weight: 15½ oz. **Length:** 4.4" over-all.
Stocks: Smooth rosewood.
Sights: Fixed.
Features: Stainless or ordnance steel. Magazines have finger extension. Introduced 1980. From American Derringer Corp.
Price: Stainless, 25 ACP $105.00
Price: Blue, matte finish, 25 ACP $89.95
Price: 250 Mag., stainless $137.50
Price: 250 Mag., blued $121.25

Arminex Trifire Pistol

ARMINEX TRIFIRE AUTO PISTOL

Caliber: 9mm. Para. (9-shot), 38 Super. (9-shot), 45 ACP (7-shot).
Barrel: 5".
Weight: 38 oz. **Length:** 8" over-all.
Stocks: Contoured smooth walnut.
Sights: Interchangeable post front, rear adjustable for windage and elevation.
Features: Single action. Slide mounted firing pin block safety. Specially contoured one-piece backstrap. Convertible by changing barrel, magazine, recoil spring. Introduced 1982. Made in U.S. by Arminex Ltd.
Price: Blue or electroless nickel $400.00
Price: With canvas case and wood presentation case $450.00

Astra A-80 Pistol

ASTRA A-80 DOUBLE-ACTION AUTO PISTOL

Caliber: 9mm Para., 38 Super (15-shot), 45 ACP (9-shot).
Barrel: 3.75".
Weight: 40 oz. **Length:** 7" over-all.
Stocks: Checkered black plastic.
Sights: Square blade front, square notch rear drift-adjustable for windage.
Features: Double or single action; loaded chamber indicator; combat-style trigger guard; optional right-side slide release (for left-handed shooters); automatic internal safety; decocking lever. Introduced 1982. Imported from Spain by Interarms.
Price: Blue. $490.00
Price: Chrome $540.00

ASTRA CONSTABLE AUTO PISTOL

Caliber: 22 LR, 10-shot, 380 ACP, 7-shot.
Barrel: 3½"
Weight: 26 oz.
Stocks: Moulded plastic
Sights: Adj. rear.
Features: Double action, quick no-tool takedown, non-glare rib on slide. 380 available in blue or chrome finish. Engraved guns also available—contact the importer. Imported from Spain by Interarms.
Price: Blue, 22 .... $370.00
Price: Chrome, 22 .... $400.00
Price: Blue, 380 .... $350.00
Price: Chrome, 380 .... $380.00

Bauer Stainless Auto

BAUER AUTOMATIC PISTOL

Caliber: 25 ACP, 6-shot.
Barrel: 2⅛".
Weight: 10 oz. **Length:** 4" over-all.
Stocks: Plastic pearl or checkered walnut.
Sights: Recessed, fixed.
Features: Stainless steel construction. Has positive manual safety as well as magazine safety.
Price: Satin stainless steel, 25 ACP $136.40

BERETTA MODEL 950 BS AUTO PISTOL

Caliber: 22 Short, 25 ACP
Barrel: 2½".
Weight: 8 oz. (22 Short, 10 oz.). **Length:** 4½" over-all.
Stocks: Checkered black plastic.
Sights: Fixed.
Features: Thumb safety and half-cock safety; barrel hinged at front to pop up for single loading or cleaning. From Beretta U.S.A.
Price: Blue. $189.95

CAUTION: PRICES CHANGE. CHECK AT GUNSHOP.

BERETTA MODEL 92 SB, 92 SB COMPACT
Caliber: 9mm Parabellum (15-shot magazine, 14-shot on Compact).
Barrel: 4.92″
Weight: 33½ oz. **Length:** 8.54″ over-all.
Stocks: Smooth black plastic; wood optional at extra cost.
Sights: Blade front, rear adj. for w.
Features: Double-action. Extractor acts as chamber loaded indicator, inertia firing pin. Finished in blue-black. Introduced 1977. Imported from Italy by Beretta USA.
Price: With plastic grips **$600.00**
Price: With wood grips **$620.00**
Price: Compact, plastic grips **$620.00**
Price: Compact, wood grips **$635.00**

Beretta Model 92 SB Compact

BERETTA MODEL 81/84 DA PISTOLS
Caliber: 32 ACP (12-shot magazine), 380 ACP (13-shot magazine).
Barrel: 3¾″
Weight: About 23 oz. **Length:** 6½″ over-all.
Stocks: Smooth black plastic (wood optional at extra cost).
Sights: Fixed front and rear.
Features: Double action, quick take-down, convenient magazine release. Introduced 1977. Imported from Italy by Beretta USA.
Price: M-81 (32 ACP) **$408.00**
Price: M-84 (380 ACP) **$408.00**
Price: Either model with wood grips **$425.00**
Price: M-82B, 32 ACP wood grips, 9-shot mag. **$483.00**
Price: M-85B, 380 ACP wood grips, 9-shot mag **$483.00**

Beretta Model 70S Pistol

BERETTA MODEL 70S PISTOL
Caliber: 22 LR, 380 ACP.
Barrel: 3.5″.
Weight: 23 oz. (Steel) **Length:** 6.5″ over-all.
Stocks: Checkered black plastic.
Sights: Fixed front and rear.
Features: Polished blue finish. Safety lever blocks hammer. Slide lever indicates empty magazine. Magazine capacity is 8 rounds for both calibers. Introduced 1977. Imported from Italy by Beretta USA.
Price: **$274.00**

Bernardelli Model 80

BERNARDELLI MODEL 80 AUTO PISTOL
Caliber: 22 LR (10-shot); 380 ACP (7-shot).
Barrel: 3½″.
Weight: 26½ oz. **Length:** 6½″ over-all.
Stocks: Checkered plastic with thumbrest.
Sights: Ramp front, white outline rear adj. for w. & e.
Features: Hammer block slide safety; loaded chamber indicator; dual recoil buffer springs; serrated trigger; inertia type firing pin. Imported from Italy by Interarms.
Price: Model 80, 22 or 380 .... **$235.00**
Price: Model 90 (22 or 32, 6″ bbl.) **$275.00**

Bren Ten Standard

BREN TEN STANDARD MODEL
Caliber: 10mm Auto, 11-shot magazine.
Barrel: 5″.
Weight: 38 oz. **Length:** 8.75″ over-all.
Stocks: Textured black nylon.
Sights: Adjustable; replaceable, 3-dot combat-type.
Features: Full-size combat pistol, with double or single action. Has reversible thumb safety and firing pin block. Blued slide, stainless frame. Introduced 1983. From Dornaus & Dixon.
Price: Standard model **$500.00**
Price: Military & Police (matte black finish) **$550.00**
Price: Dual-Master (same as Standard except comes with extra 45 ACP slide and barrel, better finish, wood grips, case) **$800.00**

Bren Ten Pocket Model
Similar to the Standard Bren Ten except smaller. Has 3.75″ barrel giving 6.90″ over-all length, and weighs 28 oz. Fires full load 10mm Auto cartridge with 8 round capacity. Has hard chrome slide, stainless frame.
Price: **$600.00**

Browning BDA-380 Pistol

BROWNING BDA-380 D/A AUTO PISTOL
Caliber: 380 ACP, 13-shot magazine.
Barrel: 3¹³⁄₁₆".
Weight: 23 oz. **Length:** 6¾" over-all.
Stocks: Smooth walnut with inset Browning medallion.
Sights: Blade front, rear drift-adj. for w.
Features: Combination safety and de-cocking lever will automatically lower a cocked hammer to half-cock and can be operated by right or left-hand shooters. Inertia firing pin. Introduced 1978. Imported from Italy by Browning.
Price: Blue $410.00
Price: Nickel $455.00

Browning Hi-Power Auto

BROWNING HI-POWER 9mm AUTOMATIC PISTOL
Caliber: 9mm Parabellum (Luger), 13-shot magazine.
Barrel: 4²¹⁄₃₂".
Weight: 32 oz. **Length:** 7¾" over-all.
Stocks: Walnut, hand checkered.
Sights: ⅛" blade front; rear screw-adj. for w. and e. Also available with fixed rear (drift-adj for w.).
Features: External hammer with half-cock and thumb safeties. A blow on the hammer cannot discharge a cartridge; cannot be fired with magazine removed. Fixed rear sight model available. Imported from Belgium by Browning.
Price: Fixed sight model $535.00
Price: 9mm with rear sight adj. for w. and e. $585.00
Price: Nickel, fixed sight $610.00
Price: Nickel, adj. sight $655.00
Price: Silver chrome, adj. sight $610.00

Browning Louis XVI Hi-Power 9mm Auto
Same as Browning Hi-Power 9mm Auto except: fully engraved, silver-gray frame and slide, gold plated trigger, finely checkered walnut grips, with deluxe walnut case.
Price: With adj. sights and walnut case $1,530.00
Price: With fixed sights $1,460.00

High Power 88 Auto Pistol II
Similar to the standard Browning High Power except available only with fixed rear sight, military parkerized finish, black checkered polyamid grips. Comes with extra magazine. Introduced 1982. Imported from Belgium by Howco Distributors, Inc.
Price: With extra magazine $499.50

Browning Challenger III Pistol

Consult our Directory pages for
the location of firms mentioned.

Browning Challenger III Pistol

BROWNING CHALLENGER III SPORTER
Caliber: 22 LR, 10-shot magazine.
Barrel: 6¾".
Weight: 29 oz. **Length:** 10⅞" over-all.
Stocks: Smooth impregnated hardwood.
Sights: ⅛" blade front on ramp, rear screw adj. for e., drift adj. for w.
Features: All steel, blue finish. Wedge locking system prevents action from loosening. Wide gold-plated trigger; action hold-open. Standard grade only. Made in U.S. From Browning.
Price: $239.95

Browning Challenger III Auto Pistol
Similar to the Challenger III except has a 5½" heavy bull barrel, new lightweight alloy frame and new sights. Over-all length is 9½", weight is 35 oz. Introduced 1982.
Price: $239.95

CAUTION: PRICES CHANGE. CHECK AT GUNSHOP.

BUSHMASTER AUTO PISTOL
Caliber: 223; 30-shot magazine.
Barrel: 11½″ (1-10″ twist).
Weight: 5¼ lbs. **Length:** 20½″ over-all.
Stocks: Synthetic rotating grip swivel assembly.
Sights: Post front, adjustable open "y" rear
Features: Steel alloy upper receiver with welded barrel assembly, AK-47-type gas system, aluminum lower receiver, one-piece welded steel alloy bolt carrier assembly. From Bushmaster Firearms.
Price: **$439.95**
Price: With matte electroless nickel finish **$479.95**

Bushmaster Auto Pistol

CHARTER EXPLORER II & SII PISTOL
Caliber: 22 LR, 8-shot magazine.
Barrel: 8″.
Weight: 28 oz. **Length:** 15½″ over-all.
Stocks: Serrated simulated walnut.
Sights: Blade front, open rear adj. for elevation.
Features: Action adapted from the semi-auto Explorer carbine. Introduced 1980. From Charter Arms.
Price: Black or satin finish **$99.00**
Price: With extra 6″ or 10″ bbl., extra magazine **$123.00**

Charter Explorer S II Pistol

COLT GOV'T MODEL MK IV/SERIES 70
Caliber: 9mm, 38 Super, 45 ACP, 7-shot.
Barrel: 5″.
Weight: 40 oz. **Length:** 8⅜″ over-all.
Stocks: Sandblasted walnut panels.
Sights: Ramp front, fixed square notch rear.
Features: Grip and thumb safeties, grooved trigger. Accurizor barrel and bushing. Blue finish or nickel in 45 only.
Price: Blue, 45 cal. **$419.95**
Price: Nickel, 45 cal. **$448.50**
Price: 9mm, blue only **$427.50**
Price: 38 Super, blue only **$434.50**
Price: 45, Satin nickel w/blue, Pachmayr grips. **$446.95**

Colt Government Model

Colt Conversion Unit
Permits the 45 and 38 Super Automatic pistols to use the economical 22 LR cartridge. No tools needed. Adjustable rear sight; 10-shot magazine. Designed to give recoil effect of the larger calibers. Not adaptable to Commander models. Blue finish.
Price: **$246.50**
Price: Fixed sight version **$235.95**

Colt Combat Grade Government Model
Same as the standard Government Model except has a higher undercut front sight, white outline rear, Colt/Pachmayr wrap-around grips, flat mainspring housing, longer trigger, bevelled magazine well, and an angled ejection port. Introduced 1983.
Price: **$506.50**

Colt Combat Grade Gov't.

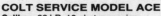

COLT SERVICE MODEL ACE
Caliber: 22 LR, 10-shot magazine.
Barrel: 5″
Weight: 42 oz. **Length:** 8⅜″ over-all.
Stocks: Checkered walnut.
Sights: Blade front, fully adjustable rear.
Features: The 22-cal. version of the Government Model auto. Based on the Service Model Ace last produced in 1945. Patented floating chamber. Original Ace Markings rolled on left side of slide. Introduced 1978.
Price: Blue only **$454.95**

Colt Service Model Ace

COLT COMBAT COMMANDER AUTO PISTOL
Caliber: 45 ACP, 7-shot; 38 Super Auto, 9-shot; 9mm Luger, 9-shot.
Barrel: 4¼".
Weight: 36 oz. **Length:** 8" over-all.
Stocks: Sandblasted walnut.
Sights: Fixed, glare-proofed blade front, square notch rear.
Features: Grooved trigger and hammer spur; arched housing; grip and thumb safeties.
Price: Blue, 9mm $427.50
Price: Blue, 45 .... $419.95
Price: Blue, 38 super $419.95
Price: Satin nickel, 45 .... $440.50

Colt Combat Commander

Colt Lightweight Commander
Same as Commander except high strength aluminum alloy frame, wood panel grips, weight 27 oz. 45 ACP only.
Price: Blue... $415.50

COONAN 357 MAGNUM PISTOL
Caliber: 357 Mag., 7-shot magazine.
Barrel: 5".
Weight: 42 oz. **Length:** 8.3" over-all.
Stocks: Smooth walnut.
Sights: Open, adjustable.
Features: Unique barrel hood improves accuracy and reliability. Many parts interchange with Colt autos. Has grip, hammer, half-cock safeties. From Coonan Arms.
Price: $549.00

Coonan 357 Auto

DETONICS 45 PISTOL
Caliber: 45 ACP, 451 Detonics Magnum, 6-shot clip; 9mm Para., 38 Super, 7-shot clip.
Barrel: 3¼".
Weight: 29 oz. (empty); MK VII is 26 oz. **Length:** 6¾" over-all, 4½" high.
Stocks: Checkered walnut.
Sights: Combat type, fixed; adj. sights avail.
Features: Has a self-adjusting cone barrel centering system, beveled magazine inlet, "full clip" indicator in base of magazine; standard 7-shot (or more) clip can be used in the 45. Throated barrel and polished feed ramp. Mark V, VI, VII available in 9mm and 38 Super; MC1 available in 9mm Para. Introduced 1977. From Detonics.
Price: MK. I, matte blue, fixed sights $497.00
Price: MK. IV, polished blue, adj. sights...................... $539.00
Price: MK. V, matte stainless, fixed sights.................... $705.00
Price: MK. VI, polished stainless, adj sights $754.00
Price: MK. VII, matte stainless, no sights $754.00
Price: MC1, non-glare combat stainless, fixed sights $632.00
Price: MC2, as above with adj. sights (9mm, 38 Super higher) $688.00
Price: MK VI and VII 451 Magnum $1,280.00

Detonics Auto Pistol

> Consult our Directory pages for
> the location of firms mentioned.

Detonics Super Compact

DETONICS SUPER COMPACT DOUBLE ACTION AUTO
Caliber: 9mm Para., 7-shot clip.
Barrel: 3".
Weight: 22 oz. **Length:** 5.7" over-all, 4" high.
Stocks: Smooth composition.
Sights: Fixed.
Features: Stainless steel construction; ambidextrous firing pin safety; trigger guard hook for two-hand shooting. Available late 1983. From Detonics.
Price: About $425.00

CAUTION: PRICES CHANGE. CHECK AT GUNSHOP.

EAGLE 357 MAGNUM PISTOL
Caliber: 357 Magnum, 9-shot clip.
Barrel: 6″, 8″, 10″, 14″ interchangeable.
Weight: 52 oz. **Length:** 10¼″ over-all (6″ bbl.).
Stocks: Wrap-around soft rubber.
Sights: Blade on ramp front, adjustable combat-style rear.
Features: Rotating six lug bolt, ambidextrous safety, combat-style trigger guard and adjustable trigger. Military epoxy finish. Contact importer for extra barrel prices. Announced 1982. Imported from Israel by Magnum Research Inc.
Price: 6″ barrel **$699.00**

Eagle 357 Magnum

ERMA KGP22 AUTO PISTOL
Caliber: 22 LR, 8-shot magazine.
Barrel: 4″.
Weight: 29 oz. **Length:** 7¾″ over-all.
Stocks: Checkered plastic.
Sights: Fixed.
Features: Has toggle action similar to original "Luger" pistol. Slide stays open after last shot. Imported from West Germany by Excam. Introduced 1978.
Price: **$216.00**

ERMA KGP38 AUTO PISTOL
Caliber: 380 ACP (5-shot).
Barrel: 4″.
Weight: 22½ oz. **Length:** 7⅜″ over-all.
Stocks: Checkered plastic. Wood optional.
Sights: Rear adjustable for windage.
Features: Toggle action similar to original "Luger" pistol. Slide stays open after last shot. Has magazine and sear disconnect safety systems. Imported from West Germany by Excam. Introduced 1978.
Price: Plastic grips. **$216.00**

Erma KGP22 Pistol

ERMA-EXCAM RX 22 AUTO PISTOL
Caliber: 22 LR, 8-shot magazine.
Barrel: 3¼″.
Weight: 21 oz. **Length:** 5.58″ over-all.
Stocks: Plastic wrap-around.
Sights: Fixed
Features: Polished blue finish. Double action. Patented ignition safety system. Thumb safety. Assembled in U.S. Introduced 1980. From Excam.
Price: **$159.00**

F.I.E. TZ-75 DA AUTO PISTOL
Caliber: 9mm Parabellum, 15-shot magazine.
Barrel: 4.72″.
Weight: 35.33 oz. **Length:** 8.25″ over-all.
Stocks: Smooth European walnut.
Sights: Undercut blade front, open rear adjustable for windage.
Features: Double action trigger system; squared-off trigger guard; rotating slide-mounted safety. Introduced 1983. Imported from Italy by F.I.E.
Price: **$399.95**

F.I.E. Tx-75 Pistol

F.I.E. "SUPER TITAN II" PISTOLS
Caliber: 32 ACP, 380 ACP.
Barrel: 3⅞″.
Weight: 28 oz. **Length:** 6¾″ over-all.
Stocks: Smooth, polished walnut.
Sights: Adjustable.
Features: Blue finish only. 12 shot (32 ACP), 11 shot (380 ACP). Introduced 1981. Imported from Italy by F.I.E. Corp.
Price: 32 ACP. **$189.95**
Price: 380 ACP. **$219.95**

F.I.E. "THE BEST" A27B PISTOL
Caliber: 25 ACP, 6-shot magazine.
Barrel: 2½″.
Weight: 13 oz. **Length:** 4⅜″ over-all.
Stocks: Checkered walnut.
Sights: Fixed.
Features: All steel construction. Has thumb and magazine safeties, exposed hammer. Blue finish only. Introduced 1978. Made in U.S. by F.I.E. Corp.
Price: **$154.95**

F.I.E. Super Titan II

F.I.E./INTERDYNAMIC KG-99 PISTOL
Caliber: 9mm Parabellum; 36 shot magazine.
Barrel: 5″.
Weight: 46 oz. **Length:** 12½″ over-all.
Stocks: High-impact nylon.
Sights: Blade front; fixed, open rear.
Features: Semi-auto only. Straight blowback action fires from closed bolt. Entire frame is high-impact black nylon. Introduced 1982. From F.I.E. Corp.
Price: About **$449.95**
Price: Extra magazine **$32.95**

Interdynamic KG-99 Pistol

F.I.E./Interdynamic KG-99K Pistol
Similar to the KG-99 except has 3″ barrel, over-all length of 10″, and weighs 44 oz. Standard magazine is 25-shot, with 36-shot optional. Introduced 1983.
Price: **$249.95**

F.I.E. TITAN II PISTOLS
Caliber: 32 ACP, 380 ACP, 6-shot magazine; 22 LR, 10-shot magazine.
Barrel: 3⅞″.
Weight: 25¾ oz. **Length:** 6¾″ over-all.
Stocks: Checkered nylon, thumbrest-type; checkered walnut optional.
Sights: Adjustable.
Features: Magazine disconnector, firing pin block. Standard slide safety. Available in blue or chrome. Introduced 1978. Imported from Italy by F.I.E. Corp.
Price: 32, blue **$136.95**
Price: 32, chrome.. **$144.95**
Price: 380, blue **$169.95**
Price: 380, chrome **$179.95**
Price: 22 LR, blue **$129.95**

F.I.E. Titan II Pistol

F.I.E. "TITAN 25" PISTOL
Caliber: 25 ACP, 6-shot magazine.
Barrel: 2⁷⁄₁₆″.
Weight: 12 oz. **Length:** 4⅝″ over-all.
Stocks: Smooth nylon.
Sights: Fixed.
Features: External hammer; fast simple takedown. Made in U.S.A. by F.I.E. Corp.
Price: Blue... **$64.95**
Price: Chrome.. **$74.95**
Price: Blue, walnut grips **$79.95**
Price: Chrome, walnut grips **$89.95**

Guardian-SS Stainless Pistol

GUARDIAN-SS AUTO PISTOL
Caliber: 380 ACP, 6-shot magazine.
Barrel: 3.25″
Weight: 20 oz. **Length:** 6″ over-all.
Stocks: Checkered walnut.
Sights: Ramp front, combat-type rear adjustable for windage.
Features: Double action, made of stainless steel. Custom Guardian has narrow polished trigger, Pachmayr grips, blue slide, hand-fitted barrel, polished feed ramp, funneled magazine well. Introduced 1982. From Michigan Armament, Inc.
Price: Standard model **$330.00**
Price: Custom Guardian...................................... **$395.00**

Heckler & Kock P7 (PSP) Pistol

HECKLER & KOCH P7 (PSP) AUTO PISTOL
Caliber: 9mm Parabellum, 8-shot magazine.
Barrel: 4.13″.
Weight: 29 oz. **Length:** 6.54″ over-all.
Stocks: Stippled black plastic.
Sights: Fixed, combat-type.
Features: Unique "squeeze cocker" in front strap cocks the action. Squared combat-type trigger guard. Blue finish. Compact size. Imported from West Germany by Heckler & Koch, Inc.
Price: **$599.00**
Price: Extra magazine....................................... **$26.00**

CAUTION: PRICES CHANGE. CHECK AT GUNSHOP.

HECKLER & KOCH HK-4 DOUBLE ACTION PISTOL
Caliber: 22 LR, 25 ACP, 32 ACP, 380 ACP, 8-shot magazine (7 in 380).
Barrel: 3¹¹/₃₂".
Weight: 16½ oz. **Length:** 6³/₁₆" over-all.
Stocks: Black checkered plastic.
Sights: Fixed blade front, rear notched drift-adj. for w.
Features: Gun comes with all parts to shoot above four calibers; polygonal (hexagon) rifling; matte black finish. Imported from West Germany by Heckler & Koch, Inc.
Price: Hk-4 380 with 22 conversion kit . . . . . . , ... $480.00
Price: HK-4 in 380 only $430.00
Price: HK-4 in four cals. $590.00
Price: Conversion units 22, 25 or 32 cal., each $101.00

Heckler & Koch HK-4

HECKLER & KOCH P9S DOUBLE ACTION AUTO
Caliber: 9mm Para., 9-shot magazine; 45 ACP, 7-shot magazine.
Barrel: 4".
Weight: 31 oz. **Length:** 7.6" over-all.
Stocks: Checkered black plastic.
Sights: Open combat type.
Features: Double action; polygonal rifling; delayed roller-locked action with stationary barrel. Loaded chamber and cocking indicators; cocking/decocking lever. Imported from West Germany by Heckler & Koch, Inc.
Price: P-9S Combat Model $550.00
Price: P-9S Target Model $630.00
Price: Walnut wrap-around competition grips $135.00
Price: Sports competition model with 4" and 5½" barrels, 2 slides . . . $990.00

Heckler & Koch P9S Pistol

Consult our Directory pages for the location of firms mentioned.

HECKLER & KOCH VP 70Z DOUBLE ACTION AUTO
Caliber: 9mm Para., 18-shot magazine.
Barrel: 4½".
Weight: 32½ oz. **Length:** 8" over-all.
Stocks: Black stippled plastic.
Sights: Ramp front, channeled slide rear.
Features: Recoil operated, double action. Only 4 moving parts. Double column magazine. Imported from West Germany by Heckler & Koch, Inc.
Price: $399.00
Price: Extra magazine $27.00

Heckler & Koch VP 70S Pistol

Helwan Auto Pistol

HELWAN 9mm AUTO PISTOL
Caliber: 9mm Parabellum, 8-shot magazine.
Barrel: 4½".
Weight: 33 oz. **Length:** 8¼" over-all.
Stocks: Grooved black plastic.
Sights: Blade front, rear drift-adjustable for windage.
Features: Updated version of the Beretta Model 951. Made by the Maadi Co. for Engineering Industries of Egypt. Introduced to U.S. market 1982. Imported from Egypt by Steyr Daimler Puch of America.
Price: $345.00

High Standard Survival Pack
Includes the High Standard Citation pistol (see Competition Handguns) finished in electroless nickel, extra magazine, and a padded canvas carrying case with three interior pockets for carrying the extra magazine, knife, compass, etc. Introduced 1982.
Price: $374.50

HIGH STANDARD SPORT-KING AUTO PISTOL
Caliber: 22 LR, 10-shot.
Barrel: 4½" or 6¾".
Weight: 39 oz. (4½" bbl.). **Length:** 9" over-all (4½" bbl.).
Stocks: Checkered walnut.
Sights: Blade front, fixed rear.
Features: Takedown barrel. Blue only. Military frame.
Price: Either bbl. length, blue finish $259.50

IVER JOHNSON MODEL X300 PONY
Caliber: 380 ACP, 6-shot magazine.
Barrel: 3".
Weight: 20 oz. **Length:** 6" over-all.
Stocks: Checkered walnut.
Sights: Blade front, rear adj. for w.
Features: Loaded chamber indicator, all steel construction. Inertia firing pin. Thumb safety locks hammer. No magazine safety. Lanyard ring. Made in U.S., available from Iver Johnson's.
Price: Blue. **$260.00**
Price: Nickel **$270.00**
Price: Military (matte finish) **$260.00**

IVER JOHNSON PP30 "SUPER ENFORCER" PISTOL
Caliber: 30 U.S. Carbine.
Barrel: 9".
Weight: 4 lbs. **Length:** 17" over-all.
Stocks: American walnut.
Sights: Blade front; click adjustable peep rear.
Features: Shortened version of the M1 Carbine. Uses 15 or 30-shot magazines. From Iver Johnson's.
Price: Blue finish **$260.00**
Price: Stainless steel. **$320.00**

JENNINGS J-22 AUTO PISTOL
Caliber: 22 LR, 6-shot magazine.
Barrel: 2½".
Weight: 13 oz. **Length:** 4¹⁵⁄₁₆" over-all.
Stocks: Walnut.
Sights: Fixed.
Features: Satin chrome finish. Introduced 1981. From Jennings Firearms.
Price: About **$69.95**

L.A.R. Grizzly Mag

LLAMA OMNI DOUBLE-ACTION AUTO
Caliber: 9mm (13-shot), 45 ACP (7-shot).
Barrel: 4¼".
Weight: 40 oz. **Length:** 9mm—8", 45—7¾" over-all.
Stocks: Checkered plastic.
Sights: Ramped blade front, rear adjustable for windage and elevation (45), drift-adjustable for windage (9mm).
Features: New DA pistol has ball-bearing action, double sear bars, articulated firing pin, buttressed locking lug and low-friction rifling. Introduced 1982. Imported from Spain by Stoeger Industries.
Price: 45 ACP. **$533.95**
Price: 9mm **$499.95**

Llama Large Frame Auto

IVER JOHNSON TP22B, TP25B AUTO PISTOL
Caliber: 22 LR, 25 ACP, 7-shot magazine.
Barrel: 2.85".
Weight: 14½ oz. **Length:** 5.39" over-all.
Stocks: Black checkered plastic.
Sights: Fixed.
Features: Double action; 7-shot magazine. Introduced 1981. From Iver Johnson's.
Price: Either caliber **$140.00**

Jennings J-22 Pistol

L.A.R. GRIZZLY WIN MAG PISTOL
Caliber: 45 Win. Mag., 7-shot magazine.
Barrel: 5⁷⁄₁₆".
Weight: 51 oz. **Length:** 8⅞" over-all.
Stocks: Checkered rubber, non-slip combat-type.
Sights: Ramped blade front, fully adjustable rear.
Features: Uses basic Browning/Colt 1911-A1 design; interchangeable calibers; bevelled magazine well; combat-type flat, checkered rubber mainspring housing; lowered and back-chamfered ejection port; polished feed ramp; throated barrel; solid barrel bushings. Announced 1983. From L.A.R. Mfg. Co.
Price: **$749.95**
Price: Conversion units (9mm Win. Mag., 45 ACP, 357 Mag., 30 Mauser, 38 Super, 38 Spec., 9mm Steyr, 9mm Browning Long, 9mm Luger). **$169.95**

Llama Omni D.A. Pistol

LLAMA LARGE FRAME AUTO PISTOLS
Caliber: 9mm Para., 45 ACP.
Barrel: 5".
Weight: 40 oz. **Length:** 8½" over-all.
Stocks: Checkered walnut.
Sights: Fixed.
Features: Grip and manual safeties, ventilated rib. Engraved, chrome engraved or gold damascened finish available at extra cost. Imported from Spain by Stoeger Industries.
Price: Blue. **$325.00**
Price: Satin chrome, 45 only **$424.95**
Price: Blue, engraved, 45 only. **$433.95**
Price: Satin chrome, engraved, 45 only. **$466.95**

CAUTION: PRICES CHANGE. CHECK AT GUNSHOP.

Llama Small Frame Auto

LLAMA SMALL FRAME AUTO PISTOLS
Caliber: 22 LR, 32 ACP and 380.
Barrel: 3¹¹⁄₁₆″.
Weight: 23 oz. **Length:** 6½″ over-all.
Stocks: Checkered plastic, thumb rest.
Sights: Fixed front, adj. notch rear.
Features: Ventilated rib, manual and grip safeties. Model XV is 22 LR, Model XA is 32 ACP, and Model IIIA is 380. Models XA and IIIA have loaded indicator; IIIA is locked breech. Imported from Spain by Stoeger Industries.
Price: Blue, 32 & 380 .... $283.95
Price: Blue, 22 LR $200.95
Price: Satin chrome, 380 .... $349.95
Price: Satin chrome, 22 LR $249.95
Price: Blue, engraved, 380 only $358.95
Price: Satin chrome, engraved, 380 .... $366.95

LONE STAR 380 AUTOMATIC PISTOL
Caliber: 380, 6-shot magazine
Barrel: 3⁷⁄₁₆″.
Weight: 20 oz. **Length:** 6″ over-all.
Stocks: Checkered walnut.
Sights: Fixed.
Features: Recreation of the 1910 Browning. Has grip, thumb and manual safeties. Comes with an extra magazine and soft case. Introduced 1983. Made in U.S. by Lone Star Arms.
Price: Blue. $275.00
Price: Electroless nickel $285.00

Lone Star 380 Auto

MAB Model P-15

Turkish MKE Pistol

O.D.I. Viking D.A. Pistol

MAB MODEL P-15 AUTO PISTOL
Caliber: 9mm Para., 15-shot magazine.
Barrel: 4½″.
Weight: 41 oz. **Length:** 8⅛″ over-all.
Stocks: Checkered black plastic.
Sights: Fixed.
Features: Rotating barrel-type locking system; thumb safety, magazine disconnector. Blue finish. Introduced 1982. Imported from France by Howco Distr., Inc.
Price: $375.00

MKE AUTO PISTOL
Caliber: 380 ACP; 7-shot magazine.
Barrel: 4″.
Weight: 23 oz. **Length:** 6½″ over-all.
Stocks: Hard rubber.
Sights: Fixed front, rear adjustable for windage.
Features: Double action with exposed hammer; chamber loaded indicator. Imported from Turkey by Mandall Shooting Supplies.
Price: $350.00

MAUSER HSc SUPER AUTO PISTOL
Caliber: 32, 380 ACP.
Barrel: 3.56″.
Weight: 29 oz. **Length:** 6″ over-all.
Stocks: Checkered walnut.
Sights: Blade front, rear drift adjustable for windage.
Features: Double or single action; low profile exposed hammer; combat-style trigger guard; blue finish. Made under license by Renato Gamba. Introduced 1983. Imported from Italy by Interarms.
Price: $415.00

O.D.I. VIKING COMBAT D.A. AUTO PISTOL
Caliber: 45 ACP.
Barrel: 5″.
Weight: 36 oz.
Stocks: Smooth teakwood standard; other materials available.
Sights: Fixed. Blade front, notched rear.
Features: Made entirely of stainless steel, brushed satin, natural finish. Features the Seecamp double action system. Spur-type hammer. Magazine holds 7 rounds in 45 ACP. Made in U.S.A. From O.D.I.
Price: $579.95

RG 26 AUTO PISTOL
Caliber: 25 ACP, 6-shot magazine.
Barrel: 2½".
Weight: 12 oz. **Length:** 4¾" over-all.
Stocks: Checkered plastic.
Sights: Fixed.
Features: Blue finish. Thumb safety. Imported by RG Industries.
Price: $69.95
Price: Nickel $74.95

RANDALL SERVICE MODEL AUTO PISTOL
Caliber: 9mm, 38 Super, 45 ACP.
Barrel: 5".
Weight: 38 ozs. **Length:** 8½" over-all.
Stocks: Checkered walnut.
Sights: Blade front, fixed or adjustable rear.
Features: All stainless steel construction, including springs and pins. Available with round-top slide and fixed sights, or ribbed slide with adjustable sights. Introduced 1983. Made in U.S. by Randall Mfg.
Price: With fixed sights, about $440.00
Price: With adjustable sights, about $490.00

Randall Service Model

Randall Compact Service Model
Similar to the Service Model except has 4½" barrel, 7¾" over-all length, and weighs 36 ozs. Same stainless steel construction, checkered walnut grips. Introduced 1983.
Price: With fixed sights, about $440.00
Price: With adjustable sights, about $490.00

RAVEN P-25 AUTO PISTOL
Caliber: 25 ACP, 6-shot magazine.
Barrel: 2⁷⁄₁₆".
Weight: 15 oz. **Length:** 4¾" over-all.
Stocks: Smooth walnut.
Sights: Ramped front, fixed rear.
Features: Available in blue, nickel or chrome finish. Made in U.S., available from EMF Co.
Price: $59.95

Raven P-25 Pistol

RUGER MARK II STANDARD AUTO PISTOL
Caliber: 22 LR, 10-shot magazine.
Barrel: 4¾" or 6".
Weight: 36 oz. (4¾" bbl.). **Length:** 8¾ (4¾" bbl.).
Stocks: Checkered hard rubber.
Sights: Fixed, wide blade front, square notch rear adj. for w.
Features: Updated design of the original Standard Auto. Has new bolt hold-open device, 10-shot magazine, magazine catch, safety, trigger and new receiver contours. Introduced 1982.
Price: Blued $168.00

Ruger Mark II Auto

SIG P-210-1 AUTO PISTOL
Caliber: 7.65mm or 9mm Para., 8-shot magazine.
Barrel: 4¾".
Weight: 31¾ oz. (9mm) **Length:** 8½" over-all.
Stocks: Checkered walnut.
Sights: Blade front, rear adjustable for windage.
Features: Lanyard loop; polished finish. Conversion unit for 22 LR available. Imported from Switzerland by Mandall Shooting Supplies.
Price: P-210-1 and P-210-2, about $1,500.00
Price: 22 Cal. Conversion unit $850.00

SIG P-210-1 Pistol

SIG P-210-6 AUTO PISTOL
Caliber: 9mm Para.; 8-shot magazine.
Barrel: 4¾".
Weight: 37 oz. **Length:** 8½" over-all.
Stocks: Checkered black plastic.
Sights: Blade front, micro. adj. rear for w. & e.
Features: Adjustable trigger stop; ribbed front stap; sandblasted finish. Conversion unit for 22 LR consists of barrel, recoil spring, slide and magazine. Imported from Switzerland by Mandall Shooting Supplies.
Price: P-210-6, about $1,750.00
Price: 22 Cal. Conversion unit $850.00

SIG-Sauer P-220 Pistol

SIG-SAUER P-220 D.A. AUTO PISTOL
Caliber: 9mm, 38 Super; 45 ACP. (9-shot in 9mm and 38 Super, 7 in 45).
Barrel: 4⅜″.
Weight: 28¼ oz. (9mm). **Length:** 7¾″ over-all.
Stocks: Checkered walnut.
Sights: Blade front, drift adj. rear for w.
Features: Double action. De-cocking lever permits lowering hammer onto locked firing pin. Squared combat-type trigger guard. Slide stays open after last shot. Imported from West Germany by Interarms.
Price: **$590.00**

SIG-SAUER P-225 D.A. AUTO PISTOL
Caliber: 9mm Parabellum, 8-shot magazine.
Barrel: 3.8″.
Weight: 26 oz. **Length:** 7³⁄₃₂″ over-all.
Stocks: Checkered black plastic.
Sights: Blade front, rear adjustable for windage.
Features: Double action; decocking lever permits lowering hammer onto locked firing pin. Squared combat-type trigger guard. Shortened, lightened version of P-220. Imported from West Germany by Interarms.
Price: **$620.00**

SIG-SAUER P-230 D.A. AUTO PISTOL
Caliber: 380 ACP (7 shot).
Barrel: 3¾″.
Weight: 16 oz. **Length:** 6½″ over-all.
Stocks: One piece black plastic.
Sights: Blade front, rear adj. for w.
Features: Double action. Same basic design as P-220. Blowback operation, stationary barrel. Introduced 1977. Imported from West Germany by Interarms.
Price: $520.00

SILE-SEECAMP II STAINLESS DA AUTO
Caliber: 25 ACP, 8-shot magazine.
Barrel: 2″, integral with frame.
Weight: About 10 oz. **Length:** 4⅛″ over-all.
Stocks: Black plastic.
Sights: Smooth, no-snag, contoured slide and barrel top.
Features: Aircraft quality 17-4 PH stainless steel. Inertia operated firing pin. Hammer fired double action only. Hammer automatically follows slide down to safety rest position after each shot—no manual safety needed. Magazine safety disconnector. Introduced 1980. From Sile Distributors.
Price: **$199.95**

SIG-Sauer P-230 D.A. Pistol

Sile-Benelli Model B76 Pistol

SILE-BENELLI B76 DA AUTO PISTOL
Caliber: 9mm Para., 8-shot magazine.
Barrel: 4¼″, 6-groove. Chrome-lined bore.
Weight: 34 oz. (empty). **Length:** 8¹⁄₁₆″ over-all.
Stocks: Walnut with cut checkering and high gloss finish.
Sights: Blade front with white face, rear adjustable for windage with white bars for increased visibility.
Features: Fixed barrel, locked breech. Exposed hammer can be locked in non-firing mode in either single or double action. Stainless steel inertia firing pin and loaded chamber indicator. All external parts blued, internal parts hard-chrome plated. All steel construction. Introduced 1979. From Sile Dist.
Price: **$349.95**

SMITH & WESSON MODEL 439 DOUBLE ACTION
Caliber: 9mm Luger, 8-shot clip.
Barrel: 4″.
Weight: 27 oz. **Length:** 7⁷⁄₁₆″ over-all.
Stocks: Checkered walnut.
Sights: ⅛″ square serrated ramp front, square notch rear is fully adj. for w. & e.
Features: Rear sight has protective shields on both sides of the sight blade. Frame is alloy. New trigger actuated firing pin lock in addition to the regular rotating safety. Magazine disconnector. New extractor design. Comes with two magazines. Introduced 1980.
Price: Blue, from **$370.50**
Price: Nickel, from **$402.00**
Price: Model 639 (stainless), from **$415.50**

Smith & Wesson Model 639

SMITH & WESSON MODEL 459 DOUBLE ACTION
Caliber: 9mm Luger, 14-shot clip.
Barrel: 4″.
Weight: 28 oz. **Length:** 7⁷⁄₁₆″ over-all.
Stocks: Checkered high-impact nylon.
Sights: ⅛″ square serrated ramp front, square notch rear is fully adj. for w. & e.
Features: Alloy frame. Rear sight has protective shields on both sides of blade. New trigger actuated firing pin lock in addition to the regular safety. Magazine disconnector; new extractor design. Comes with two magazines. Introduced 1980.
Price: Blue, from **$433.50**
Price: Nickel, from **$457.00**
Price: Model 659 (stainless), from **$431.50**

Smith & Wesson Model 659

Smith & Wesson Model 469 Mini-Gun
Basically a cut-down version of the Model 459 pistol. Gun has a 3½″ barrel, 12-round magazine, over-all length of 6⅞″, and weighs 26 oz. Also accepts the 14-shot Model 459 magazine. Cross-hatch knurling on the recurved-front trigger guard and backstrap; magazine has a curved finger extension; bobbed hammer; sandblast blue finish with pebble-grain grips. Introduced 1983.
Price: . . . . **NA**

Smith & Wesson Model 469

Star Model 28 DA

STAR MODEL 28 DOUBLE-ACTION PISTOL
Caliber: 9mm Para., 15-shot magazine.
Barrel: 4.25″.
Weight: 40 oz. **Length:** 8″ over-all.
Stocks: Checkered black plastic.
Sights: Square blade front, square notch rear click-adjustable for windage and elevation.
Features: Double or single action; grooved front and backstraps and trigger guard face; ambedextrous safety cams firing pin forward; removeable backstrap houses the firing mechanism. Introduced 1983. Imported from Spain by Interarms.
Price: **$520.00**

STAR MODEL PD AUTO PISTOL
Caliber: 45 ACP, 7-shot magazine.
Barrel: 3.94″.
Weight: 28 oz. **Length:** 7⁷⁄₁₆″ over-all.
Stocks: Checkered walnut.
Sights: Ramp front, fully adjustable rear.
Features: Rear sight milled into slide; thumb safety; grooved non-slip front strap; nylon recoil buffer; inertia firing pin; no grip or magazine safeties. Imported from Spain by Interarms.
Price: Blue. **$400.00**

Star Model PD Pistol

STAR BM, BKM AUTO PISTOLS
Caliber: 9mm Para., 8-shot magazine.
Barrel: 3.9″.
Weight: 25 oz.
Stocks: Checkered walnut.
Sights: Fixed.
Features: Blue or chrome finish. Magazine and manual safeties, external hammer. Imported from Spain by Interarms.
Price: Blue, BM and BKM. **$330.00**
Price: Chrome, BM only **$360.00**

STERLING MODEL 302
Caliber: 22 LR, 6-shot.
Barrel: 2½″.
Weight: 13 oz. **Length:** 4½″ over-all.
Stocks: Black Cycolac.
Sights: Fixed.
Features: All steel construction.
Price: Blue. **$112.95**
Price: Stainless steel. **$134.95**

Star Model BM, BKM Pistol

CAUTION: PRICES CHANGE. CHECK AT GUNSHOP.

STERLING MODEL 300
Caliber: 25 ACP, 6-shot.
Barrel: 2½".
Weight: 13 oz. **Length:** 4½" over-all.
Stocks: Black Cycolac.
Sights: Fixed.
Features: All steel construction.
Price: Blued $112.95
Price: Stainless Steel $134.95

Sterling Model 300 Pistol

STERLING MODEL 400 MK II DOUBLE ACTION
Caliber: 32, 380 ACP, 7-shot.
Barrel: 3¾".
Weight: 18 oz. **Length:** 6½" over-all.
Stocks: Checkered walnut.
Sights: Low profile, adj.
Features: All steel construction. Double action.
Price: Blued $225.95
Price: Stainless steel $260.95

Sterling Model 400 MK. II D.A.

Steyr GB D.A. Pistol

STEYR GB DOUBLE ACTION AUTO PISTOL
Caliber: 9mm Parabellum; 18-shot magazine.
Barrel: 5.39".
Weight: 33 oz. **Length:** 8.4" over-all.
Stocks: Checkered walnut.
Sights: Post front, fixed rear.
Features: Gas-operated, delayed blowback action. Measures 5.7" high, 1.3" wide. Introduced 1981. Imported by Steyr Daimler Puch.
Price: $595.00

STOEGER LUGER 22 AUTO PISTOL
Caliber: 22 LR, 10-shot.
Barrel: 4½".
Weight: 30 oz. **Length:** 8⅞" over-all.
Stocks: Checkered walnut.
Sights: Fixed.
Features: All steel construction. Action remains open after last shot and as magazine is removed. Grip and balance identical to P-08.
Price: $199.95
Price: Kit includes extra clip, charger, holster $241.95
Price: Combo (includes extra clip, holster, charger and carrying case) $249.95

Stoeger Luger 22 Auto

TARGA MODEL GT27 AUTO PISTOL
Caliber: 25 ACP, 6-shot magazine.
Barrel: 2⁷⁄₁₆".
Weight: 12 oz. **Length:** 4⅝" over-all.
Stocks: Checkered nylon.
Sights: Fixed.
Features: Safety lever take-down; external hammer with half-cock. Assembled in U.S. by Excam, Inc.
Price: Blue $58.50
Price: Chrome $64.00

TARGA GT380XE GT32XE PISTOLS
Caliber: 32 ACP or 380 ACP, 12-shot magazine.
Barrel: 3.88".
Weight: 28 oz. **Length:** 7.38" over-all.
Stocks: Smooth hardwood.
Sights: Adj. for windage.
Features: Blue or satin nickel. Ordnance steel. Magazine disconnector, firing pin and thumb safeties. Introduced 1980. Imported by Excam.
Price: 32 cal., blue $189.00
Price: 380 cal., blue $205.00

TARGA MODELS GT32, GT380 AUTO PISTOLS
Caliber: 32 ACP or 380 ACP, 6-shot magazine.
Barrel: 4⅞".
Weight: 26 oz. **Length:** 7⅜" over-all.
Stocks: Checkered nylon with thumb rest. Walnut optional.
Sights: Fixed blade front; rear drift-adj. for w.
Features: Chrome or blue finish; magazine, thumb, and firing pin safeties; external hammer; safety lever take-down. Imported from Italy by Excam, Inc.
Price: 32 cal., blue $133.00
Price: 32 cal., chrome $143.00
Price: 380 cal., blue $159.00
Price: 380 cal., chrome $167.00
Price: 380 cal., chrome, engraved, wooden grips $214.00
Price: 380 cal., blue, engraved, wooden grips $205.00

TAURUS PT-22 DOUBLE ACTION PISTOL
Caliber: 22 Long Rifle or 25 ACP
Barrel: 2.75".
Weight: 18 oz.
Stocks: Smooth Brazilian walnut.
Sights: Serrated front, fixed square notch rear.
Features: Pop-up barrel, blue finish. Introduced 1983. Made in U.S. by Taurus International Mfg. Inc.
Price: Blue only, about **$160.00**

Taurus PT-22 Pistol

TAURUS MODEL PT-92 AUTO PISTOL
Caliber: 9mm P., 15-shot magazine.
Barrel: 4.92".
Weight: 34 oz. **Length:** 8.54" over-all.
Stocks: Black plastic.
Sights: Fixed notch rear.
Features: Double action, exposed hammer, chamber loaded indicator. Inertia firing pin. Blue finish. Imported by Taurus International.
Price: About **$340.00**

Taurus PT-99 Auto Pistol
Similar to the PT-92 except has fully adjustable rear sight, smooth Brazilian walnut stocks and is available in polished or satin blue. Introduced 1983.
Price: Polished blue, about **$385.00**
Price: Satin blue, about. **$400.00**

Taurus PT-99 Pistol

Consult our Directory pages for
the location of firms mentioned.

THOMPSON 1911A1 AUTOMATIC PISTOL
Caliber: 9mm Para., 38 Super, 9-shot, 45 ACP, 7-shot magazine.
Barrel: 5".
Weight: 39 oz. **Length:** 8½" over-all.
Stocks: Checkered plastic with medallion.
Sights: Blade front, rear adj. for windage.
Features: Same specs as 1911A1 military guns—parts interchangeable. Frame and slide blued; each radius has non-glare finish. Made in U.S. by Auto-Ordnance Corp.
Price: Approximately. **$324.95**

Thompson 1911A1 Auto Pistol

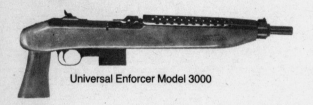

Universal Enforcer Model 3000

UNIVERSAL ENFORCER MODEL 3000 AUTO
Caliber: 30 M1 Carbine, 5-shot magazine.
Barrel: 10¼" with 12-groove rifling.
Weight: 4½ lbs. **Length:** 17¾" over-all.
Stocks: American walnut with handguard
Sights: Gold bead ramp front. Peep rear.
Features: Accepts 15 or 30-shot magazines. 4½-6 lb. trigger pull.
Price: Blue finish **$245.00**
Price: Nickel plated finish (Model 3010N) **$289.00**
Price: Gold plated finish (Model 3015G) **$328.00**
Price: Black, gray or olive Teflon-S finish **$295.00**

WALTHER PP AUTO PISTOL
Caliber: 22 LR, 8-shot; 32 ACP, 380 ACP, 7-shot.
Barrel: 3.86".
Weight: 23½ oz. **Length:** 6.7" over-all.
Stocks: Checkered plastic.
Sights: Fixed, white markings.
Features: Double action, manual safety blocks firing pin and drops hammer, chamber loaded indicator on 32 and 380, extra finger rest magazine provided. Imported from Germany by Interarms.
Price: 22 LR **$520.00**
Price: 32 and 380. . . . . **$500.00**
Price: Engraved models . . . . **On Request**
Price: 22 LR, made by Manurhin. **$460.00**
Price: 380, made by Manurhin. **$450.00**

Walther PP Auto Pistol

CAUTION: PRICES CHANGE. CHECK AT GUNSHOP.

Walther American PPK/S Auto Pistol

Similar to Walther PP except made entirely in the United States. Has 3.27″ barrel with 6.1″ length over-all. Introduced 1980.

Price: 380 ACP only **$370.00**
Price: As above, stainless **$430.00**
Price: 22 cal., Nivel (electroless finish), by Manurhin **$490.00**
Price: As above, 380 .... **$450.00**

Walther PPK/S American

WALTHER P-38 AUTO PISTOL

Caliber: 22 LR, 30 Luger or 9mm Luger, 8-shot.
Barrel: 4¹⁵⁄₁₆″ (9mm and 30), 5¹⁄₁₆″ (22 LR).
Weight: 28 oz. **Length:** 8½″ over-all.
Stocks: Checkered plastic.
Sights: Fixed.
Features: Double action, safety blocks firing pin and drops hammer, chamber loaded indicator. Matte finish standard, polished blue, engraving and/or plating available. Imported from Germany by Interarms.

Price: 22 LR **$750.00**
Price: 9mm or 30 Luger **$680.00**
Price: Engraved models .... **On Request**

Walther P-38 Auto Pistol

Walther P-38IV Auto Pistol

Same as P-38 except has longer barrel (4½″); over-all length is 8″, weight is 29 oz. Sights are non-adjustable. Introduced 1977. Imported by Interarms.
Price: **$650.00**

Walther P-5 Auto Pistol

Latest Walther design that uses the basic P-38 double-action mechanism. Caliber 9mm Luger, barrel length 3½″; weight 28 oz., over-all length 7″.
Price: **$850.00**

Walther P-5 Pistol

WILDEY AUTO PISTOL

Caliber: 45 Win. Mag. (8 shots).
Barrel: 5″, 6″, 7″, 8″, or 10″; vent. rib.
Weight: About 51 oz. (6″ bbl.).
Stock: Select hardwood, target style optional.
Sights: Blade front, rear adjustable for windage and elevation.
Features: Interchangeable barrels; patented gas operation; selective single or autoloading capability; 5-lug rotary bolt; fixed barrel; stainless steel construction; double-action trigger mechanism. Has positive hammer block and magazine safety. From Wildey Firearms.

Price: All barrel lengths **$1,295.00**

Wilkinson "Linda" Auto Pistol

Consult our Directory pages for the location of firms mentioned.

WILKINSON "LINDA" PISTOL

Caliber: 9mm Para., 31-shot magazine.
Barrel: 8⁵⁄₁₆″.
Weight: 4 lbs., 13 oz. **Length:** 12¼″ over-all.
Stocks: Checkered black plastic pistol grip, maple fore-end.
Sights: Protected blade front, Williams adjustable rear.
Features: Fires from closed bolt. Semi-auto only. Straight blowback action. Cross-bolt safety. Removable barrel. From Wilkinson Arms.

Price: **$463.00**

Arminius Revolver

ARMINIUS REVOLVERS
Caliber: 38 Special, 357 Magnum, 32 S&W, 22 Magnum, 22 LR.
Barrel: 2″, 4″, 6″.
Weight: 35 oz. (6″ bbl.). **Length:** 11″ (6″ bbl. 38).
Stocks: Checkered plastic; walnut optional for $14.95.
Sights: Ramp front, fixed rear on standard models, w. & e. adj. on target models.
Features: Thumb-release, swing-out cylinder. Ventilated rib, solid frame, swing-out cylinder. Interchangeable 22 Mag. cylinder available with 22 cal. versions. Imported from West Germany by F.I.E. Corp.
Price: . . . . **$112.95** to **$254.95**

ASTRA 357 MAGNUM REVOLVER
Caliber: 357 Magnum, 6-shot.
Barrel: 3″, 4″, 6″, 8½″.
Weight: 40 oz. (6″ bbl.). **Length:** 11¼″ (6″ bbl.).
Stocks: Checkered walnut.
Sights: Fixed front, rear adj. for w. and e.
Features: Swing-out cylinder with countersunk chambers, floating firing pin. Target-type hammer and trigger. Imported from Spain by Interarms.
Price: 3″, 4″, 6″ **$330.00**
Price: 8½″ **$340.00**

Astra Model 41, 44, 45 Double Action Revolver
Similar to the 357 Mag. except chambered for the 41 Mag., 44 Mag. or 45 Colt. Barrel length of 6″ only, giving over-all length of 11⅜″. Weight is 2¾ lbs. Introduced 1980.
Price: **$390.00**
Price: 8½″ bbl. (44 Mag. only) **$400.00**

Charter Bulldog 357

CHARTER ARMS BULLDOG
Caliber: 44 Special, 5-shot.
Barrel: 3″.
Weight: 19 oz. **Length:** 7¾″ over-all.
Stocks: Checkered walnut, Bulldog.
Sights: Patridge-type front, square-notch rear.
Features: Wide trigger and hammer; beryllium copper firing pin.
Price: Service Blue **$200.00**
Price: Stainless steel **$260.00**

Charter Arms Bulldog Tracker
Similar to the standard Bulldog except has adjustable rear sight, 2½″, 4″ or 6″ bull barrel, ramp front sight, square butt checkered walnut grips. Available in blue finish only.
Price: **$210.00**

Charter Target Bulldog 357

CHARTER TARGET BULLDOG
Caliber: 357 Mag., 44 Spec., 5-shot.
Barrel: 4″.
Weight: 20½ oz. **Length:** 8½″ over-all.
Stocks: Checkered American walnut, square butt.
Sights: Full-length ramp front, fully adj., milled channel, square notch rear.
Features: Blue finish only. Enclosed ejector rod, full length ejection of fired cases.
Price: 357 Mag. 4″ **$215.50**
Price: 44 Spec., 4″ **$225.00**

CHARTER ARMS POLICE BULLDOG
Caliber: 38 Special, 6-shot.
Barrel: 2″, 4″, 4″ straight taper bull.
Weight: 21 oz. **Length:** 9″ over-all.
Stocks: Hand checkered American walnut; square butt.
Sights: Patridge-type ramp front, notched rear.
Features: Accepts both regular and high velocity ammunition; enclosed ejector rod; full length ejection of fired cases.
Price: Blue **$185.00**
Price: "P" model, blue **$193.00**
Price: "P" model, stainless **$249.00**
Price: Regular hammer, stainless **$245.00**

Charter Arms Police Bulldog

CAUTION: PRICES CHANGE. CHECK AT GUNSHOP.

CHARTER ARMS UNDERCOVER REVOLVER
Caliber: 38 Special, 5 shot; 32 S & W Long, 6 shot.
Barrel: 2″, 3″.
Weight: 16 oz. (2″). **Length:** 6¼″ (2″).
Stocks: Smooth walnut or checkered square butt.
Sights: Patridge-type ramp front, notched rear.
Features: Wide trigger and hammer spur. Steel frame.
Price: Polished Blue $190.00
Price: 32 S & W Long, blue, 2″ $190.00
Price: Stainless, 38 Spec., 2″.......................... $245.00
Price: "P" model, blue.................................. $193.00
Price: "P" model, stainless............................. $249.00

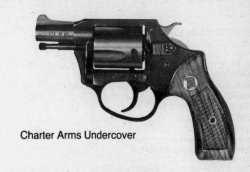

Charter Arms Undercover

Charter Arms Pathfinder
Same as Undercover but in 22 LR or 22 Mag., and has 2″, 3″ or 6″ bbl. Fitted with adjustable rear sight, ramp front. Weight 18½ oz.
Price: 22 LR, blue, 3″ $200.00
Price: 22 LR, square butt, 6″ $215.00
Price: Stainless, 22 LR, 3″ $250.00
Price: 2″, either caliber, blue only $200.00

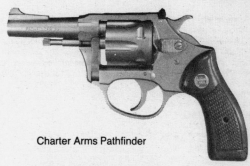

Charter Arms Pathfinder

COLT AGENT
Caliber: 38 Special, 6-shot.
Barrel: 2″.
Weight: 16¾ ozs. **Length:** 6⅞″ over-all.
Stocks: Checkered walnut.
Sights: Fixed.
Features: A no-frills, lightweight version of the Detective Special. Parkerized-type finish. Name re-introduced 1982.
Price: $199.50

COLT DETECTIVE SPECIAL
Caliber: 38 Special, 6 shot.
Barrel: 2″ or 3″.
Weight: 22 oz. **Length:** 6⅝″ over-all (2″ bbl.).
Stocks: Full, checkered walnut, round butt.
Sights: Fixed, ramp front, square notch rear.
Features: Glare-proofed sights, smooth trigger. Nickel finish, hammer shroud available as options.
Price: Blue, 2″................................... $352.95
Price: Nickel, 3″ $388.50
Price: Blue, 3″................................... $360.95
Price: Nickel, 3″ $395.95

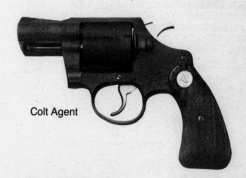

Colt Agent

Colt Detective Special

> Consult our Directory pages for
> the location of firms mentioned.

COLT PYTHON REVOLVER
Caliber: 357 Magnum (handles all 38 Spec.), 6 shot.
Barrel: 2½″, 4″, 6″ or 8″, with ventilated rib.
Weight: 38 oz. (4″ bbl.). **Length:** 9¼″ (4″ bbl.).
Stocks: Checkered walnut, target type.
Sights: ⅛″ ramp front, adj. notch rear.
Features: Ventilated rib; grooved, crisp trigger; swing-out cylinder; target hammer.
Price: Colt Blue, 2½″................................ $540.50
Price: 4″.. $551.95
Price: 6″.. $560.50
Price: 8″.. $572.50
Price: Nickeled, 4″ $585.95
Price: 6″.. $587.95
Price: 8″.. $600.50
Price: Stainless, 4″.............................. $619.50
Price: Stainless, 6″.............................. $628.50

Colt Python 357

COLT TROOPER MK III REVOLVER
Caliber: 22 LR, 22 WMR, 38 Spec., 357 Magnum, 6-shot.
Barrel: 4″, 6″ or 8″.
Weight: 39 oz. (4″ bbl.), 42 oz., (6″ bbl.). **Length:** 9½″ (4″ bbl.).
Stocks: Checkered walnut, square butt.
Sights: Fixed ramp front with ⅛″ blade, adj. notch rear.
Price: Blued with target hammer and target stocks, 4″, 357........ $244.50
Price: Nickeled 38/357 Mag. 4″................................. $250.95
Price: 22 LR, blue, 8″ $231.50
Price: 357, blue, 8″ $252.95
Price: 357, Coltguard finish, 8″ $245.95
Price: 22 LR, Coltguard finish, 4″ $239.75

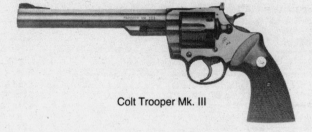

Colt Trooper Mk. III

Colt Lawman/Trooper Mark V Revolvers
Modified versions of the Lawman MK III and Trooper MK III revolvers. Internal lockwork has been redesigned to reduce trigger pull in double action and give faster lock time. Grip has been redesigned for more comfort. MK V Trooper has adjustable rear sight, and red insert front sight, vent rib 4″, 6″, 8″ barrel; MK V Lawman has 2″ or 4″ barrel, fixed sight and solid rib. Introduced 1982.
Price: Lawman, 2″, blue $269.50
Price: Lawman, 4″, nickel $286.50
Price: Trooper, 4″, blue $298.50
Price: As above, nickel $316.50
Price: As above, 6″, blue $299.50

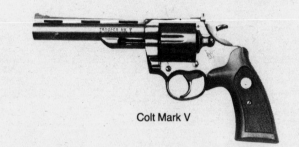

Colt Mark V

COLT DIAMONDBACK REVOLVER
Caliber: 22 LR or 38 Special, 6 shot.
Barrel: 4″ or 6″ with ventilated rib.
Weight: 24 oz. (2½″ bbl.), 28½ oz. (4″ bbl.). **Length:** 9″ (4″ bbl.)
Stocks: Checkered walnut, target type, square butt.
Sights: Ramp front, adj. notch rear.
Features: Ventilated rib; grooved, crisp trigger; swing-out cylinder; wide hammer spur.
Price: Blue, 4″ bbl. 38 Spec. or 22 .... $354.50
Price: Blue, 6″ bbl., 22 or 38................................ $362.50

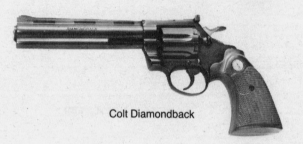

Colt Diamondback

COLT LAWMAN MK III REVOLVER
Caliber: 357 Mag., 6 shot.
Barrel: 2″ or 4″, heavy.
Weight: 33 oz. **Length:** 9⅜″.
Stocks: Checkered walnut, service style.
Sights: Fixed, glare-proofed ramp front, square notch rear.
Price: Blued $222.50
Price: Nickel $227.50
Price: With Coltguard finish $213.95

Colt Lawman Mk. III

F.I.E. MODEL N38 "Titan Tiger" REVOLVER
Caliber: 38 Special.
Barrel: 2″ or 4″.
Weight: 27 oz. **Length:** 6¼″ over-all. (2″ bbl.)
Stocks: Checkered plastic, Bulldog style. Walnut optional ($15.95).
Sights: Fixed.
Features: Thumb-release swing-out cylinder, one stroke ejection. Made in U.S.A. by F.I.E. Corp.
Price: Blue.. $129.95
Price: Chrome $144.95

HARRINGTON & RICHARDSON M622 REVOLVER
Caliber: 22 S, L or LR, 22 WMR, 6 shot.
Barrel: 2½″, 4″, round bbl.
Weight: 20 oz. (2½″ bbl.).
Stocks: Checkered black Cycolac.
Sights: Fixed, blade front, square notch rear.
Features: Solid steel, Bantamweight frame; patented safety rim cylinder; nonglare finish on frame; coil springs.
Price: Blued, 2½″, 4″ bbl. $94.50
Price: Model 632 (32 cal.)..................................... $94.50
Price: Model 642, 22 WMR $94.50

H&R Model 622

CAUTION: PRICES CHANGE. CHECK AT GUNSHOP.

HARRINGTON & RICHARDSON M686 REVOLVER
Caliber: 22 LR/22 WMRF, 6-shot.
Barrel: 4½", 5½", 7½", 10" or 12".
Weight: 31 oz. (4½"), 41 oz. (12").
Stocks: Two piece, smooth walnut-finished hardwood.
Sights: Western type blade front, adj. rear.
Features: Blue barrel and cylinder, "antique" color case-hardened frame, ejector tube and trigger. Comes with extra cylinder.
Price: 4½", 5½", 7½" bbl. $164.50
Price: 10" or 12" bbl. $185.50

H&R Model 686

Harrington & Richardson Model 649 Revolver
Similar to model 686 except has 5½" or 7½" barrel, two piece walnut-finished hardwood grips, western-type blade front sight, adjustable rear. Loads and ejects from side. Weighs 32 oz.
Price: $143.00
Price: Model 650—as above except nickel finish, 5½" only $154.00

H&R Model 649

HARRINGTON & RICHARDSON M732
Caliber: 32 S&W or 32 S&W Long, 6 shot.
Barrel: 2½" or 4" round barrel.
Weight: 23½ oz. (2½" bbl.), 26 oz. (4" bbl.).
Stocks: Checkered, black Cycolac or walnut.
Sights: Blade front; adjustable rear on 4" model.
Features: Swing-out cylinder with auto. extractor return. Pat. safety rim cylinder. Grooved trigger.
Price: Blued, 2½" or 4" bbl. $116.50
Price: Nickel, 2½" or 4" bbl. (Model 733) $127.00
Price: Blued, 2½", walnut grips $132.00
Price: Nickled, 2½", walnut grip (Model 733) $142.50

H&R Model 732

HARRINGTON & RICHARDSON MODEL 829
Caliber: 22 LR, 9-shot.
Barrel: 3", bull.
Weight: 27 ozs.
Stocks: Walnut, with H&R medallions.
Sights: Ramp and blade front, "Wind-Elv" adjustable rear.
Features: Swing-out cylinder, recessed muzzle. Introduced 1982.
Price: 22 LR or 22 Mag. (Model 826, 6-shot) $148.00
Price: As above, nickel (Model 830) $158.50
Price: Model 832 (32 S&W Long, 6-shot) $148.00
Price: As above, nickel (Model 833) $158.50

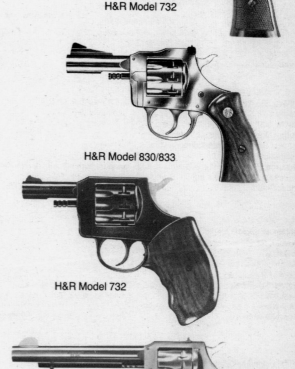

H&R Model 830/833

HARRINGTON & RICHARDSON M929
Caliber: 22 S, L or LR, 9 shot.
Barrel: 2½", 4" or 6".
Weight: 26 oz. (4" bbl.).
Stocks: Checkered, black Cycolac or walnut.
Sights: Blade front; adjustable rear on 4" and 6" models.
Features: Swing-out cylinder with auto. extractor return. Pat. safety rim cylinder. Grooved trigger. Round-grip frame.
Price: Blued, 2½", 4" or 6" bbl. $116.50
Price: Nickel (Model 930), 2½" or 4" bbl. $127.00
Price: Blued, 2½", walnut grips $132.00
Price: Nickel, 2½", walnut grips (Model 930) $142.50

H&R Model 732

HARRINGTON & RICHARDSON M949
Caliber: 22 S, L or LR, 9 shot.
Barrel: 5½" round with ejector rod.
Weight: 31 oz.
Stocks: Two-piece, smooth frontier style wrap-around, walnut-finished hardwood.
Sights: Western-type blade front, rear adj. for w.
Features: Contoured loading gate; wide hammer spur; single and double action. Western type ejector-housing.
Price: H&R Crown Luster Blue $116.50
Price: Nickel (Model 950) $127.00

H&R Model 950

H&R SPORTSMAN MODEL 999 REVOLVER
Caliber: 22 S, L or LR, 9 shot.
Barrel: 4", 6" top-break (16" twist), integral fluted vent. rib.
Weight: 34 oz. (6"). **Length:** 10½".
Stocks: Checkered walnut-finished hardwood.
Sights: Front adjustable for elevation, rear for windage.
Features: Simultaneous automatic ejection, trigger guard extension. H&R Crown Lustre Blue.
Price: Blued, 4".. $196.00
Price: Blued, 6" engraved...................................... $419.00

H&R Model 999

HARRINGTON & RICHARDSON MODELS 604, 904, 905
Caliber: 22 LR, 9-shot (M904, 905), 22 WMR, 6-shot (M604)
Barrel: 4" (M904 only), 6" target bull.
Weight: 32 oz.
Stocks: Smooth walnut.
Sights: Blade front, fully adjustable "Wind-Elv" rear.
Features: Swing-out cylinder design with coil spring construction. Single stroke ejection. Target-style bull barrel has raised solid rib giving a 7¼" sight radius.
Price: M604 or 904 .... $158.50
Price: M905, 4", H&R "Hard-Guard" finish $164.50

Harrington & Richardson Models 603, 903
Similar to 604-904 except has flat-sided barrel.
Price: $158.50

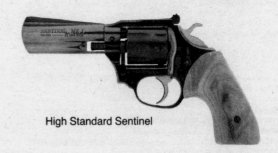

H&R Model 905

HIGH STANDARD SENTINEL
Caliber: 22 LR and 22 Mag. with extra cylinder.
Barrel: 2" or 4".
Weight: 22 oz. (2" barrel). **Length:** 7⅛" over-all (2" barrel).
Stocks: Checkered walnut.
Sights: ⅛" serrated ramp front, square notched rear.
Features: Double action, dual swing-out cylinders; steel frame; blue finish; combat-style grips. From High Standard.
Price: Model 9390 (fixed sights) $230.00
Price: Model 9392 (adj. sights) $250.00

HIGH STANDARD DOUBLE-NINE CONVERTIBLE
Caliber: 22 S, L or LR, 9-shot (22 Mag. with extra cylinder).
Barrel: 5½", dummy ejector rod fitted.
Weight: 32 oz. **Length:** 11" over-all.
Stocks: Smooth walnut, frontier style.
Sights: Fixed blade front, rear adj. for w. & e.
Features: Double-action, Western styling, rounding hammer with auto safety block; spring-loaded ejection. Swing-out cylinder.
Price: Blued $250.00

High Standard Sentinel

High Standard Long Horn Convertible
Same as the Double-Nine convertible but with a 9½" bbl., adjustable sights, blued only. Weight: 38 oz.
Price: With adjustable sights $255.00

HIGH STANDARD CAMP GUN
Caliber: 22 LR and 22 Mag., 9-shot.
Barrel: 6".
Weight: 28 oz. **Length:** 11⅛" over-all.
Stocks: Checkered walnut.
Sights: ⅛" serrated ramp front, rear adjustable for windage and elevation.
Features: Double-action; comes with two cylinders; blue finish; combat-style wrap around grips. From High Standard.
Price: Model 9393 .... $250.00

High Standard Camp Gun

HIGH STANDARD CRUSADER COMMEMORATIVE REVOLVER
Caliber: 44 Mag., 45 Long Colt.
Barrel: 6½", 8⅜".
Weight: 48 oz. (6½").
Stocks: Smooth Zrawood.
Sights: Blade front on ramp, fully adj. rear.
Features: Unique gear-segment mechanism. Smooth, light double-action trigger pull. First production devoted to the commemorative; later guns will be of plain, standard configuration.
Price: .... N.A.

HIGH STANDARD HIGH SIERRA DOUBLE ACTION
Caliber: 22 LR and 22 LR/22 Mag., 9-shot.
Barrel: 7" octagonal.
Weight: 36 oz. **Length:** 12½" over-all.
Stocks: Smooth walnut.
Sights: Blade front, adj. rear.
Features: Gold plated backstrap and trigger guard. Swing-out cylinder.
Price: Adj. sights, dual cyl...................................... $255.00

KASSNAR-SQUIRES BINGHAM MODEL 100TC REVOLVER
Caliber: 22 LR, 22 Mag., 38 Special.
Barrel: 3″, 4″, 6″.
Weight: 24 oz. **Length:** 9½″ (4″ bbl.).
Stocks: Target-type of hand checkered exotic wood.
Sights: Ramp front, fully adjustable rear.
Features: Heavy barrel with ventilated rib, full ejector rod shroud. Imported from the Philippines by Kassnar.
Price: **$149.95**

Llama Comanche

LLAMA COMANCHE REVOLVERS
Caliber: 357 Mag.
Barrel: 6″, 4″.
Weight: 28 oz. **Length:** 9¼″ (4″ bbl.).
Stocks: Checkered walnut.
Sights: Fixed blade front, rear adj. for w. & e.
Features: Ventilated rib, wide spur hammer. Chrome plating, engraved finishes available. Imported from Spain by Stoeger Industries.
Price: Blue finish **$308.95**
Price: Satin chrome.. **$391.95**

Llama Super Comanche

Llama Super Comanche Revolver
Similar to the Comanche except; large frame, 357 or 44 Mag., 4″, 6″ or 8½″ barrel only; 6-shot cylinder; smooth, extra wide trigger; wide spur hammer; over-size walnut, target-style grips. Weight is 3 lbs., 2 ozs., over-all length is 11¾″. Blue finish only.
Price: 44 Mag. **$398.95**
Price: 357 Mag. **$364.95**

ROSSI MODEL 88 STAINLESS REVOLVER
Caliber: 38 Spec., 5-shot.
Barrel: 3″.
Weight: 32 oz. **Length:** 8¾″ over-all.
Stocks: Checkered wood, service-style.
Sights: Ramp front, square notch rear drift adjustable for windage.
Features: All metal parts except springs are of 440 stainless steel; matte finish; small frame for concealability. Introduced 1983. Imported from Brazil by Interarms.
Price: **$205.00**

Rossi Model 88 Stainless

ROSSI MODELS 68, 69 & 70 DA REVOLVERS
Caliber: 22 LR (M 70), 32 S & W (M 69), 38 Spec. (M 68).
Barrel: 3″.
Weight: 22 oz.
Stocks: Checkered wood.
Sights: Ramp front, low profile adj. rear.
Features: All-steel frame. Thumb latch operated swing-out cylinder. Introduced 1978. Imported from Brazil by Interarms.
Price: 22, 32, or 38, blue **$155.00**
Price: As above, 38 Spec. only with 4″ bbl. as M 31 .... **$150.00**
Price: Model 51 (6″ bbl., 22 cal.) **$160.00**
Price: M68, M69, M70 in nickel............................... **$160.00**

Rossi Model 68

RUGER SECURITY-SIX Model 117
Caliber: 357 Mag. (also fires 38 Spec.), 6-shot.
Barrel: 2¾″, 4″ or 6″, or 4″ heavy barrel.
Weight: 33½ oz. (4″ bbl.) **Length:** 9¼″ (4″ bbl.) over-all.
Stocks: Hand checkered American walnut, semi-target style.
Sights: Patridge-type front on ramp, white outline rear adj. for w. and e.
Features: Music wire coil springs throughout. Hardened steel construction. Integral ejector rod shroud and sighting rib. Can be disassembled using only a coin.
Price: 2¾″, 6″ and 4″ heavy barrel **$247.00**
Price: 4″ HB, 6″ with Big Grip stocks. **$266.00**

Ruger Security-Six

RUGER POLICE SERVICE-SIX Models 107, 108, 109
Caliber: 357 (Model 107), 38 Spec. (Model 108), 9mm (Model 109), 6-shot.
Barrel: 2¾" or 4" and 4" heavy barrel.
Weight: 33½ oz. (4" bbl.). **Length:** 9¼" (4 bbl.) over-all.
Stocks: Checkered American walnut, semi-target style.
Sights: Patridge-type front, square notch rear.
Features: Solid frame; barrel, rib and ejector rod housing combined in one unit. All steel construction Field strips without tools.
Price: Model 107 (357) $217.50
Price: Model 108 (38) $217.50
Price: Model 109 (9mm) $236.50
Price: Mod. 707 (357), Stainless, 4" & 4" HB $239.50
Price: Mod. 708 (38), Stainless, 4" & 4" HB. $239.50

Ruger Police Service-Six

RUGER SPEED-SIX Models 207, 208, 209
Caliber: 357 (Model 207), 38 Spec. (Model 208), 9mm P (Model 209) 6-shot.
Barrel: 2¾" or 4".
Weight: 31 oz. (2¾" bbl.). **Length:** 7¾" over-all (2¾" bbl.).
Stocks: Round butt design, diamond pattern checkered American walnut.
Sights: Patridge-type front, square-notch rear.
Features: Same basic mechanism as Security-Six. Hammer without spur available on special order. All steel construction. Music wire coil springs used throughout.
Price: Model 207 (357 Mag.) $221.50
Price: Model 208 (38 Spec. only) $221.50
Price: Model 209 (9mm P) $240.50
Price: Mod. 737 (357), Stainless $246.00
Price: Mod. 738 (38), Stainless $246.00
Price: Model 739 (9mm P), Stainless $261.00

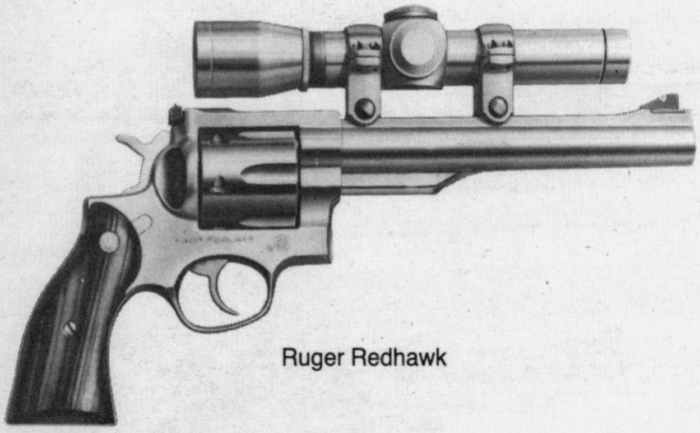

RUGER STAINLESS SECURITY-SIX Model 717
Caliber: 357 Mag. (also fires 38 Spec.), 6-shot.
Barrel: 2¾", 4" or 6".
Weight: 33 oz. (4 bbl.). **Length:** 9¼" (4" bbl.) over-all.
Stocks: Hand checkered American walnut.
Sights: Patridge-type front, fully adj. rear.
Features: All metal parts except sights made of stainless steel. Sights are black alloy for maximum visibility. Same mechanism and features found in regular Security-Six.
Price: 2¾", 6" and 4" HB. $270.50
Price: 4" HB, 6" with Big Grip stocks. $290.00

RUGER REDHAWK
Caliber: 44 Rem. Mag., 6-shot.
Barrel: 7½".
Weight: About 3¼ lbs. **Length:** 13" over-all.
Stocks: Square butt. American walnut.
Sights: Patridge-type front, rear adj. for w. & e.
Features: Stainless steel, brushed satin finish. Has a 9½" sight radius. Introduced 1979.
Price: $381.00
Price: With Ruger stainless scope rings $408.50

Ruger Redhawk

SMITH & WESSON M&P Model 10 REVOLVER
Caliber: 38 Special, 6 shot.
Barrel: 2", 4", 5" or 6".
Weight: 30½ oz. (4" bbl.). **Length:** 9¼" (4" bbl.).
Stocks: Checkered walnut, Magna. Round or square butt.
Sights: Fixed, ⅛" ramp front, square notch rear.
Price: Blued $220.00
Price: Nickeled $238.00

S&W Model 10-H.B.

Smith & Wesson 38 M&P Heavy Barrel Model 10
Same as regular M&P except: 3" or 4" ribbed bbl. with ⅛" ramp front sight, square rear, square butt, wgt. 34 oz.
Price: Blued $220.00
Price: Nickeled $238.00

S&W Model 13

SMITH & WESSON 38 M&P AIRWEIGHT Model 12
Caliber: 38 Special, 6 shot.
Barrel: 2" or 4".
Weight: 18 oz. (2" bbl.). **Length:** 6⅞" over-all.
Stocks: Checkered walnut, Magna. Round or square butt.
Sights: Fixed, ⅛" serrated ramp front, square notch rear.
Price: Blued $288.00
Price: Nickeled $326.50

SMITH & WESSON Model 13 H.B. M&P
Caliber: 357 and 38 Special, 6 shot.
Barrel: 3" or 4".
Weight: 34 oz. **Length:** 9¼" over-all (4" bbl.).
Stocks: Checkered walnut, service.
Sights: ⅛" serrated ramp front, fixed square notch rear.
Features: Heavy barrel, K-frame, square butt.
Price: Blue, M-13 . . . . $224.00
Price: Nickel $244.50
Price: Model 65, as above in stainless steel $254.00

CAUTION: PRICES CHANGE. CHECK AT GUNSHOP.

SMITH & WESSON MODEL 17 K-22 MASTERPIECE
Caliber: 22 LR, 6-shot.
Barrel: 6″, 8⅜″.
Weight: 38½ oz. (6″ bbl). **Length:** 11⅛″ over-all.
Stocks: Checkered walnut, service.
Sights: Patridge front, S&W micro. click rear adjustable for windage and elevation.
Features: Grooved tang and trigger. Polished blue finish.
Price: 6″ **$321.00**
Price: 8¾″ bbl. **$335.00**
Price: Model 48, as above in 22 Mag., 4″ or 6″ **$330.00**
Price: 8⅜″ bbl. **$345.50**

SMITH & WESSON 357 COMBAT MAGNUM Model 19
Caliber: 357 Magnum and 38 Special, 6 shot.
Barrel: 2½″, 4″, 6″.
Weight: 35 oz. **Length:** 9½″ (4″ bbl).
Stocks: Checkered Goncalo Alves, target. Grooved tangs and trigger.
Sights: Front, ⅛″ Baughman Quick Draw on 2½″ or 4″ bbl., Patridge on 6″ bbl., micro click rear adjustable for w. and e.
Price: S&W Bright Blue or Nickel, adj. sights **$277.00**

SMITH & WESSON MODEL 24 44 SPECIAL
Caliber: 44 Special, 6-shot.
Barrel: 4″ or 6½″.
Weight: 41½ oz. (4″ bbl). **Length:** 9½″ over-all (4″ bbl).
Stocks: Checkered Goncalo Alves target-type.
Sights: Ramp front on 4″, Patridge front on 6½″; fully adjustable micrometer click rear.
Features: Limited production of 7,500 pieces. Built to the original specifications. Available only in S&W bright blue with grooved top strap and barrel rib. Reintroduced 1983.
Price: 4″ barrel **$358.50**
Price: 6½″ barrel **$387.00**

SMITH & WESSON MODEL 25 REVOLVER
Caliber: 45 Colt, 6-shot.
Barrel: 4″, 6″, 8⅜″.
Weight: About 45 oz. **Length:** 11⅞″ over-all (6″ bbl).
Stocks: Checkered Goncalo Alves, target-type.
Sights: ⅛″ S&W red ramp front, S&W micrometer click rear with white outline.
Features: Available in Brite Blue or nickel finish; target trigger, target hammer. Comes with presentation case. Contact S&W for complete price list.
Price: 4″, 6″, blue or nickel **$455.00**
Price: 8⅜″, blue or nickel **$469.50**
Price: Without case, 4″, 6″, blue or nickel **$409.00**
Price: As above, 8⅜″. **$423.00**

SMITH & WESSON HIGHWAY PATROLMAN Model 28
Caliber: 357 Magnum and 38 Special, 6 shot.
Barrel: 4″, 6″.
Weight: 44 oz. (6″ bbl). **Length:** 11¼″ (6″ bbl).
Stocks: Checkered walnut, Magna. Grooved tangs and trigger.
Sights: Front, ⅛″ Baughman Quick Draw, on plain ramp, micro click rear, adjustable for w. and e.
Price: S&W Satin Blue, sandblasted frame edging and barrel top . . . **$305.50**
Price: With target stocks. **$327.00**

SMITH & WESSON 44 MAGNUM Model 29 REVOLVER
Caliber: 44 Magnum, 44 Special or 44 Russian, 6 shot.
Barrel: 4″, 6″, 8⅜″, 10⅝″.
Weight: 47 oz. (6″ bbl), 43 oz. (4″ bbl). **Length:** 11⅞″ (6½″ bbl).
Stocks: Oversize target type, checkered Goncalo Alves. Tangs and target trigger grooved, checkered target hammer.
Sights: ⅛″ red ramp front, micro click rear, adjustable for w. and e.
Features: Includes presentation case.
Price: S&W Bright Blue or Nickel 4″, 6″ **$455.00**
Price: 8⅜″ or 10⅝″ bbl., blue or nickel **$469.50**
Price: Model 629 (stainless steel), 4″, 6″ **$518.50**
Price: Model 629, 8⅜″ barrel. **$534.50**

SMITH & WESSON COMBAT MASTERPIECE
Caliber: 38 Special (M15) or 22 LR (M18), 6 shot.
Barrel: 2″ or 4″ (M15) 4″ (M18).
Weight: Loaded, 22 36½ oz., 38 34 oz. **Length:** 9⅛″ (4″ bbl).
Stocks: Checkered walnut, Magna. Grooved tangs and trigger.
Sights: Front, ⅛″ Baughman Quick Draw on ramp, micro click rear, adjustable for w. and e.
Price: Blued, M-15, 2″ or 4″ **$254.00**
Price: Nickel M-15, 2″ or 4″ **$273.00**
Price: Blued, M-18, 4″ (sq. butt, adj. sights) **$310.50**

S&W Model 19

SMITH & WESSON 357 MAGNUM M-27 REVOLVER
Caliber: 357 Magnum and 38 Special, 6 shot.
Barrel: 4″, 6″, 8⅜″.
Weight: 44 oz. (6″ bbl). **Length:** 11¼″ (6″ bbl).
Stocks: Checkered walnut, Magna. Grooved tangs and trigger.
Sights: Any S&W target front, micro click rear, adjustable for w. and e.
Price: S&W Bright Blue or Nickel, 4″, 6″ **$462.00**
Price: 8⅜″ bbl., sq. butt, target hammer, trigger, stocks **$469.00**

S&W Model 25

S&W Model 29

SMITH & WESSON 32 REGULATION POLICE Model 31
Caliber: 32 S&W Long, 6 shot.
Barrel: 2″, 3″.
Weight: 18¾ oz. (3″ bbl.). **Length:** 7½″ (3″ bbl.).
Stocks: Checkered walnut, Magna.
Sights: Fixed, 1/10″ serrated ramp front, square notch rear.
Features: Blued
Price: $263.00

S&W Model 31

SMITH & WESSON 1953 Model 34, 22/32 KIT GUN
Caliber: 22 LR, 6 shot.
Barrel: 2″, 4″.
Weight: 22½ oz. (4″ bbl.). **Length:** 8″ (4″ bbl. and round butt).
Stocks: Checkered walnut, round or square butt.
Sights: Front, 1/10″ serrated ramp, micro. click rear, adjustable for w. & e.
Price: Blued $263.00
Price: Nickeled $286.00
Price: Model 63, as above in stainless, 4″ $298.00

Smith & Wesson Model 650/651 Magnum Kit Gun
Similar to the Models 34 and 63 except chambered for the 22 WMR. Model 650 has 3″ barrel, round butt and fixed sights; Model 651 has 4″ barrel, square butt and adjustable sights. Both guns made of stainless steel. Introduced 1983.
Price: Model 650 .... $271.50
Price: Model 651 .... $298.00

S&W Model 651

SMITH & WESSON 38 CHIEFS SPECIAL & AIRWEIGHT
Caliber: 38 Special, 5 shot.
Barrel: 2″, 3″.
Weight: 19 oz. (2″ bbl.); 14 oz. (AIRWEIGHT). **Length:** 6½″ (2″ bbl. and round butt).
Stocks: Checkered walnut, Magna. Round or square butt.
Sights: Fixed, 1/10″ serrated ramp front, square notch rear.
Price: Price: Blued, standard Model 36 .... $235.00
Price: As above, nickel $254.50
Price: Blued, Airweight Model 37 .... $266.50
Price: As above, nickel $301.50

S&W Model 38

SMITH & WESSON BODYGUARD MODEL 38
Caliber: 38 Special; 5 shot, double action revolver.
Barrel: 2″.
Weight: 14½ oz. **Length:** 6⅜″.
Stocks: Checkered walnut, Magna.
Sights: Fixed 1/10″ serrated ramp front, square notch rear.
Features: Alloy frame; integral hammer shroud.
Price: Blued $277.50
Price: Nickeled $313.50

Smith & Wesson Bodyguard Model 49 Revolver
Same as Model 38 except steel construction, weight 20½ oz.
Price: Blued $247.00
Price: Nickeled $269.00

Smith & Wesson 60 Chiefs Special Stainless
Same as Model 36 except: 2″ bbl. and round butt only.
Price: Stainless steel $289.50

Consult our Directory pages for the location of firms mentioned.

S&W Model 57

SMITH & WESSON 41 MAGNUM Model 57 REVOLVER
Caliber: 41 Magnum, 6 shot.
Barrel: 4″, 6″ or 8⅜″.
Weight: 48 oz. (6″ bbl.). **Length:** 11⅜″ (6″ bbl.).
Stocks: Oversize target type checkered Goncalo Alves.
Sights: ⅛″ red ramp front, micro. click rear, adj. for w. and e.
Features: Includes presentation case.
Price: S&W Bright Blue or Nickel 4″, 6″ $455.00
Price: 8⅜″ bbl. $469.50

CAUTION: PRICES CHANGE. CHECK AT GUNSHOP.

SMITH & WESSON MODEL 64 STAINLESS M&P
Caliber: 38 Special, 6-shot.
Barrel: 4".
Weight: 30½ oz. **Length:** 9½" over-all.
Stocks: Checkered walnut, service style.
Sights: Fixed, ⅛" serrated ramp front, square notch rear.
Features: Satin finished stainless steel, square butt.
Price: **$243.50**

SMITH & WESSON MODEL 66 STAINLESS COMBAT MAGNUM
Caliber: 357 Magnum and 38 Special, 6-shot.
Barrel: 2½", 4", 6".
Weight: 35 oz. **Length:** 9½" over-all.
Stocks: Checkered Goncalo Alves target.
Sights: Front, ⅛" Baughman Quick Draw on plain ramp, micro clock rear adj. for w. and e.
Features: Satin finish stainless steel, grooved trigger with adj. stop.
Price: **$310.00**

SMITH & WESSON MODEL 67 K-38 STAINLESS COMBAT MASTERPIECE
Caliber: 38 Special, 6-shot.
Barrel: 4".
Weight: 34 oz. (loaded). **Length:** 9⅛" over-all.
Stocks: Checkered walnut, service style.
Sights: Front, ⅛" Baughman Quick Draw on ramp, micro click rear adj. for w. and e.
Features: Stainless steel. Square butt frame with grooved tangs, grooved trigger with adj. stop.
Price: **$301.00**

SMITH & WESSON MODEL 547
Caliber: 9mm Parabellum
Barrel: 3" or 4" heavy.
Weight: 34 oz. (4" barrel). **Length:** 9⅛" over-all (4" barrel).
Stocks: Checkered square butt Magna Service (4"), checkered walnut target, round butt (3").
Sights: ⅛" Serrated ramp front, fixed ⅛" square notch rear.
Features: K-frame revolver uses special extractor system—no clips required. Has ¼" half-spur hammer. Introduced 1981.
Price: Blue only **$290.00**

SMITH & WESSON MODEL 586 Distinguished Combat Magnum
Caliber: 357 Magnum.
Barrel: 4", 6", both heavy.
Weight: 46 oz. (6"), 42 oz. (4").
Stocks: Goncalo Alves target-type with speed loader cutaway.
Sights: Baughman red ramp front, S&W micrometer click rear (or fixed).
Features: Uses new L-frame, but takes all K-frame grips. Full length ejector rod shroud. Smooth combat-type trigger, semi-target type hammer. Trigger stop on 6" models; 4" models factory fitted with target hammer and trigger will have trigger stop. Also available in stainless as Model 686. Introduced 1981.
Price: Model 586 (blue only) **$294.50**
Price: Model 586, nickel **$294.50**
Price: Model 686 (stainless)....................... **$321.50**
Price: Model 581 (fixed sight, blue), 4"........... **$232.00**
Price: Model 581, nickel **$254.50**
Price: Model 681 (fixed sight, stainless) **$268.00**

TAURUS MODEL 66 REVOLVER
Caliber: 357 Magnum, 6-shot.
Barrel: 3", 4", 6".
Weight: 35 ozs.
Stocks: Checkered walnut, target-type. Standard stocks on 3".
Sights: Serrated ramp front, micro click rear adjustable for w. and e.
Features: Wide target-type hammer spur, floating firing pin, heavy barrel with shrouded ejector rod. Introduced 1978. From Taurus International.
Price: Blue, about **$226.00**
Price: Satin blue, about............................ **$226.00**
Price: Model 65 (similar to M66 except has a fixed rear sight and ramp front), blue, about.................................... **$177.00**
Price: Model 65, satin blue, about................. **$188.00**

S&W Model 64-H.B.

S&W Model 66

Smith & Wesson Accessories
Target hammers with low, broad, deeply-checkered spur, and wide-swaged, grooved target trigger. For all frame sizes, **$14.20** (target hammers not available for small frames). Target stocks: for large-frame guns, N-frame—**$21.30** to **$23.05**; K-frame—**$17.75** to **$21.30**; J-frame— **$15.95** to **$20.30**. These prices applicable only when specified on original order. Combat stocks J, K or L frame, **$11.90** to **$21.30**.

S&W Model 586

Taurus Model 66

Taurus Model 85

TAURUS MODEL 85 REVOLVER
Caliber: 38 Spec., 5-shot.
Barrel: 3″.
Weight: 21 oz.
Stocks: Smooth walnut.
Sights: Ramp front, square notch rear.
Features: Blue or satin blue finish. Introduced 1980. Imported from Brazil by Taurus International.
Price: Blue, about $188.00
Price: Satin blue, about. $201.00

Taurus Model 80

TAURUS MODEL 80 STANDARD REVOLVER
Caliber: 38 Spec., 6-shot.
Barrel: 3″ or 4″.
Weight: 31 oz. (4″ bbl.). **Length:** 9¼″ over-all (4″ bbl.).
Stocks: Checkered Brazilian walnut.
Sights: Serrated ramp front, square notch rear.
Features: Imported from Brazil by Taurus International.
Price: Blue, about $170.00
Price: Satin blue, about. $182.00

Taurus Model 82

TAURUS MODEL 82 HEAVY BARREL REVOLVER
Caliber: 38 Spec., 6-shot.
Barrel: 3″ or 4″, heavy.
Weight: 33 oz. (4″ bbl.). **Length:** 9¼″ over-all (4″ bbl.).
Stocks: Checkered Brazilian walnut.
Sights: Serrated ramp front, square notch rear.
Features: Imported from Brazil by Taurus International.
Price: Blue, about $170.00
Price: Satin blue, about. $182.00

TAURUS MODEL 73 SPORT REVOLVER
Caliber: 32 S&W Long, 6-shot.
Barrel: 3″, heavy.
Weight: 22 oz. **Length:** 8¼″ over-all.
Stocks: Oversize target-type, checkered Brazilian walnut.
Sights: Ramp front, notch rear.
Features: Imported from Brazil by Taurus International.
Price: Blue, about $186.00
Price: Satin blue, about. $198.00

TAURUS MODEL 83 REVOLVER
Caliber: 38 Spec., 6-shot.
Barrel: 4″ only, heavy.
Weight: 34½ oz.
Stocks: Over-size checkered walnut.
Sights: Ramp front, micro. click rear adj. for w. & e.
Features: Blue or nickel finish. Introduced 1977. Imported from Brazil by Taurus International.
Price: Blue, about $186.00
Price: Satin blue, about. $198.00

DAN WESSON MODEL 8-2 & MODEL 14-2
Caliber: 38 Special (Model 8-2); 357 (14-2), both 6-shot.
Barrel: 2½″, 4″, 6″, 8″; interchangeable.
Weight: 30 oz. (2½″). **Length:** 9¼″ over-all (4″ bbl.).
Stocks: Checkered, interchangeable.
Sights: ⅛″ serrated front, fixed rear.
Features: Interchangeable barrels and grips; smooth, wide trigger; wide hammer spur with short double action travel. Available in stainless or brite blue. Contact Dan Wesson for complete price list.
Price: Model 8-2, 2½″, blue $219.50
Price: As above except in stainless $253.63
Price: Model 14-2, 4″, blue $225.05
Price: As above except in stainless $259.15
Price: Model 14-2 Pistol Pac, stainless $430.65

Consult our Directory pages for the location of firms mentioned.

Dan Wesson 9-2 & 15-2 Revolvers
Same as Models 8-2 and 14-2 except they have adjustable sight. Model 9-2 chambered for 38 Special, Model 15-2 for 357 Magnum. Available in blue or stainless. Contact Dan Wesson for complete price list.
Price: Model 9-2 or 15-2, 2½″, blue $272.50
Price: As above except in stainless $306.55
Price: Model 15-2, 8″, blue. $297.90
Price: As above, with 15″ barrel, blue. $365.25

Dan Wesson Model 15-2

DAN WESSON MODEL 22 REVOLVER
Caliber: 22 LR, 22 Mag., six-shot.
Barrel: 2½", 4", 6", 8", 10"; interchangeable.
Weight: 36 oz. (2½"), 44 oz. (6"). **Length:** 9¼" over-all (4" barrel).
Stocks: Checkered; undercover, service or over-size target.
Sights: ⅛" serrated, interchangeable front, white outline rear adjustable for windage and elevation.
Features: Built on the same frame as the Dan Wesson 357; smooth, wide trigger with over-travel adjustment, wide spur hammer, with short double-action travel. Available in brite blue or stainless steel. Contact Dan Wesson for complete price list.
Price: 2½" bbl., blue **$272.50**
Price: As above, stainless **$306.55**
Price: With 4", vent. rib, blue **$301.10**
Price: As above, stainless **$335.10**
Price: Stainless Pistol Pac, 22 LR. **$598.55**

Dan Wesson 22

DAN WESSON MODEL 41V & MODEL 44V
Caliber: 41 Mag., 44 Mag., six-shot.
Barrel: 4", 6", 8", 10"; interchangeable.
Weight: 48 oz. (4"). **Length:** 12" over-all (6" bbl.).
Stocks: Smooth.
Sights: ⅛" serrated front, white outline rear adjustable for windage and elevation.
Features: Available in blue or stainless steel. Smooth, wide trigger with adjustable over-travel; wide hammer spur. Available in Pistol Pac set also.
Price: 41 Mag., 4", blue **$373.40**
Price: As above except in stainless **$416.05**
Price: 44 Mag., 4", blue, with extra unported barrel **$397.85**
Price: As above except in stainless **$440.15**

Dan Wesson 44 Magnum

HANDGUNS—SINGLE ACTION REVOLVERS

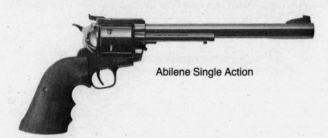

Abilene Single Action

COLT SINGLE ACTION ARMY REVOLVER
Caliber: 357 Magnum, 44 Spec., 44-40, or 45 Colt, 6 shot.
Barrel: 4¾", 5½", 7½" or 12".
Weight: 37 oz. (5½" bbl.). **Length:** 10⅞" (5½" bbl.)
Stocks: Black composite rubber with eagle and shield crest.
Sights: Fixed. Grooved top strap, blade front.
Features: See Colt catalog for variations and prices. Only basic models and prices listed here.
Price: Blued and case hardened 4¾", 5½" bbl., 44 Spec., 45 Colt... **$604.95**
Price: Nickel with walnut stocks **$700.95**
Price: With 7½" bbl., blue, 45 Colt **$620.50**

Colt Single Action Army—New Frontier
Same specifications as standard Single Action Army except: flat-top frame; high polished finish, blue and case colored; ramp front sight and target rear adj. for windage and elevation; smooth walnut stocks with silver medallion, or composition grips.
Price: 44 Special, 5½", blue.................................. **$700.95**
Price: 44 Special, 7½", blue.................................. **$720.50**
Price: 45 Colt, 4¾", blue.................................... **$700.50**
Price: 45 Colt, 7½", blue.................................... **$719.95**

ABILENE SINGLE ACTION REVOLVER
Caliber: 357 Mag., 44 Mag., 45 Colt, 6 shot.
Barrel: 4⅝", 6", 7½", 10" (44 Mag. only).
Weight: About 48 oz.
Stocks: Smooth walnut.
Sights: Serrated ramp front, click adj. rear for w. and e.
Features: Wide hammer spur. Blue or Magnaloy finish. From Mossberg.
Price: .... **NA**

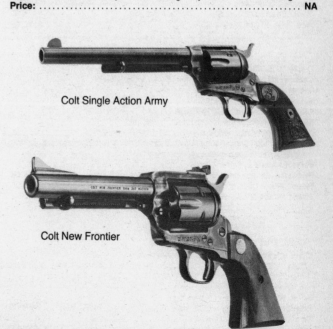

Colt Single Action Army

Colt New Frontier

COLT NEW FRONTIER 22
Caliber: 22 LR, 6-shot.
Barrel: 4¾", 6", 7½".
Weight: 29½ oz. (4¾" bbl.). **Length:** 9⅝" over-all.
Stocks: Black composite rubber.
Sights: Ramp-style front, fully adjustable rear.
Features: Cross-bolt safety. Color case-hardened frame. Available in blue only. Re-introduced 1982.
Price: 4¾", blue $276.95
Price: 6", blue $278.95
Price: 7½", blue $280.95

EMF Dakota SA

F.I.E. TEXAS RANGER REVOLVER
Caliber: 22 LR, 22 Mag.
Barrel: 4¾", 7", 9",.
Weight: 31 oz. (4¾" bbl.). **Length:** 10" over-all.
Stocks: Stained hardwood.
Sights: Blade front, notch rear.
Features: Single-action, blue/black finish. Introduced 1983. Made in the U.S. by F.I.E.
Price: 22 LR, 4¾" $59.95
Price: As above, combo (22 LR/22 Mag.) $74.95
Price: 22 LR, 7" $67.95
Price: As above, combo (22 LR/22 Mag.) $84.95
Price: 22 LR, 9" $74.95
Price: As above, combo (22 LR/22 Mag.) $89.95

F.I.E. "HOMBRE" SINGLE ACTION REVOLVER
Caliber: 357 Mag., 44 Mag., 45 LC.
Barrel: 5½" or 7½".
Weight: 45 oz. (5½" bbl.).
Stocks: Smooth walnut with medallion.
Sights: Blade front, grooved topstrap (fixed) rear.
Features: Color case hardened frame. Bright blue finish. Super-smooth action. Introduced 1979. Imported from West Germany by F.I.E. Corp.
Price: 357, 45 Colt $179.95
Price: 44 Mag. $199.95

F.I.E. E15 BUFFALO SCOUT REVOLVER
Caliber: 22 LR/22 Mag., 6-shot.
Barrel: 4¾".
Weight: 32 oz. **Length:** 10" over-all.
Stocks: Black checkered nylon, walnut optional.
Sights: Blade front, fixed rear.
Features: Slide spring ejector. Blue, chrome or blue with brass backstrap and trigger guard models available.
Price: Blued, 22 LR, 4¾" $59.95
Price: Blue, 22 combo, 4¾" $74.95
Price: Chrome or blue/brass, 22 LR, 4¾" $74.95
Price: Chrome or blue/brass, combo, 4¾" $89.95

FREEDOM ARMS 454 CASULL
Caliber: 454 Casull, 5-shot.
Barrel: 7½", 10", 12".
Weight: 50 oz. **Length:** 14" over-all (7½" bbl.).
Stocks: Smooth hardwood.
Sights: Blade front, notch rear.
Features: All stainless steel construction; sliding bar safety system. Made in U.S.A.
Price: $695.00

DAKOTA SINGLE ACTION REVOLVERS
Caliber: 22 LR, 22 Mag., 357 Mag., 30 Carbine, 44-40, 45 Colt.
Barrel: 3½", 4⅝", 5½", 7½", 12", 16¼".
Weight: 45 oz. **Length:** 13" over-all (7½" bbl.).
Stocks: Smooth walnut.
Sights: Blade front, fixed rear.
Features: Colt-type hammer with firing pin, color case-hardened frame, blue barrel and cylinder, brass grip frame and trigger guard. Available in blue or nickel plated, plain or engraved. Imported by E.M.F.
Price: 22 LR, 30 Car., 357, 44-40, 45 L.C., 4⅝", 5½", 7½".......... $295.00
Price: 22 LR/22 Mag. Combo, 5½", 7½"...................... $330.00
Price: 357, 44-40, 45, 12".................................. $330.00
Price: 357, 44-40, 45, 3½".................................. $325.00

F.I.E. Texas Ranger

F.I.E. "LEGEND" SINGLE ACTION REVOLVER
Caliber: 22 LR/22 Mag.
Barrel: 4¾".
Weight: 32 oz.
Stocks: Smooth walnut or black checkered nylon. Walnut optional ($16.95).
Sights: Blade front, fixed rear.
Features: Positive hammer block system. Brass backstrap and trigger guard. Color case hardened steel frame, rest blued. Imported from Italy by F.I.E. Corp.
Price: 22LR.. $104.95
Price: 22 combo with walnut grips $136.95

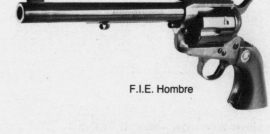

F.I.E. Hombre

Freedom 454 Casull

Freedom Arms Mini Revolver

FREEDOM ARMS MINI REVOLVER

Caliber: 22 Short, Long, Long Rifle, 5-shot, 22 Mag., 4-shot.
Barrel: 1", 1¾".
Weight: 4 oz. **Length:** 4" over-all.
Stocks: Black ebonite or simulated ivory.
Sights: Blade front, notch rear.
Features: Made of stainless steel, simple take down; half-cock safety; floating firing pin; cartridge rims recessed in cylinder. Comes in gun rug. Lifetime warranty. Also available in percussion — see black powder section. From Freedom Arms.
Price: 22 LR, 1" barrel **$131.50**
Price: 22 LR, 1¾" barrel **$136.50**
Price: 22 Mag., 1" barrel **$152.50**
Price: 22 Mag., 1¾" barrel **$152.50**

Freedom Arms Boot Gun

Similar to the Mini Revolver except has 3" barrel, weighs 5 oz. and is 5⅞" over-all. Has over-size grips, floating firing pin. Made of stainless steel. Lifetime warranty. Comes in rectangular gun rug. Introduced 1982. From Freedom Arms.
Price: 22 LR **$155.50**
Price: 22 Mag. **$176.50**

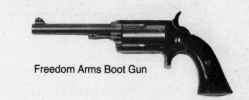

Freedom Arms Boot Gun

MITCHELL SINGLE ACTION REVOLVERS

Caliber: 22 LR/22 Mag., 357 Mag., 44 Mag., 44 Mag./44-40, 45 Colt.
Barrel: 4¾", 5½", 6", 7½", 10", 12", 18".
Weight: About 36 oz.
Stocks: One-piece walnut.
Sights: Ramp front, rear adj. for w. & e.
Features: Color case-hardened frame, grip frame is polished brass. Hammer block safety. Introduced 1980. From Mitchell Arms Corp.
Price: 22/22 Mag., 357, 44, 45, 4¾", 5½", 7½", fixed sights **$239.00**
Price: As above, adj. sights **$249.00**
Price: 44 Mag., 45 Colt, 10", 12", 18" bbl. **$295.00**
Price: Dual cyl., fixed sights **$259.00**
Price: Dual cyl., adj. sights **$275.00**
Price: Shoulder stock, for 18" bbl. only **$99.95**

Mitchell Single Action

NAM MINI REVOLVER

Caliber: 22 LR, 22 Mag., 5-shot
Barrel: 1⅛" (22 Short, LR), 1¼" (22 Mag.), 1⅝" (22 LR).
Weight: 4.5 oz. **Length:** 3.8" over-all.
Stocks: Smooth plastic; walnut on magnum model.
Sights: Blade front only.
Features: Stainless steel, single action only. Spur trugger. From North American Mfg. Corp.
Price: 22 Short **$116.50**
Price: 22 Long Rifle **$117.50**
Price: 22 Long Rifle, 1⅝" bbl. **$118.50**
Price: 22 Mag. **$134.50**

Ruger Super Single-Six

RUGER NEW MODEL SUPER SINGLE-SIX CONVERTIBLE REVOLVER

Caliber: 22 S, L, LR, 6-shot. 22 Mag. in extra cylinder.
Barrel: 4⅝", 5½", 6½" or 9½" (6-groove).
Weight: 34½ oz. (6½" bbl.). **Length:** 11¹³⁄₁₆" over-all (6½" bbl.).
Stocks: Smooth American walnut.
Sights: Improved patridge front on ramp, fully adj. rear protected by integral frame ribs.
Features: New Ruger "interlocked" mechanism, transfer bar ignition, gate-controlled loading, hardened chrome-moly steel frame, wide trigger, music wire springs throughout, independent firing pin.
Price: 4⅝", 5½", 6½", 9½" barrel **$195.00**
Price: 5½", 6½" bbl., stainless steel **$265.00**

Ruger New Model Blackhawk

RUGER NEW MODEL BLACKHAWK REVOLVER

Caliber: 357 or 41 Mag., 6-shot.
Barrel: 4⅝" or 6½", either caliber.
Weight: 42 oz. (6½" bbl.). **Length:** 12¼" over-all (6½" bbl.).
Stocks: American walnut.
Sights: ⅛" ramp front, micro click rear adj. for w. and e.
Features: New Ruger interlocked mechanism, independent firing pin, hardened chrome-moly steel frame, music wire springs throughout.
Price: Blue, 357 .... **$237.50**
Price: Stainless steel (357) **$307.50**

Ruger New Model 357/9mm Blackhawk

Same as the 357 Magnum except furnished with interchangeable cylinders for 9mm Parabellum and 357 Magnum cartridges.
Price: **$260.00**

Ruger New Model 30 Carbine Blackhawk

Specifications similar to 44 Blackhawk. Fluted cylinder, round-back trigger guard. Weight 44 oz., length 13⅛" over-all, 7½" barrel only.
Price: **$237.50**

CAUTION: PRICES CHANGE. CHECK AT GUNSHOP.

Ruger Super Blackhawk RMR

Ruger 357 Maximum

Ruger Stainless Super Blackhawk

Ruger New Model Super Blackhawk RMR

Similar to the standard N.M. Super Blackhawk except has 10½″ untapered bull barrel to provide extra weight; ejector rod and housing have been lengthened one inch to provide full-length ejection. Chambered only for 44 Mag.; target-type front and rear sights; smooth American walnut grips; weight is 54 oz. Introduced 1983.
Price: **$325.00**

Ruger New Model Blackhawk 357 Maximum

Similar to the standard N.M. Blackhawk except chambered for the 357 Maximum cartridge; available with either 7½″ or 10½″ bull barrel; weight with 7½″ is 53 oz., with 10½″ 55 oz.; over-all length with 10½″ barrel is 16⅞″. Introduced 1983.
Price: **$340.00**

RUGER NEW MODEL SUPER BLACKHAWK STAINLESS

Caliber: 44 Magnum, 6-shot. Also fires 44 Spec.
Barrel: 7½″ (6-groove, 20″ twist), 10½″.
Weight: 48 oz. (7½″ bbl.) 51 oz. (10½″ bbl.). **Length:** 13⅜″ over-all (7½″ bbl.).
Stocks: Genuine American walnut.
Sights: ⅛″ ramp front, micro click rear adj. for w. and e.
Features: New Ruger interlocked mechanism, non-fluted cylinder, steel grip and cylinder frame, square back trigger guard, wide serrated trigger and wide spur hammer.
Price: **$325.00**

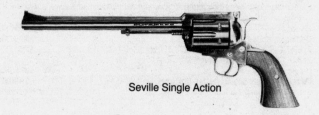

Seville Single Action

SEVILLE SINGLE ACTION REVOLVER

Caliber: 357 Mag., 9mm Win. Mag., 41 Mag., 44 Mag., 45 ACP, 45 Colt, 45 Win. Mag.
Barrel: 4⅝″, 5½″, 6½″, 7½″.
Weight: 52 oz. (4⅝″, loaded)
Stocks: Smooth walnut, thumbrest, or Pachmayr.
Sights: Ramp front with red insert, fully adj. rear.
Features: Available in blue or stainless steel. Six-shot cylinder. From United Sporting Arms of Arizona, Inc.
Price: Blue. **$300.00**
Price: Blue with brass backstrap **$320.00**
Price: Stainless, all cals. **$375.00**
Price: With "Quick Kit" bbl./caliber conversion, blue **$450.00**
Price: As above, stainless **$590.00**

Seville Stainless Super Mag

Similar to the standard Seville revolver except chambered for 357 Rem. Maximum, or 454 Magnum; 7½″ or 10½″ barrel only; grips of mesquite wood or Pachmayr rubber. Available only in stainless steel. Introduced 1983.
Price: 357 Maximum **$400.00**
Price: 454 Magnum **$500.00**

Seville Sheriff Model

SEVILLE SHERIFF'S MODEL S.A. REVOLVER

Caliber: 44-40, 44 Mag., 45 ACP, 45 Colt.
Barrel: 3½″.
Weight: 45 oz. (loaded).
Stocks: Smooth walnut. Square butt or birdshead style.
Sights: Sq. butt—ramp front, adj. rear; birdshead—blade front, fixed rear.
Features: Blue or stainless steel. Six-shot cylinder. Available with square or birdshead grip style. From United Sporting Arms of Arizona, Inc.
Price: Blue. **$300.00**
Price: Stainless steel. **$375.00**
Price: With "Quick Kit" bbl./caliber conversion, blue **$450.00**
Price: As above, stainless **$590.00**

TANARMI S.A. REVOLVER MODEL TA22S LM

Caliber: 22 LR, 22 Mag., 6-shot.
Barrel: 4¾″.
Weight: 32 oz. **Length:** 10″ over-all.
Stocks: Walnut.
Sights: Blade front, rear adj. for w. & e.
Features: Manual hammer block safety; color hardened steel frame; brass backstrap and trigger guard. Imported from Italy by Excam.
Price: 22 LR., target signts. **$105.00**
Price: 22 Mag. **$115.00**

TANARMI SINGLE ACTION MODEL TA76

Same as TA22 models except blue backstrap and trigger guard.
Price: 22 LR, blue **$67.00**
Price: Combo, blue **$81.00**
Price: 22 LR, chrome **$75.00**
Price: Combo, chrome **$89.00**

CAUTION: PRICES CHANGE. CHECK AT GUNSHOP.

Virginian Dragoon

THE VIRGINIAN DRAGOON REVOLVER
Caliber: 357 Mag., 41 Mag., 44 Mag., 45 Colt.
Barrel: 44 Mag., 6″, 7½″, 8⅜″; 357 Mag. and 45 Colt, 5″, 6″, 7½″.
Weight: 50 oz. (6″ barrel). **Length:** 10″ over-all (6″ barrel).
Stocks: Smooth walnut.
Sights: Ramp-type Patridge front blade, micro. adj. target rear.
Features: Color case-hardened frame, spring-loaded floating firing pin, coil main spring. Firing pin is lock-fitted with a steel bushing. Introduced 1977. Made in the U.S. by Interarms Industries, Inc.
Price: 6″, 7½″, 8⅜″, blue.. **$295.00**
Price: 44 Mag., 45 Colt, 6″, 7½″, 8⅜″, stainless.................. **$295.00**
Price: 41 Mag., 44 Mag., 10½″ Sil. model...................... **$425.00**

Virginian Dragoon "Deputy" Model
Similar to the standard Dragoon except comes with traditional fixed sights, blue or stainless, in 357, 44 Mag. or 45 Colt. Introduced 1983.
Price: **$285.00**

VIRGINIAN 22 CONVERTIBLE REVOLVERS
Caliber: 22 LR, 22 Mag.
Barrel: 5½″.
Weight: 38 oz. **Length:** 10¾″ over-all.
Stocks: Smooth walnut.
Sights: Ramp-type Patridge front, open fully adjustable rear.
Features: Smaller version of the big-bore Dragoon revolvers; comes with both Long Rifle and Magnum cylinders, the latter unfluted; color case-hardened frame, rest blued. Introduced 1983. Made by Uberti; imported from Italy by Interarms.
Price: Blue, with two cylinders................................. **$230.00**
Price: Stainless with two cylinders **$260.00**

Virginian 357 Single Action Revolver
A slightly smaller frame version of the Dragoon revolver. Offered only in 357 Magnum with 7½″ barrel; 13½″ over-all length, 46 oz. weight. Available in stainless steel or blue with color case-hardened frame; smooth walnut stocks; adjustable rear sight. Made in Italy by Uberti. Introduced 1983. Imported by Interarms.
Price: Blue **$230.00**
Price: Stainless **$260.00**

Virginian Dragoon Engraved Models
Same gun as the standard Dragoon except offered only in 44 Mag. or 45 Colt, 6″ or 7½″ barrel; choice of fluted or unfluted cylinder, stainless or blued. Hand-engraved frame, cylinder and barrel. Each gun comes in a felt-lined walnut presentation case. Introduced 1983.
Price: **$625.00**

Virginian 22 Convertible

> Consult our Directory pages for the location of firms mentioned.

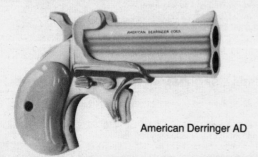

American Derringer AD

CLASSIC ARMS TWISTER
Caliber: 9mm Rimfire.
Barrel: 3¼″.
Weight: 18 oz.
Stocks: Pearlite.
Sights: None.
Features: Over-under barrels rotate on an axis for two separate shots. Spur trigger. 9mm Rimfire ammunition available. Made in U.S. by Classic Arms Ltd.
Price: **$84.95**

AMERICAN DERRINGER MODEL AD
Caliber: 22 LR, 22 Mag., 223 Rem., 25 ACP, 250 Mag., 32 Long, 32 ACP, 38 Super, 380 ACP, 38 Spec., 9 × 18, 9mm Para., 357 Mag., 41 Mag., 44-40 Win., 44 Spec., 44 Mag., 45 Colt, 45 ACP.
Barrel: 3″.
Weight: 15½ oz. (38 Spec.). **Length:** 4.82″ over-all.
Stocks: Rosewood, Zebra wood, or plastic ivory.
Sights: Blade front.
Features: Made of stainless steel with high-polish finish. Two shot capacity. Manual hammer block safety. Introduced 1980. From American Derringer Corp.
Price: 22 LR or Mag.. **$187.50**
Price: 223 Rem. or 22 Jet.................................... **$275.00**
Price: 38 Spec... **$197.50**
Price: 357 Mag. **$212.50**
Price: 9mm, 380, 38 Super **$212.00**
Price: 44 Spec... **$250.00**
Price: 44-40 Win., 45 ACP, 45 Colt **$275.00**
Price: 41, 44 Mags. **$369.00**
Price: Lightweight (7 oz.) model, 38 Spec. only **$187.50**
Price: 41, 44 Mag. single-shot (wgt. 18 oz.), rosewood grips....... **$250.00**

C. O. P. 357 MAGNUM
Caliber: 38/357 Mag., 4 shots.
Barrel: 3¼".
Weight: 28 oz. **Length:** 5.5" over-all.
Stocks: Checkered composition.
Sights: Open, fixed.
Features: Double-action, 4 barrels, made of stainless steel. Width is only one inch, height 4.1". From M & N Distributors.
Price: About $250.00
Price: In 22 Mag. $250.00
Price: In 22 LR (blued, aluminum frame) $229.95

CLASSIC ARMS SOUTHERN DERRINGER
Caliber: 22 LR or 41 Rimfire.
Barrel: 2½".
Weight: 12 oz. **Length:** 5" over-all.
Stocks: White plastic.
Sights: Blade front.
Features: Single-shot, spur-trigger derringer. Brass frame, steel barrel. The 41 RF ammunition is available from Navy Arms. Introduced in 1982. Made in U.S. by Classic Arms Ltd.
Price: Either caliber $84.95

HIGH STANDARD DERRINGER
Caliber: 22 LR, 22 Mag., 2 shot.
Barrel: 3½", over and under, rifled.
Weight: 11 oz. **Length:** 5" over-all.
Stocks: Smooth plastic.
Sights: Fixed, open.
Features: Hammerless, integral safety hammerblock, all steel unit is encased in a black, anodized alloy housing. Recessed chamber. Dual extraction. Top break, double action.
Price: Blue (M9194) $155.00
Price: Blue (M9193), 22 LR $155.00
Price: Electroless nickel (M9420), 22 Mag. $207.00

F.I.E. MODEL D-38 DERRINGER
Caliber: 38 Special.
Barrel: 3".
Weight: 14 oz.
Stocks: Checkered white nylon, walnut optional.
Sights: Fixed.
Features: Chrome finish. Spur trigger. Tip-up barrel, extractors. Made in U.S. by F.I.E. Corp.
Price: With nylon grips $81.95
Price: With walnut grips $98.95

LJUTIC LJ II PISTOL
Caliber: 22 Magnum.
Barrel: 2¾".
Stocks: Checkered walnut.
Sights: Fixed.
Features: Stainless steel; double action; ventilated rib; side-by-side barrels; positive on/off safety. Introduced 1981. From Ljutic Industries.
Price: $499.00

ARM TECH. DERRINGER
Caliber: 22 LR, 22 Mag., 4-shot.
Barrel: 2.6".
Weight: 19 ozs. **Length:** 4.6" over-all.
Stocks: Hard rubber or walnut, checkered or smooth.
Sights: Fixed, non-snagging.
Features: Four barrels with 90° rotating-indexing firing pin system. All stainless steel parts. Double-action only. Blued model available. Introduced 1983. From Armament Technologies Inc.
Price: Stainless, 22 LR, rubber grips $184.50
Price: As above, 22 Mag. $189.00
Price: Blued, 22 LR, walnut grips $174.50
Price: As above, 22 Mag. $179.00

High Standard Derringer

Ljutic LJ II Pistol

LJUTIC RECOILESS SPACE PISTOL
Caliber: 22 Mag., 357 Mag., 44 Mag., 308 Win.; single shot.
Barrel: 13½".
Weight: 5 lbs. (with scope).
Stocks: Walnut grip and fore-end.
Sights: Scope mounts furnished.
Features: Twist-bolt action; button trigger. From Ljutic Industries.
Price: $895.00

MERRILL SPORTSMAN'S SINGLE SHOT PISTOL
Caliber: 22 LR Sil., 22 Mag., 22 Hornet, 256 Win. Mag., 357 Mag., 357/44 B & D, 30-30 Win., 30 Herrett, 357 Herrett, 41 Mag., 44 Mag., 7mm Merrill, 30 Merrill, 7mm Rocket.
Barrel: 9" or 10¾", semi-octagonal; .450" wide vent. rib, matted to prevent glare; 14" barrel in all except 22 cals.
Weight: About 54 oz. **Length:** 10½" over-all (9" bbl.)
Stocks: Smooth walnut with thumb and heel rest.
Sights: Front .125" blade (.080" blade optional); rear adj. for w. and e.
Features: Polished blue finish, hard chrome optional. Barrel is drilled and tapped for scope mounting. Cocking indicator visible from rear of gun. Has spring-loaded barrel lock, positive thumb safety. Trigger adjustable for weight of pull and over-travel. For complete price list contact Rock Pistol Mfg.
Price: 9" barrel, about $575.00
Price: 10¾", 22 Sil., about $575.00
Price: 10¾" barrel, about $575.00
Price: 14" barrel, about $675.00
Price: Extra barrel, 9", 10¾", about $185.00
Price: Extra 14" bbl., about $250.00

Ljutic Space Pistol

CAUTION: PRICES CHANGE. CHECK AT GUNSHOP.

MITCHELL'S DERRINGER
Caliber: 38 Spec.
Barrel: 2¾"
Weight: 11 oz. **Length:** 5¼" over-all.
Stocks: Walnut, checkered.
Sights: Fixed, ramp front.
Features: Polished blue finish. All steel. Made in U.S. Introduced 1980. From Mitchell Arms Corp.
Price: **$149.95**

Mitchell's Derringer

Remington XP-100

STERLING X-CALIBER SINGLE SHOT
Caliber: 22, 22 Mag., 357 Mag., 44 Mag.
Barrel: 8" or 10", interchangeable.
Weight: 52 oz. (8" bbl.). **Length:** 13" over-all (8" bbl.).
Stocks: Goncolo Alves.
Sights: Patridge front, fully adj. rear.
Features: Barrels are drilled and tapped for scope mounting; hammer is notched for easy cocking with scope mounted. Finger grooved grip.
Price: Any caliber listed **$249.95**

TANARMI O/U DERRINGER
Caliber: 38 Special.
Barrel: 3".
Weight: 14 oz. **Length:** 4¾" over-all.
Stocks: Checkered white nylon.
Sights: Fixed.
Features: Blue finish; tip-up barrel. Assembled in U.S. by Excam, Inc.
Price: **$75.00**

Thompson-Center Contender

MAXIMUM SINGLE SHOT PISTOL
Caliber: 223, 22-250, 6mm BR, 243, 250 Savage, 7mm BR, 7mm TCU, 7mm-08, 30 Herrett, 308 Win.
Barrel: 10½", 14".
Weight: 61 oz. (10½" bbl.), 78 oz. (14" bbl.). **Length:** 15", 18½" over-all (with 10½" and 14" bbl., respectively).
Stocks: Smooth walnut stocks and fore-end.
Sights: Ramp front, fully adjustable open rear.
Features: Falling block action; drilled and tapped for most popular scope mounts; integral grip frame/receiver; adjustable trigger; Douglas barrel (interchangeable); Armoloy finish. Introduced 1983. Made in U.S. by M.O.A. Corp.
Price: Either barrel length **$499.00**

REMINGTON MODEL XP-100 Bolt Action Pistol
Caliber: 221 Fireball, single shot.
Barrel: 10½", ventilated rib.
Weight: 60 oz. **Length:** 16¾".
Stock: Brown nylon one-piece, checkered grip with white spacers.
Sights: Fixed front, rear adj. for w. and e. Tapped for scope mount.
Features: Fits left or right hand, is shaped to fit fingers and heel of hand. Grooved trigger. Rotating thumb safety, cavity in fore-end permits insertion of up to five 38 cal., 130-gr. metal jacketed bullets to adjust weight and balance. Included is a black vinyl, zippered case.
Price: Including case **$338.95**

SEMMERLING LM-4 PISTOL
Caliber: 45 ACP.
Barrel: 3½".
Weight: 24 oz. **Length:** 5.2" over-all.
Stocks: Checkered black plastic.
Sights: Ramp front, fixed rear.
Features: Manually operated repeater. Over-all dimensions are 5.2" x 3.7" x 1". Has a four-shot magazine capacity. Comes with manual, leather carrying case, spare stock screw and wrench. From Semmerling Corp.
Price: Complete **$894.00**
Price: Thin Version (blue sideplate instead of grips) **$894.00**

Sterling X-Caliber

THOMPSON-CENTER ARMS CONTENDER
Caliber: 221 Rem., 7mm T.C.U., 30-30 Win., 22 S, L, LR, 22 Mag., 22 Hornet, 256 Win., 6.5 T.C.U., 223 Rem., 30 & 357 Herrett, 357 Mag., also 222 Rem., 41 Mag., 44 Mag., 45 Long Colt, 45 Win. Mag., single shot.
Barrel: 10", tapered octagon, bull barrel and vent. rib.
Weight: 43 oz. (10" bbl.). **Length:** 13¼" (10" bbl.).
Stocks: Select walnut grip and fore-end, with thumb rest. Right or left hand.
Sights: Under cut blade ramp front, rear adj. for w. & e.
Features: Break open action with auto-safety. Single action only. Interchangeable bbls., both caliber (rim & centerfire), and length. Drilled and tapped for scope. Engraved frame. See T/C catalog for exact barrel/caliber availability.
Price: Blued (rimfire cals.) **$265.00**
Price: Blued (centerfire cals.) **$265.00**
Price: Extra bbls. (standard octagon) **$110.00**
Price: Bushnell Phantom scope base **$8.75**
Price: 357 and 44 Mag. vent. rib, internal choke bbl. **$125.00**

AKM Auto Rifle

AKM AUTO RIFLE
Caliber: 7.62x39, 30-shot magazine.
Barrel: 16.33".
Weight: 6.4lbs. **Length:** 34.65" over-all.
Stock: Laminated hardwood. Checkered composition pistol grip.
Sights: Protected post front, U-notch rear adjustable for elevation.
Features: Semi-auto only. Detachable box magazine. Cleaning kit, bayonet and scabbard, and sling available. Introduced to U.S. market 1982. Imported from Egypt by Steyr Daimler Puch.
Price: Standard rifle...$995.00

Auto Ordnance 27 A-1

AUTO-ORDNANCE MODEL 27 A-1
Caliber: 45 ACP, 30-shot magazine.
Barrel: 16".
Weight: 11½ lbs. **Length:** About 39½" over-all (Deluxe).
Stock: Walnut stock and vertical fore-end.
Sights: Blade front, open rear adj. for w.
Features: Re-creation of Thompson Model 1927. Semi-auto only. Deluxe model has finned barrel, adj. rear sight and compensator; Standard model has plain barrel and military sight. From Auto-Ordnance Corp.
Price: Deluxe..$489.95
Price: Standard...$469.95
Price: 1927A5 Pistol (M27A1 without stock; wgt. 7 lbs.)............$469.95
Price: Lightweight model......................................$469.95

Auto-Ordnance 1927A-3
A 22 caliber version of the 27A-1. Exact look-alike with alloy receiver. Weight is about 7 lbs., 16" finned barrel, 10-, 30- and 50-shot magazines and drum. Introduced 1977. From Auto-Ordnance Corp.
Price: $449.65

Bushmaster Auto Rifle

BUSHMASTER AUTO RIFLE
Caliber: 223; 30-shot magazine
Barrel: 18½".
Weight: 6¼ lbs. **Length:** 37.5" over-all.
Stock: Rock maple
Sights: Protected post front adj. for elevation, protected quick-flip rear peep adj. for windage; short and long range.
Features: Steel alloy upper receiver with welded barrel assembly, AK-47-type gas system, aluminum lower receiver; silent sling and swivels; bayonet lug; one-piece welded steel alloy bolt carrier assembly. From Bushmaster Firearms.
Price: With maple stock.......................................$484.95
Price: With nylon-coated folding stock..........................$494.95
Price: Matte electroless finish, maple stock.....................$524.95
Price: As above, folding stock.................................$534.95

Colt AR-15 Sporter

COLT AR-15 SPORTER
Caliber: 223 Rem.
Barrel: 20".
Weight: 7½ lbs. **Length:** 38⅜" over-all.
Stock: Reinforced polycarbonate with buttstock stowage compartment.
Sights: Post front, rear adj. for w. and e.
Features: 5-round detachable box magazine, recoil pad, flash suppressor, sling swivels.
Price: $560.50
Price: With 3x scope...$738.50

CAUTION: PRICES CHANGE. CHECK AT GUNSHOP.

CENTERFIRE RIFLES—MILITARY STYLE AUTOLOADERS

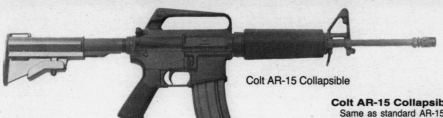

Colt AR-15 Collapsible

Colt AR-15 Collapsible Stock Model
Same as standard AR-15 except has telescoping nylon-coated aluminum buttstock and redesigned fore-end. Over-all length collapsed is 32″, extended 39″. Barrel length is 16″, weight is 5.8 lbs. Has 14½″ sight radius. Introduced 1978.
Price: **$614.50**
Price: With 3x scope **$792.50**

COMMANDO ARMS CARBINE
Caliber: 9mm or 45 ACP.
Barrel: 16½″.
Weight: 8 lbs. **Length:** 37″ over-all.
Stock: Walnut buttstock.
Sights: Blade front, peep rear.
Features: Semi-auto only. Cocking handle on left side. Choice of magazines—5, 15, 30 or 90 shot. From Commando Arms.
Price: Mark 9 or Mark 45, blue **$210.00**
Price: Nickel plated **$240.00**

> Consult our Directory pages for the location of firms mentioned.

DEMRO TAC-1M CARBINE
Caliber: 9mm (32-shot magazine), 45 ACP (30-shot magazine).
Barrel: 16⅞″.
Weight: 7¾ lbs. **Length:** 35¾″ over-all.
Stock: American walnut, removable.
Sights: Removable blade front, open rear adjustable for w. & e.
Features: Fires from open bolt. Thumb safety, integral muzzle brake. From Demro Products.
Price: **$523.25**
Price: With fitted attache case **$575.40**

Demro TAC-1M

Demro XF-7 Wasp

Demro XF-7 Wasp Carbine
Similar to the TAC-1 Carbine except has collapsible buttstock, high impact synthetic fore-end and pistol grip. Has 5, 15 or 30-shot magazine (45 ACP) or 32-shot magazine (9mm).
Price: **$619.20**
Price: With fitted attache case **$685.60**

FN-LAR Competition

FN-LAR COMPETITION AUTO
Caliber: 308 Win., 20-shot magazine.
Barrel: 21″ (24″ with flash hider).
Weight: 9 lbs. 7 oz. **Length:** 44½″ over-all.
Stock: Black composition butt, fore-end and pistol grip.
Sights: Post front, aperture rear adj. for elevation, 200 to 600 meters.
Features: Has sling swivels, carrying handle, rubber recoil pad. Consecutively numbered pairs available at additional cost. Imported by Steyr Daimler Puch of America.
Price: **$1,659.00**

FN-LAR Heavy Barrel 308 Match
Similar to FN-LAR competition except has wooden stock and fore-end, heavy barrel, folding metal bipod. Imported by Steyr Daimler Puch.
Price: With wooden, stock.................................. **$2,198.00**
Price: With synthetic stock **$2,030.00**

FN 308 Model 44
Similar to the FN-LAR except has 18″ barrel, skeleton-type folding buttstock, folding cocking handle. Introduced 1982. Imported from Belgium by HOWCO Distr., Inc.
Price: **$1,595.00**

FN-LAR Paratrooper 308 Match
Similar to FN-LAR competition except with folding skeleton stock, shorter barrel, modified rear sight. Imported by Steyr Daimler Puch.
Price: **$1,754.00**

CENTERFIRE RIFLES—MILITARY STYLE AUTOLOADERS

FNC Auto Rifle

FNC AUTO RIFLE
Caliber: 223 Rem.
Barrel: 18".
Weight: 9.61 lbs.
Stock: Synthetic stock.
Sights: Post front; flip-over aperture rear adj. for elevation.
Features: Updated version of FN-FAL in shortened carbine form. Has 30-shot box magazine, synthetic pistol grip, fore-end. Introduced 1981. Imported by Steyr Daimler Puch.
Price: Standard model $1,326.70
Price: Paratrooper, with folding stock $1,438.40

FNC-11, 22, 33 Auto Rifles
Similar to the standard FNC except has 16⅛" barrel. Model 11 has folding metal stock; Model 22 has full synthetic stock; Model 33 has full wood stock. Introduced 1982. Imported from Belgium by HOWCO Distr., Inc.
Price: $1,095.00

Galil Auto Rifle

GALIL 308 SEMI-AUTO RIFLE
Caliber: 308 Win., 25-shot magazine.
Barrel: 21".
Weight: 8.7 lbs. **Length:** 41.3" over-all (stock extended).
Stock: Tube-type metal folding stock.
Sights: Post-type front, flip-type "L" rear.
Features: Gas operated, rotating bolt. Cocking handle, safety and magazine catch can be operated from either side. Introduced 1982. Imported from Israel by Magnum Research Inc.
Price: $1,499.00
Price: As above in 223 (18.1" bbl., 38.6" o.a.l.) $1,399.00

Heckler & Koch HK-91

HECKLER & KOCH HK-91 AUTO RIFLE
Caliber: 308 Win., 5- or 20-shot magazine.
Barrel: 19".
Weight: 9½ lbs. **Length:** 40¼" over-all.
Stock: Black high-impact plastic.
Sights: Post front, aperture rear adj. for w. and e.
Features: Delayed roller lock bolt action. Sporting version of West German service rifle. Takes special H&K clamp scope mount. Imported from West Germany by Heckler & Koch, Inc.
Price: HK-91 A-2 with plastic stock $640.00
Price: HK-91 A-3 with retractable metal stock $699.00
Price: HK-91 scope mount $180.00

Heckler & Koch HK-93 Auto Rifle
Similar to HK-93 except in 223 cal., 16.13" barrel, over-all length of 35½", weighs 7¾ lbs. Slight differences in stock, fore-end.
Price: HK-93 A-2 with plastic stock $640.00
Price: HK-93 A-3 with retractable metal stock $699.00

Heckler & Koch HK-94

HECKLER & KOCH HK-94 AUTO CARBINE
Caliber: 9mm Parabellum, 15-shot magazine.
Barrel: 16".
Weight: 6½ lbs. (fixed stock). **Length:** 34¾" over-all.
Stock: High-impact plastic butt and fore-end or retractable metal stock.
Sights: Hooded post front, aperture rear adjustable for windage and elevation.
Features: Delayed roller-locked action; accepts H&K quick-detachable scope mount. Introduced 1983. Imported from West Germany by Heckler & Koch.
Price: HK94-A2 (fixed stock) $650.00
Price: HK94-A3 (retractable metal stock) $720.00
Price: 30-shot magazine $25.00
Price: Clamp to hold two magazines $27.90

Iver Johnson Survival Carbine
Similar to the stainless steel military carbine except has one-piece muzzle brake/flash hider, black DuPont Zytel stock with vertical pistol grip. Introduced 1983.
Price: $330.00
Price: With folding stock $360.00
Price: In blue steel $250.00
Price: As above with folding stock $280.00

IVER JOHNSON'S PM30G CARBINE
Caliber: 30 U.S. Carbine, 5.7 MMJ.
Barrel: 18" four-groove.
Weight: 6½ lbs. **Length:** 35½" over-all.
Stock: Glossy-finished hardwood.
Sights: Click adj. peep rear.
Features: Gas operated semi-auto carbine. 15-shot detachable magazine.
Price: Blue finish $235.00
Price: Stainless steel $300.00
Price: Paratrooper model—with telescoping wire stock, front vertical hand grip, blue finish $260.00
Price: As above, stainless $330.00

CAUTION: PRICES CHANGE. CHECK AT GUNSHOP.

Ruger Mini-14

RUGER MINI-14 223 CARBINE
Caliber: 223 Rem., 5-shot detachable box magazine.
Barrel: 18½".
Weight: 6.4 lbs. **Length:** 37¼" over-all.
Stock: American hardwood, steel reinforced.
Sights: Ramp front, fully adj. rear.
Features: Fixed piston gas-operated, positive primary extraction. 10 and 20-shot magazines available from Ruger dealers, 30-shot magazine available only to police departments and government agencies.
Price: **$335.00**
Price: As above except in stainless steel. **$375.00**
Price: As above with integral dovetails to accept Ruger steel scope rings (illus.) **$362.50**

SIG-StG 57 AUTO RIFLE
Caliber: 308 Win., 20-shot detachable box magazine.
Barrel: 18¾".
Weight: 9½ lbs. **Length:** 39" over-all.
Stock: Walnut stock and fore-end, composition vertical p.g.
Sights: Adj. post front, adj. aperture rear.
Features: Roller-lock breech, gas-assisted action; right-side cocking handle; loaded chamber indicator; no-tool take-down. Winter trigger (optional) allows firing with mittens. Spare parts, magazine, etc. available. From Mandall Shooting Supplies.
Price: **$2,100.00**

> Consult our Directory pages for the location of firms mentioned.

Springfield Armory M1A

SPRINGFIELD ARMORY M1 GARAND RIFLE
Caliber: 30-06, 8-shot clip.
Barrel: 24".
Weight: 9½ lbs. **Length:** 43½" over-all.
Stock: Walnut, military.
Sights: Military square blade front, click adjustable peep rear.
Features: Commercially-made M-1 Garand duplicates the original service rifle. Introduced 1979. From Springfield Armory.
Price: Standard, about **$560.00**
Price: National Match, about **$670.00**
Price: Ultra Match, about **$760.00**

SPRINGFIELD ARMORY M1A RIFLE
Caliber: 7.62mm Nato (308), 5-, 10- or 20-round box magazine.
Barrel: 25¹⁄₁₆" with flash suppressor, 22" without suppressor.
Weight: 8¾ lbs. **Length:** 44¼" over-all.
Stock: American walnut or birch with walnut colored heat-resistant fiberglass handguard. Matching walnut handguard available.
Sights: Military, square blade front, full click-adjustable aperture rear.
Features: Commercial equivalent of the U.S. M-14 service rifle with no provision for automatic firing. From Springfield Armory. Military accessories available including 3x-9x2 ART scope and mount.
Price: Standard M1A Rifle, about **$650.00**
Price: Match Grade, about **$795.00**
Price: Super Match (heavy Premium barrel), about **$895.50**
Price: M1A-A1 Assault Rifle, about **$775.00**

Springfield Armory BM-59

SPRINGFIELD ARMORY BM-59
Caliber: 7.62mm NATO (308 Win.); 20-round box magazine.
Barrel: 17.5".
Weight: 9¼ lbs. **Length:** 38.5" over-all.
Stock: Walnut, with trapped rubber butt pad.
Sights: Military square blade front, click adj. peep rear.
Features: Full military-dress Italian service rifle. Available in selective fire or semi-auto only. Refined version of the M-1 Garand. Accessories available include: folding alpine stock, muzzle brake/flash suppressor/grenade launcher combo, bipod, winter trigger, grenade launcher sights, bayonet, oiler. Extremely limited quantities. Introduced 1981.
Price: Standard Italian model, about **$780.00**
Price: Ital-Alpine model, about **$940.00**
Price: Alpine Paratrooper model, about **$1,100.00**
Price: Nigerian Mark IV model, about.......................... **$875.00**

Sterling Mark 6 Carbine

STERLING MARK 6 CARBINE
Caliber: 9mm Parabellum, 34-shot magazine.
Barrel: 16.1".
Weight: 7½ lbs. **Length:** 35" over-all (stock extended), 27" folded.
Stock: Folding, metal skeleton.
Sights: Post front, flip-type peep rear.
Features: Semi-auto version of Sterling submachine gun. Comes with extra 8" display barrel. Black wrinkle finish paint on exterior. Blowback operation with floating firing pin. Imported from England by Lanchester U.S.A. Introduced 1983.
Price: **$648.00**

Steyr A.U.G. Rifle

STEYR A.U.G. AUTOLOADING RIFLE
Caliber: 223 Rem.
Barrel: 16", 20", 24", interchangeable.
Weight: 7.2 lbs. (16" bbl.). **Length:** 27" over-all (16" bbl.).
Stock: Synthetic, green. One-piece moulding houses receiver group, hammer mechanism and magazine.
Sights: 1.5x scope only; scope and mount form the carrying handle.
Features: Semi-automatic, gas-operated action; can be converted to suit right or left-handed shooters, including ejection port. Transparent 30- or 40-shot magazines. Folding vertical front grip. Introduced 1983. Imported from Austria by Steyr Daimler Puch of America.
Price: **$1,175.00**

Universal 1003 Carbine

UNIVERSAL 1003 AUTOLOADING CARBINE
Caliber: 30 M1, 5-shot magazine.
Barrel: 16", 18".
Weight: 5½ lbs. **Length:** 35½" over-all.
Stock: American hardwood stock inletted for "issue" sling and oiler, blued metal handguard.
Sights: Blade front with protective wings, adj. rear.
Features: Gas operated, cross lock safety. Receiver tapped for scope mounts.
Price: **$205.00**
Price: Model 1256 "Ferret" in 256 Win. **$228.00**
Price: Model 2566 "Ferret" stainless steel, 18" bbl. **$298.00**

Universal 1006 Carbine

Universal Model 1006 Stainless Steel Carbine
Similar to the Model 1003 Carbine except made of stainless steel. Barrel length 16" or 18". Weighs 6 lbs., birch stock with satin finish walnut optional. Introduced 1982.
Price: **$275.00**

Universal 5000 Carbine

Universal Model 5000PT Carbine
Same as standard Model 1003 except comes with "Schmeisser-type paratrooper" folding stock. Barrel length 18". Over-all length open 36"; folded 26".
Price: Blue. **$248.00**
Price: As above with 16" bbl. (Model 5016) **$248.00**
Price: As above, stainless steel (Model 5006) **$312.00**

Universal Model 1005 SB Carbine
Same as Model 1003 except has "Super-Mirrored" blue finish, walnut Monte Carlo stock, deluxe barrel band. Also available finished in nickel (Model 1010N), 18K gold (Model 1015G), Raven Black Du Pont Teflon-S (Model 1020TB) or Camouflage Olive Teflon-S (Model 1025TCO).
Price: Model 1005SB **$246.00**
Price: Model 1010N **$299.00**
Price: Model 1015G **$325.00**
Price: Model 1020TB 1030 Teflon gray **$279.00**

Universal Commemorative Model 1981 Carbine
Same basic specs as Model 1003 Carbine except comes with 5-, 15- and 30-shot magazines, Weaver scope and mount, bayonet and scabbard, brass belt buckle—all in a foam-fitted case. Stock is of select black walnut with inletted medallion. Metal parts are Parkerized. Introduced 1981.
Price: Complete **$650.00**

UZI Carbine

UZI CARBINE
Caliber: 9mm Parabellum, 25-round magazine.
Barrel: 16.1".
Weight: 8½ lbs. **Length:** 24.2" (stock folded).
Stock: Folding metal stock.
Sights: Post-type front, "L" flip-type rear adj. for 100 meters and 200 meters.
Features: Adapted by Col. Uzi Gal to meet BATF regulations, this semi-auto has the same qualities as the famous submachine gun. Made by Israel Military Industries. Comes in molded Styrofoam case with sling, magazine and a short "display only" barrel. Exclusively imported from Israel by Action Arms Ltd. Introduced 1980.
Price: **$627.00**

Valmet M76 Bullpup

VALMET M82 BULLPUP CARBINE
Caliber: 223, 15- or 30-shot magazine.
Barrel: 16.5".
Weight: 7¾ lbs. **Length:** 28" over-all.
Stock: High-impact resin composition.
Sights: Post front, peep rear; both sights off-set to the left.
Features: Semi-automatic only. Uses Kalishnikov AK action. Introduced 1982. Imported by Odin International.
Price: **$998.00**

Valmet M78 Rifle

VALMET M78 STANDARD RIFLE
Caliber: 7.62 x 39.
Barrel: 24".
Weight: 10.5 lbs. **Length:** 43" over-all.
Stock: Birch buttstock, composition fore-end and pistol grip.
Sights: Hooded post front, open fully adj. rear with "night sight" blade.
Features: Semi-automatic only. Uses basic Kalishnikov action. Introduced 1982. Imported by Odin International.
Price: **$1,495.00**

Valmet M78 (NATO) Semi-Auto Rifle
Similar to M78 Standard rifle except is chambered for 7.62 x 51 NATO (308 Win.). Has straight 20-round box magazine, rubber recoil pad, folding carrying handle. Introduced 1981. Imported by Odin International. Also available as M78HV chambered for 223. Same price.
Price: **$1,495.00**

Weaver Nighthawk

WEAVER ARMS NIGHTHAWK
Caliber: 9mm Para., 25-shot magazine.
Barrel: 16.1".
Weight: 8½ lbs. **Length:** 26½" (stock retracted).
Stock: Retractable metal frame.
Sights: Hooded bead front, adjustable open V rear.
Features: Semi-auto fire only; fires from a closed bolt. Has 21" sight radius. Black plastic pistol grip and finger-groove front grip. Matte black finish. Introduced 1983. From Weaver Arms Corp.
Price: With black web sling **$395.00**

Wilkinson "Terry"

WILKINSON "TERRY" CARBINE
Caliber: 9mm Para., 30-shot magazine.
Barrel: 16³⁄₁₆".
Weight: 7 lbs. 2 oz. **Length:** 28½" over-all.
Stock: Maple stock and fore-end, grip is PVC plastic.
Sights: Williams adjustable.
Features: Closed breech, blow-back action. Bolt-type safety and magazine catch. Ejection port has spring operated cover. Receiver dovetailed for scope mount. Semi-auto only. Introduced 1977. From Wilkinson Arms.
Price: **$488.00**

Browning Auto Rifle

Browning Magnum Auto Rifle

Same as the standard caliber model, except weighs 8⅜ lbs., 45″ over-all, 24″ bbl., 3-round mag. Cals. 7mm Mag., 300 Win. Mag.

Price: Grade I	$549.95
Price: Grade III	$1,160.00
Price: Grade IV	$2,150.00

Browning Commemorative BAR

Similar to the standard BAR except has silver grey receiver with engraved and gold inlaid whitetail deer on the right side, a mule deer on the left; a gold-edged scroll banner frames "One of Six Hundred" on the left side, the numerical edition number replaces "One" on the right. Chambered only in 30-06. Fancy, highly figured walnut stock and fore-end. Introduced 1983.

Price: $3,550.00

BROWNING HIGH-POWER AUTO RIFLE

Caliber: 243, 270, 30-06, 308.
Barrel: 22″ round tapered.
Weight: 7⅜ lbs. **Length:** 43″ over-all.
Stock: French walnut p.g. stock (13⅝″x2″x1⅝″) and fore-end, hand checkered.
Sights: Adj. folding-leaf rear, gold bead on hooded ramp front.
Features: Detachable 4-round magazine. Receiver tapped for scope mounts. Trigger pull 3½ lbs. Gold plated trigger on Grade IV. Imported from Belgium by Browning.

Price: Grade I	$499.95
Price: Grade III	$1,100.00
Price: Grade IV	$2,090.00

Heckler & Koch SL7

HECKLER & KOCH SL7 AUTO RIFLE

Caliber: 308 Win., 3-shot magazine.
Barrel: 17″.
Weight: 8 lbs. **Length:** 39¾″ over-all.
Stock: European walnut, oil finished.
Sights: Hooded post front, adjustable aperture rear.

Features: Delayed roller-locked action; polygon rifling; receiver is dovetailed for H&K quick-detachable scope mount. Introduced 1983. Imported from West Germany by Heckler & Koch.

Price:	$500.00
Price: Model SL6 (as above except in 223 Rem.)	$500.00
Price: Quick-detachable scope mount	$113.00
Price: 10-shot magazine	$24.00

HECKLER & KOCH HK770 AUTO RIFLE

Caliber: 308 Win., 3-shot magazine.
Barrel: 19.6″.
Weight: 7½ lbs. **Length:** 42.8″ over-all.
Stock: European walnut. Checkered p.g. and fore-end.
Sights: Vertically adjustable blade front, open, fold-down rear adj. for w.
Features: Has the delayed roller-locked bolt system and polygonal rifling. Magazine catch located at front of trigger guard. Receiver top is dovetailed to accept clamp-type scope mount. Imported from West Germany by Heckler & Koch, Inc.

Heckler & Koch HK770

Price:	$560.00
Price: HK630, 223 Rem.	$560.00
Price: HK940, 30-06	$580.00
Price: Scope mount with 1″ rings	$113.00

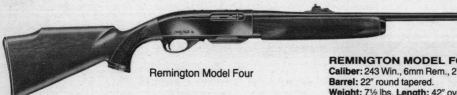

Remington Model Four

Remington Model 7400 Auto Rifle

Similar to Model Four except does not have full cheekpiece Monte Carlo stock, has slightly different fore-end design, impressed checkering, no cartridge head medallion. Introduced 1981.

Price: $461.95

REMINGTON MODEL FOUR AUTO RIFLE

Caliber: 243 Win., 6mm Rem., 270 Win., 7mm Exp. Rem., 308 Win. and 30-06.
Barrel: 22″ round tapered.
Weight: 7½ lbs. **Length:** 42″ over-all.
Stock: Walnut, deluxe cut checkered p.g. and fore-end. Full cheekpiece, Monte Carlo.
Sights: Gold bead front sight on ramp; step rear sight with windage adj.
Features: Redesigned and improved version of the Model 742. Positive cross-bolt safety. Receiver tapped for scope mount. 4-shot clip mag. Has cartridge head medallion denoting caliber on bottom of receiver. Introduced 1981.

Price:	$509.95
Price: Extra 4-shot clip magazine	$11.50

CAUTION: PRICES CHANGE. CHECK AT GUNSHOP.

CENTERFIRE RIFLES—SPORTING AUTOLOADERS

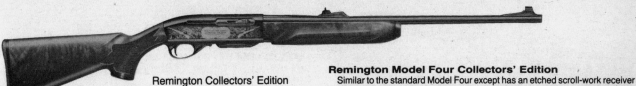

Remington Collectors' Edition

Remington Model Four Collectors' Edition

Similar to the standard Model Four except has an etched scroll-work receiver with 24K gold inlays; all metal parts are polished to a high-lustre finish. A cartridge head, denoting the rifle's 30-06 caliber is imbedded in the receiver. Stock and fore-end are specially matched high-grade walnut; fitted rosewood grip cap, brown butt pad. Serial numbers run from LE-81-001 thru LE-81-1500. Barrel length is 22″, blade-ramp front sight, adjustable sliding ramp rear sight. Only 1500 examples will be made. Introduced 1982.
Price: About. **$1,600.00**

Ruger 44 Carbine

RUGER 44 AUTOLOADING CARBINE

Caliber: 44 Magnum, 4-shot tubular magazine.
Barrel: 18½″ round tapered.
Weight: 5¾ lbs. **Length:** 36¾″ over-all.
Stock: One-piece walnut p.g. stock (13⅜″x1⅝″x2¼″).
Sights: 1/16″ front, folding leaf rear sight adj. for e.
Features: Wide, curved trigger. Sliding cross-bolt safety. Receiver tapped for scope mount, unloading button.
Price: **$332.00**

CENTERFIRE RIFLES—LEVER & SLIDE ACTIONS

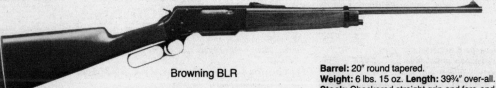

Browning B-92

BROWNING B-92 LEVER ACTION

Caliber: 357 Mag., 44 Rem. Mag., 11-shot magazine.
Barrel: 20″ round.

Weight: 5 lbs., 8 oz. **Length:** 37½″ over-all.
Stock: Straight grip stock and classic fore-end in French walnut with high gloss finish. Steel, modified crescent buttplate. (12¾″ x 2″ x 2⅞″).
Sights: Post front, classic cloverleaf rear with notched elevation ramp. Sight radius 16⅝″.
Features: Tubular magazine. Follows design of original Model 92 lever-action. Introduced 1979. Imported from Japan by Browning.
Price: **$324.95**

Browning BLR

BROWNING BLR LEVER ACTION RIFLE

Caliber: 22-250, 243, 257 Roberts, 7mm-08, 308 Win. or 358 Win. 4-shot detachable mag.

Barrel: 20″ round tapered.
Weight: 6 lbs. 15 oz. **Length:** 39¾″ over-all.
Stock: Checkered straight grip and fore-end, oil finished walnut.
Sights: Gold bead on hooded ramp front; low profile square notch adj. rear.
Features: Wide, grooved trigger; half-cock hammer safety. Receiver tapped for scope mount. Recoil pad installed. Imported from Japan by Browning.
Price: **$394.95**

Dixie Model 1873

DIXIE ENGRAVED MODEL 1873 RIFLE

Caliber: 44-40, 11-shot magazine.
Barrel: 20″, round.

Weight: 7¾ lbs. **Length:** 39″ over-all.
Stock: Walnut.
Sights: Blade front, adj. rear.
Features: Engraved and case hardened frame. Duplicate of Winchester 1873. Made in Italy. From Dixie Gun Works.
Price: **$550.00**
Price: Plain, blued carbine **$495.00**

Marlin Model 1894

MARLIN 1894 LEVER ACTION CARBINE
Caliber: 44 Magnum, 10-shot tubular magazine
Barrel: 20″ Micro-Grove®.
Weight: 6 lbs. **Length:** 37½″.
Stock: American black walnut, straight grip and fore-end. Mar-Shield® finish.
Sights: Hooded ramp front, semi-buckhorn folding rear adj. for w. & e.
Features: Receiver tapped for scope mount, offset hammer spur, solid top receiver sand blasted to prevent glare.
Price: **$262.95**
Price: Model 1894S (as above except has hammer safety) **$269.95**

Marlin Model 1894CS Carbine
Similar to the standard Model 1894S except chambered for 38 Special/357 Magnum with 9-shot magazine, 18½″ barrel, hammer block safety, brass bead front sight. Introduced 1983.
Price: **$269.95**

Marlin Model 1895S

MARLIN 1894C CARBINE 357
Caliber: 357 Magnum, 9-shot tube magazine.
Barrel: 18½″ Micro-Groove®.
Weight: 6 lbs. **Length:** 35½″ over-all.
Stock: American black walnut, straight grip and fore-end.
Sights: Bead front, adjustable semi-buckhorn folding rear.
Features: Solid top receiver tapped for scope mount or receiver sight; offset hammer spur. Receiver top sandblasted to prevent glare.
Price: About **$262.95**

MARLIN 1895S LEVER ACTION RIFLE
Caliber: 45-70, 4-shot tubular magazine.
Barrel: 22″ round.
Weight: 7½ lbs. **Length:** 40½″.
Stock: American black walnut, full pistol grip. Mar-Shield® finish; rubber butt-pad; q-d. swivels; leather carrying strap.
Sights: Bead front with Wide-Scan hood, semi-buckhorn folding rear adj. for w. and e.
Features: Solid receiver tapped for scope mounts or receiver sights, offset hammer spur.
Price: **$349.95**
Price: Model 1895SS (as above except has hammer safety) **$357.95**

Marlin Model 336ER

Marlin Model 336 Extra-Range Carbine
Similar to the standard Model 336 except chambered for 307 Win. or 356 Win.; has new hammer block safety, rubber butt pad, 5-shot magazine. Comes with detachable sling swivels and branded leather sling. Introduced 1983.
Price: **$291.95**

MARLIN 336C LEVER ACTION CARBINE
Caliber: 30-30 or 35 Rem., 6-shot tubular magazine
Barrel: 20″ Micro-Grove®.
Weight: 7 lbs. **Length:** 38½″.
Stock: Select American black walnut, capped p.g. with white line spacers. Mar-Shield® finish.
Sights: Ramp front with Wide-Scan™ hood, semi-buckhorn folding rear adj. for w. & e.
Features: Receiver tapped for scope mount, offset hammer spur; top of receiver sand blasted to prevent glare.
Price: Less scope **$249.95**
Price: Model 336CS (as above except has hammer safety) **$256.95**

Marlin Model 336T

Marlin 336T Lever Action Carbine
Same as the 336C except: straight stock; cal. 30-30 only. Squared finger lever, 18½″ barrel, weight 6¾ lbs.
Price: **$249.95**
Price: Model 336TS (as above except has hammer safety) **$256.95**

Marlin 30A Lever Action Carbine
Same as the Marlin 336C except: checkered walnut-finished hardwood p.g. stock, 30-30 only, 6-shot
Price: **$232.95**
Price: Model 30AS (as above except has hammer safety) **$239.95**

CAUTION: PRICES CHANGE. CHECK AT GUNSHOP.

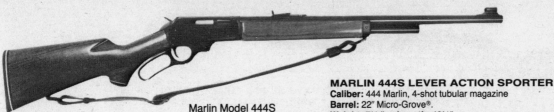

Marlin Model 444S

MARLIN 444S LEVER ACTION SPORTER
Caliber: 444 Marlin, 4-shot tubular magazine
Barrel: 22" Micro-Grove®.
Weight: 7½ lbs. **Length:** 40½".
Stock: American black walnut, capped p.g. with white line spacers, rubber rifle butt pad. Mar-Shield® finish; q.d. swivels, leather carrying strap.
Sights: Hooded ramp front, folding semi-buckhorn rear adj. for w. & e.
Features: Receiver tapped for scope mount, offset hammer spur, leather sling with detachable swivels.
Price: **$283.95**
Price: Model 444SS (as above except has hammer safety)......... **$291.95**

Marlin 375 Rifle
Similar to 444S except chambered for 375 Win., 5-shot magazine; 20" barrel; over-all length of 38½", weight of 6¾ lbs. Comes with adj. leather carrying strap and q.d. swivels
Price: **$283.95**

Mossberg Roy Rogers 479

MOSSBERG ROY ROGERS MODEL 479RR
Caliber: 30-30, 5-shot magazine.
Barrel: 18".
Weight: 6¾ lbs. **Length:** 36½" over-all.
Stock: American walnut.
Sights: Gold bead on ramp front, adjustable semi-buckhorn rear.
Features: Special edition to honor Roy Rogers and Trigger. Gold-finished trigger and barrel bands; Rogers' signature etched into right side of receiver, American eagle over stars and stripes crest on left side, both gold washed. Limited edition of 5,000 guns to be made. Introduced 1983.
Price: **$349.95**

MOSSBERG 479 PCA LEVER ACTION RIFLE
Caliber: 30-30, 6-shot.
Barrel: 20".
Weight: About 7 lbs. **Length:** 38½" over-all.
Stock: Walnut-finish hardwood.
Sights: Bead on ramp front, adjustable open rear.
Features: Blue finish; hammer block safety and rebounding hammer. Trigger built into the cocking lever. Ejection port on right side of receiver. Re-introduced 1983.
Price: About **$190.00**

NAVY ARMS HENRY CARBINE
Caliber: 44-40 or 44 rimfire.
Barrel: 21".
Weight: About 9 lbs. **Length:** About 39" over-all.
Stock: Oil stained American walnut.
Sights: Blade front, rear adj. for e.
Features: Reproduction of the original Henry carbine with brass frame and buttplate, rest blued. Will be produced in limited edition of 1,000 standard models, plus 50 engraved guns. Made in U.S. by Navy Arms.
Price: Standard **$500.00**
Price: Engraved **$1,500.00**

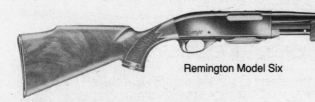

Remington Model Six

Stock: Cut-checkered walnut p.g. and fore-end, Monte Carlo with full cheekpiece.
Sights: Gold bead front sight on matted ramp, open step adj. sporting rear.
Features: Redesigned and improved version of the Model 760. Has cartridge head medallion denoting caliber on bottom of receiver. Detachable 4-shot clip. Cross-bolt safety. Receiver tapped for scope mount. Introduced 1981.
Price: **$453.95**
Price: Extra 4-shot clip **$10.75**

REMINGTON MODEL SIX SLIDE ACTION
Caliber: 6mm Rem., 243, 270, 308 Win., 30-06.
Barrel: 22" round tapered.
Weight: 7½ lbs. **Length:** 42" over-all.

Remington Model 7600

Remington Model 7600 Slide Action Rifle
Similar to Model Six except does not have Monte Carlo stock or cheekpiece, no cartridge head medallion. Slightly different fore-end design. Impressed checkering. Instroduced 1981.
Price: **$405.95**

ROSSI SADDLE-RING CARBINE
Caliber: 38 Spec., 357 Mag., 44-40, 44 Mag., 10-shot magazine.
Barrel: 20".
Weight: 5¾ lbs. **Length:** 37" over-all.
Stock: Walnut.
Sights: Blade front, buckhorn rear.
Features: Re-creation of the famous lever-action carbine. Handles 38 and 357 interchangeably. Introduced 1978. Imported by Interarms.
Price: **$230.00**
Price: Blue, engraved **$290.00**
Price: 44-40, 44 Mag. **$250.00**

Consult our Directory pages for the location of firms mentioned.

Savage Model 99E

SAVAGE 99E LEVER ACTION RIFLE
Caliber: 250 Savage, 300 Savage, 243 or 308 Win., 5-shot rotary magazine.
Barrel: 22", chrome-moly steel.
Weight: 7 lbs. **Length:** 39¾" over-all.
Stock: Walnut finished with checkered p.g.
Sights: Ramp front, adjustable ramp rear sight. Tapped for scope mounts.
Features: Grooved trigger, slide safety locks trigger and lever.
Price: $319.50

Savage Model 99C

Savage 99C Lever Action Clip Rifle
Similar to M99A except: detachable staggered clip magazine with push-button ejection. Cocking indicator. Drilled and tapped for scope mounting. Cut checkering on Monte Carlo stock and fore-end. Wgt. about 6¾ lbs., 41¾" over-all with 22" bbl. Available in cals. 243, 308, 7mm-08 Rem.
Price: $399.95

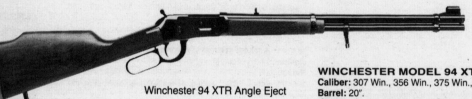

Winchester 94 XTR Angle Eject

WINCHESTER MODEL 94 XTR ANGLE EJECT
Caliber: 307 Win., 356 Win., 375 Win., 6-shot magazine.
Barrel: 20".
Weight: 7 lbs. **Length:** 38⅝" over-all.
Stock: Monte Carlo-style American walnut with fine cut checkering. Satin finish.
Sights: Hooded ramp front, semi-buckhorn rear adjustable for w. & e.
Features: All external metal parts have Winchester's deep blue high polish finish. Rifling twist 1 in 12". Rubber recoil pad fitted to buttstock. Introduced 1983. Made under license by U.S. Repeating Arms Co.
Price: With scope rings and bases $399.95

Winchester Model 94

WINCHESTER 94 LEVER ACTION CARBINE
Caliber: 30-30, (12" twist). 6-shot tubular mag.
Barrel: 16", 20".
Weight: 6½ lbs. **Length:** 37¾" over-all.
Stock: Walnut straight grip stock and fore-end (13"x1¾"x2½").
Sights: Bead front sight on ramp with removable cover; open rear. Tapped for receiver sights.
Features: Solid frame, top ejection, half-cock hammer safety. Made under license by U.S. Repeating Arms Co.
Price: $219.95
Price: Trapper model, 16" barrel $219.95

Winchester 94 Wrangler

Winchester Model 94 Wrangler
Similar to the standard Model 94 except has a 16" barrel, hoop-type finger lever, roll-engraved Western scenes on receiver. Chambered for 32 Win. Spec. only. Weighs 6⅛ lbs. and is 33¾" o.a.l. Introduced 1983.
Price: $249.95

Winchester 94 Antique Carbine
Same as M94 except: color case-hardened and scroll-engraved receiver, brass-plated loading gate and saddle ring. 30-30 only
Price: $239.95

Winchester Model 94XTR Carbine
Same as standard Model 94 except has high-grade finish on stock and fore-end with cut checkering on both. Metal has highly polished deep blue finish.
Price: $249.95

CAUTION: PRICES CHANGE. CHECK AT GUNSHOP.

Winchester 94 Crazy Horse

Winchester Model 94 Chief Crazy Horse Commemorative

Similar to the standard Model 94 except has Indian stock decorations of brass tacks and a medallion in the butt symbolizing the United Sioux Tribes. The names of the Sioux tribes are engraved on the color case-hardened re-ceiver, along with a portrait and a buffalo hunting scene. Barrel is inscribed "Chief Crazy Horse." The crescent buttplate has a polished blue finish. All decorations are authenticated by the United Sioux Tribes of South Dakota, and the issue was approved by tribal chairmen of all eleven tribes. Royalties benefit the Sioux people. Limited edition of 19,999. Chambered for 38-55 Win. Introduced 1983.
Price: **$600.00**

CENTERFIRE RIFLES—BOLT ACTIONS

Alpha 1 Rifle

ALPHA 1 BOLT ACTION RIFLE
Caliber: 243, 7mm-08, 308, 4-shot magazine.
Barrel: 20", round tapered.
Weight: 6-6¼ lbs. **Length:** 39½" over-all.
Stock: American walnut with satin finish; Monte Carlo without cheekpiece; solid rubber butt pad; swivel studs; length of pull is 13⅜".
Sights: None furnished. Receiver drilled and tapped for scope mounts.
Features: Medium-length action with three-lug locking system, 60 degree bolt rotation; side safety; cocking indicator; aluminum bedding block system; Teflon coated trigger guard/floorplate assembly. Introduced 1982. From Alpha Arms, Inc.
Price: **$450.00**
Price: Action only **$225.00**

Alpine Custom Grade

ANSCHUTZ 1432D/1532D CLASSIC RIFLES
Caliber: 22 Hornet (1432D), 5-shot clip, 222 Rem. (1532D), 2-shot clip.
Barrel: 23½"; ¹³⁄₁₆" dia. heavy.
Weight: 7¾ lbs. **Length:** 42½" over-all.
Stock: Select European walnut with checkered pistol grip and fore-end.
Sights: None furnished, drilled and tapped for scope mounting.
Features: Adjustable single stage trigger. Receiver drilled and tapped for scope mounting. Introduced 1982. Imported from Germany by Talo Distributors, Inc.
Price: 1432D (22 Hornet) **$655.00**
Price: 1532D (222 Rem.) **$655.00**

ALPINE BOLT ACTION RIFLE
Caliber: 22-250, 243 Win., 264 Win., 270, 30-06, 308, 308 Norma Mag., 7mm Rem Mag., 8mm, 300 Win. Mag., 5-shot magazine (3 for magnum).
Barrel: 23" (std. cals.), 24" (mag.).
Weight: 7½ lbs.
Stock: European walnut. Full p.g. and Monte Carlo; checkered p.g. and fore-end; rubber recoil pad; white line spacers; sling swivels.
Sights: Ramp front, open rear adj. for w. and e.
Features: Made by Firearms Co. Ltd. in England. Imported by Mandall Shooting Supplies.
Price: Standard Grade **$375.00**
Price: Custom Grade (illus.) **$395.00**

Anschutz 1432D/1532D

ANSCHUTZ 1432D/1532D Custom Rifles
Similar to the Classic models except have roll-over Monte Carlo cheekpiece, slim fore-end with Schnabel tip, Wundhammer palm swell on pistol grip, rosewood grip cap with white diamond insert. Skip-line checkering on grip and fore-end. Introduced 1982. Imported from Germany by Talo Distributors, Inc.
Price: 1432D (22 Hornet) **$698.00**
Price: 1532D (222 Rem.) **$698.00**

BSA CF-2 Rifle

BSA CF-2 BOLT ACTION RIFLE
Caliber: 222 Rem., 22-250, 243, 6.5x55, 7mm Mauser, 7x64, 270, 308, 30-06, 7mm Rem. Mag., 300 Win. Mag.
Barrel: 24".
Weight: 7¾ lbs. **Length:** 45" over-all.
Stock: European walnut with roll-over Monte Carlo, palm swell on right side of pistol grip, skip-line checkering. High gloss finish.

Sights: Open adjustable rear, hooded ramp front. Removable.
Features: Adjustable single trigger or optional double-set triggers, side safety, visible cocking indicator. Ventilated rubber recoil pad. North American-style stock has high gloss finish, European has oil. Introduced 1980. From Precision Sports.
Price: Standard calibers, North American style $660.00
Price: Magnum calibers, North American style $690.00
Price: Double-set triggers, extra $100.00
Price: Heavy barrel, extra $82.50
Price: Standard calibers, European style $715.00
Price: Magnum calibers, European style $750.00

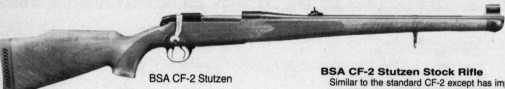

BSA CF-2 Stutzen

BSA CF-2 Stutzen Stock Rifle
Similar to the standard CF-2 except has improved bolt guide rib circlip and precision-ground striker; 20.5" barrel; full-length Stutzen-style stock with constrasting Schnabel fore-end tip and grip cap. Available in 222, 6.5 x 55, 308 Win., 30-06, 270, 7 x 64. Measures 41.3" over-all, weighs 7½ lbs. Introduced 1982. From Precision Sports.
Price: $750.00
Price: Double set triggers, add $100.00

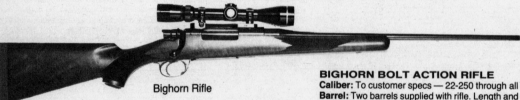

Bighorn Rifle

BIGHORN BOLT ACTION RIFLE
Caliber: To customer specs — 22-250 through all standard magnums.
Barrel: Two barrels supplied with rifle. Length and contour to customer specs.
Weight: About 6¾ lbs.
Stock: Standard grade has AA fancy claro walnut. Classic style.
Sights: None furnished. Drilled and tapped for scope mounting.
Features: Commercial Mauser action. Rifle comes with two easily interchangeable barrels, flush Pachmayr swivel sockets, black recoil pad. Available in several grades with many options. Introduced 1983. From Bighorn Rifles.
Price: With two barrels. $1,995.00

Browning BBR Rifle

BROWNING BBR BOLT ACTION RIFLE
Caliber: 25-06, 270, 30-06, 7mm Rem. Mag., 300 Win. Mag., 338 Win. Mag.
Barrel: 22" medium sporter weight with recessed muzzle.
Weight: 8 lbs. **Length:** 44½" over-all.

Stock: Select American walnut cut to lines of Monte Carlo sporter; full p.g. and high cheekpiece; 18 l.p.i. checkering. Recoil pad is standard on magnum calibers.
Features: Short throw (60°) bolt with fluted surface, 9 locking lugs, plunger-type ejector, adjustable trigger is grooved and gold plated. Hinged floorplate with detachable box magazine (4 rounds in standard cals, 3 in mags). Convenient slide safety on tang. Special anti-warp aluminum fore-end insert. Low profile swivel studs. Introduced 1978. Imported from Japan by Browning.
Price: $469.95

Browning BBR Short Action

Browning Short Action BBR
Similar to the standard BBR except has new short action for 22-250, 243, 257 Roberts, 7mm-08, 308 chamberings. Available with either 22" light barrel or 24" heavy barrel; weighs 7½ lbs. and 9½ lbs. respectively. Other specs essentially the same. Introduced 1983.
Price: Either barrel. $469.95

Colt Sauer Rifle

Colt Sauer Short Action Rifle

Same as standard rifle except chambered for 22-250, 243 and 308 Win. 24″ bbl., 43″ over-all. Weighs 7½ lbs. 3-shot magazine

Price: **$1,172.95**

CHAMPLIN RIFLE

Caliber: All std. chamberings, including 458 Win. and 460 Wea. Many wildcats on request.
Barrel: Any length up to 26″ for octagon. Choice of round, straight taper octagon, or octagon with integral quarter rib, front sight ramp and sling swivel stud.
Weight: About 8 lbs. **Length:** 45″ over-all.
Stock: Hand inletted, shaped and finished. Checkered to customer specs. Select French, Circassian or claro walnut. Steel p.g. cap, trap buttplate or recoil pad.
Sights: Bead on ramp front, 3-leaf folding rear.
Features: Right or left hand Champlin action, tang safety or optional shroud safety, Canjar adj. trigger, hinged floorplate.
Price: From **$5,400.00**

COLT SAUER RIFLE

Caliber: 25-06, 270, 30-06, (std.), 7mm Rem. Mag., 300 Wea. Mag., 300 Win. Mag. (Magnum).
Barrel: 24″, round tapered.
Weight: 8 lbs. (std.). **Length:** 43¾″ over-all.
Stock: American walnut, cast-off M.C. design with cheekpiece. Fore-end tip and p.g. cap rosewood with white spacers. Hand checkering.
Sights: None furnished. Specially designed scope mounts for any popular make scope furnished.
Features: Unique barrel/receiver union, non-rotating bolt wih cam-actuated locking lugs, tang-type safety locks sear. Detachable 3- and 4-shot magazines.
Price: Standard calibers **$1,172.95**
Price: Magnum calibers **$1,212.50**
Price: Grand Alaskan, 375 H&H **$1,245.50**

COLT SAUER GRAND AFRICAN

Caliber: 458 Win. Mag.
Barrel: 24″, round tapered.
Weight: 10½ lbs. **Length:** 44½″ over-all.
Stock: Solid African bubinga wood, cast-off M.C. with cheekpiece, contrasting rosewood fore-end and p.g. caps with white spacers. Checkered fore-end and p.g.
Sights: Ivory bead hooded ramp front, adj. sliding rear.
Price: **$1,304.95**

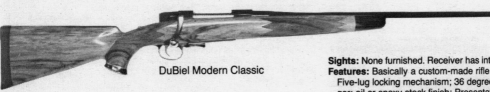

DuBiel Modern Classic

Du BIEL ARMS BOLT ACTION RIFLES

Caliber: Standard calibers 22-250 thru 458 Win. Mag. Selected wildcat calibers available.
Barrel: Selected weights and lengths. Douglas Premium
Weight: About 7½ lbs.
Stock: Five styles. Walnut, maple, laminates. Hand checkered.

Sights: None furnished. Receiver has integral milled bases.
Features: Basically a custom-made rifle. Left or right-hand models available. Five-lug locking mechanism; 36 degree bolt rotation; adjustable Canjar trigger; oil or epoxy stock finish; Presentation recoil pad; jeweled and chromed bolt body; sling swivel studs; lever latch or button floorplate release. All steel action and parts. Introduced 1978. From Du Biel Arms.
Price: Rollover Model, left or right-hand **$2,500.00**
Price: Thumbhole, left or right hand **$2,500.00**
Price: Classic, left or right hand **$2,500.00**
Price: Modern Classic, left or right hand...................... **$2,500.00**
Price: Thumbhole Mannlicher, left or right hand **$2,500.00**

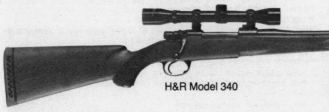

H&R Model 340

Heym SR-20 Left Hand Rifles

All Heym bolt action rifles are available with true left-hand action and stock, in all calibers listed for the right-hand version, for an additional **$160.00**.

HARRINGTON & RICHARDSON MODEL 340 RIFLE

Caliber: 243, 7x57, 308, 270, 30-06.
Barrel: 22″.
Weight: About 7¼ lbs. **Length:** 43″ over-all.
Stock: American walnut, hand checkered pistol grip and fore-end, carved and beaded cheekpiece, metal grip cap, rubber recoil pad.
Sights: None furnished. Drilled and tapped for scope mounts.
Features: Mauser-design action with hinged steel floorplate and trigger guard; adjustable trigger; high lustre blue finish. Introduced 1982. From Harrington & Richardson.
Price: **$395.00**

Heym Model SR-20L

HEYM MODEL SR-20 BOLT ACTION RIFLES

Caliber: 5.6x57, 243, 6.5x55, 6.5x57, 270, 7x57, 7x64, 308, 30-06 (SR-20L); 9.3x62 (SR-20N) plus SR-20L cals.; SR-20G—6.5x68, 7mm Rem. Mag., 300 Win. Mag., 8x68S, 375H&H.
Barrel: 20½″ (SR-20L), 24″ (SR-20N), 26″ (SR-20G).
Weight: 7-8 lbs. depending upon model.

Stock: Dark European walnut, hand-checkered p.g. and fore-end. Oil finish. Recoil pad, rosewood grip cap. Monte Carlo-style. SR-20L has full Mannlicher-style stock, others have sporter-style with schnabel tip.
Sights: Silver bead ramp front, adj. folding leaf rear.
Features: Hinged floorplate, 3-position safety,. Receiver drilled and tapped for scope mounts. Adjustable trigger. Options available include double-set triggers, left-hand action and stock, Suhler claw mounts, deluxe engraving and stock carving. Imported from West Germany by Paul Jaeger, Inc.
Price: SR-20L.. **$945.00**
Price: SR-20N **$835.00**
Price: SR-20-G... **$880.00**

Kimber Hornet Sporter

Kimber Model 82 Super America

Similar to the standard Model 82 except has the Classic stock only of specially selected, high-grade, California claro walnut, with Continental cheekpiece; borderless, full-coverage 22 lpi checkering; Niedner-type checkered steel buttplate; comes with quick-detachable, double lever scope mounts and barrel quarter-rib which has a folding leaf sight. Available in 22 Long Rifle, 22 Magnum, 22 Hornet.

Price: 22 Long Rifle, less 4x scope.............................. **$950.00**
Price: As above, with Kimber 4x Compact scope.............. **$1,135.00**
Price: 22 Mag., less scope.................................. **$969.00**
Price: As above, with Kimber 4x Compact scope.............. **$1,154.00**
Price: 22 Hornet, less scope................................ **$1,055.00**
Price: As above, with Kimber 4x Compact scope.............. **$1,240.00**

KIMBER MODEL 82 HORNET SPORTER

Caliber: 22 Hornet, 3-shot magazine.
Barrel: 22½".
Weight: About 6½ lbs. Length: 41" over-all.
Stock: Select claro walnut, Classic or Cascade (cheekpiece and Monte Carlo comb) design with hand checkered pistol grip and fore-end.
Sights: Blade front on ramp, open rear adjustable for windage and elevation; also available without sights.
Features: All steel construction. Rocker-type silent safety, checkered steel butt plate, steel grip cap. Twin locking lugs, double extractors. Receiver grooved for scope mounts. Introduced 1982.
Price: Classic stock, no sights.............................. **$618.00**
Price: Classic stock, with sights **$673.00**
Price: Cascade stock, no sights............................. **$668.00**
Price: Cascade stock, with sights **$723.00**
Price: Scope mount rings................................... **$45.00**

Kleinguenther K-15 Insta-Fire

KLEINGUENTHER K-15 INSTA-FIRE RIFLE

Caliber: 243, 25-06, 270, 30-06, 308 Win., 7x57, 308 Norma Mag., 7mm Rem. Mag., 375 H&H, 257-270-300 Weath. Mag.
Barrel: 24" (Std.), 26" (Mag.).
Weight: 7 lbs., 12 oz. Length: 43½" over-all.

Stock: European walnut M.C. with 1" recoil pad. Left or right hand. Rosewood grip cap. Hand checkered. High luster or satin finish.
Sights: None furnished. Drilled and tapped for scope mounts. Iron sights optional.
Features: Ultra-fast lock/ignition time. Clip or feed from top of receiver. Guaranteed ½" 100 yd. groups. Many optional stock features available. Imported from Germany, assembled and accurized by Kleinguenther's.
Price: All calibers, choice of European or American walnut with oil finish... **$995.00**

Krico Model 600/700L Deluxe

KRICO MODEL 400D BOLT ACTION RIFLE

Caliber: 22 Hornet, 5-shot magazine.
Barrel: 24".
Weight: 6.5 lbs. Length: 43" over-all.
Stock: Deluxe European walnut, schnabel fore-end. Ventilated rubber recoil pad.
Sights: Hooded post front, open rear adj. for windage.
Features: Detachable box magazine; action has rear locking lugs, twin extractors; checkered pistol grip and fore-end; sling swivels. Available with single or double set trigger. Imported from West Germany. Contact Krico for more data.
Price: **$569.00**
Price: With Mannlicher stock **$669.00**

KRICO MODEL 600/700E BOLT ACTION

Caliber: 17 Rem., 222, 222 Rem. Mag., 223, 243, 308, 7x57, 7x64, 270, 30-06, 7mm Rem. Mag., 300 Win Mag.; 3-shot clip magazine.
Barrel: 24" (26" in magnum calibers).
Weight: 7.2 lbs. Length: 44" over-all (24" bbl.).
Stock: Hand checkered French walnut, European style with schnabel fore-end. Classic American-style also available.
Sights: Hooded front ramp, fixed rear. Tangent rear sight optional.
Features: Adjustable single or double set trigger, silent safety, double front locking lugs. Action can be disassembled without tools. Custom versions with engraving and stock carving available. Imported from Germany by Krico.
Price: Model 600, varmint calibers............................ **$789.00**
Price: Model 700E, standard calibers......................... **$789.00**
Price: Model 700EM, magnum calibers........................ **$809.00**

Krico Model 600/700 EAC

Krico Model 600/700 EAC Bolt Action Rifle

Similar to the 600/700E except chambered for 17 Rem., 222, 223, 22-250, 243, 308, 7x57, 7x64, 270, 30-06, or 9.3x62; 24" barrel (26" in magnums); weighs 7.5 lbs.; has traditional American-style classic stock of European walnut; double front locking lugs, silent safety, sling swivels. Action may be disassembled without tools. Introduced 1983. Contact Krico for more data.
Price: **$789.00**

Krico Model 600/700L Deluxe Bolt Action

Similar to the 600/700E except chambered for 17 Rem., 222, 223, 22-250, 243, 308, 7x57, 7x64, 270, 30-06, 9.3x62, 8x68S, 7mm Rem. Mag., 300 Win. Mag., 9.3x64; has traditional European-style stock of select fancy walnut; rosewood Schnabel fore-end tip, Bavarian cheekpiece, fine 28 lpi checkering. Front sling swivel attached to the barrel with ring, gold plated single-set trigger. Introduced 1983. Contact Krico for more data.
Price: Model 600, varmint calibers............................ **$929.00**
Price: Model 700, standard calibers.......................... **$929.00**
Price: Model 700, magnum calibers.......................... **$979.00**

CENTERFIRE RIFLES—BOLT ACTIONS

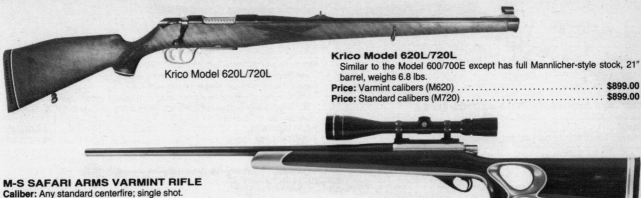

Krico Model 620L/720L

Krico Model 620L/720L
Similar to the Model 600/700E except has full Mannlicher-style stock, 21″ barrel, weighs 6.8 lbs.
Price: Varmint calibers (M620) **$899.00**
Price: Standard calibers (M720) **$899.00**

M-S SAFARI ARMS VARMINT RIFLE
Caliber: Any standard centerfire; single shot.
Barrel: 24″, stainless
Weight: To customer specs.
Stock: Fiberglass, custom painted. Thumbhole or pistol grip style.
Sights: None furnished. Drilled and tapped for scope mounting.
Features: Electronic trigger; high-speed lock time; stainless steel action. Custom built to customer specs. From M-S Safari Arms.
Price: From **$1,095.00**

M-S Safari Varmint

Mark X Marquis Carbine

MARK X MARQUIS MANNLICHER-STYLE CARBINE
Caliber: 270, 7x57, 30-06, 308 Win.
Barrel: 20″.
Weight: 7½ lbs. **Length:** 40″ over-all.
Stock: Hand checkered European walnut.
Sights: Ramp front with removable hood; open rear adj. for w. and e.
Features: Quick detachable sling swivels; fully adj. trigger; blue steel fore-end cap; white line spacers at p.g. cap and buttplate. Mark X Mauser action. Imported from Czechoslovakia by Interarms.
Price: With adj. trigger and sights **$430.00**

Interarms Mark X Alaskan

MARK X ALASKAN MAGNUM RIFLE
Caliber: 375 H&H, 458 Win Mag.; 3-shot magazine.
Barrel: 24″.
Weight: 8¼ lbs. **Length:** 44¾″ over-all.
Stock: Select walnut with crossbolt; hand checkered p.g. and fore-end; Monte Carlo; sling swivels.
Sights: Hooded ramp front; open rear adj. for w. & e.
Features: Hinged floorplate; right-hand thumb (tang) safety; adj. trigger. Imported from Czechoslovakia by Interarms.
Price: **$460.00**

MARK X CLASSIC RIFLE
Caliber: 22-250, 243, 270, 308 Win., 30-06, 25-06, 7x57, 7mm Rem. Mag., 300 Win. Mag.
Barrel: 24″.
Weight: 7½ lbs. **Length:** 44″ over-all.
Stock: Hand checkered walnut, Monte Carlo, white line spacers on p.g. cap, buttplate and fore-end tip.
Sights: Ramp front with removable hood, open rear adj. for w. and e.
Features: Sliding safety, quick detachable sling swivels, hinged floorplate. Also available as actions or bbld. actions. Imported from Czechoslovakia by Interarms.
Price: With adj. trigger and sights, from **$380.00**
Price: With adj. trigger, no sights, from **$365.00**

> Consult our Directory pages for the location of firms mentioned.

Mauser Model 66

MAUSER MODEL 66 BOLT ACTION RIFLES
Caliber: 5.6x61, 243, 6.5x57, 270, 7x64, 308 Win., 30-06, 9.3x62.
Barrel: 24″.
Weight: About 7½ lbs. **Length:** 41″ over-all.
Stock: European walnut, oil finish, Pachmayr recoil pad, rosewood fore-end and grip cap, sling swivels.

Sights: Hooded ramp front, Williams open adj. rear.
Features: Interchangeable barrels within caliber groups; silent safety locks bolt and firing pin. Double set or single trigger completely interchangeable. Contact Mauser for more data.
Price: Standard calibers, Model 66S **$1,999.00**
Price: Standard calibers, full-length stock **$2,100.00**
Price: Model 66S Ultra (21″ barrel, 7 lbs.) **$2,100.00**
Price: Model 66SM (single set trigger, special wood and finish) ... **$2,270.00**
Price: Interchangeable barrels, from **$485.00**

CENTERFIRE RIFLES—BOLT ACTIONS

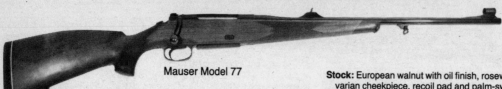

Mauser Model 77

MAUSER MODEL 77 BOLT ACTION RIFLE
Caliber: 243, 6.5x57, 270, 7x64, 308, 30-06.
Barrel: 24".
Weight: About 7½ lbs. **Length:** 44" over-all.

Stock: European walnut with oil finish, rosewood fore-end tip and grip cap. Bavarian cheekpiece, recoil pad and palm-swell p.g.
Sights: Ramp front, open rear adj. for w. & e.
Features: Detachable 3-round box magazine; same trigger system as Model 66, single set or double set; patented silent safety. Introduced 1981. Contact Mauser for more data.
Price: Half-stock **$1,890.00**
Price: Full length stock **$1,990.00**

O&L Wolverine

O&L WOLVERINE BOLT ACTION RIFLE
Caliber: 308, 270, 30-06, 300 Win. Mag., 9.3x62.
Barrel: 20".
Weight: 7 lbs. **Length:** 39.5" over-all.

Stock: Camouflaged fiberglass stock standard, walnut stock with straight fore-end on special order.
Sights: Hooded ramp front, special fixed rear sight incorporated into the quarter rib.
Features: Designed for the mountain, brush hunter on horseback. Double front locking lugs; action can be disassembled without tools; detachable box magazine. Action and barrel imported from West Germany by O&L Guns. Rifle assembled in the U.S.
Price: With fiberglass stock **$899.00**

Remington Model Seven

REMINGTON MODEL SEVEN BOLT ACTION RIFLE
Caliber: 222 Rem. (5-shot), 243, 7mm-08, 6mm, 308 (4-shot).
Barrel: 18½".
Weight: 6¼ lbs. **Length:** 37½" over-all.
Stock: Walnut, with modified Schnabel fore-end. Cut checkering.
Sights: Ramp front, adjustable open rear.
Features: New short action design; silent side safety; free-floated barrel except for single pressure point at fore-end tip. Introduced 1983.
Price: **$449.95**

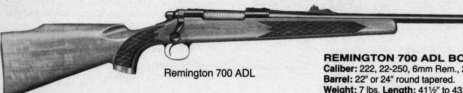

Remington 700 ADL

REMINGTON 700 ADL BOLT ACTION RIFLE
Caliber: 222, 22-250, 6mm Rem., 243, 25-06, 270, 308 and 30-06.
Barrel: 22" or 24" round tapered.
Weight: 7 lbs. **Length:** 41½" to 43½".
Stock: Walnut, RKW finished p.g. stock with impressed checkering, Monte Carlo (13⅜"x1⅝"x2⅜").
Sights: Gold bead ramp front; removable, step-adj. rear with windage screw.
Features: Side safety, receiver tapped for scope mounts.
Price: **$379.95**
Price: 7mm Rem. Mag. **$396.95**

Remington 700BDL Left Hand
Same as 700 BDL except: mirror-image left-hand action, stock. Available in 270, 30-06 only.
Price: **$463.95**
Price: 7mm Rem. Mag. **$480.95**

Remington 700 BDL

Remington 700 C Custom Rifle
Same as the 700 BDL except choice of 20", 22", or 24" bbl. with or without sights. Jewelled bolt, with or without hinged floor plate. Select American walnut stock is hand checkered, rosewood fore-end and grip cap. Hand lapped barrel. 16 weeks for delivery after placing order.
Price: . . . . **NA**

Remington 700 BDL Bolt Action Rifle
Same as 700-ADL, except: also available in 223, 7mm-08 Rem.; skip-line checkering; black fore-end tip and p.g. cap, white line spacers. Matted receiver top, quick release floorplate. Hooded ramp front sight. Q.D. swivels and 1" sling.
Price: **$446.95**
Available also in 17 Rem., 7mm Rem. Mag. and 300 Win. Mag., 8mm Rem. Mag., calibers. 44½" over-all, weight 7½ lbs.
Price: **$463.95**
Price: Peerless Grade . . . . **NA**
Price: Premier Grade . . . . **NA**

Remington 700 BDL Varmint
Same as 700 BDL, except: 24" heavy bbl., 43½" over-all, wgt. 9 lbs. Cals. 222, 223, 22-250, 6mm Rem., 243, 25-06, 7mm-08 Rem. and 308. No sights.
Price: **$467.95**

Remington 700 Safari
Same as the 700 BDL except 375 H&H or 458 Win. Magnum calibers only. Hand checkered, oil finished stock with recoil pad installed. Delivery time is about five months.
Price: **$762.95**

CAUTION: PRICES CHANGE. CHECK AT GUNSHOP.

Remington 700 Classic

REMINGTON 700 "CLASSIC" RIFLE
Caliber: 22-250, 6mm Rem., 243, 270, 30-06, 7mm Rem. Mag., 300 H&H Mag.
Barrel: 22" (6mm, 243, 270, 30-06), 24" (22-250, 7mm Rem. Mag., 300 H&H).
Weight: About 7 lbs. **Length:** 43½" over-all (24" bbl.).

Stock: American walnut, 20 l.p.i. checkering on p.g. and fore-end. Classic styling. Satin finish.
Sights: No sights furnished. Receiver drilled and tapped for scope mounting.
Features: A "classic" version of the M700ADL with straight comb stock. Fitted with rubber butt pad on all but magnum caliber, which has a full recoil pad. Sling swivel studs installed.
Price: All cals. except 7mm Rem. Mag. $404.95
Price: 7mm Rem. Mag., 300 H&H Mag. $421.95

Remington Model 788

REMINGTON 788 BOLT ACTION RIFLE
Caliber: 22-250, 222 Rem., 223 Rem., 7mm-08 Rem., 243, and 308 (4-shot).
Barrel: 18½" round tapered (24" in 223 and 22-250).
Weight: 7-7½ lbs. **Length:** 41⅝" over-all.
Stock: Walnut-finished hardwood with Monte Carlo and p.g. (13⅝"x1⅞"x2⅝").
Sights: Blade ramp front, open rear adj. for w. & e.
Features: Detachable box magazine, thumb safety, receiver tapped for scope mounts.
Price: $288.95
Price: Sling strap and swivels, installed $19.00
Price: Model 788 with Universal Model UE 4x scope, mounts and rings in cals. 222 Rem., 223 Rem., 22-250, 243 Win., 7mm-08 Rem., 308 ...... $344.95

Ruger 77 Round Top

RUGER 77 BOLT ACTION RIFLE
Caliber: 22-250, 220 Swift, 243, 6mm, 308, 358 Win. (5-shot).
Barrel: 22" round tapered (24" in 220 Swift).
Weight: 6¾ lbs. **Length:** 42" over-all.
Stock: Hand checkered American walnut (13¾"x1⅝"x2⅛"), p.g. cap, sling swivel studs and recoil pad.

Sights: Optional gold bead ramp front, folding leaf adj. rear, or scope rings.
Features: Integral scope mount bases, diagonal bedding system, hinged floor plate, adj. trigger, tang safety. Scope optional.
Price: With Ruger steel scope rings (77R) $393.00
Price: With rings and open sights (77RS) $414.00
Price: 458 Win. Mag. $496.50
Price: Barreled action only all cals. except 458, open sights $339.00
Price: Barreled action, all cals. except 458, no sights $319.00
Price: Barreled action, 458, with open sights $433.50

Ruger 77 Ultra Light

Ruger Model 77 Ultra Light
Similar to the standard Model 77 except weighs only 6 lbs., chambered only for 243 and 308; barrel tapped for target scope blocks; has 20" Ultra Light barrel. Ruger's steel 1" scope rings supplied. Introduced 1983.
Price: $455.00

Ruger Model 77 Magnum Rifle
Similar to Ruger 77 except: magnum-size action. Calibers 25-06, 270, 280, 7x57, 30-06 (5-shot), 7mm Rem. Mag., 300 Win., Mag., 338 Win. Mag., 458 Win. Mag. (3-shot). 270, 7x57, 280 and 30-06 have 22" bbl., all others have 24". Weight and length vary with caliber.
Price: $393.00

Ruger Model 77 Magnum Round Top
Same as Model 77 except: round top receiver, drilled and tapped for standard scope mounts. Open sights are standard equipment. Calibers 25-06, 270, 30-06, 7mm Rem. Mag.
Price: All cals. (Model 77ST) $393.00

Ruger International 77

Ruger International Model 77 Rifle
Same as the standard Model 77 except has 18½" barrel, full-length Mannlicher-style stock, with steel fore-end cap, loop-type sling swivel. Improved front sight. Available only in 243 or 308. Weighs 6 lbs. 4 oz. and uses the Ruger short action. Length over-all is 38½".
Price: $480.00

Ruger 77 Varmint

RUGER MODEL 77 VARMINT
Caliber: 22-250, 220 Swift, 243, 6mm, 25-06, 280, 308.
Barrel: 24″ heavy straight tapered, 26″ in 220 swift.
Weight: Approx. 9 lbs. **Length:** Approx. 44″ over-all.
Stock: American walnut, similar in style to Magnum Rifle.
Sights: Barrel drilled and tapped for target scope blocks. Integral scope mount bases in receiver.
Features: Ruger diagonal bedding system, Ruger steel 1″ scope rings supplied. Fully adj. trigger. Barreled actions available in any of the standard calibers and barrel lengths.
Price: (Model 77V) **$393.00**

SAKO STANDARD SPORTER
Caliber: 17 Rem., 222, 223 (short action); 22-250, 220 Swift, 243, 308 (medium action); 25-06, 270, 30-06, 7mm Rem. Mag., 300 Win. Mag., 338 Win. Mag., 375 H&H Mag. (long action).
Barrel: 23″ (222, 223, 243), 24″ (other cals.).
Weight: 6¾ lbs. (short); 6¾ lbs. (med.); 8 lbs. (long).
Stock: Hand-checkered European walnut.
Sights: None furnished.
Features: Adj. trigger, hinged floorplate. 222 and 223 have short action, 243 and 22-250 have medium action, others are long action. Imported from Finland by Stoeger.
Price: Short action **$725.00**
Price: Medium action **$725.00**
Price: Long action **$741.95**
Price: Magnum cals. **$758.95**
Price: 375 H&H **$775.00**

Sako Deluxe Sporter
Same action as Standard Sporter except has select wood, rosewood p.g. cap and fore-end tip. Fine checkering on top surfaces of integral dovetail bases, bolt sleeve, bolt handle root and bolt knob. Vent. recoil pad, skip-line checkering, mirror finish bluing.
Price: 222 or 223 cals. **$995.00**
Price: 22-250, 243, 308 . . . . **$995.00**
Price: 25-06, 270, 30-06 . . . . **$995.00**
Price: 7mm Rem. Mag., 300 Win. Mag., 338 Mag., 375 H&H **$1,020.00**

Sako Classic Sporter

Sako Classic Sporter
Similar to the Standard Sporter except: available in 243 (medium action), 270, 30-06 and 7mm Rem. Mag. (long action) only; straight-comb "classic-style" stock with oil finish; solid rubber recoil pad; recoil lug. No sights furnished—receiver drilled and tapped for scope mounting. Introduced 1980.
Price: 243 . . . . **$975.00**
Price: 270, 30-06 . . . . **$1,020.00**
Price: 7mm Rem. Mag. **$1,035.00**

Sako Safari Grade Bolt Action
Similar to the Standard Grade Sporter except available in long action, calibers 300 Win. Mag., 338 Win. Mag. or 375 H&H Mag. only. Stocked in French walnut, checkered 20 l.p.i., solid rubber butt pad; grip cap and fore-end tip; quarter-rib "express" rear sight, hooded ramp front. Front sling swivel band-mounted on barrel.
Price: **$1,995.00**

Sako Carbine

Sako Carbine
Same action as the Standard Sporter except has full "Mannlicher" style stock, 20″ barrel, weighs 7½ lbs., chambered for 222 Rem., 243, 270 and 30-06 only. Introduced 1977. From Stoeger.
Price: 243, 270, 30-06 only **$825.00**

Sako Super Deluxe Sporter
Similar to Deluxe Sporter except has select European Walnut with high gloss finish and deep cut oak leaf carving. Metal has super high polish, deep blue finish.
Price: **$1,995.00**

Sako Finnsport 2700 Sporter
Similar to the Standard Sporter except has Monte Carlo stock design, different checkering, comes with scope mounts. Same calibers, actions as on Standard model. Weight, 6½ to 8 lbs. Introduced 1983.
Price: **$870.00**

Sako Heavy Barrel
Same as std. Super Sporter except has beavertail fore-end; available in 222, 223 (short action) 220 Swift, 22-250, 243, 308 (medium action). Weight from 8¼ to 8½ lbs. 5-shot magazine capacity.
Price: 222, 223 (short action) **$875.00**
Price: 22-250, 243, 308 (medium action) **$875.00**

Savage Model 340

SAVAGE 340 CLIP REPEATER
Caliber: 22 Hornet, 222 Rem., 223 (4-shot) and 30-30 (3-shot).
Barrel: 24″ and 22″ respectively.
Weight: About 6½ lbs. **Length:** 40″-42″.
Stock: Walnut, Monte Carlo, checkered p.g. and fore-end.
Sights: Hooded ramp front, folding-leaf rear.
Features: Detachable clip magazine, sliding thumb safety, receiver tapped for scope mounts.
Price: **$222.00**

CAUTION: PRICES CHANGE. CHECK AT GUNSHOP.

Savage Model 110C

SAVAGE 110S, SILHOUETTE RIFLE

Caliber: 308 Win., 7mm-08 Rem., 5-shot.
Barrel: 22″, heavy tapered.
Weight: 8 lbs., 10 oz. **Length:** 43″ over-all.
Stock: Special Silhouette stock of select walnut. High fluted comb, Wundhammer swell, stippled p.g. and fore-end. Rubber recoil pad.
Sights: None. Receiver drilled and tapped for scope mounting.
Features: Receiver has satin blue finish to reduce glare. Barrel is free-floating. Top tang safety, internal magazine. Available in right-hand only. Introduced 1978.
Price: $339.50

SAVAGE 110C BOLT ACTION RIFLE

Caliber: 22-250, 243, 270, 308, 30-06, 4-shot detachable box magazine, 300 Win. Mag., 7mm Rem. Mag. (3-shot).
Barrel: 22″; 24″ in magnum calibers.
Weight: 7lbs. **Length:** 43″ over-all.
Stock: Select walnut with Monte Carlo, skip-line cut checkered p.g. and fore-end. Swivel studs.
Sights: Removable ramp front, open rear adj. for w. & e.
Features: Tapped for scope mounting, free floating barrel, top tang safety, detachable clip magazine, rubber recoil pad on all calibers. Model 110CL (left-hand) in calibers 243, 270, 30-06, 308, 7mm Rem. Mag. only.
Price: Right hand 110C...................................... $366.50
Price: Left hand 110CL..................................... $375.50
Price: Right hand, mag. cals................................ $371.50
Price: Left hand, mag. cals................................ $380.00

Savage Model 110-V Varmint Rifle
Same as the Model 110-C except chambered only for 22-250, with heavy 26″ barrel, special "varmint" stock. Introduced 1983.
Price: $339.50

Shilen DGA Varmint

SMITH & WESSON M1500 BOLT ACTION RIFLE

Caliber: 222, 223, 243, 25-06, 270, 30-06, 308, 7mm Rem. Mag., 300 Win. Mag.
Barrel: 22″ (24″ in 7mm Rem. Mag.).
Weight: 7½-7¾ lbs. **Length:** 42″ over-all (42½″ for 270, 30-06, 7mm).
Stock: American walnut with Monte Carlo comb and cheekpiece; 18-line-per-inch checkering on p.g. and fore-end.
Sights: Hooded ramp gold bead front, open round-notch rear adj. for w. & e. Drilled and tapped for scope mounts.
Features: Trigger guard and magazine box are a single unit with a hinged floorplate. Comes with q.d. swivel studs. Composition non-slip buttplate with white spacer. Magnum models have rubber recoil pad. Introduced 1979.
Price: Standard cals.. $351.95
Price: Magnum cals... $367.95

SHILEN DGA RIFLES

Caliber: All calibers.
Barrel: 24″ (sporter, #2 Weight), 25″ (Varminter, #5 weight).
Weight: 7½ lbs. (Sporter), 9 lbs., (Varminter).
Stock: Selected Claro walnut. Barrel and action hand bedded to stock with free-floated barrel, bedded action. Swivel studs installed.
Sights: None furnished. Drilled and tapped for scope mounting.
Features: Shilen Model DGA action, fully adjustable trigger with side safety. Stock finish is satin sheen epoxy. Barrel and action non-glare blue-black. From Shilen Rifles, Inc.
Price: Sporter or Varminter rifle, from.......................... $1,400.00

Smith & Wesson Model 1500 Deluxe Rifle
Similar to Standard model except comes without sights, has engine-turned bolt; floorplate has decorative scroll. Stock has skip-line checkering, pistol grip cap with inset S&W seal, white spacers. Sling, swivels and swivel posts are included. Magnum models have vent, recoil pad.
Price: Deluxe, std. cals. $401.95
Price: Deluxe, magnum cals.................................... $417.95

Smith & Wesson Mountaineer

Smith & Wesson Model 1500 Mountaineer Rifle
Similar to the standard Model 1500 except has satin-finished stock, 18 lpi checkering; no sights furnished but receiver is drilled and tapped for scope mounts. Chambered for 223, 243, 270 and 30-06 (22″ barrel), 7mm Rem. Mag. (24″ barrel). Magnum model comes with recoil pad. Introduced 1983.
Price: Standard calibers...................................... $329.95
Price: Magnum... $345.95

S&W Model 1500 Varmint

Smith & Wesson Model 1500 Varmint Deluxe Rifle
Similar to the standard 1500 except has a 22″ heavy barrel and fully adjustable trigger. Chambered for 222, 22-250 and 223. Weighs 9 lbs. 5 oz. Skip-line checkering, q.d. swivels. Introduced 1982.
Price: Blue... $426.95
Price: Parkerized, oil finished stock $439.95

Smith & Wesson Classic Hunter

Smith & Wesson Model 1700LS "Classic Hunter"
Similar to the standard Model 1500 except has classic-style stock with tapered fore-end and Schnabel tip, ribbon hand checkering, black rubber butt pad with black spacer; flush mounted sling swivels; removeable 5-shot magazine; jeweled bolt body with knurled bolt knob. Chambered only for 243, 270, 30-06. Introduced 1983.
Price: **$479.95**

STEVENS 110E BOLT ACTION RIFLE
Caliber: 270, 308, 30-06, 243, 4-shot.
Barrel: 22″ round tapered.
Weight: 6¾ lbs. **Length:** 43″ (22″barrel).
Stock: Walnut finished hardwood with Monte Carlo, checkered p.g. and fore-end, hard rubber buttplate.
Sights: Gold bead removable ramp front, step adj. rear.
Features: Top tang safety, receiver tapped for peep or scope sights.
Price: **$241.50**

Consult our Directory pages for the location of firms mentioned.

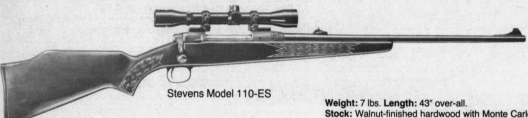

Stevens Model 110-ES

STEVENS MODEL 110-ES BOLT ACTION RIFLE
Caliber: 243, 308, 30-06; 5-shot magazine.
Barrel: 22″.

Weight: 7 lbs. **Length:** 43″ over-all.
Stock: Walnut-finished hardwood with Monte Carlo; checkered p.g. and fore-end.
Sights: Removable ramp front, removable adjustable rear.
Features: Comes with 4x scope and mounts; hard rubber buttplate; top tang safety; free-floating barrel. Introduced 1981. From Savage Arms.
Price: Model 110-ES **$296.00**

Steyr-Mannlicher S

STEYR-MANNLICHER MODELS S & S/T
Caliber: Model S—300 Win. Mag., 338 Win. Mag., 7mm Rem. Mag., 300 H&H Mag., 375 H&H Mag. (6.5x68, 8x68S, 9.3x64 optional); S/T—375 H&H Mag., 458 Win. Mag. (9.3x64 optional).
Barrel: 25.6″.

Weight: 8.4 lbs. (Model S). **Length:** 45″ over-all.
Stock: Half stock with M.C. and rubber recoil pad. Hand checkered walnut. Available with optional spare magazine inletted in butt.
Sights: Ramp front, U-notch rear.
Features: Choice of interchangeable single or double set triggers., detachable 4-shot magazine. Drilled and tapped for scope mounts. Imported by Steyr Daimler Puch of America.
Price: Model S or S/T **$962.00**
Price: With optional butt magazine (illus.) **$1,012.00**
Price: Optional cals., add **$55.00**

Steyr-Mannlicher Professional

STEYR-MANNLICHER MODEL M
Caliber: 7x64, 7x57, 25-06, 270, 30-06. Left-hand action cals.—7x64, 25-06, 270, 30-06. Optional cals.—6.5x57, 8x57JS, 9.3x62, 6.5x55, 7.5x55.
Barrel: 20″ (full stock); 23.6″ (half stock).
Weight: 6.8 lbs. to 7.5 lbs. **Length:** 39″ (full stock); 43″ (half stock).
Stock: Hand checkered walnut. Full Mannlicher or std. half stock with M.C. and rubber recoil pad.
Sights: Ramp front, open U-notch rear.
Features: Choice of interchangeable single or double set triggers. Detachable 5-shot rotary magazine. Drilled and tapped for scope mounting. Available as "Professional" model with parkerized finish and synthetic stock (right hand action only). Imported by Steyr Daimler Puch of America.
Price: Full stock **$958.00**
Price: Half stock **$893.00**
Price: For left hand action add **$127.00**
Price: Professional model with iron sights **$737.00**

Steyr-Mannlicher ML79 "Luxus"
Similar to Steyr-Mannlicher models L and M except has single-set trigger and detachable 3-shot steel magazine; 6-shot magazine optional. Same calibers as L and M. Oil finish or high gloss lacquer on stock.
Price: Full stock **$1,172.00**
Price: Half stock **$1,097.00**
Price: Optional cals., add **$55.00**
Price: Extra 3-shot magazine................................... **$41.50**
Price: Extra 6-shot magazine................................... **$77.35**

CAUTION: PRICES CHANGE. CHECK AT GUNSHOP.

CENTERFIRE RIFLES—BOLT ACTIONS

Steyr-Mannlicher L

Steyr-Mannlicher Varmint, Models SL and L

Similar to standard SL and L except chambered only for: 222 Rem. (SL), 22-250, 243, 308 and optional 5.6x57 (L). Has 26″ heavy barrel, no sights (drilled and tapped for scope mounts). Choice of single or double-set triggers. Five-shot detachable magazine.

Price:	**$965.00**
Price: Optional caliber, add	**$55.00**
Price: Spare magazine	**$25.00**

STEYR-MANNLICHER MODELS SL & L

Caliber: SL—222, 222 Rem. Mag., 223; SL Varmint—222; L—22-250, 6mm, 243, 308 Win.; L Varmint—22-250, 243, 308 Win.; L optional cal.—5.6x57.
Barrel: 20″ (full stock); 23.6″ (half stock).
Weight: 6 lbs. (full stock). **Length:** 38¼″ (full stock).
Stock: Hand checkered walnut. Full Mannlicher or standard half-stock with Monte Carlo.
Sights: Ramp front, open U-notch rear.
Features: Choice of interchangeable single or double set triggers. Five-shot detachable "Makrolon" rotary magazine, 6 rear locking lugs. Drilled and tapped for scope mounts. Imported by Steyr Daimler Puch of America.

Price: Full Stock	**$958.00**
Price: Half-stock	**$893.00**
Price: Optional caliber, add	**$55.00**

Tikka Model 55

TIKKA MODEL 55 DELUXE RIFLE

Caliber: 17 Rem., 222, 22-250, 6mm Rem., 243, 308
Barrel: 23″.
Weight: About 6½ lbs. **Length:** 41½″ over-all.

Stock: Hand checkered walnut with rosewood fore-end tip and grip cap.
Sights: Bead on ramp front, rear adjustable for windage and elevation.
Features: Detachable 3-shot magazine with 5- or 10-shot magazines available. Roll-over cheekpiece, palm swell in pistol grip. Adjustable trigger. Receiver dovetailed for scope mounting. Imported from Finland by Mandall and Armsport.

Price:	**$650.00**
Price: QD scope mounts	**$89.95**

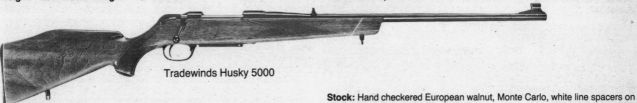

Tradewinds Husky 5000

TRADEWINDS HUSKY MODEL 5000 BOLT RIFLE

Caliber: 270, 30-06, 308, 243, 22-250.
Barrel: 23¾″.
Weight: 6 lbs. 11 oz.

Stock: Hand checkered European walnut, Monte Carlo, white line spacers on p.g. cap, fore-end tip and butt plate.
Sights: Fixed hooded front, adj. rear.
Features: Removable mag., full recessed bolt head, adj. trigger. Imported by Tradewinds.

Price:	**$395.00**

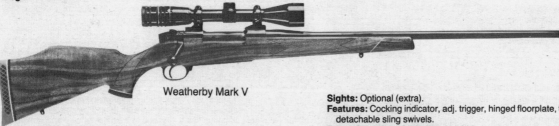

Weatherby Mark V

WEATHERBY MARK V BOLT ACTION RIFLE

Caliber: All Weatherby cals., 22-250 and 30-06
Barrel: 24″ or 26″ round tapered.
Weight: 6½-10½ lbs. **Length:** 43¼″-46½″.
Stock: Walnut, Monte Carlo with cheekpiece, high luster finish, checkered p.g. and fore-end, recoil pad.

Sights: Optional (extra).
Features: Cocking indicator, adj. trigger, hinged floorplate, thumb safety, quick detachable sling swivels.

Price: Cals. 224 and 22-250, std. bbl.	**$729.95**
Price: With 26″ semi-target bbl.	**$744.95**
Price: Cals. 240, 257, 270, 7mm, 30-06 and 300 (4″ bbl.)	**$749.95**
Price: With 26″ No. 2 contour bbl.	**$769.95**
Price: Cal. 340 (26″ bbl.)	**$769.95**
Price: Cal. 378 (26″ bbl.)	**$924.95**
Price: Cal. 460 (26″ bbl.)	**$1,063.95**

Weatherby Fibermark Rifle

Weatherby Fibermark Rifle

Same as the standard Mark V except the stock is of fiberglass; finished with a non-glare black wrinkle finish and black recoil pad; receiver and floorplate sandblasted and blued; fluted bolt has a satin finish. Currently available in right-hand model only, 24″ or 26″ barrel, 240 Weatherby Mag. through 340 Weatherby Mag. calibers. Introduced 1983.

Price: 240 W.M. through 300 W.M., 24″ bbl.	**$849.95**
Price: 240 W.M. through 340 W.M., 26″ bbl.	**$869.95**

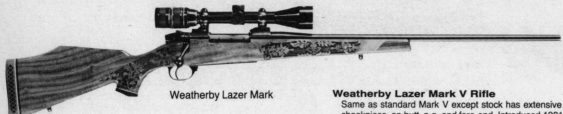

Weatherby Lazer Mark

Weatherby Lazer Mark V Rifle

Same as standard Mark V except stock has extensive laser carving under cheekpiece, on butt, p.g. and fore-end. Introduced 1981.

Price: 22-250, 224 Wea., 24″ bbl. $854.95
Price: As above, 26″ bbl. $869.95
Price: 240 Wea. thru 300 Wea., 24″ bbl. $874.95
Price: As above, 26″ bbl. $894.95
Price: 340 Wea. $894.95
Price: 378 Wea. $1,049.95
Price: 460 Wea. $1,188.95

Weatherby Mark V Rifle Left Hand

Available in all Weatherby calibers except 224 and 22-250 (and 26″ No. 2 contour 300WM). Complete left handed action; stock with cheekpiece on right side. Prices are $10 higher than right hand models except the 378 and 460WM are unchanged.

Weatherby Vanguard Rifle

WEATHERBY VANGUARD BOLT ACTION RIFLE

Caliber: 25-06, 243, 270, and 30-06 (5-shot), 7mm Rem. and 300 Win. Mag. (3-shot).
Barrel: 24″ hammer forged.
Weight: 7⅞ lbs. **Length:** 44½″ over-all.
Stock: American walnut, p.g. cap and fore-end tip, hand inletted and checkered. 13½″ pull.
Sights: Optional, available at extra cost.
Features: Side safety, adj. trigger, hinged floorplate, receiver tapped for scope mounts. Imported from Japan by Weatherby.
Price: $449.95

Whitworth Express Rifle

WHITWORTH EXPRESS RIFLE

Caliber: 22-250, 243, 25-06, 270, 7x57, 308, 30-06, 300 Win. Mag., 7mm Rem. Mag., 375 H&H, 458 Win. Mag.
Barrel: 24″.
Weight: 7½-8 lbs. **Length:** 44″.

Stock: Classic English Express rifle design of hand checkered, select European Walnut.
Sights: Three leaf open sight calibrated for 100, 200, 300 yards on ¼-rib, ramp front with removable hood (375, 458 only); other calibers have standard open sights.
Features: Solid rubber recoil pad, barrel mounted sling swivel, adjustable trigger, hinged floor plate, solid steel recoil cross bolt. Imported by Interarms.
Price: $490.00
Price: 375, 458, with express sights $590.00

Wichita Varmint Rifle

WICHITA VARMINT RIFLE

Caliber: 17 Rem. thru 308 Win., including 22 and 6mm PPC.
Barrel: 20⅛″.
Weight: 9 lbs. **Length:** 40⅛″ over-all.
Stock: AAA Fancy American walnut. Hand-rubbed finish, hand-checkered, 20 l.p.i. pattern. Hand-inletted, glass bedded steel grip cap, Pachmayr rubber recoil pad.

Sights: None. Drilled and tapped for scope mounts.
Features: Right or left-hand Wichita action with three locking lugs. Available as a single shot or repeater with 3-shot detachable magazine. Checkered bolt handle. Bolt is hand fitted, lapped and jeweled. Side thumb safety. Firing pin fall is ³⁄₁₆″. Non-glare blue finish. Shipped in hard Protecto case. From Wichita Arms.
Price: Single shot $1,075.00
Price: With blind box magazine $1,205.00

WICHITA MAGNUM STAINLESS RIFLE

Caliber: From 270 Win. through 458 Win. Mag.
Barrel: 22″ or 24″.
Weight: 8½ lbs. **Length:** 44¾″ over-all (24″ barrel).
Stock: AAA fancy walnut; hand inletted; glass bedded; steel grip cap; Pachmayr rubber recoil pad.
Sights: None. Drilled and tapped for Burris scope mounts.
Features: Stainless steel barrel and action, round contour. Target grade barrel. Available as a single shot or with a blind magazine. Fully adj. trigger. Bolt is ⅞″ in diameter with recessed face. Hand rubbed stock finish, checkered 20 l.p.i. Shipped in a hard case. Introduced 1980. From Wichita Arms.
Price: Single shot $2,155.00
Price: With blind box magazine $2,285.00

WICHITA CLASSIC RIFLE

Caliber: 17 Rem. thru 308 Win., including 22 and 6mm PPC.
Barrel: 21⅛″.
Weight: 8 lbs. **Length:** 41″ over-all.
Stock: AAA Fancy American walnut. Hand-rubbed and checkered (20 l.p.i.). Hand-inletter, glass bedded, steel grip cap. Pachmayr rubber recoil pad.
Sights: None. Drilled and tapped for scope mounting.
Features: Available as single shot or repeater. Octagonal barrel and Wichita action, right or left-hand. Checkered bolt handle. Bolt is hand-fitted, lapped and jewelled. Adjustable Canjar trigger is set at 2 lbs. Side thumb safety. Firing pin fall is ³⁄₁₆″. Non-glare blue finish. Shipped in hard Protecto case. From Wichita Arms.
Price: Single shot $1,725.00
Price: With blind box magazine $1,855.00

CENTERFIRE RIFLES—BOLT ACTIONS

Winchester 70 XTR Sporter

Winchester Model 70 XTR Sporter
Same as the Model 70 XTR Sporter Magnum except available only in 270 Win. and 30-06, 5-shot magazine.

Price: $459.95

Winchester 70 XTR Sporter Varmint Rifle
Same as 70 XTR Sporter Magnum except: 223, 22-250 and 243 only, no sights, 24″ heavy bbl., 44½″ over-all, 9¾ lbs. American walnut Monte Carlo stock with cheekpiece, black serrated buttplate, black fore-end tip, high luster finish.

Price: $459.95

WINCHESTER 70 XTR SPORTER MAGNUM
Caliber: 264 Win. Mag., 7mm Rem. Mag., 300 Win. Mag., 338 Win. Mag., 3-shot magazine.
Barrel: 24″.
Weight: 7¾ lbs. **Length:** 44½″ over-all.
Stock: American walnut with Monte Carlo cheekpiece. XTR checkering and satin finish.
Sights: Hooded ramp front, adjustable folding leaf rear.
Features: Three-position safety, detachable sling swivels, stainless steel magazine follower, rubber butt pad, epoxy bedded receiver recoil lug. Made under license by U.S. Repeating Arms Co.

Price: $459.95

Winchester Model 70 Westerner
Available in 223, 243, 270, 308, 30-06 with 22″ barrel, 7mm Rem. Mag. and 300 Win. Mag. with 24″ barrel. Iron sights and 4x scope or iron sights only.
Price: With iron sights $369.95

Winchester 70 XTR Express

WINCHESTER 70 XTR SUPER EXPRESS MAGNUM
Caliber: 375 H&H Mag., 458 Win. Mag., 3-shot magazine.
Barrel: 24″ (375), 22″ (458).
Weight: 8½ lbs.
Stock: American walnut with Monte Carlo cheekpiece. XTR wrap-around checkering and finish.
Sights: Hooded ramp front, open rear.
Features: Two steel crossbolts in stock for added strength. Front sling swivel mounted on barrel. Contoured rubber butt pad. Made under license by U.S. Repeating Arms Co.
Price: 375 H&H $699.95
Price: 458 Win $749.95

Winchester 70 XTR Featherweight

Winchester Model 70 XTR Featherweight
Available only in 243, 257 Roberts, 270, 7x57, 30-06 or 308; 22″ tapered featherweight barrel; classic-style American walnut stock with Schnabel fore-end, wraparound XTR checkering fashioned after early Model 70 custom rifle patterns. Red rubber butt pad with black spacer, detachable sling swivels included. High polish blue metal surfaces, satin finish stock. Optional ramped blade front sight, adjustable folding rear. Weighs 6¾ lbs. Introduced 1981.
Price: Without sights $469.95
Price: With sights $499.95

CENTERFIRE RIFLES—SINGLE SHOTS

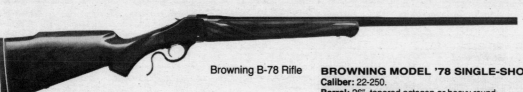

Browning B-78 Rifle

BROWNING MODEL '78 SINGLE-SHOT RIFLE
Caliber: 22-250.
Barrel: 26″, tapered octagon or heavy round.
Weight: Oct. bbl. 7¾ lbs. Heavy round bbl. 8½ lbs. **Length:** 42″ over-all.
Stock: Select walnut, hand rubbed finish, hand checkered (13⅝″x 1⅝″x2⅛″★). Rubber recoil pad. ★Bore measurement.
Sights: None. Furnished with scope mount and rings.
Features: Closely resembles M1885 High Wall rifle. Falling block action with exposed hammer, auto, ejector. Adj. trigger (3½ to 4½ lbs.), half-cock safety. Imported from Japan by Browning.
Price: $474.95

CENTERFIRE RIFLES—SINGLE SHOTS

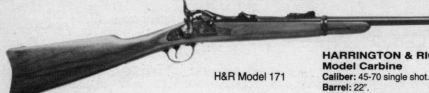

H&R Model 171

HARRINGTON & RICHARDSON Model 174.L.B.H. Commemorative Carbine
Caliber: 45-70, single shot.
Barrel: 22″.
Weight: 7 lbs., 4 oz. **Length:** 41″.
Stock: American walnut with metal grip adapter.
Sights: Blade front, tang mounted aperture rear adj. for w. and e.
Features: Replica of the 1873 Springfield carbine. Engraved breech block, side lock and hammer. Action color case hardened. Each comes with book entitled "In the Valley of the Little Big Horn".
Price: $375.00

HARRINGTON & RICHARDSON Model 171 Cavalry Model Carbine
Caliber: 45-70 single shot.
Barrel: 22″.
Weight: 7 lbs. **Length:** 41″.
Stock: American walnut with saddle ring and bridle.
Sights: Blade front, barrel mounted leaf rear adj. for e.
Features: Replica of the 1873 Springfield Carbine. Blue-black finish. Deluxe version has engraved breech block, side lock & hammer.
Price: $375.00

Harrington & Richardson Model 157 Single Shot Rifle
Same as Model 158 except has pistol grip stock, full length fore-end, and sling swivels. Scope not included; drilled and tapped for mounts. 22 Hornet or 30-30 cals.
Price: $122.00

H&R Model 158

Harrington & Richardson Model 058 Combo Gun
Same as Model 158, except fitted with accessory 20-ga. barrel (26″, Mod.).
Price: 22 Hornet, 357 Mag., 44 Mag. or 30-30 Win., plus 20-ga.... **$122.00**
Price: Model 258 (as above except nickel finish) **$149.50**

HARRINGTON AND RICHARDSON 158 TOPPER RIFLE
Caliber: 30-30, 22 Hornet, 357 Mag., 44 Mag., single shot.
Barrel: 22″ round tapered.
Weight: 6 lbs. **Length:** 37″.
Stock: Walnut finished hardwood stock and fore-end.
Sights: Blade front; folding adj. rear.
Features: Side lever break-open action with visible hammer. Easy takedown.
Price: $100.00

HECKLER & KOCH HK877 SINGLE SHOT RIFLE
Caliber: 30-06 with interchangeable 22-250 barrel.
Barrel: 24″.
Weight: 6 lbs. **Length:** 41″ over-all.
Stock: European walnut, oil finished.
Sights: Bead front, U-notch rear.
Features: Barrel grooved for clamp-type scope mount; sliding safety provides cocking/decocking and trigger setting functions; satin-finished receiver; adjustable trigger. Introduced 1983. Imported from West Germany by Heckler & Koch.
Price: .... NA

Heckler & Koch HK877

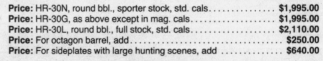

HEYM-RUGER Model HR 30/38 RIFLE
Caliber: 243, 6.5x57R, 7x64, 7x65R, 308, 30-06 (standard); 6.5x68R, 300 Win. Mag., 8x68S, 9.3x74R (magnum).
Barrel: 24″ (standard cals.), 26″ (magnum cals.).
Weight: 6½ to 7 lbs.
Stock: Dark European walnut, hand checkered p.g. and fore-end. Oil finish, recoil pad. Full Mannlicher-type or sporter-style with schnabel fore-end, Bavarian cheekpiece.
Sights: Bead on ramp front, leaf rear.
Features: Ruger No. 1 action and safety, Canjar single-set trigger, hand-engraved animal motif. Options available include deluxe engraving and stock carving. Imported from West Germany by Paul Jaeger Inc.

Heym-Ruger HR 30/38

Price: HR-30N, round bbl., sporter stock, std. cals.............. $1,995.00
Price: HR-30G, as above except in mag. cals. $1,995.00
Price: HR-30L, round bbl., full stock, std. cals. $2,110.00
Price: For octagon barrel, add.................................. $250.00
Price: For sideplates with large hunting scenes, add $640.00

Ljutic Space Rifle

LJUTIC RECOILESS SPACE RIFLE
Caliber: 22-250, 30-30, 30-06, 308; single-shot.
Barrel: 24″.

Weight: 8¾ lbs. **Length:** 44″ over-all.
Stock: Walnut stock and fore-end.
Sights: Iron sights or scope mounts.
Features: Revolutionary design has anti-recoil mechanism. Twist-bolt action uses six moving parts. Scope and mounts extra. Introduced 1981. From Ljutic Industries.
Price: $3,295.00

CAUTION: PRICES CHANGE. CHECK AT GUNSHOP.

NAVY ARMS ROLLING BLOCK RIFLE

Caliber: 45-70.
Barrel: 26½".
Stock: Walnut finished.
Sights: Fixed front, adj. rear.
Features: Reproduction of classic rolling block action. Available in Buffalo Rifle (octagonal bbl.) and Creedmore (half round, half octagonal bbl.) models. Made in U.S. by Navy Arms.
Price: 18", 26", 30" full octagon barrel $374.00
Price: Creedmore Model, 30" full octagon $399.00
Price: 30", half-round. $379.00
Price: 26", half round $374.00
Price: Half-round Creedmore. $399.00

Navy Rolling Block

Navy Creedmoor Target Rifle

Similar to standard Rolling Block rifle except has checkered pistol grip stock and fore-end and cheek rest. Full octagon barrel. Available in 45-70 and 45-90. Has a vernier peep sight on buttstock. From Navy Arms.
Price: $600.00

Ruger No. 1 International

RUGER NUMBER ONE SINGLE SHOT

Caliber: 220 Swift, 22-250, 243, 6mm Rem., 25-06, 270, 7x57mm, 30-06, 7mm Rem. Mag., 300 Win., 338 Win. Mag., 45-70, 458 Win. Mag., 375 H&H Mag.
Barrel: 26" round tapered with quarter-rib (also 22" and 24", depending upon model).

Weight: 8 lbs. **Length:** 42" over-all.
Stock: Walnut, two-piece, checkered p.g. and fore-end (either semi-beavertail or Henry style).
Sights: None, 1" scope rings supplied for integral mounts. 3 models have open sights.
Features: Under lever, hammerless falling block design has auto ejector, top tang safety. Standard Rifle 1B illus.
Price: $405.00
Price: Also available as Light Sporter, Medium Sporter, Varminter, Tropical Rifle and International $405.00
Price: Barreled action, blued only $286.50

Ruger No. 3 Carbine

RUGER NO. 3 CARBINE SINGLE SHOT

Caliber: 22 Hornet, 223, 375 Win., 45-70.
Barrel: 22" round.
Weight: 6 lbs. **Length:** 38½".
Stock: American walnut, carbine-type.
Sights: Gold bead front, adj. folding leaf rear.
Features: Same action as No. 1 Rifle except different lever. Has auto ejector, top tang safety, adj. trigger.
Price: $284.00

SHARPS "OLD RELIABLE" RIFLE

Caliber: 45-70, 45-120-3¼" Sharps.
Barrel: 28", full octagon, polished blue.
Weight: 9½ lbs. **Length:** 45" over-all.
Stock: Walnut with deluxe checkering at p.g. and fore-end.
Sights: Sporting blade front, folding leaf rear. Globe front, vernier rear optional at extra cost.
Features: Falling block, lever action. Color case-hardened hammer, buttplate and action with automatic safety. Available with engraved action for **$97.25** extra. From Shore.
Price: Old Reliable. $377.50
Price: Sporter Rifle $362.50
Price: Military Carbine $345.00
Price: Sporter Carbine $362.50

Consult our Directory pages for the location of firms mentioned.

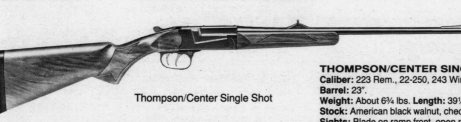

Thompson/Center Single Shot

THOMPSON/CENTER SINGLE SHOT RIFLE

Caliber: 223 Rem., 22-250, 243 Win., 7mm Rem. Mag., 30-06.
Barrel: 23".
Weight: About 6¾ lbs. **Length:** 39½" over-all.
Stock: American black walnut, checkered p.g. and fore-end.
Sights: Blade on ramp front, open rear adj. for windage only.
Features: Break-open design with interchangeable barrels. Double-set or single-stage trigger function. Cross-bolt safety. Sights removeable for scope mounting. Made in U.S. by T/C. Introduced 1983.
Price: $425.00
Price: Extra barrel $140.00

ARMSPORT "EMPEROR" 4000 DOUBLE RIFLE
Caliber: 243, 270, 284, 7.65, 308, 30-06, 7mm Rem. Mag., 9.3, 300 H&H, 375 H&H; Shotgun barrels in 12, 16 or 20-ga.
Barrel: Shotgun barrel length and chokes to customer specs.
Stock: Dimensions to customer specs. Stock and fore-end of root walnut.
Sights: Rifle barrels have blade front with bead, leaf rear adj. for w.
Features: Receiver and sideplates engraved. Gun comes with extra set of barrels fitted to action. Packaged in a hand-made, fitted luggage-type leather case lined with Scotch loden cloth. Introduced 1978. From Armsport.
Price: Complete **$16,300.00**

ARMSPORT "EMPEROR" 4010 DOUBLE RIFLE
Side-by-side version of the Model 4000 over-under rifle. Available in 243, 270, 284, 7.65, 308, 30-06, 7mm Rem. Mag., 9.3, 300 H&H, 338 Win. and 375 H&H. Shotgun barrels in 16 or 20 ga., choice of length and choke. Comes in fitted luggage-type case.
Price: **$12,750.00**

Bauer Rabbit

BAUER RABBIT
Caliber/Gauge: 22 LR over 410 (3").
Barrel: 20".
Weight: 4¾ lbs. **Length:** 38½"; disassembled 20".
Stock: Metal skeleton.
Sights: Fixed.
Features: Takes down quickly into two pieces. Single selective trigger. Rust resistant finish on stock, barrel and receiver.
Price: **$89.60**

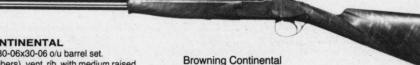

Browning Continental

BROWNING SUPERPOSED CONTINENTAL
Caliber/Gauge: 20 ga. x 20 ga. with extra 30-06x30-06 o/u barrel set.
Barrel: 20 ga.—26½" (Mod. & Full, 3" chambers), vent. rib, with medium raised German nickel silver sight bead. 30-06—24".
Weight: 6 lbs. 14 oz. (rifle barrels) 5 lbs. 14 oz. (shotgun barrels)
Stock: Select high grade American walnut with oil finish. Straight grip stock and schnabel fore-end with 26 l.p.i. hand checkering.
Sights: Rifle barrels have flat face gold bead front on matted ramp, folding leaf rear.
Features: Action is based on a specially engineered Superposed 20-ga. frame. Single selective trigger works on inertia; let-off is about 4½ lbs. Automatic selective ejectors. Manual top tang safety incorporated with barrel selector. Furnished with fitted luggage-type case. Introduced 1979. Imported from Belgium by Browning.
Price: **$6,000.00**

BROWNING EXPRESS RIFLE
Caliber: 270 or 30-06.
Barrel: 24".
Weight: About 6 lbs., 14 oz. **Length:** 41" over-all.
Stock: Select walnut with oil finish; straight grip, Schnabel fore-end; hand checkered to 25 lpi.
Sights: Gold bead on ramp front, adjustable folding leaf rear.
Features: Specially engineered superposed action with reinforced breech face. Receiver hand engraved. Single selective trigger, auto. selective ejectors, manual safety. Comes in fitted luggage case. Imported from Belgium by Browning.
Price: Either caliber **$4,300.00**

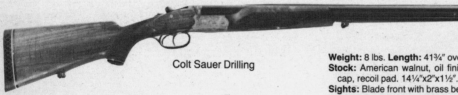

Colt Sauer Drilling

COLT SAUER DRILLING
Caliber/Gauge: 12 ga., over 30-06, 12 ga. over 243.
Action: Top lever, cross bolt, box lock.
Barrel: 25" (Mod. & Full).

Weight: 8 lbs. **Length:** 41¾" over-all.
Stock: American walnut, oil finish. Checkered p.g. and fore-end. Black p.g. cap, recoil pad. 14¼"x2"x1½".
Sights: Blade front with brass bead, folding leaf rear.
Features: Cocking indicators, tang barrel selector, automatic sight positioner, set rifle trigger, side safety. Blue finish with bright receiver engraved with animal motifs and European-style scrollwork. Imported from West Germany by Colt.
Price: **$3,945.95**

Ferlach Custom Drilling

FERLACH CUSTOM DRILLING (FRANZ SODIA)
Caliber/Gauge: Any desired.
Action: Blitz, with Greener cross-bolt.
Barrel: Any length, to customer specs.
Weight: To customer specs. **Length:** To customer specs.
Stock: Custom or standard dimensions; best wood on request.
Sights: Any style, to customer specs.
Features: Options include highly figured wood, magnum chambering, scope, fancy side plates, cartridge trap, set trigger, etc. Imported from Austria by Ferlach (Austria) of North America.
Price: **$3,950.00**

FERLACH CUSTOM DOUBLE RIFLE (FRANZ SODIA)

Caliber: Any caliber desired; metric, English or American.
Action: Boxlock or sidelock, side-by-side or over-under, with or without ejectors.
Barrel: Any length desired.
Weight: To customer specs. **Length:** To customer specs.
Stock: Best walnut; fine checkering.
Sights: Silver bead front, with folding night sight if specified. Sourdough rear with vertical inlay and 200 yd. folding leaf. Scope with claw mount available.

Ferlach Double Rifle

Features: Any desired including highly figured wood, auto ejection, set trigger, folding sights, extra barrel sets, night sights. Imported from Austria by Ferlach (Austria) of North America.
Price: Base, boxlock action. **$5,750.00**
Price: Base, sidelock action **$9,500.00**

H&R 258 Handy Gun II

HARRINGTON & RICHARDSON 258 HANDY GUN II

Caliber/Gauge: 22 Hornet, 30-30 Win., 357 Mag., 357 Maximum, 44 Mag. with interchangeable 20-ga. 3" barrel.
Barrel: 22" (rifle), 22" (Mod.) shotgun.
Weight: About 6½ lbs. **Length:** 37" over-all.
Stock: American hardwood with walnut finish.
Sights: Bead front on shotgun; ramped blade front, adjustable folding leaf rear on rifle barrel.
Features: Interchangeable barrels. All metal parts have H&R Hard-Gard electroless matte nickel finish. Comes with heavy duck case. Introduced 1982.
Price: **$149.50**

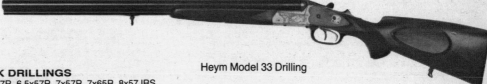

Heym Model 33 Drilling

HEYM MODEL 33 BOXLOCK DRILLINGS

Caliber/Gauge: 5.6x50R Mag., 5.6x57R, 6.5x57R, 7x57R, 7x65R, 8x57JRS, 9.3x74R, 222, 243, 270, 308, 30-06; 16x16 (2¾"), 20x20 (3").
Barrel: 25" (Full & Mod.).
Weight: About 6½ lbs. **Length:** 42" over-all.
Stock: Dark European walnut, checkered p.g. and fore-end; oil finish.
Sights: Silver bead front, folding leaf rear. Automatic sight positioner. Available with scope and Suhler claw mounts.

Features: Greener-type crossbolt and safety, double under-lugs. Double set triggers. Plastic or steel trigger guard. Engraving coverage varies with model. Imported from West Germany by Paul Jaeger Inc.
Price: Model 33, from. **$3,350.00**

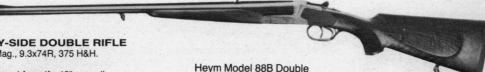

Heym Model 88B Double

HEYM MODEL 88B SIDE-BY-SIDE DOUBLE RIFLE

Caliber: 30-06, 8x57JRS, 300 Win. Mag., 9.3x74R, 375 H&H.
Barrel: 25".
Weight: 7½ lbs. (std. cals), 8½ lbs. (mag.) **Length:** 42" over-all.
Stock: Fancy French walnut, classic North American design.
Sights: Silver bead post on ramp front, fixed or 3-leaf express rear.
Features: Action has complete coverage hunting scene engraving. Comes with fitted leather case. Available as boxlock or with q.d. sidelocks. Imported from West Germany by Paul Jaeger, Inc.

Price: Boxlock, from. **$5,470.00**
Price: Sidelock, Model 88B-SS, from **$7,570.00**
Price: Disengageable ejectors, add **$190.00**

HEYM MODEL 37B DOUBLE RIFLE DRILLING

Caliber/Gauge: 7x65R, 30-06, 8x57JRS, 9.3x74R; 20 ga. (3").
Barrel: 25" (shotgun barrel choked Full or Mod.).
Weight: About 8½ lbs. **Length:** 42" over-all.
Stock: Dark European walnut, hand-checkered p.g. and fore-end. Oil finish.
Sights: Silver bead front, folding leaf rear. Available with scope and Suhler claw mounts.
Features: Full side-lock construction. Greener-type crossbolt, double under lugs, cocking indicators. Imported from West Germany by Paul Jaeger, Inc.
Price: Model 37 double rifle drilling **$6,860.00**
Price: Model 37 Deluxe (hunting scene engraving) from, ... **$7,840.00**

Heym Model 37 Side Lock Drilling

Similar to Model 37 Double Rifle Drilling except has 12x12, 16x16 or 20x20 over 5.6x50R Mag., 5.6x57R, 6.5x57R, 7x57R, 7x65R, 8x57JRS, 9.3x74R, 222, 243, 270, 308 or 30-06. Rifle barrel is manually cocked and uncocked.
Price: Model 37 with border engraving **$5,190.00**
Price: As above with engraved hunting scenes. **$6,170.00**

HEYM MODEL 22S SAFETY COMBO GUN

Caliber/Gauge: 16 or 20 ga. (2¾", 3") over 22 Hornet, 22 WMR, 222 Rem., 222 Rem. Mag., 223, 243 Win., 5.6x50R, 6.5x57R, 7x57R.
Barrel: 24", solid rib.
Weight: About 5½ lbs.
Stock: Dark European walnut, hand-checkered p.g. and fore-end. Oil finish.
Sights: Silver bead ramp front, folding leaf rear.
Features: Tang mounted cocking slide, separate barrel selector, single set trigger. Base supplied for quick-detachable scope mounts. Patented rocker-weight system automatically uncocks gun if accidentally dropped or bumped hard. Imported from West Germany. Contact Heym for more data.
Price: Model 22S **$1,390.00**
Price: Scope mounts, add **$125.00**

HEYM MODEL 55B/77B O/U DOUBLE RIFLE
Caliber: 7x65R, 308, 30-06, 8x57JRS, 9.3x74R; 375 H&H, 458 Win. Mag.
Barrel: 25″
Weight: About 8 lbs., depending upon caliber. **Length:** 42″ over-all.
Stock: Dark European walnut, hand-checkered p.g. and fore-end. Oil finish.
Sights: Silver bead ramp front, open V-type rear.
Features: Boxlock or full sidelock; Kersten double crossbolt, cocking indicators; hand-engraved hunting scenes. Options available include interchangeable barrels, Zeiss scopes in claw mounts, deluxe engravings and stock carving, etc. Imported from West Germany by Paul Jaeger, Inc.
Price: Model 55B boxlock **$3,880.00**
Price: Model 55BSS sidelock **$6,160.00**
Price: Interchangeable shotgun barrels **$1,715.00**

Heym 55B/77B O/U

Heym Model 55BF/77BF O/U Combo Gun
Similar to Model 55B/77B o/u rifle except chambered for 12, 16 or 20 ga. (2¾″ or 3″) over 5.6x50R, 222 Rem., 5.6x57R, 243, 6.5x57R, 270, 7x57R, 7x65R, 308, 30-06, 8x57JRS, 9.3x74R, or 375 H&H. Has solid rib barrel. Available as boxlock or sidelock, with interchangeable shotgun and rifle barrels.
Price: Model 55BF boxlock **$3,070.00**
Price: Model 55BFSS sidelock **$5,350.00**

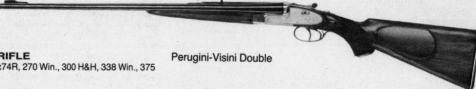

PERUGINI-VISINI DOUBLE RIFLE
Caliber: 7mm Rem. Mag., 7x65R, 9.3x74R, 270 Win., 300 H&H, 338 Win., 375 H&H, 458 Win. Mag., 470 Nitro.
Barrel: 22″-26″.
Weight: 7¼ to 8½ lbs., depending upon caliber. **Length:** 39½″ over-all (22″ bbl.).
Stock: Oil-finished walnut; checkered grip and fore-end; cheekpiece.
Sights: Bead on ramp front, express rear on ¼-rib.

Perugini-Visini Double

Features: True sidelock action with ejectors; sideplates are hand detachable; comes with trunk case. Introduced 1983. Imported from Italy by Wm. Larkin Moore & Co.
Price: **$10,000.00**

PERUGINI-VISINI O/U DOUBLE RIFLE
Caliber: 7mm Rem. Mag., 7x65R, 9.3x74R, 270 Win., 284 Win., 338 Win. Mag., 375 H&H, 458 Win. Mag.
Barrel: 24″.
Weight: 8 lbs. **Length:** 40½″ over-all.
Stock: Oil-finished walnut; checkered grip and fore-end; cheekpiece, rubber recoil pad.
Sights: Bead on ramp front, express rear on ¼-rib; scope and claw mounts optional.

Perugini-Visini O/U Double

Features: Boxlock action with ejectors; silvered receiver, rest blued; double triggers. Comes with trunk case. Introduced 1983. Imported from Italy by Wm. Larkin Moore.
Price: **$3,250.00**

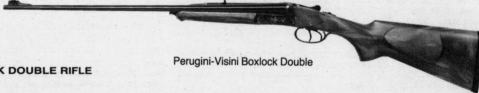

Perugini-Visini Boxlock Double

PERUGINI-VISINI BOXLOCK DOUBLE RIFLE
Caliber: 9.3x74R, 444 Marlin.
Barrel: 25″.
Weight: 8 lbs. **Length:** 41½″ over-all.
Stock: Oil-finished walnut; checkered grip and fore-end; cheekpiece; rubber recoil pad.
Sights: Bead on ramp front, express rear on ¼-rib.

Features: Boxlock, non-ejector action; color case-hardened receiver; double triggers. Comes with trunk case. Introduced 1983. Imported from Italy by Wm. Larkin Moore.
Price: **$2,000.00**

Savage Model 24-C

SAVAGE MODEL 24-C O/U
Caliber/Gauge: Top bbl. 22 S, L, LR; bottom bbl. 20 gauge cyl. bore.
Action: Take-down, low rebounding visible hammer. Single trigger, barrel selector spur on hammer.
Barrel: 20″ separated barrels.
Weight: 5¾ lbs. **Length:** 35″ (taken down 20″).
Stock: Walnut finished hardwood, straight grip.
Sights: Ramp front, rear open adj. for e.
Features: Trap door butt holds one shotshell and ten 22 cartridges, comes with special carrying case. Measures 7″x22″ when in case.
Price: **$177.50**

CAUTION: PRICES CHANGE. CHECK AT GUNSHOP.

DRILLINGS, COMBINATION GUNS, DOUBLE RIFLES

Savage Model 24-D

Savage Model 24-F.G. O/U
Same as Model 24-D except: color case hardened frame, stock is walnut finished hardwood, no checkering or M.C.
Price: **$158.00**

Savage Model 24-V
Similar to Model 24-D except: 22 Hornet, 222 Rem, or 30-30 and 20 ga., 223 or 357 Rem. Max. and 20 ga.; stronger receiver; color case-hardened frame; folding leaf rear sight; receiver tapped for scope.
Price: **$225.00**

Savage Model 24-D O/U
Caliber/Gauge: Top bbl. 22 S, L, LR or 22 Mag.; bottom bbl. 20 or 410 gauge.
Action: Bottom opening lever, low rebounding visible hammer, single trigger, barrel selector spur on hammer, separate extractors, color case-hardened frame.
Barrel: 24″, separated barrels.
Weight: 6¾ lbs. **Length:** 40″.
Stock: Walnut, checkered p.g. (14″x1½″x2½″).
Sights: Ramp front, rear open adj. for e.
Features: Receiver grooved for scope mounting.
Price: **$195.50**

Savage Model 24-VS Camper/Survival Shotgun
Similar to the standard Model 24-V except satin nickel finish, full-length, tung-oil finished stock and an accessory pistol grip stock. Chambered for 357 Rem. Max. over 20 gauge. Also available in 22 Long Rifle over 20 gauge as Model 24-CS. Introduced 1983.
Price: Model 24-VS **$266.50**
Price: Model 24-CS **$208.00**

Valmet 412 K Double

VALMET 412KE COMBINATION GUN
Caliber/Gauge: 12 over 222, 223, 243, 308, 30-06.
Barrel: 24″ (Imp. & Mod.).
Weight: 7⅝ lbs.
Stock: American walnut, with recoil pad. Monte Carlo style. Standard measurements 14″x1⅜″x2″x2⅜″.
Sights: Blade front, flip-up-type open rear.
Features: Barrel selector on trigger. Hand checkered stock and fore-end. Barrels are screw-adjustable to change bullet point of impact. Barrels are interchangeable. Introduced 1980. Imported from Finland by Valmet.
Price: **$834.00**
Price: Engraved model **$2,584.00**

VALMET 412K DOUBLE RIFLE
Caliber: 243, 308, 30-06, 375 Win.
Barrel: 24″
Weight: 8⅝ lbs.
Stock: American walnut with Monte Carlo style.
Sights: Ramp front, adjustable open rear.
Features: Barrel selector mounted in trigger. Cocking indicators in tang. Recoil pad. Valmet scope mounts available. Interchangeable barrels. Introduced 1980. Imported from Finland by Valmet.
Price: Extractors, 243, 308, 30-06 .... **$1,069.00**
Price: With ejectors, 375 Win., 9.3x74R **$1,119.00**
Price: Engraved model **$2,819.00**

Winchester Double Express

> Consult our Directory pages for
> the location of firms mentioned.

WINCHESTER DOUBLE XPRESS O/U RIFLE
Caliber: 30-06/30-06, 9.3x74R/9.3x74R, 270/270, 257 Roberts/257 Roberts.
Barrel: 23½″.
Weight: 8½ lbs. **Length:** 39⅝″ over-all.
Stock: 2½″x1¹¹⁄₁₆″x14⅜″. Fancy American walnut with hand checkered pistol grip and fore-end, solid rubber butt pad.
Sights: Bead on ramp front, folding leaf rear on quarter-rib.
Features: Integral scope bases; q.d. sling swivels. Uses Model 101 action; receiver silvered and engraved, barrels blued. Comes with hard case. Introduced 1982. Imported from Japan by Winchester Group, Olin Corp.
Price: **$2,750.00**

A. ZOLI RIFLE-SHOTGUN O/U COMBO
Caliber/Gauge: 12 ga./308 Win., 12 ga./222, 12 ga./30-06.
Barrel: Combo—24″; shotgun—28″ (Mod. & Full).
Weight: About 8 lbs. **Length:** 41″ over-all (24″ bbl.).
Stock: European walnut.
Sights: Blade front, flip-up rear.
Features: Available with German claw scope mounts on rifle/shotgun barrels. Comes with set of 12/12 (Mod. & Full) barrels. Imported from Italy by Mandall Shooting Supplies.
Price: With two barrel sets, without claw mounts **$1,395.00**
Price: With two barrel sets, with claw mounts **$1,495.00**

WINCHESTER SUPER GRADE O/U COMBO
Caliber/Gauge: 12 ga. over 30-06.
Barrel: 25″. Shot barrel uses Winchoke system.
Weight: 8½ lbs. **Length:** 41¼″ over-all.
Stock: 2½″x1¾″x14″. Fancy American walnut with hand checkered pistol grip and fore-end; ventilated rubber recoil pad.
Sights: Bead front, folding leaf rear.
Features: Single selective mechanical trigger, combination barrel selector. Full length top barrel rib with integral scope bases. Uses Model 101 frame. Silvered and engraved receiver, blued barrels. Imported from Japan by Winchester Group, Olin Corp.
Price: **$2,250.00**

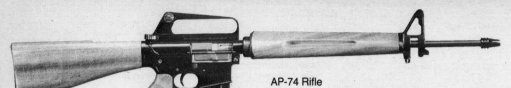

AP-74 Rifle

AP-74 AUTO RIFLE
Caliber: 22 LR, 32 ACP, 15 shot magazine.
Barrel: 20″ including flash reducer.
Weight: 6½ lbs. **Length:** 38½″ over-all.

Stock: Black plastic.
Sights: Ramp front, adj. peep rear.
Features: Pivotal take-down, easy disassembly. AR-15 look-alike. Sling and sling swivels included. Imported by EMF.
Price: $250.00
Price: With walnut stock and fore-end $275.00
Price: 32 ACP.. $265.00
Price: With wood stock and fore-end $290.00

AM-180 Auto Carbine

AM-180 AUTO CARBINE
Caliber: 22 LR, 177-round magazine.
Barrel: 16½″.
Weight: 5¾ lbs. (empty), 10 lbs. (loaded). **Length:** 36″ over-all.
Stock: High impact plastic stock and fore-end.
Sights: Blade front, peep rear adj. for w. and e.
Features: Available in selective fire version for law enforcement or semi-auto only for civilians. Imported from Austria by Christopher & Assoc.

Price: $595.00
Price: Laser sight system, about............................... $795.00
Price: Extra drum magazine................................... $80.00
Price: Winding mechanism.................................... $47.00

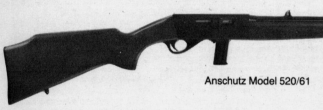

Anschutz Model 520/61

ANSCHUTZ DELUXE MODEL 520/61 AUTO
Caliber: 22 LR, 10-shot clip.
Barrel: 24″.
Weight: 6½ lbs. **Length:** 43″ over-all.
Stock: European hardwood; checkered pistol grip, Monte Carlo comb, beavertail fore-end.
Sights: Hooded ramp front, folding leaf rear.
Features: Rotary safety, empty shell deflector, single stage trigger. Receiver grooved for scope mounting. Introduced 1982. Imported from Germany by Talo Distributors, Inc.
Price: $259.00

Auto-Ordnance 1927A-3

AUTO-ORDNANCE MODEL 1927A-3
Caliber: 22 LR, 10, 30 or 50-shot magazine.
Barrel: 16″, finned.
Weight: About 7 lbs.
Stock: Walnut stock and fore-end.
Sights: Blade front, open rear adjustable for windage and elevation.
Features: Re-creation of the Thompson Model 1927, only in 22 Long Rifle. Alloy receiver, finned barrel.
Price: $449.65

Browning Auto Rifle

BROWING AUTOLOADING RIFLE
Caliber: 22 LR, 11-shot.
Barrel: 19¼″.
Weight: 4¾ lbs. **Length:** 37″ over-all.
Stock: Checkered select walnut (13¾″x1¹³⁄₁₆″x2⅝″) with p.g. and semi-beavertail fore-end.
Sights: Gold bead front, folding leaf rear.
Features: Engraved receiver is grooved for tip-off scope mount; cross-bolt safety; tubular magazine in buttstock; easy take down for carrying or storage. Imported from Japan by Browning.
Price: Grade I $267.95
Price: Grade II $380.00
Price: Grade III $815.00
Price: Also available in Grade I, 22 S (16-shot) $267.95

CAUTION: PRICES CHANGE. CHECK AT GUNSHOP.

Browning BAR-22

BROWNING BAR-22 AUTO RIFLE
Caliber: 22 LR only, 15-shot tube magazine.
Barrel: 20¼".
Weight: About 6¼ lbs. **Length:** 38¼" over-all.

Stock: French walnut. Cut checkering at p.g. and fore-end.
Sights: Gold bead front, folding leaf rear. Receiver grooved for scope mounting.
Features: Magazine tube latch locks closed from any position. Cross bolt safety in rear of trigger guard. Trigger pull about 5 lbs. Introduced 1977. Imported from Japan by Browning.
Price: Grade I $244.95
Price: Grade II $349.95

Charter AR-7 Explorer

ERMA ESG22 GAS-OPERATED CARBINE
Caliber: 22 Mag., 12-shot magazine, 22 LR, 15-shot magazine.
Barrel: 18".
Weight: 6 lbs. **Length:** 35½" over-all.
Stock: Walnut-stained beech.
Sights: Military post front, peep rear adj. for w. & e.
Features: Locked breech, gas-operated action. Styled after M-1 Carbine. Also available as standard blowback action. Receiver grooved for scope mounting. Introduced 1978. From Excam.
Price: Gas. 22 Mag.. $295.00
Price: Blowback, 22 LR (EM-1) $195.00

CHARTER AR-7 EXPLORER CARBINE
Caliber: 22 LR, 8-shot clip.
Barrel: 16" alloy (steel-lined).
Weight: 2½ lbs. **Length:** 34½"/16½" stowed.
Stock: Moulded grey Cycloac, snap-on rubber butt pad.
Sights: Square blade front, aperture rear adj. for e.
Features: Take-down design stores bbl. and action in hollow stock. Light enough to float.
Price: Black $98.00
Price: Satin chrome... $101.00

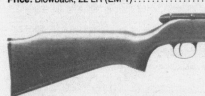

H&R Model 700 Auto

H&R Model 700 Deluxe Rifle
Same as Model 700 except has select walnut stock with cheekpiece, checkered grip and fore-end, rubber rifle recoil pad. No iron sights; comes with H&R Model 432 4x, 1" tube scope, with base and rings.
Price: $295.00

HARRINGTON & RICHARDSON Model 700 Auto Rifle
Caliber: 22 Mag., 5-shot clip.
Barrel: 22".
Weight: 6½ lbs. **Length:** 43¼" over-all.
Stock: Walnut, Monte Carlo, full p.g., composition buttplate.
Sights: Blade front, folding leaf rear.
Features: Drilled and tapped for scope mounting. 10-shot clip available. Made in U.S. by H&R.
Price: $185.00

H&K Model 270 Auto

HECKLER & KOCH HK270 AUTO RIFLE
Caliber: 22 LR, 5-shot magazine.
Barrel: 19¾".
Weight: 5.5 lbs. **Length:** 38.2" over-all.
Stock: European walnut.
Sights: Post front adj. for elevation, diopter rear adjustable for windage.
Features: Straight blow-back action; 3½ lb. trigger pull. Extra 20-shot magazine available. Receiver grooved for scope mount. Introduced 1978. Imported from West Germany by Heckler & Koch.
Price: $250.00
Price: Scope mount, rings $65.10
Price: 20-shot magazine... $24.00

HECKLER & KOCH MODEL 300 AUTO RIFLE
Caliber: 22 Mag., 5-shot box mag.
Barrel: 19¾".
Weight: 5¾ lbs. **Length:** 39½" over-all.
Stock: European walnut, Monte Carlo with cheek rest; checkered p.g. and Schnabel fore-end.
Sights: Post front adj. for elevation, V-notch rear adj. for windage.
Features: Hexagon (polygonal) rifling; comes with sling swivels; straight blow-back inertia bolt action; single-stage trigger (3½-lb. pull). Clamp scope mount with 1" rings available at extra cost. Imported from West Germany by Heckler & Koch, Inc.
Price: HK300 .... $350.00
Price: Scope mount with 1" rings $113.00

KASSNAR-SQUIRES BINGHAM MODEL M-16
Caliber: 22 LR, 15-shot magazine.
Barrel: 19½", including flash hider/muzzle brake.
Weight: 6 lbs. **Length:** 38" over-all.
Stock: Mahogany, painted black.
Sights: Post front adjustable for elevation, peep rear adjustable for windage.
Features: Replica of AR-15 rifle. Comes with carrying sling. Imported from the Philippines by Kassnar.
Price: $139.95
Price: With collapsible buttstock as M-16R $159.95

KASSNAR-SQUIRES BINGHAM MODEL 20 RIFLE
Caliber: 22 Long Rifle, 15-shot magazine.
Barrel: 20".
Weight: 6 lbs. **Length:** 41" over-all.
Stock: Philippine mahogany with walnut finish.
Sights: Blade on ramp front, V-notch rear adjustable for elevation.
Features: Receiver grooved for scope mounting. Gun comes with 4x scope installed. Imported from the Philippines by Kassnar.
Price: $69.95
Price: Model 2000 (checkered stock, adj. rear sight)............... $99.95

RIMFIRE RIFLES—AUTOLOADERS

Marlin Model 990

MARLIN MODEL 990 SEMI-AUTO RIFLE
Caliber: 22 LR, 18-shot tubular magazine.
Barrel: 22″ Micro-Groove®.
Weight: About 5½ lbs. **Length:** 40¾″ over-all.
Stock: American black walnut, Monte Carlo style with fluted comb and full pistol grip; checkered p.g. and fore-end.
Sights: Ramp bead front with Wide-Scan™ hood, adjustable folding semi-buckhorn rear.
Features: Receiver grooved for tip-off mount; bolt hold-open device; cross-bolt safety. Introduced 1979.
Price: **$125.95**

Marlin Model 995

MARLIN MODEL 995 SEMI-AUTO RIFLE
Caliber: 22 LR, 7-shot clip magazine
Barrel: 18″ Micro-Grove®.
Weight: 5½ lbs. **Length:** 36¾″ over-all.
Stock: American black walnut, Monte Carlo-style, with full pistol grip. Checkered p.g. and fore-end.
Sights: Ramp bead front with Wide-Scan hood; adjustable folding semi-buckhorn rear.
Features: Receiver grooved for tip-off scope mount; bolt hold-open device; cross-bolt safety. Introduced 1979.
Price: **$117.95**

Marlin Model 60

MARLIN 60 SEMI-AUTO RIFLE
Caliber: 22 LR, 18-shot tubular mag.
Barrel: 22″ round tapered.
Weight: About 5½ lbs. **Length:** 41″ over-all.
Stock: Walnut finished Monte Carlo.
Sights: Ramp front, open adj. rear.
Features: Matted receiver is grooved for tip-off mounts. Has new tube magazine closure system.
Price: Less scope. **$97.95**

MARLIN MODEL 75C SEMI-AUTO RIFLE
Caliber: 22 LR, 14-shot magazine.
Barrel: 18″.
Weight: 5 lbs. **Length:** 36¾″ over-all.
Stock: Walnut-finished hardwood; Monte Carlo with full p.g.
Sights: Ramp front, adj. open rear.
Features: Bolt hold-open device; cross-bolt safety; receiver grooved for scope mounting.
Price: **$97.95**

MARLIN 70 AUTO
Caliber: 22 LR, 7-shot clip magazine.
Barrel: 18″ (16-groove rifling).
Weight: 4½ lbs. **Length:** 36½″ over-all.
Stock: Walnut-finished hardwood with Monte Carlo, full p.g.
Sights: Ramp front, adj. open rear. Receiver grooved for scope mount.
Features: Receiver top has serrated, non-glare finish; chrome plated trigger; cross-bolt safety; bolt hold-open; chrome plated magazine.
Price: Less scope. **$97.95**

Mossberg Model 353

MOSSBERG MODEL 353 AUTO LOADING RIFLE
Caliber: 22 LR, 7-shot clip.
Barrel: 18″ AC-KRO-GRUV.
Weight: 5 lbs. **Length:** 38″ over-all.
Stock: Walnut, checkered at p.g. and fore-end. Black Tenite two-position fold-down fore-end.
Sights: Open step adj. U-notch rear, bead front on ramp.
Features: Sling swivels and web strap on left of stock, extension fore-end folds down for steady firing from prone position. Receiver grooved for scope mounting.
Price: About **$94.95**

MOSSBERG MODEL 380 AUTO RIFLE
Caliber: 22 LR, 15-shot tube magazine.
Barrel: 20″, tapered, with AC-KRO-GRUV.
Weight: About 5½ lbs. with scope.
Stock: Walnut-finished hardwood, with black non-slip buttplate.
Sights: Bead front, adj. open rear.
Features: Receiver grooved for scope mounting. Available with optional 4x scope, mount. Magazine feeds through buttstock. Introduced 1981.
Price: With open sights, about **$91.00**
Price: With 4x scope, about **$95.00**

CAUTION: PRICES CHANGE. CHECK AT GUNSHOP.

Mossberg 377 Plinkster

MOSSBERG 377 PLINKSTER AUTO RIFLE
Caliber: 22 LR, 15-shot tube magazine
Barrel: 20" AC-KRO-GRUV.
Weight: 6¼ lbs. **Length:** 40" over-all.
Stock: Straight line, moulded one-piece thumbhole.
Sights: No iron sights. Comes with 4x scope.
Features: Walnut texture stock finish, checkered fore-end. Tube magazine loads through port in buttstock. Has bolt hold-open.
Price: With 4x scope, about $103.00

Remington Nylon 66

REMINGTON NYLON 66MB AUTO RIFLE
Caliber: 22 LR, 14-shot tubular mag.
Barrel: 19⅝" round tapered.
Weight: 4 lbs. **Length:** 38½" over-all.
Stock: Moulded Mohawk Brown Nylon, checkered p.g. and fore-end.
Sights: Blade ramp front, adj. open rear.
Features: Top tang safety, double extractors, receiver grooved for tip-off mounts.
Price: $129.95
Price: Model 66MB With Universal UA 4x scope $142.95

Remington Nylon 66BD Auto Rifle
Same as the Model 66AB except has black stock, barrel, and receiver cover. Black diamond-shape inlay in fore-end. Introduced 1978.
Price: **$129.95**
Price: Model 66 BD with 4x scope **$142.95**

Remington Nylon 66AB Auto Rifle
Same as the Model 66MB except: Apache Black Nylon stock, chrome plated receiver.
Price: $138.95

Remington Model 552A

REMINGTON 552A AUTOLOADING RIFLE
Caliber: 22 S (20), L (17) or LR (15) tubular mag.
Barrel: 21" round tapered.
Weight: About 5¾ lbs. **Length:** 40" over-all.
Stock: Full-size, walnut-finished hardwood.
Sights: Bead front, step open rear adj. for w. & e.
Features: Positive cross-bolt safety, receiver grooved for tip-off mount.
Price: $174.95

Remington Model 552BDL Auto Rifle
Same as Model 552A except: Du Pont RKW finished walnut stock, checkered fore-end and capped p.g. stock. Blade ramp front and fully adj. rear sights.
Price: **$197.95**

Ruger 10/22 Sporter

RUGER 10/22 AUTOLOADING CARBINE
Caliber: 22 LR, 10-shot rotary mag.
Barrel: 18½" round tapered.
Weight: 5 lbs., 12 oz. **Length:** 36¾" over-all.
Stock: Birch with p.g. and bbl. band.
Sights: Gold bead front, folding leaf rear adj. for e.
Features: Detachable rotary magazine fits flush into stock, cross-bolt safety, receiver tapped and grooved for scope blocks or tip-off mount. Scope base adapter furnished with each rifle.
Price: Model 10/22 RB $134.50

Ruger 10/22 Auto Sporter
Same as 10/22 Carbine except: Walnut stock with hand checkered p.g. and fore-end with straight buttplate, no bbl. band, has sling swivels.
Price: Model 10/22 DSP $163.00

Tradewinds Model 260-A

TRADEWINDS MODEL 260-A AUTO RIFLE
Caliber: 22 LR, 5-shot (10-shot mag. avail.).
Barrel: 22½".
Weight: 5¾ lbs. **Length:** 41½".
Stock: Walnut, with hand checkered p.g. and fore-end.
Sights: Ramp front with hood, 3-leaf folding rear, receiver grooved for scope mount.
Features: Double extractors, sliding safety. Imported by Tradewinds.
Price: $250.00

U.S. Arms PMA1P

U.S. ARMS PMAI "ASSAULT" 22
Caliber: 22 LR, 25-round magazine.
Barrel: 18".
Weight: 5½ lbs. **Length:** 38½" over-all.
Stock: Hardwood stained black.
Sights: Blade front on ramp, open rear adjustable for windage and elevation.
Features: Large capacity detachable 25-shot magazine; fold-down fore-end serves as vertical grip. Introduced 1983. Made by Mossberg.
Price: .... **NA**
Price: Model PMAIP (as above with 16⅛" barrel, hand-grip stock) .... **NA**

UNIVERSAL 2200 LEATHERNECK CARBINE
Caliber: 22 LR, 10-shot.
Barrel: 18".
Weight: 5½ lbs. **Length:** 35¾" over-all.
Stock: Birch hardwood with lacquer finish.
Sights: Blade front, peep rear adj. for w. & e.
Features: Look-alike to the G.I. Carbine except in rimfire. Recoil operated. Metal parts satin-polish blue. Flip-type safety. Optional 30-shot magazine available. Receiver drilled and tapped for scope mounting. Introduced 1979. From Universal Firearms.
Price: **$246.00**

Consult our Directory pages for
the location of firms mentioned.

Weatherby Mark XXII

WEATHERBY MARK XXII AUTO RIFLE, CLIP MODEL
Caliber: 22 LR only, 5- or 10-shot clip.
Barrel: 24" round contoured.
Weight: 6 lbs. **Length:** 42¼" over-all.
Stock: Walnut, Monte Carlo comb and cheekpiece, rosewood p.g. cap and fore-end tip. Skip-line checkering.
Sights: Gold bead ramp front, 3-leaf folding rear.
Features: Thumb operated side safety also acts as single shot selector. Receiver grooved for tip-off scope mount. Single pin release for quick take-down.
Price: **$279.95**
Price: Extra 5-shot clip **$6.95**
Price: Extra 10-shot clip **$7.95**

Weatherby Mark XXII Tubular Model
Same as Mark XXII Clip Model except: 15-shot tubular magazine.
Price: **$289.95**

RIMFIRE RIFLES—LEVER & SLIDE ACTIONS

Browning BL-22

BROWNING BL-22 LEVER ACTION RIFLE
Caliber: 22 S(22), L(17) or LR(15). Tubular mag.
Barrel: 20" round tapered.
Weight: 5 lbs. **Length:** 36¾" over-all.
Stock: Walnut, 2-piece straight grip Western style.
Sights: Bead post front, folding-leaf rear.
Features: Short throw lever, ½-cock safety, receiver grooved for tip-off scope mounts. Imported from Japan by Browning.
Price: Grade I **$239.95**
Price: Grade II, engraved receiver, checkered grip and fore-end **$274.95**

Browning BPR-22 Pump

BROWNING BPR-22 PUMP RIFLE
Caliber: 22 Mag., 11-shot magazine.
Barrel: 20¼".
Weight: About 6¼ lbs. **Length:** 38¼" over-all.
Stock: French walnut. Cut checkered p.g. and fore-end.
Sights: Gold bead front, folding leaf rear. Receiver grooved for scope mount.
Features: Short, positive pump stroke, side ejection. Magazine tube latches from any position. Cross bolt safety in rear of trigger guard. Introduced 1977. Imported from Japan by Browning.
Price: 22 Magnum, Grade I **$269.95**
Price: 22 Magnum, Grade II **$379.95**

CAUTION: PRICES CHANGE. CHECK AT GUNSHOP.

ERMA EG73 LEVER ACTION CARBINE
Caliber: 22 Mag., 12-shot magazine.
Barrel: 19¼".
Weight: 6 lbs. **Length:** 37⅜" over-all.
Stock: Walnut-staned beech.
Sights: Hooded ramp front, buckhorn rear. Receiver grooved for scope mounting.
Features: Tubular magazine, side ejection. Introduced 1978. Imported by Excam.
Price: **$229.00**

Erma Lever Action Carbines
Model EG712. Similar to Magnum model except chambered for 22 S, L, LR with magazine capacity of 21, 17 and 15 respectively. Barrel length is 18½", weight is 5½ lbs. Introduced 1978.
Price: **$204.00**
Model EG712 L. As above except has European walnut stock, engraved nickel silver receiver, heavy octagonal barrel. Imported by Excam. Introduced 1978.
Price: **$300.00**

Marlin 1894M

MARLIN MODEL 1894M CARBINE
Caliber: 22 Mag., 11-shot magazine.
Barrel: 20" Micro-Groove®.
Weight: 6 lbs. **Length:** 37½" over-all.
Stock: Straight grip stock of American black walnut.
Sights: Ramp front with brass bead, adjustable semi-buckhorn folding rear.
Features: Has new hammer block safety. Side-ejecting solid-top receiver tapped for scope mount or receiver sight; squared finger lever, reversible off-set hammer spur for scope use. Scope shown is optional. Introduced 1983.
Price: **$269.95**

Marlin Golden 39A

MARLIN GOLDEN 39A LEVER ACTION RIFLE
Caliber: 22 S(26), L(21), LR(19), tubular magazine.
Barrel: 24" Micro-Groove®.
Weight: 6½ lbs. **Length:** 40" over-all.
Stock: American black walnut with white line spacers at p.g. cap and buttplate.
Sights: Bead ramp front with detachable "Wide-Scan"™ hood, folding rear semi-buckhorn adj. for w. and e.
Features: Take-down action, receiver tapped for scope mount (supplied), off-set hammer spur. Mar-Shield® stock finish.
Price: **$242.95**

Marlin Golden 39M

MARLIN GOLDEN 39M CARBINE
Caliber: 22 S(21), L(16), LR(15), tubular magazine.
Barrel: 20" Micro-Grove®.
Weight: 6 lbs. **Length:** 36" over-all.
Stock: American black walnut, straight grip, white line buttplate spacer. Mar-Shield® finish.
Sights: "Wide-Scan"™ ramp front with hood, folding rear semi-buckhorn adj. for w. and e.
Features: Squared finger lever. Receiver tapped for scope mount (supplied) or receiver sight, offset hammer spur, take-down action.
Price: **$242.95**

Remington Model 572

REMINGTON 572 FIELDMASTER PUMP RIFLE
Caliber: 22 S(20), L(17) or LR(14). Tubular mag.
Barrel: 21" round tapered.
Weight: 5½ lbs. **Length:** 42" over-all.
Stock: Walnut-finished hardwood with p.g. and grooved slide handle.
Sights: Blade ramp front; sliding ramp rear adj. for w. & e.
Features: Cross-bolt safety, removing inner mag. tube converts rifle to single shot, receiver grooved for tip-off scope mount.
Price: **$181.95**
Price: Sling and swivels installed **$17.75**

Remington Model 572 BDL Deluxe
Same as the 572 except: p.g. cap, walnut stock with RKW finish, checkered grip and fore-end, ramp front and fully adj. rear sights.
Price: **$204.95**
Price: Sling and swivels installed **$17.75**

ROSSI 62 SA PUMP RIFLE
Caliber: 22 S, L or LR, 22 Mag.
Barrel: 23", round or octagon.
Weight: 5¾ lbs. **Length:** 39¼" over-all.
Stock: Walnut, straight grip, grooved fore-end.
Sights: Fixed front, adj. rear.
Features: Capacity 20 Short, 16 Long or 14 Long Rifle. Quick takedown. Imported from Brazil by Interarms.
Price: Blue **$160.00**
Price: Nickel **$180.00**
Price: Blue, with octagon barrel **$170.00**
Price: 22 Mag., as Model 59 . . . . **$195.00**
Price: 22 Mag., octagon barrel **$205.00**

Rossi 62 SAC Carbine
Same as standard model except has 16¼" barrel. Magazine holds slightly fewer cartridges.
Price: Blue **$160.00**
Price: Nickel **$180.00**

RIMFIRE RIFLES—LEVER & SLIDE ACTIONS

Winchester 9422

WINCHESTER 9422 XTR LEVER ACTION RIFLE
Caliber: 22 S(21), L(17), LR(15). Tubular mag.
Barrel: 20½″. (16″ twist).
Weight: 6¼ lbs. **Length:** 37⅛″ over-all.
Stock: American walnut, 2-piece, straight grip (no p.g.).
Sights: Hooded ramp front, adj. semi-buckhorn rear.
Features: Side ejection, receiver grooved fro scope mounting, takedown action. Has XTR wood and metal finish. Made under license by U.S. Repeating Arms Co.
Price: **$299.95**

Winchester 9422M XTR Lever Action Rifle
Same as the 9422 except chambered for 22 Mag. cartridge, has 11-round mag. capacity.
Price: **$299.95**

Winchester 9422 Annie Oakley

Winchester Model 9422 Annie Oakley Commemorative
Similar to the standard Model 9422 except finger lever, receiver and barrel bands are antique-gold plated. Receiver is roll-engraved with Oakley's portrait and a show scene. Offered in a limited issue of 6,000 rifles. Introduced 1983.
Price: **$699.00**

RIMFIRE RIFLES—BOLT ACTIONS & SINGLE SHOTS

Anschutz 1416/1516

ANSCHUTZ DELUXE 1416/1516 RIFLES
Caliber: 22 LR (1416D), 5-shot clip, 22 Mag. (1516D), 4-shot clip.
Barrel: 22½″.
Weight: 6 lbs. **Length:** 41″ over-all.
Stock: European walnut; Monte Carlo with cheekpiece, schnabel fore-end, checkered pistol grip and fore-end.
Sights: Hooded ramp front, folding leaf rear.
Features: Uses Model 1403 target rifle action. Adjustable single stage trigger. Receiver grooved for scope mounting. Imported from Germany by Talo Distributors, Inc.
Price: 1416D, 22 LR **$370.00**
Price: 1516D, 22 Mag. **$380.00**

Anschutz 1418D/1518D Deluxe Rifles
Similar to the 1416D/1516D rifles except has full length Mannlicher-style stock, shorter 19¾″ barrel. Weighs 5½ lbs. Stock has buffalo horn schnabel tip. Double set trigger available on special order. Model 1418D chambered for 22 LR, 1518D for 22 Mag. Imported from Germany by Talo Distributors, Inc.
Price: 1418D. **$521.50**
Price: 1518D. **$533.50**

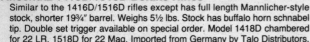

Anschutz 1422/1522

ANSCHUTZ 1422D/1522D CLASSIC RIFLES
Caliber: 22 LR (1422D), 5-shot clip, 22 Mag. (1522D), 4-shot clip.
Barrel: 24″.
Weight: 7¼ lbs. **Length:** 43″ overall.
Stock: Select European walnut; checkered pistol grip and fore-end.
Sights: Hooded ramp front, folding leaf rear.
Features: Uses Match 54 action. Adjustable single stage trigger. Receiver drilled and tapped for scope mounting. Introduced 1982. Imported from Germany by Talo Distributors, Inc.
Price: 1422D (22 LR) **$597.00**
Price: 1522D (22 Mag.). **$597.00**

Anschutz 1422D/1522D Custom Rifles
Similar to the Classic models except have roll-over Monte Carlo cheekpiece, slim fore-end with schnabel tip, Wundhammer palm swell on pistol grip, rosewood grip cap with white diamond insert. Skip-line checkering on grip and fore-end. Introduced 1982. Imported from Germany by Talo Industries.
Price: 1422D. **$634.50**
Price: 1522D. **$634.50**

Chipmunk Single Shot

CHIPMUNK SINGLE SHOT RIFLE
Caliber: 22, S, L, LR, or 22 Mag., single shot.
Barrel: 16⅛″.
Weight: About 2½ lbs. **Length:** 30″ over-all.
Stock: American walnut.
Sights: Post on ramp front, peep rear adj. for windage and elevation.
Features: Drilled and tapped for scope mounting using special Chipmunk base ($9.95). Made in U.S.A. Introduced 1982. From Chipmunk Mfg.
Price: **$119.95**
Price: Fully engraved Presentation Model with hand checkered fancy stock **$500.00**

CAUTION: PRICES CHANGE. CHECK AT GUNSHOP.

Clayco Model 4

CLAYCO MODEL 4 BOLT ACTION RIFLE
Caliber: 22 LR, 5-shot clip.
Barrel: 24".
Weight: 5¾" lbs. **Length:** 42" over-all.
Stock: Hardwood with walnut finish.
Sights: Ramp front with bead, open rear adjustable for windage and elevation.
Features: Wing-type safety on rear of bolt. Receiver grooved for tip-off scope mount. Black composition buttplate and pistol grip cap. Introduced 1983. Imported from China by Clayco Sports Ltd.
Price: **$150.00**

H&R Model 865

HARRINGTON & RICHARDSON MODEL 865 RIFLE
Caliber: 22 S, L or LR. 5-shot clip mag.
Barrel: 22" round tapered.
Weight: 5 lbs. **Length:** 39" over-all.
Stock: Walnut finished hardwood with Monte Carlo and p.g.
Sights: Blade front, step adj. open rear.
Features: Cocking indicator, sliding side safety, receiver grooved for tip-off scope mounts.
Price: **$89.50**

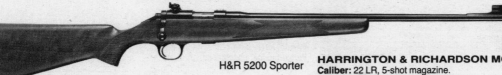

H&R 5200 Sporter

HARRINGTON & RICHARDSON MODEL 5200 SPORTER
Caliber: 22 LR, 5-shot magazine.
Barrel: 24", with recessed muzzle.
Weight: 6½ lbs. **Length:** 42" over-all.
Stock: Classic-style American walnut with hand-cut checkering, rubber butt pad.
Sights: Hooded ramp front, Lyman peep rear fully adjustable for w. & e.
Features: Adjustable tirgger, recessed magazine release, high polish blue finish. Drilled and tapped for scope mounting. Announced 1982. From Harrington & Richardson.
Price: **$375.00**

KASSNAR-SQUIRES BINGHAM MODEL 1400 RIFLE
Caliber: 22 LR, 5-shot magazine.
Barrel: 23".
Weight: 7 lbs. **Length:** 41½" over-all.
Stock: Philippine mahogany, hand checkered.
Sights: Blade on ramp front, open rear adjustable for windage and elevation.
Features: Blued metal; twin locking locks. Imported by Kassnar.
Price: **$129.95**
Price: Model 14 (no checkering, 4x scope installed) **$74.95**
Price: Model 1500 (22 Mag. version of M1400) **$149.95**

HARRINGTON & RICHARDSON MODEL 750
Caliber: 22 S, L or LR, single shot.
Barrel: 22" round tapered.
Weight: 5 lbs. **Length:** 39" over-all.
Stock: Walnut finished hardwood with Monte Carlo comb and p.g.
Sights: Blade front, step adj. open rear.
Features: Double extractors, feed platform, cocking indicator, sliding side safety, receiver grooved for tip-off scope mount.
Price: **$79.00**

Kimber Model 82

Features: High quality adult-sized bolt action rifle. All steel construction. Rocker-type silent safety. All steel parts finished in high polish blue. Available with or without sights. Barreled actions available. Scope shown optional. Made in U.S.A. Introduced 1980. From Kimber of Oregon.
Price: Classic stock without sights, 22 LR **$495.00**
Price: Classic stock with sights **$550.00**
Price: Scope mount rings **$45.00**
Price: Cascade sporter stock, no sights **$545.00**
Price: Cascade sporter stock, with sights **$600.00**
Price: Classic stock, no sights, 22 Mag. **$568.00**
Price: Classic stock, with sights, 22 Mag. **$623.00**
Price: Cascade sporter stock, no sights, 22 Mag. **$618.00**
Price: Cascade sporter stock, with sights, 22 Mag. **$673.00**
Price: Extra 5-shot magazine **$10.60**
Price: Extra 10-shot magazine **$11.25**

KIMBER MODEL 82 BOLT ACTION RIFLE
Caliber: 22 Long Rifle, 22 Mag.; 5-shot detachable magazine.
Barrel: 22½", 6-groove.
Weight: About 6½ lbs. **Length:** 41" over-all.
Stock: Select claro walnut. "Classic" style or Cascade (cheekpiece and Monte Carlo) stock. Checkered p.g. and fore-end.
Sights: Blade front on ramp, open rear adj. for w. & e.

RIMFIRE RIFLES—BOLT ACTIONS & SINGLE SHOTS

Kimber Model 82 Super America

Similar to the standard Model 82 except has the Classic stock only of specially selected, high-grade, California claro walnut, with Continental cheekpiece; borderless, full-coverage 22 lpi checkering; Niedner-type checkered steel buttplate; comes with quick-detachable, double lever scope mounts and barrel quarter-rib which has a folding leaf sight. Available in 22 Long Rifle, 22 Magnum, 22 Hornet.
Price: 22 Long Rifle, less 4x scope. **$950.00**
Price: As above, with Kimber 4x Compact scope **$1,135.00**

Kimber Super America

Price: 22 Mag., less scope. **$969.00**
Price: As above with Kimber 4x Compact scope **$1,154.00**
Price: 22 Hornet, less scope. **$1,055.00**
Price: As above, with Kimber 4x Compact scope **$1,240.00**

Krico Model 302 DRC

KRICO MODEL 302 BOLT ACTION RIFLE

Caliber: 22 LR.
Barrel: 24″.
Weight: 6½ lbs.
Stock: Select walnut with checkered pistol grip and fore-end.
Sights: Post front with hood, rear adj. for windage.
Features: High quality bolt action rifle available with 5- or 10-shot magazine, single or double-set trigger. Imported from West Germany. Contact Krico for more data.
Price: Model 302 (22 LR) **$409.00**
Price: Model 352 (22 Mag.) **$429.00**
Price: Model 302 with double-set trigger **$449.00**

KRICO MODEL 302 DR C BOLT ACTION RIFLE

Caliber: 22 Long Rifle, 22 Mag.
Barrel: 24″.
Weight: 6.5 lbs. **Length:** 43″ over-all.
Stock: European walnut in classic style.
Sights: Post front with hood, rear adjustable for windage.
Features: Polished blue finish; available with single or double-set triggers; dual extractors; 5- or 10-shot magazine. Introduced 1983. Contact Krico for more data.
Price: 22 LR **$409.00**
Price: 22 Mag. **$429.00**

Krico Model 304 Bolt Action Rifle

Same as Model 302 except has 20″ barrel, weighs 6.2 lbs., has full-length Mannlicher-style stock.
Price: Model 304 (22 LR) **$499.00**
Price: Model 354 (22 Mag.) **$529.00**

Marlin Model 780

MARLIN 780 BOLT ACTION RIFLE

Caliber: 22 S, L, or LR; 7-shot clip magazine.
Barrel: 22″ Micro-Groove.
Weight: 5½ lbs. **Length:** 41″.
Stock: Monte Carlo American black walnut with checkered p.g. and fore-end. White line spacer at buttplate. Mar-Shield® finish.
Sights: "Wide-Scan"™ ramp front, folding semi-buckhorn rear adj. for w. & e.
Features: Gold plated trigger, receiver anti-glare serrated and grooved for tip-off scope mount.
Price: **$119.95**

Marlin 781 Bolt Action Rifle

Same as the Marlin 780 except: tubular magazine holds 25 Shorts, 19 Longs or 17 Long Rifle cartirdges. Weight 6 lbs.
Price: **$124.95**

Marlin 782 Bolt Action Rifle

Same as the Marlin 780 except: 22 Rimfire Magnum cal. only, weight about 6 lbs. Sling and swivels attached
Price: **$133.95**

Marlin Model 783

Marlin 783 Bolt Action Rifle

Same as Marlin 780 except: Tubular magazine holds 12 rounds of 22 Rimfire Magnum ammunition.
Price: **$138.95**

Marlin Model 25

Marlin 25 Bolt Action Repeater

Similar to Marlin 780, except: walnut finished p.g. stock, adjustable open rear sight, ramp front.
Price: **$97.95**

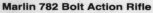

CAUTION: PRICES CHANGE. CHECK AT GUNSHOP.

Marlin Model 15

Marlin Model 25M Bolt Action Rifle
Similar to the Model 25 except chambered for 22 Mag. Has 7-shot clip magazine, 22″ Micro-Groove® barrel, walnut-finished hardwood stock. Introduced 1983.
Price: **$111.95**

MARLIN MODEL 15 BOLT ACTION RIFLE
Caliber: 22, S, L, LR, single shot.
Barrel: 22″.
Weight: 5½ lbs. **Length:** 41″ over-all.
Stock: Walnut-finished hardwood with Monte Carlo and full p.g.
Sights: Ramp front, adjustable open rear.
Features: Receiver grooved for tip-off scope mount; thumb safety; red cocking indicator.
Price: **$92.95**

Mossberg Model 341

MOSSBERG MODEL 640K CHUCKSTER
Caliber: 22 Mag. 5-shot clip mag.
Barrel: 24″ AC-KRO-GRUV.
Weight: 6¼ lbs. **Length:** 44¾″ over-all.
Stock: Walnut, checkered p.g. and fore-end, Monte Carlo comb and cheekpiece.
Sights: Ramp front with bead, fully adj. leaf rear.
Features: Grooved trigger, sliding side safety, double extractors, receiver grooved for tip-off scope mounts and tapped for aperture rear sight.
Price: About **$104.00**

MOSSBERG MODEL 341 RIFLE
Caliber: 22 S, L, LR, 7-shot clip.
Barrel: 24″ AC-KRO-GRUV.
Weight: 6½ lbs. **Length:** 43½″ over-all.
Stock: Walnut, checkered p.g. and fore-end, Monte Carlo and cheekpiece. Buttplate with white line spacer.
Sights: Bead front, U-notch rear adj. for w. and e.
Features: Sliding side safety, 8 groove rifling.
Price: About **$94.95**

Remington 541-S Custom

REMINGTON MODEL 541-S
Caliber: 22 S, L, LR; 5-shot clip.
Barrel: 24″.
Weight: 5½ lbs. **Length:** 42⅝″ over-all.
Stock: Walnut, checkered p.g. and fore end.
Sights: None. Drilled and tapped for scope mounts or receiver sights.
Features: Clip repeater. Thumb safety. Receiver and trigger guard scroll engraved.
Price: **$373.95**
Price: Extra 10-shot clip **$6.75**

Remington Model 581

Remington Model 582 Rifle
Same as M581 except: tubular magazine under bbl. holds 20 S, 15 L or 14 LR cartridges. Wgt. 5½ lbs.
Price: **$173.95**

REMINGTON MODEL 581 RIFLE
Caliber: 22 S, L or LR. 5-shot clip mag.
Barrel: 24″ round.
Weight: 4¾ lbs. **Length:** 42⅜″ over-all.
Stock: Walnut finished Monte Carlo with p.g.
Sights: Bead post front, screw adj. open rear.
Features: Sliding side safety, wide trigger, receiver grooved for tip-off scope mounts. Comes with single-shot adapter.
Price: **$148.95**
Price: Left hand action and stock **$153.95**

Ruger 22 Bolt Action

RUGER 22 RIMFIRE BOLT ACTION RIFLE
Caliber: 22 Long Rifle, 10-shot magazine.
Barrel: 20″.
Weight: About 5 lbs., 13 oz. **Length:** 39¼″ over-all.
Stock: Straight-grained American walnut.
Sights: Gold bead front, adjustable folding leaf rear.
Features: Mauser-type action uses Ruger's 10-shot rotary magazine; 3-position safety; simplified bolt stop; patented bolt locking system. Uses the dual-screw barrel attachment system of the 10/22 rifle. Integral scope mounting system with 1″ Ruger rings. Announced 1983.
Price: **$275.00**

Stevens Model 72

SAVAGE STEVENS MODEL 72 CRACKSHOT
Caliber: 22 S, L, LR, single shot.
Barrel: 22" octagonal.
Weight: 4½ lbs. **Length:** 37" over-all.
Stock: Walnut, straight grip and fore-end.
Sights: Blade front, step adj. rear.
Features: Falling block action, color case hardened frame.
Price: $126.50

Stevens Model 89

SAVAGE-STEVENS MODEL 89
Caliber: 22 LR, single shot.
Barrel: 18½".
Weight: 5 lbs. **Length:** 35" over-all.
Stock: Walnut finished hardwood.
Sights: Blade front, step adj. rear.
Features: Single-shot Martini-type breech block. Hammer must be cocked by hand independent of lever prior to firing. Automatic ejection. Satin black frame finish.
Price: $85.00

Springfield Armory M6

SPRINGFIELD ARMORY M6 SURVIVAL RIFLE
Caliber: 22 LR over 410 shotgun.
Barrel: 18".
Weight: 3½ lbs. **Length:** 31½" over-all.
Stock: Steel, folding, with magazine for nine 22 LR, four 410 cartridges.
Sights: Blade front, military aperture for 22; V-notch for 410.
Features: All metal construction. Designed for quick disassembly and minimum maintenance. Folds for compact storage. Introduced 1982. Made in U.S. by Springfield Armory.
Price: About $136.00

Stevens Model 35

STEVENS MODEL 35 BOLT ACTION RIFLE
Caliber: 22 LR or 22 Mag. (Model 35-M); detachable 5-shot clip.
Barrel: 22".
Weight: 4¾ lbs. **Length:** 41" over-all.
Stock: Walnut-finished hardwood.
Sights: Ramp front, step-adjustable open rear.
Features: Checkered pistol grip and fore-end. Receiver grooved for scope mounting. Introduced 1982. From Savage Arms.
Price: Model 35 .... $92.50
Price: Model 35-M $96.00
Price: Model 36 (22 LR, single shot)..................... $88.50

TRADEWINDS MODEL 311-A BOLT ACTION RIFLE
Caliber: 22 LR, 5-shot (10-shot mag. avail.).
Barrel: 22½".
Weight: 6 lbs. **Length:** 41¼".
Stock: Walnut, Monte Carlo with hand checkered p.g. and fore-end.
Sights: Ramp front with hood, folding leaf rear, receiver grooved for scope mt.
Features: Sliding safety locks trigger and bolt handle. Imported by Tradewinds.
Price: $185.00

COMPETITION RIFLES—CENTERFIRE & RIMFIRE

Anschutz Mark 2000

ANSCHUTZ MARK 2000 TARGET RIFLE
Caliber: 22 LR, single-shot.
Barrel: 26", heavy. ⅞" diameter.
Weight: 8 lbs. **Length:** 43" over-all.
Stock: Walnut finished hardwood.
Sights: Globe front (insert-type), micro-click peep rear.
Features: Action similar to the Anschutz Model 1403D. Stock has thumb groove, Wundhammer swell p.g., adjustable hand stop and sling swivel.
Price: Without sights $206.00
Price: Sight set $30.50

Anschutz 1813 Super Match

Anschutz 1813 Super Match Rifle

Same as the model 1811 except: International-type stock with adj. cheek-piece, adj. aluminum hook buttplate, weight 15½ lbs., 46″ over-all. Imported from West Germany by Talo Distributers, Inc.

Price: Right hand, no sights **$1,124.00**
Price: M1813-L (left-hand action and stock) **$1,235.00**

Anschutz 1807 Match Rifle

Same as the model 1811 except: 26″ bbl. (⅞″ dia.), weight 10 lbs. 44½″ over-all to conform to ISU requirements and also suitable for NRA matches.

Price: Right hand, no sights **$706.00**
Price: M1807-L (true left-hand action and stock) **$775.00**
Price: Int'l sight set **$156.00**
Price: Match sight set **$113.00**

ANSCHUTZ 1811 MATCH RIFLE

Caliber: 22 LR. Single Shot.
Barrel: 27¼″ round (1″ dia.)
Weight: 11 lbs. **Length:** 46″ over-all.
Stock: French walnut, American prone style with Monte Carlo, cast-off cheek-piece, checkered p.g., beavertail fore-end with swivel rail and adj. swivel, adj. rubber buttplate.
Sights: None. Receiver grooved for Anschutz sights (extra). Scope blocks.
Features: Single stage adj. trigger, wing safety, short firing pin travel. Imported from West Germany by Talo Distributors, Inc.

Price: Right hand, no sights **$774.00**
Price: M1811-L (true left-hand action and stock) **$850.00**
Price: Anschutz Int'l. sight set **$156.00**

Anschutz Model 1810 Super Match II

Similar to the Super Match 1813 rifle except has a stock of European hard-wood with tapered fore-end and deep receiver area. Hand and palm rests not included. Uses Match 54 action. Adjustable hook buttplate and cheekpiece. Sights not included. Introduced 1982. Imported from Germany by Talo Distributors, Inc.

Price: Right-hand **$999.50**
Price: Left-hand **$1,099.50**
Price: International sight set **$156.00**
Price: Match sight set **$113.00**

Anschutz 54.18 MS

Anschutz Model 54.18 MS Silhouette Rifle

Same basic features as Anschutz 1813 Super Match but with special metallic silhouette stock and two-stage trigger.
Price: **$682.00**
Price: Model 54.18 MSL (true left-hand version of above) **$747.00**

Anschutz 1827B Biathlon

ANSCHUTZ 1827B BIATHLON RIFLE

Caliber: 22 LR, 5-shot magazine.
Barrel: 21½″.
Weight: 9 lbs. with sights. **Length:** 42½″ over-all.
Stock: Walnut-finished hardwood; cheekpiece, stippled pistol grip and fore-end.
Sights: Globe front specially designed for Biathlon shooting, micrometer rear with hinged snow cap.
Features: Uses Match 54 action and adjustable trigger; adjustable wooden buttplate, Biathlon butt hook, adjustable hand stop rail. **Special Order Only.** Introduced 1982. Imported from Germany by Talo Distributors, Inc.

Price: Right-hand **$998.00**
Price: Left-hand **$1,137.00**

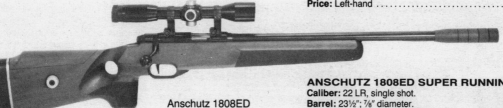

Anschutz 1808ED

ANSCHUTZ 1808ED SUPER RUNNING TARGET

Caliber: 22 LR, single shot.
Barrel: 23½″; ⅞″ diameter.
Weight: 9¼ lbs. **Length:** 42″ over-all.
Stock: European hardwood. Heavy beavertail fore-end, adjustable cheekpiece, buttplate, stippled pistol grip and fore-end.
Sights: None furnished. Receiver grooved for scope mounting.
Features: Uses Super Match 54 action. Adjustable trigger from 14 oz. to 3.5 lbs. Removable sectioned barrel weights. **Special Order Only.** Introduced 1982. Imported from Germany by Talo Distributors, Inc.

Price: Right-hand **$790.00**
Price: Left-hand, 1808EDL **$868.00**

COMPETITION RIFLES—CENTERFIRE & RIMFIRE

ANSCHUTZ MODEL 1403D MATCH RIFLE
Caliber: 22 LR only. Single shot.
Barrel: 26" round (1¹¹⁄₁₆" dia.)
Weight: 7¾ lbs. **Length:** 44" over-all.
Stock: Walnut finished hardwood, cheekpiece, checkered p.g., beavertail fore-end, adj. buttplate.
Sights: None furnished.
Features: Sliding side safety, adj. single stage trigger, receiver grooved for Anschutz sights. Imported from West Germany by Talo Distributors, Inc.
Price: **$379.00**
Price: 1403DL (left hand) **$399.00**
Price: Match sight set **$113.00**

ANSCHUTZ MODEL 64-MS
Caliber: 22 LR, single shot.
Barrel: 21¾", medium heavy, ⅞" diameter.
Weight: 8 lbs. 1 oz. **Length:** 39½" over-all.
Stock: Walnut-finished hardwood, silhouette-type.
Sights: None furnished. Receiver drilled and tapped for scope mounting.
Features: Designed for metallic silhouette competition. Stock has stippled checkering, contoured thumb groove with Wundhammer swell. Two-stage trigger is adj. for weight of pull, take-up, and over-travel. Slide safety locks sear and bolt. Introduced 1980. Imported from West Germany by Talo Distributors, Inc.
Price: **$365.00**

BSA Martini Match

BSA MARTINI ISU MATCH RIFLE
Caliber: 22 LR, single shot.
Barrel: 28".
Weight: 10¾ lbs. **Length:** 43-44" over-all.
Stock: Match type French walnut butt and fore-end; flat cheekpiece, full p.g.; spacers are fitted to allow length adjustment to suit each shooting position; adj. buttplate.
Sights: Modified PH-1 Parker-Hale tunnel front, PH-25 aperture rear with aperture variations from .080" to .030".

Features: Fastest lock time of any commercial target rifle; designed to meet I.S.U. specs. for the Standard Rifle. Fully adjustable trigger (less than ½ lb. to 3½ lbs.). Mark V has heavier barrel, weighs 12¼ lbs. Imported from England by Freelands Scope Stands.
Price: I.S.U., Standard weight **$950.00**
Price: Mark V heavy bbl. **$1,000.00**

Beeman Mini-Match 2000

BEEMAN/FEINWERKBAU 2000 TARGET RIFLE
Caliber: 22 LR.
Barrel: 26¼"; 22" for Mini-Match.
Weight: 9 lbs. 12 oz. **Length:** 43¾" over-all (26¼" bbl.).
Stock: Standard match. Walnut with stippled p.g. and fore-end; walnut-stained birch for the Mini-Match.
Sights: Globe front with interchangeable inserts; micrometer match aperture rear.
Features: Meets ISU standard rifle specifications. Shortest lock time of any small bore rifle. Trigger fully adjustable for weight, release point, length, lateral position, etc. Available in Standard and Mini-Match models. Introduced 1979. Imported from West Germany by Beeman's Inc.

Price: Right-hand **$795.00**
Price: Left-hand **$855.00**
Price: Mini-Match, right-hand **$765.00**
Price: Mini-Match, left-hand **$798.00**

Beeman/FWB Free Rifle

Stock: Anatomically correct thumbhole stock of laminated wood.
Sights: Globe front with interchangeable inserts, micrometer match aperture rear.
Features: Fully adjustable mechanical or new electronic trigger; accessory rails for moveable weights and adjustable palm rest; adjustable cheekpiece and hooked buttplate. Right or left hand. Introduced 1983. Imported by Beeman.

BEEMAN/FEINWERKBAU ULTRA MATCH 22 FREE RIFLE
Caliber: 22 LR, single shot.
Barrel: 26.4".
Weight: 17 lbs. (with accessories).

Price: Right hand, electronic trigger **$1,505.00**
Price: As above, mechanical trigger **$1,285.00**
Price: Left hand, electronic trigger **$1,650.00**
Price: As above, mechanical trigger **$1,400.00**

Beeman/Weihrauch HW60

Weight: 10.8 lbs. **Length:** 45.7" over-all.
Stock: Walnut with adjustable buttplate. Stippled p.g. and fore-end. Rail with adjustable swivel.
Sights: Hooded ramp front, match-type aperture rear.
Features: Adj. match trigger with push-button safety. Left-hand version also available. Introduced 1981. Imported from West Germany by Beeman's, Inc.
Price: Right-hand. **$495.00**
Price: Left-hand **$545.00**

BEEMAN/WEIHRAUCH HW60 TARGET RIFLE
Caliber: 22 LR, single shot.
Barrel: 26.8".

CAUTION: PRICES CHANGE. CHECK AT GUNSHOP.

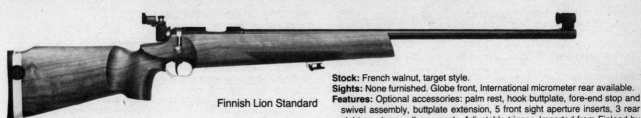

Finnish Lion Standard

FINNISH LION STANDARD TARGET RIFLE
Caliber: 22 LR, single-shot.
Barrel: 27⅝".
Weight: 10½ lbs. **Length:** 44⁹⁄₁₆" over-all.

Stock: French walnut, target style.
Sights: None furnished. Globe front, International micrometer rear available.
Features: Optional accessories: palm rest, hook buttplate, fore-end stop and swivel assembly, buttplate extension, 5 front sight aperture inserts, 3 rear sight apertures, allen wrench. Adjustable trigger. Imported from Finland by Mandall Shooting Supplies.

Price:	**$500.00**
Price: Thumbhole stock model	**$695.00**
Price: Heavy barrel model (either stock)	**$535.00**
Price: Sight set (front and rear)	**$100.00**

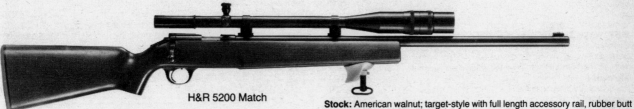

H&R 5200 Match

HARRINGTON & RICHARDSON MODEL 5200 RIFLE
Caliber: 22 LR, single shot.
Barrel: 28" target-weight with recessed muzzle.
Weight: 11 lbs. **Length:** 46" over-all.

Stock: American walnut; target-style with full length accessory rail, rubber butt pad. Comes with hand stop.
Sights: None supplied. Receiver drilled and tapped for receiver sight, barrel for front sight.
Features: Fully adj. trigger (1.1 to 3.5 lbs.), heavy free-floating target weight barrel, "Fluid-Feed" loading platform, dual extractors. Polished blue-black metal finish. Introduced 1981. From Harrington & Richardson.
Price: **$325.00**

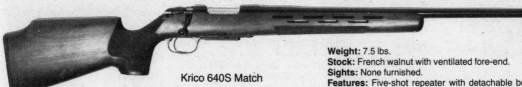

Krico 640S Match

KRICO MODEL 640S MATCH SPORTER
Caliber: 17 Rem., 222, 223, 22-250, 243, 308.
Barrel: 20", semi-bull.

Weight: 7.5 lbs.
Stock: French walnut with ventilated fore-end.
Sights: None furnished.
Features: Five-shot repeater with detachable box magazine. Available with single or double-set trigger. Imported from West Germany. Contact Krico for more data.

Price: 17 Rem., 222, 223 cals	**$849.00**
Price: 22-250, 243, 308 cals	**$849.00**
Price: Model 440S, 22 Hornet	**$619.00**

Krico Model 340S

KRICO MODEL 340S (MS) SILHOUETTE RIFLE
Caliber: 22 Long Rifle, 5-shot clip.
Barrel: 21", match quality.

Weight: 8.1 lbs. **Length:** 39.5" over-all.
Stock: European walnut match-style designed for off-hand shooting. Suitable for right- or left-hand shooters. Stippled grip and fore-end.
Sights: None furnished. Receiver grooved for tip-off mounts.
Features: Free-floated heavy barrel; fully adjustable two-stage match trigger or double-set trigger. Meets NRA official MS rules. Introduced 1983. Contact Krico for more data.
Price: **$599.00**

Krico Model 630S

KRICO MODEL 630S TARGET MATCH RIFLE
Caliber: 17 Rem., 222, 223, 22-250, 243, 308; single-shot.
Barrel: 23.5", semi-bull.
Weight: 9.5 lbs. **Length:** 43.3" over-all.
Stock: French walnut, special match style with stippled pistol grip and fore-end.
Sights: None furnished; drilled and tapped for scope mounts.
Features: Comes with choice of match trigger or double set triggers; high polish blue finish. Introduced 1983. Contact Krico for more data.

Price:	**$899.00**
Price: Model 360S — as above except in 22 LR, 8.3 lbs., 42.5" o.a.l.	**$589.00**
Price: Model 430S — as above except in 22 Hornet	**$599.00**

COMPETITION RIFLES—CENTERFIRE & RIMFIRE

Krico Model 650SS Sniper

KRICO MODEL 650SS SNIPER RIFLE
Caliber: 222, 223, 243, 308.
Barrel: 26". Specially designed match bull barrel, matte blue finish, with muzzle brake/flash hider.
Weight: 10.6 lbs. **Length:** 46" over-all.
Stock: Select walnut with oil finish. Spring-loaded, adj. cheekpiece, adjustable recoil pad.
Sights: None furnished. Drilled and tapped for scope mounts.
Features: Match trigger with 10mm wide shoe; single standard or double set trigger available. All metal has matte blue finish. Bolt knob has ¾" diameter. Scope mounts available for special night-sight devices. Imported from West Germany. Contact Krico for more data.
Price: Without scope, mount. $1,249.00
Price: Model 640S, as above but without moveable cheekpiece. $929.00
Price: With Schmidt & Bender 1.5-6x42 sniper scope $2,249.00

KRICO MODEL 430S TARGET MATCH RIFLE
Caliber: 22 Hornet.
Barrel: 24".
Weight: 8.8 lbs. **Length:**
Stock: Walnut. Target style with stippled p.g. and fore-end.
Sights: None furnished. Drilled and tapped for scope mounts.
Features: Comes with either double set or match trigger. Has 11mm dovetail rail for scope mounting. Imported from West Germany. Contact Krico for more data.
Price: Single shot, set trigger. $499.00
Price: Repeater, set trigger $559.00

KRICO MODEL 330S MATCH RIFLE
Caliber: 22 LR, single shot.
Barrel: 25.6", heavy.
Weight: 9.9 lbs.
Stock: Special match stock of walnut finished beech; built-in hand-stop; adjustable recoil pad.
Sights: Hooded front with interchangeable inserts; diopter match rear with rubber eye-cup.
Features: Match trigger set at factory for 4 oz. pull. Stippled pistol grip area. Imported from West Germany. Contact Krico for more data.
Price: $629.00

M-S Silhouette Rifle

M-S SAFARI ARMS SILHOUETTE RIFLE
Caliber: 22 LR or any standard centerfire cartridge; single shot.
Barrel: 23" (rimfire); 24" (centerfire). Fluted or smooth.
Weight: 10 lbs., 2 oz. (with scope).
Stock: Fiberglass, silhouette-design; custom painted.
Sights: None furnished. Drilled and tapped for scope mounting.
Features: Electronic trigger, stainless steel action, high-speed lock time. Custom built to customer specs. From M-S Safari Arms.
Price: 22 LR. $1,095.00
Price: Centerfire, from $1,095.00

M-S Safari Match

M-S SAFARI ARMS 1000 YARD MATCH RIFLE
Caliber: 30-338, 300 Win. Mag.; single shot.
Barrel: 28", heavy.
Weight: 18½ lbs. with scope.
Stock: Fiberglass, custom painted to customer specs.
Sights: None furnished. Drilled and tapped for scope mounting.
Features: Sleeved stainless steel action, high-speed lock time. Fully adjustable prone stock. Electronic trigger. From M-S Safari Arms.
Price: $1,995.00

Mauser Model 66SP

MAUSER MODEL 66 SP MATCH RIFLE
Caliber: 308 Win.
Barrel: 27.5" with muzzle brake.
Weight: 12 lbs. (without scope).
Stock: Special walnut match design with broad fore-end, thumbhole pistol grip, spring-loaded cheekpiece, Morgan adj. recoil pad.
Features: Uses the Mauser telescopic short action. Other calibers available upon request. Has 3-shot magazine, match trigger adjustable for pull and travel. Contact Mauser for more data.
Price: . . . . P.O.R.

CAUTION: PRICES CHANGE. CHECK AT GUNSHOP.

MOSSBERG MODEL 144 TARGET RIFLE
Caliber: 22 LR only. 7-shot clip.
Barrel: 27″ round (¹⁵⁄₁₆″ dia.)
Weight: About 8 lbs. **Length:** 43″ over-all.
Stock: Target-style walnut with high thick comb, cheekpiece, p.g., beavertail fore-end, adj. handstop and sling swivels.
Sights: Lyman 17A hooded front with inserts, Mossberg S331 receiver peep with ¼-minute clicks.
Features: Wide grooved trigger adj. for wgt. of pull, thumb safety, receiver grooved for scope mounting.
Price: About **$175.00**

Remington 540-XRJR Junior Rimfire Position Rifle
Same as 540-XR except fitted with 1¾″ shorter stock to fit the junior shooter. Over-all length adjustable from 41¾″ to 45″. Length of pull adjustable from 11″ to 14¼″.
Price: **$358.95**

REMINGTON 540-XR RIMFIRE POSITION RIFLE
Caliber: 22 LR, single-shot.
Barrel: 26″ medium weight target. Countersunk at muzzle.
Weight: 8 lbs., 13 oz. **Length:** Adj. from 43½″ to 46¾″.
Stock: Position-style with Monte Carlo, cheekpiece and thumb groove. 5-way adj. buttplate and full length guide rail.
Sights: None furnished. Drilled and tapped for target scope blocks. Fitted with front sight base.
Features: Extra-fast lock time. Specially designed p.g. to eliminate wrist twisting. Adj. match trigger. Match-style sling with adj. swivel block ($18.00) and sight set ($69.95) available.
Price: **$358.95**

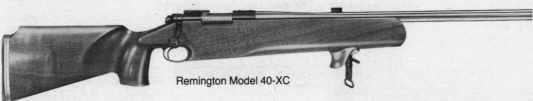

Remington Model 40-XC

REMINGTON 40-XC NAT'L MATCH COURSE RIFLE
Caliber: 7.62 NATO, 5-shot.
Barrel: 23¼″, stainless steel.
Weight: 10 lbs. without sights. **Length:** 42½″ over-all.
Stock: Walnut, position-style, with palm swell.

Sights: None furnished.
Features: Designed to meet the needs of competitive shooters firing the national match courses. Position-style stock, top loading clip slot magazine, anti-bind bolt and receiver, bright stainless steel barrel. Meets all I.S.U. Army Rifle specifications. Adjustable buttplate, adjustable trigger.
Price: **$916.95**

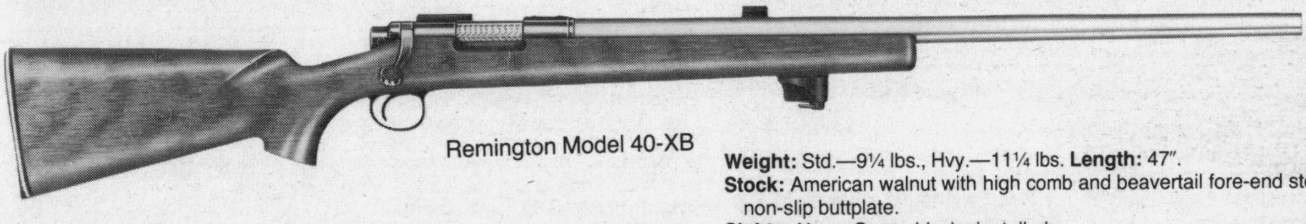

Remington Model 40-XB

REMINGTON 40-XB RANGEMASTER TARGET Centerfire
Caliber: 222 Rem., 22-250, 6mm Rem., 243, 25-06, 7mm Rem. Mag. (30-338 (30-7mm Rem. Mag.), 300 Win. Mag., 7.62 NATO (308 Win.), 30-06. Single shot.
Barrel: 27¼″ round (Stand. dia.—¾″, Hvy. dia.—⅞″)

Consult our Directory pages for the location of firms mentioned.

Weight: Std.—9¼ lbs., Hvy.—11¼ lbs. **Length:** 47″.
Stock: American walnut with high comb and beavertail fore-end stop. Rubber non-slip buttplate.
Sights: None. Scope blocks installed.
Features: Adjustable trigger pull. Receiver drilled and tapped for sights.
Price: Standard s.s., stainless steel barrel **$847.95**
Price: Repeating model **$903.70**
Price: Extra for 2 oz. trigger **$93.95**

REMINGTON 40-XR RIMFIRE POSITION RIFLE
Caliber: 22 LR, single-shot.
Barrel: 24″, heavy target.
Weight: 10 lbs. **Length:** 43″ over-all.
Stock: Position-style with front swivel block on fore-end guide rail.
Sights: Drilled and tapped. Furnished with scope blocks.
Features: Meets all I.S.U. specifications. Deep fore-end, buttplate vertically adjustable, wide adjustable trigger.
Price: **$664.95**

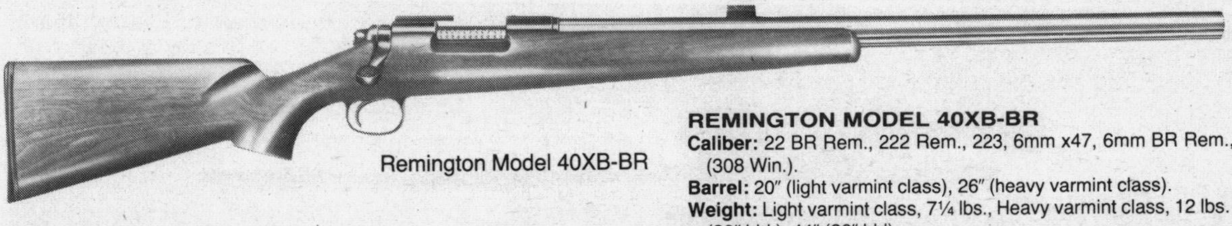

Remington Model 40XB-BR

REMINGTON MODEL 40XB-BR
Caliber: 22 BR Rem., 222 Rem., 223, 6mm x47, 6mm BR Rem., 7.62 NATO (308 Win.).
Barrel: 20″ (light varmint class), 26″ (heavy varmint class).
Weight: Light varmint class, 7¼ lbs., Heavy varmint class, 12 lbs. **Length:** 38″ (20″ bbl.), 44″ (26″ bbl).
Stock: Select walnut.
Sights: None. Supplied with scope blocks.
Features: Unblued stainless steel barrel, trigger adj. from 1½ lbs. to 3½ lbs. Special 2 oz. trigger at extra cost. Scope and mounts extra.
Price: **$893.95**

SHILEN DGA BENCHREST SINGLE SHOT RIFLE
Caliber: 22, 22-250, 6x47, 308.
Barrel: Select/Match grade stainless. Choice of caliber, twist, chambering, contour or length shown in Shilen's catalog.
Weight: To customer specs.
Stock: Fiberglass. Choice of Classic or thumbhole pattern.
Sights: None furnished. Specify intended scope and mount.
Features: Fiberglass stocks are spray painted with acrylic enamel in choice of basic color. Comes with Benchrest trigger. Basically a custom-made rifle. From Shilen Rifles, Inc.
Price: From **$1,400.00**

Steyr SSG Marksman

STEYR-MANNLICHER SSG MARKSMAN
Caliber: 308 Win.
Barrel: 25.6".
Weight: 8.6 lbs. **Length:** 44.5" over-all.
Stock: Choice of ABS "Cycolac" synthetic half stock or walnut. Removable spacers in butt adjusts length of pull from 12¾" to 14".
Sights: Hooded blade front, folding leaf rear.
Features: Parkerized finish. Choice of interchangeable single or double set triggers. Detachable 5-shot rotary magazine (10-shot optional). Drilled and tapped for scope mounts. Imported from Austria by Steyr Daimler Puch of America.
Price: Synthetic half stock **$765.35**
Price: Walnut half stock **$887.30**
Price: Synthetic half stock with Kahles ZF69 scope **$1,482.00**
Price: Optional 10-shot magazine **$66.00**

Steyr-Mannlicher SSG Match
Same as Model SSG Marsksman except has heavy barrel, match bolt, Walther target peep sights and adj. rail in fore-end to adj. sling travel. Weight is 11 lbs.
Price: Synthetic half stock **$996.00**
Price: Walnut half stock **$1,106.00**

Swiss K-31 Target

SWISS K-31 TARGET RIFLE
Caliber: 308 Win., 6-shot magazine.
Barrel: 26".
Weight: 9½ lbs. **Length:** 44" over-all.
Stock: Walnut.
Sights: Protected blade front, ladder-type adjustable rear.
Features: Refined version of the Schmidt-Rubin straight-pull rifle. Comes with sling and muzzle cap. Imported from Switzerland by Mandall Shooting Supplies.
Price: **$1,000.00**

TIKKA MODEL 65 WILD BOAR RIFLE
Caliber: 7x64, 308, 30-06, 7mm Rem. Mag., 300 Win. Mag.; 5-shot detachable clip.
Barrel: 20½".
Weight: About 7½ lbs. **Length:** 41" over-all.
Stock: Hand checkered walnut; vent. rubber recoil pad.
Sights: Bead on post front, special ramp-type open rear.
Features: Adjustable trigger; palm swell in pistol grip. Sight system developed for low-light conditions. Imported from Finland by Mandall Shooting Supplies.
Price: **$595.00**

Walther U.I.T. Match
Same specifications and features as standard U.I.T. Super rifle but has scope mount bases. Fore-end had new tapered profile, fully stippled. Imported from Germany by Interarms.
Price: **$925.00**

WALTHER U.I.T. SUPER
Caliber: 22 LR, single shot.
Barrel: 25½".
Weight: 10 lbs., 3 oz. **Length:** 44¾".
Stock: Walnut, adj. for length and drop; fore-end guide rail for sling or palm rest.
Sights: Globe-type front, fully adj. aperture rear.
Features: Conforms to both NRA and U.I.T. requirements. Fully adj. trigger. Left hand stock available on special order. Imported from Germany by Interarms.
Price: **$850.00**

WALTHER RUNNING BOAR MATCH RIFLE
Caliber: 22 LR, single shot.
Barrel: 23.6".
Weight: 8 lbs. 5 oz. **Length:** 42" over-all.
Stock: Walnut thumb-hole type. Fore-end and p.g. stippled.
Features: Especially designed for running boar competition. Receiver grooved to accept dovetail scope mounts. Adjustable cheekpiece and butt plate. 1.1 lb. trigger pull. Left hand stock available on special order. Imported from Germany by Interarms.
Price: **$825.00**

Walther GX-1 Match Rifle
Same general specs as U.I.T. except has 25½" barrel, over-all length of 44½", weight of 15½ lbs. Stock is designed to provide every conceivable adjustment for individual preference and anatomical compatibility. Left-hand stock available on special order. Imported from Germany by Interarms.
Price: **$1,250.00**

Wichita Silhouette

WICHITA SILHOUETTE RIFLE
Caliber: All standard calibers with maximum over-all cartridge length of 2.800".
Barrel: 24" free-floated Matchgrade.
Weight: About 9 lbs.
Stock: Metallic gray fiberthane with ventilated rubber recoil pad.
Sights: None furnished. Drilled and tapped for scope mounts.
Features: Legal for all NRA competitions. Single shot action. Fluted bolt, 2-oz. Canjar trigger; glass-bedded stock. Comes with hard case. Introduced 1983. From Wichita Arms.
Price: **$1,185.00**
Price: Left-hand **$1,285.00**

CAUTION: PRICES CHANGE. CHECK AT GUNSHOP.

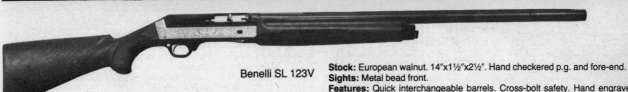

Benelli SL 123V

Stock: European walnut. 14"x1½"x2½". Hand checkered p.g. and fore-end.
Sights: Metal bead front.
Features: Quick interchangeable barrels. Cross-bolt safety. Hand engraved receiver on higher grades. Imported from Italy by Heckler & Koch, Inc.

Price: Standard model, SL 121V	$449.00
Price: Engraved, SL 123V	$525.00
Price: Slug gun, 121V	$492.00
Price: Model SL 201, 20 ga.	$453.00
Price: Extra barrels	$236.00

BENELLI AUTOLOADING SHOTGUN
Gauge: 12 ga. (5-shot, 3-shot plug furnished).
Barrel: 26" (Skeet, Imp. Cyl., Mod.); 28" (Full, Imp. Mod., Mod.). Vent. rib.
Weight: 6¾ lbs.

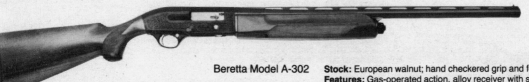

Beretta Model A-302

Stock: European walnut; hand checkered grip and fore-end.
Features: Gas-operated action, alloy receiver with scroll engraving; magazine cut-off, push-button safety. Multi-choke models come with four interchangeable screw-in choke tubes. Introduced 1983. Imported from Italy by Beretta U.S.A.

Price: 12 or 20 ga., standard chokes	$565.00
Price: Multi-choke, 12 ga. only	$650.00
Price: 12 ga. trap with Monte Carlo stock	$590.00
Price: 12 or 20 ga. Skeet	$580.00

BERETTA A-302 AUTO SHOTGUN
Gauge: 12 or 20, 2¾" or 3".
Barrel: 12 ga. — 22" (Slug); 26" (Imp. Cyl., Skeet); 28" (Mod., Full, Multi-choke); 30" (Full, Full Trap); 20 ga. — 26" (Imp. Cyl., Skeet); 28" (Mod., Full).
Weight: About 6½ lbs. (20 ga.).

Browning Auto-5

BROWNING AUTO-5 LIGHT 12 and 20
Gauge: 12, 20; 5-shot; 3-shot plug furnished; 2¾" chamber.
Action: Recoil operated autoloader; takedown.
Barrel: 26" (Skeet boring in 12 & 20 ga., Cyl., Imp. Cyl., Mod in 20 ga.); 28" (Skeet in 12 ga., Mod., Full); 30" (Full in 12 ga.).
Weight: 12 ga. 7¼ lbs., 20 ga. 6⅜ lbs.
Stock: French walnut, hand checkered half-p.g. and fore-end. 14¼" x 1⅝" x 2½".
Features: Receiver hand engraved with scroll designs and border. Double extractors, extra bbls. interchangeable without factory fitting; mag. cut-off; cross-bolt safety. Imported from Japan by Browning.

Price: Vent. rib only	$559.95
Price: Extra barrels, vent. rib only	$175.00

Browning Auto-5 Magnum 12
Same as Std. Auto-5 except: chambered for 3" magnum shells (also handles 2¾" magnum and 2¾" HV loads). 28" Mod., Full; 30" and 32" (Full) bbls. 14"x1⅝"x2½" stock. Recoil pad. Wgt. 8¾ lbs.
Price: Vent. rib only $569.95

Browning Auto-5 Magnum 20
Same as Magnum 12 except barrels 28" Full or Mod., or 26" Full, Mod. or Imp. Cyl. With ventilated rib, 7½ lbs.
Price: $569.95

Browning A-5 Buck Special

Browning Auto-5 Light 12, 20 or 12 Buck Special
Same as A-5 Light model except: 24" bbl. choked for slugs, gold bead front sight on contoured ramp, rear sight adj. for w.&e. Wgt. 12 ga., 7 lbs.; 20 ga., 6 lbs. 2 oz.; 3" Mag. 12, 8¼ lbs. All Buck Specials are available with carrying sling, detachable swivels and swivel attachments for $20.00 extra.

Price:	$569.95
Price: 12 or 20 ga. Magnum	$584.95

Browning Auto-5 Light Skeet
Same as Light Standard except: 12 and 20 ga. only, 26" or 28" bbl. (Skeet). With vent. rib. Wgt. 6⅜-7½ lbs.
Price: $559.95

Browning B-80 Auto

Weight: About 6½ lbs.
Stock: 14¼" x 1⅝" x 2½". Hand checkered French walnut. Solid black recoil pad.
Features: Vent. rib barrels have non-reflective rib; steel receiver with high-polish blue; cross-bolt safety; interchangeable barrels. Introduced 1981. Imported from Belgium by Browning.

Price: 12 or 20 ga., 2¾" or 3", vent. rib	$549.95
Price: Buck Special, 12 or 20 ga., 2¾" or 3"	$559.95
Price: Buck Special, with accessories (carrying strap, swivels)	$579.95
Price: Extra barrels	$179.95

BROWNING B-80 AUTO SHOTGUN
Gauge: 12 (2¾" & 3"), 20 (2¾" & 3")
Barrel: 22" (Slug), 26" (Imp. Cyl., Cyl., Skeet, Full, Mod.), 28" (Full, Mod.), 30" (Full), 32" (Full).

Franchi Model 48/AL

FRANCHI 48/AL AUTO SHOTGUN
Gauge: 12 or 20, 5-shot. 2¾" or 3" chamber.
Action: Recoil-operated automatic.
Barrel: 24" (Imp. Cyl. or Cyl.); 26" (Imp. Cyl. or Mod); 28" (Skeet, Mod. or Full); 30", 32" (Full). Interchangeable barrels.
Weight: 12 ga. 6¼ lbs., 20 ga. 5 lbs. 2 oz.
Stock: Epoxy-finished walnut, with cut-checkered pistol grip and fore-end.
Features: Chrome-lined bbl., easy takedown, 3-round plug provided. Ventilated rib barrel. Imported from Italy by F.I.E.
Price: Vent. rib 12, 20 .... $394.95

Franchi Slug Gun
    Same as Standard automatic except 22" Cylinder bored plain barrel, adj. rifle-type sights, sling swivels.
Price: 12 or 20 ga., standard $394.95
Price: As above, Hunter grade $419.95
Price: Extra barrel $154.95

Price: Hunter model (engraved) $419.95
Price: 12 ga. Magnum $419.95
Price: Extra barrel $154.95

Ithaca Model 51A

ITHACA MODEL 51A AUTOMATIC
Gauge: 12 or 20 ga., 2¾" chamber.
Action: Gas-operated, rotary bolt has three locking lugs. Takedown. Self-compensating for high or low base loads.
Barrel: Roto-Forged, 30" (Full), 28" (Full, Mod.), 26" (Imp. Cyl. or Skeet). Extra barrels available. Raybar front sight.
Weight: About 7½ lbs.
Stock: 14"x1⅝"x2½". Hand checkered walnut, white spacers on p.g. and under recoil pad.
Features: Hand fitted, engraved receiver, 3 shot capacity, safety is reversible for left hand shooter.
Price: With vent, rib $477.00
Price: Presentation Series $1,658.00

Ithaca Model 51A Magnum
    Same Standard Model 51 except has 3" chamber.
Price: With vent rib $525.00

Ithaca Model 51A Supreme Skeet
    Same gun as Model 51 Skeet with fancy American walnut stock, 26" (Skeet) barrel, 12 or 20 ga..
Price: $604.00

Ithaca Model 51A Trap

ITHACA MODEL 51A DEERSLAYER
Gauge: 12 or 20 ga., 2¾" chamber.
Action: Gas-operated, semi-automatic.
Barrel: 24", special bore.
Weight: 7½ lbs. (12 ga.), 7¼ lbs. (20 ga.).
Stock: 14"x1½"x2¼", American walnut. Checkered p.g. and fore-end.
Sights: Raybar front, open rear adj. for w. and e.
Features: Sight base grooved for scope mounts. Easy takedown, reversible safety. Scope optional.
Price: $475.00

Ithaca Model 51A Supreme Trap
    Same gun as standard Model 51 with fancy American walnut trap stock, 30" (Full).
Price: $614.00
Price: With Monte Carlo stock $650.00

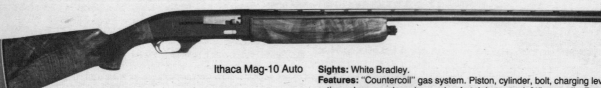

Ithaca Mag-10 Auto

Sights: White Bradley.
Features: "Countercoil" gas system. Piston, cylinder, bolt, charging lever, action release and carrier made of stainless steel. ⅜" vent. rib. Reversible cross-bolt safety. Low recoil force. Supreme and Presentation models have full fancy claro American black walnut.
Price: Standard, plain barrel $670.00
Price: Deluxe, vent. rib $860.00
Price: Standard, vent. rib $730.00
Price: Supreme, vent. rib $925.00
Price: Presentation Series $1,727.00

ITHACA MAG-10 GAS OPERATED SHOTGUN
Gauge: 10, 3½" chamber, 3-shot.
Barrel: 26", 28" (Full, Mod.), 32".
Weight: 11¼ lbs.
Stock: American walnut, checkered p.g. and fore-end (14⅛"x2⅜"x1½"), p.g. cap, rubber recoil pad.

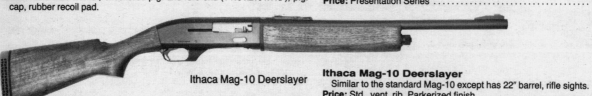

Ithaca Mag-10 Deerslayer

Ithaca Mag-10 Deerslayer
    Similar to the standard Mag-10 except has 22" barrel, rifle sights.
Price: Std., vent. rib, Parkerized finish $730.00
Price: Deluxe, blue finsih $860.00
Price: Supreme grade $995.00

K.F.C. Model 250

Weight: 7 lbs. 6 oz. **Length:** 48″ over-all (28″ barrel).
Stock: 14⅛″x1½″x2½″. American walnut, hand checkered p.g. and fore-end.
Features: Gas-operated, ventilated barrel rib. Has only 79 parts. Cross-bolt safety is reversible for left-handed shooters. Introduced 1980. Imported from Japan by La Paloma Marketing.
Price: Standard Grade **$485.00**
Price: Deluxe Grade (silvered, etched receiver). **$520.00**
Price: With choke tubes, Standard Grade **$565.00**
Price: As above, Deluxe Grade **$599.00**

KAWAGUCHIYA K.F.C. M-250 AUTO SHOTGUN
Gauge: 12, 2¾″.
Barrel: 24½″ (Imp. Cyl. Mod., Full, interchangeable choke tubes); or 26″ (Imp. Cyl.), 28″ (Mod.), 30″ (Full) for standard choke models.

Ljutic Bi-Matic Auto

LJUTIC BI-MATIC AUTO SHOTGUN
Gauge: 12 only, 2¾″ chamber.
Barrel: 26″ to 32″ (30″ standard); choked to customer specs.
Weight: About 10 lbs.
Stock: To customer specs. Oil finish, hand checkered.
Features: Two-shot, low recoil auto designed for trap and Skeet. One-piece actuating rod, pull or release trigger. Available with right or left-hand ejection. Many options available. Custom made. From Ljutic Industries.
Price: **$3,595.00**

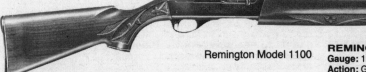

Mossberg Model 5500

MOSSBERG 5500 AUTO SHOTGUN
Gauge: 12 only, 2¾″ or 3″ chamber.
Barrel: 18½″ (Cyl.), 24″ (Slugster), 26″ (Imp. Cyl.), 28″ (Mod.), 30″ (Full, 2¾″ or 3″).
Weight: 7½ lbs. **Length:** 48″ over-all (with 28″ barrel).
Stock: 14″x1½″x2½″. Walnut-finished hardwood.
Sights: Bead front.
Features: Safety located on top of receiver. Interchangeable barrels and ACCU-CHOKE choke tubes. Introduced 1983.
Price: About **$340.00**
Price: Slug gun, about **$291.00**

Remington Model 1100

Remington 1100 Magnum
Same as 1100 except: chambered for 3″ magnum loads. Available in 12 ga. (30″) or 20 ga. (28″) Mod. or Full, 14″x1½″x2½″ stock with recoil pad, Wgt. 7¾ lbs.
Price: **$497.95**
Price: With vent. rib **$542.95**
Price: Left hand model with vent. rib **$573.95**

REMINGTON MODEL 1100 AUTO
Gauge: 12, 3-shot plug furnished.
Action: Gas-operated autoloader.
Barrel: 26″ (Imp. Cyl.), 28″ (Mod., Full), 30″ Full in 12 ga. only.
Weight: 12 ga. 7½ lbs.
Stock: 14″x1½″x2½″ American Walnut, checkered p.g. and fore-end.
Features: Quickly interchangeable barrels within gauge. Matted receiver top with scroll work on both sides of receiver. Crossbolt safety.
Price: **$453.95**
Price: With vent. rib **$497.95**
Price: Left hand model with vent. rib **$528.95**

Remington 1100 Special Field

Remington 1100 "Special Field"
Similar to standard Model 1100 except comes with 21″ barrel only, choked Imp. Cyl., Mod., Full; 12 ga. weighs 7¼ lbs., LT-20 version 6½ lbs.; has straight-grip stock, shorter fore-end, both with cut checkering. Comes with vent rib only; matte finish receiver without engraving. Introduced 1983.
Price: **$524.95**

Remington 1100 Small Gauge
Same as 1100 except: 28 ga. 2¾″ (5-shot) or 410, 3″ (except Skeet, 2½″ 4-shot). 45½″ over-all. Available in 25″ bbl. (Full, Mod., or Imp. Cyl.) only.
Price: With vent. rib **$509.95**

Remington 1100 LT-20
Basically the same design as Model 1100, but with special weight-saving features that retain strength and dependability of the standard Model 1100.
Barrel: 28″ (Full, Mod.), 26″ (Imp. Cyl.).
Weight: 6½ lbs.
Price: **$453.95**
Price: With vent. rib **$497.95**
Price: LT-20 magnum **$497.95**
Price: With vent. rib **$542.95**
Price: LT-20 Deer Gun (20″ bbl.). **$497.95**
Price: LT-20 Ltd. has 23″ (Mod. or Imp. Cyl.) bbl., 1″ shorter stock.. **$497.95**

SHOTGUNS—AUTOLOADERS

Remington 1100 TA Trap

Remington 1100 TA Trap
Same as the standard 1100 except: recoil pad. 14⅜"x1⅜"x1¾" stock. Right- or left-hand models. Wgt. 8¼ lbs. 12 ga. only. 30" (Mod. Trap, Full) vent. rib bbl. Ivory bead front and white metal middle sight.
Price:	**$524.95**
Price: With Monte Carlo stock	**$534.95**
Price: 1100TA Trap, left hand	**$555.95**
Price: With Monte Carlo stock	**$565.95**
Price: Tournament Trap	**$617.95**
Price: Tournament Trap with M.C. stock, better grade wood, different checkering, cut checkering	**$629.95**

Remington 1100D Tournament Auto
Same as 1100 Standard except: vent, rib, better wood, more extensive engraving.
Price: **$2,000.00**

Remington 1100F Premier Auto
Same as 1100D except: select wood, better engraving
Price: **$4,000.00**
Price: With gold inlay **$6,000.00**

Remington 1100 Extra bbls. 12 and 20 ga.: Plain **$101.95** (20, 28 & 410, **$110.95**). Vent., rib 12 and 20 **$145.95** (20, 28 & 410, **$154.95**). Vent. rib Skeet **$155.95**. Vent. rib Trap **$155.95**. Deer bbl. **$120.95**. Available in the same gauges and chokes as shown on guns. **Prices are approximate.**

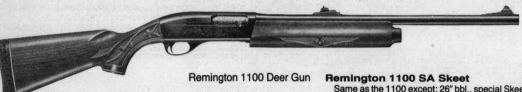

Remington 1100 Deer Gun

Remington 1100 SA Skeet
Same as the 1100 except: 26" bbl., special Skeet boring, vent. rib (high rib on LT-20), ivory bead front and metal bead middle sights. 14"x1½"x2½" stock. 12, 20, 28, 410 ga. Wgt. 7½ lbs., cut checkering, walnut, new receiver scroll.
Price: 12 ga., Skeet SA	**$513.95**
Price: 12 ga. Left hand model with vent. rib	**$544.95**
Price: 28 & 410 ga., 25" bbl.	**$525.95**
Price: 20 ga. LT-20 Skeet SA	**$513.95**
Price: Tournament Skeet (28, 410)	**$620.95**
Price: Tournament Skeet (12 or 20)	**$608.95**

Remington 1100 Deer Gun
Same as 1100 except: 12 ga. only, 22" bbl. (Imp. Cyl.), rifle sights adjustable for w. and e.; recoil pad with white spacer. Weight 7¼ lbs.
Price: **$497.95**
Price: Left-hand Deer Gun **$528.95**

S & W Model 1000 Auto

SMITH & WESSON MODEL 1000 AUTO
Gauge: 12, 2¾" or 3" chamber, 4-shot.
Action: Gas-operated autoloader.
Barrel: 26" (Skeet, Imp. Cyl.), 28" (Mod. Full). Also available with screw-in Multi-Choke tubes.
Weight: 7½ lbs. (28" bbl.). **Length:** 48" over-all (28" bbl.).
Stock: 14"x1½"x2⅜", American walnut.
Features: Interchangeable crossbolt safety, vent. rib with front and middle beads, engraved alloy receiver, pressure compensator and floating piston for light recoil.
Price:	**$469.95**
Price: Extra barrels (as listed above)	**$139.95**
Price: Extra 22" barrel (Cyl. bore) with rifle sights	**$115.95**
Price: With 3" chamber, 30" (Mod., Full) barrel	**$511.95**
Price: With Multi-Choke system	**$496.95**
Price: Extra Multi-Choke barrel	**$166.95**

Smith & Wesson Model 1000 20 Gauge & 20 Magnum
Similar to 12 ga. model except slimmed down to weigh only 6½ lbs. Has self-cleaning gas system. Choice of four interchangeable barrels (26", Imp. Cyl. or Skeet, 28" Mod., Full) or Multi-Choke system which includes tubes for Imp. Cyl., Mod., Full.
Price: **$469.95**
Price: Extra barrels **$139.95**
Price: With 3" chamber, (Mod., Full) **$511.95**
Price: With Multi-Choke system, ... **$496.95**

Smith & Wesson 1000 Trap

Smith & Wesson Model 1000 Trap Shotgun
Similar to the standard Model 1000 except has Monte Carlo trap stock, medium width stepped rib with white middle bead, Bradley front; integral wire shell catcher; specially tuned trigger; 30" Multi-Choke barrel with Full, Mod. and Imp. Mod. tubes. Steel receiver. Introduced 1983.
Price: **$564.95**

Smith & Wesson Model 1000 Waterfowler Auto
Similar to the standard Model 1000 except all exterior metal is Parkerized to reduce glare, bolt is black oxidized, stock has a dull oil finish. Comes with q.d. swivels and a padded, camouflaged sling. Available with 30" (Full) barrel with 3" chamber. Introduced 1982.
Price: **$538.95**

CAUTION: PRICES CHANGE. CHECK AT GUNSHOP.

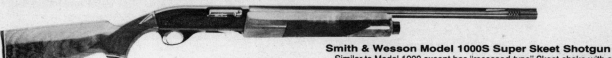

S & W Model 1000 S

Smith & Wesson Model 1000S Super Skeet Shotgun

Similar to Model 1000 except has "recessed-type" Skeet choke with a compensator system to soften recoil and reduce muzzle jump. Stock has right-hand palm swell. Trigger is contoured (rounded) on right side; pull is 2½ to 3 lbs. Vent. rib has double sighting beads with a "Bright Point" fluorescent red front bead. Fore-end cap weights (included) of 1 and 2 oz. can be used to change balance. Select-grade walnut with oil finish. Barrel length is 25", weight 8¼ lbs., over-all length 45.7". Stock measures 14"x1½"x2½" with .08" cast-off at butt, .16" at toe.
Price: **$709.95**
Price: Super Skeet interchangeable barrel **$229.95**

Tradewinds Model H-170

TRADEWINDS H-170 AUTO SHOTGUN

Gauge: 12 only, 2¾" chamber.
Action: Recoil-operated automatic.
Barrel: 26", 28" (Mod.) and 28" (Full), chrome lined.
Weight: 7 lbs.
Stock: Select European walnut stock, p.g. and fore-end hand checkered.
Features: Light alloy receiver, 5-shot tubular magazine, ventilated rib. Imported from Italy by Tradewinds.
Price: **$395.00**

Weatherby Eighty-Two Auto

WEATHERBY EIGHTY-TWO AUTO

Gauge: 12 only, 2¾" and 3" chamber.
Action: Gas operated autoloader with "Floating Piston."
Barrel: 26" (Mod., Imp. Cyl., Skeet), 28" (Full, Mod.), 30" (Full, Full Trap, Full 3" Mag.). Vent. Rib. Also available with Multi-choke interchangeable choke tubes.

Weight: About 7½ lbs. **Length:** 48¼" (28").
Stock: Walnut, hand checkered p.g. and fore-end, rubber recoil pad with white line spacer.
Features: Cross bolt safety, fluted bolt, gold plated trigger. Imported from Japan by Weatherby. Introduced 1982.
Price: Field or Skeet grade **$439.95**
Price: Trap Grade **$469.95**
Price: Extra interchangeable barrels, from **$164.95**
Price: Multi-Choke models **$459.95**

Winchester Model 1500 XTR

WINCHESTER 1500 XTR AUTO SHOTGUN

Gauge: 12 and 20, 2¾" chamber, 2-shot magazine.
Barrel: 28" vent. rib Winchoke with Full, Mod., Imp. Cyl. tubes.
Weight: 7 to 7¼ lbs. **Length:** 45⅝" over-all.
Stock: American walnut, cut-checkered p.g. and fore-end.
Sights: Metal bead front.

Features: Winchester XTR fit and finish. Gas-operated action; front locking, rotating bolt. Interchangeable barrels. Engine turned bolt, nickel plated carrier, cross-bolt safety. Introduced 1978. Made under license by U.S. Repeating Arms Co.
Price: Vent. rib barrel with Winchoke **$449.95**
Price: Extra barrel, plain field **$108.95**
Price: As above, with Winchoke **$130.20**
Price: Extra barrel, vent. rib **$139.95**
Price: As above, with Winchoke **$161.20**
Price: Deer Slug barrel **$122.95**

Winchester Ranger

WINCHESTER RANGER AUTO SHOTGUN

Gauge: 12 and 20, 2¾" chamber.
Barrel: 28" vent. rib with Winchoke tubes (Imp. Cyl., Mod., Full), or 28" plain barrel (Mod.).
Weight: 7 to 7¼ lbs. **Length:** 48⅝" over-all.
Stock: Walnut-finished hardwood with ribbed fore-end.
Sights: Metal bead front.
Features: Cross-bolt safety, front-locking rotating bolt, black serrated butt-plate, gas-operated action. Made under license by U.S. Repeating Arms. Co.
Price: Vent. rib with Winchoke **$279.95**
Price: Plain barrel **$259.95**

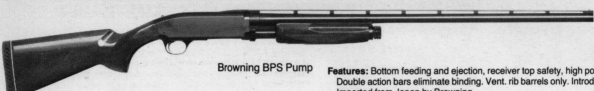

Browning BPS Pump

BROWNING BPS PUMP SHOTGUN

Gauge: 12 only, 3″ chamber (2¾″ in target guns), 5-shot magazine.
Barrel: 26″, 28″, 30″, 32″ (Imp. Cyl., Mod. or Full). Also available with Invector choke tubes.
Weight: 7 lbs. 12 oz. (28″ barrel). **Length:** 48¾″ over-all (28″ barrel).
Stock: 14¼″x1½″x2½″. Select walnut, semi-beavertail fore-end, full p.g. stock.

Features: Bottom feeding and ejection, receiver top safety, high post vent. rib. Double action bars eliminate binding. Vent. rib barrels only. Introduced 1977. Imported from Japan by Browning.
Price: Grade I, Hunting **$374.95**
Price: As above, with Invector chokes **$394.95**
Price: Grade I, Trap **$399.95**
Price: Invector Trap, vent. rib **$414.95**
Price: Extra Trap barrel **$139.95**
Price: As above, Invector chokes **$149.95**
Price: Extra hunting barrel **$129.95**
Price: As above, Invector chokes **$149.95**
Price: BPS, Buck Special, no accessories **$399.95**
Price: As above with accessories **$419.95**

Ithaca Model 37

ITHACA MODEL 37 FEATHERLIGHT

Gauge: 12, 20 (5-shot; 3-shot plug furnished).
Action: Slide; takedown; bottom ejection.
Barrel: 26″, 28″, 30″ in 12 ga.; 26″ or 28″ in 20 ga. (Full, Mod. or Imp. Cyl.)
Weight: 12 ga. 6½ lbs., 20 ga. 5¾ lbs.
Stock: 14″x1⅝″x2⅝″. Checkered walnut p.g. stock and fore-end.
Features: Ithaca Raybar front sight; decorated receiver, crossbolt safety; action release for removing shells.
Price: Standard **$345.00**
Price: Standard Vent Rib **$396.00**
Price: 2500 Series **$919.00**
Price: Presentation Series **$1,727.00**

Ithaca Model 37 Ultralite
Weighs five pounds. Same as standard Model 37 except 20 ga. comes only with 25″ vent. rib barrel choked Full, Mod. or Imp. Cyl.; 12 ga., 26″ barrel with same chokes as 20 ga. Has recoil pad, gold plated trigger, Sid Bell-designed grip cap. Also available as Ultra-Deerslayer with 20″ barrel, 20 ga. only.
Price: **$435.00**
Price: Deerslayer model **$414.00**

Ithaca 37 English Ultra

Ithaca Model 37 Magnum
Same as standard Model 37 except chambered for 3″ shells with resulting longer receiver. Stock dimensions are 14″x1⅞″x1½″. Grip cap has a Sid Bell-designed flying mallard on it. Has a recoil pad, vent. rib barrel with Raybar front sight. Available in 12 or 20 ga. with 30″ (Full), 28″ (Mod.) and 26″ (Imp. Cyl.) barrel. Weight about 7¼ lbs. Introduced 1978.
Price: **$435.00**

Ithaca Model 37 English Ultralite
Similar to the standard Model 37 Ultralite except vent. rib barrel has straight-grip stock with better wood, cut-checkered pump handle, grip area and butt, oil finished wood. Introduced 1981.
Price: **$496.00**

Ithaca Model 37 Supreme
Same as Model 37 except: hand checkered fore-end and p.g. stock, Ithaca recoil pad and vent. rib. Model 37 Supreme also with Skeet (14″x1½″x2¼″) or Trap (14½″x1½″x1⅞″) stocks available at no extra charge. Other options available at extra charge.
Price: **$650.00**

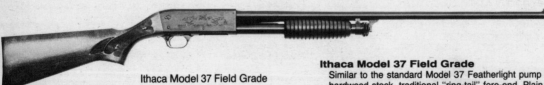

Ithaca Model 37 Field Grade

Ithaca Model 37 Deerslayer
Same as Model 37 except: 26″ or 20″ bbl. designed for rifled slugs; sporting rear sight, Raybar front sight: rear sight ramp grooved for Redfield long eye relief scope mount. 12, or 20 gauge. With checkered stock, beavertail fore-end and recoil pad.
Price: **$385.00**
Price: Super Deluxe model **$435.00**

Ithaca Model 37 De Luxe Featherlight
Same as Model 37 except: checkered stock with p.g. cap; beavertail fore-end; vent. rib; recoil pad. Wgt. 12 ga. 6¾ lbs.
Price: With vent. rib **$414.00**

Ithaca Model 37 Field Grade
Similar to the standard Model 37 Featherlight pump except has American hardwood stock, traditional "ring-tail" fore-end. Plain or vent. rib, 12 or 20 gauge, 2¾″ chamber only. Raybar front sight. Introduced 1983.
Price: Standard **$292.00**
Price: Vent. rib **$333.00**

KASSNAR-SQUIRES BINGHAM MODEL 30 D SHOTGUN
Gauge: 12 only, 2¾″ chamber.
Barrel: 20″ (Imp. Cyl., Slug); 24″ (Slug); 26″ (Imp. Cyl.); 28″ (Mod.); 30″ (Full).
Weight: 7 lbs. **Length:** 48″ over-all (30″ bbl.).
Stock: Philippine mahogany.
Features: Checkered grip and fore-end; slug guns have ramp front, open rear sights. Imported from the Philippines by Kassnar.
Price: Slug gun or field model **$149.95**

Marlin Model 120

MARLIN 120 MAGNUM PUMP GUN
Gauge: 12 ga. (2¾" or 3" chamber) 5-shot; 3-shot plug furnished.
Action: Hammerless, side ejecting, slide action.
Barrel: 20" slug, 26" (Imp. Cyl.), 28" (Mod.), 30" (Full), with vent. rib or 38" MXR plain.
Weight: 8 lbs. **Length:** 50½" over-all (30" bbl.).
Stock: 14"x1½"x2⅜". Hand-checkered walnut, capped p.g., semi-beavertail fore-end. Mar-Shield® finish.
Features: Interchangeable bbls., slide lock release; large button cross-bolt safety.
Price: **$355.00**
Price: Extra barrels, about **$103.95**

MARLIN GLENFIELD 778 PUMP GUN
Gauge: 12 (2¾" or 3" chamber). 5-shot, 3-shot plug furnished.
Barrel: 20" slug (with sights), 26" (Imp. Cyl.), 28" (Mod.), 30" (Full), all with or without rib; 38" MXR (Full), no rib.
Weight: 7¾ lbs. **Length:** 50½" over-all (30" bbl.).
Stock: Walnut-finished hardwood. Semi-beavertail fore-end, vent. recoil pad.
Features: Machined steel receiver, double action bars, engine-turned bolt, shell carrier and bolt slide. Interchangeable barrel. Introduced 1978.
Price: Plain barrel **$244.95**
Price: Vent. rib barrel **$277.95**

Mossberg Model 500

MOSSBERG MODEL 500 AGVD, CGVD
Gauge: 12, 20, 3".
Action: Takedown.
Barrel: 28" ACCU-CHOKE (interchangeable tubes for Imp. Cyl., Mod., Full). Vent. rib only.
Weight: 6¾ lbs. (20-ga.), 7¼ lbs. (12-ga.) **Length:** 48" over-all.
Stock: Walnut-finished hardwood; checkered p.g. and fore-end; recoil pad. (14"x1½"x2½").
Features: Side ejection; top tang safety; trigger disconnector prevents doubles. Easily interchangeable barrels within gauge.
Price: Vent rib, either gauge, about **$206.00**
Price: Extra barrels, from **$24.95**
Price: Youth model, 20 ga., 13" buttstock, 25" (Mod.), about **$180.00**

Mossberg 500 Medallion Series
Same as standard Model 500, AGVD, CGVD, except has medallion in receiver for one of four game birds — Quail, Pheasant, Grouse, and Duck. Pheasant and Duck guns are in 12 gauge, others in 20 gauge, all with ACCU-CHOKE. Limited to 5,000 guns for each category. All guns have 28" vent. rib barrels with Full, Mod. and Imp. Cyl. choke tubes. Introduced 1983.
Price: About **$225.00**

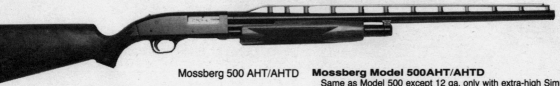

Mossberg 500 AHT/AHTD

Mossberg Model 500AHT/AHTD
Same as Model 500 except 12 ga. only with extra-high Simmons Olympic-style free floating rib and built-up Monte Carlo trap-style stock. 30" barrel (Full), 28" ACCU-CHOKE with 3 interchangeable choke tubes (Mod., Imp. Mod., Full).
Price: Price: With 30" barrel, fixed choke .... **NA**
Price: With ACCU-CHOKE barrel, 28" or 30" .... **NA**

Mossberg Model 500EGV
Similar to Mossberg Model 500 except: 410 bore only, 26" bbl. (Full); 2½", 3" shells; holds six 2¾" or five 3" shells. Walnut-finished stock with checkered p.g. and fore-end, fluted comb and recoil pad (14"x1¼"x2½"). Weight about 6 lbs., length over-all 45¾".
Price: With vent. rib barrel .... **N.A.**

Mossberg Model 500ASG Slugster
Same as standard Mossberg Model 500 except has Slugster barrel with ramp front sight, open adj. folding-leaf rear, running deer scene etched on receiver. 12 ga.—18½", 24", 20-ga.—24" bbl.
Price: .... **N.A.**

Remington Model 870

REMINGTON 870 WINGMASTER PUMP GUN
Gauge: 12, 20, (5-shot; 3-shot wood plug).
Action: Takedown, slide action
Barrel: 12, 20, ga., 26" (Imp. Cyl.); 28" (Mod. or Full); 12 ga., 30" (Full).
Weight: 7 lbs., 12 ga. (7¾ lbs. with Vari-Weight plug); 6½ lbs., 20 ga.
Length: 48½" over-all (28" bbl.).
Stock: 14"x1⅝"x2½". Checkered walnut, p.g.; fluted extension fore-end; fitted rubber recoil pad.
Features: Double action bars, crossbolt safety. Receiver machined from solid steel. Hand fitted action.
Price: Plain bbl. **$342.95**
Price: With vent. rib **$386.95**
Price: Left hand, vent. rib., 12 ga. only **$412.95**
Price: Lt. Wt. Limited, 23" vent. rib, Imp. Cyl., Mod **$386.95**

SHOTGUNS—SLIDE ACTIONS

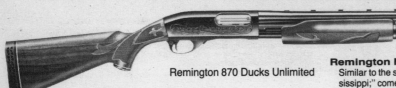

Remington 870 Ducks Unlimited

Remington Model 870 DU Commemorative
Similar to the standard Model 870, this DU special edition is called "The Mississippi;" comes only in 12 gauge 3" Magnum with 32" Full-choke barrel; distinctive engraving on both sides of the receiver; special DU serial number. Introduced and made only in 1983.
Price: **$453.95**

Remington 870 Magnum
Same as the M870 except 3" chamber, 12 ga. 30" bbl. (Mod. or Full), 20 ga. 28" bbl. (Mod. or Full). Recoil pad installed. Wgt., 12 ga. 8 lbs., 20 ga. 7½ lbs.
Price: Plain bbl. **$369.95**
Price: With vent. rib **$413.95**
Price: Left hand model, vent rib. bbl. **$439.95**

Remington 870 Small Gauges
Exact copies of the large ga. Model 870, except that guns are offered in 28 and 410 ga. 25" barrel (Full., Mod., Imp. Cyl.). D and F grade prices same as large ga. M870 prices.
Price: With vent. rib barrel **$398.95**
Price: Lightweight Magnum, 20 ga. plain bbl. (5¾ lbs.) **$369.95**
Price: Lightweight Magnum, 20 ga., vent. rib bbl. **$413.95**

Remington 870F Premier
Same as M870, except select walnut, better engraving
Price: **$4,000.00**
Price: With gold inlay **$6,000.00**

Remington 870 Deer Gun

Remington Model 870 Brushmaster Deluxe
Carbine version of the M870 with 20" bbl. (Imp. Cyl.) for rifled slugs. 40½" over-all, wgt. 6½ lbs. Recoil pad. Adj. rear, ramp front sights, 12 or 20 ga. Deluxe.
Price: **$364.95**
Price: Left-hand model **$390.95**

Remington Model 870 Competition Trap
Same as standard 870 except single shot, gas reduction system, select wood. Has 30" (Full choke) vent. rib barrel
Price: **$624.95**

Remington 870D Tournament
Same as 870 except: better walnut, hand checkering. Engraved receiver and bbl. Vent. rib. Stock dimensions to order.
Price: **$2,000.00**

Remington 870 Lightweight

Remington Model 870 20 Ga. Lt. Wt.
Same as standard Model 870 except weighs 6 lbs.; 26" (Imp. Cyl.), 28" (Full, Mod.), 30" (Full).
Price: Plain barrel **$342.95**
Price: Vent. rib barrel **$386.95**

Remington 870 TA Trap

Remington 870 TA Trap
Same as the M870 except: 12 ga. only, 30" (Mod., Full) vent. rib. bbl., ivory front and white metal middle beads. Special sear, hammer and trigger assy. 14⅜"x1½"x1⅞" stock with recoil pad. Hand fitted action and parts. Wgt. 8 lbs.
Price: Model 870TA Trap **$396.95**
Price: TA Trap with Monte Carlo stock. **$406.95**

Remington 870 Extra Barrels
Plain **$86.95**. Vent. rib **$130.95**. Vent. rib Skeet **$140.95**. Vent. rib Trap **$140.95**. 34" Trap **$156.95**. With rifle sights **$106.95**. Available in the same gauges and chokes as shown on guns. **Prices are approximate.**

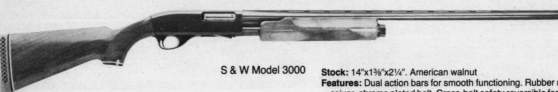

S & W Model 3000

SMITH & WESSON MODEL 3000 PUMP
Gauge: 12 or 20 ga., 3" chamber.
Barrel: 22" (Cyl.) with rifle sights, 26" (Imp. Cyl.), 28" (Mod.), 30" (Full), vent. rib or plain. Also available with Multi-Choke system.
Weight: About 7½ lbs. **Length:** 48½" over-all (28" bbl.).

Stock: 14"x1⅜"x2¼". American walnut
Features: Dual action bars for smooth functioning. Rubber recoil pad, steel receiver, chrome plated bolt. Cross-bolt safety reversible for left-handed shooters. Introduced 1980.
Price: With vent. rib barrel **$378.95**
Price: Extra vent. rib barrel. **$125.95**
Price: Slug barrel with rifle sights **$102.95**
Price: With Multi-Choke system **$405.95**
Price: Extra Multi-Choke barrel **$152.95**

CAUTION: PRICES CHANGE. CHECK AT GUNSHOP.

SHOTGUNS—SLIDE ACTIONS

Consult our Directory pages for the location of firms mentioned.

Smith & Wesson Model 3000 Waterfowler Pump
Similar to the standard Model 3000 except all exterior metal is Parkerized to reduce glare, bolt is black oxidized, stock has a dull oil finish. Comes with q.d. swivels and a padded, camouflaged sling. Available with 30″ (Full) barrel with 3″ chamber. Introduced 1982.
Price: **$405.95**

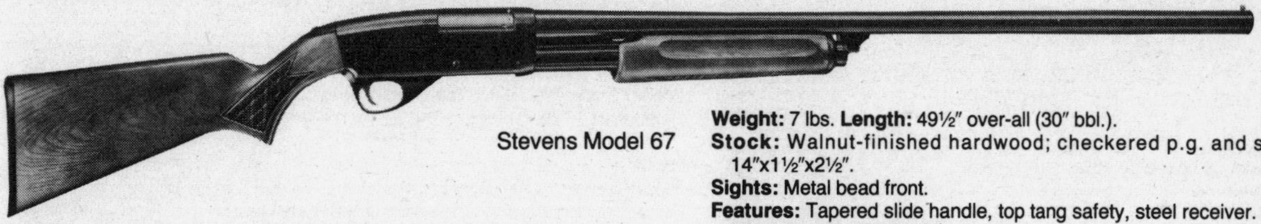

Stevens Model 67

Weight: 7 lbs. **Length:** 49½″ over-all (30″ bbl.).
Stock: Walnut-finished hardwood; checkered p.g. and slide handle. 14″x1½″x2½″.
Sights: Metal bead front.
Features: Tapered slide handle, top tang safety, steel receiver. From Savage Arms. Introduced 1981.

STEVENS MODEL 67 PUMP SHOTGUN
Gauge: 12, 20 (2¾″ & 3″), 410 (2½″ & 3″).
Barrel: 26″ (Full, 410 ga.), 28″ (Mod., Full), 30″ (Full, 12 ga.), or interchangeable choke tubes.

Price: Model 67 .... **$168.50**
Price: Model 67VR (vent. rib)............................. **$186.00**
Price: Model 67 Slug Gun (21″ barrel, rifle sights) **$171.50**
Price: Model 67-T (with 3 choke tubes) **$202.50**
Price: Model 67-VRT (as above with vent. rib) **$219.95**

Weatherby Ninety-Two

Weight: About 7½ lbs. **Length:** 48⅛″ (28″ bbl.)
Stock: Walnut, hand checkered p.g. and fore-end, white line spacers at p.g. cap and recoil pad.
Features: Short stroke action, crossbolt safety. Introduced 1982. Imported from Japan by Weatherby.

WEATHERBY NINETY-TWO PUMP
Gauge: 12 only, 3″ chamber.
Action: Short stroke slide action.
Barrel: 26″ (Mod., Imp. Cyl., Skeet), 28″ (Full, Mod.), 30″ (Full, Full Trap, 3″ Mag. Full). Vent. Rib; or Multi-Choke barrel with interchangeable tubes.

Price: Field or Skeet grade, fixed chokes **$399.95**
Price: Trap grade **$429.95**
Price: Extra interchangeable bbls. **$164.95**
Price: Multi-Choke models **$419.95**

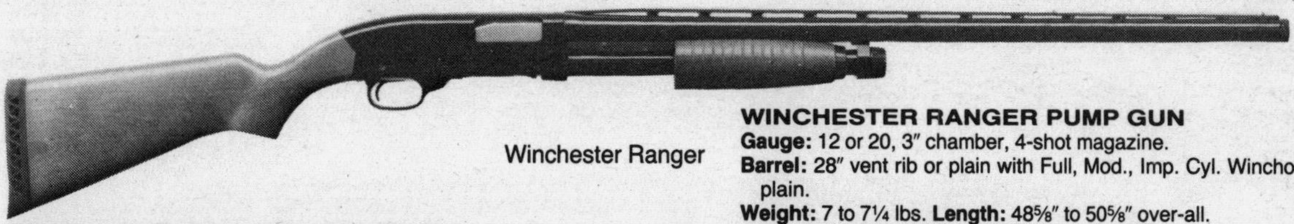

Winchester Ranger

WINCHESTER RANGER PUMP GUN
Gauge: 12 or 20, 3″ chamber, 4-shot magazine.
Barrel: 28″ vent rib or plain with Full, Mod., Imp. Cyl. Winchoke tubes, or 30″ plain.
Weight: 7 to 7¼ lbs. **Length:** 48⅝″ to 50⅝″ over-all.
Stock: Walnut finished hardwood with ribbed fore-end.
Sights: Metal bead front.
Features: Cross-bolt safety, black rubber butt pad, twin action slide bars, front-locking rotating bolt. Made under license by U.S. Repeating Arms Co.

Winchester Ranger Youth Pump Gun
Similar to the standard Ranger except chambered only for 3″ 20 ga., 22″ plain barrel with Winchoke tubes (Full, Mod., Imp. Cyl.) or 22″ plain barrel with fixed Mod. choke. Weighs 6½ lbs., measures 41⅝″ o.a.l. Stock has 13″ pull length and gun comes with discount certificate for full-size stock. Introduced 1983. Made under license by U.S. Repeating Arms Co.
Price: Plain barrel, Winchoke........................ **$179.95**
Price: Plain barrel, Mod. choke **$164.95**

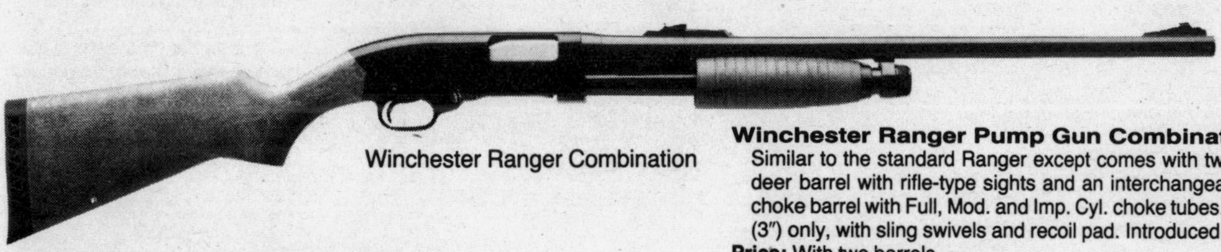

Price: Plain barrel **$164.95**
Price: Vent. rib barrel, Winchoke........................ **$189.95**
Price: Vent. rib. Mod. choke............................. **$179.95**

Winchester Ranger Combination

Winchester Ranger Pump Gun Combination
Similar to the standard Ranger except comes with two barrels: 24⅛″ (Cyl.) deer barrel with rifle-type sights and an interchangeable 28″ vent. rib Winchoke barrel with Full, Mod. and Imp. Cyl. choke tubes. Available in 12 gauge (3″) only, with sling swivels and recoil pad. Introduced 1983.
Price: With two barrels **$219.95**

WINCHESTER 1300 XTR PUMP GUN
Gauge: 12 and 20, 3″ chamber, 4-shot.
Barrel: 28″, vent. rib with Full, Mod., Imp. Cyl. Winchoke tubes.
Weight: 7¼ lbs. **Length:** 48⅝″ over-all.
Stock: American walnut, cut-checkered p.g. and fore-end. XTR finish.
Sights: Metal bead front.
Features: Winchester XTR fit and finish. Has twin action bars, cross-bolt safety, alloy receiver and trigger guard. Front-locking, rotating bolt, engine-turned bolt. Introduced 1978. Made under license by U.S. Repeating Arms Co.
Price: Vent. rib with Winchoke................................. **$359.95**
Price: Extra field barrel, plain................................ **$104.95**
Price: As above with Winchoke................................ **$125.20**
Price: Extra field barrel with vent. rib **$135.95**
Price: As above with Winchoke................................ **$156.20**
Price: 1300 Deer Slug barrel **$118.95**

Winchester 1300 XTR Deer Gun
Similar to the 1300 XTR except available only in 12 gauge with 24⅛″ barrel (Cyl.) and rifle-type sights. Weight is 6½ lbs.
Price: **$339.95**

Winchester 1300 XTR Waterfowl Pump Gun
Similar to the 1300 XTR except available only in 12 ga. with 30″ vent rib barrel and Winchoke.
Price: **$359.95**

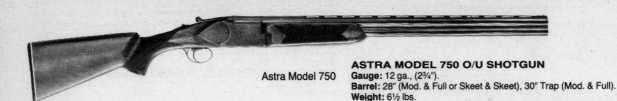

Astra Model 750

Astra Model 650 O/U Shotgun

Same as Model 750 except has double triggers.
Price: With extractors $493.00
Price: With ejectors $630.00

ARMSPORT MODEL 2500 O/U

Gauge: 12 or 20 ga.
Barrel: 26″ (Imp. Cyl. & Mod.); 28″ (Mod. & Full); vent. rib.
Weight: 8 lbs.
Stock: European walnut, hand checkered p.g. and fore-end.
Features: Single selective trigger, automatic ejectors, engraved receiver. Imported by Armsport.
Price: $695.00
Price: With extractors only $595.00

ASTRA MODEL 750 O/U SHOTGUN

Gauge: 12 ga., (2¾″).
Barrel: 28″ (Mod. & Full or Skeet & Skeet), 30″ Trap (Mod. & Full).
Weight: 6½ lbs.
Stock: European walnut, hand-checkered p.g. and fore-end.
Features: Single selective trigger, scroll-engraved receiver, selective auto ejectors, vent. rib. Introduced 1980. From L. Joseph Rahn, Inc.
Price: $733.00
Price: With extractors only $600.00
Price: Trap or Skeet (M.C. stock and recoil pad.). $850.00

> Consult our Directory pages for
> the location of firms mentioned.

Beretta Model 686

BERETTA SERIES 680 OVER-UNDER

Gauge: 12 (2¾″).
Barrel: 29½″ (Imp. Mod. & Full, Trap), 28″ (Skeet & Skeet).
Weight: About 8 lbs.
Stock: Trap—14⅜″x1¼″x2⅛″; Skeet—14⅜″x1⅜″x2⅞₁₆″. European walnut with hand checkering.

Sights: Luminous front sight and center bead.
Features: Trap Monte Carlo stock has deluxe trap recoil pad, Skeet has smooth pad. Imported from Italy by Beretta U.S.A. Corp.
Price: Skeet or Trap gun $1,580.00
Price: As above with fitted case $1,580.00
Price: M686 Field gun (illus.) $980.00
Price: M685 Field gun $820.00
Price: M687EL, Field $2,212.00
Price: M680 Single bbl. Trap, 32″ or 34″ $1,580.00
Price: M680 Combo Trap O/U, with single bbl. $2,200.00

Beretta Model SO-3EELL

BERETTA SO-3 O/U SHOTGUN

Gauge: 12 ga. (2¾″ chambers).
Action: Back-action sidelock.
Barrel: 26″, 27″, 28″, 29″ or 30″, chokes to customer specs.
Stock: Standard measurements—14⅛″x1⁷₁₆″x2⅜″. Straight "English" or p.g.-style. Hand checkered European walnut.
Features: SO-3—"English scroll" floral engraving on action body, sideplates and trigger guard. Stocked in select walnut. SO-3EL—as above, with full engraving coverage. Hand-detachable sideplates. SO-3EELL—as above with deluxe finish and finest full coverage engraving. Internal parts gold plated. Top lever is pierced and carved in relief with gold inlaid crown. Introduced 1977. Imported from Italy by Beretta U.S.A. Corp.
Price: SO-3 .... $6,245.00
Price: SO-3EL $7,440.00
Price: SO-3EELL $10,000.00

Beretta Model SO-4

Beretta SO-4 Target Shotguns

Target guns derived from Model SO-3EL. Light engraving coverage. Single trigger. Skeet gun has 28″ (Skeet & Skeet) barrels, 10mm rib, p.g. stock (14⅛″x2⁹₁₆″x1⅜″), fluted beavertail fore-end. "Skeet" is inlaid in gold into trigger guard. Weight is about 7 lbs. 10 ozs. Trap guns have 30″ (Imp. Mod. & Full or Mod. & Full) barrels, trap stock dimensions, fitted recoil pad, fluted beavertail fore-end. Weight is about 7 lbs. 12 ozs. "Trap" is inlaid in gold into trigger guard. Special dimensions and features, within limits, may be ordered. Introduced 1977.
Price: Skeet $7,285.00
Price: Trap $7,285.00

CAUTION: PRICES CHANGE. CHECK AT GUNSHOP.

Browning Citori Field

Browning Citori O/U Trap Models

Similar to standard Citori except: 12 gauge only; 30", 32" (Full & Full, Imp. Mod. & Full, Mod. & Full), 34" single barrel in Combo Set (Full, Imp. Mod., Mod.); Monte Carlo cheekpiece (14⅜"x1⅜"x1⅜"x2"); fitted with trap-style recoil pad; conventional target rib and high post target rib.

Price: Grade I, (high post rib)................................ **$865.00**
Price: Grade II (high post rib)................................ **$1,410.00**
Price: Grade V (high post rib)................................ **$2,095.00**
Price: Grade I Combo (32" O/U & 34" single bbl., high post ribs) incl. luggage case.......................... **$1,450.00**
Price: Grade I with Invector tubes.......................... **$892.00**

BROWNING CITORI O/U SHOTGUN

Gauge: 12, 20, 28 and 410.
Barrel: 26", 28" (Mod. & Full, Imp. Cyl. & Mod.), in all gauges, 30" (Mod. & Full, Full & Full) in 12 ga. only. Also offered with Invector choke tubes.
Weight: 6 lbs. 8 oz. (26" 410) to 7 lbs. 13 oz. (30" 12-ga.).
Length: 43" over-all (26" bbl.).
Stock: Dense walnut, hand checkered, full p.g., beavertail fore-end. Field-type recoil pad on 12 ga. field guns and trap and Skeet models.
Sights: Medium raised beads, German nickel silver.
Features: Barrel selector integral with safety, auto ejectors, three-piece takedown. Imported from Japan by Browning.
Price: Grade I, 12 and 20 .... **$775.00**
Price: Grade I, 28 and 410................................... **$800.00**
Price: Grade II, 12 and 20 .... **$1,300.00**
Price: Grade V, 12 and 20 .... **$1,960.00**
Price: Grade II, 28 and 410................................ **$1,345.00**
Price: Grade V, 28 and 410 .... **$2,010.00**
Price: Grade VI, 28 and 410, high post rib **$2,050.00**
Price: Grade I, Invector................................... **$802.00**

Browning Citori Skeet

Browning Citori O/U Sporter

Similar to standard Citori except; comes with 26" (Mod. & Full, Imp. Cyl. & Mod.) only; straight grip stock with schnabel fore-end; satin oil finish.

Price: Grade I, 12 and 20 .... **$775.00**
Price: Grade I, 28 and 410................................... **$800.00**
Price: Grade II, 12 and 20 .... **$1,300.00**
Price: Grade V, 12 and 20 .... **$1,960.00**
Price: Grade II, 28 and 410................................ **$1,345.00**
Price: Grade V, 28 and 410 .... **$2,010.00**

Browning Citori O/U Skeet Models

Similar to standard Citori except: 26", 28" (Skeet & Skeet) only; stock dimensions of 14⅜"x1½"x2", fitted with Skeet-style recoil pad; conventional target rib and high post target rib.

Price: Grade I, 12 & 20 (high post rib) **$865.00**
Price: Grade I, 28 & 410 (high post rib) **$900.00**
Price: Grade II, all gauges (high post rib)............... **$1,410.00**
Price: Grade V, all gauges (high post rib) **$2,095.00**
Price: Grade VI, all gauges, (high post rib) **$2,150.00**
Price: Four barrel Skeet set — 12, 20, 28, 410 barrels, with case, Grade I only **$2,900.00**

Browning Citori Superlight

Browning Citori Sideplate 20 Gauge

Same as the Citori Sporter except available only in 20 gauge with 26" barrels (Imp. Cyl. & Mod. or Mod. & Full). The satin steel sideplates, receiver and long trigger guard tang have etched upland game scenes. Wood and checkering of Grade V style.

Price: **$1,960.00**
Price: Four barrel Skeet set — 12, 20, 28, 410 barrels, with case, Grade I only **$2,900.00**

Browning Superlight Citori Over-Under

Similar to the standard Citori except availiable in 12 or 20 gauge (3" chambers) with 26" barrels choked Imp. Cyl. & Mod. or 28" choked Mod. & Full. Has straight grip stock, schnabel fore-end tip. Superlight 12 weighs 6 lbs., 9 oz. (26" barrels); Superlight 20, 5 lbs., 12 oz. (26" barrels). Introduced 1982.

Price: Grade I only, 12 or 20 .... **$800.00**
Price: Grade VI.. **$2,050.00**

Browning Presentation One

Browning Presentation Superposed Combinations

Standard and Lightning models are available with these factory fitted extra barrels: 12 and 20 ga., same gauge bbls.; 12 ga., 20 ga. bbls.; 20 ga., extra sets 28 and/or 410 gauge; 28 ga., extra 410 bbls. Extra barrels may be had in Lightning weights with Standard models and vice versa. Prices range from **$6,275.00** (12, 20 ga., one set extra bbls. same gauge) for the Presentation I Standard to about **$18,800.00** for the Presentation 4 grade in a 4-barrel matched set (12, 20, 28 and 410 gauges).

BROWNING SUPERPOSED SUPER-LIGHT Presentation Series

Gauge: 12 & 20, 2¾" chamber.
Action: Boxlock, top lever, single selective trigger. Bbl. selector combined with manual tang safety.
Barrel: 26½" (Mod. & Full, or Imp. Cyl. & Mod.)
Weight: 6⅜ lbs., average
Stock: Straight grip (14¼"x1⅝"x2½") hand checkered (fore-end and grip) select walnut.
Features: The Presentation Series is available in four grades and covers the Superposed line. Basically this gives the buyer a wide choice of engraving styles and designs and mechanical options which would place the gun in a "custom" bracket. Options are too numerous to list here and the reader is urged to obtain a copy of the latest Browning catalog for the complete listing. Series introduced 1977. Imported from Belgium by Browning.
Price: From **$4,560.00**

Browning Presentation Superposed Magnum 12
Browning Superposed 3″ chambers; 30″ (Full & Full or Full & Mod.) barrels. Stock, 14¼″x1⅝″x2½″ with factory fitted recoil pad. Weight 8 lbs.
Price: From **$4,500.00**

Superposed Presentation Broadway Trap 12
Same as Browning Lightning Superposed except: ⅝″ wide vent. rib; stock, 14⅜″x1⁷⁄₁₆″x1⅝″. 30″ or 32″ (Imp. Mod, Full; Mod., Full; Full, Full). 8 lbs. with 32″ bbls.
Price: From **$4,680.00**

Browning Limited Edition Waterfowl Superposed
Same specs as the Lightning Superposed. Available in 12 ga. only, 28″ (Mod. & Full). Limited to 500 guns, the edition number of each gun is inscribed in gold on the bottom of the receiver with "Black Duck" and its scientific name. Sides of receiver have two gold inlayed black ducks, bottom has two, and one on the trigger guard. Receiver is completely engraved and grayed. Stock and fore-end are highly figured dark French walnut with 24 lpi checkering, hand-oiled finish, checkered butt. Comes with form fitted, velvet-lined, black walnut case. Introduced 1983.
Price: **$8,000.00**
Price: Similar treatment as above except for the Pintail Duck Issue **$7,700.00**

Browning Presentation Superposed Lightning Skeet
Same as Standard Superposed except: Special Skeet stock, fore-end; center and front ivory bead sights. Wgt. 6½-7¾ lbs.
Price: All gauges, from **$4,570.00**

Browning Presentation Superposed Lightning Trap 12
Same as Browning Lightning Superposed except: semi-beavertail fore-end and ivory sights; stock, 14⅜″x1⁷⁄₁₆″x1⅝″. 7¾ lbs. 30″ (Full & Full, Full & Imp. Mod. or Full & Mod.)
Price: From **$4,570.00**

Browning Presentation Superposed All-Gauge Skeet Set
Consists of four matched sets of barrels in 12, 20, 28 and 410 ga. Available in either 26½″ or 28″ length. Each bbl. set has a ¼″ wide vent. rib with two ivory sight beads. Grade I receiver is hand engraved and stock and fore-end are checkered. Weight 7 lbs., 10 oz. (26½″ bbls.), 7 lbs., 12 oz. (28″ bbls.). **Contact Browning for prices.**

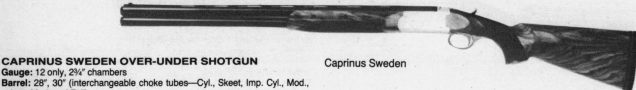

CAPRINUS SWEDEN OVER-UNDER SHOTGUN
Gauge: 12 only, 2¾″ chambers
Barrel: 28″, 30″ (interchangeable choke tubes—Cyl., Skeet, Imp. Cyl., Mod., Imp. Mod. and Full)
Weight: 6.8 lbs. (Game model).
Stock: 14″x1¾″x2⅛″ (Game model). High-grade walnut with rubber pad or checkered butt. Monte Carlo optional. Tru-oil or linseed oil finish.
Features: Made completely of stainless steel. Single selective trigger; barrel selector in front of the trigger; gas pressure activated auto. ejectors; firing pins set by top lever action; double safety system. Six standard choke tubes, plus optional tubes to change point of impact. Imported from Sweden by Caprinus U.S.A. Introduced 1982.
Price: Skeet Special, from **$5,500.00**
Price: Skeet Game, from **$5,800.00**
Price: Game, from **$5,800.00**
Price: Trap, from **$5,840.00**

Caprinus Sweden

ERA "THE FULL LIMIT" O/U SHOTGUN
Gauge: 12 or 20 ga., 2¾″.
Barrel: 28″ (Mod. & Full); vent. top and middle ribs.
Weight: 7¾ lbs.
Stock: Walnut-finished hardwood, hand checkered.
Features: Auto. safety; extractors; double triggers; engraved receiver. Imported from Brazil by F.I.E.
Price: **$399.95**

Clayco Model 6

Franchi Alcione Super Deluxe
Similar to the Falconet Super except has best quality hand engraved, silvered receiver, 24K gold plated trigger, elephant ivory bead front sight. Comes with luggage-type fitted case. Has 14K gold inlay on receiver. Same barrel and chokes as on Falconet Super. Introduced 1982.
Price: Alcione Super Deluxe. **$1,595.00**

CLAYCO MODEL 6 OVER-UNDER SHOTGUN
Gauge: 12, 2¾″ chambers.
Barrel: 26″ (Imp. Cyl. & Mod.), 28″ (Mod. & Full).
Weight: 7 lbs. 15 oz. (26″ bbls.). **Length:** 43″ over-all (26″ bbls.).
Stock: 14¼″ x 1⅝″ x 2½″. Walnut finished hardwood. Checkered pistol grip and fore-end.
Features: Mechanical single trigger, automatic safety; ventilated rubber recoil pad. Scroll-engraved blued receiver. Ventilated top rib. Introduced 1983. Imported from China by Clayco Sports Ltd.
Price: **$295.00**

Franchi Falconet Super

Franchi Falconet Super
Similar to the Diamond Grade except has a lightweight alloy receiver, single selective mechanical trigger with the barrel selector button on the trigger, and a rubber butt pad. Higher quality hand engraved receiver. Available in 12 ga. only, 27″ (Imp. Cyl. & Mod.) or 28″ (Mod. & Full) barrels. Translucent front sight bead. Introduced 1982.
Price: Falconet Super **$1,015.00**

FRANCHI DIAMOND GRADE OVER-UNDER
Gauge: 12 ga. only, 2¾″ chambers.
Barrel: 28″ (Mod. & Full).
Weight: 6 lbs. 13 oz.
Stock: French walnut with cut checkered pistol grip and fore-end.
Features: Top tang safety, automatic ejectors, single selective trigger. Chrome plated bores. Decorative scroll on silvered receiver. Introduced 1982. Imported from Italy by F.I.E. Corp.
Price: Diamond Grade **$850.00**

IGA Over-Under

HEYM MODEL 55/77 O/U SHOTGUN
Gauge: 12, 16, 20 ga. (2¾" or 3").
Barrel: 28" (Full & Mod.) standard; other lengths and chokes to customer specs.
Weight: 6¾-7½ lbs.
Stock: European walnut, hand-checkered p.g. and fore-end.
Features: Boxlock or full sidelock action; Kersten double cross bolt, double under lugs; cocking indicators. Arabesque or hunting engraving. Options include interchangeable barrels, front trigger that functions as a single non-selective trigger, deluxe engraving and stock carving. Imported from West Germany by Paul Jaeger, Inc.
Price: Model 55F or 77F boxlock **$3,070.00**
Price: Model 55FSS or 77FSS sidelock **$5,350.00**
Price: Interchangeable o/u rifle barrels **$2,570.00**
Price: Interchangeable rifle-shotgun barrels **$1,715.00**

IGA OVER-UNDER SHOTGUN
Gauge: 12, 20, 28 (2¾"), 410 (3").
Barrel: 26" (Full & Full, 410 only, Imp. Cyl. & Mod.), 28" (Mod. & Full).
Weight: 6¾ to 7 lbs.
Stock: 14½" x 1½" x 2½". Oil finished hardwood with checkered pistol grip and fore-end.
Features: Manual safety, double triggers, extractors only, ventilated top rib. Introduced 1983. Imported from Brazil by Stoeger Industries.
Price: Double triggers **$417.00**
Price: Single trigger **$499.95**

K.F.C. OT-Skeet Shotguns
Skeet versions of FG model. Model E-1 has 26" or 28" (Skeet & Skeet) barrels with 13mm vent. rib, middle and front bead sights, gold colored wide trigger. Stock dimensions are 14"x1½"x2½". Plastic buttplate, push-button fore-end release. Weight is about 7½ lbs.
Price: E-1 . . . . **$1,070.00**
Price: E-2 . . . . **$1,660.00**

K.F.C. "FG" Standard

K.F.C. OT-Trap-E2 Shotgun
Same as E-1 model except chromed receiver has high grade scroll engraving, super deluxe French walnut stock and fore-end.
Price: **$1,660.00**

K.F.C. "FG" OVER-UNDER SHOTGUN
Gauge: 12 only (2¾").
Barrel: 26", 28" (Imp. Cyl. & Imp. Mod.); vent. rib.
Weight: About 6.8 lbs.
Stock: 14"x1½"x2⅜". High grade French walnut.
Sights: Sterling silver front bead.
Features: Selective single trigger, selective auto ejectors, non-automatic safety; chrome lined bores, chrome trigger. Introduced 1981. Imported from Japan by La Paloma Marketing.
Price: **$748.00**

K.F.C. OT-E1

K.F.C. OT-Trap-E1 Shotgun
Trap version of FG over-under. Has 30" (Imp. Mod. & Full) barrels, 13mm vent. rib, bone white middle and front beads, scroll-engraved, blued receiver, wide gold-colored trigger. Stock dimensions are 14"x1¼"x1¼"x2"; high grade French walnut; rubber recoil pad; oil finish. Weight is about 7.9 lbs. Introduced 1981. From La Paloma Marketing.
Price: **$1,070.00**

Kassnar/Fias SK-4D O/U Shotgun
Same as SK-4 except has deluxe receiver engraving, sideplates, better wood.
Price: **$499.95**

KASSNAR/FIAS SK-1 O/U SHOTGUN
Gauge: 12 or 20 ga. (3" chambers).
Action: Top lever break open, boxlock, Greener cross bolt.
Barrel: 26" (Imp. Cyl. & Mod.), 28" (Mod. & Full), 30" (Mod. & Full), 32" (Full & Full).
Weight: 6-6½ lbs.
Stock: Select European walnut. 14"x2¼"x1¼".
Features: Double triggers and non-automatic extractors. Checkered p.g. and fore-end. Imported by Kassnar Imports.
Price: **$429.95**

Kassnar/Fias SK-3 O/U Shotgun
Same as SK-1 except has single selective trigger.
Price: **$449.95**

Lanber Model 844

LANBER MODEL 844 OVER-UNDER
Gauge: 12, 2¾" or 3".
Barrel: 28" (Imp. Cyl. & Imp. Mod.), 30" (Mod. & Full).
Weight: About 7 lbs. **Length:** 44⅜" (28" bbl.).
Stock: 14¼" x 1⅝" x 2½". European walnut; checkered pg. and fore-end.
Features: Single non-selective or selective trigger, double triggers on magnum model. Available with or without ejectors. Imported from Spain by Lanbar Arms of America. Introduced 1983.
Price: Field, with selective trigger, extractors $475.00
Price: As above, 3" Mag. $499.00
Price: As above, with ejectors $569.00

Lanber Model 2009

Lanber Model 2004 Over-Under

Same basic specifications as Model 844 except fitted with LanberChoke interchangeable choke tube system. Available in trap, Skeet, pigeon and field models; ejectors only; single selective trigger; no middle rib on target guns (2008, 2009).
Price: Model 2004 . . . . **$698.00**
Price: Model 2008 . . . . **$859.00**
Price: Model 2009 (30″ bbl., illus.) **$859.00**

LJUTIC BI-GUN O/U SHOTGUN

Gauge: 12 ga only.
Barrel: 28″ to 34″; choked to customer specs.   Ljutic Bi-Gun Skeet
Weight: To customers specs.
Stock: To customer specs. Oil finish, hand checkered.
Features: Custom-made gun. Hollow-milled rib, choice of pull or release trigger, pushbutton opener in front of trigger guard. From Ljutic Industries.
Price: **$7,995.00**
Price: Bi-Gun Combo (interchangeable single barrel, two trigger guards, one for single trigger, one for doubles) **$9,995.00**
Price: Extra barrels with screw-in chokes or O/U barrel sets **$3,000.00**

Ljutic Four Barrel Skeet Set

Similar to Bi Gun except comes with matched set of four 28″ barrels in 12, 20, 28 and 410. Ljutic Paternator chokes and barrel are integral. Stock is to customer specs, of American or French walnut with fancy checkering.
Price: Four barrel set **$16,000.00**

Marocchi America

MAROCCHI AMERICA TARGET SHOTGUN

Gauge: 12 or 20, 2¾″ chambers.
Barrel: 26″ to 29″ (Skeet), 27″ to 32″ (trap), 32″ (trap mono, choice of top single or high rib under), 30″ (over-under with extra 32″ single).
Weight: 7¼ to 8 lbs.
Stock: Hand checkered select walnut with left or right-hand palm swell; choice of beavertail or Schnabel fore-end.
Features: Designed specifically for American target sports. Frame has medium engraving coverage with choice of three finishes. No extra charge for special stock dimensions or stock finish. Comes with fitted hard shell case. Custom engraving and inlays available. Introduced 1983. Imported from Italy by Marocchi U.S.A.
Price: From **$2,300.00**

> Consult our Directory pages for
> the location of firms mentioned.

Marocchi Contrast Cup

MAROCCHI CONTRAST TARGET SHOTGUN

Gauge: 12 or 20 ga., 2¾″ chambers.
Barrel: 26″ to 29″ (Skeet), 27″ to 32″ trap.
Weight: 7¼ to 8 lbs.
Stock: Select walnut with hand rubbed wax finish; hand checkered p.g. and fore-end; beavertail or Schnabel fore-end; grip has right or left palm swell.
Features: Lightly engraved frame on standard grade, or can be ordered with custom engraving and inlays in choice of three finishes. Optional different buttstock available. Gun comes with fitted hard shell case. Introduced 1983. Imported from Italy by Marocchi U.S.A.
Price: From **$2,000.00**

Marocchi SM28 SXS Shotgun

Similar to the Model Contrast except gun is totally custom made to the customer's specifications. Introduced 1983.
Price: **$11,000.00**

Remington 3200 Trap

REMINGTON 3200 COMPETITION TRAP

Gauge: 12 ga. (2¾″ chambers).
Barrel: 30″ (Full & Full, Full & Imp. Mod., Full & Mod.), 32″ (Full & Imp. Mod.).
Weight: 8¼ lbs. (30″ bbl.). **Length:** 48″ over-all (30″ bbl.).
Stock: Fancy walnut checkered 20 l.p.i. Full beavertail fore-end. Satin finish.14⅜″x2″x1½″. Optional 1⅜″ or 1½″ drop on Monte Carlo stocks.
Features: Super-fast lock time, separated barrels, engraved receiver. Combination manual safety and barrel selector on top tang. Single selective trigger. Ivory bead front sight, white-metal middle.
Price: Competition Trap with or without M.C. stock **$1,925.00**
Price: Pigeon (28″, Imp. Mod. & Full) **$1,925.00**

Remington 3200 Competition Skeet

Same as Trap except 26″ or 28″ (Skeet & Skeet) barrels, stock measures 14″x2⅛″x1½″. Over-all length is 43″ with 26″ barrels, weight is 7¾ lbs.
Price: Competition Skeet **$1,925.00**
Price: Competition Skeet 4-bbl. set (with bbls. for 12, 20, 28 and 410 in luggage case **$6,875.00**

CAUTION: PRICES CHANGE. CHECK AT GUNSHOP.

ROTTWEIL OLYMPIA '72 SKEET SHOTGUN

Gauge: 12 ga. only.
Action: Boxlock.
Barrel: 27″ (special Skeet choke), vent. rib. Chromed lined bores, flared chokes.
Weight: 7¼ lbs. **Length:** 44½″ over-all.
Stock: French walnut, hand checkered, modified beavertail fore-end. Oil finish.
Sights: Metal bead front.
Features: Inertia-type trigger, interchangeable for any system. Frame and lock milled from steel block. Retracting firing pins are spring mounted. All coil springs. Selective single trigger. Action engraved. Extra barrels are available. Introduced 1976. Imported from West Germany by Dynamit Nobel.
Price: **$2,145.00**
Price: Trap model (Montreal) is similar to above except has 30″ (Imp. Mod. & Full) bbl., weighs 8 lbs., 48½″ over-all. **$2,145.00**

ROTTWEIL 72 AMERICAN SKEET

Gauge: 12, 2¾″.
Barrel: 26¾″ (Skeet & Skeet).
Weight: About 7½ lbs.
Stock: 14½″ x 1⅜″ x 1⅜″ x ¼″. Select French walnut with satin oil finish; hand checkered grip and fore-end; double ventilated recoil pad.
Sights: Plastic front in metal sleeve, center bead.
Features: Interchangeable trigger groups with coil springs; interchangeable buttstocks; special .433″ ventilated rib; matte finish silvered receiver with light engraving. Introduced 1978. Imported from West Germany by Dynamit Nobel.
Price: **$2,145.00**

Rottweil Olympia '72

ROTTWEIL AAT TRAP GUN

Gauge: 12, 2¾″.
Barrel: 32″ (Imp. Mod. & Full).
Weight: About 8 lbs.
Stock: 14½″x1⅜″x1⅜″x1⅞″. Monte Carlo style of selected French walnut with oil finish. Checkered fore-end and p.g.
Features: Has infinitely variable point of impact via special muzzle collar. Extra single lower barrels available—32″ (Imp. Mod.) or 34″ (Full). Special trigger groups—release/release or release/pull—also available. Introduced 1979. From Dynamit Nobel.
Price: With single lower barrel **$2,145.00**
Price: Combo (single and o/u barrels) **$2,795.00**
Price: Interchangeable trap trigger group **$345.00**

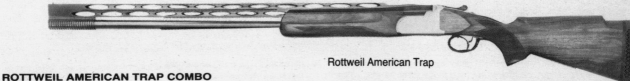

Rottweil American Trap

ROTTWEIL AMERICAN TRAP COMBO

Gauge: 12 ga. only.
Action: Boxlock
Barrel: Separated o/u, 32″ (Imp. Mod. & Full); single is 34″ (Full), both with high vent. rib.
Weight: 8½ lbs. (o/u and single)
Stock: Monte Carlo style, walnut, hand checkered and rubbed. Unfinished stocks available. Double vent. recoil pad. Choice of two dimensions.
Sights: Plastic front in metal sleeve, center bead.

Features: Interchangeable inertia-type trigger groups. Trigger groups available: single selective; double triggers;, release/pull; release/release selective. Receiver milled from block steel. Chokes are hand honed, test fired and reworked for flawless patterns. All coil springs, engraved action. Introduced 1977. Imported from West Germany by Dynamit Nobel.
Price: **$2,795.00**
Price: American Trap O/U (as above except only with o/u bbls.) . . . **$2,145.00**

Rottweil Field Supreme

ROTTWEIL FIELD SUPREME O/U SHOTGUN

Gauge: 12 only.
Action: Boxlock.
Barrel: 28″ (Mod. & Full, Imp. Cyl. & Imp. Mod.), vent. rib.
Weight: 7¼ lbs. **Length:** 47″ over-all.
Stock: Select French walnut, hand checkered and rubbed. Checkered p.g. and fore-end, plastic buttplate. Unfinished stocks available.
Sights: Metal bead front.

Features: Removable single trigger assembly with button selector (same trigger options as on American Trap Combo); retracting spring mounted firing pins; engraved action. Extra barrels available. Imported from West Germany by Dynamit Nobel.
Price: **$2,145.00**
Price: Live Pigeon (28″ Mod. & Full) **$2,145.00**

Ruger Red Label

RUGER "RED LABEL" O/U SHOTGUN

Gauge: 20, 3″ chambers, 12, 2¾″ and 3″ chambers.
Barrel: 26″, (Skeet & Skeet, Imp. Cyl. & Mod.) 12 and 20 ga.; 28″ (20 ga. only, Skeet & Skeet, Imp. Cyl. & Mod., Full & Mod.).
Weight: About 7 lbs. **Length:** 43″ (26″ barrels).
Stock: 14″x1½″x2½″. Straight grain American walnut. Checkered p.g. and fore-end, rubber recoil pad.
Features: Automatic safety/barrel selector, stainless steel trigger. Patented barrel side spacers may be removed if desired. 20 ga. introduced 1977; 12 ga. introduced 1982.
Price: About **$798.00**

FRANCISCO SARRIUGARTE MODEL 101E O/U
Gauge: 12, 2¾" chambers.
Barrel: 26" (Imp. Cyl. & Mod.), 28" (Mod. & Full).
Weight: About 7 lbs. **Length:** 43" over-all (26" barrels).
Stock: Hand checkered European walnut with full pistol grip.
Sights: Medium bead front.
Features: Single trigger, automatic ejectors. Receiver has border engraving. Introduced 1982. Imported from Spain by Toledo Armas.
Price: Model 101E **$585.00**
Price: Model 101E DS (selective trigger) **$623.00**
Price: Model 101 DS (selective trigger and extractors) **$495.00**

Francisco Sarriugarte Model 200 Trap
Similar to the Model 101E except has 30" (Full & Full) barrels, weighs 8 lbs., Monte Carlo stock. Automatic ejectors, single trigger, ventilated middle rib. Introduced 1982.
Price: **$872.00**

Francisco Sarriugarte Model 400 Trap, 501E Special
True sidelock over-under. Barrel length and chokes to order. Stock dimensions, engraving to customer specifications. Introduced 1982.
Price: From **$1,975.00**
Price: Model 501E Special **$1,660.00**
Price: Model 501E Special "Niger" **$2,116.00**
Price: Model 501E Special "Excelsior" **$2,215.00**

Secolo Model 250

SECOLO MODEL 550 TRAP OVER-UNDER
Gauge: 12 ga., 2¾" chambers.
Barrel: 30", 32", five interchangeable choke tubes, standard chokes.
Stock: European walnut, with Monte Carlo.
Features: Silvered or color case-hardened receiver; 9mm or 12mm rib height; ventilated middle rib. Imported from Spain by L. Joseph Rahn.
Price: Model 550 .... **$925.00**
Price: Model 540 Mono-Trap, upper barrel **$1,115.00**
Price: Model 530 Mono-Trap, under barrel **$1,150.00**
Price: Model 560 Skeet **$900.00**

SECOLO MODEL 250 O/U SHOTGUN
Gauge: 12 ga., 2¾" chambers.
Barrel: 28" (Mod. & Full).
Weight: About 7 lbs.
Stock: European walnut; checkered pistol grip and fore-end.
Features: Single or double triggers, extractors only (ejectors optional); silvered frame, rest blued; light engraving; sling swivels. Imported from Spain by L. Joseph Rahn.
Price: **$425.00**

VALMET MODEL 412K OVER-UNDER
Gauge: 12 or 20 ga. (2¾" or 3").
Barrel: 26" (Imp. Cyl. & Mod.), 28" (Mod. & Full), 30" (Mod. & Full); vent. rib.
Weight: About 7½ lbs.
Stock: American walnut. Standard dimensions-$13\frac{9}{10}$"x1½"x2⅖". Checkered p.g. and fore-end.
Features: Model 412K is extractor (basic) model. Free interchangeability of barrels, stocks and fore-ends into KE (auto. ejector) model, double rifle model, combination gun, etc. Barrel selector in trigger; auto. top tang safety; barrel cocking indicators. Double triggers optional. Introduced 1980. Imported from Finland by Valmet.
Price: Model 412K (extractors), from **$719.00**
Price: Model 412 KE (ejectors), from **$749.00**
Price: Extra barrels from **$339.00**
Price: Engraved model **$2,499.00**

Valmet 412KE Target Series
Trap and Skeet versions of 412 gun. Auto. ejectors only; 12 ga., 2¾", 3" chambers, 30" barrels (Imp. & Full.—Trap, Skeet & Skeet—Skeet). 20 ga., 3" chambers. Trap stock measures $14\frac{3}{10}$"x1⅖"x1⅗"x2½"; Skeet stock measures $13\frac{9}{10}$"x1⅘"x2⅖"x1⅘". Trap weight 7⅝ lbs.: Skeet weight 7½ lbs. Non-automatic safety. Introduced 1980. Imported from Finland by Valmet.
Price: Trap **$759.00**
Price: Skeet **$759.00**

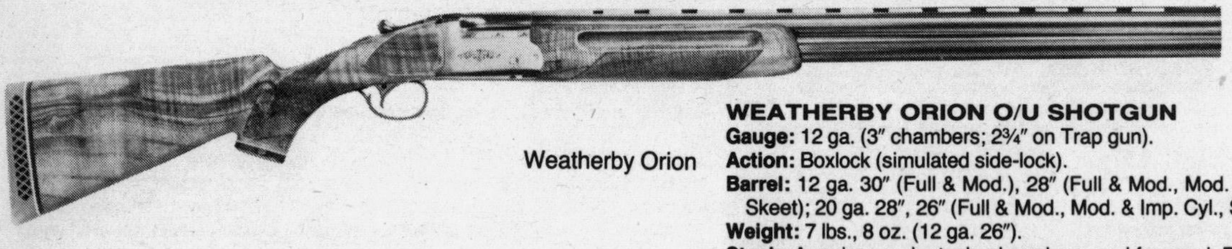
Weatherby Orion

WEATHERBY ORION O/U SHOTGUN
Gauge: 12 ga. (3" chambers; 2¾" on Trap gun).
Action: Boxlock (simulated side-lock).
Barrel: 12 ga. 30" (Full & Mod.), 28" (Full & Mod., Mod. & Imp. Cyl., Skeet & Skeet); 20 ga. 28", 26" (Full & Mod., Mod. & Imp. Cyl., Skeet & Skeet).
Weight: 7 lbs., 8 oz. (12 ga. 26").
Stock: American walnut, checkered p.g. and fore-end. Rubber recoil pad. Dimensions for field and Skeet models, 20 ga. 14"x1½"x2½".
Features: Selective auto ejectors, single selective mechanical trigger. Top tang safety, Greener cross-bolt. Introduced 1982. Imported from Japan by Weatherby.
Price: 12 ga. Field **$749.95**
Price: Skeet **$789.95**
Price: 12 ga. Trap **$799.95**

Weatherby Athena

WEATHERBY ATHENA O/U SHOTGUN
Gauge: 12 or 20 ga. (3" chambers; 2¾" on Trap gun).
Action: Boxlock (simulated side-lock) top lever break-open. Selective auto ejectors, single selective trigger (selector inside trigger guard).
Barrel: 28" with vent rib and bead front sight, Full & Mod., Mod. & Imp. Cyl. or Skeet & Skeet.
Weight: 12 ga. 7⅜ lbs., 20 ga. 6⅞ lbs.
Stock: American walnut, checkered p.g. and fore-end (14¼"x1½"x2½").
Features: Mechanically operated trigger. Top tang safety, Greener cross-bolt, fully engraved receiver, recoil pad installed.
Price: 12 or 20 ga. Field **$1,099.95**
Price: Skeet **$1,109,00**
Price: 12 ga. Trap Model **$1,119.00**

CAUTION: PRICES CHANGE. CHECK AT GUNSHOP.

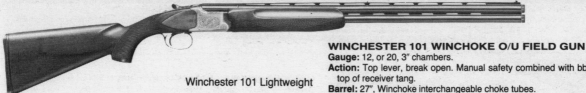

Winchester 101 Lightweight

Winchester 101 Diamond Grade Target Guns

Similar to the Model 101 except designed for trap and Skeet competition, with tapered and elevated rib, anatomically contoured trigger and internationally-dimensioned stock. Receiver has deep-etched diamond-pattern engraving. Skeet guns available in 12, 20, 28 and 410 with ventilated muzzles to reduce recoil. Trap guns in 12 ga. only; over-under, combination and single-barrel configurations in a variety of barrel lengths with Winchoke system. Straight or Monte Carlo stocks available. Introduced 1982. Imported from Japan by Winchester Group, Olin Corp.

Price: Trap, o/u, standard and Monte Carlo, 30″, 32″ **$1,500.00**
Price: Trap, single barrel, 32″ or 34″ **$1,595.00**
Price: Trap, o/u-single bbl. combo sets **$2,350.00**
Price: Skeet, 12 and 20 . . . . **$1,450.00**
Price: Skeet, 28 and 410 . . . . **$1,475.00**

WINCHESTER 101 WINCHOKE O/U FIELD GUN

Gauge: 12, or 20, 3″ chambers.
Action: Top lever, break open. Manual safety combined with bbl. selector at top of receiver tang.
Barrel: 27″, Winchoke interchangeable choke tubes.
Weight: 12 ga. 7 lbs. Others 6½ lbs. **Length:** 44¾″ over-all.
Stock: 14″x1½″x2½″. Checkered walnut p.g. and fore-end; fluted comb.
Features: Single selective trigger, auto ejectors. Hand engraved satin gray receiver. Comes with hard gun case. Imported from Japan by Winchester Group, Olin Corp.
Price: **$1,195.00**

> Consult our Directory pages for
> the location of firms mentioned.

Winchester Model 101 Waterfowl Winchoke

Same as Model 101 Field Grade except in 12 ga. only, 3″ chambers, 32″ barrels. Comes with four Winchoke tubes: Mod., Imp. Mod., Full, Extra-Full. Blued receiver with hand etching and engraving. Introduced 1981. Imported from Japan by Winchester Group, Olin Corp.
Price: **$1,195.00**

Winchester 101 Pigeon Grade

Winchester Model 101 Pigeon Grade

Similar to the Model 101 Field except comes in three styles: Lightweight (12 or 28 ga., Mod. & Full, Mod. & Imp. Cyl., 28″), Lightweight-Winchoke (12 or 20 ga., six choke tubes for 12 ga., four for 20 ga., 27″), Featherweight (12 or 20 ga., Imp. Cyl. & Mod., 25½″), all with 3″ chambers. Vent. rib barrel with middle bead, fancy American walnut. Featherweight has English-style stock. Hard case included. Introduced 1983. Imported from Japan by Winchester Group, Olin Corp.
Price: Lightweight and Featherweight **$1,400.00**
Price: Lightweight-Winchoke **$1,450.00**

Winchester 501 Grand European

A. ZOLI DELFINO S.P. O/U

Gauge: 12 or 20 (3″ chambers).
Barrel: 28″ (Mod. & Full); vent. rib.
Weight: 5½ lbs.
Stock: Walnut. Hand checkered p.g. and fore-end; cheekpiece.
Features: Color case hardened receiver with light engraving; chrome lined barrels; automatic sliding safety; double triggers; ejectors. From Mandall Shooting Supplies.
Price: $795.00

WINCHESTER MODEL 501 GRAND EUROPEAN O-U

Gauge: 12 ga. (Trap), 12 and 20 ga. (Skeet). 2¾″ chambers.
Barrel: 27″ (Skeet & Skeet), 30″ (Imp. Mod. & Full), 32″ (Imp. Mod. & Full).
Weight: 7½ lbs. (Skeet), 8½ lbs. (Trap) **Length:** 47⅛″ over-all (30″ barrel).
Stock: 14⅛″x1½″x2½″ (Skeet). Full fancy walnut, hand-rubbed oil finish.
Features: Silvered, engraved receiver; engine-turned breech interior. Slide-button selector/safety, selective auto. ejectors. Chrome bores, tapered vent. rib. Trap gun has Monte Carlo or regular stock, recoil pad; Skeet gun has rosewood buttplate. Introduced 1981. Imported from Japan by Winchester Group, Olin Corp.
Price: Trap or Skeet **$1,800.00**

Zoli Silver Snipe

ZOLI SILVER SNIPE O/U SHOTGUN

Gauge: 12, 20 (3″ chambers).
Action: Purdey-type double boxlock, crossbolt.
Barrel: 26″ (Imp. Cyl. & Mod.), 28″ (Mod. & Full), 30″, 12 only (Mod. & Full); 26″ Skeet (Skeet & Skeet), 30″ Trap (Full & Full).
Weight: 6½ lbs. (12 ga.).
Stock: Hand checkered p.g. and fore-end, European walnut.
Features: Auto. safety (exc. Trap and Skeet), vent rib, single trigger, chrome bores. Imported from Italy by Mandall Shooting Supplies.
Price: Field $795.00

Zoli Golden Snipe O/U Shotgun

Same as Silver Snipe except selective auto. ejectors.
Price: Field $875.00

Union Armera Winner

ARMSPORT WESTERN DOUBLE
Gauge: 12 only (3″ chambers).
Barrel: 20″.
Weight: 6½ lbs.
Stock: European walnut, checkered p.g. and beavertail fore-end.
Sights: Metal front bead on matted solid rib.
Features: Exposed hammers. Imported by Armsport.
Price: $500.00

AYA MODEL 117 DOUBLE BARREL SHOTGUN
Gauge: 12 (2¾″), 20 (3″).
Action: Holland & Holland sidelock, Purdey treble bolting.
Barrel: 26″ (Imp. Cyl. & Mod.) 28″ (Mod. & Full).
Stock: 14½″x2⅜″x1½″. Select European walnut, hand checkered p.g. and beavertail fore-end.
Features: Single selective trigger, automatic ejectors, cocking indicators; concave barrel rib; hand-detachable lockplates; hand engraved action. Imported from Spain by Precision Sports, Inc.
Price: $1,650.00

AyA Model No. 2

AYA No. 2 SIDE-BY-SIDE
Gauge: 12, 16, 20, 28, 410.
Barrel: 26″, 27″, 28″, choked to customer specs.

AYA No. 4 DELUXE SIDE-BY-SIDE
Gauge: 12, 16, 20, 28 & 410.
Barrel: 26″, 27″, 28″ (Imp. Cyl. & Mod. or Mod. & Full).
Weight: 5 lbs. 2 oz. to 6½ lbs.
Stock: 14½″x2¼″x1½″. European walnut. Straight grip with checkered butt, classic fore-end.
Features: Boxlock action, color case-hardened, automatic ejectors, double triggers (single trigger available). Imported from Spain by William Larkin Moore & Co. and Precision Sports, Inc.
Price: 12, 16 ga., about.................................... $2,195.00
Price: 20 ga., about $2,195.00
Price: 28, 410 ga., about..................................... $2,255.00

AYA MODEL XXV BL, SL DOUBLE
Gauge: 12, 16, 20.
Barrel: 25″, chokes as specified.
Weight: 5 lbs., 15 oz. to 7 lbs., 8 oz.
Stock: 14½″x2¼″x1½″. European walnut. Straight grip stock with classic pistol grip, checkered butt.
Features: Boxlock (Model BL), sidelock (Model SL). Churchill rib, auto ejectors, double triggers (single available), color case-hardened action (coin-finish available). Imported from Spain by Wm. Larkin Moore & Co. and Precision Sports, Inc.
Price: BL, 12 ga., about...................................... $1,995.00
Price: BL, 20 ga., about...................................... $1,995.00
Price: SL, 12 ga., about...................................... $3,295.00
Price: SL, 20 ga., about...................................... $3,295.00
Price: SL, 28 or 410, about.................................. $3,395.00

UNION ARMERA "WINNER" DOUBLE
Gauge: 12 and 20 ga., 2¾″ chambers.
Barrel: Length and choking to customer specs.
Weight: To customer specs.
Stock: Ultra deluxe European walnut; dimensions to customer specs.
Features: Hand engraved action, automatic ejectors. All options available. Introduced 1982. Imported from Spain by Toledo Armas.
Price: Winner, from $3,055.00
Price: Luxe, from $5,622.00

ARMSPORT GOOSEGUN SIDE-BY-SIDE
Gauge: 10 ga. (3½″ chambers).
Barrel: 32″ (Full & Full). Solid matted rib.
Weight: 11 lbs.
Stock: European walnut, checkered p.g. and fore-end.
Features: Double triggers, vent. rubber recoil pad with white spacer. Imported by Armsport.
Price: $595.00

Weight: 5 lbs. 15 oz. to 7½ lbs.
Stock: 14½″x2¼″x1½″. European walnut. Straight grip stock, checkered butt, classic fore-end. Can be made to custom dimensions.
Features: Sidelock action with auto. ejectors, double triggers standard, single trigger optional. Hand-detachable locks. Color case-hardened action. Imported from Spain by Wm. Larkin Moore & Co. and Precision Sports, Inc.
Price: 12, 16, 20 ga., from.................................... $2,175.00
Price: 28 ga., from $2,365.00
Price: 410 ga., from $2,365.00

AYA Model 56 Side-By-Side
Similar to the No. 1 except in 12, 16 or 20 ga. only, available with raised, level or vent rib. Does not have hand-detachable locks. Imported from Spain by Wm. Larkin Moore & Co. and Precision Sports, Inc.
Price: About... $5,250.00

AYA No. 1 Side-by-Side
Similar to the No. 2 except barrel lengths to customer specifications. Barrels are of chrome-nickel steel. Imported from Spain by Wm. Larkin Moore & Co. and Precision Sports, Inc.
Price: 12, 16, 20 ga., from.................................... $4,895.00
Price: 28 ga., from $5,495.00
Price: 410 ga., from $5,495.00

AyA Model XXVSL

BERNARDELLI XXVSL DOUBLE
Gauge: 12.
Action: Holland & Holland-style sidelock with double sears.
Barrel: Demi-block (chopper lump), 25″, choice of choke.
Weight: About 6½ lbs. **Length:** To customer specs.
Stock: Best walnut with dimensions to customer specs.
Features: Firing pins removable from face of standing breech; manual or auto safety; selective auto ejectors; classic or beavertail fore-end. Imported from Italy by Knight & Knight.
Price: With fitted luggage case................................ $1,865.00

CAUTION: PRICES CHANGE. CHECK AT GUNSHOP.

SHOTGUNS—SIDE-BY-SIDES

Beretta Model 424

BERETTA M-424 SIDE-BY-SIDE

Gauge: 12 (2¾"), 20 (3").
Action: Beretta patent boxlock; double underlugs and bolts.
Barrel: 12 ga.—26" (Imp. Cyl. & Mod.), 28" (Mod. & Full); 20 ga.—26" (Imp. Cyl. & Mod.), 28" (Mod. & Full).
Weight: 6 lbs. 14 oz. (20 ga.).
Stock: 14⅛"x1⁹⁄₁₆"x2⁹⁄₁₆". "English" straight-type, hand checkered European walnut.
Features: Coil springs throughout action; double triggers (front is hinged); automatic safety; extractors. Concave matted barrel rib. Introduced 1977. Imported by Beretta U.S.A. Corp.
Price: $900.00

Beretta M-426 Side-By-Side
Same as M-424 except action body is engraved; pistol grip stock; a silver pigeon is inlaid into top lever; single selective trigger; selective automatic ejectors. Introduced 1977. Imported by Beretta U.S.A. Corp.
Price: $1,115.00

Browning B-SS

Weight: 6¾ lbs. (26" bbl., 20 ga.); 7½ lbs. (30" bbl., 12 ga.).
Stock: 14¼"x1⅝"x2½". French walnut, hand checkered. Full p.g., full beavertail fore-end.
Features: Automatic safety, automatic ejectors. Hand engraved receiver, mechanical single selective trigger with barrel selector in rear of trigger guard. Imported from Japan by Browning.
Price: Grade I, 12 or 20 ga. $760.00
Price: Grade II, 12 or 20 ga. $1,275.00

BROWNING B-SS
Gauge: 12 (2¾"), 20 (3").
Action: Top lever break-open action, top tang safety, single trigger.
Barrel: 26" (Mod. and Full or Imp. Cyl. and Mod.), 28" (Mod. and Full), 30" (Full & Full or Mod. & Full).

Browning B-SS Sporter

Browning B-SS Sporter
Similar to standard B-SS except has straight-grip stock and full beavertail fore-end with traditional oil finish. Introduced 1977.
Price: Grade I, 12 or 20 ga. $760.00
Price: Grade II, 12 or 20 ga. $1,275.00

Hermanos Model 150

Barrel: 20", 26", 28", 30", 32" (Cyl. & Cyl., Full & Full, Mod. & Full, Mod. & Imp. Cyl., Imp. Cyl. & Full, Mod. & Mod.).
Weight: 5 to 7¼ lbs.
Stock: Hand checkered walnut, beavertail fore-end.
Features: Exposed hammers; double triggers; color casehardened receiver; sling swivels; chrome lined bores. Imported from Spain by Mandall Shooting Supplies.
Price: $299.50
Price: Model 225 (hammerless version) $295.00

CRUCELEGUI HERMANOS MODEL 150 DOUBLE
Gauge: 12 or 20 (2¾" chambers).
Action: Greener triple crossbolt.

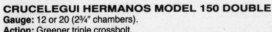

Danok Red Prince

INDUSTRIAS DANOK "RED PRINCE" DOUBLE
Gauge: 12 only, 2¾" chambers.
Barrel: 28" (Mod. & Full).
Weight: About 7 lbs. **Length:** 45" over-all.
Stock: Hand checkered European walnut; straight grip stock.
Sights: Medium bead front.
Features: Automatic ejectors, double triggers, hand engraved action. Introduced 1982. Imported from Spain by Toledo Armas.
Price: $896.00

Erbi Model 76

Weight: About 7 lbs. **Length:** 45" over-all.
Stock: Hand checkered European walnut.
Sights: Medium bead front.
Features: Straight grip stock, silvered, engraved receiver, double triggers. Introduced 1982. Imported from Spain by Toledo Armas.
Price: Model 76ST (extractors) $590.00
Price: Model 76AJ (auto. ejectors) $668.00
Price: Model 80 (sidelock) $1,003.00

ERBI MODEL 76 DOUBLE
Gauge: 10, 12, 20, 28.
Barrel: 28" (Mod. & Full); 28-ga. in 26" only.

Ferlib Model FVII

GALEF'S DOUBLE BARREL SHOTGUN
Gauge: 10 (3½"); 12, 20, 410 (3"); 16, 20 (2¾").
Action: Modified Anson & Deeley boxlock, case hardened.
Barrel: 32" 10, 12 only (Full & Full); 30" 12 only (Mod. & Full); 28" all exc. 410 (Mod. & Full); 26" 12, 20, 28 (I.C. & Mod.); 26" 410 only (Mod. & Full); 22" 12 only (I.C. & I.C.).
Weight: 10½ lbs. (10), 7¾ lbs. (12) to 6 lbs. (410).
Stock: Hand checkered European walnut, p.g., beavertail fore-end, rubber recoil pad. Dimensions vary with gauge.
Features: Auto safety, plain extractors. Imported from Spain by Galef.
Price: 10 ga. $439.00
Price: 12 - 410 .... $298.90

FERLIB MODEL F VII DOUBLE SHOTGUN
Gauge: 12, 20, 28, 410.
Barrel: 25" to 28".
Weight: 5½ lbs. (20 ga.).
Stock: Oil-finished walnut, checkered straight grip and fore-end.
Features: Boxlock action with fine scroll engraved, silvered receiver. Double triggers standard. Introduced 1983. Imported from Italy by Wm. Larkin Moore.
Price: 12 or 20 ga. $2,950.00
Price: 28 or 410 ga. $3,250.00
Price: Extra for single trigger, beavertail fore-end $300.00

F.I.E. "THE BRUTE" DOUBLE BARREL
Gauge: 12, 16, 20 (2¾" chambers), 410 (3" chambers).
Action: Boxlock.
Barrel: 18" (Cyl.), 28" (Mod. & Full).
Weight: 5 lbs. 2 oz. **Length:** 30" over-all.
Stock: Hand checkered walnut with full beavertail fore-end.
Features: The smallest, lightest double barrel shotgun available. Introduced 1979. Imported from Brazil by F.I.E. Corp.
Price: With 28" barrels $229.95
Price: "Riot" model with 18" barrels $242.95
Price: "Brute" model with 18" barrels $259.95

GIB Magnum

GIB 10 GAUGE MAGNUM SHOTGUN
Gauge: 10 ga. (3½" chambers).
Action: Boxlock.
Barrel: 32" (Full).
Weight: 10 lbs.
Stock: 14½"x1½"x2⅝". European walnut, checkered at p.g. and fore-end.
Features: Double triggers; color hardened action, rest blued. Front and center metal beads on matted rib; ventilated rubber recoil pad. Fore-end release has positive Purdey-type mechanism. Imported from Spain by Mandall Shooting Supplies.
Price: $500.00

Garbi Model 60

GARBI MODEL 60 SIDE-BY-SIDE
Gauge: 12, 16, 20 (2¾" chambers).
Barrel: 26", 28", 30"; choked to customers specs.
Weight: 5½ to 6½ lbs.
Stock: Select walnut. Dimensions to customer specs.
Features: Sidelock action. Scroll engraving on receiver. Hand checkered stock. Double triggers. Extractors. Imported from Spain by L. Joseph Rahn, Inc.
Price: Model 60A, 12 ga. only $830.00
Price: With demi-bloc barrels and ejectors, 12, 16, 20 ga. $1,139.00

GARBI MODEL 51 SIDE-BY-SIDE
Gauge: 12, 16, 20 (2¾" chambers).
Barrel: 28" (Mod. & Full).
Weight: 5½ to 6½ lbs.
Stock: Walnut, to customer specs.
Features: Boxlock action; hand-engraved receiver; hand-checkered stock and fore-end; double triggers; extractors. Introduced 1980. Imported from Spain by L. Joseph Rahn, Inc.
Price: Model 51A, 12 ga., extractors $515.00
Price: Model 51B, 12, 16, 20 ga., ejectors....................... $890.00

Garbi Model 62
Similar to Model 60 except choked Mod. & Full, plain receiver with engraved border, demi-bloc barrels, gas exhaust valves, jointed triggers, extractors. Imported from Spain by L. Joseph Rahn.
Price: Model 62A, 12 ga., only.................................. $830.00
Price: Model 62B, 12, 16, 20 ga., ejectors $1,115.00

Garbi Model 71

GARBI MODEL 71 DOUBLE
Gauge: 12, 16, 20.
Barrel: 26", 28", choked to customer specs.
Weight: 5 lbs., 15 oz., (20 ga.).
Stock: 14½"x2¼"x1½". European walnut. Straight grip, checkered butt, classic fore-end.
Features: Sidelock action, automatic ejectors, double triggers standard. Color case-hardened action, coin finish optional. Five other models are available. Imported from Spain by Wm. Larkin Moore.
Price: Model 71, from...................................... $1,675.00

SHOTGUNS—SIDE-BY-SIDES

Garbi Model 110 Double
True sidelock available in 12, 20 and 28 ga. with barrel length, chokes and stock dimensions made to customer specifications. Introduced 1982. Imported from Spain by Toledo Armas.
Price: Model 110 . . . . **$2,433.00**
Price: Model 300 . . . . **$5,980.00**

Garbi Model 101 Side-by-Side
Similar to the Garbi Model 71 except is available with optional level, file-cut, Churchill or ventilated top rib, and in a 12-ga. pigeon or wildfowl gun. Has Continental-style floral and scroll engraving, select walnut stock. Better over-all quality than the Model 71. Imported from Spain by Wm. Larkin Moore.
Price: **$2,800.00**

GARBI MODEL 102 SHOTGUN
Gauge: 12, 16, 20.
Barrel: 12 ga.-25″ to 30″; 16 & 20 ga.-25″ to 28″. Chokes as specified.
Weight: 20 ga.-5 lbs., 15 oz. to 6 lbs., 4 oz.
Stock: 14½″x2¼x1½″; select walnut.
Features: Holland pattern sidelock ejector with chopper lump barrels, Holland-type large scroll engraving. Double triggers (hinged front) std., non-selective single trigger available. Many options available. Imported from Spain by Wm. Larkin Moore.
Price: From **$2,800.00**

Garbi Model 103A, B Side-by-Side
Similar to the Garbi Model 71 except has Purdey-type fine scroll and rosette engraving. Better over-all quality than the Model 101. Model 103B has nickel-chrome steel barrels, H&H-type easy opening mechanism; other mechanical details remain the same. Imported from Spain by Wm. Larkin Moore.
Price: Model 103A **$2,800.00**
Price: Model 103B **$3,800.00**

Garbi Model 200 Side-by-Side
Similar to the Garbi Model 71 except has barrels of nickel-chrome steel, heavy duty locks, magnum proofed. Very fine continental-style floral and scroll engraving, well figured walnut stock. Other mechanical features remain the same. Imported from Spain by Wm. Larkin Moore.
Price: **$4,300.00**

Garbi Model Special Side-by-Side
Similar to the Garbi Model 71 except has best quality wood and metal work. Special game scene engraving with or without gold inlays, fancy figured walnut stock. Imported from Spain by Wm. Larkin Moore.
Price: **$4,400.00**

IGA Side-by-Side

IGA SIDE-BY-SIDE SHOTGUN
Gauge: 12, 20, 28 (2¾″), 410 (3″).
Barrel: 26″ (Full & Full, 410 only, Imp. Cyl. & Mod.), 28″ (Mod. & Full).
Weight: 6¾ to 7 lbs.
Stock: 14½″ x 1½″ x 2½″. Oil-finished hardwood. Checkered pistol grip and fore-end.
Features: Automatic safety, extractors only, solid matted barrel rib. Double triggers only. Introduced 1983. Imported from Brazil by Stoeger Industries.
Price: **$325.00**
Price: Coach Gun, 12 or 20 ga., 20″ bbls. **$283.95**

Larranaga Traditional

MIGUEL LARRANAGA "THE TRADITIONAL" DOUBLE
Gauge: 12 or 20 ga., 2¾″ chambers.
Barrel: 28″ (Mod. & Full). **Length:** 45″ over-all.
Weight: About 6½ lbs. **Length:** 45″ over-all.
Stock: Hand engraved European walnut, straight grip.
Sights: Medium bead front.
Features: Exposed hammers, hand engraved locks, checkered butt. Introduced 1982. Imported from Spain by Toledo Armas.
Price: **$497.00**

Mercury Magnum

Weight: 7¼ lbs. (12 ga.); 6½ lbs. (20 ga.); 10⅛ lbs. (10 ga.). **Length:** 45″ (28″ bbls.).
Stock: 14″x1⅝″x2¼″ walnut, checkered p.g. stock and beavertail fore-end, recoil pad.
Features: Double triggers, front hinged, auto safety, extractors; safety gas ports, engraved frame. Imported from Spain by Tradewinds.
Price: (12, 20 ga.) **$295.00**
Price: (10 ga.) **$480.00**

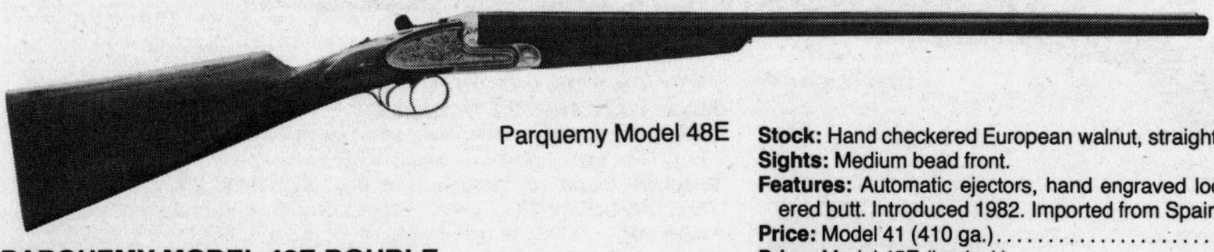

MERCURY MAGNUM DOUBLE BARREL SHOTGUN
Gauge: 10 (3½″), 12 or 20 (3″) magnums.
Action: Triple-lock Anson & Deeley type.
Barrel: 28″ (Full & Mod.), 12 and 20 ga.; 32″ (Full & Full), 10 ga.

Parquemy Model 48E

Stock: Hand checkered European walnut, straight grip.
Sights: Medium bead front.
Features: Automatic ejectors, hand engraved locks, double triggers, checkered butt. Introduced 1982. Imported from Spain by Toledo Armas.
Price: Model 41 (410 ga.) **$336.00**
Price: Model 45E (boxlock) **$507.00**
Price: Model 48 (410 ga., extractors) **$608.00**
Price: Model 48E **$718.00**
Price: Model 50 . . . . **$858.00**

PARQUEMY MODEL 48E DOUBLE
Gauge: 12, 20, 28 (2¾″ chambers), 410 (3″).
Barrel: 28″ (Mod. & Full).
Weight: 5½ to 7 lbs. **Length:** 45″ over-all.

Piotti King No. 1

PIOTTI MODEL PIUMA SIDE-BY-SIDE
Gauge: 12, 16, 20, 28, 410.
Barrel: 25″ to 30″ (12 ga.), 25″ to 28″ (16, 20, 28, 410).
Weight: 5½ to 6¼ lbs. (20 ga.).
Stock: Dimensions to customer specs. Straight grip stock with checkered butt, classic splinter fore-end, hand rubbed oil finish are standard; pistol grip, beavertail fore-end, satin luster finish optional.
Features: Anson & Deeley boxlock ejector double with chopper lump barrels. Level, file-cut rib, light scroll and rosette engraving, scalloped frame. Double triggers with hinged front standard, single non-selective optional. Coin finish standard, color case hardened optional. Imported from Italy by Wm. Larkin Moore.
Price: **$4,700.00**

PIOTTI KING NO. 1 SIDE-BY-SIDE
Gauge: 12, 16, 20, 28, 410.
Barrel: 25″ to 30″ (12 ga.), 25″ to 28″ (16, 20, 28, 410). To customer specs. Chokes as specified.
Weight: 6½ lbs. to 8 lbs. (12 ga., to customer specs.)
Stock: Dimensions to customer specs. Finely figured walnut; straight grip with checkered butt with classic splinter fore-end and hand-rubbed oil finish standard. Pistol grip, beavertail fore-end, satin luster finish optional.
Features: Holland & Holland pattern sidelock action, auto. ejectors. Double trigger with front trigger hinged standard; non-selective single trigger optional. Coin finish standard; color case-hardened optional. Top rib: level, file cut standard; concave, ventilated optional. Very fine, full coverage scroll engraving with small floral bouquets, gold crown in top lever, name in gold, and gold crest in fore-end. Imported from Italy by Wm. Larkin Moore.
Price: **$11,000.00**

Piotti Model Monte Carlo Side-by-Side
Similar to the Piotti King No. 1 except has Purdey-style scroll and rosette engraving, no gold inlays, over-all workmanship not as finely detailed. Other mechanical specifications remain the same. Imported from Italy by Wm. Larkin Moore.
Price: **$9,200.00**

Piotti Model Lunik Side-by-Side
Similar to the Piotti King No. 1 except better over-all quality. Has Renaissance-style large scroll engraving in relief, gold crown in top lever, gold name, and gold crest in fore-end. Best quality Holland & Holland-pattern sidelock ejector double with chopper lump (demi-bloc) barrels. Other mechanical specifications remain the same. Imported from Italy by Wm. Larkin Moore.
Price: **$11,500.00**

Piotti Model Lunik

ROSSI "SQUIRE" DOUBLE BARREL
Gauge: 20, 410 (3″ chambers).
Barrel: 20 ga.—26″ (Imp. Cyl. & Mod.), 28″ (Mod. & Full); 410—26″ (Full & Full).
Weight: About 7½ lbs.
Stock: Walnut finished hardwood.
Features: Double triggers, raised matted rib, beavertail fore-end. Massive twin underlugs mesh with synchronized sliding bolts. Introduced 1978. Imported by Interarms.
Price: 20 ga. **$205.00**
Price: 410 . . . . **$300.00**

Piotti Model King EELL Side-by-Side
Similar to the Piotti King No. 1 except highest quality wood and metal work. Choice of either bulino game scene engraving or game scene engraving with gold inlays. Engraved and signed by a master engraver. Exhibition grade wood. Other mechanical specifications remain the same. Imported from Italy by Wm. Larkin Moore.
Price: **$16,000.00**

ROSSI OVERLAND DOUBLE BARREL
Gauge: 12, 20, 410 (3″ chambers).
Action: Sidelock with external hammers; Greener crossbolt.
Barrel: 12 ga., 20″ (Imp. Cyl., Mod.) 28″ (Mod. & Full), 20 ga., 20″ (Mod., Full), 410 ga., 26″ (Full & Full).
Weight: 6½ to 7 lbs.
Stock: Walnut p.g. with beavertail fore-end.
Features: Solid raised matted rib. Exposed hammers. Imported by Interarms.
Price: 12 or 20 . . . . **$270.00**
Price: 410 . . . . **$285.00**

Sarasqueta Model 119E

J. J. SARASQUETA MODEL 119E DOUBLE
Gauge: 12 ga., 2¾″ chambers.
Barrel: 28″ (Mod. & Full, Imp. Cyl. & Mod.).
Weight: About 7 lbs. **Length:** 45″ over-all.
Stock: Hand checkered European walnut, straight grip.
Sights: Medium bead front.
Features: Automatic ejectors, hand engraved locks, double triggers. Introduced 1982. Imported from Spain by Toledo Armas.
Price: Model 119E **$732.00**
Price: Model 130 (made to order only) **$1,445.00**

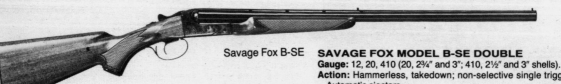

Savage Fox B-SE

SAVAGE FOX MODEL B-SE DOUBLE
Gauge: 12, 20, 410 (20, 2¾″ and 3″; 410, 2½″ and 3″ shells).
Action: Hammerless, takedown; non-selective single trigger; auto. safety. Automatic ejectors.
Barrel: 12, 20 ga., 26″ (Imp. Cyl., Mod.); 12 ga. (Mod., Full); 410, 26″ (Full, Full). Vent. rib on all.
Weight: 12 ga. 7 lbs., 16 ga. 6¾ lbs., 20 ga. 6½ lbs., 410 ga. 6¼ lbs.
Stock: 14″x1½″x2½″. Walnut, checkered p.g. and beavertail fore-end.
Features: Decorated, case-hardened frame; white bead front and middle sights.
Price: **$398.50**

SHOTGUNS—SIDE-BY-SIDES

W&C Scott Chatsworth

W&C SCOTT CHATSWORTH GRANDE LUXE DOUBLE
Gauge: 12, 16, 20, 28.
Barrel: 25″, 26″, 27″, 28″, 30″ (Imp. Cyl. & Mod., or to order); concave rib standard, Churchill or flat rib optional.
Weight: About 6½ lbs. (12 ga.).
Stock: 14¾″ x 1½″ x 2¼″, or made to customer specs. French walnut with 32 lpi checkering.
Features: Entirely hand fitted; boxlock action (sideplates optional); English scroll engraving; gold name plate shield in stock. Imported from England by L. Joseph Rahn.
Price: 12 or 16 ga. **$7,000.00**
Price: 20 ga. **$8,025.00**
Price: 28 ga. **$8,425.00**

SAVAGE-STEVENS MODEL 311 DOUBLE
Gauge: 12, 16, 20, 410 (12, 20 and 410, 3″ chambers).
Action: Top lever, hammerless; double triggers, auto. top tang safety.
Barrel: 12, 16, 20 ga. 26″ (Imp. Cyl., Mod.); 12 ga. 28″ (Mod., Full); 12 ga. 30″ (Mod., Full); 410 ga. 26″ (Full, Full).
Weight: 7-8 lbs. (30″ bbl.). **Length:** 45¾″ over-all.
Stock: 14″x1½″x2½″. Walnut finish, p.g., fluted comb.
Features: Box type frame, case-hardened finish.
Price: **$248.50**

W&C Scott Bowood DeLuxe Game Gun
Similar to the Chatsworth Grand Luxe except less ornate metal and wood work; checkered 24 lpi at fore-end and pistol grip. Imported from England by L. Joseph Rahn.
Price: 12 or 16 ga. **$4,780.00**
Price: 20 ga. **$5,480.00**
Price: 28 ga. **$5,750.00**

W&C Scott Kinmount Game Gun
Similar to the Bowood DeLuxe Game Gun except less ornate engraving and wood work; checkered 20 lpi; other details essentially the same. Imported from England by L. Joseph Rahn.
Price: 12 or 16 ga. **$3,435.00**
Price: 20 ga. **$3,935.00**
Price: 28 ga. **$4,105.00**

Toledo Armas Valezquez

TOLEDO ARMAS "VALEZQUEZ" DOUBLE
Gauge: 12 ga., 2¾″ chambers.
Barrel: Length and choking to customer specs.
Weight: To customer specs.
Stock: Exhibition grade European walnut; dimensions to customer specs.
Features: Hand engraved action. Automatic ejectors. All options available. Introduced 1982. Imported from Spain by Toledo Armas.
Price: From **$3,275.00**

Urbiola Model 160E

URBIOLA MODEL 160E DOUBLE
Gauge: 12 and 20 ga., 2¾″ chambers.
Barrel: 12 ga.—28″ (Mod. & Full), 20 ga.—26″ (Imp. Cyl. & Full).
Weight: About 7 lbs. **Length:** 45″ over-all (28″ barrels).
Stock: Hand checkered European walnut, straight grip, checkered butt.
Sights: Medium bead front.
Features: Hand engraved locks, automatic ejectors, double triggers. Introduced 1982. Imported from Spain by Toledo Armas.
Price: Model 160E **$727.00**
Price: Model 165 .... **$825.00**

Ventura 66/66 XXV-SL

VENTURA 66/66 XXV-SL DOUBLES
Gauge: 12 ga. (2¾″), 20 ga. (3″), 28 ga. (2¾″).
Action: H&H sidelock with double underlugs.
Barrel: 25″, 27½″, 30″ (12 ga. only), with chokes according to use.
Weight: 12 ga.—6½ lbs.; 28 ga.—5¾ lbs.
Stock: Select French walnut, hand checkered. Straight English stock, slender beavertail fore-end.

Features: Single selective or double triggers, auto. ejectors, gas escape valves, and intercepting safeties. Extensive hand engraving and finishing. Can be made to customer specs. Accessories, extra barrels also available. Imported from Spain by Ventura Imports.
Price: From .... **$1,260.00 to 1,496.00**

Ventura 53/53 XXV-BL

VENTURA 53/53XXV-BL DOUBLES
Gauge: 12 ga. (2¾″), 20 ga. (3″), 28 ga. (2¾″), 410 (3″).
Action: Anson & Deeley with double underlugs.
Barrel: 25″, 27½″, 30″ (12 ga. only), with chokes according to use.
Weight: 12 ga.—6½ lbs.; 28 ga.—5¼ lbs.
Stock: Select French walnut, hand checkered. Straight English stock with slender beavertail fore-end.
Features: Single selective or double triggers, auto ejectors, hand-engraved scalloped frames. Accessories also available. Imported from Spain by Ventura Imports.
Price: From .... **$776.00 to 976.00**

Ventura Model 51

VENTURA MODEL 51 DOUBLE
Gauge: 12 ga. (2¾"), 20 ga. (3").
Action: Anson & Deeley with double underlugs.
Barrel: 27½", 30" (12 ga. only) with chokes according to use.
Weight: 6 to 6½ lbs.
Stock: Select French walnut, hand checkered pistol grip stock with slender beavertail fore-end.
Features: Single selective trigger, auto ejectors, hand-engraved action. Leather trunk cases, wood cleaning rods and brass snap caps available. Imported from Spain by Ventura Imports.
Price: From **$724.00**

Winchester Model 23

WINCHESTER MODEL 23 PIGEON GRADE DOUBLE
Gauge: 12, 20, 3" chambers.
Barrel: 26", (Imp. Cyl. & Mod.), 28" (Mod. & Full). Vent. rib.
Weight: 7 lbs. (12 ga.); 6½ lbs. (20 ga.). **Length:** 46¾" over-all (28" bbls.).
Stock: 14"x1½"x2½" High grade American walnut, beavertail fore-end. Hand cut checkering.
Features: Mechanical trigger; tapered ventilated rib; selective ejectors. Receiver, top lever and trigger guard have silver gray satin finish and fine line scroll engraving. Introduced 1978. Imported from Japan by Winchester Group, Olin Corp.
Price: **$1,195.00**

Winchester Model 23 XTR Lightweight
Similar to standard Pigeon Grade except has 25½" barrels, English-style straight grip stock, thinner semi-beavertail fore-end. Available in 12 or 20 gauge (Imp. Cyl. & Mod.). Silver-gray frame has engraved bird scenes. Comes with hard case. Introduced 1981. Imported from Japan by Winchester Group, Olin Corp.
Price: **$1,275.00**

Winchester Model 23 Heavy Duck
Same basic features as the standard Model 23 Pigeon Grade except has plain, blued receiver, 30" barrels choked Full and Extra Full, 3" chambers. Comes with hard case. Introduced 1983.
Price: **$1,450.00**

Winchester Model 23 Pigeon Grade Winchoke
Same features as standard Model 23 Pigeon Grade except has 25½" barrels with interchangeable Winchoke tubes. Six are supplied with 12 ga. (Skeet, Imp. Cyl., Mod., Imp. Mod., Full, Extra Full), four with 20 ga. (Skeet, Imp. Cyl., Mod., Full). Comes with hard case. Introduced 1983.
Price: **$1,300.00**

SHOTGUNS—BOLT ACTIONS

Marlin Model 55

MARLIN MODEL 55 GOOSE GUN BOLT ACTION
Gauge: 12 only, (3" mag. or 2¾").
Action: Bolt action, thumb safety, detachable 2-shot clip. Red cocking indicator.
Barrel: 36", Full choke.
Weight: 8 lbs. **Length:** 57" over-all.
Stock: Walnut-finished hardwood, p.g., ventilated recoil pad, leather strap & swivels. Mar-Shield® finish.
Features: Tapped for receiver sights. Swivels and leather carrying strap. Brass bead front sight, U-groove rear sight.
Price: **$160.95**

MARLIN SUPERGOOSE 10 M5510
Gauge: 10, 3½" Magnum or 2⅞" regular, 2-shot clip.
Barrel: 34" (Full), bead front sight, U-groove rear sight.
Weight: About 10½ lbs. **Length:** 55½" over-all.
Stock: Extra long walnut-finished hardwood with p.g., Pachmayr vent. pad., white butt spacer.
Features: Bolt action, removable 2-shot clip magazine. Positive thumb safety, red cocking indicator. Comes with quick-detachable swivels and leather carrying strap.
Price: **$263.95**

MOSSBERG MODEL 183K BOLT ACTION
Gauge: 410, 3-shot (3" chamber).
Action: Bolt; top-loading mag.; thumb safety.
Barrel: 25" with C-Lect-Choke.
Weight: 5¾ lbs. **Length:** 45¼" over-all.
Stock: Walnut finish, p.g., Monte Carlo comb., rubber recoil pad w/spacer.
Features: Moulded trigger guard with finger grooves, gold bead front sight.
Price: About **$102.00**

Mossberg Model 395K

MOSSBERG MODEL 395K BOLT ACTION
Gauge: 12, 3-shot (3" chamber).
Action: Bolt; takedown; detachable clip.
Barrel: 26" with C-Lect-Choke.
Weight: 7½ lbs. **Length:** 45¾" over-all.
Stock: Walnut finish, p.g. Monte Carlo comb; recoil pad.
Features: Streamlined action; top safety; grooved rear sight.
Price: About **$110.00**
Price: 20 ga., 3" chamber, 28" bbl., 6¼ lbs., as M 385K . . . . **NA**
Price: 12 ga., 38" bbl., Full choke (Model 395 SPL), about **$126.00**

Beretta Model 680

BERETTA 680 MONO SINGLE BARREL
Gauge: 12 only (2¾").
Barrel: 32", 34" (Full).
Weight: About 8 lbs.
Stock: 14⅜"x1⅜"x1⅝". Premium walnut with Monte Carlo, checkered p.g. and fore-end.
Features: Low profile boxlock action, auto ejector, manual safety. High rib, two sight beads, chrome lined bores. Ventilated recoil pad. Comes with fitted case. Imported from Italy by Beretta U.S.A. Corp.
Price: **$1,580.00**

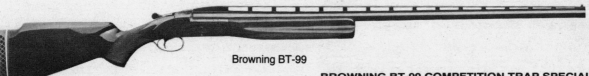

Browning BT-99

BROWNING BT-99 COMPETITION TRAP SPECIAL
Gauge: 12 gauge only (2¾").
Action: Top lever break-open, hammerless.
Barrel: 32" or 34" (Mod., Imp. Mod. or Full) with 1½₂" wide high post floating vent. rib. Also comes with Invector choke tubes.
Weight: 8 lbs. (32" bbl.).
Stock: French walnut; hand checkered, full pistol grip, full beavertail fore-end; recoil pad. Trap dimensions with M.C. 14⅜"x1⅜"x1⅜"x2".
Sights: Ivory front and middle beads.
Features: Gold plated trigger with 3½-lb. pull, deluxe trap-style recoil pad, auto ejector, no safety. Also available in engraved Pigeon Grade. Imported from Japan by Browning.
Price: Grade I Competition **$724.95**
Price: Grade I Competition with extra bbl. **$1,030.00**
Price: Pigeon Grade Competition **$1,650.00**
Price: Grade I Invector **$744.95**

FIE "S.O.B." SINGLE BARREL
Gauge: 12, 20 (2¾"), 410 (3").
Action: Button-break on trigger guard.
Barrel: 12 & 20 ga. 18½" (Cyl.), 28" (Full); 410 ga. 26" (Full).
Weight: 6½ lbs.
Stock: Walnut finished hardwood, full beavertail fore-end.
Sights: Metal bead front.
Features: Exposed hammer. Automatic ejector. Imported from Brazil by F.I.E. Corp.
Price: **$69.95**
Price: With 18½" bbl., short stock **$89.95**

FIE "C.B.C" SINGLE BARREL SHOTGUN
Gauge: 12, 16, 20 (2¾"), 410 (3").
Barrel: 12 ga. & 20 ga. 28" (Full); 410 ga. (Full).
Weight: 6½ lbs.
Stock: Walnut stained hardwood, beavertail fore-end.
Sights: Metal bead front.
Features: Trigger guard button is pushed to open action. Exposed hammer, auto ejector, three-piece takedown. Imported from Brazil by F.I.E. Corp.
Price: **$84.95**

GALEF COMPANION SINGLE BARREL SHOTGUN
Gauge: 12, 20, 410 (3"); 16, 28 (2¾").
Action: Folding boxlock.
Barrel: 28" exc. 12 (30") and 410 (26"), all Full.
Weight: 5½ lbs. (12) to 4½ lbs. (410).
Stock: 14"x1½"x2⅝" hand checkered walnut, p.g.
Features: Non-auto safety, folds. Imported from Italy by Galef.
Price: Plain bbl. **$138.00**
Price: Vent. rib **$167.20**

H&R Model 099

HARRINGTON & RICHARDSON MODEL 099 DELUXE
Gauge: 12, 20, 410 (3" chamber); 16 (2¾").
Barrel: 12 ga. 28" (Full, Mod.); 16 ga. 28" (Mod.); 20 ga. 26" (Full, Mod.); 410 ga. 25" (Full).
Weight: About 5½ lbs. **Length:** 43" over-all (28" barrel).
Stock: Semi-pistol grip walnut finished hardwood; semi-beavertail fore-end. 13¾"x1½"x2½".
Sights: Bead front.
Features: All metal finished with H & R's "Hard-Guard" electroless matte nickel. Introduced 1982. From Harrington & Richardson.
Price: **$95.00**

H & R Model 088
Same features as Model 099 except has semi-pistol grip stock, different finish. Available in most popular gauge and choke combinations, including 12 ga. with 30", 32" or 36" (Full) barrel. Junior model also available (does not have recoil pad).
Price: **$80.00**
Price: 12 ga., 30", 32" (Full) **$82.00**
Price: 12 ga., 36" (Full) **$84.50**

H & R Model 162
Same as the 099 except 12 or 20 ga., 24" Cyl. bored bbl., adj. folding leaf rear sight, blade front, 5½ lbs.; over-all 40". Cross bolt safety; push-button action release.
Price: **$100.00**

H&R 490 Greenwing

H & R Model 490 Greenwing
Same as Model 490 except specially polished blue finish with gold-finish trigger and gold-filled inscription on frame.
Price: **$95.00**

H&R Model 176

H & R Model 490

Like the 099 except ideally proportioned stock for the smaller shooter. Can be cheaply changed to full size. 20 ga. (Mod.), or 410 (Full) 26″ bbl. Weight 5 lbs., 40½″ over-all.

Price: **$84.50**

ITHACA 5E GRADE SINGLE BARREL TRAP GUN

Gauge: 12 only.

Action: Top lever break open hammerless, dual locking lugs.

Barrel: 32″ or 34″, rampless vent. rib.

Stock: (14½″x1½″x1⅞″). Select walnut, checkered p.g. and beavertail fore-end, p.g. cap, recoil pad, Monte Carlo comb, cheekpiece. Cast-on, cast-off or

H & R Model 176 Magnum

Similar to the Model 099 except in 10 gauge (3½″ chamber) only with 36″ (Full) barrel. Also available with 32″ (Full) barrel. All barrels specially designed for steel shot use. Special long fore-end and recoil pad.

Price: From **$105.50**

H & R Model 176 10 Ga. Slug Gun

Similar to standard Model 176 magnums except chambered for 10 ga. slugs. Ramp front sight, adjustable folding leaf rear sight, recoil pad, sling swivels. Has 28″ barrel (Cyl.), 3½″ chamber. Extra length magnum-type fore-end. Weighs 9¼ lbs. Introduced 1982.

Price: **$122.00**

extreme deviation from standard stock dimensions $100 extra. Reasonable deviation allowed without extra charge.

Features: Frame, top lever and trigger guard extensively engraved and gold inlaid. Gold name plate in stock.

Price: Custom made **$7,000.00**
Price: Dollar Grade.. **$9,700.00**

Ljutic Mono Gun

LJUTIC MONO GUN SINGLE BARREL

Gauge: 12 ga. only.

Barrel: 34″, choked to customer specs; hollow-milled rib, 35½″ sight plane.

Weight: Approx. 9 lbs.

Stock: To customer specs. Oil finish, hand checkered.

Features: Totally custom made. Pull or release trigger; removable trigger guard contains trigger and hammer mechanism; Ljutic pushbutton opener on front of trigger guard. From Ljutic Industries

Price: **$3,395.00**
Price: With Olympic Rib, custom 32″ barrel **$3,550.00**
Price: As above with screw-in chokes.. **$3,755.00**

Ljutic Dyna Trap II

Ljutic Dyna Trap II Shotgun

Similar to the Mono Gun Single Barrel except has 33″ single barrel, choice of Monte Carlo or straight stock.

Price: Pull or release trigger.. **$2,495.00**

Ljutic Space Gun

LJUTIC RECOILLESS SPACE GUN SHOTGUN

Gauge: 12 only, 2¾″ chamber.

Barrel: 30″ (Full).

Weight: 8½ lbs.

Stock: 14½″ to 15″ pull length; universal comb; medium or large p.g.

Sights: Choice of front sight or vent. rib model.

Features: Choice of pull or release button trigger; anti-recoil mechanism. Revolutionary new design. Introduced 1981. From Ljutic Industries.

Price: From **$3,295.00**

Savage-Stevens Model 94

Stevens M94-Y Youth's Gun

Same as Model 94-C except: 26″ bbl., 20 ga. Mod. or 410 Full, 12½″ stock with recoil pad. Wgt. about 5½ lbs. 40½″ over-all.

Price: **$98.50**

SAVAGE-STEVENS MODEL 94 Single Barrel Gun

Gauge: 12, 16, 20, 410 (12, 20 and 410, 3″ chambers).

Action: Top lever break open; hammer; auto. ejector.

Barrel: 12 ga. 28″, 30″, 32″, 36″; 16, 20 ga. 28″; 410 ga. 26″. Full choke only.

Weight: About 6 lbs. **Length:** 42″ over-all (26″ bbl.).

Stock: 14″x1½″x2½″. Walnut finish, checkered p.g. and fore-end.

Features: Color case-hardened frame, low rebounding hammer.

Price: 26″ to 32″ bbls. **$92.00**
Price: With 36″ bbl. **$98.50**

CAUTION: PRICES CHANGE. CHECK AT GUNSHOP.

SHOTGUNS—SINGLE SHOTS

Snake Charmer

"SNAKE CHARMER" SHOTGUN
Gauge: 410, 3" chamber.
Barrel: 18⅛" (Cyl.).
Weight: 3½ lbs. **Length:** 28⅛" over-all.
Stock: Moulded plastic, thumbhole type.
Sights: None.
Features: Measures 19" when taken apart. All stainless steel construction. Storage compartment in buttstock holds four spare rounds of 410. Introduced 1978. From H. Koon, Inc.
Price: $110.00
Price: Vinyl carrying case $7.00
Price: Leather scabbard $32.00

Stevens 9478 Single

STEVENS 9478 SINGLE BARREL
Gauge: 10, 12, 20 or 410.
Barrel: 26" (Full, Mod.), 28" (Full), 30" (Full), 32" (Full), 36" (Full).
Weight: 6¼ lbs. (9½ lbs. for 10 ga.) **Length:** 42" to 52" over-all.
Stock: Walnut finished hardwood. 14"x1½"x2½".
Features: Bottom opening action "lever", manually cocked hammer, auto. ejection. Color case-hardened frame. Youth Model available in 20 or 410, 26" (Mod.) barrel, 12½" pull stock, weighs 5½ lbs.
Price: 9478 .... $84.50
Price: 10 ga., 36" (Full) $116.50

SHOTGUNS—MILITARY & POLICE

Benelli Model 121-M1

BENELLI MODEL 121-MI POLICE SHOTGUN
Gauge: 12, 2¾" chamber.
Barrel: 20" (Cyl.).
Weight: About 7½ lbs.
Stock: Oil-finished Beech.
Sights: Post front, buckhorn-type rear.
Features: All metal parts black Parkerized, including bolt; smooth, non-checkered stock, swivel stud on butt. Imported by Heckler & Koch.
Price: $499.00

FIE SPAS 12

FIE SPAS 12 PUMP/AUTO SHOTGUN
Gauge: 12, 2¾".
Barrel: 21½". Barrel threaded for SPAS choke tubes.
Weight: 9.6 lbs. **Length:** 31¾" (stock folded).
Stock: Folding, metal.
Sights: Blade front, aperture rear.
Features: Functions as pump or gas-operated auto. Has 9-shot magazine. Parkerized alloy receiver, chrome lined bore, resin pistol grip and pump handle. Made in Italy by Franchi. Introduced 1983. Imported by FIE Corp.
Price: $599.95

Ithaca 37 Hand Grip

ITHACA MODEL 37 M & P SHOTGUN
Gauge: 12, 2¾" chamber, 5-shot magazine.
Barrel: 18" (Cyl.), 20" (Cyl. or Full).
Weight: 6½ lbs.
Stock: Oil-finished walnut with grooved walnut pump handle.
Sights: Bead front.
Features: Metal parts are Parkerized or matte chrome. Available with vertical hand grip instead of full butt.
Price: 5-shot, Parkerized $328.50
Price: 8-shot, Parkerized $343.50
Price: 8-shot, chrome $383.50
Price: Hand Grip stock, 5-shot $351.75
Price: Hand Grip stock, 8-shot $366.75

Ithaca Model 37 "Bear Stopper"
Compact, handgrip version of the 12 gauge Model 37 M&P. Choice of 5-shot, 18½" (Cyl.), or 8-shot 20" (Cyl.) barrel. Comes with sling and swivels. Introduced 1983.
Price: Blued, 5-shot, 18½" $315.00
Price: Parkerized, 5-shot, 18½" $351.75
Price: Parkerized, 8-shot, 20" $366.75
Price: Chrome, 8-shot, 20" $406.75

Ithaca 37 DSPS

Ithaca Model 37 DSPS Shotgun

Law enforcement version of the Model 37 Deerslayer. Designed primarily for shooting rifled slugs but equally effective with buckshot. Available in either 5- or 8-shot models in blue, Parkerized or matte chrome finishes. Has 20″ barrel with Full choke, oil-finished stock, adjustable rifle-type sights.

Price: Parkerized, 5-shot **$363.50**
Price: Blue, 5-shot **$363.50**
Price: Matte chrome, 8-shot **$418.50**
Price: Parkerized or blue, 8-shot **$378.50**

Ithaca Model 37 LAPD

Similar to the Model 37 DSPS except comes with sling swivels, sling, rubber recoil pad. RIfle-type sights, checkered pistol grip stock, 5-shot magazine.
Price: **$405.00**

Ithaca Mag-10 Roadblocker

ITHACA MAG-10 ROADBLOCKER
Gauge: 10, 3½″ chamber.
Barrel: 22″ (Cyl.).
Weight: 10¾ lbs.
Stock: Walnut stock and fore-end, oil finish.
Sights: Bead front.
Features: Non-glare finish on metal parts. Uses Ithaca's Countercoil gas system. Rubber recoil pad. Vent. rib or plain barrel.
Price: Plain barrel **$696.75**
Price: Vent rib barrel **$725.50**

Mossberg 500 Security

MOSSBERG MODEL 500 SECURITY SHOTGUNS
Gauge: 12, 20 (2¾″), 410 (3″).
Barrel: 18½″, 20″ (Cyl.).
Weight: 5½ lbs. (410), 7 lbs. (12 ga.).
Stock: Walnut-finished hardwood.
Sights: Rifle-type front and rear or metal bead front.
Features: Available in 6- or 8-shot models. Top-mounted safety, double action slide bars, sling swivels, rubber recoil pad. Blue, Parkerized or electroless nickel finishes. Price list not complete—contact Mossberg for full list.
Price: 12 ga., 6-shot, 18½″, blue, bead sight, about **$178.95**
Price: As above, Parkerized, about **$215.00**
Price: As above, nickel, about **$240.00**
Price: 12 ga., 8-shot, 20″ Parkerized, rifle sights, about **$218.00**
Price: 20 ga., 6-shot, 18½″, blue, bead sight, about **$202.00**
Price: Model 500 US, parkerized finish, handguard, about **$220.00**
Price: Model 500 ATP, blued, bayonet lug, sling, about **$245.00**

Mossberg Cruiser Persuader Shotgun

Similar to the Model 500 Security guns except fitted with the "Cruiser" pistol grip. Grip and fore-end are solid black. Available in either blue or electroless nickel; 12 gauge only with 18½″ (6-shot) or 20″ (8-shot) barrel. Comes with extra long black web sling. Weight is 5¾ lb. (18½″), 6 lb. (20″). Over-all length is 28″ with 18½″ barrel.
Price: 6-shot, 18½″, blue, about **$200.00**
Price: As above, nickel, about **$240.00**
Price: 8-shot, 20″, blue, about **$215.00**
Price: As above, nickel, about **$240.00**

Mossberg 5500 AP5

MOSSBERG 5500 AP5 GUARDIAN SHOTGUN
Gauge: 12, 2¾″ chamber.
Barrel: 18½″ (Cyl.).
Weight: 7½ lbs. **Length:** 38½″ over-all.
Stock: Hardwood.
Sights: Bead front.
Features: Matte blue finish, grooved fore-end. Also available with Cruiser pistol grip. Introduced 1983.
Price: . . . . **NA**

Mossberg 595 AP5

MOSSBERG 595 AP5 BOLT ACTION SHOTGUN
Gauge: 12 ga., 2¾″ chamber.
Barrel: 18½″.
Weight: 7½ lbs. **Length:** 38½″ over-all.
Stock: Hardwood.
Sights: Bead front, open rear.
Features: Detachable 5-shot box magazine, rubber recoil pad, grooved fore-end. Comes with sling swivel studs. Introduced 1983.
Price: . . . . **NA**

CAUTION: PRICES CHANGE. CHECK AT GUNSHOP.

SHOTGUNS—MILITARY & POLICE

Remington 870 Police

REMINGTON MODEL 870P POLICE SHOTGUN
Gauge: 12, 2¾" chamber.
Barrel: 18", 20" (Police Cyl.), 20" (Imp. Cyl.).
Weight: About 7 lbs.
Stock: Lacquer-finished hardwood or folding stock.
Sights: Metal bead front or rifle sights.
Features: Solid steel receiver, double-action slide bars.
Price: Wood stock, 18" or 20", bead sight $319.95
Price: Wood stock, 20", rifle sights $344.95

Sile Model TP-8

SILE TP8 POLICE/SURVIVAL SHOTGUN
Gauge: 12, 2¾" chamber, 7-shot magazine.
Barrel: 19¾".
Weight: 6¾ lbs. **Length:** 39½" over-all with stock, 29½" without.
Stock: Hollow, plastic coated, steel tube, plastic fore-end.
Sights: Bead on ramp front, open bar rear.
Features: Dual action bars, non-reflective electroless nickel finish. Stock holds spare ammunition or survival equipment. Rotating sling swivels. Hard chrome lined barrel. Introduced 1982. Imported from Italy by Sile.
Price: $255.00

Savage 69-R/69-RXL

SAVAGE MODEL 69-R/69-RXL PUMP SHOTGUN
Gauge: 12 only, 3" chamber.
Barrel: M69-R — 18¼" (Cyl.), M69-RXL — 20" (Cyl.).
Weight: 6½ lbs. **Length:** 38" over-all.
Stock: Hardwood, tung-oil finish.
Sights: Bead front.
Features: Top tang safety, 5-shot (69-R) or 7-shot (69-RXL). Stock has fluted comb and full pistol grip, ventilated rubber pad. QD swivel studs. Introduced 1982.
Price: Either model $171.50
Price: Model 69-N (satin nickel finish) $231.00

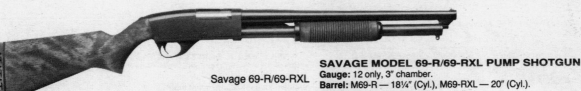

Stevens 311-R Guard Gun

STEVENS MODEL 311-R GUARD GUN DOUBLE
Gauge: 12 or 20 ga.
Barrel: 18¼" (Cyl. & Cyl.).
Weight: 6¾ lbs. **Length:** 35¼" over-all.
Stock: Hardwood, tung-oil finish.
Sights: Bead front.
Features: Top tang safety, double triggers, color case-hardened frame, blue barrels. Ventilated rubber recoil pad. Introduced 1982.
Price: $248.50

Winchester Defender

WINCHESTER DEFENDER PUMP GUN
Gauge: 12, 3" chamber, 7-shot capacity.
Barrel: 18" (Cyl.).
Weight: 6¾ lbs. **Length:** 38⅝" over-all.
Stock: Walnut finished hardwood stock and ribbed fore-end.
Sights: Metal bead front.
Features: Cross-bolt safety, front-locking rotating bolt, twin action slide bars. Black rubber butt pad. Made under license by U.S. Repeating Arms Co.
Price: $189.95

Winchester "Stainless Marine" Pump Gun
Same as the Defender except has bright chrome finish, stainless-steel barrel, rifle-type sights only. Has special fore-end cap for easy cleaning and inspection.
Price: $354.95

Winchester Stainless Police Pump Gun
Same as the Defender except has satin chrome finish, 7-shot capacity, stainless steel barrel, detachable sling swivels. Metal bead front sight or rifle-type front and rear sights.
Price: With bead front sight $339.95
Price: With rifle-type sights. $354.95

CAUTION: PRICES CHANGE. CHECK AT GUNSHOP.

The following pages catalog the black powder arms currently available to U.S. shooters. These range from quite precise replicas of historically significant arms to totally new designs created expressly to give the black powder shooter the benefits of modern technology.

Most of the replicas are imported, and many are available from more than one source. Thus examples of a given model such as the 1860 Army revolver or Zouave rifle purchased from different importers may vary in price, finish and fitting. Most of them bear proof marks, indicating that they have been test fired in the proof house of their country of origin.

A list of the importers and the retail price range are included with the description for each model. Many local dealers handle more than one importer's products, giving the prospective buyer an opportunity to make his own judgment in selecting a black powder gun. Most importers have catalogs available free or at nominal cost, and some

are well worth having for the useful information on black powder shooting they provide in addition to their detailed descriptions and specifications of the guns.

A number of special accessories are also available for the black powder shooter. These include replica powder flasks, bullet moulds, cappers and tools, as well as more modern devices to facilitate black powder cleaning and maintenance. Ornate presentation cases and even detachable shoulder stocks are also available for some black powder pistols from their importers. Again, dealers or the importers will have catalogs.

The black powder guns are arranged in four sections: Single Shot Pistols, Revolvers, Muskets & Rifles, and Shotguns. The guns within each section are arranged roughly by date of the original, with the oldest first. Thus the 1847 Walker replica leads off the revolver section, and flintlocks precede percussion arms in the other sections.

BLACK POWDER SINGLE SHOT PISTOLS—FLINT & PERCUSSION

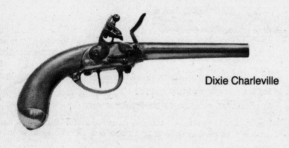

Dixie Charleville

CHARLEVILLE FLINTLOCK PISTOL
Caliber: 69, (.680″ round ball).
Barrel: 7½″.
Weight: 48 oz. **Length:** 13½″ over-all.
Stock: Walnut.
Sights: None.
Features: Brass frame, polished steel barrel, iron belt hook, brass buttcap and backstrap. Replica of original 1777 pistol. Imported by Dixie.
Price: $135.00

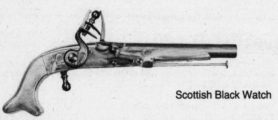

Scottish Black Watch

BLACK WATCH SCOTCH PISTOL
Caliber: 577 (.550″ round ball).
Barrel: 7″, smoothbore.
Weight: 1½ lbs. **Length:** 12″ over-all.
Stock: Brass.
Sights: None.
Features: Faithful reproduction of this military flintlock. From Dixie.
Price: $135.00

TOWER FLINTLOCK PISTOL
Caliber: 45, 69.
Barrel: 8¼″.
Weight: 40 oz. **Length:** 14″ over-all.
Stock: Walnut.
Sights: Fixed.
Features: Engraved lock, brass furniture. Specifications, including caliber, weight and length may vary with importers. Available as flint or percussion. Imported by Toledo Armas.
Price: $59.95

CVA TOWER PISTOL
Caliber: 45.
Barrel: 9″, octagon at breech, tapering to round at muzzle. Rifled.
Weight: 36 oz. **Length:** 15¼″ over-all.
Stock: Selected hardwood.
Sights: None.
Features: Color case-hardened and engraved lock plate; early-style brass trigger; brass trigger guard, nose cap, thimbles, grip cap; blued barrel and ramrod. Introduced 1981.
Price: Complete, percussion $99.95
Price: Kit form, percussion $69.95
Price: Kit form, flintlock $79.95

Dixie Queen Anne

DIXIE QUEEN ANNE FLINTLOCK PISTOL
Caliber: 50.
Barrel: 7½″, smoothbore.
Stock: Walnut.
Sights: None.
Features: Browned steel barrel, fluted brass trigger guard, brass mask on butt. Lockplate left in the white. Made by Pedersoli in Italy. Introduced 1983. Imported by Dixie Gun Works.
Price: $99.95

CAUTION: PRICES CHANGE. CHECK AT GUNSHOP.

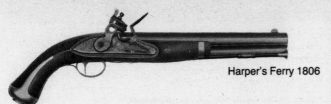

Harper's Ferry 1806

HARPER'S FERRY 1806 PISTOL
Caliber: 54.
Barrel: 10″.
Weight: 40 oz. **Length:** 16″ over-all.
Stock: Walnut.
Sights: Fixed.
Features: Case hardened lock, brass mounted browned bbl. Replica of the first U.S. Gov't.-made flintlock pistol. Imported by Navy Arms, Dixie.
Price: **$165.00**

Dixie Pennsylvania Pistol

DIXIE PENNSYLVANIA PISTOL
Caliber: 44 (.430″ round ball).
Barrel: 10″ (⅞″ octagon).
Weight: 2½ lbs.
Stock: Walnut-stained hardwood.
Sights: Blade front, open rear drift-adj. for windage; brass.
Features: Available in flint or percussion. Brass trigger guard, thimbles, nose-cap, wedgeplates; high-lustre blue barrel. Imported from Italy by Dixie Gun Works.
Price: Flint, finished **$119.95**
Price: Percussion, finished **$105.00**
Price: Flint, kit **$85.00**
Price: Percussion, kit **$72.50**

Lyman Plains Pistol

LYMAN PLAINS PISTOL
Caliber: 50 or 54.
Barrel: 8″, 1-in-66″ twist.
Weight: 50 oz. **Length:** 15″ over-all.
Stock: Walnut half-stock.
Sights: Blade front, V-notch rear adj. for windage.
Features: Polished brass trigger guard and ramrod tip, color case-hardened lock, spring-loaded target hammer, blackened iron furniture. Hooked patent breech, detachable belt hook. Introduced 1981. From Lyman Products.
Price: Finished **$159.95**
Price: Kit **$119.95**

Kentucky Flintlock Pistol

KENTUCKY FLINTLOCK PISTOL
Caliber: 44, 45.
Barrel: 10⅛″.
Weight: 32 oz. **Length:** 15½″ over-all.
Stock: Walnut.
Sights: Fixed.
Features: Specifications, including caliber, weight and length may vary with importer. Case hardened lock, blued bbl.; availble also as brass bbl. flint Model 1821 ($136.75, Navy). Imported by Navy Arms, The Armoury, CVA (kit only), Hopkins & Allen, Sile.
Price: . . . . **$40.95 to $142.00**
Price: In kit form, from . . . . **$90.00 to $112.00**
Price: Brass barrel (Navy Arms) **$153.00**
Price: Single cased set (Navy Arms) **$225.00**
Price: Double cased set (Navy Arms) **$370.00**
Price: Brass bbl., single cased set (Navy Arms) **$240.00**
Price: Brass bbl., double cased set (Navy Arms) **$400.00**

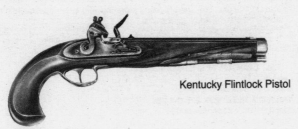

J & S Hawken Pistol

Kentucky Percussion Pistol
Similar to flint version but percussion lock. Imported by The Armoury, Navy Arms, F.I.E., CVA, Armsport, Sile, Hopkins & Allen, Toledo Armas.
Price: About **$120.00**
Price: Brass barrel (Navy Arms) **$136.75**
Price: In kit form . . . . **$35.95 to $102.00**
Price: Single cased set (Navy Arms) **$208.00**
Price: Double cased set (Navy Arms) **$335.00**
Price: Brass bbl. single cased set (Navy Arms) **$225.00**
Price: Brass bbl., double cased set (Navy Arms) **$370.00**

CVA COLONIAL PISTOL
Caliber: 45 (.451″ bore).
Barrel: 6¾″, octagonal, rifled.
Length: 12¾″ over-all.
Stocks: Selected hardwood.
Features: Case hardened lock, brass furniture, fixed sights. Steel ramrod. Available in either flint or percussion. Imported by CVA.
Price: Percussion **$69.95**
Also available in kit form, either flint or percussion. Stock 95% inletted.
Price: Flint **$59.95**
Price: Percussion **$49.95**

J&S HAWKEN PERCUSSION PISTOL
Caliber: 50, uses 50-cal. mini; 54, uses 54-cal. mini.
Barrel: 9″.
Weight: 41 oz. **Length:** 14″ over-all.
Stock: European walnut with checkered grip.
Sights: Fixed.
Features: Blued steel barrel with swivel-type rammer, three-quarter stocked, adj. single set trigger, German silver furniture, scroll engraved lock. From Navy Arms.
Price: Finished, either cal. **$200.00**

BLACK POWDER SINGLE SHOT PISTOLS—FLINT & PERCUSSION

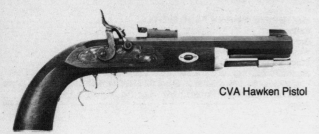

CVA Hawken Pistol

CVA HAWKEN PISTOL
Caliber: 50.
Barrel: 9¾", octagonal, 1" flats; rifled.
Weight: 50 oz. **Length:** 16½" over-all.
Stock: Select walnut.
Sights: Beaded blade front, fully adjustable rear.
Features: Hooked breech, early-style brass trigger. Color case-hardened lock plate; brass wedge plate, nose cap, ramrod thimbles, trigger guard, grip cap; blue barrel and sights.
Price: Finished, percussion **$106.95**
Price: Finished, flintlock **$116.95**
Price: Kit, percussion. **$69.95**
Price: Kit, flintlock. **$79.95**

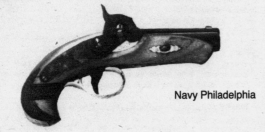

Dixie Overcoat Pistol

CVA MOUNTAIN PISTOL
Caliber: 45 or 50 cal.
Barrel: 9", octagon. ¹⁵/₁₆" across flats.
Weight: 40 oz. **Length:** 14" over-all.
Stock: Select hardwood.
Sights: German silver blade front, fixed primitive rear.
Features: Engraved color case-hardened lock. Adjustable sear engagement. Fly and bridle. Hooked breech. Browned steel on finished pistol. German silver wedge plates. Stainless steel nipples. Hardwood ramrod. Belt hook optional. Introduced 1978. From CVA.
Price: **$124.95**
Price: Kit form **$109.95**

Navy Philadelphia

DIXIE OVERCOAT PISTOL
Caliber: 39.
Barrel: 4", smoothbore.
Weight: 13 oz. **Length:** 8" over-all.
Stock: Walnut-finished hardwood. Checkered p.g.
Sights: Bead front.
Features: Shoots .380" balls. Breech plug and engraved lock are burnished steel finish; barrel and trigger guard blued.
Price: Engraved model **$34.50**

Dixie Philadelphia

DIXIE LINCOLN DERRINGER
Caliber: 41.
Barrel: 2", 8 lands, 8 grooves.
Weight: 7 oz. **Length:** 5½" over-all.
Stock: Walnut finish, checkered.
Sights: Fixed.
Features: Authentic copy of the "Lincoln Derringer." Shoots .400" patched ball. German silver furniture includes trigger guard with pineapple finial, wedge plates, nose, wrist, side and teardrop inlays. All furniture, lockplate, hammer, and breech plug engraved. Imported from Italy by Dixie Gun Works.
Price: With wooden case **$159.95**
Price: Kit (not engraved) **$59.95**

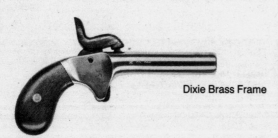

Dixie Brass Frame

PHILADELPHIA DERRINGER PERCUSSION PISTOL
Caliber: 45.
Barrel: 3⅛".
Weight: 14 oz. **Length:** 7" over-all.
Stock: Walnut, checkered grip.
Sights: Fixed.
Features: Engraved wedge holder and bbl. Also available in flintlock version (Armoury, $29.95). Imported by Sile (45-cal. only), CVA (45-cal. percussion only), Navy Arms, Toledo Armas.
Price: . . . . **$18.37 to $131.00**
Price: Kit form (CVA, Navy Arms) **$98.50**

DIXIE BRASS FRAME DERRINGER
Caliber: 41.
Barrel: 2½".
Weight: 7 oz. **Length:** 5½" over-all.
Stocks: Walnut.
Features: Brass frame, color case hardened hammer and trigger. Shoots .395" round ball. Engraved model available. From Dixie Gun Works.
Price: Plain model **$49.95**
Price: Engraved model **$59.95**
Price: Kit form, plain model **$37.50**

DIXIE PHILADELPHIA DERRINGER
Caliber: 41.
Barrel: 3½", octagon.
Weight: 8 oz. **Length:** 5½" over-all.
Stock: Walnut, checkered p.g.
Sights: Fixed.
Features: Barrel and lock are blued; brass furniture. From Dixie Gun Works.
Price: **$45.00**

CAUTION: PRICES CHANGE. CHECK AT GUNSHOP.

BLACK POWDER SINGLE SHOT PISTOLS—FLINT & PERCUSSION

Dixie Abilene

DIXIE ABILENE DERRINGER
Caliber: 41.
Barrel: 2½", 6-groove rifling.
Weight: 8 oz. **Length:** 6½" over-all.
Stocks: Walnut.
Features: All steel version of Dixie's brass-framed derringers. Blued barrel, color case hardened frame and hammer. Shoots .395" patched ball. Comes with wood presentation case.
Price: $54.95
Price: Kit form $45.00

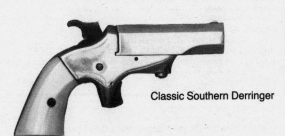

Classic Southern Derringer

CLASSIC ARMS SOUTHERN DERRINGER
Caliber: 44.
Barrel: 2½".
Weight: 12 oz. **Length:** 5" over-all.
Stock: White plastic.
Sights: Blade front.
Features: Percussion, uses .440" round ball. Brass frame, steel barrel. Introduced 1982. Made in U.S. by Classic Arms Ltd.
Price: $84.95
Price: Kit $54.00

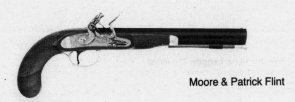

Le Page Dueling Pistol

NAVY ARMS LE PAGE DUELING PISTOL
Caliber: 44.
Barrel: 9", octagon.
Weight: 34 oz. **Length:** 15" over-all.
Stock: European walnut.
Sights: Adjustable rear.
Features: Single set trigger. Silvered metal finish. From Navy Arms.
Price: $300.00
Price: Single cased set $400.00
Price: Double cased set $700.00

BRITISH DRAGOON FLINT PISTOL
Caliber: .615".
Barrel: 12", polished steel.
Weight: 3 lbs., 2 oz. **Length:** 19" over-all.
Stock: Walnut, with brass furniture.
Features: Lockplate marked "Willets 1761." Brass trigger guard and butt cap. Made in U.S. by Navy Arms.
Price: $395.00
Price: Kit $295.00

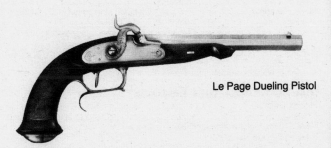

British Dragoon Flint

MOORE & PATRICK FLINT DUELING PISTOL
Caliber: 45.
Barrel: 10", rifled.
Weight: 32 oz. **Length:** 14½" over-all.
Stock: European walnut, checkered.
Sights: Fixed.
Features: Engraved, silvered lock plate, blue barrel. German silver furniture. Imported from Italy by Dixie and Navy Arms.
Price: .... $200.00 to $225.00

Moore & Patrick Flint

H & A ENGLISH FLINTLOCK TARGET PISTOL
Caliber: 45.
Barrel: 10".
Weight: 2 lbs. 4 oz. **Length:** 15" over-all.
Stock: English walnut with checkered grip.
Sights: Fixed.
Features: Engraved lock in white, browned barrel, German silver furniture. Special roller bearing frizzen spring. Also available in percussion lock. From Hopkins & Allen.
Price: $254.30

F. Rochatte Pistol

F. ROCHATTE PERCUSSION PISTOL
Caliber: 45, uses .440" round ball.
Barrel: 10".
Weight: 32 oz. **Length:** 16½" over-all.
Stock: European walnut.
Sights: Dovetailed front and rear, adj. for windage.
Features: Single adj. trigger, highly polished lock and round barrel with top flat; all steel furniture. French-style finial on butt. From Navy Arms.
Price: Finished gun $250.00

John Manton Pistol

W. Parker Pistol

H & A 1810 Dueller

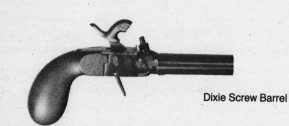

Dixie Screw Barrel

JOHN MANTON MATCH PISTOL
Caliber: 45, uses .440" round ball.
Barrel: 10", rifled.
Weight: 36 oz. **Length:** 15½" over-all.
Stock: European walnut; checkered grip.
Sights: Bead front.
Features: Highly polished steel barrel and lock, brass furniture. From Navy Arms.
Price: Finished gun **$225.00**

W. PARKER PERCUSSION PISTOL
Caliber: 45, uses .440" round ball.
Barrel: 10", rifled.
Weight: 40 oz. **Length:** 16" over-all.
Stock: European walnut; checkered grip.
Sights: Dovetailed front and rear, adj.for windage.
Features: Fully adj. double set triggers, German silver furniture; lock engraved "London." From Navy Arms.
Price: Finished gun **$250.00**
Price: As above from Dixie, 11" bbl........................... **$250.00**

H&A 1810 ENGLISH DUELING PISTOL
Caliber: 45.
Barrel: 11".
Weight: 2 lbs., 5 oz. **Length:** 15" over-all.
Stock: European walnut, checkered, with German silver inlays.
Sights: Fixed.
Features: Double set triggers, precision "match" barrel, silver plated furniture, browned barrel. Percussion lock only. From Hopkins & Allen.
Price: **$265.30**

DIXIE SCREW BARREL PISTOL
Caliber: .445".
Barrel: 2½".
Weight: 8 oz. **Length:** 6½" over-all.
Stocks: Walnut.
Features: Trigger folds down when hammer is cocked. Close copy of the originals once made in Belgium. Uses No. 11 percussion caps.
Price: **$79.95**

T.G.A. LIEGE DERRINGER
Caliber: 451".
Barrel: 2⅜".
Weight: 7 oz. **Length:** 6½" over-all.
Stock: Walnut.
Sights: None.
Features: Removable round, rifled barrel. All metal parts case-hardened. Folding trigger. Introduced 1980. From Trail Guns Armory.
Price: Deluxe engraved model with case and flask **$99.00**

CLASSIC ARMS ELGIN CUTLASS PISTOL
Caliber: 44 (.440").
Barrel: 4¼".
Weight: 21 oz. **Length:** 12" over-all.
Stock: Walnut.
Sights: None.
Features: Replica of the pistol used by the U.S. Navy as a boarding weapon. Smoothbore barrel. Available as a kit or finished. Made in U.S. by Navy Arms.
Price: Kit **$78.50**
Price: Finished **$104.95**

Elgin Cutlass Pistol

H & A Target Boot

HOPKINS & ALLEN BOOT PISTOL
Caliber: 36 or 45.
Barrel: 6".
Weight: 42 oz. **Length:** 13" over-all.
Stock: Walnut.
Sights: Silver blade front; rear adj. for e.
Features: Under-hammer design. From Hopkins & Allen.
Price: **$71.50**
Price: Kit form.. **$55.20**
Price: Target version with wood fore-end, ramrod, hood front sight, elevator rear **$89.80**

CAUTION: PRICES CHANGE. CHECK AT GUNSHOP.

BLACK POWDER SINGLE SHOT PISTOLS—FLINT & PERCUSSION

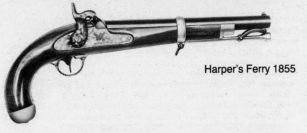

Harper's Ferry 1855

HARPER'S FERRY MODEL 1855 PERCUSSION PISTOL
Caliber: 58.
Barrel: 11¾", rifled.
Weight: 56 oz. **Length:** 18" over-all.
Stock: Walnut.
Sights: Fixed.
Features: Case hardened lock and hammer; brass furniture; blued bbl. Shoulder stock available, priced at $35.00. Imported by Navy Arms and Dixie.
Price: $218.50
Price: From Dixie $135.00
Price: With detachable shoulder stock $263.50

Thompson/Center Patriot

THOMPSON/CENTER PATRIOT PERCUSSION PISTOL
Caliber: 36, 45.
Barrel: 9¼".
Weight: 36 oz. **Length:** 16" over-all.
Stock: Walnut.
Sights: Patridge-type. Rear adj. for w. and e.
Features: Hook breech system; double set triggers; coil mainspring. From Thompson/Center Arms.
Price: $185.00

Dixie Tornado Target

> Consult our Directory pages for the location of firms mentioned.

DIXIE TORNADO TARGET PISTOL
Caliber: 45 (.445" round ball).
Barrel: 10", octagonal
Stock: Walnut, target-style. Left unfinished for custom fitting. Walnut fore-end.
Sights: Blade on ramp front, micro-type open rear adjustable for windage and elevation.
Features: Grip frame style of 1860 Colt revolver. Improved model of the Tingle and B.W. Southgate pistol. Trigger adjustable for pull. Frame, barrel, hammer and sights in the white, brass trigger guard. Comes with solid brass, walnut-handled cleaning rod with jag and nylon muzzle protector. Introduced 1983. From Dixie Gun Works.
Price: $145.00

BUCCANEER DOUBLE BARREL PISTOL
Caliber: 44.
Barrel: 9½".
Weight: 40 oz. **Length:** 15½" over-all.
Stock: Walnut, one piece.
Sights: Fixed.
Features: Case hardened and engraved lockplate, solid brass fittings. Percussion or flintlock. Imported by The Armoury. Available as the "Corsair" from Armsport, Sile.
Price: Complete $103.75
Price: Kit form $92.50
Price: Corsair, complete .... $99.00 Kit $86.00

BLACK POWDER REVOLVERS

Colt 1847 Walker

COLT 1847 WALKER PERCUSSION REVOLVER
Caliber: 44.
Barrel: 9", 7 groove, RH twist.
Weight: 73 oz.
Stocks: One-piece walnut.
Sights: German silver front sight, hammer notch rear.
Features: Made in U.S. by Colt. Faithful reproduction of the original gun, including markings. Color cased frame, hammer, loading lever and plunger. Blue steel backstrap, brass square-back trigger guard. Blue barrel, cylinder, trigger and wedge. Accessories available. Re-introduced 1979. Limited supplies available.
Price: $449.50

WALKER 1847 PERCUSSION REVOLVER
Caliber: 44, 6-shot.
Barrel: 9".
Weight: 72 oz. **Length:** 15½" over-all.
Stocks: Walnut.
Sights: Fixed.
Features: Case hardened frame, loading lever and hammer; iron backstrap; brass trigger guard; engraved cylinder. Imported by Sile, Navy Arms, Dixie, Armsport, Allen Firearms.
Price: .... $125.00 to $229.00
Price: Single cased set (Navy Arms) $264.00

Walker 1847

CAUTION: PRICES CHANGE. CHECK AT GUNSHOP.

BLACK POWDER REVOLVERS

Colt First Dragoon

COLT 1st MODEL DRAGOON
Caliber: 44.
Barrel: 7½", part round, part octagon.
Weight: 66 oz.
Stocks: One piece walnut.
Sights: German silver blade front, hammer notch rear.
Features: First model has oval bolt cuts in cylinder, square-back flared trigger guard, V-type mainspring, short trigger. Ranger and Indian scene on cylinder. Color cased frame, loading lever, plunger and hammer; blue barrel, cylinder, trigger and wedge. Polished brass backstrap and trigger guard. Re-introduced in 1979. From Colt. Limited supplies available.
Price: **$358.50**
Price: Same gun except markings, from Allen Firearms **$224.00**

Colt 3rd Model Dragoon Revolver
Similar to the 1st Model except has oval trigger guard, long trigger, flat mainspring and rectangular bolt cuts. Limited supplies available.
Price: **$358.50**
Price: Same gun except markings, from Allen Firearms **$224.00**
Price: With silver plated guard and backstrap or as Confederate Tucker & Sherrard, Allen Firearms **$240.00**

Colt 2nd Model Dragoon Revolver
Similar to the 1st Model except this model is distinguished by its rectangular bolt cuts in the cylinder, straight square-back trigger guard, short trigger and flat mainspring with roller in hammer. Limited supplies available.
Price: **$358.50**
Price: Same gun except markings, from Allen Firearms **$224.00**

Dixie Third Dragoon

DIXIE THIRD MODEL DRAGOON
Caliber: 44 ((.454" round ball).
Barrel: 7⅜".
Weight: 4 lbs., 2½ oz.
Stocks: One-piece walnut.
Sights: Brass pin front, hammer notch rear, or adjustable folding leaf rear.
Features: Cylinder engraved with Indian fight scene; steel backstrap with polished brass backstrap; color case-hardened steel frame, blue-black barrel. Imported by Dixie Gun Works.
Price: **$140.00**

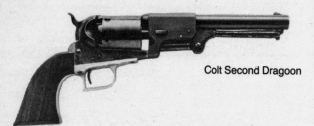

Colt Second Dragoon

COLT BABY DRAGOON REVOLVER
Caliber: 31.
Barrel: 4", 7 groove, RH twist.
Weight: About 21 oz.
Stocks: Varnished walnut.
Sights: Brass pin front, hammer notch rear.
Features: Unfluted cylinder with Ranger and Indian scene; cupped cylinder pin; no grease grooves; one safety pin on cylinder and slot in hammer face; straight (flat) mainspring. Silver backstrap and trigger guard. Re-introduced in 1979. From Colt.
Price: **$324.50**
Price: Same gun except markings, with choice of 3", 4", 5" barrel, from Allen Firearms **$190.00**

Dixie Baby Dragoon

BABY DRAGOON 1848 PERCUSSION REVOLVER
Caliber: 31, 5-shot.
Barrel: 4", 5", 6".
Weight: 24 oz. (6" bbl.). **Length:** 10½" (6" bbl.).
Stocks: Walnut.
Sights: Fixed.
Features: Case hardened frame; safety notches on hammer and safety pin in cylinder; engraved cylinder scene; octagonal bbl. Imported by F.I.E., Dixie (5" only), Allen.
Price: . . . . **$59.95 to $184.00**

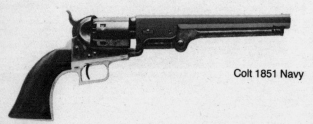

Colt 1851 Navy

COLT 1851 NAVY PERCUSSION REVOLVER
Caliber: 36.
Barrel: 7½", octagonal, 7 groove, LH twist.
Weight: 42 oz.
Stocks: One-piece varnished walnut.
Sights: Brass pin front, hammer notch rear.
Features: Faithful reproduction of the original gun. Color cased frame, loading lever, plunger, hammer and latch. Blue cylinder, trigger, barrel, screws, wedge. Silver plated brass backstrap and square-back trigger guard. Accessories available. Re-introduced in 1979. Limited supplies available.
Price: **$335.95**
Price: London model, from Allen Firearms **$201.00**

CAUTION: PRICES CHANGE. CHECK AT GUNSHOP.

BLACK POWDER REVOLVERS

Dixie 1851 Navy

1851 NAVY-SHERIFF
Same as 1851 Sheriff model except: 4" barrel, fluted cylinder, belt ring in butt. Imported by Richland, Sile, Euroarms of America.
Price: .... **$50.00 to $114.95**

1851 SHERIFF MODEL PERCUSSION REVOLVER
Caliber: 36, 44, 6-shot.
Barrel: 5".
Weight: 40 oz. **Length:** 10½" over-all.
Stocks: Walnut.
Sights: Fixed.
Features: Brass backstrap and trigger guard; engraved navy scene; case hardened frame, hammer, loading lever. Available with brass frame from some importers at slightly lower prices. Imported by Sile, The Armoury.
Price: Steel frame .... **$41.95 to $110.00**
Price: Brass frame .... **$34.95 to $102.00**
Price: Kit, brass or steel frame (Sile) **$66.15**

1851 Squareback Navy 36
Same as standard Colt model except 36 cal. only, has earlier square-back trigger guard, nickel plated backstrap, color case hardened frame. From Lyman, Euroarms, Allen.
Price: **$200.00**
Price: Kit form. **$119.95**
Price: Stainless steel (Allen) **$250.00**

Colt 1861 Navy

Dixie New Model Army

Colt 1860 Army

NAVY MODEL 1851 PERCUSSION REVOLVER
Caliber: 36 or 44, 6-shot.
Barrel: 7½".
Weight: 44 oz. **Length:** 13" over-all.
Stocks: Walnut finish.
Sights: Post front, hammer notch rear.
Features: Brass backstrap and trigger guard; some have engraved cylinder with navy battle scene; case hardened frame, hammer, loading lever. Imported by Shore, (36 cal. only), The Armoury, Navy Arms, F.I.E., Dixie, (illus.) Richland, Euroarms of America, Sile, Armsport, Hopkins & Allen, CVA.
Price: Brass frame .... **$31.50 to $119.95**
Price: Steel frame .... **$40.95 to $140.95**
Price: Kit form .... **$30.95 to $93.00**
Price: Engraved model (Dixie) **$97.50**
Price: Also as "Hartford Pistol," Kit (Richard) ...... **$59.95** Complete **$79.95**
Price: Also as "Hartford Dragoon Buntline" (Hopkins & Allen) **$166.95**
Price: Navy-Civilian model (Navy Arms) **$124.50**
Price: Single cased set, steel frame (Navy Arms) **$207.00**
Price: Double cased set, steel frame (Navy Arms) **$339.75**
Price: As above, civilian model (Navy Arms) **$212.00**
Price: Double cased set, civilian model (Navy Arms) **$350.00**
Price: Shoulder stock (Navy Arms) **$45.00**

ARMY 1851 PERCUSSION REVOLVER
Caliber: 44, 6-shot.
Barrel: 7½".
Weight: 45 oz. **Length:** 13" over-all.
Stocks: Walnut finish.
Sights: Fixed.
Features: 44 caliber version of the 1851 Navy. Imported by Sile, The Armoury.
Price: .... **$33.50 to $138.00**

Colt 1861 Navy Percussion Revolver
Similar to 1851 Navy except has round 7½" barrel, rounded trigger guard, German silver blade front sight, "creeping" loading lever. Limited supplies available.
Price: **$335.95**
Price: Same gun except markings, from Allen Firearms **$210.00**

NEW MODEL 1858 ARMY PERCUSSION REVOLVER
Caliber: 36 or 44, 6-shot.
Barrel: 6½" or 8".
Weight: 40 oz. **Length:** 13½" over-all.
Stocks: Walnut.
Sights: Blade front, groove-in-frame rear.
Features: Replica of Remington Model 1858. Also available from some importers as Army Model Belt Revolver in 36 cal., shortened and lightened version of the 44. Target Model (Iver Johnson, Navy) has fully adj. target rear sight, target front, 36 or 44 ($74.95-$209.00). Imported by CVA, (as 1858 Remington Army), Dixie, Navy Arms, F.I.E., Iver Johnson, The Armoury, Shore (44 cal., 8" bbl. only), Richland, Euroarms of America (engraved, stainless and plain), Armsport, Sile, Allen.
Price: .... **$49.95 to $198.00**
Price: Single cased set (Navy Arms) **$225.00**
Price: Double cased set (Navy Arms) **$375.00**
Price: Kit form .... **$66.95 to $123.95**
Price: Nickel finish (Navy Arms) **$152.75**
Price: Single cased set (Navy Arms) **$240.00**
Price: Double cased set (Navy Arms) **$400.00**
Price: Stainless steel (Euroarms, Navy Arms, Sile, Allen) **$140.00 to $200.00**
Price: Target model (Sile, Euroarms, Navy Arms, Allen) .. **$95.95 to $185.00**

COLT 1860 ARMY PERCUSSION REVOLVER
Caliber: 44.
Barrel: 8", 7 grooves, LH twist.
Weight: 42 oz.
Stocks: One-piece walnut.
Sights: German silver front sight, hammer notch rear.
Features: Made in U.S. by Colt. Steel backstrap cut for shoulder stock; brass trigger guard. Cylinder has Navy scene. Color case hardened frame, hammer, loading lever. Basically a continuation of production with all original markings, etc. Original-type accessories available. Re-introduced 1979. Limited supplies available.
Price: Unfluted cylinder. **$344.50**
Price: Fluted cylinder model. **$364.50**

BLACK POWDER REVOLVERS

Dixie 1860 Army

CVA 1860 ARMY REVOLVER
Caliber: 44, 6-shot.
Barrel: 8″ round.
Weight: 44 oz. **Length:** 13½″ over-all.
Stocks: One-piece walnut.
Sights: Blade front, hammer-notch rear.
Features: Engraved cylinder, creeping-style loading lever, solid brass trigger guard, blued barrel. Introduced 1982. From CVA.
Price: Finished $157.95
Price: Kit $121.95

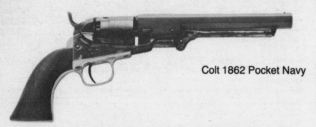

Colt 1862 Pocket Navy

Dixie Spiller & Burr

Dixie "Wyatt Earp"

DIXIE "WYATT EARP" REVOLVER
Caliber: 44.
Barrel: 12″ octagon.
Weight: 46 oz. **Length:** 18″ over-all.
Stocks: Two piece walnut.
Sights: Fixed.
Features: Highly polished brass frame, backstrap and trigger guard; blued barrel and cylinder; case hardened hammer, trigger and loading lever. Navy-size shoulder stock ($45.00) will fit with minor fitting. From Dixie Gun Works.
Price: $99.95

SPILLER & BURR REVOLVER
Caliber: 36 (.375″ round ball).
Barrel: 7″, octagon.
Weight: 2½ lbs. **Length:** 12½″ over-all.
Stocks: Two-piece walnut.
Sights: Fixed.
Features: Reproduction of the C.S.A. revolver. Brass frame and trigger guard. Also available as a kit. From Dixie, Navy Arms.
Price: .... $69.95 to $109.00
Price: Kit form .... $39.95 to $65.00

1860 ARMY PERCUSSION REVOLVER
Caliber: 44, 6-shot.
Barrel: 8″.
Weight: 40 oz. **Length:** 13⅝″ over-all.
Stocks: Walnut.
Sights: Fixed.
Features: Engraved navy scene on cylinder; brass trigger guard; case hardened frame, loading lever and hammer. Some importers supply pistol cut for detachable shoulder stock, have accessory stock available. Imported by Navy Arms, Shore, The Armoury, Dixie (half-fluted cylinder, not roll engraved), Lyman, Iver Johnson, Richland, Euroarms of America (engraved, stainless steel or burnished steel model), Armsport, Sile, Hopkins & Allen, Allen.
Price: .... $44.95 to $178.00
Price: Single cased set (Navy Arms) $220.00
Price: Double cased set (Navy Arms) $365.00
Price: 1861 Navy: Same as Army except 36 cal., 7½″ bbl., wt. 41 oz., cut for stock; round cylinder (fluted avail.), from Navy $142.00
Price: Single cased set (Navy Arms) $230.00
Price: Double cased set (Navy Arms) $386.50
Price: Kit (Lyman, Sile) $134.95
Price: Stainless steel (Euroarms, Allen)........... $200.00 to $260.00
Price: Brass frame (Allen) $125.00

1861 NAVY MODEL REVOLVER
Caliber: 36, 44, 6-shot.
Barrel: 7½″.
Weight: 2½ lbs. **Length:** 13″ over-all.
Stocks: One piece smooth walnut.
Sights: Blade front, hammer notch rear.
Features: Shoots .380″ ball. Case hardened frame, loading lever and hammer. Cut for shoulder stock. Non-fluted cylinder. From CVA (brass frame, 44-cal.), Navy Arms, Armsport, Euroarms of America, Allen.
Price: .... $100.00 to $155.95
Price: Blued steel backstrap, trigger guard (Navy Arms) $142.00
Price: With full fluted cyl. .... $100.00 to $142.00
Price: Single cased set (Navy Arms) $230.00
Price: Double cased set (Navy Arms) $386.50
Price: Kit form (CVA) $114.95
Price: 44 cal. (CVA) $99.95
Price: 44 cal. kit (CVA) $79.95
Price: Stainless steel (Allen) $260.00

COLT 1862 POCKET NAVY PERCUSSION REVOLVER
Caliber: 36.
Barrel: 5½″, octagonal, 7 groove, LH twist.
Weight: 27 oz.
Stocks: One piece varnished walnut.
Sights: Brass pin front, hammer notch rear.
Features: Rebated cylinder, hinged loading lever, silver plated backstrap and trigger guard, color cased frame, hammer, loading lever, plunger and latch, rest blued. Has original-type markings. Re-introduced 1979. Limited supplies available.
Price: $315.50
Price: Same gun except markings, from Allen Firearms $205.00

Colt 1862 Pocket Police Revolver
Similar to 1862 Pocket Navy except has 5½″ round barrel, fluted cylinder, different markings and loading lever. Faithful reproduction of the original gun.
Price: $315.50

1862 POCKET POLICE PERCUSSION REVOLVER
Caliber: 36, 5-shot.
Barrel: 5½″, 7½″.
Weight: 26 oz. **Length:** 12″ (6½″ bbl.).
Stocks: Walnut.
Sights: Fixed.
Features: Half-fluted and rebated cylinder; case hardened frame, loading lever and hammer; silver trigger guard and backstrap. Imported by Navy Arms (5½″ only), Euroarms of America, Allen.
Price: $205.00
Price: Cased with accessories (Navy Arms) $180.00
Price: Stainless steel (Allen) $255.00

CAUTION: PRICES CHANGE. CHECK AT GUNSHOP.

BLACK POWDER REVOLVERS

ROGERS & SPENCER PERCUSSION REVOLVER
Caliber: 44.
Barrel: 7½".
Weight: 47 oz. **Length:** 13¾" over-all.
Stocks: Walnut.
Sights: Cone front, integral groove in frame for rear.
Features: Accurate reproduction of a Civil War design. Solid frame; extra large nipple cut-out on rear of cylinder; loading lever and cylinder easily removed for cleaning. Comes with six spare nipples and wrench/screwdriver. From Euroarms of America, (engraved, burnished, target models) Navy Arms, Dixie, Sile.
Price: .... $120.00 to $169.00
Price: Nickel plated $120.00
Price: Kit version $95.00
Price: Target version $200.00

Consult our Directory pages for the location of firms mentioned.

NAVY ARMS 1862 LEECH & RIGDON REVOLVER
Caliber: 375".
Barrel: 7½".
Weight: 2 lbs., 10 oz. **Length:** 13½" over-all.
Stocks: Smooth walnut.
Sights: Fixed.
Features: Modern version of the famous Civil War revolver. Brass backstrap and trigger guard. Color case hardened frame. Copy of the Colt Navy but with round barrel. From Navy Arms.
Price: $136.50

GRISWOLD & GUNNISON PERCUSSION REVOLVER
Caliber: 36, 44, 6-shot.
Barrel: 7½".
Weight: 44 oz. (36 cal.). **Length:** 13" over-all.
Stocks: Walnut.
Sights: Fixed.
Features: Replica of famous Confederate pistol. Brass frame, backstrap and trigger guard; case hardened loading lever; rebated cylinder (44 cal. only). Imported by Navy Arms, Sile, Allen.
Price: $125.00
Price: As above from Sile (1851 Confederate) $75.90
Price: Kit (Navy Arms) $76.75
Price: Single cased set (Navy Arms) $180.00
Price: Double cased set (Navy Arms) $288.00
Price: Shoulder stock (Navy Arms) $45.00

Ruger Old Army

RUGER 44 OLD ARMY PERCUSSION REVOLVER
Caliber: 44, 6-shot. Uses .457" dia. lead bullets.
Barrel: 7½" (6-groove, 16" twist).
Weight: 46 oz. **Length:** 13½" over-all.
Stocks: Smooth walnut.
Sights: Ramp front, rear adj. for w. and e.
Features: Stainless steel standard size nipples, chrome-moly steel cylinder and frame, same lockwork as in original Super Blackhawk. Also available in stainless steel in very limited quantities. Made in USA. From Sturm, Ruger & Co.
Price: Stainless steel (Model KBP-7) $285.00
Price: Blued steel (Model BP-7) $216.50

Freedom Mini Percussion

FREEDOM ARMS PERCUSSION MINI REVOLVER
Caliber: 22, 5-shot.
Barrel: 1", 1¾", 3".
Weight: 4¾ oz. (1" bbl.).
Stocks: Simulated ivory or ebony, or rosewood (optional).
Sights: Fixed.
Features: Percussion version of the 22 RF gun. All stainless steel; spur trigger. Gun comes with leather carrying pouch, bullet setting tool, powder measure, 20 29-gr. bullets. Introduced 1983. From Freedom Arms.
Price: 1" barrel $146.85
Price: 1¾" barrel $151.85
Price: 3" barrel $167.90

BLACK POWDER MUSKETS & RIFLES

Dixie Brown Bess

DIXIE SECOND MODEL BROWN BESS
Caliber: 74.
Barrel: 41¾" smoothbore.
Weight: 9½ lbs. **Length:** 57¾".
Stock: Walnut-finished hardwood.
Sights: Fixed.
Features: All metal finished bright. Brass furniture. Lock marked "Tower" and has a crown with "GR" underneath. From Dixie Gun Works.
Price: $275.00
Price: Kit form $245.00
Price: "Musketoon" (same as above but with 30" bbl., brown finish on metal) $295.00

BLACK POWDER MUSKETS & RIFLES

Dixie Indian Gun

DIXIE INDIAN GUN
Caliber: 75.
Barrel: 31″, round tapered.
Weight: About 9 lbs. **Length:** 47″ over-all.
Stock: Hardwood.
Sights: Blade front.
Features: Modified Brown Bess musket; brass furniture, browned lock and barrel. Lock is marked "GRICE 1762" with crown over "GR." Serpent-style sideplate. Introduced 1983.
Price: Complete $375.00
Price: As above, in kit form $360.00

NAVY ARMS BROWN BESS MUSKET
Caliber: 75, uses .735″ round ball.
Barrel: 42″, smoothbore.
Weight: 9½ lbs. **Length:** 59″ over-all.
Stock: Walnut.
Sights: Fixed.
Features: Polished barrel and lock with brass trigger guard and buttplate. Bayonet and scabbard available. From Navy Arms.
Price: Finished $450.00
Price: Kit $342.00
Price: Finished gun with maple stock $295.00

NAVY ARMS CHARLEVILLE MUSKET
Caliber: 69
Barrel: 44⅝″.
Weight: 8¾ lbs. **Length:** 59⅜″ over-all.
Stock: Walnut.
Sights: Blade front.
Features: Replica of Revolutionary War 1763 musket. Bright metal, walnut stock. From Navy Arms.
Price: Finished $380.00
Price: Kit $310.00

CVA Squirrel Rifle

CVA SQUIRREL RIFLE
Caliber: 32.
Barrel: 25″, octagonal; 1¹⁄₁₆″ flats.
Weight: 5 lbs., 12 oz. **Length:** 40¾″ over-all.
Stock: Hardwood.
Sights: Beaded blade front, fully adjustable hunting-style rear.
Features: Color case-hardened lock plate, brass buttplate, trigger guard, wedge plates, thimbles; double-set triggers; hooked breech; authentic V-type mainspring. Introduced 1983. From CVA.
Price: Finished, percussion $189.95
Price: Finished, flintlock $199.95
Price: Kit, percussion $134.95
Price: Kit, flintlock $144.95

> Consult our Directory pages for
> the location of firms mentioned.

CVA FRONTIER RIFLE
Caliber: 50.
Barrel: 28″, octagon; ¹⁵⁄₁₆″ flats, 1-66″ twist.
Weight: 6 lbs., 14 oz. **Length:** 44″ over-all.
Stock: American hardwood.
Sights: Brass blade front, fully adjustable hunting-style rear.
Features: Available in flint or percussion. Solid brass nosecap, trigger guard, buttplate, thimbles and wedge plates; blued barrel; color case-hardened lock and hammer. Double set triggers, patented breech plug bolster, V-type mainspring. Hooked breech. Introduced 1980.
Price: 50 cal., percussion, complete rifle $204.95
Price: 50-Cal. flint, complete rifle $214.95
Price: 50 cal., percussion, kit $149.95
Price: 50 cal. flint, kit $159.95

CVA KENTUCKY RIFLE
Caliber: 45 (.451″ bore).
Barrel: 33½″, rifled, octagon (⅞″ flats).
Length: 48″ over-all.
Stock: Select hardwood.
Sights: Brass Kentucky blade type front, dovetail open rear.
Features: Available in either flint or percussion. Stainless steel nipple included. From CVA.
Price: Percussion.. $184.95
Price: Flint.. $194.95
Price: Percussion Kit...................................... $109.95
Price: Flint Kit... $117.95

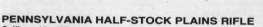

Hatfield Squirrel Rifle

HATFIELD SQUIRREL RIFLE
Caliber: 32, 36, 45, 50
Barrel: 39½″, octagon, 32″ on half-stock.
Weight: 8 lbs. (32 cal.).
Stock: American fancy maple (full-stock); Missouri black walnut (half-stock).
Sights: Silver blade front, buckhorn rear
Features: Recreation of the traditional squirrel rifle. Available in flint or percussion with browned steel or brass trigger guard and buttplate. Half-stock in percussion only with brass furniture. From Hatfield Rifle Works. Introduced 1983.
Price: Full-stock... $699.95
Price: Half-stock, 45-cal. only $499.95
Price: Full-stock, 36-cal., percussion $599.95

PENNSYLVANIA HALF-STOCK PLAINS RIFLE
Caliber: 45 or 50.
Barrel: 32″ rifled, ¹⁵⁄₁₆″ dia.
Weight: 8½ lbs.
Stock: Walnut.
Sights: Fixed.
Features: Available in flint or percussion. Blued lock and barrel, brass furniture. Offered complete or in kit form. From The Armoury.
Price: Flint.. $235.00
Price: Percussion.. $210.00

CAUTION: PRICES CHANGE. CHECK AT GUNSHOP.

Dixie Tennessee Rifle

DIXIE TENNESSEE MOUNTAIN RIFLE

Caliber: 32 or 50.
Barrel: 41½", 6-groove rifling, brown finish.
Length: 56" over-all.
Stock: Walnut, oil finish; Kentucky-style.
Sights: Silver blade front, open buckhorn rear.
Features: Re-creation of the original mountain rifles. Early Schultz lock, interchangeable flint or percussion with vent plug or drum and nipple. Tumbler has fly. Double-set triggers. All metal parts browned. From Dixie.
Price: Flint or Percussion, finished rifle, 50 cal. $250.00
Price: Kit, 50 cal. $195.00
Price: Left-hand model, flint or perc.. . . . . $250.00
Price: Left-hand kit, flint or perc., 50 cal. $225.00
Price: Squirrel Rifle (as above except in 32 cal. with ¹³⁄₁₆" barrel), flint or percussion $295.00
Price: Kit, 32 cal., flint or percussion $255.00

CVA MOUNTAIN RIFLE

Caliber: 50.
Barrel: 32", octagon; ¹⁵⁄₁₆" across flats; 1-66" twist.
Weight: 7 lbs., 14 oz. **Length:** 48" over-all.
Stock: Select hardwood with cheekpiece.
Sights: German silver blade front, screw-adj. rear.
Features: Available in percussion or flintlock. Engraved lock with adj. sear engagement; hooked breech with two barrel tenons; rifled 1-in-66"; double set triggers; German silver patch box, tenon plates, pewter-type nosecap; browned iron furniture. From CVA.
Price: Kit, percussion $189.95
Price: Kit, flintlock $199.95
Price: Finished rifle, percussion $284.95
Price: Finished rifle, flintlock $294.95

CVA Big Bore Mountain Rifle

Similar to the standard Mountain Rifle except comes in 54 or 58 cal. only. Barrel flats measure 1" across. Stock does not have a patch box. Introduced 1980.
Price: 54 cal., percussion, complete rifle $294.95
Price: 54 cal., percussion, kit. $209.95
Price: 58 cal. percussion, 1-72" twist, kit only $209.95

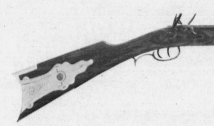

CVA Pennsylvania

CVA PENNSYLVANIA LONG RIFLE

Caliber: 50.
Barrel: 40", octagonal; ⅞" flats.
Weight: 8 lbs., 3 ozs. **Length:** 55¾" over-all.
Stock: Select walnut.
Sights: Brass blade front, fixed semi-buckhorn rear.
Features: Color case-hardened lock plate, brass buttplate, toe plate, patchbox, trigger guard, thimbles, nosecap; blued barrel, double-set triggers; authentic V-type mainspring. Introduced 1983. From CVA.
Price: Finished, percussion $289.95
Price: Finished, flintlock $299.95
Price: Kit, percussion $249.95
Price: Kit, flintlock $259.95

Dixie York County

YORK COUNTY RIFLE

Caliber: 45 (.445" round ball).
Barrel: 36", rifled, ⅞" octagon, blue.
Weight: 7½ lbs. **Length:** 51½" over-all.
Stock: Maple, one piece.
Sights: Blade front, V-notch rear, brass.
Features: Adjustable double-set triggers. Brass trigger guard, patchbox, buttplate, nosecap and sideplate. Case-hardened lockplate. From Dixie Gun Works.
Price: Percussion. $175.00
Price: Flint $190.00
Price: Percussion Kit $139.95
Price: Flint Kit $149.95

Dixie Trade Gun

DIXIE NORTHWEST TRADE GUN

Caliber/Gauge: 20 (.600" round ball or 1 oz.#6 shot).
Barrel: 36", smoothbore.
Weight: 7½ lbs. **Length:** 53½" over-all.
Stock: Walnut, 13½" pull.
Sights: Brass blade front only.
Features: Flintlock. Brass buttplate, serpentine sideplate; browned barrel, Wheeler flint lock, triggerguard; hickory ramrod with brass tip. From Dixie Gun Works.
Price: $450.00

BLACK POWDER MUSKETS & RIFLES

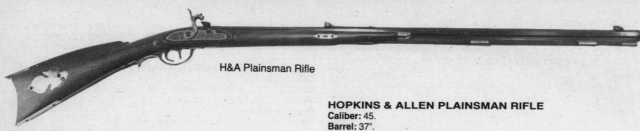

H&A Plainsman Rifle

KENTUCKY FLINTLOCK RIFLE
Caliber: 44 or 45.
Barrel: 35".
Weight: 7lbs. **Length:** 50" over-all.
Stock: Walnut stained, brass fittings.
Sights: Fixed.
Features: Available in Carbine model also, 28" bbl. Some variations in detail, finish. Kits also available from some importers. Imported by Navy Arms, The Armoury, F.I.E., CVA, Armsport, Hopkins & Allen, Sile, Shore (45-cal. only).
Price: .... $59.95 to $273.75
Price: Kit form (CVA, Numrich, F.I.E., Sile) .... $72.95 to 189.95
Price: Deluxe model, flint or percussion (Navy Arms, Sile), about ... $400.00
Price: As above, 50-cal. (Navy Arms) $273.75

MOWREY ETHAN ALLEN SQUIRREL RIFLE
Caliber: 32, 36, or 45.
Barrel: 28", 8-groove rifling, octagon, 1:60 twist.
Weight: 7½ lbs. **Length:** 43" over-all.
Stock: Curly maple.
Sights: Open, fully adj.
Features: Box-lock action, cut-rifled barrel, hand-rubbed oil finish. Available with either brass or browned steel furniture, action. Made in U.S.
Price: Complete $328.00
Price: Kit $237.00

HOPKINS & ALLEN PLAINSMAN RIFLE
Caliber: 45.
Barrel: 37".
Weight: 7½ lbs. **Length:** 53" over-all.
Stock: Walnut.
Sights: Blade front, rear adjustable for w. & e.
Features: Double set triggers, blued barrel has ¹³/₁₆" flats, solid brass barrel rib, engraved percussion lockplate. From Hopkins & Allen.
Price: $292.60

Kentucky Percussion Rifle
Similar to flintlock except percussion lock. Finish and features vary with importer. Imported by Navy Arms, F.I.E. Corp., The Armoury, CVA, Hopkins & Allen, Armsport (rifle-shotgun combo), Shore, Sile.
Price: .... $54.95 to 250.00
Price: Kit form (F.I.E., Sile) $169.95
Price: Armsport combo $295.00
Price: Deluxe model (Navy Arms) $375.00
Price: 50 cal. (Navy Arms) $246.00

Mowrey Ethan Allen Plains Rifle
Similar to Squirrel Rifle except in 50 or 54 caliber, 32" barrel, weighs 9½ lbs.
Price: Complete $328.00
Price: Kit $237.00

Lyman Great Plains

LYMAN GREAT PLAINS RIFLE
Caliber: 50 or 54 cal.
Barrel: 32", 1-66" twist.

Weight: 9 lbs.
Stock: Walnut.
Sights: Steel blade front, buckhorn rear adj. for w. & e. or fixed.
Features: Blued steel furniture. Coil spring lock, Hawken-style trigger guard and double set triggers. Round thimbles recessed and sweated into rib. Steel wedge plates and toe plates. Introduced 1980. From Lyman.
Price: Percussion... $354.95
Price: Flintlock $369.95
Price: Percussion Kit $249.95

Kentuckian Rifle

KENTUCKIAN RIFLE & CARBINE
Caliber: 44.
Barrel: 35" (Rifle), 27½" (Carbine).

Weight: 7 lbs. (Rifle), 5½ lbs. (Carbine). **Length:** 51" (Rifle) over-all, Carbine 43".
Stock: Walnut stain.
Sights: Brass blade front, steel V-Ramp rear.
Features: Octagon bbl., case hardened and engraved lock plate. Brass furniture. Imported by Dixie.
Price: Rifle or carbine, flint $185.00
Price: As above, percussion $175.00

Lyman Trade Rifle

LYMAN TRADE RIFLE
Caliber: 50 or 54.
Barrel: 28" octagon, 1-48" twist.

Weight: 8¾ lbs. **Length:** 45" over-all.
Stock: European walnut.
Sights: Blade front, open rear adj. for w. or optional fixed sights.
Features: Polished brass furniture with blue steel parts. Hook breech, single trigger, coil spring percussion lock. Steel barrel rib and ramrod ferrules. Introduced 1979. From Lyman.
Price: Percussion.. $269.95
Price: Kit, percussion $199.95
Price: Flintlock $279.95
Price: Kit, flintlock $214.95

CAUTION: PRICES CHANGE. CHECK AT GUNSHOP.

H&A Pa. Hawken

HOPKINS & ALLEN PA. HAWKEN RIFLE
Caliber: 50.
Barrel: 29″.
Weight: 7½ lbs. **Length:** 44″ over-all.
Stock: Walnut.
Sights: Blade front, open rear adjustable for windage.
Features: Single trigger, dual barrel wedges. Convertible ignition system. Brass patch box.
Price: With percussion lock $199.50
Price: Conversion kit (percussion to flint) $39.95

TRYON RIFLE
Caliber: 50, 54 cal.
Barrel: 34″, octagon; 1-63″ twist.
Weight: 9 lbs. **Length:** 49″ over-all.
Stock: European walnut with steel furniture.
Sights: Blade front, fixed rear.
Features: Reproduction of an American plains rifle with double set triggers and back-action lock. Imported from Italy by Trail Guns Armory and Dixie.
Price: Percussion only $350.00
Price: From Dixie Gun Works $299.00

ALAMO LONG RIFLE
Caliber: 38, 45, 50 cal.
Barrel: 35″.
Weight: 7½ lbs. **Length:** 51″ over-all.
Stock: European walnut.
Sights: Blade front, fixed rear.
Features: Double set trigger. Blued octagon barrel, bright lock, brass trigger guard, patch box, buttplate, thimbles. Has Alamo battle scene engraved on patch box. Imported from Italy by Trail Guns Armory.
Price: Percussion.. $265.00
Price: Flintlock $275.00

H&A Brush Rifle

Weight: 7 lbs.
Stock: Hardwood.
Sights: Silver blade front, notch rear.
Features: Convertible ignition system. Brass furniture. Introduced 1983.
Price: Percussion.. $189.00
Price: Flint... $200.10
Price: Pre-assembled kit, percussion............................ $129.00
Price: As above, flint.. $140.10
Price: Kit, percussion.. $99.50
Price: Kit, flint $110.60

HOPKINS & ALLEN BRUSH RIFLE
Caliber: 36 or 45.
Barrel: 25″, octagon, $^{15}/_{16}$″ flats.

H & A Buggy Rifle

HOPKINS & ALLEN BUGGY RIFLE
Caliber: 45.
Barrel: 20″, 25″ or 32″, octagonal.
Weight: 6½ lbs. **Length:** 37″ over-all.
Stock: American walnut.
Features: A short under-hammer rifle. Blued barrel and receiver, black plastic buttplate.
Price: 20″ or 25″ bbl. $208.47
Price: 32″ bbl.. $223.47

Thompson/Center Hawken

Stock: American walnut.
Sights: Blade front, rear adj. for w. & e.
Features: Solid brass furniture, double set triggers, button rifled barrel, coil-type main spring. From Thompson/Center Arms.
Price: Percussion Model (45, 50 or 54 cal.) $270.00
Price: Flintlock model (45, 50, or 54 cal.) $282.50
Price: Percussion kit $190.00
Price: Flintlock kit.. $202.50

THOMPSON/CENTER HAWKEN RIFLE
Caliber: 45, 50 or 54.
Barrel: 28″ octagon, hooked breech.

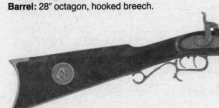

T/C Hawken Cougar

Thompson/Center Hawken Cougar
Similar to the standard T/C Hawken except stock is of highly figured walnut; all furniture—lock plate, hammer, triggers, trigger plate, trigger guard, fore-end cap, thimbles escutcheons, etc. are of stainless steel with matte finish. Replacing the patch box is a stainless steel medallion cast in deep relief depicting a crouching cougar. Internal parts, breech plug, tang, barrel, sights and under rib are ordnance steel. Barrel, sights and under rib are blued. Buttplate is solid brass, hard chromed to match the stainless parts. Limited production. Introduced 1982. From Thompson/Center Arms.
Price: $350.00

BLACK POWDER MUSKETS & RIFLES

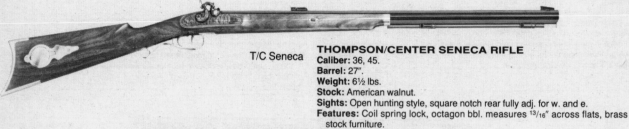

T/C Renegade

THOMPSON/CENTER RENEGADE RIFLE
Caliber: 50 and 54 plus 56 cal., smoothbore.
Barrel: 26″, 1″ across the flats.
Weight: 8 lbs.
Stock: American walnut.
Sights: Open hunting (Patridge) style, fully adjustable for w. and e.
Features: Coil spring lock, double set triggers, blued steel trim.
Price: Percussion model $215.00
Price: Flintlock model, 50 and 54 cal. only $227.50
Price: Percussion kit $165.00
Price: Flintlock kit $177.50

T/C Seneca

THOMPSON/CENTER SENECA RIFLE
Caliber: 36, 45.
Barrel: 27″.
Weight: 6½ lbs.
Stock: American walnut.
Sights: Open hunting style, square notch rear fully adj. for w. and e.
Features: Coil spring lock, octagon bbl. measures ¹³/₁₆″ across flats, brass stock furniture.
Price: $270.00

Buffalo Hunter Rifle

BUFFALO HUNTER PERCUSSION RIFLE
Caliber: 58.
Barrel: 25½″.
Weight: 8 lbs. **Length:** 41½″ over-all.
Stock: Walnut finished, hand checkered, brass furniture.
Sights: Fixed.
Features: Designed for primitive weapons hunting. 20 ga. shotgun bbl. also available $90.00. Imported by Navy Arms, Dixie.
Price: . . . . $215.00 to $264.00

SILE HAWKEN HUNTER CARBINE
Caliber: 45, 50, 54.
Barrel: 22″, full octagon with hooked breech and hard chrome rifled or smooth bore.
Weight: 7 lbs. **Length:** 38″ over-all.
Stock: Walnut with checkered p.g. and fore-end, rubber recoil pad.
Sights: Blade front, fully adjustable open rear.
Features: Black oxidized brass hardware, engraved case hardened lock plate, sear fly and coil spring mechanism. Stainless steel nipple. Adjustable double set triggers. From Sile Dist.
Price: Percussion, rifle or carbine $261.00
Price: Flintlock $271.80

ARMOURY R140 HAWKIN RIFLE
Caliber: 45, 50 or 54.
Barrel: 29″.
Weight: 8¾ to 9 lbs. **Length:** 45¾″ over-all.
Stock: Walnut, with cheekpiece.
Sights: Dovetail front, fully adjustable rear.
Features: Octagon barrel, removable breech plug; double set triggers; blued barrel, brass stock fittings, color case hardened percussion lock. From Armsport, The Armoury, Sile (hard chrome bore).
Price: . . . . $175.00 to $282.00
Price: Kit . . . . $205.70 to $210.00

Navy Hawken Mark I

NAVY ARMS MARK I HAWKEN RIFLE
Caliber: 50 and 54.
Barrel: 26″.
Weight: 9 lbs. **Length:** 43″ over-all.
Stock: American walnut with cheek rest.
Sights: Blade front, adjustable Williams rear.
Features: Designed specifically for maxi-ball shooting. Double set triggers, blued barrel, polished brass furniture. Stainless steel chamber insert. Flint or percussion. Made in U.S. by Navy Arms.
Price: Finished, percussion, 50 or 54 . . . . $263.00
Price: True left-hand model, 50-cal. only, finished $263.00
Price: As above, kit $175.95
Price: Finished, flintlock, 50 or 54 . . . . $275.00
Price: As above, kit $186.00

HAWKEN RIFLE
Caliber: 45, 50, 54 or 58.
Barrel: 28″, blued, 6-groove rifling.
Weight: 8¾ lbs. **Length:** 44″ over-all.
Stock: Walnut with cheekpiece.
Sights: Blade front, fully adj. rear.
Features: Coil mainspring, double set triggers, polished brass furniture. Also available with chrome plated bore or in flintlock model from Sile. Introduced 1977. From Kassnar, Sile, Dixie (45 or 50 only, walnut stock), Armsport, Toledo Armas, Shore and Hopkins & Allen, 50-cal. only.
Price: . . . . $175.00 to $252.95
Price: Hard chrome bore, Sile, about $238.95
Price: True left-hand rifle, flint and percussion (Kassnar) $299.95

Armsport Hawken Rifle-Shotgun Combo
Similar to Hawken above except 50-cal only, with 20 gauge shotgun barrel. From Armsport.
Price: $250.00

CAUTION: PRICES CHANGE. CHECK AT GUNSHOP.

BLACK POWDER MUSKETS & RIFLES

Dixie Wesson Rifle

Dixie Wesson Rifle

Similar to the Richland version except barrel is fitted with a false muzzle, hand checkered stock and fore-end. Comes with loading rod and loading accessories. From Dixie Gun Works.

Price: $325.00

ITHACA-NAVY HAWKEN RIFLE

Caliber: 50 and 54.
Barrel: 32″ octagonal, 1-inch dia.
Weight: About 9 lbs.
Stock: Black walnut.
Sights: Blade front, rear adj. for w.
Features: Completely made in U.S. Hooked breech, 1⅞″ throw percussion lock. Attached twin thimbles and under-rib. German silver barrel key inlays, Hawken-style toe and buttplates, lock bolt inlays, barrel wedges, entry thimble, trigger guard, ramrod and cleaning jag, nipple and nipple wrench. American made. Introduced 1977. Made in U.S. by Navy Arms.

Price: Complete, percussion $435.00
Price: Kit, percussion $295.00
Price: Complete, flint....................................... $460.00
Price: Kit, flint $330.00

DELUXE HAWKEN RIFLE

Caliber: 50.
Barrel: 28″.
Weight: 7 lbs. **Length:** 43½″ over-all.
Stock: Dark polished walnut.
Sights: Blade front, open rear adj. for w.
Features: Brass patchbox, trigger guard, buttplate and furniture; color case hardened lock, rest blued. From F.I.E. Corp., Toledo Armas.

Price: $174.95
Price: Kit form. $159.95
Price: Finished flintlock model............................. $239.95

RICHLAND PERCUSSION WESSON RIFLE

Caliber: 50.
Barrel: 28″; 1⅛″ octagon.
Length: 45″ over-all.
Stock: Walnut.
Sights: Blade front, rear adj. for e.
Features: Adjustable double set triggers, color case hardened frame. Introduced 1977. From Richland Arms.

Price: With false muzzle $295.00
Price: Engraved version $412.00

CVA HAWKEN RIFLE

Caliber: 50 or 54.
Barrel: 28″, octagon; 1″ across flats; 1-66″ twist.
Weight: 7 lbs. 15 oz. **Length:** 44″ over-all.
Stock: Select walnut.
Sights: Beaded blade front, fully adj. open rear.
Features: Fully adj. double set triggers; brass patch box, wedge plates, nose cap, thimbles, trigger guard and buttplate; blued barrel; color case-hardened, engraved lockplate. Percussion or flintlock. Hooked breech. Introduced 1981.

Price: Finished rifle, percussion $249.95
Price: Finished rifle, flintlock $259.95
Price: Kit, percussion $167.95
Price: Kit, flintlock $177.95

Mississippi Model 1841 Percussion Rifle

Similar to Zouave Rifle but patterned after U.S. Model 1841. Imported by Navy Arms, Dixie.

Price: .... $225.00 to $275.00.

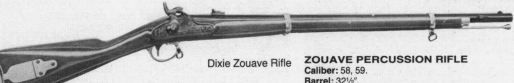

Dixie Zouave Rifle

ZOUAVE PERCUSSION RIFLE

Caliber: 58, 59.
Barrel: 32½″.
Weight: 9½ lbs. **Length:** 48½″ over-all.
Stock: Walnut finish, brass patch box and buttplate.
Sights: Fixed front, rear adj. for e.
Features: Some small details may vary with importers. Also available from Navy Arms as carbine, with 22″ bbl. Extra 20 ga. shotgun bbl. $45.00. Imported by Navy Arms, Dixie.

Price: .... $87.95 to $265.00
Price: Deluxe Model (Navy Arms)................................. $355.00

Parker-Hale Whitworth

PARKER-HALE WHITWORTH MILITARY TARGET RIFLE

Caliber: 45.
Barrel: 36″.
Weight: 9¼ lbs. **Length:** 52½″ over-all.
Stock: Walnut. Checkered at wrist and fore-end.
Sights: Hooded post front, open step-adjustable rear.
Features: Faithful reproduction of the Whitworth rifle, only bored for 45-cal. Trigger has a detented lock, capable of being adjusted very finely without risk of the sear nose catching on the half-cock bent and damaging both parts. Introduced 1978. Imported from England by Navy Arms.

Price: $575.00

PARKER-HALE VOLUNTEER RIFLE

Caliber: .451″.
Barrel: 32″.
Weight: 9½ lbs. **Length:** 49″ over-all.
Stock: Walnut, checkered wrist and fore-end.
Sights: Globe front, adjustable ladder-type rear.
Features: Recreation of the type of gun issued to volunteer regiments during the 1860's. Rigby-pattern rifling, patent breech, detented lock. Stock is glass bedded for accuracy. Comes with comprehensive accessory/shooting kit. From Navy Arms.

Price: $575.00

BLACK POWDER MUSKETS & RIFLES

Parker-Hale 1853

PARKER-HALE ENFIELD 1853 MUSKET
Caliber: .577″.
Barrel: 39″, 3-groove cold-forged rifling.
Weight: About 9 lbs. **Length:** 55″ over-all.
Stock: Seasoned walnut.
Sights: Fixed front, rear step adj. for elevation.
Features: Three band musket made to original specs from original gauges. Solid brass stock furniture, color hardened lock plate, hammer; blued barrel, trigger. Imported from England by Navy Arms.
Price: $400.00

PARKER-HALE ENFIELD PATTERN 1858 NAVAL RIFLE
Caliber: .577″.
Barrel: 33″.
Weight: 8½ lbs. **Length:** 48½″ over-all.
Stock: European walnut.
Sights: Blade front, step adj. rear.
Features: Two-band Enfield percussion rifle with heavy barrel. 5-groove progressive depth rifling, solid brass furniture. All parts made exactly to original patterns. Imported from England by Navy Arms.
Price: $370.00

Navy Arms 3-Band Musket
Faithful reproduction of the Confederate-used rifle. Blued barrel, brass buttplate, trigger guard, nose cap. From Navy Arms.
Price: $280.00

NAVY ARMS 2-BAND ENFIELD 1858
Caliber: .577 Minie, .575 round ball.
Barrel: 33″.
Weight: 10 lbs. **Length:** 49″ over-all.
Stock: Walnut.
Sights: Folding leaf rear adjustable for elevation.
Features: Blued barrel, color case-hardened lock and hammer, polished brass buttplate, trigger guard, nose cap. From Navy Arms, Euroarms of America.
Price: $305.00

Parker-Hale 1861

PARKER-HALE ENFIELD 1861 CARBINE
Caliber: 577.
Barrel: 24″.
Weight: 7½ lbs. **Length:** 40¼″ over-all.
Stock: Walnut.
Sights: Fixed front, adj. rear.
Features: Percussion muzzle loader, made to original 1861 English patterns. Imported from England by Navy Arms.
Price: $300.00

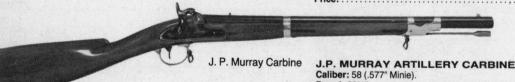

London Armory 3-Band Enfield

LONDON ARMORY 3-BAND 1853 ENFIELD
Caliber: 58 (577 Minie, 575 round ball, 580 maxi ball).
Barrel: 39″.
Weight: 9½ lbs. **Length:** 54″ over-all.
Stock: European walnut.
Sights: Inverted "V" front, traditional Enfield folding ladder rear.
Features: Re-creation of the famed London Armory Company Pattern 1862 Enfield Musket. One-piece walnut stock, brass buttplate, trigger guard and nosecap. Lockplate marked "London Armoury Co." and with a British crown. Blued Baddeley barrel bands. From Dixie, Euroarms of America.
Price: $315.00

J. P. Murray Carbine

J.P. MURRAY ARTILLERY CARBINE
Caliber: 58 (.577″ Minie).
Barrel: 23½″.
Weight: 7 lbs., 9 oz. **Length:** 39″ over-all.
Stock: Walnut.
Sights: Blade front, rear drift adj. for windage.
Features: Browned barrel, color case-hardened lock, blued swivel and band springs, polished brass buttplate, trigger guard, barrel bands. From Navy Arms.
Price: $263.00

ERMA-EXCAM GALLAGER CARBINE
Caliber: 54 (.540″ ball).
Barrel: 22⅓″.
Weight: 7¼ lbs. **Length:** 39″ over-all.
Stock: European walnut.
Sights: Post front, rear adjustable for w. & e.
Features: Faithful reproduction of the 1860 breech-loading carbine. Made in West Germany. Imported by Excam. Introduced 1978.
Price: $325.00

U.S. M-1862 REMINGTON CONTRACT RIFLE
Caliber: 58.
Barrel: 33″.
Weight: 9½ lbs. **Length:** 48½″ over-all.
Stock: Walnut, brass furniture.
Sights: Blade front, folding 3-leaf rear.
Features: Re-creation of the 1862 military rifle. Each rifle furnished with two stainless steel nipples. From Euroarms of America.
Price: About $200.00

CAUTION: PRICES CHANGE. CHECK AT GUNSHOP.

BLACK POWDER MUSKETS & RIFLES

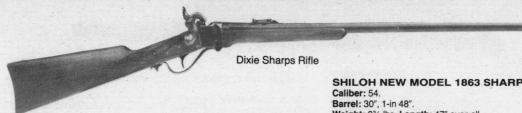

Dixie Sharps Rifle

Dixie Sharps Rifle
Similar to the Shiloh Sharps except has 28½" barrel, checkered half-stock fore-end and stock wrist, flat lockplate. Carbine-style case hardened butt-plate. Imported from Italy by Dixie Gun Works.
Price: $349.95
Price: Military Carbine (22" barrel) $329.95

COOK & BROTHER CONFEDERATE CARBINE
Caliber: 58.
Barrel: 24".
Weight: 7½ lbs. **Length:** 40½" over-all.
Stock: Select walnut.
Features: Re-creation of the 1861 New Orleans-made artillery carbine. Color case-hardened lock, browned barrel. Buttplate, trigger guard, barrel bands, sling swivels and nosecap of polished brass. From Euroarms of America.
Price: $190.00

SHILOH NEW MODEL 1863 SHARPS RIFLE
Caliber: 54.
Barrel: 30", 1-in 48".
Weight: 8¾ lbs. **Length:** 47" over-all.
Stock: Black walnut, oil finish.
Sights: Blade front, rear leaf adj. for e.
Features: Duplicate of original percussion rifle. Receiver, sideplate, hammer, buttplate, patch box color hardened; barrel is blue-black. Twelve different models of the Sharps now available in many original chamberings. Made in U.S. by C. Sharps Arms Co.
Price: Sporting Rifle... $599.00
Price: Military Rifle.. $630.00

Shiloh New Model 1863 Sharps Carbine
Shortened, carbine version of the 1863 rifle. Caliber 54. Has 22" barrel, black walnut stock without patch box, single barrel band. Weighs 8 lbs., 12 oz., over-all length is 39⅛". Made in U.S. by C. Sharps Arms Co.
Price: $499.00

Dixie 1863 Musket

DIXIE 1863 SPRINGFIELD MUSKET
Caliber: 58 (.570" patched ball or .575 Minie).
Barrel: 50", rifled.
Stock: Walnut stained.
Sights: Blade front, adjustable ladder-type rear.
Features: Bright-finish lock, barrel, furniture. Reproduction of the last of the regulation muzzle loaders. Imported from Japan by Dixie Gun Works.
Price: Finished $265.00
Price: Kit $225.00

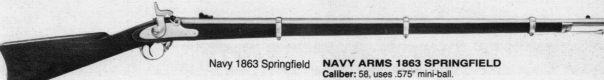

Navy 1863 Springfield

NAVY ARMS 1863 SPRINGFIELD
Caliber: 58, uses .575" mini-ball.
Barrel: 40", rifled.
Weight: 9½ lbs. **Length:** 56" over-all.
Stock: Walnut.
Sights: Open rear adj. for elevation.
Features: Full-size 3-band musket. Polished bright metal, including lock. From Navy Arms.
Price: Finished rifle $380.00
Price: Kit $310.00

SHILOH SHARPS 1874 MILITARY RIFLE
Caliber: 45-70, 50-70.
Barrel: 30", Round.
Weight: 8¾ lbs.
Stock: American walnut.
Sights: Blade front, Lawrence-style open rear.
Features: Military-style fore-end with three barrel bands and 1¼" sling swivels. Color case-hardened receiver, buttplate and barrel bands, blued barrel. Re-creation of the original Sharps rifles. Five other models in many original chamberings available. From C. Sharps Arms Co.
Price: 1874 Military Rifle...................................... $630.00
Price: 1874 Carbine... $499.00
Price: 1874 Business Rifle..................................... $575.00
Price: 1874 Sporting Rifle No. 1............................... $699.00
Price: 1874 Sporting Rifle No. 3............................... $599.00
Price: 1874 Long Range Express Sporting Rifle $749.00

> Consult our Directory pages for
> the location of firms mentioned.

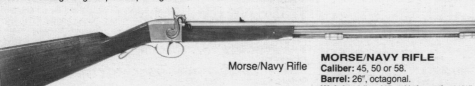

Morse/Navy Rifle

MORSE/NAVY RIFLE
Caliber: 45, 50 or 58.
Barrel: 26", octagonal.
Weight: 6 lbs. (45 cal.). **Length:** 41½" over-all.
Stock: American walnut, full p.g.
Sights: Blade front, open fixed rear.
Features: Brass action, trigger guard, ramrod pipes. Made in U.S. by Navy Arms.
Price: $167.00
Price: Kit $100.00

BLACK POWDER MUSKETS & RIFLES

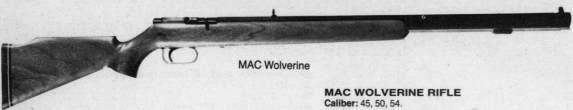

MAC Wolverine

KODIAK DOUBLE RIFLE
Caliber: 58x58, 50x50 and 58-cal./12 ga. optional.
Barrel: 28″, 5 grooves, 1-in-48″ twist.
Weight: 9½ lbs. **Length:** 43¼″ over-all.
Stock: Czechoslovakian walnut, hand checkered.
Sights: Adjustable bead front, adjustable open rear.
Features: Hooked breech allows interchangeability of barrels. Comes with sling and swivels, adjustable powder measure, bullet mould and bullet starter. Engraved lock plates, top tang and trigger guard. Locks and top tang polished, rest blued. Imported from Italy by Trail Guns Armory, Inc.
Price: 58 cal. SxS $495.00
Price: 50 cal. SxS $495.00
Price: 50 cal. x 12 ga., 58x12................................... $495.00
Price: Spare barrels, 58 cal. SxS, 50 cal. SxS $294.25
Price: Spare barrels, 58x12 ga................................. $294.25
Price: Spare barrels, 12 ga. x 12 ga. $160.00

MAC WOLVERINE RIFLE
Caliber: 45, 50, 54.
Barrel: 26″, octagon, 1″ flats.
Weight: 7¾ lbs.
Stock: Choice of walnut, cherry or maple; soft recoil pad.
Sights: Brass-bead front, Lyman adjustable folding leaf rear.
Features: New design uses straight-line ignition with #209 shotshell primer. Fires from an open bolt; has positive safety notch. Fully adjustable trigger. Introduced 1983. Made in U.S. by Michigan Arms Corp.
Price: $365.00
Price: Friendship Special (select barrel, Lyman globe front, Williams target peep rear, adjustable recoil pad, custom stock, special breech block) $599.00

Sanftl Schuetzen Rifle

SANFTL SCHUETZEN PERCUSSION TARGET RIFLE
Caliber: 45 (.445″ round ball).
Barrel: 29″, ⅞″ octagon.
Weight: 9 lbs. **Length:** 43″ over-all.
Stock: Walnut, Schuetzen-style.
Sights: Open tunnel front post, peep rear adjustable for windage & elevation.
Features: True back-action lock with ''backward'' hammer; screw-in breech plug; buttplate, trigger guard and stock inlays are polished brass. Imported from Italy by Dixie Gun Works, Hopkins & Allen.
Price: $595.00

BLACK POWDER SHOTGUNS

Beretta O/U Shotgun

BERETTA MODEL 1000 MUZZLE LOADING O-U SHOTGUN
Gauge: 12 only.
Barrel: 30″.
Weight: About 7 lbs. **Length:** 46½″ over-all.
Stock: Walnut; English-style with checkpiece.
Features: Special limited production replica of an early Beretta over-under. Silvered, engraved lockplates, trigger guard, hammers, barrel bands. Ramrod fits on right side of blued barrels. Introduced 1981. Imported from Italy by Beretta U.S.A. Corp.
Price: $840.00

CVA Shotgun

CVA PERCUSSION SHOTGUN
Gauge: 12.
Barrel: 28″.
Weight: 6 lbs., 10 oz. **Length:** 44½″over-all.
Stock: Select hardwood; checkered pistol grip and fore-end.
Sights: Brass bead front.
Features: Hooked breech system. Blued barrels and thimbles, polished steel wedge plates, trigger guard, triggers, tang, lock and hammers; engraved lock, hammers, tang and trigger guard. Introduced 1983. From CVA.
Price: Finished $249.95
Price: Kit $189.95

BLACK POWDER SHOTGUNS

Mowrey A & T Shotgun

TRAIL GUNS KODIAK 10 GAUGE DOUBLE
Gauge: 10.
Barrel: 20″, 30¾″ (Cyl. bore).
Weight: About 9 lbs. **Length:** 47⅛″ over-all.
Stock: Walnut, with cheek rest. Checkered wrist and fore-end.
Features: Chrome plated bores; engraved lockplates, brass bead front and middle sights; sling swivels. Introduced 1980. Imported from Italy by Trail Guns Armory.
Price: $379.95

MOWREY A. & T. 12 GAUGE SHOTGUN
Gauge: 12 ga. only.
Barrel: 32″, octagon.
Weight: 8 lbs. **Length:** 48″ over-all.
Stock: Curly maple, oil finish, brass furniture.
Sights: Bead front.
Features: Available in percussion only. Steel or brass action. Uses standard 12 ga. wadding. Made by Mowrey.
Price: Complete $328.00
Price: Kit form... $237.00

SILE DELUXE DOUBLE BARREL SHOTGUN
Gauge: 12.
Barrel: 28″ (Cyl. & Cyl.); hooked breech, hard chrome lining.
Weight: 6 lbs. **Length:** 44½″ over-all.
Stock: Walnut, with checkered grip.
Features: Engraved, polished blue and color case-hardened hardware; locks are color case-hardened and engraved. Steel buttplate; brass bead front sight. From Sile.
Price: Percussion only $299.00
Price: Confederate Cavalry Model (shortened version of above model with 14″ bbl. 30½″ o.a.l., checkered stock, swivels, brass ramrod)......... $299.00

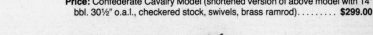

Navy Terry Texas Ranger

NAVY ARMS TERRY TEXAS RANGER SHOTGUN
Gauge: 12 only.
Barrel: 14″.
Weight: 6 lbs. **Length:** 30″ over-all.
Stock: Walnut; checkered pistol grip.
Features: Replica of a Confederate Civil War gun. Color case-hardened lock plates and hammers. Imported by Navy Arms.
Price: $342.00

Navy Classic Double

NAVY CLASSIC DOUBLE BARREL SHOTGUN
Gauge: 10, 12.
Barrel: 28″.
Weight: 7 lbs., 12 ozs. **Length:** 45″ over-all.
Stock: Walnut.
Features: Color case-hardened lock plates and hammers; hand checkered stock. Imported by Navy Arms.
Price: 12 ga.. $342.00
Price: 10 ga.. $360.00
Price: Kit, 12 ga.. $265.00
Price: Kit, 10 ga.. $280.00
Price: As "Texas Ranger," 12 ga., 14″ bbls........................ $342.00

MORSE/NAVY SINGLE BARREL SHOTGUN
Gauge: 12 ga.
Barrel: 26″.
Weight: 5 lbs. **Length:** 41½″ over-all.
Stock: American walnut, full p.g.
Sights: Front bead
Features: Brass receiver, black buttplate. Made in U.S. by Navy Arms.
Price: $167.00
Price: Kit $105.00

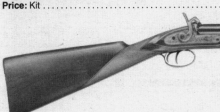

Dixie Double Barrel

DOUBLE BARREL PERCUSSION SHOTGUN
Gauge: 12.
Barrel: 30″ (I.C.&Mod.).
Weight: 6¼ lbs. **Length:** 45″ over-all.
Stock: Hand checkered walnut, 14″ pull.
Features: Double triggers, light hand engraving. Details vary with importer. Imported by The Armoury, Dixie, Euroarms of America, Toledo Armas, Hopkins & Allen.
Price: Upland .... $125.00 to $299.85
Price: 12 ga. kit (Dixie, magnum) $235.00
Price: 10 ga. (Dixie, magnum)................................. $335.00
Price: 10 ga. kit (Dixie, magnum) $285.00

Guns in this section are powered by: A) disposable CO_2 cylinders, B) hand-pumped compressed air released by trigger action, C) air compressed by a spring-powered piston released by trigger action. Calibers are generally 177 (BB or pellet) and 22 (ball or pellet); a few guns are made in 20 or 25 caliber. Pellet guns are usually rifled, those made for BB's only are smoothbore.

BSA Scorpion

BSA SCORPION AIR PISTOL
Caliber: 177 or 22, single shot.
Barrel: 7⅞", rifled.
Weight: 3.6 lbs. **Length:** 15¾" over-all.
Power: Spring-air, barrel cocking.
Stock: Moulded black plastic contoured with thumbrest.
Sights: Interchangeable bead or blade front with hood, open rear adjustable for w. & e.
Features: Muzzle velocity of 510 fps (177) and 380 fps (22). Comes with pellets, oil, targets and steel target holder. Scope and mount optional. Introduced 1980. Imported from England by Precision Sports.
Price: 177 or 22 cal. **$139.95**
Price: 1.5x15 scope and mount. **$59.95**

Beeman/Webley Hurricane

BEEMAN/WEBLEY HURRICANE PISTOL
Caliber: 177 or 22, single shot.
Barrel: 8", rifled.
Weight: 2.4 lbs. **Length:** 11½" over-all.
Power: Spring piston.
Stocks: Thumbrest, checkered high-impact synthetic.
Sights: Hooded front, micro-click rear adj. for w. and e.
Features: Velocity of 470 fps (177-cal.). Single stroke cocking, adjustable trigger pull, manual safety. Rearward recoil like a firearm pistol. Steel piston and cylinder. Scope base included; 1.5x scope **$39.95** extra. Shoulder stock available. Introduced 1977. Imported from England. Available from Beeman's, Great Lakes Airguns.
Price: **$129.95**

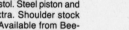

BEEMAN/WEBLEY TEMPEST AIR PISTOL
Caliber: 177 or 22, single shot.
Barrel: 6.75", rifled ordnance steel.
Weight: 32 oz. **Length:** 9" over-all.
Power: Spring piston.
Stocks: Checkered black epoxy with thumbrest.
Sights: Post front; rear has sliding leaf adjustable for w. and e.
Features: Adjustable trigger pull, manual safety. Velocity 470 fps (177 cal.). Steel piston in steel liner for maximum performance and durability. Unique rearward spring simulates firearm recoil. Shoulder stock available. Introduced 1979. Imported from England. Available from Beeman, Great Lakes Airguns.
Price: **$99.95**

Beeman/Webley Tempest

BEEMAN/WISCHO S-20 STANDARD
Caliber: 177, single shot.
Barrel: 7".
Weight: 2 lbs., 2 oz.
Power: Spring piston.
Stocks: Walnut.
Sights: Hooded front, open rear adj. for elevation.
Features: Stocks suitable for right or left-handed shooters; 450 fps; 24 oz. trigger pull. Introduced 1980. Imported by Beeman.
Price: **$119.50**

Beeman/FWB Model 2

BEEMAN/FEINWERKBAU MODEL 2 CO² PISTOL
Caliber: 177, single shot
Barrel: 10.1".
Weight: 2.5 lbs. **Length:** 16¼" over-all.
Power: Special CO² cylinder.
Stocks: Stippled walnut with adjustable palm shelf.
Sights: Blade front with interchangeable inserts; open micro. click rear with adjustable notch width.
Features: Power adjustable from 360 fps to 525 fps. Fully adjustable trigger; three weights for balance and weight adjustments. Introduced 1983. Imported by Beeman.
Price: Right hand **$555.00**
Price: Left hand **$595.00**

BEEMAN/FEINWERKBAU MODEL 90 PISTOL
Caliber: 177, single shot.
Barrel: 7.5", 12-groove rifling.
Weight: 3.0 lbs. **Length:** 16.4" over-all.
Power: Spring piston, single stroke sidelever cocking.
Stocks: Stippled walnut with adjustable palm shelf.
Sights: Interchangeable blade front, fully adjustable open notch rear.
Features: Velocity of 475 to 525 fps. Has new adjustable electronic trigger. Recoilless action, metal piston ring and dual mainsprings. Cocking effort is 12 lbs. Introduced 1983. Imported by Beeman.
Price: **$625.00**

CAUTION: PRICES CHANGE. CHECK AT GUNSHOP.

BEEMAN/FEINWERKBAU MODEL 80 MATCH PISTOL
Caliber: 177, single shot.
Barrel: 7.5"; 12 groove rifling.
Weight: 2.8 to 3.2 lbs. (varies with weight selection). **Length:** 16.4" over-all.
Power: Spring piston, single-stroke sidelever cocking.
Stocks: Stippled walnut with adjustable palm shelf.
Sights: Interchangeable-blade front, rear notch micro. adj. for w. and e.
Features: Four-way adjustable match trigger. Recoilless operation. Metal piston ring and dual mainsprings. Interchangeable weights attach to frame, not barrel. Weights may be arranged to suit balance preference. Cocking effort 12 lbs. Muzzle velocity 475-525 fps. Introduced 1978. Imported by Beeman.
Price: Right-hand **$595.00**
Price: Left-hand **$625.00**

FWB Model 80

Weihrauch HW-70

BEEMAN/WEIHRAUCH HW-70 AIR PISTOL
Caliber: 177, single shot.
Barrel: 6¼", rifled.
Weight: 38 oz. **Length:** 12¾" over-all.
Power: Spring, barrel cocking.
Stocks: Plastic, with thumbrest.
Sights: Hooded post front, square notch rear adj. for w. and e.
Features: Adj. trigger. 24-lb. cocking effort, 410 f.p.s. M.V.; automatic barrel safety. Available from Beeman, Great Lakes Airguns.
Price: **$109.95**

BEEMAN/WISCHO BSF S-20 PISTOL
Caliber: 177, single shot.
Barrel: 7" rifled.
Weight: 45 oz. **Length:** 15.8" over-all.
Power: Spring piston barrel cocking.
Stocks: Walnut with thumbrest.
Sights: Bead front, rear adj. for e.
Features: Cocking effort of 17 lbs.; M.V. 450 f.p.s.; adj. trigger. Optional scope and mount available. Detachable aluminum stock optional. Available from Beeman, Great Lakes Airguns.
Price: **$149.50**

Beeman/Wischo S-20

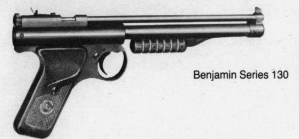

Benjamin Series 130

BENJAMIN SUPER S. S. TARGET PISTOL SERIES 130
Caliber: BB, 22 and 177; single shot.
Barrel: 8"; BB smoothbore; 22 and 177, rifled.
Weight: 2 lbs. **Length:** 11" over-all.
Power: Hand pumped.
Features: Bolt action; fingertip safety; adj. power.
Price: M130, BB **$78.10**
Price: M132, 22 . . . . **$78.10**
Price: M137, 177 . . . . **$78.10**

CROSMAN MODEL 357 SIX AIR PISTOL
Caliber: 177, 6-shot.
Barrel: 6" or 4" (Model 357 Four), rifled steel.
Weight: 32 oz. (6") **Length:** 11⅜" over-all.
Power: CO_2 Powerlet.
Stocks: Checkered wood-grain plastic.
Sights: Ramp front, fully adjustable rear.
Features: Average 430 fps (Model 357 Six). Break-open barrel for easy loading. Single or double action. Vent rib barrel. Wide, smooth trigger. Two speed loaders come with each gun. Introduced 1983.
Price: 4" or 6", about **$40.00**

Crosman Model Four

Crosman 1861 Shiloh

CROSMAN MODEL 1861 SHILOH REVOLVER
Caliber: 177 pellets or BBs, 6-shot.
Barrel: 6" rifled.
Weight: 1 lb., 14 oz. **Length:** 12¾" over-all.
Power: CO_2 Powerlet.
Stocks: Wood-grained plastic.
Sights: Fixed.
Features: Modeled after the 1861 Remington revolver. Averages 42 shots per CO_2 Powerlet. Velocity of 330 to 350 fps with pellets. Introduced 1981.
Price: About **$28.00**

AIR GUNS—HANDGUNS

Crosman 1322/1377

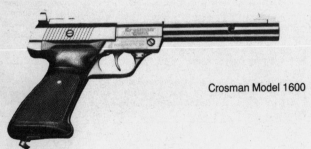

Crosman Model 1600

CROSMAN MODEL 1322 AIR PISTOL
Caliber: 22, single shot.
Barrel: 8″, button rifled.
Weight: 37 oz. **Length:** 13⅝″.
Power: Hand pumped.
Sights: Blade front, rear adj. for w. and e.
Features: Moulded plastic grip, hand size pump forearm. Cross bolt safety. Also available in 177 Cal. as **Model 1377** (same price).
Price: About **$45.00**

CROSMAN 1600 BB PISTOL
Caliber: BB, 17-shot.
Barrel: 7¾″.
Weight: 29 oz. **Length:** 11⅜″ over-all.
Power: Standard CO₂.
Stocks: Contoured with thumbrest.
Sights: Patridge-type front, fully adj. rear.
Features: Gives about 80 shots per powerlet, slide-action safety, steel barrel, die-cast receiver. Introduced 1983.
Price: About **$27.00**

Crosman Mark I

Crosman Model 38T

Daisy Model 188

Daisy Model 179

CROSMAN MARK I TARGET PISTOL
Caliber: 22, single shot.
Barrel: 7¼″, button rifled.
Weight: 42 oz. **Length:** 11″.
Power: Crosman Powerlet CO₂ cylinder.
Features: New system provides same shot-to-shot velocity of 370-420 fps. Checkered thumbrest grips, right or left. Patridge front sight, rear adj. for w. & e. Adj. trigger.
Price: About **$49.00**

Crosman Mark II Target Pistol
Same as Mark I except 177 cal.
Price: About **$49.00**

CROSMAN 38T TARGET REVOLVER
Caliber: 177, 6-shot.
Barrel: 6″, rifled.
Weight: 40 oz. **Length:** 11″ over-all.
Power: CO₂ Powerlet cylinder.
Features: Double action, revolving cylinder. Adj. rear sight.
Price: About **$44.00**

Crosman 38C Combat Revolver
Same as 38 Target except 3½″ bbl., 36 oz.
Price: About **$44.00**

DAISY MODEL 188 BB/PELLET PISTOL
Caliber: 177.
Barrel: 9.9″.
Weight: 1.67 lbs. **Length:** 12″ over-all.
Stocks: Die-cast metal; checkered with thumbrest.
Sights: Blade and ramp front, notched rear.
Features: Single shot for pellets, 24-shot for BBs. Spring action with under-barrel cocking lever. Grip and receiver of die-cast metal. Introduced 1979.
Price: About **$21.00**

DAISY 179 SIX GUN
Caliber: BB, 12-shot.
Barrel: Steel lined, smoothbore.
Weight: NA **Length:** 11½″ over-all.
Power: Spring.
Features: Forced feed from under-barrel magazine. Single action, molded wood grained grips.
Price: About **$28.00**

CAUTION: PRICES CHANGE. CHECK AT GUNSHOP.

FEINWERKBAU FWB-65 MKII AIR PISTOL
Caliber: 177, single shot.
Barrel: 6.1"; fixed bbl. wgt. avail.
Weight: 42 oz. **Length:** 14.1" over-all.
Power: Spring, sidelever cocking.
Stocks: Walnut, stippled thumbrest.
Sights: Front, interchangeable post element system, open rear, click adj. for w. & e. and for sighting notch width. Scope mount avail.
Features: New shorter barrel for better balance and control. Cocking effort 9 lbs. 2-stage trigger, 4 adjustments. Quiet firing, 525 fps. Programs instantly for recoil or recoilless operation. Permanently lubricated. Steel piston ring. Special switch converts trigger from 17.6 oz. pull to 42 oz. let-off. Available from Beeman, Great Lakes Airguns.
Price: Right-hand...$485.00
Price: Left-hand..$499.50
Price: Model 80 (Great Lakes Airguns), std. grip..................$570.00

FWB-65 Mk. I

GAMO CENTER AIR PISTOL
Caliber: 177, single shot.
Barrel: 7", rifled.
Weight: 46 oz. **Length:** 13.8" over-all.
Power: Underlever spring air.
Sights: Hooded front, micro-adjustable rear.
Features: Velocity of 400 to 435 fps on single stroke of the lever. Sight radius of 13". Adjustable trigger. Blued metal finish. Introduced 1981. Imported from Spain by Stoeger Industries.
Price: $110.00
Price: With ambidextrous grip and safety, non-adj. trigger...........$90.00

Feinwerkbau Model 65 International Match Pistol
Same as FWB 65 MKI pistol except: new adj. wood grips to meet international regulations, optional 3 oz. barrel sleeve weight. Available from Beeman.
Price: Right-hand...$545.00
Price: Left-hand..$575.00

Gamo Center

Consult our Directory pages for the location of firms mentioned.

HAMMERLI "MASTER" CO₂ TARGET PISTOL
Caliber: 177, single shot.
Barrel: 6.4", 12-groove.
Weight: 38.4 oz. **Length:** 16" over-all.
Power: 12 gram cylinder.
Stocks: Plastic with thumbrest and checkering.
Sights: Ramp front, micro rear, click adj. Adj. sight radius from 11.1" to 13.0".
Features: Single shot, manual loading. Residual gas vented automatically. 5-way adj. trigger. Available from Mandall Shooting Supplies.
Price: $495.00

MARKSMAN PLAINSMAN 1049 CO₂ PISTOL
Caliber: BB, 100-shot repeater.
Barrel: 5⅞", smooth.
Weight: 28 oz. **Length:** 9½" over-all.
Stocks: Simulated walnut with thumbrest.
Power: 8.5 or 12.5 gram CO₂ cylinders.
Features: 3 position power switch. Auto. ammunition feed. Positive safety.
Price: $32.95

Marksman Plainsman

Marksman 1010

Marksman 1050

MARKSMAN #1010 REPEATER PISTOL
Caliber: 177, 20-shot repeater.
Barrel: 2½", smoothbore.
Weight: 24 oz. **Length:** 8¼".
Power: Spring
Features: Thumb safety. Uses BBs, darts or pellets. Repeats with BBs only.
Price: Black finish..$14.95
Price: With self-contained target/backstop........................$24.95

MARKSMAN 1050 AIR PISTOL
Caliber: 177, single-shot.
Weight: 28 oz.
Power: Spring.
Stocks: Checkered black plastic.
Sights: Fixed.
Features: Velocity about 280 fps. Cross-bolt safety. Also shoots 177-cal. darts. Introduced 1983.
Price: $23.95

POWER LINE 717 PELLET PISTOL
Caliber: 177, single shot.
Barrel: 9.61″.
Weight: 48 oz. **Length:** 13½″ over-all.
Stocks: Molded wood-grain plastic, with thumbrest.
Sights: Blade and ramp front, micro. adjustable notch rear.
Features: Single pump pneumatic pistol. Rifled brass barrel. Cross-bolt trigger block. Muzzle velocity 360 fps (177 cal.), 290 fps (22 cal.). From Daisy. Introduced 1979.
Price: Either model, about **$68.00**

Power Line 717

POWER LINE MODEL 790
Caliber: 177 cal. pellet, single-shot.
Barrel: 8½″, rifled steel.
Weight: 42 oz.
Power: 12 gram CO₂ cartridge.
Stocks: Simulated walnut, checkered. Thumbrest. Left or right hand.
Sights: Patridge front, fully adj. rear with micro. click windage adjustment.
Features: Pull-bolt action, crossbolt safety. High-low power adjustment.
Price: About **$68.00**
Price: Model 41 Magnum (as above but nickel plated, black grips), about **$75.00**

Power LIne 780/790

POWER LINE MATCH 777 PELLET PISTOL
Caliber: 177, single shot.
Barrel: 9.61″ rifled steel.
Weight: 49 oz. **Length:** 13½″ over-all.
Power: Sidelever, single pump pneumatic.
Stocks: Smooth hardwood, fully contoured; right or left hand.
Sights: Blade and ramp front, match-grade open rear with adj. width notch, micro. click adjustments.
Features: Adjustable trigger; manual cross-bolt safety. MV of 360 fps. Comes in foam-filled carrying case and complete cleaning kit, adjustment tool and pellets.
Price: About **$250.00**

Power Line 777

POWER LINE CO₂ 1200 CUSTOM TARGET PISTOL
Caliber: BB, 177.
Barrel: 10½″, smooth.
Weight: 30 oz. **Length:** 11¼″ over-all.
Power: Daisy CO₂ cylinder.
Stocks: Contoured, checkered moulded wood-grain plastic.
Sights: Blade ramp front, fully adj. square notch rear.
Features: 60-shot BB reservoir, gravity feed. Cross bolt safety. Velocity of 420-450 fps for more than 100 shots.
Price: About **$35.00**

Precise RO-72

PRECISE/RO-72 BULLSEYE AIR PISTOL
Caliber: 177, single shot.
Barrel: 7¼″, rifled.
Weight: 35 oz.
Power: Spring air, barrel cocking.
Stock: Molded plastic with thumbrest.
Sights: Hooded front, micro. adj. open rear for w. and e.
Features: Four interchangeable front sights—triangle, bead, narrow post, wide post. Rear sight rotates to give four distinct sight pictures. Muzzle velocity 325 fps. Precise International, importer.
Price: **$40.00**

Precise Minuteman Micron

PRECISE MINUTEMAN® MICRON AIR PISTOL
Caliber: 177, single shot.
Barrel: 6¼″, rifled.
Weight: 28 oz. **Length:** 12½″ over-all.
Power: Spring air, barrel cocking.
Stocks: Contoured plastic
Sights: Hooded front, fixed rear.
Features: Blue finish. Comes with 250 pellets. Introduced 1983. Imported by Precise International.
Price: **$16.00**

RWS MODEL 5G AIR PISTOL
Caliber: 177, single shot.
Barrel: 7″.
Weight: 2¾ lbs. **Length:** 16″ over-all.
Power: Spring air, barrel cocking.
Stocks: Plastic, thumbrest design.
Sights: Tunnel front, micro click open rear.
Features: Velocity of 410 fps. Two-stage trigger with automatic safety. Imported from West Germany by Dynamit Nobel of America, Great Lakes Airguns.
Price: **$120.00**

RWS Model 5G

RWS MODEL 5GS AIR PISTOL
Same as the Model 5G except comes with 1.5×15 pistol scope with ramp-style mount, muzzle brake/weight. No open sights supplied. Introduced 1983.
Price: **$145.00**

RWS Model 6M

> Consult our Directory pages for the location of firms mentioned.

RWS MODEL 6G AIR PISTOL
Caliber: 177, single shot.
Barrel: 7″.
Weight: 3 lbs. **Length:** 16″ over-all.
Power: Spring air, barrel cocking.
Stocks: Plastic, thumbrest design.
Sights: Tunnel front with interchangeable inserts, micro click open rear.
Features: Velocity of 410 fps. Recoilless double piston system, two-stage adjustable trigger. Comes with sight inserts. Imported from West Germany by Dynamit Nobel of America, Great Lakes Airguns.
Price: **$175.00**

RWS MODEL 6M MATCH AIR PISTOL
Caliber: 177, single shot.
Barrel: 7″.
Weight: 3 lbs. **Length:** 16″ over-all.
Power: Spring air, barrel cocking.
Stocks: Walnut-finished hardwood with thumbrest.
Sights: Adjustable front, micro click open rear.
Features: Velocity of 410 fps. Recoilless double piston system, moveable barrel shroud to protect front sight during cocking. Imported from West Germany by Dynamit Nobel of America, Great Lakes Airguns.
Price: **$205.00**

RWS Model 10 Match Air Pistol
Refined version of the Model 6M. Has special adjustable match trigger, oil finished and stippled match grips, barrel weight. Also available in left-hand version, and with fitted case.
Price: Model 10 .... **$400.00**
Price: Model 10, left hand. **$445.00**
Price: Model 10, with case **$445.00**
Price: Model 10, left hand, with case **$480.00**

RWS Model 10

Record Model 3

RECORD MODEL 3 AIR PISTOL
Caliber: 177, single shot.
Barrel: 5.25″, rifled.
Weight: 1.9 lbs. **Length:** 11.42″ over-all.
Power: Spring-air, barrel cocking.
Stocks: Checkered plastic with thumbrest.
Sights: Hooded front, fully adjustable rear.
Features: Velocity of about 300 fps. Matte blue/black finish. Introduced 1983. Imported from West Germany by Great Lakes Airguns.
Price: **$39.95**

RECORD MODEL 68 AIR PISTOL
Caliber: 177, single shot.
Barrel: 7″, rifled.
Weight: 2.91 lbs. **Length:** 14.37″ over-all.
Power: Spring-air, barrel cocking.
Stocks: Checkered plastic with thumb rest.
Sights: Hooded front with square post, fully adjustable rear.
Features: Velocity of about 300 fps. Easily accessible trigger adjustment knob. Introduced 1983. Imported from West Germany by Great Lakes Airguns.
Price: **$64.50**

Record Model 68

Record "Jumbo"

RECORD "JUMBO" DELUXE AIR PISTOL

Caliber: 177, single shot.
Barrel: 6″, rifled.
Weight: 1.9 lbs. **Length:** 7.25″ over-all.
Power: Spring-air, lever cocking.
Stocks: Smooth walnut.
Sights: Fixed.
Features: Thumb safety. Grip magazine compartment for extra pellet storage. Introduced 1983. Imported from West Germany by Great Lakes Airguns.
Price: $66.50

Sheridan Model HB

SHERIDAN MODEL HB PNEUMATIC PISTOL

Caliber: 5mm; single shot.
Barrel: 9⅜″, rifled.
Weight: 36 oz. **Length:** 12″ over-all.
Power: Underlever pneumatic pump.
Stocks: Checkered simulated walnut; forend is walnut.
Sights: Blade front, fully adjustable rear.
Features: "Controller-Power" feature allows velocity and range control by varying the number of pumps—3 to 10. Maximum velocity of 400 fps. Introduced 1982. From Sheridan Products.
Price: $80.40

SHERIDAN MODEL EB CO₂ PISTOL

Caliber: 20 (5mm).
Barrel: 6½″, rifled, rust proof.
Weight: 27 oz. **Length:** 9″ over-all.
Power: 12 gram CO_2 cylinder.
Stocks: Checkered simulated walnut. Left- or right-handed.
Sights: Blade front, fully adjustable rear.
Features: Turn-bolt single-shot action. Gives about 40 shots at 400 fps per CO_2 cylinder.
Price: $60.35

Sheridan Model EB

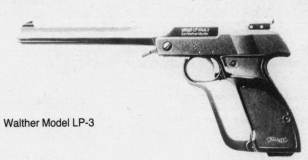

Walther Model LP-3

WALTHER MODEL LP-3

Caliber: 177, single shot.
Barrel: 9⅜″, rifled.
Weight: 45½ oz. **Length:** 13³⁄₁₆″ over-all.
Power: Compressed air, lever cocking.
Features: Recoilless operation, cocking in grip frame. Micro-click rear sight, adj. for w. & e., 4-way adj. trigger. Plastic thumbrest grips. Imported by Interarms.
Price: $385.00

Walther Model LP-3 Match Pistol

Same specifications as LP-3 except for grips, frame shape and weight. Has adjustable walnut grips to meet international shooting regulations. Imported by Interarms.
Price: $465.00

WALTHER CP-2 CO₂ AIR PISTOL

Caliber: 177, single shot.
Barrel: 9″.
Weight: 40 oz. **Length:** 14¾″ over-all.
Power: CO_2.
Stocks: Full target type stippled wood with adjustable hand-shelf.
Sights: Target post front, fully adjustable target rear.
Features: Velocity of 520 fps. CO_2 powered; target-quality trigger; comes with adaptor for charging with standard CO_2 air tanks, case, and accessories. Introduced 1983. Imported from West Germany by Interarms.
Price: $795.00

Walther Model LP-53

WALTHER MODEL LP-53 PISTOL

Caliber: 177, single shot.
Barrel: 9⅜″.
Weight: 40.5 oz. **Length:** 12⅜″ over-all.
Power: Spring air.
Features: Micrometer rear sight. Interchangeable rear sight blades. Target grips. Bbl. weight availble at extra cost. Inported from West Germany by Interarms.
Price: $215.00

CAUTION: PRICES CHANGE. CHECK AT GUNSHOP.

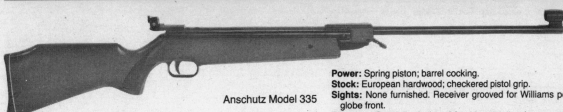

Anschutz Model 335

ANSCHUTZ MODEL 335 AIR RIFLE
Caliber: 177, single shot.
Barrel: 18½".
Weight: 7¼ lbs. **Length:** 43¼" over-all.

Power: Spring piston; barrel cocking.
Stock: European hardwood; checkered pistol grip.
Sights: None furnished. Receiver grooved for Williams peep rear, Anschutz globe front.
Features: Specially designed for 10 meter "novice-expert" shooters. Adjustable two-stage trigger. Introduced 1982. Imported from Germany by Talo Distributors, Inc.
Price: Without sight $161.50
Price: Magnum model, no sights............................... $171.50
Price: Sight set $28.35

Anschutz Model 380

ANSCHUTZ MODEL 380 AIR RIFLE
Caliber: 177, single shot.
Barrel: 20¼".

Weight: 10.8 lbs. (including sights). **Length:** 42⅛" over-all.
Power: Spring piston; sidelever cocking.
Stock: European hardwood with stippled pistol grip and fore-end. Adjustable cheekpiece and rubber buttpad.
Sights: Globe front; match aperture rear.
Features: Recoilless and vibration free. Two-stage adjustable match trigger. Introduced 1982. Imported from Germany by Talo Distributors, Inc.
Price: With sights.. $886.00
Price: Left-hand, with sights.................................. $948.00

BSA Airsporter-S

BSA AIRSPORTER-S AIR RIFLE
Caliber: 177 or 22.
Barrel: 19.5", rifled.
Weight: 8 lbs. **Length:** 44.7" over-all.
Power: Spring air, underlever action.
Stock: Oil-finished walnut, high comb Monte Carlo cheekpiece.
Sights: Ramp front with interchangeable bead and blade, adjustable for height; tangent-type rear adj. for w. & e.

Features: Muzzle velocity of 825 fps (177) and 635 fps (22). Fully adj. trigger. Cylinder is a large diameter, one-piece impact extrusion. Scope and mount optional. Introduced 1980. Imported from England by Precision Sports.
Price: 177 or 22 cal. $399.95
Price: Standard Airsporter $329.95
Price: 4x20 scope and mount $59.95

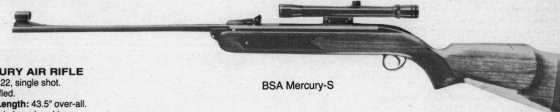

BSA Mercury-S

BSA MERCURY AIR RIFLE
Caliber: 177 or 22, single shot.
Barrel: 18.5", rifled.
Weight: 7 lbs. **Length:** 43.5" over-all.
Power: Spring-air, barrel cocking.
Stock: European hardwood. Monte Carlo cheekpiece, ventilated butt pad.
Sights: Adjustable bead/blade front, tangent rear adj. for w. & e.
Features: Muzzle velocity of 700 fps (177) and 550 fps (22). Reversible "V" and "U" notch rear sight blade. Single stage match-type trigger, adj. for weight of pull and sear engagement. Scope and mount optional. Introduced 1980. Imported from England by Precision Sports.
Price: 177 or 22 cal. $229.95
Price: 4x20 scope and mount $59.95

BSA Mercury-S Air Rifle
Similar to the standard Mercury model except weighs 7¼ lbs., has European walnut stock with oil finish, checkered fore-end and pistol grip. Muzzle velocity of 825 fps (177), 635 fps (22). Introduced 1982. From Precision Sports.
Price: $289.95

BSA AIRSPORTER-S COMMEMORATIVE
Commemorates BSA's 100-year anniversary in 1982. Similar to standard Airsporter-S except has a new cocking lever concealed in the fore-end, new hand-checkered Stutzen stock with Schnabel tip, grip cap. Comes with 4×40 scope and mount, leather sling and swivels, pile-lined case, BSA patch, shooting kit, and registration certificate. Only 1000 made. Introduced 1983.
Price: $650.00

AIR GUNS—LONG GUNS

BSA Meteor Super

BSA METEOR/METEOR SUPER AIR RIFLES

Caliber: 177 or 22, single shot.
Barrel: 18.5″, rifled.
Weight: 6 lbs. **Length:** 42″ over-all.
Power: Spring air, barrel cocking.
Stock: European hardwood.
Sights: Adj. bead/blade front, adj. tangent rear with reversible "U" and "V" notch blade.

Features: Muzzle velocity of 650 fps (177) and 500 fps (22). Aperture rear sight element supplied. Cylinder is dovetailed for scope mounting. Adjustable trigger mechanism. Meteor Super has M.C. cheekpiece, vent. rubber recoil pad. Introduced 1980. Imported from England by Precision Sports.
Price: Meteor **$149.95**
Price: Meteor Super **$169.95**

BSF Model 55D

BSF MODEL 55D AIR RIFLE

Caliber: 177, single shot.
Barrel: 16″, rifled.
Weight: 6.5 lbs. **Length:** 40.7″ over-all.
Power: Spring-air, barrel cocking.
Stock: Walnut stained hardwood.
Sights: Hooded front, open rear adjustable for elevation.
Features: Velocity of 870 fps. Adjustable trigger, receiver grooved for scope. Rubber butt pad. Imported from West Germany by Great Lakes Airguns.
Price: **$159.50**

Beeman FWB 124/127

BEEMAN/FEINWERKBAU 124/127 MAGNUM

Caliber: 177 (FWB-124); 22 (FWB-127); single shot.
Barrel: 18.3″, 12-groove rifling.
Weight: 6.8 lbs. **Length:** 43½″ over-all.
Power: Spring piston air; single stroke barrel cocking.
Stock: Walnut finished hardwood.
Sights: Tunnel front; click-adj. rear for w., slide-adj. for e.
Features: Velocity 680-820 fps, cocking effort of 18 lbs. Forged steel receiver; nylon non-drying piston and breech seals. Auto. safety, adj. trigger. Standard

model has no checkering, cheekpiece. Deluxe has hand-checkerd p.g. and fore-end, high comb cheekpiece, and buttplate with white spacer. Imported by Beeman, Great Lakes Airguns (124 only).
Price: Standard model **$269.50**
Price: Deluxe model (illus.) **$299.50**

FWB 300-S

BEEMAN/FEINWERKBAU F300-S RUNNING BOAR (TH)

Caliber: 177, single shot.
Barrel: 19.9″, rifled.
Weight: 10.9 lbs. **Length:** 43″ over-all.
Power: Single stroke sidelever, spring piston.

Stock: Walnut with adjustable buttplate, grip cap and comb. Designed for fixed and moving target use.
Sights: None furnished; grooved for optional scope.
Features: Recoilless, vibration free. Permanent lubrication and seals. Barrel stabilizer weight included. Crisp single-stage trigger. Available from Beeman.
Price: Right-hand **$698.00**
Price: Left-hand **$760.00**

BEEMAN/FEINWERKBAU 300-S "UNIVERSAL" MATCH

Caliber: 177, single shot.
Barrel: 19.9″.
Weight: 10.2 lbs. (without barrel sleeve). **Length:** 43.3″ over-all.
Power: Spring piston, single stroke sidelever.
Stock: Walnut, stippled p.g. and fore-end. Detachable cheekpieces (one std., high for scope use.) Adjustable buttplate, accessory rail. Buttplate and grip cap spacers included.
Sights: Two globe fronts with interchangeable inserts. Rear is match aperture with rubber eyecup and sight viser. Front and rear sights move as a single unit.
Features: Recoilless, vibration free. Grooved for scope mounts. Steel piston ring. Cocking effort about 9½ lbs. Barrel sleeve optional. Left-hand model available. Introduced 1978. Imported by Beeman.
Price: Right-hand **$789.50**
Price: Left-hand **$850.00**

BEEMAN/FEINWERKBAU 300-S SERIES MATCH RIFLE

Caliber: 177, single shot.
Barrel: 19.9″, fixed solid with receiver.
Weight: Approx. 10 lbs. with optional bbl. sleeve. **Length:** 42.8″ over-all.
Power: Single stroke sidelever, spring piston.
Stock: Match model—walnut, deep fore-end, adj. buttplate.
Sights: Globe front with interchangeable inserts. Click micro. adj. match aperture rear. Front and rear sights move as a single unit.
Features: Recoilless, vibration free. Five-way adjustable match trigger. Grooved for scope mounts. Permanent lubrication, steel piston ring. Cocking effort 9 lbs. Optional 10 oz. bbl. sleeve. Available from Beeman.
Price: Right hand **$678.50**
Price: Left hand **$749.50**

CAUTION: PRICES CHANGE. CHECK AT GUNSHOP.

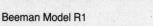

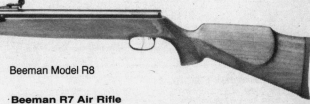

Beeman Model R1

BEEMAN R1 AIR RIFLE

Caliber: 177 or 22, single shot.
Barrel: 19.6″, 12-groove rifling.
Weight: 8.5 lbs. **Length:** 45.2″ over-all.
Power: Spring-piston, barrel cocking.
Stock: Walnut-stained beech; cut checkered pistol grip Monte Carlo comb and cheekpiece; rubber butt pad.
Sights: Tunnel front with interchangeable inserts, open rear click adjustable for windage and elevation. Grooved for scope mounting.
Features: Velocity of 940 fps (177), 800 fps (22). Non-drying nylon piston and breech seals. Adjustable metal trigger. Right or left hand stock. Imported by Beeman.

Price: Right hand, 177 .... $329.50
Price: Left hand, 177 .... $359.50
Price: Right hand, 22 .... $329.50
Price: Left hand, 22 .... $359.50

Beeman Model R8

BEEMAN R8 AIR RIFLE

Caliber: 177, single shot.
Barrel: 18.3″.
Weight: 7.2 lbs. **Length:** 43.1″ over-all.
Power: Barrel cocking, spring-piston.
Stock: Walnut with Monte Carlo cheekpiece; checkered pistol grip.
Sights: Globe front, fully adjustable rear; interchangeable inserts.
Features: Velocity of 735 fps. Nylon piston and breech seals. Adjustable match-grade, two-stage, grooved metal trigger. Rubber butt pad. Imported by Beeman.
Price: $249.50

Beeman R7 Air Rifle

Similar to the R8 model except has double-jointed cocking lever, match grade trigger block; velocity of 680-700 fps; barrel length 17″; weights 5.8 lbs. Imported by Beeman.
Price: $159.50

Weihrauch Model 35EB

BEEMAN HW 35L/35EB SPORTER RIFLES

Caliber: 177 (35L), 177 or 22 (35EB), single shot.
Barrel: 19½″.
Weight: 8 lbs. **Length:** 43½″ over-all (35L).
Power: Spring, barrel cocking.
Stock: Walnut finish with high comb, full pistol grip.
Sights: Globe front with five inserts, target micrometer rear with rubber eye-cup.

Features: Fully adjustable trigger, manual safety. Thumb-release barrel latch. Model 35L has Bavarian cheekpiece stock, 35EB has walnut, American-style stock with cheekpiece, sling swivels, white spacers. Imported by Beeman, Great Lakes Airguns.
Price: Model 35L $269.50
Price: Model 35EB.. $350.00

Weihrauch Model 55T

BEEMAN HW 55 TARGET RIFLES

Model:	55SM	55MM	55T
Caliber:	177	177	177
Barrel:	18½″	18½″	18½″
Length:	43½″	43½″	43½″
Wgt. lbs.:	7.8	7.8	7.8
Rear sight:	All aperture		
Front sight:	All with globe and 4 interchangeable inserts.		
Power:	All spring (barrel cocking). 660-700 fps.		
Price:	$369.50	$450.50	$449.50

Features: Trigger fully adj. and removable. Micrometer rear sight adj. for w. and e. on all. Pistol grip high comb stock with beavertail fore-end, walnut finish stock on 55SM. Walnut stock on 55MM, Tyrolean stock on 55T. Imported by Beeman.

Beeman Falcon 1

BEEMAN FALCON 1 AIR RIFLE

Caliber: 177, single shot.
Barrel: 18″, rifled.
Weight: 6.6 lbs. **Length:** 43″ over-all.
Power: Spring-piston, barrel cocking.
Stock: Walnut-stained hardwood.
Sights: Tunnel front with interchangeable inserts; rear with rotating disc to give four sighting notches.
Features: Velocity 680 fps. Match-type adjustable trigger. Receiver grooved for scope mounting. Imported by Beeman.
Price: $139.95

Beeman Falcon 2 Air Rifle

Similar to the Falcon 1 except weighs 5.8 lbs., 41″ over-all; front sight is hooded post on ramp, rear sight has two-way click adjustments. Adjustable trigger. Imported by Beeman.
Price: $109.95

 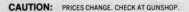

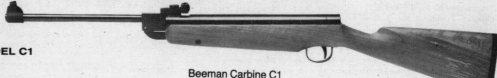

BEEMAN/WEBLEY VULCAN II DELUXE
Caliber: 177 or 22, single shot.
Barrel: 17", rifled.
Weight: 7.6 lbs. **Length:** 43.7" over-all.
Power: Spring piston air, barrel cocking.
Stock: Walnut. Cut checkering, rubber butt pad, checkpiece. Standard version has walnut-stained beech.
Sights: Hooded front, micrometer rear.
Features: Velocity of 830 fps (177), 675 fps (22). Single stage adjustable trigger; receiver grooved for scope mounting. Self-lubricating piston seal. Introduced 1983. Imported by Beeman.
Price: Standard **$189.50**
Price: Deluxe **$229.50**

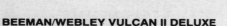

Webley Vulcan II

BEEMAN/NORICA AIR RIFLE KIT
Caliber: 177, single shot.
Barrel: 17.9", rifled.
Weight: 4.9 lbs. **Length:** 40" over-all.
Power: Spring-piston, barrel cocking.
Stock: Beech, unfinished.
Sights: Hooded ramp front, adjustable rear.
Features: Velocity 600 fps. World's only air rifle kit. Metal parts are factory blued. Stock may be finished to individual taste. Imported by Beeman.
Price: **$89.95**

BEEMAN CARBINE MODEL C1
Caliber: 177, single shot.
Barrel: 14", 12-groove rifling.
Weight: 6¼ lbs. **Length:** 38" over-all.
Power: Spring-piston, barrel cocking.
Stock: Walnut-stained beechwood with rubber butt pad.
Sights: Blade front, rear click-adjustable for windage and elevation.
Features: Velocity 830 fps. Adjustable trigger. Receiver grooved for scope mounting. Imported by Beeman.
Price: **$169.50**

Beeman Carbine C1

Benjamin Series 340

BENJAMIN SERIES 3100 SUPER REPEATER RIFLES
Caliber: BB, 100-shot; 22, 85-shot.
Barrel: 23", rifled or smoothbore.
Weight: 6¼ lbs. **Length:** 35" over-all.
Power: Hand pumped.
Features: Bolt action. Piggy back full view magazine. Bar V adj. rear sight. Walnut stock and pump handle.
Price: M3100, BB **$92.60**
Price: M3120, 22 rifled **$92.60**

BENJAMIN SERIES 340 AIR RIFLE
Caliber: 22 or 177, pellets or BB; single shot.
Barrel: 23", rifled and smoothbore.
Weight: 6 lbs. **Length:** 35" over-all.
Power: Hand pumped.
Features: Bolt action, walnut Monte Carlo stock and pump handle. Ramp-type front sight, adj. stepped leaf type rear. Push-pull safety.
Price: M340, BB **$96.20**
Price: M343, 22 .... **$96.20**
Price: M347, 177 .... **$96.20**

CROSMAN MODEL 6100 CHALLENGER RIFLE
Caliber: 177, single shot.
Weight: 7 lbs., 12 oz. **Length:** 46" over-all.
Power: Spring air, barrel cocking.
Stock: Stained hardwood with checkered pistol grip, rubber recoil pad.
Sights: Globe front, open fully adjustable rear.
Features: Average velocity 820 fps. Automatic safety, two-stage adjustable trigger. Receiver grooved for scope mounting. Introduced 1982. Imported from West Germany by Crosman Air Guns.
Price: About **$202.25**

Crosman 6100 Challenger

CROSMAN MODEL 66 POWERMASTER
Caliber: 177 (single shot) or BB
Barrel: 20", rifled, solid steel.
Weight: 3 lbs., 14 oz. **Length:** 38½" over-all.
Stock: Wood-grained plastic; checkered p.g. and fore-end.
Sights: Ramp front, fully adjustable open rear.
Features: Velocity about 675 fps. Bolt action, cross-bolt safety. Introduced 1983.
Price: About **$40.00**

Crosman Model 66

CAUTION: PRICES CHANGE. CHECK AT GUNSHOP.

Crosman 2100 Classic

CROSMAN MODEL 2100 CLASSIC AIR RIFLE

Caliber: 177 pellets or BBs, 180-shot BB magazine.
Barrel: 21", rifled.
Weight: 4 lbs., 13 oz. **Length:** 39¾" over-all.
Power: Pump-up, pneumatic.
Stock: Wood-grained checkered ABS plastic.
Features: Three pumps gives about 450 fps, 10 pumps about 700 fps. Cross-bolt safety; concealed reservoir holds over 180 BBs.
Price: About **$45.00**

Crosman 2200 Magnum

CROSMAN MODEL 2200 MAGNUM AIR RIFLE

Caliber: 22, single-shot.
Barrel: 19", rifled steel.
Weight: 4 lbs., 13 oz. **Length:** 39¾" over-all.
Stock: Full-size, wood-grained plastic with checkered p.g. and fore-end.
Sights: Ramp front, open step-adjustable rear.
Features: Variable pump power—3 pumps give 395 fps, 6 pumps 530 fps, 10 pumps 620 fps (average). Full-size adult air rifle. Has white line spacers at pistol grip and buttplate. Introduced 1978.
Price: About **$54.00**

Crosman Model 73

CROSMAN MODEL 73 SADDLE PAL CO_2

Caliber: 177 pellets or BBs, 16-shot magazine.
Barrel: 18", steel.
Weight: 3 lbs., 3 oz. **Length:** 34¾" over-all.
Stock: Simulated wood.
Sights: Ramp front, rear adj. for e.
Features: Positive lever safety. Velocity is 475 fps (pellets), 525 fps (BBs). 100 shots per CO_2 cartridge.
Price: About **$28.00**

CROSMAN MODEL 1 RIFLE

Caliber: 22, single shot.
Barrel: 19", rifled brass.
Weight: 5 lbs., 1 oz. **Length:** 39" over-all.
Power: Pneumatic, variable power.
Stock: Walnut stained American hardwood.
Sights: Blade front, Williams rear with micrometer click settings.
Features: Precision trigger mechanism for light, clean pull. Metal receiver grooved for scope mounting. Bolt action with cross-bolt safety. Muzzle velocities range from 365 fps (three pumps) to 625 fps (10 pumps). Introduced 1981.
Price: About **$79.00**

CROSMAN MODEL 788 BB SCOUT RIFLE

Caliber: 177, BB.
Barrel: 14", steel.
Weight: 2 lbs. 7 oz. **Length:** 31" over-all.
Stock: Wood-grained ABS plastic.
Sights: Blade on ramp front, open adj. rear.
Features: Variable pump power—3 pumps give MV of 330 fps, 6 pumps 437 fps, 10 pumps 470 fps (BBs, average). Steel barrel, cross-bolt safety. Introduced 1978.
Price: About **$26.00**

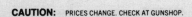

Crosman Model 760

CROSMAN MODEL 760 PUMPMASTER

Caliber: 177 pellets or BB, 200 shot.
Barrel: 19½", rifled steel.
Weight: 4 lbs., 3 oz. **Length:** 35" over-all.
Power: Pneumatic, hand pump.
Features: Short stroke, power determined by number of strokes. Walnut finished plastic checkered stock and fore-end. Post front sight and adjustable rear sight. Cross-bolt safety. Introduced 1983.
Price: About **$30.00**

Daisy Model 850

DAISY MODEL 850/851 PNEUMATIC RIFLE

Caliber: BB or 177, 100-shot BB reservoir.
Barrel: 20.8", rifled steel.
Weight: 4.3 lbs. **Length:** 33⅜" over-all.
Power: Single pump pneumatic.
Stock: Moulded plastic with woodgrain finish.
Sights: Ramp front, fully adjustable open rear.
Features: Shoots either BB's or pellets at 520 fps (BB) and 480 fps (pellet). Manual cross-bolt trigger block safety. Introduced 1981.
Price: About **$64.00**
Price: Model 851 (as above with wood stock and fore-end) **$90.00**

Daisy Model 1894

DAISY 1894 SPITTIN' IMAGE CARBINE
Caliber: BB, 40-shot.
Barrel: 17½", smoothbore.
Length: 38⅜" over-all.
Power: Spring.
Features: Cocks halfway on forward stroke of lever, halfway on return.
Price: About **$41.00**

Daisy Model 840

DAISY MODEL 840
Caliber: 177 pellet (single-shot) or BB (350-shot).
Barrel: 19", smoothbore, steel.
Weight: 3¼ lbs. **Length:** 37⅛" over-all.
Stock: Moulded wood-grain stock and fore-end.
Sights: Ramp front, open, adj. rear.
Features: Single pump pneumatic rifle. Muzzle velocity 325 fps (BB), 300 fps (pellet). Steel buttplate; straight pull bolt action; cross-bolt safety. Fore-end forms pump lever. Introduced 1978.
Price: About **$35.00**

Daisy Model 95

DAISY RIFLES

Model:	95	111	105
Caliber:	BB	BB	BB
Barrel:	18"	18"	13½"
Length:	35"	35"	30½"
Power:	Spring	Spring	Spring
Capacity:	700	700	450
Price: About	$32.75	$28.00	$23.00

Features: Model 95 stock and fore-end are wood; 105 and 111 have plastic stocks.

Daisy Red Ryder

DAISY 1938 RED RYDER COMMEMORATIVE
Caliber: BB, 650-shot repeating action.
Barrel: Sturdy steel, under-barrel loading port.
Weight: 3½ lbs. **Length:** 35" over-all.
Stock: Wood stock burned with Red Ryder lariat signature.
Sights: Post front, adjustable V-slot rear.
Features: Wood fore-end. Saddle ring with leather thong. Lever cocking. Gravity feed. Controlled velocity. Commemorates one of Daisy's most popular guns, the Red Ryder of the 1940s and 1950s.
Price: About **$39.95**

Erma ELG 10

ERMA ELG 10 AIR RIFLE
Caliber: 177, single shot.
Barrel: 17.7", rifled.
Weight: 6.4 lbs. **Length:** 38.2".
Power: Spring-piston, lever-action cocking.
Stock: Walnut-stained beechwood.
Sights: Hooded ramp post front, open rear adjustable for windage and elevation.
Features: Velocity to 550 fps. Sliding manual safety. Dummy magazine tube under barrel contains a brass cleaning rod. Imported by Beeman.
Price: **$279.50**

BEEMAN/FEINWERKBAU 300-S MINI-MATCH
Caliber: 177, single shot.
Barrel: 17⅛".
Weight: 8.8 lbs. **Length:** 40" over-all.
Power: Spring piston, single stroke sidelever cocking.
Stock: Walnut. Stippled grip, adjustable buttplate. Scaled-down for youthful or slightly built shooters.
Sights: Globe front with interchangeable inserts, micro. adjustable rear. Front and rear sights move as a single unit.
Features: Recoilless, vibration free. Grooved for scope mounts. Steel piston ring. Cocking effort about 9½ lbs. Barrel sleeve optional. Left-hand model available. Introduced 1978. Imported by Beeman.
Price: Right-hand... **$649.50**
Price: Left-hand.. **$695.00**

GAMO GAMATIC AIR RIFLE
Caliber: 177, repeater.
Weight: 6.5 lbs. **Length:** 38" over-all.
Power: Barrel cocking spring type.
Stock: Aluminum buttstock with polymer fore-end.
Sights: Hooded front, micro-adj. rear.
Features: Velocity over 660 fps. Blued metal finish. Introduced 1981. Imported from Spain by Stoeger Industries.
Price: **$178.00**

Gamo Expomatic

GAMO MODEL 600 AIR RIFLE
Caliber: 177, 22, single shot.
Weight: 7 lbs. **Length:** 44″ over-all.
Power: Barrel cocking spring type.
Stock: Lacquered beechwood.
Sights: Hooded front, micro-adj. open rear.
Features: Velocity over 660 fps. Blued metal finish. Introduced 1981. Imported from Spain by Stoeger Industries.
Price: **$144.00**

GAMO EXPO AIR RIFLE
Caliber: 177, 22.
Weight: 5.5 lbs. **Length:** 42″ over-all.
Power: Barrel cocking spring type.
Stock: Lacquered beechwood.
Sights: Hooded front, open micro-adj. rear.
Features: Velocity of 600 fps. Blued metal finish. Introduced 1981. Imported from Spain by Stoeger Industries.
Price: **$110.00**

GAMO CADET AIR RIFLE
Caliber: 177 only.
Weight: 5 lbs. **Length:** 37″ over-all.
Power: Barrel cocking spring type.
Stock: Lacquered beechwood.
Sights: Hooded front, micro-adj. open rear.
Features: Velocity of 570 fps. Blued metal finish. Receiver grooved for scope mounting. Introduced 1981. Imported from Spain by Stoeger Industries.
Price: **$94.00**

GAMO EXPOMATIC AIR RIFLE
Caliber: 177 only, repeater.
Weight: 5.5 lbs. **Length:** 42″ over-all.
Power: Barrel cocking spring type.
Stock: Lacquered beechwood.
Sights: Hooded front, micro-adj. rear.
Features: Velocity of 600 fps. Blued metal finish. Introduced 1981. Imported from Spain by Stoeger Industries.
Price: **$144.00**

GAMO 68 AIR RIFLE
Caliber: 177, 22, single shot.
Weight: 6.5 lbs. **Length:** 38″ over-all.
Power: Barrel cocking spring type.
Stock: Aluminum buttstock with polymer fore-end.
Sights: Hooded front, micro-adj. rear.
Features: Velocity of 600 fps. Blued metal finish. Introduced 1981. Imported from Spain by Stoeger Industries.
Price: **$144.00**

Gamo Cadet

Marksman Model 1750

MARKSMAN 1750 AIR RIFLE
Caliber: 177, single-shot.
Weight: 5 lbs., 4 ozs.
Power: Spring.
Stock: Stained beechwood.
Sights: Blade on ramp front, adjustable open rear.
Features: Shoots BBs, pellets, or darts. Break-action cocking. Automatic safety. Introduced 1983.
Price: **$69.95**

Marksman Model 1740

Weight: 5 lbs., 1 oz. **Length:** 36½″ over-all.
Power: Spring, barrel cocking.
Stock: Moulded high-impact ABS plastic.
Sights: Ramp front, open rear adj. for e.
Features: Automatic safety; fixed front, adj. rear sight; shoots 177 cal. BB's pellets and darts. Velocity about 450 fps.
Price: **$29.50**

MARKSMAN 1740 AIR RIFLE
Caliber: 177, 100-shot.
Barrel: 15½″, smoothbore.

POWER LINE MODEL 922
Caliber: 22 pellets, 5-shot clip.
Barrel: 20.8″. Decagon rifled brass barrel.
Weight: 5 lbs. **Length:** 37¾″ over-all.
Stock: Moulded wood-grained plastic with checkered p.g. and fore-end.
Sights: Ramp front, full adj. open rear.
Features: Muzzle velocity from 285 fps (two pumps) to 555 fps. (ten pumps). Straight pull bolt action. Separate buttplate and grip cap with white spacers. Introduced 1978.
Price: About **$70.00**

Power Line Model 922

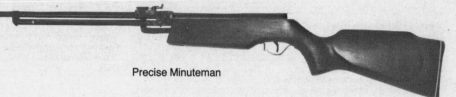

Power Line 880

POWER LINE 880 PUMP-UP AIR GUN
Caliber: 177 pellets, BB.
Barrel: Smooth bore, steel.
Weight: 6 lbs. **Length:** 37¾" over-all.
Power: Spring air.
Stock: Wood grain moulded plastic.
Sights: Ramp front, open rear adj. for e.
Features: Crafted by Daisy. Variable power (velocity and range) increase with pump strokes. 10 strokes for maximum power. 100-shot BB magazine. Cross-bolt trigger safety. Positive cocking valve.
Price: About $53.00

POWER LINE 881 PUMP-UP AIR GUN
Caliber: 177 pellets, BB.
Barrel: Decagon rifled.
Weight: 6 lbs. **Length:** 37¾" over-all.
Power: Spring air.
Stock: Wood grain moulded plastic with Monte Carlo cheekpiece.
Sights: Ramp front, step-adj. rear for e.
Features: Crafted by Daisy. Accurized version of Model 880. Checkered fore-end and p.g.
Price: About $64.00

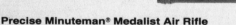

Precise Minuteman

PRECISE MINUTEMAN® MAGNUM
Caliber: 177, single shot.
Barrel: 19.4", rifled.
Weight: 7¼ lbs. **Length:** 44" over-all.
Power: Spring, under-lever cocking.
Stock: Stained hardwood, with cheek rest.
Sights: Hooded front, open rear adj. for w. and e.
Features: Velocity of 575 fps. Blued finish. Receiver grooved for scope mounting. Precise International, importer.
Price: $100.00

Precise Minuteman® Middleweight
Similar to the Minuteman Magnum except has 19" barrel, weighs 5½ lbs., has over-all length of 43". Velocity of 785 fps. Introduced 1983. Imported by Precise International.
Price: $60.00

Precise Medalist

Precise Minuteman® Medalist Air Rifle
Same as the Minuteman Middleweight except has ratchet-adjustable open rear sight, barrel lock/release to ease cocking. Introduced 1983. Imported by Precise International.
Price: $65.00

RWS Model 25

RWS MODEL 25 AIR RIFLE
Caliber: 177, single shot.
Weight: 5¼ lbs. **Length:** 38" over-all.
Power: Spring air, barrel cocking.
Stock: Walnut-finished hardwood.
Sights: Globe front, micro click open rear.
Features: Velocity of 541 fps. Two-stage trigger. Small dimensions for young shooters. Imported from West Germany by Dynamit Nobel of America, Great Lakes Airguns.
Price: $105.00

RWS Model 27 Air Rifle
Similar to the Model 25 except has a fully adjustable two stage trigger, micro click rear sight with four-way blade, dovetail base for peep sight or scope mounting. Available in 177 or 22 caliber. Measures 42" over-all and weighs 6 lbs.
Price: 177 or 22 .... $145.00

RWS Model 35 Air Rifle
Similar to the Model 27 except slightly heavier and needs less cocking effort. Has hardwood stock with cheekpiece, checkered pistol grip, rubber butt pad. Globe front sight uses optional interchangeable inserts. Available in 177 or 22 caliber. Weighs 6½ lbs.
Price: $180.00

RWS Model 35

RWS MODEL 45 AIR RIFLE
Caliber: 177 or 22, single shot.
Weight: 7¾ lbs. **Length:** 46" over-all.
Power: Spring air, barrel cocking.
Stock: Walnut-finished hardwood with rubber recoil pad.
Sights: Globe front with interchangeable inserts, micro click open rear with four-way blade.
Features: Velocity of 820 fps (177 cal.), 689 fps (22 cal.). Dovetail base for either micrometer peep sight or scope mounting. Automatic safety. Imported from West Germany by Dynamit Nobel of America, Great Lakes Airguns.
Price: 177 or 22 .... $199.00
Price: With deluxe walnut stock. $220.00

RWS Model 45S Air Rifle
Same as the standard Model 45 except comes without sights and has a 4×20 scope, ramp-type mount, muzzle brake/weight, sling and swivels. Introduced 1983.
Price: $240.00
Price: As above, without scope, mount, sling, swivels $190.00

CAUTION: PRICES CHANGE. CHECK AT GUNSHOP.

RWS Model 50

RWS MODEL 50 AIR RIFLE

Caliber: 177, single shot.
Weight: 8 lbs. **Length:** 45″ over-all.
Power: Spring air, underlever cocking.
Stock: Walnut-finished hardwood with cheekpiece, checkered grip, rubber butt pad.
Sights: Globe front, micro click open rear.
Features: Velocity of 750 fps. Automatic safety. Dovetail base for scope or peep sight mounting. Imported from West Germany by Dynamit Nobel of America, Great Lakes Airguns.
Price: **$250.00**

RWS Model 75

RWS MODEL 75 MATCH AIR RIFLE

Caliber: 177, single shot.
Barrel: 19″.
Weight: 11 lbs. **Length:** 43.7″ over-all.
Power: Spring air, side-lever cocking.
Stock: Oil finished walnut with stippled grip, adjustable buttplate, accessory rail, Conforms to I.S.U. rules.
Sights: Globe front with 5 inserts, fully adjustable match peep rear.
Features: Velocity of 574 fps. Fully adjustable trigger. Model 75 HV has stippled fore-end, adjustable cheekpiece. Uses double opposing piston system for recoilless operation. Imported from West Germany by Dynamit Nobel of America.
Price: Model 75 .... **$600.00**
Price: Model 75 HV **$710.00**
Price: Model 75 left hand **$640.00**
Price: Model 75 HV left hand **$750.00**
Price: Model 75 U (adj., cheekpiece, buttplate, M82 sight) **$890.00**

RWS Model 75K Running Boar Air Rifle

Similar to the Model 75 Match except has adjustable cheekpiece and buttplate, different stock, sandblasted barrel sleeve, detachable barrel weight, elevated-grip cocking lever, and a 240mm scope mount. Introduced 1983.
Price: **$790.00**

SIG-Hammerli 420

SIG-HAMMERLI MILITARY LOOK 420

Caliber: 177 or 22, single shot.
Barrel: 19″, rifled.
Weight: About 7 lbs. **Length:** 44¼″ over-all.
Stock: Synthetic stock and handguard.
Sights: Open, fully adj.
Features: Side lever cocking; adjustable trigger; rifled steel barrel. Introduced 1977. Imported by Mandall Shooting Supplies.
Price: **$295.00**

SIG-Hammerli 403

SIG-HAMMERLI MODELS 401 & 403 AIR RIFLES

Caliber: 177, single shot.
Weight: 7.8 lbs. **Length:** 44″ over-all.
Power: Spring air, sidelever cocking.
Stock: Beechwood.
Sights: Globe front accepts interchangeable inserts; fully adj. open rear (Model 401) or match aperture rear (Model 403).
Features: Sidelever cocking effort of 20 lbs. Automatic safety. Model 403 has a 2-lb. barrel sleeve and adj. buttplate. Fully adj. trigger. Introduced 1980. Imported by Mandall Shooting Supplies, Great Lakes Airguns.
Price: Model 401 .... **$379.00**
Price: Model 403, target model **$399.50**

Sharp-Innova Rifle

SHARP-INNOVA AIR RIFLE

Caliber: 177 and 22, single shot.
Barrel: 19.5″, rifled.
Weight: 4.4 lbs. **Length:** 34.6″ over-all.
Power: Pneumatic, multi-stroke.
Stock: Mahogany.
Sights: Hooded front, adjustable aperture rear.
Features: Velocity of 960 fps with 8 pumps (177). Adjustable trigger. Receiver grooved for scope mount. Introduced 1983. Imported from Japan by Great Lakes Airguns.
Price: **$129.50**

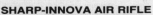

Sheridan Blue Streak

SHERIDAN BLUE AND SILVER STREAK RIFLES
Caliber: 5mm (20 cal.), single shot.
Barrel: 18½", rifled.
Weight: 5 lbs. **Length:** 37" over-all.
Power: Hand pumped (swinging fore-end).
Features: Rustproof barrel and piston tube. Takedown. Thumb safety. Mannlicher type walnut stock. Left-hand models same price.
Price: Blue Streak $101.55
Price: Silver Streak $105.40

SHERIDAN CO₂ AIR RIFLES
Caliber: 5mm (20 cal.), single shot.
Barrel: 18½", rifled.
Weight: 6 lbs. **Length:** 37" over-all.
Power: Standard 12.5 gram CO_2 cylinder.
Stock: Walnut sporter.
Sights: Open, adj. for w. and e. Optional Sheridan-Williams 5D-SH receiver sight or Weaver D4 scope.
Features: Bolt action single shot, CO_2 powered. Velocity approx. 514 fps., manual thumb safety. Blue or Silver finish. Left-hand models avail. at same prices.
Price: CO_2 Blue Streak $101.55
Price: CO_2 Silver Streak $105.40
Price: CO_2 Blue Streak with receiver sight $118.15
Price: CO_2 Blue Streak with scope $134.15

Sterling HR-81 Rifle

STERLING HR-81 AIR RIFLE
Caliber: 177 or 22, single-shot.
Barrel: 19½".
Weight: 8½ lbs. **Length:** 31½" over-all.
Power: Spring air, (barrel cocking).
Stock: Stained hardwood, with checkpiece, checkered pistol grip.
Sights: Tunnel-type front with four interchangeable elements, open adjustable V-type rear.
Features: Velocity of 900 fps (177), 660 fps (22). Bolt action with easily accessible loading port; adjustable single-stage match trigger; rubber recoil pad. Integral scope mount rails. Scope and mount optional. Introduced 1983. Imported from England by Lanchester U.S.A.
Price: $229.00

WALTHER LGV SPECIAL
Caliber: 177, single shot.
Barrel: 16", rifled.
Weight: 10¼ lbs. **Length:** 41⅜" over-all.
Power: Spring air (barrel cocking).
Features: Micro. click adj. aperture receiver sight; Adj. trigger. Walnut match stock, adj. buttplate. Double piston provides vibration-free shooting. Easily operated bbl. latch. Removable heavy bbl. sleeve. 5-way adj. trigger. Imported from Germany by Interarms.
Price: $550.00

Walther LGV Special

WALTHER LGR RIFLE
Caliber: 177, single-shot.
Barrel: 19½", rifled.
Weight: 10.2 lbs. **Length:** 44¼" over-all.
Power: Side lever cocking, compressed air.
Stock: French walnut.
Sights: Replaceable insert hooded front, Walther micro. adjustable rear.
Features: Recoilless operation. Trigger adj. for weight, pull and position. High comb stock with broad stippled fore-end and p.g. Imported from Germany by Interarms.
Price: $660.00

WALTHER LGR UNIVERSAL MATCH AIR RIFLE
Caliber: 177, single shot.
Barrel: 25.5".
Weight: 13 lbs. **Length:** 44¾" over-all.
Power: Spring air, barrel cocking.
Stock: Walnut match design with stippled grip and fore-end, adjustable cheekpiece, rubber butt pad.
Features: Has the same weight and contours as the Walther U.I.T. rimfire target rifle. Comes complete with sights, accessories and muzzle weight. Imported from West Germany by Interarms.
Price: $770.00

Walther LGR Match Air Rifle
Same basic specifications as standard LGR except has a high comb stock, sights are mounted on riser blocks. Introduced 1977.
Price: $750.00

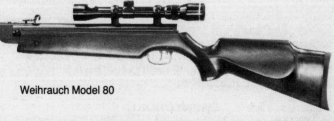

WEIHRAUCH MODEL 80 AIR RIFLE
Caliber: 177, single shot.
Barrel: 19.5", rifled.
Weight: 8.82 lbs. **Length:** 45.28" over-all.
Power: Spring-air, barrel cocking.
Stock: Walnut stained hardwood.
Sights: Globe front, open rear adjustable for windage and elevation.
Features: Velocity of 900 fps. Adjustable trigger, checkered p.g., rubber butt pad. Imported from West Germany by Great Lakes Airguns.
Price: $289.50

Weihrauch Model 80

CAUTION: PRICES CHANGE. CHECK AT GUNSHOP.

Chokes & Brakes

Baker Superior Choke Tubes

Stan Baker's Superior choke tubes can be installed only in single-barrel guns. The external diameter of the barrel is enlarged by swaging, allowing enough for reaming and threading to accept the screw-in WinChoke-style tube. Installation on a single-barrel gun without rib is **$85.00**; with vent rib, cost is **$110.00.** Prices are higher for target guns, so contact Baker for specifics. Price includes honing the bore. Extra choke tubes are **$15.95** each. One tube and wrench are provided. Baker also installs WinChoke tubes.

Briley Screw-In Chokes

Installation of these choke tubes requires that all traces of the original choking be removed, the barrel threaded internally with square threads and then the tubes are custom fitted to the specific barrel diameter. The tubes are thin and, therefore, made of stainless steel. Cost of installation for single-barrel guns (pumps, autos) runs **$75.00**; un-single target guns run **$150.00**; over-unders and side-by-sides cost **$150.00** per barrel. Prices include one choke tube and a wrench for disassembly. Extra tubes are **$40.00** each.

Briley also makes "Eccentric" choke tubes that allow horizontal or vertical movement of the pattern up to 11". Add **$35.00** to the prices above. Installation available only from Briley.

Cellini Recoil Reducer

Designed for handgun and rifle applications, the Cellini Reducer is available as a removable factory-installed accessory. Over-all length is 2½", weight is 3.5 ounces, and the unit must be installed by the maker. It is said to reduce muzzle jump to zero, even for automatic weapons. Cost starts at $150. Contact Cellini for full details.

Cutts Compensator

The Cutts Compensator is one of the oldest variable choke devices available. Manufactured by Lyman Gunsight Corporation, it is available with a steel body. A series of vents allows gas to escape upward and downward. For the 12-ga. Comp body, six fixed-choke tubes are available: the Spreader—popular with Skeet shooters; Improved Cylinder; Modified; Full; Superfull, and Magnum Full. Full, Modified and Spreader tubes are available for 12, or 20, and an Adjustable Tube, giving Full through Improved Cylinder chokes, is offered in 12, or 20 gauges. Cutts Compensator, complete with wrench, adaptor and any single tube **$63.35;** with adjustable tube **$80.80.** All single choke tubes **$17.50** each. No factory installation available.

Emsco Choke

E. M. Schacht of Waseca, Minn., offers the Emsco, a small diameter choke which features a precision curve rather than a taper behind the 1½" choking area. 9 settings are available in this 5 oz. attachment. Its removable recoil sleeve can be furnished in dural if desired. Choice of three sight heights. For 12, 16 or 20 gauge. Price installed, **$29.95.** Not installed, **$18.50.**

Lyman CHOKE

The Lyman CHOKE is similar to the Cutts Comp in that it comes with fixed-choke tubes or an adjustable tube, with or without recoil chamber. The adjustable tube version sells for **$34.95** with recoil chamber, in 12 or 20 gauge. Lyman also offers Single-Choke tubes at **$17.50.** This device may be used with or without a recoil-reduction chamber; cost of the latter is **$7.95** extra. Available in 12 or 20 gauge only, no factory installation offered.

Mag-Na-Port

Electrical Discharge Machining works on any firearm except those having shrouded barrels. EDM is a metal erosion technique using carbon electrodes that control the area to be processed. The Mag-na-port venting process utilizes small trapezoidal openings to direct powder gases upward and outward to reduce recoil.

No effect is had on bluing or nickeling outside the Mag-na-port area so no refinishing is needed. Cost for the Mag-na-port treatment is **$49.00** for handguns, **$65.00** for rifles, plus transportation both ways, and **$2.00** for handling.

Poly-Choke

The Poly-Choke Co., manufacturers of the original adjustable shotgun choke, now offers two models in 12, 16, 20 and 28 gauge, the Deluxe Ventilated and the Deluxe Standard. Each provides 9 choke settings including Xtra-Full and Slug. The Ventilated model reduces 20% of a shotgun's recoil, the company claims, and is priced at **$52.25.** The Standard model is **$49.95,** postage not included.

Pro-Choke

Pro-Choke is a system of interchangeable choke tubes that can be installed in any single or double-barreled shotgun, including over-unders. The existing chokes are bored out, the muzzles over-bored and threaded for the tubes. A choice of three Pro-Choke tubes are supplied—Skeet, Imp. Cyl., Mod., Imp. Mod., or Full. Cost of the installation is **$159.95** for single-barrel guns, **$209.95** for doubles. Extra tubes cost **$40** each. Postage and handling charges are **$8.50.**

Pro-Port

A compound ellipsoid muzzle venting process similar to Mag-na-porting, only exclusively applied to shotguns. Like Mag-na-porting, this system reduces felt recoil, muzzle jump, and shooter fatigue. Very helpful for Trap doubles shooters. Pro-Port is a patented process and installation is available in both the U.S. and Canada. Cost for the Pro-Port process is **$110.00** for over-unders (both barrels); **$80.00** for only the bottom barrel; and **$65.00** for single barrel shotguns. Prices do not include shipping and handling.

Walker Choke Tubes

This interchangeable choke tube system uses an adaptor fitted to the barrel without swaging. Therefore, it can be fitted to any single-barreled gun. The choke tubes use the conical-parallel system as used on all factory-choked barrels. These tubes can be used in Winchester, Mossberg, Smith & Wesson, Weatherby, or similar barrels made for the standard screw-in choke system. Available for 10 gauge, 12, 16 and 20. Factory installation with choice of Standard Walker Choke tube is **$70.00;** with ventilated (muzzle brake) tube **$75.70.** A full range of constriction is available. Contact Walker Arms for more data.

Micrometer Receiver Sights

BEEMAN/WEIHRAUCH MATCH APERTURE SIGHT
Micrometer ¼-minute click adjustment knobs with settings indicated on scales. Price **$69.95**

BEEMAN/FEINWERKBAU MATCH APERTURE SIGHTS
Locks into one of four eye-relief positions. Micrometer ¼-minute click adjustments; may be set to zero at any range. Extra windage scale visible beside eyeshade. Primarily for use at 5 to 20 meters. Price.......... **$99.95**

BEEMAN SPORT APERTURE SIGHT
Positive click micrometer adjustments. Standard units with flush surface screwdriver adjustments. Deluxe version has target knobs.
Price: Standard **$24.98**
Price: Deluxe **$29.98**

BUEHLER
"Little Blue Peep" auxiliary rear sight used with Buehler scope mounts. Price **$3.75**

FREELAND TUBE SIGHT
Uses Unertl 1″ micrometer mounts. For 22-cal. target rifles, inc. 52 Win., 37, 40X Rem. and BSA Martini. Price.................. **$123.00**

LYMAN No. 57
¼-min. clicks. Target or Stayset knobs. Quick release slide, adjustable zero scales. Made for almost all modern rifles. Price............ **$43.95**

LYMAN No. 66
Fits close to the rear of flat-sided receivers, furnished with target or Stayset knobs. Quick release slide, ¼-min. adj. For most lever or slide action or flat-sided automatic rifles. Price **$43.95**

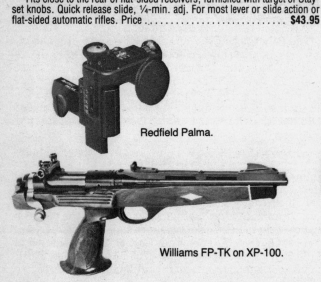

Redfield Palma.

Williams FP-TK on XP-100.

REDFIELD "PALMA" TARGET SIGHT
Windage and elevation adjustments are ¼-MOA and can be adjusted for "hard" or "soft" feel. Repeatability error limited to .001″ per click. Windage latitude 36 MOA, elevation 60 MOA. Mounting arm has three positions, providing ample positioning latitude for other sighting aids such as variable diopter correction, adjustable filters. An insert in the sighting disc block accepts either the standard American sighting disc thread or the European 9.5mm × 1 metric thread. Elevation staff and the sighting disc block have dovetail construction for precise travel. Price.................. **$205.55**

WILLIAMS FP
Internal click adjustments. Positive locks. For virtually all rifles, T/C Contender, plus Win., Rem. and Ithaca shotguns. Price **$32.67**
With Twilight Aperture.................................. **$33.60**
With Target Knobs..................................... **$38.85**
With Target Knobs & Twilight Aperture.................... **$39.80**
With Square Notched Blade.............................. **$34.35**
With Target Knobs & Square Notched Blade **$40.60**

WILLIAMS 5-D SIGHT
Low cost sight for shotguns, 22's and the more popular big game rifles. Adjustment for w. and e. Fits most guns without drilling or tapping. Also for Br. SMLE. Price **$18.55**
With Twilight Aperture.................................. **$19.50**
Extra Shotgun Aperture **$4.90**

WILLIAMS GUIDE
Receiver sight for .30 M1 Car., M1903A3 Springfield, Savage 24's, Savage-Anschutz rifles and Wby. XXII. Utilizes military dovetail; no drilling. Double-dovetail W. adj., sliding dovetail adj. for e. Price............ **$17.75**
With Twilight Aperture.................................. **$18.70**
With Open Sight Blade.................................. **$16.35**

Sporting Leaf and Open Sights

BINGHAM SPORTING RIFLE SIGHTS
All-steel sights are imported from Europe. Many styles of both front and rear sights available; random sampling listed here.
European express gold bead for European express ramp **$4.25**
European express ramp **$7.50**
Semi-buckhorn rear, with elevator **$6.50**
Rocky Mountain front, blue or bright **$3.95**
European 2-leaf folding express rear (V and U notch)........ **$12.50**

BINGHAM CLASSIC SIGHTS
All-steel sights for "classic" rifles. Rear sights only. This listing not complete; contact Bingham for full list.
Model 66 folding ladder-type.......................... **$19.95**
Model Saddle Ring Carbine (73, 92, 94, etc.)............. **$14.95**
Elevator, Winchester-type, early series (1876-WW II) **$4.95**

BURRIS SPORTING REAR SIGHT
Made of spring steel, supplied with multi-step elevator for coarse adjustments and notch plate with lock screw for finer adjustments. Price **$10.95**

LYMAN No. 16
Middle sight for barrel dovetail slot mounting. Folds flat when scope or peep sight is used. Sight notch plate adjustable for e. White triangle for quick aiming. 3 heights: A—.400″ to .500″, B—.345″ to .445″, C—.500″ to .600″. Price **$9.95**

MARBLE FALSE BASE
New screw-on base for most rifles replaces factory base. ⅜″ dovetail slot permits installation of any Marble rear sight. Can be had in sweat-on models also. Price **$3.60**

MARBLE CONTOUR RAMP
For late model Rem. 725, 740, 760, 742 rear sight mounting. ⁹⁄₁₆″ between mounting screws. Price **$8.00**

Lyman No. 66

Williams Dovetail Open.

MARBLE FOLDING LEAF
Flat-top or semi-buckhorn style. Folds down when scope or peep sights are used. Reversible plate gives choice of "U" or "V" notch. Adjustable for elevation. Price **$7.20**
Also available with both w. and e. adjustment **$8.40**

MARBLE SPORTING REAR
With white enamel diamond, gives choice of two "U" and two "V" notches of different sizes. Adjustment in height by means of double step elev,2a,2t,2o,2r
and sliding notch piece. For all rifles; screw or dovetail installation. Price .... **$7.40-$8.40**

WICHITA MULTI RANGE SIGHT SYSTEM
Designed for silhouette shooting. System allows you to adjust the rear sight to four repeatable range settings, once it is pre-set. Sight clicks to any of the settings by turning a serrated wheel. Front sight is adjustable for weather and light conditions with one adjustment. Specify gun when ordering.
Price: Rear sight **$69.95**
Front sight **$39.95**

WILLIAMS DOVETAIL OPEN SIGHT
Open rear sight with w. and e. adjustment. Furnished with "U" notch or choice of blades. Slips into dovetail and locks with gib lock. Heights from .281″ to .531″. Price with blade **$10.15**
Less Blade **$6.65**
Extra Blades.. **$3.50**

WILLIAMS GUIDE OPEN SIGHT
Open rear sight with w. and e. adjustment. Bases to fit most military and commercial barrels. Choice of square "U" or "V" notch blade, ³⁄₁₆″, ¼″, ⁵⁄₁₆″, or ⅜″ high. Price with blade **$12.25**
Extra blades, each **$3.50**
Price, less blade **$8.75**

Front Sights

LYMAN BLADE & DOVETAIL SIGHTS
Made with gold or ivory beads $\frac{1}{16}$" to $\frac{3}{32}$" wide and in varying heights for most military and commercial rifles. Price $6.95

MARBLE STANDARD
Ivory, red, or gold bead. For all American made rifles, $\frac{1}{16}$" wide bead with semi-flat face which does not reflect light. Specify type of rifle when ordering. Price $4.25

Marble's Standard Blade, Sheard, Contour, Standard

MARBLE-SHEARD "GOLD"
Shows up well even in darkest timber. Shows same color on different colored objects; sturdily built. Medium bead. Various models for different makes of rifles so specify type of rifle when ordering. Price $5.25

MARBLE CONTOURED
Same contour and shape as Marble-Sheard but uses standard $\frac{1}{16}$" or $\frac{3}{32}$" bead, ivory, red or gold. Specify rifle type. Price $4.80

WILLIAMS GUIDE BEAD SIGHT
Fits all shotguns, $\frac{1}{8}$" ivory, red or gold bead. Screws into existing sight hole. Various thread sizes and shank lengths. Price $3.45

Globe Target Front Sights

FREELAND SUPERIOR
Furnished with six 1" plastic apertures. Available in $4\frac{1}{2}$"-$6\frac{1}{2}$" lengths. Made for any target rifle. Price $35.00
Price with 6 metal insert apertures $37.00
Price, front base $8.00

FREELAND TWIN SET
Two Freeland Superior or Junior Globe Front Sights, long or short, allow switching from 50 yd. to 100 yd. ranges and back again without changing rear sight adjustment. Sight adjustment compensation is built into the set; just interchange and you're "on" at either range. Set includes 6 plastic apertures. Price with 6 metal apertures $56.00

FREELAND MILITARY
Short model for use with high-powered rifles where sight must not extend beyond muzzle. Screw-on base; six plastic apertures. Price . . $33.00
Price with 6 metal apertures $37.00
Price, front base $8.00

LYMAN No. 17A
7 interchangeable inserts which include 4 apertures, one transparent amber and two posts .50" and .100" in width. Price $18.95

REDFIELD Nos. 63 and 64
For rifles specially stocked for scopes where metallic sights must be same height as scopes. Instantly detachable to permit use of scope. Two styles and heights of bases. Interchangeable inserts. No. 64 is $\frac{1}{4}$" higher. Price with base, ... $33.70
No. 64 . . . . $39.70

REDFIELD No. 65
1" long, $\frac{5}{8}$" diameter. Standard dovetail base with 7 aperture or post inserts which are not reversible. For any rifle having standard barrel slot. $\frac{13}{32}$" height from bottom of base to center of aperture. No. 65NB ($26.30) same as above with narrow base for Win. 64 N.R.A., 70, and Savage 40, 45, and 99 with ramp front sight base. Price $27.50

REDFIELD No. 66
Replaces entire removable front sight stud, locked in place by screw in front of barrel band. $\frac{3}{4}$" from bottom of base to center of aperture. For Spgfld. 1903. Price $30.10

REDFIELD No. 68
For Win. 52, heavy barrel, Sav. 19 and 33, and other rifles requiring high front sight. $\frac{17}{32}$" from bottom of base to center of aperture. Standard dovetail size only. Price $25.50

REDFIELD OLYMPIC FRONT
Detachable. 10 inserts—5 steel, sizes .090", .110", .120", .140", .150"; one post insert, size .100"; four celluloid, sizes .090", .110", .120", .140". Celluloid inserts in clear, green, or amber, with or without cross hairs. For practically all rifles and with any type rear sight. Fits all standard Redfield, Lyman, or Fecker scope blocks. Price with base, ... $50.10

REDFIELD INTERNATIONAL SMALLBORE FRONT
Similar to Olympic. Drop-in insertion of eared inserts. Outer sleeve prevents light leakage. Comes complete with 6 clear inserts and 6 skeleton inserts. Price $53.50

REDFIELD INTERNATIONAL MILITARY BIG BORE
Same as International Match except tube only $2\frac{1}{4}$" long. For 30 cal. use. Price $53.50

Ramp Sights

LYMAN SCREW-ON RAMP AND SIGHT
Used with 8-40 screws but may also be brazed on. Heights from .10" to .350". Ramp without sight $10.95

MARBLE FRONT RAMPS
Available in either screw-on or sweat-on style. 5 heights; $\frac{3}{16}$", $\frac{5}{16}$", $\frac{3}{8}$", $\frac{7}{16}$", $\frac{9}{16}$". Standard $\frac{3}{8}$" dovetail slot. Price $7.50
Hoods for above ramps $1.65

WILLIAMS SHORTY RAMP
Companion to "Streamlined" ramp, about $\frac{1}{2}$" shorter. Screw-on or sweat-on. It is furnished in $\frac{1}{8}$", $\frac{3}{16}$", $\frac{9}{32}$", and $\frac{3}{8}$" heights without hood only.
Price $8.75

WILLIAMS STREAMLINED RAMP
Hooded style in screw-on or sweat-on models. Furnished in $\frac{9}{16}$", $\frac{7}{16}$", $\frac{3}{8}$", $\frac{5}{16}$", $\frac{3}{16}$" heights. Price with hood $13.80
Price without hood $11.45

WILLIAMS SHOTGUN RAMP
Designed to elevate the front bead for slug shooting or for guns that shoot high. Diameters to fit most 12, 16, 20 ga. guns. Fastens by screw-clamp, no drilling required. Price, with Williams gold bead $8.50
Price, without bead $6.25
Price, with Guide Bead $9.70

Handgun Sights

BINGHAM PISTOL SIGHTS
All-steel sights of various designs for Colt Government Model and Browning Hi-Power. Low profile "battle sights" (front and rear) for either Colt G.M. or Browning HP. Price $16.95
Combat sight set, low profile, white outline for Colt G.M., front and rear $21.95
National Match front sight, Colt G.M. $3.75
Camp Perry front sight, Colt G.M. $4.95

BO-MAR DE LUXE
Gives $\frac{3}{8}$" w. and e. adjustment at 50 yards on Colt Gov't 45, sight radius under 7". For GM and Commander models only. Uses existing dovetail slot. Has shield-type rear blade. Price $45.00

BO-MAR LOW PROFILE RIB
Streamlined rib with front and rear sights; $7\frac{1}{8}$" sight radius. Brings sight line closer to the bore than standard or extended sight and ramp. Weighs 4 oz. Made for Ruger Mark I Bull Barrel, Colt Gov't 45, Super 38, and Gold Cup 45 and 38. Price $55.00
Rib & Tuner—inserted in Low Profile Rib—accuracy tuner. Adjustable for barrel positioning. $64.00

BO-MAR COMBAT RIB
For S&W Model 19 revolver with 4" barrel. Sight radius $5\frac{3}{4}$"; weight $5\frac{1}{2}$ oz. Price $55.00

BO-MAR FAST DRAW RIB
Streamlined full length rib with integral Bo-Mar micrometer sight and serrated fast draw sight. For Browning 9mm, S&W 39, Colt Commander 45, Super Auto and 9mm. Price $55.00

Wichita Grand Master Deluxe Rib.

BO-MAR WINGED RIB
For S&W 4" and 6" length barrels—K-38, M10, HB 14 and 19. Weight for the 6" model is about $7\frac{1}{4}$ oz. Price $63.00

BO-MAR COVER-UP RIB
Adj. rear sight, winged front guards. Fits right over revolver's original front sight. For S&W 4" M-10HB, M-13, M-58, M-64 & 65, Ruger 4" models SDA-34, SDA-84, SS-34, SS-84, GF-34, GF-84. Price $60.00

MICRO
Click adjustable w. and e. rear with plain or undercut front sight in ⅛"
widths. Standard model available for 45, Super 38 or Commander autos.
Low model for above pistols plus Colt Service Ace. Also for Ruger with 4¾"
or 6" barrel. Price for sets... **$35.00**
    Price with ramp front sight... **$43.00**
    Adjustable rear sight only... **$29.50**
    Front ramp only, with blade... **$19.00**

MICRO
All-steel replacement for Ruger single-action and double-action revolvers. Two styles: MR-44 for square front end of sight leaf. Price ... **$18.00**

MMC "BAR CROSS" SIGHT SYSTEM
Provides a quick, clear sight picture in a variety of lighting conditions.
Black oxide finish is non-reflective. Front sight has a horizontal white bar with
vertical white bar, gives illusion of cross hair in poor light. Fixed rear comes
with or without white outline. Various front blades available.
    White outline rear sight.. **$17.30**
    Plain rear... **$13.50**
    Ramp Bar Cross front.. **$12.40**

MMC COMBAT DESIGN
Available specifically for Colt M1911 and descendants, High Standard autos, Ruger standard autos. Adaptable to other pistols. Some gunsmithing required. Not necessary to replace front sight. Contact MMC for complete details.
    Price, less leaf... **$26.15**
    Plain leaf.. **$7.75**
    White outline leaf... **$11.40**
    Extra for satin nickel finish (base only)........................... **$8.50**
    With reflector beads, add... **$2.25**

MILLETT SERIES 100 SIGHTS
Replacement sights for revolvers and auto pistols. Positive click adjust-
ments for windage and elevation. Designed for accuracy and ruggedness.
Made to fit S&W, Colt, High Standard, Ruger, Dan Wesson, Browning, AMT
Hardballer and Abilene handguns. Rear blades are available in white outline
or positive black target. All steel construction and easy to install.
Price .... **$39.95 to $56.95**

MILLETT MARK SERIES PISTOL SIGHTS
Mark I and Mark II replacement combat sights for government-type auto
pistols. Mark I is high profile, Mark II low profile. Both have horizontal light
deflectors.
    Mark I, front and rear.. **$27.95**
    Mark II, front and rear... **$39.95**

OMEGA OUTLINE SIGHT BLADES
Replacement rear sight blades for Colt and Ruger single action guns and
the Interarms Virginian Dragoon. Standard Outline available in gold or white
notch outline on blue metal. Price....................................... **$5.95**

OMEGA MAVERICK SIGHT BLADES
Replacement "peep-sight" blades for Colt, Ruger SAs, Virginian Dra-
goon. Three models available—No. 1, Plain, No. 2, Single Bar, No. 3 Double
Bar Rangefinder. Price, each... **$6.95**

WICHITA SIGHT SYSTEMS
For 45 auto pistols. Target and Combat styles available. Designed by Ron
Power. All-steel construction, click adjustable. Each sight has two traverse
pins, a large hinge pin and two elevation return springs. Sight blade is serrated and mounted on an angle to deflect light. Patridge front for target, ramp
front for combat. Both are legal for ISPC and NRA competitons.
    Rear sight, target or combat.. **$49.50**
    Front sight, patridge or ramp....................................... **$8.95**

Wichita Combat V Rib

WICHITA GRAND MASTER DELUXE RIBS
Ventilated rib has wings machined into it for better sight acquisition.
Made of stainless steel, sights blued. Uses Wichita Multi-Range rear sight,
adjustable front sight. Made for revolvers with 6" barrel.
    Price: Model 301 (adj. sight K-frames with custom bbl. of 1.000"-1.032"
dia., L and N frames with 1.062"-1.100" bbl.)....................... **$129.95**
    Price: Model 302 (fixed-sight K-frames; M10, 65, 13 with 1.000" bbl. N-
frame with 1.062" bbl.).. **$129.95**
    Price: Model 303 (Model 29, 629 with factory bbl., adj. sight K, L, N
frames).. **$129.95**
    Price: Extra for white outline rear sight............................. **$6.00**

WICHITA COMBAT V RIBS
Designed by Ron Power, the ventilated rib has a lengthwise V-groove that
emphasizes the front sight and reduces glare and distortion. Over-size rear
sight blade for the click-adjustable sight. Made for Browning Hi-Power, Colt
Commander, Govt. and Gold Cup models, Ruger Mark I, 4" S&W K-
frames—models 10HB, 13, 64HB, 65, 58 with 4" barrel. From Wichita Arms
Inc. Price: With sights... **$89.95**
    Price: Extra for white outline rear sight............................. **$6.00**

Sight Attachments

FREELAND LENS ADAPTER
Fits 1⅛" O.D. presciption ground lens to all standard tube and receiver
sights for shooting without glasses. Price without lens.......... **$44.00**
    Clear lens ground to prescription.................................. **$21.00**
    Yellow or green prescription lens.................................. **$21.00**

MERIT ADAPTER FOR GLOBE FRONT SIGHTS
An Iris Shutter Disc with a special adapter for mounting in Lyman or Redfield globe front sights. Price.. **$42.00**

MERIT IRIS SHUTTER DISC
Eleven clicks gives 12 different apertures. No. 3 and Master, primarily
target types, 0.22" to .125"; No. 4, ½" dia. hunting type, .025" to .155".
Available for all popular sights. The Master Disc, with flexible rubber light
shield, is particularly adapted to extension, scope height, and tang sights. All
Merit Deluxe models have internal click springs; are hand fitted to minimum
tolerance.
    Std. Master... **$45.00**
    Master Deluxe.. **$54.30**
    No. 4 Hunting Disc... **$37.50**

MERIT LENS DISC
Similar to Merit Iris Shutter (Model 3 or Master) but incorporates provision for mounting prescription lens integrally. Lens may be obtained locally,
or prescription sent to Merit. Sight disc is ⁷⁄₁₆" wide (Mod. 3), or ¾" wide
(Master). Lens, ground to prescription, **$19.00** Standard tints, **$23.50** Model 3 Deluxe. Price.. **$57.75**
    Master Deluxe.. **$67.50**

MERIT OPTICAL ATTACHMENT
For revolver and pistol shooters, instantly attached by rubber suction cup
to regular or shooting glasses. Any aperture .020" to .156". Price, Deluxe
(swings aside)... **$54.75**

REDFIELD SURE-X SIGHTING DISC
Eight hole selective aperture. Fits any Redfield target sight. Each click
changes aperture .004". Price... **$21.10**

REDFIELD SIGHTING DISCS
Fit all Redfield receiver sights. .046" to .093" aperture. ⅜", ½" and ⅞"
O.D. Price, each... **$4.70**

WILLIAMS APERTURES
Standard thread, fits most sights. Regular series ⅜" to ½" O.D., .050" to
.125" hole. "Twilight" series has white reflector ring. .093" to .125" inner
hole. Price, regular series... **$3.00.** Twilight series............ **$3.15**
New wide open ⁵⁄₁₆" aperture for shotguns fits 5-D and Foolproof sights.
Price.. **$4.30**

Shotgun Sights

ACCURA-SITE
For shooting shotgun slugs. Three models to fit most shotguns—"A" for
vent. rib barrels, "B" for solid ribs, "C" for plain barrels. Rear sight has
windage and elevation provisions. Easily removed and replaced. Includes
front and rear sights. Price.................................... **$25.95 to $27.95**

FOR DOUBLE BARREL SHOTGUNS (PRESS FIT)
Marble 214—Ivory front bead, ¹¹⁄₆₄"... **$2.40; 215**—same with .080"
rear bead and reamers... **$8.15. Marble 220**—Bi-color (gold and ivory)
front bead, ¹¹⁄₆₄" and .080" rear bead, with reamers... **$9.25; Marble
221**—front bead only... **$3.50. Marble 223**—Ivory rear .080"... **$2.20.
Marble 224**—Front sight reamer for 214-221 beads... **$2.25; Marble
226**—Rear sight reamer for 223. Price....................... **$1.75**

FOR SINGLE OR DB SHOTGUNS (SCREW-ON FIT)
Marble 217—Ivory front bead ¹¹⁄₆₄"... **$2.65; Marble 216**... **$5.50;
Marble 218**—Bi-color front, ¹¹⁄₆₄"... **$3.85; Marble 219**... **$6.70 Marble
223T**—Ivory rear .080" Price.. **$3.65**
    Marble Bradley type sights 223BT—⅛", ⁵⁄₆₄" and ¹¹⁄₆₄" long. Gold, Ivory
or Red bead.. **$2.50**

SLUG SITE
A combination V-notch rear and bead front sight made of adhesive-
backed formed metal approx. 7" over-all. May be mounted, removed and re-
mounted as necessary, using new adhesive from the pack supplied.
Price.. **$10.00**

CAUTION: PRICES CHANGE. CHECK AT GUNSHOP.

SCOPES & MOUNTS
HUNTING, TARGET ■ & VARMINT ■ SCOPES

Maker and Model	Magn.	Field at 100 Yds (feet)	Relative Brightness	Eye Relief (in.)	Length (in.)	Tube Diam. (in.)	W&E Adjustments	Weight (ozs.)	Price	Other Data
Aimpoint										
Mark II	0	—	—	—	6	—	Int.	12	$189.95	Projects variable intensity aiming dot. Unlimited eye relief. 3x magnification lens, $94.95, 1.5-4x lens $135.95. Imported by Aimpoint USA, Inc.
Mark III	0	—	—	—	6	—	Int.	12	219.95	
American Import Co.										
Dickson 200[1]	4	19	13.7	3.5	11.5	¾	Int.	6	12.50	[1]Complete with mount for 22-cal. RF rifles. [2]Standard crosshair reticle, coated lenses. [3]Anodized finish. [4]Wide angle. [5]Super wide angle. [6]Post and crosshair, 3 post,, tapered post, crosshair and 4-post crosshair all available as options. 2, 3, apply to all models.[7] Complete with bridge mount.
Dickson 218 32mm	2½	32	164	3.7	12	1	Int.	9.3	47.95	
Dickson 220 32mm[2]	4	29	64	3.6	12	1	Int.	9.1	46.95	
Dickson 224 40mm	4	30	100	3.5	12½	1	Int.	10	54.95	
Dickson 226 40mm[3]	6	20	44.7	3.7	13	1	Int.	10	54.95	
Dickson 228 32mm[4]	4	37	64	3.3	12	1	Int.	10.5	73.95	
Dickson 230 40mm[4]	4	37	100	3.8	12.4	1	Int.	12	78.95	
Dickson 231 40mm[4]	6	24½	44.5	3.8	12.4	1	Int.	12	81.00	
Dickson 232 32mm[4]	3-9	42-14	112.4-13	3.1-2.5	12.9	1	Int.	12	93.95	
Dickson 233 20mm[5]	4	42	25	3	9.8	1	Int.	10.2	73.95	
Dickson 240 32mm	3-9	37-12.3	112-13	3	12.8	1	Int.	13.8	62.95	
Dickson 242 40mm	3.9	37-12.3	177-19.4	3	12.8	1	Int.	15.2	78.95	
Dickson 244 20mm	1½-5	46	177	4.3	11.3	1	Int.	10.3	67.95	
Dickson Pistol 250[7]	1½	15.3	100	11-16	8½	¾	Int.	6	19.95	
Bausch & Lomb										
3x-9x 40mm	3-9	36-12	267	3.2	13	1	Int.	17	339.95	Contact Bushnell for details.
4x 40 mm	4	28	150	3.2	12¾	1	Int.	14½	219.95	
Beeman										
Blue Ribbon 20[1]	1.5	14	150	11-16	8.3	¾	Int.	3.6	46.95	All scopes have 5-pt. reticle, all glass, fully coated lenses. [1]Pistol scope; cast mounts included. [2]Pistol scope; silhouette knobs. [3]Rubber armor coating; built-in double adj. mount, parallax-free setting. [4]Objective focus, built-in double-adj. mount; matte finish. [5]Objective focus. [6]Has 8 lenses; objective focus; milled mounts included. [7]Includes cast mounts. [8]Objective focus; silhouette knobs; matte finish. [9]Has 9 lenses; objective focus.
Blue Ribbon 25[2]	2	19	150	10-24	9 1/16	1	Int.	7.4	127.50	
SS-1[3]	2.5	30	61	3.25	5½	1	Int.	7	119.95	
SS-2[4]	3	34.5	74	3.5	6.8	1.38	Int.	13.6	189.50	
50R[5]	2.5	33	245	3.5	12	1	Int.	11.8	89.50	
35R[6]	3	25	67	2.5	11¼	¾	Int.	5.1	39.95	
30A[7]	4	21	21	2	10.2	¾	Int.	4.5	21.95	
Blue Ribbon 66R[8]	2-7	62-16	384-31	3	11.4	1	Int.	14.9	159.50	
45R[9]	3-7	26-12	67-9	2.5	10 5/8	¾	Int.	6	63.95	
Burris										
4x Fullfield[1]	3.8	37	49	3¼	11¼	1	Int.	11	159.95	Dot reticle $10 extra. Target knobs $15 extra. ½-minute dot $10 extra. LER = Long Eye Relief—ideal for forward mounting on handguns. Plex or crosshair only. Matte "Safari" finish avail. on 4x, 6x, 2-7x, 3-9x with Plex reticle, $10 extra, [1]3" dot $10 extra. [2]1"-3" dot $10 extra. [3]1"-3" dot $10 extra. [4]With parallax adjustment $135.95. [5]With parallax adjustment $142.95. [6]With parallax adjustment $151.95. [7]With parallax adjustment $158.95. Parallax adjustment adds 5 oz. to weight.
2x-7x Fullfield[2] HiLume	2.5-6.8	50-19	81-22	3¼	11 7/8	1	Int.	14	213.95	
3x-9x Fullfield[3] HiLume	3.3-8.6	40-15	72-17.6	3¼	12¾	1	Int.	15	229.95	
2¾ Fullfield	2.7	53	49	3¼	10½	1	Int.	9	150.95	
6x Fullfield	5.8	24	36	3¼	13	1	Int.	12	172.95	
1¾-5x Fullfield HiLume	2.5-6.8	70-27	121-25	3¼	10¾	1	Int.	13	188.95	
4x-12x Fullfield	4.4-11.8	28-10½	—	3-3¼	15	1	Int.	18	263.95	
■ 6x-18x Fullfield	6.5-17.6	17-7.5	—	3-3¾	15.8	12	Int.	18.5	267.95	
■ 10x Fullfield	9.8	12½	—	3¼	15	1	Int.	15	224.95	
■ 12x Fullfield	11.8	11	—	3¼	15	1	Int.	15	231.95	
2x LER	1.7	21	—	10-24	8¾	1	Int.	6.8	117.95	
3x LER	2.7	17	—	10-20	8 7/8	1	Int.	6.8	124.95	
4x LER[6]	3.7	11	—	10-22	9 5/8	1	Int.	8.5	133.95	
5x LER[7]	4.5	8.7	—	12-22	10 7/8	1	Int.	9.5	140.95	
7x IER	6.5	6.5	—	10-16	11¼	1	Int.	10	172.95	
1½x-4x LER	1.6-3.8	16-11	—	11-24	10½	1	Int.	11	213.95	
2x-7x Mini	2.5-6.9	32-14	—	3¾	9 3/8	1	Int.	10.5	159.95	
4x Mini	3.6	24	—	3¾	8¼	1	Int.	7.8	116.95	
6x Mini	5.5	17	—	3¾	9	1	Int.	7.8	124.95	
3x-9x Mini	3.6-8.8	25-11	—	3¾	9 7/8	1	Int.	11.5	168.95	
Bushnell										
Scope Chief VI	4	37.3	150	3	12.3	1	Int.	12	159.95	All ScopeChief, Banner and Custom models come with Multi-X reticle, with or without BDC (bullet drop compensator) that eliminates hold-over. Prismatic Rangefinder (PRF) on some models. Contact Bushnell for data on full line. Prices include BDC—deduct $5 if not wanted. Add $30 for PRF. BDC feature available in all Banner models, except 2.5x. [1]Wide angle. [2]Complete with mount rings. [3]Equipped with Wind Drift Compensator and Parallax-free adjustment. [4]Parallax focus adjustment. [5]Wide angle. [6]Wide angle. [7]Parallax focus adjustment. [8]Phantoms intended for handgun use. [9]Mount separate. [10]Has battery-powered, lighted reticle. [11]With mounts.
Scope Chief VI	4	29	96	3½	12	1	Int.	9.3	119.95	
Scope Chief VI	3-9	35-12.6	267-30	3½-3⅓	12.6	1	Int.	14.3	191.95	
Scope Chief VI	3-9	43-14.6	241-26.5	3	12.1	1	Int.	15.4	239.95	
Scope Chief VI	2½-8	45-14	247-96	3.7-3.3	11.2	1	Int.	12.1	169.95	
Scope Chief VI	1½-4½	73.7-24.5	267-30	3.5-3.5	9.6	1	Int.	9.5	159.95	
Scope Chief VI	4-12	29-10	150-17	3.2	13.5	1	Int.	17	234.95	
Centurion Handgun 4x32mm	4	10.2	96	10-20	8¾	1	Int.	9.3	169.95	
Custom 22	4	28.4	—	2½	10 5/16	7/8	Int.	5¼	41.95	
Custom 22	3-7	29-13.6	28-5	2¼-2½	10	7/8	Int.	6½	51.95	
Banner	2½	45	96	3½	10.9	1	Int.	8	86.95	
Banner 32mm	4	29	96	3½	12	1	Int.	10	100.95	
Banner 40mm	4	37⅓	150	3	12⅓	1	Int.	12	131.95	
Banner Lite-Site 4x[10]	4	28	150	3.3	12.9	1	Int.	11½	199.95	
Banner 40mm	6	19.5	67	3	13.5	1	Int.	11.5	109.95	
Banner[1]	6	19½	42	3	13½	1	Int.	10½	109.95	
Banner 22[2]	4	27.5	37.5	3	11 5/8	1	Int.	8	64.95	
■ Banner Silhouette[3]	10	12	24	3	14½	1	Int.	14.6	167.95	
■ Banner	10	12	24	3	14½	1	Int.	14.6	167.95	
Banner[4]	1½-4	63-28	294-41	3½	10½	1	Int.	10.3	123.95	
Banner[5]	1¾-4½	71-27	216-33	3	10.2	1	Int.	11½	143.95	
Banner Lite-Site 3x-9x[10]	3.9	36-12	267	3.5-3.3	13.6	1	Int.	14	239.95	
Banner 32mm	3-9	39-13	171-19	3½	11.5	1	Int.	11	137.95	
Banner 38mm[6]	3-9	43-14.6	241-26½	3	12	1	Int.	14	160.95	
Banner 40mm	3-9	35-12.6	267-30	3½	13	1	Int.	13	180.95	
Banner[7]	4-12	29-10	150-17	3.2	13½	1	Int.	15½	163.95	
Magnum Phantom[8]	1.3	17	441	7-21	7.8	15/16	Int.	5½	71.95	
Magnum Phantom[9]	2½	9	100	8-21	9.7	15/16	Int.	6½	79.95	
Sportview	3-9	41.5-13.6	241-26.5	3	12.5	1	Int.	14	86.95	(continued)

HUNTING, TARGET ■ & VARMINT ■ SCOPES

Maker and Model	Magn.	Field at 100 Yds (feet)	Relative Brightness	Eye Relief (in.)	Length (in.)	Tube Diam. (in.)	W&E Adjustments	Weight (ozs.)	Price	Other Data
Bushnell (cont'd.)										
Sportview	4	34.5	135	3	12.5	1	Int.	11.5	66.95	
Sportview 22	3-7	26-12	67.4-12.6	2.5	11.5	1	Int.	5.5	39.95	
Sportview 4x32mm	4	28	96	4	11.8	1	Int.	11.3	59.95	
Sportview 4x15mm[11]	4	17	21	2.3	10.2	7/8	Int.	6	13.95	
Colt										
AR-15 3x	3	40	—	—	6	—	Int.	—	$171.95	All Colt scopes come complete with mount and allow use of iron sights. Reflex sighting system provides a variable intensity red dot; battery operated, batteries not included.
AR-15 4x	4	30	—	—	6	—	Int.	—	191.50	
Reflex Sight	1	—	—	—	7½	—	Int.	—	205.50	
Davis Optical										
Spot Shot 1½"	10,12 15,20 25,30	10-4	—	2	25	.75	Ext.	—	116.00	Focus by moving non-rotating obj. lens unit. Ext. mounts included. Recoil spring $4.50 extra.
Spot Shot 1¼"	10,12, 15,20	10.6	—	2	25	.75	Ext.	—	90.00	
Fontaine										
4x32 Wide Angle	4	38	64	3.0	11.8	1	Int.	10.0	104.45	Non-waterproof also available. Scopes listed have Jennison TCS with Optima system. Extra TCS drums $5.50 ea. Scopes with TCS also avail. Also with duplex reticle.
4 x 40 Wide Angle	4	38	100	3.0	12.0	1	Int.	11.6	127.00	
3-9 x 32 Wide Angle	3-9	43.5-15	114-12.8	3.3-3.0	12.2	1	Int.	12.0	156.20	
3-9 x 40 Wide Angle	3-9	43.5-15	177.3-19.6	3.3-3.0	12.2	1	Int.	12.5	175.40	
Jason										
860	4	29	64	3	11.8	1	Int.	9.2	50.00	Constantly centered reticles, ballbearing click stops, nitrogen filled tubes, coated lenses. 4-Post crosshair about $3.50 extra on models 860, 861, 864, 865.
861	3-9	35-13	112-12	3	12.7	1	Int.	10.9	76.00	
862	4	19	14	2	11	3/4	Int.	5.5	13.50	
863C	3-7	23-10	43-8	3	11	3/4	Int.	8.4	44.00	
Jason										
865	3-9	35-13	177-19	3	13	1	Int.	12.2	80.00	
869	4	19	25	2	11.4	3/4	Int.	6	23.00	
873	4	29	100	3	12.7	1	Int.	11.1	75.00	
875	3-9	35-13	177-19	3	13	1	Int.	12.2	80.00	
877	4	37	100	3	11.6	1	Int.	11.6	85.00	
878	3-9	42.5-13.6	112-12	2.7	12.7	1	Int.	12.7	110.00	
Kahles										
Helia Super 2.5 x 20[1]	2.5	50	64	3.25	9.8	1	Int.	12.6	279.00	[1]Lightweight model weighs 10.1 oz. [2]Lightweight—11.2 oz. [3]Lightweight—13 oz. [4]Lightweight—16 oz. [5]Lightweight—12.6 oz. [6]Lightweight—15.4 oz. [7]Lightweight—15.7 oz. [8]Lightweight—17.8 oz. [9]Calibrated for 7.62 NATO ammo, 100 to 800 meters. [10]Avail. with key adj., std. click adj., or calibrated for 7.62 or 5.56 NATO ammo. Also avail. with integral bases for standard (STANAG) mountings. All scopes have constantly centered reticles except ZF69; all come with lens caps. Imported from Austria by Kahles of America. (Del-Sports, Inc.).
Helia Super 4 x 32[2]	4	30	60	3.25	11.6	1	Int.	15	319.00	
Helia 6 x 42[3]	6	21.1	49	3.25	12.8	1	Int.	17.5	349.00	
Helia 8 x 56[4]	8	15.6	49	3.25	14.8	1	Int.	23	389.00	
Helia 1.1-4.5 x 20[5]	1.1-4.5	72.2-27	328-18	3.25	10.8	30mm	Int.	15	369.00	
Helia 1.5-6 x 20[6]	1.5-6	55.6-19.5	784-49	3.25	12.8	30mm	Int.	20	399.00	
Helia 2.2-9 x 42[7]	2.2-9	36.1-13.5	364-21	3.25	13.7	30mm	Int.	20.3	449.00	
Helia 3-12 x 56[8]	3-12	27.1-10	347-21	3.25	15.6	30mm	Int.	24.8	499.00	
ZF69 Sniper[9]	6	22.5	49	3.25	12.2	26mm	Int.	16.8	499.00	
Kobra 1.5 x 14[10]	1.5	45	87	4	7.7	26mm	Int.	11	299.00	
Kassnar										
2x-7x Wide Angle	2-7	49-19	258-21	3-2.7	11	1	Int.	12.8	94.95	Other models avail., including ¾" and 7/8" tubes for 22-cal. rifles. Contact Kassnar for details. [1]Also in 3x-9x40—$109.95 [2]Also in 4x40—$79.95. [3]Also in 3x-9x40—$89.95.
3x-9x Wide Angle[1]	3-9	42-15	112-13	3-2.7	12.2	1	Int.	13	99.95	
4x32 Wide Angle[2]	4	36	64	3.5	12	1	Int.	9.2	69.95	
6x40 Wide Angle	6	24	44	3	12.8	1	Int.	12	84.95	
1.5-4x Std.	1.5-4	52-27	177-25	4.4-3	10	1	Int.	9.5	79.95	
2x-7x Std.	2-7	42-16	256-21	3.1-3	11	1	Int.	12.5	84.95	
3x-9x Std.[3]	3-9	36-13	112-13	3.1-3	12.2	1	Int.	13.5	87.95	
4x-12x40 Std.	4-12	27-9.6	100-11	3-2.7	13.5	1	Int.	16	159.95	
2.5x32 Std.	2.5	36	164	3.6	12	1	Int.	9.3	64.95	
Kimber										
4x Compact	3.6	26.5	—	4.1	10.3	1	Int.	8.5	185.00	Duplex reticle with fine crosshair, parallax free at 75 yds.
Leatherwood										
ART II	3.0-8.8	31-12	—	3.5	13.9	1	Int.	42	675.00	
ART/MPC	3.0-8.7	31-12	—	3.7	14.1	1	Int.	33	349.50	
4x	4.1	27	—	4	12.25	1	Int.	12.3	125.00	
Leupold										
M8-2X EER[1]	1.8	22.0	—	12-24	8.1	1	Int.	6.8	150.55	Constantly centered reticles, choice of Duplex, tapered CPC, Leupold Dot, Crosshair and Dot. CPC and Dot reticles extra. [1]2x and 4x scope have from 12"-24" of eye relief and are suitable for handguns, top ejection arms and muzzleloaders. [2]8x, 12x, 3x9, 3.5x10 and 6.5x20 come with Adjustable Objective. [3]Silhouette/Target scopes have 1-min divisions with ¼-min clicks, and Adjustable Objectives. 50-ft. Focus Adaptor available for indoor target ranges, $37.50. Sunshade available for all Adjustable Objective scopes, $10.35. [4]Also available in matte finish for about $18.00 extra.
M8-2X EER Silver[1]	1.8	22.0	—	12-24	8.1	1	Int.	6.8	159.45	
M8-4X EER[1]	3.5	9.5	—	12-24	8.4	1	Int.	7.6	183.75	
M8-4X EER Silhouette[1]	3.5	9.5	—	12-24	8.4	1	Int.	8.5	200.30	
M8-2.5X Compact	2.3	42	—	4.3	8.5	1	Int.	7.4	160.90	
M8-4X Compact	3.6	26.5	—	4.1	10.3	1	Int.	8.5	183.75	
6x Compact	5.7	16	—	3.9	10.7	1	Int.	8.5	187.50	
3-9x Compact	3.2-8.5	34.5-13.5	—	3.8-3.1	11	1	Int.	9.5	250.00	
3-9x Compact Sil.	3.2-8.5	34.5-13.5	—	3.8-3.1	11	1	Int.	9.5	258.95	
M8-4X[4]	3.6	28	—	4.4	11.4	1	Int.	8.8	183.75	
M8-6X	5.9	18.0	—	4.3	11.4	1	Int.	9.9	195.25	
M8-8X[2]	7.8	14.5	—	4.0	12.5	1	Int.	13.0	261.60	
M8-12X[2]	11.6	9.2	—	4.2	13.0	1	Int.	13.5	265.10	
6.5 x 20 Sil. AO	6.5-19.2	14.8-5.7	—	5.3-3.7	14.2	1	Int.	16	394.80	
M8-12X Silhouette[3]	11.6	9.2	—	4.2	13.0	1	Int.	14.5	297.25	
M8-24X[3]	24.0	4.7	—	3.2	13.6	1	Int.	14.5	369.30	
M8-36X[3]	36.0	3.2	—	3.4	13.9	1	Int.	15.5	369.30	
Vari-X-II 1X4	1.6-4.2	70.5-28.5	—	4.3-3.8	9.2	1	Int.	9.0	225.05	
Vari-X-II 2X7	2.5-6.6	44.0-19.0	—	4.1-3.7	10.7	1	Int.	10.4	245.70	
Vari-X-II 3X9[4]	3.5-9.0	32.0-13.5	—	4.1-3.7	12.3	1	Int.	13.1	263.95	
Vari-X-II 3X9[2]	3.5-9.0	32.0-13.5	—	4.1-3.7	12.3	1	Int.	14.5	297.20	
Vari-X-III 1.5X5	1.5-4.6	66.0-24.0	—	4.7-3.5	9.4	1	Int.	9.3	259.55	
Vari-X-III 2.5X8[4]	2.7-7.9	38.0-14.0	—	4.2-3.4	11.3	1	Int.	11.0	292.95	
Vari-X-III 3.5X10	3.4-9.9	29.5-10.5	—	4.6-3.6	12.4	1	Int.	13.0	306.25	
Vari-X-III 3.5X10[2]	3.4-9.9	29.5-10.5	—	4.6-3.6	12.4	1	Int.	14.4	336.35	
Vari-X-III 6.5X20[2]	6.5-19.2	14.8- 5.7	—	5.3-3.7	14.2	1	Int.	16	362.70	
Lyman										
Lyman 4x	4	30	—	3¼	12	1	Int.	10	149.95	
Variable	1¾-5	47-18	—	3	12¼	1	Int.	12¼	159.95	(continued)

HUNTING, TARGET ■ & VARMINT ■ SCOPES

Maker and Model	Magn.	Field at 100 Yds (feet)	Relative Brightness	Eye Relief (in.)	Length (in.)	Tube Diam. (in.)	W&E Adjustments	Weight (ozs.)	Price	Other Data
Lyman (cont'd.)										
■ 20x LWBR[1]	20	5.5	—	2¼	17⅛	1	Int.	15¼	**339.95**	Choice of standard CH, tapered post, or tapered post and CH reticles. All-weather reticle caps. All Lyman scopes have Perma-Center reticle which remains in optical center regardless of changes in w&e. Adj. for parallax. [1]⅛ or ¼ MOA clicks. [2]Non-rotating objective lens focusing. ¼ MOA click adjustments. 5 different dot reticles, $12.50 extra. [3]Standard crosswire, 4 Center-Range reticles. [4]Std. Fine, Extra Fine, 1 Min. Dot, ½-Min. Dot reticles. External adjustment knobs; hand lapped zero repeat w. and e. systems. Choice of 4 reticles.
■ All-American[2]	3-9	39-13	—	3¾-3¼	10½	1	Int.	14	**179.95**	
2x-7x Var.	1.9-6.8	49-19	—	3¼	11⅝	1	Int.	10½	**169.95**	
■ 25x LWBR	25	4.8	—	3	17	1	Int.	19	**369.95**	
■ 35x LWBR	35	3.8	—	3	17	1	Int.	19	**399.95**	
Metallic Silhouette[3] 6x-SL	6.2	20	—	3¼	13⅞	1	Int.	14¼	**249.95**	
Metallic Silhouette[4] 8x-SL	8.1	14	—	3¼	14⅝	1	Int.	15¼	**259.95**	
Metallic Silhouette 10x-SL	10	12	—	3¼	15⅜	1	Int.	15¼	**269.95**	
RWS										
100 4x32	4	20	—	—	10⅞	¾	Int.	6	**38.00**	Air gun scopes. All have Dyna-Plex reticle. Imported from Japan by Dynamit Nobel of America.
200 3-7x-20	3-7	24-17	—	—	11¼	¾	Int.	6	**60.80**	
300 4x32	4	28	—	—	12¾	1	Int.	11	**95.00**	
400 2-7x32	2-7	56-17	—	—	12¾	1	Int.	12	**149.00**	
800 1.5x20	1.5	19	—	—	8¾	1	Int.	6½	**99.95**	
Redfield										
Illuminator Trad. 3-9x	2.9-8.7	33-11	—	3½	12¾	1	Int.	17	**330.30**	*Accutrac feature avail. on these scopes at extra cost. Traditionals have round lenses. 4-Plex reticle is standard. [1]"Magnum Proof." Specially designed for magnum and auto pistols. Uses "Double Dovetail" mounts. [2]Mounts solidly on receiver. CH or dot. 20x—$308.20, 24x—$317.65.
Illuminator Widefield 3-9x*	2.9-8.7	38-13	—	3½	12¾	1	Int.	17	**366.05**	
Tracker 4x	3.9	28.9	—	3½	11.02	1	Int.	9.8	**89.20**	
Tracker 2-7x	2.3-6.9	36.6-12.2	—	3½	12.20	1	Int.	11.6	**133.85**	
Tracker 3-9x	3.0-9.0	34.4-11.3	—	3½	14.96	1	Int.	13.4	**151.70**	
Traditional 4x¾"	4	24½	27	3½	9⅜	¾	Int.	—	**98.15**	
Traditional 2½x	2½	43	64	3½	10¼	1	Int.	8½	**135.65**	
Traditional 4x	4	28½	56	3½	11⅜	1	Int.	9¾	**153.50**	
Traditional 6x	6	19	—	3½	12½	1	Int.	11½	**178.50**	
Traditional 3x-9x* Royal	3-9	34-11	—	3½-4¼	12½	1	Int.	13	**267.86**	
Traditional 2x-7x*	2-7	42-14	207-23	3½	11¼	1	Int.	12	**210.65**	
Traditional 3x-9x*	3-9	34-11	163-18	3½	12½	1	Int.	13	**232.10**	
Traditional 8xMS	8	16.6	—	3-3¾	14⅛	1	Int.	17⅕	**244.60**	
Traditional 10xMS	10	12.6	—	3-3¾	14⅛	1	Int.	17½	**255.30**	
Traditional 12xMS	12.4	8.1	—	3-3¾	14⅛	1	Int.	17½	**267.80**	
Pistol Scopes										
1½xMP[1]	1.5	14	—	19-32	9 13/16	1	Int.	10.5	**128.50**	
2½xMP	2.5	9	—	14-24	9 13/16	1	Int.	10.5	**135.65**	
4xMP	3.6	9	—	12-22	9 11/16	1	Int.	11.1	**169.75**	
Traditional 4x-12x*	4-12	26-9	112-14	3½	13⅞	1	Int.	14	**332.40**	
Traditional 6x-18x*	6-18	18-6	50-6	3½	13 15/16	1	Int.	18	**369.95**	
Low Profile Scopes										
Widefield 2¾xLP	2¾	55½	69	3½	10½	1	Int.	8	**169.60**	
Widefield 4xLP	3.6	37½	84	3½	11½	1	Int.	10	**189.40**	
Widefield 6xLP	5.5	23	—	3½	12¾	1	Int.	11	**207.25**	
Widefield 1¾x5xLP	1¾-5	70-27	136-21	3½	10¾	1	Int.	11½	**223.15**	
Widefield 2x7xLP*	2-7	49-19	144-21	3½	11¾	1	Int.	13	**243.00**	
Widefield 3x-9xLP*	3-9	39-15	112-18	3½	12½	1	Int.	14	**269.95**	
■ 6400 Target[4]	16, 20, 24	6½, 5, 4½	5¾, 3½, 2½	3	17	1	Int.	18	**298.70**	
Sanders										
Bisley 2½x20	2½	42	64	3	10¾	1	Int.	8¼	**48.50**	Alum. alloy tubes, ¼" adj. coated lenses. Five other scopes are offered; 6x45 at $68.50, 8x45 at $70.50, 2½x7x at $69.50, 3-9x33 at $72.50 and 3-9x40 at $78.50. Rubber lens covers (clear plastic) are $3.50. Write to Sanders for details. Choice of reticles in CH, PCH, 3-post.
Bisley 4x33	4	28	64	3	12	1	Int.	9	**52.50**	
Bisley 6x40	6	19	45	3	12½	1	Int.	9½	**56.50**	
Bisley 8x40	8	18	25	3¼	12½	1	Int.	9½	**62.50**	
Bisley 10x40	10	12½	16	2½	12½	1	Int.	10¼	**64.50**	
Bisley 5-13x40	5-13	29-10	64-9	3	14	1	Int.	14	**86.50**	
Shepherd										
3 x 9 40mm	3-9	43.5-15.0	—	3.3	13	1	Int.	13½	**NA**	Instant range finding and bullet drop compensating; choice of plain, range finding or bullet drop reticle by turning cover cap; built-in collimator. From Shepherd Scope Ltd.
Swarovski Habicht										
1.5x20 DV SD	1.5	69	—	3⅛	10	26mm	Int.	12.0	**290.00**	All models steel except LD model light alloy. All-weather scopes. 4x & 6x scopes have centered reticles—7 different designs. NOVA has eyepiece recoil mechanism and rubber ring shield to protect face. FIve Year warranty. For spirit Level, add $47. Importer-distributor: Strieter Corp.
Nova 4x32 DV LD	4	30	—	3⅛	11	26mm	Int.	15.9	**330.00**	
Nova 4x32 DV SD	4	30	—	3⅛	11	26mm	Int.	16.6	**330.00**	
Nova 6x42 DV SD	6	20	—	3¼	11	26mm	Int.	18.7	**350.00**	
Swift										
Mark I 4x15	4	16.2	—	2.4	11	¾	Int.	4.7	**22.00**	All Swift Mark I scopes, with the exception of the 4x15, have Quadraplex reticles and are fog-proof and waterproof. The 4x15 has crosshair reticle and is non-waterproof. (continued)
Mark I 4x32	4	29	—	3½	12	1	Int.	9	**68.00**	
Mark I 4x32 WA	4	37	—	3½	11¾	1	Int.	10½	**74.00**	
Mark I 4x40 WA	4	35½	—	3¾	12¼	1	Int.	12	**86.00**	
Mark I 3-9x32	3-9	35¾-12¾	—	3	12¾	1	Int.	13¾	**89.50**	
Mark I 3-9x40 WA	3-9	42½-13½	—	2¾	12¾	1	Int.	14	**99.50**	
Mark I 6x40	6	18	—	3¾	13	1	Int.	10	**76.00**	
Mark I 1½-4½x32	1½-4½	55-22	—	3½	12	1	Int.	13	**94.50**	
Tasco										
1860 Tube Sight[1]	4	12½	14	3	32½	¾	Ext.	25	**124.95**	[1]Brass tube for many black powder guns. [2]Supercon®, fully coated lenses; waterproof, shockproof, fogproof; includes haze filter caps, lifetime warranty. [3]Trajectory-Range Finding scopes. [4]30/30 range finding reticle; rubber covered; built-in mounting rings. Also avail. in wide angle models. [5]Waterproof; anodized finish; ¼-min. click stops; R.F. reticle. [6]R.F. reticle, fully coated lenses; ¼-min. clicks; waterproof. [7]Integral mount for 22 RF, airguns with grooved receiver. Also avail. in brushed aluminum finish. [8]Adj., built-in mount; adj. rheostat, polarizer; ½-min. clicks. Avail. to fit Rem. 870, 1100, also with side mounts, in wide angle. Contact Tasco for complete list of models offered. (continued)
WA 4 x 40 Wide Angle[2]	4	36	100	3¼	12⅝	1	Int.	12½	**114.95**	
WA 3-9 x 40 Wide Angle[2]	3-9	43½-15	178-20	3¼	12⅝	1	Int.	11½	**139.95**	
WA 2.5 x 32 Wide Angle[2]	2.5	52	44	3¼	12	1	Int.	9½	**109.95**	
WA 2-7 x 32 Wide Angle[2]	2-7	56-17	256-21	3¼	11½	1	Int.	11½	**134.95**	
WA 1¾-5 x 20 Wide Angle[2]	1.75-5	72-24	131-16	3¼	10⅝	1	Int.	10¾	**119.95**	
RC 3-9 x 40 WA[2,4]	3-9	43½-15	178-20	3¼	—	1	Int.	12⅝	**179.95**	
RC 4 x 40 WA[2,4]	4	36	100	3¼	11⅞	1	Int.	11	**159.95**	
TR 3-9 x 32 TRF[3]	3-9	35-14	114-13	3¼	12	1	Int.	12	**124.95**	
TR 6-18 x 40 TRF[3]	6-18	16-5	44-5	3	16¼	1	Int.	16½	**189.95**	
W 4 x 32[5]	4	28	64	3¼	11¾	1	In.t	9½	**56.95**	

HUNTING, TARGET ■ & VARMINT ■ SCOPES

Maker and Model	Magn.	Field at 100 Yds (feet)	Relative Bright-ness	Eye Relief (in.)	Length (in.)	Tube Diam. (in.)	W&E Adjust-ments	Weight (ozs.)	Price	Other Data
Tasco (cont'd.)										
W 4-12 x 40[5]	4-12	29-9	100-11	3	13¾	1	Int.	15	**139.95**	
PM 4 x 18[6,7]	4	—	20	3	16¼	⅞	Int.	—	**69.95**	
BDICFV Battery Dot[8]	1	—	—	—	7½	—	Int.	10	**239.95**	
Thompson/Center										
Lobo 1½ x[1]	1.5	16	127	11-20	7¾	⅞	Int.	5	**75.00**	[1]May be used on light to medium recoil guns, including muzzleloaders. Coated lenses, nitrogen filled, lifetime warranty. [2]For heavy recoil guns. Nitrogen filled. Duplex reticle only. Target turrets avail. on 1½x, 3x models.
Lobo 3x[1]	3	9	49	11-20	9	⅞	Int.	6.3	**80.00**	
RP 1½ x[2]	1.5	28	177	11-20	7½	1	Int.	5.1	**99.00**	
RP 2½x[2]	2.5	15	64	11-20	8½	1	Int.	6.5	**99.00**	
RP 3x[2]	3	13	44	11-20	8¾	1	Int.	5.4	**99.00**	
RP 4x[2]	4	10	71	12-20	9¼	1	Int.	10.4	**120.00**	
Unertl										
■ 1" Target	6,8,10	16-10	17.6-6.25	2	21½	¾	Ext.	21	**155.00**	[1]Dural ¼ MOA click mounts. Hard coated lenses. Non-rotating objective lens focusing. [2]¼ MOA click mounts. [3]With target mounts. [4]With calibrated head. [5]Same as 1" Target but without objective lens focusing. [6]Price with ¼ MOA click mounts. [7]With new Posa mounts. [8]Range focus until near rear of tube. Price is with Posa mounts. Magnum clamp. With standard mounts and clamp ring **$266.00.**
■ 1¼" Target[1]	8,10,12,14	12-16	15.2-5	2	25	¾	Ext.	21	**203.00**	
■ 1½" Target	8,10,12,14 16,18,20	11.5-3.2	—	2¼	25½	¾	Ext.	31	**230.00**	
■ 2" Target[2]	8,10,12, 14,16,18, 24,30,36	8	22.6-2.5	2¼	26¼	1	Ext.	44	**310.00**	
■ Varmint, 1¼"[3]	6,8,10,12	1-7	28-7.1	2½	19½	⅞	Ext.	26	**204.00**	
■ Ultra Varmint, 2"[4]	8,10 12,15	12.6-7	39.7-11	2½	24	1	Ext.	34	**291.00**	
■ Small Game[5]	4,6	25-17	19.4-8.4	2¼	18	¾	Ext.	16	**120.00**	
■ Vulture[6]	8 10	11.2 10.9	29 18½	3-4 —	15⅝ 16⅛	1	Ext.	15½	**226.00**	
■ Programmer 200[7]	8,10,12 14,16,18, 20,24,30,36	11.3-4	39-1.9	—	26½	1	Ext.	45	**385.00**	
■ BV-20[8]	20	8	4.4	4.4	17⅞	1	Ext.	21¼	**278.00**	
Weatherby										
Mark XXII[1]	4	25	50	2½-3½	11¾	⅞	Int.	9¼	**85.35**	[1]Focusing in top turret. [2]Centered, non-magnifying reticles. Binocular focusing. Lumi-Plex $10 extra.
Premier Standard	2¾	45	212	3½	11¾	1	Int.	12¼	**149.95**	
Premier Standard[2]	4	31	100	3½	12¾	1	Int.	12¼	**154.95**	
Premier Standard	3-9	43½-14½	177-19	3	12	1	Int.	14¾	**164.95**	
Premier Wide Angle	4	35¾	100	3	11¾	1	Int.	14	**179.95**	
Premier Wide Angle	3-9	43½-14¾	177-19	3	12	1	Int.	14¾	**199.95**	
Weaver										
K1.5[1]	1½	55	—	5¼	9⅜	1	Int.	9¾	**110.00**	Steel-Lite II (lighter weight, glossy finish) in K, V and Wider View scopes. Crosshair and Dual-X reticle optional on all K and V scopes (except no RF on K1.5, K2.5, K3 and K3W; no post in K8, 10, 12; no post or RF in T models). Dot, post and RF $18 extra in T models. [1]Avail. with mount for Rem. 1100 or 870, Dual-X reticle. K1.5—$147, K2.5—$147. [2]Stainless (K4S) $190. K4M (matte finish) $167. [3]56mm objective gives big 7mm exit pupil. Excellent for low light conditions. German post reticle $18 extra. [4]Micro-Trac standard on all K and V models. ¼" Graduated adjustments .V9M has matte finish, $224. [5]¼-minute adj. [6]¼-minute adj. [7]¼" click stops. Crosshair and Dual-X Standard on T models. [8]Commemorative version of K4. Has gold ocular and obj. rings, scroll engraving, turret cap medallions. Comes with engraved mount rings. Dual-X reticle only. [9]Dual-X reticle only. Stainless steel. [10]$2.50 extra for Dual-X on V22, D4 or D6. D model prices include N or Tip-Off mount. [11]Projects red dot aiming point. [12]KT models have fast focus front ends, SL-II finish, smaller, covered knobs. [13]Stainless steel. Dual-X only. [14]AR models intended for airguns. [15]Dual-X reticle only. Large 56mm exit pupil for low-light hunting.
K2.5[1]	2.6	38	—	4½	10⅜	1	Int.	10¼	**110.00**	
K3	3.2	34	—	4	10⅝	1	Int.	10¼	**119.00**	
K4•50[8]	4.1	27	—	4	11.8	1	Int.	12	**209.00**	
K4[2]	4.1	27	—	4	11¾	1	Int.	12	**124.00**	
K6	5.9	19	—	3⅞	13½	1	Int.	13½	**153.00**	
K-856[3]	7.7	15	—	3½	15	1	Int.	18.7	**239.00**	
K3-W	2.9	48	—	3½	11	1	Int.	11	**147.00**	
K4-W	3.7	38	—	3⅝	11 13/16	1	Int.	13	**161.00**	
K6-W	6	24	—	3½	13¼	1	Int.	14½	**190.00**	
KT6[12]	6	17	—	3.7	13¾	1	Int.	16.5	**229.00**	
KT10	10	11	—	3.1	14.3	1	Int.	17	**247.00**	
KT 16	16	6.4	—	3.5	15	1	Int.	17½	**267.00**	
P2S[13]	1.9	14	—	10-24	10	1	Int.	—	**157.00**	
P4S[9]	4.0	7	—	12-20	9.9	1	Int.	12.5	**190.00**	
V4.5-W	1.6-4.2	74-27	—	4¼-3¾	10⅜	1	Int.	14¼	**200.00**	
V7-W	2.6-6.9	43-17	—	3⅝-3¾	12⅜	1	Int.	15¼	**210.00**	
V9-W	3.3-9	35-13	—	3⅝	14⅛	1	Int.	18¼	**219.00**	
V9-WF[5]	3.3-9	35-13	—	3⅝	14	1	Int.	18¼	**239.00**	
V4.5	1.6-4.3	63-24	—	4⅜-3⅞	10⅜	1	Int.	13½	**161.00**	
V7	2.5-6.7	40-15	—	4-3⅞	12⅜	1	Int.	14½	**171.00**	
V856[15]	3.1-8.3	35-13	—	3.8	14.3	1	Int.	21.5	**335.00**	
V9	3.3-8.8	31-12	—	3¾	14⅛	1	Int.	17½	**181.00**	
V9F[4]	3.3-8.8	31-12	—	3¾	14	1	Int.	17½	**200.00**	
V12F	4.4-11.8	23-9	—	3⅞-4¼	14	1	Int.	17½	**210.00**	
T6[7]	6	19	—	3½	14¼	1	Int.	17¾	**267.00**	
T10	10	11	—	3½	15	1	Int.	18	**286.00**	
T16	16	7	—	3⅝	15¾	1	Int.	18¾	**304.00**	
T25[5]	25	4.2	—	3¾	19⅛	1	Int.	20	**353.00**	
V22[10]	3-5.8	31-16	—	1⅝-2¼	12⅜	⅞	Int.	7¾	**45.00**	
D4	4.2	29	—	2¼	11⅞	⅞	Int.	6½	**34.50**	
D6	6.2	20	—	2¼	12 5/16	⅞	Int.	6¾	**38.00**	
Qwik-Point[11]	1	—	—	6	—	—	Int.	8	**86.00**	
Williams										
Twilight Crosshair	2½	32	64	3¾	11¼	1	Int.	8½	**104.75**	TNT models
Twilight Crosshair	4	29	64	3½	11¾	1	Int.	9½	**111.40**	
Twilight Crosshair	2-6	45-17	256-28	3	11½	1	Int.	11½	**151.50**	
Twilight Crosshair	3-9	36-13	161-18	3	12¾	1	Int.	13½	**159.00**	
Zeiss										
Diatal C 4x32	4	30	—	3.5	10.6	1	Int.	11.3	**305.00**	All scopes have ¼-minute click-stop adjustments. Choice of Z-Plex or fine crosshair reticles. Rubber armored objective bell, rubber eyepiece ring. Lenses have T-Star coating for highest light transmission. Imported from West Germany by Carl Zeiss, Inc.
Diatal C 6x32	6	20	—	3.5	10.6	1	Int.	11.3	**340.00**	
Diatal C 10x36	10	12	—	3.5	12.7	1	Int.	14.1	**395.00**	
Diavari C 3-9x36	3-9	36-13	—	3.5	11.2	1	Int.	15.2	**540.00**	

■ Signifies target and/or varmint scope. Hunting scopes in general are furnished with a choice of reticle—crosshairs, post with crosshairs, tapered or blunt post, or dot crosshairs, etc. The great majority of target and varmint scopes have medium or fine crosshairs but post or dot reticles may be ordered. W—Windage E—Elevation MOA—Minute of angle or 1" (approx.) at 100 yards, etc.

SCOPE MOUNTS

Maker, Model, Type	Adjust.	Scopes	Price	Suitable for
B-Square				[1]Clamp-on, blue finish. Stainless finish **$59.95**. [2]For Bushnell Phantom only. [3]Blue finish; stainless finish **$59.95**. [4]For solid rib—requires drilling & tapping. [5]Clamp-on. [6]Clamp-on, blue; stainless finish **$49.95**. [7]Clamp-on, for Bushnell Phantom only, blue; stainless finish **$49.95**. [8]Requires drilling & tapping. [9]No gunsmithing, no sight removal; blue; stainless finish **$59.95**. [10]Clamp-on. [11]Also M600, 660.
Pistols				
Colt Python[1]	W&E	1"	$ 49.95	
Daisy 717/722 Champion[2]	No	1"	19.95	
Dan Wesson Clamp-On[3]	W&E	1"	49.95	
Dan Wesson Integral[4]	W&E	1"	39.95	
Hi-Standard Mono-Mount[5]	No	1"	39.95	
Hi-Standard Victor	W&E	1"	49.95	
Ruger 22 Auto Mono-Mount[6]	No	1"	39.95	
Ruger Single-Six[7]	No	1"	39.95	
T-C Contender	W&E	1"	49.95	
Sterling X-Caliber	W&E	1"	49.95	
Rifles				
Mini-14[8]	W&E	1"	49.95	
Mini-14[9]	W&E	1"	49.95	
M-94 Side Mount	W&E	1"	49.95	
Ruger 77[10]	W&E	1"	49.95	
SMLE Side Mount	W only	1"	49.95	
T-C Single-Shot Rifle	W&E	1"	49.95	
Rem. Model Seven[11]	W&E	1"	39.95	
Military				
M1-A	W&E	1"	59.95	
AR-15/16	W&E	1"	49.95	
FN-LAR	W only	1"	149.95	
HK-91/93	W only	1"	49.95	
Valmet M71S	W&E	1"	129.95	
AK-47	W&E	1"	149.95	
Shotguns				
Rem. 870/1100	W&E	1"	59.95	
S&W 1000P	W&E	1"	59.95	
Beeman				
Double Adjustable	W&E	1"	$19.98	All grooved receivers and scope bases on all known air rifles and 22-cal. rimfire rifles (½" to ⅝"—6mm to 15mm).
Deluxe Ring Mounts	No	1"	17.98	
Professional Mounts	W&E	1"	79.95	
Buehler				
One Piece (T)[1]	W only	1" split rings, 3 heights.	Complete—57.25	[1]Most popular models. [2]Most popular models. [3]Most popular models. [4]Sako dovetail receivers. [5]15 models. [6]No drilling & tapping.
		1" split rings, 3 heights, engraved	Rings only—80.25	
		26mm, 2 heights	Rings only—41.25	
One Piece Micro Dial (T)[2]	W&E	1" split rings.	Complete—70.25	
Two Piece (T)[3]	W only	1" split rings.	Complete—57.25	
Two Piece Dovetail (T)[4]	W only	1" split rings.	Complete—70.75	
One Piece Pistol (T)[5]	W only	1" split rings.	Complete—57.25	
One Piece Pistol Stainless (T)[1]	W only	1" split rings. Stainless steel	Complete—74.75	
One Piece Ruger Mini 14 (T)[6]	W only	1" split rings.	Complete—70.75	
Burris				
Supreme One Piece (T)[1]	W only	1" split rings, 3 heights.	25.95	[1]Most popular rifles. Universal, rings, mounts fit Burris, Universal, Redfield, Leupold and Browning bases. Comparable prices. [2]Browning Standard 22 Auto rifle. [3]Most popular rifles. [4]Grooved receivers. [5]Universal dovetail; accept Burris, Universal, Redfield, Leupold rings. For Dan Wesson, S&W, Virginian, Ruger Blackhawk, Win. 94. [6]Medium standard front, extension rear, per pair. Low standard front, extension rear, per pair.
			1 piece-base—18.95	
Trumount Two Piece (T)	W only	1" split rings, 3 heights.	2 piece base—16.95	
Browning Auto Mount[2]	No	¾", 1" split rings.	14.95	
Sight-Thru Mount[3]	No	1" split rings.	16.95	
Rings Mounts[4]	No	¾", 1" split rings.	¾" rings—12.95	
			1" rings—12.95	
L.E.R. Mount Bases[5]	No	1" split rings.	16.95	
Extension Rings[6]	No	1" scopes.	29.95	
Bushnell				
Detachable (T) mounts only[1]	W only	1" split rings, uses Weaver base.	Rings—15.95	[1]Most popular rifles. Includes windage adj. [2]V-block bottoms lock to chrome-moly studs seated into two 6-48 holes. Rem. XP-100. [3]Heavy loads in Colt, S&W, Ruger revolvers, Ruger Hawkeye, [4]M94 Win., center dovetail.
22 mount	No	1" only.	Rings— 7.95	
All Purpose[2]	No	Phantom.	17.95	
Rigid[3]	No	Phantom.	17.95	
94 Win.[4]	No	Phantom.	17.95	
Clearview				
Universal Rings (T)[1]	No	1" split rings.	19.95	[1]All popular rifles including Sav. 99. Uses Weaver bases. [2]Allows use of open sights. [3]For 22 rimfire rifles, with grooved receivers or bases.
Mod 101, & 336[2]	No	1" split rings.	19.95	
Broad-View[4]	No		19.95	
Model 22[3]	No	¾", ⅞", 1"	11.95	
Conetrol				
Hunter[1]	W only	1", 26mm, 26.5mm solid or split rings, 3 heights.	48.93	[1]All popular rifles, including metric-drilled foreign guns. Price shown for base, two rings. Matte finish. [2]Gunnur grade has mirror-finished rings, satin-finish base. Price shown for base, two rings. [3]Custom grade has mirror-finished rings and mirror-finished, contoured base. Price shown for base, 2 rings. [4]Win. 94, Krag, older split-bridge Mannlicher-Schoenauer, Mini-14, M-1 Garand, etc. Prices same as above. [5]For all popular guns with integral mounting provision, including Sako, BSA, Ithacagun, Ruger, H&K and many others. Also for grooved-receiver rimfires and air rifles. Prices same as above. [6]For XP-100, T/C Contender, Colt SAA, Ruger Blackhawk, S&W.
Gunnur[2]	W only	1", 26mm, 26.5mm solid or split rings, 3 heights.	59.91	
Custum[3]	W only	1", 26mm, 26.5mm solid or split rings, 3 heights.	74.91	
One Piece Side Mount[4]	W only	1", 26mm, 26.5mm solid or split rings, 3 heights.		
Daptar Bases[5]	W only	1", 26mm, 26.5mm solid or split rings, 3 heights.		
Pistol Bases[6]	W only	1" split rings.		
Pistol Bases, 3-Ring[7]	W only	1" scopes.		
EAW				
Pivot[1]	W&E	1"/26mm	150.00	[1]Most popular magazine rifles. Optional 30mm. [2]For Sako; also for mounting Kahles ZF69 on Steyr SSG rifle. [3]For Kahles 30mm scope. Bases by Redfield, Leupold, Burris. Two heights. Imported by Kahles of America (Del-Sports, Inc.).
Slide On[2]	W only	1"/26mm	100.00	
Kahles[3]	W only	30mm	50.00	
Griffin & Howe				
Standard Double Lever (S).	No	1" or 26mm split rings.	110.00	All popular models (Garand $110; Win. 94 $110). All rings $45.
Holden				
Wide Ironsighter[1][3]	No	1" Split rings.	19.95	[1]Most popular rifles including Ruger Mini-14, H&R M700, and muzzleloaders. Rings have oval holes to permit use of iron sights. [2]For 1" dia. scopes. [3]For ¾" or ⅞" dia. scopes. [4]For 1" dia. extended eye relief scopes.
Ironsighter Center Fire[1]	No	1" Split rings.	19.95	
Ironsighter S-94	No	1" split rings	24.95	
Ironsighter 22 cal. rimfire				
Model #500[2]	No	1" Split rings.	10.95	
Model #600[3]	No	⅞" Split rings also fits ¾".	10.95	
Ironsighter Handguns[4]	No	1" Split rings.	21.95	
Jaeger				
QD, with windage (S)	W only	1", 3 heights.	150.00	All popular models
Kimber				
Standard[1]	No	1", split rings	48.90	[1]High rings; low rings—**$45.00**; both only for Kimber rifles. [2]For Kimber rifles only. Also avail. for Mauser (Std., FN, small-ring), Rem. 700, 721, 722, Weatherby MK.V, Win. 70, **$110.00** (incl. bases).
Double Lever	No	1", split rings	75.00	

SCOPE MOUNTS

Maker, Model, Type	Adjust.	Scopes	Price	Suitable for
Kris Mounts				
Side-Saddle[1]	No	1", 26mm split rings.	11.98	[1]One-piece mount for Win. 94. [2]Most popular rifles and Ruger. [3]Blackhawk revolver. Mounts have oval hole to permit use of iron sights.
Two Piece (T)[2]	No	1", 26mm split rings.	7.98	
One Piece (T)[3]	No	1", 26mm split rings.	11.98	
Kwik-Site				
KS-See-Thru[1]	No	1"	18.95	[1]Most rifles. Allows use of iron sights. [2]22-cal. rifles with grooved receivers. Allows use of iron sights. [3]Model 94, 94 Big Bore. No drilling or tapping. [4]Most rifles. One-piece solid construction. Use on Weaver bases. 32mm obj. lens or larger. [5]Non-see-through model; for grooved receivers.
KS-22 See-Thru[2]	No	1"'	15.95	
KS-W94[3]	Yes	1"	32.95	
KSM Imperial[4]	No	1"	25.95	
KS-WEV	No	1"	19.95	
KS-WEV-HIGH	No	1"	19.95	
KS-T22 1"[5]	No	1"	15.95	
Leatherwood				
M-1A, M-14	W only	ART II, ART/MPC (Weaver rings)	75.00	[1]Popular bolt actions. [2]With M-16 adaptor. [3]Adaptor base for H&K rail mounts.
AR-15, M-16	No	As above	17.95	
FN-FAL	No	As above	175.00	
SSG	No	As above	50.00	
One-piece Bridge[1]	No	As above	9.95	
Night Vision Adaptor[2]	No	Night vision scopes	37.50	
H&K Adaptor[3]	No	ART II, ART/MPC (Weaver rings)	59.95	
Leupold				
STD Bases (T)[1]	W only	One piece base (dovetail front, windage rear)	Base—18.70	[1]Most popular rifles. Also available in 2-piece version, same price. [2]Ruger revolvers, Thompson/Center Contender, S&W K&N Frame revolvers and Colt .45 "Gold Cup" N.M. Available with silver or blue finish. [3]Reversible extended front; regular rear rings, in two heights.
STD Handgun mounts[2] Base and two rings[2]	No	1"	47.80	
STD Rings		1" & 26mm, 3 ring heights interchangeable with other mounts of similar design.	1" rings—27.00 26mm rings—29.50	
Extension-Ring Sets[3]		1"	37.40	
Marlin				
One Piece QD (T)	No	1" split rings.	12.10	Most Marlin and Glenfield lever actions.
Millett				
Diamond-Facet		1" Low, medium, high	26.95	Rem. 40X, 700, 722, 725, Ruger 77 (round top) Weatherby, etc. FN Mauser, FN Brownings, Colt 57, Interarms MKX, Parker-Hale, Sako (round receiver), many others.
		Engraved Black Onyx	39.95	
Universal Two Piece Bases				
700 Series	W only	Two-piece bases	20.95	
FN Series	W only	Two-piece bases	20.95	
T/C Contender	W only	One-piece base	21.95	
XP-100 Base	W only	Two-piece base	20.95	
Numrich				
Side Mount	No	1" split rings.	7.95	M-1 carbine.
Pachmayr				
Lo-Swing (S)[1]	Yes	3/4", 7/8", 1", 26mm solid or split loops.	65.00	[1]All popular rifles, including Ruger Mini-14, Browning BBR. Scope swings aside for instant use of iron sights. [2]Adjustable base. Win. 70, 88; Rem. 721, 722, 725, 740, 760; Mar. 336; Sav. 99, New Model for Colt Sauer.
Lo-Swing (T)[2]	Yes	3/4", 7/8", 1", 26mm split rings.	65.00	
Redfield				
JR-SR(T)[1]	W only	3/4", 1", 26mm.	JR—18.90-22.20 SR—21.90-25.70	[1]Low, med. & high, split rings. Reversible extension front rings for 1". 2-piece bases for Sako. Colt Sauer bases $63.90. [2]Split rings for grooved 22's. See-thru mounts $23.30. [3]Used with MP scopes for: S&W K or N frame. XP-100, Colt J or I frame. T/C Contender, Colt autos, black powder rifles.
Ring (T)[2]	No	3/4" and 1".		
Double Dovetail MP[3]	No	1", split rings.	51.50	
S&K				
Insta-Mount (T) base only[1]	No	Use S&K rings only.	18.00-81.00	[1]1903, A3, M1 Carbine, Lee Enfield #1, MK. III, #4, #5, M1917, M98 Mauser, FN Auto, AR-15, AR-180, M-14, M-1, Ger. K-43, Mini-14, M1-A, Krag, AKM, AK-47. [2]Most popular rifles. For "see through underneath" risers, add $10.00.
Conventional rings and bases[2]	No	1" split rings.	32.00	
Sako				
QD Dovetail	W only	1" only.	82.00	Sako, or any rifle using Sako action, 3 heights available, Stoeger, importer.
Tasco				
790BA and 792BA series[1]	No	1", regular or high.	9.95	[1]Many popular rifles. Also in brushed aluminum. [2]For 22s with grooved receivers. [3]Most popular rifles. [4]Most popular rifles. [5]"Quick Peep" 1" ring mount; fits all 22-cal. rifles with grooved receivers. [6]For Ruger Mini-14; also in brushed aluminum. [7]Side mount for Win. 94. [8]Side mount rings and base for Win. 94 in 30-30, 375 Win.
794[2]	No	Split rings.	9.95	
795 Quick Peep[3]	No	1" only.	9.95	
796[5]	No	1" only	9.95	
885 BK[8]	No	1" only	23.95	
895[7]	No	1" only	5.95	
896[6]	No	1" only	39.95	
800L Series (with base)[4]	No	1" only.	13.95	
Thompson/Center				
Contender 9746[1]	No	T/C Lobo	8.75	[1]All Contenders except vent. rib. [2]T/C rail mount scopes; all Contenders except vent. rib. [3]All S&W K and Combat Masterpiece, Hi-Way Patrolman, Outdoorsman, 22 Jet, 45 Target 1955. Requires drilling, tapping. [4]Blackhawk, Super Blackhawk, Super Single-Six. Requires drilling, tapping. [5]45 or 50 cal.; replaces rear sight. [6]Rail mount scopes; 54-cal. Hawken, 50, 54, 56-cal. Renegade. Replaces rear sight.
Contender 9741[2]	No	2 1/2, 4 RP	8.75	
Contender 7410	No	Bushnell Phantom 1.3, 2.5x	8.75	
S&W 9747[3]	No	Lobo or RP	8.75	
Ruger 9748[4]	No	Lobo or RP	8.75	
Hawken 9749[5]	No	Lobo or RP	8.75	
Hawken/Renegade 9754[6]	No	Lobo or RP	8.75	
Unerti				
Posa (T)[1]	Yes	3/4", 7/8, 1".scopes.	Per set 63.00	[1]Unerti target or varmint scopes. [2]Any with regular dovetail scope bases.
1/4 Click (T)[2]	Yes	3/4", 1" target scopes.	Per set 59.00	
Weaver				
Detachable Mount (T & S)[1]	No	3/4", 7/8", 1", 26mm.	20.00	[1]Nearly all modern rifles. Extension rings, 1" $23.45. [2]Most modern big bore rifles. [3]22s with grooved receivers. [4]Same. Adapter for Lee Enfield—$9.65. 5 7/8"—$13.45. 1" See-Thru extension—$23.45. [6]Colt Officer's Model, Python, Ruger B'hawk, Super B'hawk, Security Six, 22 Autos, Mini-14, Ruger Redhawk, S&W N frames. No drilling or tapping. Also in stainless steel—$58.95.
Pivot Mount (T)[2]	No	1"	25.75	
Tip-Off (T)[3]	No	3/4", 7/8".	11.15	
Tip-Off (T)[4]	No	1", two-piece.	20.00	
See-Thru Mount[5]	No	1" Split rings and 7/8"-tip-off. Fits all top mounts.	20.00	
Mount Base System[6]	No	1"	44.95	
Williams				
Offset (S)[1]	No	3/4", 7/8", 1" 26mm solid, split or extension rings.	47.05	[1]Most rifles, Br. S.M.L.E. (round rec) $3.85 extra. [2]Same. [3]Most rifles. [4]Most rifles. [5]Many modern rifles. [6]Most popular rifles.
QC (T)[2]	No	Same.	38.60	
QC (S)[3]	No	Same.	38.60	
Low Sight-Thru[4]	No	1", 7/8", sleeves $1.80.	17.75	
Sight-Thru[5]	No	1", 7/8", sleeves $1.80.	17.75	
Streamline[6]	No	1" (bases form rings).	17.75	

(S)—Side Mount   (T)Top Mount   22mm—.866"   25.4mm = 1"1.024"   26.5mm = 1.045"   30mm = 1.81"

SPOTTING SCOPES

BAUSCH & LOMB DISCOVERER—15X to 60X zoom, 60mm objective. Constant focus throughout range. Field at 1000 yds. 40 ft (60X), 156 ft. (15X). Comes with lens caps. Length 17½", wgt. 48½ oz.
Price: **$399.95**

BUSHNELL SPACEMASTER—60MM objective. Field at 1000 yds., 158' to 37'. Relative brightness, 5.76. Wgt., 36 oz. Length closed, 11⅝". prism focusing, without eyepiece.
Price: **$254.95**
15X, 20X, 40X and 60X eyepieces, each **$49.95**
22X wide angle eyepiece **$54.95**

BUSHNELL SPACEMASTER 45°—Same as above except: Wgt., 43 oz., length closed 13". Eyepiece at 45°, without eyepiece.
Price: **$319.95**

BUSHNELL ZOOM SPACEMASTER—20X-45X zoom. 60mm objective. Field at 1000 yards 120'-72'. Relative brightness 9-1.7. Wgt. 36 oz., length 11⅝".
Price: **$379.95**

BUSHNELL SENTRY®—50mm objective. Field at 1000 yards 120'-45'. Relative brightness 6.25. Wgt., 25½ oz., length 12⅝", without eyepiece.
Price: **$139.95**
20X, 32X and 48X eyepieces, each **$44.95**

BUSHNELL ZOOM SPOTTER—40mm objective. 9X-30X var. power.
Price: **$99.95**

BUSHNELL COMPETITOR—40mm objective. Prismatic. Field at 1000 yards 140'. Minimum focus 33'. Length 12½", weight 18½ oz.
Price: **$91.95**

BUSHNELL TROPHY—16X-36X zoom. Rubber armored, prismatic. 50mm objective. Field at 1000 yards 131' to 90'. Minimum focus 20'. Length with caps 13⅝", weight 38 oz.
Price: **$319.95**
With interchangeable eyepieces—20x, 32x, 48x **$244.95**

BUSHNELL—10x30mm hand telescope. Field 183 ft. at 1000 yards. Weight 11 ozs.; 10" long. Tripod mount
Price: **$34.95**

DICKSON 270—20x to 60x variable, 60mm objective, achromatic coated objective lens, complete with metal table tripod with 5 vertical and horizontal adjustments. Turret type, 20x, 30x, 40x 60x
Price: **$249.95**

DICKSON 274A—20x to 60x variable zoom. 60mm achromatic coated objective lens, complete with adjustable metal table tripod.
Price: **$150.00**

DICKSON 274B—As above but with addition of 4 × 16 Finder Scope.
Price: **$161.95**

HUTSON CHROMATAR 60—63.4mm objective. 22.5X eyepiece at 45°. Wgt. 24 oz., 8" over-all. 10½ foot field at 100 yards.
Price: **$119.00**
15X or 45X eyepieces, each **$22.00**

OPTEX MODEL 420—15x-60x-60 Zoom; 18" overall; weighs 4 lbs. with folding tripod (included). From Southern Precision Instrument
Price: **$135.00**

OPTEX MODEL 421—15x-45x-50 Zoom; 18" over-all; weighs 4 lbs. with folding tripod (included). From Southern Precision Instrument
Price: **$110.00**

OPTEX MODEL 422—8x-25x-30 Zoom. Armour coated; 18" over-all; weighs 3 lbs. with tripod (included). From Southern Precision Instrument
Price: **$100.00**

OPTEX MODEL 423—Same as Model 422 except 12x-40x-40
Price: **$120.00**

REDFIELD 30x SPOTTER—60mm objective, 30x. Field of view 9.5 ft. at 100 yds. Uses catadioptric lens system. Length over-all is 7.5", weight is 11.5 oz. Eye relief 0.5".
Price: **$390.40**

SWAROVSKI HABICHT HAWK 30x75 IRALIN TELESCOPE—75mm objective, 30X. Field at 1,000 yds. 90ft. Minimum, focusing distance 90 ft. Length: closed 13 in., extended 20½". Weight: 47 oz. Precise recognition of smallest details even at dusk. Leather or rubber covered, with caps and carrying case.
Price: **$895.00**
Same as above with short range supplement. Minimum focusing distance 24 to 30 ft. **$935.00**

SWIFT TELEMASTER M841—60mm objective. 15X to 60X variable power. Field at 1000 yards 160 feet (15X) to 40 feet (60X). Wgt. 3.4 lbs. 17.6" over-all.
Price: **$415.00**
Tripod for above **$79.95**
Photo adapter **$19.00**
Case for above **$57.50**

SWIFT TELEMASTER JR. M842—25-50mm zoom spotting scope. Smaller version of M841 with same features. 14.9" over-all, wgt. 2.2 lbs.
Price: **$255.00**

SWIFT M844 COMMANDO PRISMATIC SPOTTING SCOPE, MK.II—60mm objective. Comes with 20X eyepiece; 15X, 30X, 40X, 50X, 60X available. Built-in sunshade. Field at 1000 yds. with 20X, 120 ft. Length 13.7", wgt. 2.1 lbs.
Price: **$245.00**

SWIFT M847 SCANNER—50mm objective. Comes with 25x eyepiece; 20x, 30x, 35x eyepieces available. Field of view at 1000 yds. is 112 ft. (25x). Length 13.6", weight 23 oz.
Price: **$147.50**
Each additional eyepiece **$25.50**
Tubular case **$25.00**
Tripod **$79.95**

SWIFT M700 SCOUT—9X-30X, 30mm spotting scope. Length 15½", weighs 2.1 lbs. Field of 204 ft. (9X), 60 ft. (30X).
Price: **$96.00**

TASCO 31T SQUARE SPOTTING SCOPE—40mm objective. 12X and 20X. Field at 1000 yds. 185 ft. (12X) and 120 ft. (20X). Built-in tripod and swivel turret. Weight 29.5 oz. Length 8¼".
Price: **$109.95**

TASCO 32T SQUARE SPOTTING SCOPE—50mm objective. 17X and 30X. Field at 1000 yds. 133 ft. (17X) and 89 ft. (30X). Built-in tripod and swivel turret. Weight 25.9 oz. Length 11½".
Price: **$129.95**

TASCO 33T ZOOM SQUARE SPOTTING SCOPE—60mm objective. Prismatic. 20X to 45X. Field at 1000 yds. 104 ft. (20X) to 70 ft. (45X). With tripod and 45° angle swivel turret. Weight 52 oz. Length 15".
Price: **$359.95**

TASCO 34T RUBBER COVERED SPOTTING SCOPE—50mm objective. 25X. Field at 1000 yds. 136 ft. With tripod and built-in tripod adapter. Weight 29.9 oz. Length 13¾".
Price: **$199.95**

TASCO 21T SPOTTING SCOPE—40mm objective. 20X. Field at 1000 yds. 136 ft. With Tasco 8P tripod. Weight 18.2 oz. Length 12⅜".
Price: **$109.95**

TASCO 26T SPOTTING SCOPE—50mm objective. 25X. Field at 1000 yds. 109 ft. With Tasco 8P tripod. Weight 23.6 oz. Length 13¾".
Price: **$179.95**

TASCO 25T/25P RUBBER COVERED SPOTTING SCOPE—60mm objective. 25X. Field at 1000 yds. 94 ft. Prismatic. With Tasco 25P deluxe tripod, olive green to match rubber covering. Weight 38.3 oz. Length 11½".
Price: **$529.95**

TASCO 18T ZOOM—60mm objective. 20X to 60X variable power. Field at 100 yards 9 feet (20X) to 3 feet (60X). Wgt. 4 lbs. 16" overall
Price: **$219.95**

UNERTL RIGHT ANGLE—63.5mm objective, 24X. Field at 100 yds., 7 ft. Relative brightness, 6.96. Eye relief, ½". Wgt., 41 oz. Length closed, 19". Push-pull and screw-focus eyepiece. 16X and 32X eyepieces **$35.00** each.
Price: **$242.00**

UNERTL STRAIGHT PRISMATIC—Same as Unertl Right Angle except: straight eyepiece and wgt. of 40 oz.
Price: **$205.00**

UNERTL 20X STRAIGHT PRISMATIC—54mm objective. 20X. Field at 100 yds., 8.5 ft. Relative brightness, 6.1. Eye relief, ½". Wgt. 36 oz. Length closed, 13½". Complete with lens covers.
Price: **$172.00**

UNERTL TEAM SCOPE—100mm objective. 15X, 24X, 32X eyepieces. Field at 100 yds. 13 to 7.5 ft. Relative brightness, 39.06 to 9.79. Eye relief, 2" to 1½". Weight 13 lbs. 29⅞" overall. Metal tripod, yoke and wood carrying case furnished (total weight, 67 lbs.)
Price: **$900.00**

WEATHERBY—60mm objective, 20X-45X zoom
Price: **$323.95**
Tripod for above **$69.95**

WEAVER TS4 SPOTTING SCOPE—50mm objective. Power determined by choice of eyepiece—12x, 16x, 20x, 32x. Field of view (20x) 117 ft. at 1000 yds. Uses 45° sighting angle. Length 12.6", weight 37.4 oz.
Price: Body only **$225.00**
12x eyepiece **$65.00**
16x eyepiece **$75.00**
20x eyepiece **$75.00**
32x eyepiece **$80.00**

WEAVER TS6 SPOTTING SCOPE—60mm objective. Power determined by choice of eyepiece—15x, 20x, 25x, 40x. Field of view (15x) of 150 ft. at 1000 yds. Straight-through sighting. Length 12.4", weight 37.4" oz.
Price: Body only **$280.00**
15x eyepiece **$65.00**
20x eyepiece **$75.00**
25x eyepiece **$75.00**
40x eyepiece **$80.00**
15x-45x variable eypiece (TS 6 only) **$167.00**

PERIODICAL PUBLICATIONS

Airgun World
10 Sheet St., Windsor, Berks., SL4 1BG, England.£11 for 12 issues. Monthly magazine catering exclusively to the airgun enthusiast.

Alaska Magazine
Alaska Northwest Pub. Co., Box 4-EEE, Anchorage, AK 99509. $18.00 yr. Hunting and fishing articles.

American Field†
222 W. Adams St., Chicago, IL. 60606. $18.00 yr. Field dogs and trials, occasional gun and hunting articles.

American Firearms Industry
Nat'l. Assn. of Federally Licensed Firearms Dealers, 2801 E. Oakland Park Blvd., Ft. Lauderdale, FL 33306. $20 yr. For firearms dealers & distributors.

The American Handgunner*
591 Camino de la Reina, San Diego, CA 92108. $11.95 yr. Articles for handgun enthusiasts, collectors and hunters.

American Hunter (M)
Natl. Rifle Assn., 1600 Rhode Island Ave. N.W., Washington, DC 20036. $15.00 yr. Wide scope of hunting articles.

American Rifleman (M)
National Rifle Assn., 1600 Rhode Island Ave., N.W., Wash., DC 20036. $15.00 yr. Firearms articles of all kinds.

The American Shotgunner
P.O. Box 3351, Reno, NV 89505. $15.00 yr. Official publ. of the Amercan Assn. of Shotgunning. Shooting, reloading, hunting, investment collecting, new used gun classifieds. Membership and benefits w. yrly. subscr.

American West*
Amer. West Publ. Co., 3033 No. Campbell, Tucson, AZ 85719. $15.00 yr.

AMI
Action Press, Avenue Louis 60, B1050 Brussels, Belgium. Belg. Franc 325, 12 issues. Arms, shooting information; French text.

Arms Collecting (Q)
Museum Restoration Service P.O. Drawer 390, Bloomfield, Ont., Canada K0K IG0. $10.00 yr. $27.50 3 yrs.

Australian Shooters' Journal
U.S. distr.: Blacksmith Corp., P.O. Box 424, Southport, CT 06490; $35 yr., samples $3.50. Hunting and shooting articles.

Black Powder Times*
P.O. Box 842, Mount Vernon, WA 98273. $10.00 for 6 issues. Magazine for blackpowder activities; test reports.

The Blade Magazine*
P.O. Box 22007, Chattanooga, TN 37422. $14.99 yr. Add $10 f. foreign subscription. A magazine for all enthusiasts of the edged blade.

The Buckskin Report
The Buckskin Press, P.O. Box 789, Big Timber, MT 59011. $18.00 yr. Articles for the blackpowder shooter.

Deer Unlimited*
P.O. Box 509, Clemson, SC 29631. $12.00 yr.

Deutsches Waffen Journal
Journal-Verlag Schwend GmbH, Postfach 100340, D7170 Schwäbisch Hall, Germany. DM65.00 yr. plus DM16.80 for postage. Antique and modern arms. German text.

Ducks Unlimited, Inc. (M)
1 Waterfowl Way at Gilmer, Long Grove, IL 60047

Enforcement Journal (Q)
Frank J. Schira, editor, Natl. Police Officers Assn., 609 West Main St., Louisville, KY 40202 $6.00 yr.

The Field†
The Harmsworth Press Ltd., Carmelite House, London EC4Y OJA, England. $88.00 yr. Hunting and shooting articles, and all country sports.

Field & Stream
CBS Publications, 1515 Broadway, New York, NY 10036. $11.94 yr. Articles on firearms plus hunting and fishing.

Fur-Fish-Game
A.R. Harding Pub. Co., 2878 E. Main St., Columbus, OH 43209. $8.00 yr. "Gun Rack" column by Don Zutz.

Gray's Sporting Journal
Gray's Sporting Journal Co., 42 Bay Rd., So. Hamilton, MA 01982. $23.50 per yr. f. 4 consecutive issues. Hunting and fishing journals.

Gun Owner*
Gun Owners of California, Inc., 1121 L St., Suite 810, Sacramento, CA 95814. With membership $15 yr.; single copy $3. A California magazine for sportsmen everywhere.

The Gun Report
World Wide Gun Report, Inc., Box 111, Aledo, IL 61231. $20.00 yr. For the gun collector.

The Gunrunner
Div. of Kexco Publ. Co. Ltd., Box 565, Lethbridge, Alb., Canada T1J 3Z4. $10.00 yr. Newspaper, listing everything from antiques to artillery.

Gun Show Gazette
P.O. Box 2685, Warner Robins, GA 31099. $10 yr. Extensive gun show listings, with articles on guns, knives and hunting.

Gun Week†
Hawkeye Publishing, Inc., P.O. Box 411, Station C, Buffalo NY 14209. $15.00 yr. U.S. and possessions; $19.00 yr. other countries. Tabloid paper on guns, hunting, shooting and collecting.

Gun World
Gallant Publishing Co., 34249 Camino Capistrano, Capistrano Beach, CA 92624. $14.00 yr. For the hunting, reloading and shooting enthusiast.

Guns & Ammo
Petersen Pub. Co., 8490 Sunset Blvd., Los Angeles, CA 90069. $11.94 yr. Guns, shooting, and technical articles.

Guns
Guns Magazine, 591 Camino de la Reina, San Diego, CA 92108. $14.95 yr. Articles for gun collectors, hunters and shooters.

Guns Review
Ravenhill Pub. Co. Ltd., Box 35, Standard House, Bonhill St., London E.C. 2A 4DA, England. £11.55 sterling (approx. U.S. $24) USA & Canada yr. For collectors and shooters.

Handloader*
Wolfe Pub. Co. Inc., Box 3030, Prescott, AZ 86302 $13.00 yr. The journal of ammunition reloading.

INSIGHTS*
NRA, 1660 Rhode Island Ave. N.W., Washington, DC 20036. Editor Mary E. Shelsby. $5.00 yr. (6 issues). Plenty of details for the young target shooter.

International Shooting Sport*
International Shooting Union (UIT), Bavariaring 21, D-8000 Munich 2, Germany. Europe: (Deutsche Mark) DM39.00 yr., p.p.; outside Europe: DM45.00. For the International target shooter.

The Journal of the Arms & Armour Society (M)
Joseph G. Rosa (Secy.), 17 Woodville Gardens, Ruislip, Middlesex, HA4 7NB, England. $16.00 yr. Articles for the historian and collector.

Journal of the Historical Breechloading Smallarms Assn.
Publ. annually, Imperial War Museum, Lambeth Road, London SE1 6HZ, England. $8.00 yr. Articles for the collector plus mailings of lecture transcripts, short articles on specific arms, reprints, newsletter, etc.; a surcharge is made f. airmail.

Knife World
Knife World Publications, P.O. Box 3395, Knoxville, TN 37917. $8.00 yr., $14.00 2 yrs. Published monthly f. knife enthusiasts and collectors. Articles on custom and factory knives; other knife related interests.

Law and Order
Law and Order Magazine, 5526 N. Elston Ave., Chicago, IL 60630. $12.00 yr. Articles on weapons for law enforcement, etc.

Man At Arms*
222 West Exchange St., Providence, RI 02903. $18.00 yr. The magazine of arms collecting-investing, with excellent brief articles for the collector of antique and modern firearms.

MAN/MAGNUM
S.A. Man (1982) (Pty) Ltd., P.O. Box 35204, Northway, Durban 4065, Rep. of South Africa. R19 f. 12 issues. Africa's only publication on hunting, shooting, firearms, bushcraft, knives, etc.

The Marlin Collector (M)
R.W. Paterson, 407 Lincoln Bldg., 44 Main St., Champaign, IL 61820. Publ. 4 times a yr. $5.00 one-time initiation fee; $7.00 yr.

Muzzle Blasts (M)
National Muzzle Loading Rifle Assn., P.O. Box 67, Friendship, IN 47021. $16.00 yr. For the black powder shooter.

The Muzzleloader Magazine*
Rebel Publishing Co., Inc., Route 5, Box 347-M, Texarkana, TX 75503. $8.50 U.S., $10.50 foreign yr. The publication for black powder shooters.

National Defense (M)*
American Defense Preparedness Assn., Rosslyn Center, Suite 900, 1700 North Moore St., Arlington, VA 22209. $25.00 yr. Articles on military-related topics, including weapons, materials technology, management and policy.

National Knife Collector (M)
7201 Shallowford Rd., Chattanooga, TN 37421. Membership $15 yr.

National Rifle Assn. Journal (British) (Q)
Natl. Rifle Assn. (BR.), Bisley Camp, Brookwood, Woking, Surrey, England. GU24, OPB. $14.00 inc. air postage.

National Wildlife*
Natl. Wildlife Fed., 1412 16th St. N.W., Washington, DC 20036. $10.50 yr. (6 issues); *International Wildlife*, 6 issues, $10.50 yr. Both, $17.50 yr., plus membership benefits. Write to this addr., attn.: Promotion Dept., for the proper information.

New Zealand Wildlife (Q)
New Zealand Deerstalkers Assoc. Inc., P.O. Box 6514, Wellington, N.Z. $12.00 (N.Z.). Hunting and shooting articles.

North American Hunter* (M)
7901 Flying Cloud Dr., P.O. Box 35557, Minneapolis, MN 55435. $18.00 yr. (6 issues). Articles on North American game hunting.

Northwestern Sportsman
Box 1208, Big Timber, MT 59011. $10.00 yr.

Outdoor Life
Times Mirror Magazines, Inc., 380 Madison Ave., New York, NY 10017. $11.94 yr. Shooting columns by Jim Carmichel, and others.

Point Blank
Citizens Committee for the Right to Keep and Bear Arms (sent to contributors) Liberty Park, 12500 NE 10th Pl., Bellevue, WA 98005

The Police Marksman*
6000 E. Shirley Lane, Montgomery, AL 36117. $15.00 yr.

Police Times/Command (M)
1100 N.E. 125th St., No. Miami, FL 33161

Popular Mechanics
Hearst Corp., 224 W. 57th St., New York, NY 10019. $11.97 yr. Hunting, shooting and camping articles.

Precision Shooting
Precision Shooting, Inc., 37 Burnham St., East Hartford, CT 06108. $12.50 yr. Journal of the International Benchrest Shooters, National Benchrest Shooting Assn., and target shooting in general.

Rendezvous & Longrifles (M)
Canadian Black Powder Federation Newsletter, P.O. Box 2876, Postal Sta. "A", Moncton, N.B. E1C, 8T8, Canada. 6 issues per yr. w. $15.00 membership.

Rifle*
Wolfe Publishing Co. Inc., Box 3030, Prescott, AZ 86302. $13.00 yr. The magazine for shooters.

Rod & Rifle Magazine
Lithographic Serv. Ltd., P.O. Box 38-138, Petone, New Zealand. $20.00 yr. (6 issues) Hunting and shooting articles.

Safari* (M)
Safari Magazine, 5151 E. Broadway, Tucson, AZ 85711. $20 (6 times). Official journal of Safari Club International; the journal of big game hunting.

Saga
Lexington Library, Inc., 355 Lexington Ave., New York, NY 10017. Currently annual. No subscription. $1.75 p. issue U.S.

Second Amendment Reporter
Second Amendment Fdn., James Madison Bldg., 12500 NE 10th Pl., Bellevue, WA 98005. $15.00 yr. (non-contributors).

The Shooting Industry
Publisher's Dev. Corp., 591 Camino de la Reina, Suite 200, San Diego, CA 92108. $25.00 yr. To the trade $12.50

Shooting Magazine
10 Sheet St., Windsor, Berks. SL4 1BG England. £11.00 for 12 issues. Monthly journal catering mainly to claypigeon shooters.

The Shooting Times & Country Magazine (England)†
10 Sheet St., Windsor, Berkshire SL4 1BG, England. $49.40 yr. (52 issues). Game shooting, wild fowling, hunting, game fishing and firearms articles.

Shooting Times
PJS Publications, News Plaza. P.O. Box 1790, Peoria, IL 60656. $15.00 yr. Guns, shooting, reloading; articles on every gun activity.

The Shotgun News‡
Snell Publishing Co., Box 669, Hastings, NE 68901. $15.00 yr. Sample copy $3.00. Gun ads of all kinds.

Shotgun Sports
P.O. Box 5400, Reno, NV 89513. $20. yr.

Shotgun West
2052 Broadway, Santa Monica, CA 90404. $8.50 yr. Trap, Skeet and international shooting, scores; articles, schedules.

The Sixgunner (M)
Handgun Hunters International, P.O. Box 357, MAG. Bloomingdale, OH 43910

The Skeet Shooting Review
National Skeet Shooting Assn., P.O. Box 28188, San Antonio, TX 78228. $15.00 yr. (Assn. membership of $20.00 includes mag.) Competition results, personality profiles of top Skeet shooters, how-to articles, technical, reloading information.

Soldier of Fortune
Subscription Dept., P.O. Box 310, Martinsville, NJ 08836. $26.00 yr. U.S., Can., Mex.; $33.00 all other countries surface.

Sporting Goods Business
Gralla Publications, 1515 Broadway, New York, NY 10036. Trade journal.

The Sporting Goods Dealer
1212 No. Lindbergh Blvd., St. Louis, Mo. 63132. $30.00 yr. The sporting goods trade journal.

Sporting Gun
Bretton Court, Bretton, Peterborough PE3 8DZ, England £15.00 (approx. U.S. $28.00) (airmail £24.00) yr. For the game and clay enthusiasts.

Sports Afield
The Hearst Corp., 250 W. 55th St., New York, NY 10019. $11.97 yr. Grits Gresham on firearms, ammunition and Thomas McIntyre, Dave Harbour, Dave Bowring on hunting.

Sports Merchandiser
A W.R.C. Smith Publication, 1760 Peachtree Rd. NW, Atlanta, GA 30357. Trade Journal.

Survival Guide
McMullen Publishing, Inc., 2145 LaPalma Ave., Anaheim, CA 92801. 12 issues $19.98.

TACARMI
Via Vespri Siciliani 25, 20146 Milano, Italy. $33.00 yr. Antique and modern guns. (Italian text.).

Trap & Field
1100 Waterway Blvd., Indianapolis, IN 46202. $16.00 yr. Official publ. Amateur Trapshooting Assn. Scores, averages, trapshooting articles.

Turkey Call* (M)
Natl. Wild Turkey Federation, Inc., P.O. Box 530, Edgefield, SC 29824. $15.00 w. membership (6 issues p. yr.)

The U.S. Handgunner* (M)
U.S. Revolver Assn., 59 Alvin St., Springfield, MA 01104. $5.00 yr. General handgun and competition articles. Bi-monthly sent to members.

Waterfowler's World*
P.O. Box 38306, Germantown, TN 38183. $12.00 yr.

Wisconsin Sportsman*
Wisconsin Sportsman, Inc., P.O. Box 2266, Oshkosh, WI 54903. $7.95.

*Published bi-monthly † Published weekly ‡ Published three times per month. All others are published monthly.
M = Membership requirements; write for details. Q = Published Quarterly.

Shooting Sports Booklets & Pamphlets

Basic Pistol Marksmanship—Textbook for basic courses in pistol shooting. 50¢[2]

Basic Rifle Marksmanship—Text for a basic course in shooting the rifle. 50¢[2]

The Cottontail Rabbit—56-page rundown on America's most popular hunting target. Where to find him, how to hunt him, how to help him. Bibliography included. $2 ea.[4]

The Elk—125-page report on the hunting and management of this game animal, more properly called *wapiti*. Extensive biblio. $2 ea.[4]

Fact Pact II—Authoritative and complete study on gun use and ownership. This is a valuable 102-page reference. $2ea[1].

For The Young Hunter—A 32-page booklet giving fundamental information on the sport. 50¢ each.[4]

Free Films—Brochure listing outdoor movies available to sportsmen's clubs. Free[1]

Fundamentals of Claybird Shooting—A 39-page booklet explaining the basics of Skeet and trap in non-technical terms. Many diagrams. 25¢[5]

Game, Gunners and Biology—A thumbnail history of American wildlife conservation. $2 ea.[4]

Gray Fox and Squirrels—112-page paperbound illustrated book giving full rundown on the squirrel families named. Extensive bibliography. $2 ea.[4]

Hunting Dogs—An excellent primer on hunting dogs for the novice hunter. 50¢ ea.[4]

The Mallard—80-page semi-technical report on this popular duck. Life cycle, laws and management, hunting—even politics as they affect this bird—are covered. Bibliography. $2 ea.[4]

The Mourning Dove—Illustrated booklet includes life history, conservation and hunting of the mourning dove. $2[4]

NRA Air Gun Training Program—A "self-teaching" precision air rifle and pistol manual. $1[2]

NRA Hunter Safety & Conservation Program Instructor's Manual—Teaching outlined and sources of information for hunter safety and conservation instructor, including exercises and demonstrations. 50¢[2]

NRA Hunter Safety & Conservation Program Student Manual (Revised)—Textbook for use in creating safer hunting environment and explain hunter's involvement in wildlife conservation. 50¢[2]

NRA Illustrated International Shooting Handbook—18 major articles detailing shooting under ISU rules, training methods, etc. NRA, Washington, DC, 1964. $2.50 ea. ($1.50 to NRA members.)[2]

Principles of Game Management—A 25-page booklet surveying in popular manner such subjects as hunting regulations, predator control, game refuges and habitat restoration. Single copies free, 25¢ each in bulk[4]

The Ring-Necked Pheasant—Popular distillation of much of the technical literature on the "ringneck." 104-page paperbound book, appropriately illustrated. Bibliography included. $2 ea.[2]

Ruffed Grouse, by John Madson—108-page booklet on the life history, management and hunting of *Bonasa umbellus* in its numerous variations. Extensive biblio. $2[4]

Trap or Skeet Fundamentals—Handbooks explaining fundamentals of these two sports, complete with explicit diagrams to start beginners off right. Free[3]

The White-Tailed Deer—Interesting fact-filled booklet gives life history, conservation and hunting information on this popular game animal. $2 [4]

---

[1]National Shooting Sports Foundation, Inc., 1075 Post Road, Riverside, CT 06878
[2]National Rifle Association of America, 1600 Rhode Island Ave., Washington, DC 20036

[3]Remington Arms Company, Dept. C, Bridgeport, CT. 06602
[4]Olin Corp., Conservation Dept., East Alton, IL 62024
[4]Winchester-Western, Shotgun Shooting Promotion, P.O. Box 30-275, New Haven, CT 06511

The Arms Library for
COLLECTOR·HUNTER·SHOOTER·OUTDOORSMAN

A selection of books—old, new and forthcoming—for everyone in the arms field, with a brief description by . . . JOE RILING

NEW BOOKS
(Alphabetically, no categories)

African Hunting and Adventure, by William Charles Baldwin, Books of Zimbabwe, Bulawayo, 1981. 451 pp., illus. $50.00

Facsimile reprint of the scarce 1863 London edition. African hunting and adventure from Natal to the Zambesi.

All About Varmint Hunting, by Nick Sisley, The Stone Wall Press, Inc., Wash., DC, 1982. 182 pp., illus. Paper covers. $8.95.

The most comprehensive up-to-date book on hunting common varmints found throughout North America.

Arms & Accoutrements of the Mounted Police 1873-1973, by Roger F. Phillips and Donald J. Klancher, Museum Restoration Service, Ontario, Canada, 1982. 224 pp., illus. $49.95.

A definitive history of the revolvers, rifles, machine guns, cannons, ammunition, swords, lances, saddlery, holsters, etc. used by the NWMP, the RNWMP and the RCMP during the first 100 years of the Force.

Arms & Equipment of the Civil War, by Jack Coggins, Outlet Books, New York, NY, 1983. 160 pp., illus. $7.98.

Lavishly illustrated guide to the principal weapons and equipment used by the army and naval forces of the Blue and the Gray.

Bell of Africa, by Walter (Karamojo) D.M. Bell, Ray Riling Arms Books Co., Phila., PA, 1983. 236 pp., illus. $35.00.

Autobiography of the greatest elephant hunter of them all.

The Best of Jack O'Connor, by Jack O'Connor, Amwell Press, Clinton, NJ, 1980. 192 pp., illus. Limited edition, signed and numbered. $150.00.

A collection of the finest selections from O'Connor's writings.

Big Rack, Texas All-Time Largest Whitetails 1892-1975, by Robert Rogers, et al, Outdoor Worlds of Texas, Inc., 1980. 167 pp., illus. $19.95.

Pictures and stories of all classifications of Texas trophy whitetail deer.

Browning Hi-Power Pistol, Desert Publications, Cornville, AZ, 1982. 20 pp., illus. Paper covers. $4.95

Covers all facets of the various military and civilian models of this gun.

Catalogue of the Enfield Pattern Room: British Rifles, Herbert Wooden, Her Majesty's Stationery Office, London, England, 1981. 80 pp., illus. Paper covers. $14.95.

The first exhaustive catalogue of a specific section of the collection in the Pattern Room at the Royal Small Arms Factory at Enfield Lock.

Colt's SAA Post War Models, George Garton, Gun Room Press, Highland Park, NJ, 1979. 166 pp., illus. $21.95.

Details all guns produced and their variations.

The Complete Book of Combat Handgunning, by Chuck Taylor, Desert Publications, Cornville, AZ, 1982. 168 pp., illus. Paper covers. $12.95.

Covers virtually every aspect of combat handgunning.

Complete Book of Shooting: Rifles, Shotguns, Handguns, by Jack O'Connor, Stackpole Books, Harrisburg, PA, 1983. 392 pp., illus. $24.95.

A thorough guide to each area of the sport, appealing to those with a new or ongoing interest in shooting.

The Deer Book, edited by Lamar Underwood, Amwell Press, Clinton, NJ, 1982. 480 pp., illus. $25.00

An anthology of the finest stories on North American deer ever assembled under one cover.

Deer Hunter's Yearbook, by the editors of Outdoor Life magazine, Stackpole Books, Harrisburg, PA, 1983. 192 pp., illus. $16.95.

A collection of the choicest stories on deer hunting to be published by the ever-popular Outdoor Life magazine.

Elephant Hunting in East Equatorial Africa, by Arthur H. Neumann, Books of Zimbabwe, Bulawayo, 1982. 455 pp., illus. $65.00.

Facsimile reprint of the scarce 1898 London edition. An account of three years ivory hunting under Mount Kenya.

The Golden Age of Shotgunning, by Bob Hinman, Wolfe Publishing Co., Inc., Prescott, AZ, 1982. $17.95.

A valuable history of the late 1800's detailing that fabulous period of development in shotguns, shotshells and shotgunning.

Great Whitetails of North America, by Robert Rogers, Texas Hunting Services, Corpus Christi, TX, 1981. 223 pp., illus. $24.95.

Pictures and stories of over 100 of the largest whitetail deer ever taken in North America.

The Grizzly Book/The Bear Book, two volume set edited by Jack Samson, Amwell Press, Clinton, NJ, 1982. 304 pp.; 250 pp., illus. Slipcase. $37.50.

A delightful pair of anthologies. Stories by men such as O'Connor, Keith, Fitz, Pope, and many others.

Grouse Magic by Nick Sisley, Nick Sisley, Apollo, PA, 1981. 240 pp., illus. Limited edition, signed and numbered. Slipcase. $30.00.

A book that will enrich your appreciation for grouse hunting and all the aura that surrounds the sport.

Gun Digest, 1984, 38th Edition, edited by Ken Warner, DBI Books, Inc., Northfield, IL 1983. 472 pp., illus. Paper covers. $13.95.

The world's greatest gun book in its 38th annual edition.

Guns Illustrated, 1984, 16th Edition, edited by Harold A. Murtz, DBI Books, Inc., Northfield, IL, 1983. 344 pp., illus. Paper covers. $11.95.

Technical articles for gun enthusiasts plus a complete illustrated catalog of all current guns, ammo, and accessories including specifications and prices. A must for the modern gun buff.

The Gun Digest Black Powder Loading Manual, by Sam Fadala, DBI Books, Inc., Northfield, IL, 1982. 224 pp., illus. Paper covers. $9.95.

450 loads for 86 of the most popular black powder rifles, handguns and shotguns.

Gun Digest Book of Shotgun Gunsmithing, by Ralph Walker, DBI Books, Inc., Northfield, IL, 1983. 256 pp., illus. Paper covers. $9.95.

The principles and practices of repairing, individualizing and accurizing modern shotguns by one of the world's premier shotgun gunsmiths.

The Gun Digest Book of Single Action Revolvers, by Jack Lewis, DBI Books, Inc., Northfield, IL, 1982. 256 pp., illus. Paper covers. $9.95.

A fond, in-depth look at the venerable "wheelgun" from its earliest days through today's latest developments.

Gun Owner's Book of Care, Repair and Improvement, by Roy Dunlap. Outdoor Life/Harper & Row, New York, NY, 1977. 336 pp., illus. $12.95.

The basic guide to repair and maintenance of guns. Over 350 step-by-step photographs.

Gun Traders Guide 10th Edition, by Paul Wahl, Stoeger Publishing Co., So. Hackensack, NJ, 1983. 415 pp., illus. Paper covers. $10.95.

Complete fully illustrated guide to identification of modern firearms with current market values.

The Gunsmiths and Gunmakers of Eastern Pennsylvania, by James Biser Whisker and Roy Chandler, Old Bedford Village Press, Bedford, PA, 1982. 130 pp., illus. Limited, numbered edition. Paper covers. $17.50.

Locates over 2000 gunsmiths before 1900, with references and documentation.

The Gunmakers and Gunsmiths of Western Pennsylvania, by James B. Whisker and Vaughn E. Whisker, Old Bedford Village Press, Bedford, PA, 1982. 103 pp., illus. Limited, numbered and signed edition. Paper covers. $17.50.

Lists over 650 names before 1900.

The History and Development of Small Arms Ammunition, Vol. 2, by George A. Hoyem, Armory Publications, Tacoma, WA, 1982. 303 pp., illus. $34.50.

Small arms and ammunition of 31 nations and dominions covered in detail together for the first time.

A History of the John M. Browning Semi-Automatic .22 Caliber Rifle, by Homer C. Tyler, Homer C. Tyler, Jefferson City, MO, 1982. 58 pp., illus. Paper covers. $10.00.

All models and variations are shown. Includes engraved guns.

How to Make Practical Pistol Leather, by J. David McFarland, Desert Publications, Cornville, AZ, 1982. 68 pp., illus. Paper covers. $6.95.

A guide for designing and making holsters and accessories for law enforcement, security, survival and sporting use.

The Hunter's Book of the Pronghorn Antelope, by Bert Popowski and Wilf E. Pyle, Winchester Press, Piscataway, NJ, 1982. 376 pp., illus. $16.95.

A comprehensive, copiously illustrated volume and a valuable guide for anyone interested in the pronghorn antelope.

A Hunter's Life in South Africa, by R. Gordon Cumming, 2 volumes, Books of Zimbabwe, Bulawayo, 1980. 389;381 pp., illus. $80.00.

Five years of a hunter's life deep in the interior of South Africa. A facsimile reprint of the 1850 London edition.

A Hunter's Wanderings in Africa, by F.C. Selous, Books of Zimbabwe, Bulawayo, 1981. 455 pp., illus. $50.00.

A facsimile reprint of the 1881 London edition. A narrative of nine years spent among the game of the interior of South Africa.

The Hunting Rifle, by Jack Lewis, DBI Books, Inc., Northfield, IL, 1983. 256 pp., illus. Paper covers. $10.95.

A thorough and knowledgeable account of today's hunting rifles.

Hunting and Stalking Deer Throughout the World, by Kenneth G. Whitehead, Batsford Books, London, England, 1982. 336 pp., illus. $19.95.

A comprehensive coverage of deer hunting areas on a country-by-country basis, dealing with every species in any given country.

Hunting on Safari in East and Southern Africa, by Aubrey Wynne-Jones, Macmillan South Africa, Johannesburg, S. Africa, 1980. 180 pp., illus. $35.00.

Every aspect of hunting in East and Southern Africa is covered, from the early planning stages of the hunt itself.

Hunting Wild Turkeys in the Everglades, by Frank P. Harben, Harben Publishing Co., Safety Harbor, FL. 341 pp., illus. Paper covers. $8.95.

Describes techniques, ways and means of hunting this wary bird.

Jim Corbett's India, edited by R.E. Hawkins, Oxford University Press, London, England, 1978. 250 pp., illus. $19.95.

A selection of stories from Jim Corbett's big game hunting books.

Knives '84, edited by Ken Warner, DBI Books, Inc., Northfield, IL, 1983. 256 pp., illus. Paper covers. $10.95.

The fourth edition of this increasingly popular knife book.

L'Incisione Delle Armi Sportive (Engraving of Sporting Arms), by Mario Abbiatico, Edizioni Artistiche Italiane, Famars, Brescia, Italy, 1983. 536 pp., illus. Italian text. $105.00.

An encyclopedia of Italian engraving on sporting arms. 1000 black and white and 200 full color illustrations.

Major Ned. H. Roberts and the Schuetzen Rifle, edited by Gerald O. Kelver, Brighton, CO, 1982. 99 pp., illus. $10.00.

A compilation of the writings of Major Ned H. Roberts which appeared in various gun magazines.

Matching the Gun to the Game, by Clair Rees, Winchester Press, Piscataway, NJ, 1982. 272 pp., illus. $26.95.

Covers selection and use of handguns, black-powder firearms for hunting, matching rifle type to the hunter, calibers for multiple use, tailoring factory loads to the game.

Military Pistols of Japan, by Fred L. Honeycutt, Jr., Julin Books, Lake Park, FL, 1982. 167 pp., illus. $24.00.

Covers every aspect of military pistol production in Japan through WWII.

Modern Gun Values, 4th Edition, by Jack Lewis, ed. by Harold A. Murtz, DBI Books, Northfield, IL, 1983. 400 pp., illus. Paper covers. $12.95.

An updated and expanded edition of the book that has become the standard for valuing modern firearms.

The Modern Gunsmith, by James V. Howe, Bonanza Books, NY, 1982. 415;424;68 pp., illus. $14.98.

Two volumes and supplement in one. The most authoritative work ever written on gunsmithing and gunmaking.

Muzzle Loading Today, by Andrew Courtney, London, England, 1981. 87 pp., illus. Paper covers. $5.95.

History, ignition systems, weapons and accessories.

The Mysteries of Shotgun Patterns, by George G. Oberfell and Charles E. Thompson, Oklahoma State University Press, Stillwater, OK, 1982. 164 pp., illus. Soft covers. $25.00.

Shotgun ballistics for the hunter in non-technical language, with information on improving effectiveness in the field.

Nosler Reloading Manual Number Two, Nosler Bullets, Inc., Bend, OR, 1981. 308 pp., illus. $8.95.

Thorough coverage of powder data, specifically tailored to the well known Nosler partition and solid base bullets.

The Old Pro Turkey Hunter, by Gene Nunnery, Gene Nunnery, Meridian, MS, 1980. 144 pp., illus. $12.95.

True facts and old tales of turkey hunters.

The P-08 Parabellum Luger Automatic Pistol, edited by J. David McFarland, Desert Publications, Cornville, AZ, 1982. 20 pp., illus. Paper covers. $4.95.

Covers every facet of the Luger, plus a listing of all known Luger models.

The Recollections of an Elephant Hunter 1864-1875, by William Finaughty, Books of Zimbabwe, Bulawayo, 1980. 244 pp., illus. $40.00.

Reprint of the scarce 1916 privately published edition. The early big game hunting exploits of William Finaughty in Matabeleland and Nashonaland.

Records of Exotics, Volume 2, 1978 Edition, compiled by Thompson B. Temple, Thompson B. Temple, Ingram, TX, 1978. 243 pp., illus. $15.00.

Lists almost 1,000 of the top exotic trophies bagged in the United States. Gives complete information on how to score.

Reloading Tools, Sights and Telescopes for Single Shot Rifles, by Gerald O. Kelver, Gerald O. Kelver, Brighton, CO, 1982. 163 pp., illus. Paper covers. $10.00.

A listing of most of the famous makers of reloading tools, sights and telescopes with a brief description of the products they manufactured.

Rifle Shooting as a Sport, by Bernd Klingner, A.S. Barnes and Co., Inc, San Diego, CA, 1980. 186 pp., illus. Paper covers. $15.00.

Basic principles, positions and techniques by an international expert.

The Ruger No. 1, by J.D. Clayton, edited by John T. Amber, Blacksmith Corp., Southport, CT, 1983. 200 pp., illus. $39.50.

Covers this famous rifle from original conception to current production.

Ruger Rimfire Handguns 1949-1982, by J.C. Munnell, G.D.G.S., Inc., McKeesport, PA, 1982. 189 pp., illus. Paper covers. $12.00.

Updated edition with additional material on the semiautomatic pistols and the new model .22 revolver.

Score Better at Trap, by Fred Missildine, Winchester Press, New York, NY, 1976. 159 pp., illus. $10.00.

An essential book for all trap shooters.

Sharps Firearms, by Frank Seller, Frank M. Seller, Denver, CO, 1982. 358 pp., illus. $39.95.

Traces the development of the Sharps firearms with full range of guns made including all martial varieties.

The Springfield Rifle M1903, M1903A1, M1903A3, M1903A4, Desert Publications, Cornville, AZ, 1982. 100 pp., illus. Paper covers. $5.95.

Covers every aspect of disassembly & assembly, inspection, repair & maintenance.

L.C. Smith Shotguns, by Lt. Col. William S. Brophy, The Gun Room Press, Highland Park, NJ, 1979. 244 pp., illus. $39.95.

The first work on this very important American gun and manufacturing company.

Strayed Shots and Frayed Lines, edited by John E. Howard, Amwell Press, Clinton, NJ, 1982. 425 pp., illus. $24.95.

An anthology of some of the finest, funniest stories on hunting and fishing ever assembled.

Tanzania Safaris, by Brian Herne, Amwell Press, Clinton, NJ, 1982. 259 pp., illus. Limited, signed and numbered edition. Slipcase. $75.00.

The story of Tanzania and hunting safaris, professional hunters, and a little history too.

Target Pistol Shooting, by K.B. Hinchliffe, David and Charles, London, 1981. 235 pp., illus. $25.00.

A complete guide to target shooting designed to give the novice and expert guidance on the correct techniques for holding, aiming, and firing pistols.

Target Rifle Shooting, by David Parish and John Anthony, E.P. Publishing, Ltd., West Yorkshire, England, 1981. 120 pp., illus. $12.95.

Explains all factors for correct shooting methods.

Target Rifle Shooting, by Major E.G.B. Reynolds and Robin Fulton, 2nd edition, Barrie & Jenkins Ltd., London, England, 1976. 239 pp., illus. $15.00.

A comprehensive manual on the sport of target rifle shooting.

Thompson Guns 1921-1945, Anubis Press, Houston, TX, 1980. 215 pp., illus. Paper covers. $7.95.

Facsimile reprinting of five complete manuals on the Thompson submachine gun.

A Treasury of Outdoor Life, edited by William E. Rae, Stackpole Books, Harrisburg, PA, 1983. 520 pp., illus. $24.95.

The greatest hunting, fishing, and survival stories from America's favorite sportsman's magazine.

U.S. Rifle, M14 from John Garand to the M1, by R. Blake Stevens, Collector Grade Publications, Toronto, Canada, 1983. 400 pp., illus. $34.95.

The complete history of the M14 rifle.

Walther P-38 Pistol, by Maj. George Nonte, Desert Publications, Cornville, AZ, 1982. 100 pp., illus. Paper covers. $5.95.

Complete volume on one of the most famous handguns to come out of WWII. All models covered.

Whitetail Hunting, by Jim Dawson, Stackpole Books, Harrisburg, PA, 1982. 224 pp., illus. $14.95.

New angles on hunting the whitetail deer.

The Wild Sheep of the World, by Raul Valdez, Wild Sheep and Goat International, Mesilla, NM, 1983. 150 pp., illus. $40.00.

The first comprehensive survey of the world's wild sheep written by a zoologist.

You Can't Miss, by John Shaw and Michael Bane, Paladin Press, Boulder, CO, 1983. 152 pp., illus. Paper covers. $8.95.

The secrets of a successful combat shooter. How to better your defensive shooting skills.

ballistics *and* handloading

ABC's of Reloading, 2nd Edition, by Dean A. Grennell, DBI Books, Inc., Northfield, IL, 1980. 288 pp., illus. Paper covers. $9.95.

A natural, logical, thorough set of directions on how to prepare shotgun shells, rifle and pistol cases prior to reloading.

American Ammunition and Ballistics, by Edward A. Matunas, Winchester Press, New York, NY, 1979. 288 pp., illus. $15.95.

A complete reference book covering all presently manufactured and much discontinued American rimfire, centerfire, and shotshell ammunition.

The Art of Bullet Casting from Handloader & Rifle Magazines 1966-1981, compiled by Dave Wolfe, Wolfe Publishing Co., Prescott, AZ, 1981. 258 pp., illus. Paper covers. $12.95. Deluxe hardbound. $19.50.

Articles from "Handloader" and "Rifle" magazines by authors such as Jim Carmichel, John Wootters, and the late George Nonte.

Ballistic Science for the Law Enforcement Officer, by Charles G. Wilber, Ph.D., Charles C. Thomas, Springfield, IL, 1977. 309 pp., illus. $33.00.

A scientific study of the ballistics of civilian firearms.

Basic Handloading, by George C. Nonte, Jr., Outdoor Life Books, New York, NY, 1982. 192 pp., illus. Paper covers. $4.50.

How to produce high-quality ammunition using the safest, most efficient methods known.

The Bullet's Flight, by Franklin Mann, Wolfe Publishing Co., Inc., Prescott, AZ, 1980. 391 pp., illus. $22.00.

The ballistics of small arms. A reproduction of Harry Pope's personal copy of this classic with his marginal notes.

Cartridges of the World 4th Edition, by Frank C. Barnes, DBI Books, Inc., Northfield, IL. 352 pp., illus. Paper covers. $12.95.

Gives the history, dimensions, performance and physical characteristics for more than 1,000 different cartridges.

Cast Bullets, by Col. E. H. Harrison, A publication of the National Rifle Association of America, Washington, DC, 1979. 144 pp., illus. Paper covers. $8.95.

An authoritative guide to bullet casting techniques and ballistics.

Computer for Handloaders, by Homer Powley. A Slide rule plus 12 page instruction book for use in finding charge, most efficient powder and velocity for any modern centerfire rifle. $6.95.

Discover Swaging, by David Corbin, Stackpole Books, Harrisburg, PA, 1980. 288 pp., illus., $18.95.

A book for the serious rifle and handgun reloading enthusiast.

Firearms Identification, by Dr. J. H. Mathews, Charles C. Thomas, Springfield, IL, 1973 3 vol. set. A massive, carefully researched, authoritative work published as:

Vol. I **The Laboratory Examination of Small Arms** 400 pp., illus. $56.75.
Vol. II **Original Photographs and Other Illustrations of Handguns** 492 pp., illus. $56.75.
Vol. III **Data on Rifling Characteristics of Handguns and Rifles** 730 pp., illus. $88.00.

Firearms Investigation, Identification and Evidence, by J. S. Hatcher, Frank J. Jury and Jac Weller. Stackpole Books, Harrisburg, PA, 1977. 536 pp., illus. $26.95.

Reprint of the 1957 printing of this classic book on forensic ballistics. Indispensable for those interested in firearms identification and criminology.

Game Loads and Practical Ballistics for The American Hunter, by Bob Hagel, Alfred A. Knopf, NY, NY, 1978. 315 pp., illus., hardbound. $13.95.

Everything a hunter needs to know about ballistics and performance of commercial hunting loads.

Handbook for Shooters and Reloaders, by P.O. Ackley, Salt Lake City, UT, 1970, *Vol. I,* 567 pp., illus. $12.50. *Vol. II,* a new printing with specific new material. 495 pp., illus. $9.95.

Handbook of Metallic Cartridge Reloading, by Edward Matunas, Winchester Press, Tulsa, OK, 1981. 272 pp., illus. $14.95.

Up-to-date, comprehensive loading tables prepared by the four major powder manufacturers.

Handloader's Digest, 9th Edition, edited by Ken Warner, DBI Books, Inc., Northfield, IL, 1982. 320 pp., illus. Paper covers. $10.95.

Latest edition of the book no handloader should be without.

Handloader's Digest Bullet and Powder Update, edited by Ken Warner, DBI Books, Inc., Northfield, IL, 1980. 128 pp., illus. Paper covers $5.95.

An update on the 8th ed. of "Handloader's Digest". Included is a round-up piece on new bullets, another on new primers and powders plus five shooters' reports on the various types of bullets.

Handloading, by Bill Davis, Jr., NRA Books, Wash., D.C., 1980. 400 pp., illus. Paper covers. $12.95.

A complete update and expansion of the NRA Handloader's Guide.

Handloading for Handgunners, by Geo. C. Nonte, DBI Books, Inc., Northfield, IL, 1978. 288 pp., illus. Paper covers. $9.95.

An expert tells the ins and outs of this specialized facet of reloading.

Handloading for Hunters, by Don Zutz, Winchester Press, NY, 1977. 288 pp., illus. Paper covers $9.95.

Precise mixes and loads for different types of game and for various hunting situations with rifle and shotgun.

The Home Guide to Cartridge Conversions, by Maj. George C. Nonte Jr., The Gun Room Press, Highland Park, NJ, 1976. 404 pp., illus. $19.95.

Revised and updated version of Nonte's definitive work on the alteration of cartridge cases for use in guns for which they were not intended.

Hornady Handbook of Cartridge Reloading, Hornady Mfg. Co., Grand Island, NE, 1981. 650 pp., illus. $11.95.

New edition of this famous reloading handbook. Latest loads, ballistic information, etc.

Lyman Cast Bullet Handbook, 3rd Edition, edited by C. Kenneth Ramage, Lyman Publications, Middlefield, CT, 1980. 416 pp., illus. Paper covers. $16.95.

Information on more than 5,000 tested cast bullet loads and 19 pages of trajectory and wind drift tables for cast bullets.

Lyman Centennial Journal 1878-1978, edited by C. Kenneth Ramage and Edward R. Bryant, Lyman Publications, Middlefield, CT, 1980. 222 pp., illus. Paper covers. $10.95.

The history of the Lyman company and its products in both words and pictures.

Lyman Black Powder Handbook, ed. by C. Kenneth Ramage, Lyman Products for Shooters, Middlefield, CT, 1975. 239 pp., illus. Paper covers $11.95.

The most comprehensive load information ever published for the modern black powder shooter.

Lyman Pistol & Revolver Handbook, edited by C. Kenneth Ramage, Lyman Publications, Middlefield, CT, 1978. 280 pp., illus. Paper covers. $11.95.

An extensive reference of load and trajectory data for the handgun.

Lyman Reloading Handbook No.46, edited by C. Kenneth Ramage, Lyman Publications, Middlefield, CT, 1982. 300 pp., illus. $16.95.

A large and comprehensive book on reloading. Extensive list of loads for jacketed and cast bullets.

Lyman Shotshell Handbook, 2nd ed., edited by C. Kenneth Ramage, Lyman Gunsight Corp., Middlefield, CT, 1976. 288 pp., illus., paper covers. $11.95.

Devoted exclusively to shotshell reloading, this book considers: gauge, shell length, brand, case, loads, buckshot, etc. plus an excellent reference section. Some color illus.

Metallic Cartridge Reloading, edited by Robert S.L. Anderson, DBI Books, Inc., Northfield, IL, 1982. 320 pp., illus. Paper covers. $12.95.

A true reloading manual with a wealth of invaluable technical data provided by outstanding reloading experts. A must for any reloader. Extensive load tables.

Metallic Reloading Basics, edited by C. Kenneth Ramage, Lyman Publications, Middlefield, CT, 1976. 60 pp., illus. Paper covers. $1.95.

Provides the beginner with loading data on popular bullet weights within the most popular calibers.

Modern Handloading, by Maj. Geo. C. Nonte, Winchester Press, NY, 1972. 416 pp., illus. $15.00.

Covers all aspects of metallic and shotshell ammunition loading, plus more loads than any book in print; state and Federal laws, reloading tools, glossary.

Pet Loads, by Ken Waters, Wolfe Publ. Co., Inc., Prescott, AZ, 1979. Unpaginated. In looseleaf form. $29.50.

A collection of the last 13 years' articles on more than 70 metallic cartridges. Most calibers featured with updated material.

Practical Handgun Ballistics, by Mason Williams, Charles C. Thomas, Publisher, Springfield, IL, 1980. 215 pp., illus. $19.50.

Factual information on the practical aspects of ammunition performance in revolvers and pistols.

Reloading for Shotgunners, edited by Robert S.L. Anderson, DBI Books, Inc., Northfield, IL, 1981. 224 pp., illus. Paper covers. $8.95.

Articles on wildcatting, slug reloading, patterning, skeet and trap loads, etc., as well as extensive reloading tables.

Sierra Bullets Reloading Manual, Second Edition, by Robert Hayden et al, The Leisure Group, Inc., Santa Fe Springs, CA, 1978. 700 pp., illus. Looseleaf binder. $16.95.

Includes all material in the original manual and its supplement updated, plus a new section on loads for competitive shooting.

Speer Reloading Manual Number 10 , Omark Industries, Inc., Lewiston, ID, 1979, 560 pp., illus. Paper covers. $10.00.

Expanded version with facts, charts, photos, tables, loads and tips.

Why Not Load Your Own? by Col. T. Whelen, A. S. Barnes, New York, 1957, 4th ed., rev. 237 pp., illus, $7.95.

A basic reference on handloading, describing each step, materials and equipment. Loads for popular cartridges are given.

Yours Truly, Harvey Donaldson, by Harvey Donaldson, Wolfe Publ. Co., Inc., Prescott, AZ, 1980. 288 pp., illus. $19.50.

Reprint of the famous columns by Harvey Donaldson which appeared in "Handloader" from May 1966 through December 1972.

COLLECTORS

American Boys' Rifles 1890-1945, by Jim Perkins, RTP Publishers, Pittsburg, PA, 1976. 245 pp., illus. $17.50.

The history and products of the arms companies who made rifles for the American boy, 1890-1945.

The American Cartridge, by Charles R. Suydam, Borden Publ. Co., Alhambra, CA, rev. ed., 1973. 184 pp., illus. $8.50.

An illus. study of the rimfire cartridge in the U.S.

American Handguns & Their Makers, compiled by J.B. Roberts, Jr. and Ted Bryant, NRA Books, Wash., DC, 1981. 248 pp., illus. Paper covers. $11.95.

First in a series of manuals on gun collecting and the history of firearms manufacturing.

" . . . And Now Stainless", by Dave Ecker with Bob Zwirz, Charter Arms Corp., Bridgeport, CT, 1981. 165 pp., illus. $15.00.

The Charter Arms story. Covers all models to date.

Arms Makers of Maryland, by Daniel D. Hartzler, George Shumway, York, PA, 1975. 200 pp., illus. $35.00.

A thorough study of the gunsmiths of Maryland who worked during the late 18th and early 19th centuries.

Ballard Rifles in the H.J. Nunnemacher Coll., by Eldon G. Wolff. Milwaukee Public Museum, Wisc., 2nd ed., 1961. Paper, 77 p. plus 4 pp. of charts and 27 plates. $5.00.

A thoroughly authoritative work on all phases of the famous rifles, their parts, patent and manufacturing history.

Basic Documents on U.S. Marital Arms, commentary by Col. B. R. Lewis, reissue by Ray Riling, Phila., PA., 1956 and 1960. *Rifle Musket Model 1855.* The first issue rifle of musket caliber, a muzzle loader equipped with the Maynard Primer, 32 pp. $2.50. *Rifle Musket Model 1863.* The Typical Union muzzle-loader of the Civil War, 26 pp. $1.75. *Breech-Loading Rifle Musket Model 1866.* The first of our 50 caliber breechloading rifles, 12 pp. $1.75. *Remington Navy Rifle Model 1870.* A commercial type breech-loader made at Springfield, 16 pp. $1.75 *Lee Straight Pull Navy Rifle Model 1895.* A magazine cartridge arm of 6mm caliber. 23 pp. $3.00. *Breech-Loading Arms* (five models)-27pp. $2.75. *Ward-Burton Rifle Musket 1871*-16 pp. $2.50. *U.S. Magazine Rifle and Carbine (cal. 30) Model 1892*(the Krag Rifle) 36 pp. $3.00.

Basic Manual of Military Small Arms, by W.H.B. Smith, Stackpole Books, Harrisburg, PA, 1980. 216 pp., illus. $22.95.

Reprint of the scarce 1943 original edition. An extensive source representing the small arms of 14 countries.

The Breech-Loader in the Service, 1816-1917, by Claud E. Fuller, N. Flayderman, New Milford, Conn., 1965. 381 pp., illus. $14.50.

Revised ed. of a 1933 historical reference on U.S. Standard and experimental military shoulder arms. Much patent data, drawings, and photographs of the arms.

A voluminous work that covers handloading-and other things-in great detail. Replete with data for all cartridge forms.

British Military Pistols 1603-1888, by R. E. Brooker, Jr., Le Magazine Royal Press, Coral Gables, FL, 1978. 139 pp., illus. $20.00.

Covers flintlock and percussion pistols plus cartridge revolvers up to the smokeless powder period.

The British Service Lee, Lee-Metford, and Lee-Enfield, by Ian Skennerton, Arms & Armour Press, London, England, 1982. 380 pp., illus. $32.50.

A very comprehensive and authoritative book on these famous military arms. A must for the Enfield collector.

California Gunsmiths 1846-1900, by Lawrence P. Sheldon, Far Far West Publ., Fair Oaks, CA, 1977. 289 pp., illus. $29.65.

A study of early California gunsmiths and the firearms they made.

Carbines of the Civil War, by John D. McAulay, Pioneer Press, Union City, TN, 1981. 123 pp., illus. Paper covers. $7.95.

A guide for the student and collector of the colorful arms used by the Federal cavalry.

Cartology Savalog, by Gerald Bernstein, Gerald Bernstein, St. Louis, MO, 1976. 177 pp., illus. Paper covers. $8.95.

An infinite variations catalog of small arms ammunition stamps.

The Cartridge Guide, by Ian V. Hogg, Stackpole Books, Harrisburg, PA, 1982. 160 pp., illus. $21.95.

The small arms ammunition identification manual.

Civil War Carbines, by A.F. Lustyik. World Wide Gun Report, Inc., Aledo, Ill, 1962. 63 pp., illus. Paper covers. $2.00.

Accurate, interesting summary of most carbines of the Civil War period, in booklet form, with numerous good illus.

Civil War Guns, by William B. Edwards, Castle Books, NY, 1976. 438 pp., illus. $15.00.

Describes and records the exciting and sometimes romantic history of forging weapons for war and heroism of the men who used them.

A Collector's Guide to Air Rifles, by Dennis E. Hiller, London, England, 1980. 170 pp., illus. Paper covers. $15.95.

Valuations, exploded diagrams and many other details of air rifles, old and new.

Colt Engraving, by R.L. Wilson, The Gun Room Press, Highland Park, NJ, 1982. 560 pp., illus. $69.95.

New and completely revised edition of the author's original work on finely engraved Colt firearms.

The Collector's Handbook of U.S. Cartridge Revolvers, 1856 to 1899, by W. Barlow Fors, Adams Press, Chicago, IL, 1973. 96 pp., illus. $10.95.

Concise coverage of brand names, patent listings, makers' history, and essentials of collecting.

Colt Firearms from 1836, by James E. Serven, new 8th edition, Stackpole Books, Harrisburg, PA, 1979. 398 pp., illus. $29.95. Deluxe ed. $49.95.

Excellent survey of the Colt company and its products. Updated with new SAA production chart and commemorative list.

The Colt Heritage, by R.L. Wilson, Simon & Schuster, 1979. 358 pp., illus. $50.00.

The official history of Colt firearms 1836 to the present.

Colt Pistols 1836-1976, by R.L. Wilson in association with R.E. Hable, Jackson Arms, Dallas, TX, 1976. 380 pp., illus. $100.00.

A magnificently illustrated book in full-color featuring Colt firearms from the famous Hable collection.

Colt's SAA Post War Models, by George Garton, Beinfield Publishing, Inc., No. Hollywood, CA, 1978. 176 pp., illus. $21.95.

Complete story on these arms including charts, tables and production information.

Colt's Variations of the Old Model Pocket Pistol, 1848 to 1872, by P.L. Shumaker, Borden Publishing, Co., Alhambra, CA, 1966, a reprint of the1957 edition. 150 pp., illus. $8.95.

A useful tool for the Colt specialist and a welcome return of a popular source of information that had been long out-of-print.

Confederate Longarms and Pistols, "A Pictorial Study", by Richard Taylor Hill and Edward W. Anthony, Taylor Publishing Co., Dallas, TX, 1978. $29.95.

A reference work identifying over 175 Confederate arms through detailed photography, and a listing of information.

Contemporary Makers of Muzzleloading Firearms, by Robert Weil, Screenland Press, Burbank, CA, 1981. 300 pp., illus. $39.95.

Illustrates the work of over 30 different contemporary makers.

Early Indian Trade Guns:1625-1775, by T.M. Hamilton, Museum of the Great Plains, Lawton, OK, 1968. 34 pp., illus. Paper covers. $7.95.

Detailed descriptions of subject arms, compiled from early records and from the study of remnants found in Indian country.

Fifteen Years in the Hawken Lode, by John D. Baird, The Gun Room Press, Highland Park, NJ, 1976. 120 pp., illus. $15.00.

A collection of thoughts and observations gained from many years of intensive study of the guns from the shop of the Hawken brothers.

'51 Colt Navies, by N.L. Swayze. Gun Hill Publ. Co., Yazoo City, MS, 1967. 243 pp., well illus. $15.00.

The first major effort devoting its entire space to the 1851 Colt Navy revolver. There are 198 photos of models, sub-models, variations, parts, markings, documentary material, etc. Fully indexed.

Firearms in Colonial America: The Impact on History and Technology 1492-1792, by M.L. Brown, Smithsonian Institution Press, Wash., D.C., 1980. 449 pp., illus. $45.00.

An in-depth coverage of the history and technology of firearms in Colonial North America.

Firearms of the Confederacy, by Claud R. Fuller & Richard D. Steuart, Quarterman Publ., Inc., Lawrence, MA, 1977. 333 pp., illus. $25.00.

The shoulder arms, pistols and revolvers of the Confederate soldier, including the regular United States Models, the imported arms and those manufactured within the Confederacy.

The Firearms Price Guide, 2nd Edition, by D. Byron, Crown Publishers, New York, NY, 1981. 448 pp., illus. Paper covers. $9.95.

An essential guide for every collector and dealer.

Flayderman's Guide to Antique American Firearms . . .And Their Values, Third Edition, by Norm Flayderman, DBI Books, Inc., Northfield, IL, 1983. 624 pp., illus. Paper Covers. $18.95.

Updated and expanded third edition of this bible of the antique gun field.

The .45-70 Springfield, by Albert J. Frasca and Robert H. Hall, Springfield Publishing Co., Northridge, CA, 1980. 380 pp., illus. $39.95.

A carefully researched book on the trapdoor Springfield, including all experimental and very rare models.

The 45/70 Trapdoor Springfield Dixie Collection, compiled by Walter Crutcher and Paul Oglesby, Pioneer Press, Union City, TN, 1975. 600 pp., illus. Paper covers. $9.95.

An illustrated listing of the 45-70 Springfields in the Dixie Gun Works Collection. Little known details and technical information is given, plus current values.

Gun Collector's Digest, 3rd Edition, edited by Joseph J. Schroeder, DBI Books, Inc., Northfield, IL, 1981. 256 pp., illus. Paper covers. $9.95.

Excellent reading by some of the world's finest collector/writers. The best book on general gun collecting available.

The Gun Collector's Handbook of Values 1980-81, by C. E. Chapel, Coward, McCann & Geoghegan, Inc., New York, NY, 1980. 462 pp., illus. $17.95.

Thirteenth rev. ed. of the best-known price reference for collectors.

Gunmarks, by David Byron, Crown Publishers, Inc., New York, NY, 1979. 185 pp., illus. $20.00.

Trade names, codemarks, and proofs from 1870 to the present.

Gun Traders Guide, 10th Edition, by Paul Wahl, Stoeger Publ. Co., S. Hackensack, NJ, 1983. 256 pp., illus. Paper covers. $10.95.

A fully illustrated and authoritative guide to identification of modern firearms with current market values.

Gunsmiths of Ohio—18th & 19th Centuries: Vol. I, Biographical Data, by Donald A. Hutslar, George Shumway, York, PA, 1973. 444 pp., illus. $35.00.

An important source book, full of information about the old-time gunsmiths of Ohio.

The Hand Cannons of Imperial Japan, 1543-1945, by Harry Derby, Harry Derby, Charlotte, NC, 1982. 300 pp., illus. $37.00.

Superb, comprehensive and definitive study of Japanese handguns beginning with the introduction of the matchlock in Japan and continuing into the post-WW II period.

The Hawken Rifle: Its Place in History, by Charles E. Hanson, Jr., The Fur Press, Chadron, NE, 1979. 104 pp., illus. Paper covers. $6.00.

A definitive work on this famous rifle.

Hawken Rifles, The Mountan Man's Choice, by John D. Baird, The Gun Room Press, Highland Park, NJ, 1976. 95 pp., illus. $15.00.

Covers the rifles developed for the Western fur trade. Numerous specimens are described and shown in photographs.

High Standard Automatic Pistols, 1932-1950, by Charles E. Petty, American Ordnance Publications, Charlotte, NC, 1976. 124 pp., illus. $12.95.

Describes and illustrates the early history of the company and many details of the various popular pistols. Includes dates and serial numbers.

Historical Hartford Hardware, by William W. Dalrymple, Colt Collector Press, Rapid City, SD, 1976. 42 pp., illus. Paper covers. $5.50.

Historically associated Colt revolvers.

A History of the Colt Revolver, by Charles T. Haven and Frank A. Belden, Outlet Books, New York, NY, 1978. 711 pp., illus. $25.00.

A giant of a book packed with information and pictures about the most cherished American revolver.

The History and Development of Small Arms Ammunition, Vol. 1, by George A. Hoyem, Armory Publications, Tacoma, WA, 1981. 230 pp., illus. $27.50.

Describes and illustrates ammunition from military long arms—flintlock through rimfire.

History of Modern U.S. Military Small Arms Ammunition, Vol. 2, 1940-1945, by F.W. Hackley, W.M. Woodin and E.L. Scranton, The Gun Room Press, Highland Park, NJ, 1976. 300 pp., illus. $25.00.

A unique book covering the entire field of small arms ammunition developed during the critical World War II years.

The History of Winchester Firearms 1866-1980, edited by Duncan Barnes, et al, Winchester Press, Tulsa, OK, 1980. 237 pp., illus. $21.95.

Specifications on all Winchester firearms. Background information on design, manufacture and use.

The Kentucky Rifle, by Merrill Lindsay, Arma Press, NY/the Historical Society of York County, York, PA, 1972. 100 pp., 81 large colored illustrations. $17.95.

Presents in precise detail and exact color 77 of the finest Kentucky rifles ever assembled in one place. Also describes the conditions which led to the development of this uniquely American arm.

Kentucky Rifles and Pistols 1756-1850, compiled by members of the Kentucky Rifle Association, Wash., DC, Golden Age Arms Co., Delaware, OH, 1976. 275 pp., illus. $29.50.

Profusely illustrated with more than 300 examples of rifles and pistols never before published.

Know Your Ruger Single Action Revolvers 1953-1963, by John C. Dougan, edited by John T. Amber, Blacksmith Corp., Southport, CT, 1981. 199 pp., illus. $35.00.

A definitive reference work for the Ruger revolvers produced in the period 1953-1963.

The Krag Rifle Story, by Franklin B. Mallory and Ludwig Olson, Springfield Research Service, Silver Spring, MD, 1979. 224 pp., illus. $20.00.

Covers both U.S. and European Krags. Gives a detailed description of U.S. Krag rifles and carbines and extensive data on sights, bayonets, serial numbers, etc.

Krag Rifles, by William S. Brophy, Beinfeld Pub. Inc., No. Hollywood, CA, 1980. 200 pp., illus. $29.95.

The first comprehensive work detailing the evolution and various models, both military and civilian.

The Krieghoff Parabellum, by Randall Gibson, Randall Gibson, Midland, TX, 1980. 280 pp., illus. $30.00.

A definitive work on the most desirable model Luger pistol.

Lever Action Magazine Rifles Derived from the Patents of Andrew Burgess by Samuel L. Maxwell Sr., Samuel L. Maxwell, Bellevue, WA, 1976. 368 pp., illus. $29.95.

The complete story of a group of lever action magazine rifles collectively referred to as the Burgess/Morse, the Kennedy or the Whitney.

Manual of Pistol and Revolver Cartridges, Volume 2, Centerfire U.S. and British Calibers, by Hans A. Erlmeier and Jakob H. Brandt, Journal-Verlag, Weisbaden, Germany, 1981. 270 pp., illus. $12.95.

Catalog system allows cartridges to be traced either by caliber or alphabetically.

Mauser Bolt Rifles, by Ludwig Olson, F. Brownell & Son, Inc., Montezuma, IA, 1976. 364 pp., illus. $29.95.

The most complete, detailed, authoritative and comprehensive work ever done on Mauser bolt rifles.

The Metric FAL, by R. Blake Stevens and Jean E. Van Rutten, Collector Grade Publications, Toronto, Canada, 1981. 372 pp., illus. Paper covers. $50.00.

Volume three of the FAL series. The free world's right arm.

Military Small Arms Ammunition of the World, 1945-1980, by Peter Labbett, Presidio Press, San Rafael, CA, 1980. 129 pp., illus. $18.95.

An up-to-date international guide to the correct identification of ammunition by caliber, type, and origin.

M1 Carbine, Design, Development and Production, by Larry Ruth, Desert Publications, Cornville, AZ. 300 pp., illus. Paper covers. $20.00.

The complete history of one of the world's most famous and largest produced firearms.

Modern Guns Identification and Values, 3rd Edition, edited by Russell and Steve Quertermous, Collector Books, Paducah, KY, 1981. 432 pp., illus. Paper covers. $11.95.

A catalog of well over 20,000 guns with important identifying information and facts.

More Single Shot Rifles, by James C. Grant, The Gun Room Press, Highland Park, NJ, 1976. 324 pp., illus. $15.00.

Details the guns made by Frank Wesson, Milt Farrow, Holden, Borchardt, Stevens, Remington, Winchester, Ballard and Peabody-Martini.

The Muzzle-Loading Cap Lock Rifle, by Ned H. Roberts, George Shumway Publisher, York, PA and Track of the Wolf Co., Osseo, MN, 1978. 308 pp., illus. $24.50.

Reprint of the revised and enlarged privately printed edition of this general survey of its subject and of the makers of the rifles.

The New England Gun, by Merrill Lindsay, David McKay Co., NY, 1976. 155 pp., illus. Paper covers. $12.50. Cloth, $20.00.

A study of more than 250 New England guns, powder horns, swords and polearms in an exhibition by the New Haven Colony Historical Society.

Simeon North: First Official Pistol Maker of the United States, by S. North and R. North, Rutgers Book Center, Highland Park, NJ, 1972. 207 pp., illus. $9.95.

Exact reprint of the original. Includes chapters on New England pioneer manufacturers and on various arms.

The Northwest Gun, by Charles E. Hanson, Jr., Nebraska State Historical Society, Lincoln, NB, 1976. 85 pp., illus., paper covers. $6.

Number 2 in the Society's "Publications in Anthropology." Historical survey of rifles which figured in the fur trade and settlement of the Northwest.

The Official 1981 Price Guide to Antique and Modern Firearms, edited by Thomas E. Hudgeons, House of Collectibles, Inc., Orlando, FL, 1981. 450 pp., illus. Paper covers. $9.95.

Over 10,000 current collectors values for over 650 manufacturers of American and foreign made firearms.

Paterson Colt Pistol Variations, by R.L. Wilson and R. Phillips, Jackson Arms Co., Dallas, TX, 1979. 250 pp., illus. $35.00.

A tremendous book about the different models and barrel lengths in the Paterson Colt story.

Peacemaker Evolutions & Variations, by Keith A. Cochran, Colt Collectors Press, Rapid City, SD, 1975. 47 pp., illus. Paper covers. $10.00.

Corrects many inaccuracies found in other books on the Peacemaker and gives much new information regarding this famous arm.

The Pennsylvania-Kentucky Rifle, by Henry J. Kauffman, Crown Publishers, New York, NY 1981. 293 pp., illus. $9.98.

A colorful account of the history and gunsmiths who produced the first American rifle superior to those brought from the Old Country.

Pennsylvania Longrifles of Note, by George Shumway, George Shumway, Publisher, York, PA, 1977. 63 pp., illus. Paper covers. $6.95.

Illustrates and describes samples of guns from a number of Pennsylvania rifle-making schools.

The Plains Rifle, by Charles E. Hanson, Jr., The Gun Room Press, Highland Park, NJ, 1977. 171 pp., illus. $15.00.

Historical survey of popular civilian arms used on the American frontiers, their makers, and their owners.

The Rare and Valuable Antique Arms, by James E. Serven, Pioneer Press, Union City, TN, 1976. 106 pp., illus. Paper covers. $4.95.

A guide to the collector in deciding which direction his collecting should go, investment value, historic interest, mechanical ingenuity, high art or personal preference.

Rifles in Colonial America, Vol. I, by George Shumway, George Shumway, Publisher, York, PA, 1980. 353 pp., illus. $49.50.

An extensive photographic study of American longrifles made in the late Colonial, Revolutionary, and post-Revolutionary periods.

Rifles in Colonial America, Vol. II, by George Shumway, George Shumway, Publisher, York, PA, 1980. 302 pp., illus. $49.50.

Final volume of this study of the early evolution of the rifle in America.

Samuel Colt's New Model Pocket Pistols; The Story of the 1855 Root Model Revolver, by S. Gerald Keogh, S.G. Keogh, Ogden, UT, 1974. 31 pp., illus., paper covers. $5.00.

Collector's reference on various types of the titled arms, with descriptions, illustrations, and historical data.

Savage Automatic Pistols, by James R. Carr. Publ. by the author, St. Charles, Ill., 1967. A reprint. 129 pp., illus. with numerous photos. $20.00.

Collector's guide to Savage pistols, models 1907-1922, with features, production data, and pictures of each.

Small Arms of the Sea Services, by Robert H. Rankin. N. Flayderman & Co., New Milford, CT, 1972. 227 pp., illus. $14.50.

Encyclopedic reference to small arms of the U.S. Navy, Marines and Coast Guard. Covers edged weapons, handguns, long arms and others, from the beginnings.

Southern Derringers of the Mississippi Valley, by Turner Kirkland. Pioneer Press, Tenn., 1971. 80 pp., illus., paper covers. $2.00.

A guide for the collector, and a much-needed study.

The Standard Directory of Proof-Marks, ed. by R.A. Steindler, The John Olson Company, Paramus, NJ, 1976. 144 pp., illus. Paper covers. $5.95.

A comprehensive directory of the proof-marks of the world.

Still More Single Shot Rifles, by James J. Grant, Pioneer Press, Union City, TN, 1979. 211 pp., illus. $17.50.

A sequel to the author's classic works on single shot rifles.

The 36 Calibers of the Colt Single Action Army, by David M. Brown. Publ. by the author at Albuquerque, NM, new reprint 1971. 222 pp., well-illus. $20.00.

Edited by Bev Mann of *Guns Magazine.* This is an unusual approach to the many details of the Colt S.A. Army revolver. Halftone and line drawings of the same models make this of especial interest.

The Trapdoor Springfield, by M.D. Waite and B.D. Ernst, Beinfeld Publ. Co., Inc., No. Hollywood, CA, 1979. 250 pp., illus. $29.95.

The first comprehensive book on the famous standard military rifle of the 1873-92 period.

Underhammer Guns, by H.C. Logan. Stackpole Books, Harrisburg, PA, 1965. 250 pp., illus. $10.00.

A full account of an unusual form of firearm dating back to flintlock days. Both American and foreign specimens are included.

U.S. Cartridges and Their Handguns, by Charles R. Suydam, Beinfeld Publ., Inc., No. Hollywood, CA, 1977. 200 pp., illus. Paper covers. $9.95.

The first book ever showing which gun used what cartridge. A must for the gun and cartridge collector.

The Virginia Manufactory of Arms, by Giles Cromwell, University Press of Virginia, Charlottesville, VA, 1975. 205 pp., illus. $29.95.

The only complete history of the Virginia Manufactory of Arms which produced muskets, pistols, swords, and cannon for the state's militia from 1802 through 1821.

Walther Models PP and PPK, 1929-1945, by James L. Rankin, assisted by Gary Green, James L. Rankin, Coral Gables, FL, 1974. 142 pp., illus. $20.00.

Complete coverage on the subject as to finish, proof marks and Nazi Party inscriptions.

Walther Volume II, Engraved, Presentation and Standard Models, by James L. Rankin, J.L. Rankin, Coral Gables, FL, 1977. 112 pp., illus. $20.00.

The new Walther book on embellished versions and standard models. Has 88 photographs, including many color plates.

Walther, Volume III, 1908-1980, by James L. Rankin, Coral Gables, FL, 1981. 226 pp., illus. $24.50.

Covers all models of Walther handguns from 1908 to date, includes holsters, grips and magazines.

The Whitney Firearms, by Claud Fuller. Standard Publications, Huntington, W. Va., 1946. 334 pp., many plates and drawings. $30.00.

An authoritative history of all Whitney arms and their maker. Highly recommended. Available with Ray Riling Arms Books Co.

The William M. Locke Collection, compiled by Robert B. Berryman, et al, The Antique Armory, Inc., East Point, GA, 1973. 541 pp., illus. $40.00.

A magnificently produced book illustrated with hundreds of photographs of guns from one of the finest collection of American firearms ever assembled.

Winchester, Dates of Manufacture, by George Madis, Art & Reference House, Lancaster, TX, 1982. 51 pp. $4.95.

Dates, serial numbers and number of each model made.

The Winchester Book, by George Madis, Art & Reference House, Lancaster, TX, 1980. 638 pp., illus. $39.50.

A greatly enlarged edition of this most informative book on these prized American arms.

The Winchester Handbook, by George Madis, Art & Reference House, Lancaster, TX, 1982. 287 pp., illus. $19.95.

The complete line of Winchester guns, with dates of manufacture, serial numbers, etc.

Winchester—The Gun That Won the West, by H.F. Williamson. Combat Forces Press, Washington, D.C., 1952. Later eds. by Barnes, NY. 494 pp., profusely illus., paper covers. $20.00.

A scholarly and essential economic history of an honored arms company, but the early and modern arms introduced will satisfy all but the exacting collector.

EDGED WEAPONS

The Robert Abels Collection of Bowie Type Knives of American Interest, by Robert Abels, Robert Abels, Hopewell Junction, NY, 1974. 20 pp., illus. Paper covers. $1.95.

A selection of American Bowie-type knives from the collection of Robert Abels.

American Axes, by Henry Kauffman, The Stephen Green Press, Brattleboro, VT, 1972. 200 pp., illus. $25.00.

A definitive work on the subject. Contains a roster of American axe makers, glossary and notes on the care and use of axes.

American Knives; The First History and Collector's Guide, by Harold L. Peterson, The Gun Room Press, Highland Park, NJ, 1980. 178 pp., illus. $15.00.

A reprint of this 1958 classic. Covers all types of American knives.

American Polearms 1526-1865, by Rodney Hilton Brown, H. Flayderman & Co., New Milford, CT, 1967. 198 pp., illus. $14.50.

The lance, halbred, spontoon, pike and naval boarding weapons used in the American military forces through the Civil War.

The American Sword, 1775-1945, by Harold L. Peterson, Ray Riling Arms Books, Co., Phila., PA, 1980. 286 pp. plus 60 pp. of illus. $29.95.

1977 reprint of a survey of swords worn by U.S. uniformed forces, plus the rare "American Silver Mounted Swords, (1700-1815)."

The Art of Blacksmithing, by Alex W. Bealer, Funk & Wagnalls, New York, NY, revised edition, 1976. 438 pp., illus. $16.95.

Required reading for anyone who makes knives or is seriously interested in the history of cutlery.

Basic Manual of Knife Fighting, by William L. Cassidy, Paladin Press, Boulder, CO, 1978. 41 pp., illus. Paper covers. $4.

A manual presenting the best techniques developed by the experts from 1930 to date.

The Best of Knife World, Volume I, edited by Knife World Publ., Knoxville, TN, 1980. 92 pp., illus. Pater covers. $3.95.

A collection of articles about knives. Reprinted from monthly issues of Knife World.

Blacksmithing for the Home Craftsman, by Joe Pehoski, Joe Pehoski, Washington, TX, 1973. 44 pp., illus. Paper covers. $3.50.

This informative book is chock-full of drawings and explains how to make your own forge.

Blades and Barrels, by H. Gordon Frost, Wallon Press, El Paso, TX, 1972. 298 pp., illus. $16.95.

The first full scale study about man's attempts to combine an edged weapon with a firearm.

Bowie Knives, by Robert Abels, Robert Abels, NY, 1960. 48 pp., illus. Paper covers. $3.00.

A booklet showing knives, tomahawks, related trade cards and advertisements.

Custom Knife...II, by John Davis Bates, Jr., and James Henry Schippers, Jr., Custom Knife Press, Memphis, TN, 1974. 112 pp., illus. $20.00.

The book of pocket knives and folding hunters. A guide to the 20th century makers' art.

The Cutlery Story: From Stone Age to Steel Age, by Lewis D. Bement, Custom Cutlery Co., Dalton, GA, 1972. 36 pp., illus. Paper covers. $3.50.

A classic booklet about the history, romance, and manufacture of cutlery from the earliest times to modern methods of manufacture.

Edge of the Anvil, by Jack Andrews, Rodale Press, Emmaus, PA, 1978. 224 pp., illus. Paper covers. $10.95.

A basic blacksmith book.

The Fighting Knife, by W.D. Randall, Jr. and Col.Rex Applegate, W.D. Randall, Orlando, FL, 1975. 60 pp., illus. Paper covers. $2.75.

Manual for the use of Randall-made fighting knives and similar types.

Fighting Knives, by Frederick J. Stephens, Arco Publishing Co., Inc., New York, NY, 1980. 127 pp., illus. $14.95.

An illustrated guide to fighting knives and military survival weapons of the world.

For Knife Lovers Only, by Harry K. McEvoy, Knife World Publ., Knoxville, TN, 1979. 67 pp., illus. Paper covers. $4.95.

A fascinating and unusual approach to the story of knives.

A Guide to Handmade Knives, edited by Mel Tappan, The Janus Press, Inc., Los Angeles, CA, 1977. No paper covers. Deluxe hardbound. $19.50.

The official directory of the Knifemakers Guild.

Gun Digest Book of Knives, 2nd Edition, by Jack Lewis and Roger Combs, DBI Books, Inc., Northfield, IL, 1982. 288 pp., illus. Paper covers. $10.95.

Covers the complete spectrum of the fascinating world of knives.

How to Make Knives, by Richard W. Barney & Robert W. Loveless, Beinfield Publ., Inc., No. Hollywood, CA, 1977. 178 pp., illus. $15.00.

A book filled with drawings, illustrations, diagrams, and 500 how-to-do-it photos.

How to Make Your Own Knives, by Jim Mayes, Everest House, New York, NY, 1978. 191 pp., illus. $7.95.

An illustrated step-by-step guide for the sportsman and home hobbyist.

Kentucky Knife Traders Manual No. 6, by R.B. Ritchie, Hindman, KY, 1980. 217 pp., illus. Paper covers. $10.00.

Guide for dealers, collectors and traders listing pocket knives and razor values.

The Knife Album Price Guide 1976 Edition, by Robert Mayes, Robert Mayes, Middlesboro, KY, 1976. 174 pp. Paper covers. $6.00.

The only book on identification and accurate pricing.

Knife Digest, Second Annual Edition, edited by William L. Cassidy, Knife Digest Publ. Co., Berkeley, CA, 1976. 178 pp., illus. $15.00.

The second annual edition of the internationally known book on blades.

Knife Throwing, Sport...Survival...Defense, by Blackie Collins, Knife World Publ., Knoxville, TN, 1979. 31 pp., illus. Paper covers. $3.00.

How to select a knife, how to make targets, how to determine range and how to survive with a knife.

Knife Throwing a Practical Guide, by Harry K. McEvoy, Charles E. Tuttle Co., Rutland, VT, 1973. 108 pp., illus. Paper covers. $3.95.

If you want to learn to throw a knife this is the "bible".

Knifecraft: A Comprehensive Step-by-Step Guide to the Art of Knifemaking, by Sid Latham, Stackpole Books, Harrisburg, PA, 1978. 224 pp., illus. $24.95.

An exhaustive volume taking both amateur and accomplished knifecrafter through all the steps in creating a knife.

Knifemakers of Old San Francisco, by Bernard R. Levine, Badger Books, San Francisco, CA, 1978. 240 pp., illus. $12.95.

The story about the knifemakers of San Francisco, the leading cutlers of the old West.

The Knife Makers Who Went West, by Harvey Platts, Longspeak Press, Longmont, CO, 1978. 200 pp., illus. $19.95.

Factual story of an important segment of the American cutlery industry. Primarily about Western knives and the Platts knife makers.

Knives '83, edited by Ken Warner, DBI Books, Inc., Northfield, IL, 1982. 224 pp., illus. Paper covers. $8.95.

The third edition of the world's greatest knife book.

Knives and Knifemakers, by Sid Latham, Winchester Press, NY, 1973. 152 pp., illus. $17.50.

Lists makers and suppliers of knife-making material and equipment.

Light But Efficient, by Albert N. Hardin, Jr. and Robert W. Hedden, Albert N. Hardin, Jr., Pennsauken, NJ, 1973. 103 pp., illus. $7.95.

A study of the M1880 Hunting and M1890 intrenching knives and scabbards.

Marble Knives and Axes, by Konrad F. Schreier, Jr., Beinfeld Publ., Inc., No. Hollywood, CA, 1978. 80 pp., illus. Paper covers. $5.95.

The first work ever on the knives and axes made by this famous old, still-in-business, manufacturer.

The Modern Blacksmith, by Alexander G. Weygers, Van Nostrand Reinhold Co., NY, 1977. 96 pp., illus. $10.95.

Shows how to forge objects out of steel. Use of basic techniques and tools.

Nathan Starr Arms Maker 1776-1845, by James E. Hicks, The Restoration Press, Phoenix, AZ, 1976. 166 pp., illus. $12.95.

Survey of the work of Nathan Starr of Middletown, CT, in producing edged weapons and pole arms for the U.S., 1799-1840, also some firearms.

Naval Swords, by P.G.W. Annis, Stackpole Books, Harrisburg, PA, 1970. 80 pp., illus. $5.50.

British and American naval edged weapons 1660-1815.

The Official 1981 Price Guide to Collector Knives, by James F. Parker and J. Bruce Voyles, House of Collectibles, Orlando, FL, 1981. 533 pp., illus. Paper covers. $9.95.

Buying and selling prices on collector pocket and sheath knives.

A Photographic Supplement of Confederate Swords with Addendum, by William A. Albaugh III, Moss Publications, Orange, VA, 1979. 259 pp., illus. $20.00.

A new updated edition of the classic work on Confederate edged weapons.

Pocket Knife Book 1 & 2—Price Guide, by Roy Ehrhardt, Heart of America Press, Kansas City, MO, 1974. 96 pp., illus. Spiral bound stiff paper covers. $6.95.

Reprints from the pocket knife sections of early manufacturers and sporting goods catalogs.

Pocket Knife Book 3—Price Guide, by Roy and Larry Ehrhardt, Heart of America Press, Kansas City, MO, 1974. Spiral bound stiff paper covers. $6.95.

Compiled from sections of various product sales catalogs of both Winchester and Marble Co. dating from the '20s and '30s.

The Pocketknife Manual, by Blackie Collins, Blackie Collins, Rock Hill, SC, 1976. 102 pp., illus. Paper covers. $5.50.

Building, repairing and refinishing pocketknives.

Practical Blacksmithing, edited by J. Richardson, Outlet Books, NY, 1978. four volumes in one, illus. $7.98.

A reprint of the extremely rare, bible of the blacksmith. Covers every aspect of working with iron and steel, from ancient uses to modern.

The Practical Book of Knives, by Ken Warner, Winchester Press, New York, NY, 1976. 224 pp., illus. $12.95.

All about knives for sport and utility.

Rice's Trowel Bayonet, reprinted by Ray Riling Arms Books, Co., Phila., PA, 1968. 8 pp., illus. Paper covers. $3.00.

A facsimile reprint of a rare circular originally published by the U.S. Government in 1875 for the information of U.S. Troops.

The Samurai Sword, by John M. Yumoto, Charles E. Tuttle Co., Rutland, VT, 1958. 191 pp., illus. $11.00.

A must for anyone interested in Japanese blades, and the first book on this subject written in English.

Scottish Swords from the Battlefield at Culloden, by Lord Archibald Campbell, The Mowbray Co., Providence, RI, 1973. 63 pp., illus. $5.00.

A modern reprint of an exceedingly rare 1894 privately printed edition.

Secrets of Modern Knife Fighting, by David E. Steele, Phoenix Press, Arvada, CO, 1974. 149 pp., illus. $17.50.

Details every facet of employing the knife in combat, including underwater fighting.

Step-by-Step Knifemaking, by Davis Boye, Rodale Press, Emmous, PA, 1978. 288 pp.,illus. $12.95.

Gives the fundamentals of knifemaking and shows how to make knives either as a hobby or as a business.

Swords and Other Edged Weapons, by Robert Wilkinson-Latham, Arco Publishing Co., New York, NY, 1978. 227 pp., illus. $8.95.

Traces the history of the "Queen of Weapons" from its earliest forms in the stone age to the military swords of the Twentieth century.

Tomahawks Illustrated, by Robert Kuck, Robert Kuck, New Knoxville, OH, 1977. 112 pp., illus. Paper covers. $8.50.

A pictorial record to provide a reference in selecting and evaluating tomahawks.

U.S. Military Knives, Bayonets and Machetes, Book III, by M. H. Cole, M.H. Cole, Birmingham, AL, 1979. 219 pp., illus. $23.00.

The most complete text ever written on U.S. military knives, bayonets, machetes and bolo's.

GENERAL

The Airgun Book, by John Walter, Stackpole Books, Harrisburg, PA, 1981. 320 pp., illus. $21.95.

Provides the airgun enthusiast with a much-needed basic book on his subject.

All About Airguns, by Robert J. Traister, TAB Books, Blue Ridge, Summit, PA, 1981. 304 pp., illus. $14.95.

A complete guide to airguns as a hobby, with special information and easy-to-follow directions on how to use them.

American Tools of Intrigue, by John Minnery & Jose Ramos, Desert Publications, Cornville, AZ, 1981. 128 pp., illus. Paper covers. $8.95.

Clandestine weapons which the Allies supplied to resistance fighters.

An Illustrated Guide to Rifles and Automatic Weapons, by Major Frederick Myatt, Arco Publishing Co., Inc., New York, NY, 1981. 160 pp., illus. $14.95.

Stories of gun designs, combat efficiency, production records, etc.

Bannerman Catalogue of Military Goods—1927, replica edition, DBI Books, Inc., Northfield, IL 1981. 384 pp., illus. Paper covers. $12.95.

Fascinating insights into one of the more colorful American arms merchants.

Black Powder Gun Digest, 3rd Edition, edited by Jack Lewis, DBI Books, Inc., Northfield, IL, 1982. 256 pp., illus. Paper covers. $10.95.

All new articles, expressly written for the black powder gun buff.

The Book of Shooting for Sport and Skill, edited by Frederick Wilkinson, Crown Publishers, Inc., New York, NY, 1980. 348 pp., illus. $19.95.

A comprehensive and practical encyclopedia of gunmanship by a squad of over twenty experts from both sides of the Atlantic.

Carbine; The Story of David Marshall "Carbine" Williams, by Ross E. Beard, Jr., The Sandlapper Store, Inc., Lexington, SC, 1977. 315 pp., illus. Deluxe limited edition, numbered and signed by the author and "Carbine". $25.

The story of the man who invented the M1 Carbine and holds 52 other firearms patents.

Colonial Frontier Guns, by T.M. Hamilton, The Fur Press, Chadron, NE, 1980. 176 pp., illus. Paper covers. $12.00.

French, Dutch, and English trade guns before 1780.

Colonial Riflemen in the American Revolution, by Joe D. Huddleston, George Shumway Publisher, York, PA, 1978. 70 pp., illus. $18.00.

This study traces the use of the longrifle in the Revolution for the purpose of evaluating what effects it had on the outcome.

The Complete Black Powder Handbook, by Sam Fadala, DBI Books, Inc. Northfield, IL, 1979. 288 pp., illus. Paper covers. $9.95.

Everything you want to know about black powder firearms and their shooting.

The Complete Book of Thompson Patents, compiled by Don Thomas, Desert Publications, Cornville, AZ, 1981. 482 pp., illus. Paper covers. $19.95.

From John Blish's breech closure patented in 1915 to Charles W. Robin's automatic sear release of 1947. Includes all other firearm patents granted to the developers of the famed "Tommy Gun."

The Complete Book of Trick & Fancy Shooting, by Ernie Lind, The Citadel Press, Secaucus, NJ, 1977. 159 pp., illus. Paper covers. $6.00.

Step-by-step instructions for acquiring the whole range of shooting skills with rifle, pistol and shotgun.

The Complete Survival Guide, edited by Mark Thiffault, DBI Books, Inc., Northfield, IL, 1983. 256 pp., illus. Paper covers. $10.95.

Covers all aspects of survival from manmade and natural disasters—equipment, techniques, weapons, etc.

Dead Aim, by Lee Echols, Acme Printing Co., San Diego, CA, a reprint, 1972. 116 pp., illus. $9.95.

Nostalgic antics of hell-raising pistol shooters of the 1930's.

Eli Whitney and the Whitney Armory, by Merrill Lindsay, Arma Press, North Branford, CT, 1979. 95 pp., illus. Paper covers. $4.95. Cloth $9.95.

History of the Whitney Armory 1767-1862, with notes on how to identify Whitney flintlocks.

The Encyclopedia of Infantry Weapons of World War II, by Ian V. Hogg, Harper & Row, New York, NY, 1977. 192 pp., illus. $15.95.

A fully comprehensive and illustrated reference work including every major type of weapon used by every army in the world during World War II.

Encyclopedia of Modern Firearms, Vol. 1, compiled and publ. by Bob Brownell, Montezuma, IA, 1959. 1057 pp. plus index, illus. $50.00. Dist. by Bob Brownell, Montezuma, IA 50171.

Massive accumulation of basic information of nearly all modern arms pertaining to "parts and assembly". Replete with arms photographs, exploded drawings, manufacturers' lists of parts, etc.

The FP-45 Liberator Pistol, 1942-1945, by R.W. Koch, Research, Arcadia, CA, 1976. 116 pp., illus. $15.00.

A definitive work on this unique clandestine weapon.

Famous Guns & Gunners, by George E. Virgines, Leather Stocking Press, West Allis, WI, 1980. 113 pp., illus. $12.95.

Intriguing and fascinating tales of men of the West and their guns.

Frankonia Jagd Catalogue, 1980-81, Waffen-Frankonia, Wurzburg, Germany, 1980. 372 pp., illus. Paper covers. $12.00.

Latest catalogue from this famous German sporting goods supplier. Rifles, shotguns, handguns, and accessories.

The German Sniper, 1914-1945, by Peter R. Senich, Paladin Press, Boulder, CO, 1982. 468 pp., illus. $49.95.

The development and application of Germany's sniping weapons systems and tactics traced from WW I through WW II.

Great Sporting Posters, by Sid Latham, Stackpole Books, Harrisburg, PA, 1980. 48 pp., illus. Paper covers. $14.95.

Twenty-three full-color reproductions of beautiful hunting and fishing poster art, mostly of the early 1900s.

Guns & Ammo, 1984 Annual, edited by Craig Boddington, Petersen Publishing Co., Los Angeles, CA, 1982. 288 pp., illus. Paper covers. $6.95.

Annual catalog of sporting firearms and accessories along with articles for the gun enthusiast.

Gun Digest Book of Metallic Silhouette Shooting, by Elgin Gates, DBI Books, Inc., Northfield, IL, 1979. 256 pp., illus. Paper covers. $8.95.

Examines all aspects of this fast growing sport including history, rules and meets.

Gun Digest Book of Holsters and Other Gun Leather, edited by Roger Combs, DBI Books, Inc., Northfield, IL, 1983. 256 pp., illus. Paper covers. $9.95.

An in-depth look at all facets of leather goods in conjunction with guns. Covers design, manufacture, uses, etc.

Gun Digest Book of Scopes and Mounts, by Bob Bell, DBI Books, Inc., Northfield, IL, 1983. 224 pp., illus. Paper covers. $9.95.

Traces the complete history, design, development of scopes and mounts from their beginnings to the current high-tech level of today. Covers the various uses and applications for the modern shooter/hunter.

Gun Talk, edited by Dave Moreton. Winchester Press, NY, 1973. 256 pp., illus. $9.95.

A treasury of original writing by the top gun writers and editors in America. Practical advice about every aspect of the shooting sports.

The Gun That Made the Twenties Roar, by Wm. J. Helmer, rev. and enlarged by George C. Nonte, Jr., The Gun Room Press, Highland Park, NJ, 1977. Over 300 pp., illus. $16.95.

Historical account of John T. Thompson and his invention, the infamous "Tommy Gun."

The Gunfighter, Man or Myth? by Joseph G. Rosa, Oklahoma Press, Norman, OK, 1969. 229 pp., illus. (including weapons). Paper covers. $9.95.

A well-documented work on gunfights and gunfighters of the West and elsewhere. Great treat for all gunfighter buffs.

The Gunfighters, by Dale T. Schoenberger, The Caxton Printers, Ltd., Caldwell, ID, 1971. 207 pp., illus. $12.95.

Startling expose of our foremost Western folk heroes.

Guns of the Gunfighters, by the editors of Guns & Ammo, Crown Publishing Co., New York, NY, 1982. 50 pp., illus. Paper covers. $6.98.

A must for Western buffs and gun collectors alike.

The Guns of Harpers Ferry, by S.E. Brown Jr. Virginia Book Co., Berryville, VA, 1968. 157 pp., illus. $20.00.

Catalog of all known firearms produced at the U.S. armory at Harpers Ferry, 1798-1861, with descriptions, illustrations and a history of the operations there.

The Gunsmith in Colonial Virginia, by Harold B. Gill, Jr., University Press of Virginia, Charlottesville, VA, 1975. 200 pp., illus. $11.95.

The role of the gunsmith in colonial Virginia from the first landing at Jamestown through the Revolution is examined, with special attention to those who lived and worked in Williamsburg.

Guns, Pistols, Revolvers, by Heinrich Muller, St. Martin's Press, New York, NY, 1980. 224 pp., illus. $29.95.

A comprehensive overview of the various types of hand and small arms in use from the 14th to the 19th century.

Guns & Shooting: A Selected Bibliography, by Ray Riling, Ray Riling Arms Books Co., Phila., PA, 1982. 434 pp., illus. Limited, numbered edition. $75.00.

A limited edition of this superb bibliographical work, the only modern listing of books devoted to guns and shooting.

Hatcher's Notebook, by Maj. Gen. J. S. Hatcher. Stackpole Books, Harrisburg, Pa., 1952. 2nd ed. with four new chapters, 1957. 629 pp., illus. $19.95.

A dependable source of information for gunsmiths, ballisticians, historians, hunters, and collectors.

Home Guide to Muzzle Loaders, by George C. Nonte, Jr., Stackpole Books, Harrisburg, PA, 1982. 224 pp., illus. Paper covers. $14.95.

From the basics of muzzleloading, to the differences between the modern and replica muzzle loader, plus how to make one.

The Identification and Registration of Firearms, by Vaclav "Jack" Krcma, C. C. Thomas, Springfield, IL, 1971. 173 pp., illus. $21.50.

Analysis of problems and improved techniques of recording firearms data accurately.

The Illustrated Encyclopedia of 19th Century Firearms, by Major Frederick Myatt, Crescent Books, New York, NY, 1980. 216 pp., illus. $12.95.

An illustrated history of the development of the world's military firearms during the 19th century.

Kill or Get Killed, by Col. Rex Applegate, new rev. and enlarged ed. Paladin Press, Boulder, CO, 1976. 421 pp., illus. $19.95.

For police and military forces. Last word on mob control.

The Law Enforcement Book of Weapons, Ammunition and Training Procedures, Handguns, Rifles and Shotguns, by Mason Williams, Charles C. Thomas, Publisher, Springfield, IL, 1977. 496 pp., illus. $35.00.

Data on firearms, firearm training, and ballistics.

Law Enforcement Handgun Digest, 3rd Edition, by Jack Lewis, DBI Books, Inc., Northfield, IL, 1980. 288 pp., illus. Paper covers. $9.95.

Covers such subjects as the philosophy of a firefight, SWAT, weapons, training, combat shooting, etc.

Lyman Muzzleloader's Handbook, 2nd Edition, edited by C. Kenneth Ramage, Lyman Publications, Middlefield, CT, 1982. 248 pp., illus. Paper covers. $11.95.

Hunting with rifles and shotguns, plus muzzle loading products.

Medicolegal Investigation of Gunshot Wounds, by Abdullah Fatteh, J.B. Lippincott Co., Phila., PA, 1977. 272 pp., illus. $25.75.

A much-needed work, clearly written and easily understood, dealing with all aspects of medicolegal investigation of gunshot wounds and deaths.

Military Small Arms of the 20th Century, 4th Edition, by Ian V. Hogg and John Weeks, DBI Books, Inc., Northfield, IL, 1981. 288 pp., illus. Paper covers. $12.95.

A comprehensive illustrated encyclopedia of the world's small-caliber firearms.

Modern Airweapon Shooting, by Bob Churchill & Granville Davis, David & Charles, London, England, 1981. 196 pp., illus. $18.95.

A comprehensive, illustrated study of all the relevant topics, from beginnings to world championship shooting.

No Second Place Winner, by Wm. H. Jordan, publ. by the author, Shreveport, LA (Box 4072), 1962. 114 pp., illus. $10.00.

Guns and gear of the peace officer, ably discussed by a U.S. Border Patrolman for over 30 years, and a first-class shooter with handgun, rifle, etc.

Old Time Posters from the Great Sporting Days, Stackpole Books, Harrisburg, PA, 1982. 48 pp., illus. Paper covers. $19.95.

Quality reproductions of 22 fine sporting posters in full color. 11"x16".

Olympic Shooting, by Colonel Jim Crossman, NRA, Washington, DC, 1978. 136 pp., illus. $12.95.

The complete, authoritative history of U.S. participation in the Olympic shooting events from 1896 until the present.

The Practical Book of Guns, by Ken Warner, Winchester Press, New York, NY, 1978. 261 pp., illus. $14.95.

A book that delves into the important things about firearms and their use.

E.C. Prudhomme, Master Gun Engraver, A Retrospective Exhibition: 1946-1973, intro. by John T. Amber, The R.W. Norton Art Gallery, Shreveport, LA, 1973. 32 pp., illus., paper covers. $5.00.

Examples of master gun engraving by Jack Prudhomme.

The Quiet Killers II: Silencer Update, by J. David Truby, Paladin Press, Boulder, CO, 1979. 92 pp., illus. Paper covers. $8.00.

A unique and up-to-date addition to your silencer bookshelf.

Sam Colt: Genius, by Robt. F. Hudson, American Archives Publ. Co., Topsfield, MA, 1971. 160 pp., illus. Plastic spiral bound. $6.50.

Historical review of Colt's inventions, including facsimiles of patent papers and other Colt information.

The Shooter's Workbench, by John A. Mosher, Winchester Press, NY, 1977. 256 pp., illus. $13.95.

Accessories the shooting sportsman can build for the range, for the shop, for transport and the field, and for the handloading bench.

Small Arms of the World, 11th Edition, a complete revision of W.H.B. Smith's firearms classic by Edward Clinton Ezell, Stackpole Books, Harrisburg, PA, 1977. 667 pp., illus. $29.95.

A complete revision of this firearms classic now brings all arms enthusiasts up to date on global weapons production and use.

Sporting Arms of the World, by Ray Bearse, Outdoor Life/Harper & Row, N.Y., 1977. 500 pp., illus. $15.95.

A mammoth, up-to-the-minute guide to the sporting world's favorite rifles, shotguns, handguns.

Survival Guns, by Mel Tappan, The Janus Press, Inc., Los Angeles, CA, 1976. 458 pp., illus. Paper covers. $9.95.

A guide to the selection, modification and use of firearms and related devices for defense, food gathering, etc. under survival conditions.

Triggernometry, by Eugene Cunningham. Caxton Printers Lt., Caldwell, ID, 1970. 441 pp., illus. $12.95.

A classic study of famous outlaws and lawmen of the West—their stature as human beings, their exploits and skills in handling firearms. A reprint.

Weapons of the American Revolution, and Accoutrements, by Warren Moore. A & W Books, NY, 1974. 225 pp., fine illus. $15.

Revolutionary era shoulder arms, pistols, edged weapons, and equipment are described and shown in fine drawings and photographs, some in color.

Gunsmithing

The Art of Engraving, by James B. Meek, F. Brownell & Son, Montezuma, IA, 1973. 196 pp., illus. $24.95.

A complete, authoritative, imaginative and detailed study in training for gun engraving. The first book of its kind—and a great one.

Artistry in Arms, The R.W. Norton Gallery, Shreveport, LA., 1970. 42 pp., illus. Paper, $5.00.

The art of gunsmithing and engraving.

Building the Kentucky Pistol, by James R. Johnston, Golden Age Arms Co., Worthington, OH, 1974. 36 pp., illus. Paper covers. $4.00.

A step-by-step guide for building the Kentucky pistol. Illus. with full page line drawings.

Building the Kentucky Rifle, by J.R. Johnston. Golden Age Arms Co., Worthington, OH, 1972. 44 pp., illus. Paper covers. $5.00.

How to go about it, with text and drawings.

Checkering and Carving of Gun Stocks, by Monte Kennedy. Stackpole Books, Harrisburg, PA, 1962. 175 pp., illus. $27.95.

Rev., enlarged clothbound ed. of a much sought-after, dependable work.

Clyde Baker's Modern Gunsmithing, revised by John E. Traister, Stackpole Books, Harrisburg, PA, 1981. 530 pp., illus. $24.95.

A revision of the classic work on gunsmithing.

The Complete Rehabilitation of the Flintlock Rifle and Other Works, by T.B. Tyron. Limbo Library, Taos, NM, 1972. 112 pp., illus. Paper covers. $6.95.

A series of articles which first appeared in various issues of the *American Rifleman* in the 1930s.

Do-It-Yourself Gunsmithing, by Jim Carmichel, Outdoor Life-Harper & Row, New York, NY, 1977. 371 pp., illus. $16.95.

The author proves that home gunsmithing is relatively easy and highly satisfying.

Firearms Assembly 3: The NRA Guide to Rifle and Shotguns, NRA Books, Wash., D.C., 1980. 264 pp., illus. Paper covers. $8.95.

Text and illustrations explaining the takedown of 125 rifles and shotguns, domestic and foreign.

Firearms Assembly 4: The NRA Guide to Pistols and Revolvers, NRA Books, Wash., D.C., 1980. 253 pp., illus. Paper covers. $8.95.

Text and illustrations explaining the takedown of 124 pistol and revolver models, domestic and foreign.

Firearms Blueing and Browning, by R.H. Angier. Stackpole Books, Harrisburg, PA, 151 pp., illus. $12.95.

A useful, concise text on chemical coloring methods for the gunsmith and mechanic.

First Book of Gunsmithing, by John E. Traister, Stackpole Books, Harrisburg, PA, 1981. 192 pp., illus. $18.95.

Beginner's guide to gun care, repair and modification.

Gun Digest Book of Exploded Firearms Drawings, 3rd Edition edited by Harold A. Murtz, DBI Books, Inc., Northfield, IL, 1982. 480 pp., illus. Paper covers. $12.95.

Contains 470 isometric views of modern and collector's handguns and long guns, with parts lists. A must for the gunsmith or tinkerer.

Gun Digest Book of Riflesmithing, by Jack Mitchell, DBI Books, Inc., Northfield, IL, 1982. 256 pp., illus. Paper covers. $9.95.

The art and science of rifle gunsmithing. Covers tools, techniques, designs, finishing wood and metal, custom alterations.

Gunsmithing: The Tricks of the Trade, by J.B. Wood, DBI Books, Inc., Northfield, IL, 1982. 256 pp., illus. Paper covers. $9.95.

How to repair and replace broken gun parts using ordinary home workshop tools.

Gun Care and Repair, by Monte Burch, Winchester Press, NY, 1978. 256 pp., illus. $15.95.

Everything the gun owner needs to know about home gunsmithing and firearms maintenance.

Gun Digest Book of Firearms Assembly/Disassembly Part I: Automatic Pistols, by J.B. Wood, DBI Books, Inc., Northfield, IL, 1979. 320 pp., illus. Paper covers. $10.95.

A thoroughly professional presentation on the art of pistol disassembly and reassembly. Covers most modern guns, popular older models, and some of the most complex pistols ever produced.

Gun Digest Book of Firearms Assembly/Disassembly Part II: Revolvers, by J. B. Wood, DBI Books, Inc., Northfield, IL, 1979. 320 pp., illus. Paper covers. $10.95.

How to properly dismantle and reassemble both the revolvers of today and of the past.

The Gun Digest Book of Firearms Assembly/Disassembly Part III: Rimfire Rifles, by J. B. Wood, DBI Books, Inc., Northfield, IL, 1980. 288 pp., illus. Paper covers. $9.95.

A most comprehensive, uniform, and professional presentation available for disassembling and reassembling most rimfire rifles.

The Gun Digest Book of Firearms Assembly/Disassembly Part IV: Centerfire Rifles, by J. B. Wood, DBI Books, Inc., Northfield, IL, 1980. 288 pp., illus. Paper covers. $9.95.

A professional presentation on the assembly and reassembly of centerfire rifles.

The Gun Digest Book of Firearms Assembly/Disassembly, Part V: Shotguns, by J.B. Wood, DBI Books, Inc., Northfield, IL, 1980. 288 pp., illus. Paper covers. $9.95.

A professional presentation on the complete disassembly and assembly of 26 of the most popular shotguns, new and old.

The Gun Digest Book of Firearms Assembly/Disassembly Part VI: Law Enforcement Weapons, by J.B. Wood, DBI Books, Inc., Northfield, IL, 1981. 288 pp., illus. Paper covers. $9.95.

Step-by-step instructions on how to completely dismantle and reassemble the most commonly used firearms found in law enforcement arsenals.

Gun Digest Book of Gunsmithing Tools and Their Uses, by John E. Traister, DBI Books, Inc., Northfield, IL, 1980. 256 pp., illus. Paper covers. $8.95.

The how, when and why of tools for amateur and professional gunsmiths and gun tinkerers.

The Gun Digest Book of Pistolsmithing, by Jack Mitchell, DBI Books, Inc., Northfield, IL, 1980. 288 pp., illus. Paper covers. $9.95.

An expert's guide to the operation of each of the handgun actions with all the major functions of pistolsmithing explained.

Gun Digest Review of Custom Guns, edited by Ken Warner, DBI Books, Inc., Northfield, IL, 1980. 256 pp., illus. Paper covers. $9.95.

An extensive look at the art of custom gun making. This book is a must for anyone considering the purchase of a custom firearm.

Gun Owner's Book of Care, Repair & Improvement, by Roy Dunlap, Outdoor Life-Harper & Row, NY, 1974. 336 pp., illus. $12.95.

A basic guide to repair and maintenance of guns, written for the average firearms owner.

Gunsmith Kinks, by F.R. (Bob) Brownell. F. Brownell & Son, Montezuma, I. 1st ed., 1969. 496 pp., well illus. $12.95.

A widely useful accumulation of shop kinks, short cuts, techniques and pertinent comments by practicing gunsmiths from all over the world.

Gunsmithing, by Roy F. Dunlap. Stackpole Books, Harrisburg, PA, 714 pp., illus. $27.50.

Comprehensive work on conventional techniques, incl. recent advances in the field. Valuable to rifle owners, shooters, and practicing gunsmiths.

Gunsmiths and Gunmakers of Vermont, by Warren R. Horn, The Horn Co., Burlington, VT, 1976. 76 pp., illus. Paper covers. $5.00.

A checklist for collectors, of over 200 craftsmen who lived and worked in Vermont up to and including 1900.

The Gunsmith's Manual, by J.P. Stelle and Wm.B. Harrison, The Gun Room Press, Highland Park, NJ, 1982. 376 pp., illus. $12.95.

For the gunsmith in all branches of the trade.

Gunstock Finishing and Care, by A. Donald Newell, Stackpole Books, Harrisburg, PA, 1982. 512 pp., illus. $27.95.

The most complete resource imaginable for finishing and refinishing gun wood.

Home Gun Care & Repair, by P.O. Ackley, Stackpole Books, Harrisburg, PA, 1969. 191 pp., illus. Paper covers. $6.95.

Basic reference for safe tinkering, fixing, and converting rifles, shotguns, handguns.

How to Build Your Own Wheellock Rifle or Pistol, by George Lauber, The John Olson Co., Paramus, NJ, 1976. Paper covers. $6.95.

Complete instructions on building these arms.

How to Build Your Own Flintlock Rifle or Pistol, by Georg Lauber, The John Olson Co., Paramus, NJ, 1976. Paper covers. $6.95.

The second in Mr. Lauber's three-volume series on the art and science of building muzzle-loading black powder firearms.

"How to Build Your Own Percussion Rifle or Pistol", by Georg Lauber, The John Olson Co., Paramus, NJ, 1976. Paper covers, $6.95.

The third and final volume of Lauber's set of books on the building of muzzle-loaders.

Learn Gunsmithing, by John Traister, Winchester Press, Tulsa, OK, 1980. 202 pp., illus. $15.95.

The troubleshooting method of gunsmithing for the home gunsmith and professional alike.

Lock, Stock and Barrel, by R.H. McCrory. Publ. by author at Bellmore, NY, 1966. Paper covers. 122 pp., illus. $6.00.

A handy and useful work for the collector or the professional with many helpful procedures shown and described on antique gun repair.

The Modern Kentucky Rifle, How to Build Your Own, by R.H. McCrory. McCrory, Wantagh, NY, 1961. 68 pp., illus., paper bound. $6.00.

A workshop manual on how to fabricate a flintlock rifle. Also some information on pistols and percussion locks.

Pistolsmithing, by George C. Nonte, Jr., Stackpole Books, Harrisburg, PA, 1974. 560 pp., illus. $19.95.

A single source reference to handgun maintainence, repair, and modification at home, unequaled in value.

Professional Gunsmithing, by W.J. Howe, Stackpole Books, Harrisburg, PA, 1968 reprinting. 526 pp., illus. $24.95.

Textbook on repair and alteration of firearms, with detailed notes on equipment and commercial gunshop operation.

Respectfully Yours H.M. Pope, compiled and edited by G.O. Kelver, Brighton, CO, 1976. 266 pp., illus. $16.50.

A compilation of letters from the files of the famous barrelmaker, Harry M. Pope.

The Trade Gun Sketchbook, by Charles E. Hanson, The Fur Press, Chadron, NB, 1979. 48 pp., illus. Paper covers. $4.00.

Complete full-size plans to build seven different trade guns from the Revolution to the Indian Wars and a two-thirds size for your son.

The Trade Rifle Sketchbook, by Charles E. Hanson, The Fur Press, Chadron, NB, 1979. 48 pp., illus. Paper covers. $4.00.

Includes full scale plans for ten rifles made for Indian and mountain men; from 1790 to 1860, plus plans for building three pistols.

Troubleshooting Your Rifle and Shotgun, by J.B. Wood, DBI Books, Inc., Northfield, IL, 1978. 192 pp., illus. Paper covers. $6.95.

A gunsmiths advice on how to keep your long guns shooting.

handguns

American Pistol and Revolver Design and Performance, by L.R. Wallack, Winchester Press, NY, 1978. 224 pp., illus. $16.95.

How different types and models of pistols and revolvers work, from trigger pull to bullet impact.

American Police Handgun Training, by Charles R. Skillen and Mason Williams, Charles C. Thomas, Springfield, IL, 1980. 216 pp., illus. $17.50.

Deals comprehensively with all phases of current handgun training procedures in America.

Askins on Pistols and Revolvers, by Col. Charles Askins, NRA Books, Wash., D.C., 1980. 144 pp., illus. Paper covers. $8.95.

A book full of practical advice, shooting tips, technical analysis and stories of guns in action.

The Black Powder Handgun by Sam Fadala, DBI Books, Inc., Northfield, IL, 1981. 288 pp., illus. Paper covers. $9.95.

The author covers this oldtimer in all its forms: pistols and six-shooters in both small and large bore, target and hunting.

Blue Steel and Gun Leather, by John Bianchi, Beinfeld Publishing, Inc., No. Hollywood, CA, 1978. 200 pp., illus. $12.00.

A complete and comprehensive review of holster uses plus an examination of available products on today's market.

Colt Automatic Pistols, by Donald B. Bady, Borden Publ. Co., Alhambra, CA, 1974. 368 pp., illus. $16.95.

The rev. and enlarged ed. of a key work on a fascinating subject. Complete information on every automatic marked with Colt's name.

The Colt .45 Auto Pistol, compiled from U.S. War Dept. Technical Manuals, and reprinted by Desert Publications, Cornville, AZ, 1978. 80 pp., illus. Paper covers. $5.95.

Covers every facet of this famous pistol from mechanical training, manual of arms, disassembly, repair and replacement of parts.

Combat Handgun Shooting, by James D. Mason, Charles C. Thomas, Springfield, IL, 1976. 256 pp., illus. $27.50.

Discusses in detail the human as well as the mechanical aspects of shooting.

Combat Handguns, edited by Edward C. Ezell, Stackpole Books, Harrisburg, PA, 1980. 288 pp., illus. $19.95.

George Nonte's last great work, edited by Edward C. Ezell. A comprehensive reference volume offering full coverage of automatic handguns vs. revolvers, custom handguns, combat autoloaders and revolvers—domestic and foreign, and combat testing.

Combat Shooting for Police, by Paul B. Weston. Charles C. Thomas, Springfield, IL, 1967. A reprint. 194 pp., illus. $15.00.

First publ. in 1960 this popular self-teaching manual gives basic concepts of defensive fire in every position.

Defensive Handgun Effectiveness, by Carroll E. Peters, Carroll E. Peters, Manchester, TN, 1977. 198 pp., charts and graphs. $10.00.

A systematic approach to the design, evaluation and selection of ammunition for the defensive handgun.

The Defensive Use of the Handgun for the Novice, by Mason Williams, Charles C. Thomas, Publisher, Springfield, IL, 1980. 226 pp., illus. $15.00.

This book was developed for the home owner, housewife, elderly couple, and the woman who lives alone. Basic instruction for purchasing, loading and firing pistols and revolvers.

Flattops & Super Blackhawks, by H.W. Ross, Jr., H.W. Ross, Jr., Bridgeville, PA, 1979. 93 pp., illus. Paper covers. $9.95.

An expanded version of the author's book "Ruger Blackhawks" with an extra chapter on Super Blackhawks and the Mag-Na-Ports with serial numbers and approximate production dates.

Hallock's .45 Auto Handbook, by Ken Hallock, The Mihan Co., Oklahoma City, OK, 1981. 178 pp., illus. Paper covers. $11.95.

For gunsmiths, dealers, collectors and serious hobbyists.

A Handbook on the Primary Identification of Revolvers & Semi-automatic Pistols, by John T. Millard, Charles C. Thomas, Springfield, IL, 1974. 156 pp., illus. $15.00.

A practical outline on the simple, basic phases of primary firearm identification with particular reference to revolvers and semi-automatic pistols.

Handgun Competition, by Maj. Geo. C. Nonte, Jr., Winchester Press, NY, 1978. 288 pp., illus. $14.95.

A comprehensive source-book covering all aspects of modern competitive pistol and revolver shooting.

Handguns of the World, by Edward C. Ezell, Stackpole Books, Harrisburg, PA., 1981. 704 pp., illus. $39.95.

Encyclopedia for identification and historical reference that will be appreciated by gun enthusiasts, collectors, hobbyists or professionals.

High Standard Automatic Pistols 1932-1950, by Charles E. Petty, American Ordnance Publ., Charlotte, NC, 1976. 124 pp., illus. $12.95.

A definitive source of information for the collector of High Standard pistols.

The Illustrated Encyclopedia of Pistols and Revolvers, by Major Frederick Myatt, Crescent Books, New York, NY, 1980. 208 pp., illus. $14.98.

An illustrated history of handguns from the 16th century to the present day.

The Illustrated Book of Pistols, by Frederick Wilkinson, Hamlyn Publishing Group, Ltd. London, England, 1979. 192 pp., illus. $10.98.

A carefully researched study of the pistol's evolution and use in war and peace.

Japanese Hand Guns, by F.E. Leithe, Borden Publ. Co., Alhambra, CA, 1968. Unpaginated, well illus. $9.95.

Identification guide, covering models produced since the late 19th century. Brief text material gives history, descriptions, and markings.

Jeff Cooper on Handguns, by Jeff Cooper, Petersen Publishing Co., Los Angeles, CA, 1979. 96 pp., illus. Paper covers. $2.50.

An expert's guide to handgunning. Technical tips on actions, sights, loads, grips, and holsters.

Know Your 45 Auto Pistols—Models 1911 & A1, by E.J. Hoffschmidt, Blacksmith Corp., Southport, CT, 1974. 58 pp., illus. Paper covers. $5.95.

A concise history of the gun with a wide variety of types and copies.

Know Your Walther P.38 Pistols, by E.J. Hoffschmidt, Blacksmith Corp., Southport, CT, 1974. 77 pp., illus. Paper covers. $5.95. variations.

Covers the Walther models Armee, M.P., H.P., P.38—history and variations.

Know Your Walther P.P. & P.P.K. Pistols, by E.J. Hoffschmidt, Blacksmith Corp., Southport, CT, 1975. 87 pp., illus. Paper covers. $5.95.

A concise history of the guns with a guide to the variety and types.

The Luger Pistol (Pistole Parabellum), by F.A. Datig, Borden Publ. Co., Alhambra, CA, 1962. 328 pp., well illus. $12.95.

An enlarged, rev. ed. of an important reference on the arm, its history and development from 1893 to 1945.

Luger Variations, by Harry E. Jones, Harry E. Jones, Torrance, CA, 1975. 328 pp., 160 full page illus., many in color. $30.00.

A rev. ed. of the book known as "The Luger Collector's Bible".

Lugers at Random, by Charles Kenyon, Jr. Handgun Press, Chicago, IL. 1st ed., 1970. 416 pp., profusely illus. $20.00.

An impressive large side-opening book carrying throughout alternate facing-pages of descriptive text and clear photographs. A new boon to the Luger collector and/or shooter.

Mauser Pocket Pistols 1910-1946, by Roy G. Pender, Collectors Press, Houston, TX, 1971. 307 pp. $14.95.

Comprehensive work covering over 100 variations, including factory boxes and manuals. Over 300 photos. Limited, numbered ed.

The Mauser Self-Loading Pistol, by Belford & Dunlap, Borden Publ. Co., Alhambra, CA. Over 200 pp., 300 illus., large format. $13.50.

The long-awaited book on the "Broom Handles", covering their inception in 1894 to the end of production. Complete and in detail: pocket pistols, Chinese and Spanish copies, etc.

Modern American Centerfire Handguns, by Stanley W. Trzoniec, Winchester Press, Tulsa, OK, 1981. 260 pp., illus. $24.95.

The most comprehensive reference on handguns in print.

The New Handbook of Handgunning, by Paul B. Weston, Charles C. Thomas, Publisher, Springfield, IL, 1980. 102 pp., illus. $15.00.

A step-by-step, how-to manual of handgun shooting.

The Pistol Guide, by George C. Nonte, Stoeger Publ. Co., So. Hackensack, NJ, 1980. 256 pp., illus. Paper covers. $8.95.

A unique and detailed examination of a very specialized type of gun: the autoloading pistol.

Pistol & Revolver Guide, 3rd Ed., by George C. Nonte, Stoeger Publ. Co., So. Hackensack, NJ, 1975. 224 pp., illus. Paper covers. $6.95.

The standard reference work on military and sporting handguns.

Pistols of the World, Revised Edition, by Ian V. Hogg and John Weeks, DBI Books, Inc., Northfield, IL, 1982. 306 pp., illus. $12.95.

A valuable reference for collectors and everyone interested in guns.

Pistol & Revolver Digest, 3rd Edition, by Dean A. Grennell, DBI Books, Inc., Northfield, IL, 1982. 288 pp., illus. Paper covers. $9.95.

The latest developments in handguns, shooting, ammunition, and accessories, with catalog.

Quick or Dead, by William L. Cassidy, Paladin Press, Boulder, CO, 1978. 178 pp., illus. $12.95.

Close-quarter combat firing, with particular reference to prominent twentieth-century British and American methods of instruction.

Report of Board on Tests of Revolvers and Automatic Pistols. From the *Annual Report* of the Chief of Ordnance, 1907. Reprinted by J.C. Tillinghast Marlow, NH, 1969. 34 pp., 7 plates, paper covers. $5.00.

A comparison of handguns, including Luger, Savage, Colt, Webley-Fosbery and other makes.

Revolver Guide, by George C. Nonte, Jr., Stoeger Publishing Co., So. Hackensack, NJ, 1980. 288 pp., illus. Paper covers. $8.95.

Fully illustrated guide to selecting, shooting, caring for and collecting revolvers of all types.

System Mauser, a Pictorial History of the Model 1896 Self-Loading Pistol, by J.W. Breathed, Jr., and J.J. Schroeder, Jr. Handgun Press, Chicago, IL, 1967. 273 pp., well illus., 1st limited ed. hardbound. $17.50.

10 Shots Quick, by Daniel K. Stern. Globe Printing Co., San Jose, CA, 1967. 153 pp., photos. $12.50.

History of Savage-made automatic pistols, models of 1903-1917, with descriptive data for shooters and collectors.

The Walther P-38 Pistol, by Maj. Geo. C. Nonte, Paladin Press, Boulder, CO, 1975. 90 pp., illus. Paper covers. $5.00.

Covers all facets of the gun—development, history, variations, technical data, practical use, rebuilding, repair and conversion.

The Walther Pistols 1930-1945, by Warren H. Buxton, Warren H. Buxton, Los Alamos, NM, 1978. 350 pp., illus. $29.95.

Volume I of a projected 4 volume series "The P.38 Pistol". The histories, evolutions, and variations of the Walther P.38 and its predecessors.

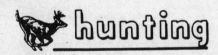

NORTH AMERICA

After Your Deer Is Down, by Josef Fischl and Leonard Lee Rue, III, Winchester Press, Tulsa, OK, 1981. 160 pp., illus. Paper covers. $9.95.

The care and handling of big game, with a bonus of venison recipes.

All About Deer in America, ed. by Robert Elman, Winchester Press, NY, 1976. 256 pp., illus. $13.95.

Twenty of America's great hunters share the secrets of their hunting success.

All Season Hunting, by Bob Gilsvik, Winchester Press, NY, 1976. 256 pp., illus. $13.95.

A guide to early-season, late-season and winter hunting in America.

All About Small-Game Hunting in America, ed. by Russell Tinsley, Winchester Press, NY, 1976. 308 pp., illus. $14.95.

Collected advice by the finest small-game experts in the country.

All About Wildfowling in America, by Jerome Knap, Winchester Press, NY, 1977. 256 pp., illus. $13.95.

More than a dozen top writers provide new and controversial ideas on how-to and where-to hunt wildfowl successfully.

The Art of Hunting Big Game in North America, by Jack O'Connor, Random House, NY, 1978. 418 pp., illus. $17.95.

A revised and updated edition on technique, planning, skill, outfitting, etc.

The Best of Nash Buckingham, by Nash Buckingham, selected, edited and annotated by George Bird Evans. Winchester Press, NY, 1973. 320 pp., $15.95.

Thirty pieces that represent the very cream of Nash's output on his whole range of outdoor interests—upland shooting, duck hunting, even fishing.

Bird Hunting Know-How, by D.M. Duffey. Van Nostrand, Princeton, NJ, 1968. 192 pp., illus. $9.95.

Game-getting techniques and sound advice on all aspects of upland bird hunting, plus data on guns and loads.

Black Powder Hunting, by Sam Fadala, Stackpole Books, Harrisburg, PA, 1978. 192 pp., illus. $10.95.

The author demonstrates successful hunting methods using percussion firearms for both small and big game.

The Bobwhite Quail Book, Compiled by Lamar Underwood, Amwell Press, Clinton, NJ, 1981. 442 pp., illus. $25.00.

An anthology of the finest stories on Bobwhite quail ever assembled under one cover.

Bobwhite Quail Hunting, by Charley Dickey, printed for Stoeger Publ. Co., So. Hackensack, NH, 1974. 112 pp., illus., paper covers. $3.95.

Habits and habitats, techniques, gear, guns and dogs.

The Bobwhite Quail, Its Life and Management, by Walter Rosene. Rutgers University Press, New Brunswick, NJ. 1st ed., 1969. 418 pp., photographs, maps and color plates. $50.00.

An exhaustive study of an important species which has dimished under the impact of changing agricultural and forestry practices.

The Book of the Wild Turkey, by Lovett E. Williams, Jr. Winchester Press, Tulsa, OK, 1981. 204 pp., illus. $19.95.

A definitive reference work on the wild turkey for hunter, game manager, conservationist, or amateur naturalist.

The Complete Book of Hunting, by Rober Elman, Abbeville Press, New York, NY, 1982. 320 pp., illus. $49.95.

A compendium of the world's game birds and animals, handloading, international hunting, etc.

The Complete Book of Deer Hunting, by Byron W. Dalrymple, Winchester Press, NY, 1973. 247 pp., illus. $12.95.

Practical "how-to" information. Covers the 20 odd North-American subspecies of deer.

The Complete Book of the Wild Turkey, by Roger M. Latham, Stackpole Books, Harrisburg, Pa., 1978. 228 pp., illus. $12.95.

A new revised edition of the classic on American wild turkey hunting.

The Complete Guide to Bird Dog Training, by John R. Falk, Winchester Press, NY, 1976. 256 pp., illus. $12.95.

How to choose, raise, train, and care for a bird dog.

The Complete Guide to Game Care and Cookery, by Sam Fadala, DBI Books, Inc., Northfield, IL., 1981. 288 pp., illus. Paper covers. $9.95.

How to dress, preserve and prepare all kinds of game animals and birds.

Coveys and Singles: The Handbook of Quail Hunting, by Robert Gooch, A.S. Barnes, San Diego, CA, 1981. 196 pp., illus. $11.95.

The story of the quail in North America.

Death in the Silent Places, by Peter Hathaway Capstick, St. Martin's Press, New York, NY, 1981. 243 pp., illus. $13.95.

The author recalls the extraordinary careers of legendary hunters such as Corbett, Karamojo Bell, Stigand and others.

Deer Hunting, by R. Smith, Stackpole Books, Harrisburg, PA, 1978. 224 pp., illus. Paper covers. $9.95.

A professional guide leads the hunt for North America's most popular big game animal.

The Desert Bighorn, edited by Gale Monson and Lowell Sumner, University of Arizona Press, Tucson, AZ, 1980. 392 pp., illus. $35.00.

Life history, ecology and management of the Desert Bighorn.

The Dove Shooter's Handbook, by Dan M. Russell, Winchester Press, NY, 1974. 256 pp., illus. $9.95.

A complete guide to America's top game bird—natural history, hunting methods, equipment, conservation and future prospects.

Dove Hunting, by Charley Dickey, Galahad Books, NY, 1976. 112 pp., illus. $6.00.

This indispensable guide for hunters deals with equipment, techniques, types of dove shooting, hunting dogs, etc.

Drummer in the Woods, by Burton L. Spiller, Stackpole Books, Harrisburg, PA, 1980. 240 pp., illus. $13.95.

Twenty-one wonderful stories on grouse shooting by "the Poet Laureate of Grouse".

The Duck Hunter's Handbook, by Bob Hinman, Winchester Press, NY, 1974. 252 pp., illus. $12.95.

Down-to-earth, practical advice on bagging ducks and geese.

The Duck-Huntingest Gentlemen, by Keith C. Russell et al, Winchester Press, Tulsa, OK, 1980. 284 pp., illus. $14.95.

A collection of stories on waterfowl hunting.

Ducks of the Mississippi Flyway, ed. by John McKane, North Star Press, St. Cloud, MN, 1969. 54 pp., illus. Paper covers. $4.50.

A duck hunter's reference. Full color paintings of some 30 species, plus descriptive text.

Expert Advice on Gun Dog Training, ed. by David M. Duffey, Winchester Press, NY, 1977. 256 pp., illus. $11.95.

Eleven top pros talk shop, revealing the techniques and philosophies that account for their consistent success.

A Gallery of Waterfowl and Upland Birds, by Gene Hill, with illustrations by David Maass, Pedersen Prints, Los Angeles, CA, 1978. 132 pp., illus. $39.95.

Gene Hill at his best. Liberally illustrated with fifty-one full-color reproductions of David Maass' finest paintings.

The Game Trophies of the World, edited and compiled by G. Kenneth Whitehead, Paul Parey, Hamburg, W. Germany. 215 pp., illus. Paper covers. $29.00.

Covers all the game trophies of the world using the Boone & Crockett method of scoring. Text in English, French and German.

Getting the Most out of Modern Waterfowling, by John O. Cartier, St. Martin's Press, NY, 1974. 396 pp., illus. $17.95.

The most comprehensive, up-to-date book on waterfowling imaginable.

Goose Hunting, by Charles L. Cadieux, Stackpole Books, Harrisburg, PA, 1979. 197 pp., illus. $16.95.

Personal stories of goose hunting from Quebec to Mexico.

Grizzly Country, by Andy Russell. A.A. Knopf, NYC, 1973, 302 pp., illus. $10.95.

Many-sided view of the grizzly bear and his world, by a noted guide, hunter and naturalist.

Grizzlies Don't Come Easy, by Ralph Young, Winchester Press, Tulsa, OK, 1981. 200 pp., illus. $15.95.

The life story of a great woodsman who guided famous hunters such as O'Connor, Keith, Fitz, Page and others.

1984 Gun Digest Hunting Annual, edited by Robert S.L. Anderson, DBI Books, Inc., Northfield, IL, 1983. 224 pp., illus. Paper covers. $9.95.

The top writers in their fields of shooting and hunting give the reader technical and factual information on how to hunt, where, when, and more.

Grouse and Woodcock, An Upland Hunter's Book, by Nick Sisley, Stackpole Books, Harrisburg, PA, 1980. 192 pp., illus. $13.95.

Latest field techniques for effective grouse and woodcock hunting.

Hal Swiggett on North American Deer, by Hal Swiggett, Jolex, Inc., Oakland, NJ, 1980. 272 pp., illus. Paper covers. $8.95.

Where and how to hunt all species of North American deer.

Handgun Hunting, by Maj. George C. Nonte, Jr. and Lee E. Jurras, Winchester Press, NY, 1975. 245 pp., illus. $10.95.

A book with emphasis on the hunting of readily available game in the U.S. with the handgun.

Hard Hunting, by Patrick Shaughnessy and Diane Swingle, Winchester Press, New York, NY, 1978. $12.95.

A couple explores a no-frills, low-cost, highly successful, adventurous approach to wilderness hunting.

The History of Wildfowling, by John Marchington, Adam and Charles Black, London, England, 1980. 288 pp., illus. $27.50.

Covers decoys, punting, and punt guns.

Horns in the High Country, by Andy Russell, Alfred A. Knofp, NY, 1973. 259 pp., illus. $15.50.

A many-sided view of wild sheep and their natural world.

How to Hunt, by Dave Bowring, Winchester Press, Tulsa, OK, 1982. 208 pp., illus. Cloth. $15.00. Paper covers. $10.95.

A basic guide to hunting big game, small game, upland birds, and waterfowl.

A Hunter's Fireside Book, by Gene Hill Winchester Press, NY, 1972. 192 pp., illus. $12.95.

An outdoor book that will appeal to every person who spends time in the field—or who wishes he could.

The Hunter's Shooting Guide, by Jack O'Connor, Outdoor Life Books, New York, NY, 1982. 176 pp., illus. Paper covers. $4.50.

A classic covering rifles, cartridges, shooting techniques for shotguns/rifles/handguns.

Hunting the American Wild Turkey, by Dave Harbour, Stackpole Books, Harrisburg, PA, 1975. 256 pp., illus. $14.95.

The techniques and tactics of hunting North America's largest, and most popular, woodland game bird.

Hunting America's Game Animals and Birds, by Robert Elman and George Peper, Winchester Press, NY, 1975. 368 pp., illus. $15.95.

A how-to, where-to, when-to guide—by 40 top experts—covering the continent's big, small, upland game and waterfowl.

Hunting America's Mule Deer, by Jim Zumbo, Winchester Press, Tulsa, OK, 1981. 272 pp., illus. $14.95.

The best ways to hunt mule deer. The how, when, and where to hunt all seven subspecies.

Hunting Dog Know-How, by D.M. Duffey, Van Nostrand, Princeton, NJ, 1965. 177 pp., illus. $15.95.

Covers selection, breeds, and training of hunting dogs, problems in hunting and field trials.

Hunting Moments of Truth, by Eric Peper and Jim Rikhoff, Winchester Press, NY, 1973. 208 pp., illus. $12.95.

The world's most experienced hunters recount 22 most memorable occasions.

Hunting with Bow and Arrow, by George Laycock and Erwin Bauer, Arco Publ. Co., Inc., NYC, 1966. $3.95.

A practical guide to archery as a present-day sport. Mentions equipment needed and how to select it. Illus. instructions on how to shoot with ease and accuracy.

Hunting Trophy Deer, by John Wootters, Winchester Press, NY, 1977. 288 pp., illus. $15.95.

One of America's most experienced and respected hunting writers provides all the specialized advice you need to succeed at bagging trophy deer.

Hunting Upland Birds, by Chas. F. Waterman. Winchester Press, NY, 1972. 320 pp., illus. $10.95.

Excellent treatment of game habits and habitat, hunting methods, and management techniques for each of the 18 major North American game-bird species.

Hunting the Uplands with Rifle and Shotgun, by Luther A. Anderson, Winchester Press, NY, 1977. 224 pp., illus. $12.95.

Solid practical know-how to help make hunting deer and every major species of upland game bird easier and more satisfying.

Hunting Whitetail Deer, by Robert E. Donovan, Winchester Press, NY, 1978. 256 pp., illus. $15.95.

For beginners and experts alike, this book is the key to successful whitetail hunting.

Hunting the Woodlands for Small and Big Game, by Luther A. Anderson, A. S. Barnes & Co., New York, NY, 1980. 256 pp., illus. $12.00.

A comprehensive guide to hunting in the United States. Chapters on firearms, game itself, marksmanship, clothing and equipment.

In Search of the Wild Turkey, by Bob Gooch, Greatlakes Living Press, Ltd., Waukegan, IL, 1978. 182 pp., illus. $9.95.

A state-by-state guide to wild turkey hot spots, with tips on gear and methods for bagging your bird.

The Market Hunter, by David and Jim Kimball, Dillon Press Inc., Minneapolis, MN, 1968. 132 pp., illus. $6.95.

The market hunter, one of the "missing chapters" in American history, is brought to life in this book.

Mixed Bag, by Jim Rikhoff, National Rifle Association of America, Wash., DC, 1981. 284 pp., illus. Paper covers. $9.95.

Reminiscences of a master raconteur.

Modern Hunting with Indian Secrets, by Allan A. Macfarlan. Stackpole Books, Harrisburg, PA, 1971. 222 pp., illus. $12.95.

How to acquire the new-old skills of the Redman, how to apply them to modern hunting.

Modern Pheasant Hunting, by Steve Grooms, Stackpole Books, Harrisburg, PA, 1982. 224 pp., illus. $16.95.

New look at pheasants and hunters from an experienced hunter who respects this splendid gamebird.

Modern Turkey Hunting, by James F. Brady, Crown Publ., N.Y.C., NY, 1973. 160 pp., illus. $12.95.

A thorough guide to the habits, habitat, and methods of hunting America's largest game bird.

Modern Wildfowling, by Eric Begbie, Saiga Publishing Co., Ltd., Surrey, England, 1980. 171 pp., illus. $27.50.

History of wildfowling, guns and equipment.

More Grouse Feathers, by Burton L. Spiller. Crown Publ., NY, 1972. 238 pp., illus. $15.00.

Facsimile of the original Derrydale Press issue of 1938. Guns and dogs, the habits and shooting of grouse, woodcook, ducks, etc. Illus by Lynn Bogue Hunt.

Mostly Tailfeathers, by Gene Hill, Winchester Press, NY, 1975. 192 pp., illus. $12.95.

An interesting, general book about bird hunting.

The Muzzleloading Hunter, by Rick Hacker, Winchester Press, Tulsa, OK, 1981. 283 pp., illus. $16.95.

A comprehensive guide for the black powder sportsman.

The Nash Buckingham Library, compiled by Douglas C. Mauldin, Delta Arms Sporting Goods, Indianola, MS 1980. 7 volume set in slipcase. $150.00.

Seven outdoor hunting classics by Nash Buckingham, the 20th century's greatest sporting writer.

North American Big Game Hunting, by Byron W. Dalrymple, Winchester Press, New York, NY, 1974. 384 pp., illus. $15.00.

A comprehensive, practical guide, with individual chapters devoted to all native species.

North American Elk: Ecology and Management, edited by Jack Ward Thomas and Dale E. Toweill, Stackpole Books, Harrisburg, PA, 1982. 576 pp., illus. $39.95.

The definitive, exhaustive, classic work on the North American Elk.

The North American Waterfowler, by Paul S. Bernsen, Superior Publ. Co., Seattle, WA, 1972. 206 pp., Paper covers. $4.95.

The complete inside and outside story of duck and goose shooting. Big and colorful, illus. by Les Kouba.

1001 Hunting Tips, by Robert Elman, Winchester Press, N.Y.,NY, 1978. 256 pp., illus. $17.95.

A post-graduate course in big-game hunting, small-game hunting, wild-fowling, and hunting upland birds.

The Old Man's Boy Grows Older, by Robert Ruark, Holt, Rinehart and Winston, New York, NY, 1961. 302 pp., illus. $35.00.

A classic by a big-game hunter and world traveler.

One Man's Wilderness, by Warren Page, Holt, Rinehart and Winston, NY, 1973. 256 pp., illus. $30.00.

A world-known writer and veteran sportsman recounts the joys of a lifetime of global hunting.

The Outlaw Gunner, by Harry M. Walsh, Tidewater Publishers, Cambridge, MD, 1973. 178 pp., illus. $12.50.

A colorful story of market gunning in both its legal and illegal phases.

Pinnell and Talifson: Last of the Great Brown Bear Men, by Marvin H. Clark, Jr., Great Northwest Publishing and Distributing Co., Spokane, WA, 1980. 224 pp., illus. $20.00.

The story of these famous Alaskan guides and some of the record bears taken by them.

The Practical Hunter's Dog Book, by John R. Falk, Winchester Press, NY, 1971. 314 pp., illus. $10.95.

Helps to choose, train and enjoy your gun dog.

The Practical Hunter's Handbook, by Anthony J. Acerrano, Winchester Press, New York, NY, 1978. 224 pp., illus. Paper covers. $9.95.

How the time-pressed hunter can take advantage of every edge his hunting situation affords him.

The Practical Wildfowler, by John Marchington, Adam and Charles Black, London, England, 1977. 143 pp., illus. $21.95.

Advice on both the practical and ethical aspects of the sport.

Predator Caller's Companion, by Gerry Blair, Winchester Press, Tulsa, OK, 1981. 280 pp., illus. $13.95.

Predator calling techniques and equipment for the hunter and trapper.

Ranch Life and the Hunting Trail, by Theodore Roosevelt, Readex Microprint Corp., Dearborn, MI. 1966 186 pp. With drawings by Frederic Remington. $15.00.

A facsimile reprint of the original 1899 Century Co., edition. One of the most fascinating books of the West of that day.

Ringneck! Pheasants & Pheasant Hunting, by Ted Janes, Crown Publ., NY, 1975. 120 pp., illus. $8.95.

A thorough study of one of our more popular game birds.

Sheep and Sheep Hunting, by Jack O'Connor, Winchester Press, Tulsa, OK, 1980. 308 pp., illus. $14.95.

Memorial edition of the definitive book on wild sheep.

Shooting Pictures, by A.B. Frost, with 24 pp. of text by Chas. D. Lanier. Winchester Press, NY, 1972. 12 color plates. Enclosed in a board portfolio. Ed. limited to 750 numbered copies. $175.00.

Frost's twelve superb 12" by 16" pictures have often been called the finest sporting prints published in the U.S. A facsimile of the 1895-6 edition printed on fine paper with superb color fidelity.

Shots at Mule Deer, by Rollo S. Robinson, Winchester Press, New York, NY, 1970. 209 pp., illus. $15.

Description, strategies for bagging it, the correct rifle and cartridge to use.

Small Game Hunting, by Tom Brakefield, J.B. Lippincott Co., Phila., PA, 1978. 244 pp., illus. $10.

Describes where, when, and how to hunt all major small game species from coast to coast.

Squirrels and Squirrel Hunting, by Bob Gooch. Tidewater Publ., Cambridge, MD, 1973. 148 pp., illus. $6.

A complete book for the squirrel hunter, beginner or old hand. Details methods of hunting, squirrel habitat, management, proper clothing, care of the kill, cleaning and cooking.

Successful Deer Hunting, by Sam Fadala, DBI Books, Inc., Northfield, IL, 1983. 288 pp., illus. Paper covers. $10.95.

Here's all the dope you'll need—where, why, when and how—to have a successful deer hunt.

Successful Waterfowling, by Zack Taylor, Crown, Publ., NY, 1974. 276 pp., illus. Paper covers. $15.95.

The definitive guide to new ways of hunting ducks and geese.

Timberdoodle, by Frank Woolner, Crown Publ., Inc., NY, 1974. 168 pp., illus. $10.95.

A thorough, practical guide to the American woodcock and to woodcock hunting.

Topflight; A Speed Index to Waterfowl, by J.A. Ruthven & Wm. Zimmerman, Moebius Prtg. Co., Milwaukee, WI, 1968. 112 pp. $7.50.

Rapid reference for specie identification. Marginal color band of book directs reader to proper section. 263 full color illustrations of body and feather configurations.

The Trophy Hunter, by Col. Allison, Stackpole Books, Harrisburg, 1981. 240 pp., illus. $24.95.

Action-packed tales of hunting big game trophies around the world—1860 to today.

Trouble With Bird Dogs...and What to do About Them, by George Bird Evans, Winchester Press, NY, 1979. 288 pp., illus. $15.95.

How to custom-train your dog for specific kinds of hunting.

Turkey Hunting with Charlie Elliot, by Charles Elliot, David McKay Co., Inc., New York, NY 1979. 275 pp., illus. $14.95.

The old professor tells you all about America's big-game bird.

Turkey Hunter's Guide, by Byron W. Dalrymple, et al, a publication of The National Rifle Association, Washington, DC, 1979. 96 pp., illus. Paper covers. $4.95.

Expert advice on turkey hunting hotspots, guns, guides, and calls.

The Whispering Wings of Autumn, by Gene Hill and Steve Smith, Amwell Press, Clinton, NJ, 1982. 192 pp., illus. $17.50.

A collection of both fact and fiction on two of North America's most famous game birds, the Ruffed Grouse and the Woodcock.

The Whitetail Deer Hunter's Handbook, by John Weiss, Winchester Press, New York, NY, 1979. 256 pp., illus. Paper covers. $9.95.

Wherever you live, whatever your level of experience, this brand-new handbook will make you a better deer hunter.

Whitetail: Fundamentals and Fine Points for the Hunter, by George Mattis, World Publ. Co. New York, NY, 1976. 273 pp., illus. $9.95.

A manual of shooting and trailing and an education in the private world of the deer.

The Wild Turkey Book, edited and with special commentary by J. Wayne Fears, Amwell Press, Clinton, NJ, 1982. 303 pp., illus. $22.50.

An anthology of the finest stories on wild turkey ever assembled under one cover.

The Wings of Dawn, by George Reiger, Stein and Day, New York, NY, 1980. 320 pp., illus. $29.95.

The complete book of North American waterfowling.

20 Great Trophy Hunts, by John O. Cartier, David McKay Co., Inc., New York, NY, 1981. 320 pp., illus. $22.50.

The cream of outstanding true-life hunting stories.

AFRICA/ASIA

African Rifles & Cartridges, by John Taylor. The Gun Room Press, Highland Park, NJ, 1977. 431 pp., illus. $21.95.

Experiences and opinions of a professional ivory hunter in Africa describing his knowledge of numerous arms and cartridges for big game. A reprint.

Big Game Hunting Around the World, by Bert Klineburger and Vernon W. Hurst, Exposition Press, Jericho, NY, 1969. 376 pp., illus. $30.00.

The first book that takes you on a safari all over the world.

Death in the Long Grass, by Peter Hathaway Capstick, St. Martin's Press, New York, NY, 1977. 297 pp., illus. $11.95.

A big game hunter's adventures in the African bush.

The Elephant Hunters of the Lado, by Major W. Robert Foran, Amwell Press, Clinton, NJ, 1981. 311 pp., illus. Limited, numbered, and signed edition, in slipcase. $85.00.

From a previously unpublished manuscript by a famous "white hunter."

Green Hills of Africa, by Ernest Hemingway. Charles Scribner's Sons, NY, 1963. 285 pp., illus. Paper covers. $5.95.

A famous narrative of African big-game hunting, first published in 1935.

Horned Death, by John F. Burger. Standard Publications, Huntington, WV, 1947. 340 pp., illus. $100.00.

Hunting the African cape buffalo.

Hunting in Africa, by Bill Morkel, Howard Timmins, Publishers, Capetown, South Africa, 1980. 252 pp., illus. $25.00.

An invaluable guide for the inexperienced hunter contemplating a possible safari.

Hunting the Big Cats, two volume set, edited by Jim Rikhoff, Amwell Press, Clinton, NJ, 1981. Total of 808 pp., illustrated by Bob Kuhn. Limited, numbered, and signed edition. In slipcase. $150.00.

The most definitive work on hunting the world's largest wild cats ever compiled. A collection of 70 articles on hunting in Africa, Asia, North and South America.

The Recollections of an Elephant Hunter 1864-1875, by William Finaughty, Books of Zimbabwe, Bulawayo, Zimbabwe, 1980. 244 pp., illus. $40.00.

Reprint of a very scarce book on elephant hunting.

Uganda Safaris, by Brian Herne, Winchester Press, Tulsa, OK, 1979. 236 pp., illus. $12.95.

The chronicle of a professional hunter's adventures in Africa.

The Wanderings of an Elephant Hunter, by W.D.M. Bell, Neville Spearman, Suffolk, England, 1981. 187 pp., illus. $35.00.

The greatest of elephant books by perhaps the greatest elephant hunter of all times, 'Karamojo' Bell.

The Accurate Rifle, by Warren Page. Winchester Press, NY, 1973. 256 pp., illus. $13.95.

A masterly discussion. A must for the competitive shooter hoping to win, and highly useful to the practical hunter.

The AK-47 Assault Rifle, Desert Publications, Cornville, AZ, 1981. 150 pp., illus. Paper covers. $6.95.

Complete and practical technical information on the only weapon in history to be produced in an estimated 30,000,000 units.

American Rifle Design and Performance, by L.R. Wallack, Winchester Press, NY, 1977. 288 pp., illus. $16.95.

An authoritative, comprehensive guide to how and why every kind of sporting rifle works.

The Bolt Action: A Design Analysis, by Stuart Otteson, ed. by Ken Warner, Winchester Press, NY, 1976. 320 pp., illus. $12.95.

Precise and in-depth descriptions, illustrations and comparisons of 16 bolt actions. A new approach.

The Book of the Garand, by Maj.-Gen. J.S. Hatcher, The Gun Room Press, Highland Park, NJ, 1977. 292 pp., illus. $15.00.

A new printing of the standard reference work on the U.S. Army M1 rifle.

Carbines Cal. .30 M1, M1A1, M2 and M3, by D.B. McLean, Normount Armament Co., Wickenburg, AZ, 1964. 221 pp., well illus., paperbound $7.95.

U.S. field manual reprints on these weapons, edited and reorganized.

The Commerical Mauser '98 Sporting Rifle, by Lester Womack, Womack Associates, Publishers, Prescott, AZ, 1980. 69 pp., illus. $20.00.

The first work on the sporting rifles made by the original Mauser plant in Oberndorf.

The Deer Rifle, by L.R. Wallack, Winchester Press, New York, NY, 1978. 256 pp., illus. $12.95.

Everything the deer hunter needs to know to select and use the arms and ammunition appropriate to his needs.

Description and Instructions for the Management of the Gallery-Practice Rifle Caliber .22—Model of 1903. Inco., 1972. 12 pp., 1 plate. Paper, $2.50.

Reprint of 1907 War Dept. pamphlet No. 1925.

Description of Telescopic Musket Sights, Inco, 1972. 10 pp. 4 plates. Paper, $2.50.

Reprint of 1917 War Dept. pamphlet No. 1957, first publ. in 1908.

F.N.-F.A.L. Auto Rifles, Desert Publications, Cornville, AZ, 1981. 130 pp., illus. Paper covers. $6.95.

A definitive study of one of the free world's finest combat rifles.

The First Winchester, by John E. Parsons. Winchester Press, New York, NY, 1977. 207 pp., well illus. $24.95.

This new printing of *The Story of the 1866 Repeating Rifle* (1st publ. 1955) is revised, and additional illustrations included.

A Forgotten Heritage; The Story of a People and the Early American Rifle, by Harry P. Davis, The Gun Room Press, Highland Park, NJ, 1976. 199 pp., illus. $9.95.

Reprint of a very scarce history, originally published in 1941, the Kentucky rifle and the people who used it.

Garand Rifles M1, M1C, M1D, by Donald B. McLean, Normount Armament Co., Wickenburg, AZ, 1968. Over 160 pp., 175 illus., paper wrappers. $7.95.

Covers all facets of the arm: battlefield use, disassembly and maintenance, all details to complete lock-stock-and-barrel repair, plus variations, grenades, ammo., and accessories; plus a section on 7.62mm NATO conventions.

The Golden Age of Single-Shot Rifles, by Edsall James, Pioneer Press, Union City, TN, 1975. 33 pp., illus. Paper covers. $2.75.

A detailed look at all of the fine, high quality sporting single-shot rifles that were once the favorite of target shooters.

The Gun Digest Book of the .22 Rimfire, by John Lachuk, DBI Books, Northfield, IL, 1978. 224 pp., illus. Paper covers. $7.95.

Everything you want to know about the .22 rimfire cartridge and the arms that use it.

Gun Digest Book of the Hunting Rifle, by Jack Lewis, DBI Books, Inc., Northfield, IL, 1983. 256 pp., illus. Paper covers. $10.95.

Covers all aspects of the hunting rifle—design, development, different types, uses, and more.

The Hunting Rifle, by Jack O'Connor. Winchester Press, NY, 1970. 352 pp., illus. $14.95.

An analysis, with wit and wisdom, of contemporary rifles, cartridges, accessories and hunting techniques.

Know Your M1 Garand, by E. J. Hoffschmidt, Blacksmith Corp., Southport, CT, 1975, 84 pp., illus. Paper covers. $5.95.

Facts about America's most famous infantry weapon. Covers test and experimental models, Japanese and Italian copies, National Match models.

The Model 70 Winchester 1937-1964, by Dean H. Whitaker, Taylor Publishing Co., Dallas, TX, 1978. 210 pp., illus. $24.95.

An authoritative reference book on this model. Gives production history, changes, dimensions, specifications on special-order guns, etc.

The M-14 Rifle, facsimile reprint of FM 23-8, Desert Publications, Cornville, AZ, 50 pp., illus. Paper $5.95.

In this well illustrated and informative reprint, the M-14 and M-14E2 are covered thoroughly.

The Modern Rifle, by Jim Carmichel, Winchester Press, NY, 1975. 320 pp., illus. $13.95.

The most comprehensive, thorough, up-to-date book ever published on today's rifled sporting arms.

North American FALS, by R. Blake Stevens, Collector Grade Publications, Toronto, Canada, 1979. 166 pp., illus. Paper covers. $20.00.

NATO's search for a standard rifle.

100 Years of Shooters and Gunmakers of Single Shot Rifles, by Gerald O. Kelver, Brighton, CO, 1975. 212 pp., illus. Paper covers $10.00.

The Schuetzen rifle, targets and shooters, primers, match rifles, original loadings and much more. With chapters on famous gunsmiths like Harry Pope, Morgan L. Rood and others.

The '03 Springfields, by Clark S. Campbell, Ray Riling Arms Books Co., Phila., PA, 1978. 320 pp., illus. $29.95.

The most authoritative and definitive work on this famous U.S. rifle, the 1903 Springfield and its 30-06 cartridge.

The Pennsylvania Rifle, by Samuel E. Dyke, Sutter House, Lititz, PA, 1975. 61 pp., illus. Paper covers. $5.00.

History and development, from the hunting rifle of the Germans who settled the area. Contains a full listing of all known Lancaster, PA, gunsmiths from 1729 through 1815.

Position Rifle Shooting, by Bill Pullum and F.T. Hanenkrat. Winchester Press, NY, 1973. 256 pp., illus. Paper covers, $5.95.

The single most complete statement of rifle shooting principles and techniques, and the means of learning, teaching and using them, ever to appear in print.

The Revolving Rifles, by Edsall James, Pioneer Press, Union City, TN, 1975. 23 pp., illus. Paper covers $2.50.

Valuable information on revolving cylinder rifles, from the earliest matchlock forms to the latest models of Colt and Remington.

The Rifle Book, by Jack O'Connor, Random House, NY, 1978. 337 pp., illus. Paper covers $10.95.

The complete book of small game, varmint and big game rifles.

Rifle Guide, by Robert A. Steindler, Stoeger Publishing Co., South Hackensack, NJ, 1978. 304 pp., illus. Paper covers. $7.95.

Complete, fully illustrated guide to selecting, shooting, caring for, and collecting rifles of all types.

Rifles AR15, M16, and M16A1, 5.56 mm, by D.B. McLean. Normount Armament Co., Wickenburg, AZ, 1968. Unpaginated, illus., paper covers. $8.95.

Descriptions, specifications and operation of subject models are set forth in text and picture.

Rifle Shooting as a Sport, by Bernd Klingner, A.S. Barnes & Co., Inc., San Diego, CA, 1980. 186 pp., illus. Paper covers. $15.00.

All factors for correct and incorrect shooting methods explained by an international expert marksman.

Schuetzen Rifles, History and Loading, by Gerald O. Kelver, Gerald O. Kelver, Publisher, Brighton, CO, 1972. Illus. $7.50.

Reference work on these rifles, their bullets, loading, telescopic sights, accuracy, etc. A limited, numbered ed.

Single Shot Rifles and Actions, by Frank de Haas, ed. by John T. Amber, DBI Books, Northfield, IL, 1969. 352 pp., illus. $9.95.

The definitive book on over 60 single shot rifles and actions. Covers history, parts photos, design and construction, etc.

The Sporting Rifle and its Projectiles, by Lieut. James O Forsyth, The Buckskin Press, Big Timber, MT, 1978. 132 pp., illus. $10.00.

Facsimile reprint of the 1863 edition, one of the most authoritative books ever written on the muzzle-loading round ball sporting rifle.

The .22 Rifle, by Dave Petzal. Winchester Press, NY, 1972. 244 pp., illus. $9.95.

All about the mechanics of the .22 rifle. How to choose the right one, how to choose a place to shoot, what makes a good shot, the basics of small-game hunting.

The American Shotgun, by David F. Butler, Lyman Publ., Middlefield, CT, 1973. 256 pp. illus. Paper covers. $11.95.

A comprehensive history of the American smoothbore's evolution from Colonial times to the present day.

American Shotgun Desgin and Performance, by L.R. Wallack, Winchester Press, NY 1977. 184 pp., illus. $16.95.

An expert lucidly recounts the history and development of American shotguns and explains how they work.

The Best Shotguns Ever Made in America, by Michael McIntosh, Charles Scribner's Sons, New York, NY, 1981. 185 pp., illus. $17.95.

Seven vintage doubles to shoot and to treasure.

The British Shotgun, Vol. One, 1850-1870, by I.M. Crudgington and D.J. Baker, Barrie & Jenkins, London, England, 1979. 256 pp., illus $30.00.

The evolution of the shotgun during its formative years in Great Britain.

The Double Shotgun, by Don Zutz, Winchester Press, New York, NY 1978. 288 pp., illus. $17.50.

The history and development of the most classic of all sporting arms.

How to be a Winner Shooting Skeet & Trap, by Tom Morton, Tom Morton, Knoxville, MD, 1974. 144 pp., illus. Paper covers. $8.95.

The author explains why championship shooting is more than a physical process.

The Parker Gun, by Larry L. Baer, Beinfeld Publ., Inc., No. Hollywood, CA, 1980. 240 pp., illus. $29.95.

Originally published as two separate volumes. This is the only comprehensive work on the subject of America's most famous shotgun. Incuded are new material and new photographs.

Plans and Specifications of the L.C. Smith Shotgun, by Lt. Col. William S. Brophy, USAR Ret., F. Brownell & Son, Montezuma, IA, 1982. 247 pp., illus. $19.95.

The only collection ever assembled of all the drawings and engineering specifications on the incomparable and very collectable L.C. Smith shotgun.

The Police Shotgun Manual, by Robert H. Robinson, Charles C. Thomas, Springfield, IL 1973. 153 pp., illus. $17.50.

A complete study and analysis of the most versatile and effective weapon in the police arsenal.

Score Better at Skeet, by Fred Missildine, with Nick Karas. Winchester Press, NY 1972. 160 pp., illus. $10.00.

The long-awaited companion volume to *Score Better at Trap.*

75 Years with the Shotgun, by C.T. (Buck) Buckman, Valley Publ., Fresno, CA, 1974. 141 pp., illus. $7.50.

An expert hunter and trapshooter shares experiences of a lifetime.

The Shotgun Book, by Jack O'Connor, Alfred A. Knopf, New York, NY, 1978. 341 pp., illus. $16.95.

An indispensable book for every shotgunner containing up-to-the-minute authoritative information on every phase of the shotgun.

The Shotgun in Combat, by Tony Lesce, Desert Publications, Cornville, AZ, 1979. 148 pp., illus. Paper covers $6.95.

A history of the shotgun and its use in combat.

Shotgun Digest, 2nd Edition, edited by Jack Lewis and Jack Mitchell, DBI Books, Inc., Northfield, IL 1980. 288 pp., illus. Paper covers. $9.95.

All-new look at shotguns by a double-barreled team of writers.

Shotgunners Guide, by Monte Burch, Winchester Press, New York, NY, 1980. 208 pp., illus. $15.95.

A basic book for the young and old who want to try shotgunning or who want to improve their skill.

Shotgunning: The Art and the Science, by Bob Brister, Winchester Press, NY 1976. 321 pp., illus. $15.95.

Hundreds of specific tips and truly novel techniques to improve the field and target shooting of every shotgunner.

Shotguns & Shooting, by E.S. McCawley, Jr., Van Nostrand Reinhold Co., NY 1965. 146 pp., illus. Paper covers. $5.95.

Covers the history and development, types of shotguns and ammunition, shotgun shooting, etc.

Sure-Hit Shotgun Ways, by Francis E. Sell, Stackpole Books, Harrisburg, PA, 1967. 160 pp., illus. $15.00.

On guns, ballistics and quick skill methods.

Skeet Shooting with D. Lee Braun, edited by R. Campbell, Grosset & Dunlap, NY, 1967. 160 pp., illus. Paper covers $3.95.

Thorough instructions on the fine points of Skeet shooting.

Trapshooting with D. Lee Braun and the Remington Pros., ed. by R. Campbell. Remington Arms Co., Bridgeport, CT. 1969. 157 pp., well illus., Paper covers. $3.95.

America's masters of the scattergun give the secrets of professional marksmanship.

Wing & Shot, by R.G. Wehle, Country Press, 167. 190 pp., illus. $12.

Step-by-step account on how to train a fine shooting dog.

The World's Fighting Shotguns, by Thomas F. Swearengen, T. B. N. Enterprises, Alexandria, VA 1979. 500 pp., illus. $29.95.

The complete military and police reference work from the shotgun's inception to date, with up-to-date developments.

You and the Target, by Kay Ohye, Kay Ohye Enterprises, No. Brunswick, NJ, 1978. 83 pp., illus. Paper cover. $9.95.

All new trapshooting handbook to better scores.

ARMS ASSOCIATIONS IN AMERICA AND ABROAD

UNITED STATES

ALABAMA

Alabama Gun Collectors Assn.
Dick Boyd, Secy., P.O. Box 5548, Tuscaloosa, AL 35405

ARIZONA

Arizona Arms Assn.,
Clay Fobes, Secy., P.O. Box 17061, Tucson, AZ 85731

CALIFORNIA

Calif. Hunters & Gun Owners Assoc.
V.H. Wacker, 2309 Cipriani Blvd., Belmont, CA 94002
Greater Calif. Arms & Collectors Assn.
Donald L. Bullock, 8291 Carburton St., Long Beach, CA 90808
Los Angeles Gun & Ctg. Collectors Assn.
F.H. Ruffra, 20810 Amie Ave., Apt. #9, Torrance, CA 90503

COLORADO

Pikes Peak Gun Collectors Guild
Charles Cell, 406 E. Uintah St., Colorado Springs, CO 80903

CONNECTICUT

Ye Conn. Gun Guild, Inc.
Robert L. Harris, P.O. Box 8, Cornwall Bridge, CT 06754

FLORIDA

Florida Gun Collectors Assn., Inc.
John D. Hammer, 5700 Mariner Dr., 304-W, Tampa, FL 33609
Tampa Bay Arms Collectors' Assn.
John Tuvell, 24611 — 67th Ave. S., St. Petersburg, FL 33712
Unified Sportsmen of Florida
P.O. Box 6565, Tallahassee, FL 32314

GEORGIA

Georgia Arms Collectors
Cecil W. Anderson, P.O. Box 218, Conley, GA 30027

HAWAII

Hawaii Historic Arms Assn.
John A. Bell, P.O. Box 1733, Honolulu, HI 96806

IDAHO

Idaho State Rifle and Pistol Assn.
Tom Price, 3631 Pineridge Dr., Coeur d'Alene, ID 83814

ILLINOIS

Fox Valley Arms Fellowship, Inc.
P.O. Box 301, Palatine, IL 60067
Illinois State Rifle Assn.
224 S. Michigan Ave., Room 200, Chicago, IL 60604
Illinois Gun Collectors Assn.
P.O. Box 1694, Kankakee, IL 60901
Little Fort Gun Collectors Assn.
Ernie Robinson, P.O. Box 194, Gurnee, IL 60031

Mississippi Valley Gun & Cartridge Coll. Assn.
Lawrence Maynard, R.R. 2, Aledo, IL 61231
NIPDEA
c/o Phil Stanger, 1029 Castlewood Lane, Deerfield, IL 60015
Sauk Trail Gun Collectors
Gordell M. Matson, 3817-22 Ave., Moline, IL 61265
Wabash Valley Gun Collectors Assn., Inc.
Eberhard R. Gerbsch, 416 South St., Danville, IL 61832

INDIANA

Indiana Sportsmen's Council-Legislative
Maurice Latimer, P.O. Box 93, Bloomington, IN 47402
Indiana State Rifle & Pistol Assn.
Thos. Glancy, P.O. Box 552, Chesterton, IN 46304
Southern Indiana Gun Collectors Assn., Inc.
Harold M. McClary, 509 N. 3rd St., Boonville, IN 47601

IOWA

Central States Gun Collectors Assn.
Avery Giles, 1104 S. 1st Ave., Marshtown, IA 50158

KANSAS

Four State Collectors Assn.
M.G. Wilkinson, 915 E. 10th, Pittsburg, KS 66762
Kansas Cartridge Coll. Assn.
Bob Linder, Box 84, Plainville, KS 67663
Missouri Valley Arms Collectors Assn.
Chas. F. Samuel, Jr., Box 8204, Shawnee Mission, KS 66208

KENTUCKY

Kentuckiana Arms Coll. Assn.
Tony Wilson, Pres., Box 1776, Louisville, KY 40201
Kentucky Gun Collectors Assn., Inc.
Ruth Johnson, Box 64, Owensboro, KY 42302
Kentucky Rifle Assn.
Ronald Gabel, 158 W. Unionville, RD 1, Schnecksville, PA 18078

LOUISIANA

Washitaw River Renegades
Sandra Rushing, P.O. Box 256, Main St., Grayson, LA 71435

MARYLAND

Baltimore Antique Arms Assn.
Stanley I. Kellert, E-30, 2600 Insulator Dr., Baltimore, MD 21230

MASSACHUSETTS

Bay Colony Weapons Collectors, Inc.
Ronald B. Santurjian, 47 Homer Rd., Belmont, MA 02178
Massachusetts Arms Collectors
John J. Callan, Jr., P.O. Box 1001, Worcester, MA 01613

MICHIGAN

Royal Oak Historical Arms Collectors, Inc.
Nancy Stein, 25487 Hereford, Huntingdon Woods, MI 48070

MINNESOTA

Minnesota Weapons Coll. Assn., Inc.
Box 662, Hopkins, MN 55343

MISSISSIPPI

Mississippi Gun Collectors Assn.
Mrs. Jack E. Swinney, P.O. Box 1332, Hattiesburg, MS 39401

MISSOURI

Mineral Belt Gun Coll. Assn.
D.F. Saunders, 1110 Cleveland Ave., Monett, MO 65708

MONTANA

Montana Arms Collectors Assn.
Lewis E. Yearout, 308 Riverview Dr. East, Great Falls, MT 59404
The Winchester Arms Coll. Assn.
Lewis E. Yearout, 308 Riverview Dr. East, Great Falls, MT 59404

NEW HAMPSHIRE

New Hampshire Arms Collectors, Inc.
Frank H. Galeucia, Rte. 28, Box 44, Windham, NH 03087

NEW JERSEY

Englishtown Benchrest Shooters Assn.
Tony Hidalgo, 6 Capp St., Carteret, NJ 07008
Experimental Ballistics Associates
Ed Yard, 110 Kensington, Trenton, NJ 08618
Jersey Shore Antique Arms Collectors
Joe Sisia, P.O. Box 100, Bayville, NJ 08721
New Jersey Arms Collectors Club, Inc.
Angus Laidlaw, 230 Valley Rd., Montclair, NJ 07042

NEW YORK

Empire State Arms Coll. Assn.
P.O. Box 2328, Rochester, NY 14623
Hudson-Mohawk Arms Collectors Assn., Inc.
Bennie S. Pisarz, 6 Lamberson St., Dolgeville, NY 13329
Iroquois Arms Collectors Assn.
Dennis Freeman, 12144 McNeeley Rd., Akron, NY 14001
Mid-State Arms Coll. & Shooters Club
Jack Ackerman, 24 S. Mountain Terr., Binghamton, NY 13903

NORTH CAROLINA

North Carolina Gun Collectors Assn.
Jerry Ledford, Rt. 10, Box 144, Hickory, NC 28601

OHIO

Central Ohio Gun and Indian Relic Coll. Assn.
Coyt Stookey, 134 E. Ohio Ave., Washington C.H., OH 43160
Ohio Gun Collectors, Assn., Inc.
Drawer 24F, Cincinnati, OH 45224
The Stark Gun Collectors, Inc.
William I. Gann, 5666 Waynesburg Dr., Waynesburg, OH 44688

OKLAHOMA

Indian Territory Gun Collectors Assn.
P.O. Box 4491, Tulsa, OK 74104

OREGON

Oregon Cartridge Coll. Assn.
Richard D. King, 3228 N.W. 60th, Corvallis, OR 97330

Oregon Arms Coll. Assn., Inc.
Ted Dowd, P.O. Box 25103, Portland, OR 97225

PENNSYLVANIA

Presque Isle Gun Coll. Assn.
James Welch, 156 E. 37 St., Erie, PA 16504

SOUTH CAROLINA

Belton Gun Club, Inc.
J.K. Phillips, Route 1, Belton, SC 29627
South Carolina Arms Coll. Assn.
P.O. Box 115, Irmo, SC 29063

SOUTH DAKOTA

Dakota Territory Gun Coll. Assn., Inc.
Curt Carter, Castlewood, SD 57223

TENNESSEE

Memphis Antique Weapons Assn.
Jan Clement, 1886 Lyndale #1, Memphis TN 38107
Smoky Mountain Gun Coll. Assn., Inc.
Hugh W. Yarbro, P.O. Box 286, Knoxville, TN 37901
Tennessee Gun Collectors Assn., Inc.
M.H. Parks, 3556 Pleasant Valley Rd., Nashville, TN 37204

TEXAS

Houston Gun Collectors Assn., Inc.
P.O. Box 37369, Houston, TX 77237
Texas State Rifle Assn.
P.O. Drawer 340809, Dallas, TX 75234

UTAH

Utah Gun Collectors Assn.
Nick Davis, 5676 So. Meadow Lane #4,Ogden, UT 84403

VIRGINIA

Virginia Arms Collectors & Assn.
Clinton E. Jones, P.O. Box 333, Mechanicsville, VA 23111

WASHINGTON

Washington Arms Collectors, Inc.
J. Dennis Cook, P.O. Box 7335, Tacoma, WA 98407

WISCONSIN

Great Lakes Arms Coll. Assn., Inc.
E. Warnke, 1811 N. 73rd St. Wauwatosa, WI 53213
Wisconsin Gun Collectors Assn., Inc.
Rob. Zellmer, P.O. Box 181, Sussex, WI 53089

WYOMING

Wyoming Gun Collectors
Bob Funk, Box 1805, Riverton, WY 82501

NATIONAL ORGANIZATIONS

Amateur Trap Shooting Assn.
P.O. Box 458, Vandalia, OH 45377
American Association of Shotgunning
P.O. Box 3351, Reno, NV 89505
American Defense Preparedness Assn.
Rosslyn Center, Suite 900, 1700 N. Moore St., Arlington, VA 22209
American Police Pistol & Rifle Assn.
1100 N.E. 125th St., No. Miami, FL 33161
American Single Shot Rifle Assn.
L.B. Thompson, 987 Jefferson Ave., Salem, OH 44460
American Society of Arms Collectors, Inc.
Robt. F. Rubendunst, 6550 Baywood Lane, Cincinnati, OH 45224
Armor & Arms Club
J.K. Watson, Jr., c/o Lord, Day & Lord, 25 Broadway, New York, NY 10004

Association of Firearm and Toolmark Examiners
Eugenia A. Bell, Secy., 7857 Esterel Dr., LaJolla, CA 92037
Boone & Crockett Club
205 South Patrick, Alexandria, VA 22314
Cast Bullet Assn., Inc.
Ralland J. Fortier, 14193 Van Doren Rd., Manassas, VA 22111
Citizens Committee for the Right to Keep and Bear Arms
Natl. Hq.: 12500 N.E. Tenth Pl., Bellevue, WA 98005
Deer Unlimited of America, Inc.
P.O. Box 509, Clemson, SC 29631
Ducks Unlimited, Inc.
One Waterfowl Way, Long Grove, IL 60047
Experimental Ballistics Associates
Ed Yard, 110 Kensington, Trenton, NJ 08618
Handgun Hunters International
J. D. Jones, Dir., P. O. Box 357 MAG, Bloomingdale, OH 43910
International Benchrest Shooters
Evelyn Richards, 411 N. Wilbur Ave. Sayre, PA 18840
International Cartridge Coll. Assn., Inc.
Victor v. B. Engel, 1211 Walnut St., Williamsport, PA 17701
International Handgun Metallic Silhouette Assoc.
Box 1609, Idaho Falls, ID 83401
Marlin Firearms Coll. Assn., Ltd.
Dick Paterson, Secy., 407 Lincoln Bldg., 44 Main St., Champaign, IL 61820
Miniature Arms Collectors/Makers Society Ltd.
Joseph J. Macewicz, 104 White Sand Lane, Racine, WI 53402
National Assn. of Federally Licd. Firearms Dealers
Andrew Molchan,2801 E. Oakland Park Blvd., Ft. Lauderdale, Fl 33306
National Automatic Pistol Collectors Assn.
Tom Knox, P.O. Box 15738, Tower Grove Station, St. Louis, MO 63163
National Bench Rest Shooters Assn., Inc.
Stella Buchtel, 5735 Sherwood Forest Dr., Akron, OH 44319
National Deer Hunter Assn.
1415 Fifth St. So., Hopkins, MN 55343
National Muzzle Loading Rifle Assn.
Box 67, Friendship, IN 47021
National Police Officers Assn. of America
Frank J. Schira, Ex. Dir., 609 West Main St., Louisville, KY 40202
National Reloading Mfrs. Assn., Inc.
4905 S.W. Griffith Dr., Suite 101, Beaverton, OR 97005
Nationel Rifle Assn.
1600 Rhode Island Ave., N.W., Washington, DC 20036
National Shooting Sports Fdtn., Inc.
Arnold H. Rohlfing, Exec. Director, 1075 Post Rd., Riverside, Ct 06878
National Skeet Shooting Assn.
Ann Myers, Exec. Director, P.O. Box 28188, San Antonio, TX 78228
National Wild Turkey Federation, Inc.
P.O. Box 530, Edgefield, SC 29824
North-South Skirmish Assn., Inc.
T.E. Johnson, Jr., 9700 Royerton Dr., Richmond, VA 23228
Remington Society of America
Fritz Baehr, 3125 Fremont Ave., Boulder, CO 80302
Ruger Collector's Assn., Inc.
Nancy J. Padua, P.O. Box 211, Trumbull, CT 06611
SAAMI, Sporting Arms and Ammunition Manufacturers' Institute, Inc.
P.O. Box 218, Wallingford, CT 06492
Safari Club International
Holt Bodinson, 5151 E. Broadway, Suite 1680, Tucson, AZ 85711
Second Amendment Foundation
James Madison Building, 12500 N.E. 10th Pl., Bellevue, WA 98005
Southern California Schuetzen Society
Thomas Trevor, 13621 Sherman Way, Van Nuys, CA 91405
U.S. Revolver Assn.
Stanley A. Sprague, 59 Alvin St., Springfield, MA 01104
Winchester Arms Collectors Assoc.
Lewis E. Yearout, 308 Riverview Dr., E., Great Falls, MT 59404
World Fast Draw Assn.
Gene Cozzitorto, 1026 Llagas Rd., Morgan Hill, CA 95037

AUSTRALIA

Sporting Shooters' Assn. of Australia Inc.
Mr. K. MacLaine, P.O. Box 210, Belgrave, Vict. 3160, Australia

CANADA

Alberta

Canadian Historical Arms Society
P.O. Box 901, Edmonton, Alb., Canada T5J 2L8

BRITISH COLUMBIA

B.C. Historical Arms Collectors
Ron Tyson, Box 80583, Burnaby, B.C. Canada V5H 3X9

NEW BRUNSWICK

Canadian Black Powder Federation
Mrs. Janet McConnell, P.O. Box 2876, Postal Sta. ''A'', Moncton, N.B. E1C 8T8, Can.

ONTARIO

Ajax Antique Arms Assn.
Monica A. Wright, P.O. Box 145, Millgrove, Ont., L0R 1V0, Canada
The Anglers and Hunters of Ontario
P.O. Box 15141, Peterborough, Ont., K9J 7H7, Canada
Glengarry Antique Arms
P.O. Box 122, R.R. #1, North Lancaster, Ont., Canada
National Firearms Assn.
P.O. Box 4610 Sta. F, Ottawa, Ont., K1S 5H8 Canada
The Ontario Handgun Assn.
135 Centre St. East, Richmond Hill, Ont., L4C 1A5, Canada
Oshawa Antique Gun Coll. Inc.
Monica A. Wright, P.O. Box 145, Millgrove, Ont., L0R 1V0, Canada

EUROPE

ENGLAND

Arms and Armour Society of London
A.R.E. North. Dept. of Metalwork, Victoria & Albert Museum, South Kensington, London SW7 2RL
British Cartridge Collectors Club
Peter F. McGowan, 15 Fuller St., Ruddington, Nottingham
Historical Breechloading Smallarms Assn.
D.J. Penn, M.A., Imperial War Museum, Lambeth Rd., London SE1 6HZ, England.Journal and newsletter are $8 a yr. seamail; surcharge for airmail
National Rifle Assn. (British)
Bisley Camp, Brookwood, Woking, Surrey, GU24 0PB, England

FRANCE

Syndicat National de l'Arquebuserie du Commerce de l'Arme Historique
B.P. No 3, 78110 Le Vesient, France

GERMANY (WEST)

Deutscher Schützenbund
Lahnstrasse, 6200 Wiesbaden-Klarenthal, West Germany

NEW ZEALAND

New Zealand Deerstalkers Assn.
Mr. Shelby Grant, P.O. Box 6514, Wellington, New Zealand

SOUTH AFRICA

Historical Firearms Soc. of South Africa
P.O. Box 145, 7725 Newlands, Republic of South Africa
South African Reloaders Assn.
Box 27128, Sunnyside, Pretoria 0132, South Africa

Directory of the Arms Trade

AMMUNITION (Foreign)

Beeman Inc., 47 Paul Drive, San Rafael, CA 94903/415-472-7121
Dynamit Nobel of America, Inc., 105 Stonehurst Court, Northvale, NJ 07647/210-767-1660(RWS, Geco, Rottweil)
Fiocchi of America, Inc., P.O. Box 7067, Jewell Station, Springfield, MO 65801/417-869-0786
Fiocchi Munizioni, Via S. Barbara 4, 22053 Lecco (Como), Italy
Hansen Cartridge Co., 246 Old Post Rd., Southport, CT 06490/203-259-5454
Norma, (See Outdoor Sports Headquarters, Inc.)
Hirtenberger Patronen-, Zündhütchen- & Metallwarenfabrik, A.G., Leobersdorfer Str. 33, A2552 Hirtenberg, Austria
Kendall International, Inc., 501 East North, Carlisle, KY 40311/606-298-7336 (Lapua)
Lapua (See Kendall International, Inc.)
PMC (See Patton and Morgan Corp.)
Patton and Morgan Corp., 6 East 45th St., New York, NY 10017/212-370-5777 (PMC ammo)
Paul Jaeger Inc., 211 Leedom St., Jenkintown, PA 19046/215-884-6920
RWS (Rheinische-Westfälische Sprengstoff) [See Dynamit Nobel of America]

AMMUNITION (Commercial)

BBM Corp., 221 Interstate Dr., West Springfield, MA 01089/413-736-0371 (45 ACP shotshell)
Bingham Ltd., 1775-C Wilwat Dr., Norcross, GA 30093
Cascade Cartridge Inc., (See Omark)
Dynamit Nobel of America, Inc., 105 Stonehurst Court, Northvale, NJ 07647/201-767-1660(RWS)
Eclipse Cartridge, Inc., 26407 Golden Valley Rd., Saugus, CA 91350/805-251-6610
Eley-Kynoch, ICI-America, Wilmington, DE 19897/302-575-3000
Estate Cartridge Inc., P.O. Box 3702, Conroe, TX 77305 (shotshell)
Federal Cartridge Co., 2700 Foshay Tower, Minneapolis, MN 55402/612-333-8255
Frontier Cartridge Division-Hornady Mfg. Co., Box 1848, Grand Island, NE 68801/308-382-1390
Hansen Cartridge Co., 246 Old Post Rd., Southport, CT 06490/203-259-5454
ICI-America, Wilmington, DE 19897/302-575-3000(Eley-Kynoch)
Midway Arms, Inc., R. R. #5, Box 298, 7450 Old Hwy. 40 West, Columbia, MO 65201/314-445-3030
Omark Industries, Box 856, Lewiston, ID 83501
Precision Prods. of Wash., Inc., N. 311 Walnut Rd., Spokane, WA 99206/509-928-0604 (Exammo)
RWS, (See Dynamit Nobel of America)
Remington Arms Co., 939 Barnum Ave., P. O. Box #1939, Bridgeport, CT 06601
Service Armament, 689 Bergen Blvd., Ridgefield, NJ 07657
Super Vel, Hamilton Rd., Rt. 2, P. O. Box 1398, Fond du Lac, WI 54935/414-921-2652
U.S. Ammunition Co., 19014 Des Moines Way So., Seattle, WA 98148
Weatherby's, 2781 E. Firestone Blvd., South Gate, CA 90280
Winchester, Shamrock St., East Alton, IL 62024

AMMUNITION (Custom)

American Pistol Bullet, 133 Blue Bell Rd., Greensboro, NC 27406/919-272-6151
Ballistek, Weapons Systems Div., 3450 Antelope Dr., Lake Havasu City, AZ 86403/602-855-0997
Beal's Bullets, 170 W. Marshall Rd., Lansdowne, PA 19050 (Auto Mag Specialists)
Bell's Gun & Sport Shop, 3309-19 Mannheim Rd., Franklin Park, IL 60131
Brass Extrusion Labs. Ltd., 800 W. Maple Lane, Bensenville, IL 60106
C.W. Cartridge Co., 71 Hackensack St., Wood-Ridge, NJ 07075 (201-438-5111)
Russell Campbell Custom Loaded Ammo, 219 Leisure Dr., San Antonio, TX 78201/512-735-1183
Crown City Arms, P.O. Box 1126, Cortland, NY 13045/607-753-8238

Cumberland Arms Rt. 1, Shafer Rd., Blantons Chapel, Manchester, TN 37355
Denali Bullet Co., P.O. Box 82217, Fairbanks, AK 99701/907-479-8227
Eagle Cap Custom Bullets, P.O. Box 659, Enterprise, OR 97828/503-426-4282
E.W. Ellis Sport Shop, RFD 1, Box 315, Corinth, NY 12822
Ellwood Epps Northern Ltd., 210 Worthington St. W., North Bay, Ont. PIB 3B4, Canada
Estate Cartridge Inc., P.O. Box 3702, Conroe, TX 77305/409-539-9144 (shotshell)
Jack First Distributors, Inc., 44633 Sierra Hwy., Lancaster, CA 93534/805-945-6981
Ramon B. Gonzalez, P.O. Box 370, Monticello, NY 12701
Gussert Bullet & Cartridge Co., Inc., P.O. Box 3945, Green Bay, WI 54303
Jensen's Custom Ammunition, 5146 E. Pima, Tucson, AZ 85716
R.H. Keeler, 817 "N" St., Port Angeles, WA 98362/206-457-4702
KTW Inc., 710 Foster Park Rd., Lorain, OH 44053 216/233-6919 (bullets)
Dean Lincoln, P.O. Box 1886, Farmington, NM 87401
Lindsley Arms Cartridge Co., Inc., P.O. Box 1287, 408 N.E. 3rd St., Boynton Beach, FL 33435/305-737-8562 (inq. S.A.S.E.)
Lomont Precision Bullets, 4421 S. Wayne Ave., Ft. Wayne, IN 46807/219-694-6792 (custom cast bullets only)
McConnellstown Reloading & Cast Bullets, Inc., R.D. 3, Box 40, Huntingdon, PA 16652/814-627-5402
Numrich Arms Corp., 203 Broadway, W. Hurley, NY 12491
Pearl Armory, Revenden Springs, AR 72460
Robert Pomeroy, Morison Ave., Corinth, ME 04427/207-285-7721 (custom shells)
Precision Ammo Co., P.O. Box 63, Garnerville, NY 10923/914-947-2720
Precision Prods. of Wash., Inc., N. 311 Walnut Rd., Spokane, WA 99206/509-928-0604 (Exammo)
Anthony F. Sailer-Ammunition, 707 W. Third St., P. O. Box L, Owen, WI 54460/715-229-2516
Sanders Cust. Gun Serv., 2358 Tyler Lane, Louisville, KY 40205
Senica Run, Inc., P.O. Box 3032, Greeley, CO 80633
Geo. Spence, 202 Main St., Steele, MO 63877/314-695-4926 (boxer-primed cartridges)
The 3-D Company, Box J, Main St., Doniphan, NE 68832/402-845-2285 (reloaded police ammo)

AMMUNITION COMPONENTS—BULLETS, POWDER, PRIMERS

Accurate Arms Co., Inc., (Propellents Div.), Rt. 1, Box 167, McEwen, TN, 37101/615-729-5301 (powders)
The Alberts Corp., P.O. Box 233, Budd Lake, NJ 07828/201-691-8575 (swaged bullets)
Ammo-O-Mart Ltd., P.O. Box 125, Hawkesbury, Ont., Canada K6A 2R8 (Curry bullets; Nobel powder)
Austin Powder Co. (See Red Diamond Dist. Co.)
Ballistic Prods., Inc., Box 488, 2105 Shaughnessy Circle, Long Lake, MN 55356
Ballistic Research Industries (BRI), 6000 B Soquel Ave., Santa Cruz, CA 95062/408-476-7981 (12-ga. Sabo shotgun slug)
Barnes Bullets, P.O. Box 215, American Fork, UT 84003/801-756-4222
Bell's Gun & Sport Shop, 3309-19 Mannheim Rd., Franklin Pk., IL 60131
Bitterroot Bullet Co., Box 412, Lewiston, ID 83501/208-743-5635 (Coin or stamps) f.50¢ U.S.; 75¢ Can. & Mex.; intl. $3.00 and #10 SASE for lit.
B.E.L.L., Brass Extrusion Laboratories, Ltd., 800 W. Maple Lane, Bensenville, IL 60106
Milton Brynin, 214 E. Third St., Mount Vernon, NY 10550/914-664-1311 (cast bull.)
CCI, (See: Omark Industries)
Cabin Enterprises, 3424 - 4th St., Kenosha, WI 53142/414/553-9441 (Green Bay bullets)
Kenneth E. Clark, 18738 Highway 99, Madera, CA 93637/209-674-6016 (Bullets)
Denali Bullet Co., P.O. Box 82217, Fairbanks, AK 99701/907-479-8227 (bullets)
Division Lead, 7742 W. 61 Pl., Summit, IL 60502
DuPont, Explosives Dept., Wilmington, DE 19898
Dynamit Nobel of America, Inc., 105 Stonehurst Court, Northvale, NJ 07647/201-767-1660 (RWS percussion caps)
Eagle Cap Custom Bullets, P.O. Box 659, Enterprise, OR 97828/503-426-4282
Elk Mountain Shooters Supply Inc., 1719 Marie, Pasco, WA 99301 (Alaskan bullets)
Farmer Bros., 1102 N. Washington, Eldora, IA 50627/515-858-3651 (Lage wad)

Federal Cartridge Co., 2700 Foshay Tower, Minneapolis, MN 55402/612-333-8255 (nickel cases)
Forty Five Ranch Enterprises, 119 S. Main, Miami, OK 74354/918-542-9307
Godfrey Reloading Supply, Hi-Way 67-111, Brighton, IL 62012 (cast bullets)
Lynn Godfrey, (See: Elk Mtn. Shooters Supply)
Green Bay Bullets, see: Cabin Enterprises*
GTM Co., George T. Mahaney, 15915B E. Main St., La Puente, CA 91744 (all brass shotshells)
Gussert Bullet & Cartridge Co., Inc., P.O. Box 3945, Green Bay, WI 54303
Hardin Specialty Distr., P. O. Box 338, Radcliff, KY 40160/502-351-6649 (empty, primed cases)
Hepplers Gun Shop, 6000 B Soquel Ave., Santa Cruz, CA 95062/408-475-1235 (BRI 12-ga. slug)
Hercules Powder Co., 910 Market St.,Wilmington, DE 19899
Hodgdon Powder Co. Inc., 7710 W. 63rd St., Shawnee Mission, KS 66202/913-362-5410
Hornady Mfg. Co., Box 1848, Grand Island, NE 68801/308-382-1390
Kendall International, Inc., 501 East North, Carlisle, KY 40311/606-298-7336 (Lapua bull.)
NORMA (See Outdoor Sports Headquarters, Inc.)
N.E. House Co., 195 West High St., E. Hampton, CT 06424/203-267-2133 (zinc bases in 30, 38, 44 and 45-cal. only)
Jaro Manuf., P.O. Box 6125, 206 E. Shaw, Pasadena, TX 77506/713-472-0471 (bullets)
L.L.F. Die Shop, 1281 Highway 99 North, Eugene, OR 97402/503-688-5753
Lage Uniwad Co., 1102 Washington St., Eldora, IA 50627/515-858-3651
Ljutic Ind., Inc., Box 2117,Yakima, WA 98902 (Mono-wads)
Lomont Precision Bullets, 4421 S. Wayne Ave., Ft. Wayne, IN 46807/219-694-6792 (custom cast bullets)
Lyman Products Corp., Rte. 147, Middlefield, CT 06455
Michael's Antiques, Box 233, Copiague, L.I., NY 11726 (Balle Blondeau)
Miller Trading Co., 20 S. Front St., Wilmington, NC 28401/919-762-7107 (bullets)
Nosler Bullets, P.O. Box 688, Beaverton, OR 97005
Omark Industries, Box 856, Lewiston, ID 83501/208-746-2351
The Oster Group, 50 Sims Ave., Providence, RI 02909 (alloys f. casting bull.)
Outdoor Sports Headquarters, Inc., 2290 Arbor Blvd., Dayton, OH 45439/513-294-2811
Pyrodex, Inc., 7710 W. 63rd St., Shawnee Mission, KS 66202 (black powder substitute)
Robert Pomeroy, Morison Ave., East Corinth, ME 04427
Red Diamond Distributing Co., 1304 Snowdon Dr., Knoxville, TN 37912 (black powder)
Remington-Peters, 939 Barnum Ave., P.O. Box #1939, Bridgeport, CT 06601
Sierra Bullets Inc., 10532 So. Painter Ave., Santa Fe Springs, CA 90670
Speer Products, Box 856, Lewiston, ID 83501
C.H. Stocking, Rte. 3, Box 195, Hutchinson, MN 55350 (17 cal. bullet jackets)
Supreme Products Co., 1830 S. California Ave., Monrovia, CA 91016/800-423-7159 (rubber bullets)
Taracorp Industries, 16th & Cleveland Blvd., Granite City, IL 62040/618-451-4524 (Lawrence Brand lead shot)
Taylor Bullets, P.O. Box 21254, San Antonio, TX 78221 (cast)
United Cartridge Co., P.O. Box 604, Valley Industrial Park, Casa Grande, AR 85222/602-836-2510 (P.C. wads)
Vitt & Boos, 2178 Nichols Ave., Stratford, CT 06497/203-375-6859 (Aerodynamic shotgun slug, 12-ga. only)
Winchester, Shamrock St., East Alton, IL 62024
Worthy Products, Inc., R.D. #3, Box 268, Gillette Rd., Mexico, NY 13114/315-963-7413 (slug loads)
Xelex Ltd., P.O. Box 543, Renfrow, Ont. K7V 4B1, Canada (powder, Curry bullets)
Zero Bullet Co., P.O. Box 1188, Cullman, AL 35055

ANTIQUE ARMS DEALERS

Robert Abels, 2881 N.E. 33 Ct., Ft. Lauderdale, FL 33306/305-564-6985 (Catalog $1.00)
Beeman Inc., 47 Paul Dr., San Rafael, CA 94903/415-472-7121 (airguns only)
Wm. Boggs, 1243 Grandview Ave., Columbus, OH 43212
Dave Chicoine, d/b/a Liberty A.S.P., P.O. Box 385, Cos Cob, CT 06807/203-357-1893
Ed's Gun House, Rte. 1, Minnesota City, MN 55959/507-689-2925
Ellwood Epps Northern Ltd., 210 Worthington St. W., North Bay, Ont. PlB 3B4 Canada
William Fagan, 126 Belleview, Mount Clemens, MI 48043/313-465-4637
Jack First Distributors, Inc., 44633 Sierra Hwy., Lancaster, CA 93534/805-945-6981
N. Flayderman & Co., Squash Hollow, New Milford, CT 06776
Fulmer's Antique Firearms, Chet Fulmer, P.O. Box 792, Detroit Lakes, MN 56501/218-847-7712
Garcia National Gun Traders, Inc., 225 S.W. 22nd Ave., Miami, FL 33135
Herb Glass, Bullville, NY 10915/914-361-3021
James Goergen, Rte. 2, Box 182BB, Austin, MN 55912/507-433-9280
Goodman's for Guns, 1002 Olive St., St. Louis, MO 63101/314-421-5300
Griffin's Guns & Antiques, R.R. 4, Peterborough, Ont., Canada K9J 6X5/705-748-3220
The Gun Shop, 6497 Pearl Rd., Parma Heights (Cleveland), OH 44130/216-884-7476
Hansen & Company, 244 Old Post Rd., Southport, CT 06490
Holbrook Antique Militaria, 4050 S.W. 98th Ave., Miami, FL 33165/305-223-6500
Jackson Arms, 6209 Hillcrest Ave., Dallas, TX 75205
Lever Arms Serv. Ltd., 572 Howe St., Vancouver, B.C., Canada V6C 2E3/604-685-6913
Lone Pine Trading Post, Jct. Highways 61 and 248, Minnesota City, MN 55959/507-689-2922

Charles W. Moore, R.D. 2, Box 276, Schenevus, NY 12155/607-278-5721
Museum of Historical Arms, 1038 Alton Rd., Miami Beach, FL 33139/305-672-7480 (ctlg $5)
New Orleans Arms Co., 5001 Treasure St., New Orleans, LA 70186/504-944-3371
O.K. Hardware, Westgate Shopping Center, Great Falls, MT 59404
Old Western Scrounger, 3509 Carlson Blvd., El Cerrito, CA 94530/415-527-3872 (write for list; $2)
Pioneer Guns, 5228 Montgomery, (Cincinnati) Norwood, OH 45212/513-631-4871
Pony Express Sport Shop, Inc., 17460 Ventura Blvd., Encino, CA 91316/213-788-0123
Martin B. Retting, Inc., 11029 Washington, Culver City, CA 90230/213-837-6111
Ridge Guncraft, Inc., 125 E. Tyrone Rd., Oak Ridge, TN 37830/615-483-4024
San Francisco Gun Exch., 124 Second St., San Francisco, CA 94105/415-982-6097
Santa Ana Gunroom, P.O. Box 1777, Santa Ana, CA 92701/714-541-3035
Ward & Van Valkenburg, 114-32nd Ave. N., Fargo, ND 58102
M.C. Wiest, 125 E. Tyrone Rd., Oak Ridge, TN 37830/615-483-4024
J. David Yale, Ltd., 2618 Conowingo Rd., Bel Air, MD 21014/301-838-9479
Lewis Yearout, 308 Riverview Dr. E., Great Falls, MT 59404

BOOKS (ARMS), Publishers and Dealers

Arms & Armour Press, 2-6 Hampstead High Street, London NW3 1QQ, England
Beeman Inc., 47 Paul Dr., San Rafael, CA 94903/415-472-7121 (airguns)
Beinfeld Publishing, Inc., 12767 Saticoy St., No. Hollywood, CA 91605/213-982-3700
Blacksmith Corp., P.O. Box 424, Southport, CT 06490/203-367-4041
Blacktail Mountain Books, 42 First Ave. West, Kalispell, MT 59901/406-257-5573
DBI Books, Inc., One Northfield Plaza, Northfield, IL 60093/312-441-7010
Dove Press, P.O. Box 3882, Enid, OK 73701/405-234-4347
EPCO Publ. Co., 62-19 Cooper Ave., Glendale, NY 11385/212-497-1100
Empire Co.,P.O. Box 2902, Santa Fe, NM 87501/505-983-2381
Fairfield Book Co., Inc., P.O. Box 289, Brookfield Center, Ct. 06805/800-243-1318/203-775-0053
Fortress Publications Inc., P.O. Box 241, Stoney Creek, Ont. L8G 3X9, Canada/416-662-3505
Guncraft Books, Div. of Ridge Guncraft, Inc., 125 E. Tyrone Rd., Oak Ridge, TN 37830/615-483-4024
Gunnerman Books, P.O. Box 4292, Auburn Heights, MI 48057/313-879-2779
Handgun Press, 5832 S. Green, Chicago, IL 60621
Jackson Arms, 6209 Hillcrest Ave., Dallas, TX 75205
Jolex Inc., 294 W. Oakland, Oakland, NJ 07436/201-337-3356
Long Survival Publications, 718 Lincoln Ave., Wamego, KS 66547/913-456-7387
Lyman, Route 147, Middlefield, CT 06455
John Olson Co., 294 W. Oakland Ave., Oakland, NJ 07436
Pachmayr Gun Works, Inc., 1220 S. Grand Ave., Los Angeles, CA 90015/213-748-7271
Personal Firearms Record Book Co., P.O. Box 2800, Santa Fe, NM 87501/505-983-2381
Gerald Pettinger Arms Books, Route 2, Russell, IA 50238/515-535-2239
Ray Riling Arms Books Co., 114 Greenwood Ave., Box 135, Wyncote, PA 19095/215-438-2456
Rutgers Book Center, Mark Aziz, 127 Raritan Ave., Highland Park, NJ 08904
Stackpole Books, Cameron & Kelker Sts., Telegraph Press Bldg., Harrisburg, PA 17105
Stoeger Publishing Co., 55 Ruta Court, South Hackensack, NJ 07606
James C. Tillinghast, Box 405, Hancock, NH 03449/603-525-6615
Ken Trotman, 2-6 Hampstead High St., London, NW3, 1QQ, England
Winchester Press, 1421 S. Sheridan Rd., P.O. Box 1260, Tulsa, OK 74101/918-835-3161
Wolfe Publishing Co., Inc., Box 30-30, Prescott, AZ 86302/602-445-7810

BULLET & CASE LUBRICANTS

Cabin Enterprises, 3424-4th St., Kenosha, WI 53142 (EZE-Size case lube)
Chopie Mfg. Inc., 700 Copeland Ave., La Crosse, WI 54601/608-784-0926 (Black-Solve)
Cooper-Woodward, Box 972, Riverside, CA 92502/714-683-5952 (Perfect Lube)
Corbin Mfg. & Supply Inc., P.O. Box 758, Phoenix, OR 97535/503-826-5211
Gussert Bullet & Cartridge Co., Inc., P.O. Box 3945, Green Bay, WI 54303 (Super Lube)
Hodgdon Powder Co., Inc., 7710 W. 63rd St., Shawnee Mission, KS 66202/913-362-5410
Javelina Products, Box 337, San Bernardino, CA 92402/714-882-5847 (Alox beeswax)
Jet-Aer Corp., 100 Sixth Ave., Paterson, NJ 07524
LeClear Industries, 1126 Donald Ave., Royal Oak, MI 48073/313-588-1025
Lenz Prod. Co., Box 1226, Sta. C, Canton, OH 44708 (Clenzoil)
Lyman Products Corp., Rte. 147, Middlefield, CT. 06455 (Size-Ezy)
Marmel Prods., P.O. Box 97, Utica, MI 48087/313-731-8029 (Marvellube, Marvelux)
Micro Ammunition Co., P.O. Box 117, Mesilla Park, NM 88047/505-522-2674 (Micro-Lube)

Mirror Lube, American Speclty. Lubricants, P.O. Box 693, San Juan Capistrano, CA 92693/714-496-1098
M&N Bullet Lube, Box 495, Jefferson St., Madras, OR 97741/503-475-2992
Northeast Industrial, Inc., 2516 Wyoming, El Paso, TX 79903/915-532-8344 (Ten X-Lube; NEI mold prep)
Pacific Tool Co., P.O. Box 2048, Ordnance Plant Rd., Grand Island, NE 68801/308-384-2308
RCBS, Inc., Box 1919, Oroville, CA 95965
SAECO Rel. Inc., 525 Maple Ave., Carpinteria, CA 93103/805-684-6925
Shooters Accessory Supply (SAS) (See Corbin Mfg. & Supply)
Tamarack Prods., Inc., Box 224, Barrington, IL 60010 (Bullet lube)
Testing Systems, Inc., 220 Pegasus Ave., Northvale, NJ 07647/201-767- 7300

CARTRIDGES FOR COLLECTORS

AD Hominem, R.R. 3, Orillia, Ont., Canada L3V 6H3/705-689-5303
Antique Arsenal, 365 S. Moore, Lakewood, CO 80226
Cameron's, 16690 W. 11th Ave., Golden CO 80401/303-279-7365
Centrefire Sports Dunedin, P.O. Box 1293, 41 Dowling St., Dunedin, New Zealand
Chas. E. Duffy, Williams Lane, West Hurley, NY 12419
Tom M. Dunn, 1342 So. Poplar, Casper, WY 82601
Ellwood Epps (Orillia) Ltd., Hwy. 11 North, Orillia, Ont. L3V 6H3, Canada/705-689-5333
Jack First Distributors, Inc., 44633 Sierra Hwy., Lancaster, CA 93534/805-945-6981
"Gramps" Antique Cartridges, Box 341, Washago, Ont., Canada L0K 2B0
Hansen Cartridge Co., 246 Old Post Rd., Southport, CT 06490/203-259-5454
Idaho Ammunition Service, 410 21st Ave., Lewiston, ID 83501
San Francisco Gun Exchange, 124 Second St., San Francisco, CA 94105/415-982-6097
Ernest Tichy, 365 So. Moore, Lakewood, CO 80226
James C. Tillinghast, Box 405, Hancock, NH 03449/603-525-6615 (list $1)
Lewis Yearout, 308 Riverview Dr. E., Great Falls, MT 59404

CASES, CABINETS AND RACKS—GUN

Action Co., P.O. Box 528, McKinney, TX 75069
Alco Carrying Cases, 601 W. 26th St., New York, NY 10001/212-675-5820
Bob Allen Sportswear, 214 S.W. Jackson, Des Moines, IA 50315/515-283-1988 (carrying)
Allen Co., Inc., 640 Compton St., Broomfield, CO 80020/303-469-1857
Art Jewel Ltd., 421A Irmen Dr., Addison, IL 60101/312-628-6220
Assault Systems of St. Louis, 869 Horan, St. Louis, MO 63026/314-343-3575 (canvas carrying case)
Morton Booth Co., Box 123, Joplin, MO 64801
Boyt Co., Div. of Welsh Sportg. Gds., Box 1108, Iowa Falls, IA 50126
Brenik, Inc., 925 W. Chicago Ave., Chicago, IL 60622
Browning, Rt. 4, Box 624-B, Arnold, MO 63010
Cap-Lex Gun Cases, Capitol Plastics of Ohio, Inc., 333 Van Camp Rd., Bowling Green, OH 43402
Challanger Mfg. Corp., 30 South St., Mt. Vernon, NY 10550/914-664-7134
Dara-Nes Inc., see: Nesci
Dart Mfg. Co., 4012 Bronze Way, Dallas, TX 75237/214-333-4221
Doskocil Mfg. Co., Inc., jP.O. Box 1246, Arlington, TX 75010/817-467-5116 (Gun Guard carrying)
East-Tenn Mills, Inc., 2300 Buffalo Rd., Johnson City, Tn 37601 (gun socks)
Ellwood Epps (Orillia) Ltd., R.R. 3, Hwy, 11 North, Orillia, Ont. L3V 6H3, Canada/705-689-5333 (custom gun cases)
Norbert Ertel, P.O. Box 1150, Des Plaines, IL 60018/312-825-2315 (cust. gun cases)
Flambeau Plastics Corp., 801 Lynn, Baraboo, WI 53913
Fort Knox Security Products, 1051 N. Industrial Park Rd., Orem, UT 84057/801-224-7233 (safes)
Gun-Ho Case Mfg. Co., 110 East 10th St., St. Paul, MN 55101
Hansen Cartridge Co., 246 Old Post Rd., Southport, CT 06490/203-259-5454
Harbor House Gun Cabinets, 12508 Center St., South Gate, CA 90280
Marvin Huey Gun Cases, Box 98, Reed's Spring, MO 65737/417-538-4233 (handbuilt leather cases)
Jumbo Sports Prods., P.O. Box 280-Airport Rd., Frederick, MD 21701
Kalispel Metal Prods. (KMP), Box 267, Cusick, WA 99119 (aluminum boxes)
Kane Products Inc., 5572 Brecksville Rd., Cleveland, OH 44131/216-524-9962 (GunChaps)
Kolpin Mfg., Inc., Box 231, Berlin, WI 54923/414-361-0400
Marble Arms Corp., 420 Industrial Park, Gladstone, MI 49837/906-428-3710
Bill McGuire, 1600 No. Eastmont Ave., East Wenatchee, WA 98801 (custom cases)
Merchandise Brokers, P.O. Box 491, Lilburn, GA 30247/404-923-0015 (GunSlinger portable rack)
W.A. Miller Co., Inc., (Wamco), Mingo Loop, Oguossoc, ME 04964 (wooden handgun cases)
Nesci Enterprises, Inc., P.O. Box 119, East Hampton, CT 06424/203-267-2588 (firearms security chests)
Nortex Industrial Fan Co., 2821 Main St., Dallas TX 75226/214-748-1157 (automobile gun rack)
Paul-Reed, Inc., P.O. Box 227, Charlevoix, MI 49720
Penguin Industries, Inc., Airport Industrial Mall, Coatesville, PA 19320/215-384-6000
Precise, 3 Chestnut, Suffern, NY 10901
Protecto Plastics, Div. of Penquin Ind., Airport Industrial Mall, Coatesville, PA 19320/215-384-6000 (carrying cases)
Provo Steel & Supply Co., P.O. Box 977, Provo, UT 84601 (steel gun cases)

Randall Manufacturing, 7965 San Fernando Rd., Sun Valley, CA 91352/213-875-2045
Red Head Brand Corp., 4949 Joseph Hardin Dr., Dallas, TX 75236/214-333-4141
Richland Arms Co., 321 W. Adrian, Blissfield, MI 49228
Saf-T-Case Mfg. Co., Inc., P.O. Box 5472, Irving, TX 75062
San Angelo Co. Inc., P.O. Drawer 5820, San Angelo, TX 76902/915-655-7126
Buddy Schoellkopf, 4949 Joseph Hardin Dr., Dallas, TX 75236/214-333-2121
Se-Cur-All Cabinet Co., K-Prods., P.O. Box 2052, Michigan City, IN 46360/219-872-7957
Security Gun Chest, (See Tread Corp.)
Spitz & Blauvelt, Inc., P.O. Box 643/1100 W. South, Hastings, NE 68901/402-462-4178 (cases)
Stearns Mfg. Co., P.O. Box 1498, St. Cloud, MN 56301
Stowline Inc., 811 So. 1st Kent, WA 98031/206-852-9200 (vaults)
Tread Corp., P.O. Box 13207, Roanoke, VA 24032/703-982-6881 (security gun chest)
Trik Truk, P.O. Box 3760, Kent, WA 98301 (P.U. truck cases)
Weather Shield Sports Equipm. Inc., Rte. #3, Petoskey Rd., Charlevoix, MI 49720
Woodstream Corp., Box 327, Lititz, PA 17543
Yield House, Inc., RFD, No. Conway, NH 03860

CHOKE DEVICES, RECOIL ABSORBERS & RECOIL PADS

Action Products Inc., 22 N. Mulberry St., Hagerstown, MD 21740/301-707-1414 (rec. shock eliminator)
Arms Ingenuity Co., Box 1; 51 Canal St., Weatogue, CT 06089/203-658-5624 (Jet-Away)
Stan Baker, 5303 Roosevelt Way NE, Seattle, WA 98105/206-522-4575 (shotgun)
Jes Briley Mfg. Co., 1085-C Gessner, Houston, TX 77055/713-932-6995 (choke tubes)
C&H Research, 115 Sunnyside Dr., Lewis, KS 67552/316-324-5445 (Mercury recoil suppressor)
Vito Cellini, P. O. Box 17792, San Antonio, TX 78217/512-826-2584
Dahl's Gun Shop, 6947 King Ave., Route 4, Billings, MT 59102/406-656-6132
Defense Technology Associates, 3333 Midway Dr., Suite 102, San Diego, CA 92110/714-223-5339 (Muzzle-Mizer rec. abs.)
Diverter Arms, Inc., P.O. Box 22084, Houston, TX 77027 (shotgun diverter)
Edwards Recoil Reducer, 269 Herbert St., Alton, IL 62002/618-462-3257
Emsco Variable Shotgun Chokes, 101 Second Ave., S.E., Waseca, MN 56093/507-835-1779
Griggs Recreational Prods. Inc., P.O. Box 324, Twin Bridges, MT 59754/406-684-5202 (recoil director)
La Paloma Marketing, 4500 E. Speedway Blvd., Suite 93, Tucson, AZ 85712/602-881-4750 (Action rec. shock eliminator)
Lyman Products Corp., Rte. 147, Middlefield, CT. 06455 (Cutts Comp.)
MBM Enterprises, Rt. 4, Box 265, 715 E. 46th St., Stillwater, OK 70474/405-377-0296 (Counter-Coil rec. abs.)
Mag-Na-Port Arms, Inc., 30016 S. River Rd., Mt. Clemens, MI 48043 (muzzle-brake system)
Mag-Na-Port of Canada, 1861 Burrows Ave., Winnipeg, Manitoba R2X 2V6, Canada
Don Mitchell Corp., 200 N. Tustin Ave., Suite 200, Santa Ana, CA 92705 (muzzle brakes)
Multi-Gauge Enterprises, 433 W. Foothill Blvd., Monrovia, CA 91016/213-358-4549 (chokes)
Pachmayr Gun Works, Inc., 1220 So. Grand Ave., Los Angeles, CA 90015/213-748-7271 (recoil pads)
Poly-Choke Co., Inc., 150 Park Ave., East Hartford, CT 06108/203-289-2743
Pro-Choke, Inc., 2760 N.E. 7th Ave., Pompano Beach, FL 33064/305-946-5718
Pro-Port Canada, 1861 Burrows Ave., Winnipeg, Manitoba R2X 2V6, Canada
Pro-Port U.S.A., 30016 South River Rd., Mt. Clemens, MI 48045/313-469-7323
Purbaugh, see: Multi-Gauge Enterprises
Supreme Products Co., 1830 S. California Ave., Monrovia, CA 91016/800-423-7159 (recoil pads)

CHRONOGRAPHS AND PRESSURE TOOLS

B-Square Co., Box 11281, Ft. Worth, TX 76110
Custom Chronograph Co., Box 1061, Brewster, WA 98812/509-689-2004
Diverter Arms, Inc., P.O. Box 22084, Houston, TX 77027 (press. tool)
Oehler Research, P.O. Box 9135, Austin, TX 78756
Telepacific Electronics Co., Inc., P.O. Box 1329, San Marcos, CA 92069/714-744-4415
Tepeco, P.O. Box 919, Silver City, NM 88062/505-388-2070 (Tepeco Speed-Meter)
M. York, 5508 Griffith Rd., Gaithersburg, MD 20760/301-253-4217 (press. tool)

CLEANING & REFINISHING SUPPLIES

A 'n A Co., Box 571, King of Prussia, PA 19406 (Valet shotgun cleaner)
Armite Labs., 1845 Randolph St., Los Angeles, CA 90001/213-587-7744 (pen oiler)
Armoloy Co. of Ft. Worth, 204 E. Daggett St., Ft Worth, TX 76104/817-461-0051
Beeman Inc., 47 Paul Dr., San Rafael, CA 94903/415-472-7121

Belltown, Ltd., 33 Belltown Rd., Stamford, CT 06905/203-348-0911 (gun clg. cloth kit)
Birchwood-Casey, 7900 Fuller Rd., Eden Prairie, MN 55344/612-927-7933
Bisonite Co., Inc., P.O. Box 84, Kenmore Station, Buffalo, NY 14217
Blue and Gray Prods., Inc., R.D. #6, Box 348, Wellsboro, PA 16901/717-724-1383
Break-Free, a Div. of San/Bar Corp., 9999 Muirlands Blvd., Irvine, CA 92714/714-855-9911
Jim Brobst, 299 Poplar St., Hamburg, PA 19526/215-562-2103 (J-B Bore Cleaning Compound)
GB Prods. Dept., H & R, Inc., Industrial Rowe, Gardner, MA 01440
Browning Arms, Rt. 4, Box 624-B, Arnold, MO 63010
J.M. Bucheimer Co., P.O. Box 280, Airport Rd., Frederick, MD 21701/301-662-5101
Burnishine Prod. Co., 8140 N. Ridgeway, Skokie, IL 60076 (Stock Glaze)
Call 'N, Inc., 1615 Bartlett Rd., Memphis, TN 38134/901-372-1682 (Gunskin)
Chem-Pak, Inc., Winchester, VA 22601/703-667-1341 (Gun-Savr.protect. & lubricant)
Chopie Mfg. Inc., 700 Copeland Ave., La Crosse, WI 54601/608-784-0926 (Black-Solve)
Clenzoil Co., Box 1226, Sta. C, Canton, OH 44708/216-833-9758
Clover Mfg. Co., 139 Woodward Ave., Norwalk, Ct. 06856/800-243-6492 (Clover compound)
J. Dewey Mfg. Co., 186 Skyview Dr., Southbury, CT 06488/203-264-3064 (one-piece gun clg. rod)
Diah Engineering Co., 5177 Haskell St., La Canada, CA 91011/213-625-2184 (barrel lubricant)
Dri-Slide, Inc.,413 N. Darling, Fremont, MI 49412/616-924-3950
Forty-Five Ranch Enterpr., 119 S. Main St., Miami, OK 74354/918-542-9307
Gun-All Products, Box 244, Dowagiac, MI 49047
Frank C. Hoppe Div., Penguin Ind., Inc., Airport Industrial Mall, Coatesville, PA 19320/215-384-6000
Jet-Aer Corp., 100 Sixth Ave., Paterson, NJ 07524 (blues & oils)
Kellog's Professional Prods., Inc., P.O. Box 1201, Sandusky, OH 44870
K.W. Kleinendorst, R.D. #1, Box 113B, Hop Bottom, PA 18824/717-289-4687 (rifle clg. cables)
Terry K. Kopp, Highway 13, Lexington, MO 64067/816-259-2636 (stock rubbing compound; rust preventative grease)
LPS Chemical Prods., Holt Lloyd Corp., 4647 Hugh Howell Rd., Tucker, GA 30048/404-934-7800
LEM Gun Spec., Box 31, College Park, GA 30337/404-761-9054 (Lewis Lead Remover)
Liquid Wrench, Box 10628, Charlotte, NC 28201 (pen. oil)
Lynx Line Gun Prods. Div., Protective Coatings, Inc., 20626 Fenkell Ave., Detroit, MI 48223/313-255-6032
Marble Arms Co., 420 Industrial Park, Gladstone, MI 49837/906-428-3710
Micro Sight Co., 242 Harbor Blvd., Belmont, CA 94002/415-591-0769 (bedding)
Mirror-Lube, American Speclty. Lubricants, P.O. Box 693, San Juan Capistrano, CA 92693/714-496-1098
New Method Mfg. Co., Box 175, Bradford, PA 16701/814-262-6611 (gun blue; Minute Man gun care)
Northern Instruments, Inc., 6680 North Highway 49, Lino Lake, MN 55014 (Stor-Safe rust preventer)
Numrich Arms Co., West Hurley, NY 12491 (44-40 gun blue)
Old World Oil Products, 3827 Queen Ave. No., Minneapolis, MN 55412
Original Mink Oil, Inc., P.O. Box 20191, 10652 N.E. Holman, Portland, OR 97220/503-255-2814
Outers Laboratories, Route 2, Onalaska, WI 54650/608-783-1515 (Gunslick kits)
Radiator Spec. Co., 1400 Independence Blvd., Charlotte, NC 28201 (liquid wrench)
Reardon Prod., 103 W. Market St., Morrison, IL 61270 (Dry-Lube)
Rice Protective Gun Coatings, 235-30th St., West Palm Beach, FL 33407/305-845-2383
Rig Products, 87 Coney Island Dr., Sparks, NV 89431/703-331-5666
Rusteprufe Labs., Rte. 5, Sparta, WI 54656/608-269-4144
Rust Guardit, see: Schwab Industries
San/Bar Corp., Break-Free Div., 9999 Muirlands Blvd, Irvine, CA 92714/714-855-9911
Saunders Sptg. Gds., 338 Somerset, No. Plainfield, NJ 07060 (Sav-Bore)
Schultea's Gun String 67 Burress, Houston, TX 77022 (pocket-size rifle cleaning kit)
Schwab Industries, Inc., P.O. Box 1269, Sequim, WA 98382/206-683-2944 (Rust Guardit)
Service Armament, 689 Bergen Blvd., Ridgefield, NJ 07657 (Parker-Hale)
Silicote Corp., Box 359, Oshkosh, WI 54901 (Silicone cloths)
Silver Dollar Guns, P.O. Box 475, 10 Frances St., Franklin, NH 03235/603-934-3292 (Silicone oil)
Sportsmen's Labs., Inc., Box 732, Anoka, MN 55303 (Gun Life lube)
Taylor & Robbins, Box 164, Rixford, PA 16745 (Throat Saver)
Testing Systems, Inc., 220 Pegasus Ave., Northgale, NJ 07647/201-767-7300 (gun lube)
Texas Platers Supply Co., 2453 W. Five Mile Parkway, Dallas, TX 75233 (plating kit)
Totally Dependable Prods., Inc., (TDP Ind.), P.O. Box 277, Zieglerville, PA 19492/215-287-7851
Treso Inc., P.O. Box 4640, Pagosa Springs, CO 81157/303-264-2295 (mfg. Durango Gun Rod)
C. S. Van Gorden, 1815 Main St., Bloomer, WI 54724/715-568-2612 (Instant Blue)
WD-40 Co., P.O. Box 80607, San Diego, CA 92138-9021
West Coast Secoa, 3915 U S Hwy 98S, Lakeland, FL 33801 (Teflon coatings)
Williams Gun Sight, 7389 Lapeer Rd., Davison, MI 48423 (finish kit)
Winslow Arms Inc., P.O. Box 783, Camden, SC 29020 (refinishing kit)
Wisconsin Platers Supply Co., (See Texas Platers Supply Co.)
Woodstream Corp., P.O. Box 327, Lititz, PA 17543 (Mask)
Zip Aerosol Prods., 21320 Deering Court, Canoga Park, CA 91304

CUSTOM GUNSMITHS

Ahlman's Inc., R.R. 1, Box 20, Morristown, MN 55052/507-685-4244
Don Allen Inc., R.R. 4, Northfield, MN 55057/507-645-9216
Amrine's Gun Shop, 937 Luna Ave., Ojai, CA 93023
Andy's Gun Shop, A. Fleury, Burke, NY 12917
Antique Arms Co., D. F. Saunders, 1110 Cleveland Ave., Monett, MO 65708/417-235-6501 (Hawken copies)
R. J. Anton, 874 Olympic Dr., Waterloo, IA 50701/319-233-3666
Armament Gunsmithing Co., Inc., 525 Route 22, Hillside, NJ 07205/201-686-0960
John & Mary Armbrust, John's Gun Shop, 823 S. Union St., Mishawaka, IN 46544/219-255-0973
Armurier Hiptmayer, P.O. Box 136, Eastman, Que. JOE 1P0, Canada/514-297-2492
Armuriers Liegeois-Artisans Reunis "ALAR," rue Masset 27, 4300 Ans, Belgium
Atkinson Gun Co., P.O. Box 512, Prescott, AZ 86301
Ed von Atzigen, The Custom Shop, 890 Cochrane Crescent, Peterborough, Ont., K9H 5N3 Canada/705-742-6693
Creighton Audette, 19 Highland Circle, Springfield, VT 05156/802-885-2331
Richard W. Baber, Hanson's Gun Center, 1440 N. Hancock Ave., Colorado Springs, CO 80903/303-634-4220
Bain and Davis Sptg. Gds., 599 W. Las Tunas Dr., San Gabriel, CA 91776/213-284-2264
Stan Baker, 5303 Roosevelt Way NE, Seattle, WA 98105/206-522-4575 (shotgun specialist)
Joe J. Balickie, Rte. 2, Box 56-G, Apex, NC 27502
Barta's Gunsmithing, 10231 US Hwy., #10, Cato, WI 54206/414-732-4472
Roy L. Bauer, c/o C-D Miller Guns, St. Onge, SD 57779
George Beitzinger, 116-20 Atlantic Ave., Richmond Hill, NY 11419/212-846-2753
Bell's Custom Shop, David Norin, 3319 Mannheim Rd., Franklin Park, IL 60131/312-678-1900 (handguns)
Bennett Gun Works, 561 Delaware Ave., Delmar, NY 12054/518-439-1862
Gordon Bess, 708 River St., Canon City, CO 81212/303-275-1073
Al Biesen, 5021 Rosewood, Spokane, WA 99208/509-328-9340
Roger Biesen, W. 2039 Sinto Ave., Spokane, WA 99201
Billingsley & Brownell, Box 25, Wyarna, WY 82845/307-737-2468 (cust. rifles)
John Bivins, Jr., 200 Wicklow Rd., Winston-Salem, NC 27106
Bob's Gun & Tackle Shop, 746 Granby St., Norfolk, VA 23510/804-627-8311
Boone Mountain Trading Post, 118 Sunrise Rd., Saint Marys, PA 15857/814-834-4879
Victor Bortugno, Atlantic & Pacific Arms Co., 4859 Virginia Beach Blvd., Virginia Beach, VA 23462
Art Bourne, (See Guncraft)
Larry D. Brace, 771 Blackfoot Ave., Eugene, OR 97404/503-688-1278
Breckheimers, Rte. 69-A, Parish, NY 13131
L. H. Brown, Brown's Rifle Ranch, 1820 Airport Rd., Kalispell, MT 59901
Lenard M. Brownell, (See Billingsley & Brownell)
Ted Buckland, 361 Flagler Rd., Nordland, WA 98358/206-385-2142 (ML)
David Budin, Main St., Margaretville, NY 12455/914-568-4103
George Bunch, 7735 Garrison Rd., Hyattsville, MD 20784
Ida I. Burgess, Sam's Gun Shop, 25 Squam Rd., Rockport, MA 01966/617-546-6839 (bluing repairs)
Leo Bustani, P.O. Box 8125, W. Palm Beach, FL 33407
Cache La Poudre Rifleworks, 168 No. College Ave., Ft. Collins, CO 80524/303-482-6913 (cust. ML)
Cameron's Guns, 16690 W. 11th Ave., Golden, CO 80401
Lou Camilli, 4700 Oahu Dr. N.E., Albuquerque, NM 87111/505-293-5259 (ML)
Ralph L. Carter, Carter's Gun Shop, 225 G St., Penrose, CO 81240/303-372-6240
R. MacDonald Champlin, P.O. Box 693, Manchester, NH 03105/603-622-1420 (ML rifles and pistols)
Mark Chanlynn, Bighorn Trading Co., 1704-14th St., Boulder, CO 80302
Dave Chicoine, d/b/a Liberty A.S.P., P.O. Box 385, Cos Cob, CT 06807/203-357-1893
Claude Christopher, 1606 Berkley Rd., Greenville, NC 27834/919-756-0872 (ML)
Classic Arms Corp., P.O. Box 8, Palo Alto, CA 94302/415-321-7243
John Edward Clark, R.R. #4, Tottenham, Ont. L0G 1W0 Canada/416-936-2131 (ML)
Kenneth E. Clark, 18738 Highway 99, Madera, CA 93637/209-674-6016
Combat Weapons, 1265 Balsam St., Lakewood, CO 80215 (shotgun/riot)
John Corry, P.O. Box 109, Deerfield, IL 60015/312-541-6250 (English doubles & repairs)
The Country Gun Shoppe Ltd., 251 N. Front St., Monument, CO 80132
Raymond A. Cover, Rt. 1, Box 101A, Mineral Point, MO 63660/314-749-3783
Crest Carving Co., 14849 Dillow St., Westminster, CA 92683
Crocker, 1510 - 42nd St., Los Alamos, NM 87544 (rifles)
J. Lynn Crook, Rt. 7, Box 119-A, Lebanon, TN 37087/615-449-1930
Philip R. Crouthamel, 513 E. Baltimore, E. Lansdowne, PA 19050/215-623-5685
Curt Crum, c/o Dave Miller, 3131 E. Greenlee Rd., Tucson, AZ 85716/602-326-3117
Jim Cuthbert, 715 S. 5th St., Coos Bay, OR 97420
Dahl's Custom Stocks, Rt. 4, Box 558, Schofield Rd., Lake Geneva, WI 53147/414-248-2464
Dahl's Gunshop, 6947 King Ave., Route 4, Billings, MT 59102/406-656-6132
Homer L. Dangler, Box 254, Addison, MI 49220/517-547-6745 (Kentucky rifles; brochure $3)
Jack Dever, 8520 N.W. 90, Oklahoma City, OK 73132/405-721-6393
R. H. Devereaux, The Custom Gunsmith, 475 Trucky St., St. Igance, MI 49781/906-643-8625
Dominic DiStefano, 4303 Friar Lane, Colorado Springs, CO 80907
Dixon Muzzleloading Shop, Inc., RD #1, Box 175, Kempton, PA 19529/215-756-6271 (ML)

William Dixon, Buckhorn Gun Works, Rt. 4 Box 200, Rapid City, SD 57701/787-6289

Bill Dowtin, P.O. Box 72, Celina, TX 75009

Charles Duffy, Williams Lane, W. Hurley, NY 12491

David R. Dunlop, Rte. 1, Box 199, Rolla, ND 58367

D. W. Firearms, D. Wayne Schlumbaum, 1821 - 200th S.W., Alderwood Manor, WA 98036

John H. Eaton, 8516 James St., Upper Marlboro, MD 20870

Jere Eggleston, 400 Saluda Ave., Columbia, SC 29205/803-799-3402

Elko Arms, Dr. L. Kortz, 28 rue Ecole Moderne, B-7400 Soignies, H.T., Belgium

Bob Emmons, 238 Robson Rd., Grafton, OH 44044/216-458-5890

Bill English, 4411 S.W. 100th, Seattle, WA 98146/206-932-7345

Armas ERBI, S. coop., Avda. Eulogio Estarta, Elgoibar (Guipuzcoa), Spain

Ken Eyster, Heritage Gunsmiths Inc., 6441 Bishop Rd., Centerburg, OH 43011/614-625-6131

N. B. Fashingbauer, P.O. Box 366, Lac Du Flambeau, WI 54538/715-588-7116

Andy Fautheree, P.O. Box 863, Pagosa Springs, CO 81147/303-264-2892 (cust. ML)

Ted Fellowes, Beaver Lodge, 9245-16th Ave., S.W., Seattle, WA 98106/206-763-1698 (muzzleloaders)

Jack First Distributors Inc., 44633 Sierra Highway, Lancaster, CA 93534/805-945-6981

Fischer Sports Center, 221 E. Washington, Ann Arbor, MI 48104/313-769-4166

Clyde E. Fischer, P.O. Box 1437, Three Rivers, TX 78071/512-786-4125

Marshall F. Fish, Rt. 22 North, Westport, NY 12993

Jerry A. Fisher, 1244-4th Ave. West, Kalispell, MT 59901/406-755-7093

Flynn's Cust. Guns, P.O. Box 7461, Alexandria, LA 71306/318-445-7130

John Fordham, Box 9 Dial Star Rt., P.O. Box 1093, Blue Ridge, GA 30513/404-632-3602

Larry L. Forster, Box 212, Gwinner, ND 58040/701-678-2475

Jay Frazier, S.R. Box 8644, Bird Creek, AK 99540/903-653-8302

Freeland's Scope Stands, 3737—14th Ave., Rock Island, IL 61201/309-788-7449

Fredrick Gun Shop, 10 Elson Drive, Riverside, RI 02915/401-433-2805

R. L. Freshour, P.O. Box 2837, Texas City, TX 77590

Frontier Arms, Inc., 420 E. Riding Club Rd., Cheyenne, WY 82001

Frontier Shop & Gallery, The Depot, Main St., (Box 1805), Riverton, WY 82501/307-856-4498

Fuller Gunshop, Cooper Landing, AK 99572

Karl F. Furr, 76 East 350 No., Orem, UT 84057/801-225-2603

Garcia Natl. Gun Traders, Inc., 225 S.W. 22nd Ave., Miami, FL 33135

Jim Garrett, 2820 East NaniLoa Circle, Salt Lake City, UT 84117/801-277-6930

Gentry's Bozeman Gunsmith, David O. Gentry, 218 No. 7th, Bozeman, MT 59715/406-586-1405 (cust. Montana Mtn. Rifle)

Gentry's Gun Shop, 314 N. Hoffman, Belgarde, MT 59715

Edwin Gillman, R.R. 6, Box 195, Hanover, PA 17331/717-632-1662

Gilman-Mayfield, 752 N. Abby, Fresno, CA 93701/209-268-5085

Dale Goens, Box 224, Cedar Crest, NM 87008

Dave Good, 14906 Robinwood St., Lansing, MI 48906/517-321-5392

A. R. Goode, 12845 Catoctin Furnace Rd., Thurmont, MD 21788/301-271-2228

Goodling's Gunsmithing, R.D. #1, Box 1097, Spring Grove, PA 17362/717-225-3350

Gordie's Gun Shop, Gordon Mulholland, 1401 Fulton St., Streator, IL 61364/815-672-7202

Charles E. Grace, 10144 Elk Lake Rd., Williamsburg, MI 49690/616-264-9483

Roger M. Green, 315 S. 2nd St., P.O. Box 984, Glenrock, WY 82637/307-436-9804

Griffin & Howe, 589 Broadway, New York, NY 10012

H. L. "Pete" Grisel, 61912 Skyline View Dr., Bend, OR 97701/503-389-2649 (rifles)

Karl Guenther, 43-32 160th St., Flushing, NY 11372/212-461-7325

Gun City, 504 East Main Ave., Bismarck, ND 58501/701-223-2304

Guncraft, 117 W. Pipeline, Hurst, TX 76053/817-268-2887

Guncraft (Kamloops) Ltd., 127 Victoria St., Kamloops, B.C. V2C 1Z4, Canada/604-374-2151

Guncraft (Kelowna) Ltd., 1771 Harvey Ave., Kelowna, B.C. V1Y 6G4, Canada/604-860-8977

The Gunshop, R.D. Wallace, 320 Overland Rd., Prescott, AZ 86301

H & R Custom Gun Serv., 68 Passaic Dr., Hewitt, NJ 07421

H-S Precision, Inc., 112 N. Summit, Prescott, AZ 85302/602-445-0607

Paul Haberly, 2364 N. Neva, Chicago, IL 60635/312-889-1114

Martin Hagn, Herzogstandweg 41, 8113 Kochel a. See, W. Germany (s.s. actions & rifles)

Chas. E. Hammans, Box 788, Stuttgart, AR 72160

Dick Hanson, Hanson's Gun Center, 1440 No. Hancock, Colorado Springs, CO 80903/303-634-4220

Harkrader's Cust. Gun Shop, 825 Radford St., Christiansburg, VA 24073

Harp's Gun Repair Shop, 3349 Pio-Nono Circle, Macon, GA 31206 (cust. rifles)

Rob't W. Hart & Son Inc., 401 Montgomery St., Nescopeck, PA 18635/717-752-3481 (actions, stocks)

Hal Hartley, 147 Blairs Fork Rd., Lenoir, NC 28645

Hartmann & Weiss KG, Rahlstedter Str. 139, 2000 Hamburg 73, W. Germany

Hubert J. Hecht, Waffen-Hecht, 724-K St., Sacramento, CA 95814/916-448-1177

Edw. O. Hefti, 300 Fairview, College Station, TX 77840/715-846-4959

Stephen Heilmann, P.O. Box 657, Grass Valley, CA 95945/916-272-8758

Iver Henriksen, 1211 So. 2nd St. W., Missoula, MT 59801

Wm. Hobaugh, Box M, Philipsburg, MT 59858/406-859-3515

Richard Hodgson, 5589 Arapahoe, Unit 104, Boulder, CO 80301

George Hoenig, 6521 Morton Dr., Boise, ID 83705/208-375-1116

Dick Holland, 422 N.E. 6th St., Newport, OR 97365/503-265-7556

Hollingsworth's Guns, Route 1, Box 55B, Alvaton, KY 42122/502-842-3580

Hollis Gun Shop, 917 Rex St., Carlsbad, NM 88220/505-835-3782

Bill Holmes, Rt. 2, Box 242, Fayetteville, AR 72701/501-521-8958

Al Hunkeler, Buckskin Machine Works, 3235 So. 358th St., Auburn, WA 98002/206-927-5412 (ML)

Huntington's, P.O. Box 991, Oroville, CA 95965

Hyper-Single Precision SS Rifles, 520 E. Beaver, Jenks, OK 74037/918-299-2391

Independent Machine & Gun Shop, 1416 N. Hayes, Pocatello, ID 83201

Paul Jaeger, Inc. 211 Leedom St., Jenkintown, PA 19046/215-884-6920

R. L. Jamison, Jr., Route 4, Box 200, Moses Lake, WA 98837/206-762-2659

J. J. Jenkins Ent. Inc., 375 Pine Ave. No. 25, Goleta, CA 93017/805-967-1366

Jerry's Gun Shop, 9220 Ogden Ave., Brookfield, IL 60513/312-485-5200

Neal G. Johnson, Gunsmithing Inc., 111 Marvin Dr., Hampton, VA 23666/804-838-8091

Peter S. Johnson, The Orvis Co., Inc., Manchester, VT 05254/802-362-3622

Bruce Jones, 389 Calla Ave., Imperial Beach, CA 92032

Joseph & Associates, 4810 Riverbend Rd., Boulder, CO 80301/303-332-6720

Jos. Jurjevic, Gunshop, 605 Main St., Marble Falls, TX 78654/512-693-3012

Ken's Gun Specialties, K. Hunnell, Box 241, Lakeview, AR 72642/501-431-5606

Kennedy Gun Shop, Rte. 12, Box 21, Clarksville, TN 37040/615-647-6043

Monty Kennedy, P.O. Box 214, Kalispell, MT 59901/406-857-3596

Kennon's Custom Rifles, 5408 Biffle, Stone Mtn., GA 30083/404-469-9339

Stanley Kenvin, 5 Lakeville Lane, Plainview, NY 11803/516-931-0321

Kesselring Gun Shop, 400 Pacific Hiway No., Burlington, WA 98233/206-724-3113

Benjamin Kilham, Kilham & Co., Main St., Box 37, Lyme, NH 03768/603-795-4112

Don Klein Custom Guns, P.O. Box 277, Camp Douglas, WI 54618/608-427-6948

K. W. Kleinendorst, R.D., Box 113B, Hop Bottom, PA 18824/717-289-4687

Terry K. Kopp, Highway 13, Lexington, MO 64067/816-259-2636

J. Korzinek, R.D. #2, Box 73, Canton, PA 17724/717-673-8512 (riflesmith) (broch. $1.50)

L & W Casting Co., 5014 Freeman Rd. E., Puyallup, WA 98371

Sam Lair, 520 E. Beaver, Jenks, OK 74037/918-299-2391 (single shots)

Maynard Lambert, Kamas, UT 84036

Harry Lawson Co., 3328 N. Richey Blvd., Tucson, AZ 85716/602-326-1117

John G. Lawson, (The Sight Shop), 1802 E. Columbia, Tacoma, WA 98404/206-474-5465

Mark Lee, 2333 Emerson Ave., N., Minneapolis, MN 55411/612-521-0673

Bill Leeper, (See Guncraft)

Art LeFeuvre, 1003 Hazel Ave., Deerfield, IL 60015/312-945-0073

LeFever Arms Co. Inc., R.D. #1, Box 31, Lee Center, NY 13363/315-337-6722

Leland Firearms Co., 13 Mountain Ave., Llewellyn Park, West Orange, NJ 07052/201-964-7500 (shotguns)

Lenz Firearms Co., 310 River Rd., Eugene, OR 97404/503-689-6900

Al Lind, 7821—76th Ave. S.W., Tacoma, WA 98498/206-584-6363

Max J. Lindauer, R.R. 2, Box 27, Washington, MO 63090

Robt. L. Lindsay, J & B Enterprises, 9416 Emory Grove Rd., Gaithersburg, MD 20760/301-948-2941 (services only)

Ljutic Ind., Box 2117, Yakima, WA 98904 (shotguns)

Llanerch Gun Shop, 2800 Township Line, Upper Darby, PA 19082/215-789-5462

James W. Lofland, 2275 Larkin Rd., Boothwyn, PA 19061/215-485-0391 (SS rifles)

London Guns, 1528—20th St., Santa Monica, CA 90404/213-828-8486

McCann's Muzzle-Gun Works, Tom McCann, 200 Federal City Rd., Pennington, NJ 08534/609-737-1707 (ML)

John I. McCann, 2911 N. 5th St., Coeur d'Alene, ID 83814/208-667-3919

McCormick's Gun Bluing Service, 609 N.E. 104th Ave., Vancouver, WA 98664/206-256-0579

Stan McFarland, 2221 Idella Ct., Grand Junction, CO 81506/303-243-4704 (cust. rifles)

Bill McGuire, 1600 N. Eastmont Ave., East Wenatchee, WA 98801

R. J. Maberry, 511 So. K, Midland, TX 79701

Harold E. MacFarland, Route #4, Box 1249, Cottonwood, AZ 86326/602-634-5320

Frank E. Malin, Charles Boswell (Gunmakers) Ltd., 5 Queen St., Melbourne, Ont., Canada/519-289-2361

Monte Mandarino, 136 Fifth Ave. West, Kalispell, MT 59901/406-257-6208 (Penn. rifles)

Lowell Manley, 3684 Pine St., Deckerville, MI 48427/313-376-3665

Dale Marfell, 107 N. State St., Litchfield, IL 62056/217-327-3832

Marquart Precision Co., P.O. Box 1740, Prescott, AZ 86302/602-445-5646

Marsh Al's, Rt. #3, Box 729, Preston, ID 83263/208-852-2437

Elwyn H. Martin, Martin's Gun Shop, 937 S. Sheridan Blvd., Lakewood, CO 80226/303-922-2184

Mashburn Arms Co., 1218 N. Pennsylvania, Oklahoma City, OK 73107/405-236-5151 (special orders only)

Seely Masker, Custom Rifles, 261 Washington Ave., Pleasantville, NY 10570/914-769-2627

E. K. Matsuoka, 2801 Kinohou Place, Honolulu HI 96822/808-988-3008

Geo. E. Matthews & Son Inc., 10224 S. Paramount Blvd., Downey, CA 90241

Maurer Manchester Arms, Inc., 6858 Manchester Rd., Clinton, OH 44216/216-882-3133 (muzzleloaders)

John E. Maxson, Box 332, Dumas, TX 79029/806-935-5990 (high grade rifles)

Eric Meitzner, c/o Don Allen, Inc., Rt. 1, Timberlane, Northfield, MN 55057/507-645-9216

Miller Custom Rifles, 655 Dutton Ave., San Leandro, CA 94577/415-568-2447

Miller Gun Works, S. A. Miller, P.O. Box 7326, Tamuning, Guam 96911

C-D Miller Guns, Purl St., Box 260, St. Onge, SD 57779/605-578-1790

David Miller Co., 3131 E. Greenlee Rd., Tucson, AZ 85716/602-326-3117 (classic rifles)

Earl Milliron, 1249 N.E. 166th Ave., Portland, OR 97230/503-252-3725

Wm. Larkin Moore & Co., 31360 Via Colinas, Suite 109, Westlake Village, CA 91360/213-889-4160

Mitch Moschetti, P.O. Box 27065, Cromwell, CT 06416/203-632-2308

Mountain Bear Rifle Works, Inc., Wm. Scott Bickett, 100-B Ruritan Rd., Sterling, VA 22170/703-430-0420

Larry Mrock, R.F.D. 3, Box 207, Woodhill-Hooksett Rd., Bow, NH 03301/603-224-4096 (broch. $3)

Newman Gunshop, 119 Miller Rd., Agency, IA 52530/515-937-5775

Paul R. Nickels, Interwest Gun Service, P.O. Box 243, 52 N. 100 W., Providence, UT 84332/801-753-4260

Ted Nicklas, 5504 Hegel Rd., Goodrich, MI 48438/313-797-4493

William J. Nittler, 290 More Drive, Boulder Creek, CA 95006/408-338-3376 (shotgun repairs)

Jim Norman, Custom Gunstocks, 11230 Calenda Rd., San Diego, CA 92127/619-487-4173

Nu-Line Guns, 1053 Caulkshill Rd., Harvester, MO 63303/314-441-4500

O'Brien Rifle Co., 324 Tropicana No. 128, Las Vegas, NV 89109/702-736-6082 (17-cal. Rifles)

Vic Olson, 5002 Countryside Dr., Imperial, MO 63052/314-296-8086

The Orvis Co., Inc., Peter S. Johnson, Manchester, VT 05254/802-362-3622

Maurice Ottmar, Box 657, 113 East Fir, Coulee City, WA 99115/509-632-5717

Pachmayr Gun Works, 1220 S. Grand Ave., Los Angeles, CA 90015

Paterson Gunsmithing, 438 Main St., Paterson, NJ 07501/201-345-4100

C. R. Pedersen & Son, 2717 S. Pere Marquette, Ludington, MI 49431/616-843-2061

John Pell, 410 College Ave., Trinidad, CO 81082/303-846-9406

A. W. Peterson Gun Shop, 1693 Old Hwy. 441, Mt. Dora, FL 32757 (ML rifles, also)

Eugene T. Plante, Gene's Custom Guns, 3890 Hill Ave., P.O. Box 8534, White Bear Lake, MN 55110/612-429-5105

R. Neal Rice, 5152 Newton, Denver, CO 80221

Ridge Guncraft, Inc., 125 E. Tyrone Rd., Oak Ridge, TN 37830/615-483-4024

Rifle Ranch, Jim Wilkinson, Rte. 5, Prescott, AZ 86301/602-778-7501

Rifle Shop, Box M, Philipsburg, MT 59858

Wm. A. Roberts Jr., Rte. 4, Box 75, Athens, AL 35611/205-232-7027 (ML)

Bob Rogers Guns, P.O. Box 305, Franklin Grove, IL 61031/815-456-2685

Carl Roth, 4728 Pine Ridge Ave., Cheyenne, WY 82001/307-634-3958 (rust bluing)

Royal Arms, 1210 Bert Costa, El Cajon, CA 92020/619-448-5466

R.P.S. Gunshop, 11 So. Haskell, Central Point, OR 97502/503-664-5010

Murray F. Ruffino, c/o Neal G. Johnson, 111 Marvin Dr., Hampton, VA 23666/804-838-8091

Rush's Old Colonial Forge, 106 Wiltshire Rd., Baltimore, MD 21221 (Ky.-Pa. rifles)

Russell's Rifle Shop, Route 5, Box 92, Georgetown, TX 78626/512-778-5338 (gunsmith services)

Lewis B. Sanchez, Cumberland Knife & Gun Works, 5661 Bragg Blvd., Fayetteville, NC 28303

Sanders Custom Gun Serv., 2358 Tyler Lane, Louisville, KY 40205

Sandy's Custom Gunshop, Rte. #1, Box 20, Rockport, IL 62370/217-437-4241

Saratoga Arms Co., 1752 N. Pleasantview Rd., Pottstown, PA 19464/215-323-8326

Roy V. Schaefer, 965 W. Hilliard Lane, Eugene, OR 97404/503-688-4333

N. H. Schiffman Cust. Gun Serv., 963 Malibu, Pocatello, ID 83201

SGW, Inc. (formerly Schuetzen Gun Works), 624 Old Pacific Hwy. S.E., Olympia, WA 98503/206-456-3471

Schumaker's Gun Shop, Rte. 4, Box 500, Colville, WA 99114/509-684-4848

Schwartz Custom Guns, 9621 Coleman Rd., Haslett, MI 48840/517-339-8939

David W. Schwartz Custom Guns, 2505 Waller St., Eau Claire, WI 54701/715-832-1735

Schwarz's Gun Shop, 41-15th St., Wellsburg, WV 26070/304-737-0533

Shane's Gunsmithing, P.O. Box 321, Hwy. 51 So., Minocqua, WI 54548/715-356-9631

Shaw's, Finest in Guns, 9447 W. Lilac Rd., Escondido, CA 92025/619-728-7070

Shell Shack, 113 E. Main, Laurel, MT 59044

George H. Sheldon, P.O. Box 489, Franklin, NH 03235 (45 autos & M-1 carbines only)

Lynn Shelton Custom Rifles, 1516 Sherry Court, Elk City, OK 73644/405-225-0372

Shilen Rifles, Inc., 205 Metropark Blvd., Ennis, TX 75119/214-875-5318

Harold H. Shockley, 204 E. Farmington Rd., Hanna City, IL 61536/309-565-4524 (hot bluing & plating)

Shootin' Shop, Inc., 1169 Harlow Rd., Springfield, OR 97477/503-747-0175

Walter Shultz, 1752 N. Pleasantview Rd., Pottstown, PA 19464

Silver Dollar Guns, P.O. Box 475, 10 Frances St., Franklin, NH 03235/603-934-3292 (45 autos & M-1 carbines only)

Simmons Gun Spec., 700 Rogers Rd., Olathe, KS 66061

Simms Hardware Co., 2801 J St., Sacramento, CA 95816/916-442-3800

Sklany's Shop, 566 Birch Grove Dr., Kalispell, MT 59901/406-755-4527 (Ferguson rifle)

Markus Skosples, Ziffren's,224 W. Third, Davenport, IA 52801

Jerome F. Slezak, 1290 Marlowe, Lakewood (Cleveland), OH 44107/216-221-1668

John Smith, 912 Lincoln, Carpentersville, IL 60110

Snapp's Gunshop, 6911 E. Washington Rd., Clare, MI 48617/517-386-9226

Fred D. Speiser, 2229 Dearborn, Missoula, MT 59801/406-549-8133

Sport Service Center, 2364 N. Neva, Chicago, IL 60635

Sportsman's Bailiwick, 5306 Broadway, San Santonio, TX 78209/512-824-9649

Sportsmen's Equip. Co., 915 W. Washington, San Diego, CA 92103/619-296-1501

Sportsmen's Exchange & Western Gun Traders, Inc., P.O. Box 111, 560 S. "C" St., Oxnard, CA 93032/805-483-1917

Jess L. Stark, Stark Mach. Co., 12051 Stroud, Houston, TX 77072/713-498-5882

Ken Starnes, Rt. 1, Box 269, Scroggins, TX 75480/214-365-2312

Keith Stegall, Box 696, Gunnison, CO 81230

Victor W. Strawbridge, 6 Pineview Dr., Dover Point, Dover, NH 03820/603-742-0013

W. C. Strutz, Rifle Barrels, Inc., P.O. Box 611, Eagle River, WI 54521/715-479-4766

Suter's House of Guns, 332 N. Tejon, Colorado Springs, CO 80902

A. D. Swenson's 45 Shop, P.O. Box 606, Fallbrook, CA 92028

T-P Shop, 212 E. Houghton, West Branch, MI 48661

Tag Gun Works, 236 Main, Springfield, OR 97477/503-741-4118 (ML)

Talmage Ent., 43197 E. Whittier, Hemet, CA 92343

Taylor & Robbins, Box 164, Rixford, PA 16745

James A. Tertin, c/o Gander Mountain, P.O. Box 128 - Hwy. W, Wilmot, WI 53192/414-862-2344

Larry R. Thompson, Larry's Gun Shop, 440 E. Lake Ave., Watsonville, CA 95076/408-724-5328

Gordon A. Tibbitts, 1378 Lakewood Circle, Salt Lake City, UT 84117/801-272-4126

Daniel Titus, 872 Penn St., Bryn Mawr, PA 19010/215-525-8829

Tom's Gunshop, 4435 Central, Hot Springs, AR 71913/501-624-3856

Todd Trefts, 1290 Story Mill Rd., Bozeman, MT 59715/406-586-6003

Trinko's Gun Serv., 1406 E. Main, Watertown, WI 53094

Herb G. Troester's Accurizing Serv., 2292 W. 1000 North, Vernal, UT 84078/801-789-2158

Dennis A. "Doc" Ulrich, 2511 S. 57th Ave., Cicero, IL 60650

Brent Umberger, Sportsman's Haven, R.R. 4, Cambridge, OH 43725

Upper Missouri Trading Co., Inc., Box 181, Crofton, MO 68730

Chas. VanDyke Gunsmith Service, 201 Gatewood Cir. W., Burleson, TX 76028/817-295-7373 (shotgun & recoil pad specialist)

Milton Van Epps, Rt. 69-A, Parish, NY 13131/313-625-7498

Gil Van Horn, P.O. Box 207, Llano, CA 93544

J. W. Van Patten, Box 145, Foster Hill, Milford, PA 18337

Vic's Gun Refinishing, 6 Pineview Dr., Dover, NH 03820/603-742-0013

Walker Arms Co., Rt. 2, Box 73, Selma, AL 36701

Walker Arms Co., 127 N. Main St., Joplin, MO 64801

R. D. Wallace, 320 Overland Rd., Prescott, AZ 86301/602-445-0568

R. A. Wardrop, Box 245, 409 E. Marble St., Mechanicsburg, PA 17055

Weatherby's, 2781 Firestone Blvd., South Gate, CA 90280/213-569-7186

Weaver Arms Co., P.O. Box 8, Dexter, MO 63841/314-624-3218 (ambidextrous bolt action)

J. S. Weeks & Son, 4748 Bailey Rd., Dimondale, MI 48821 (custom rifles)

Terry Werth, 1203 Woodlawn Rd., Lincoln, IL 62656/217-732-3870

Charles Westbrook, 80 Park Creek Ct., Roswell, GA 30076

Jerry Wetherbee, 63470 Hamehook Rd., Bend, OR 97701/503-389-6080 (ML)

Cecil Weems, Box 657, Mineral Wells, TX 76067

Wells Sport Store, Fred Wells, 110 N. Summit St., Prescott, AZ 86301/602-445-3655

R. A. Wells, 3452 N. 1st, Racine, WI 53402

Robert G. West, 27211 Huey Lane, Eugene, OR 97402/503-689-6610

Western Gunstocks Mfg. Co., 550 Valencia School Rd., Aptos, CA 95003

Duane Wiebe, P.O. Box 497 Lotus, CA 95651/916-626-6240

M. Wiest & Son, 125 E. Tyrone Rd., Oak Ridge, TN 37830/615-483-4024

Dave Wills, 2776 Brevard Ave., Montgomery, AL 36109/205-272-8446

Williams Gun Sight Co., 7389 Lapeer Rd., Davison, MI 48423

Bob Williams, P.O. Box 143, Boonsboro, MD 21713

Williamson-Pate Gunsmith Service, 117 W. Pipeline, Hurst, TX 76053/817-268-2887

Thomas E. Wilson, 644 Spruce St., Boulder, CO 80302 (restorations)

Robert M. Winter, Box 484, Menno, SD 57045

J. David Yale, Ltd., 2618 Conowingo Rd., Bel Air, MD 21014/301-838-9479 (ML work)

Mike Yee, 4732-46th Ave. S.W., Seattle, WA 98116/206-935-3682

York County Gun Works, RR 4, Tottenham, Ont., LOG 1WO Canada (muzzleloaders)

Russ Zeeryp, 1601 Foard Dr., Lynn Ross Manor, Morristown, TN 37814

CUSTOM METALSMITHS

Billingsley & Brownell, Box 25, Wyarno, WY 82845/307-737-2468

Ted Blackburn, 85 E., 700 South, Springville, UT 84663/801-489-7341 (precision metalwork; steel trigger guard)

Gregg Boeke, Rte. 2, Cresco, IA 52136/319-547-3746

Larry D. Brace, 771 Blackfoot Ave., Eugene, OR 97404/503,688-1278

Tom Burgess, 180 McMannamy Draw, Kalispell, MT 59901/406-755-4110

Dave Cook, c/o Marble Arms Corp., 420 Industrial Park, Gladstone, MI 49837/906-425-2841

John H. Eaton, 8516 James St., Upper Marlboro, MD 20870

Ken Eyster Heritage Gunsmiths Inc., 6441 Bishop Rd., Centerburg, OH 43011/614-625-43031

Phil Fischer, 7333 N.E. Glisan, Portland, OR 97213/503-255-5678

Geo. M. Fullmer, 2499 Mavis St., Oakland, CA 94601/415-533-4193 (precise chambering—300 cals.)

Roger M. Green, P.O. Box 984, 315 S. 2nd St., Glenrock, WY 82637/307-436-9804

Harkrader's Custom Gun Shop, 825 Radford St., Christiansburg, VA 24073

Huntington's, P.O. Box 991, Oroville, CA 95965

Paul Jaeger, Inc., 211 Leedom St., Jenkintown, PA 19046/215-884-6920

Ken Jantz, Rt. 1, Sulphur, OK 73086/405-622-3790

Benjamin Kilham, Kilham & Co., Main St., Box 37, Lyme, NH 03768/603-795-4112

Terry K. Kopp, Highway 13, Lexington, MO 64067/816-259-2636

R. H. Lampert, Rt. 1, Box 61, Guthrie, MN 56451/218-854-7345

Mark Lee, 2333 Emerson Ave., N., Minneapolis, MN 55411/612-521-0673

Dave Talley, Rte. 10, Box 249-B, Easley, SC 29640/803-295-2012

Herman Waldron, Box 475, Pomeroy, WA 99347/509-843-1404

R. D. Wallace/The Gun Shop, 320 Overland Rd., Prescott, AZ 86301/602-445-0568

Edward S. Welty, R.D. 2, Box 25, Cheswick, PA 15024

Terry Werth, 1203 Woodlawn Rd., Lincoln, IL 62656/217-732-3870

John Westrom, Precise Firearm Finishing, 25 N.W. 44th Ave., Des Moines, IA 50313/515-288-8680

Dick Willis, 141 Shady Creek Rd., Rochester, NY 14623

DECOYS

Carry-Lite, Inc., 5203 W. Clinton Ave., Milwaukee, WI 53223

Deeks, Inc., P.O. Box 2309, Salt Lake City, UT 84114

Ted Devlet's Custom Purveyors, P.O. Box 886, Fort Lee, NJ 07024/201-886-0196

Flambeau Plastics Corp., P.O. Box 97, Middlefield, OH 44062/216-632-1631

G & H Decoy Mfg. Co., P.O. Box 1208, Henryetta, OK 74437/918-652-3314

Penn's Woods Products, Inc., 19 W. Pittsburgh St., Delmont, PA 15626/412-468-8311

Sports Haven Inc., P.O. Box 88231, Seattle, WA 98188

Tex Wirtz Ent., Inc., 1925 Hubbard St., Chicago, IL 60622

Woodstream Corp., P.O. Box 327, Lititz, PA 17543

ENGRAVERS, ENGRAVING TOOLS

Abominable Engineering, P.O. Box 1904, Flagstaff, AZ 86002/602-779-3025

John J. Adams, 47 Brown Ave., Mansfield, MA 02048/617-339-4613

Aurum Etchings, P.O. Box 401059, Garland, TX 75040/214-276-8551 (acid engraving)

Paolo Barbetti, c/o Stan's Gunshop, 53103 Roosevelt Way N.E., Seattle, WA 98105/206-522-4575

Billy R. Bates, 2905 Lynnwood Circle S.W., Decatur, AL 35603/205-355-3690

Joseph C. Bayer, 439 Sunset Ave., Sunset Hill Griggstown, RD 1, Princeton, NJ 08540/201-359-7283

Angelo Bee, 10703 Irondale Ave., Chatsworth, CA 91311/213-882-1567

Sid Bell Originals Inc., R.D. 2, Tully, NY 13159/607-842-6431

Robert Bernard, P.O. Box 93, Fordyce, AR 71742/501-352-5861

Weldon Bledsoe, 6812 Park Place Dr., Fort Worth, TX 76118/817-589-1704

Carl Bleile, Box 11285, Cincinnati, OH 45211/513-662-0802

C. Roger Bleile, Box 5112, Cincinnati, OH 45205/513-251-0249

Erich Boessler, Gun Engraving Intl., Am Vogeltal 3, 8732 Münnerstadt, W. Germany

Henry "Hank" Bonham, 218 Franklin Ave., Seaside Heights, NJ 08751

D. Boone Trading Co., P.O. Box 284, Brinnon, WA 98320/206-796-4330 (ivory, scrimshaw tools)

Bryan Bridges, 6350 E. Paseo San Andres, Tucson, AZ 85710

Dennis B. Brooker, RR #3, Indianola IA 50125

Burgess Vibrocrafters (BVI), Rt. 83, Grayslake, IL 60030

Byron Burgess, 1941 Nancy, Los Osos, CA 93402/805-528-3349

Brian V. Cannavaro, Box 173, Route 4, Smyrna, TN 37167/615-355-2028

Winston Churchill, Twenty Mile Stream Rd., RFD Box 29B, Proctorsville, VT 05153/802-226-7772

Ron Collings, See: John Corry

John Corry, P.O. Box 109, Deerfield, IL 60015/312-541-6250

Crocker Engraving, 1510 - 42nd St., Los Alamos, NM 87544

W. Daniel Cullity, 209 Old County Rd., East Sandwich, MA 02537/617-888-1147

Art A. Darakis, RD #2, Box 165D, Fredericksburg, OH 44627/216-695-4271

Tim Davis, 230 S. Main St., Eldorado, OH 45321

James R. DeMunck, 3012 English Rd., Rochester, NY 14616/716-225-0626 (SASE)

C. Gregory Dixon, RD 1, Box 175, Kempton, PA 19529/215-756-6271

Howard M. Dove, 52 Brook Rd., Enfield, CT 06082/203-749-9403

Michael W. Dubber, 3107 E. Mulberry, Evansville, IN 47714/812-476-4036

Ernest Dumoulin-Deleye, 8 rue Florent Boclinville, 4410 Herstal (Vottem), Belgium

Henri Dumoulin & Fils, rue du Tilleul 16, B-4411 Milmoret (Herstal), Belgium

Ken Eyster, Heritage Gunsmiths Inc., 6441 Bishop Rd., Centerburg, OH 43011/614-625-6131

John Fanzoi, P.O. Box 25, Ferlach, Austria 9170

Jacqueline Favre, 3111 So. Valley View Blvd., Suite B-214, Las Vegas, NV 89102/702-876-6278

Armi FERLIB, 46 Via Costa, 25063 Gardone V.T. (Brescia), Italy

L. R. Fliger, 3616 78th Ave. N., Brooklyn Park, MN 55443/612-566-3808

Heinrich H. Frank, 210 Meadow Rd., Whitefish, MT 59937/406-862-2681

Leonard Francolini, P.O. Box 32, West Granby, CT 06090/203-651-9422

J. R. French, 2633 Quail Valley, Irving TX 75060

GRS Corp., P.O. Box 748, Emporia, KS 66801/316-343-1084 (Gravermeister tool)

Donald Glaser, 1520 West St., Emporia, KS 66801

Eric Gold, Box 1904, Flagstaff, AZ 86002

Daniel Goodwin, P.O. Box 1619, Kalispell, MT 59901/406-752-1116

Howard V. Grant, P.O. Box 396, Lac Du Flambeau, WI 54538

Griffin & Howe, 589 Broadway, New York, NY 10012

The Gunshop, R. D. Wallace, 320 Overland Rd., Prescott, AZ 86301/602-445-0568

F. R. Gurney Engraving Method Ltd., 11440 Kingsway Ave., Edmonton, Alberta, Canada T5G 0X4/403-451-4097

Hand Engravers Supply Co., P.O. Box 3001, Overlook Branch, Dayton, OH 45431/513-426-6762

Frank E. Hendricks, Inc., Rt. 2, Box 189J, San Antonio, TX 78229/512-696-2876

Neil Hermsen, 505 Pepperidge Rd., Lewisville, NC 27023/919-945-9304

Heidemarie Hiptmayer, R.R. 112, #750, P.O. Box 136, Eastman, Que. J0E 1PO, Canada/514-297-2492

Ken Hunt, c/o Hunting World, Inc., 16 E. 53rd St., New York, NY 10022/212-755-3400

Ken Hurst/Firearms Engraving Co., Suite 200, Krise Building, Lynchburg, VA 24504/804-847-0636

Ralph W. Ingle, #4 Missing Link, Rossville, GA 30741/404-866-5589 (color broch. $3)

Paul Jaeger, Inc., 211 Leedom, Jenkintown, PA 19046/215-884-6920

Bill Johns, 1113 Nightingale, McAllen, TX 78501/512-682-2971

Ann N. Jordan, 733 Santa Lucia, Los Osos, CA 93402/805-528-7398 (scrimshaw)

Joseph, 100 Whitney Ave., New Haven, CT 06511

Steven Kamyk, 9 Grandview Dr., Westfield, MA 01085/413-568-0457

T. J. Kaye, P.O. Box 4, Telegraph, TX 76883

Lance Kelly, 1824 Royal Palm Dr., Edgewater, FL 32032/904-423-4933

Jim Kelso, Rt. 1, Box 5300, Worcester, VT 05682/802-229-4254

Kleinguenther's, P.O. Box 1261, Seguin, TX 78155

E. J. Koevenig, Engraving Service, P.O. Box 55, Hill City, SD 57745/605-574-2239

John Kudlas, 622-14th St. S.E., Rochester, MN 55901/507-288-5579

Ben Lane, Jr., 2118 Lipscomb St., Amarillo, TX 79109/806-372-3771

Beth Lane, Pontiac Gun Co., 815 N. Ladd, Pontiac, IL 61764/815-842-2402

Herb Larsen, 35276 Rockwell Dr., Abbotsford, B.C. V2S 4N4, Canada/604-853-5151

Terry Lazette, 142 N. Laurens Dr., Bolivar, OH 44612/216-874-4403

Franz Letschnig, Master-Engraver, 210 Chemin Marieville, Richelieu, P. Queb. J3L 3V8, Canada

W. Neal Lewis, 9 Bowers Dr., Newnan, GA 30263/404-251-3045

Frank Lindsay, 1326 Tenth Ave., Holdrege, NE 68949/308-995-4623

Steve Lindsay, P.O. Box 1413, Kearney, NE 68847/308-236-7885

London Guns, 1528-20th St., Santa Monica, CA 90404/213-828-8486

Ed. J. Machu, Jr., Sportsman's Bailiwick, 5306 Broadway, San Antonio, TX 78209

Harvey McBurnette, Rt. 4, Box 337, Piedmont, AL 36272

Lynton S.M. McKenzie, 6940 N. Alvernon Way, Tucson, AZ 85718/602-299-5090

Wm. H. Mains, 3111 S. Valley View Blvd., Suite B-214, Las Vegas, NV 89102/702-876-6278

Robert E. Maki, P.O. Box 947, Northbrook, IL 60062/312-724-8238

George Marek, 454 State Rd., Mendon, IL 62351/217-936-2687

Rudy Marek, Rt. 1, Box 1A, Banks, OR 97106

S. A. Miller, Miller Gun Works, P.O. Box 7326, Tamuning, Guam 96911

Cecil J. Mills, 2265 Sepulveda Way, Torrance, Ca 90501/213-328-8088

Frank Mittermeier, 3577 E. Tremont Ave., New York, NY 10465

Mitch Moschetti, P.O. Box 27065, Denver, CO 80227/303-936-1184

Gary N. Nelson, 975 Terrace Dr., Oakdale, CA 95361/209-847-4590

NgraveR Co., 879 Raymond Hill Rd., Oakdale, CT 06370/203-848-8031 (engr. tool)

New Orleans Jewelers Supply, 206 Chartres St., New Orleans, LA 70130/504-523-3839 (engr. tool)

Hans Obiltschnig, 12. November St. 7, 9170 Ferlach, Austria

Oker's Engraving, 365 Bell Rd., Bellford Mtn. Hts., P.O. Box 126, Shawnee, CO 80475/303-838-6042

Gale Overbey, 612 Azalea Ave., Richmond, VA 23227

Pachmayr Gun Works, Inc., 1220 S. Grand Ave., Los Angeles, CA 90015/213-748-7271

Rex Pedersen, C. R. Pedersen & Son, 2717 S. Pere Marquette, Ludington, MI 49431/616-843-2061

Marcello Pedini, 5 No. Jefferson Ave., Catskill, NY 12414/518-943-5257

Paul R. Piquette, 40 Royalton St., Chicopee, MA 01020/413-592-1057

Arthur Pitetti, Hawk Hollow Rd., Denver, NY 12421

Jeremy W. Potts, 912 Poplar St., Denver, CO 80220/303-355-5462

Wayne E. Potts, 912 Poplar St., Denver, CO 80220/303-355-5462

Ed Pranger, 1414-7th St., Anacortes, WA 98221/206-293-3488

E. C. Prudhomme, 513 Ricou-Brewster Bldg., Shreveport, LA 71101/318-425-8421

Puccinelli Design, 114 Gazania Ct., Novato, CA 94947/415-892-7977

Martin Rabeno, Spook Hollow Trading Co., Box 37F, RD #1, Ellenville, NY 12428/914-647-4567

Wayne Reno, c/o Blackhawk Mtn., P.O. Box 1983, Englewood, CO 80150/303-985-5447

Jim Riggs, 206 Azalea, Boerne, TX 78006/512-249-8567 (handguns)

Hans Rohner, Box 224, Niwot, CO 80544/303-652-2659

John R. Rohner, Sunshine Canyon, Boulder, CO 80302/303-444-3841

Richard D. Roy, 87 Lincoln Way, Windsor, CT 06095/203-688-0304

Joe Rundell, 6198 Frances Rd., Clio, MI 48420/313-687-0559

Robert P. Runge, 94 Grove St., Ilion, NY 13357/315-894-3036

Shaw-Leibowitz, Rt. 1, Box 421, New Cumberland, WV 26047/304-564-3108 (etchers)

George Sherwood, Box 735, Winchester, OR 97495/503-672-3159

Ben Shostle, The Gun Room, 1201 Burlington Dr., Muncie, IN 47302/317-282-9073

W. P. Sinclair, 36 South St., Warminster, Wiltsh. BA12 8DZ, England

Ron Skaggs, 508 W. Central, Princeton, IL 61536/815-872-1661

Russell J. Smith, 231 Springdale Rd., Westfield, MA 01085/413-568-5476

R. Spinale, 3415 Oakdale Ave., Lorain, OH 44055/216-246-5344

Ray Swan, 885 French Rd., Cheektowaga, NY 14227/716-668-3430

Robt. Swartley, 2800 Pine St., Napa, CA 94559

George W. Thiewes, 1846 Allen Lane, St. Charles, IL 60174/312-584-1383

Denise Thirion, Box 408, Graton, CA 95444/707-829-1876

Anthony Tuscano, 1473 Felton Rd., South Euclid, OH 44121

Robert Valade, Rte. 1, Box 30-A, Cove, OR 97824

John Vest, 6715 Shasta Way, Klamath Falls, OR 97601

Ray Viramontez, 4348 Newberry Ct., Dayton, OH 45432/513-426-6762

Louis Vrancken, 30-rue sur le bois, 4531 Argenteau (Liege), Belgium

Vernon G. Wagoner, 2325 E. Encanto, Mesa, AZ 85203/602-835-1307

R. D. Wallace/The Gun Shop, 320 Overland Rd., Prescott, AZ 86301/602-445-0568

Terry Wallace, 385 San Marino, Vallejo, CA 94590

Floyd E. Warren, 1273 State Rt. 305 N.E., Cortland, OH 44410/216-637-3429

David W. Weber Custom Engraving, 420 E. 57th, #125, Loveland, CO 80537/303-663-1182

Rachel Wells, 110 N. Summit St., Prescott, AZ 86301/602-445-3655

Sam Welch, Box 2152, Kodiak, AK 99615/907-486-5085

Claus Willig, c/o Paul Jaeger, Inc., 211 Leedom St., Jenkintown, PA 19046

Mel Wood, Star Route, Box 364, Elgin, AZ 85611/602-455-5541

GAME CALLS

Black Duck, 1737 Davis Ave., Whiting, IN 46394/219-659-2997

Burnham Bros., Box 669, 912 Main St., Marble Falls, TX 78654/512-693-3112

Call'N, Inc., 1615 Bartlett Rd., Memphis, TN 38134/901-372-1682

Faulk's, 616 18th St., Lake Charles, LA 70601

Lohman Mfg. Co., P.O. Box 220, Neosho, MO 64850/417-451-4438

Mallardtone Game Calls, 2901 16th St., Moline, IL 61265/309-762-8089

Phil. S. Olt Co., Box 550, Pekin, IL 61554/309-348-3633

Penn's Woods Products, Inc., 19 W. Pittsburgh St., Delmont, PA 15626

Scotch Game Call Co., Inc., 60 Main St., Oakfield, NY 14125

Johnny Stewart Game Calls, Box 7954, Waco, TX 76710/817-772-3261

Sure-Shot Game Calls, Inc., P.O. Box 816, Groves, TX 77619

Thomas Game Calls, P.O. Box 336, Winnsboro, TX 75494

Weems Wild Calls, P.O. Box 7261, Ft. Worth, TX 76111/817-531-1051

Tex Wirtz Ent., Inc., 1925 W. Hubbard St., Chicago, IL 60622

GUN PARTS, U.S. AND FOREIGN

Badger Shooter's Supply, 106 So. Harding, Owen, WI 54460/715-229-2101

Behlert Custom Guns, Inc., Box 227, Monmouth Junction, NJ 08852/201-329-2284 (handgun parts)

Dave Chicoine, d/b/a Liberty A.S.P., P.O. Box 385, Cos Cob, CT 06807/203-357-1893 (S&W only; ctlg. $5)

Philip R. Crouthamel, 513 E. Baltimore, E. Lansdowne, PA 19050/215-623-5685

Charles E. Duffy, Williams Lane, West Hurley, NY 12491

Christian Magazines, P.O. Box 184, Avoca, PA 18641

Federal Ordnance Inc., 1443 Potrero Ave., So. El Monte, CA 91733/213-350-4161

Jack First Distributors Inc., 44633 Sierra Highway, Lancaster, CA 93534/805-945-6981

Gun City, 504 E. Main, Bismarck, ND 58501/701-223-2304 (magazines, gun parts)

Gun-Tec, P.O. Box 8125, W. Palm Beach, FL 33407 (Win. mag. tubing; Win. 92 conversion parts)

Hansen & Co., 244 Old Post Rd., Southport, CT 06490/203-259-7337

Hunter's Haven, Zero Prince St., Alexandria, VA 22314

Walter H. Lodewick, 2816 N.E. Halsey, Portland, OR 97232/503-284-2554 (Winchester parts)

Marsh Al's, Rte. #3, Box 729, Preston, ID 83263/208-852-2437 (Contender rifle)

Michigan Armament, Inc., P.O. Box 146, 135 Sumner, Lake Elsinore, CA 92330/714-674-5750 (handgun parts; magazines)

Morgan Arms Co., Inc., 2999 So. Highland Dr., Las Vegas, NV 89109/702-737-5247 (MK-I kit)

Numrich Arms Co., West Hurley, NY 12491

Pacific Intl. Merch. Corp., 2215 "J" St., Sacramento, CA 95816/916-446-2737 (Vega 45 Colt mag.)

Potomac Arms Corp. (See Hunter's Haven)

Pre-64 Winchester Parts Co., P.O. Box 8125, West Palm Beach, FL 33407 (send stamped env. w. requ. list)

Martin B. Retting, Inc., 11029 Washington Blvd., Culver City, CA 90230/213-837-6111

Rock Island Armory, Inc., 111 E. Exchange St., Geneseo, IL 61254/309-944-2109

Royal Ordnance Works Ltd., P.O. Box 3245, Wilson, NC 27893/919-237-0515

Sarco, Inc., 323 Union St., Stirling, NJ 07980

Sherwood Intl. Export Corp., 18714 Parthenia St., Northridge, CA 91324

Simms, 2801 J St., Sacramento, CA 95816/916-442-3800

Clifford L. Smires, R.D. 1, Box 100, Columbus, NJ 08022/609-298-3158 (Mauser rifle parts)

Springfield Sporters Inc., R.D. 1, Penn Run, PA 15765/412-254-2626

Tomark Industries, 12043 S. Paramount Blvd., Downey, CA 90242 (Cherokee gun accessories)

Triple-K Mfg. Co., 568-6th Ave., San Diego, CA 92101/619-232-2066 (magazines, gun parts)

GUNS (Foreign)

Abercrombie & Fitch, 2302 Maxwell Lane, Houston, TX 77023 (Ferlib)

Action Arms, P.O. Box 9573, Philadelphia, PA 19124/215-744-0100

Alpha Arms, Inc., 1602 Stemmons, Suite "D," Carrollton, TX 75006/214-245-3115

American Arms International, P.O. Box 11717, Salt Lake City, UT 84147/801-531-0180

Anschutz (See Talo Distributors, Inc.)

AYA (Aguirre y Aranzabal) See IGI Domino or Wm. L. Moore (Spanish shotguns)

Armoury Inc., Rte. 202, New Preston, CT 06777

Armsport, Inc., 3590 N.W. 49th St., Miami, FL 33142/305-635-7850

Armurier Liegeois-Artisans Reunis (A.L.A.R.), 27, rue Lambert Masset, 4300 Ans, Belgium

Baikal International, 12 Fairview Terrace, Paramus, NJ 07652/201-845-8710 (Russian shotguns)

Pedro Arrizabalaga, Eibar, Spain

Beeman, Inc., 47 Paul Dr., San Rafael, CA 94903/415-472-7121 (FWB, Weihrauch, FAS firearms)

Benelli Armi, S.p.A., via della Staziona 50, 61029 Urbino, Italy

Beretta U.S.A., 17601 Indian Head Highway, Accokeek, MD 20607/301-283-2191

M. Braun, 32, rue Notre-Dame, 2240 Luxemburg, Luxemburg (all types)

Britarms/Berdan (Gunmakers Ltd.), see: Action Arms

Bretton, 21 Rue Clement Forissier, 42-St. Etienne, France

Browning (Gen. Offices), Rt. 1, Morgan, UT 84050/801-876-2711

Browning, (parts & service), Rt. 4, Box 624-B, Arnold, MO 63010/314-287-6800

Caprinus U.S.A., Inc., 100 Prospect St., Stamford, CT 06901/203-359-3773 (stainl. steel shotguns)

Century Arms Co., 3-5 Federal St., St. Albans, VT 05478

Champlin Firearms, Inc., Box 3191, Enid, OK 73701

Ets. Chapuis, 42380 St. Bonnet-le-Chateau, France (See R. Painter)

Christopher & Associates, 5636 San Fernando Rd., Glendale, CA 91202/213-725-7221 (SAM 180 rifle)

Clayco Sports Ltd., 625 W. Crawford, Clay Center, KS 67432/913-632-2180

Conco Arms, P.O. Box 159, Emmaus, PA 18049/215-967-5477 (Larona)

Connecticut Valley Arms Co., Saybrook Rd., Haddam, CT 06438 (CVA)

Walter Craig, Inc., Box 927, Selma, AL 36701/205-875-7989

Creighton & Warren, P.O. Box 15723, Nashville, TN 37215 (Krieghoff combination guns)

Morton Cundy & Son, Ltd., P.O. Box 315, Lakeside, MT 59922

Charles Daly (See Outdoor Sports HQ)

Dikar s. Coop. (See Connecticut Valley Arms Co.)

Dixie Gun Works, Inc., Hwy 51, South, Union City, TN 38261/901-885-0561 ("Kentucky" rifles)

Dynamit Nobel of America, Inc., 105 Stonehurst Court, Northvale, NJ 07647/201-767-1660 (Rottweil)

E.M.F. Co. Inc. (Early & Modern Firearms), 1900 E. Warner Ave. 1-D, Santa Ana, CA 92705/714-966-0202

Ernest Dumoulin-Deleye, 8 rue Florent Boclinville, 4410 Herstal (Vottem), Belgium

Henri Dumoulin & Fils, rue du Tilleul 16, B-4411 Milmort (Herstal), Belgium

Peter Dyson Ltd., 29-31 Church St., Honley, Huddersfield, Yorkshire HD7 2AH, England (accessories f. antique gun collectors)

Elko Arms, 28 rue Ecole Moderne, 7400 Soignes, Belgium

Euroarms of American, Inc., P.O. Box 3277, 1501 Lenoir Dr., Winchester, VA 22601/703-661-1863 (ML)

Excam Inc., 4480 E. 11 Ave., P.O. Box 3483, Hialeah, FL 33013

Famars, Abbiatico & Salvinelli, Via Cinelli 29, Gardone V.T. (Brescia), Italy 25063

J. Fanzoj, P.O. Box 25, Ferlach, Austria 9170

Armi FERLIB, 46 Via Costa, 25063 Gardone V.T. (Brescia), Italy

Ferlach (Austria) of North America, 2320 S.W. 57th Ave., Miami, FL 33155/305-266-3030

Firearms Imp. & Exp. Corp., (F.I.E.), P.O. Box 4866, Hialeah Lakes, Hialeah, FL 33014/305-685-5966

Flaig's Inc., Babcock Blvd. & Thompson Rd., Millvale, PA 15209/412-821-1717

Auguste Francotte & Cie, S.A., 61 Mont St. Martin, 4000 Liege, Belgium

Frankonia Jagd, Hofmann & Co., Postfach 6780, D-8700 Wurzburg 1, West Germany

Freeland's Scope Stands, Inc., 3737 14th Ave., Rock Island, IL 61201/309-788-7449

J. L. Galef & Son, Inc., 85 Chambers, New York, NY 10007

Renato Gamba, S.p.A., Gardone V.T. (Brescia), Italy (See Steyr Daimier Puch of America Corp.)

Armas Garbi, Urki #12, Eibar (Guipuzcoa) Spain (shotguns, See W. L. Moore)

Gastinne Renette, P.O. Box 3395, College Sta.; 225 Industrial Dr., Fredericksburg, VA 22401/703-898-1524

George Granger, 66 Cours Fauriel, 42 St. Etienne, France

Heckler & Koch Inc., 933 N. Kenmore St., Suite 218, Arlington, VA 22201/703-243-3700

A. D. Heller, Inc., Box 56, 2322 Grand Ave., Baldwin, NY 11510/516-868-6300

Heym, Friedr. Wilh., see: Paul Jaeger, Inc.

HOWCO Dist. Inc., 122 Lafayette Ave., Laurel, MD 20707/301-953-3301

Hunting World, 16 E. 53rd St., New York, NY 10022

IGI Domino Corp., 200 Madison Ave., New York, NY 10016/212-889-4889 (Breda)

Incor, Inc., P.O. Box 132, Addison, TX 75001/214-931-3500 (Cosmi auto shotg.)

Interarmco, See Interarms (Walther)

Interarms Ltd., 10 Prince St., Alexandria, VA 22313 (Mauser, Valmet M-62/S)

Italguns, Via Voltabo, 20090 Cusago (Milano), Italy

Paul Jaeger Inc., 211 Leedom St., Jenkintown, PA 19046/215-884-6920 (Heym)

Jenkins Imports Corp., 462 Stanford Pl., Santa Barbara, CA 93111/805-967-5092 (Gebrüder Merkel)

Kassnar Imports, 5480 Linglestown Rd., Harrisburg, PA 17110

Kawaguchiya Firearms, c/o La Paloma Marketing, 4500 E. Speedway Blvd., Suite 93, Tucson, AZ 85712/602-881-4750

Kimel Industries, Box 335, Matthews, NC 28105/704-821-7663

Kleinguenther's, P.O. Box 1261, Seguin, TX 78155

Knight & Knight, 5930 S.W. 48 St., Miami, FL 33155 (made-to-order only)

Krico-North America, P.O. Box 266, Bolton, Ont. LOP 1AO, Canada/416-880-5267

L. A. Distributors, 4 Centre Market Pl., New York, NY 10013
Lanber Arms of America, Inc., 377 Logan St., Adrian, MI 49221/518-263-7444 (Spanish o-u shotguns)
Lanchester U.S.A., Inc., P.O. Box 47332, Dallas, TX 75247/214-688-0073 (Sterling)
La Paloma Marketing, 4500 E. Speedway Blvd., Suite 93, Tucson, AZ 85712/602-881-4750 (K.F.C. shotguns)
Leland Firearms Co., 13 Mountain Ave., Llewellyn Park, West Orange, NJ 07052/201-325-3379 (Spanish shotguns)
Lever Arms Serv. Ltd., 572 Howe St., Vancouver, B.C., Canada V6C 2E3/604-685-6913
Liberty Arms Organization, Box 306, Montrose, CA 91020/213-248-0618
Llama (See Stoeger)
Magnum Research, Inc., 2825 Anthony Lane So., Minneapolis, MN 55418/612-781-3446 (Israeli Galil)
Mandall Shtg. Suppl. 7150 East 4th St., Scottsdale, AZ 85252/602-945-2553
Mannlicher (See Steyr Daimler Puch of Amer.)
Manu-Arm, B.P. No. 8, Veauche 42340, France
Manufrance, 100-Cours Fauriel, 42 St. Etienne, France
Marocchi USA Inc., 5939 W. 66th St., Bedford Park, IL 60638
Mauser-Werke Oberndorf, P. O. Box 1349, 7238 Oberndorf/Neckar, West Germany
Mendi s. coop. (See Connecticut Valley Arms Co.)
Merkuria, FTC, Argentinska 38, 17005 Prague 7, Czechoslovakia (BRNO)
Mitchell Arms Corp., 116 East 16th St., Costa Mesa, CA 92627/714-548-7701 (Uberti pistols)
Moore Supply Co., 3000 So. Main, Salt Lake City, UT 84115/801-487-1671 (Nikko)
Wm. Larkin Moore & Co., 31360 Via Colinas, Suite 109, Westlake Village, CA 91360/213-889-4160 (AYA, Garbi, Ferlib, Piotti, Lightwood, Perugini Visini)
Navy Arms Co., 689 Bergen Blvd., Ridgefield, NJ 07657
NIKKO (See Moore Supply)
O&L Guns Inc., P.O. Box 1146, Seminole, TX 79360/915-758-2933 (Wolverine rifle)
Odin International, Ltd., 818 Slaters Lane, Alexandria, VA 22314/703-339-8005 (Valmet/military types; Zastava)
Osborne Shooting Supplies, Rte. 3, Box 254H, Roscommon, MI 48653/517-821-5603 (Hammerli)
Outdoor Sports Headquarters, Inc., 2290 Arbor Blvd., Dayton, OH 45439/513-294-2811 (Charles Daly shotguns)
P.M. Air Services, Ltd., P.O. Box 1573, Costa Mesa, CA 92626
Pachmayr Gun Works, 1220 S. Grand Ave., Los Angeles, CA 90015
Pacific Intl. Merch. Corp., 2215 "J" St., Sacramento, CA 95816/916-446-2737
Painter Co., 2901 Oakhurst Ave., Austin, TX 78703/512-474-2824 (Chapuis)
Parker-Hale, Bisleyworks, Golden Hillock Rd., Sparbrook, Birmingham B11 2PZ, England
Perazzi U.S.A. Inc., 206 S. George St., Rome, NY 13440/315-337-8566
Picard-Fayolle, 42-rue du Vernay, 42100 Saint Etienne, France
Precise, 3 Chestnut, Suffern, NY 10901
Precision Sports, P.O. Box 219, 123 Lake St., Ithaca, NY 14850/607-273-2993 (BSA CF rifle; AYA side-by-side shotgun)
Puccinelli Co., 114 Gazania Ct., Novato, CA 94947/415-892-7977 (I.A.B., Rizzini, Bernardelli shotguns of Italy)
Quantetics Corp., Imp.-Exp. Div., 582 Somerset St. W., Ottawa, Ont. K1R 5K2 Canada/613-237-0242 (Unique pistols-Can. only)
RG Industries, Inc., 2485 N.W. 20th St., Miami, FL 33142 (Erma)
L. Joseph Rahn, Inc., 3940 Trade Center Dr., Ann Arbor, MI 48104/313-971-1195 (Garbi, Astra shotguns)
Ravizza Caccia Pesca Sport, s.p.a., Via Volta 60, 20090 Cusago, Italy
Richland Arms Co., 321 W. Adrian St., Blissfield, MI 49228
F. lli Rizzini, 25060 Magno di Gardone V.T., (Bs.) Italy
Rottweil, (See Dynamit Nobel of America)
Victor Sarasqueta, S.A., P.O. Box 25, 3 Victor Sarasqueta St., Eibar, Spain
Sarco, Inc., 323 Union St., Stirling, NJ 07980/201-647-3800
Savage Industries, Inc., Springdale Rd., Westfield, MA 01085/413-562-2361
Thad Scott, P.O. Box 412, Indianola, MS 38751 (Perugini Visini)
Security Arms Co., (See Heckler & Koch)
Service Armament, 689 Bergen Blvd., Ridgefield, NJ 07657 (Greener Harpoon Gun)
Sherwood Intl. Export Corp., 18714 Parthenia St., Northridge, CA 91324
Shore Galleries, Inc., 3318 W. Devon Ave., Chicago, IL 60645
Shotguns of Ulm, P.O. Box 253, Milltown, NJ 08850/201-297-0573
Sile Distributors, 7 Centre Market Pl., New York, NY 10013/212-925-4111
Simmons Spec., Inc., 700 Rogers Rd., Olathe, KS 66061
Sloan's Sprtg. Goods, Inc., 10 South St., Ridgefield, CT 06877
Franz Sodia Jagdgewehrfabrik, Schulhausgasse 14, 9170 Ferlach, (Kärnten) Austria
Solersport, 23629 7th Ave. West, Bothell, WA 98011/206-483-9607 (Unique)
Steyr-Daimler-Puch of America Corp., Gun South, Inc., Box 6607, 7605 Eastwood Mall, Birmingham, AL 35210 (rifles)
Stoeger Industries, 55 Ruta Ct., S. Hackensack, NJ 07606/201-440-2700
Talo Distributors, Inc., P.O. Box 177, Westfield, MA 01086/800-343-1111 (Anschutz)
Taurus International Mfg. Inc., P.O. Box 558567, Ludlam Br., Miami, FL 33155/305-662-2529
Toledo Armas, S.A., 922 S.W. Cashew Circle, Sebastian, FL 32958/305-589-2180
Tradewinds, Inc., P.O. Box 1191, Tacoma, WA 98401
Uberti, Aldo & Co., Via G. Carducci 41 or 39, Ponte Zanano (Brescia) Italy
Ignacio Ugartechea, Apartado 21, Eibar, Spain
Valmet Sporting Arms Div., 7 Westchester Plaza, Elmsford, NY 10523/914-347-4440 (sporting types)
Valor of Florida Corp., P.O. Box 10116, Hialeah, FL 33010/305-633-0127 (Valmet)
Ventura Imports, P.O. Box 2782, Seal Beach, CA 90740 (European shotguns)
Verney-Carron, B.P. 72, 54 Boulevard Thiers, 42002 St. Etienne Cedex, France
Perugini Visini & Co. s.r.l., Via Camprelle, 126, 25080 Nuvolera (Bs.), Italy

Waffen-Frankonia, see: Frankonia Jagd
Weatherby's, 2781 Firestone Blvd., So. Gate, CA 90280/213-569-7186
Winchester, Olin Corp., 120 Long Ridge Rd., Stamford, CT 06904
Fabio Zanotti di Stefano, Via XXV Aprile 1, 25063 Gardone V.T. (Brescia) Italy
Zavodi Crvena Zastava, 29 Novembra St., No. 12, Belgrade, Yugosl.
Antonio Zoli & Co., 39 Via Zanardelli, 25063 Gardone V.T., Brescia, Italy

GUNS & GUN PARTS, REPLICA AND ANTIQUE

Antique Gun Parts, Inc., 1118 S. Braddock Ave., Pittsburgh, PA 15218/412-241-1811 (ML)
Armoury Inc., Rte. 202, New Preston, CT 06777
Artistic Arms, Inc., Box 23, Hoagland, IN 46745 (Sharps-Borchardt replica)
Bob's Place, Box 283J, Clinton, IA 52732 (obsolete Winchester parts only)
Dave Chicoine, d/b/a Liberty A.S.P., P.O. Box 385, Cos Cob, CT 06807 (S&W only; ctlg. $5)
Collector's Armoury, Inc., 800 Slaters Lane, Alexandria, VA 22314/703-339-8005
Dixie Gun Works, Inc., Hwy 51, South, Union City, TN 38261/901-885-0561
Federal Ordnance Inc., 1443 Portrero Ave., So. El Monte, CA 91733/213-350-4161
Jack First Distributors, Inc., 44633 Sierra Hwy., Lancaster, CA 93534/805-945-6981
Fred Goodwin, Goodwin's Gun Shop, Sherman Mills, ME 04776/207-365-4451 (antique guns & parts)
Hansen & Co., 244 Old Post Rd., Southport, CT 06490/203-259-7337
Terry K. Kopp, Highway 13, Lexington, MO 64067/816-259-2636 (restoration & pts. 1890 & 1906 Winch.)
The House of Muskets, Inc., 120 N. Pagosa Blvd., Pagosa Springs, CO 81147/303-264-2295 (ML guns)
Log Cabin Sport Shop, 8010 Lafayette Rd., Lodi, OH 44254/216-948-1082 (ctlg. $30)
Edw. E. Lucas, 32 Garfield Ave., East Brunswick, NJ 08816/201-251-5526 (45/70 Springfield parts; some Sharps, Spencer parts)
Lyman Products Corp., Middlefield, CT 06455
Tommy Munsch Gunsmithing, Rt. 2, Box 248, Little Falls, MN 56345/612-632-5835 (parts list $1.50; oth. inq. SASE)
Numrich Arms Co., West Hurley, NY 12491
Replica Models, Inc., 800 Slaters Lane, Alexandria, VA 22314/703-339-8005
S&S Firearms, 88-21 Aubrey Ave., Glendale, NY 11385/212-497-1100
Sarco, Inc., 323 Union St., Stirling, NJ 07980/201-647-3800
C. H. Stoppler, 1426 Walton Ave., New York, NY 10452 (miniature guns)
Upper Missouri Trading Co., 3rd & Harold Sts., Crofton, NE 68730/402-388-4844
C. H. Weisz, Box 311, Arlington, VA 22210/703-243-9161
W. H. Wescombe, P.O. Box 488, Glencoe, CA 95232 (Rem. R.B. parts)

GUNS (Pellet)

Barnett International, Inc., P.O. Box 934, Odessa, FL 33556/813-847-1254
Beeman Precision Airguns, 47 Paul Dr., San Rafael, CA 94903/415-472-7121
Benjamin Air Rifle Co., 1525 So. 8th St., Louis, MO 63104
Crosman Airguns, 980 Turk Hill Rd., Fairport, NY 14450/716-223-6000
Daisy Mfg. Co., Rogers, AR 72756 (also Feinwerkbau)
Dynamit Nobel of America, Inc., 105 Stonehurst Ct., Northvale, NJ 07647/201-767-1660 (Dianawerk)
J. L. Galef & Son, Inc., 85 Chambers St., New York, NY 10007 (B.S.A.)
Great Lakes Airguns, 6175 So. Park Ave., Hamburg, NY 14075/716-648-6666
Harrington & Richardson Arms Co., Industrial Rowe, Gardner, MA 01440 (Webley)
Gil Hebard Guns, Box 1, Knoxville, IL 61448
Interarms, 10 Prince, Alexandria, VA 22313 (Walther)
Lanchester U.S.A., Inc., P.O. Box 47332, Dallas, TX 75247/214-688-0073 (Sterling HR-81)
Marksman Products, see: S/R Industries
Paragon Sales & Services, Inc., P.O. Box 2022, Joliet, IL 60434/815-725-9212
Phoenix Arms Co., Little London Rd., Horam, Nr. Heathfield, East Sussex TN21 OBJ, England (Jackal)
Power Line (See Daisy Mfg. Co.)
Precise, 3 Chestnut, Suffern, NY 10901
Precision Sports, P.O. Box 219, 123 Lake St., Ithaca, NY 14850/607-273-2993 (B.S.A.)
S/R Industries, Inc., 2133 Donguez St., P.O. Box 2983, Torrance, CA 90509/213-320-8004 (Marksman)
Service Armament, 689 Bergen Blvd., Ridgefield, NJ 07657 (Webley)
Sheridan Products, Inc., 3205 Sheridan, Racine, WI 53403
Smith & Wesson, 2100 Roosevelt Ave., Springfield, MA 01104
Target Airgun Supply, 11552 Knott St., Suite 2, Garden Grove, CA 92641/714-892-4473

GUNS, SURPLUS—PARTS AND AMMUNITION

Can Am Enterprises, Fruitland, Ont. LOR ILO, Canada/416-643-4357 (Enfield rifles)
Century Arms, Inc., 3-5 Federal St., St. Albans, VT 05478
Walter Craig, Inc., Box 927, Selma, AL 36701/205-875-7989
Eastern Firearms Co., 790 S. Arroyo Pkwy., Pasadena, CA 91105
J. M. Emringer, Armurier, 3A, rue de Bettembourg, L-3346 Leudelange, Grand-Duchy of Luxemburg

Garcia National Gun Traders, 225 S.W. 22nd, Miami, FL 33135
Hansen Cartridge Co., 246 Old Post Rd., Southport, CT 06490/203-259-5424
Lever Arms Serv. Ltd., 572 Howe St., Vancouver, B.C., Canada V6C 2E3/604-685-6913
Paragon Sales & Services, Inc., P.O. Box 2022, Joliet, IL 60434 (ammunition)
Sarco, Inc., 323 Union St., Stirling, NJ 07980/201-647-3800
Service Armament Co., 689 Bergen Blvd., Ridgefield, NJ 07657
Sherwood Intl. Export Corp., 18714 Parthenia St., Northridge, CA 91324
Springfield Sporters Inc., R.D. 1, Penn Run, PA 15765/412-254-2626

GUNS, U.S.-made

AMT (Arcadia Machine & Tool), 536 N. Vincent Ave., Covina, CA 91722/213-915-7803
Accuracy Systems, Inc., 2105 S. Hardy Dr., Tempe, AZ 85282
Advantage Arms USA, Inc., 840 Hampden Ave., St. Paul, MN 55114/612-644-5197
Alpha Arms (See H. Koon, Inc.)
American Derringer Corp., 127 N. Lacy Dr., Waco, TX 76705/817-799-9111
ArmaLite, 118 E. 16th St., Costa Mesa, CA 92627
Armament Systems and Procedures, Inc., Box 356, Appleton, WI 54912/414-731-8893 (ASP pistol)
Arminex, 7882 E. Gray Rd., Scottsdale Airpark, Scottsdale, AZ 85260/602-998-5774 (Excalibur s.a. pistol)
Arm Tech, Armament Technologies Inc., 240 Sargent Dr., New Haven, CT 06511/203-562-2543 (22-cal. derringers)
Arnett Guns (See Gary DelSignore Weaponry)
Artistic Arms, Inc.,Box 23, Hoagland, IN 46745 (Sharps-Borchardt)
Artistic Firearms Corp., John Otteman, 4005 Hecker Pass Hwy., Gilroy, CA 95020/408-842-4278 (A.F.C. Comm. Rife 1881-1981)
Auto-Ordnance Corp., Box ZG, West Hurley, NY 12491
Bauer Firearms, 34750 Klein Ave., Fraser, MI 48026
Bighorn Rifle Co., P.O. Box 892, Orem, UT 84057/801-224-2764
Bogun Inc., 15125 Garfield Ave., P.O. Box 740, Paramount, CA 90723/213-531-2211 (conv. rifle/shotgun)
Brown Precision Co., P.O. Box 270W; 7786 Molinos Ave., Los Molinos, CA 96055/916-384-2506 (High Country rifle)
Browning (Gen. Offices), Rt. 1, Morgan, UT 84050/801-876-2711
Browning (Parts & Service), Rt. 4, Box 624-B, Arnold, MO 63010/314-287-6800
Buffalo Arms Inc., 10 Tonawanda St., Tonawanda, NY 14150/716-693-7970
Bushmaster Firearms Co., 309 Cumberland Ave., Portland ME 04101/207-775-3339 (police handgun)
CB Arms, Inc., 65 Hathaway Court, Pittsburgh, PA 15235/412-795-4621 (Double Deuce h'gun)
Challanger Mfg. Corp., 118 Pearl St., Mt. Vernon, NY 10550 (Hopkins & Allen)
Champlin Firearms, Inc., Box 3191, Enid, OK 73701
Charter Arms Corp., 430 Sniffens Ln., Stratford, CT 06497
Chipmunk Manufacturing Inc., 114 E. Jackson, Medford, OR 97501/503-826-7329 (22 S.S. rifle)
Classic Arms, 815-22nd St., Union City, NJ 08757/201-863-1493
Colt Firearms, P.O. Box 1868, Hartford, CT 06102/203-236-6311
Commando Arms, Inc., Box 10214, Knoxville, TN 37919
Coonan Arms, Inc., 326 Chester St., St. Paul, MN 55107/612-224-1702 (357 Mag. Autom.)
Crown City Arms, P.O. Box 1126, Cortland, NY 13045/607-753-8238 (45 auto handgun)
Cumberland Arms, Rt. 1, Shafer Rd., Blanton Chapel, Manchester, TN 37355
Davis Industries, 13748 Arapahoe Pl., Chino, CA 91710/714-591-4727 (derringer)
Leonard Day & Co., P.O. Box 723, East Hampton, MA 01027/413-527-7990 (ML)
Gary DelSignore Weaponry, 3675 Cottonwood, Cedar City, UT 84720/801-586-2505 (Arnett Guns)
Demro Products Inc., 345 Progress Dr., Manchester, CT. 06040/203-649-4444 (wasp, Tac guns)
Detonics 45 Associates, 2500 Seattle Tower, Seattle, WA 98101 (auto pistol)
Deutsch Waffen und Maschine Fabriken, Inc., 113 N. 2nd St., Whitewater, WI 53190/414-473-4848 (Ugly gun)
Dornaus & Dixon Enterprises, Inc., 15896 Manufacture Lane, Huntingdon Beach, CA 92649/714-891-5090
DuBiel Arms Co., 1724 Baker Rd., Sherman, TX 75090/214-893-7313
El Dorado Arms, 35 Gilpin Ave., Happauge, NY 11787/516-234-0212
Excalibur (See Arminex)
FTL Marketing Corp., 12521-3 Oxnard St., No. Hollywood, CA 91601/213-985-2939
Falling Block Works, P.O. Box 3087, Fairfax, VA 22038/703-476-0043
Firearms Imp. & Exp. Corp., P.O. Box 4866, Hialeah Lakes, Hialeah, FL 33014/305-685-5966 (FIE)
Fraser Firearms Corp., 34575 Commerce Rd., Fraser, MI 48026/313-293-9545
Freedom Arms Co., Freedom, WY 83120 (mini revolver, Casull rev.)
Golden Age Arms Co., 14 W. Winter St., Delaware, OH 43015
Franklin C. Green, 530 W. Oak Grove Rd., Montrose, CO 81401/303-249-7003 (Green Free Pistol)
Harrington & Richardson, Industrial Rowe, Gardner, MA 01440
Hatfield Rifle Works, 2028 Frederick Ave., St. Joseph, MO 64501/816-233-9106 (squirrel rifle)
Hawken Armory, P.O. Box 2604, Hot Springs, AR 71901/501-268-8296 (ML)

A.D. Heller, Inc., Box 268, Grand Ave., Baldwin, NY 11510
Heritage Arms Corp., 11281 Leo Lane, Dallas, TX 75229/214-247-6420
High Standard Sporting Firearms, 31 Prestige Park Circle, East Hartford, CT 06108
Holmes Firearms Corp., Rte. 6, Box 242, Fayetteville, AR 72701
Hopkins & Allen Arms, 3 Ethel Ave., P.O. Box 217, Hawthorne, NJ 07507/201-427-1165 (ML)
Hyper-Single Precision SS Rifles, 520 E. Beaver, Jenks, OK 74037/918-299-2391
Ithaca Gun Co., Ithaca, NY 14850
Iver Johnson, 2202 Redmond Rd., Jacksonville, AR 72076/501-982-9491
Paul Jaeger, Inc., 211 Leedom St., Jenkintown, Pa 19046
Jennings Firearms, 4510 Carter Ct., Chino, CA 91710/714-591-3921
Kimber of Oregon, Inc., 9039 S.E. Jannsen Rd., Clackamas, OR 97015/503-656-1704
Kimel Industries, Box 335, Matthews, NC 28105/704-821-7663
H. Koon, Inc., 12523 Valley Branch, Dallas, TX 75234/214-243-8124
Krupp KK Arms Co,, Star Route, Box 671, Kerrville, TX 78028/512-257-4718 (handguns)
L.A.R. Manufacturing Co., 4133 West Farm Rd., West Jordan, UT 84084/801-255-7106 (Grizzly Win Mag pistol)
Ljutic Ind., Inc., P.O. Box 2117, 918 N. 5th Ave., Yakima, WA 98902/509-248-0476 (Mono-Gun)
Lone Star Armaments, Inc., 1701 No. Greenville Ave., Suite 202, Richardson, TX 75081 (semi-auto pistols)
M & N Distributors, 23535 Telo St., Torrance, CA 90505/213-530-9000 (Budischowsky)
MS Safari Arms, P.O. Box 23370, Phoenix, AZ 85062/602-269-7283
Marlin Firearms Co., 100 Kenna Drive, New Haven, CT 06473
Matteson Firearms Inc., Otsego Rd., Canajoharie, NY 13317/607-264-3744 (SS rifles)
Merrill Co., 704 E. Commonwealth, Fullerton, CA 92631/714-879-8922
Michigan Armament, Inc., P.O. Box 146, Lake Elsinore, CA 92330/714-674-5750 (pistols)
Michigan Arms Corp., 479 W. 14 Mile Rd., Clawson, MI 48017/313-435-0160 (ML)
The M.O.A. Corp., 110 Front St., Dayton, OH 45402/513-223-6401 (Maximum pistol)
O.F. Mossberg & Sons, Inc., 7 Grasso St., No. Haven, CT 06473
Mowrey Gun Works, Box 38, Iowa Park, TX 76367
Navy Arms Co., 689 Bergen Blvd., Ridgefield, NJ 07657
North American Arms, P.O. Box 280, Spanish Fork, UT 84660/801-798-9893
Numrich Arms Corp., W. Hurley, NY 12491
ODI, Inc., 124A Greenwood Ave., Midland Park, NJ 07432/201-444-4557
Pecos Valley Armory, 1022 So. Canyon, Carlsbad, NM 88220/505-887-6023 (ML)
Provider Arms, Inc., 261 Haglund Dr., Chesterton, IN 46304/219-879-5590 (ML Predator rifle)
R.B. Industries, Ltd. (See Fraser Firearms Corp.)
R G Industries, 2485 N.W. 20th St., SE., Miami, FL 33142
Randall Manufacturing, 7965 San Fernando Rd., Sun Valley, CA 91352/213-875-2045
Raven Arms, 1300 Bixby Dr., Industry, CA 91745/213-961-2511 (P-25 pistols)
Remington Arms Co., 939 Barnum Ave., P.O. Box #1939, Bridgeport, CT 06601
Rock Pistol Mfg., Inc., 704 E. Commonwealth, Fullerton, CA 92631/714-870-8530 (Merrill pistol, etc.)
Ruger (See Sturm, Ruger & Co.)
Savage Industries, Inc., Springdale Rd., Westfield, MA 01085/413-562-2361
Sceptre, Inc., P.O. Box 1282, Marietta, GA 30061/404-428-5513
Semmerling Corp., P.O. Box 400, Newton, MA 02160
Serrifile, Inc., 210 E. Avjenue L, Lancaster, CA 93535/805-945-0713 (derringer)
Shepherd & Turpin Dist. Co., P.Q. Box 40, Washington, UT 84780/801-635-2001
Shiloh Products, 37 Potter St., Farmingdale, NY 11735 (Sharps)
Six Enterprises, 6564 Hidden Creek Dr., Dan Jose, CA 95120/408-268-8296 (Timberliner rifle)
Smith & Wesson, Inc., 2100 Roosevelt Ave., Springfield, MA 01101
Springfield Armory, 111 E. Exchange St., Geneseo, IL 61254
SSK Industries, Rt. 1, Della Dr., Bloomingdale, OH 43910/614-264-0176
Sterling Arms Corp., 211 Grand St., Lockport, NY 14094/716-434-6631
Sturm, Ruger & Co., Southport, CT 06490
Tennessee Valley Arms, P.O. Box 2022, Union City, TN 38261/901-885-4456
Texas Gun & Machine Co., P.O. Box 2837, Texas City, TX 77590/713-945-0070 (Texas rifles)
Thompson-Center Arms, Box 2405, Rochester, NH 03867
Trail Guns Armory, 1634 E. Main St., League City, TX 77573 (muzzleloaders)
Trapper Gun, Inc., 18717 E. 14 Mile Rd., Fraser, MI 48026/313-792-0133 (handguns)
United Sporting Arms of Arizona, Inc, 2021 E. 14th St., Tucson, AZ 85719/602-632-4001 (handguns)
U.S. Repeating Arms Co., P.O. Box 30-300, New Haven, CT 06511/203-789-5000
Universal Firearms, 3740 E. 10th Ct., Hialeah, FL 33013
Weatherby's, 2781 E. Firestone Blvd., South Gate, CA 90280
Weaver Arms Corp., 344 No. Vinewood St., Escondido, CA 92026/714-745-4342
WSI, P.O. Box 66, Youngstown, OH 44501/216-743-9666 (9mm Viking)
Dan Wesson Arms, 293 So. Main St., Monson, MA 01057
Western Arms/Allen Arms, 1107 Pen Rd., Santa Fe, NM 87501/505-982-3399 (ML)
Wichita Arms, 444 Ellis, Wichita, KS 67211/316-265-0661
Wildey Firearms Co., Inc., P.O. Box 4264, New Windsor, NY 12250/203-272-7215
Wilkinson Arms, Rte. #2, Box 2166, Parma, ID 83660/208-722-6771
Winchester, (See U.S. Repeating Arms)

GUNSMITHS, CUSTOM (see Custom Gunsmiths)

GUNSMITHS, HANDGUN (see Pistolsmiths)

GUNSMITH SCHOOLS

Colorado School of Trades, 1575 Hoyt, Lakewood, CO 80215/303-233-4697
Lassen Community College, P.O. Box 3000, Hiway 139, Susanville, CA 96130/916-257-6161
Modern Gun Repair School, 2538 No. 8th St., Phoenix, AZ 85006/602-990-8346 (home study)
Montgomery Technical College, P.O. Drawer 487, Troy, NC 27371/919-572-3691
Murray State College, Gunsmithing Program, Tishomingo, OK 73460/405-371-2371
North American School of Firearms, Curriculum Development Ctr., 4401 Birch St., Newport Beach, CA 92663/714-546-7360 (correspondence)
North American School of Firearms, Education Service Center, Oak & Pawnee St., Scranton, PA 18515/717-342-7701
Oregon Institute of Technology, Small Arms Dept., Klamath Falls, OR 97601
Penn. Gunsmith School, 812 Ohio River Blvd., Avalon, Pittsburgh, PA 15202
Pine Technical Institute, 1100 Fourth St., Pine City, MN 55063/612-629-6764
Police Sciences Institute, 4401 Birch St., Newport Beach, CA 92660/714-546-7360 (General Law Enforcement Course)
Southeastern Community College, Gunsmithing Dept., Drawer F, West Burlington, IA 52655/319-752-2731
Trinidad State Junior College, 600 Prospect, Trinidad, CO 81082/303-846-5621
Yavapai College, 1100 East Sheldon St., Prescott, AZ 86301/602-445-7300

GUNSMITH SUPPLIES, TOOLS, SERVICES

Acoustic Trap Co., 34 Bay Ridge Ave., Brooklyn, NY 11220/212-745-9311 (test bullet trap)
Albright Prod. Co., P. O. Box 1144, Portola, CA 96122 (trap buttplates)
Alley Supply Co., Carson Valley Industrial Park, P.O. Box 848, Gardnerville, NV 89410/702-782-3800 (JET line lathes, mills, etc.)
Ametek, Hunter Spring Div., One Spring Ave., Hatfield, PA 19440/215-822-2971 (trigger gauge)
Anderson Mfg. Co., Union Gap Sta., P.O. Box 3120, Yakima, WA 98903/509-453-2349 (tang safe)
Answer Stocking Systems, 113 N. 2nd St., Whitewater, WI 53190/414-473-4848 (urethane hammers, vice jaws, etc.)
Armite Labs., 1845 Randolph St., Los Angeles, CA 90001/213-587-7744 (pen oiler)
B-Square Co., Box 11281, Ft. Worth, TX 76110
Jim Baiar, 490 Halfmoon Rd., Columbia Falls, MT 59912 (hex screws)
Behlert Custom Guns, Inc., Box 227, Monmouth Junction, NJ 08852/201-329-2284
Dennis M. Bellm Gunsmithing, Inc., dba P.O. Ackley Rifle Barrels, 2376 S. Redwood Rd., Salt Lake City, UT 84119/801-974-0697 (rifles only)
Al Biesen, W. 2039 Sinto Ave., Spokane, WA 99201 (grip caps, buttplates)
Roger Biesen, 5021 W. Rosewood, Spokane, WA 99208/509-328-9340 (grip caps, buttplates)
Billingsley & Brownell, Box 25, Wyarno, WY 82845/307-737-2468 (cust. grip caps, bolt handle, etc.)
Blue Ridge Machine and Tool, P.O. Box 536, Hurricane, WV 25526/304-562-3538 (machinery, tools, shop suppl.)
Bonanza Sports Mfg. Co., 412 Western Ave., Faribault, MN 55021/507-332-7153
Briganti Custom Gun-Smithing, P.O. Box 56, 475-Route 32, Highland Mills, NY 10930/914-928-9816 (cold rust bluing, hand polishing, metal work)
Brookstone Co., 125 Vose Farm Rd., Peterborough, NH 03458
Brownell's, Inc., Rt. 2, Box 1, Montezuma, IA 50171/515-623-5401
Lenard M. Brownell (See Billingsley & Brownell)
W.E. Brownell Co., 1852 Alessandro Trail, Vista, CA 92083 (checkering tools)
Burgess Vibrocrafters, Inc. (BVI), Rte. 83, Grayslake, IL 60030
M.H. Canjar, 500 E. 45th Denver, CO 80216/303-623-5777 (triggers, etc.)
Chapman Mfg. Co., Rte. 17 at Saw Mill Rd., Durham, CT 06422
Chase Chemical Corp., 3527 Smallman St., Pittsburgh, PA 15201/412-681-6544 (Chubb Multigauge for shotguns)
Chicago Wheel & Mfg. Co., 1101 W. Monroe St., Chicago, IL 60607/312-226-8155 (Handee grinders)
Dave Chicoine, d/b/a Liberty A.S.P., P.O. Box 385, Cos Cob, CT 06807/203-357-1893 (spl. S&W tools)
Christy Gun Works, 875-57th St., Sacramento, CA 95819
Classic Arms Corp., P.O. Box 8, Palo Alto, CA 94302/415-321-7243 (floorplates, grip caps)
Clover Mfg. Co., 139 Woodward Ave., Norwalk, CT 06856/800-243 6492 (Clover compound)
Clymer Mfg. Co., Inc., 14241 W. 11 Mile Rd., Oak Park, MI 48237/313-541-5533 (reamers)
Dave Cook, 720 Hancock Ave., Hancock, MI 49930 (metalsmithing only)
Dayton-Traister Co., 9322-900th West, P.O. Box 593, Oak Harbor, WA 98277/206-675-5375 (triggers)
Delta Arms Sporting Goods, Highway 82 West, Indianola, MS 38751/601-887-5566 (Lightwood/England)

Dem-Bart Checkering Tools, Inc., 6807 Hiway #2, Snohomish, WA 98290/206-568-7536
Dremel Mfg. Co., 4915-21st St., Racine, WI 53406 (grinders)
Chas. E. Duffy, Williams Lane, West Hurley, NY 12491
Peter Dyson Ltd., 29-31 Church St., Honley, Huddersfield, Yorksh. HD7 2AH, England (accessories f. antique gun coll.)
Edmund Scientific Co., 101 E. Glouster Pike, Barrington, NJ 08007
Emco-Lux, 2050 Fairwood Ave., P.O. Box 07861, Columbus, OH 43207/614-445-8328
Jack First Distributors, Inc., 44633 Sierra Hwy., Lancaster, CA 93534/805-945-6981
Forster Products, Inc., 82 E. Lanark Ave., Lanark, IL 61046/815-493-6360
Francis Tool Co., (f'ly Keith Francis Inc.), P.O. Box 7861, Eugene, OR 97401/503-746-4831 (reamers)
G. R. S. Corp., P.O. Box 748, Emporia, KS 66801/316-343-1084 (Grarermeister)
Gilmore Pattern Works, P.O. Box 50084, Tulsa, OK 74150/918-245-9627 (Wagner safe-T-planer)
Glendo Corp., P.O. Box 1153, Emporia, KS 66801/316-343-1084 (Accu-Finish tool)
Gold Lode, Inc., 1305 Remington Rd., Suite A, Schaumburg, IL 60195 (gold inlay kit)
Grace Metal Prod., 115 Ames St., Elk Rapids, MI 49629 (screw drivers, drifts)
Gunline Tools, Box 478, Placentia, CA 92670/714-528-5252
Gun-Tec, P.O. Box 8125, W. Palm Beach, Fl 33407
Half Moon Rifle Shop, 490 Halfmoon Rd., Columbia Falls, MT 59912/406-892-4409 (hex screws)
Henriksen Tool Co., Inc., P.O. Box 668, Phoenix, OR 97535/503-535-2309 (reamers)
Huey Gun Cases (Marvin Huey), Box 98, Reed's Spring, MO 65737/417-538-4233 (high grade English ebony tools)
Paul Jaeger Inc., 211 Leedom St., Jenkintown, PA 19046
Jeffredo Gunsight Co., 1629 Via Monserate, Fallbrook, CA 92028 (trap buttplate)
K&D Grinding Co., P.O. Box 1766, Alexandria, LA 71301/318-487-0823 (cust. tools f. pistolsmiths)
Kasenit Co., Inc., 3 King St., Mahwah, NJ 07430/201-529-3663 (surface hrdng. comp.)
Terry K. Kopp, Highway 13, Lexington, MO 64067/816-359-2636 (stock rubbing compound)
J. Korzinek, RD#2, Box 73, Canton, PA 17724/717-673-8512 (stainl. steel bluing; broch. $1.50)
John G. Lawson, (The Sight Shop) 1802 E. Columbia Ave., Tacoma, WA 98404/206-474-5465
Lea Mfg. Co., 237 E. Aurora St., Waterbury, CT 06720/203-753-5116
Lightwood (Fieldsport) Ltd., Britannia Rd., Banbury, Oxfordsh. OX16 8TD, England
Lock's Phila. Gun Exch., 6700 Rowland Ave., Philadelphia, PA 19149/215-332-6225
Longbranch Gun Bluing Co., 2415 Los Osos Valley Rd., Los Osos, CA 93401/805-528-1792
John McClure, 4549 Alamo Dr., San Diego, CA 92115 (electric checkering tool)
McIntrye Tools, P.O. Box 491/State Road #1144, Troy, NC 27371/919-572-2603 (shotgun bbl. facing tool)
Michaels of Oregon Co., P.O. Box 13010, Portland, OR 97213/503-255-6890
Viggo Miller, P.O. Box 4181, Omaha, NE 68104 (trigger attachment)
Miller Single Trigger Mfg. Co., R.D. 1, Box 99, Millersburg, PA 17061/717-692-3704
Frank Mittermeier, 3577 E. Tremont, New York, NY 10465
Moderntools, 1671 W. McNab Rd., Ft. Lauderdale, FL 33309/305-979-3900
N&J Sales Co., Lime Kiln Rd., Northford, CT 06472/203-484-0247 (screwdrivers)
Karl A. Neise, Inc., 1671 W. McNab Rd., Ft. Lauderdale, FL 33309/305-979-3900
Palmgren Prods., Chicago Tool & Eng. Co., 8383 South Chicago Ave., Chicago, IL 60167/312-721-9675 (vises, etc.)
Panavise Prods., Inc., 2850 E. 29th St., Long Beach, CA 90806/213-595-7621
C.R. Pedersen & Son, 2717 S. Pere Marquette, Ludington, MI 49431/616-843-2061
Pilkington Gun Co., P.O. Box 1296, Mukogee, OK 74401/918-683-9418 (Q.D. scope mt.)
Richland Arms Co., 321 W. Adrian St., Blissfield, MI 49228
Riley's Inc., 121 No. Main St., P.O. Box 139, Avilla, IN 46710/219-897-2351 (Niedner buttplates, grip caps)
A.G. Russell, 1705 Hiway 71N, Springdale, AR 72764 (Arkansas oilstones)
Schaffner Mfg. Co., Emsworth, Pittsburgh, PA 15202 (polishing kits)
SGW, Inc. (formerly Schuetzen Gun Works), 624 Old Pacific Hwy, S.E. Olympia, WA 98503/206-456-3471
Shaw's, 9447 W. Lilac Rd., Escondido, CA 92025/619-728-7070
Shooters Specialty Shop, 5146 E. Pima, Tucson, AZ 85712/602-325-3346
L.S. Starrett Co., 121 Crescent St., Athol, MA 01331/617-249-3551
Texas Platers Supply Co., 2453 W. Five Mile Parkway, Dallas, TX 75233 (plating kit)
Timney Mfg. Inc., 3106 W. Thomas Rd., Phoenix, AZ 85017/602-269-6937
Stan de Treville, Box 33021, San Diego, CA 92103/619-298-3393 (checkering patterns)
Turner Co., Div. Cleanweld Prods., Inc., 821 Park Ave., Sycamore, IL 60178/815-895-4545
Twin City Steel Treating Co., Inc. 1114 S. 3rd, Minneapolis, MN 55415/612-332-4849 (heat treating)
Walker Arms Co., Rt. 2, Box 73, Hwy. 80 W, Selma, AL 36701/205-872-6231 (tools)
Will-Burt Co., 169 So. Main, Orrville, OH 44667 (vises)
Williams Gun Sight Co., 7389 Lapeer Rd., Davison, MI 48423
Wilson Arms Co., 63 Leetes Island Rd., Branford, CT 06405
Wisconsin Platers Supply Co. (See Texas Platers)
W.C. Wolff Co., Box 232, Ardmore, PA 19003 (springs)
Woodcraft Supply Corp., 313 Montvale, Woburn, MA 01801

HANDGUN ACCESSORIES

Baramie Corp., 6250 E. 7 Mile Rd., Detroit, MI 48234 (Hip-Grip)
Bar-Sto Precision Machine, 13377 Sullivan Rd., Twentynine Palms, CA 92277/619-367-2747
Behlert Custom Guns, Inc., Box 227, Monmouth Junction, NJ 08852/201-329-2284
Belt Slide, Inc, 1301 Brushy Bend Dr., Round Rock, TX 78664/512-255-1805
Bingham Ltd., 1775-C Wilwat Dr., Norcross, GA 30093 (magazines)
C'Arco, P.O. Box 308, Highland, CA 92346 (Ransom Rest)
Central Specialties Co., 6030 Northwest Hwy., Chicago, IL 60631/312-774-5000 (trigger lock)
Dave Chicoine, d/b/a Liberty A.S.P., P.O. Box 385, Cos Cob, CT 06807/203-357-1893 (shims f. S&W revs.)
D&E Magazines Mfg., P.O. Box 4876, Sylmar, CA 91342 (clips)
Doskocil Mfg. Co., Inc, P.O. Box 1246, Arlington, TX 75010/817-467-5116 (Gun Guard cases)
Essex Arms, Box 345, Island Pond, VT 05846/802-723-4313 (45 Auto frames)
Frielich Police Equipment, 396 Broome St., New York, NY 10013/212-254-3045 (cases)
R. S. Frielich, 211 East 21st St., New York, NY 10010/212-777-4477 (cases)
Laka Tool Co., 62 Kinkel St., Westbury, L.I., NY 11590/516-334-4620 (stainless steel 45 Auto parts)
Lee's Red Ramps, 7252 E. Ave. U-3, Littlerock, CA 93543/805-944-4487 (ramp insert kits; spring kits)
Lee Precision Inc., 4275 Hwy. U, Hartford, WI 53027 (pistol rest holders)
Kent Lomont, 4421 So. Wayne Ave., Ft. Wayne, In 46807/219-694-6792 (Auto Mag only)
Los Gatos Grip & Specialty Co., P.O. Box 1850, Los Gatos, CA 95030 (custom-made)
Mascot rib sight (See Travis R. Strahan)
W. A. Miller Co., Inc., Mingo Loop, Oguossoc, ME 04964 (cases)
No-Sho Mfg. Co., 10727 Glenfield Ct., Houston, TX 77096/713-723-0966
Harry Owen (See Sport Specialties)
Pachmayr, 1220 S. Grand, Los Angeles, CA 90015 (cases)
Pacific Intl. Mchdsg. Corp., 2215 "J" St., Sacramento, CA 95818/916-446-2737 (Vega 45 Colt comb. mag.)
Randall Manufacturing, 7965 San Fernando Rd. Sun Valley, CA 91352/213-875-2045 (magazines, carrying rugs)
Sile Distributors, 7 Centre Market Pl., New York, NY 10013
Sport Specialties, (Harry Owen), Box 5337, Hacienda Hts., CA 91745/213-968-5806 (.22 rimfire adapters; .22 insert bbls. f. T/C Contender, autom. pistols)
Sportsmen's Equipment Co., 415 W. Washington, San Diego, CA 92103/619-296-1501
Travis R. Strahan, Rt. 7,Townsend Circle, Ringgold, GA 30736/404-937-4495 (Mascot rib sights)
Turkey Creek Enterprises, Rt. 1, Box 10, Red Oak, CA 74563/918-754-2884 (wood handgun cases)
M. Tyler, 1326 W. Britton, Oklahoma City, OK 73114 (grip adaptor)
Whitney Sales, Inc., P.O. Box 875, Reseda, CA 91335

HANDGUN GRIPS

Ajax Custom Grips, Inc., 12229 Cox Lane, Dallas, TX 75234/214-241-6302
Art Jewel Enterprises Ltd., 421A Irmen Dr., Addison, IL 60101/312-628-6220
Beeman Inc., 47 Paul Dr., San Rafael, CA 94903/415-472-7121 (airguns only)
Bingham Ltd., 1775-C Wilwat Dr., Norcross, GA 30093
Dave Chicoine, d/b/a Liberty A.S.P., P.O. Box 385, Cos Cob, CT 06807/203-357-1893 (orig. S&W 1855-1950)
Fitz Pistol Grip Co., P.O. Box 55, Grizzly Gulch, Whiskeytown, CA 96055/916-778-3136
Gateway Shooters' Supply, Inc., 10145-103rd St., Jacksonville, FL 32210 (Rogers grips)
The Gunshop, R.D. Wallace, 320 Overland Rd., Prescott, AZ 86301
Herrett's , Box 741, Twin Falls, ID 83301
Hogue Combat Grips, P.O. Box 2036, Atascadero, CA 93423/805-466-6266 (Monogrip)
Paul Jones Munitions Systems, (See Fitz Co.)
Russ Maloni, 40 Sigman Lane, Elma, NY 14059/716-652-7131
Millett Industries, 16131 Gothard St., Huntington Beach, CA 92647/714-842-5575 (custom)
Monogrip, (See Hogue)
Monte Kristo Pistol Grip Co., P.O. Box 55 Grizzly Gulch, Whiskeytown, CA 96095/916-778-3136
Mustang Custom Pistol Grips, see: Supreme Products Co.
Pachmayr Gun Works, Inc., 1220 S. Grand Ave., Los Angeles, CA 90015/213-748-7271
Robert H. Newell, 55 Coyote, Los Alamos, NM 87544/505-662-7135 (custom stocks)
Rogers Grips (See Gateway Shooters' Supply)
A. Jack Rosenberg & Sons, 12229 Cox Lane, Dallas, TX 75234/214-241-6302 (Ajax)
Royal Ordnance Works Ltd., P.O. Box 3254, Wilson, NC 27893/919-237-0515
Russwood Custom Pistol Grips, 40 Sigma Lane, Elma, NY 14059/716-652-7131 (cust. exotic woods)
Jean St. Henri, 6525 Dume Dr., Malibu, CA 90265 (custom)
Jay Scott, Inc., 81 Sherman Place, Garfield, NJ 07026/201-340-0550
Sile Dist., 7 Centre Market Pl., New York, NY 10013/212-925-4111
Sports Inc., P.O. Box 683, Park Ridge, IL 60068/312-825-8952 (Franzite)
Supreme Products Co., 1830 S. California Ave., Monrovia, CA 91016/800-423-7159

HEARING PROTECTORS

AO Safety Prods., Div. of American Optical Corp., 14 Mechanic St., Southbridge, MA 01550/617-765-9711 (ear valves, ear muffs)
Bausch & Lomb, 635 St. Paul St., Rochester, NY 14602
David Clark Co., Inc., 360 Franklin St., Worcester, MA 01604
Norton Co., see: Siebe
Safety Direct, 23 Snider Way, Sparks, NV 89431/702-354-4451 (Silencio)
Siebe Norton, Inc., 16624 Edwards Rd., P.O. Box 7500, Cerritos, CA 90701/213-926-0545 (Lee Sonic ear valve)
Smith & Wesson, 2100 Roosevelt Ave., Springfield, MA 01101
Willson Safety Prods. Div., P.O. Box 622, Reading, PA 19603 (Ray-O-Vac)

HOLSTERS & LEATHER GOODS

Alessi Custom Concealment Holsters, 2465 Niagara Falls Blvd., Tonawanda, NY 14150/716-691-5615
American Sales & Mfg. Co., P.O. Box 677, Laredo, TX 78040/512-723-6893
Andy Anderson, P.O. Box 225, North Hollywood, CA 91603/213-877-2401 (Gunfighter Custom Holsters)
Armament Systems & Procedures, Inc., P.O. Box 356, Appleton, WI 54912/414-731-8893 (ASP)
Rick M. Bachman, 1840 Stag Lane, Kalispell, MT 59901/406-755-6902
Beeman Inc., 47 Paul Dr., San Rafael, CA 94903/415-472-7121
Belt Slide, Inc., 1301 Brushy Bend, Round Rock, TX 78664/512-255-1805
Bianchi Leather Prods. Co., Inc., 100 Calle Cortez, Temecula, CA 92390/714-676-5621
Ted Blocker's Custom Holsters, Box 821, Rosemead, CA 91770/213-442-5772 (shop: 4945 Santa Anita Ave., Temple City, CA 91780)
Edward H. Bohlin, 931 N. Highland Ave., Hollywood, CA 90038/213-463-4888
Bo-Mar Tool & Mfg. Co., P.O. Box 168, Carthage, TX 75633/214-693-5220
Boyt Co., Div. of Welch Sptg., Box 1108, Iowa Falls, IA 51026
Brauer Bros. Mfg. Co., 2012 Washington Ave., St. Louis, MO 63103/314-231-2864
Browning, Rt. 4, Box 624-B, Arnold, MO 63010
J.M. Bucheimer Co., P.O. Box 280, Airport Rd., Frederick, MD 21701/301-662-5101
Cathey Enterprises, Inc., 9516 Neils Thompson Dr., Suite 116, Austin, TX 78758/512-837-7150
Chace Leather Prods., Longhorn Div., 507 Alden St., Fall River, MA 02722/617-678-7556
Cobra Ltd., 1865 New Highway, Farmingdale, NY 11735/516-752-8544
Colt, P.O. Box 1868, Hartford, CT. 06102/203-236-6311
Daisy Mfg. Co., Rogers, AR 72756
Davis Leather Co., G. Wm. Davis, P.O. Box 446, Arcadia, CA 91006/213-445-3872
Eugene DeMayo & Sons, Inc., 2795 Third Ave., Bronx, NY 10455/212-665-7075
Ellwood Epps Northern Ltd., 210 Worthington St. W., North Bay, Ont. P1B 3B4, Canada (custom made)
The Eutaw Co., Box 608, U.S. Highway 176W, Holly Hill, SC 29059
GALCO International Ltd., 7383 N. Rogers Ave., Chicago, IL 60626/312-338-2800
Gunfighter (See Anderson)
Hoyt Holster Co., P.O. Box 69, Coupeville, WA 98239/206-678-6640
Don Hume, Box 351, Miami, OK 74354/918-542-6604
The Hunter Corp., 3300 W. 71st Ave., Westminster, CO 80030/303-427-4626
John's Custom Leather, 525 S. Liberty St., Blairsville, PA 15717/412-459-6802
Jumbo Sports Prods., P.O. Box 280, Airport Rd., Frederick, MD 21701
Kirkpatrick Leather, Box 3150, Laredo, TX 89041/512-723-6631
Kolpin Mfg. Inc., P.O. Box 231, Berlin, WI 54923/414-361-0400
Morris Lawing, 150 Garland Ct., Charlotte, NC 28202/704-375-1740
George Lawrence Co., 306 S. W. First Ave., Portland, OR 97204
Liberty Organization Inc., P.O. Box 306, Montrose, CA 91020/213-248-0618
Mixson Leathercraft Inc., 1950 W. 84th St., Hialeah, FL 33014/305-820-5190 (police leather products)
Nordac Mfg. Corp., Rt 12, Box 124, Fredericksburg, VA 22405/703-752-2552
Kenneth L. Null-Custom Concealment Holsters, R.D. #5, Box 197, Hanover, PA 17331 (See Seventrees)
Arvo Ojala, 3960 S.E. 1st, Gresham, OR 97030
Old West Inc. Leather Prods., P.O. Box 2030, Chula Vista, CA 92012/714-429-8050
Pioneer Products, 1033 W. Amity Rd., Boise, ID 83075/208-345-2003
Pony Express Sport Shop Inc., 17460 Ventura Blvd., Encino, CA 91316/213-788-0123
Red Head Brand Corp., 4949 Joseph Hardin Dr., Dallas, TX 75236/214-333-4141
Red River Outfitters, P.O. Box 241, Tujunga, CA 91042/213-352-0177
Rogers Holsters, 1736 St. Johns Bluff Rd., Jacksonville, FL 32216/904-641-9434
Roy's Custom Leather Goods, Hwy, 1325 & Rawhide Rd., P.O. Box G, Magnolia, AR 71753/501-234-1566
Safariland Leather Products, 1941 So. Walker Ave., Monrovia, CA 91016/213-357-7902
Safety Speed Holster, Inc., 910 So. Vail, Montebello, CA 90640/213-723-4140
Buddy Schoellkopf Products, Inc., 4949 Joseph Hardin Dr., TX 75236/214-333-2121
Seventrees Systems Ltd., R.D. 5, Box 197, Hanover, PA 17331/717-632-6873 (See Null)
Sile Distr., 7 Centre Market Pl., New York NY 10013/212-925-4111
Smith & Wesson, 2100 Roosevelt Ave., Springfield, MA 01101
Milt Sparks, Box 187, Idaho City, ID 83631/208-392-6695 (broch. $2)
Robert A. Strong Co., 105 Maplewood Ave., Gloucester, MA 01930/617-281-3300
Torel, Inc., 1053 N. South St., Yoakum, TX 77995 (gun slings)

Triple-K Mfg. Co., 568 Sixth Ave., San Diego, CA 92101/619-232-2066
Viking Leathercraft, P.O. Box 2030, Chula Vista, CA 92012/619-429-8050
Whitco, Box 1712, Brownsville, TX 78520 (Hide-A-Way)
Wyman Corp., P.O. Box 8644, Salt Lake City, UT 84104/801-359-0368 (Cannon Packer f. rifle, shotgun)

HUNTING AND CAMP GEAR, CLOTHING, ETC.

Bob Allen Sportswear, P.O. Box 477, Des Moines, IA 50302
Eddie Bauer, 15010 NE 36th St., Redmond, WA 98052
L. L. Bean, Freeport, ME 04032
Bear Archery, R.R. 4, 4600 Southwest 41st Blvd., Gainesville, FL 32601/904-376-2327 (Himalayan backpack)
Bernzomatic Corp., 740 Driving Pk. Ave., Rochester, NY 14613 (stoves & lanterns)
Big Beam, Teledyne Co., 290 E. Prairie St., Crystal Lake, IL 60014 (lamp)
Browning, Rte. 1, Morgan, UT 84050
Camp Trails, P.O. Box 23155, Phoenix, AZ 85063/602-272-9401 (packs only)
Camp-Ways, 12915 S. Spring St., Los Angeles, CA 90061/213-532-0910
Challanger Mfg. Co., Box 550, Jamaica, NY 11431 (glow safe)
Chippewa Shoe Co., 925 First Ave., Chippewa Falls, WI 54729/715-723-5571 (boots)
Coleman Co., Inc., 250 N. St. Francis, Wichita, KS 67201
Converse Rubber Co., 55 Fordham Rd., Wilmington, MA 01887 (boots)
Dana Safety Heater, J. L. Galef & Son, Inc., 85 Chamber St., New York, NY 10007
Danner Shoe Mfg. Co., 5188 S.E. International Way, Milwaukie, OR 97222/503-653-2920 (boots)
DEER-ME Prod. Co., Box 345, Anoka, MN 55303 (tree steps)
Dunham Co., P.O. Box 813, Brattleboro, VT 05301/802-254-2316 (boots)
Durango Boot, see: Georgia/Northlake
Frankonia Jagd, Hofmann & Co., Postfach 6780, D-8700 Wurzburg 1, West Germany
Freeman Ind., Inc., 100 Marblehead Rd., Tuckahoe, NY 10707 (Trak-Kit)
French Dressing Inc., 15 Palmer Heights, Burlington, VT 05401/802-658-1434 (boots)
Game-Winner, Inc., 2690 Cumberland Parkway, Suite 440, Atlanta, GA 30339/404-588-0401 (camouflage suits)
Gander Mountain, Inc., Box 128, Hwy. "W", Wilmot, WI 53192/414-862-2331
Georgia Boot Div., U.S. Industry, 1810 Columbia Ave., Franklin, TN 37064/615-794-1556
Georgia/Northlake Boot Co., P.O. Box 10, Franklin, TN 37064/615-794-1556 (Durango)
Gokeys, 84 So. Wabasha, St. Paul, MN 55107/612-292-3933
Gun Club Sportswear, Box 477, Des Moines, IA 50302
Gun-Ho Case Mfg. Co., 110 E. 10th St., St. Paul, MN 55101
Joseph M. Herman Shoe Co., Inc., 114 Union St., Millis, MA 02054/617-376-2601 (boots)
Himalayan Industries, Inc., P.O. Box 7465, Pine Bluff, AR 71611/501-534-6411
Bob Hinman Outfitters, 1217 W. Glen, Peoria, IL 61614
Hunting World, 16 E. 53rd St., New York, NY 10022
Jung Shoe Mfg. Co., 620 S. 8th St., Sheboygan, WI 53081/414-458-3483 (boots)
Kelty Pack, Inc., 9281 Borden Ave., Sun Valley, CA 91352/213-768-1922
La Crosse Rubber Mills Co., P.O. Box 1328, La Crosse, WI 54601/608-782-3020 (boots)
Peter Limmer & Sons Inc., Box 66, Intervale, NH 03845 (boots)
Marathon Rubber Prods. Co. Inc., 510 Sherman St., Wausau, WI 54401 (rain gear)
Marble Arms Corp., 420 Industrial Park, Gladstone, MI 49837
Nimrod & Wayfarer Trailers, 500 Ford Blvd., Hamilton, OH 45011
The Orvis Co., Manchester, VT 05254/802-362-3622 (fishing gear; clothing)
PGB Assoc., 310 E. 46th St., Suite 3E, New York, NY 10017/212-867-9560
Prime Leather Finishes Co., 205 S. Second St., Milwaukee, WI 53204 (leath. waterproofer; Boot n' Saddle Soap)
Quabaug Rubber Co./Vibram U.S.A., 17 School St. N. Brookfield, MA 01535/617-867-7731 (boots)
Quoddy Moccasins, Div. R. G. Barry Corp., 67 Minot Ave., Auburn, ME 04210/207-784-3555
Ranger Mfg. Co., Inc., P.O. Box 3676, Augusta, GA 30904
Ranger Rubber Co., 1100 E. Main St., Endicott, NY 13760/607-757-4260 (boots)
Red Ball, P.O. Box 3200, Manchester, NH 03105/603-669-0708 (boots)
Red Head Brand Corp., 4949 Joseph Hardin Dr., Dallas, TX 75236/214-333-4141
Red Wing Shoe Co., Rte 2, Red Wing, MN 55066
Refrigiwear, Inc., 71 Inip Dr., Inwood, Long Island, NY 11696
Reliance Prod. Ltd., 1830 Dublin Ave., Winnipeg 21, Man. R3H 0H3 Can. (tent peg)
W. R. Russell Moccasin Co., 285 S.W. Franklin, Berlin, WI 54923
Safariland Hunting Corp., P.O. Box NN, McLean, VA 22101/703-356-0622 (camouflage rain gear)
Servus Rubber Co., 1136 2nd St., Rock Island, IL 61201 (footwear)
The Ski Hut-Trailwise, 1615 University Ave., P.O. Box 309, Berkeley, CA 94710
Stearns Mfg. Co., P.O. Box 1498, St. Cloud, MN 56301
Sterno Inc., 300 Park Ave., New York, NY 10022 (camp stoves)
Teledyne Co., Big Beam, 290 E. Prairie St., Crystal Lake, IL 60014
10-X Mfg. Co., 316 So. Lexington Ave., Cheyenne, WY 82001/307-635-9192
Thermos Div., KST Co., Norwich, CT 06361 (Pop Tent)
Norm Thompson, 1805 N.W. Thurman St., Portland, OR 97209
Trim Unlimited, 2111 Glen Forest, Plano, TX 75023/214-596-5059 (electric boat)
Utica Duxbak Corp., 1745 S. Acoma St., Denver, CO 80223/303-778-0324

Waffen-Frankonia, see: Frankonia Jagd
Walker Shoe Co., P.O. Box 1167, Asheboro, NC 27203-1167/919-625-1380 (boots)
Weinbrenner Shoe Corp., Polk St., Merrill, WI 54452
Wenzel Co., 1280 Research Blvd., St. Louis, MO 63132
Wolverine Boots & Shoes Div., Wolverine World Wide, 9341 Courtland Dr., Rockford, MI 49351/616-866-1561 (footwear)
Woods Bag & Canvas Co., Ltd., 90 River St., P.O. Box 407, Ogdensburg, NY 13669/315-393-3520
Woodstream Corp., Box 327, Lititz, PA 17543 (Hunter Seat)
Woolrich Woolen Mills, Mill St., Woolrich, PA 17779/717-769-6464
Yankee Mechanics, RFD No. 1, Concord, NH 03301/603-225-3181 (hand winches)

KNIVES AND KNIFEMAKER'S SUPPLIES—FACTORY and MAIL ORDER

Alcas Cutlery Corp., Olean, NY 14760/716-372-3111 (Cutco)
Atlanta Cutlery, Box 839, Conyers, GA 30207/404-922-3700 (mail order, supplies)
Bali-Song Inc., 3039 Roswell St., Los Angeles, CA 90085/213-258-7021
L. L. Bean, 386 Main St., Freeport, ME 04032/207-865-3111 (mail order)
Benchmark Knives, P.O. Box 998, Gastonia, NC 28052/704-867-1307
Crosman Blades™, The Coleman Co., 250 N. St. Francis, Wichita, KS 67201
Boker, The Cooper Group, P.O. Box 728, Apex, NC 27502/919-362-7510
Bowen Knife Co., Box 1929, Waycross, GA 31501/912-287-1200
Browne and Pharr Inc., 1775-I Wilwat Dr., Norcross, GA 30091/404-447-9285
Browning, Rt. 1, Morgan, UT 84050/801-876-2711
Buck Knives, Inc., P.O. Box 1267; 1900 Weld Blvd., El Cajon, CA 92022/619-449-1100 or 800-854-2557
Camillus Cutlery Co., 52-54 W. Genesee St., Camillus, NY 13031/315-672-8111 (Sword Brand)
W. R. Case & Sons Cutlery Co., 20 Russell Blvd., Bradford, PA 16701/814-368-4123
Charter Arms Corp., 430 Sniffens Lane, Stratford, CT 06497/203-377-8080 (Skatchet)
Chicago Cutlery Co., 5420 N. County Rd. 18, P.O. Box 9494, Minneapolis, MN 55440/612-533-0472
E. Christopher Firearms, Rt. #128, Box 303, Miamitown, OH 45041/513-353-1321 (supplies)
Collins Brothers Div. (belt-buckle knife), See Bowen Knife Co.
Colonial Knife Co., P.O. Box 3327, Providence, RI 02909/401-421-1600 (Master Brand)
Custom Purveyors, Ted Devlet's, P.O. Box 886, Fort Lee, NJ 07024/201-886-0196 (mail order)
Dixie Gun Works, Inc., P.O. Box 130, Union City, TN 38261/901-885-0700 (supplies)
Eze-Lap Diamond Prods., Box 2229, 15164 Weststate St., Westminster, CA 92683/714-847-1555 (knife sharpeners)
Gerber Legendary Blades, 14200 S.W. 72nd St., Portland, OR 99223/503-639-6161
Golden Age Arms Co., 14 W. Winter St., Delaware, OH 43015/614-369-6513 (supplies)
Gutmann Cutlery Co., Inc., 900 S. Columbus Ave., Mt. Vernon, NY 10550/914-699-4044
H & B Forge Co., Rte. 2, Box 24, Shiloh, OH 44878/419-896-3435 (throwing knives, tomahawks)
Russell Harrington Cutlery, Inc., Subs. of Hyde Mfg. Co., 44 River St., Southbridge, MA 01550/617-764-4371 (Dexter, Green River Works)
J. A. Henckels Zwillingswerk, Inc., 1 Westchester Plaza, Elmsford, NY 10523/914-592-7370
Imperial Knife Associated Companies, 1776 Broadway, New York, NY 10019/212-757-1814
Indian Ridge Traders, Box 869, Royal Oak, MI 48068/313-399-6034 (mostly blades)
Jet-Aer Corp., 100 Sixth Ave., Paterson, NJ 07524/201-278-8300
KA-BAR Cutlery Inc., 5777 Grant Ave., Cleveland, OH 44105/216-271-4000
KA-BAR Knives, Collectors Division, 434 No. 9th St., Olean, NY 14760/716-372-5611
Keene Corp., Cutting Serv. Div., 1569 Tower Grove Ave., St. Louis, MO 63110/314-771-1550
Kershaw Cutlery Co., 6024 Jean Rd., Suite D, Lake Oswego, OR 97034/503-636-0111
Knife and Gun Supplies, P.O. Box 13522, Arlington, TX 76013/817-261-0569
Koval Knives, P.O. Box 14130, Columbus, OH 43214/614-888-6486 (supplies)
Lakota Corp., 30916 Agoura Rd., Suite 311, Westlake Village, CA 91361/213-889-7177
Lamson & Goodnow Mfg. Co., Shelburne Falls, MA 03170/413-625-6331
Lansky Sharpeners, P.O. Box 800, Buffalo, NY 14221/716-634-6333 (sharpening devices)
Al Mar Knives, Inc., 5861 S.W. Benfield Ct., Lake Oswego, OR 97034/503-639-8554
Marttiini Knives, 30 East 40 St., New York, NY 10016/212-532-3239
Matthews Cutlery, P.O. Box 33095, Decatur, GA 30033/404-636-7923 (mail order)
R. Murphy Co., Inc., 13 Groton-Harvard Rd., Ayer, MA 01432/617-772-3481 (StaySharp)
Nordic Knives, 1643-C-Z Copenhagen Dr., Solvang, CA 93463 (mail order)
Normark Corp., 1710 E. 78th St., Minneapolis, MN 55423/612-869-3291
Olsen Knife Co., Inc., 7 Joy St., Howard City, MI 49329/616-937-4373
Ontario Knife Co., Subs. of Servotronics, Inc., P.O. Box 145, Franklinville, NY 14737/716-676-5527 (Old Hickory)
Parker Cutlery, 6928 Lee Highway, Chattanooga, TN 37415/615-894-1782
Plaza Cutlery Inc., 3333 Bristol, #161, Costa Mesa, CA 92626/714-549-3932 (mail order)
Queen Cutlery Co., P.O. Box 500, Franklinville, NY 14737/617-676-5540

R & C Knives and Such, P.O. Box 32631, San Jose, CA 95152/408-923-5728 (mail order)
Randall-Made Knives, Box 1988, Orlando, FL 32802/305-855-8075 (ctlg. $1)
Rigid Knives, P.O. Box 816, Hwy. 290E, Lake Hamilton, AR 71951/501-525-1377
A. G. Russell Co., 1705 Hiwy. 71 N., Springdale, AR 72764/501-751-7341
Bob Sanders, 2358 Tyler Olane, Louisville, KY 40205 (Bahco steel)
San Diego Knives, 2785 Kurtz No. 8, San Diego, CA 92110/714-297-4530 (mail order)
Schrade Cutlery Corp., 1776 Broadway, New York, NY 10019/212-757-1814
Bob Schrimsher, Custom Knifemaker's Supply, P.O. Box 308, Emory, TX 75440/214-328-2453
Paul Sheffield, P.O. Box 141, Deland, FL 32720/904-736-9356 (supplies)
Smith & Wesson, 2100 Roosevelt Ave., Springfield, MA 01101/413-781-8300
Jesse W. Smith Saddlery, E. 3024 Sprague, Spokane, WA 99201 (sheath-makers)
Swiss Army Knives, Inc., P.O. Box 846, Shelton, CT 06484/203-929-6391 (Victorinox; folding)
Tekna, 3549 Haven Ave., Menlo Park, CA 94025/415-365-5112
Thompson/Center, P.O. Box 2405, Rochester, NH 03867/603-332-2394
Tommer-Bordein Corp., 220 N. River St., Delano, MN 55328/612-972-3901
Tru-Balance Knife Co., 2115 Tremond Blvd., Grand Rapids, MI 49504/616-453-3679
Utica Cutlery Co., 820 Noyes St., Utica, NY 13503/315-733-4663 (Kutmaster)
Valor Corp., 5555 N.W. 36th Ave., Miami, FL 33142
Washington Forge, Inc., Englishtown, NJ 07727/201-446-7777 (Carriage House)
Wenoka Cutlery, 85 North Ave., Natick, MA 01760/617-453-3679
Western Cutlery Co., 1800 Pike Rd., Longmont, CO 80501/303-772-5900 (Westmark)
Walt Whinnery, Walts Cust. Leather, 1947 Meadow Creek Dr., Louisville, KY 40281/502-458-4351 (sheathmaker)
Wilkinson Sword, 1316 W. Main St., Richmond, VA 23220/804-353-1812
J. Wolfe's Knife Works, Box 1056, Larkspur, CA 94939 (supplies)
Wyoming Knife Co., 14054 N. 95th St., Longmont, CO 80511/308-776-9254

LABELS, BOXES, CARTRIDGE HOLDERS

Milton Brynin, 214 E. Third St., Mount Vernon, NY 10710/914-667-6549 (cartridge box labels)
E-Z Loader, Del Rey Products, P.O. Box 91561, Los Angeles, CA 90009
Peterson Label Co., P.O. Box 186, 23 Sullivan Dr., Redding Ridge, CT 06876/203-938-2349 (cartridge box labels; Targ-Dots)
N. H. Schiffman, 963 Malibu, Pocatello, ID 83201 (cartridge carrier)

LOAD TESTING and PRODUCT TESTING, (CHRONOGRAPHING, BALLISTIC STUDIES)

Hutton Rifle Ranch, 1802 S. Oak Park Dr., Rolling Hills, Tucson, AZ 85710
Kent Lomont, 4421 S. Wayne Ave., Ft. Wayne, IN 46807/219-694-6792 (handguns, handgun ammunition)
Plum City Ballistics Range, Norman E. Johnson, Rte. 1, Box 29A, Plum City, WI 54761/715-647-2539
Russell's Rifle Shop,' Rte. 5, Box 92, Georgetown, TX 78626/512-778-5338 (load testing and chronographing to 300 yds.)
John M. Tovey, 4710 - 104th Lane NE, Circle Pines, MN 55014
H. P. White Laboratory, Inc., 3114 Scarboro Rd., Street, MD 21154/301-838-6550

MISCELLANEOUS

Accurizing Service, Herbert G. Troester, 2292 W. 1000 North, Vernal, UT 84078/801-789-2158
Action, Mauser-style only, Crandell Tool & Machine Co., 1540 N. Mitchell St., Cadillac, MI 49601/616-775-5562
Activator, B.M.F. Activator, Inc., 3705 Broadway, Houston, TX 77017/713-645-6726
Adapters, Sage Industries, P.O. Box 2248, Hemet, CA 92342/714-925-1006 (12-ga. shotgun; 38 S&W blank)
Adjusta-Targ, Inc., 1817 Thackeray N.W., Massillon, OH 44646
Archery, Bear, R.R. 4, 4600 Southwest 41st Blvd., Gainesville, FL 32601/904-376-2327
Arms Restoration, J. J. Jenkins Ent. Inc., 375 Pine Ave. No. 25, Goleta, CA 93017/805-967-1366
Assault Rifle Accessories, Cherokee Gun Accessories, 830 Woodside Rd., Redwood City, CA 94061
Barrel Band Swivels, Phil Judd, 83 E. Park St., Butte, MT 59701
Bedding Kit, Bisonite Co., P.O. Box 84, Kenmore Station, Buffalo, NY 14217
Bedding Kit, Fenwal, Inc., Resins Systems Div., 400 Main St., Ashland, MA 01721
Belt Buckles, Adina Silversmiths Corp., P.O. Box 348, 3195 Tucker Rd., Cornwell Heights, PA 19020/215-639-7246
Belt Buckles, Bergamot Brass Works, 820 Wisconsin St., Delavan, WI 53115/414-728-5572
Belt Buckles, Just Brass Inc., 21 Filmore Place, Freeport, NY 11520 (ctlg. $2)
Belt Buckles, Sports Style Associates, 148 Hendrickson Ave., Lynbrook, NY 11563/516-599-5080
Belt Buckles, Pilgrim Pewter Inc., R.D. 2, Tully, NY 13159/607-842-6431
Benchrest & Accuracy Shooters Equipment, Bob Pease Accuracy, P.O. Box 787, Zipp Road, New Braunfels, TX 78130/512-625-1342
Blowgun, PAC Outfitters, P.O. Box 56, Mulvane, KS 67110/316-777-4909

Bootdryers, Baekgaard Ltd., 1855 Janke Dr., Northbrook, IL 60062
Breech Plug Wrench, Swaine Machine, 195 O'Connell, Providence, RI 02905
Bulletproof Clothing, EMGO USA Ltd., 115 E. 57th St., Suite 1430, New York NY 10022/1-800-223-5801
Cannons, South Bend Replicas Ind., 61650 Oak Rd., S. Bend, IN 44614/219-289-4500 (ctlg. $5)
Cartridge Adapters, Sport Specialties, Harry Owen, Box 5337, Hacienda Hts., CA 91745/213-968-5806
Case Gauge, Plum City Ballistics Range, Rte. 1, Box 29A, Plum City, WI 54761/715-647-2539
Cased, high-grade English tools, Marvin Huey Gun Cases, Box 98, Reed's Spring, MO 65737/417-538-4233 (ebony, horn, ivory handles)
Cherry Converter, Amimex Inc., 2660 John Montgomery Dr., San Jose, CA 95148/408-923-1720 (shotguns)
Clips, D&E Magazines Mfg., P.O. Box 4876, Sylmar, CA 91342 (handgun and rifle)
CO2 Cartridges, Nittan U.S.A. Inc., 4901 Morena Blvd., Suite 307, San Diego, CA 92117/714-272-6113
Deer Drag, D&H Prods. Co., Inc., P.O. Box 22, Glenshaw, PA 15116/412-443-2190
Defendor, Ralide, Inc., P.O. Box 131, Athens, TN 37303/615-745-3525
Dryer, Thermo-Electric, Golden-Rod, Buenger Enterprises, Box 5286, Oxnard, CA 93030/805-985-9596
E-Z Loader, Del Rey Prod., P.O. Box 91561, Los Angeles, CA 90009/213-823-04494
Ear-Valve, Norton Co., Siebe Norton, 16624 Edwards Rd., Cerritos, CA 90701/213-926-0545 (Lee-Sonic)
Farrsight, Farr Studio, 1231 Robinhood Rd., Greenville, TN 37743
Flares, Colt Industries, P.O. Box 1868, Hartford, CT 06102
Flares, Smith & Wesson Chemical Co., 2399 Forman Rd., Rock Creek, OH 44084
Frontier Outfitters, Red River Outfitters, P.O. Box 241, Tujunga, CA 91042/213-352-0177 (frontier, western, military Americana clothing)
Game Hoist, Cam Gear Ind., P.O. Box 1002, Kalispell, MT 59901 (Sportsmaster 500 pocket hoist)
Game Hoist, Precise, 3 Chestnut, Suffern, NY 10901
Game Scent, Buck Stop Lure Co., Inc., 3015 Grow Rd. N.W., Stanton, MI 48888/517-762-5091
Game Scent, Pete Rickard, Rte. 1, Cobleskill, NY 12043/518-234-2731 (Indian Buck lure)
Game Scent, Safariland Hunting Corp., P.O. Box NN, McLean, VA 22101/703-356-0622 (buck lure)
Gargoyles, Pro-tec Inc., 11108 Northrup Way, Bellevue, WA 98004/306-828-6595
Gas Pistol, Penguin Ind., Inc., Airport Industrial Mall, Coatesville, PA 19320/215-384-6000
Grip Caps, Classic Arms Corp., P.O. Box 8, Palo Alto, CA 94301/415-321-7243
Grip Caps, Knickerbocker Enterprises, 16199 S. Maple Ln. Rd., Oregon City, OR 97045
Grip Caps, Philip D. Letiecq, AQ 18 Wagon Box Rd., P.O. Box 251, Story, WY 82842/307-683-2817
Gun Bedding Kit, Fenwal, Inc., Resins System Div., 400 Main St., Ashland, MA 01721/617-881-2000
Gun Jewelry, Sid Bell Originals, R.D. 2, Tully, NY 13159/607-842-6431
Gun Jewelry, Pilgrim Pewter Inc., R.D. 2, Tully, NY 13159/607-842-6431
Gun Jewelry, Al Popper, 614 Turnpike St., Stoughton, MA 02072/617-344-2036
Gun Jewelry, Sports Style Assoc., 148 Hendricks Ave., Lynbrook, NY 11563
Gun photographer, Mustafa Bilal, 727 Belleview Ave. East, Suite 103, Seattle, WA 98102/206-322-5449
Gun photographer, Art Carter, 818 Baffin Bay Rd., Columbia, SC 29210/803-772-2148
Gun photographer, John Hanusin, 3306 Commercial, Northbrook, IL 60062/312-564-2706
Gun photographer, Jim Weyer, 224½ Huron St., Toledo, OH 43604/419-241-5454
Gun photographer, Steve White, 1920 Raymond Dr., Northbrook, IL 60062/312-564-2720
Gun Record Book, B. J. Co., Bridge St., Bluffton, SC 29910
Gun Sling, Kwikfire, Wayne Prods. Co., P.O. Box 247, Camp Hill, PA 17011
Gun Slings, Torel, Inc., 1053 N. South St., Yoakum, TX 77995
Hugger Hooks, Roman Products, 4363 Loveland St., Golden, CO 80403/303-279-6959
Insect Repellent, Armor, Div. of Buck Stop, Inc., 3015 Grow Rd., Stanton, MI 48888
Insert Barrels and Cartridge Adapters, Sport Specialties, Harry Owen, Box 5337, Hacienda Hts., CA 91745/213-968-5806
Kentucky Rifle Drawings, New England Historic Designs, P.O. Box 171, Concord, NH 03301/603-224-2096
Knife Sharpeners, Lansky Sharpeners, P.O. Box 800, Buffalo, NY 14221/716-634-6333
Light Load, Jacob & Tiffin Inc., P.O. Box 547, Clanton, AL 35045
Locks, Gun, Bor-Lok Prods., 105 5th St., Arbuckle, CA 95912
Locks, Gun, Master Lock Co., 2600 N. 32nd St., Milwaukee, WI 53245
Miniature Cannons, Karl J. Furr, 76 East, 350 North, Orem, UT 84057/801-225-2603 (replicas)
Miniature Guns, Charles H. Stoppler, 5 Minerva Place, New York, NY 10468
Monte Carlo Pad, Frank A. Hoppe Div., Penguin Ind., Airport Industrial Mall, Coatesville, PA 19320/215-384-6000
Muzzle Rest, Meadow Industries, Dept. 450, Marlton, NJ 08053/609-234-1210
Muzzle-Top, Allen Assoc., Box 532, Glenside, PA 19038 (plastic gun muzzle cap)
Old Gun Industry Art, Hansen & Co., 244 Old Post Rd., Southport, CT 06490/203-259-7337
Patterning Data, Whits Shooting Stuff, P.O. Box 1340, Cody, WY 82414
Pell Remover, A. Edw. Terpening, 838 E. Darlington Rd., Tarpon Springs, FL 33589
Powderhorns, Kirk Olson, Ft. Woolsey Guns, P.O. Box 2122, Prescott, AZ 86302/602-778-3035

Powderhorns, Tennessee Valley Mfg., P.O. Box 1125, Corinth, MS 38834
Powderhorns, Thomas F. White, 5801 Westchester Ct., Worthington, OH 43085/614-888-0128
Practice Ammunition, Hoffman New Ideas Inc., 821 Northmoor Rd., Lake Forest, IL 60045/312-234-4075
Pressure Testg. Machine, M. York, 5508 Griffith Rd., Gaithersburg, MD 20760/301-253-4217
Ram-Line accessories, Chesco, Inc., 406 Violet St., Golden, CO 80401/303-279-0886
Ransom Handgun Rests, C'Arco, P.O. Box 308, Highland, CA 92346
Retriev-R-Trainer, Scientific Prods. Corp., 426 Swann Ave., Alexandria, VA 22301
Rifle Magazines, Butler Creek Corp., Box GG, Jackson Hole, WY 83001/307-733-3599 (30-rd. Mini-14)
Rifle Magazines, Condor Mfg. Co., 418 W. Magnolia Ave., Glendale, CA 91204/213-240-1745 (25-rd. 22-cal.)
Rifle Magazines, Miller Gun Works, P.O. Box 7326, Tamuning, Guam 96911 (30-cal. M1 15&30-round)
Rifle Slings, Bianchi Leather Prods., 100 Calle Cortez, Temecula, CA 92390/714-676-5621
Rifle Slings, Chace Leather Prods., Longhorn Div., 507 Alden St., Fall River, MA 02722/617-678-7556
Rifle Slings, John's Cust. Leather, 525 S. Liberty St., Blairsville, PA 15717/412-459-6802
Rifle Slings, Kirkpatrick Leather Co., Box 3150, Laredo, TX 78041/512-723-6631
RIG, NRA Scoring Plug, Rig Products, 87 Coney Island Dr., Sparks, NV 89431/702-331-5666
Rubber Cheekpiece, W. H. Lodewick, 2816 N.E. Halsey, Portland, OR 97232/503-284-2554
Saddle Rings, Studs, Fred Goodwin, Sherman Mills, ME 04776
Safeties, William E. Harper, The Great 870 Co., P.O. Box 6309. El Monte, CA 91734/213-579-3077 (f. Rem. 870P)
Safeties, Williams Gun Sight Co., 7389 Lapeer Rd., Davison, MI 48423
Salute Cannons, Naval Co., R.D. 2, 4747 Cold Spring Creamery Rd., Doylestown, PA 18901
Sav-Bore, Saunders Sptg. Gds., 338 Somerset St., N. Plainfield, NJ 07060
Scrimshaw Engraving, C. Milton Barringer, 217-2nd Isle N., Port Richey, FL 33568/813-868-3777
Sharpening Stones, Russell's Arkansas Oilstones, 1705 Hiway 71N., Springdale, AR 72764
Shell Catcher, Auto Strip Pak, 419 W. Magnolia Ave., Glendale, CA 91204/213-240-1745
Shell Shrinker Mfg. Co., P.O. Box 462, Fillmore, CA 93015
Shooter's Porta Bench, Centrum Industries, Inc., 443 Century, S.W., Grand Rapids, MI 49503/616-454-9424
Shooters Rubber Stamps, Craft Haven, 828 N. 70th, Lincoln, NE 68505/402-466-5739
Shooting Coats, 10-X Mfg. Co., 316 So. Lexington Ave., Cheyenne, WY 82001/307-635-9192
Shooting Glasses, Willson Safety Prods. Division, P.O. Box 622, Reading, PA 19603
Shotgun Barrel, Pennsylvania Arms Co., Box 128, Duryea, PA 18642/717-457-0845 (rifled)
Shotgun Case Accessories, AC Enterprises, 507 N. Broad St., Edenton, NC 27932 (British-made Charlton)
Shotgun Converter, Amimex Inc., 2660 John Montgomery Dr., San Jose, CA 95148/408-923-1720
Shotgun/riot, Combat Weapons, 1265 Balsam St., Lakewood, CO 80215
Shotgun Sight, bi-ocular, Trius Prod., Box 25, Cleves, OH 45002
Shotshell Adapter, PC Co., 5942 Secor Rd., Toledo, OH 43623/419-472-6222 (Plummer 410 converter)
Single Shot Action, John Foote, Foote-Shephard Inc., P.O. Box 6473, Marietta, GA 30065
Snap Caps, Edwards Recoil Reducer, 269 Herbert St., Alton, IL 62002/618-462-3257
Sportsman's Chair, Ted Devlet's Custom Purveyors, P.O. Box 886, Fort Lee, NJ 07024/201-886-0196
Springfield Safety Pin, B-Square Co., P.O. Box 11281, Ft. Worth, TX 76110
Springs, W. C. Wolff Co., Box 232, Ardmore, PA 19003/215-647-3461
Stock pad, variable, Meadow Industries, Dept. 450, Marlton, NJ 08053/609-234-1210
Supersound, Edmund Scientific Co., 101 E. Gloucester Pike, Barrington, NJ 08007 (safety device)
Swivel base (f. lever actions), Lautard Tool Works, 2570 Rosebery Ave., W. Vancouver, B.C., Canada V7V 2Z9/604-926-7150
Swivels, Michaels, P.O. Box 13010, Portland, OR 97213/503-255-6890
Swivels, Sile Dist., 7 Centre Market Pl., New York, NY 10013/212-925-4111
Swivels, Williams Gun Sight Co., 7389 Lapeer Rd., Davison, MI 48423
Tomahawks, H&B Forge Co., Rt. 2, Shiloh, OH 44878/419-896-2075
Tree Stand, Advanced Hunting Equipment Inc., P.O. Box 1277, Cumming, GA 30130/404-887-1171 (tree lounge)
Tree Stand, Climbing, Amacker Prods., P.O. Box 1432; 602 Kimbrough Dr., Tallulah, LA 71282/318-574-4903
Trophies, Blackinton & Co., 140 Commonwealth, Attleboro Falls, MA 02763
Trophies, F. H. Noble & Co., 888 Tower Rd., Mundelein, IL 60060
Warning Signs, Delta Ltd., P.O. Box 777, Mt. Ida, AR 71957
W&E target tang sight, Lautard Tool Works, 2570 Rosebery Ave., W. Vancouver, B.C., Canada V7V 2Z9/604-926-7150
World Hunting Info., Jack Atcheson & Sons, Inc., 3210 Ottawa St., Butte, MT 59701
World Hunting Info., J/b adventures & Safaris, Inc., 800 E. Girard, Suite 603, Denver, CO 80231/303-696-0261
World Hunting Info. Klineburger, 12 & East Pine, Seattle, WA 98122/206-329-1600
World Hunting Info., Wayne Preston, Inc., 3444 Northhaven Rd., Dallas, TX 75229/214-358-4477

MUZZLE-LOADING GUNS, BARRELS or EQUIPMENT

Luther Adkins, Box 281, Shelbyville, IN 46176/317-392-3795 (breech plugs)
Anderson Mfg. Co., Union Gap Sta. P.O. Box 3120, Yakima, WA 98903/509-453-2349
Armoury, Inc., Rte. 202, New Preston, CT 06777
Arm Tech, Armament Technologies Inc., 240 Sargent Dr., New Haven, CT 06511/203-562-2543 (22-cal. derringers)
Beaver Lodge, 9245 16th Ave. S.W., Seattle, WA 98106/206-763-1698
John Bivins, Jr., 200 Wicklow Rd., Winston-Salem, NC 27106
Blackhawk East, C2274 POB, Loves Park, IL 61131/815-633-7784
Blackhawk Mtn., 1337 Delmar Parkway, Aurora, CO 80010
Blackhawk West, Box 285, Hiawatha, KS 66434
Blue and Gray Prods., Inc. RD #6, Box 348, Wellsboro, PA 16901/717-724-1383
Jim Brobst, 299 Poplar St., Hamburg, PA 19526/215-562-2103 (ML rifle bbls.)
Ted Buckland, 361 Flagler Rd., Nordland, WA 98358/206-385-2142 (custom only)
G. S. Bunch, 7735 Garrison, Hyattsville, MD 20784/301-577-6598 (flask repair)
Butler Creek Corp., Box GG, Jackson Hole, WY 83001/307-733-3599 (poly & maxi patch)
C.N.S. Co., P.O. Box 238, Mohegan Lake, NY 10547
Cache La Poudre Rifleworks, 168 N. College, Ft. Collins, CO 80521/303-482-6913 (custom muzzleloaders)
Challanger Mfg. Co., 118 Pearl St., Mt. Vernon, NY 10550
R. MacDonald Champlin, P.O. Box 693, Manchester, NH 03105/603-622-1420 (custom muzzleloaders)
Chopie Mfg. Inc., 700 Copeland Ave., LaCrosse, WI 54601/608-784-0926 (nipple wrenches)
Connecticut Valley Arms Co. (CVA), Saybrook Rd., Haddam, CT 06438 (kits also)
Earl T. Cureton, Rte. 2, Box 388, Willoughby Rd., Bulls Gap, TN 37711/615-235-2854 (powder horns)
Leonard Day & Co., P.O. Box 723, East Hampton, MA 01027/413-527-7990
Dixie Gun Works, Inc., P.O. Box 130, Union City, TN 38261
Dixon Muzzleloading Shop, Inc., RD #1, Box 175, Kempton, PA 19529/215-756-6271
EMF Co., Inc., 1900 E. Warner Ave. 1-D, Santa Ana, CA 92705/714-966-0202
Euroarms of America, Inc., P.O. Box 3277, 1501 Lenoir Dr., Winchester, VA 22601/703-662-1863
The Eutaw Co., Box 608, U.S. Highway 176W, Holly Hill, SC 29059 (accessories)
Excam, Inc., 4480 E. 11th Ave., Hialeah, FL 33012
Andy Fautheree, P.O. Box 863, Pagosa Springs, CO 81147/303-264-2892 (cust. ML)
Ted Fellowes, Beaver Lodge, 9245 16th Ave. S.W., Seattle, WA 98106/206-763-1698
Firearms Imp. & Exp. Corp., (F.I.E.), P.O. Box 4866, Hialeah Lakes, Hialeah, FL 33014/305-685-5966
Marshall F. Fish, Rt. 22 N., Westport, NY 12993 (antique ML repairs)
Flamingo Co., 29 Tiburon Lane, Lake Havasu City, AZ 86403/602-855-4856 (Flame-N-Go fusil; Accra-Shot)
The Flintlock Muzzle Loading Gun Shop, 1238 "G" So. Beach Blvd., Anaheim, CA 92804/714-821-6655
C. R. & D. E. Getz, Box 88, Beavertown, PA 17813 (barrels)
Golden Age Arms Co., 14 W. Winter St., Delaware, OH 43015 (ctlg. $2.50)
A. R. Goode, 12845 Catoctin Furnace Rd., Thurmont, MD 21788/301-271-2228 (ML rifle bbls.)
Green Mountain Rifle Barrel, RFD 1, Box 184, Center Ossipee, NH 03814
Guncraft Inc., 117 W. Pipeline, Hurst, TX 76053/817-268-2887
Hatfield Rifle Works, 2028 Frederick Ave., St. Joseph, MO 64501/816-233-9106 (squirrel rifle)
Hawken Armory, P.O. Box 2604, Hot Springs, AR 71901/501-268-8296
Hopkins & Allen, 3 Ethel Ave., P.O. Box 217, Hawthorne, NJ 07507/201-427-1165
The House of Muskets, Inc., 120 N. Pagosa Blvd., Pagosa Springs, CO 81147/303-264-2295 (ML bbls. & supplies)
JJJJ Ranch, Wm. Large, Rte. 1, State Route 243, Ironton, OH 45638/614-532-5298
Jerry's Gun Shop, 9220 Odgen Ave., Brookfield, IL 60513/312-485-5200
Kern's Gun Shop, 319 E. Main St., Ligonier, PA 15658/412-238-7651 (ctlg. $1.50)
LaChute Ltd., Box 48B, Masury, OH 44438/216-448-2236 (powder additive)
Art LeFeuvre, 1003 Hazel Ave., Deerfield, IL 60015/312-945-0073 (antique gun restoring)
Les' Gun Shop (Les Bauska), 105-9th West, P.O. Box 511, Kalispell, MT 59901/406-755-2635
Lever Arms Serv. Ltd., 572 Howe St., Vancouver, BC V6C 2E3, Canada
Log Cabin Sport Shop, 8010 Lafayette Rd., Lodi, OH 44254/216-948-1082 (ctlg. $3)
Lyman Products Corp., Rte. 147, Middlefield, CT 06455
McCann's Muzzle-Gun Works, 200 Federal City Rd., Pennington, NJ 08534/609-737-1707
McKenzie River Arms, P.O. Box 766, Springfield, OR 97477
McKeown's Sporting Arms, R.R. 4, Pekin, IL 61554/309-347-3559 (E-Z load rev. stand)
Mike Marsh, 6 Stanford Rd., Dronfield Woodhouse, Nr. Sheffield S18 SQJ, England (accessories)
Maurer Manchester Arms Inc., 6858 Manchester Rd., Clinton, OH 44216/216-882-3133 (cust. muzzleloaders)
Michigan Arms Corp., 479 W. 14 Mile Rd., Clawson, MI 48017/313-435-0160
Mountain State Muzzleloading Supplies, Box 154-1, Williamstown, WV 26187/304-375-7842
Mowrey Gun Works, FM 368, Box 28, Iowa Park, TX 76367/817-592-2331
Muzzleloaders Etc., Inc., Jim Westberg, 9909 Lyndale Ave. S., Bloomington, MN 55420/612-884-1161

Numrich Corp., W. Hurley, NY 12491 (powder flasks)
Kirk Olson, Ft. Woolsey Guns, P.O. Box 2122, Prescott, AZ 86302/602-778-3035 (powderhorns)
Ox-Yoke Originals, 130 Griffin Rd., West Suffield, CT 06093/203-668-5110 (dry lubr. patches)
Orrin L. Parsons, Jr., Central Maine Muzzle-Loading & Gunsmithing, RFD #1, Box 787, Madison, ME 04950
Ozark Mountain Arms Inc., S.R. 4, Box 4000-W, Branson, MO 65616/417-334-6971
Pecos Valley Armory, 1022 So. Canyon, Carlsbad, NM 88220/505-887-6023
A. W. Peterson Gun Shop, 1693 Old Hwy. 441 N., Mt. Dora, FL 32757 (ML guns)
Phyl-Mac, 609 N.E. 104th Ave., Vancouver, WA 98664/206-256-0579 (cust. charger)
Provider Arms, Inc., 261 Haglund Rd., Chesterton, IN 46304/219-879-5590 (Predator rifle)
Richland Arms, 321 W. Adrian St., Blissfield, MI 49228
Rush's Old Colonial Forge, 106 Wiltshire Rd., Baltimore, MD 21221
Salish House, Inc., P.O. Box 383, Lakeside, MT 55922/406-844-3625
H. M. Schoeller, 569 So. Braddock Ave., Pittsburgh, PA 15221
Sharon Rifle Barrel Co., P.O. Box 106, Kalispell, MT 59901
Shiloh Products, 37 Potter St., Farmingdale, NY 11735 (4-cavity mould)
Shore Galleries, Inc., 3318 W. Devon Ave., Chicago, IL 60645/312-676-2900
Sile Distributors, 7 Centre Market Pl., New York, NY 10013/213-925-4111
C. E. Siler Locks, Rt. 6, Box 5, Candler, NC 28715/704-667-2376 (flint locks)
Ken Steggles, see: Mike Marsh
The Swampfire Shop, 1693 Old Hwy. 441 N., Mt. Dora, FL 32757/904-383-0595
Tag Gun Works, 236 Main, Springfield, OR 97477/503-741-4118 (supplies)
Tennessee Valley Arms, P.O. Box 2022, Union City, TN 38261/901-885-4456
Tennessee Valley Mfg., P.O. Box 1125, Corinth, MS 38834 (powderhorns)
Ten-Ring Precision, Inc., 1449 Blue Crest Lane, San Antonio, TX 78232/512-494-3063
Treso Inc., P.O. Box 4640, Pagosa Springs, CO 81157 (accessories)
Upper Missouri Trading Co., 3rd and Harold Sts., Crofton, NB 68730/402-388-4844
R. Watts, 826 Springdale Rd., Atlanta, GA 30306 (ML rifles)
J. S. Weeks & Son, 4748 Bailey Rd., Dimondale, MI 48821/517-636-0591 (supplies)
Western Arms/Allen Arms, 1107 Pen Rd., Santa Fe, NM 87501/505-982-3399 (guns)
W. H. Wescomb, P.O. Box 488, Glencoe, CA 95232 (parts)
Thos. F. White, 5801 Westchester Ct., Worthington OH 43085/614-888-0128 (powder horn)
Williamson-Pate Gunsmith Serv., 117 W. Pipeline, Hurst, TX 76053/817-268-2887
Winchester Sutler, Siler Route, Box 393-E, Winchester, VA 22601/703-888-3595 (haversacks)
York County Gun Works, R.R. #4, Tottenham, Ont. LOG 1WO, Canada (locks)

PISTOLSMITHS

Allen Assoc., Box 532, Glenside, PA 19038 (speed-cock lever for 45 ACP)
Armament Gunsmithing Co., Inc., 525 Route 22, Hillside, NJ 07205/201-686-0960
Bain and Davis Sptg. Gds., 559 W. Las Tunas Dr., San Gabriel, CA 91776/213-284-2264
Lee Baker, 7252 East Ave. U-3, Littlerock, CA 93543/805-944-4487 (cust. blue)
Bar-Sto Precision Machine, 73377 Sullivan Rd., Twentynine Palms, CA 92277/619-367-2747(S.S. bbls. f. 45 ACP)
Behlert Custom Guns, Inc., Box 227, Monmouth Junction, NJ 08852/201-329-2284 (short actions)
Bell's Custom Shop, 3319 Mannheim Rd., Franklin Park, IL 60131/312-678-1900/312-678-1900
F. Bob Chow, Gun Shop, Inc., 3185 Mission, San Francisco, CA 94110/415-282-8358
Brown Custom Guns, Inc., Steven N. Brown, 8810 Rocky Ridge Rd., Indianapolis, IN 46217/317-881-2771 aft. 5 PM
Dick Campbell, 3268 S. Downing, Englewood, CO 80110/303-789-4995 (PPC guns)
Dave Chicoine, d/b/a Liberty A.S.P., P.O. Box 385, Cos Cob, CT 06807/203-357-1893 (rep. & rest. of early S&W prods.)
J. E. Clark, Rte. 2, Box 22A, Keithville, LA 71047
Davis Co., 2793 Del Monte St., West Sacramento, CA 95691/916-372-6789
Day Arms Corp., 2412 S.W. Loop 410, San Antonio, TX 78227
Dominic DiStefano, 4303 Friar Lane, Colorado Springs, CO 80907/303-599-3366 (accurizing)
Dan Dwyer, 915 W. Washington, San Diego, CA 92103/619-296-1501
Ken Eversull Gunsmith, Inc., P.O. Box 1766, Alexandria, LA 71301/318-487-0823
Jack First Distributors, Inc., 44633 Sierra Hwy., Lancaster, CA 93534/805-945-6981
John Fordham, Box 9 Dial Star Rte., P.O. Box 1093, Blue Ridge, GA 30513/404-632-3602
Giles' 45 Shop, 8614 Tarpon Springs Rd., Odessa, FL 33556/813-920-5366
The Gunshop, R. D. Wallace, 320 Overland Rd., Prescott, AZ 86301
Gil Hebard Guns, Box 1, Knoxville, IL 61448
Paul Jaeger, Inc., 211 Leedom St., Jenkintown, PA 19046/215-884-6920
J. D. Jones, Rt. 1, Della Dr., Bloomingdale, OH 43910/614-264-0176
Kart Sptg. Arms Corp., 1190 Old Country Rd., Riverhead, NY 11901/516-727-2719 (handgun conversions)
Benjamin Kilham, Kilham & Co., Main St., Box 37, Lyme, NH 03768/603-795-4112

Terry K. Kopp, Highway 13, Lexington, MO 64067/816-259-2636 (rebblg., conversions)
John G. Lawson, The Sight Shop, 1802 E. Columbia Ave., Tacoma, WA 98404/206-474-5465
Lenz Firearms Co., 310 River Rd., Eugene, OR 97404/503-689-6900
Kent Lomont, 4421 So. Wayne Ave., Ft. Wayne, IN 46807/219-694-6792 (Auto Mag only)
Mag-Na-Port Arms, Inc., 30016 S. River Rd., Mt. Clemens, MI 48043/313-469-6727
Robert A. McGrew, 3315 Michigan Ave., Colorado Springs, CO 80910/303-636-1940
Rudolf Marent, 9711 Tiltree, Houston, TX 77075/713-946-7028 (Hammerli)
Nu-Line Guns, 1053 Caulks Hill Rd., Harvester, MO 63303/314-441-4501
Pachmayr Gun Works, 1220 S. Grand Ave., Los Angeles, CA 90015
SSK Industries (See: J. D. Jones)
L. W. Seecamp Co., Inc., Box 255, New Haven, CT 06502/203-877-3429 (DA Colt auto conversions)
Silver Dollar Guns, P.O. Box 475, 10 Frances St., Franklin, NH 03235/603-934-3292 (45 ACP)
Spokhandguns Inc., Vern D. Ewer, East 1911 Sprague Ave., Spokane, WA 99202/509-325-3992
Sportsmens Equipmt. Co., 915 W. Washington, San Diego, CA 92103/619-296-1501 (specialty limiting trigger motion in autos)
Irving O. Stone, Jr., 73377 Sullivan Rd., Twentynine Palms, CA 92277/619-367-2747
Victor W. Strawbridge, 6 Pineview Dr., Dover Pt., Dover, NH 03820
A. D. Swenson's 45 Shop, P.O. Box 606, Fallbrook, CA 92028
Trapper Gun, 18717 East 14 Mile Rd., Fraser, MI 48026/313-792-0134
Dennis A. "Doc" Ulrich, 2511 S. 57th Ave., Cicero, IL 60650
Vic's Gun Refinishing, 6 Pineview Dr., Dover, NH 03820/603-742-0013
Walters Industries, 6226 Park Lane, Dallas, TX 75225/214-691-5150

REBORING AND RERIFLING

P.O. Ackley (See Dennis M. Bellm Gunsmithing, Inc.)
Atkinson Gun Co., P.O. Box 512, Prescott, AZ 86301
Dennis M. Bellm Gunsmithing Inc., 2376 So. Redwood Rd., Salt Lake City, UT 84119/801-974-0697; price list $3 (rifle only)
Dave Chicoine, d/b/a Liberty A.S.P., P.O. Box 385, Cos Cob, CT 06807/203-357-1893 (reline handgun bbls.)
H-S Precision, Inc., 112 N. Summit, Prescott, AZ 85302/602-445-0607
Bruce Jones, 389 Calla Ave., Imperial Beach, CA 92032
Terry K. Kopp, Highway 13, Lexington, MO 64067/816-259-2636 (Invis-A-Line bbl.; relining)
Les' Gun Shop, (Les Bauska), 105-9th West, P.O. Box 511, Kalispell, MT 59901/406-755-2635
Nu-Line Guns, 1053 Caulks Hill Rd., Harvester, MO 63303/314-441-4500 (handguns)
Redman's Gun Shop, P.O. Box 647, Okanogan, WA 98840/509-422-5512
SGW, Inc. (formerly Schuetzen Gun Works), 624 Old Pacific Hwy. S.E., Olympia, WA 98503/206-456-3471
Sharon Gun Specialties, 14587 Peaceful Valley Rd., Sonora, CA 95370
Siegrist Gun Shop, 2689 McLean Rd., Whittemore, MI 48770/517-873-3929
Snapp's Gunshop, 6911 E. Washington Rd., Clare, MI 48617
J. W. Van Patten, Box 145, Foster Hill, Milford, PA 18337
Robt. G. West, 27211 Huey Lane, Eugene, OR 97402

RELOADING TOOLS AND ACCESSORIES

Advance Car Mover Co., Inc., P.O. Box 1181, Appleton, WI 54911/414-734-1878 (bottom pour lead casting ladles)
Accessory Specialty Co., 2711 So. 84th St., West Allis, WI 53227/414-545-0879 (Reload-a-stand)
Advanced Precision Prods. Co., 5183 Flintrock Dr., Westerville, OH 43081/614-895-0560 (case super luber)
American Wad Co., P&P Tool, 125 W. Market St., Morrison, IL 61270/815-772-7618 (12-ga. shot wad)
Anderson Mfg. Co., R.R.1, Royal, IA 51357/712-933-5542 (Shotshell Trimmers)
C'Arco, P.O. Box 308, Highland, CA 92346/714-862-8311 (Ransom "Grand Master" progr. loader)
Creighton Audette, 19 Highland Circle, Springfield, VT 05156/802-885-2331 (Universal Case Selection gauge)
Aurands, 229 E. 3rd St., Lewistown, PA 17044
B-Square Eng. Co., Box 11281, Ft. Worth, TX 76110
Ballistic Prods., P.O. Box 488, 2105 Shaughnessy Circle, Long Lake, MN 55356/612-473-1550
Ballistic Research Industries (BRI), 600 B Soquel Ave., Santa Cruz, CA 95062/408-476-7981
Bear Machine Co., 2110 1st Natl. Tower, Akron, OH 44308/216-253-4039
Belding & Mull, P.O. Box 428, 100 N. 4th St., Philipsburg, PA 16866/814-342-0607
Berdon Machine Co., Box 483, Hobart, WA 98025/206-392-1866 (metallic press)
Blackhawk East, Dowman Greene, C2274 POB, Loves Park, IL 61131/815-633-7784
Blackhawk Mtn., Richard Miller, 1337 Delmar Parkway, Aurora, CO 80010/303-366-3659
Blackhawk West, R. L. Hough, Box 285, Hiawatha, KS 66434/303-366-3659
Bonanza Sports, Inc., 412 Western Ave., Faribault, MN 55021/507-332-7153
Gene Bowlin, Rt. 1, Box 890, Snyder, TX 79549/915-573-2323 (arbor press)

Brown Precision Co., P.O. Box 270W, 7786 Molinos Ave., Los Molinos, CA 96055/916-384-2506 (Little Wiggler)

C-H Tool & Die Corp., 106 N. Harding St., Owen, WI 54461/715-229-2146

Camdex, Inc., 2228 Fourteen Mile Rd., Warren, MI 48092/313-977-1620

Carbide Die & Mfg. Co., Box 226, Covina, CA 91724

Carter Gun Works, 2211 Jefferson Pk. Ave., Charlottesville, VA 22903

Cascade Cartridge, Inc., (See: Omark)

Cascade Shooters, 60916 McMullin Dr., Bend, OR 97702/503-389-5872 (bull. seating depth gauge)

Central Products f. Shooters, 435 Route 18, East Brunswick, NJ 08816 (neck turning tool)

Chevron Case Master, R.R. 1, Ottawa, IL 61350

Lester Coats, 416 Simpson St., No. Bend, OR 97459/503-756-6995 (core cutter)

Container Development Corp., 424 Montgomery St., Watertown, WI 53094

Continental Kite & Key Co., (CONKKO) Box 40, Broomall, PA 19008/215-353-1443 (primer pocket cleaner)

Cooper-Woodward, Box 972, Riverside, CA 92502/714-683-5952 (Perfect Lube)

Corbin Mfg. & Supply Inc., P.O. Box 758, Phoenix, OR 97535/503-826-5211

Custom Products, RD #1, Box 483A, Saegertown, PA 16443/814-763-2769 (decapping tool, dies, etc.)

J. Dewey Mfg. Co., 186 Skyview Dr., Southbury, CT 06488/203-264-3064

Dillon Precision Prods., Inc., 7755 E. Gelding Dr., Suite 106, Scottsdale, AZ 85260/602-948-8009

Diverter Arms, Inc., P.O. Box 22084, Houston, TX 77027 (bullet puller)

Division Lead Co., 7742 W. 61st Pl., Summit, IL 60502

Eagle Products Co., 1520 Adelia Ave., So. El Monte, CA 91733

Edmisten Co. Inc., P.O. Box 1293, Hwy 105, Boone, NC 28607/704-264-1490

Efemes Enterprises, P.O. Box 122M, Bay Shore, NY 11706 (Berdan decapper)

W. H. English, 4411 S. W. 100th, Seattle, WA 98146 (Paktool)

Farmer Bros., 1102 N. Washington, Eldora, IA 50627/515-858-3651 (Lage)

Fitz, P.O. Box 55, Grizzly Gulch, Whiskey Town, CA 96095/916-778-3136 (Fitz Flipper)

Flambeau Plastics Corp., P.O. Box 97 Middlefield, OH 44062/216-632-1631

Forster Products Inc., 82 E. Lanark Ave., Lanark IL 61046/815-493-6360

Francis Tool Co., P.O. Box 7861, Eugene, OR 97401/503-746-4831 (powder measure)

Geo. M. Fullmer, 2499 Mavis St., Oakland, CA 94601 (seating die)

Gene's Gun Shop, Rt. 1, Box 890, Snyder, TX 79549/915-573-2323 (arbor press)

Gopher Shooter's Supply, Box 278, Faribault, MN 55021

Hart Products, Rob W. Hart & Son Inc., 401 Montgomery St., Nescopeck, PA 18635

Hensley & Gibbs, Box 10, Murphy, OR 97533

Richard Hoch, The Gun Shop, 62778 Spring Creek Rd., Montrose, CO 81401/303-249-3625 (custom Schuetzen bullet moulds)

Hoffman New Ideas Inc., 821 Northmoor Rd., Lake Forest, IL 60045/312-234-4075 (spl. gallery load press)

Hollywood Reloading, (See Whitney Sales, Inc.)

Hornady (See Pacific)

Hulme see: Marshall Enterprises (Star case feeder)

Independent Mach. & Gun Shop, 1416 N. Hayes, Pocatello, ID 83201

Ivy Armament, P.O. Box 10, Greendale, WI 53129

Javelina Products, Box 337, San Bernardino, CA 92402 (Alox beeswax)

Neil Jones, RD #1, Box 483A, Saegertown, PA 16433/814-763-2769 (decapping tool, dies)

Paul Jones Munitions Systems (See Fitz Co.)

Kexplore, P.O. Box 22084, Houston, TX 77027/713-789-6943

Kuharsky Bros. (See Modern Industries)

Lac-Cum Bullet Puller, Star Route, Box 240, Apollo, PA 15613/412-478-1794

Lage Uniwad Co., 1102 N. Washington St., Eldora, IA 50627 (Universal Shotshell Wad)

Lee Custom Engineering, Inc. (See Mequon Reloading Corp.)

Lee Precision, Inc., 4275 Hwy. U, Hartford, WI 53027/414-673-3075

Lewisystems, Menasha Corp., 426 Montgomery St., Watertown, WI 53094

L. L. F. Die Shop, 1281 Highway 99 N., Eugene, OR 97402/503-688-5753

Dean Lincoln, P.O. Box 1886, Farmington, NM 87401 (mould)

Ljutic Industries, 918 N. 5th Ave., Yakima, WA 98902

Lock's Phila. Gun Exch., 6700 Rowland, Philadelphia, PA 19149/215-332-6225

Lyman Products Corp., Rte. 147, Middlefield, CT 06455

McKillen & Heyer Inc., 37603 Arlington Dr., Box 627, Willoughby, OH 44094/216-942-2491 (case gauge)

Paul McLean, 2670 Lakeshore Blvd., W., Toronto, Ont. M8V 1G8 Canada/416-259-3060 (Universal Cartridge Holder)

MEC, Inc. (See Mayville Eng. Co.)

MTM Molded Prod., 5680 Webster St., P.O. Box 1438, Dayton, OH 45414/513-890-7461

Magma Eng. Co., P.O. Box 881, Chandler, AZ 85224

Marmel Prods., P.O. Box 97, Utica, MI 48087/313-731-8029 (Marvelube, Marvelux)

Marquart Precision Co., P.O. Box 1740, Prescott, AZ 86302/602-445-5646 (precision case-neck turning tool)

Marshall Enterprises, P.O. Box 83, Millbrae, CA 94030/415-365-1230 (Hulme autom. case feeder f. Star rel.)

Mayville Eng. Co., 715 South St., Mayville, WI 53050/414-387-4500 (shotshell loader)

Mequon Reloading Corp., P.O. Box 253, Mequon, WI 53092/414-673-3060

Merit Gun Slight Co., P.O. Box 995, Sequim, WA 98382

Multi-Scale Charge Ltd., 3269 Niagara Falls Blvd., North Tonawanda, NY 14120/416-967-5305

Normington Co., Box 6, Rathdrum, ID 83858 (powder baffles)

NorthEast Industrial Inc., N.E.I., 2516 Wyoming, El Paso, TX 79903/915-532-8344 (bullet mould)

J. Northcote, Box 5158, Hacienda Heights, CA 91745/213-968-5806 (hollow pointer)

Ohaus Scale, (See RCBS)

Omark Industries, Box 856, Lewiston, ID 83501/208-746-2351

P&P Tool Co., 125 W. Market St., Morrison, IL 61270/815-772-7618 (12-ga. shot wad)

Pacific Tool Co., P.O. Box 2048, Ordnance Plant Rd., Grand Island, NE 68801/308-384-2308

Pak-Tool Co., 4411 S.W. 100th, Seattle, WA 98146

Pem's Manufacturing Co., 5063 Waterloo Rd., Atwater, OH 44201/216-947-2202 (pedestal cranks, primer pocket cleaner)

Plum City Ballistics Range, Rte. 1, Box 29A, Plum City, WI 54761

Ponsness-Warren, Inc., P.O. Box 8, Rathdrum, ID 83858/208-687-1331

Marian Powley, Petra Lane, R.R.1, Eldridge, IA 52748/319-285-9214

Precise Alloys Inc., 406 Hillside Ave., New Hyde Park, NY 11040/516-354-8860 (chilled lead shot; bullet wire)

Quinetics Corp., P.O. Box 29007, San Antonio, TX 78229/516-684-8561 (kinetic bullet puller)

RCBS, Inc., Box 1919, Oroville, CA 95965/916-533-5191

Redding Inc., 114 Starr Rd., Cortland, NY 13045

Reloaders Equipment Co., 4680 High St., Ecorse, MI 48229 (bullet puller)

Rifle Ranch, Rte. 5, Prescott, AZ 86301

Rochester Lead Works, 76 Anderson Ave., Rochester, NY 14607/716-442-8500 (leadwire)

Rorschach Precision Prods., P.O. Box 1613, Irving, TX 75060/214-254-9762 (carboloy bull. dies)

Rotex Mfg. Co. (See Texan)

SAECO Rel. 525 Maple Ave., Carpinteria, CA 93013/805-684-6925

SSK Industries, Rt. 1, Della Drive, Bloomingdale, OH 43910/614-264-0176 (primer tool)

Sandia Die & Cartridge Co., Rte. 5, Box 5400, Albuquerque, NM 87123/505-298-5729

Shassere, Box 35865, Houston, TX 77096/713-780-7041 (cartridge case caddy/loading block)

Shiloh Products, 37 Potter St., Farmingdale, NY 11735 (4-cavity bullet mould)

Shooters Accessory Supply, (See Corbin Mfg. & Supply)

Sil's Gun Prod., 490 Sylvan Dr., Washington, PA 15301 (K-spinner)

Jerry Simmons, 715 Middlebury St., Goshen, IN 46526/219-533-8546 (Pope de- & recapper)

J. A. Somers Co., P.O. Box 49751, Los Angeles, CA 90049 (Jasco)

Sport Flite Mfg., Inc., 2520 Industrial Row, Troy, MI 48084/313-280-0648 (swaging dies)

Star Machine Works, 418 10th Ave., San Diego, CA 92101/619-232- 3216

TEK Ind., Inc., 2320 Robinson St., Colorado Springs, CO 80904/303-630-1295 (Vibra Tek Brass Polisher & Medium, Vibra Brite Rouge)

T&T Products, Inc., 6330 Hwy. 14 East, Rochester, MN 55901 (Meyer shotgun slugs)

Texan Reloaders, Inc., 444 So. Cips St., Watseka, IL 60970/815-432-5065

Trico Plastics, 590 S. Vincent Ave., Azusa, CA 91702

WAMADET, Silver Springs, Goodleigh, Barnstaple, Devon, England

Walker Mfg. Inc., 8296 So. Channel, Harsen's Island, MI 48028 (Berdan decapper)

Wammes Guns Inc., 236 N. Hayes St., Bellefontaine, OH 43311 (Jim's powder baffles)

Weatherby, Inc., 2781 Firestone Blvd., South Gate, CA 90280/213-569-7186

Weaver Arms Corp., 344 No. Vinewood St., Escondido, CA 92025/714-745-4342 (progr. loader)

Webster Scale Mfg. Co., Box 188, Sebring, FL 33870

Whits Shooting Stuff, P.O. Box 1340, Cody, WY 82414

Whitney Sales, Inc., P.O. 875, Reseda, CA 91335 (Hollywood)

L. E. Wilson, Inc. P.O. Box 324, 404 Pioneer Ave., Cashmere, WA 98815

Xelex, Ltd., P.O. Box 543, Renfrow K7V 4B1, Canada (powder)

Zenith Enterprises, 5781 Flagler Rd., Nordland, WA 98358/206-385-2142

RESTS—BENCH, PORTABLE, ETC.

A&A Design & Manufacturing, 361 SW "K" St., Grants Pass, OR 97526/503-474-1026 (Tour de Force bench rest)

B-Square Co., P.O. Box 11281, Ft. Worth, TX 76109/817-923-0964 (handgun)

Jim Brobst, 299 Poplar St., Hamburg, PA 19526/215-562-2103 (bench rest pedestal)

Bullseye Shooting Bench, 6100 - 40th St. Vancouver, WA 98661/206-694-6141 (portable)

C'Arco, P.O. Box 2043, San Bernardino, CA 92401 (Ransom handgun rest)

Centrum kIndustries, Inc. 443 Century S.W., Grand Rapids, MI 49503/616-454-9424 (Porta Bench)

Cravener's Gun Shop, 1627 - 5th Ave., Ford City, PA 16226/412-763-8312 (portable)

Decker Shooting Products, 1729 Laguna Ave., Schofield, WI 54476 (rifle rests)

The Gun Case, 11035 Maplefield, El Monte, CA 91733

Joe Hall's Shooting Products, Inc., 443 Wells Rd., Doylestown, PA 18901/215-345-6354 (adj. portable)

Harris Engineering, Inc., Barlow, KY 42024/502-334-3633 (bipods)

Rob. W. Hart & Son, 401 Montgomery St., Nescopeck, PA 18635

Tony Hidalgo, 6 Capp St., Carteret, NJ 07008/201-541-5894 (shooters stools)

North Star Devices, Inc., P.O. Box 2095, North St. Paul, MN 55109 (Gun Slinger)

Progressive Prods., Inc., P.O. Box 67, Holmen, WI 54636/608-526-3345 (Sandbagger rifle rest)

Rec. Prods., Res., Inc., 158 Franklin Ave., Ridgewood, NJ 07450 (Butts Bipod)

Suter's House of Guns, 332 N. Tejon, Colorado Springs, CO 80902/303-635-1475

Tuller & Co., Basil Tuller 29 Germania, Galeton, PA 16922/814-435-2442 (Protector sandbags)

Turkey Creek Enterprises, Rt. 1, Box 10, Red Oak, CA 74563/918-754-2884 (portable shooting rest)

Wichita Arms, 444 Ellis, Wichita, KS 67211/316-265-06612

RIFLE BARREL MAKERS

P.O. Ackley Rifle Barrels (See Dennis M. Bellm Gunsmithing Inc.)
Luther Adkins, P.O. Box 281, Shelbyville, IN 46176/317-392-3795
Atkinson Gun Co., P.O. Box 512, Prescott, AZ 86301
Jim Baiar, 490 Halfmoon Rd., Columbia Falls, MT 59912/406-892-4409
Bauska Rifle Barrels, Inc., 105-9th Ave. West, Kalispell, MT 59901/406-755-2635
Dennis M. Bellm Gunsmithing Inc., 2376 So. Redwood Rd., Salt Lake City, UT 84119/801-974-0697; price list $3 (new rifle bbls., incl. special & obsolete)
Leo Bustani, P.O. Box 8125, West Palm Beach, FL 33407/305-622-2710 (Win.92 take-down; Trapper 357-44 mag. bbls.)
Ralph L. Carter, Carter's Gun Shop, 225 G St., Penrose, CO 81240/303-372-6240
Christy Gun Works, 875 57th St., Sacramento, CA 95819
Cuthbert Gun Shop, 715 So. 5th Coos Bay, OR 97420
Charles P. Donnelly & Son, Siskiyou Gun Works, 405 Kubli Rd., Grants Pass, OR 97526/503-846-6604
Douglas Barrels, Inc., 5504 Big Tyler Rd., Charleston, WV 25312/304-776-1341
Douglas Jackalope Gun & Sport Shop, Inc., 1048 S. 5th St., Douglas, WY 82633/307-358-3854
Federal Firearms Co., Inc., P.O. Box 145, Thoms Run Rd., Oakdale, PA 15071/412-221-0300
C. R. & D. E. Getz, Box 88, Beavertown, PA 17813
A. R. Goode, 12845 Catoctin Furnace Rd., Thurmont, MD 21788/301-271-2228
Half Moon Rifle Shop, 490 Halfmoon Rd., Columbia Falls, MT 59912/406-892-4409
H-S Precision, Inc., 112 N. Summit, Prescott, AZ 85302/602-445-0607
Hart Rifle Barrels, Inc., RD 2, Lafayette, NY 13084/315-677-9841
H&H Barrels Works, Inc., 1520 S.W. 5th Ave., Ocala, FL 32674/904-351-4200
Wm. H. Hobaugh, Box M, Philipsburg, MT 59858/406-859-3515
Huntington Precision Arms Inc., David R. Huntington, 670 So. 300 West, Heber City, UT 84032/801-654-2953
Terry K. Kopp, Highway 13, Lexington, MO 64067/816-259-2636 (22-cal. blanks)
Les' Gun Shop, (Les Bauska), 105-9th West, P.O. Box 511, Kalispell, MT 59901/406-755-2635
Marquart Precision Co., P.O. Box 1740, Prescott, AZ 86302/602-445-5646
Nu-Line Guns, 1053 Caulkshill Rd., Harvester, MO 63303/314-441-4500
Numrich Arms, W. Hurley, NY 12491
John T. Pell Octagon Barrels, (KOGOT), 410 College Ave., Trinidad, CO 81083/303-846-9406
Pennsylvania Arms Co., Box 128, Duryea, PA 18642/717-457-0845 (rifled shotgun bbl. only)
Sanders Cust. Gun Serv., 2358 Tyler Lane, Louisville, KY 40205
SGW, Inc., D. A. Schuetz, 624 Old Pacific Hwy. S.E., Olympia, WA 98503/206-456-3471
Sharon Gun Specialties, 14587 Peaceful Valley Rd., Sonora, CA 95370/209-532-4139
E. R. Shaw, Inc., Prestley & Thoms Run Rd., Bridgeville, PA 15017/412-221-3636
Shilen Rifles, Inc., 205 Metropark Blvd., Ennis, TX 75119/214-875-5318
W. C. Strutz, Rifle Barrels, Inc., P.O. Box 611, Eagle River, WI 54521/715-479-4766
Titus Barrel & Gun Co., R.F.D. #1, Box 23, Herber City, UT 84032
Bob Williams, P.O. Box 143, Boonsboro, MD 21713
Wilson Arms, 63 Leetes Island Rd., Branford, CT 06405

SCOPES, MOUNTS, ACCESSORIES, OPTICAL EQUIPMENT

Aimpoint U.S.A., 201 Elden St., Suite 103, Herndon, VA 22070/703-471-6828 (electronic sight)
The American Import Co., 1167 Mission, San Francisco, CA 94103/415-863-1506
Anderson Mfg. Co., Union Gap Sta. P.O. Box 3120, Yakima, WA 98903/509-453-2349 (lens cap)
Armsport, Inc., 3590 N.W. 49th St., Miami, FL 33122/305-635-7850
Armson O.E.G. (See Leadership Keys, Inc.)
B-Square Co., Box 11281, Ft. Worth, TX 76109 (Mini-14 mount)
Bausch & Lomb Inc., 1400 Goodman St., Rochester, NY 14602/716-338-6000
Beeman Inc., 47 Paul Dr., San Rafael, CA 94903/415-472-7121
Bennett, 561 Delaware, Delmar, NY 12054/518-439-1862 (mounting wrench)
Billingsley & Brownell, Box 25, Wyarno, WY 82845/307-737-2468 (cust. mounts)
Lenard M. Brownell (See Billingsley & Brownell)
Browning Arms, Rt. 4, Box 624-B, Arnold, MO 63010
Maynard P. Buehler, Inc., 17 Orinda Highway, Orinda, CA 94563/415-254-3201 (mounts)
Burris Co. Inc., 331 E. 8th St., Box 1747, Greeley, CO 80631/303-356-1670
Bushnell Optical Co., 2828 E. Foothill Blvd., Pasadena, CA 91107
Butler Creek Corp., Box GG, Jackson Hole, WY 83001 (lens caps)
Chesco, Inc., 406 Violet St., Golden, CO 80401/303-279-0886 (Ram-Line see thru mt. f. Mini 14)
Kenneth Clark, 18738 Highway 99, Madera, CA 93637/209-674-6016
Clearview Mfg. Co., Inc. 20821 Grand River Ave., Detroit, MI 48219/313-535-0033 (mounts)
Colt Firearms, P.O. Box 1868, Hartford CT 06102/203-236-6311
Compass Instr. & Optical Co., Inc., 104 E. 25th St., New York, NY 10010
Conetrol Scope Mounts, Hwy 123 South, Seguin, TX 78155
D&H Prods. Co., Inc., P. O. Box 22, Glenshaw, PA 15116/412-443-2190 (lens covers)
Davis Optical Co., P.O. Box 6, Winchester, IN 47934/317-584-5311

Del-Sports Inc., Main St., Margaretville, NY 12455/914-586-4103 (Kahles; EAW mts.)
Dickson (See American Import Co.)
Eder Instrument Co., 5115 N. Ravenswood, Chicago, IL 60640 (borescope)
Flaig's, Babcock Blvd., Millvale, PA 15209
Fontaine Ind., Inc., 11552 Knott St., Suite 2, Garden Grove, CA 92641/714-892-4473
Freeland's Scope Stands, Inc., 3737 14th, Rock Island, IL 61201/309-788-7449
Griffin & Howe, Inc., 589 Broadway, New York, NY 10012
H&H Assoc., P.O. Box 447, Strathmore, CA 93267 (target adj. knobs)
Heckler & Koch, Inc., 933 N. Kenmore St., Suite 218, Arlington, VA 22201/703-243-3700
H.J. Hermann Leather Co., Rt. 1, Skiatook, OK 74070 (lens caps)
J.B. Holden Co., 295 W. Pearl, Plymouth, MI 48170/313-455- 4850
The Hutson Corp., 105 Century Dr., No., Mansfield, TX 76063/817-477-3421
Import Scope Repair Co., P.O. Box 2633, Durango, CO 81301/303-247-1422
Interarms, 10 Prince St., Alexandria, VA 22313
Paul Jaeger, Inc., 211 Leedom St., Jenkintown, PA 19046/215-884-6920
Jason Empire Inc., 9200 Cody, P.O. Box 14930, Overland Park, KS 66214/913-888-0220
Jennison TCS (See Fontaine Ind., Inc.)
Kahles of America, Div. of Del-Sports, Inc., Main St., Margaretville, NY 12455/914-586-4103
Kris Mounts, 108 Lehigh St., Johnstown, PA 15905
Kuharsky Bros. (See Mondern Industries)
Kwik-Site, 5555 Treadwell, Wayne, MI 48185/313-326-1500 (rings, mounts only)
Leadership Keys, Inc., P.O. Box 2130, Farmington Hills, MI 48018/313-478-2577 (Armson O.E.G.)
Leatherwood Enterprises, Suite 4B The Mall, P.O. Box 111, Stephenville, TX 76401/817-968-2719
T.K. Lee, 2830 S. 19th St., Off. #4, Birmingham, AL 35209/205-871-6065 (reticles)
E. Leitz, Inc., Rockleigh, NJ 07647
Leupold & Stevens Inc., P.O. Box 688, Beaverton, OR 97075/503-646-9171
Jake Levin and Son, Inc., 9200 Cody, Overland Park, KS 66214
W.H. Lodewick, 2816 N.E. Halsey, Portland, OR 97232/503-284-2554 (scope safeties)
Lyman Products Corp., Route 147, Middlefield, CT. 06455
Mandall Shooting Supplies, 7150 E. 4th St., Scottsdale, AZ 85252
Marble Arms Co., 420 Industrial Park, Gladstone, MI 49837/906-428-3710
Marlin Firearms Co., 100 Kenna Dr., New Haven, CO 06473
Robert Medaris, P.O. Box 309, Mira Loma, CA 91752/714-685-5666 (side mount f. H&K 91 & 93)
Millet Industries, 16131 Gothard St., Huntington Beach, CA 92647/714-842-5575 (mounts)
O.F. Mossberg & Sons, Inc., 7 Grasso Ave., North Haven, CT 06473
Orchard Park Enterprise, P.O. Box 563, Orchard Park, NY 14127/716-662-2255 (Saddleproof mount)
Nite-Site, Inc., P.O. Box O, Rosemount, MN 55068/612-890-7631
Numrich Arms, West Hurley, NY 12491
Nydar, (See Swain Nelson Co.)
PEM's Mfg. Co., 5063 Waterloo Rd., Atwater, OH 44201/216-947-2202 (rings, mounts)
Pachmayr Gun Works, 1220 S. Grand Ave., Los Angeles, CA 90015/213-748-7271
Pilkington Gun Co., P.O. Box 1296, Muskogee, OK 74401/918-693-9418 (Q. D. mt.)
Precise, 3 Chestnut, Suffern, NY 10901
Ranging, Inc., 90 Lincoln Rd. North, East Rochester, NY 14445/716-385-1250
Ray-O-Vac, Willson Prod. Div., P.O. Box 622, Reading, PA 19603 (shooting glasses)
Redfield Gun Sight Co., 5800 E. Jewell Ave., Denver, CO 80222/303-757-6411
S & K Mfg. Co., Box 247, Pittsfield, PA 16340/814-563-7803 (Insta-Mount)
SSK Industries, Rt. 1, Della Dr., Bloomingdale, OH 43910/614-264-0176 (bases)
Sanders Cust. Gun Serv., 2358 Tyler Lane, Louisville, KY 40205 (MSW)
Sears, Roebuck & Co., 825 S. St. Louis, Chicago, IL 60607
Shepherd Scope Ltd., R.R. #1, P.O. Box 23, Waterloo, NE 68069/402-779-2424 (autom. range finding scope)
Sherwood Intl. Export Corp., 18714 Parthenia St., Northridge, CA 91324 (mounts)
W.H. Siebert, 22720 S.E. 56th Pl., Issaquah, WA 98027
Singlepoint (See Normark)
Southern Precision Inst. Co., 3419 E. Commerce St., San Antonio, TX 78219
Spacetron Inc., Box 84, Broadview, IL 60155(bore lamp)
Stoeger Industries, 55 Ruta Ct., S. Hackensack, NJ 07606/201-440-2700
Strieter Corp., 2100-18th Ave., Rock Island, IL 61201/309-794-9800 (Swarovski)
Supreme Lens Covers, Box GG, Jackson Hole, WY 83001 (lens caps)
Swain Nelson Co., Box 45, 92 Park Dr., Glenview, IL 60025 (shotgun sight)
Swift Instruments, Inc., 952 Dorchester Ave., Boston, MA 02125
Tasco, 7600 N.W. 26th St., Miami, FL 33122/305-591-3670
Ted's Sight Aligner, Box 1073, Scottsdale, AZ 85252
Thompson-Center Arms, P.O. Box 2405, Rochester, NH 03867 (handgun scope)
Tradewinds, Inc., Box 1191, Tacoma, WA 98401
John Unertl Optical Co., 3551-5 East St., Pittsburgh, PA 15214
United Binocular Co., 9043 S. Western Ave., Chicago, IL 60620
Vissing (See Supreme Lens Covers)
Wasp Shooting Systems, Box 241, Lakeview, AR 72642/501-431-5606 (mtg. system f. Ruger Mini-14 only)
Weatherby's, 2781 Firestone, South Gate, CA 90280/213-569-7186
W.R. Weaver Co., 7125 Industrial Ave., El Paso, TX 79915
Wide View Scope Mount Corp., 26110 Michigan Ave., Inkster, MI 48141
Williams Gun Sight Co., 7389 Lapeer Rd., Davison, MI 48423

Boyd Williams Inc., 8701-14 Mile Rd. (M-57),Cedar Springs, MI 49319 (BR)
Willrich Precision Instrument Co., 95 Cenar Lane, Englewood, NJ 07631/201-567-1411 (borescope)
Carl Zeiss Inc.,Consumer Prods. Div., Box 2010, 1015 Commerce St., Petersburg, VA 23803/804-861-0033

SIGHTS, METALLIC

Accura-Site Co., Inc., Box 114, Neenah, WI 54956/414-722-0039
B-Square Eng. Co., Box 11281, Ft. Worth, TX 76110
Beeman Inc., 47 Paul Dr., San Rafael, CA 94903/415-472-7121 (airguns only)
Behlert Custom Sights, Inc., Box 227, Monmouth Junction, NJ 08852/201-329-2284
Bingham Ltd., 1775-C Wilwat Dr., Norcross, GA 30093/404-448-1440
Bo-Mar Tool & Mfg. Co., Box 168, Carthage, TX 75633
Maynard P. Buehler, Inc., 17 Orinda Highway, Orinda, CA 94563/415-254-3201
Christy Gun Works, 875 57th St., Sacramento, CA 95819
Andy Fautheree, P.O. Box 863, Pagosa Springs, CO 81147/303-264-2892 ("Calif. Sight" f. ML)
Freeland's Scope Stands, Inc., 3734-14th Ave., Rock Island, IL 61201/309-788-7449
Paul T. Haberly, 2364 N. Neva, Chicago, IL 60635
Paul Jaeger, Inc., 211 Leedom St., Jenkintown, PA 19046/215-884-6920
Lautard Tool Works, 2570 Rosebery Ave., W. Vancouver, B.C., Canada V7V 2Z9/604-926-7150 (W&E adj. target tang sight)
Lee's Red Ramps, 7252 E. Ave. U-3, Littlerock, CA 93543/805-944-4487 (white outline rear sight)
James W. Lofland, 2275 Larkin Rd., Boothwyn, PA 19061/215-485-0391
Lyman Products Corp., Rte. 147, Middlefield, CT 06455
Marble Arms Corp., 420 Industrial Park, Gladstone, MI 49837/906-428-3710
Merit Gunsight Co., P.O. Box 995, Sequim, WA 98382
Micro Sight Co., 242 Harbor Blvd., Belmont, CA 94002/415-591-0769
Millet Industries, 16131 Gothard St., Huntington Beach, CA 92647/714-842-5575
Miniature Machine Co., 210 E. Poplar, Deming, NM 88030/505-546-2151
Omega Sights, 30016 S. River Rd., Mt. Clemens, MI 48043/313-469-6727
C.R. Pedersen & Son, 2717 S. Pere Marquette, Ludington, MI 49431/616-843-2061
PEM's Manufacturing Co., 5063 Waterloo Rd., Atwater, OH 44201/216-947-2202
Poly Choke Co., Inc., 150 Park Ave., East Hartford, CT 06108/203-289-2743
Redfield Gun Sight Co., 5800 E. Jewell St., Denver, CO 80222
S&M Tang Sights, P.O. Box 1338, West Babylon, NY 11704/516-226-4057
Schwarz's Gun Shop, 41-15th St., Wellsburg, WV 26070
Simmons Gun Specialties, Inc., 700 Rodgers Rd., Olathe, KS 66061
Slug Site Co., Whitetail Wilds, Lake Hubert, MN 56469/218-963-4617
Sport Service Center, 2364 N. Neva, Chicago, IL60635/312-889-1114
Tradewinds, Inc., Box 1191, Tacoma, WA 98401
Wichita Arms, 444 Ellis, Wichita, KS 67211/316-265-0661
Williams Gun Sight Co., 7389 Lapeer Rd., Davison, MI 48423

STOCKS (Commercial and Custom)

Accuracy Products, 9004 Oriole Trail, Wonder Lake, IL 60097
Adams Custom Gun Stocks, 13461 Quito Rd., Saratoga, CA 95070
Ahlman's Inc., R.R. 1, Box 20, Morristown, MN 55052
Don Allen Inc., R.R. 4, Northfield, MN 55057/507-645-9216 (blanks)
Answer Stocking Systems, 113 N. 2nd St., Whitewater, WI 53190/414-473-4848 (synthetic)
R.J. Anton, 874 Olympic Dr., Waterloo, IA 50701/319-233-3666
Creighton Audette, 19 Highland Circle, Springfield, VT 05156/802-885-2331 (custom)
Jim Baiar, 490 Halfmoon Rd., Columbia Falls, MT 599123
Joe J. Balickie, Custom Stocks, Rte. 2, Box 56-G, Apex, NC 27502
Bartas Gunsmithing, 10231 U.S.H.#10, Cato, WI 54206/414-732-4472
Donald Bartlett, 16111 S.E. 229th Pl., Kent, WA 98031/206-630-2190 (cust.)
Beeman Inc., 47 Paul Dr., San Rafael, CA 94903/415-472-7121 (airguns only)
Al Biesen, West 2039 Sinto Ave., Spokane, WA 99201
Roger Biesen, 5021 W. Rosewood, Spokane, WA 99208/509-328-9340
Stephen L. Billeb, Box 219, Philipsburg, MT 59858/406-859-3919
Billingsley & Brownell, Box 25, Wyarno, WY 82845/307-737-2468 (cust.)
E.C. Bishop & Son Inc., 119 Main St., Box 7, Warsaw MO 65355/816-438-5121
Gregg Boeke, Rte. 2, Cresco, IA 52136/319-547-3746
John M. Boltin, 2008 Havens Dr., North Myrtle Beach, SC 29582/803-272-6581
Border Gun Shop, Gary Simmons, 2760 Tucson Hiway, Nogales, AZ 85621/602-281-0045 (spl. silueta stocks, complete rifles)
Garnet D. Brawley, P.O. Box 668, Prescott, AZ 86301/602-445-4768 (cust.)
Brown Precision Co., P.O. Box 270W; 7786 Molinos Ave., Los Molinos, CA 96055/916-384-2506
Lenard M. Brownell, (See Billingsley & Brownell)
Jack Burres, 10333 San Fernando Road, Pacoima, CA 91331 (English, Claro, Bastogne Paradox walnut blanks only)
Calico Hardwoods, Inc., 1648 Airport Blvd., Windsor, CA 95492/707-546-4045 (blanks)
Dick Campbell, 3268 S. Downing, Englewood, CO 80110/303-789-4995
Shane Caywood, 321 Hwy. 51 So., Minocqua, WI 54548/715-356-9631 (cust.)
Claude Christopher, 1606 Berkley Rd., Greenville, NC 27834/919-756-0872 (rifles)
Winston Churchill, Twenty Mile Stream Rd., Rt. 1, Box 29B, Proctorsville, VT 05153

Crane Creek Gun Stock Co., 25 Shephard Terr., Madison, WI 53705
Reggie Cubriel, 15502 Purple Sage, San Antonio, TX 78255/512-695-8401 (cust. stockm.)
Bill Curtis, 4919 S. Spade, Murray, UT 84107/801-262-8413
Dahl's Custom Stocks, Rt. 4, Box 558, Schofield Rd., Lake Geneva, WI 53147/414-248-2464 (Martin Dahl)
Sterling Davenport, 9611 E. Walnut Tree Dr., Tucson, AZ 85715/602-749-5590 (custom)
Jack Dever, 8520 N.W. 90, Oklahoma City, OK 73132/405-721-6393
Charles De Veto, 1087 Irene Rd., Lyndhurst, OH 44124/216-442-3188
Bill Dowtin, 3919 E. Thrush Lane, Flagstaff, AZ 86001/602-779-1898 (Calif. Engl., black walnut blanks only)
Gary Duncan, 1118 Canterbury, Enid, OK 73701 (blanks only)
David R. Dunlop, Rte. 1, Box 199, Rolla, ND 58367
D'Arcy A. Echols, P.O. Box 532, Broomfield, CO 80020/303-466-7788 (custom)
Jere Eggleston, 400 Saluda Ave., Columbia, SC 29205/803-799-3402 (cust.)
Bob Emmons, 238 Robson Road, Grafton, OH 44044 (custom)
Ken Eyster Heritage Gunsmiths Inc., 6441 Bishop Rd., Centerburg, OH 43011/614-625-6131 (cust.)
Reinhart Fajen, Box 338, Warsaw, MO 65355/816-438-5111
N.B. Fashingbauer, P.O. Box 366, Lac Du Flambeau, WI 54538/715-588-7116
Ted Fellowes, Beaver Lodge, 9245 16th Ave. S.W., Seattle WA 98106/206-763-1698
Phil Fischer, 7333 N.E. Glisan, Portland, OR 97213/503-255-5678 (cust.)
Clyde E. Fischer, P.O. Box 1437, Three Rivers, TX 78071/512-786-4125 (Texas Mesquite)
Jerry A. Fisher, 1244-4th Ave. W., Kalispell, MT 59901/406-755-7093
Flaig's Lodge, Millvale, PA 15209
Donald E. Folks. 205 W. Lincoln St., Pontiac, IL 61764/815-844-7901 (custom trap, Skeet, livebird stocks)
Larry L Forster, Box 212, Gwinner, ND 58040/701-678-2475
Freeland's Scope Stands, Inc., 3737 14th Ave., Rock Island, IL 61201/309-788-7449
Jim Garrett, 2820 East NaniLoa Circle, Salt Lake City, UT 84117/801-227-6930 (fiberglass)
Dale Goens, Box 224, Cedar Crest, NM 87008
Gordie's Gun Shop, Gordon Mulholland, 1401 Fulton St., Streator, IL 61364/815-672-7202 (cust.)
Gary Goudy, 263 Hedge Rd., Menlo Park, CA 94025/415-322-1338 (cust.)
Gould's Myrtlewood, 1692 N. Dogwood, Coquille, OR 97423 (gun blanks)
Charles E. Grace, 10144 Elk Lake Rd., Williamsburg, MI 49690/616-264-9483
Rolf R. Gruning, 315 Busby Dr., San Antonio, TX 78209
Karl Guenther, 43-32 160th St., Flushing, NY 11372/212-461-7325
Guncraft, Inc., 117 W. Pipeline, Hurst, TX 76053/817-268-2887
The Gunshop, R.D. Wallace, 320 Overland Rd., Prescott, AZ 86301 (custom)
Half Moon Rifle Shop, 490 Halfmoon Rd., Columbia Falls, MT 59912
Harper's Custom Stocks, 928 Lombrano St., San Antonio, TX 78207
Hal Hartley, 147 Blairsfork Rd., Lenoir, NC 28645
Hayes Gunstock Service Co., 914 E. Turner St., Clearwater, FL 33516
Hubert J. Hecht, Waffen-Hecht, 724-K St., Sacramento, CA 95814/916-448-1177
Edward O. Hefti, 300 Fairview, College Station, TX 77840/715-846-4959
Warren Heydenberk, P.O. Box 339, Richlandtown, PA 18955/215-536-0798 (custom)
Doug Hill, 4312 Unruh Dr., Enid, OK 73701/405-242-4455 (cust.)
Klaus Hiptmayer, P.O. Box 136, Eastman, Que., J0E 1P0 Canada/514-297-2492
Richard Hodgson, 5589 Arapahoe, Unit 104, Boulder, CO 80301
Hoenig & Rodman, 6521 Morton Dr., Boise, ID 83705/208-375-1116 (stock duplicating machine)
George Hoenig, 6521 Morton Dr., Boise, ID 83705/208-375-1116
Hollis Gun Shop, 917 Rex St., Carlsbad, NM 88220
Paul Jaeger, Inc., 211 Leedom St., Jenkintown, PA 19046/215-884-6920
Johnson Wood Products, I.D. Johnson & Sons, Rte. #1, Strawberry Point, IA 52076/319-933-4930 (blanks)
Monty Kennedy, P.O. Box 214, Kalispell, MT59901/406-857-3596
Don Klein, P.O. Box 277, Camp Douglas, WI 54618/608-427-6948
LeFever Arms Co., Inc., R.D.#1, Box 31, Lee Center, NY 13363/315-337-6422
Lenz Firearms Co., 310 River Rd., Eugene, OR 97404/503-689-6900
Stanley Kenvin, 5 Lakeville Lane, Plainview, NY 11803/516-931-0321 (custom)
Philip D. Letiecq, AQ, 18 Wagon Box Rd., P.O. Box 251, Story, WY 82842/307-683-2817
Al Lind, 7821 76th Ave. S. W., Tacoma, WA 98498/206-584-6361 (cust. stockm.)
Earl K. Matsuoika, 2801 Kinohou Pl., Honolulu, HI 96822/808-988-3008 (cust.)
John I. McCann, 2911 N. 5th St., Coeur d'Alene, ID 83814/208-667-3919
Bill McGuire, 1600 N. Eastmont Ave., East Wenatchee, WA 98801
Gale McMillan, 28638 N. 42 St., Box 7870-Cave Creek Stage, Phoenix, AZ 85020/602-585-4684
Maurer Manchester Arms Inc., 6858 Manchester Rd., Clinton, OH 44216/216-882-3133
John E. Maxson, Box 332, Dumas, TX 79029/806-935-5990 (custom)
R. M. Mercer, 216 S. Whitewater Ave., Jefferson, WI 53549/414-674-3839 (custom)
Robt. U. Milhoan & Son, Rt. 3, Elizabeth, WV 26143
C-D Miller Guns, Purl St., Box 260, St. Onge, SD 57779/605-578-1790
Earl Milliron Custom Guns & Stocks, 1249 N.E. 166th Ave., Portland, OR 97230/503-252-3725
Ted Nicklas, 5504 Hegel Rd., Goodrich, MI 48438/313-797-4493 (custom)
Nelsen's Gun Shop, 501 S. Wilson, Olympia, WA 98501
Paul R. Nickels, Interwest Gun Service, P.O. Box 243, Providence, UT 84332/801/753-4260
Oakley and Merkley, Box 2446, Sacramento, CA 95811 (blanks)
Jim Norman, Custom Gunstocks, 11230 Calenda Road, San Diego, CA 92127/619-487-4173

Maurice Ottmar, Box 657, 113 E. Fir, Coulee City, WA 99115/509-632-5717 (cust.)

Pachmayr Gun Works, 1220 S. Grand Ave., Los Angeles, CA 90015 (blanks and custom jobs)

Paulsen Gunstocks, Rte. 71, Box 11, Chinook, MT 59523/406-357-3403 (blanks)

Peterson Mach. Carving, Box 1065, Sun Valley, CA 91352

Rely-A Outfitters Corp., P.O. Box 697, Saratoga Springs, NY 12866/518-584-6964 (Rely-A gunstock)

R. Neal Rice, 5152 Newton, Denver, CO 80221

Richards Micro-Fit Stocks, P.O. Box 1066, Sun Valley, CA 91352 (thumbhole)

Carl Roth, Jr., 4728 Pineridge Ave., Cheyenne, WY 82001/309-634-3958

Matt Row, Lock, Stock 'N Barrel, 8972 East Huntington Dr., San Gabriel, CA 91775/213-287-0051

Royal Arms, 1210 Bert Costa, El Cajon, CA 92020/619-448-5466

Sage International Ltd., 1856 Star Batt Dr., Rochester, MI 38063/313-852-8733 (telescoping shotgun stock)

Sanders Cust. Gun Serv., 2358 Tyler Lane, Louisville, KY 40205 (blanks)

Saratoga Arms Co., 1752 N. Pleasantview RD., Pottstown, PA 19464/215-323-8386

Roy Schaefer, 965 W. Hilliard Lane, Eugene, OR 97404/503-688-43333 (blanks)

Schwartz Custom Guns, 9621 Coleman Rd., Haslett, MI 48840/517-339-8939

David W. Schwartz, 2505 Waller St., Eau Claire, WI 54701/715-832-1735 (custom)

Shaw's, The Finest in Guns, 9447 W. Lilac Rd., Escondido, CA 92025/619-728-7070

Hank Shows, The Best,1078 Alice Ave., Ukiah, CA 95482/707-462-9060

Walter Shultz, 1752 N. Pleasantview Rd., Pottstown, PA 19464

Sile Dist., 7 Centre Market Pl., New York, NY 10013/213-925-4111 (shotgun stocks)

Six Enterprises, 6564 Hidden Creek Dr., San Jose, CA 95120/408-268-8296 (fiberglass)

Ed Sowers, 8331 DeCelis Pl., Sepulveda, CA 91343 (hydro-coil gunstocks)

Fred D. Speiser, 2229 Dearborn, Missoula, MT 59801/406-549-8133

Sport Service Center, 2364 N. Neva, Chicago, IL 60635/312-889-1114 (custom)

Sportsmen's Equip. Co., 915 W. Washington, San Diego, CA 92103/714-296-1501 (carbine conversions)

Keith Stegall, Box 696, Gunnison, CO 81230

Stinhour Rifles, Box 84, Cragsmoor, NY 12420/914-647-4163

Surf N' Sea, Inc., 62-595 Kam Hwy., Box 268, Haleiwa, HI 96712 (custom gunstocks blanks)

Talmage Enterpr., 43197 E. Whittier, Hemet, CA 92343

Brent L. Umberger, Sportsman's Haven, R.R. 4, Cambridge, OH 43725

Milton van Epps, Rt. 69-A, Parish, NY 13131

Gil Van Horn, P.O. Box 207, Llano, CA 93544

John Vest, 6715 Shasta Way, Klamath Falls, OR 97601/503-884-5585 (classic rifles)

Weatherby's, 2781 Firestone, South Gate, CA 90280/213-569-7186

Cecil Weems, Box 657, Mineral Wells, TX 76067

Frank R. Wells, 4733 N. Tonalea Trail, Tucson, AZ 85749/602-749-4563 (custom stocks)

Western Gunstocks Mfg. Co., 550 Valencia School Rd., Aptos, CA 95003

Duane Wiebe, P.O. Box 497, Lotus, CA 95651

Bob Williams, P.O. Box 143, Boonsboro, MD 21713

Williamson-Pate Gunsmith Service, 117 W. Pipeline, Hurst, TX 76053/817-268-2887

Jim Windish, 2510 Dawn Dr., Alexandria, VA 22306/703-765-1994 (walnut blanks)

Dave Wills, 2776 Brevard Ave., Montgomery, AL 36109/305-272-8446

Robert M. Winter, Box 484, Menno, SD 57045

Mike Yee, 4732-46th Ave. S.W., Seattle, WA 98116/206-935-3682

Russell R. Zeryp, 1601 Foard Dr., Lynn Ross Manor, Morristown, TN 37814

TARGETS, BULLET & CLAYBIRD TRAPS

Beeman Inc., 47 Paul Dr., San Rafael, CA 94903/415-472-7121 (airgun targets, silhouettes and traps)

Bulletboard Target Systems Laminations Corp., Box 469, Neenah, WI 54956/414-725-8368

Caswell Equipment Co., Inc., 1221 Marshall St. N.E., Minneapolis, MN 55413/612-379-2000 (target carriers; commercial shooting ranges)

J.G. Dapkus Co., P.O. Box 180, Cromwell, CT 06416/203-632-2308 (live bullseye targets)

Data-Targ, (See Rocky Mountain Target Co.)

Detroit Bullet Trap Co., 2233 N. Palmer Dr., Schaumburg, IL 60195/312-397-4070

Electro Ballistic Lab., 616 Junipero Serva Blvd., Stanford, CA 94305 (Electronic Trap Boy)

Ellwood Epps Northern Ltd., 210 Worthington St., W., North Bay, Ont. P1B 3B4, Canada (hand traps)

Jaro Manuf., 206 E. Shaw, Pasadena, TX 77506/713-472-0417 (paper targets)

Laminations Corp. ("Bullettrap"), Box 469, Neenah, WI 54956/414-725-8368

Laporte S.A., B.P. 212, 06603 Antibes, France (claybird traps)

MCM (Mathalienne de Construction de Mecanique), P.O. Box 18, 17160 Matha, France (claybird traps)

Millard F. Lerch, Box 163, 10842 Front St., Mokena, IL 60448 (bullet target)

National Target Co., 4960 Wyaconda Rd., Rockville, MD 20852

Outers Laboratories, Inc., Rte. 2, Onalaska, WI 54650/608-783-1515 (claybird traps)

Peterson Label Co., P.O. Box 186, 23 Sullivan Dr., Redding Ridge, CT 06876/203-938-2349 (paste-ons; Targ-Dots)

Recreation Prods. Res. Inc., 158 Franklin Ave., Ridgewood, NJ 07450 (Butts Bullet trap)

Remington Arms Co., Bridgeport, CT 06602 (claybird traps)

Reproductions West, Box 6765, Burbank, CA 91510 (silhouette targets)

Rocky Mountain Target Co., P.O. Box 700, Black Hawk, SD 57718/605-787-5946 (Data-Targ)

Scientific Prod. Corp., 426 Swann Ave., Alexandria, VA 22301 (Targeteer)

Sheridan Products, Inc., 3205 Sheridan, Racine, WI 54303 (traps)

South West Metallic Silhouettes, Rt. 7, Box 82, Abilene, TX 79605/915-928-4463

Trius Prod., Box 25, Cleves, OH 45002/513-914-5682 (claybird, can thrower)

U.S. Repeating Arms Co., P.O. Box 30-300, New Haven, CT 06511/203-789-5000 (claybird traps)

Winchester, Olin Corp., 120 Long Ridge Rd., Stamford, CT 06904

TAXIDERMY

Jack Atcheson & Sons, Inc., 3210 Ottawa St., Butte, MT 59701

Dough's Taxidermy Studio, Doug Domedion, 2027 Lockport-Olcott Rd., Burt, NY 14028/716-778-7790 (deer head specialist)

Jonas Bros., Inc., 1037 Broadway, Denver, CO 80203 (catlg. $2)

Kulis Freeze-Dry Taxidermy, 725 Broadway Ave., Bedford, OH 44146

Mark D. Parker, 1233 Sherman Dr., Longmont, CO 80501/303-772-0214

TRAP & SKEET SHOOTERS EQUIP.

D&H Prods. Co., Inc., P.O. Box 22, Glenshaw, PA 15116/412-443-2190 (snap shell)

Griggs Recreational Prods. Inc., 200 S. Main, Twin Bridges, MT 59754/406-684-5202 (recoil redirector)

Ken Eyster Heritage Gunsmiths, Inc., 6441 Bishop Rd., Centerburg, OH 43011/614-625-6131 (shotgun competition choking)

LaPorte S.A., B.P. 212, Pont de la Brague, 06603 Antibes, France (traps, claybird)

MCM (Mathalienne de Construction de Mecanique), P.O. Box 18, 17160 Matha, France (claybird traps)

Wm. J. Mittler, 290 Moore Dr., Boulder Creek, CA 95006 (shotgun choke specialist)

Multi-Gauge Enterprises, 433 W. Foothill Blvd., Monrovia, CA 91061/213-358-4549; 357-6117 (shotgun specialists)

William J. Mittler, 290 Moore Dr., Boulder Creek, CA 95006/408-338-3376 (shotgun repairs)

Outers Laboratories, Inc., Route 2, Onalaska, WI 54650/608-783-1515 (trap, claybird)

Purbaugh & Sons (See Multi-Gauge) (shotgun barrel inserts)

Remington Arms Co., P.O. Box 1939, Bridgeport, Ct. 06601 (trap, claybird)

Super Pigeon Corp., P.O. Box 428, Princeton, MN 55371 (claybird target)

Daniel Titus, Shooting Specialties, 872 Penn St., Bryn Mawr, PA 19010/215-525-8829 (hullbag)

Trius Products, Box 25, Cleves, OH 45002/513-941-5682 (can thrower; trap, claybird)

Winchester-Western, New Haven, CT 06504 (trap, claybird)

TRIGGERS, RELATED EQUIP.

Ametek, Hunter Spring Div., One Spring Ave., Hatfield, PA 19440/215-822-2971 (trigger gauge)

NOC, Cadillac Industrial Park, 1610 Corwin St., Cadillac, MI 49601/616-775-3425 (triggers)

M.H. Canjar Co., 500 E. 45th Ave., Denver, CO 80216/303-623-5777 (triggers)

Central Specialties Co., 6030 Northwest Hwy., Chicago,IL 60631/312-774-5000 (trigger lock)

Custom Products, Neil A. Jones, RD #1, Box 483A, Saegertown, PA 16433/814-763-2769 (trigger guard)

Dayton-Traister Co., 9322-900th West, P.O. Box 593, Oak Harbor, WA 98277/206-675-5375 (triggers)

Electronic Trigger Systems, 4124 Thrushwood Lane, Minnetonka, MN 55343/612-935-7829

Flaig's, Babcock Blvd. & Thompson Run Rd., Millvale, PA 15209 (trigger shoes)

Bill Holmes, Rt. 2, Box 242, Fayetteville, AR 72701/501-521-8958 (trigger release)

Neil A. Jones, see: Custom Products

Michaels of Oregon Co., P.O. Box 13010, Portland, OR 97213/503-255-6890 (trigger guards)

Miller Single Trigger Mfg. Co., R.D. 1, Box 99, Millersburg, PA 17061/717-692-3704

Viggo Miller, P.O. Box 4181, Omaha, NB 68104 (trigger attachment)

Ohaus Corp., 29 Hanover Rd., Florham Park, NJ 07932 (trigger pull gauge)

Pachmayr Gun Works, 1220 S. Grand Ave., Los Angeles, CA 90015 (trigger shoe)

Pacific Tool Co., P.O. Box 2048, Ordnance Plant Rd., Grand Island, NE 68801 (trigger shoe)

Richland Arms Co., 321 W. Adrian St., Blissfield, MI 49228 (trigger pull gauge)

Sport Service Center, 2364 N. Neva, Chicago, IL 60635 (release triggers)

Timney Mfg. Co., 3106 W. Thomas Rd., Suite 1104, Phoenix, AZ 85017/602-269-6937 (triggers)

Melvin Tyler, 1326 W. Britton Ave., Oklahoma City, OK 73114 (trigger shoe)

Williams Gun Sight Co., 7389 Lapeer Rd., Davison, MI 48423 (trigger shoe)

Highlights of This Issue

Handgun power can be rated and compared, rationally and completely. See how beginning on page **6**.

When the French build a revolver, they don't fool around—this is what they do to make a police model into a target gun. Story starts on page **50**.

American air power today? Yes, but we're talking pellet guns, lots of them, starting on page **83**.

Even if everyone's serious about assault rifles and survival, they're still fun. A 16-page special feature starts on page **31**.

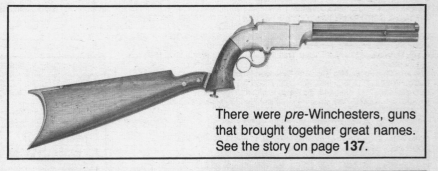

There were *pre*-Winchesters, guns that brought together great names. See the story on page **137**.

Books are part of the fun in guns, and a lot of books are a lot of fun. See how to get in on it, beginning page **118**.

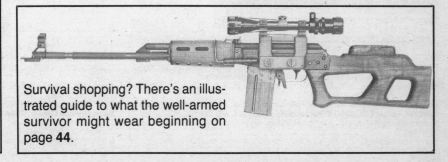

Survival shopping? There's an illustrated guide to what the well-armed survivor might wear beginning on page **44**.

Highlights of This Issue Con't.

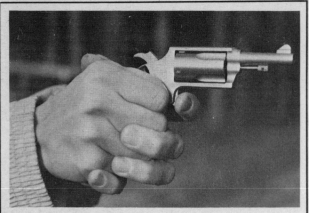

The mini-revolvers can be shot well, can group in 2 inches at 50 feet, in fact. See how it's done beginning page **64**.

Les Bowman was there when the Sharps rifle almost made it again. He tells all beginning page **18**.

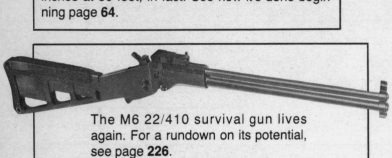

The M6 22/410 survival gun lives again. For a rundown on its potential, see page **226**.

Big bores make sense on deer for old-timers who don't want to track them far. See page **178**.

Is the Benelli B76 the thinking man's 9mm? Articles begin on pages **123** and **227**.

Being chaired off the range is not the least of the joys for top shooters in England. Story: page **216**.

A good rough rifle is there in almost any military bolt rifle. See article, page **114**.